S0-DOR-434

Linn's World Stamp Almanac

Fifth Edition

Compiled and Edited by the Staff of Linn's Stamp News

Published by *Linn's Stamp News*, the largest and most informative stamp newspaper in the world. *Linn's* is owned by Amos Press, 911, Vandemark Road, Sidney, Ohio 45365. Amos Press also publishes *Scott Stamp Monthly* and the Scott line of catalogs, albums and mounts.

033041

ISSN 0146-6887

With Gratitude . . .

The assembling of facts in this Almanac would have been impossible without the generous assistance of many people. Our special thanks to the follows:

Stanley Bierman
George Brett
Herbert R. Collins
Peter H. Daly
James T. DeVoss
Fredelle Fishburn
Richard C. Frajola
Bruce Hecht
Richard Helbock
Bernard A. Hennig
Doug Holl
Otto Hornung
John Hotchner
Donald M. McDowell
Steven Rod
Sheldon Ruckens
Richard C. Sennett
William F. Sharpe
Clark Timmins
Herbert A. Trenchard
Varro Tyler
Les Winick
Charles Yeager

Introduction

The first edition of *Linn's World Stamp Almanac*, published in 1977, was an almost instant sellout. A second edition was published a year later, a third in 1980 and a fourth in 1982. Each succeeding edition was an improvement over its predecessor.

Seven years in the making, this fifth edition is a complete revision of the basic format established in the previous four. Vast amounts of new material — most of it specifically related to stamps, especially U.S. stamps — have been added. All the remaining text has been screened, corrected, revised and updated.

The resultant work represents literally years of labor on the part of the *Linn's* editorial staff — with the valuable help of a large and knowledgeable group of expert contributors. This book makes accessible to hobbyists, researchers and dealers a vast storehouse of facts and figures that has never before been available in one place. Simply stated, this fifth edition of *Linn's World Stamp Almanac* is the most useful single reference source a collector can own.

So much new material has been added that we can't even list all the additions. Here are some of the highlights:

New in this edition are a listing of the first stamps of the various nations of the world, as well as country-by-country details (from the German *Michel Runsdschau*) on the proliferating number of new stamps issued in recent years.

Collectors of U.S. stamps will appreciate the detailed data in the all-new Chapter 3, listing designers, engravers, first-day facts and quantities issued for most U.S. stamps. This chapter also describes the components of various U.S. stamp series and provides detailed information on such recently popular collecting areas as state duck stamps and plate number coils.

To the section on Postal Regulations has been added all the information needed to enable a collector to use precanceled stamps on first-class mail. The chapter on expertizing now contains a comprehensive listing of expert committees.

Stamp-show participants will welcome the extensive additions in the chapter on exhibiting. New are tips on what judges look for, listings of international grand prix winners and listings of all the U.S. winners at FIP-sponsored international stamp exhibitions.

Reflecting increasing collector interest in how stamps are used, we've added three detailed charts of domestic postal rates, from the Colonial era up to the present day. Like so much in this almanac, this rate information existed before, but it had never been assembled in a way that allows collectors to make easy use of it.

This fifth edition of our almanac is as complete and as accurate as we could make it. But given its size and its complexity, errors and oversights have surely crept in. We welcome corrections and suggestions from readers.

— Michael Laurence

Contents

Chapter 1

History of the Posts
World Postal Chronology

The following is a chronological presentation of significant events in the development of postal communications throughout the world. It has been formulated with an eye towards events of significance to stamp collectors and postal historians, and includes a number of postal and philatelic "firsts" of the world. There is also an intentional emphasis on the events of the century and a half since the general introduction of the adhesive postage stamp in Great Britain in 1840. This is widely esteemed as a pivotal event in encouraging the public use of postal services that eventually gave rise to the worldwide mail-carrying system we take for granted today.

As in any other sphere of human endeavor, there are multiple claimants for some honors, among which we have tried to select the one most commonly acknowledged. Where multiple dates were available, we have chosen the earliest of those presented.

Some important events or "firsts" may not have been listed, either inadvertently or for lack of a specific citation. For example, the date of the first facsimile transmission by telephone line arguably belongs on this list, but could not be found. The editors will seriously consider any documented suggestions for qualified additions to this listing.

4000 B.C. — Postal service established in China.

3000 B.C. — Postal service established in Egypt (Third Dynasty) and Assyria. The earliest postal markings are letters from Egyptian court officials of this period, with the exhortation "In the name of the living king, speed." in red and blue markings.

1200 B.C. — Egyptians produce papyrus, a coarse translucent paper made from overlapped reed fiber.

539 B.C. — Persian Emperor Cyrus the Great establishes postal relay service, stationing fresh relays of men and horses, called angareion, along key routes in his empire.

250 B.C. — Roman postal system, or Cursus Publicus, uses small, two-wheeled vehicles to carry mail.

200 B.C. — Chinese use paper as writing material.

549 — historical records note the use of kites to carry letters from a Chinese city under seige.

645 — Japan establishes a mounted relay messenger service between major towns and cities.

1150 — the guild of butchers in Germany organizes the Metzger Post, recorded as the first of many international trade guild posts of the Middle Ages.

1150 — Bremen municipal post organized by the Hanseatic League.

1276 — first European paper mills get under way at Fabriano, Italy.

1282 — European papermakers introduce the use of watermarks as a control and papermaker identification device.

1290 — Amadeo Tassis establishes the Correiri Bergamaschie, a courier service in the Venetian Republic.

1402 — China's Imperial Courier Service is made available for public use.

1450 — Count Roger I of Thurn and Taxis is knighted by Emperor Frederick III for establishing a postal relay service linking northern Italy and the Tyrol.

1463 — houses in the Parisian district of Pont Notre Dame are the first to be numbered to facilitate mail delivery.

1464 — June 19: King Louis XI passes edict permitting use of French state post for private correspondence.

1487 — Venetians in Cyprus organize public postal service for use of the Knights Templar and Mediterranean merchants.

1505 — Jan. 18: Spain contracts with Franz von Taxis to maintain a postal system between Belgium and the Netherlands, Emperor Maximilian of Germany, the kings of France and Spain and several key French and Spanish cities.

1574 — Thurn and Taxis postal service made available to the public.

1574 — during the Spanish seige of Leiden, Holland, an organized carrier pigeon post carried messages to and from the city.

1588 — markings denoting the amount of postage paid or due are required by regulations on letters carried by the Toulouse-Paris messengers.

1633 — weekly packet boat service is inaugurated between Dover, England, and Calais, France.

1639 — Nov. 5: Richard Fairbanks of Boston appointed as postmaster of the Massachusetts Bay Colony, inaugurating the first public postal service in America.

1650 — the Thurn and Taxis postal service of Europe introduces the first horse-drawn mail coaches since Roman times.

1652 — first specification of a free franking privilege made in a decree of the Council of State that allowed letters to pass without charge through the mails between British Members of Parliament and specified government officials. The following year a related decree stated that such letters be endorsed "These are for the Service of the Commonwealth."

1653 — April 8: Under a mandate from King Louis XIV, Renouard de Villayer issued small slips of gummed paper with an inscription that translates as "Postage paid on ____ the ____ day of the year 1653." These were sold to various institutions for 1 sou each, and the sender was to fill in the spaces, affix the label to a letter and deposit the letter in another de Villayer innovation, the public mailbox. Though Renouard's Petite Poste was limited to Paris and ended in a failure, the postage paid labels are widely acknowledged as the first postage stamps.

1657 — Oliver Cromwell's Post Office Act gives the British Post Office a monopoly on the carriage of mail.

1661 — Aug. 12: Henry Bishop, the postmaster general of Britain, introduces the first postal datestamp, the so-called Bishop mark, which could be used to track the amount of time between the receipt of a letter at a post office and its delivery.

1661 — the first slogan postmark is applied in London to letters to addressees along the road to Kent: "THE POST FOR ALL KENT GOES EVERY NIGHT FROM THE ROUND HOUSE IN LOVE LANE & COMES EVERY MORNING."

1663 — first handstamped postage due markings were introduced at the Foreign Post Office in London, England.

1680 — April 1: William Dockwra establishes the London Penny Post to carry letters and small parcels between London and Westminster. His service also introduced the first handstamps to show prepayment and the first handstamps to indicate the hour of posting. It was suppressed in November 1682, and shortly afterward was re-opened under the aegis of the British Post Office.

1683 — "D'JARSEY" straightline postmarks are applied to mail from Jersey received at St. Malo, the earliest European postmark to indicate a town or place of origin.

1691 — mail is carried by boat on the Canal du Midi in France, the first use of canals to expedite postal service.

1693 — Duncan and John Campbell organize the first internal postal network in America to circulate their newspaper, *The Boston Newsletter*, to New York.

1745 — first censor marking, the manuscript endorsement "OPENED BY THE REBELS," is applied by the British Post Office to letters delayed in transit from Scotland to England during the Jacobite Rebellion.

1784 — Sept. 15: letters are carried, dropped and recovered from a balloon piloted by Vincent Lunardi in Hertfordshire, England.

1790 — the first blue papers are introduced, as is the first batonne-watermarked paper.

1792 — June 1: letters from Canada could be prepaid all the way to their destinations in the United States, the first time that a letter mailed in one country was accepted as prepaid correspondence by another.

1800 — mailboxes for the posting of unpaid letters appear in France and Prussia.

1802 — British Board of Customs and Excise introduces adhesive labels to show prepayment of taxes on various dutiable items, such as patent medicines.

1812—Jan. 23: the first river steamer mail is carried by the steamboat *New Orleans* up the Mississippi from Louisiana to Natchez.

1818 — Nov. 7: sale of prestamped lettersheets begins in Sardinia, as mandated by royal edict. Three different denominations and handstamped designs showing a mounted messenger blowing a horn are produced, reflecting three different distances that the lettersheets could be sent without the prepayment of further fees.

1821 — said to be the year of use of a red oval adhesive label on a parcel from Dublin, Ireland, to Ludlow, England, inscribed "FROM C & R ELLIOTT'S LONDON & DUBLIN PARCEL OFFICE, 33 SACKVILLE ST OPPOSITE THE GENERAL POST OFFICE DUBLIN," and rated 6/6d.

1825 — a dandy roll watermarking device is patented in England.

1826 — John Marshall of England introduces the use of wire bits with the dandy roll, by which any desired watermark could be produced.

1830 — Nov. 11: first unofficial railway mail is carried on the route from Liverpool to Manchester, England.

1833 — Aug. 4: the SS *Royal William* leaves Quebec City for London, England, via Pictou, Nova Scotia, carrying the first unofficial transatlantic mail to travel by steamship.

1838 — Jan. 24: first railway mail-sorting car is introduced on the run from Birmingham to Liverpool, England.

1838 — April 4: first official transatlantic steamship mail carried from Cork, Ireland, to New York City by the British steamer *Sirius*.

1838 — Oct. 27: the first device to transfer mailbags to and from a moving train is installed on the London to Liverpool line in England.

1838 — Nov. 1: 1-penny lettersheets embossed with the seal of the colony are issued by the postmaster general at Sydney to prepay local correspondence. The first unambiguous item of postal stationery also received the first postal cancellation, a handstamp showing the time of delivery across the colorless embossed design.

1838 — first overland mail run in Australia between Melbourne and Sydney.

1839 — February: William Frederick Harnden founds the first North American private express mail service operating between New York City and Boston.

1840 — May 1: First day of issue for the Penny Black of Great Britain, the world's first adhesive postage stamp. The stamps became valid for postage on May 6, though usages before that date are known. Accompanying the stamp into service were the first stamp cancellation devices, brass handstamps in the so-called Maltese Cross pattern. These imperforate stamps were also the first watermarked issue.

1840 — the first forged stamps appear, crude counterfeits of the Penny Black made from a wood engraving. An electrotyped forgery of the same stamp was discovered the following March as well, which lead to the first prosecution and conviction for stamp forgery.

1842 — Feb. 1: first adhesive postage stamps for a local postal service issued by the New York City Despatch Post.

1843 — March 1: first lithographic postage stamps issued by the Swiss canton of Zurich on red-lined security paper.

1843 — Aug. 1: first South American postage stamps are issued by Brazil.

1844 — May: the British Post Office introduces the first numeral cancels, which indicated the country and office of origin by a combination of their shape and the numeral in the design.

1847 — April 19: the first stamp error is produced, a Penny Red from plate 77 with the right-hand letter "A" omitted at position BA.

1847 — Sept. 21: first colonial postage stamps are issued by Mauritius.

1847 — Oct. 1: Henry Archer submits proposal to the British postmaster general for the construction of experimental machines to facilitate the separation of individual stamps from stamp sheets. An experimental perforator and a rouletting machine are later constructed.

1849 — the British security printing firm Perkins Bacon pioneers the use of interchangeable designs for different nations with the Seated Britannia issues of Mauritius (1849), Trinidad (1851) and Barbados (1852) in which only the inscription and color changed.

1850 — Jan. 1: first Australian postage stamps are issued by the colony of New South Wales.

1850 — German-Austrian convention between the Austro-Hungarian Empire, nine German states or services and three Austrian-dominated principalities in northern Italy marks first international postal union.

1851 — first bisects are created when 3-penny and 6d stamps of New Brunswick are cut in half and combined to pay combination rates for which no stamps of the correct denomination were available.

1852 — July 1: first Asian postage stamps are issued for use in the Indian district of Sind.

1853 — June: first duplex cancellations, combining the functions of canceling the stamp and identifying the post office and date of posting, are introduced by the London district post for use on letters posted too late for the last run of the day.

1854 — Jan. 28: Great Britain introduces the first general issue of perforated stamps, the Penny Red in perf gauge 16.

1854 — July: Spain issues the first Official postage stamps.

1855 — first special event postmark introduced for the Exposition Universelle in Paris, France.

1857 — September: first trials of an experimental mechanized stamp cancellation machine in London, England.

1857 — Great Britain officially adopts black as the standard ink for postal cancellations.

1859 — Jan. 1: France issues the first postage due stamp, a 10-centime denomination.

1859 — Aug. 17: John Wise in the balloon *Jupiter* carries prepaid letters

1860 — Oct. 1: first shipboard mail-sorting begins with the inauguration of the Holyhead and Kingstown packet service.

1860 — Oct. 1: first shipboard mail sorting begins with the inauguration of the Holyhead and Kingstown packet service.

1863 — May 11: opening of the first Paris Postal Conference under chairman Montgomery Blair, postmaster general of the United States.

1864 — March 1: following a successful invasion by Austrian and Prussian forces, the duchy of Holstein is the site of the first occupation postage stamps.

1866 — Dr. Jacques Amable Le Grand invents the perforation gauge in Paris, France.

1866 — India overprints regular stamps "Service" for Official use and overprints revenue stamps "POSTAGE" for postal use.

1867 — Straits Settlements creates the first surcharged stamps, overprinting Indian issues with a crown and a new value in Straits Settlements currency.

1867 — Frances Wirth invents the first high-speed canceling machine in Germany.

1868 — the first stamps provisionally overprinted to denote a political change are issues of Spain, Cuba and Puerto NACION" when the monarchy was overthrown by a junta.

1870 — Sept. 5: first of 31 unmanned balloon carrying messages from the besieged French city of Metz is launched. Also under siege by the Prussians, Paris witnessed the departure of its first manned mail-carrying balloon, *Le Neptune*, piloted by Jules Duruof, on Sept. 23.

1874 — Sept. 15: opening of postal conference at Bern, Switzerland, attended by delegates from 22 countries. An agreement to create a worldwide postal union was reached on Oct. 9, ratified the following May 5, and came into effect in most participating nations on July 1, 1875.

1874 — UPU regulations require some form of identification on the country of issue on all stamps issued by member-nations.

1874 — Hong Kong sanctions use of 1867 revenue stamps as postage stamps as well, the first postal-fiscal issues.

1876 — May: the first unequivocal commemorative is issued in the form of two 3¢ pictorial stamped envelopes produced by the United States for the Centennial Exposition in Philadelphia.

1877 — June 19: 5¢ stamps specially printed for the occasion are used with regular United States stamps on mail carried on the flight of the balloon *Buffalo* from Nashville to Gallatin, Tenn.

1878 — May 2: second Paris Postal Conference convened. Delegates from 38 nations name the organization for the worldwide regulation of international mail the Universal Postal Union.

1879 — July: full shipboard postal service is first inaugurated on *SS Columba* and *SS Iona* on the route between Greenock and Ardrishaig, Scotland.

1879 — the British security printing firm De La Rue produces a 2 1/2-penny Victoria definitive for Nevis and the same design, color and denomination later the same year for Antigua, changing only the name of the colony. This so-called keyplate concept, in which a single design could be used to furnish many denominations for many different countries, was adopted widely, especially for colonial issues, and used on British Commonwealth stamps as late as the mid-1950s.

1879 — the practice of circulating specimens of new postal issues among UPU member-nations is inaugurated.

1880 — first fully automated steam-powered canceling machine is invented by Thomas and Martin Leavitt of Boston, Mass.

1886 — mailboxes installed on New York City streetcars.

1887 — July: the first adhesive commemorative postage stamp is issued, a 2-pfennig private local post issue by the Private Letter Co. of Frankfurt-am-Main, Germany, for the Ninth German Federal and Jubilee Shooting Competition.

1887 — Precancels first authorized in the United States.

1888 — the first government-authorized commemorative set is a series of six designs produced by New South Wales to mark the 100th anniversary of settlement at Sydney Cove.

1890 — July 2: the first item of semi-postal stationery is issued, a 1-penny pictorial stamped envelope for the golden jubilee of penny postage. It sold for 1/-, the remaining 11d going to the Rowland Hill Benevolent Fund for Post Office Widows and Orphans.

1892 — the 400th anniversary of the arrival of Columbus in the New World becomes the first event to spark related commemoratives in different countries, including many Latin American nations, followed by the United States in 1893 and Grenada and Trinidad in 1898.

1893 — the first machine cancellation to use a promotional slogan instead of canceling bars is used to advertise Chicago's Columbian Exposition.

1895 — the first stamp booklet is issued by Luxembourg.

1897 — June: first semipostal stamps are produced by New South Wales to aid a tuberculosis sanatorium.

1897 — the first self-propelled mail truck, a steam-powered van, is inaugurated by the British Post Office in service between London and Surrey. Also in 1897, a gasoline-powered mail vehicle was used experimentally at the main post office in London.

1898 — a Daimler mail truck powered by a gasoline-driven engine enters British mail service between Reading and Newbury.

1898 — November: stamps are issued by the Original Great Barrier Pigeongram Service to frank mail borne by carrier pigeon from Great Barrier Island and Auckland, New Zealand.

1898 — UPU Congress at Washington, D.C., sets forth plan for the international color coding of stamps: green to signify international printed matter, red for postcard and blue for letter-rate stamps.

1898 — first omnibus issue in which one design is used by more than one nation is produced by Portugal and the Portuguese colonies to mark the 400th anniversary of Vasco de Gama's discovery of an oceanic route to India.

1904 — first meter franking machine enters service in Christchurch, New Zealand.

1905 — June 1: a Daimler bus of the Bavarian Post Office makes the first postal bus run between Bad Tolz and Longgries.

1908 — August: an unofficial flight from Paris to St. Nazaire marks the first mail flown by a heavier-than-air vehicle.

1909 — Sept. 25: the collecting of first-day covers is prefigured with the preparation by a private stationery firm of special souvenir envelopes for the 2¢ Hudson-Fulton commemorative issued by the United States.

1910 — Sept. 23: a few cards are unofficially carried on the first international heavier-than-air airmail flight from Brig, Switzerland, across the Alps to Domodossola, Italy, where Peruvian pilot Jorge Chavez crashed and died.

1911 — Feb. 18: first official airmail carried from Allahabad to Naini, India, during the United Provinces Exhibition.

1912 — Feb. 26: first semiofficial airmail stamps are issued in Germany for a flight from Bork to Bruck.

1917 — May 16: first airmail stamp issued by a government is an Italian 25-centesimo Express Delivery stamp with a special overprint for experimental airmail flights between Rome and Turin that began six days later.

1918 — May 13: first regular issue airmail stamps go on sale, the 24¢ Jenny airmail intended for use on the Washington, Philadelphia and New York route that was inaugurated on May 15.

1919 — June 14: Alcock and Brown complete the first non-stop mail-carrying transatlantic flight from St. John's, Newfoundland, to Clifden, Ireland.

1922 — the Geneva-based League of Nations becomes the first international organization to issue its own stamps.

1922 — Jan. 1: use of meters to frank international mail is sanctioned by UPU member-nations.

1923 — Jan. 3: Luxembourg issues the first souvenir sheet, containing a single 10-franc definitive in green instead of the black of the sheet-format issue on the occasion of the birth of Princess Elizabeth.

1923 — Sept. 1: George W. Linn creates the first cacheted first-day cover for the 2¢ Harding Memorial issue, consisting of a black-bordered mourning envelope with a five line inscription.

1928 — Aug. 23: first catapult mail from French liner *Ile de France* to French coast, saving one day in mail transit time. Experimental flights had been conducted on Aug. 8 and Aug. 12.

1930 — the first automated high-speed pre-delivery mail sorting machine is installed at the head post office in Rotterdam, the Netherlands.

1934 — first experiments to produce an automatic high-speed facing and cancellation machine are begun at the Dollis Hill post office research station in London, England.

1939 — May 17: Pitney-Bowes in New York City introduces its Mailomat combination franking and mailing machine that included a coin-operated postage meter and was intended to function as a fully automated post office.

1942 — Germany adopts the first national postal code system a simple two-digit marking.

1952 — May: a BOAC Comet-1 inaugurates the first jet airmail service between London, England, and Johannesburg, South Africa.

1956 — Sept. 15: the six member-nations of the European Coal and Steel Community each produce a pair of stamps of uniform design with the word "EUROPA" as the central design feature, thus beginning a series that has continued ever since.

1957 — Nov. 19: Great Britain tests automated mail-sorting equipment at Southampton using current definitives with graphite lines on the reverse side.

1957 — Dec. 19: automatic letter facing machine is installed in Southampton, England.

1958 — Oct. 4: first transatlantic jet airmail service inaugurated by BOAC between London and New York. Pan-Am begins similar service between New York and Paris on Oct. 26.

1959 — Nov. 18: Phosphored bands are printed on British stamps in a further test of automated mail-sorting equipment.

1962 — Jan. 13: Phosphor-tagged stamps are issued by Canada for trial use with experimental mail-sorting equipment installed in Winnipeg, Manitoba, with tests commencing March 13.

1963 — June 17: Tonga introduces first self-adhesive postage stamps.

1968 — number of worldwide post offices peaks at 437,168, as recorded in a three-volume compendium by the Universal Postal Union.

1974 — Sept. 6: *Westar*, a U.S. communications satellite, relays the first message from New Jersey to California in a new Mailgram service, a joint venture of the United States Postal Service and Western Union. Messages could be electronically relayed over great distances for rapid prepaid delivery by either telegraph or regular mail.

1975 — June 23: The first coin-operated postage label vending machine is installed at a post office in Shibuyai, Japan. Similar machines manufactured by Frama are introduced in Switzerland on Aug. 8, 1976.

1982 — Jan. 4: Electronic Computer-Originated Mail service (E-COM) is inaugurated by the USPS, enabling bulk mailers to transmit text to any of 25 major mail centers for printing and forwarding to recipients.

1982 — Feb. 15: Western Airlines issues the first of a number of what are essentially intercity airmail carrier adhesives, enabling customers to prepay next-day delivery of a letter to a designated city where it would be placed in the mail stream for regular delivery by USPS requiring the usual stamps.

1983 — July 18: USPS inaugurates Express Mail next day service and stamps for prepayment of two-pound packages. The service had been in development since mid-1970.

1983 — Nov. 21: Canada Post tests labels allowing Christmas card mailers to precode envelopes for sorting by optical scanner in exchange for a discount on postage rates with its "Stick 'n Tick" labels. The test, confined to Winnipeg, Manitoba, is expanded to seven additional cities in 1984 and later introduced on a national basis with some modifications.

1986 — May 18: USPS inaugurates international priority airmail service from New York, Chicago, Boston and Washington, D.C.

1987 — Dec. 14: On this, the peak day of the Christmas season, the USPS handles 168,000,000 pieces of mail, believed the largest one-day total handled by any postal administration ever.

1988 — Jan. 1: British Post Office introduces new insured two-day business-to-business International Datapost service between London and Moscow.

1989 — Aug. 23: USPS inaugurates Autopost service in Washington, D.C. The Autopost system automatically weighs mail and dispenses a self-adhesive postage label indicating the amount of postage, date, class of mail service, weight of piece, ZIP code of the post office, identification of the automat machine and a transaction number.

Stamp-Issuing Entities

Since Great Britain issued the Penny Black and Two-Pence Blue in 1840, postage stamps have been issued in the name of more than 700 geopolitical entities. This has resulted in an array of stamps that may bewilder the beginning stamp collector, especially the collector whose study of history has somehow not included such areas as Alaouites or Trebizond.

In the following listing, we have attempted to provide a compilation of the nations, provinces, cities, armies and other entities that have, at one point or another, issued postage stamps.

For the purposes of this listing, we have limited listings of stamp-issuing entities to those authorities exercising de facto political control of an area or territory, which have issued stamps for other than strictly local use. We have omitted issues produced purely for municipal or private use.

We have attempted to provide brief geographical and historical sketches for each of these entities, so that the reader may obtain a general idea of where the country issuing a given stamp is located and its general circumstances and background.

We have not attempted to give complete philatelic background of all stamp-issuing entities. All entities are listed as active or inactive, the dates in the parentheses following the name of the country indicating the period of time during which stamps have been issued. A perusal of any of the leading catalogs and general non-philatelic reference sources will supply additional information, and is highly recommended.

We have also attempted to indicate population where possible, including the most current figures we could find for territories that are now issuing stamps. For so-called dead countries, those entities no longer producing stamps, we have tried to supply the latest population estimate available from the period during which stamps were issued.

Numbers of stamps issued have been indicated for most nations, with estimates for those currently issuing stamps and an absolute number of varieties for those listed in the major catalogs. For the interest of the reader, we have also indicated the average number of stamps issued per year circa 1975-88 or the portion thereof during which stamps have been issued.

- A -

ABU DHABI (1964-72)

Stamp-issuing status: inactive; Population: 25,000 (1971 estimate); Stamps issued: 83.

A sheikdom in the former Trucial States in eastern Arabia, bordering on the Persian Gulf.

Under British protection 1862-1971, Abu Dhabi joined with the other Trucial States to form the independent United Arab Emirates on Dec. 2, 1971.

Long undeveloped, with few resources, Abu Dhabi's medieval existence began to change dramatically with the discovery of oil in 1958. By the 1970s, it had become a major oil exporter and enjoyed one of the highest per capita incomes in the world.

ADEN (1937-65)

Stamp-issuing status: inactive; Population: 220,000; Stamps issued: 173.

Former British colony and protectorate in southwest Arabia. The colony of Aden was attached to India 1839-1937, and Indian stamps were used.

Stamps of the colony were first issued in 1937, being used in most of the Aden protectorate area, as well as within the Aden colony itself.

In 1963, the two districts, except for the eastern Kathiri and Qu'aiti states, united to form the Federation of South Arabia.

Aden stamps were replaced by those of the Federation on April 1, 1965.

AEGEAN ISLANDS (Individual Islands' Issues) (1912-32)

Stamp-issuing status: inactive; Stamps issued: less than 125.

A number of Italian issues were

overprinted with names of the various Aegean islands including Calchi, Calino, Caso, Coo, Fero, Fisso, Nisiro, Patmo, Piscopi, Rhodes (Rodi), Scarpanto, Simi and Stampalia.

AEGEAN ISLANDS (DODECANESE) (1912-47)

Stamp-issuing status: inactive.

A group of 12 islands in the southeastern Aegean Sea.

Under Turkish rule since the early 16th century, the islands declared their independence in 1912, during the Italo-Turkish War, but were soon occupied by Italy. Greece recognized Italian control of the islands in 1920, and Turkey formally ceded them to Italy in 1923.

Occupied by Germany after the Italian collapse in 1943, they were liberated by the British in 1945.

Italy issued a large number of stamps for use in the islands from 1912-43, while the Germans overprinted a few issues from 1943-45.

During 1945-47, stamps of the British Middle East Forces were used. In 1947, specially overprinted Greek stamps were used. Regular Greek issues have been used since 1947, when the islands were annexed by Greece.

AFARS AND ISSAS, FRENCH TERRITORY OF THE (1967-1977)

Stamp-issuing status: inactive; Stamps issued: 189.

A French overseas territory in northeast Africa bordering on the Gulf of Aden. Formerly the Somali Coast, a French colony.

On June 27, 1977, on the occasion of this territory becoming independent, the name was changed to Djibouti.

AFGHANISTAN (1871-)

Stamp-issuing status: active; Population: 15 million; Stamps issued: more than 1,200; Issues per year for last decade: 21.

A republic in central Asia. Long divided and ruled by neighboring states, Afghanistan's history as a unified nation began in 1747, when Afghanistan was freed and established a large empire in east Persia and northwest India.

During the 19th century, Afghani power declined, and during 1881-1919, the country was dominated by the British.

After 1919, Afghanistan broke away from British influence. In 1973, the monarchy was replaced by a republican government.

The republic was overthrown in a pro-Soviet coup in 1978. The new regime was unable to unify the country or to quell conservative resistance in the countryside.

In December 1979, the U.S.S.R. invaded Afghanistan, establishing what it hoped would be a more effective government. During 1980-81, the 60,000-100,000 Soviet troops and the regular Afghan army were unable to defeat the rebels, who remained in control of much of the country.

AGUERA, LA (1920-24)

Stamp-issuing status: inactive; Stamps issued: 26.

District in the western Sahara on the Atlantic coast. A Spanish possession, La Aguera issued its own stamps until 1924, when it was attached to the Spanish Sahara.

AITUTAKI (1903-32, 1972-)

Stamp-issuing status: active; Population: 3,000; Stamps issued: more than 400; Issues per year for last decade: 32.

One of the Cook Islands in the South Pacific Ocean, northeast of New Zealand. Aitutaki issued its own stamps until 1932, when these were replaced by those of the Cook Islands. In August 1972, Aitutaki resumed issuing its own stamps.

AJMAN (1964-72)

Stamp-issuing status: inactive.

One of the Trucial States in eastern Arabia. A sheikdom under British protection from 1892-1971, Ajman joined the independent United Arab Emirates on Dec. 2, 1971.

UAE issues replaced those of Ajman in 1972. Subsequent Ajman issues came on to the philatelic market after 1972, but these were not recognized as valid by the government.

ALAND (1984-)

Stamp-issuing status: active; Population: 21,211 (1978); Stamps issued: more than 30; Issues per year since 1984: 8.

Island group of 572 square miles in the Gulf of Bothnia between Finland and Sweden.

On Feb. 5, 1982, the Finnish government gave the self-governing territory of Aland the right to propose stamps and denominations to Finnish postal authorities. The first Aland issues appeared on March 1, 1984. Although Finnish stamps remain valid for use on the islands, and mixed Finnish and Aland frankings do occur there, Aland stamps may not be used in Finland.

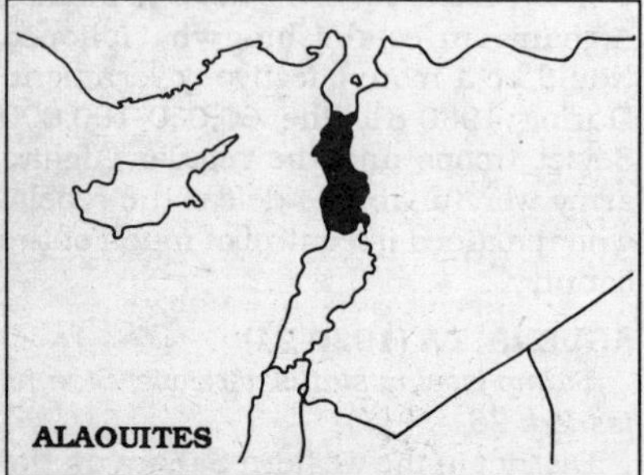

ALAOUITES (1925-30)

Stamp-issuing status: inactive; Stamps issued: 73.

A district of Syria, bordering on the Mediterranean Sea. Alaouites was under Turkish rule until 1918, when it was occupied by the French.

During 1920-41, it was ruled by France under mandate from the League of Nations.

In 1930, the name of the province was changed to Latakia, and stamps so inscribed came into use. In 1941, Latakia was annexed by Syria, and its issues were replaced by Syrian stamps.

ALBANIA (1913-)

Stamp-issuing status: active; Population: 3 million; Stamps issued: more than 2,200; Issues per year for last decade: 56.

A republic in southeast Europe, bordering on the Adriatic Sea. Under Turkish rule from 1478-1912, Albania became independent after the first Balkan War.

Overrun by German, Serbian, Montenegrin, Greek, Bulgarian, Italian, French and Austrian troops during World War I, foreign forces remained in Albania until 1921.

In 1939, the country was occupied by Italy and, later, Germany. In 1944, British-supported Communist guerrillas drove the Germans from the country and established a provisional government.

In 1946, a Communist people's republic was proclaimed. At first it appeared that Albania would become a satellite of Yugoslavia, but it has stubbornly maintained its independence. In 1960, because of the Soviet Union's de-Stalinization campaign, Albania broke with the U.S.S.R. and aligned its foreign policy with that of the People's Republic of China. In 1978 China's liberalization brought a break between that country and Albania.

Albania is the most economically undeveloped of the Eastern European nations.

ALDERNEY (1983-)

Stamp-issuing status: active; Population: 2,086 (1981 estimate); Stamps issued: more than 40; Issues per year since 1983: 8.

A small English Channel island just off the French coast near the tip of the Cherbourg peninsula.

Alderney is part of the Bailiwick of Guernsey, which has been a British crown territory since the mid-13th century. After it began issuing stamps in 1969, Guernsey handled Alderney's postal affairs. Alderney's request to produce separate issues was rejected by Guernsey in 1975, but a later compromise allowed Alderney to issue occasional sets of stamps. Alderney's issues — typically about one set each year — are produced under the aegis of the Bailiwick of Guernsey Post Office in consultation with Alderney's parliamentary finance committee.

ALEDSCHEN (ALSEDZIAI) (1941)

Stamp-issuing status: inactive; Stamps issued: 36.

A city in Lithuania. In 1941, the local German military commander overprinted Russian stamps "Laisvi/Alsedziai/24-VI-41" for use in the area.

ALEXANDERSTADT (BOLSCHAJA ALEXANDROWKA) (1941-42)

Stamp-issuing status: inactive; Stamps issued: 16.

A city in the Ukraine. During 1941-42, the local German military authorities issued Russian stamps surcharged with a "16.8.41/B.ALEX." swastika overprint and surcharged with new values for use in the district.

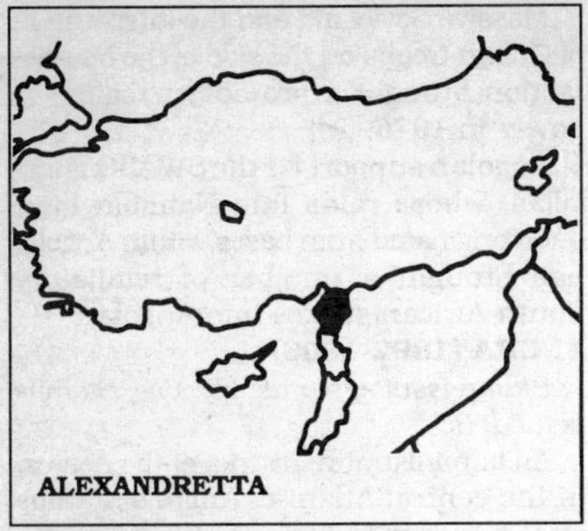

ALEXANDRETTA (1938)

Stamp-issuing status: inactive; Stamps issued: 31.

A district of southern Turkey, bordering on the Mediterranean Sea. Alexandretta was part of the Ottoman Turkish Empire for several hundred years, until its occupation by the French in 1918.

It was administered as part of the French mandate of Syria until 1938, when it became autonomous from Syria, its name being changed to Hatay.

Stamps of Hatay replaced those of Alexandretta. In 1939, the territory was returned to Turkey, and Turkish stamps have since been in use.

ALEXANDRIA (1899-1931)

Stamp-issuing status: inactive; Stamps issued: 105.

An Egyptian port on the Mediterranean Sea.

The French Post Office in Alexandria operated from 1830 through March 31, 1931. Regular French issues were used until 1899, when separate issues were begun for Alexandria.

ALGERIA (1924-58, 1962-)

Stamp-issuing status: active; Population: 21.5 million; Stamps issued: more than 1,025; Issues per year for last decade: 25.

A republic in Northern Africa. Under Turkish rule from 1518-1830, Algeria was occupied by France after 1830.

During World War II, it was under the pro-Nazi Vichy regime until 1943, when it was occupied by U.S.-Free French forces.

In 1958, Algeria became an integral part of France, and French stamps replaced those of the colony. In 1962, Algeria became independent and resumed issuing its own stamps.

During 1967-74, Algeria maintained close ties with the U.S.S.R., but in recent years, it has moved into a more neutral position.

Despite oil earnings and attempts at land reform and industrialization, Algeria is plagued by endemic poverty and unemployment.

ALLENSTEIN (1920)

Stamp-issuing status: inactive; Population: 540,000 (1920 estimate); Stamps issued: 28.

A district of East Prussia, Allenstein was one of those territories administered by the Allies until 1920, when a local plebiscite resulted in the area's return to Germany.

German stamps overprinted for Allenstein were used during the plebiscite period. Since the end of World War II, this area has been a part of Poland.

ALSACE AND LORRAINE (1870-72, 1940-41)

Stamp-issuing status: inactive; Stamps issued: 28.

Two districts lying between France and Germany. Long disputed, these areas were annexed by Germany in 1871, retaken by France in 1918, retaken by Germany in 1939, and finally re-occupied by France in 1945.

German occupation issues for Alsace and Lorraine were used throughout occupied France from 1870-71 and in the two provinces from 1870-72.

Individual overprints on German stamps were produced for Alsace and for Lorraine in 1940. On Jan. 1, 1942, they were replaced by regular German stamps.

ALWAR (1877-1902)

Stamp-issuing status: inactive; Stamps issued: 4.

A former feudatory state in Northern India, southwest of Delhi. Separate issues were used until 1902, after which they were replaced by Indian stamps.

AMIENS (1909)

Stamp-issuing status: inactive.

A city in northern France. During May 13-19, 1909, local provisionals were issued by the Chamber of Commerce during a strike by postal employees.

AMUR PROVINCE (1920)

Stamp-issuing status: inactive.

Between February and April 1920, a People's Revolutionary Committee ruled at Blagoveschensk, in southeastern Siberia. The Amur Province was absorbed by the Far Eastern Republic, when that state was formed on April 6, 1920.

ANDAMAN AND NICOBAR ISLANDS (1942)

Stamp-issuing status: inactive.

Located in the Indian Ocean, these islands were first settled by the British in 1789. Subsequently, they fell under the administration of the governor-general of India and now form part of the Indian republic.

During World War II, the islands were occupied by the Japanese. At this time, contemporary British Indian stamps were crudely surcharged for use in the islands.

ANDORRA (1928-)

Stamp-issuing status: active; Population: 45,000; Stamps issued: (French) more than 425, (Spanish) more than 175; Issues per year for last decade: (French) 13, (Spanish) 8.

An autonomous enclave in the Pyrenees Mountains, jointly administered by France and the Spanish bishop of Urgel. Stamps are issued by both France and Spain for use in the principality.

ANGOLA (1870-)

Stamp-issuing status: active; Population: 8.5 million; Stamps issued: more than 800; Issues per year for last decade: 14.

A former Portuguese colony in southwestern Africa. The Angolan coast came under Portuguese control in the 16th century, while the interior was conquered during the late 19th century.

Angolan nationalist groups waged a guerrilla war against the Portuguese during 1961-74. In 1974 Portugal agreed to the independence of the country, and on Nov. 11, 1975, Angola became an independent nation.

With the withdrawal of Portugal, the three largest of the nationalist groups quickly fell out over the composition of the new government.

The ensuing civil war caused most of the whites remaining in Angola to emigrate and brought the economic collapse of the country.

Massive Soviet aid and the intervention of Cuban troops on the side of the Marxist faction brought a pro-Soviet regime to power in 1976.

Angolan support for the SWAPO guerrillas, whose raids into Namibia have often originated from bases within Angola, has brought a number of retaliatory South African strikes into Angola.

ANGRA (1892-1906)

Stamp-issuing status: inactive; Stamps issued: 35.

An administrative district of the Azores, in the central Atlantic. Angra's stamps were replaced by those of the Azores in 1906. Since 1931, regular Portuguese stamps have been used in the district.

ANGUILLA (1967-)

Stamp-issuing status: active; Population: 7,000; Stamps issued: more than 760; Issues per year for last decade: 45.

A small island in the Caribbean, formerly attached to St. Kitts-Nevis-Anguilla. In September 1967, Anguilla declared its independence from both that state and Great Britain. In 1971 direct British control was re-established.

ANJOUAN (1892-1914)

Stamp-issuing status: inactive; Population: 22,000 (1987 estimate); Stamps issued: 30.

One of the Comoro Islands in the Indian Ocean near Madagascar. The sultanate of Anjouan came under French protection in 1886, and separate stamp issues began in 1892. Stamps of Anjouan were replaced by those of Madagascar in 1914. In 1950, issues of the Comoro Islands came into use.

ANNAM AND TONKIN (1888-92)

Stamp-issuing status: inactive; Stamps issued: 6.

Roughly, the area of Tonkin and Annam Protectorates corresponds with modern Vietnam. From 1892, regular issues of French Indo-China were used, although in 1936, Indo-China issued a separate set for Annam.

Since 1945, stamps of the People's Democratic Republic of Vietnam have been used in the north, while those of the republic of Vietnam were used in the south from 1954-75.

ANTEQUERA (1936)

Stamp-issuing status: inactive.

A city in the province of Malaga, in southern Spain.

Contemporary Spanish stamps were overprinted for local use on the authority of the Falangist military commander in October 1936.

ANTIGUA (1862-)

Stamp-issuing status: active; Population: 79,000; Stamps issued: more than 1,100; Issues per year for last decade: 59.

A state in association with Great Britain, comprising the island of Antigua and several smaller islands in the eastern Caribbean, southeast of Puerto Rico.

Under British rule since 1632, Antigua became a separate colony in 1956. In 1967 Antigua became self-governing and became the independent state of Antigua-Barbuda in 1981.

Stamp-issuing dependencies of Antigua are Barbuda and Redonda.

ARAD (1919)

Stamp-issuing status: inactive; Stamps issued: 55.

A district of pre-World War I Hungary, occupied by France in 1919, at which time overprinted Hungarian stamps were issued. The district is now a part of Romania.

ARBE (RAB) (1920)

Stamp-issuing status: inactive.

An island in the Mali Kvarner, off the northwestern coast of Yugoslavia. During d'Annunzio's occupation of Fiume, issues were overprinted for Arbe.

ARGENTINA (1858-)

Stamp-issuing status: active; Population: 30.6 million; Stamps issued: more than 2,000; Issues per year for last decade: 51.

A republic in southern South America. Independent from Spain in 1816, Argentina was torn by regional separatism through much of the 19th century. This is reflected in the issuing of separate stamps by several Argentine provinces during 1858-80.

Large-scale European immigration and investment after the 1880s made Argentina the most economically advanced nation in South America.

Since 1930, Argentina has, more often than not, been ruled by authoritarian military regimes. During World War II, the government was sympathetic to the Axis, and after the war, a large number of ex-Nazis found sanctuary in Argentina.

In 1946, Juan Domingo Peron was elected president, and he dominated the country's political life until his death in 1974, although he was in exile 1955-73.

Chronic, unresolved economic and social tensions erupted into virtual civil war during 1976-80. Both leftist guerrillas, and the military government used terror and violence to further their ends. Thousands died in the conflict.

Although the government suppressed the radical terrorists and restored some semblance of order, Argentina's economy had deteriorated badly. High unemployment and spiraling inflation have provoked intense popular dissatisfaction with the ruling junta. Argentina's seizure of the Falkland Islands in early April 1982, was, at least in part, an attempt to unify the nation behind the regime.

ARGYROKASTRON (GJINOKASTER) (1914)

Stamp-issuing status: inactive; Stamps issued: 16.

A city in Southern Albania. Turkish stamps were surcharged for use during the area's occupation by Greece.

ARMAVIR (1920)

Stamp-issuing status: inactive.

A city in northern Caucasus, Russia. Two Russian stamps were surcharged by the local authorities.

ARMENIA (1919-23)

Stamp-issuing status: inactive; Population: 1.2 million (1923 estimate); Stamps issued: 310.

The westernmost area of the Caucasus. Long under a vague Turkish suzerainty, Armenia was conquered by the Russians during the 19th century.

During World War I Armenia was occupied by Turco-German forces. Between May 1918 and December 1920, and again between February and April 1921, it existed as an independent republic, issuing its own stamps.

In 1923, it joined the Transcaucasian Federation of Soviet Republics. Transcaucasian issues were soon superseded by those of the Soviet Union.

ARMY OF THE NORTH (1919)

Stamp-issuing status: inactive; Stamps issued: 5.

During 1919, the Army of the North, under Gen. Rodzianko, fought against the Soviet forces in the Petrograd (Leningrad) area. This army was subsequently incorporated into Gen. Nikolai N. Yudenitch's Army of the Northwest.

ARMY OF THE NORTHWEST (1919)

Stamp-issuing status: inactive; Stamps issued: 14.

An anti-Bolshevik force under the command of General Yudenitch, which operated in northwestern Russia around the city of Pskov. Between June and November 1919, this army threatened the Soviets in Petrograd (Leningrad). In November it was defeated by the Red Army and dissolved.

ARMY OF THE WEST (1919)

Stamp-issuing status: inactive; Stamps issued: 12.

The Western Army was formed in Courland in 1919 to maintain German influence in the Baltic States. It was primarily an instrument of the German High Command, which was forbidden to operate directly in the region.

The Army of the West was concerned less with the threat of the Bolsheviks in Russia than with restoring the domination of German landholders in the area, and so refused to cooperate with Yudenitch in fighting the Russians.

In November 1919, the army attacked Riga, but was thrown back by an Anglo-Latvian counter-offensive which brought about the force's dissolution.

ARUBA (1986-)

Stamp-issuing status: active; Population: 66,500; Stamps issued: more than 40; Issues per year since 1986: 20.

Southwesternmost of the six islands in the Netherlands Antilles of which it was formerly a part, Aruba is an island of 69 square miles east of Curacao and north of Venezuela's Paraguayana Peninsula. Aruba achieved a separate status within the kingdom of the Netherlands that will give the island complete independence by the mid-1990s. Aruba began issuing its own stamps Jan. 1, 1986.

ASCENSION (1922-)

Stamp-issuing status: active; Population: 1,700; Stamps issued: more than 420; Issues per year for last decade: 20.

An island in the South Atlantic Ocean. Occupied by the British in 1815, Ascension was attached to the crown colony of St. Helena in 1922.

ASCH (1938)

Stamp-issuing status: inactive; Stamps issued: 5.

A city in the Sudetenland (Czechoslovakia). Local authorities overprinted Czech stamps in 1938, upon the area's cession to Germany.

AUNUS (1919)

Stamp-issuing status: inactive; Stamps issued: 8.

Aunus, the Finnish name for Olonets, a Russian town, was occupied by Finnish forces in 1919. Finnish stamps overprinted with the town name were used during the occupation.

AUSTRALIA (1902-)

Stamp-issuing status: active; Population: 16 million (1986); Stamps issued: more than 1,150; Issues per year for last decade: 38.

An island continent between the Pacific and Indian Oceans, southeast of Asia. British settlement began in the late 18th century, with six colonies developing — New South Wales, Victoria, Queensland, South Australia, Western Australia and Tasmania. Each of these states initially issued its own stamps.

These colonies united to form the Commonwealth of Australia on Jan. 1, 1901, although each continued to issue its own stamps for a number of years.

Australia has rich natural resources and, since World War II, has developed into one of the major economic powers of the region. It has maintained close ties with the United States since 1945, although in recent years Japan has replaced the United States as Australia's main economic partner.

Australia administers a number of island groups in the South Pacific and plays a leading role in the region.

AUSTRALIAN ANTARCTIC TERRITORY (1957-)

Stamp-issuing status: active; Stamps issued: more than 55.

A large portion of Antarctica is claimed by Australia, which maintains scientific research stations there. Stamps of the Australian Antarctic Territory are also valid for postage in Australia.

AUSTRIA (1850-)

Stamp-issuing status: active; Population; 7.5 million (1986); Stamps issued: more than 2,200; Issues per year for last decade: 37.

A republic in central Europe, Austria was the center of the Hapsburg Empire, which during the 16th to 19th centuries controlled (at one time or another) Hungary, Czechoslovakia, Belgium, the Netherlands and large portions of Yugoslavia, Poland, Romania, Italy and Germany.

After 1815, Austrian power declined with the growth of nationalism among its subjects. In 1867, the Austro-Hungarian dual monarchy was created to appease Hungarian nationalists, but the government resisted similar concessions to other national groups.

The assassination of the Archduke Francis Ferdinand, heir to the Austro-Hungarian throne, in Sarajevo, Bosnia, on June 28, 1914, began the series of events that quickly led to World War I.

During World War I, Austrian troops were active in the Balkans, Romania, Poland, Russia and Italy, but by October 1918, Austria's armies were routed, and the monarchy collapsed.

The empire dissolved rapidly, and Austria emerged much reduced in size, representing the German-speaking area of the empire. In 1918 the republic of "German Austria" was formed, and there was considerable sentiment for annexation by Germany.

By the Treaty of St. Germain (1922), Austria was expressly forbidden to unite with Germany and the country's name became simply "Austria."

During the 1930s, an Austrian fascist regime attempted to maintain independence, but in March 1938, Germany invaded and quickly occupied the country, merging it into the Third Reich with only a token protest from the Allies.

In 1945, the Allies liberated Austria, and the republic was re-established.

In 1955, foreign troops were withdrawn, and Austria proclaimed its political neutrality.

Austria maintains close economic ties with much of western Europe.

AUSTRIAN OFFICES IN CRETE (1903-14)

Stamp-issuing status: inactive; Stamps issued: 24.

Like several other European nations, Austria maintained its own post offices in Crete, using stamps valued in French centimes and francs.

Although intended for use in Crete, these issues were available for use at Austrian post offices throughout the Turkish Empire.

AUSTRIAN OFFICES IN THE TURKISH EMPIRE (1867-1914)

Stamp-issuing status: inactive; Stamps issued: 85.

Austria began using special stamps for its offices in the Turkish Empire in 1867, having previously used its issues for Lombardy-Venetia for these offices.

Austrian post offices in the Turkish Empire were closed Dec. 15, 1914.

AVILA (1937)

Stamp-issuing status: inactive.

The capital city of the province of the same name, in central Spain.

A Nationalist overprint was applied to contemporary Spanish stamps by the local authorities.

AZERBAIJAN (IRANIAN) (1945-46)

Stamp-issuing status: inactive.

A province in northwestern Iran. Occupied by Soviet forces during World War II, a puppet government was established in May 1945, at which time contemporary Iranian stamps were overprinted for use.

In March 1946, Soviet troops withdrew, and Azerbaijan became an "autonomous" government. In December 1946, full Iranian administration was restored.

AZERBAIJAN (RUSSIAN) (1919-24)

Stamp-issuing status: inactive; Population: 2.1 million (1923 estimate); Stamps issued: 100.

The eastern portion of the Caucasus. Occupied by Russia in the 19th century, Azerbaijan declared its independence in 1917, after the Russian Revolution. Turkish and British occupation was followed by the establishment of a Communist regime in 1920.

Azerbaijan was incorporated into the Transcaucasian Federated Republic in 1923. Soviet stamps have been used since 1924.

AZORES (1868-1931, 1980-)

Stamp-issuing status: active; Population: 252,000; Stamps issued: more than 460; Issues per year for last decade: 8.

A group of islands in the North Atlantic. The islands used Portuguese stamps until 1868, when overprinted stamps came into use.

Separate Azores issues were replaced by regular Portuguese stamps in 1931. In 1980 Portugal again began to issue separate stamps for the Azores.

- B -

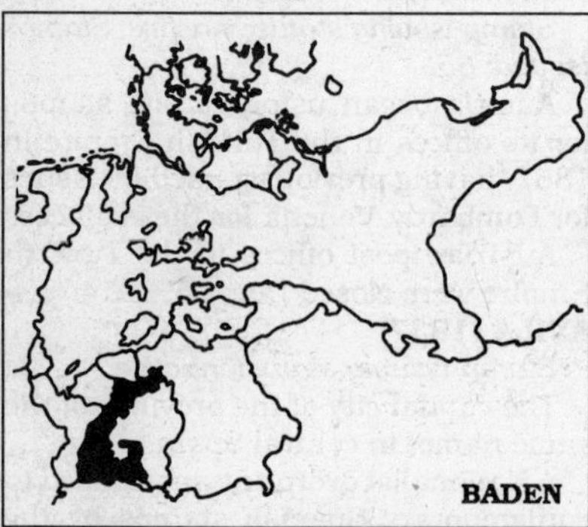

BADEN (1851-71, 1946-49)

Stamp-issuing status: inactive; Stamps issued: (1851-71) 33; (1946-49) 60.

A former grand duchy in southwestern Germany on the Rhine River. In 1870, it joined the German Empire.

After World War II, Baden was included in the French zone of occupation, and separate issues were again in use from 1945-49, with some issues valid for use in the German Federal Republic until March 31, 1950.

BAENA (1937)

Stamp-issuing status: inactive.

A city in the province of Cordoba in southern Spain.

In July 1937, contemporary Spanish stamps were overprinted to commemorate the anniversary of the Nationalist landing at Cadiz and the Nationalist occupation of Baena.

BAHAMAS (1859-)

Stamp-issuing status: active; Population: 238,000; Stamps issued: more than 600; Issues per year for last decade: 22.

A scattered group of some 700 islands and 2,000 islets in the Atlantic Ocean, east of Florida.

One of the Bahamian islands (San Salvador, now Watling Island) was the site of Columbus' first landfall in the New World. The Bahamas were largely bypassed by Europeans, however, until British settlement began in 1647. In 1783, the Bahamas became a British colony.

The Bahamas became self-governing in 1964 and fully independent in 1973. International banking and tourism are the country's major industries.

BAHAWALPUR (1945-50)

Stamp-issuing status: inactive; Stamps issued: 56.

A state of Pakistan. In 1947, the Moslem amir declared independence from India and joined Bahawalpur to Pakistan.

BAHRAIN (1933-)

Stamp-issuing status: active; Population: 400,000; Stamps issued: more than 330; Issues per year for last decade: 7.

An archipelago in the Persian Gulf. Under British protection 1861-1971, Bahrain used a variety of stamps: unoverprinted Indian stamps from 1884 to 1933; overprinted Indian issues 1933-48; overprinted British issues 1948-60; and its own designs from 1960.

Oil was first discovered in 1932 and has become, with international banking, the economic mainstay of a very prosperous Bahrain.

Tensions between the Sunnite majority (60 percent) and Shi'ite minority (40 percent) have grown since the establishment of the fundamentalist Shi'ite regime in Iran.

BAMRA (1888-94)

Stamp-issuing status: inactive; Stamps issued: 19.

A feudatory state in eastern India. Bamra issued separate stamps until 1894, when its issues were replaced by those of India.

BANAT, ("BANAT, BACSKA") BACSKA (1919)

Stamp-issuing status: inactive; Stamps issued: 52.

A district of south central Europe, formerly under Hungarian rule. In 1919, postal authorities at Temesvar overprinted Hungarian stamps, which were used largely to pay the salaries of postal workers.

The area is now divided between Yugoslavia and Romania.

BANGKOK (1882-85)

Stamp-issuing status: inactive; Stamps issued: 22.

The capital of Thailand. During 1855-85, Britain exercised extraterritorial privileges in Bangkok, which included the right to use her own stamps.

Straits Settlements stamps overprinted "B" were used until July 1, 1885.

BANGLADESH (1971-)

Stamp-issuing status: active; Population: 104 million; Stamps issued: more than 250; Issues per year for last decade: 18.

A republic in the Bengal region of south Asia. Formerly East Pakistan, Bangladesh declared its independence in April 1971.

After a bitter civil war, Pakistan was defeated by India and the rebels, and Bangladesh independence was recognized in December 1971.

Since independence, Bangladesh has suffered continuing economic problems and political instability. In foreign affairs, it is closely linked to India and the Soviet Union.

Before the issue of Bangladesh's first definitive set (and for some time thereafter), existing stocks of Pakistani stamps were overprinted locally, creating so many varieties that, at this time, no general catalog has attempted to list them.

BANJA LUKA (1941)

Stamp-issuing status: inactive; Stamps issued: 2.

A city in northern Bosnia (Yugoslavia). During World War II, two Yugoslavian stamps were overprinted by the local partisans for use in the area.

BARANYA (1919)

Stamp-issuing status: inactive; Stamps issued: 64.

A Hungarian district briefly occupied by Serbia after World War I.

BARBADOS (1852-)

Stamp-issuing status: active; Population: 253,000; Stamps issued: more than 725; Issues per year for last decade: 25.

An island in the West Indies. A British colony from 1628-1966. On Nov. 30, 1966, Barbados became an independent state within the British Commonwealth.

BARBUDA (1922, 1968-)

Stamp-issuing status: active; Population: 1,250; Stamps issued: more than 8,675.

A small island in the Leeward group in the West Indies. A dependency of Antigua.

BARWANI (1921-48)

Stamp-issuing status: inactive; Stamps issued: 37.

A former feudatory state in western India. Barwani stamps were replaced by those of India on July 1, 1948.

BASE ATLANTICA (1943-44)

Stamp-issuing status: inactive; Stamps issued: 29.

During World War II, the Supreme Commander of Italian submarine forces authorized the overprinting of a number of Italian stamps for use by Italian military personnel stationed in Bordeaux, France.

BASEL (1845)

Stamp-issuing status: inactive; Stamps issued: 1.

Capital of the canton of the same name, in northern Switzerland. Basel is situated on the Rhine and borders on both France and Germany. In 1845 the famous "Basel Dove" was issued. Since regarded as one of the most beautiful of the classic issues, it was not popular among the townspeople and was soon withdrawn.

BASUTOLAND (1933-66)

Stamp-issuing status: inactive; Population: 750,000 (1964 estimate); Stamps issued: 113.

A former British crown colony surrounded by South Africa. Under British control after 1871, Basutoland became the independent state of Lesotho on Oct. 4, 1966.

Stamps of the Cape of Good Hope were used 1871-1910, and those of the Union of South Africa 1910-33, when the colony began to use its own issues.

BATUM (1919-20)

Stamp-issuing status: inactive; Stamps issued: 65.

A Georgian port on the Black Sea, Batum was annexed by Russia from Turkey in 1878 and became a major Russian naval base.

During World War I, it was occupied by the Germans and the Turks, and in December 1918, Batum was occupied by British forces. The port was evacuated by the British in July 1920.

During the British occupation, three series of lithographed stamps (two overprinted "British Occupation"), as well as a number of Russian stamps overprinted and surcharged, were in use.

After the British evacuation, stamps of Georgia were used, these being replaced by Russian stamps in 1923.

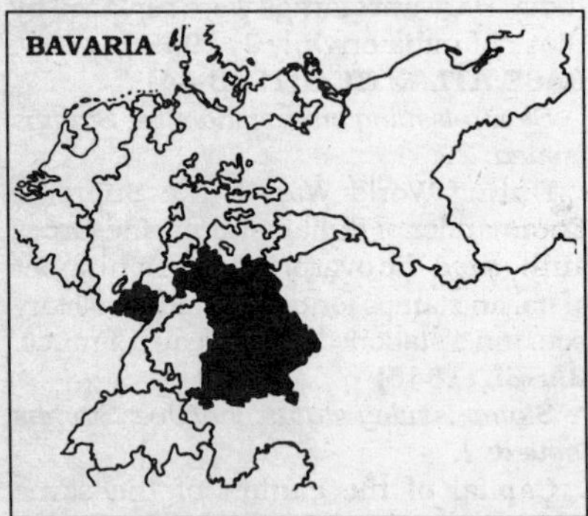

BAVARIA (1849-1920)

Stamp-issuing status: inactive; Stamps issued: 340.

Former kingdom in southern Germany. Bavaria joined the German Empire in 1870, retaining its own monarchy. The country was briefly independent following World War I.

Bavarian stamps were replaced by German issues in 1920.

BECHUANALAND PROTECTORATE (1888-1966)

Stamp-issuing status: inactive; Population: 550,000; Stamps issued: 207.

District in south central Africa, directly north of the Republic of South Africa. A British protectorate was established over the region in 1885, ending with the area becoming independent as the Republic of Botswana in 1966.

BEIRUT (1909-14)

Stamp-issuing status: inactive.

The capital of Lebanon. Prior to World War I, a number of European nations maintained their own postal systems in Beirut.

The Russian post office used stamps of the Russian Levant overprinted "Beyrouth" after 1909. In January 1905, the French authorities overprinted a contemporary French Offices in Turkey stamp for provisional use in Beirut. In July 1906, a similar provisional was used by the British authorities in Beirut. Both are scarce.

BEJUMA (1854)

Stamp-issuing status: inactive.

A small town near Valencia, Venezuela. In 1854, the postmaster issued local stamps to frank mail to Valencia.

BELGIAN CONGO (1886-1960)

Stamp-issuing status: inactive; Population 19 million (1971 estimate); Stamps issued: 410.

A former Belgian colony in central Africa. In 1885, the Congo Free State was established under the personal rule of Leopold II.

In 1908, the Belgian government assumed control of the area, withdrawing after the establishment of the independent Republic of the Congo in 1960.

BELGIUM (1849-)

Stamp-issuing status: active; Population 9.8 million; Stamps issued: more than 2,200; Issues per year for last decade: 39.

A constitutional monarchy in northwest Europe, bordering on the English Channel.

Conquered by Julius Caesar in the 1st century B.C., Belgium was ruled by a succession of foreign nations for nearly 2,000 years. In 1830, Belgium became independent from the last of these foreign rulers, the Dutch. Because of its strategic position, Belgian independence and neutrality was guaranteed by the major European powers.

In 1914, Germany occupied most of the country, although Belgium's spirited resistance throughout the war earned worldwide respect. Germany again occupied Belgium during World War II.

Since 1945, Belgium has aligned itself with the West and is a member of both NATO and the Common Market.

BELIZE (1973-)

Stamp-issuing status: active; Population: 158,000; Stamps issued: more than 300; Issues per year for last decade: 25.

A former British colony in Central America.

Formerly known as British Honduras, the name "Belize" was adopted in 1973. Belize became independent on Sept. 20,

1981.

A total of 1,800 British troops remain stationed in Belize to protect the country from Guatemala, which has long exerted a rather dubious claim to the territory.

In 1984-85 stamps were produced for the Cayes of Belize, some sparsely populated offshore islands. The stamps served no legitimate postal need, and were intended simply to raise money through sales to stamp collectors.

BENIN (1892-99, 1976-)

Stamp-issuing status: active; Population: 3.9 million; Stamps issued: more than 350; Issues per year for last decade: 31.

The coastal area of Dahomey, on the Gulf of Guinea, Benin was occupied by the French in the 19th century.

Separate stamps were issued from 1892. In 1895, the area was grouped with recently conquered inland territories to form the French colony of Dahomey.

In November 1975, Dahomey changed its name to the People's Republic of Benin.

BEQUIA (1984-)

Stamp-issuing status: active; Stamps issued: more than 200; Issues per year 1984-86: 100.

Bequia is the nearest neighbor of St. Vincent and the northernmost in a group of small subsidiary islands in the Lesser Antilles north of Trinidad and South America.

Following the proliferation of Grenadines of St. Vincent issues that began in the early 1970s, stamps began to be issued for Bequia in 1984.

BERGEDORF (1861-68)

Stamp-issuing status: inactive; Stamps issued: 5.

A town in northern Germany, originally owned by Hamburg and the Free City of Lubeck (1420-1867). In 1867, it passed into the sole possession of Hamburg.

Bergedorf began issuing stamps in 1861, these being replaced by those of the North German Confederation in 1868.

BERLIN (1948-)

Stamp-issuing status: active; Population: 1.8 million; Stamps issued: more than 850; Issues per year for last decade: 27.

The capital of Prussia and, after 1871, of Germany. Surrounded by the Soviet Zone of Occupation, Berlin was divided into U.S., British, French and Soviet zones in 1945.

In 1948, political tension brought the creation of the zones of West (Allied) Berlin and East (Soviet) Berlin.

In 1949, East Berlin became the capital of the German Democratic Republic.

BERMUDA (1848-)

Stamp-issuing status: active; Population: 57,600; Stamps issued: more than 530; Issues per year for last decade: 17.

A group of islands in the west central Atlantic Ocean. A British colony since 1609, Bermuda was granted internal self-government in 1968.

BHOPAL (1876-1950)

Stamp-issuing status: inactive; Stamps issued: 149.

A former feudatory state in central India. Bhopal issued separate stamps for ordinary use until 1908, when they were replaced by Indian stamps.

Bhopal continued to issue its own official stamps until 1950, when these, too, were replaced by Indian issues.

BHOR (1879-1902)

Stamp-issuing status: inactive; Stamps issued: 3.

A former feudatory state in western India. Bhor issues were replaced by those of India in 1902.

BHUTAN (1955-)

Stamp-issuing status: active; Population: 1.25 million; Stamps issued: more than 1,300; Issues per year for last decade: 40.

Kingdom in the eastern Himalayas between India and Tibet.

Bhutan was under British influence during the 19th century and was a British protectorate after 1910. In 1949 it became independent, although it is guided in foreign relations by India, with whom it carries on 99 percent of its commerce.

Since 1966 Bhutan has issued large numbers of attractive (and philatelically inspired) stamps. Among the novel forms these issues have taken are: gold, silver and steel foil, designs printed on silk, 3-D plastic stamps and souvenir sheets, miniature plastic records, plastic bas-relief, and designs printed on rose-scented paper.

BIAFRA (1968-70)

Stamp-issuing status: inactive; Population: 14 million (1968 estimate); Stamps issued: 44.

The eastern region of Nigeria, in which is concentrated the Ibo tribe. On May 30, 1967, the Ibos proclaimed the independent Republic of Biafra, and on Feb. 5, 1968, the first Biafran postage stamps were issued.

On Jan. 9, 1970, after a bitter civil war, Biafra surrendered to armies of the central government. Since that time, stamps of Nigeria have been in use.

During 1968-70, some 68 major varieties were issued, as well as several overprinted sets that appeared on the market after Biafra's defeat. These latter sets were not issued for postal use and so are excluded from most major catalogs.

BIALYSTOK (1916)

Stamp-issuing status: inactive; Stamps issued: 2.

A city and province in northeastern Poland. In 1916, the local German military commander issued stamps for use in the area.

BIJAWAR (1935-39)

Stamp-issuing status: inactive; Stamps issued: 10.

A former feudatory state in central India. Bijawar issued stamps from 1935-39, after which they were replaced by Indian stamps.

BILBAO (1937)

Stamp-issuing status: inactive.

The major port of northern Spain, located on the Bay of Biscay.

Spanish stamps were overprinted in July 1937, to celebrate the occupation of the city by Franco's Nationalist forces.

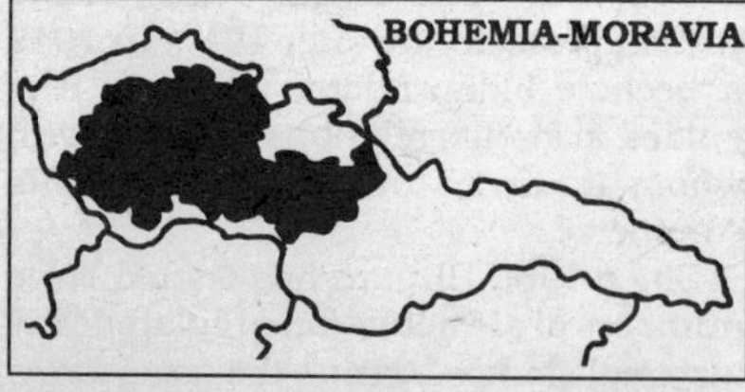

BOHEMIA AND MORAVIA (1939-45)

Stamp-issuing status: inactive; Stamps issued: 180.

A German puppet-state created from the western provinces of Czechoslovakia prior to World War II. Bohemia and Moravia were re-incorporated into Czechoslovakia following the war.

BOLIVIA (1867-)

Stamp-issuing status: active; Population 5.6 million; Stamps issued: more than 1,100; Issues per year for last decade: 14.

A land-locked republic in South America, Bolivia was part of the Inca empire during the 13th-16th centuries. It was conquered by Spain in the 1530s and, as the Presidency of Charcas, was attached to the vice-royalty of Rio de la Plata. Notable primarily for its rich silver mines, which were exploited and depleted by the Spanish, Bolivia was an imperial backwater for three centuries.

In 1825, the Spanish were expelled, and Bolivia, taking its name from the Great Liberator Simon Bolivar, became independent.

Bolivia has been beset by numerous wars and revolutions. In the first hundred years of its independence, Bolivia lost territory to Chile, Brazil and Paraguay, three of its four neighbors. Its only coastal territory was lost to Chile in the War of the Pacific (1879-84).

Chronic internal instability has given Bolivia one of the lowest standards of living in Latin America. Its government has been a bewildering succession of military dictatorships.

Because of frequent shortages of regular postal issues, one often finds revenues, postage dues and bisects used provisionally by Bolivian post offices.

BOPHUTHATSWANA (1977-)

Stamp-issuing status: active; Stamps issued: more than 200; Issues per year during last decade: 20.

One of South Africa's so-called Bantustans or Bantu homelands, a scattering of nominally semi-autonomous states for otherwise disenfranchised black South Africans located on the sites of reserves set up under the policies of the white-run apartheid government prior to World War II.

Bophuthatswana is in fact a scattering of seven small independent tracts of territory within the eastern half of South Africa, six of which are in the northern part of the nation near the border with Botswana.

Although not accorded international recognition as a sovereign state, Bophuthatswana's stamps have generally been accepted on international mail. Stamp-issuing policies have remained conservative.

BOSNIA AND HERZEGOVINA (1879-1918)

Stamp-issuing status: inactive; Population: 2 million (1918 estimate); Stamps issued: 199.

Located in southwestern Yugoslavia, the provinces of Bosnia and Herzegovina were placed under Austria protection in 1878, and a year later, their first separate stamps appeared.

Formally Ottoman provinces, Bosnia and Herzegovina were only nominally under Turkish rule after this, and in 1908, Austria-Hungary annexed the area.

In 1914, the Austrian Archduke Ferdinand, heir to the aging Austrian emperor, was assassinated at Sarajevo, the capital, setting off the series of events that culminated in World War I.

Since 1918, Bosnia and Herzegovina have formed part of Yugoslavia.

BOTSWANA (1966-)

Stamp-issuing status: active; Population: 67,000; Stamps issued: more than 450; Issues per year during last decade: 24.

A republic in central southern Africa, directly north of the Republic of South Africa. Formerly the British Bechuanaland Protectorate, the republic became independent as Botswana on Sept. 30, 1966.

Many Botswanans are migrant workers in South Africa, with which Botswana is closely linked.

BRAC (BRAZZA) (1944)

Stamp-issuing status: inactive; Stamps issued: 6.

An island in the Adriatic Sea, off the coast of Yugoslavia. In 1944, Yugoslavian stamps were overprinted by the German military authorities for use in the island.

BRAZIL (1843-)

Stamp-issuing status: active; Population: 137.3 million; Stamps issued: more than 2,400; Issues per year for last decade: 54.

A large republic, occupying nearly half of South America. Brazil was discovered by Europeans in 1500, and Portugal soon began colonizing the coastal areas. During 1808-21, after Napoleon had occupied Portugal, Brazil was the seat of the Portuguese empire. In 1821, the Portuguese king returned to Lisbon, leaving his son, Dom Pedro, to act as regent in Brazil.

In 1822, Dom Pedro declared the independence of the Empire of Brazil. Although Dom Pedro and his son, Dom Pedro II, were popular, the feeling grew that an American monarchy was an anachronism, and in 1889 a bloodless coup established the republic.

Since 1930, except for the period 1956-64, Brazil has been ruled by a succession of military regimes. During the 1970s, the government eased repressive policies and, since 1979, has liberalized political conditions considerably.

Ambitious industrial and agricultural programs since 1930 have capitalized on the country's enormous natural resources, and Brazil has become the leading industrial nation of Latin America. Economic growth has been slowed in recent years by the enormous increases in prices for petroleum, which Brazil must import.

BREMEN (1855-68)

Stamp-issuing status: inactive; Population: 122,402 (1871 estimate); Stamps issued: 16.

A major German seaport in northwestern Germany. Bremen was a free city and a member of the German and, later, the North German Confederations, joining the German Empire in 1870.

Bremen used its own stamps from 1855-68, after which issues of the North German Confederation came into use.

BRITISH ANTARCTIC TERRITORY (1963-)

Stamp-issuing status: active; Population: 300; Stamps issued: more than 140; Issues per year for last decade: 7.

A British territory in the south Atlantic Ocean, forming part of the Falkland Islands Dependencies.

BRITISH BECHUANALAND (1886-98)

Stamp-issuing status: inactive; Population: 84,210 (1904 estimate); Stamps issued: 41.

Located in southern Africa, British Bechuanaland was a British crown colony until 1895, when it was annexed to Cape Colony. It is now part of the Republic of South Africa.

Overprinted stamps of Cape Colony were in use from 1886 to 1898, when they were replaced by regular Cape Colony stamps.

Since 1910, stamps of South Africa have been used, although most Cape Colony stamps remained valid until 1937.

BRITISH CENTRAL AFRICA (1891-1908)

Stamp-issuing status: inactive; Population: 1.6 million (1907 estimate); Stamps issued: 73.

A former British territory in central Africa. In 1907, British Central Africa adopted the name Nyasaland Protectorate, which subsequently became independent as the Republic of Malawi.

BRITISH COLUMBIA AND VANCOUVER ISLAND (1860-71)

Stamp-issuing status: inactive; Population: 650,000 (1869 estimate); Stamps issued: 18.

A Canadian province on the northwest coast of North America, bordering on the Pacific Ocean. The two British colonies of Vancouver (established 1849) and British Columbia (established 1858) united in 1866 and joined the Canadian Confederation in 1871.

BRITISH EAST AFRICA (1890-1903)

Stamp-issuing status: inactive; Stamps issued: 102.

Territories originally under control of the British East Africa Co., after 1895 directly under British administration.

In 1903, the area was reformed as the East Africa and Uganda protectorates.

During 1895-1903, this area used overprinted stamps of Britain, India and Zanzibar, as well as its own issues. In 1903, East Africa and Uganda issues came into use.

BRITISH GUIANA (1850-1966)

Stamp-issuing status: inactive; Population: 630,000 (1966 estimate); Stamps issued: 317.

A former colony on the northern coast of South America, British Guiana became an independent republic in 1966, assuming the name Guyana.

Early issues of British Guiana include a number of major rarities, among them "The World's Most Valuable Stamp," the 1¢ black on magenta of 1856. This stamp is unique and has passed through the hands of some of the giants of philately.

BRITISH HONDURAS (1866-1973)

Stamp-issuing status: inactive; Population: 135,000 (1973 estimate); Stamps issued: 322.

Located in Central America on the Caribbean Sea, this area was contested by the British and Spanish until 1798, when British authority was secured.

In 1862, it became a British colony under Jamaican administration, and in 1884 became a separate colony. In 1973, British Honduras changed its name to Belize.

BRITISH INDIAN OCEAN TERRITORY (1968-80)

Stamp-issuing status: inactive; Population: 550 (1976 estimate); Stamps issued: 89.

A group of British-owned islands in the Indian Ocean. Formerly dependencies of Mauritius and the Seychelles, these islands were organized as a crown colony on Nov. 8, 1965. In 1980, the name of the colony was changed to Zil Eloigne Sesel. (later changed to Zil Elevagne Sesel).

BRITISH OFFICES IN CHINA (1917-30)

Stamp-issuing status: inactive; Stamps issued: 27.

Britain long maintained post offices in various Chinese cities. Stamps of Hong Kong were used in these offices until Dec. 31, 1916, after which Hong Kong stamps overprinted "China" were used.

On Nov. 30, 1922, all British post

offices in China were closed, except in the leased territory of Wei-hai-wei, which used British Offices in China issues until Sept. 30, 1930.

BRITISH OFFICES IN MOROCCO (1898-1957)

Stamp-issuing status: inactive; Stamps issued: 339.

British post offices in Morocco used overprinted contemporary stamps of Gibraltar (1898-1906) and Britain.

Separate issues were used in the Spanish Zone, the French Zone, and Tangier, as well as the general issues used throughout the country.

Regular British stamps were also often used.

BRITISH OFFICES IN THE TURKISH EMPIRE (1885-1914, 1919-23)

Stamp-issuing status: inactive; Stamps issued: 64.

Until 1885, regular British stamps were used by British post offices in the Ottoman Empire. After that date, British stamps surcharged in Turkish currency or overprinted "LEVANT" were used.

British post offices in the area were closed Oct. 1, 1914, reopened March 1919, and finally closed Sept. 27, 1923.

BRITISH VIRGIN ISLANDS (1866-)

Stamp-issuing status: active; Population: 12,034 (1980 estimate).

A group of islands in the West Indies, southeast of Puerto Rico. The western portion of the Virgin Islands were under Danish rule until 1917, and under the United States since. The 30 eastern islands, which comprise the British Virgin Islands, were under Dutch control until 1666, when they passed to Britain.

Until 1956, they were administered as part of the Leeward Islands colony. In 1956 the British Virgin Islands became a separate crown colony and in 1967 became an Associated State, with Britain retaining control of foreign affairs and defense.

BRUNEI (1906-)

Stamp-issuing status: active; Population: 226,000; Stamps issued: more than 300; Issues per year for last decade: 12.

A sultanate on the northwest coast of Borneo, situated between the Malaysian states of Sabah and Sarawak. Under British protection since 1888, Brunei secured full self-government in 1971. Britain retains control of foreign affairs. Complete independence is targeted for 1983.

BRUNSWICK (1852-68)

Stamp-issuing status: inactive; Stamps issued: 26.

A former duchy in northern Germany, joining the German Empire in 1870. Brunswick's issues were used from 1852-68, when they were replaced by those of the North German Confederation.

BUENOS AIRES (1858-64)

Stamp-issuing status: inactive; Stamps issued: 13.

Buenos Aires, long the chief port and commercial center of Argentina, was at various times in the 19th century independent from the rest of the country.

Since 1862, however, it has formed a province of Argentina, whose stamps have been in use since 1864. A British post office in the city used regular British stamps (canceled "B-32") from 1860 to 1873.

BULGARIA (1879-)

Stamp-issuing status: active; Population: 9 million; Stamps issued: more than 3,100; Issues per year for last decade: 87.

A communist People's Republic in southeastern Europe.

During the 10th and 12th centuries, the Bulgars ruled much of the Balkan peninsula but subsequently declined in power, falling under Turkish control in 1396. In 1878 Bulgaria became an autonomous principality, under nominal Turkish rule. In fact, Bulgaria was independent — more closely aligned with Russia than with Turkey — and this independence was formalized in 1908.

The Treaty of San Stefano (1878) established a "Greater Bulgaria," which included all Bulgars and encompassed territory that now forms parts of Yugoslavia, Greece, Romania and Turkey. The powers, fearing the expansion of Russian influence in the Balkans through such a large client-state, overturned that treaty at the Congress of Berlin, later in the year. Bulgaria's foreign policy from 1878 through 1944 was based on the creation of this Greater Bulgaria.

In 1885, Bulgaria absorbed Eastern Rumelia, and in the Balkan Wars (1912-13) further expanded its borders. Its defeat by the Allies in World War I cost Bulgaria its Aegean coastline, and its defeat in World War II brought the overthrow of the monarchy and the establishment of the communist regime.

Bulgaria is one of the most reliable of the Soviet satellites in eastern Europe.

BUNDI (1894-1948)

Stamp-issuing status: inactive; Stamps issued: 105.

A former feudatory state in northwestern India, Bundi issued stamps from 1894 to 1902 and from 1915 to 1948. During 1902-15 and after 1950, stamps of India were used. From 1948-50, stamps of Rajasthan were in use.

BURGOS (1936-38)

Stamp-issuing status: inactive.

A province in north central Spain. Burgos was occupied by the Nationalists early in the Spanish Civil War, and a large number of overprinted Spanish postage and fiscal stamps were used in the province during this period.

BURKINA FASO (1984-)

Stamp-issuing status: active; Population: 8.3 million (1989 estimate); Stamps issued: more than 125; Issues per year since 1984: 43.

A poor, landlocked republic in the savannah region of West Africa, the former French colony of Upper Volta is bounded by the states of Mali, Niger, Benin, Togo, Ghana and Ivory Coast.

Following a 1983 coup d'etat, Upper Volta's name was changed to Burkina Faso on Aug. 4, 1984. The name is a transliteration of indigenous words meaning "country of incorruptible men." The first stamps bearing the new name were in an airmail set issued on May 23, 1984.

BURMA (1937-)

Stamp-issuing status: active; Population: 36 million; Stamps issued: more than 250; Issues per year for last decade: 5.

A republic in southeast Asia. Burma was a part of British India until 1937, when it became a separate territory under Britain.

Occupied by Japan, 1942-45, Burma was re-occupied by Britain, which granted independence on Jan. 4, 1948.

Burma maintains a staunch nationalist socialism and keeps relations with other countries to a minimum. In 1978, government repression drove 150,000 Moslem Burmese to flee the country, settling in neighboring Bangladesh.

BURUNDI (1962-)

Stamp-issuing status: active; Population: 4.9 million; Stamps issued: more than 1,000; Issues per year for last decade: 16.

A republic in Central Africa. As Urundi, it was administered by Belgium, under a United Nations mandate, until it became an independent kingdom in 1962. In 1966, the monarchy was overthrown by a military coup.

Traditionally, Burundi has been ruled by the Tutsi (Watusi) tribe, which comprises only 14 percent of the population. In 1972-73, the Bantu Hutus, who make up 85 percent of Burundi's population, revolted, sparking a genocidal civil war in which 100,000 Hutsi and 10,000 Tutsi were killed. Another 100,000 Hutsi fled to Tanzania and Zaire. The government is presently attempting to undo the effects of this struggle and is committed to a policy of ethnic reconciliation.

BUSHIRE (1915)

Stamp-issuing status: inactive; Stamps issued: 30.

An Iranian port on the Persian Gulf. Bushire was occupied by British forces from Aug. 8, 1915, to Oct. 16, 1915.

BUSSAHIR (BASHAHR) (1895-1901)

Stamp-issuing status: inactive; Stamps issued: 35.

A former feudatory state in northern India, Bussahir stamps were replaced by those of India. With the closing of the state post office, large numbers of remainders and reprints were released to the philatelic market. These exist both unused and canceled "19 MA 1900."

- C -

CABO GRACIAS A DIOS (1904-12)

Stamp-issuing status: inactive; Stamps issued: 77.

A cape and seaport in the extreme northeast of Nicaragua. The circulation of two radically different currencies in the country necessitated the overprinting of Nicaraguan stamps for use in the province.

CADIZ (1936-37)

Stamp-issuing status: inactive.

A major Spanish port on the Atlantic Ocean, located in Southern Spain.

Contemporary Spanish stamps were overprinted by the Nationalist local authorities during the Spanish Civil War.

CAICOS ISLANDS (1981-)

Stamp-issuing status: active; Stamps issued: more than 100.

The northwesternmost six principal islands of the Turks and Caicos Islands, located in the West Indies, south of the Bahamas.

Stamps overprinted "Caicos Islands" appeared in mid-1981, followed by purpose-inscribed issues in 1983 and since. These have been accompanied by a continuing steady flow of emissions from Turks and Caicos Islands.

CALIMNO (1912-32)

Stamp-issuing status: inactive; Stamps issued: 26.

One of the Turkish Dodecanese Islands in the eastern Aegean Sea. Occupied by Italy in 1912, Italian stamps overprinted "Calimno" were used from 1912-29, when they were replaced by the Aegean Island's general issues.

Sets overprinted with the island's name were released in 1930 and 1932.

CAMBODIA (Kampuchea) (1951-74)

Stamp-issuing status: active; Population: 6.5 million; Stamps issued: 392 (1951-74 estimate).

A communist republic in southeast Asia. It lies in Indo-China and borders Vietnam, Laos and Thailand.

During the 9th-13th centuries, Cambodia was the center of the Khmer empire, which ruled Thailand, Cambodia, Laos and southern Vietnam. By the 19th century, Khmer power had long been declining, and in 1863, a French protectorate was established over Cambodia.

A constitutional monarchy was established in 1941. In 1951, Cambodia became a separate member of the French Union, and in 1955, it became fully independent.

During the Vietnamese War, Cambodia attempted to maintain its independence and neutrality. In 1965, relations were broken with the United States, after ARVN forces attacked Viet-Cong bases in Cambodia. By 1969, the Viet-Cong-supported Khmer Rouge rebels posed such a threat that relations were restored.

In 1970, the monarchy was deposed, and a pro-western republic was established. In 1971, the name Khmer Republic was adopted.

There followed several years of intense fighting between the North Vietnamese and Khmer Rouge and the U.S.-backed forces of the republic. More than 100,000 died during 1971-75. The communists quickly defeated government forces after the U.S. withdrawal from South Vietnam.

There followed one of the more bizarre and horrifying episodes in recent history. The Khmer Rouge broke with the Vietnamese allies and began a systematic reign of terror that claimed one million lives during 1975-78. During this period (1977-78), Cambodia was renamed Democratic Kampuchea.

In 1978, border skirmishes with Vietnam erupted into war, and in January 1979, a Vietnamese-backed regime was established. Continuing civil war and widespread famine during 1979-80, following three years of Khmer Rouge atrocities, devastated the country.

CAMEROUN (1897-)

Stamp-issuing status: active; Population: 8.5 million; Stamps issued: (French) more than 1,050, (German) 38; Issues per year for last decade: 27.

A republic in West Africa. Cameroun was a German protectorate until 1915, when it was occupied by the British and French.

In 1922, it was mandated to these countries by the League of Nations. The French portion became the independent State of Cameroun in 1960, with the southern portion of the British mandate joining it in 1961.

The northern portion of the British mandate joined Nigeria. In 1972, Cameroun changed its official designation to the United Republic of Cameroon.

Politically stable, Cameroon has enjoyed considerable development in agriculture and transportation since independence.

CAMPECHE (1876)

Stamp-issuing status: inactive; Stamps issued: 3.

A Mexican state occupying the western part of the Yucatan peninsula. Provisional stamps were produced for use there during the struggle by Juarez against Emperor Maximilian.

CAMPIONE D'ITALIA (1944-52)

Stamp-issuing status: inactive.

A small Italian enclave in Switzerland, which for a time issued stamps valid for postage to Switzerland and Italy.

These issues were used during the period when northern Italy was controlled by the Italian Social Republic, while Campione remained loyal to the royalist government, from which it was unable to secure supplies of stamps.

CANADA (1851-)

Stamp-issuing status: active; Population: 25.5 million; Stamps issued: more than 1,300; Issues per year for last decade: 91.

An independent state within the British Commonwealth, occupying the northern portion of North America.

Under French rule until 1763, when it was transferred to Britain, modern Canada was formed with the union of the various individual British colonies in North America in 1867. British Columbia and Vancouver Island were added in 1871, Prince Edward Island in 1873, and Newfoundland in 1949.

Canada possesses rich natural resources, but her harsh climate and small population have slowed development.

Canada has encouraged the differences among its people, socially and politically, so that rather than a melting pot, the country more resembles a patchwork quilt. This has produced a richness and variety among the various ethnic groups in Canada.

It has also encouraged the development of regionalism and separatism: The western provinces are largely Conservative, while the East is largely Liberal; the majority of the population is English-speaking and of British descent, while in Quebec, 80 percent are of French descent.

CANAL ZONE (1904-79)

Stamp-issuing status: inactive; Stamps issued: 270.

A strip of land 10 miles wide lying on either side of the Panama Canal, from the Atlantic to Pacific oceans, dividing the Republic of Panama into two parts.

Thwarted by Colombia from building the Panama Canal through its territory, the U.S. supported the Panamanian revolution of 1903, and almost immediately received a perpetual lease to the territory.

In 1978, the United States and Panama agreed to a revised treaty, allowing for the gradual transfer of control of the Canal to Panama by the end of the century. On Sept. 30, 1979, the U.S. Canal Zone Postal Service ceased operation, and on Oct. 1, the Panamanian Postal Service took charge.

CANARY ISLANDS (1936-39)

Stamp-issuing status: inactive.

A group of islands in the Atlantic Ocean, located off the northwestern coast of Africa.

Under Spanish rule since the 15th century, the Canary Islands have normally used regular Spanish issues.

During the Spanish Civil War, however, a large number of overprinted stamps were used on mail carried by a provisional airline service linking Las Palmas with Seville, where it was linked to the rest of Europe. These issues were in use until the re-establishment of the Spanish state service in May 1938.

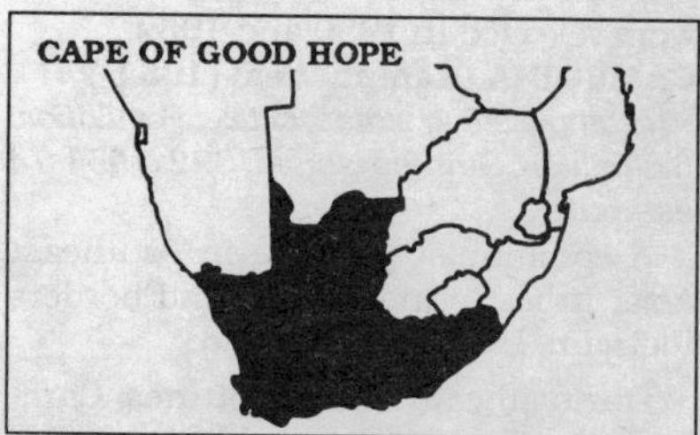

CAPE OF GOOD HOPE (1853-1910)

Stamp-issuing status: inactive; Stamps issued: 95.

Located at the southern tip of Africa, the Cape of Good Hope was originally a Dutch colony, passing to the British after the Napoleonic Wars. Conflict between English immigrants and established Dutch settlers (Boers) led to the withdrawal of the Boers into the interior after 1936.

These tensions, intensified by the discovery of rich diamond and gold deposits, increasing English immigration and Britain's imperialistic policy, resulted in the Boer War of 1899-1902, which ended with British occupation of the formerly independent Boer republics.

In 1910, Cape Colony joined with Natal, Transvaal and the Orange River Colony to form the Union of South Africa.

During the Boer War, a number of provisionals appeared, the most famous of which were issued at Mafeking, where the defending British force was commanded by Gen. Robert S.S. Baden-Powell, who later established the Boy Scouts.

CAPE JUBY (1916-48)

Stamp-issuing status: inactive; Stamps issued: 172.

A Spanish possession in the western Sahara on the Atlantic coast, opposite the Canary Islands. Secured by agreement with France, Spanish troops occupied Cape Juby in 1916, at which time overprinted stamps of Rio de Oro were issued.

From 1916 to 1919, stamps of Rio de Oro and Spanish Morocco were used in the area. In January 1919, overprinted stamps again appeared, and these remained in use until 1948, when they were replaced by those of the Spanish Sahara.

CAPE VERDE (1877-)

Stamp-issuing status: active; Population: 350,000; Stamps issued: more than 550; Issues per year for last decade: 13.

A group of islands in the Atlantic Ocean, west of Senegal.

Cape Verde was uninhabited when first discovered by the Portuguese in 1456 or 1460. The first Portuguese settlers arrived in 1462, and black slaves were introduced soon thereafter. The modern Cape Verdeans are descendents of the two groups.

In 1975, Cape Verde became independent, with close ties to Guinea-Bissau (the former Portuguese Guinea). Drought and famine in recent years have created major difficulties for this already impoverished nation.

CAROLINE ISLANDS (1900-14)

Stamp-issuing status: inactive; Population: 30,000 (1915 estimate); Stamps issued: 29.

A large group of islands in the western Pacific Ocean. The Carolines were purchased by Germany from Spain in 1899. They were captured by Japan in 1914 and subsequently administered by the Japanese under a mandate from the League of Nations.

In 1944 they were occupied by the United States and since 1947 have been administered by the United States, under a mandate from the United Nations, as part of the Pacific Islands Trusteeship.

Japanese stamps were used from 1914 to 1944, and U.S. issues since 1944.

CARPATHO-UKRAINE (1939, 1944-45)

Stamp-issuing status: inactive; Stamps issued: 1.

The easternmost province of pre-Munich Czechoslovakia. It was created as an autonomous state and swiftly annexed by Hungary in 1939.

With the Axis withdrawal in 1944, the area became independent for a brief time, reverting to Hungary in 1945. In 1949, it was annexed by the U.S.S.R.

CARCHI (1912-32)

Stamp-issuing status: inactive; Stamps issued: 26.

One of the Turkish Dodecanese Islands in the eastern Aegean Sea. Carchi was occupied by Italy in 1912.

Italian stamps overprinted "Karki," "Calchi," or "Carchi" were used until 1929, when the general Aegean Islands' issues came into use. Two sets overprinted with the island's name were issued in 1930 and 1932.

CARUPANO (1902-03)

Stamp-issuing status: inactive; Stamps issued: 13.

A port of Venezuela, near Trinidad. During the Anglo-German-Italian occupation of La Guaira, Carupano was isolated and soon ran out of stamps, necessitating the issue of provisional issues, until regular stocks could be obtained.

CASO (1912-32)

Stamp-issuing status: inactive; Stamps issued: 26.

One of the Turkish Dodecanese Islands in the eastern Aegean Sea. Caso was occupied by Italy in 1912, at which time Italian issues overprinted "Caso" were placed in use. These were replaced in 1929 by the general Aegean Islands' issues, although two sets overprinted for the island were issued in 1930 and 1932.

CASTELLORIZO (1920-32)

Stamp-issuing status: inactive; Population: 2,238 (1936 estimate); Stamps issued: 73.

Small island in the Mediterranean off the southwest coast of Turkey. Occupied by France in 1915, Castellorizo was transferred to Italy in 1920. After World War II, the island, along with the rest of the Dodecanese Islands, passed to Greece.

CATTARO (1944)

Stamp-issuing status: inactive; Stamps issued: 10.

A Yugoslavian province on the Adriatic, occupied by the Italians from 1941-43, and Germans, 1943-45, during World War II.

In 1944, Italian and Yugoslavia issues were overprinted for use in Cattaro by the German Occupation Authorities.

CAVALLA (1893-1914)

Stamp-issuing status: inactive; Stamps issued 11.

A town in northern Greece. The French post office in Cavalla used unoverprinted French stamps (canceled "5156" within a diamond-shaped grid of dots) after 1874. During 1893-1914, it used stamps overprinted or inscribed "Cavalle."

Seized by Bulgaria from Turkey in 1912, Cavalla was taken by the Greeks in 1913. Bulgarian stamps overprinted by the Greek occupation authorities were used pending the arrival of regular Greek stocks.

CAYMAN ISLANDS (1901-)

Stamp-issuing status: active; Population: 18,500; Stamps issued: more than 600; Issues per year for last decade: 20.

Three islands in the Caribbean Sea, northwest of Jamaica. The Cayman Islands have been a British colony since its settlement in the 18th century.

During the 1970s, the Caymans became a tax-free haven for banking, and many Western banks have branches in the colony.

CENTRAL AFRICAN REPUBLIC (1959-)

Stamp-issuing status: active; Population: 3 million; Stamps issued: more than 1,300; Issues per year for last decade: 71.

A landlocked nation in central Africa, surrounded by Chad, Cameroon, Congo, Zaire, and the Sudan.

Formerly the French colony of Ubangi-Shari, the Central African Republic was established Dec. 1, 1958, and became fully independent Aug. 13, 1960.

Although possessed of substantial mineral resources, the country has been unable to develop economically and has been politically unstable since independence.

During 1960-65, the CAR was a center of Chinese influence in Africa. In 1965 the pro-Chinese regime was overthrown, and Jean-Bedel Bokassa came to power. On Dec. 4, 1976, Bokassa proclaimed the country the Central African Empire, with himself as Emperor Bokassa I.

Bokassa's rule was marked by almost unrelenting cruelty and barbarism, characterized by rumors that the emperor himself practiced cannibalism.

On Sept. 20, 1979, Bokassa was overthrown in a bloodless coup supported by 800-1,000 French troops, flown in from bases in Gabon and Chad. A republic was re-established under David Dacko, who had been president of the country 1960-66.

CENTRAL ALBANIA (1915)

Stamp-issuing status: inactive.

During World War I, Albania was overrun by various foreign armies. From January 1914 to February 1916, the central portion of the country was controlled by a provisional regime under Essad Pasha. Essad was supplanted by the Austrians in 1916.

CENTRAL CHINA (1949-50)

Stamp-issuing status: inactive; Stamps issued: 113.

The Communist Central Chinese Liberation Area included the provinces of Honan, Hupeh, Hunan and Kiangsi.

Separate issues for the region were used after the occupation of Hankow from the Nationalists.

CENTRAL LITHUANIA (1920-22)

Stamp-issuing status: inactive; Stamps issued: 53.

Historically a part of Lithuania, this territory was under Russian rule until 1915, when it was occupied by the Germans.

German stamps overprinted for Lithuania were used until December 1918, when regular Lithuanian stamps were issued. In October 1920, the area was occupied by Polish forces, who established an autonomous state, which issued its own stamps during 1920-22.

In 1922, it was annexed by Poland, but in 1939, it was occupied by Soviet forces and returned to Lithuania.

Central Lithuania was soon occupied by the Germans in 1941 and was held until 1945. Since World War II, Soviet stamps have been in use.

CEPHALONIA AND ITHACA (1941)

Stamp-issuing status: inactive; Stamps issued: 29.

Two of the Ionian Islands, off the western coast of Greece. The islands were occupied by Italian forces in 1941, when Greek stamps were overprinted for use in the two islands by the local Italian military authorities.

These were soon superseded by the general occupation issues for the Ionian Islands.

CEYLON (1857-1972)

Stamp-issuing status: inactive; Population: 12.5 million; Stamps issued: 511.

Island in the Indian Ocean, off the southeast coast of India. Much of the island was under Portugal during the 16th and 17th centuries, succeeded by the Dutch.

From 1795-1815, the British ruled Ceylon. In 1948, Ceylon became a self-governing dominion, and in 1972, it became independent as the Republic of Sri Lanka.

CHAD (1922-36, 1959-)

Stamp-issuing status: active; Population: 4.7 million; Stamps issued: more than 1,150; Issues per year for last decade: 38.

A republic in central Africa. A former dependency of Ubangi-Shari, Chad was occupied by the French during 1897-1914, after defeating fierce native resistance.

In 1920, Chad became a separate colony, joining in French Equatorial Africa in 1934. In 1958 the Chad Republic became an independent state in the French Union, and in 1960 it became fully independent.

Following independence, Chad retained close ties with France, which provided economic aid and support in the government's civil war with Libyan-backed Arab guerrillas after 1966.

In 1981, Libyan forces occupied Chad at the request of a coalition government. Libya's efforts to merge the two nations, however, alarmed even the pro-Libyan elements of the regime, and international pressure brought a rapid Libyan withdrawal. The political situation remains tense, and renewed civil war is likely.

CHAMBA (1886-1950)

Stamp-issuing status: active; Population: 168,908 (1941 estimate); Stamps issued: 182.

A state in northern India, Chamba became independent of Kashmir in 1846. In 1886, its postal service was joined to that of India, and overprinted Indian stamps came into use.

These overprinted issues were replaced by Indian stamps April 1, 1950, although they continued to be postally valid until Jan. 1, 1951.

CHARKARI (CHARKHARI) (1894-1950)

Stamp-issuing status: inactive; Stamps issued: 44.

A former feudatory state in north-central India, Charkari's stamps were replaced by those of India on May 1, 1950.

CHECINY (1919)

Stamp-issuing status: inactive.

A city in southern Poland. Local stamps were issued in 1919 under the authority of the municipal authorities.

CHELYABINSK (1920-22)

Stamp-issuing status: inactive.

A city in southwestern Siberia. Russian stamps were overprinted for local use by the municipal authorities during 1920-22.

CHIAPAS (1866)

Stamp-issuing status: inactive; Stamps issued: 5.

A state of southern Mexico, bordering on Guatemala and the Pacific Ocean.

CHIHUAHUA (1872)

Stamp-issuing status: inactive; Stamps issued: 2.

The capital city of the State of Chihuahua in northern Mexico.

CHILE (1853-)

Stamp-issuing status: active; Population: 12.9 million; Stamps issued: more than 1,225; Issues per year for last decade: 25.

A republic in southwest South America. Chile was settled by Spain as early as 1540, although Indian resistance in the south was not overcome until the late 19th century. During 1817-18, Chile secured its independence, with the aid of Argentine forces under San Martin.

During the 19th century, Chile aggressively expanded its borders, acquiring nitrate-rich northern districts from Peru and Bolivia during the War of the Pacific, 1879-84, and subduing Indian resistance in the south.

After 1891, Chile was a liberal republic, but economic problems in recent years have produced social unrest and radical regimes, both Leftist and Rightist.

CHIMARRA (HIMERA) (1914, 1920)

Stamp-issuing status: inactive; Stamps issued: 12.

A city in the southern coast of Albania. Philatelically inspired issues were released during the Greek occupation of the port.

CHINA (1878-)

Stamp-issuing status (People's Republic) active, (Empire and Republic) inactive; Population: (People's Republic) 1.06 billion, (Empire and Republic) 422 million; Stamps issued: (People's Republic) more than 2,150, (Empire and Republic) 2,481; Issues per year for last decade: (People's Republic) 78.

An ancient country occupying a large area in eastern Asia, between Turkestan and the China Sea and stretching from Siberia to Indo-China. Chinese civilization appeared in the 3rd millennium B.C., producing one of the earliest sophisticated cultures. China was long divided into numerous states, within a feudal system.

China was unified under the Chin and Han dynasties (255 B.C.-220 A.D.), but again broke into contending states after the fall of the Hans.

Unification was achieved under the Sui and T'ang dynasties (589-907), but internal division again appeared.

In the early 13th century, the Mongols overran China, establishing the Yuan dynasty, which at its height (circa 1300) ruled China, Turkestan, Korea and Indo-China.

In 1368, the Ming dynasty expelled the Yuan and inaugurated a period of dynamic growth. In 1644, the Manchu dynasty overthrew the Ming and created a vast and powerful empire.

During 1840-1900, China was defeated in a series of wars, which secured for the European powers numerous concessions within the Chinese empire.

In 1892, Dr. Sun Yat-sen founded the Regenerate China Society, which began to foment revolution. In 1911, the empress-dowager was deposed, and a republic proclaimed.

A period of civil war and internal division under local warlords ensued, until Chiang Kai-shek, commanding the Nationalist armies, was able to re-establish some unity during the 1920s.

In 1927, Chiang moved against Soviet influence in the Nationalist government, and the Communists split with the regime, launching a guerrilla war against the central government.

In 1931, Japan occupied Manchuria and began to expand into China, openly invading the country in 1937. The Nationalists and Communists maintained an uneasy truce during World War II, but with the defeat of Japan and the occupation of Manchuria by the Soviets, the civil war began in earnest.

By 1949, the Nationalists had been defeated and driven to the island of Formosa (Taiwan). Since that time, the Chinese People's Republic on the mainland and the Republic of China on Taiwan have both claimed to represent the rightful government of China.

The Chinese People's Republic was closely linked with the U.S.S.R. during the 1950s, but by the 1960s this relationship had deteriorated. Conflicting nationalisms became identified with ideological differences, and the two nations have each come to regard the other as its principal enemy.

U.S. relations with the mainland regime, broken in 1950, have become increasingly close since 1971. On Dec. 15, 1978, the United States formally recognized the People's Republic as the sole legal government of China.

The Nationalist regime on Taiwan has been politically isolated in recent years. In 1971, it was expelled from the United Nations, in favor of the People's Republic, and in 1978, the United States, its principal ally and supporter, severed formal diplomatic relations. Taiwan has been able, however, to maintain extensive informal contacts abroad through its active international commercial operations.

CHINA EXPEDITIONARY FORCES (1900-21)

Stamp-issuing status: inactive.

A total of 33 stamps of British India overprinted "C.E.F." were used by the British Expeditionary Force in China in 1900-21.

CHINESE TREATY PORTS (1865-97)

Stamp-issuing status: inactive.

Before the establishment of the imperial posts in 1897, a number of Chinese treaty ports issued local stamps. These include Chungking (1894), Foochow (1895), Hankow (1893), Ichang (1895), Kewkiang (1894), Nanking (1896), Wuhu (1894) and Shanghai (1865).

CHIOS (1913)

Stamp-issuing status: inactive.

Island in the Aegean Sea. Chios was captured by Greece from Turkey in 1912. In 1913, an overprinted Greek stamp was issued. Stamps of Greece have since been used.

CHRISTMAS ISLAND (1958-)

Stamp-issuing status: active; Population: 3,018; Stamps issued: more than 200; Issues per year for last decade: 12.

An island in the Indian Ocean. Under the British colony of Singapore from 1900-58, Christmas Island was transferred to Australian administration in 1958.

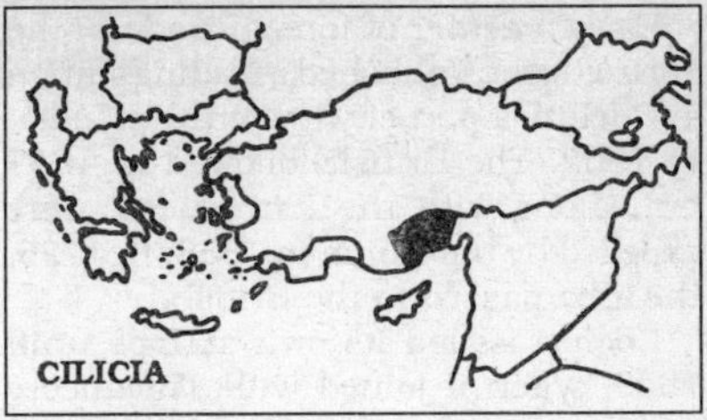
CILICIA

CILICIA (1919-21)

Stamp-issuing status: inactive; Stamps issued: 117.

A district of southern Turkey, northwest of Syria. Cilicia was occupied by the British and French from Turkey in 1918.

In 1919, France assumed sole control and in 1920 received the territory as a mandate from the League of Nations. In 1921, however, Turkish forces expelled the French, and in 1923, France gave up its claims to the area.

During 1919, Cilicia used Palestinian stamps, and during 1919-21, the French regime issued overprinted stamps of Turkey and France.

CISKEI (1981-)

Stamp-issuing status: active; Stamps issued: more than 60; Issues per year 1981-84: 20.

One of South Africa's so-called Bantustans or Bantu homelands, a scattering of nominally semi-autonomous states for otherwise disenfranchised black South Africans located on the sites of reserves set up under the policies of the white-run apartheid government prior to World War II.

Ciskei is the most southerly of these, consisting of a wedge of coastal territory southwest of the city of East London.

Although not accorded international recognition as a sovereign state, Ciskei's stamps have generally been accepted on international mail. Stamp-issuing policies have been conservative.

COAMO (1898)

Stamp-issuing status: inactive; Stamps issued: 1.

A city in Puerto Rico. U.S. forces issued a stamp for provisional use in August-September 1898 after the city was wrested from Spanish control.

COCHIN (1892-1949)

Stamp-issuing status: inactive; Stamps issued: 201.

Early a center of foreign traders, the Portuguese established a trading station at Cochin, a port city in southern India, in 1502. The British followed in 1635 but, along with the Portuguese, were expelled by the Dutch in 1663. In 1795, the area passed to the British.

Cochin issued its own stamps until 1949, when it joined with Travancore and the coastal towns of Tangasseri and Anjengo to form the United State of Travancore-Cochin, whose issues then came into use. Indian stamps replaced these issues on April 1, 1951.

COCHIN CHINA (1886-92)

Stamp-issuing status: inactive; Stamps issued: 5.

The southernmost area of Vietnam. Occupied by France from 1863-67, Cochin China served as the base for French expansion in the region.

In 1887, Cochin China was incorporated into French Indo-China, whose stamps were used after 1892.

COCOS ISLANDS (KEELING ISLANDS) (1963-)

Stamp-issuing status: active; Population: 569; Stamps issued: more than 150; Issues per year for last decade: 12.

A group of tiny islands in the Indian Ocean under Australian administration. Stamps of the Cocos Islands are also valid in Australia.

COLOMBIA (1859-)

Stamp-issuing status: active; Population: 29 million; Stamps issued: more than 1,600; Issues per year for last decade: 25.

A republic in northwest South America. The seat of the Spanish viceroyalty of New Granada after 1718, Colombia declared its independence in 1810, finally ousting the Spanish in 1824.

Colombia, Venezuela and Ecuador comprised the State of Greater Colombia until 1830 when the three nations separated.

In 1903 the northern province of Panama broke away from Colombia and, with U.S. support, became independent.

Colombia is one of the few democracies in Latin America, although it has been plagued by chronic violence and disorder. "La Violencia" of 1948-58 claimed 200,000 lives, and political violence, albeit much abated, continues.

Colombia has been officially named the Republic of New Granada (1831-58), the Grenadine Confederation (1858-61), the United States of New Granada (1861), the United States of Colombia (1861-85), and the Republic of Colombia (since 1885).

COLOMBIA—STATES' ISSUES (1863-1904)

Stamp-issuing status: inactive; Stamps issued: 452 (combined).

Until 1885, the various Colombia states were sovereign, possessing the right to issue their own stamps.

In 1886, a national convention abolished most of the states' rights, transferring sovereignty to the central government. The states, however, retained the right to issue stamps, and did so as late as 1904.

The states that used their own stamps, along with national issues, were Antioquia, Bolivar, Boyaca, Canca, Cundinamarca, Panama, Santander, the city of Cucuta and Tolima.

COMORO ISLANDS (1950-)

Stamp-issuing status: active; Population: 456,000; Stamps issued: more than 550; Issues per year for last decade: 44.

A group of islands in the Mozambique Channel between Mozambique and Madagascar. Under French rule since the 19th century, the Comoros were attached to Madagascar from 1911-46, being re-organized as an Overseas Territory in 1946. Since 1950, the Comoros have issued their own stamps.

The Comoros became independent in 1975, except for Mayotte, which voted to remain French. A coup soon after independence placed a leftist regime in power, but its increasingly eccentric rule brought another coup in 1978, which replaced it with a pro-French government.

CONFEDERATE STATES OF AMERICA (1861-65)

Stamp-issuing status: inactive; Population: 9 million (1865 estimate); Stamps issued: 14.

The southern states of the United States, seceded from the Union in 1861 and attempted to establish an independent confederation.

After initial successes against the U.S.

forces, the Confederacy was on the defensive after 1863. By early 1865, the rebellious areas had been overrun, and the states were re-incorporated within the United States.

CONFEDERATE STATES OF AMERICA — PROVISIONAL ISSUES (1861)

Stamp-issuing status: inactive.

In the early months of the Civil War, many southern post offices were without regular stocks of stamps. U.S. stamps in rebel territory were demonetized after June 1, 1861, and general Confederate issues were not available until October 1861.

During the interim, many local postmasters issued provisional stamps and postal stationery. Occasionally, such provisionals appeared later during the war, when regular Confederate stamps were unavailable.

CONGO DEMOCRATIC REPUBLIC (1960-71)

Stamp-issuing status: inactive; Stamps issued: 431.

In January 1960, Belgium agreed to grant independence to the Belgian Congo, and general elections were held May 31. On June 30, the country became independent.

The Congo was immediately torn by domestic violence, causing most whites to flee and two of the richest regions, Katanga and South Kasai, to secede. In August, Belgian troops were replaced by United Nations forces, which gradually restored order and suppressed the independence movements in the south.

In 1963 Katanga was re-united with the Congo, and on June 30, 1964, its president, Moise Tshombe, became president of the Congo.

Within months of the U.N. withdrawal (June 1964), yet another separatist movement broke out, when leftists proclaimed a people's republic in Stanleyville. The central government suppressed this uprising, with the support of Belgian and white mercenary troops.

In 1965, General Joseph D. Mobutu became president. He began an Africanization program, wherein all Congolese with Christian names were required to adopt African names (he became Mobutu Sese Seko), Congolese place names were changed, and in 1971, the Congo itself was renamed the Republic of Zaire.

CONGO PEOPLE'S REPUBLIC (1959-)

Stamp-issuing status: active; Population: 2.14 million; Stamps issued: More than 1,125; Issues per year for last decade: 51.

A republic on the north bank of the Congo River, in west central Africa. The former French colony of Middle Congo, the Congo became a member state in the French community in 1958 and gained independence in 1960.

After 1963, the Congo adopted a Marxist-Leninist stance, with ties to both the U.S.S.R. and China. U.S. relations, severed in 1965, were restored in 1977.

While French economic ties remain strong, the Congo is politically aligned with the U.S.S.R. with whom a treaty of friendship and cooperation was signed in May 1981.

CONSTANTINOPLE (1909-14, 1921-23)

Stamp-issuing status: inactive.

The capital of the Ottoman Empire, situated on the Hellespont between the Black Sea and the Aegean Sea.

During 1873-81, Turkish stamps were overprinted for local use within the city, and a number of private posts issued stamps.

Italian stamps overprinted "Constantinopoli" were used by the Italian post in the city from 1909-14. These issues were again used from 1921-23 by the Italian garrison in Constantinople.

Stamps of the Russian Levant overprinted with the name of the city were used by the Russian postal service in Constantinople from 1909-14. During 1919, Romanian forces in the city used contemporary Romanian stamps overprinted "Posta Romana Constantinopl" with the emblem of the Romanian PTT.

COOK ISLANDS (1892-)

Stamp-issuing status: active; Population: 17,754; Stamps issued: more than 950; Issues per year for last decade: 56.

A group of islands in the South Pacific Ocean, northeast of New Zealand. In 1901, the Cook Islands became a dependency of New Zealand, gaining internal self-government in 1965.

CORDOBA (1858-65)

Stamp-issuing status: inactive; Stamps

issued: 2.

A province in central Argentina, Cordoba issued its own stamps from 1858 to 1865, when they were replaced by the issues of the central government.

CORFU (1923, 1941)

Stamp-issuing status: inactive; Stamps issued: 60.

The major island of the Ionian Islands, off the western coast of Greece in the Ionian Sea. Corfu, under Greek control since 1864, was occupied by Italy in 1923 and 1941-43.

Stamps of Italy and Greece were overprinted by the Italians for use on the island.

CORRIENTES (1856-80)

Stamp-issuing status: inactive; Stamps issued: 8.

The northeast province of Argentina, Corrientes issued its own stamps until 1880, when they were replaced by regular Argentine issues.

COS (1912-32)

Stamp-issuing status: inactive; Stamps issued: 26.

One of the Turkish Dodecanese Islands in the eastern Aegean Sea. Cos was occupied by Italy in 1912, at which time overprinted Italian stamps were issued.

These were superseded by the general Aegean Islands' issues in 1929, although two sets overprinted "Coo" were issued in 1930 and 1932.

COSTA RICA (1863-)

Stamp-issuing status: active; Population: 2.6 million; Stamps issued: more than 1,200; Issues per year for last decade: 36.

A republic in Central America, located between Nicaragua and Panama. Under Spain until 1821, Costa Rica's subsequent history has been mostly peaceful, enabling it to develop a relatively high standard of living. Still chiefly an agricultural country, individual ownership of land is common.

COUDEKERQUE (1940)

Stamp-issuing status: inactive.

A city in northern France, near Dunkerque. For a time after the German occupation in World War II, overprinted French stamps were used in the city.

COURLAND (1945)

Stamp-issuing status: inactive; Stamps issued: 4.

In October 1944, German forces in the Courland peninsula were cut off from Germany by the advancing Soviet army. In April 1945, the local German commander overprinted four German stamps for use in the area.

CRETE (1898-1910, 1944)

Stamp-issuing status: inactive; Population: 335,000 (1910 estimate); Stamp issued: 145.

A large island in the Aegean Sea, Crete was originally a province of Turkey. Continuous religious civil strife between the Christian and Moslem natives brought the intervention of the Great Powers in 1898.

In 1899, the island was declared an autonomy under Prince George of Greece. In 1908, the Cretan Assembly voted for union with Greece, which finally occurred in 1913.

Crete used Turkish stamps until 1899. Stamps of Crete were used until 1913, when Greek stamps came into use. During 1898-1914, various stamps were issued by the Powers for use in their districts of Crete, including Britain (1898-99), Russia (1899), Austria (1903-14), France (1903-13) and Italy (1900-12).

During World War II, German military air parcel post stamps were overprinted "Inselpost" for use by German troops on Crete and nearby islands, after their isolation following the German withdrawal from Greece.

CRIMEA (1919)

Stamp-issuing status: inactive.

A large peninsula on the Black Sea, south of the Ukraine. From the Crimea, the Krim Tatars ruled a powerful state during the 15th-17th centuries. They later came under Turkish rule, which was supplanted by Russian rule in 1783.

During World War I, the Crimea was occupied by the Germans, who in June 1918, set up a Tatar government in the area. With the German withdrawal in November, a provisional government was established and several stamps were issued. The Crimea was subsequently occupied by the French, the Bolsheviks, Gen. Denikin's Volunteer Army, and finally by the Bolsheviks a second (and final) time.

During World War II, the Crimea was

again occupied by the Germans and was included in the Ukraine administrative district.

CROATIA (1941-45)

Stamp-issuing status: inactive; Population: 7 million (1945 estimate); Stamps issued: 221.

A district of northern Yugoslavia, bordering on the Adriatic Sea. Croatia was a province of Hungary until 1918, when it became a part of Yugoslavia.

In 1941, a German puppet state was created in Croatia. Nominally a kingdom under an Italian prince, in fact the state was ruled by the Croat fascist party.

Croatia was overrun by Russian and Yugoslavian partisan forces in 1945 and re-incorporated into Yugoslavia.

CUAUTLA (1867)

Stamp-issuing status: inactive; Stamps issued: 1.

A town in the State of Morelos in central Mexico, a simple provisional issue was produced there during the struggle against Emperor Maximilian.

CUBA (1855-)

Stamp-issuing status: active; Population: 9.9 million; Stamps issued: more than 2,750; Issues per year for last decade: 80.

The largest island of the West Indies, located south of Florida.

Under Spanish rule from 1511-1898, Cuba was the scene of intense revolutionary activity after 1868. In 1898, the sinking of the *USS Maine* in Havana harbor precipitated the Spanish-American War, which ended with the U.S. assuming trusteeship of the island.

In 1902, the Cuban republic became independent, although the United States actively intervened in Cuban affairs until the 1930s.

In 1959 a liberal guerrilla movement, led by Fidel Castro, overthrew the repressive government of Fulgencio Batista, who had ruled Cuba since 1952. Castro, influenced by his brother Raul and Che Guevera, soon began to purge the revolution of its non-Marxist elements.

The regime nationalized foreign holdings and began the program of collectivization that has since taken most agricultural sectors out of private hands. A large number of Cubans preferred exile to the new order, and many hundreds of thousands have fled the island, most settling in the United States.

Castro linked Cuban policy closely with that of the U.S.S.R., which soon established a strong military presence on the island. U.S.-Cuban relations deteriorated rapidly. In 1961, the United States backed an abortive invasion by a Cuban exile force, and in 1962, the discovery of nuclear missiles at Soviet bases in Cuba brought the United States and the Soviet Union to the brink of war. The United States imposed a total trade embargo on Cuba in 1962, which was supported by the Organization of American States in 1963.

In the years since, the Castro regime has improved the standard of living in Cuba and has largely overcome illiteracy. The Cuban economy is dependent on massive Soviet aid, however.

Since 1975, Cuban troops and advisors have actively supported pro-Soviet factions in Africa and, more recently, in Central America.

The U.S. Treasury Department prohibits the importation of Cuban postage stamps into the United States through the mail.

CUERNAVACA (1867)

Stamp-issuing status: inactive; Stamps issued: 1.

The capital city of the State of Morelos in central Mexico. A simple provisional issue was produced there during the struggle against Emperor Maximilian.

CYPRUS (1880-)

Stamp-issuing status: active; Population: 675,000; Stamps issued: more than 650; Issues per year for last decade: 21.

A large island in the eastern Mediterranean. Long ruled by foreigners, Cyprus was a Turkish possession from

1571 to 1878.

In 1878, the British occupied the island, formally annexing it in 1914. In 1960, the British withdrew and Cyprus became an independent republic.

Tension between Greek and Turkish elements, each of which seeks union with the respective mother country, led to a Turkish invasion of northeastern Cyprus in 1974. Turkey currently occupies about 40 percent of the island, issuing stamps as the Turkish Republic of Northern Cyprus.

Since the invasion, Greek and Turkish regimes have maintained an uneasy truce, dividing the island between them along a buffer zone patrolled by United Nations peacekeeping troops.

CYRENAICA (1923-35, 1950-51)

Stamp-issuing status: inactive; Population: 225,000 (1934 estimate); Stamps issued: 157.

A district of north Africa, west of Egypt. Cyrenaica was under Turkish control until 1912, when it was ceded to Italy and incorporated with Tripolitania to form the colony of Libia. In 1942, it was occupied by the British, becoming part of the independent kingdom of Libya in 1951.

CZECHOSLOVAK LEGION POST (1918-20)

Stamp-issuing status: inactive; Stamps issued: 14.

During World War I, many Czech nationalists fought against Austria on the Russian front. After the Russian Revolution, these units attempted to move to the western front to continue fighting, but clashes with the Bolsheviks en route to Vladivostok led to the Czechs' involvement in the Russian Civil War.

The Czechs achieved notable successes, for a time holding large areas along the Trans-Siberian Railroad. News of these successes created sympathy for the cause of Czechoslovak independence.

During this period, the Czech Legion issued a number of stamps for use by its forces in Russia.

CZECHOSLOVAKIA (1918-)

Stamp-issuing status: active; Population: 15.5 million (1986); Stamps issued: more than 3,100; Issues per year for last decade: 55.

A republic in central Europe. The medieval kingdom of Bohemia, long a power in central Europe, passed to the Hapsburgs of Austria in 1526.

Nationalism grew in strength throughout the 19th century, and in 1918, Czechoslovakia became independent. In 1938, Czechoslovakia lost border territories to Germany, Hungary and Poland, and in 1939, the balance of the country was occupied by Germany.

In 1945, the country was liberated by Allied forces and the Czechoslovak republic was re-established. In February 1948, the Communists seized power and by September had effectively suppressed opposition. There followed a long period of violent repression and purges of liberal party leaders.

In January 1968, Alexander Dubeck replaced Antonin Novotny as party leader and launched a program aimed at establishing a democratic Communist system. The Soviet Union feared that the success of such reforms would weaken its control over its Eastern European satellites, and relations between the two governments became increasingly cool. In August, Soviet, Polish, East German, Hungarian and Bulgarian forces invaded Czechoslovakia and put an end to the liberalization. Nearly a third of the Czechoslovak Communist Party members were expelled, and some 40,000 Czechs fled the country. The government has since maintained a repressive, staunchly pro-Soviet policy.

- D -

DAHOMEY (1899-1945, 1960-76)

Stamp-issuing status: inactive; Population: 3.1 million (1975 estimate); Stamps issued: 652.

A former republic on the Gulf of Guinea in West Africa.

During 1863-92 France occupied the area, consolidating its holdings as the colony of Dahomey in 1899.

In 1958 Dahomey became an autonomous republic within the French Community, and in 1960 it became an independent republic.

After a series of coups following independence, the present government assumed power in 1972. In 1974, it announced the formation of a Marxist-

Leninist socialist state, and in November 1975, changed the name of the country to the People's Republic of Benin.

DALMATIA (1919-22)

Stamp-issuing status: inactive; Stamps issued: 14.

Area on the coast of Yugoslavia around the port of Zara. Dalmatia was occupied by Italy in 1918 and became part of Yugoslavia after World War II.

DANISH WEST INDIES (1855-1917)

Stamp-issuing status: inactive; Population: 27,500 (1917 estimate); Stamps issued: 65.

A small group of islands east of Puerto Rico. Having passed through the hands of Spain, France, The Netherlands, Great Britain, the Knights of Malta and Brandenburg (Prussia), the islands finally came under Danish rule in 1733 and 1754 (St. Thomas).

In 1916 the colony was sold to the United States, which took possession on April 1, 1917. They were renamed the U.S. Virgin Islands, and U.S. stamps replaced those of the colony.

DANUBE STEAM NAVIGATION COMPANY (1866-80)

Stamp-issuing status: inactive.

This company carried mail along the Danube, serving all countries through which the river passed, as well as the Russian port of Odessa on the Black Sea.

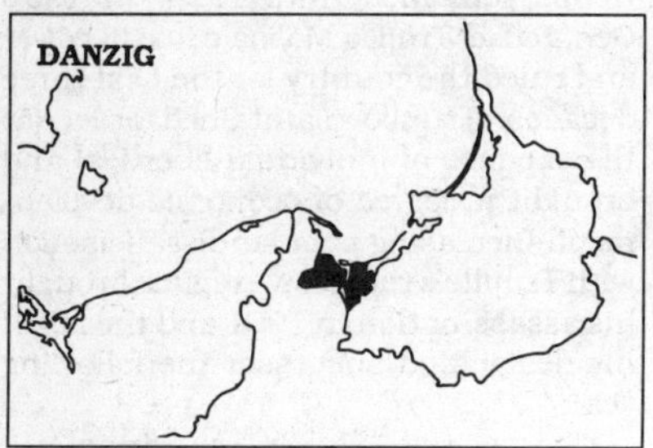

DANZIG (1920-39)

Stamp-issuing staus: inactive; Population: 407,000 (1939 estimate); Stamps issued: 427.

A port on the Baltic Sea. Part of Prussia until after World War I, Danzig and adjacent territory was made a "Free City and State" under the protection of the League of Nations in 1920.

In 1939, the district was occupied by Germany and, in 1945, was annexed by Poland.

DARDANELLES (1904-14)

Stamp-issuing status: inactive; Stamps issued: 9.

A port on the strait of the same name between the Aegean and Mamara Seas. Issues of the Russian Levant were overprinted for use at its post office at Dardanelles.

DEBRECEN (1919-20)

Stamp-issuing status: inactive; Stamps issued: 129.

A Hungarian district occupied by Romania after World War I, but later returned to Hungary.

DEDEAGATCH (1893-1914)

Stamp-issuing status: inactive; Stamps issued: 15 (French), 22 (Greek).

A seaport in northern Greece. The French post office in Dedeagatch used unoverprinted French issues (canceled "5155" in a diamond-shaped grid of dots) from 1874-93 and stamps overprinted or inscribed "Dedeagh" from 1893 until August 1914.

During the first Balkan War (1912), Dedeagatch was occupied by Bulgaria from Turkey. In 1913, Greece occupied the city from Bulgaria, and overprinted Bulgarian stamps, along with a typeset provisional issue, were used pending the arrival of regular Greek stamps.

DENMARK (1851-)

Stamp-issuing status: active; Population: 5.1 million; Stamps issued: more than 1,075; Issues per year for last decade: 25.

A kingdom in northwestern Europe, located strategically between the North Sea and the Baltic Sea.

Denmark was one of the chief Viking centers and for centuries was one of the leading powers in northern Europe. At one time or another during the Middle Ages, Denmark ruled Norway, Sweden, Finland, Iceland and England.

During the 17th-19th centuries, Danish power declined, and defeats by Sweden, Britain and Prussia forced it back to, roughly, its present boundaries.

After 1815, Denmark adopted a policy of neutrality, which it maintained for 130 years.

This policy was abandoned after World

War II, during which the country was occupied by Germany. Denmark was a charter member of NATO and joined the Common Market in 1960.

A rich country agriculturally, Denmark has undergone an industrial boom since 1945. A long tradition of democracy and social cooperation mark the country's political life.

DHAR (1897-1901)

Stamp-issuing status: inactive; Stamps issued: 1.

A former feudatory state in west-central India, Dhar issues were replaced by those of India on April 1, 1901.

DIEGO-SUAREZ (1890-96)

Stamp-issuing status: inactive; Population: 12,000 (1896); Stamps issued: 63.

A port at the north end of Madagascar, Diego Suarez was a French colony from 1885 to 1896, when it was attached to Madagascar.

DJIBOUTI (1977-)

Stamp-issuing status: active; Population: 387,000 (1987 estimate); Stamps issued: more than 325; Issues per year for last decade: 33.

The former French overseas territory of Afars and Issas in northeast Africa became independent on June 17, 1977.

Somali Coast and Obock issues also received Djibouti overprints and surcharges in 1894-1902.

Djibouti is supported by French aid, and a French garrison remains in the country.

DOBRUDJA (1916-18)

Stamp-issuing status: inactive; Stamps issued: 10.

A Romanian territory on the Black Sea, comprising the area south of the Danube River. Dobrudja was occupied by Bulgaria during World War I, during which time overprinted Bulgarian stamps were used in the district.

DODECANESE ISLANDS (1947)

Stamp-issuing status: inactive; Stamps issued: 10.

The former Italian Aegean Islands, occupied by Greece after World War II. Overprinted Greek stamps were used until their replacement by regular Greek issues.

DOMINICA (1874-)

Stamp-issuing status: active; Population: 81,000; Stamps issued: more than 1,000; Issues per year for last decade: 50.

An island in the Caribbean southeast of Puerto Rico. Dominica was a British Crown Colony 1833-1968 and an Associate State 1968-78. On Nov. 3, 1978, it became independent.

DOMINICAN REPUBLIC (1865-)

Stamp-issuing status: active; Population: 6.4 million; Stamps issued: more than 1,720; Issues per year for last decade: 40.

A republic occupying the eastern two-thirds of the island of Hispaniola in the West Indies. The Dominican Republic was ruled by Spain until c.1800, thereafter falling under periods of Spanish, French and Haitian rule until 1844.

In 1861-65, the republic was again occupied by Spain. A Dominican request for annexation by the U.S. was rejected in 1865.

The first stamps used in the country were Spanish colonial issues for Cuba and Puerto Rico. After the Spanish withdrawal, the Dominican Republic began issuing its own stamps.

The rest of the 19th century was marked by political instability. From 1916 to 1922, the country was under U.S. military administration, and U.S. troops remained until 1924. In 1930 Gen. Rafael Trujillo Molina came to power and ruled the country for the next three decades. Trujillo maintained order (at the expense of individual liberties) and brought a degree of economic development. Increasing popular dissatisfaction with Trujillo's repressive regime brought his assassination in 1961 and the fall of his designated successor the following year.

Free elections were held in 1962, but the president was deposed in 1963. In 1965 the ousted leader's followers staged a revolt, bringing U.S. intervention. U.S. troops, along with small contingents from five South American countries, remained as a peacekeeping force until September 1966, presiding over new elections. Since that time, the Dominican Republic has enjoyed relative stability and economic progress.

DON COSSACK GOVERNMENT (1918-19)

Stamp-issuing status: inactive; Stamps issued: 80.

On June 5, 1918, the Don Cossacks established a republic at Rostov, in southern Russia. Allied with Gen. Denikin's Volunteer Army, the government fell to the Soviets after Denikin's withdrawal from Rostov in February 1920.

DUBAI (1963-72)

Stamp-issuing status: inactive.

A sheikdom in the Trucial States in east Arabia in the Persian Gulf. Dubai was under British protection from 1892-1971 when it became a part of the independent United Arab Emirates.

DUNKERQUE (1940)

Stamp-issuing status: inactive.

A French port on the English Channel. During July 1-Aug. 9, 1940, 15 French stamps overprinted locally by the German military authorities were in use in the area around Dunkerque.

DURANGO (1937)

Stamp-issuing status: inactive.

A city in the province of Vizcaya in northern Spain. A 16-value set was overprinted by local authorities in 1937 to commemorate the occupation of the city by the Nationalists.

DURAZZO (1909-11, 1916-18)

Stamp-issuing status: inactive; Stamps issued: 9.

An Albanian port. Italian stamps overprinted "Durazzo" and surcharged in Turkish currency were used by the Italian post office in the city from February 1909 to 1911.

DUTTIA (DATIA) (1893-1921)

Stamp-issuing status: inactive; Stamps issued: 137.

A former feudatory state in north-central India, Duttia's stamps were replaced by Indian issues in 1921.

- E -

EAST AFRICA FORCES (1943-50)

Stamp-issuing status: inactive.

A total of nine British stamps were overprinted "E.A.F." or "Somalia" for use in Italian Somalia under the British occupation.

EAST AFRICA AND UGANDA PROTECTORATES (1903-21)

Stamp-issuing status: inactive; Population: 6.5 million; Stamps issued: 62.

A former British administrative unit in eastern Africa, comprising Kenya and Uganda.

EAST CHINA (1938-50)

Stamp-issuing status: inactive; Stamps issued: 125.

The Communist East China Liberation Area included the provinces of Shantung, Kiangsu, Chekiang, Anhwei and Fukien. Fourteen postal districts within East China issued stamps during 1938-49.

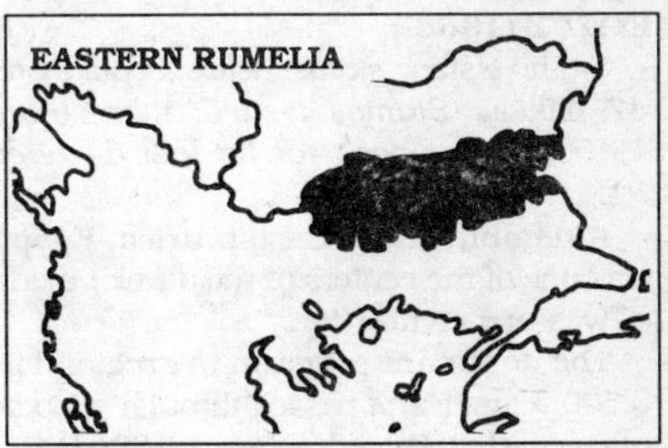

EASTERN RUMELIA (1880-85)

Stamp-issuing status: inactive; Stamps issued: 40.

A Bulgarian district in the southeast Balkan Peninsula. After Turkey's defeat by Russia in 1877-78, Eastern Rumelia became autonomous.

In 1885, a coup overthrew the vestiges of Turkish control and South Bulgaria was established.

EASTERN SILESIA (1920)

Stamp-issuing status: inactive; Stamps issued: 59.

A former Austrian territory in central Europe. After World War I, it was disputed between Czechoslovakia and Poland, being divided between the two countries in 1920.

ECUADOR (1865-)

Stamp-issuing status: active; Population: 9.6 million; Stamps issued: more than 1,900; Issues per year for last decade: 41.

Republic on the western coast of South America. Ecuador was the site of a number of early Indian cultures and was the center of the northern Inca empire at the time of its conquest by Spain (1533).

In 1822, Ecuador became independent as part of Bolivar's Great Colombia. In 1830, it withdrew to form a separate nation.

Despite substantial petroleum deposits (it is an OPEC member), Ecuador remains an underdeveloped nation.

A series of military and civilian regimes have alternated control in recent years. Since 1979, a democratic civilian government has ruled the country.

A long-standing border dispute between Ecuador and Peru remains unresolved. Armed hostilities occasionally erupt between the two countries, most recently in January/February 1981.

EGYPT (1866-)

Stamp-issuing status: active; Population: 47 million; Stamps issued: more than 1,400; Issues per year for last decade: 31.

A republic in northeast Africa. Egypt was one of the centers of the development of western civilization.

The dominant power in the region for 3,500 years, Egypt passed through periods of strength and weakness until 330 B.C., after which it was ruled by foreign states and dynasties until modern times.

After 1517, Egypt was under Turkish control. In 1882, Britain occupied Egypt, although a nominal Turkish suzerainty remained until 1914.

Egypt was a British protectorate until 1922, after which time it was virtually independent. British troops remained until 1951, when Egypt became completely independent.

The corruption and extravagance of the monarchy brought the overthrow of King Farouk in 1952 and the establishment of a republic in 1953. In 1954, Lt. Col. Gamel Abdel Nasser, one of the leaders in the 1952 coup, came to power and ruled until his death in 1970.

Nasser pursued a pan-Arab policy and attempted to unite the Arab world under his leadership. The United Arab Republic joined Egypt and Syria 1958-61, but attempts to maintain the union or to include Iraq and Yemen during this period failed.

Nasser's foreign policy, technically neutral, was in most instances aligned with that of the U.S.S.R., and by the time of his death, thousands of Soviet advisors were in Egypt.

Nasser was succeeded by Anwar Sadat, who expelled Soviet advisors in 1971 and who pursued an increasingly pro-Western policy after 1974. Egypt has fought wars with Israel in 1948, 1956, 1967 and 1973. In each instance, Israel has won.

In 1979, Egypt and Israel signed a formal peace treaty, establishing formal diplomatic relations, setting a timetable for Israeli withdrawal from Egyptian territory occupied since 1967, and providing for an as yet undetermined Palestinian state.

Egypt's attempt to make peace with Israel brought its ostracism by other Arab nations. Although the issue of a Palestinian state remains a major point of dispute, Egypt has, however, continued to work within the framework of its 1979 treaty with Israel.

In October 1981, Sadat was assassinated. He was quickly succeeded by his vice president, Hosni Mubarak, who has continued Sadat's peace initiative with Israel while working toward restoring normal relations with other Arab states.

Mubarak's firm support of Iraq in its war with Iran, which has included the dispatch of several hundred key Egyptian military personnel to the front, has done much to bring Egypt back into the Arab fold.

ELOBEY, ANNOBON AND CORISCO (1903-09)

Stamp-issuing status: inactive; Population: 3,000 (1910 estimate); Stamps issued: 62.

A group of islands near the Guinea coast off west Africa. The islands were acquired by Spain in 1778. Stamps of Fernando Po were used from 1868 to 1903.

In 1909, the islands were attached to Spanish Guinea, now the Republic of Equatorial Guinea.

ELWA (1941)

Stamp-issuing status: inactive.

A city in Estonia. Some 58 Russian stamps were provisionally overprinted "Eesti"/"Post" by the German military authorities for use in the city.

EPIRUS (1914-16)

Stamp-issuing status: inactive; Stamps issued: 61.

A region in southeast Albania. Inhabitants set up a provisional government in February 1914, and were united with Greece in December 1914.

In 1916, Franco-Italian forces occupied the area, giving it to Albania after World War I.

EQUATORIAL GUINEA (1968-)

Stamp-issuing status: active; Population: 304,000 (1983 estimate); Stamps issued: more than 1,200; Issues per year for last decade: 10.

A republic in the Gulf of Guinea, in West Africa, comprising the former Spanish colonies of Fernando Po and Rio Muni. Equatorial Guinea became independent Oct. 12, 1968.

In 1972 Masie Ngeuma Biyogo became president for life. He ruled by terror, reviving slavery, killing some 50,000 people, and driving tens of thousands more into exile.

The U.S. suspended relations with the Biyogo government in 1976. The U.S.S.R., China, and North Korea maintained close relations, and Cuba maintained a military advisory mission in the country.

On Aug. 5, 1979, Masie was overthrown, and a junta assumed power. The coup halted the production of vast numbers of brightly colored stamps (perfs, imperfs, souvenir sheets, gold-foil sheets) that were issued by Equatorial Guinea in the 1970s.

ERSEKA (1914)

Stamp-issuing status: inactive.

A city in southeastern Albania, occupied by Greece in 1914. During the Greek occupation, the local authorities issued a set of seven stamps for use in the area.

ERITREA (1892-1937, 1948-52)

Stamp-issuing status: inactive; Population: 600,000 (1931 estimate); Stamps issued: 323.

A district in northeast Africa, bordering on the Red Sea. Long under general Ethiopian domination, the area was occupied by Italy during 1870-85. In 1890, Italian possessions in the region were consolidated into Eritrea.

In 1936, the colony was absorbed into Italian East Africa. It was occupied by the British in 1941, after which overprinted British stamps were used. In 1950, Eritrea became an autonomous part of Ethiopia, whose issues have been in use since 1952. Eritrea has not willingly accepted Ethiopian rule and since 1970 has waged a guerrilla war, aided by Arab states.

ESTONIA (1918-40)

Stamp-issuing status: inactive; Stamps issued: 202.

A district in northern Europe bordering on the Baltic Sea and the Gulf of Finland. Estonia declared independence from Russia in 1917.

In 1939, Soviet forces occupied the country, absorbing it in 1940. Occupied by Germany from 1941-44 and administered as part of Ostland, Estonia was re-occupied by the U.S.S.R. after World War II.

ETHIOPIA (ABYSSINIA) (1894-1938, 1942-)

Stamp-issuing status: active; Population: 45.7 million; Stamps issued: more than 1,350; Issues per year for last decade: 33.

A republic in northeast Africa. Ethiopia was an ancient empire, isolated from the rest of the Christian world after the Moslem conquests of the 7th century.

During the 19th century, the country was again united out of the petty states into which it had disintegrated. An Italian invasion was crushed in 1896, but many outlying areas were gradually lost to the British, French and Italians.

In 1935-36, Ethiopia was defeated by Italy and in 1936, with Eritrea and Italian Somaliland, incorporated into the colony of Italian East Africa.

In 1941, Ethiopia was liberated with the help of British forces, and independence was restored.

In 1975, the Emperor Haile Selassie I, who had reigned since 1922, was deposed, and a socialist military regime assumed power.

In 1978 Soviet advisors and 20,000 Cuban troops helped Ethiopia defeat Somalia in a border war in the Ogaden. Ethiopia is the center of Soviet influence in northern Africa.

EUPEN AND MALMEDY (1920-25)

Stamp-issuing status: inactive.

Two towns in western Germany annexed by Belgium after World War I. A total of 68 overprinted stamps of Belgium were used until 1925, when regular

Belgian issues came into use.

- F -

FALKLAND ISLANDS (1878-)

Stamp-issuing status: active; Population: 1,900; Stamps issued: more than 500; Issues per year for last decade: 20.

The Falkland Islands (with its dependencies) comprise some 200 islands off the southeastern coast of South America. Only the two main islands, East and West Falkland, are inhabited. Ninety-eight percent of the Falklanders are of British descent and have British nationality.

The Falklands were discovered by the British in 1592 but were uninhabited until a French settlement was established in 1764 and a British settlement in 1765. The two countries disputed sovereignty until 1770 when France sold her claim to Spain. Spain and Britain disputed ownership of the islands until 1806, when the Spanish withdrew their settlement.

Although Spain ceased pressing its claim at that time, the newly independent United Provinces of Rio de la Plata claimed the Falklands after 1816. A settlement was maintained 1820-33, when the British re-occupied the islands and peacefully expelled the Argentine garrison.

Argentina has maintained its claim to the Falklands and, on April 2, 1982, seized the islands. A British fleet was immediately dispatched to oust the Argentines, and successfully recaptured the islands.

FALKLAND ISLANDS DEPENDENCIES (1946-85)

Stamp-issuing status: inactive; Stamps issued: 127.

Several island groups in the South Atlantic Ocean and the British sector of Antarctica. In 1944, Graham Land, South Georgia, the South Orkneys and South Shetlands received separate stamp sets, overprinted on Falkland issues, and in 1946, general issues for the territory began. In 1962 this area was re-organized as the British Antarctic Territory, with South Georgia remaining attached to the Falklands.

In October 1985 two of the principal dependencies, South Georgia and South Sandwich Islands, ceased to be dependencies of the Falkland Islands and began to issue their own stamps.

FAR EASTERN REPUBLIC (1920-22)

Stamp-issuing status: inactive; Population: 1.5 million (1920 estimate); Stamps issued: 58.

The Far Eastern Republic, comprising eastern Siberia from Lake Baikal to the Pacific Ocean, was formed on April 6, 1920, to act as a buffer between the Soviet Union and Japan. The state was immediately beset by intrigues between pro- and anti- Bolshevik factions, with the former finally gaining the upper hand. Japanese forces were forced to withdraw from Vladivostock in November 1922, and soon thereafter the Far Eastern Republic joined the Soviet Union.

FARIDKOT (1879-1901)

Stamp-issuing status: inactive; Stamps issued: 20.

A former principality in the Punjab area of India. Faridkot issued stamps and maintained its own postal system until Jan. 1, 1887, when it signed a postal convention uniting its postal system to that of India.

Overprinted Indian stamps were used until March 31, 1901, when they were replaced by regular Indian issues.

FAROE ISLANDS (1919, 1940-41, 1975-)

Stamp-issuing status: active; Population: 46,500; Stamps issued: more than 180; Issues per year for last decade: 14.

A group of islands in the North Atlantic Ocean. The Faroe Islands, long a Danish possession, are now a self-governing part of the kingdom of Denmark. The islands were occupied by Britain during World War II, after Denmark's occupation by Germany.

FERNANDO PO (1868-1909, 1929, 1960-68)

Stamp-issuing status: inactive; Population: 63,000 (1968 estimate); Stamps issued: 265.

An island in the Gulf of Guinea, off the west coast of Africa. Fernando Po was acquired by Spain in 1778 and was incorporated into Spanish Guinea in 1909.

In 1960, it became an overseas province of Spain, but in 1968 united with Rio

Muni to form the independent republic of Equatorial Guinea.

FEZZAN-GHADAMES (1943-51)

Stamp-issuing status: inactive; Stamps issued: 160.

Districts in the interior of Libya, occupied by French forces during 1942-43. The districts were transferred to the kingdom of Libya in December 1951.

FIJI (1870-)

Stamp-issuing status: active; Population: 700,000; Stamps issued: more than 600; Issues per year for last decade: 20.

A group of islands in the South Pacific Ocean. Fiji was a British colony from 1874 to 1970 when it became an independent dominion within the British Commonwealth.

FINLAND (1856-)

Stamp-issuing status: active; Population: 4.9 million; Stamps issued: more than 1,000; Issues per year for last decade: 17.

A republic in northern Europe. Under Swedish rule from 1187 to 1809, Finland became a grand duchy with the Russian tsar as grand duke in 1809.

In 1899, Finland was incorporated into the Russian Empire, but in July 1917, the Finnish Diet proclaimed independence. After several years of warfare, Russia accepted Finnish independence in 1919.

In 1939, Finland was invaded by the U.S.S.R. and, in 1940, was compelled to cede extensive eastern territories to the Soviets. Finland subsequently allied herself with Germany in an attempt to regain these territories, but her defeat cost even further concessions.

Although economically and culturally oriented toward the West, Finland has since World War II pursued a policy of acquiescence to the Soviet Union.

FIUME (1918-24)

Stamp-issuing status: inactive; Population: 44,956 (1924 estimate); Stamps issued: 270.

A city on the Adriatic Sea. A former Hungarian port, Fiume was disputed by Italy and Yugoslavia after World War I.

An Italian private army occupied the city in 1919, and a free state was subsequently established during 1920-22. A fascist coup brought Italian occupation in 1922.

In 1924, Fiume was annexed to Italy, while adjacent territory was annexed to Yugoslavia.

In May 1945, Fiume was occupied by Yugoslav partisans. Italian stamps were overprinted for use in the area during 1945-46, after which regular Yugoslavian issues came into use.

FRANCE (1849-)

Stamp-issuing status: active; Population: 55.5 million; Stamps issued: more than 3,000; Issues per year for last decade 67.

A republic in western Europe. France was overrun by the German Franks in the 5th century. During the 8th century, the Frankish kingdom stopped the Arab advance into Europe and by c. A.D. 800, the Frankish Empire, under Charlemagne, ruled most of western and central Europe.

In 843, the empire was partitioned, and the western kingdom became the foundation of modern France. During the Middle Ages, France lacked any strong central government, being divided among numerous feudal states.

The English dominated much of the area during the 11th-15th centuries, but they were finally expelled after 1453.

The French Revolution (1789) began a series of wars in Europe that lasted until the final defeat of Napoleon Bonaparte in 1815.

During the second half of the 19th century, France built a far-flung overseas empire.

During World War I, France suffered greatly, and most of the bitterest fighting was on French soil. France emerged from the war the pre-eminent power on the continent, but in the 1930s it lost ground to a re-emerging Germany.

France quickly crumbled before Germany's invasion in May and June 1940. The northern and western portions of the country were occupied by Germany, and a German puppet regime was established in the south. A Free French government, based in Africa, continued to war against the Axis overseas.

Following World War II, France rapidly rebuilt its economy and again played a major role in world affairs. During 1958-70, Gen. Charles de Gaulle's policies of economic and technological development and independence in foreign affairs were aimed at re-establishing France's greatness. De Gaulle disengaged France from its colonial commitments, and during 1958-62, most of French Africa became independent. France, however, retains close economic and political ties with many of its former colonies.

FRENCH COLONIES (1859-1906, 1944-45)

Stamp-issuing status: inactive; Stamps issued: 100.

During 1859-92, general French colonial issues were used in French possessions not issuing their own stamps. General postage dues were in use until 1906 and during 1944-45.

The French colonial semipostal issues of 1943-44 were intended for use in the colonies, but were actually used in parts of France occupied by the Free French.

FRENCH CONGO (1891-1906)

Stamp-issuing status: inactive; Stamps issued: 52.

The territory occupied by France, north of the Congo River, at times including Gabon, Ubangi and Chad, as well as the area now included in the Congo People's Republic.

The French Congo issued stamps from 1891 until 1906 when the administrative area was broken up into the separate colonies of Gabon and Middle Congo.

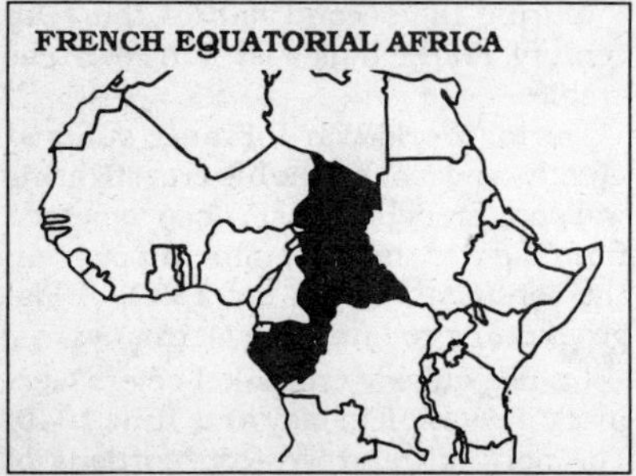

FRENCH EQUATORIAL AFRICA (1936-58)

Stamp-issuing status: inactive; Population: 4.5 million (1958 estimate); Stamps issued: 312.

The French possessions north of the Congo River, formerly included in the French Congo. Stamps inscribed French Equatorial Africa were used from 1936 to 1958, when the area was divided into four republics — Chad, Congo, Gabon and Central African Republic, which have since issued their own stamps.

FRENCH GUIANA (1886-1946)

Stamp-issuing status: inactive; Population: 29,000 (1947 estimate); Stamps issued: 274.

A former French colony on the northeastern coast of South America, north of Brazil. Separate issues were used in French Guiana from 1886 until 1946, when the area became an overseas department of France, using regular French issues.

FRENCH GUINEA (1892-1944)

Stamp-issuing status: active; Population: 5.8 million; Stamps issued: 229; Issues per year for last decade: 34.

A former French colony on the western coast of Africa. During 1892-1944, French Guinea used its own stamps. In 1944, these were replaced by those of French West Africa.

In 1958, the colony became independent as the republic of Guinea, and again began issuing its own stamps.

FRENCH INDIA (1892-1954)

Stamp-issuing status: inactive; Population: 400,000 (1954 estimate); Stamps issued: 308.

Several French enclaves on the east coast of India, dating from the period of French domination of the region in the 18th century.

Separate stamp issues were in use from 1892 until 1954, when the last of the French holdings were transferred to India, and Indian stamps came into use.

FRENCH MOROCCO (1891-1956)

Stamp-issuing status: inactive; Population: 8.3 million (1956 estimate); Stamps issued: 542.

Former French protectorate in northwest Africa. The greater part of Morocco became a French protectorate in 1912.

In 1956, the French and Spanish zones were united as the independent kingdom of Morocco.

FRENCH OFFICES IN CHINA (1894-1922)

Stamp-issuing status: inactive.

Until Dec. 31, 1922, France maintained an extensive postal system in China. In addition to a general series of stamps for these offices, individual issues were used at French post offices in Canton, Hoi Hao, Mongtsen, Pakhoi, Tch'ong K'ing (Chunking), and Yunnan Fou (Kunming).

In addition, stamps were issued for Kwangchowan, a leased territory administered by French Indo-China.

FRENCH OFFICES IN CRETE (1902-14)

Stamp-issuing status: inactive.

France issued two series of stamps for use in its post offices in Crete during the period of that country's autonomous regime.

FRENCH OFFICES IN EGYPT (1899-1931)

Stamp-issuing status: inactive.

Until April 1, 1931, France maintained post offices in Alexandria and Port Said, issuing stamps for use in both cities.

FRENCH OFFICES IN TURKEY (1885-1914, 1921-23)

Stamp-issuing status: inactive.

Like many other European nations, France maintained its own postal services within the Ottoman Empire. Aside from a general issue, individual issues were used in Cavalle (Cavalla), Dedeagh (Dedeagatch), Port Lagos and Vathy (Samos).

FRENCH OFFICES IN ZANZIBAR (1894-1906)

Stamp-issuing status: inactive.

During the late 19th century, France competed with England for influence in East Africa, including Zanzibar.

French post offices in Zanzibar were closed in 1906 when Britain assumed direct control over the sultanate.

FRENCH POLYNESIA (1892-)

Stamp-issuing status: active; Population: 163,000; Stamps issued: more than 600; Issues per year for last decade: 23.

After 1842, France expanded its holdings in the South Pacific, consolidating these into the Oceanic Settlements in 1885. This group was renamed the French Oceanic Settlements in 1903.

In 1957 the colony was renamed French Polynesia and in the following year became an Overseas Territory of the French Republic.

FRENCH SOUTHERN AND ANTARCTIC TERRITORIES (1955-)

Stamp-issuing status: active; Population: 200; Stamps issued: more than 200; Issues per year for last decade: 11.

The French overseas territory comprising its holdings in the Antarctic area. Formerly dependencies of Madagascar, this administrative unit was established in 1955 to strengthen France's claims in the region.

FRENCH SUDAN (1894-1943)

Stamp-issuing status: inactive; Population: 3.8 million (1941 estimate); Stamps issued: 164.

Former French colony in northwest Africa. Separate issues were in use from 1894-1943, when they were replaced by those of French West Africa. In 1959, this area joined with Senegal to form the independent republic of Mali.

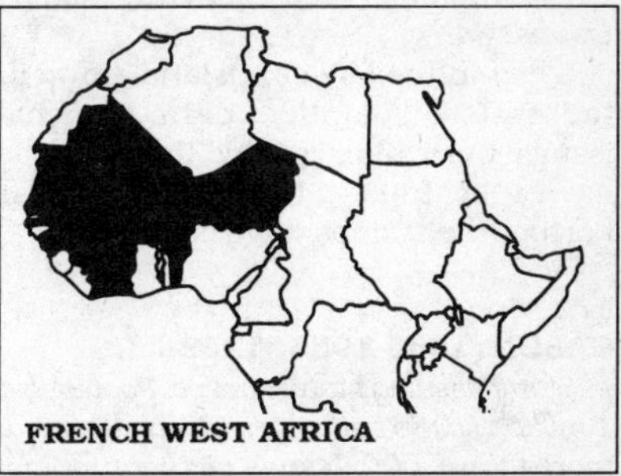

FRENCH WEST AFRICA

FRENCH WEST AFRICA (1943-59)

Stamp-issuing status: inactive; Population: 18 million (1959 estimate); Stamps issued: 138.

Former French administrative unit comprising the African colonies of Senegal, French Guinea, Ivory Coast, Dahomey, French Sudan, Mauritania, Niger and Upper Volta.

Although French West Africa was formed in 1895 as an administrative unit, the various colonies continued to issue their own stamps until 1943, when French West African issues came into use. These, in turn, were replaced by the separate issues of the territories as they became republics during 1958-59.

FUJEIRA (1964-72)

Stamp-issuing status: inactive.

Sheikdom in the Trucial States in southeast Arabia, in the Persian Gulf. Fujeira was under British protection from 1892 to 1971, when it became a member of the independent United Arab

Emirates.

FUNAFUTI (1984-)

Stamp-issuing status: active; Stamps issued: more than 100; Issues per year 1984-87: 33.

One of nine small islands in the Tuvalu Islands, formerly the Ellice Island group in the Gilbert and Ellice Islands. The island chain is located east of the Solomon Islands and north of Fiji in the south-eastern central Pacific Ocean.

Like the other Tuvalu Islands, Funafuti issued a flurry of stamps depicting such diverse subjects as cars, locomotives, cricket players and the British Royal Family in the mid-1980s.

FUNCHAL (1892-1905)

Stamp-issuing status: inactive; Population: 150,000 (1905 estimate); Stamps issued: 34.

A city in the Madeira island group in the eastern Atlantic Ocean. Funchal issues were replaced by those of the Azores in 1905. Since 1931, regular Portuguese stamps have been in use.

- G -

GABON (1886-1936, 1959-)

Stamp-issuing status: active; Population: 1 million (1986 estimate); Stamps issued: more than 1,000; Issues per year for last decade: 35.

Republic in western Equatorial Africa, north of the Congo region. Gabon was one of the four French colonies comprising French Equatorial Africa. In 1958, Gabon became a republic and, in 1960, gained independence from France.

Gabon possesses abundant natural resources, and through foreign aid and government development, it has become one of the most prosperous Black African nations.

GALAPAGOS ISLANDS (1957-59)

Stamp-issuing status: inactive; Stamps issued: 7.

A group of islands in the eastern South Pacific Ocean. Ecuador issued stamps for this province from 1957 to 1959. Although intended for use in the Galapagos, these issues were commonly used throughout Ecuador.

GAMBIA (1869-)

Stamp-issuing status: active; Population: 740,000; Stamps issued: more than 700; Issues per year for last decade: 35.

Republic in West Africa. British influence was dominant on the coast after the early 17th century, with the inland area occupied in 1902.

In 1965, Gambia became independent, and in 1970, it became a republic. It is one of the few African states to remain truly democratic.

Early in 1982, Gambia formed a federation, Sene-Gambia, with Senegal, which, except for a small length of coastline, surrounds it.

GENEVA (1843-50)

Stamp-issuing status: inactive; Stamps issued: 8.

A canton of Switzerland, almost surrounded by France. Geneva issued several stamps, which were used until the issue of national Swiss stamps in 1850.

GEORGIA (1919-20)

Stamp-issuing status: inactive; Population: 2.3 million (1920 estimate); Stamps issued: less than 75.

A region in the western Caucasus, south of Russia and north of Turkey. Long under Turkish influence, the region of Georgia was conquered by Russia during 1810-78.

In May 1918, following the withdrawal of German forces that had occupied the area during World War I, Georgia declared its independence. Georgia was recognized by the League of Nations, but on Feb. 25, 1921, it was occupied by Soviet forces. The Georgian Soviet Republic was merged into the Transcaucasian Federation of Soviet Republics in March 1922, and issues of the federation replaced those of Georgia on Oct. 1, 1923.

Georgian nationalist sentiment remains strong, provoking strong repression and massive purges since 1972. Despite this, illegal private enterprise and nationalism remain potent forces.

GERMAN EAST AFRICA (1893-1916)

Stamp-issuing status: inactive; Population: 7.7 million (1916 estimate); Stamps issued: 78.

A former German colony in eastern Africa, on the Indian Ocean. The area was long dominated by the Arab Sultanate of Zanzibar, but German influence in the area was recognized after 1886.

Stamps for the colony were in use from 1893 to 1916. After World War I, the colony was divided into Tanganyika (British), Ruanda-Urundi (Belgian) and Kionga (Portuguese).

GERMAN NEW GUINEA (1888-1914)

Stamp-issuing status: inactive; Population: 600,000 (1919 estimate); Stamps issued: 23.

A former German protectorate, comprising the northeastern portion of New Guinea and the adjacent islands. Regular German stamps were used from 1888 to 1898 when they were replaced by separate issues.

In 1914, the area was occupied by Australian forces, and stamps of New Guinea replaced those of the German administration.

GERMAN SOUTH-WEST AFRICA (1897-1915)

Stamp-issuing status: inactive; Population: 95,000 (1919 estimate); Stamps issued: 34.

A former German colony on the southwestern coast of Africa. Regular German stamps were used from 1888 to 1897, and stamps of the colony from 1897 to 1915.

In 1915, South African forces occupied the area, and stamps of the Union of South Africa came into use. In 1919, South Africa was granted a mandate over the territory. Since 1923, stamps of South-West Africa have been used.

GERMANY (1872-)

Stamp-issuing status: active; Population: 61 million; Stamps issued: more than 2,250; Issues per year for last decade: 38.

State in central Europe. Traditionally divided into numerous petty sovereignties, German unification began with the growth of Prussian power in the 19th century.

French occupation during the Napoleonic Wars brought the dissolution of many of the smaller states and stimulated German nationalism, which looked more and more to Prussia for leadership.

The German Confederation (1815-66) and North German Confederation (1867-71) paved the way for unification. The Franco-Prussian War of 1870-71 brought the German states (except Austria) together to defeat France, and the German victory saw the creation of the German Empire with the Prussian king as emperor.

Germany quickly emerged as the dominant military power on the continent.

In August 1914, after many years of tension, war between the major powers finally erupted, with the Central Powers (Germany and Austria-Hungary; later Bulgaria and Turkey) pitted against the Allies (Britain, France, and Russia, later joined by many other nations, including the United States and Japan). Both sides anticipated a short war and quick victory, but stalemates arose on all major fronts, and both sides settled in for years of trench warfare. During 1916-17, the Central Powers advanced in Russia, and the Russian front collapsed. The Treaty of Brest-Litovsk (March 3, 1918) gave Germany large areas of European Russia and much of the country's industry and mineral resources.

The Central Powers were less successful elsewhere: during the fall of 1918, Turkey surrendered to advancing British and Arab forces, Bulgaria surrendered, and Austria-Hungary collapsed. By this point, Germany itself was near economic collapse. The kaiser abdicated in November 1918, and a republic was established, soon after which Germany surrendered unconditionally.

The Treaty of Versailles (1919) stripped Germany of its overseas empire and transferred German European territories to France, Belgium, Poland and, after plebiscites, to Denmark and Lithuania. The harshness of the treaty's terms and the economic dislocation following the war provided fertile ground for political extremism, which culminated in the naming of Adolph Hitler as chancellor in 1933.

Hitler's National Socialist German Workers' Party quickly suppressed all political freedoms and began openly to re-arm. In 1936, Germany remilitarized the Rhineland, and in 1938, Austria and the Sudetenland (German-speaking Czechoslovakia) were annexed.

In 1939, Germany signed a non-aggression pact with the U.S.S.R., and on Sept. 1, German forces invaded Poland, precipitating World War II. Through 1942, Germany enjoyed an almost unbroken string of military successes. The entry of the United States into the war, however, gradually began to tell, and during 1944-45, Germany was on the retreat. In April 1945, soon after Hitler's suicide, Germany surrendered unconditionally.

Germany lost all territory acquired after 1919, as well as much of that which had been left to her after her defeat in World War I. The country was divided into four zones of occupation, administered by the U.S., Great Britain, France and U.S.S.R.

In 1949, the German Federal Republic was formed from the three western zones, and the German Democratic Republic was created out of the Soviet zone. The German Federal Republic became fully independent in 1955.

During the 1950s and 1960s, West Germany underwent a major economic boom, which has continued at a slower pace. West Germany now ranks as the fourth greatest economic power in the world and leads most other nations in worker participation in industry.

During the 1970s, West Germany normalized relations with its communist neighbors and has dramatically expanded its trade with Eastern Europe.

GERMAN DEMOCRATIC REPUBLIC (1949-)

Stamp-issuing status: active; Population: 16.7 million; Stamps issued: more than 2,800; Issues per year for last decade: 81.

During 1945-49, the U.S.S.R. occupied the eastern zone of Germany, which included the provinces of Saxony-Anhalt, Saxony, Brandenburg, Mecklenburg and Thuringia. On Oct. 7, 1949, the Russian zone was united as the German Democratic Republic. Although East Germany became fully independent in 1954, some 400,000 Soviet troops remain in the country.

The East German economy was held back by heavy-handed central planning until the mid-1960s. A relaxation of controls brought rapid industrialization, and by the early 1970s, East Germany was the ninth ranked economic power in the world.

GERMANY (SOVIET ZONE LOCAL ISSUES) (1945-46)

Stamp-issuing status: inactive; Stamps issued: 221.

During 1945-46, the Soviet-occupation postal authorities authorized issues for a number of localities — Berlin-Brandenburg (Berlin Postal Administration); Mecklenburg-Western Pomerania (Mecklenburg-Vorpommern); Saxony (Hall Postal Administration); East Saxony (Dresden Postal Administration); Thuringia (Erfurt Postal Administration); and Western Saxony (Leipzig Postal Administration).

GERMAN OFFICES IN CHINA (1898-1917)

Stamp-issuing status: inactive: Stamps issued: 55.

Germany maintained post offices in various Chinese cities after 1886, with specially overprinted German stamps in use from 1898 to 1917.

GERMAN OFFICES IN MOROCCO (1899-1919)

Stamp-issuing status: inactive; Stamps issued: 58.

German post offices in Morocco began using overprinted German stamps in 1899. In 1914, these offices were closed in the French zone and, in 1919, were closed in the Spanish zone.

GERMAN OFFICES IN TURKEY (1870-1914)

Stamp-issuing status: inactive; Stamps issued: 59.

German post offices began operating in Turkish cities in 1870, using unoverprinted stamps of the North German Postal District.

In 1872, these were replaced by regular German issues, and in 1884, overprinted German stamps came into use.

GHANA (1957-)

Stamp-issuing status: active; Population: 12.2 million; Stamps issued: more than 1,000; Issues per year for last decade: 44.

A republic in west Africa, on the Gulf of Guinea. Formed from the former British colony of the Gold Coast and the mandated territory of British Togoland in 1957, Ghana became fully independent in 1960.

During 1957-66, Ghana was ruled by Kwame Nkrumah, one of the leaders of its independence movement. Nkrumah launched major economic projects but, in the process, built up a huge foreign debt. His economic mismanagement and repression of political opposition created popular dissatisfaction, and in 1966, he was overthrown in a military coup.

The new regime expelled Chinese and East German advisors, and in 1969, civilian government was restored.

Political instability — the military has ousted civilian governments in 1972, 1978, 1979 and 1982 — and economic stagnation make Ghana's future uncertain.

GIBRALTAR (1886-)

Stamp-issuing status: active; Population: 7 million; Stamps issued: more than 440; Issues per year for last decade: 25.

A fortified promontory on the European side of the Strait of Gibraltar. Strategically located, Gibraltar has passed under a number of rulers.

Britain occupied the area in 1704 and has held it since, although Spain maintains its claim to the colony.

GILBERT ISLANDS (1976-79)

Stamp-issuing status: inactive; Population: 52,000 (1973 estimate); Stamps issued: 72.

A group of islands in the Pacific Ocean, northeast of Australia. Formerly part of the Gilbert and Ellice Islands, the Gilberts became a separate British crown colony in 1976. The Gilbert Islands became the independent Republic of Kiribati on July 12, 1979.

GILBERT AND ELLICE ISLANDS (1911-75)

Stamp-issuing status: inactive; Population: 58,000 (1975 estimate); Stamps issued: 260.

Two groups of islands in the Pacific Ocean northeast of Australia. A British colony after 1915, the groups were separated in 1975, the Ellice Islands renaming themselves Tuvalu.

GOLD COAST (1875-1957)

Stamp-issuing status: inactive; Population: 3.1 million; Stamps issued: 165.

Former British colony in Africa on the Gulf of Guinea. Originally held by a variety of European powers, control of the coastal area was consolidated by Britain by 1871. The interior was conquered by 1901. In 1957, the Gold Coast became the independent state of Ghana.

The first separate stamps for the Gold Coast were issued in 1875. Gold Coast issues continued in use until their replacement by Ghanan stamps in 1957.

GRANADA (1936)

Stamp-issuing status: inactive.

A city and province in southern Spain.

During the siege of Granada in July 1936, the Nationalist administration issued a stamp for local use. After the siege was lifted, this stamp was used in other parts of Spain occupied by the Nationalists.

GRAND COMORO (1897-1911)

Stamp-issuing status: inactive; Stamps issued: 29.

One of the Comoro Islands in the Mozambique Channel near Madagascar. In 1911, it was attached to the French colony of Madagascar, whose stamps were used until 1947 when the Comoro Islands were separated, issuing their own stamps in 1950.

GREAT BRITAIN (1840-)

Stamp-issuing status: active; Population: 56.4 million; Stamps issued: more than 1,200; Issues per year for last decade: 37.

Kingdom in northwest Europe comprised of England, Wales, Scotland and Northern Ireland.

After the accession of the Tudor dynasty (1485), Britain became unified and began to develop into a world power. British overseas expansion began in the late 16th century, and in the following 200 years, Britain emerged as the dominant European naval and colonial power, supplanting the Spanish and Dutch.

After her victory in the Napoleonic wars, Britain emerged as the dominant world power, building an empire that, by 1900, included large areas throughout the world.

Although victorious in World War I, Britain suffered severe losses in manpower and resources. The postwar period saw the loss of Ireland (1921) and the development of nationalism in India.

During World War II, Britain again suffered. For a year following the fall of France (June 1940), Britain was the only major power to stand against Germany. After Germany's invasion of Russia (June 1941) and Japan's attack on Pearl Harbor (December 1941), she gained powerful allies but continued to bear the brunt of German air attacks.

Britain emerged from World War II victorious, but battered and exhausted. Industrial growth has continued, although she has lost her former predominant economic position. The two decades following World War II saw the dissolution of the empire, and Britain's overseas dominion today is mostly comprised of small scattered island possessions in the West Indies and in the Atlantic, Indian and Pacific oceans.

One major result of this process has been the redirection of Britain's focus from the Commonwealth to Europe. In 1973 Britain joined the Common Market.

Britain issued the world's first regular adhesive postage stamp in 1840.

GREAT BRITAIN-REGIONALS (1958-)

In 1958, Britain began issuing regional definitive issues for various areas within the country. Such regionals are sold only at the post offices within the respective regions, but are valid for postage throughout the country.

Regional issues have been released for Guernsey (1958-69); Jersey (1958-69); Isle of Man (1958-73); Northern Ireland (1958-); Scotland (1958-); and Wales and Monmouthshire (1958-).

GREECE (1861-)

Stamp-issuing status: active; Population: 9.95 million; Stamps issued: more than 1,900; Issues per year for last decade: 39.

Republic in southeastern Europe. Greece was the center of the Minoan civilization of Crete during the 2nd millennium B.C., and of the Hellenic civilization after c. 800 B.C.

After the 7th and 8th centuries B.C., Greek colonies were established throughout the Mediterranean, producing a civilization that greatly influenced subsequent European development.

The conquests of Alexander the Great spread Greek culture throughout western Asia, and Alexandrine successor states maintained Greek cultural dominance in the Middle East and northern India for two centuries.

After 146 B.C., Greece was conquered by Rome, although the Romans soon became thoroughly Hellenized and so perpetuated Greece's cultural influence.

Greece remained under the Eastern Roman Empire until it was occupied by the French and Italian crusaders. In 1456, the country was conquered by the Turks.

Greek nationalism began to emerge in the late 18th century, culminating in revolution in 1821. By 1832, Greece had become an independent kingdom.

Greece has since expanded to include Greek-speaking territories in the southern Balkans, as well as Crete and the Aegean Islands. The period 1912-19 saw the rapid expansion of Greece's borders, producing many occupation issues.

Greece successfully resisted an Italian invasion in 1940, but German intervention in 1941 brought the country's rapid defeat and occupation by Germany, Italy and Bulgaria. Communist elements, defeated by the royalist government and Britain in 1944-45, waged a guerrilla war against the regime during 1947-49. The communists were suppressed, with U.S. assistance.

In the postwar years, Greece experienced rapid economic growth. Increasing tension between liberal and conservative factions, however, brought a military coup in 1967. After unsuccessfully attempting to moderate the harshness of the regime, King Constantine and the royal family fled the country.

In 1973, this government was overthrown in a second military coup. The new government, in turn, was overthrown in 1974, and democratic civilian government was restored.

GREENLAND (1905-)

Stamp-issuing status: active; Population: 53,000; Stamps issued: more than 160; Issues per year for last decade: 7.

The world's largest island, located in the Arctic, northeast of Canada. Greenland was occupied by the Norsemen during the 10th-15th centuries, but the deteriorating climate and increasingly aggressive Eskimo inroads finally wiped out the European settlements.

In 1721, Denmark again began colonization. In 1953, the colony became an integral part of the kingdom of Denmark.

In 1979, home rule was extended to Greenland, and a socialist-dominated legislature was elected. Native place names have come into use, and the official name for Greenland is now Nalatdlit Nunat.

Greenland was a U.S. protectorate from 1940-45, during the German occupation of Denmark.

GRENADA (1861-)

Stamp-issuing status: active; Population: 92,500; Stamps issued: more than 1,650; Issues per year for last decade: 7.

An island in the West Indies. A British colony since the 18th century, Grenada became an independent state in 1974.

GRENADA-GRENADINES (1973-)

Stamp-issuing status: active; Population: 6,000; Stamps issued: more than 930; Issues per year for last decade: 68.

A small group of islands in the West Indies administered by Grenada.

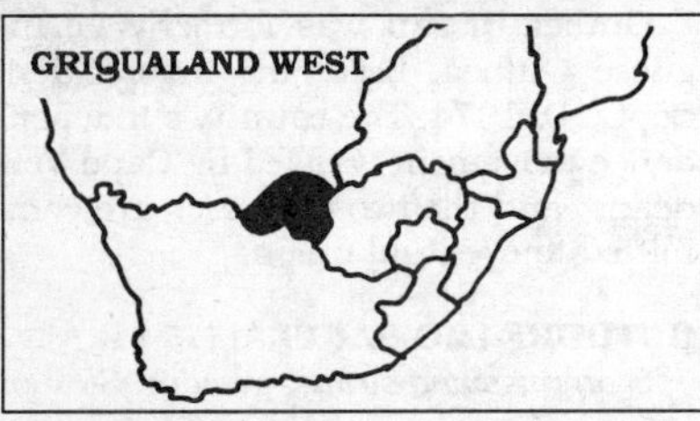

GRIQUALAND WEST (1874-80)

Stamp-issuing status: inactive; Stamps issued: 101.

Located in South Africa, north of the Orange River, this territory was occupied by the British in 1871, and established as a British crown colony in 1873.

It was annexed to Cape Colony in 1880 and since 1910 has been part of South Africa.

Griqualand West issued one provisional at Kimberley in 1874 and many varieties of the overprint "G" on various Cape Colony stamps during 1877-78. From 1871 to 1877 and after 1880, Cape Colony stamps were in use.

GRODNO (1919)

Stamp-issuing status: inactive; Stamps issued: 5.

A city in the White Russian Soviet Socialist Republic (U.S.S.R.), formerly part of Poland. After World War I, the German military commander issued stamps overprinted on Ukrainian and Russian stamps.

GUADALAJARA (1867-68)

Stamp-issuing status: inactive; Stamps issued: 55.

The capital of the state of Jalisco in northwestern Mexico. Guadalajara is one of the major cities of the country and, during the war against the French-supported Emperor Maximilian, issued a number of provisional postage stamps.

GUADELOUPE (1884-1947)

Stamp-issuing status: inactive; stamps issued: 276.

An island in the West Indies, under French rule since 1635. From 1775 to 1946, Guadeloupe was a French colony and since 1946 has been an overseas department of France. French stamps replaced those of Guadeloupe in 1947.

GUAM (1899-1901, 1930-31)

Stamp-issuing status: inactive; Population: 9,500; Stamps issued: 14.

The largest of the Mariana Islands in the western Pacific, Guam was ceded to the U.S. by Spain in 1898, after its capture by U.S. forces during the Spanish-American War.

Occupied by the Japanese in 1941, the island was recaptured and served as a base for U.S. bomber attacks on Japan during the last months of World War II. Guam is now administered by the U.S. Department of the Interior.

U.S. stamps overprinted "GUAM" were used from 1899 to 1901, when they were replaced by regular U.S. stamps, although the overprinted stamps remained in use for several years.

During 1930-31, Philippine stamps overprinted "GUAM GUARD MAIL" were used by the local military forces.

GUANACASTE (1885-91)

Stamp-issuing status: inactive; Stamps issued: 61.

A province of Costa Rica. During 1885-91, the government granted a substantially larger discount on stamps purchased by this province, in order to encourage additional sales to offset the high transportation costs to the area.

Stamps used in the province during this period were overprinted to prevent their purchase in Guanacaste and resale elsewhere.

GUATEMALA (1871-)

Stamp-issuing status: active; Population: 8 million; Stamps issued: more than 1,250; Issues per year for last decade: 32.

Republic in Central America on the southern border of Mexico. The center of the Maya-Quiche Indian civilization, Guatemala was conquered by the Spanish in the early 16th century.

The center of the Audiencia of Guatemala, which included all of Central America and the Mexican state of Chiapas, Guatemala remained under Spanish rule until 1821 when it declared its independence.

During 1822-23, it was under Mexico, and during 1823-39, it formed part of the Republic of the United States of Central America. Since 1839, Guatemala has been completely independent.

Guatemala's economy is land-based, with ownership concentrated in the hands of a relatively small Spanish-descended oligarchy. Most menial labor is done by Indian laborers. The standard of living is very low for most Guatemalans, and illiteracy is high.

Since independence, Guatemala has been ruled by an almost unbroken succession of military dictatorships. For the past two decades, the country has been wracked by terrorism from both left- and right-wing elements.

GUAYANA (1903)

Stamp-issuing status: inactive; Stamps issued: 20.

A state in eastern Venezuela. In 1903, a revolutionary group issued stamps for use in the area.

GUERNSEY (1941-45, 1958-)

Stamp-issuing status: active; Population: 54,500; Stamps issued: more than 350; Issues per year for last decade: 20.

An island in the English Channel. A bailiwick under the British crown, Guernsey was occupied by Germany from 1940-45, during which time bisected British issues and locally printed stamps were used.

During 1958-69, regional issues, valid throughout Britain but sold only in Guernsey, were in use along with regular British stamps.

On Oct. 1, 1969, the Guernsey postal administration was separated from that of Britain, and the bailiwick has issued its own stamps since that time.

GUIDIZZOLO (1945)

Stamp-issuing status: inactive.

A city in northern Italy. Overprinted Italian stamps were used provisionally, following the collapse of the Italian Social Republic.

GUINEA (1959-)

Stamp-issuing status: active; Population: 6.6 million; Stamps issued: more than 1,125; Issues per year for last decade: 36.

Republic in West Africa. Formerly the colony of French Guinea, Guinea became independent on Sept. 28, 1958.

GUINEA-BISSAU (1974-)

Stamp-issuing status: active; Population: 870,000 (1985 estimate); Stamps issued: more than 525.

Independent republic on the coast of Africa, bordered by Senegal and Guinea.

Guinea-Bissau was formerly Portuguese Guinea, becoming independent Sept. 10, 1974. The country's independence movement was led by Cape Verdeans, and the two countries are committed to eventual union.

GUTDORF (MOISAKULA) (1941)

Stamp-issuing status: inactive; Stamps issued: 7.

A city in Estonia. Overprinted Russian and Estonian stamps were used for a time during the German occupation in World War II.

GUYANA (1966-)

Stamp-issuing status: active; Population: 794,000; Stamps issued: more than 850; Issues per year for last decade: 67.

A republic on the northeast coast of South America. Formerly the colony of British Guiana, which became independent in 1966. The republic was established in 1970. Guyana's boundaries with Venezuela (which claims half of the country) and Surinam are in dispute.

GWALIOR (1885-1950)

Stamp-issuing status: inactive; Stamps issued: 188.

A state in north central India, Gwalior united its postal system with that of India through a postal convention. Overprinted Indian stamps were used 1885-1950 when they were replaced by regular Indian issues.

- H -

HAITI (1881-)

Stamp-issuing status: active; Population: 6 million; Stamps issued: more than 1,300; Issues per year for last decade: 22.

A republic occupying the western third of the island of Hispaniola in the West Indies. The Spanish occupied the island after its discovery by Columbus in 1492, enslaving the Indian population, which was soon exterminated.

In time, the Spanish partially abandoned the island, and the western portion became a base for pirates. This area gradually came under French control, which was recognized by Spain in 1697.

Under the French, African slaves were imported to work the sugar plantations, which were the mainstay of the colony's economy. In 1804 the descendants of these slaves expelled their French masters.

The Republic of Haiti split into two parts in 1811, but in 1820, it was reunited and enlarged by the conquest of the eastern portion of the island (lost in 1844).

During the 19th century, anarchy and foreign indebtedness increased, finally bringing U.S. occupation in 1915. U.S. troops withdrew in 1934, and the last U.S. controls ended in 1941.

Since 1957, Haiti has been ruled by the Duvaliers, first by Dr. Francois Duvalier ("Papa Doc") and, since his death in 1971, by his son, Jean-Claude ("Baby Doc").

Haiti is a miserably poor country, the result of years of civil disorder and dictatorial rule. Although Jean-Claude's rule has been less oppressive than that of his father, economic conditions have shown little improvement. In recent years, thousands of Haitians have illegally immigrated to the United States.

HAMBURG (1859-67)

Stamp-issuing status: inactive; Stamps issued: 22.

A seaport and former Free City in northern Germany. Hamburg's stamps (1859-67) were replaced by those of the North German Confederation on Jan. 1, 1868.

HANOVER (1850-1866)

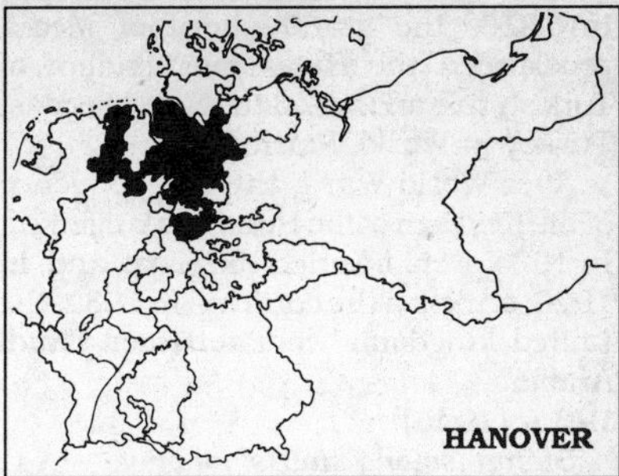

Stamp-issuing status: inactive; Stamps issued: 25.

A former kingdom in northern Germany. United with Britain from 1714 to 1837 through a common monarch, Hanover supported Austria in the Austro-Prussian War (1866) and was annexed by Prussia.

Hanover's stamps were first issued in 1850, being replaced by those of Prussia in 1866.

HATAY (1939)

Stamp-issuing status: inactive; Stamps issued: 50.

As a semi-autonomous district of Syria under French mandate, this area issued stamps as Alexandretta. In 1938, it was renamed Hatay, and in 1939, it was absorbed by Turkey.

HAWAII (1851-1900)

Stamp-issuing status: inactive; Population: 150,000 (1900 estimate); Stamps issued: 91.

An island group in the north-central Pacific, Hawaii became a united kingdom in the late 18th century. After a period of constitutional unrest, the native monarchy was overthrown in 1893.

The provisional government, unsuccessful in securing annexation by the U.S., proclaimed Hawaii a republic. In 1898, the area was annexed by the U.S., and the Territory of Hawaii was established in 1900. In 1959, Hawaii became the 50th state of the U.S.

Hawaiian stamps continued in use after the islands' annexation, being finally replaced by regular U.S. stamps in 1900.

HEJAZ (1916-25)

Stamp-issuing status: inactive; Stamps issued: 188.

Located on the western coast of the Arabian Peninsula, Hejaz includes the Moslem holy cities of Mecca and Medina.

In 1916, the grand sherif of Mecca proclaimed the Hejaz independent of Turkish rule and joined the British against Turkey in World War I.

After World War I, the independence of the Kingdom of the Hejaz was confirmed. In 1924, Nejd invaded the Hejaz and, in 1926, annexed the country. In 1932, the united kingdoms were renamed Saudi Arabia.

HELA (1945)

Stamp-issuing status: inactive.

A peninsula on the Gulf of Danzig in northern Europe. German forces on the peninsula were cut off by the advancing Russians and issued a provisional stamp for use on mail to be carried back to Germany proper.

This "U-Boat" stamp was used briefly, although it never actually became necessary to use U-boats to carry this mail.

HELIGOLAND (1867-90)

Stamp-issuing status: inactive; Population: 12,307 (1900 estimate); Stamps issued: 26.

A strategically located island in the North Sea, Heligoland was ceded to Great Britain by Denmark in 1807. Britain transferred the island to Germany in 1890, in exchange for some German claims in East Africa.

The Germans built a major naval base on the island. The base was destroyed by the British after World War II. Heligoland was returned to Germany in 1952.

Stamps of Hamburg were used in Heligoland from 1859 to 1867, when separate issues came into use. These were among the most attractive of British colonial issues. The plates used in printing Heligoland's stamps passed into private hands, and many reprintings were made.

Since 1890, German stamps have been used on the island.

HELSINGFORS (HELSINKI) (1866-91)

Stamp-issuing status: inactive.

The capital of Finland. Stamps were issued by the local postmaster and were valid throughout the district.

HONAN (1941-42)

Stamp-issuing status: inactive.

A province in central China. Overprinted Chinese stamps were issued by the Japanese during World War II.

HONDURAS (1866-)

Stamp-issuing status: active; Population: 4.5 million; Stamps issued: more than 1,000; Issues per year for last decade: 15.

Republic in Central America. Originally dominated by the Mayas, Honduras was conquered by Spain in the early 16th century, and until 1838, its history follows that of Guatemala. In 1838, it became independent.

Honduras' chief export is bananas, and the country has been the stereotypical "banana republic" since the last century. In 1975, Gen. Oswaldo Lopez Arellano, president since 1963, was ousted by the Army over charges of widespread bribery. Since that time, the Honduran government has pursued a number of ambitious social programs, and free elections were held in 1981.

In recent years, tensions have increased between Honduras and El Salvador over the presence of some 300,000 Salvadoreans in Honduras. A brief war was fought in 1969, and border clashes occurred in 1970 and 1976.

HONG KONG (1862-)

Stamp-issuing status: active; Population: 5.4 million; Stamps issued: more than 550; Issues per year for last decade: 18.

A peninsula and island at the mouth of the Canton River in southeast China. Hong Kong has been a British possession since 1841, except for its occupation by Japan from 1941 to 1945.

Hong Kong is highly industrialized, and its annual exports of $9 billion plus are led by textiles, clothing and electronics.

HOPEI (1941-42)

Stamp-issuing status: inactive.

A province in northern China, surrounding Peking and Tientsin. Regular Chinese stamps were overprinted by occupying Japanese forces during World War II.

HORTA (1892-1905)

Stamp-issuing status: inactive; Population: 49,000 (estimate); Stamps issued: 34.

A district of the Azores. From 1868 to 1892 and from 1905 to 1931, stamps of the Azores were used. Since 1931, regular Portuguese stamps have been in use.

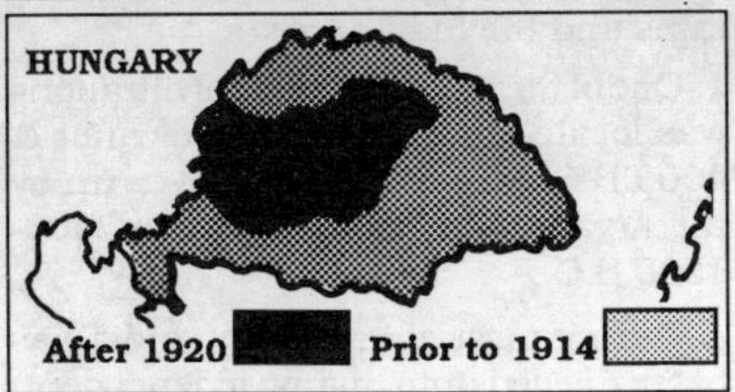

HUNGARY (1871-)

Stamp-issuing status: active; Population: 10.8 million; Stamps issued: more than 3,775; Issues per year for last decade: 70.

A people's republic in East Central Europe. This area of flat plains and grasslands, bisected by the Danube River, was a favorite route of eastern tribes invading southern and western Europe. From the 4th to the 9th centuries, succeeding immigrations of Germans, Huns, Avars and other peoples passed through the region.

Toward the end of the 9th century, Hungary was settled by the Magyars, who for nearly a century raided throughout central Europe. Under Stephen I (977-1038), the Magyars were converted to Christianity and thereafter served as Europe's eastern bulwark against the Asian tribes.

In the early 16th century, the Ottoman Turks destroyed Hungarian power. Most of the country was conquered by the Turks, and the remaining northern and western fringe came under the rule of Hapsburg Austria. During 1686-1718, the Austrians expelled the Turks from Hungary.

Austria completely dominated Hungary until the mid-19th century. Magyar nationalism forced the creation of the Austro-Hungarian Monarchy in 1867, after which Hungary was an equal partner with Austria. Having achieved its own nationalist goals, Hungary denied similar nationalist ambitions among its subject peoples.

The Dual Monarchy's defeat in World War I brought the disintegration of the empire and of the Kingdom of Hungary. During 1918-20, the country was overrun by Serbian, French and Romanian armies and was torn by civil war between royalist and Bolshevik factions. Hungary emerged in 1920 as a nationalist state, having lost 50 percent of its population and 75 percent of its territory to Yugoslavia, Romania and Czechoslovakia.

In 1938, Hungary participated in the dismemberment of Czechoslovakia and, during World War II, joined the Axis, regaining much of its former territory. In 1944-45, it was defeated by the U.S.S.R. and reduced to its pre-1938 boundaries. On Feb. 1, 1946, a republic was established, but in 1947 the communists ousted the president and purged non-communist elements from the government.

Demonstrations in October 1956, turned into open revolt against the regime. In early November, some 200,000 Soviet troops crushed the uprising, and a hard-line regime was re-established. Some 40,000 Soviet troops remained in Hungary, and Hungarian forces participated in the 1968 Warsaw Pact invasion of Czechoslovakia.

The present Hungarian government has pursued cautiously liberal internal policies since 1968. Elements of small private enterprise and a degree of cultural freedom have been restored, without provoking Soviet reaction.

HVAR (LESINA) (1944)

Stamp-issuing status: inactive.

An island in the Adriatic Sea, off the coast of Yugoslavia. In 1944, Yugoslavian stamps were overprinted for use on the island by the German military commander of the Dalmatian Province.

HYDERABAD (1869-1950)

Stamp-issuing status: inactive; Population: 16.3 million (1941 estimate); Stamps issued: 114.

The largest of the princely states, Hyderabad (Deccan) was the most powerful of the native states in southern India. Hyderabad became independent from the Mogul Empire in the early 18th century and allied itself to Britain after c.1760.

After Britain's withdrawal from the subcontinent in 1947, the Moslem rulers of the state resisted domination by Hindu India, but Indian authority was firmly established in September 1948. Hyderabad maintained separate stamp issues until April 1, 1950, since which time Indian stamps have been used.

- I -

ICARIA (NICARIA) (1912-13)

Stamp-issuing status: inactive; Stamps issued: 53.

An island in the Aegean Sea. In July 1912, Icaria declared its independence from Turkey. In November the island was occupied by Greece, and Icarian issues were replaced by overprinted Greek stamps, which, in turn, were replaced by regular Greek stamps.

ICELAND (1873-)

Stamp-issuing status: active; Population: 241,750; Stamps issued: more than 780; Issues per year for last decade: 16.

A large island in the North Atlantic. Iceland was colonized from Norway after c. 870, and after 1380 was under Danish rule.

In 1918, Iceland became independent, united with Denmark only in the person of the Danish monarch. In 1944, Iceland severed this last tie with Denmark and became a republic.

Since 1949, Iceland has been a member of NATO, and the U.S. maintains a sizable base on the island.

IDAR (1939-44)

Stamp-issuing status: inactive; Population: 262,660; Stamps issued: 6.

A former feudatory state in western India.

IFNI (1941-1969)

Stamp-issuing status: inactive; Population: 52,000 (1968 estimate); Stamps issued: 250.

A Spanish enclave on the western coast of Morocco. Ceded to Spain in 1860, Ifni was occupied in 1934. In 1969, Spain returned the area to Morocco, whose stamps replaced those of the colony.

ILI REPUBLIC (1945-1949)

Stamp-issuing status: inactive.

A short-lived state established by the Uighurs in northwestern Sinkiang. At the end of 1949, the state was integrated into the Chinese People's Republic.

INDIA (1854-)

Stamp-issuing status: active; Population: 846 million; Stamps issued: more than 1,550; Issues per year for last decade: 46.

Republic in south-central Asia, occupying the greater part of the Indian subcontinent between the Himalaya Mountains and the Indian Ocean.

One of the world's earliest civilizations was located in the Indus valley after c. 4000 B.C. This culture was overrun by the Aryans who conquered India 2400-1500 B.C.

During most of its history, India has been divided into many independent, frequently warring states.

In 1498, the Portuguese reached India and quickly began building a commercial empire that dominated the coastal areas for a century.

The Portuguese were supplanted by the Dutch in the early 17th century, who in turn were succeeded by the British in the late 17th century.

Anglo-French rivalry for influence over the local princes was intense until Britain's military defeat of the French forces in 1760.

During the next 100 years, the British East India Co. constantly expanded Britain's holdings in the subcontinent.

In 1857, the British government took over the governing of India directly. In 1877, the empire of India was proclaimed with Queen Victoria as empress.

In the early 20th century, Indian nationalism became an increasingly powerful force. After World War I, Mohandas K. Gandhi organized the All-India Congress Party, which assumed the leadership of the Indian independence movement. Later, the Moslem nationalists withdrew from the predominantly Hindu Congress Party to form the Moslem League under Mohammed Ali Jinnah.

After years of agitation and negotiation, the British gave up control of India on Aug. 15, 1947, and the country was partitioned into Hindu (India) and Moslem (Pakistan) states.

Religious riots and war between the two nations began almost immediately. Settled only with great difficulty, war has erupted several times since, most recently in 1971-72.

India absorbed the remaining French holdings in 1956 and seized Portugal's Indian territory in 1961. In 1962, Communist Chinese forces occupied disputed areas in the north.

INDIA-CONVENTION STATES (1884-1950)

Stamp-issuing status: inactive; Stamps issued (total): 960.

During 1864-86, six Indian states joined their postal services to that of British India, using overprinted Indian stamps. The states entering into such postal conventions were Chamba, Faridkot, Gwalior, Jhind, Nabha and Patiala.

The stamps of the convention states were valid throughout India. They were replaced by those of the Republic of India on Jan. 1, 1951.

INDIA-FEUDATORY STATES (1864-1951)

Stamp-issuing status: inactive; Stamps issued (total): 1,631.

After 1862, many rulers of the semi-autonomous native princely states began to establish modern public postal systems, utilizing their own stamps.

These systems existed alongside that of British India, with the stamps normally valid only within the state where they were issued.

The Indian feudatory states issuing their own stamps were: Alwar (1877-1902); Bamra (1888-94); Barwani (1921-48); Bhopal (1876-1950); Bhor (1879-1902); Bijawar (1935-39); Bundi (1894-1920, 1940-48); Bussahir (1895-1901); Charkhari (1894-1950); Cochin (1892-1949); Dhar (1897-1901); Duttia (1893-1921); Hyderabad (1869-1950); Idar (1939-44); Indore (1886-1950); Jaipur (1904-49); Jammu and Kashmir (1866-94); Jasdan (1942-50); Jhalawar (1887-1900); Jind (1874-85); Kishangarh (1899-1949); Las Bela (1897-1907); Morvi (1931-50); Nandgaon (1892-95); Nawanagar (1875-95); Orchha (1913-50); Poonch (1876-94); Rajasthan (1948-50); Rajpeepla (1880-86); Saurashtra (1864-1950); Sirmoor (1879-1902); Travancore (1888-1949); Travancore-Cochin (1949-51); and Wadhwan (1888-95).

INDIAN EXPEDITIONARY FORCES (1914-22)

During and after World War I, Indian forces fighting with the Allies used 10 stamps of British India overprinted "I.E.F." An "I.E.F. D/i" overprint was similarly applied to eight Turkish stamps used by the British during the occupation of Mesopotamia.

INDO-CHINA (1889-1949)

Stamp-issuing status: inactive; Population: 27 million (1949 estimate); Stamps issued: 453.

Former French administrative unit in southeast Asia, comprising Cochin-China, Cambodia, Annam and Tonkin, and Kwangchowan.

The area broke up in 1949 to form the states of Cambodia, Laos and Vietnam, within the French Union, with the issues of the separate states replacing those of Indo-China.

INDONESIA (1945-)

Stamp-issuing status: active; Population: 173 million; Stamps issued: more than 1,550; Issues per year for last decade: 32.

A republic occupying the great part of the Malay Archipelago in southeastern Asia; formerly the Netherlands East Indies.

Portugal dominated the area during the 16th century but was supplanted by the Dutch after 1595. Except for a period of British occupation during the Napoleonic wars (1811-16), the area remained under Dutch control until its occupation by Japan in 1942.

After the surrender of Japan in August 1945, Indonesian nationalists under Achmed Sukarno proclaimed the independent Republic of Indonesia in central Java and throughout most of Sumatra.

The ensuing civil war was finally ended by the withdrawal of the Dutch in December 1949. In 1950, Indonesia was unified as a republic.

In 1963, Western New Guinea (West Irian) was absorbed by Indonesia.

During the early 1960s, Indonesia was aligned with the U.S.S.R., but an abortive communist uprising in 1965 brought massive retaliation by the military. President Sukarno, who had ruled as a dictator since 1960, was deposed, and some 300,000 communists executed.

The new regime, under Gen. Suharto, restored peaceful relations with Indonesia's neighbors, restored popular elections and has actively promoted economic development.

In 1976 the former Portuguese Timor was annexed by Indonesia.

INDORE (HOLKAR) (1886-1949)

Stamp-issuing status: inactive; Stamps issued: 47.

A former feudatory state in west-central India. Indore used its own stamps from 1886 to 1949. With its merger into Rajasthan, stamps of that state were used from 1949 to April 1, 1950. Stamps of India are now in use.

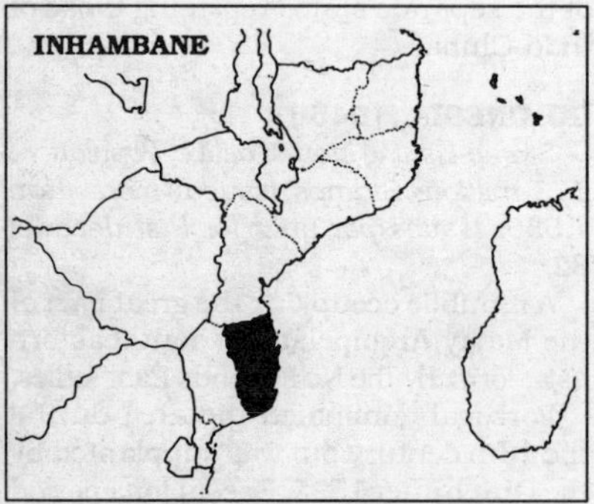

INHAMBANE (1895-1914)

Stamp-issuing status: inactive; Population: 248,000 (1917 estimate); Stamps issued: 101.

A district of southern Mozambique. Its stamps were superseded by those of Mozambique.

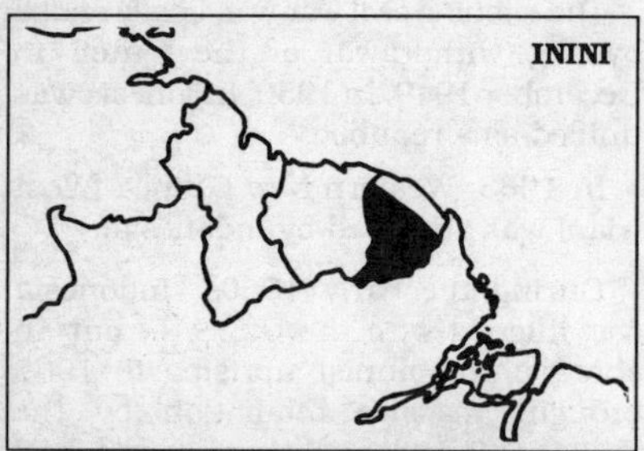

ININI (1932-46)

Stamp-issuing status: inactive; Population: 5,024 (1941 estimate); Stamps issued: 53.

The interior of French Guiana, on the northeastern coast of South America. During 1930-46, this area was separated from French Guiana, being reunited when the area was absorbed by France.

IONIAN ISLANDS (1859-64, 1941-43)

Stamp-issuing status: inactive; Stamps issued: 16.

A group of islands off the western coast of Greece. Occupied at various times by the Greeks, Romans, Byzantines, Venetians, Turks, French and British, the islands were united with Greece in 1864.

Three stamps were issued by the British (1859-64), and an additional 13 during World War II, by the occupying Italian forces (1941-43).

IRAN (PERSIA until 1935) (1870-)

Stamp-issuing status: active; Population: 49.8 million; Stamps issued: more than 2,500; Issues per year for last decade: 33.

Kingdom in western Asia. Iran was the seat of the ancient kingdom of Elam (c. 3000-640 B.C.), which competed with the Mesopotamian states to its west.

The area was settled by the Iranians, an Aryan people, c.1800 B.C., from whom arose the Medes, Persians and Parthians. At various times from the 7th century B.C. to the 7th century A.D., Persian states dominated the Middle East, at times ruling territory from Egypt and Thrace to India.

Debilitating wars with Rome weakened Persia, making it easy prey to the Arabs in the 7th century. With the decline of the caliphate after 1040, Persia was torn by centuries of war and anarchy, complicated by Turkish immigration and Mongol invasions (13th-15th centuries).

National unity was re-established under the Safawid dynasty (1502-1722).

After the mid-18th century, Persia declined, losing its outlying provinces (Afghanistan, the Caucasus, etc.) and falling under European influence.

Russia and Britain carved out spheres of influence in the 19th century and occupied portions of the country in World War I and World War II.

In 1921, Riza Pahlavi, a military chief, led a coup and assumed virtual control of the government, becoming shah in 1925. He began to radically modernize Persia, a program continued by his son and successor, Mohammed Riza Pahlavi.

Mohammed Riza Pahlavi attempted to modernize Iran rapidly and used the country's substantial oil revenues toward this end. While his policies brought a social and economic transformation of Iran, the shah ruled absolutely, and political opposition was suppressed.

Increasing dissatisfaction with the regime brought the coalition of many disparate elements in Iranian society. Anti-government riots brought martial law in September 1978, but the government's position deteriorated rapidly. On Jan. 16, 1979, the shah left Iran, and in mid-February, the caretaker regime of Shahpur Baktiar, a long-time opponent of the shah, was overthrown amid popular demonstrations by supporters of Ayatollah Ruhollah Khomeini. On April 1, the Ayatollah declared Iran an Islamic republic and immediately set about creating a theocratic regime, reflecting staunchly conservative Islamic values.

Khomeini accused the United States, which had strongly supported the shah, of fomenting most of the country's problems. Relations between the two countries quickly deteriorated, and in November 1979, student demonstrators seized U.S. embassy personnel in Teheran. The embassy staff was held hostage, pending the return of the shah to Iran, where he was to be tried by revolutionary courts. The death of the shah in July 1980 did not bring a resolution of the problem, which continued until the captives' release in January 1981.

In September 1980, Iraq attacked Iran, beginning a bitter war that has drained the resources of both nations.

Political and economic instability have become the norm in Iran. Political terrorism and government repression, as bad or worse than under the shah, are everyday occurrences.

IRAQ (1923-)

Stamp-issuing status: active; Population: 16 million; Stamps issued: more than 1,300; Issues per year for last decade: 46.

A republic in western Asia, occupying the Tigris and Euphrates valley, north of Arabia. Occupied from Turkey by British forces during World War I, Iraq became a British mandated territory in 1920.

In 1921, a kingdom was established under Faisal I, son of King Hussein of Hejaz and leader of the Arab Army in World War I.

Britain withdrew from Iraq in 1932, although it intervened during World War II to overthrow a pro-Axis ministry. In 1958, the monarchy was deposed, and a pan-Arab, pro-Soviet republic was established. The new regime nationalized most Iraqi industry and broke up large land holdings.

Iraq has maintained close ties with Syria, which is ruled by another branch of the same Baathist political party. A number of national disputes have come between the two countries.

In 1978, Iraq executed a number of communists and has since expanded trade with the West.

In September 1980, Iraq, prompted by a long-standing border dispute and by the new Iranian regime's attempts to foment revolution among Iraq's Shi'ite minority, invaded Iran. Strong Iranian resistance soon brought the war to a standstill, despite periodic heavy fighting. Although both nations are on the verge of bankruptcy because of the war, no negotiated settlement appears likely.

IRELAND (1922-)

Stamp-issuing status: active; Population: 36 million; Stamps issued: more than 725; Issues per year for last decade: 17.

An island in northwestern Europe, west of Britain. Long restive under British rule, Ireland revolted in 1916, securing independence as a dominion.

In 1949, the Irish Free State became the independent Republic of Ireland. The northern counties, where the Protestants are in the majority, remain under British rule, although they are claimed by the republic.

ISRAEL (1948-)

Stamp-issuing status: active; Population: 4.2 million; Stamps issued: more than 1,030; Issues per year for last decade: 33.

Republic in western Asia, occupying Palestine and (since 1967) border areas of Syria and Egypt.

Under the British mandate, Jewish and Arab elements in Palestine came into bitter conflict over the future of the nation. The Jews wished to create a homeland for their people, while the Arabs advocated the creation of a secular Palestinian state in which the rights of the Jewish minority would be respected.

On May 14, 1948, British troops were withdrawn from Palestine, and the Jewish National Council immediately proclaimed the state of Israel in areas of the country under Jewish control.

Israel was immediately attacked by its Arab neighbors but defeated their forces, emerging from the 1949 cease-fire with its territory approximately 50 percent larger than that initially allocated for it by the U.N. partition plan.

In 1956, Egypt nationalized the Suez Canal and barred Israeli shipping. Israel invaded Egypt and occupied Gaza and the Sinai. After U.N. intervention, Israel withdrew.

In 1967, after a year of Arab guerrilla raids from Jordan and bombardment of Israeli settlements from Syria, war again broke out.

Israel defeated Egypt, Syria and Jordan in the Six-Day War, occupying the West Bank from Jordan, the Golan Heights from Syria, and Sinai and Gaza from Egypt.

On Oct. 6, 1973, after several years of failure to negotiate a settlement, Arab forces attacked Israel again, re-occupying some lost territory in the Sinai. After initial Arab gains, Israel counterattacked quickly, occupying territory on the west bank of the Suez Canal and advancing in Syria. A cease-fire was negotiated Oct. 24.

Peace negotiations proceeded very slowly during 1973-77, but began to move rapidly after November 1977, when Egyptian President Anwar Sadat visited Jerusalem in an attempt to break the deadlock.

On March 26, 1979, Egypt and Israel signed a formal peace treaty, ending hostilities and establishing diplomatic relations.

Under the terms of the peace treaty, Israel has returned the Sinai to Egypt. Continuing hostility between Israel and the Palestine Liberation Organization make real peace unlikely in the near future.

ISTRIA-SLOVENE COAST (1945-47)

Stamp-issuing status: inactive: 51.

Former Italian provinces on the Adriatic Sea, occupied by Yugoslavia after World War II.

ITALIAN COLONIES (1932-34)

Stamp-issuing status: inactive; Stamps issued: 87.

General issues released for all Italian colonies.

ITALIAN EAST AFRICA (1938-41)

Stamp-issuing status: inactive; Population: 12 million (1941 estimate); Stamps issued: 76.

A former Italian colony in East Africa, formed from Eritrea, Italian Somaliland, and Ethiopia. It was occupied by the British in 1941 and, after World War II, was dissolved.

ITALIAN OFFICES ABROAD (1861-1923)

Stamp-issuing status: inactive; Stamps issued: 17.

Italy maintained many post offices abroad, utilizing a general overprint on Italian stamps (1874-90), overprints for specific cities or territories, and unoverprinted stamps distinguishable only by their cancellations.

Italian post offices were maintained in Egypt, Tunisia, Tripolitania, Eritrea, China, Crete, and many cities in the Turkish Empire and Albania.

ITALIAN OFFICES IN ALBANIA (1902-09)

Stamp-issuing status: inactive; Stamps issued: 6.

During the 19th century, Italy operated her own post offices in a number of Albanian cities, using regular Italian stamps.

In 1883, the Turkish government suppressed these offices, but in 1902, they were re-opened using Italian stamps overprinted "Albania" and surcharged in Turkish currency.

In 1909, these issues were replaced by those of the various cities where Italian post offices were in operation.

ITALIAN OFFICES IN CHINA (1917-22)

Stamp-issuing status: inactive; Stamps issued: 70.

During 1901-17, Italian troops in China, as well as legation and consular personnel, were permitted to use unoverprinted Italian stamps. From September 1917, to Dec. 31, 1922, Italian stamps overprinted for Peking and Tientsin were used.

ITALIAN SOCIAL REPUBLIC (1943-45)

Stamp-issuing status: inactive; Stamps issued: 64.

The Italian puppet state under Mussolini, which nominally ruled those areas under German occupation during the final days of World War II.

ITALY (1862-)

Stamp-issuing status: active; Population: 57.3 million; Stamps issued: more than 1,900; Issues per year for last decade: 45.

A republic in western Europe. Italy was the center of the Roman Empire, which until the 5th century ruled southern and western Europe, North Africa and much of the Middle East.

After the collapse of Rome, Italy was ruled by a succession of foreign powers: Ostrogoths, Lombards, Franks, Arabs, Normans, Germans, Spanish, Byzantines, and French. By 1815, the country was roughly divided into several spheres: the Sardinian kingdom, which ruled the island of Sardinia and northwestern Italy; the Lombardo-Venetian Kingdom, which was ruled by Austria, in the north; the Papal States, which controlled the central portion of the peninsula; and the Kingdom of the Two Sicilies in the south.

During the 19th century, Italian nationalism grew in strength, and there was increasing sentiment for unification.

During 1859-61, nationalist uprisings deposed local rulers and united most of Italy with Sardina. On March 17, 1861, the united Kingdom of Italy was proclaimed under the House of Savoy.

Italy acquired several African colonies during the late 19th century and, in the Italo-Turkish War (1911-12) and World War I, acquired territory from Turkey and Austria.

Domestic unrest after World War I brought the Fascist party to power in 1922, although the monarchy was retained. The Fascists, under Benito Mussolini, built up Italy's military forces and pursued an aggressive foreign policy, conquering Ethiopia (1935) and Albania (1939).

Italy entered World War II in 1940 as an ally of Germany, but military reverses brought German domination and, in 1943, the invasion of Italy by the Allies.

Mussolini was deposed in 1943, although he was put in charge of the northern Italian Social Republic, a German puppet-state until its collapse in 1945.

The royalist government, in the meantime, declared war on Germany and fought with the Allies to free Italy from German occupation.

In 1946, the monarchy was abolished, and Italy became a republic.

Since World War II, Italy has enjoyed dynamic industrial growth, and its standard of living has improved greatly. The huge increase in petroleum prices during the 1970s has caused serious economic upsets in recent years.

IVORY COAST (1892-1944, 1959-)

Stamp-issuing status: active; Population: 8.8 million; Stamps issued: more than 950; Issues per year for last decade: 44.

A republic in West Africa, bordering on the Gulf of Guinea. French influence was strong along the coast from 1700. After 1842, France began to occupy territory in the area.

The boundaries of the colony were fixed between 1892 and 1898, and native resistance was crushed by 1919. During World War II, the Ivory Coast remained under control of the Vichy regime until November 1942.

After 1944, it used stamps of French West Africa. In 1958, the Ivory Coast became a republic, achieving independence in 1960.

The Ivory Coast is the most prosperous of the tropical African nations and is the leader of the pro-Western bloc in Africa.

- J -

JAFFA (1909-14)

Stamp-issuing status: inactive.

Israeli port on the Mediterranean Sea. Prior to World War I, a number of European nations maintained their own postal systems in the city.

After 1909, the Russian post used 10 stamps of the Russian Levant overprinted "Jaffa."

JAIPUR (1904-49)

Stamp-issuing status: inactive; Stamps issued: 103.

A former feudatory state in north-central India. Jaipur merged into the United State of Rajasthan in 1948. Jaipur's issues were replaced by those of Rajasthan in 1949, which were in turn replaced by those of India on April 1, 1950.

JAMAICA (1860-)

Stamp-issuing status: active; Population: 2.3 million; Stamps issued: more than 690; Issues per year for last decade: 24.

A republic occupying the island of Jamaica in the West Indies, south of Cuba. Jamaica was discovered by Columbus in 1494 and was occupied by Spain until 1655, when it became a British possession.

The original Arawak inhabitants soon died out under the Spanish, who began the importation of African slaves to work the sugar plantations.

Jamaica became an independent republic on Aug. 6, 1962.

Economic dissatisfaction brought a socialist regime to power 1972-80. Attempts to expand Jamaican ownership in bauxite mining operations and to expand welfare programs failed to improve the economy, and a pro-Western government was elected in 1980. Jamaica has since moved away from Cuba and toward the West.

JAMMU AND KASHMIR (1866-94)

Stamp-issuing status: inactive; Stamps issued: 143.

These north Indian states were united in 1846. From 1866 to 1878, each state issued its own stamps. Common issues began in 1878.

From 1894 to 1948, Indian issues were used. Since Indian independence, this predominantly Moslem area has been disputed between India and Pakistan, and stamps of these nations have been used in the territories under their control.

JANINA (1902-11, 1913-14)

Stamp-issuing status: inactive; Stamps issued: 12.

A city in northwest Greece. Janina was part of the Turkish province of Albania until occupied by Greece in 1913. During 1902-11 and 1913, an Italian post office, utilizing overprinted Italian stamps, operated in the city.

JAPAN (1871-)

Stamp-issuing status: active; Population: 121.2 million; Stamps issued: more than 1,900; Issues per year for last decade: 45.

A group of islands off the eastern coast of Asia. Japan pursued an isolationist policy until 1854, when a U.S. fleet forced it to admit limited foreign trade.

In 1867, internal dissension caused the restoration of imperial power and centralization within the country. Japan embarked on a program of rapid modernization and, by the early 20th century, was a world power.

During 1871-1910, Japan expanded her territory through an aggressive imperialistic foreign policy, gaining Formosa, Korea, etc.

Her victory over Russia in 1905 established her as a major military power and encouraged the growth of nationalism throughout Asia.

During World War I, Japan sided with the Allies, acquiring former German Pacific holdings after the war. During 1918-25, Japan occupied portions of Russian Siberia and Sakhalin and, in the 1930s, began to aggressively expand at the expense of China, which was invaded in 1937.

In 1940, Japan joined the Axis and invaded French Indo-China and, in 1941, attacked British and U.S. territories in the Pacific.

After initial successes, the tide turned against Japan in 1943, ending with her defeat in 1945. All territory, except the home islands, was taken from her by the Allies, who occupied Japan itself until 1952.

Since World War II, Japan has enjoyed an economic boom, making it the World's third greatest industrial power.

JAPANESE OFFICES IN CHINA (1900-22)

Stamp-issuing status: inactive.

Unoverprinted Japanese stamps were used at a number of Japanese post offices in China from 1876 to 1900. From Jan. 1, 1900, through Dec. 31, 1922, 49 overprinted Japanese stamps were used.

JAPANESE OFFICE IN KOREA (1900-01)

Stamp-issuing status: inactive.

For a short time, Japanese post offices in Korea used 15 overprinted Japanese stamps. These were withdrawn in April 1901.

JASDAN (1942-50)

Stamp-issuing status: inactive; Stamps issued: 1.

A former feudatory state in western India. Indian stamps replaced Jasdan's single issue in 1950.

JERSEY (1941-45, 1958-)

Stamp-issuing status: active; Population: 75,000; Stamps issued: more than 400; Issues per year for last decade: 25.

An island in the English Channel united with the British Commonwealth. Local issues were used during the World War II German occupation, regional issues from 1958-69, and issues of the independent Jersey Postal Administration since Oct. 1, 1969.

JERUSALEM (1909-14, 1948)

Stamp-issuing status: inactive.

The capital of Palestine and a holy city of Judaism, Christianity and Islam. Prior to World War I, a number of European nations maintained their own postal systems in Jerusalem.

Separate issues were made for their posts in the city by Italy (1909-11) and Russia (1909-14).

In 1948, the French consulate operated a postal service in Jerusalem, utilizing overprinted French Consular Service stamps.

JHALAWAR (1887-90)

Stamp-issuing status: inactive; Stamps issued: 2.

A former princely state in western India. Jhalawar's stamps were replaced by regular Indian issues on Nov. 1, 1900.

JHIND (1874-1950)

Stamp-issuing status: inactive; Stamps issued: 252.

A former feudatory state in the northern Punjab of India. Jhind issued 32 stamps from 1874 to 1885, when a postal convention united its postal system to that of India.

From July 1885 to April 1, 1950, a total of 220 different overprinted Indian stamps were used. Regular Indian issues replaced these overprinted issues on April 1, 1950, although the overprinted stamps remained valid until Jan. 1, 1951.

JOHORE (1876-)

Stamp-issuing status: active; Population: 1 million (1960 estimate); Stamps issued: 212; Issues per year for past decade: 1.

A former non-federated British Malay state. Johore was under British protection from 1914 to 1957. The area joined the Federation of Malaya in 1957.

JORDAN (1920-)

Stamp-issuing status: active; Population: 3.2 million; Stamps issued: more than 1,000; Issues per year for last decade: 28.

A kingdom occupying the territory east of the Jordan River in western Asia. Under Turkish control from 1516 to 1918, the area was occupied from 1918 to 1946 by Great Britain.

Abdullah, second son of King Hussein of Hejaz, became amir of the Trans-Jordan in 1921 and king when the area became independent in 1946.

Jordan seized a large territory on the western bank of the Jordan River in 1948, but the area was occupied by Israel in 1967.

By 1970, the growing power of Palestinian guerrillas in Jordan provoked a reaction by King Hussein and his Bedouin supporters. After a bitter campaign, Palestinian strength in the country was broken by mid-1971.

King Hussein's government is supported by subsidies from the Arab oil states. Because of this, and because of his opposition to the 1979 Israeli-Egyptian peace treaty, Hussein has moved away from Jordan's traditional pro-Western posture to adopt a non-aligned position. He has warmly supported Iraq in its war with Iran.

- K -

KAMPUCHEA (1977-)

Cambodia's name was officially changed to Kampuchea in 1977. Importation of Kampuchean stamps into the United States was prohibited effective on April 17, 1975.

KARELIA (1922, 1941-43)

Stamp-issuing status: inactive; Population: 270,000 (1923 estimate); Stamps issued: 15.

A Soviet district east of Finland. During 1921-22, an autonomous government briefly issued stamps until its suppression by the Soviets.

During 1941-43, the area was occupied by Finland, at which time overprinted Finnish issues and one semipostal were used.

KARLSBAD (1938)

Stamp-issuing status: inactive.

A city in the Sudetenland (Czechoslovakia). In 1938 the local authorities overprinted 68 Czechoslovakian stamps to commemorate the area's cession to Germany.

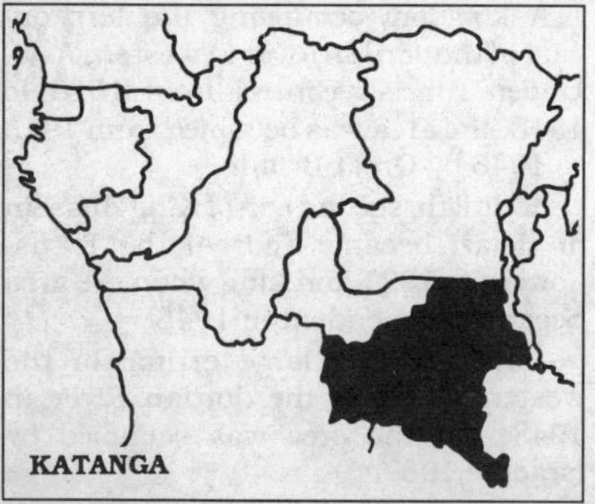

KATANGA (1960-63)

Stamp-issuing status: inactive.

The southernmost province of Zaire. When Belgium granted independence to the Belgian Congo in 1960, Katanga seceded from the new state. After a bitter struggle, the Katangan regime was crushed by the central government with U.N. support.

In early 1977, Katangan forces, based in Angola, launched an invasion of the province. After a rapid initial advance, the Katangese were defeated by forces of the Zairean government, with the support of Moroccan troops and aid from the U.S. and other Western powers.

KEDAH (1912-)

Stamp-issuing status: active; Population: 752,700 (1960 estimate); Stamps issued: 151; Issues per year for past decade: 2.

A sultanate in southwest Malayan peninsula. Kedah was under British protection from 1909 to 1942, Japanese occupation 1942-43, Siamese occupation 1943-45, British administration 1945-57. Since 1948, Kedah has been a member of the Federation of Malaya.

KELANTAN (1911-)

Stamp-issuing status: active; Population: 545,600 (1960 estimate); Stamps issued: 158; Issues per year for past decade: 2.

A sultanate in the northeast Malaya peninsula. The area was under British protection after 1909, and was occupied by Japan (1942-43) and Siam (1943-45) during World War II.

KENYA (1963-)

Stamp-issuing status: active; Population: 19.7 million; Stamps issued: more than 400; Issues per year for last decade: 33.

Republic in East Africa. Formerly a British protectorate, the inroads of European settlers provoked the nationalist Mau Mau movement in 1952.

After years of fighting, Great Britain agreed to grant Kenyan independence, which was declared Dec. 12, 1963. During 1968-72, the government mounted a campaign against Asians with British passports, who controlled the commerce of the nation, and many were forced to leave the country.

Kenya has shown steady economic growth since independence and enjoys a relatively free political life.

A 1980 military and economic aid accord gives the United States access to Kenyan air and naval bases.

KENYA AND UGANDA (1922-35)

Stamp-issuing status: inactive; Stamps

issued: 31.

The postal union comprising the colony of Kenya (coastal area), the protectorate of Kenya (inland) and Uganda, all British colonial territories.

KENYA, UGANDA AND TANGANYIKA (1935-64)

Stamp-issuing status: inactive; Population: 42.7 million (1976 estimate); Stamps issued: 102.

Postal union of Kenya, Uganda and the mandated territory of Tanganyika, British possessions in East Africa. The area was renamed Kenya, Uganda and Tanzania, after Tanganyika and Zanzibar merged to form Tanzania in 1964.

KERASSUNDE (1909-14)

Stamp-issuing status: inactive.

A Turkish port on the Black Sea, now Giresun. After 1909, the Russian post office in Kerassunde used stamps of the Russian Levant overprinted with the name of the city.

KHOR FAKKAN (1965-69)

Stamp-issuing status: inactive.

A dependency of the sheikdom of Sharjah in the Trucial States of eastern Arabia.

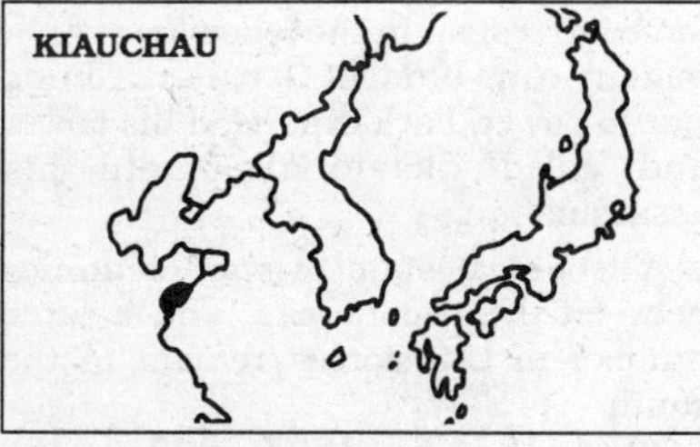

KIAUCHAU (1900-1914)

Stamp-issuing status: inactive; Population: 190,000 (1909 estimate); Stamps issued; 42.

Former German colony on the southern side of the Shantung peninsula in China. The area was seized by Germany in 1897 and subsequently leased to Germany by China. It was occupied by Japan in 1914 and returned to China in 1922.

KIEV (1918, 1920)

Stamp-issuing status: inactive.

Capital of the Ukraine. Kiev issued stamps during the confused period of the Russian Civil War. In 1918, Russian stamps were overprinted with the trident device of the Ukraine. In 1920, Kievan authorities issued surcharged Russian savings stamps for provisional postage use.

KILIS (1921)

Stamp-issuing status: inactive.

A city in southern Turkey. After World War I, this area was included in the French-occupied territory of Syria. It was restored to Turkey in 1923.

In 1921, a shortage of regular stamps necessitated a single provisional issue.

KING EDWARD VII LAND (1908)

Stamp-issuing status: inactive.

In 1908, Sir Ernest Henry Shackleton led a British expedition to explore King Edward VII Land in Antarctica. A contemporary New Zealand stamp was overprinted for use by the members of the expedition.

KIONGA (1916)

Stamp-issuing status: inactive; Stamps issued: 4.

A small area in northern Mozambique in the Indian Ocean. Kionga was part of German East Africa until World War I, when it was occupied by Portuguese forces from Mozambique, to which it was joined by the Treaty of Versailles.

KIRIBATI (1979-)

Stamp-issuing status: active; Population: 60,300 (1982 estimate); Stamps issued: more than 200.

The British protectorate of the Gilbert Islands became the independent republic of Kiribati on July 12, 1979.

KIRIN AND HEILUNGCHANG (1927-31)

Stamp-issuing status: inactive; Stamps issued: 32.

A district of Manchuria. After 1927, Chinese stamps were overprinted for sale in the area. These issues were replaced by those of Manchukuo in 1931, after Japanese forces overran Manchuria.

KISHANGARH (1899-1949)

Stamp-issuing status: inactive; Stamps issued: 118.

A former princely state in northwestern India. In 1948, it joined Rajasthan, whose stamps were used from 1949 to 1950. Since 1950, Indian issues have been used.

KONSTANTINSBAD (1938)

Stamp-issuing status: inactive.

A city in the Sudetenland (Czechoslovakia). In 1938 the municipal authorities overprinted 35 different Czechoslovakian stamps to commemorate union with Germany.

KORCE (KORYTSA, also KORYTZA, KORCA, KORITSA OR CORITSA) (1914-18)

Stamp-issuing status: inactive; Stamps issued: 19.

The center of the short-lived Eastern Albanian Republic during World War I. Supported by French troops, the republic collapsed upon their withdrawal in 1918.

During its existence, however, the Korce regime issued a number of stamps, which are listed under "Albania" in the standard U.S. catalogs.

Forgeries of the 1917-18 issues abound, and collectors should use caution when buying them.

KOREA, DEMOCRATIC PEOPLE'S REPUBLIC OF (NORTH KOREA) (1946-)

Stamp-issuing status: active; Population: 20 million (1985 estimate); Stamps issued: more than 3,000; Issues per year for past decade: 150.

A Communist state occupying the northern half of the Korean peninsula.

After World War II, Korea was occupied from Japan, with U.S. forces holding the southern half of the country. Soviet troops occupied the north.

In 1948, this partition was made permanent, and separate regimes were established in the two zones. The Democratic People's Republic of Korea was established on May 1, 1948, under the leadership of Kim Il Sung.

In 1950, North Korea attacked South Korea, but three years of fighting, with U.S.,U.N. and Chinese intervention, ended with a cease-fire that left the boundary between the two Koreas essentially unchanged.

The greatest part of Korea's resources and pre-war industry were in the north, and the North Korean government has actively developed these into a substantial industrial plant.

North Korea is a totalitarian state, built upon a personality cult centered around Kim Il Sung. It maintains ties with both China and the U.S.S.R.

KOREA, REPUBLIC OF (SOUTH KOREA) (1946-)

Stamp-issuing status: active; Population: 43 million; Stamps issued: 1,450; Issues per year for last decade: 41.

After the establishment of the Democratic People's Republic of Korea in 1948, the Republic of Korea was established in the southern portion of the peninsula occupied by the U.S. The regime in the south was recognized as the legal government of Korea on Dec. 12, 1948.

On June 25, 1950, North Korea attacked South Korea, quickly pushing the South Korean forces back to a small pocket of resistance in the southeast.

Massive U.N. intervention brought a North Korean rout, but the invasion of the North by Communist China brought the retreat of the U.N. forces to below the 38th parallel.

On July 10, 1951, after renewed U.N. advances, peace talks began, and on July 27, 1953, an armistice was achieved.

From 1948 to 1960, Dr. Syngman Rhee was president of South Korea. The corruption of the regime alienated many South Koreans, and in 1960 Rhee was forced to resign. In the following year, a military coup brought Gen. Park Chung Hee to power. Park expanded his power and ruled dictatorially until his assassination.

A technical state of war continues between the two Koreas, and a large number of U.S. forces remain in the south.

KOREA (1884-85, 1895-1905, 1946)

Stamp-issuing status: inactive; Population: 22.8 million (1938 estimate); Stamps issued: 69.

A peninsula in east Asia, surrounded on three sides by the Sea of Japan and the Yellow Sea and bounded on the north by Manchuria and the U.S.S.R.

Korea was under Chinese control until 1895, when it passed under Japanese influence. In 1910, Japan annexed Korea, ruling it until 1945.

After World War II, Korea was divided at the 38th parallel into two zones of occupation — the north under the Soviets and the south under the U.S. In 1948, separate regimes were established in the two zones.

KUBAN COSSACK GOVERNMENT (1918-20)

Stamp-issuing status: inactive; Stamps issued: 24.

In late 1917, the Kuban Cossacks in southern Russia established a republic in opposition to the Bolshevik forces. In the spring of 1918, this republic declared its independence.

The Kuban Cossacks were recognized by the White Russian government of Gen. Denikin, but after his withdrawal from the area in March 1920, the republic was quickly occupied by the Red Army.

A number of Russian stamps were surcharged by this regime.

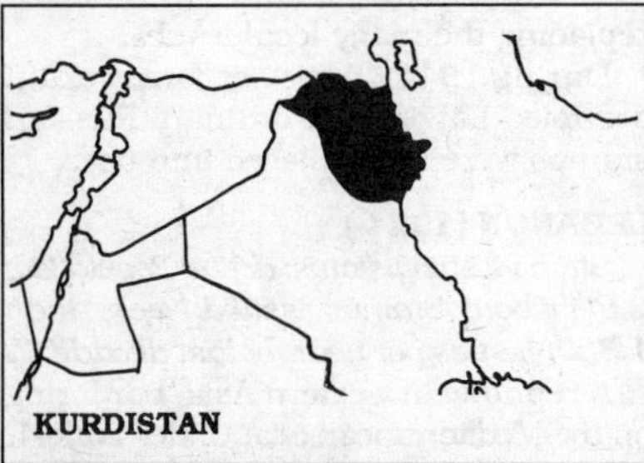

KURDISTAN

KURDISTAN (1923)

Stamp-issuing status: inactive.

The region of western Asia occupied by the Kurds, divided between Iraq, Iran and Turkey. In 1923, stamps were issued by rebel forces in northern Iraq.

KURLAND (1945)

Stamp-issuing status: inactive; Stamps issued: 4.

Four German stamps were overprinted for use in Kurzeme in April 1945, by German forces cut off by the Soviet advance.

KUSTANAI (1920)

Stamp-issuing status: inactive.

A city in the Kazakh Soviet Socialist Republic. In 1920, the local authorities overprinted Russian stamps for use in the area.

KUWAIT (1923-)

Stamp-issuing status: active; Population: 1.7 million; Stamps issued: more than 1,100; Issues per year for last decade: 32.

A sheikdom at the northern end of the Persian Gulf. Kuwait was under British protection from 1899 to 1961, becoming independent June 19, 1961.

Kuwait is rich in oil and one of the more active members of OPEC. During the 1970s, Kuwait led the push for increasing petroleum prices and became extremely wealthy.

Education, medical care and social security are free to Kuwaiti citizens, and internal taxation has been abolished.

KWANGCHOWAN (1906-44)

Stamp-issuing status: inactive; Stamps issued: 144.

A Chinese port south of Canton leased by France from 1898 to 1945. Kwangchowan was administered as part of French Indo-China. Occupied by Japan during World War II, the city was re-occupied by the Chinese after the war.

KWANGTUNG (1942-50)

Stamp-issuing status: inactive; Stamps issued: 70.

A province in southern China, centered around its capital, Canton. Japanese forces occupying Kwangtung overprinted 60 Chinese stamps for use in the province from 1942 to 1945.

Some 10 regular Chinese (Nationalist) issues were used during 1945-49. In October 1949, Canton, which had briefly become the Nationalist capital, fell to the Communists, and Communist issues for South China came into use, to be replaced by national issues in 1950.

- L -

LABUAN (1879-1906)

Stamp-issuing status: inactive; Stamps issued: 136.

An island off the northwest coast of Borneo. Labuan was ceded by Brunei to Britain in 1848 and administered by the British North Borneo Co. from 1890 to 1906.

In 1907, Labuan was attached to the Straits Settlements and, since 1945, has been part of British North Borneo (Sabah).

LAGOS (1874-1906)

Stamp-issuing status: inactive; Stamps issued: 59.

A territory in south Nigeria. Lagos was occupied by Great Britain in 1861 and, during 1886-1906, was a separate protectorate.

The territory merged with the Southern Nigerian Protectorate in 1906.

LAOS (1951-)

Stamp-issuing status: active; Population: 3.6 million (1985 estimate); Stamps issued: more than 1000; Issues per year for last decade: 54.

A state in northwestern Indo-China. Formerly a kingdom of some influence, by the early 19th century Laos was under Siamese rule. In 1893, Siam renounced its claims, and in 1899, Laos became a French protectorate.

During 1941-45, Laos was occupied by Japan. After World War II, Laos was re-established as a kingdom (1947), under French protection. In 1953 it became independent within the French Union, and in 1956 it became fully independent.

During the Vietnamese War, Laos maintained a precarious neutrality, with troops of both sides active within the country. With the U.S. withdrawal from Indo-China, the neutralist regime collapsed. In May 1975, the Lao Democratic People's Republic, a Vietnamese satellite, was established.

LAS BELA (1897-1907)

Stamp-issuing status: inactive; Population: 63,000; Stamps issued: 6.

A former feudatory state of India, now a part of Pakistan.

LATAKIA (1931-37)

Stamp-issuing status: inactive; Population: 280,000 (1936 estimate); Stamps issued: 35.

This area, orginally called Alaouites, was a district of western Syria under French mandate. Its stamps were replaced by those of Syria in 1937, after its merger with Syria in December 1936.

LATVIA (1918-41)

Stamp-issuing status: inactive; Population: 2 million (1940 estimate); Stamps issued: 338.

A former republic on the Baltic and the Gulf of Riga. Although the majority of Latvians are Slavic, the area was long dominated by a German land-owning class, descendants of the Knights of the Tuetonic Order, who conquered the region during the Middle Ages. Latvia was ruled by Poland and Sweden until Russia occupied the territory in the 18th century.

During 1917-18, Latvia was occupied by Germany, and in 1918 it declared its independence from Russia. During 1919, the Latvian government fought both the Red Army, which sought to re-establish Russian control, and the Army of the West, which sought to maintain German influence. By the end of 1919, Latvia was able to secure its independence.

In 1939, as part of the Soviet-German Non-Aggression Pact, the U.S.S.R. established military bases in Latvia. In June 1940, Soviet forces seized the country, and in July it was absorbed into the Soviet Union.

In July 1941, Germany occupied the country, and many cities overprinted their stocks of Russian stamps for provisional use. In November, German "Ostland" issues were introduced, replacing the many local issues.

During 1944-45, Soviet forces again occupied Latvia, and ordinary Russian stamps were again placed into use.

LEBANON (1924-)

Stamp-issuing status: active; Population: 2.6 million; Stamps issued: more than 1,300; Issues per year for last decade: 7.

A republic in western Asia, bordering on the Mediterranean Sea. Under Turkish rule until 1918, Lebanon was occupied by the French after World War I under a League of Nations mandate. It was declared independent in 1941, and in 1944, its independence was implemented.

Lebanon's population is 57 percent Moslem and 40 percent Christian, and from 1943, the two groups co-existed through a constitutional apportioning of key government posts. During 1969-75, Palestinian commando groups became increasingly powerful in Lebanon, which they used as a base for raids against Israel.

Efforts of the government to restrain Palestinian activities, with which many Lebanese Moslems sympathized, and after 1970, Israeli counterattacks against Palestinian bases in southern Lebanon, destabilized the Lebanese government.

During 1965-76, these tensions erupted in civil war. Generally, Arab nations supported the Palestinians and leftist Moslem factions, while Israel supported the various Christian groups. In 1976, Syria intervened, suppressed PLO activity, and attempted to mediate the conflict. Although sporadic clashes continue, the presence of foreign troops has prevented the resumption of full-scale civil war.

LEEWARD ISLANDS (1890-1956)

Stamp-issuing status: inactive; Population: 109,000 (1954 estimate); Stamps issued: 134.

A group of islands in the West Indies, southeast of Puerto Rico. The Leeward Islands was a former administrative unit of British island possessions in the Caribbean — Antigua, Montserrat, St. Kitts, Nevis and Anguilla, British Virgin Islands, and Dominica (until 1940).

Leeward issues were used throughout the colony, while the issues of the individual presidencies were valid only within their own territories.

LEMNOS (1912-13)

Stamp-issuing status: inactive.

A Greek island in the Aegean Sea. Lemnos utilized 38 overprinted Greek stamps during its occupation by Turkey.

LEROS (1912-32)

Stamp-issuing status: inactive; Stamps issued: 26.

One of the Dodecanese Islands in the eastern Aegean Sea. Leros was claimed from Turkey by Italy in 1912, at which time Italian stamps overprinted "Leros" were issued.

In 1929, these were superseded by general issues for the Aegean Islands, although two sets overprinted "Lero" were released in 1930 and 1932.

LESOTHO (1966-)

Stamp-issuing status: active; Population: 1.6 million; Stamps issued: more than 620; Issues per year for last decade: 38.

A kingdom in southern Africa, surrounded by the Republic of South Africa. Until it became independent as Lesotho in 1966, this territory was the British crown colony of Basutoland.

Lesotho is completely surrounded by South Africa, and the majority of its work force is employed in that country.

LIBERIA (1860-)

Stamp-issuing status: active; Population: 2 million (1986 estimate); Stamps issued: more than 1,550; Issues per year for the last decade: 27.

A republic on the west coast of Africa, which after 1822 was colonized by freed slaves from the United States. In 1847, Liberia was proclaimed independent.

Liberian political and economic life has been dominated by the descendants of these freed slaves, who constitute less than 3 percent of the country's population.

LIBYA (1912-)

Stamp-issuing status: active; Population: 3.7 million; Stamps issued: more than 1,150; Issues per year for last decade: 59.

A republic in northern Africa, bordering on the Mediterranean Sea. Occupied until 1912 by Turkey, the area that is now Libya passed to Italy after its victory in the Turko-Italian War of 1912.

The colonies of Tripolitania and Cyrenaica were united into Libya in 1934. During World War II, the colony was occupied by the Allies with Tripolitania and Cyrenaica under British administration, using "M.E.F." stamps (Middle Eastern Forces), while Fezzan-Ghadames was under French administration, using its own issues.

On Dec. 24, 1951, the independent Kingdom of Libya was established. In September 1969, the monarchy was deposed and the Libyan Arab Republic was established.

The Libyan Arab Republic is ruled by a military junta headed by Col. Muammar al-Qadhafi. Qadhafi's policies are a blend of socialism, fundamentalist Islam and ardent pan-Arabism. Libya has led the movement within OPEC for constantly higher petroleum prices and has used its huge oil income for sweeping social programs and to support radical movements throughout the world.

Libya has actively funded and trained leftist movements, including the Japanese "Red Army," the Irish Republican Army, Black September (the radical arm of the PLO), Philippine Moslem terrorists and others. Since 1975, Libya has been closely linked with the U.S.S.R.

Qadhafi's long-range goal is to assume leadership of the Arab world, and his ambitions have brought problems with a number of Libya's neighbors. In 1976 he was accused of attempting the overthrow of the Sudanese government.

In 1977 Libya and Egypt fought several battles on their common border. During 1977-79, Libyan troops supported Arab guerrillas in their attempt to transfer northern Chad to Libyan control. In 1979, Libya attempted to overthrow the government of Tunisia.

LIECHTENSTEIN (1912-)

Stamp-issuing status: active; Population: 27,825; Stamps issued: more than 970; Issues per year for last decade: 25.

A principality in central Europe between Switzerland and Austria. Liechtenstein, founded in 1719, became a sovereign state in 1806, and became independent in 1866. Until 1918, it retained close ties with Austria, which until 1920 operated the Liechtenstein postal service.

Since 1920, it has been associated with Switzerland, its post office having been under Swiss administration since 1921.

In 1868, Liechtenstein abolished its army and has since remained free of foreign entanglements. It remains the only European nation denying women the right to vote.

Liechtenstein is one of the major tax havens of the world, and many international corporations have headquarters there. The country's major exports include postage stamps and plastic postage stamp mounts.

LISSO (1912-32)

Stamp-issuing status: inactive; Stamps issued: 26.

One of the Dodecanese Islands in the eastern Aegean Sea. Lisso was occupied from Turkey by Italy in 1912, at which time Italian stamps overprinted "Lipso" were issued.

In 1929, Lisso's issues were superseded by the general issues for the Aegean Islands, although two sets overprinted "Lisso" or "Lipso" were released in 1930 and 1932.

LITHUANIA (1918-40)

Stamp-issuing status: inactive; Population: 2.88 million (1940 estimate); Stamps issued: 452.

A country of eastern Europe, northeast of Poland and south of Latvia.

Lithuania ruled a large empire in the later Middle Ages, stretching from the Baltic to the Black Seas. In 1385 Lithuania was united with the Kingdom of Poland. Initially the dominant partner, Lithuania was gradually eclipsed by Poland. It was absorbed by Russia in 1793 and remained under Russian control until World War I.

In 1915 the country was occupied by Germany, which supported its declaration of independence from Russia in 1918. German troops remained in Lithuania until the end of 1919. In 1920 the border district of Central Lithuania was lost to Poland, but this was somewhat offset by Lithuania's seizure of the German port of Memel from the Allies in 1923.

In October 1939, Lithuania re-occupied Central Lithuania, in return for which she allowed the Soviet Union to establish military bases. In June 1940, Lithuania was seized by Soviet forces and in July was annexed to the U.S.S.R.

In June 1941, German forces occupied the country, and a number of local overprints on Russian stamps were used, as well as general overprints for Lithuania as a whole. From November 1941 to 1944, German issues overprinted "Ostland" were used.

In 1944, the U.S.S.R. re-occupied Lithuania, and Soviet issues have since been used.

LIVORNO (1930)

Stamp-issuing status: inactive.

A city in Liguria, Italy. On May 11, 1930, Mussolini visited Livorno, and a local stamp, valid only on that day, was issued by the municipal authorities to commemorate Il Duce's visit.

LJADY (1942)

Stamp-issuing status: inactive.

A Russian city near Leningrad. The German military commander surcharged two stamps of Germany and Ostland for use in the area.

LJUBLJANA (LUBIANA, LAIBACH) (1941-45)

Stamp-issuing status: inactive; Stamps issued: 131.

Western Slovenia, separated and established as an Italo-German puppet state during World War II.

LOGRONO (1937)

Stamp-issuing status: inactive.

The capital of the province of Logrono in north-central Spain. In 1937 a set of stamps was issued by the local Nationalist authorities.

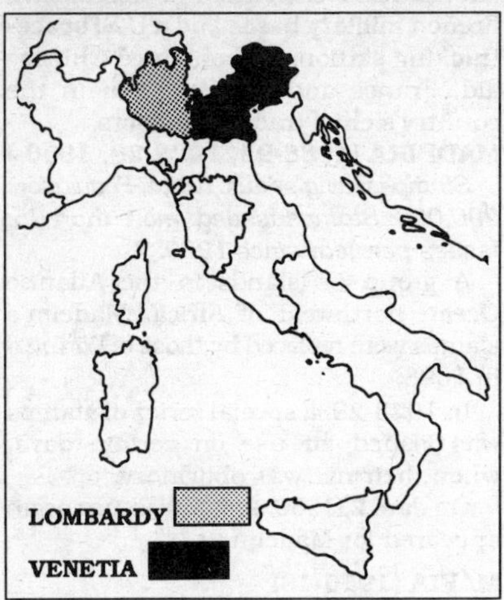

LOMBARDY-VENETIA (1850-66)

Stamp-issuing status: inactive; Stamps issued: 26.

The Lombardy-Venetian Kingdom was created in 1815, comprising northeastern Italy, under the Austrian emperor. In 1859, Milan was conquered by Sardinia, and in 1866, Austria relinquished Venetia to the Kingdom of Italy.

The Austrian administration issued separate stamps for this kingdom, inscribed in Italian currency, which were also used in Austrian post offices in the Ottoman Empire.

Since 1866, Italian stamps have been in use.

LONG ISLAND (1916)

Stamp-issuing status: inactive.

An island (Cheustan or Makronsi) in the Gulf of Smyrna. Long Island was occupied by British forces in 1916, at which time the British commander issued Turkish fiscal stamps overprinted "G.R.I. Postage" and provisional typewritten stamps, used until the British withdrawal from the island.

LORIENT (1945)

Stamp-issuing status: inactive.

In February 1945, 27 French stamps were overprinted by the German military authorities for local use.

LOURENCO MARQUES (1895-1920)

Stamp-issuing status: inactive; Population: 474,000; Stamps issued: 175.

A district of southern Mozambique. Its stamps were replaced by those of Mozambique in 1920.

LUBECK (1859-68)

Stamp-issuing status: inactive; Population: 136,413; Stamps issued: 14.

A former Free City and State in northern Germany on the Baltic Sea. Lubeck's stamps were replaced by those of the North German Confederation.

LUBOML (1919)

Stamp-issuing status: inactive; Stamps issued: 9.

A city in southern Poland. The local authorities issued a series of stamps during the German occupation. This issue was very speculative and may be found with many so-called errors.

LUGA (1941)

Stamp-issuing status: inactive; Stamps issued: 5.

A city in northwestern Russia, south of Leningrad. Surcharged Russian stamps were issued by the German military commander.

LUXEMBOURG (1852-)

Stamp-issuing status: active; Population: 366,000; Stamps issued: more than 1,400; Issues per year for last decade: 22.

A grand duchy in western Europe, strategically located between Germany, France and Belgium.

Until 1890, Luxembourg was ruled by a succession of foreign powers, although from 1815, it was technically independent, joined in personal union with the Netherlands. With the death of William III, king of the Netherlands and grand duke of Luxembourg, the country became completely independent.

Luxembourg was occupied by Germany in both world wars. In 1949, it abandoned its traditional neutrality to become a charter member of NATO. It is a member of the Common Market and is an enthusiastic promoter of European co-operation.

Luxembourg is a prosperous, highly industrialized nation.

- M -

MACAO (1884-)

Stamp-issuing status: active; Population: 390,000; Stamps issued: more than 500; Issues per year for last decade: 8.

A Chinese port occupied by Portugal since 1557. In 1849, Portugal assumed full sovereignty over the territory, which includes two small, adjacent islands.

MACEDONIA (1944)

Stamp-issuing status: inactive; Stamps issued: 8.

A region in the central Balkans, Macedonia became part of Serbia after 1913, and so became part of Yugoslavia when Serbia merged into that nation.

Bulgaria annexed the territory in 1941. On Sept. 8, 1944, Macedonia declared its independence from Bulgaria. After withdrawal of German troops in November 1944, the area was returned to Yugoslavia.

Overprinted Bulgarian stamps were in use for a few weeks before the collapse of the German puppet government.

MADAGASCAR (MALAGASY REPUBLIC) (1889-)

Stamp-issuing status: active; Population: 10.28 million (1986 estimate); Stamps issued: more than 1,100; Issues per year for last decade: 26.

A large island in the Indian Ocean off the southeast coast of Africa. During the 19th century, most of the island was united under the Hova tribe, which was placed under French protection in 1885.

In 1896, the native monarchy was abolished and Madagascar became a French colony, at times administering French island possessions in the area.

In 1958, Madagascar, renamed the Malagasy Republic, became autonomous within the French Union. In 1960 it became fully independent.

French influence remained strong until a 1972 coup brought a socialist regime to power. The new government nationalized French holdings, closed down French military bases and a U.S. space-tracking station, and obtained Chinese aid. France and the U.S. remain the country's chief trading partners.

MADEIRA (1868-98, 1928-29, 1980-)

Stamp-issuing status: active; Population: 290,000; Stamps issued: more than 75; Issues per year since 1980: 7.

A group of islands in the Atlantic Ocean northwest of Africa. Madeira's stamps were replaced by those of Portugal in 1898.

In 1928-29, a special series of stamps was issued for use on certain days, when their use was obligatory.

On Jan. 2, 1980, separate issues again appeared for Madeira.

MAFIA (1915-18)

Stamp-issuing status: inactive.

A small island off the coast of German East Africa, occupied by the British in December 1914. In January 1915, 32 captured German East African stamps were overprinted for use on the island.

Later, German fiscal stamps and Indian issues overprinted "I.E.F." were overprinted "Mafia" or "G.R.I.-Mafia" for local use.

In August 1918, the island was transferred to Tanganyikan administration, and issues of Tanganyika (Tanzania) have since been used.

MAHRA (1967)

Stamp-issuing status: inactive.

A sultanate in the Aden Protectorate in southwest Arabia. Mahra briefly issued stamps before its absorption into the People's Republic of Southern Yemen.

MAJORCA (1936-37)

Stamp-issuing status: inactive.

The largest of the Balearic Islands, in the western Mediterranean Sea.

Two sets of overprinted Spanish stamps were issued in 1936 and 1937 under the authority of the Nationalist Civil Governor of the Balearic Islands.

MAJUNGA (1895)

Stamp-issuing status: inactive.

Province and seaport on the coast of Madagascar. Stamps of France provisionally surcharged were used briefly in February 1895.

MALACCA (MELAKA) (1948-)

Stamp-issuing status: active; Population: 318,110 (1960 estimate); Stamps issued: more than 95; Issues per year for last decade: 1.

Formerly part of the British colony of Straits Settlements. Malacca was under British control since the early 19th century, except for Japanese occupation from 1942 to 1945.

The area is now a part of Malaya within the Malaysian Federation. Stamps recently issued for use there are inscribed "Melaka."

MALAGA (1937)

Stamp-issuing status: inactive.

A province of southern Spain, located on the Mediterranean Sea.

Two sets of stamps, overprinted on Spanish issues, were issued by the Nationalist Civil Governor in 1937.

MALAWI (1964-)

Stamp-issuing status: active; Population: 7.2 million; Stamps issued: more than 450; Issues per year for last decade: 23.

A republic in south-central Africa. Until it became independent on July 6, 1964, Malawi was the British Nyasaland Protectorate. Generally pro-Western, Malawi is closely linked economically with Zimbabwe and South Africa.

MALAYA, FEDERATION (1957-63)

Stamp-issuing status: inactive; Population: 7.4 million (1961 estimate); stamps issued: 35.

A formerly independent federation comprising the Malayan states in the southern part of the Malayan Peninsula. The federation merged with Singapore, Sarawak and Sabah to form Malaysia in 1963.

MALAYA-FEDERATED MALAY STATES (1900-35)

Stamp-issuing status: inactive; Stamps issued: more than 1,500.

A group of native states in the south portion of the Malayan Peninsula in southeast Asia, under British protection.

The federated states were Perak, Selangor, Negri Sembilan and Pahang.

In 1935, the federation issues were replaced by those of the individual states. In 1945, the Federated Malay States were incorporated into the Malayan Union.

MALAYSIA (1963-)

Stamp-issuing status: active; Population: 15.7 million; Stamps issued: more than 350; Issues per year for last decade: 20.

Federation within the British Commonwealth. Malaysia was formed Sept. 16, 1963, with the union of the former British territories of the Federation of Malaya, Singapore (until 1965), Sarawak and Sabah (North Borneo).

Malaysia is rich in natural resources and has enjoyed substantial industrial development since independence.

MALDIVE ISLANDS (1906-)

Stamp-issuing status: active; Population: 185,000; Stamps issued: more than 1,000; Issues per year for last decade: 49.

A group of islands in the Indian Ocean, southwest of Ceylon. The Maldives came under British protection in 1887 and were attached to the Ceylon colony until 1948.

During 1948-64, the islands were closely associated with Great Britain, becoming completely independent in July 1965.

In 1968, the 800-year-old sultanate was abolished, and a republic was established. In recent years, the Maldives have maintained close ties with India and the U.S.S.R.

MALI (1959-)

Stamp-issuing status: active; Population: 7.5 million (1985 estimate); Stamps issued: more than 1,175; Issues per year for last decade: 48.

A republic in West Africa. Formerly the French Sudan, Mali joined Senegal in 1959 to form the independent Federation of Mali.

Senegal withdrew from the federation in 1960, and Mali, which called itself the Sudanese Republic during its union with Senegal, proclaimed its independence as the Republic of Mali.

Mali maintained a carefully neutralist policy until 1968, accepting economic aid from both the Western and Communist blocs.

Since 1968, however, conservative elements have been purged, and Mali has strengthened her ties with Red China.

Since 1973, Mali has suffered terribly from drought and famine.

MALTA (1860-)

Stamp-issuing status: active; Population: 332,000; Stamps issued: more than 780; Issues per year for last decade: 20.

A group of islands in the central Mediterranean Sea, south of Sicily. Strategically located, Malta has been ruled by a long succession of foreign powers, from the Phoenicians through the British, who occupied the islands during the Napoleonic Wars.

Malta became independent in 1964 and a republic in 1974. In 1979 the last British military personnel were withdrawn. Malta maintains a non-aligned foreign policy and receives economic aid from both the Eastern and Western blocs.

MAN, ISLE OF (1973-)

Stamp-issuing status: active; Population: 61,000; Stamps issued: more than 350; Issues per year for last decade: 24.

An island in the Irish Sea, west of Britain. A self-governing crown possession, the Isle of Man used British stamps, along with its own regional issues after 1958, until July 5, 1973, when its postal administration separated from that of Britain.

MANAMA (1966-72)

Stamp-issuing status: inactive.

A dependency of the sheikdom of Ajman in the Trucial States of eastern Arabia.

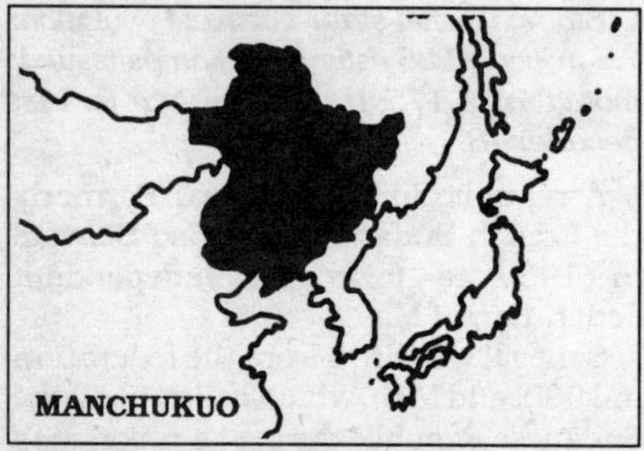

MANCHUKUO (1932-45)

Stamp-issuing status: inactive; Population: 43.2 million (1940 estimate); Stamps issued: 166.

A former Japanese satellite, comprising Manchuria and Jehol. Established in 1932 under Henry Pu-yi, who as Hsuan Tung had been the last Manchu emperor of China.

In 1934, Pu-yi became Emperor Kang Teh of Manchukuo. The area was occupied by the Soviets in July 1945, and was turned over to the Chinese Communist regime in May 1946.

Nationalist forces held the southern portion of Manchukuo until November 1948, and during 1946-48 issued stamps for this area (North-Eastern Provinces).

MARIANA ISLANDS (1899-1914)

Stamp-issuing status: inactive; Population: 40,000 (1919 estimate); Stamps issued: 27.

A group of islands in the western Pacific. Under Spanish rule from 1668-1898, when, except for Guam, they were sold to Germany.

Japan occupied the Marianas in 1914, and Japanese stamps replaced those of the German colony. In 1945, U.S. forces occupied the islands. U.S. stamps have since been in use.

MARIENWERDER (1920)

Stamp-issuing status: inactive; Stamps issued: 42.

A former Prussian district, which was occupied by the Allies after World War I. A plebiscite in 1920 returned the area to Germany. It was occupied by Poland after World War II.

MARINO (1930)

Stamp-issuing status: inactive.

A district of northeastern Venezuela, which was controlled by a revolutionary group for a short time during 1903.

MARSHALL ISLANDS (1889-1916; 1984-)

Stamp-issuing status: active; Population: 15,000 (1916 estimate), 33,000 (1984); Stamps issued: 27 (1897-1916), more than 225 since 1984; Issues per year since 1984: 48.

The easternmost island group in Micronesia, consisting of two roughly parallel chains of coral-capped islets and atolls in the western Pacific. Totaling only 70 square miles, the principal atolls are Majuro, Jaluit and Kwajalein.

Spain sold the Caroline Islands in 1898 to Germany, which renamed them the Marshall Islands and issued stamps for use there. The islands were seized by the Japanese during World War I and administered by them under a 1919 League of Nations mandate.

Invaded and conquered by United States

forces in World War II, the Marshall Islands were made part of the United Nations-mandated U.S. Trust Territory of the Pacific in 1947.

On May 1, 1981, the Marshall Islands received its own constitution, president and legislature. Stamps ascribed to the island appeared that October, but these originated privately in Japan. The Marshall Islands began issuing its own stamps in May 1984, although its mail continues to be handled by the U.S. Postal Service.

MARTINIQUE (1886-1947)

Stamp-issuing status: inactive; Population: 261,595 (1946 estimate); Stamps issued: 303.

A former French island colony in the West Indies, southeast of Puerto Rico. The island became an integral part of the French republic on Jan. 1, 1947. French stamps are now used.

MATURIN (1903)

Stamp-issuing status: inactive.

The capital of the state of Monagas in northeastern Venezuela. A revolutionary group in control of the region issued stamps for a short time during 1903.

MAURITANIA (1906-44, 1960-)

Stamp-issuing status: active; Population: 1.85 million (1986 estimate); Stamps issued: more than 975; Issues per year for last decade: 34.

A republic in northwestern Africa, bordering on the Atlantic Ocean. A former French colony, Mauritania was part of French West Africa from 1904 to 1958 and used French West African stamps 1945-49.

In 1958, Mauritania, as the Islamic Republic of Mauritania, became autonomous within the French Union, and in 1960, it became fully independent.

At one time, the territory of Mauritania was ruled by Morocco, and Morocco claimed the area until 1970. In 1976, the mineral-rich Spanish Sahara was divided between the two countries.

In 1980, Mauritania, after four years of war with the Polsario Front, renounced its share of the former Spanish Sahara, which was then occupied by Morocco.

MAURITIUS (1847-)

Stamp-issuing status: active; Population: 1.04 million; Stamps issued; more than 680; Issues per year for last decade: 23.

An island in the Indian Ocean. Mauritius was a British colony after 1810 and became independent in 1968.

Mauritius enjoys a free political life and a high literacy rate. The country's economy has expanded during the past decade.

MAYOTTE (1892-1914)

Stamp-issuing status: inactive; Population: 14,000 (1912 estimate); Stamps issued: 31.

One of the Comoro Islands, Mayotte was occupied by France in 1841 and attached to the colony of Madagascar in 1911.

The Comoros were separated from Madagascar in 1947 and began issuing their own stamps in 1950.

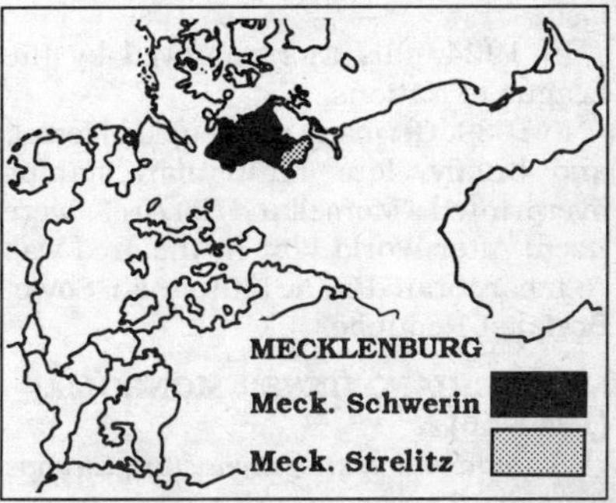

MECKLENBURG-SCHWERIN (1856-67)

Stamp-issuing status: inactive; Stamps issued: 8.

A former grand duchy in northern Germany, bordering the Baltic Sea. In 1868, issues of the North German Confederation came into use.

MECKLENBURG-STRELITZ (1864-67)

Stamp-issuing status: inactive; Stamps issued: 6.

A former grand duchy in northern Germany, divided into two parts by Mecklenburg-Schwerin, with which it was joined until 1701.

Its stamps were replaced by those of the North German Confederation in 1868.

MELILLA (1936)

Stamp-issuing status: inactive.

A port in northern Morocco. Occupied by Spain since 1470, Melilla was a military stronghold administered separately from Spanish Morocco, which was not occupied by Spain until the late 19th and early 20th centuries.

Melilla, along with Cueta, remains a part of metropolitan Spain.

In 1936, the military authorities in Melilla overprinted two Spanish stamps for local use.

MEMEL (1920-24, 1939)

Stamp-issuing status: inactive; Stamps issued: 241.

A district in northern Europe, on the Baltic Sea. German until after World War I, when the area was occupied by the French, who issued 123 surcharged and overprinted stamps. In 1923, frustrated by the League of Nations' failure to decide the disposition of sovereignty over the area, Lithuania seized Memel. They created 11¢ occupation issues.

In 1924, this was approved by the League of Nations.

In 1939, Germany re-occupied Memel, and briefly, four Lithuanian stamps overprinted "Memelland/Ist/frei" were used. After World War II, the area was re-incorporated in the Lithuanian Soviet Socialist Republic.

MENG CHIANG (INNER MONGOLIA) (1941-45)

Stamp-issuing status: inactive; Stamps issued: 127.

Regular Chinese stamps were overprinted by the Japanese in 1941, and separate issues for this area continued until the end of World War II.

This area was held by the Communist forces at the end of the war and was included in the North China postal district, which issued stamps from 1946 to 1949.

Regular issues of the central government came into use after 1950.

MERANO (1918)

Stamp-issuing status: inactive.

A city in northern Italy, formerly under Austrian rule. Local stamps were issued by the authorities in 1918, while the area was still a part of Austria.

MERIDA (1916)

Stamp-issuing status: inactive.

The capital of the state of Yucatan in southern Mexico. A single issue received a 25-centavo surcharge for local use there in 1916.

MESOPOTAMIA (1917-22)

Stamp-issuing status: inactive; Population 2.85 million (1920 estimate); stamps issued: 75.

Former Turkish province in western Asia. Mesopotamia was occupied by British forces during World War I. It became the kingdom of Iraq under British mandate in 1921.

MEXICO (1856-)

Stamp-issuing status: active; Population: 78.8 million; Stamps issued: more than 2,400; Issues per year for last decade: 47.

A republic in North America, situated between the United States and Central America, bordering on the Caribbean Sea and the Pacific Ocean.

Mexico was the center of a number of Indian cultures dating from c. 800 B.C. By the 15th century, the central portion of the country was ruled by the Aztec Empire, which was conquered by the Spanish in 1519-21.

Mexico, as the viceroyalty of New Spain, was the center of Spain's North American Empire for 300 years.

The Mexican revolution against Spain began in 1810 and finally succeeded in 1821. The Mexican Empire of 1822-23 included Central America, but this area soon became independent. The republican government that succeeded the empire was marked by instability and strife.

The weakened condition of the country cost it Texas (1836) and the large northern area that now comprises the southwestern United States (1848). An additional area in the north was sold to the United States in 1853.

During 1861-67, Mexico was torn by a civil war between the aristocracy, supported by France, and the lower classes, led by Benito Juarez.

The French were finally expelled from Mexico, and Juarez came to power.

During most of the period between 1877 and 1911, the country was ruled by the dictator Porfirio Diaz, who restored stability and secured foreign investment.

After Diaz's death, Mexico entered a period of civil war, which lasted from 1913-20. During this period, the United States intervened in Veracruz (1914) and sent a punitive expedition into northern Mexico (1916-17).

Since 1929, Mexico has been ruled by the Institutional Revolutionary Party. The PRI is a broad-based political confederation, encompassing a wide political spectrum.

Mexico has rich natural resources, including what may be the world's largest petroleum reserves, but its rugged topography and arid climate have been major obstacles to economic development.

Considerable economic and social progress has been made since 1940, but unemployment remains extremely high, and many Mexicans have yet to share in the benefits of the country's development.

MEXICO-REVOLUTIONARY OVERPRINTS (1914)

With the seizure of power in 1913 by Gen. Huerta following the assassination of President Madero, a group of Madero's former supporters launched a revolution.

This group, led by Carranza and including such leaders as Obregon, Villa, and Zapata, called themselves the "Constitutional Government."

During 1914, a number of Mexican cities and states under Constitutionalist control, provisionally overprinted stocks of regular Mexican stamps: Acambaro (Guanajuato State); Aguascalientes (Aguascalientes); Chihuahua (Chihuahua); Colima (Colima); Culiacan (Sinoloa); Guaymas (Sonora); Juarez (Chihuahua); Leon (Guanajuato); Lower California; Coahuila; Gonzales (Guanajuato); Matehuala (San Luis Potosi); Monterrey (Nuevo Leon); Queretaro; Salamanca (Guanajuato); San Juan de Allende (Coahuila); San Luis Potosi (San Luis Potosi); San Pedro; Sinaloa (Sinaloa); Sonora; Torreon (Coahuila); Tuxtla; Viezca; Yucatan; and Zacatecas.

MICRONESIA (1984-)

Stamp-issuing status: active; Population: 73,750 (1980); Stamps issued: more than 100; Issues per year 1984-88: 26.

A group of more than 600 islands totaling only 270 square miles, located in the western Pacific Ocean north of the equator.

These islands, along with what is now Palau, were part of the Spanish Caroline Islands until 1899, when they were sold to Germany, which issued stamps for use there. The Caroline Islands were seized by the Japanese during World War I and administered by them under a 1919 mandate of the League of Nations.

Invaded and conquered by United States forces in the Pacific campaigns of World War II, the islands were made part of the United Nations-mandated U.S. Trust Territory of the Pacific in 1947, using U.S. stamps since that time.

The islands were proclaimed the Federated States of Micronesia and began issuing stamps in July 1984. Mail continues to be handled by the U.S. Postal Service.

MIDDLE CONGO (1907-36)

Stamp-issuing status: inactive: Population: 747,000 (1933 estimate); Stamps issued: 123

Former French colony on the northern side of the Congo River. Created from existing French territory in 1907, it was confederated with Gabon, Ubangi-Shari and Chad to form French Equatorial Africa.

After 1936, issues of French Equatorial Africa replaced those of the individual colonies.

MIDDLE EAST FORCES (1942-50)

Stamp-issuing status: inactive.

During World War II, British and New Zealand forces occupied Italian colonies in East Africa, North Africa and the Aegean Sea.

British stamps overprinted "M.E.F." were used in these areas until 1950, after which the remainders were used in Great Britain.

MILAN (1897)

Stamp-issuing status: inactive.

A city in northern Italy. For a time, local stamps were issued by the municipal authorities.

MINORCA (1939)

Stamp-issuing status: inactive.

One of the Balearic Islands, in the western Mediterranean Sea.

Locally typeset stamps were used provisionally after the occupation of the island by the Nationalists in February 1939.

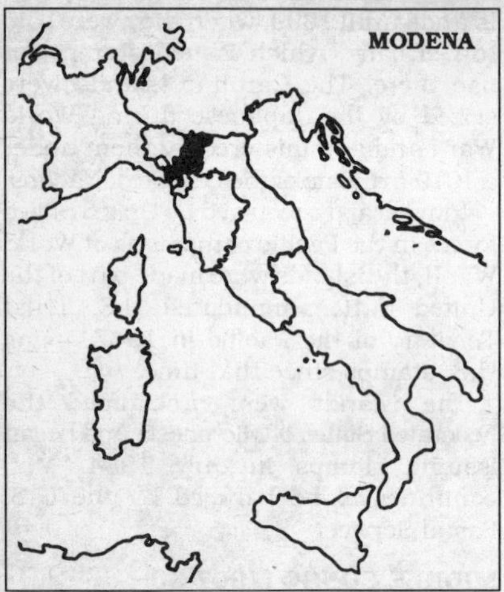

MODENA (1852-60)

Stamp-issuing status: inactive; Stamps issued: 19.

Former duchy in northern Italy. In 1859, the duchy was overthrown, and in 1860, the area merged with Sardinia, whose issues came into use.

MOHELI (1906-12)

Stamp-issuing status: inactive; Population: 4,000 (1916 estimate); Stamps issued: 22.

One of the Comoro Islands in the Mozambique Channel near Madagascar. Moheli was attached to Madagascar in 1911 and was again separated, as one of the Comoro Islands, in 1947.

Comoro stamps have been in use since 1950.

MOLDAVIA (1858-61)

Stamp-issuing status: inactive; Stamps issued: 10.

Former principality in northeastern Romania. Under Turkish suzerainty after the 16th century, Moldavia united with Wallachia in 1861 to form the Kingdom of Romania.

MOLDAVIA-WALLACHIA (1862-65)

Stamp-issuing status: inactive; Stamps issued: 11.

The united principalities that came to form Romania.

MONACO (1885-)

Stamp-issuing status: active; Population: 29,000; Stamps issued: more than 1,920; Issues per year for last decade: 56.

A principality on the southern coast of France. Long autonomous under the protection, at various times, of France, Spain and Sardinia, Monaco is independent, except for the right of France to approve the successor to the throne.

By the treaty of 1918, Monaco will be annexed by France, should the ruling Grimaldi family fail to provide an heir.

MONGOLIA (1924-)

Stamp-issuing status: active; Population: 1.9 million (1987 estimate); Stamps issued: more than 1,875; Issues per year: 75.

A republic in central Asia, located between China and Soviet Siberia. The homeland of the Mongol Empire that in the 13th-14th centuries stretched from Poland to Korea. By 1689, Mongol power had declined to the point where the region came under Chinese control.

In 1911, Mongolia declared its independence but, in 1921, was occupied by Soviet troops. In 1924, a pro-Soviet republic was established, and in 1945, after China renounced all claims in the country, the Mongolian People's Republic was established.

In recent years, the Mongolian government has carried out an active program to transform the country's economy from nomadic to a more modern, settled form.

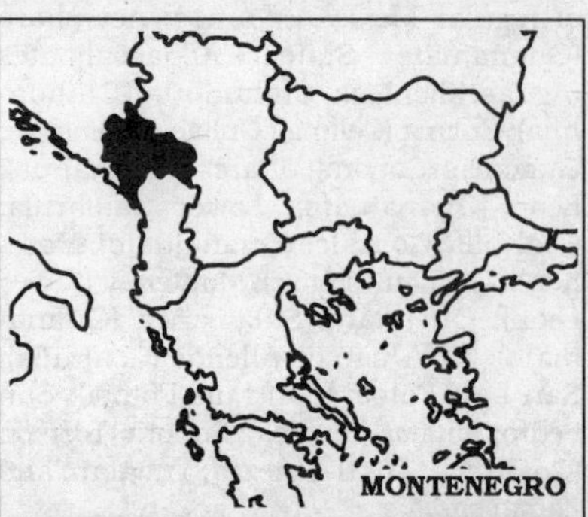

MONTENEGRO (1874-1918, 1941-45)

Stamp-issuing status: inactive; Population: 516,000 (esimated); Stamps issued: 264.

A former kingdom in the Balkans, situated north of Albania. Montenegro became independent in 1452 and for centuries successfully resisted the Turks, who held the rest of southeastern Europe.

In January 1916, the Austrians occupied Montenegro, and the government fled to Bordeaux, France, where overprinted French stamps were used for a time.

In November 1918, King Nicholas was deposed in a pro-Serbian coup, and Montenegro was united with Serbia.

During World War II, Montenegro was re-established as an Italian protectorate. In 1943-44, it was occupied by Germany, which overprinted Yugoslavian stamps and issues of the Italian administration. After the German defeat, Montenegro was again occupied by Yugoslavia, which initially overprinted issues of the Italian Montenegrin regime. Since 1945, regular Yugoslavian stamps have been used.

MONTSERRAT (1876-)

Stamp-issuing status: active; Population: 12,000; Stamps issued: more than 725; Issues per year for last decade: 26.

An island in the Leeward group in the West Indies, southeast of Puerto Rico. Montserrat was under British control after 1632 and attached to the Leeward Island colony until 1956.

MOROCCO (1956-)

Stamp-issuing status: active; Population: 22.4 million; Stamps issued: more than 725; Issues per year for last decade: 26.

A kingdom in northwestern Africa, bordering on the Atlantic Ocean and the Mediterranean Sea. Once a powerful state embracing much of Spain and North Africa in the 12th century, Moroccan power declined thereafter.

European encroachment led to the division of the country into French (southern) and Spanish (northern) protectorates in 1912.

In 1956, the two zones were reunited and Morocco again became independent. Morocco has since expanded by absorbing Tangier (1956), Ifni (1969), the northern two-thirds of the Spanish Sahara (1976) and the southern portion of the Spanish Sahara in 1980.

Morocco is closely linked to the United States and France by military and economic agreements. In recent years, Moroccan troops have aided against leftist uprisings in Mauritania and Zaire.

Morocco continues to wage a bitter war in the former Spanish Sahara against the Polisario Front, supported by Algeria, which claims independence for the region.

MORVI (1931-51)

Stamp-issuing status: inactive; Stamps issued: 13.

A former feudatory state in western India. Morvi's issues were replaced by Indian stamps in 1950.

MOSCHOPOLIS (1914)

Stamp-issuing status: inactive.

A town in southern Albania. Stamps were issued by local authorities during the Greek occupation of the area.

MOUNT ATHOS (1909-13)

Stamp-issuing status: inactive.

The holy mountain of the Orthodox Church, located in northern Greece, near Salonika. In 1909-13, 17 Russian Levant stamps were overprinted "Mount Athos" in French or Russian for use in the Russian consular post office at Daphne, the seaport at the foot of the mountain.

This post office was closed when Greece occupied the area in 1913.

MOZAMBIQUE (1877-)

Stamp-issuing status: active; Population: 14.1 million; Stamps issued: more than 1,200; Issues per year for last decade: 45.

A republic on the southeast coast of Africa. Portuguese settlements began in the 16th century, and the colony remained a Portuguese possession until June 25, 1975, when it became independent as the People's Republic of Mozambique.

Closely linked to the U.S.S.R. and Cuba, Mozambique provided bases for rebels fighting the white Rhodesian regime. Since the end of the civil war and the establishment of a majority government, Mozambique has made a number of tentative overtures to the West.

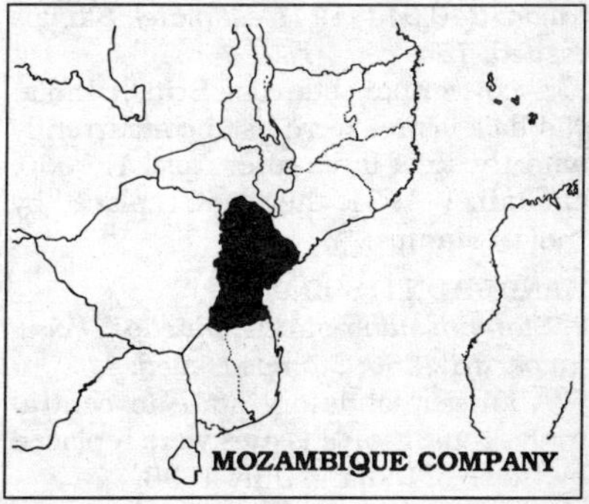

MOZAMBIQUE COMPANY (1892-1942)

Stamp-issuing status: inactive; Population: 368,000 (1939 estimate); Stamps issued: 275.

A private company that, by royal charter, acquired extensive rights in the Mozambique districts of Manica and Sofala.

Most rights, including the direct administration of the territories and the issuing of stamps, reverted to Portugal in 1942.

MUSTIQUE ISLAND (1986-)

Stamp-issuing status: active; Stamps issued: 2.

An island in the Grenadines of St. Vincent, a group of small subsidiary islands in the Lesser Antilles, north of Trinidad and South America.

Mustique Island issued a single se-tenant pair of stamps for the Royal Wedding in 1986, accompanying similar pairs issued by St. Vincent, St. Vincent Grenadines, Bequia and Union Island. Its stamp-issuing status since is uncertain.

MYTILENE (1909-13)

Stamp-issuing status: inactive.

The chief port of the Greek island of Lesbos in the eastern Aegean Sea, off the coast of Turkey. The Russian post office in Mytilene used stamps of the Russian Levant overprinted "Metelin" after 1909.

In 1912, Mytilene was occupied by Greece, and 20 overprinted Turkish stamps were used, being superseded by regular Greek issues in 1913.

- N -

NABHA (1885-1951)

Stamp-issuing status: inactive; Population: 340,044 (1941 estimate); Stamps issued: 154.

A convention state of British India. Nabha's issues were used concurrently with those of India after April 1, 1950. On Jan. 1, 1951, they were replaced by Indian stamps.

NANDGAON (1892-95)

Stamp-issuing status: inactive; Population: 182,380; Stamps issued: 11.

A former feudatory state in central India. Nandgaon's issues were replaced by those of India in July 1895.

NANUMAGA (1984-)

Stamp-issuing status: active; Stamps issued: more than 100; Issues per year 1984-87: 36.

One of nine small islands in the Tuvalu Islands, formerly the Ellice Island group in the Gilbert and Ellice Islands. The island chain is located east of the Solomon Islands and north of Fiji in the southeastern central Pacific Ocean.

Like the other Tuvalu Islands, Nanumaga issued a flurry of stamps depicting such diverse subjects as cars, locomotives, cricket players and the British Royal Family in the mid-1980s.

NANUMEA (1984-)

Stamp-issuing status: active; Stamps issued: more than 100; Issues per year 1984-87: 33.

One of nine small islands in the Tuvalu Islands, formerly the Ellice Island group in the Gilbert and Ellice Islands. The island chain is located east of the Solomon Islands and north of Fiji in the southeastern central Pacific Ocean.

Like the other Tuvalu Islands, Nanumea issued a flurry of stamps depicting such diverse subjects as cars, locomotives, cricket players and the British Royal Family in the mid-1980s.

NATAL (1857-1909)

Stamp-issuing status: inactive; Population: 1.2 million (1909 estimate); Stamps issued: 130.

A former British crown colony on the southeast coast of Africa. A short-lived Boer republic, Natal came under British control in 1843. It was incorporated into the Union of South Africa in 1910.

NAURU (1916-)

Stamp-issuing status: active; Population: 8,000; Stamps issued: more than 275; Issues per year for last decade: 18.

An island in the west central Pacific Ocean. Nauru was a German possession from 1888-1914 and was occupied by Australian forces during World War I.

From 1920-68, Nauru was a mandate under Australia, New Zealand and Great Britain. It became an independent republic on Jan. 31, 1968.

This 8-square-mile island is rich in phosphates, giving the 4,000 plus Naureans one of the highest per capita incomes in the world.

NAWANAGAR (1875-95)

Stamp-issuing status: inactive; Population: 402,192; Stamps issued: 14.

A former feudatory state in western India. Nawanagar's issues were replaced by those of India in December 1895.

NEAPOLITAN PROVINCES (1861-62)

Stamp-issuing status: inactive; Stamps issued: 8.

In October 1860, Garibaldi deposed the ruling Bourbon dynasty in the Kingdom of the Two Sicilies, and the country was annexed to Sardinia.

Sardinia issued a separate series of stamps for the Neapolitan Provinces in 1861, similar to contemporary Sardinian stamps but inscribed in Neapolitan currency. This set was superseded by regular Italian issues in 1862.

NEGRI SEMBILAN (1891-)

Stamp-issuing status: active; Population: 401,742 (1960 estimate); Stamps issued: 138; Issues per year for last decade: 1.

Sultanate on the west coast of the Malay Peninsula. Placed under British protection in 1891, the sultanate was occupied by Japan 1942-45.

Negri Sembilan joined the Federation of Malaya in 1948 and is now part of the Malaysian Federation.

NEJD (1925-26)

Stamp-issuing status: inactive.

A region in central Arabia united by the puritanical Wahhabi Moslem movement, led by the Saud family, in the 18th century.

During 1914-25, Nejd conquered the Hasa, Asir and Hejaz regions and expanded the kingdom to include most of the Arabian Peninsula.

In 1925, the Kingdom of Hejaz, Nejd and Dependencies was formed, and in 1932, the kingdom was renamed Saudi Arabia.

NEPAL (1881-)

Stamp-issuing status: active; Population: 16.5 million; Stamps issued: 475; Issues per year for last decade: 13.

Kingdom in the Himalaya Mountains between India and Tibet. United in 1768, Nepal remained independent during the British occupation of India and has since maintained that independence, enjoying good relations with both India and China.

NETHERLANDS (1852-)

Stamp-issuing status: active; Population: 14.6 million; Stamps issued: 1,275; Issues per year for last decade: 22.

Constitutional monarchy in northwest Europe, bordering on the North Sea.

Originally under Spanish rule, the Netherlands declared independence in 1581 and, during the 17th century, became one of the predominant naval and commercial powers, controlling a far-flung empire in the Caribbean, North and South America, Africa, India and the East Indies.

Conflict with England weakened Dutch power until, in 1794, it was overrun by France. The Netherlands again became independent in 1815.

Neutral during World War I, it was occupied by Germany from 1940 to 1945. The last major remnant of the Netherlands' once vast overseas empire was lost in 1950, when Indonesia became independent.

The Netherlands abandoned its policy of neutrality after World War II and aligned itself with the West. It is a member of NATO and of the Common Market.

Although it has undergone substantial industrialization since World War II, the agricultural sector of the country's economy remains strong.

NETHERLANDS ANTILLES (CURACAO) (1873-)

Stamp-issuing status: active; Population: 70,000; Stamps issued: more than 830; Issues per year for last decade; 26.

Two groups of islands in the West Indies, north of Venezuela. They were originally occupied by Spain, but have been in Dutch possession since 1634.

In 1954, the colony was made an integral part of the Kingdom of the Netherlands. Aruba separated from the Netherlands Antilles and began issuing its own stamps at the beginning of 1986.

NETHERLANDS INDIES (1845-1949)

Stamp-issuing status: inactive; Population: 76 million (1949 estimate); Stamps issued: 510.

A former Dutch colony occupying the greater portion of the East Indies. The area was originally dominated by Hindus, who were supplanted by Moslems after the 14th-15th centuries.

During the 16th century, Portugal dominated the region until forced out by the Dutch and British. After the 17th century, the Dutch ruled most of the area.

The Netherlands Indies were occupied by Japan from 1942 to 1945, during which time a great variety of occupation issues were used.

Two days after Japan's surrender, Indonesian nationalists declared independence, starting the revolution that ended with Dutch withdrawal in 1949.

NETHERLANDS NEW GUINEA (1950-62)

Stamp-issuing status: inactive; Population: 730,000 (1958 estimate); Stamps issued: 87.

The western half of the island of New Guinea, retained by the Dutch after Indonesian independence. An Indonesian invasion in 1962 caused the U.N. to assume temporary executive authority in the area, which was transferred to Indonesia in 1963.

NEVIS (1861-90)

Stamp-issuing status: inactive; Population: 11,864 (1883 estimate); Stamps issued: 33.

A former presidency in the British Leeward Islands, southeast of Puerto Rico.

NEW BRITAIN (1914-15)

Stamp-issuing status: inactive; Population: 50,600; Stamps issued: 48.

An island off the northeast coast of New Guinea, in the Pacific Ocean. Formerly part of German New Guinea, New Britain was occupied by Australian forces in 1914.

After World War I, it became part of the mandated territory of New Guinea.

NEW BRUNSWICK (1851-68)

Stamp-issuing status: inactive; Population: 286,000 (1871 estimate); Stamps issued: 11.

Former British colony in eastern Canada. New Brunswick joined the Canadian Confederation in 1867.

NEW CALEDONIA (1859-)

Stamp-issuing status: active; Population: 150,000; Stamps issued: more than 750; Issues per year for last decade: 22.

An island in the southwest Pacific Ocean. In 1853, New Caledonia became a French Colony, and in 1946, it was designated a French Overseas Territory.

NEWFOUNDLAND (1857-1949)

Stamp-issuing status: inactive; Population: 320,000 (1945 estimate); Stamps issued: 286.

An island off the eastern coast of Canada. With the mainland territory of Labrador, Newfoundland formed a British dominion until its incorporation into Canada in 1949.

NEW GREECE (1912-13)

Stamp-issuing status: inactive.

The districts of Turkey occupied by Greece in the First Balkan War. Overprinted Greek issues and one specially printed set were used in Chios, Icaria, Lemnos, Mytilene, Samos, Cavalla, Dedeagatch and other occupied Turkish territory, until they were replaced by regular Greek stamps.

NEW GUINEA (1925-42)

Stamp-issuing status: inactive; Population: 676,500 (1948 estimate); Stamps issued: 139.

The territory formerly constituting German New Guinea, the northeast portion of the island of New Guinea, in the South Pacific Ocean.

New Guinea was occupied by Australia in 1914 and administered by Australia under a mandate from the League of Nations and, after 1947, under a mandate from the United Nations.

New Guinea joined with Papua in 1949 to form the territory of Papua and New Guinea. The name later was changed to Papua New Guinea.

NEW HEBRIDES (1908-1980)

Stamp-issuing status: inactive; Population: 100,000 (1980 estimate); Stamps issued: 296.

A group of islands in the South Pacific Ocean, north of New Caledonia. New Hebrides was declared neutral by Great Britain and France in 1878 and was administered jointly by the two nations from 1906 to 1980. On July 30, 1980, the islands became independent as the Republic of Vanuatu.

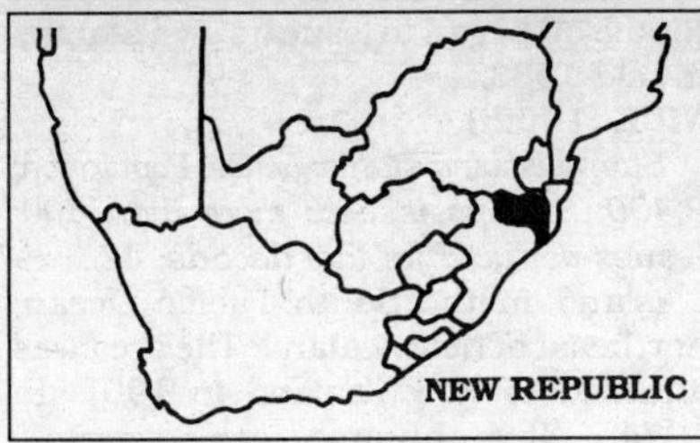

NEW REPUBLIC (1886-88)

Stamp-issuing status: inactive; Stamps issued: 68.

A short-lived Boer republic in southern Africa. It was absorbed by Transvaal in 1888.

NEW SOUTH WALES (1850-1913)

Stamp-issuing status: inactive; Population: 1.5 million (1906 estimate); Stamps issued: 190.

Former British crown colony in southeast Australia. In 1901, New South Wales merged into the Commonwealth of Australia.

NEW ZEALAND (1855-)

Stamp-issuing status: active; Population: 3.3 million; Stamps issued: more than 1,250; Issues per year for last decade: 28.

Two large islands and a number of smaller islands in the South Pacific Ocean. New Zealand was annexed by Great Britain in 1840 and, since 1907, has been a self-governing dominion within the British Commonwealth of Nations.

New Zealand has a number of dependencies in the South Pacific, among them the Cook Islands, Niue, the Tokelau Islands, and Ross Dependency in the Antarctic.

NICARAGUA (1862-)

Stamp-issuing status: active; Population: 3.3 million; Stamps issued: more than 2,200; Issues per year for last decade: 50.

A republic in Central America. Independent since 1838, Nicaragua's political history has been turbulent.

The British controlled the eastern coast until 1893, and the U.S. effectively controlled the country from 1912 to 1933.

During 1934-79, the Somoza family ruled Nicaragua. The Somoza regime brought order and considerable economic progress to the country. It also brought widespread corruption and ruthless political repression. In 1974, in response to the activities of the Marxist Sandinista guerrillas, the government imposed martial law. The subsequent excesses of the National Guard alienated virtually all elements of Nicaraguan society, and in August 1978, civil war erupted.

The United States, which had unsuccessfully attempted to moderate the government's policies, withdrew its support. In May 1979, a Sandinista force invaded Nicaragua and, by July, had overthrown the Somozas.

The Sandinista regime has consolidated its position and has suppressed political opposition. It maintains close ties with Cuba and supports Marxist revolutionary movements in neighboring countries.

NIGER (1921-45, 1959-)

Stamp-issuing status: active; Population: 6.2 million (1986 estimate); Stamps issued: more than 1,200; Issues per year for last decade: 45.

A republic in northern Africa, directly north of Nigeria.

Under French control after 1890, Niger underwent several administrative incarnations, finally emerging as the Niger Territory in 1920. The Niger Territory became the Niger Colony two years later.

Niger became part of French West Africa in 1904 and used French West African stamps during 1944-59.

In 1958, Niger became an autonomous republic and became fully independent in 1960. It has since maintained close ties with France.

NIGER COAST PROTECTORATE (1892-1900)

Stamp-issuing status: inactive; Stamps issued: 64.

Former British holdings in southern Nigeria. The area was absorbed into the Southern Nigeria Protectorate in 1900.

NIGERIA (1914-)

Stamp-issuing status: active; Population: 100 million; Stamps issued: more than 500; Issues per year for last decade: 17.

Republic in West Africa, on the Gulf of Guinea. Nigeria was formed from the union of the British protectorates of Northern Nigeria and Southern Nigeria in 1914.

Nigeria became an independent federation in 1960 and a republic in 1963.

Inter-tribal tensions have been strong since independence. A period of political strife during 1966-67 brought the secession of Biafra, which comprised the mineral-rich southeastern portion of the country. In the ensuing civil war, one million people died, most of them Biafran Ibos. In January 1970, Biafra surrendered and was re-absorbed into Nigeria.

Nigeria has rich petroleum deposits and is a member of OPEC. The massive oil price increases of the 1970s has enabled Nigeria to launch an ambitious campaign of economic development. Drastic cutbacks in oil exports during 1981-82, however, have made it increasingly difficult to maintain these programs.

NIKLASDORF (1938)

Stamp-issuing status: inactive; Stamps issued: 129.

A city in the Sudetenland (Czechoslovakia). In 1938 the municipal authorities overprinted a large number of Czechoslovak stamps to commemorate the union with Germany.

NISIROS (1912-32)

Stamp-issuing status: inactive; Stamps issued: 26.

One of the Dodecanese Islands in the eastern Aegean Sea. Nisiros was obtained from Turkey by Italy in 1912, at which time Italian stamps overprinted "Nisiros" were issued.

These were superseded by the general Aegean Islands issues in 1929, although two sets overprinted "Nisiro" were released in 1930 and 1932.

NIUAFO'OU (1983-)

Stamp-issuing status: active; Population: 900 (1983 estimate); Stamps issued: more than 60; Issues per year 1983-85: 30.

A volcanic rim island of six square miles, Niuafo'ou is part of the kingdom of Tonga, located in the southern Pacific Ocean between Fiji and Samoa, 400 miles north of the Tongatupa island group.

The island was better known as Tin Can Island, famed for the pickup and delivery of mail in sealed cans by swimmers and canoes to and from ships waiting offshore in the 1930s and '40s. Niuafo'ou began to issue its own stamps in mid-1983.

NIUE (1902-)

Stamp-issuing status: active; Population: 3,400; Stamps issued: more than 600; Issues per year for last decade: 42.

Island in the South Pacific Ocean, northeast of New Zealand. The area was annexed to New Zealand in 1901. In 1974, Niue became self-governing, although New Zealand retains responsibility for defense and foreign affairs.

NIUTAO (1984-)

Stamp-issuing status: active; Stamps issued: more than 80; Issues per year 1984-87: 27.

One of nine small islands in the Tuvalu Islands, formerly the Ellice Island group in the Gilbert and Ellice Islands. The island chain is located east of the Solomon Islands and north of Fiji in the southeastern central Pacific Ocean.

Like the other Tuvalu Islands, Niutao issued a flurry of stamps depicting such diverse subjects as cars, locomotives, cricket players and the British Royal Family in the mid-1980s.

NORFOLK ISLAND (1947-)

Stamp-issuing status: active; Population: 1,700; Stamps issued: 400; Issues per year for last decade: 20.

Island in the South Pacific Ocean, east of Australia, under Australian administration.

The inhabitants of Norfolk Island are largely descendants of the Bounty mutineers, whose ancestors immigrated to Norfolk from the Pitcairns in 1856.

NORTH BORNEO (1883-1964)

Stamp-issuing status: inactive; Population: 460,000 (1962 estimate); Stamps issued: 455.

Former British colony, occupying the northeast portion of the island of Borneo in the Malay Archipelago.

Renamed Sabah, British North Borneo joined with Malaya, Sarawak and Singapore to form the Malaysian Federation in 1963.

NORTH CHINA (1937-49)

Stamp-issuing status: inactive; Stamps issued: 127.

The North China Liberation Area comprised Chahar, Hopeh, Shansi and Suiyan. Seven postal districts issued stamps during this period.

NORTHEAST CHINA (1946-51)

Stamp-issuing status: inactive.

Communist administrative area comprising the provinces of Liaoning, Kirin, Jehol and Heilungkiang and, after 1948, all of Manchuria.

In 1951, the issues of the regional postal administration were replaced by the general issues of the People's Republic of China.

NORTH EPIRUS (1914-16, 1940-41)

Stamp-issuing status: inactive; Stamps issued: 69.

That portion of southern Albania occupied by Greece in 1914-16 and 1940-41. During 1914-16, 32 issues of Epirus and Greek stamps overprinted "Northern Epirus" were used, and in 1940-41, some 37 overprinted Greek stamps were used.

NORTH GERMAN CONFEDERATION (1868)

Stamp-issuing status: inactive; Stamps issued: 35.

A confederation of German states, formed under the leadership of Prussia in 1868, after Austria's defeat in the Austro-Prussian War.

On Jan. 1, 1868, the stamps of all member nations were replaced by those of the confederation, with the area forming the North German Postal District.

NORTH INGERMANLAND (1920)

Stamp-issuing status: inactive; Stamps issued: 14.

A district in Russia, lying between the Neva River and Finland. In 1920, the area revolted, established a provisional government and sought union with Finland.

Soviet troops quickly suppressed the revolt.

NORTHERN NIGERIA (1900-13)

Stamp-issuing status: inactive.

Former British protectorate comprising holdings in northern Nigeria. Northern Nigeria merged with the Southern Nigeria Protectorate in 1914.

NORTHERN RHODESIA (1925-64)

Stamp-issuing status: inactive; Population: 3.6 million (1963 estimate); Stamps issued: 98.

Former British protectorate in southern Africa. Northern Rhodesia became the independent republic of Zambia in 1964.

NORTHWEST CHINA (1946-49)

Stamp-issuing status: inactive; Stamps issued: 68.

The northwestern area of China proper, which after the "Long March to Yenan" was the center of the Communist revolution in China. It included the provinces of Kansu, Ninghsia, Tsinghai and, after 1949, Sinkiang. General Chinese issues replaced those of the region in 1949.

NORTHWEST CHINA (SHENSI-KANSU-NINGHSIA) (1935-49)

Stamp-issuing status: inactive.

The center of the Communist revolution in China after the "long march to Yenan."

In 1949, Sinkiang was added to the region. The regional issues were replaced by the general issues of the People's Republic of China in 1949.

NORTH WEST PACIFIC ISLANDS (1914-24)

Stamp-issuing status: inactive; Population: 636,563; Stamps issued: 38.

During World War I, Australian forces occupied the German possessions in New Guinea and the adjacent islands.

Australian stamps overprinted "N.W. Pacific Islands" were used on Nauru from 1915 to 1916 and in former German New Guinea from 1915 to 1924.

NORWAY (1855-)

Stamp-issuing status: active; Population: 4.12 million; Stamps issued: more than 950; Issues per year for last decade: 23.

A constitutional monarchy occupying the western portion of the Scandinavian Peninsula in northern Europe. A powerful kingdom in the Middle Ages, Norway later came under the domination of Denmark and, after 1814, Sweden.

In 1905, Norway became completely independent. The country was occupied by the Germans from 1940 to 1945.

Following World War II, Norway abandoned its traditional neutrality and joined NATO.

The country's abundant hydroelectric resources have produced an ongoing economic boom that has given Norway one of the highest standards of living in the world.

NOSSI-BE (1889-98)

Stamp-issuing status: inactive: Popu-

lation: 9,000 (1900 estimate); Stamps issued: 57.

An island in the Indian Ocean, lying off the northwestern coast of Madagascar, to which it was attached in 1898.

NOVA SCOTIA (1851-68)

Stamp-issuing status: inactive; Population: 387,000 (1871 estimate); Stamps issued: 13.

Former British colony in east Canada. Nova Scotia joined the Canadian Confederation in 1867.

NUGGEN (NOO) (1941)

Stamp-issuing status: inactive.

A city in Estonia. During July-Aug. 13, 1941, five Russian stamps were surcharged in red, in green and in black for use in the city by the German military commander.

NUI (1984-)

Stamp-issuing status: active; Stamps issued: more than 110; Issues per year 1984-87: 37.

One of nine small islands in the Tuvalu Islands, formerly the Ellice Island group in the Gilbert and Ellice Islands. The island chain is located east of the Solomon Islands and north of Fiji in the southeastern central Pacific Ocean.

Like the other Tuvalu Islands, Nui issued a flurry of stamps depicting such diverse subjects as cars, locomotives, cricket players and the British Royal Family in the mid-1980s.

NUKUFETAU (1984-)

Stamp-issuing status: active; Stamps issued: more than 100; Issues per year 1984-87: 34.

One of nine small islands in the Tuvalu Islands, formerly the Ellice Island group in the Gilbert and Ellice Islands. The island chain is located east of the Solomon Islands and north of Fiji in the southeastern central Pacific Ocean.

Like the other Tuvalu Islands, Nukufetau issued a flurry of stamps depicting such diverse subjects as cars, locomotives, cricket players and the British Royal Family in the mid-1980s.

NUKULAELAE (1984-)

Stamp-issuing status: active; Stamps issued: more than 100; Issues per year 1984-87: 36.

One of nine small islands in the Tuvalu Islands, formerly the Ellice Island group in the Gilbert and Ellice Islands. The island chain is located east of the Solomon Islands and north of Fiji in the southeastern central Pacific Ocean.

Like the other Tuvalu Islands, Nukulaelae issued a flurry of stamps depicting such diverse subjects as cars, locomotives, cricket players and the British Royal Family in the mid-1980s.

NYASALAND PROTECTORATE (1907-54, 1963-64)

Stamp-issuing status: inactive; Population: 3 million (1964 estimate); Stamps issued: 143.

Former British protectorate in south-central Africa. Established as British Central Africa in 1890, the name Nyasaland Protectorate was adopted in 1907.

During 1953-63, it was a member of the Federation of Rhodesia and Nyasaland. Nyasaland became independent in 1964, changing its name to Malawi.

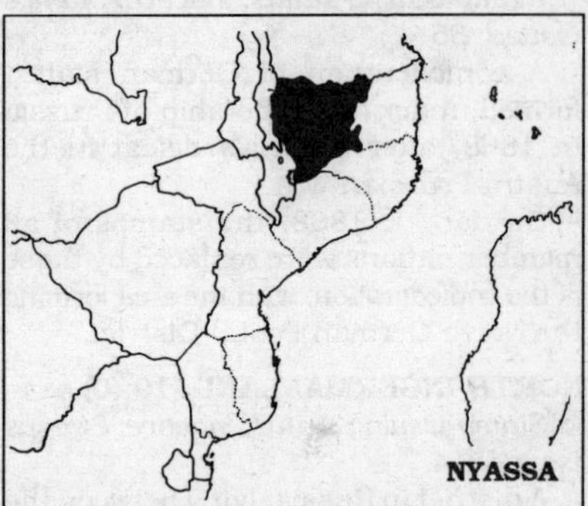

NYASSA (1897-1929)

Stamp-issuing status: inactive; Population: 3 million (1923 estimate); Stamps issued: 140.

A district in northwestern Mozambique. Nyassa was administered by the private Nyassa Co. until 1929, when the company's rights reverted to Portugal.

- O -

OAXACA (1914)

Stamp-issuing status: inactive; Stamps issued: 6.

A state in central Mexico, which issued its own stamps during the Mexican Civil War.

OBOCK (1892-94)

Stamp-issuing status: inactive; Stamps

issued: 82.

A seaport in eastern Africa, on the Gulf of Aden. Acquired by France in 1862 and actively occupied after 1884, it was merged with other French holdings in the area to form the French Somali Coast in 1902.

ODENPAH (1941)

Stamp-issuing status: inactive.

A city in Estonia. In 1941, the German military commander issued two stamps for use in the city.

ODESSA (1918-20)

Stamp-issuing status: inactive.

A Russian port on the northern coast of the Black Sea. In 1918, Odessa overprinted Russian stamps with the Ukrainian trident for use in its postal district.

During 1919, the Polish Consulate at Odessa overprinted contemporary Polish stamps "ODESA" for use on mail carried from Odessa to Poland through the cooperation of Gen. Denikin. This postal agency was closed Jan. 31, 1920.

OIL RIVERS PROTECTORATE (1892-93)

Stamp-issuing status: inactive; Stamps issued: 64.

Former British protectorate in southern Nigeria. In 1893, the name of the territory was changed to Niger Coast Protectorate.

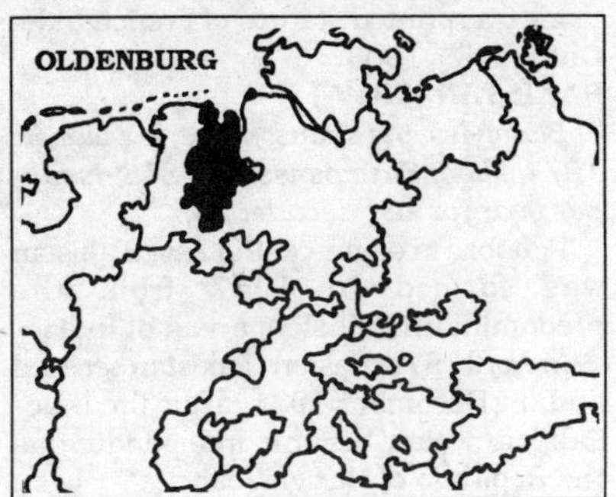

OLDENBURG (1852-67)

Stamp-issuing status: inactive; Population: 483,042 (1910 estimate); Stamps issued: 24.

A former grand duchy in northern Germany. Oldenburg's issues were replaced by those of the North German Confederation in 1868.

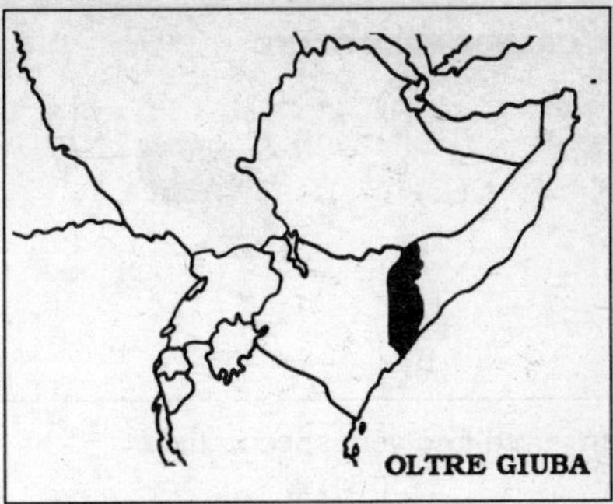

OLTRE GIUBA (1925-26)

Stamp-issuing status: inactive; Population: 12,000; Stamps issued: 35.

A district in eastern Africa, northeast of Kenya. In 1924, Britain ceded the area to Italy, and in 1926, it was incorporated into Italian Somaliland.

OMAN (MUSCAT AND OMAN) (1944-)

Stamp-issuing status: active; Population: 1.3 million (1986 estimate); Stamps issued: more than 350; Issues per year for last decade: 13.

Independent sultanate on the southeast coast of Arabia. During the first half of the 19th century, Oman ruled an empire stretching from the coast of Persia to Zanzibar, but its power declined until it came under British protection in the late 19th century.

Rebellious tribesmen in the interior fought the central government in the 1950s but were suppressed with British support. Later uprisings were quelled by 1975, with Iranian help.

In 1964, petroleum was discovered and has since become Oman's major export.

In 1979, leftist guerrilla activities resumed in the southwestern portion of the country, supported by the South Yemen People's Republic.

Accords signed with the United States in 1980 give American forces access to bases in Oman, which has become one of the cornerstones of U.S. military policy in the region.

OPATOW (1918)

Stamp-issuing status: inactive.

A city in southern Poland. Local stamps were issued by the municipal authorities in 1918. The series was philatelically

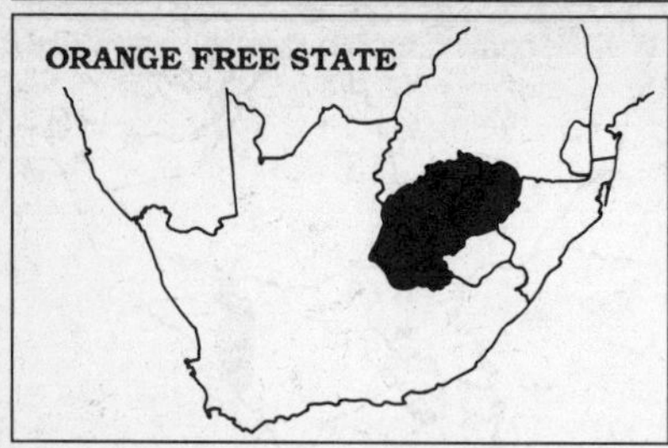

inspired and very speculative.

ORANGE FREE STATE (1868-1900)

Stamp-issuing status: inactive; Population: 528,174 (1911 estimate); Stamps issued: 84.

A former independent republic in South Africa. The Orange Free State became the British Orange River Colony in 1900 and was incorporated into the Union of South Africa in 1910.

ORCHHA (1913-50)

Stamp-issuing status: inactive; Population 314,661; Stamps issued: 20.

A former feudatory state in the Bundelkhand agency in central India. On May 1, 1950, Orchha's issues were replaced by those of India.

ORENSE (1936)

Stamp-issuing status: inactive; Stamps issued: 23.

A province of northwestern Spain. In October 1936, two sets of overprinted Spanish stamps were issued under the authority of the National Civil Governor of the province.

ORLEANS (1953)

Stamp-issuing status: inactive.

A city in northern France. During a postal strike, in August 1953, the Orleans Chamber of Commerce issued stamps for use in the city.

OSTLAND (1941-43)

Stamp-issuing status: inactive; Stamps issued: 20.

The German military district comprising Estonia, Latvia, Lithuania and adjacent portions of occupied Russia. German issues overprinted "Ostland" were used in the district.

OSTROVA (MAHRISCH-OSTRAU) (1939)

Stamp-issuing status: inactive.

A city in Moravia (Czechoslovakia). In 1939 the municipal authorities overprinted 64 Czechoslovakian stamps to commemorate union with Germany.

- P -

PAHANG (1889-)

Stamp-issuing status: active; Population: 338,210 (1960 estimate); Stamps issued: more than 140; Issues per year for last decade: 2.

The largest Malay state, under British protection after 1888. Pahang was occupied by Japan from 1942 to 1945 and joined the Federation of Malaya in 1948. It is now a part of Malaysia.

PAKHOI (1903-22)

Stamp-issuing status: inactive; Stamps issued: 67.

A port in the province of Kwangtung in southern China. France maintained a post office in Pakhoi from 1902 to 1922, using overprinted stamps of French Indo-China after 1903.

PAKISTAN (1947-)

Stamp-issuing status: active; Population: 107 million; Stamps issued: 868; Issues per year for last decade: 29.

Republic in south-central Asia. Pakistan was formed in 1947 from the predominantly Moslem areas of India.

In April 1971, Eastern Pakistan seceded and, in December 1971, after the Indo-Pakistani War, became independent as the Republic of Bangladesh.

Since 1977, Pakistan has been ruled by a repressive military dictatorship.

Tension with India has remained at a high level since the two countries became independent, and a number of wars have resolved little. Both nations maintain relatively large military forces.

PALAU (1983-)

Stamp-issuing status: active; Population: 16,000 (1983 estimate); Stamps issued:

more than 225; Issues per year 1983-88: 46.

A republic comprising about 100 islands and islets at the western end of the Caroline Islands chain in the western Pacific Ocean. Palau is about 800 miles east southeast of the Philippine Islands.

These islands were part of the Spanish Caroline Islands until 1899, when they were sold to Germany, which issued stamps for use there. The Caroline Islands were seized by the Japanese during World War I and administered by them under a 1919 mandate of the League of Nations.

Invaded and conquered by United States forces in 1944, the islands were made part of the United Nations-mandated U.S. Trust Territory of the Pacific in 1947. Palau became a republic in 1981 and began to issue its own stamps in 1983, although its mail continues to be handled by the U.S. Postal Service.

PALESTINE-BRITISH MILITARY ADMINISTRATION (1918-20)

Stamp-issuing status: inactive; Population: 1,605,816 (estimated); Stamps issued: 14.

In 1918, British and Arab forces occupied the Turkish Asian provinces bordering on the eastern Mediterranean.

Britain's military administration issued stamps inscribed "E.E.F." (Egyptian Expeditionary Forces) that were used in Palestine, Trans-Jordan, Lebanon, Syria and in parts of Cilicia and northeast Egypt.

PALESTINE-BRITISH ADMINISTRATION (1920-47)

Stamp-issuing status: inactive; Stamps issued: 109.

In 1920, British civil administration was established in Palestine, the southernmost of the formerly Turkish provinces bordering on the Mediterranean.

In 1923, the League of Nations formally placed the territory under a British mandate. The Zionist Movement brought increasing Jewish immigration into Palestine, causing an increasingly bitter rivalry between Jewish Palestinians seeking to recreate the ancient Jewish homeland and Arab Palestinians, who wished to create an independent Arab Palestinian state.

In 1948, Britain partitioned the country between the two groups and withdrew her forces, precipitating the first Arab-Israeli War.

PANAMA (1878-)

Stamp-issuing status: active; Population: 2 million (1984 estimate); Stamps issued: more than 1,300; Issues per year for last decade: 21.

A republic occupying the Isthmus of Panama, between North and South America.

The area was a department of the Republic of Colombia until 1903 when U.S. intervention enabled the Panamanians to secure their independence.

The new Panamanian government immediately conceded to the U.S. a 10-mile wide strip of land bisecting the isthmus. Construction of the Panama Canal began the following year and was completed in 1914.

While the Panamanian economy benefited greatly from the Canal, the presence of a foreign sovereignty on their soil was a constant irritant to Panamanians' national pride.

During 1964-77, U.S.-Panamanian relations deteriorated over the status of the Canal, which became an emotionally charged issue throughout Latin America.

In 1978 a revised Canal treaty was ratified by the U.S. Senate. Implemented in 1979, this treaty provides for the gradual transfer of authority, with full Panamanian ownership by the end of the century. Panama assumed political sovereignty in the Canal Zone on Oct. 1, 1979.

PAPUA NEW GUINEA (1952-)

Stamp-issuing status: active; Population: 3.2 million; Stamps issued: more than 675; Issues per year for last decade: 21.

Independent state occupying the eastern half of the island of New Guinea, in the western Pacific Ocean, north of Australia.

The southern portion of the country, Papua, was united administratively with the northern U.N. mandate of New Guinea in 1949, as Papua and New Guinea.

In 1972, the name of the territory became simply Papua New Guinea. In 1974, it achieved self-government under Australian authority and, in 1975, became independent. The country retains close ties with Australia.

Papua New Guinea has numerous tribal divisions, with 750 local languages, so the maintenance of the country's territorial integrity is a major priority. A secession movement in Bougainville brought violence in 1973 and 1976, and Indonesian incursions from West Irian occurred in 1978.

PARAGUAY (1870-)

Stamp-issuing status: active; Population: (1986 estimate); Stamps issued: more than 3,710; Issues per year during last decade: 78.

A republic in central South America. Paraguay became independent from Spain in 1811 and from La Plata in 1813.

In 1865, its territorial ambitions precipitated the War of the Triple Alliance (1865-70), in which Argentina, Brazil and Uruguay united to defeat Paraguay, annexing large areas of the country.

In 1935, Paraguay defeated Bolivia in the Chaco War, securing most of the disputed Gran Chaco region.

Paraguay has been ruled by Gen. Alfredo Stroessner since 1954. His regime is one of the most repressive in Latin America.

From 1961-83, Paraguay issued a huge number of attractive, philatelically inspired stamps. Most of these issues are omitted by the major catalogs, though the Scott catalog lists almost 2,300 of these in its For The Record listings.

PARMA (1852-60)

Stamp-issuing status: inactive: Population: 500,000 (1860 estimate); Stamps issued: 18.

Former duchy in northern Italy. Parma was annexed to Sardinia in 1860.

PARNU (PERNAU) (1941)

Stamp-issuing status: inactive; Stamps issued: 20.

A city in Estonia. Overprinted Russian stamps were issued by the German military commander.

PATIALA (1884-1951)

Stamp-issuing status: inactive; Population: 1,936,259 (1941 estimate); Stamps issued: 185.

A former convention state of British India. Patiala's issues were used concurrently with those of India after April 1, 1950. They were replaced by those of India on Jan. 1, 1951.

PATMOS (1912-32)

Stamp-issuing status: inactive; Stamps issued: 26.

One of the Dodecanese Islands in the eastern Aegean Sea. The area was obtained from Turkey by Italy in 1912, at which time Italian stamps overprinted "Patmos" were issued.

In 1929, Patmos' issues were superseded by the general Aegean Islands issues, although two sets overprinted "Patmo" were released in 1930 and 1932.

PEKING (1917-22)

Stamp-issuing status: inactive.

The capital of China. Italian post offices in the city used 38 Italian stamps overprinted "Pechino."

PENANG (PULAU PENANG) (1948-)

Stamp-issuing status: active; Population: 616,254 (1960 estimate); Stamps issued: more than 90; Issues per year for last decade: 1.

A former British possession on the west coast of the Malay Peninsula. Penang has been a member of the Federation of Malaya since 1948. Recent stamps used there are inscribed "Pulau Penang."

PENRHYN ISLAND (1902-32, 1973-)

Stamp-issuing status: active; Population: 2,050; Stamps issued: more than 400; Issues per year for last decade: 29.

A small island in the South Pacific Ocean, administered by New Zealand as part of the Cook Islands.

Penrhyn was annexed by Britain in 1888 and placed under New Zealand in

1901. Cook Islands stamps were used in Penrhyn prior to 1902 and from 1932 to 1973.

Since 1973, stamps inscribed "Penrhyn Northern Cook Islands" have been in use on the island and on six neighboring islands.

PERAK (1878-)

Stamp-issuing status: active; Population: 1.33 million (1960 estimate); Stamps issued: more than 180; Issues per year for last decade: 2.

A sultanate on the west coast of the Malay Peninsula. Under British influence after 1795, Perak was incorporated into the Federated Malay States in 1895.

Perak joined the Federation of Malaya in 1948.

PERLIS (1948-)

Stamp-issuing status: active; Population: 97,645 (1960 estimate); stamps issued: 70; Issues per year: 1.

Former Siamese tributary state in the south Malay Peninsula. Perlis was under British control after 1909, joining the Federation of Malaya in 1948.

PERU (1857-)

Stamp-issuing status: active; Population: 20.2 million (1986 estimate); Stamps issued: more than 1,575; Issues per year: 30.

A republic on the west coast of South America. Peru was the center of numerous early Indian cultures. During the 14th-15th centuries, the Inca empire, expanding from its heartland in southeastern Peru, conquered an area stretching from northern Ecuador to central Chile, including Bolivia and northwestern Argentina.

In 1532-33, Spanish adventurers overthrew the Incas, and for three centuries, Peru was the center of Spanish power in South America.

Peru became independent from Spain in 1824, although independence did little to improve the condition of the lower classes of the country. A few wealthy families, along with foreign mining interests, controlled the economic life of Peru until recent years, often ruling through military juntas.

During 1968-80, Peru was ruled by a socialistic military regime, which pursued an arduous program of nationalization and social reform. This program slowed after 1976, when popular dissatisfaction with the regime's economic policies brought a new military government to power.

In 1980, democratic civilian rule replaced the military dictatorship.

PERU-PROVISIONAL ISSUES (1881-85)

Stamp-issuing status: inactive; Stamps issued (total): 112.

During the Chilean-Peruvian War of 1879-84, Lima and Callao, the two chief cities of Peru, were occupied by Chile. Since stamps were supplied from these cities, outlying areas soon ran out of regular stamps and were forced to issue provisional stamps.

The post offices that issued such provisionals were Ancachs, Apurimac, Arequipa, Ayacucho, Chachapoyas, Chala, Chiclayo, Cuzco, Huacho, Moquegua, Paita, Pasco, Pisco, Piura, Puno and Yca.

PETAH TIQVA (1908-9)

Stamp-issuing status: inactive.

A city in Israel, near Tel-Aviv. Jewish National Fund labels were used for a time by the Austrian post office in the city.

PETROVSK (1920)

Stamp-issuing status: inactive.

A city in the Caucasus, southern Russia. Russian stamps surcharged with new values were issued by the local authorities.

PHILIPPINES (1854-)

Stamp-issuing status: inactive; Population: 17 million (1946 estimate); Stamps issued: 437.

A large group of islands in the Malay Archipelago, north of Borneo. Occupied by Spain since the 16th century, the Philippines were ceded to the United States in 1898.

Nationalist resistance was suppressed by the U.S. by mid-1902, but local self-government was expanded until 1935, when the Philippine Commonwealth was established.

During World War II, the Philippines were occupied by Japan.

Following the defeat of the Japanese in September 1945, prewar plans for independence were resumed, and on July 4, 1946, the Republic of the Philippines was declared.

Communist Huk guerrillas fought the central government after 1946 but were defeated by 1954.

Increasing leftist terrorism and student riots during 1970-71 led to a declaration of martial law by President Ferdinand Marcos. Marcos continued to rule by decree until he was ousted from the Philippines by Corazon Aquino in 1986, following a hotly contested election.

PISCOPI (1912-32)

Stamp-issuing status: inactive; Stamps issued: 46.

One of the Dodecanese Islands in the eastern Aegean Sea. Piscopi was obtained from Turkey by Italy in 1912, at which time Italian stamps overprinted "Piscopi" were issued.

Piscopi's issues were superseded by those of the Aegean Islands in 1929, although two sets overprinted for the island were issued in 1930 and 1932.

PITCAIRN ISLANDS (1940-)

Stamp-issuing status: active; Population: 50; Stamps issued: more than 275; Issues per year for last decade: 12.

A group of small islands in the South Pacific Ocean. Originally settled in 1790 by mutineers from *HMS Bounty*, Pitcairn, the only inhabited island in the group, has been a British colony since the 19th century.

POLA (1945)

Stamp-issuing status: inactive.

A city on the Adriatic coast of Yugoslavia. Stamps of Italy and the Italian Social Republic were surcharged for use under the authority of the Yugoslavia military forces.

POLAND (1860-65, 1918-)

Stamp-issuing status: active; Population: 37.5 million; Stamps issued: more than 3,000; Issues per year for last decade: 60.

A republic in eastern Europe, between Germany and Russia. During the Middle Ages, Poland was the dominant Christian power in eastern Europe, but after about 1700, its power declined.

Between 1772 and 1795, it was absorbed by Russia, Prussia and Austria and did not re-appear as an independent nation until 1918.

In the aftermath of World War I, Poland fought both Germany and Russia, acquiring large territories from both, as well as from Austria and Lithuania. During this period, many locals were used.

In 1939, Poland was invaded by Germany and the Soviet Union, igniting World War II. The two powers divided Poland between them, Germany occupying all of the country after its invasion of Russia in 1941. During the war, Poland suffered terribly, and some six million Poles, half of them Jews, were killed.

A Polish Government in Exile was established in London and was recognized by the Western Allies, but after Soviet forces occupied Poland during 1944-45, a more malleable government was established by the Russians.

The U.S.S.R.'s 1939 acquisitions were recognized by the new Polish regime. In return for this loss of about 70,000 square miles in the east, Poland was awarded about 40,000 square miles of German territory in the west.

In 1947, the Communist regime was finally established and began a thorough program of socialization. Declining farm production and harsh working conditions sparked riots in 1956, which brought a moderation of government policy. In 1970, a new series of riots brought a change of government and increased emphasis on the production of consumer goods.

Although more moderate than many other Communist states, Poland is closely linked with the U.S.S.R. It joined in the 1968 invasion of Czechoslovakia.

In the summer of 1980, the Polish labor movement, Solidarity, launched a series of strikes that brought major concessions from the government. Increasing democratization brought intense Soviet pressure to bear on the Polish leadership, resulting in a government crackdown in late 1981. The domestic situation has made slow but graded improvement since.

POLISH CORPS IN RUSSIA (1918)

Stamp-issuing status: inactive.

In 1917, Polish prisoners of war, captured by the Germans, were formed into the Polish Corps to fight, under German Command, against the Russians.

A number of Russian stamps were overprinted for use by this unit.

POLISH GOVERNMENT IN EXILE (1941-45)

Stamp-issuing status: inactive; Stamps issued: 21.

After the German-Soviet invasion of 1939, the Polish Government in Exile operated from London. During 1941-45, stamps were issued for use on letters posted from Free Polish merchant vessels and warships fighting against the Axis powers.

POLISH MILITARY POST IN RUSSIA (1917-18)

After the Russian Revolution of 1917, the Polish forces fighting with the Russian Army regrouped into a separate army corps. Contemporary Russian stamps were overprinted for their use.

POLISH OFFICES ABROAD (1919-21, 1925-39)

Poland maintained post offices in Constantinople from 1919-21 and Danzig from 1925-39, overprinting 36 and 19 Polish stamps, respectively.

PONCE (1898)

Stamp-issuing status: inactive.

A town in Puerto Rico. U.S. forces issued a provisional stamp for use after the occupation of the city from Spain in August 1898.

PONEWESCH (PANEVEZYS) (1941)

Stamp-issuing status: inactive.

A city in central Lithuania. A total of nine overprinted Russian stamps were issued by the German military commander.

PONTA DELGADA (1892-31)

Stamp-issuing status: inactive; Population: 125,000 (1905 estimate); Stamps issued: 34.

An administrative district of the Azores. Stamps of Ponta Delgada were replaced by issues of the Azores in 1905, which in turn were replaced by regular Portuguese issues in 1931.

PONTEVEDRA (1937)

Stamp-issuing status: inactive.

A province of northwestern Spain, bordering the Atlantic Ocean and Portugal.

The Nationalist authorities overprinted contemporary Spanish stamps for use in the province in 1937.

POONCH (1876-94)

Stamp-issuing status: inactive; Population: 287,000 (estimated); Stamps issued: 36.

A former tributary state of Jammu and Kashmir in northern India. Poonch's issues were replaced by those of India in 1894.

PORT ARTHUR AND DAIREN (1946-51)

Stamp-issuing status: inactive; Stamps issued: 76.

Port and peninsula in southern Manchuria, bordering on the Strait of Pohai. Under Japanese rule from 1895-1945, the area was occupied by the Soviets after World War II and turned over to the Chinese Communists in 1946.

In 1951, the regional issues were overprinted by the general issues of the People's Republic of China in 1951.

PORT LAGOS (1893-98)

Stamp-issuing status: inactive; Stamps issued: 6.

A port in northern Greece. Unoverprinted French stamps were used by the French post office in the city after 1870. During 1893-98, stamps of France, overprinted "Port-Lagos" and new values in Turkish currency were used.

PORT SAID (1899-1931)

Stamp-issuing status: inactive; Stamps issued: 102.

A major Egyptian port on the Mediterranean Sea. The French post office in the city operated from 1867 through March 31, 1931.

PORTUGAL (1853-)

Stamp-issuing status: active; Population: 10 million; Stamps issued: more than 1,600; Issues per year for last decade: 41.

A republic on the western coast of the Iberian Peninsula in southwest Europe. Independence was established in 1095. During the 15th and 16th centuries, Portugal built an overseas empire.

Portuguese power declined rapidly after 1580, although Portugal maintained much of her colonial empire until 1975. Portugal was a kingdom from 1139 until 1910 when the republic was established.

From 1932 to 1968, Portugal was ruled by Premier Antonio de Oliveira Salazar, an authoritarian dictator. After

1968, Salazar's policies were continued by his successors. The regime became increasingly unpopular, largely because of the country's debilitating wars against nationalist movements in the African colonies.

In 1974, a military coup overthrew the government, and the new liberal regime quickly granted independence to Angola, the Cape Verde Islands, Guinea-Bissau, Mozambique and Sao Tome-Principe. Autonomy was granted to Macao, Madeira and the Azores. The collapse of authority in Portuguese Timor brought that territory's occupation by Indonesia in 1976.

The government moved increasingly to the left during 1975, and the Communists, despite setbacks at the polls, increased their influence. In November, a counter-coup halted this trend, and free elections in 1976 gave Portugal a Socialist government.

Portugal's swift change from a rigidly controlled rightist dictatorship, through a flirtation with communism, to a socialist democracy has brought enormous economic strains. Despite considerable Western aid, Portugal's economic and political life remains in disarray.

PORTUGUESE AFRICA (1898, 1919, 1945)

Stamp-issuing status: inactive; Stamps issued: 20.

Three general issues were released by Portugal for use in its African colonies (Angola, Cape Verde, Portuguese Guinea, St. Thomas and Prince Islands, and Mozambique).

These were used concurrently with the issues of the separate colonies.

PORTUGUESE CONGO (CABINDA) (1893-1920)

Stamp-issuing status: inactive; Stamps issued: 137.

A district of Angola lying north of the Congo River, separated from Angola by Zaire. It was administered as the Portuguese Congo until its incorporation with the colony of Angola.

PORTUGUESE GUINEA (1881-1974)

Stamp-issuing status: inactive; Population: 565,000 (1973 estimate); Stamps issued: 400.

Former Portuguese colony in West Africa. The area was explored by the Portuguese in the 15th century but was not colonized until the 19th century. In the 1960s, an independence movement in the interior of the colony began a guerrilla war that culminated in the country's independence in 1974.

PORTUGUESE INDIA (1871-1962)

Stamp-issuing status: inactive; Population: 650,000; Stamps issued: 704.

A number of Portuguese holdings on the west coast of India. Occupied by Portugal since the 16th century, these territories were seized by India in 1961 and absorbed into the Indian republic.

Existing stocks of Portuguese Indian stamps were sold for about 10 days following the invasion and were valid until Jan. 7, 1962.

Two sets for the colony were issued in early 1962 by Portugal, which did not recognize India's action. The stamps were never used in the territories.

PRAGUE (1918)

Stamp-issuing status: inactive.

Capital city of Czechoslovakia. During November 1918, the Czech Revolutionary Committee operated a local postal service in Prague, staffed by Boy Scouts.

PRIAMUR AND MARITIME PROVINCES (1921-22)

Stamp-issuing status: inactive; Stamps issued: 60.

A region in southeastern Siberia, west of Manchuria. In May 1921, a monarchist, anti-Bolshevik regime was established, with Japanese support. This government was never secure, and with the Japanese withdrawal from Siberia in October 1922, it collapsed.

PRINCE EDWARD ISLAND (1861-73)

Stamp-issuing status: inactive; Population: 90,000 (1872 estimate); Stamps issued: 16.

An island in the Gulf of St. Lawrence, in northeastern North America. Prince Edward Island was a British colony until 1873 when it joined the Canadian Confederation.

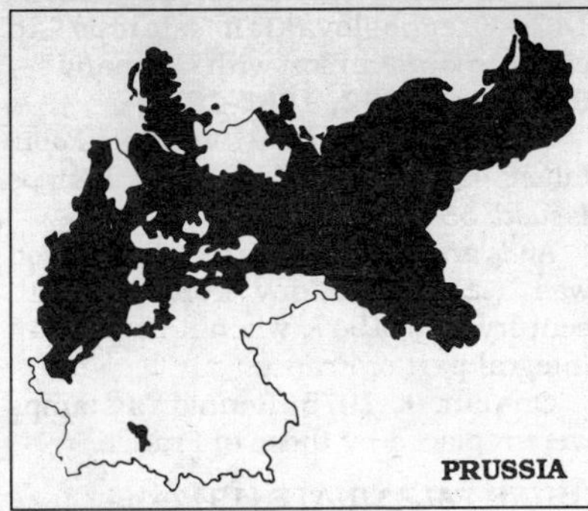

PRUSSIA (1850-67)

Stamp-issuing status: inactive; Population: 40.17 million (1910 estimate); Stamps issued: 26.

Former kingdom in northern Germany. By the early 18th century, Prussia was a major European power, and by 1870, she occupied most of northern Germany and ruled two-thirds of the German population.

Prussia dominated the German Empire established in 1870.

Stamps of Prussia were issued from 1850-67 and were replaced on Jan. 1, 1868, by issues of the North German Postal District.

PRZEDBORZ (1917-18)

Stamp-issuing status: inactive.

A city in south-central Poland. Several series of stamps were issued during World War I by the municipal authorities under the authority of the Austrian military commander.

PSKOW (PLESKAU) (1941-42)

Stamp-issuing status: inactive.

A city in northwestern Russia. During World War II, 17 stamps were issued for the district by the German military commander.

PUERTO RICO (1855-1900)

Stamp-issuing status: inactive; Population: 955,000 (1900 estimate); Stamps issued: 212.

A large island east of Hispaniola in the West Indies, Puerto Rico was discovered by Columbus on his second voyage in 1493.

Puerto Rico remained a Spanish colony until 1898, when it was occupied by the United States during the Spanish-American War. The island was subsequently ceded to the United States and since 1952, has been a commonwealth in association with the United States.

Puerto Rican issues of 1855-73 were issued in Cuba as well as Puerto Rico. Separate issues appeared after 1873. In 1898, two provisional stamps were issued by the U.S. military forces in Puerto Rico, followed by 10 overprinted U.S. stamps during 1899-1900. Since 1900, regular U.S. issues have been in use.

- Q -

QATAR (1957-)

Stamp-issuing status: active; Population: 291,000; Stamps issued: more than 650; Issues per year for last decade: 26.

An Arab sheikdom on the Persian Gulf.

Long under Persian rule, Qatar became independent in the 19th century. It was occupied by the Ottoman Turks from 1871 to 1913 and came under British protection in 1916.

In 1971, Qatar declared its independence, after considering and rejecting a plan to join in a federation with the United Arab Emirates.

Qatar is oil-rich, and its sole economic weakness is a lack of skilled labor. Its oil earnings give it one of the highest per capita incomes in the world.

QU'AITI STATE (1942-67)

Stamp-issuing status: inactive; Stamps issued: 52.

Former British protectorate in South Arabia. The Qu'aiti sultan was recognized as ruler of the entire Hadhramaut, Shirh and Mukalla, although the Kathiri State of Seiyun maintained a measure of autonomy.

The region was absorbed by the People's Republic of Southern Yemen in 1967.

QUEENSLAND (1860-1913)

Stamp-issuing status: inactive; Population: 500,000 (1909 estimate); Stamps issued: 163.

A state in northeast Australia. A British crown colony from 1859-1901, Queensland joined with five other British colonies to form the Commonwealth of Australia in 1901.

QUELIMANE (1914-22)

Stamp-issuing status: inactive; Population: 877,000 (estimate); Stamps issued: 40.

A province of Mozambique. Quelimane issues were superseded by those of Mozambique in 1922.

- R -

RAJASTHAN (1948-50)

Stamp-issuing status: inactive; Population: 13.1 million; Stamps issued: 154.

A state in northern India created by the merger of 18 Rajput states, several of which had hitherto issued their own stamps.

RAJPEEPLA (1880-86)

Stamp-issuing status: inactive; Population: 206,086; Stamps issued: 3.

A former feudatory state in western India.

RAS AL KHAIMA (1964-72)

Stamp-issuing status: inactive.

A sheikdom in the Trucial States, in eastern Arabia, bordering on the Persian Gulf. Under British protection from 1892-1971, Ras al Khaima joined the United Arab Emirates in 1972.

RASEINIAI (ROSSINGEN) (1919, 1941)

Stamp-issuing status: inactive.

A city in central Lithuania. A local stamp was issued by the municipal authorities in January 1919. For a period after the city's occupation by Germany in June 1941, 11 overprinted Russian stamps were used.

REDONDA (1979-)

Stamp-issuing status: active; Population: 0; Stamps issued: 215; Issues per year since 1979: 24.

A steep, guano-covered rock one-half mile square in the eastern Caribbean between Montserrat and Nevis, owned by Antigua.

Antiguan stamps overprinted "REDONDA" were introduced in 1979, with purpose-designed issues on a variety of popular topics following later that year. These are postally valid on Antigua, since Redonda has neither postal service nor inhabitants.

Although Redonda's stamps are not numerous, about one-third of them are $1 to $5 values. Redonda's current stamp-issuing status is questionable.

REICHENBERG-MAFFERSDORF (1938)

Stamp-issuing status: inactive.

Two cities in the Sudetenland (Czechoslovakia). In 1938 they overprinted 147 Czechoslovakian stamps to commemorate union with Germany.

REUNION (1852, 1885-1974)

Stamp-issuing status: inactive; Population: 490,000 (1974 estimate); Stamps issued: 556.

An island in the Indian Ocean. Reunion was a French colony from the 17th century until 1947, when it became an integral part of France.

On Jan. 1, 1975, Reunion's stamps were replaced by those of France.

RHINE PALATINATE (1947-49)

Stamp-issuing status: inactive; Stamps issued: 53.

A district of western Germany occupied by France after World War II.

RHINELAND (1923)

Stamp-issuing status: inactive.

The area of Germany lying west of the Rhine River. After World War I, France attempted to establish a satellite state in the region, which contained rich mineral deposits and much of Germany's heavy industry. An abortive Rhineland Republic (October 1923-January 1924) produced a number of overprints on contemporary German issues.

RHODES (1912-45)

Stamp-issuing status: inactive; Stamps issued: 131.

The largest of the Dodecanese Islands in the eastern Aegean Sea. The center of a prehistoric civilization from c. 3500 B.C., Rhodes' strategic position in the eastern Mediterranean area brought many foreign masters, including the Greeks, Romans, Arabs, Crusaders and, after 1522, the Turks.

In 1912, Rhodes was obtained from Turkey by Italy, and Italian stamps overprinted "Rodi" were issued. Rhodes continued to issue its own stamps, which were used throughout the Dodecanese Islands concurrently with the general issues of the Aegean Islands.

During 1943-45, Rhodes was occupied by the Germans. Occupied by British forces in 1945, Rhodes, along with the rest of the island group, was annexed to Greece in 1947.

RHODESIA (1890-1924, 1965-78)

Stamp-issuing status: inactive; Population: 10 million (1978 estimate); Stamps issued: 379.

A former British administrative unit in southeastern Africa. The area was under the British South Africa Co. until 1924, when Rhodesia was divided into Northern Rhodesia and Southern Rhodesia, under direct British rule.

During 1953-63, these two colonies were united with the Nyasaland Protectorate to form the Federation of Rhodesia and Nyasaland.

With the dissolution of the federation, the three colonies were again separated. Northern Rhodesia became independent as Zambia in 1964, and in 1965, Southern Rhodesia assumed the name Rhodesia and declared its independence from Great Britain. Rhodesia became Zimbabwe on Dec. 31, 1978.

RHODESIA AND NYASALAND (1954-63)

Stamp-issuing status: inactive; 8.51 million (1961 estimate); Stamps issued: 56.

A former federation comprising the British territories of Northern Rhodesia, Southern Rhodesia and Nyasaland in southeast Africa.

RIO DE ORO (1905-24)

Stamp-issuing status: inactive; Population: 24,000 (1922 estimate); Stamps issued: 148.

A former Spanish colony on the northwest coast of Africa. Rio de Oro was incorporated into the Spanish Sahara in 1924.

RIO MUNI (1960)

Stamp-issuing status: inactive; Population: 185,000 (1968 estimate); Stamps issued: 85.

Former Spanish colony on the Gulf of Guinea, bordering on Cameroon and Gabon.

Rio Muni was claimed by Spain in 1885 and formed part of Spanish Guinea from 1909 to 1959. In 1959 it became an overseas province of Spain. In 1968 it merged with Fernando Po to form the independent Republic of Equatorial Guinea.

RIOUW ARCHIPELAGO (1954-60)

Stamp-issuing status: inactive.

A group of islands in Indonesia, south of Singapore. Because of differing rates of exchange between the currency used in the islands with that used in the rest of Indonesia, 41 Dutch Indies and Indonesian stamps were overprinted for use in the area.

RIZEH (1909-14)

Stamp-issuing status: inactive.

A Turkish port on the Black Sea. After 1909, nine stamps of the Russian Levant overprinted "Rizeh" were used by the Russian postal service in the city.

ROKISKIS (RAKISCHKI) (1941)

Stamp-issuing status: inactive.

A city in Lithuania. Seven overprinted Russian stamps were issued by the German military authorities after Rokiskis' occupation in June 1941.

ROMAGNA (1859-60)

Stamp-issuing status: inactive; Population: 1,341,091 (1853 estimate); Stamps issued: 9.

A territory in north-central Italy, under Papal rule after 1503. In 1859 a provisional government replaced the Papal authorities, and in 1860 Romagna was annexed to the Kingdom of Sardinia.

ROMAN STATES

ROMAN STATES (1852-70)

Stamp-issuing status: inactive; Population: 3.12 million (1853 estimate); Stamps issued: 25.

The greater part of central Italy, over which the Pope acted as temporal and religious ruler.

During 1859-61, most of the area joined Sardinia. The districts around Rome remained under Papal control, which was maintained by French troops. In 1870, the French withdrew, and Italy absorbed the remaining Papal territory, except for the enclave of Vatican City.

ROMANIA (1865-)

Stamp-issuing status: active; Population: 22.4 million; Stamps issued: more than 4,300; Issues per year for last decade: 79.

A republic in southeastern Europe, bordering on the Danube River and the Black Sea.

Under Turkish rule since the 15th century, Romania was formed from the union of the principalities of Wallachia and Moldavia in 1861, under Ottoman suzerainty. In 1878, as a result of the Russo-Turkish war, Romania became independent.

Although ruled by a Hohenzollern dynasty, related to the ruling family of Germany, Romania did not enter World War I until August 1916, and then joined the Allies. After initial successes, Romanian forces were routed, and by January 1917, almost all of the country had been overrun by Germany, Austria and Bulgaria.

Romania enjoyed considerably greater military success after the armistice, overrunning a large part of Hungary and occupying territories from Austria, Russia and Bulgaria. By the final peace (1920), Romania doubled in size.

During the 1930s, the Iron Guard, a Romanian fascist movement, gained control of the government, and in 1941, Romania entered World War II as an ally of Germany. In 1944, the regime was overthrown by King Michael, with Soviet support, and Romania joined the Allies.

Soviet troops occupied the country after World War II, forcing Michael to abdicate and establishing the people's republic on Dec. 30, 1947.

From the 1950s, Romania has pursued an increasingly independent foreign policy. In 1959, Soviet troops were refused entry into the country, and during the 1960s, political ties were strengthened with China, Israel and the West.

ROMANIAN OFFICES IN TURKEY (1896-1914, 1919)

Stamp-issuing status: inactive.

During 1896-1919, Romania maintained a post office in Constantinople, surcharging or overprinting 11 regular issues for use there.

ROSS DEPENDENCY (1957-87)

Stamp-issuing status: inactive; Stamps issued: 20.

The sector of Antarctica under New Zealand administration. New Zealand closed its post office there and withdrew Ross Dependency stamps from sale at the end of 1987.

ROUAD, ILE (1916-20)

Stamp-issuing status: inactive; Stamps issued: 16.

An island in the Mediterranean, off the coast of Latakia. Ile Rouad was occupied by the French from Turkey in 1916, after which stamps of the French offices in Levant were overprinted "Ile Rouad." The area was attached to Syria in 1920.

RUANDA-URUNDI (1924-62)

Stamp-issuing status: inactive; Population: 4.7 million (1958 estimate); Stamps issued: 203.

Two areas of central Africa, between Zaire and Tanzania. Formerly part of German East Africa, they were occupied by Belgian Congo forces during World War I and subsequently were administered by Belgium under a League of Nations (later U.N.) mandate.

They became independent in 1962 as the Republic of Rwanda and the Kingdom of Burundi.

RUMBERG (1938)

Stamp-issuing status: inactive.

A city in the Sudetenland (Czechoslovakia). Municipal authorities overprinted Czechoslovakian stamps to commemorate the union with Germany.

RUSSIA (1857-)

Stamp-issuing status: active; Population: 283 million; Stamps issued: more than 6,000; Issues per year for last decade: 100.

A country comprising the greater portion of eastern Europe and northern Asia. European Russia was ruled by Norse dynasties until the Mongol conquest in the 13th century.

After the 16th century, Muscovy (Moscow) became the center of a resurgent Russian state, which for several hundred years steadily expanded its borders.

A major European power after 1700, Russian strength deteriorated in the late 19th and early 20th centuries. Mounting frustrations with the autocratic rule of the tsars and military defeats in World War I brought the fall of the monarchy in March 1917.

In November, the liberal Kerensky regime was overthrown by the Bolsheviks (Communists) who made peace with Germany and began consolidation of their power.

Anti-Bolshevik forces (the "White Russians") quickly formed throughout the country. White Russian regimes were established in western and southern Russia and throughout Siberia. Bolshevik control was limited to northern and central Europe and Russia. Britain, France, Japan and the United States became involved in the civil war, but the inability of the various White Russian governments to cooperate with each other, or to meet the legitimate needs of the people, made it possible for the Bolshevik Red Army to have generally established Soviet authority by the end of 1920.

During 1920-23, the government consolidated its position. Although a number of border provinces (Poland, Finland, the Baltic States and Bessarabia) were lost, the newly formed Union of Soviet Socialist Republics included almost all of the territory of the old empire.

Lenin's death in 1924 precipitated a power struggle within the Communist leadership, with Josef Stalin ultimately emerging as the absolute ruler of the country. During the 1920s and early 1930s, Stalin exiled his opponents within the party. From the mid-1930s through 1953, he purged any suspected opposition through show trials and executions. Millions of Russians died.

Following World War I, when both Germany and Russia were ostracized by the powers, the two countries worked closely and secretly, the Russians supplying Germany with armaments forbidden by the Treaty of Versailles, while German officers trained the Red Army. Alarmed by the German threat after Hitler's rise to power, the U.S.S.R. at first attempted to take a strong stand against German expansionism in the 1930s.

By 1938, however, Russia was convinced that the Allies would not fight, and in 1939 the Soviet-German Non-Aggression Pact was signed. A few months later, Germany invaded Poland, while the Soviets occupied southern Poland, the Baltic States and Bessarabia.

In 1941, Germany attacked Russia, and the U.S.S.R. joined the Allies. At first successful, the Germans were pushed back after the end of 1942, and during 1944-45, Soviet forces occupied most of Eastern Europe.

With the peace, the Soviets retained their 1939-40 acquisitions, and Soviet troops forced the establishment of satellite regimes in the rest of the area during 1945-48.

Since World War II, the U.S.S.R. has concentrated on economic and military development. It has exercised an aggressive foreign policy and has not hesitated to use military force as an accepted instrument of policy.

After 1956, the brutal policies of Stalin were officially denounced, and under his successor, Nikita Khrushchev, the government was less harsh. Krushchev was himself deposed in 1964, and his successors have become increasingly rigid and totalitarian.

A new era under Mikhail Gorbachov of openness, economic restructuring and what many see as the democratization of the U.S.S.R. appears now to be under way.

RUSSIA-ARMY OF THE NORTHWEST (1919)

Stamp-issuing status: inactive; Stamps issued: 14.

Overprinted Russian stamps were used briefly in 1919 by Gen. Nicolai N. Yudenich's White Russian Army operating in the Baltic area, southwest of Leningrad.

RUSSIAN COMPANY FOR STEAM SHIPPING AND TRADE (ROPIT) (1865-68)

Stamp-issuing status: inactive; Stamps issued: 7.

The offices of this private company were used as postal branches under agreement with the Russian government. The company issued several stamps for this service, which were supplanted by official issues for the Russian Levant in May 1868.

In 1918, a number of the company's agencies in the Turkish Empire were re-opened. Anticipating the revival of business following World War I, ROPIT overprinted its stocks of Russian Levant stamps with its initials and new values. The collapse of Gen. Denikin's South Russian government, however, brought the closing of the agencies, and the overprinted stamps were never placed in use.

RUSSIAN OFFICES IN CHINA (1899-1920)

Stamp-issuing status: inactive.

During 1899-1920, Russia maintained post offices in a number of Chinese cities. Russian stamps overprinted "China" in Russian or surcharged in cents and dollars were used for these post offices.

RUSSIAN OFFICES IN THE TURKISH EMPIRE (1863-1923)

Stamp-issuing status: inactive.

Russia, along with many other European nations, maintained post offices in the Ottoman Empire until the Treaty of Lausanne (1923) abolished their extraterritorial postal privileges.

RWANDA (1962-)

Stamp-issuing status: active; Population: 6.5 million; Stamps issued: more than 1,200; Issues per year for last decade: 49.

A republic in East Africa. Until 1916, it was part of German East Africa. The territory, along with Burundi, was administered by Belgium under a League of Nations (later U.N.) mandate as the Trust Territory of Ruanda-Urundi.

On July 1, 1962, Rwanda became an independent republic.

Rwanda is one of the most densely populated countries in Africa and is very poor. The government is attempting to implement ambitious economic and social improvement programs.

RYUKYU ISLANDS (1947-72)

Stamp-issuing status: inactive; Population: 950,000 (1972 estimate); Stamps issued: 257.

A chain of islands located between Japan and Taiwan, the Ryukyus were under Japanese rule until 1945, when they were occupied by the United States after one of the bloodiest campaigns in the Pacific Theater of World War II.

They remained under U.S. administration until May 15, 1972, when they reverted to Japan.

Japanese stamps, overprinted by local postmasters, and one crude printed provisional were used until 1948, when the occupation authorities began issuing stamps for general use.

Since the return of the islands to Japan, regular Japanese stamps have been in use.

- S -

SAAR (1920-35, 1947-59)

Stamp-issuing status: inactive; Population: 1.4 million (1959 estimate); Stamps issued: 500.

A coal-rich district of Germany, southeast of Luxembourg. The Saar was occupied by France after World War I and was placed under League of Nations administration, with France controlling the mines as part of the German war reparations.

In 1935, a plebiscite resulted in the reunion of the area with Germany. The Saar was reoccupied by France in 1945, returning to the German Federal Republic in 1957.

Saar stamps continued to be used until their final replacement by German issues in 1959.

SABAH (1964-)

Stamp-issuing status: inactive; Population: 700,000 (1979 estimate); Stamps issued: 38.

A state in northeastern Borneo. Formerly British North Borneo, the territory assumed the name Sabah in 1963 when it joined with Malaya, Sarawak and Singapore to form the Federation of Malaysia.

ST. CHRISTOPHER (1870-90)

Stamp-issuing status: inactive; Population: 18,500 (1890 estimate); Stamps issued: 24.

An island in the West Indies, southeast of Puerto Rico. Formerly a presidency of the Leeward Islands, St. Kitts was united with Nevis in 1903 to form the presidency of St. Kitts-Nevis.

In 1952, this designation was changed to St. Christopher-Nevis-Anguilla.

ST. CHRISTOPHER-NEVIS-ANGUILLA (1952-80)

Stamp-issuing status: inactive; Population: 50,000 (estimate); Stamps issued: 304.

An associated state in the British Commonwealth, St. Christopher-Nevis-Anguilla came into being in 1952. Stamps of St. Kitts-Nevis and Leeward Islands continued in concurrent use there until 1956.

In 1967, Anguilla separated unilaterally and began issuing its own stamps, although "Anguilla" continued to appear on St. Christopher-Nevis-Anguilla issues for 13 years thereafter. Nevis and St. Kitts (St. Christopher) parted company in 1980.

ST. HELENA (1856-)

Stamp-issuing status: active; Population: 5,895; Stamps issued: more than 480; Issues per year for last decade: 18.

An island in the southern Atlantic Ocean. Under British rule since 1673, the colony includes the dependencies of Ascension and Tristan da Cunha.

ST. KITTS-NEVIS (1903-50)

Stamp-issuing status: inactive; Stamps issued: 97.

A group of islands in the West Indies, southeast of Puerto Rico. Formed in 1903 as a presidency of the British Leeward Islands colony, the designation of St. Christopher-Nevis-Anguilla was adopted in 1952.

In 1956, this became a separate British colony, securing independence in 1967 as St. Kitts-Nevis-Anguilla. Soon after independence, Anguilla seceded from the union, declaring its independence from both St. Kitts-Nevis and Great Britain.

ST. LUCIA (1860-)

Stamp-issuing status: active; Population: 124,000; Stamps issued: more than 950; Issues per year for last decade: 50.

An island in the West Indies. The island was disputed between France and Britain from 1627-1803, with Britain acquiring control after 1803.

On March 1, 1967, St. Lucia became an independent associated state in the British Commonwealth. It became fully independent on Feb. 22, 1979.

Funded by foreign aid, St. Lucia is pursuing an ambitious economic development program.

ST. MARIE DE MADAGASCAR (1894-98)

Stamp-issuing status: inactive; Population: 8,000 (1894 estimate); Stamps issued: 13.

An island off the east coast of Madagascar. Occupied by the French in the 17th century, it was a French colony until 1898, when it was attached to Madagascar.

ST. NAZAIRE (1945)

Stamp-issuing status: inactive.

A city in northern France, at the mouth of the Loire River. In 1945, Allied advances cut St. Nazaire off from the rest of German-occupied France. During this period, the local Chamber of Commerce issued three provisional stamps for local use.

ST. PIERRE AND MIQUELON (1885-1976, 1986-)

Stamp-issuing status: active; Population: 6,200; Stamps issued: more than 650.

Two small islands off the southern coast of Newfoundland. Originally occupied by the French in 1604, they are the only remnants of a once-vast French North American empire.

Separate stamps issued for St. Pierre and Miquelon were discontinued in late 1976, but were reintroduced in 1986.

ST. THOMAS AND PRINCE ISLANDS (1869-1978)

Stamp-issuing status: inactive; Population: 88,000; Stamps issued: 574.

Two small islands in the Gulf of Guinea. Portuguese possessions since 1490, St. Thomas and Prince became the independent Democratic Republic of Sao Tome and Principe on July 12, 1975.

ST. VINCENT (1861-)

Stamp-issuing status: active; Population: 109,000; Stamps issued: more than 1,030; Issues per year for last decade: 52.

An island in the West Indies. St. Vincent was a British colony from 1763 to 1969. On Oct. 27, 1969, St. Vincent became an independent associated state in the British Commonwealth. It became fully independent on Oct. 27, 1979.

ST. VINCENT-GRENADINES (1973-)

Stamp-issuing status: active; Stamps issued: more than 550; Issues per year for last decade: 44.

A small group of islands administered by St. Vincent, including Bequia, Mustique, Canouan and Union Island. A host of expensive topical issues were produced for the Grenadines, Bequia and Union Island during 1984-88, almost exclusively for consumption by stamp collectors.

SALONICA (1909-13, 1944)

Stamp-issuing status: inactive.

A major port in northern Greece, on the Aegean Sea. The Russian post office in Salonica used overprinted Russian Levant stamps after 1909, along with the general issues of the Russian offices in Turkey.

The Russian set was quickly followed by a similar series issued by Italy for its post office in Salonica.

During 1916, British issues overprinted "Levant" were used by the British forces in Salonica.

During the last stages of World War II, Italian stamps were overprinted by the German military commander for use in Salonica.

SALVADOR, EL (1867-)

Stamp-issuing status: active; Population: 5.3 million (1984 estimate); Stamps issued: more than 2,225; Issues per year for the last decade: 40.

A republic in Central America, bordering on the Pacific Ocean.

El Salvador was conquered by the Spanish in the 1520s and was ruled as part of the captaincy-general of Guatemala until 1821. It came under Mexican rule briefly, then formed part of the Central American Confederation until 1839.

Since independence, El Salvador's history has been marked by political instability. Coups, countercoups, inequitable land ownership and a long-running civil war between Marxist guerrillas and right-wing elements of the military make the country's future extremely uncertain.

SAMOA (1877-)

Stamp-issuing status: active; Population: 160,000; Stamps issued: more than 650; Issues per year for last decade: 20.

A group of islands in the South Pacific Ocean, east of Fiji. The native kingdom of Samoa was under the influence of the United States, Britain and Germany until 1899 when the islands were partitioned between the United States and Germany with Great Britain withdrawing her claims.

The eastern islands were ceded to the United States by the local chiefs from 1900-04. American Samoa has since been administered by the United States, using regular U.S. stamps.

Western Samoa was seized from Germany by New Zealand forces in 1914, and New Zealand subsequently administered the western islands under a mandate from the League of Nations (later the United Nations).

Western Samoa became independent on Jan. 1, 1962. In 1977 the country's name was changed to Samoa. Ties to New Zealand remain strong.

SAMOS (1878-1915)

Stamp-issuing status: inactive; Stamps issued (total): 33.

An island in the Aegean Sea. Under Turkish rule since the 15th century, Samos became an autonomous principality in 1832, under British, French and Russian protection. France overprinted and surcharged a set of nine stamps "Vathy" for use in 1894-1900.

In September 1912, a provisional government was established, and Turkish troops withdrew. The government issued 2¢ stamps. In 1913, Samos was united with Greece.

SAN MARINO (1877-)

Stamp-issuing status: active; Population: 23,100; Stamps issued: more than 1,275; Issues per year for last decade: 27.

A tiny independent republic in central Italy. Surrounded on all sides by Italy, San Marino has maintained its independence since the 4th century A.D. It is the world's smallest republic and claims to be Europe's oldest state.

Postage stamps and tourism are the country's major industries.

SAN SEBASTIAN (1936-37)

Stamp-issuing status: inactive.

The capital of the province of Guipuzcoa in northern Spain.

Nationalist authorities overprinted a number of Spanish stamps for use in the city during the Spanish Civil War.

SANTA CRUZ DE TENERIFE (1937)

Stamp-issuing status: inactive.

A province of Spain in the Canary Islands.

A set of overprinted Spanish stamps was issued in 1937 by the Nationalist authorities.

SANTA MARIA DE ALBARRACIA (1937)

Stamp-issuing status: inactive.

A city in the province of Teruel in northern Spain.

Two overprinted Spanish stamps were issued in 1937 under the authority of the Nationalist Inspector-General of Posts.

SAO TOME AND PRINCIPE (1975-)

Stamp-issuing status: active; Population: 114,025 (1987 estimate); Issues per year 1975-83: 60.

The Portuguese colony of St. Thomas and Prince became the independent Democratic Republic of Sao Tome and Principe on July 12, 1975. It now issues large numbers of topically oriented stamps primarily intended for stamp collectors.

SARAWAK (1869-)

Stamp-issuing status: inactive; Population: 975,918 (1970); Stamps issued: 247.

A state on the northwestern coast of Borneo. In 1893, the area was ceded to Sir James Brooke by the sultan of Brunei. Sarawak remained an independent state until 1888, when it accepted British control of its foreign affairs.

The Brooke dynasty ruled until 1946, when the last rajah ceded Sarawak to Britain. In 1963, the colony joined with Malaya, Singapore and Sabah (North Borneo) to form the Federation of Malaysia.

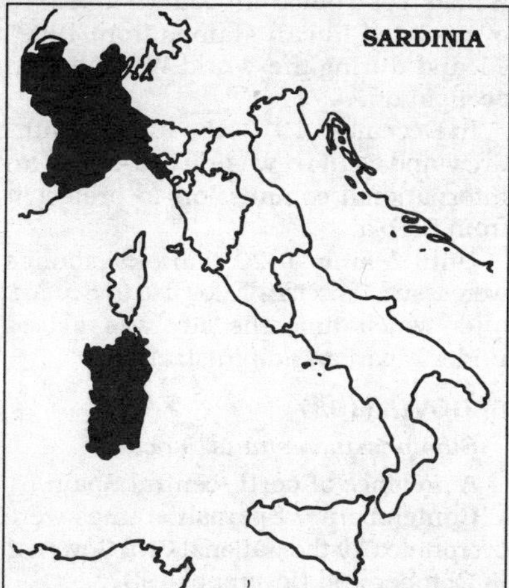

SARDINIA (1851-62)

Stamp-issuing status: inactive; Stamps issued: 15.

A former kingdom in northwestern Italy. The Sardinian House of Savoy led the Italian nationalist movement, absorbing most of the many Italian states during 1859-61.

In 1861, the Sardinian kingdom became the Kingdom of Italy, which began to issue stamps in 1862.

SARNY (1941)

Stamp-issuing status: inactive.

A city in the western Ukraine. After the German occupation of the city in 1941, six stamps were issued by the German military commander.

SASENO (1923)

Stamp-issuing status: inactive.

A small island off the coast of Albania. Occupied by Italy in 1914, eight Italian stamps were overprinted for use there in 1923. Saseno was formally returned to Albania in 1947.

SAUDI ARABIA (1932-)

Stamp-issuing status: active; Population: 9.6 million; Stamps issued: more than 1,300; Issues per year for last decade: 32.

Nejd, in northern Arabia, was long the center of the fundamentalist Wahabbi Moslem sect. Under Turkish control until 1913, Nejd was freed by Ibn Saud, a warrior king who immediately set about the enlargement of his domain. He conquered the Turkish province of Hasa in 1913, the Kingdom of the Hejaz in 1925, and most of Asir in 1926. In 1932 the kingdom adopted the name Saudi Arabia.

Oil was discovered in 1936, and petroleum soon became the country's major export and economic mainstay. Saudi Arabia has played a leading role in OPEC.

Saudi Arabia is an absolute monarchy, ruled by the Saud family. Mecca and Medina, the holy cities of Islam, are within the country, and the Koran is the law of the land.

Saudi Arabia has been an active force in the Arab movement for a Palestinian state. Since the 1967 Arab-Israeli War, it has given annual subsidies to the Arab frontline states, as well as to the various

Palestinian political groups. The Saudis were among the leaders in the 1973-74 oil boycott of the West.

SAURASHTRA (SORUTH) (1864-1949)

Stamp-issuing status: inactive; Population: 670,719; Stamps issued: 34.

A former feudatory state, actually named Junagadh, in western India. Its stamps were replaced by those of the United State of Saurashtra in 1949.

SAURASHTRA, UNITED STATE OF (1949-50)

Stamp-issuing status: inactive; Stamps issued: 26.

A state formed in 1948 with the merger of over 400 states and territories in western India. Indian stamps have been used in the state since April 1, 1950.

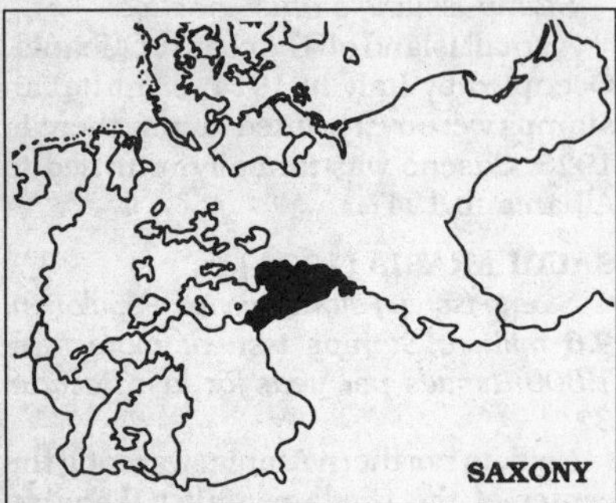

SAXONY (1850-67)

Stamp-issuing status: inactive; Population: 2.5 million (estimate); Stamps issued: 19.

Former kingdom in central Germany. Saxon issues were replaced by those of the North German Confederation in 1868.

SCARPANTO (1912-32)

Stamp-issuing status: inactive; Stamps issued: 26.

The Greek island of Karpathos in the Dodecanese Islands in the eastern Aegean Sea.

The island was obtained from Turkey by Italy in 1912. At that time, Italian stamps overprinted "Scarpanto," the Italian name for the island, were issued.

Scarpanto's issues were superseded by those of the Aegean Islands in 1929, although two sets were overprinted for the island in 1930 and 1932.

SCHLESWIG (1920)

Stamp-issuing status: inactive; Stamps issued: 42.

An area of the central Jutland Peninsula, in Germany and Denmark. Under German rule from 1864-1918, the province was divided into two districts after World War I.

A plebiscite in 1920 resulted in the northern portion voting to join Denmark and the southern district voting for reunion with Germany.

SCHLESWIG-HOLSTEIN (1850-67)

Stamp-issuing status: inactive; Population: 1.52 million (estimate); Stamps issued: 25.

Former duchies in northern Germany, forming the southern portion of the Jutland Peninsula. Under Danish control until 1864, the duchies were seized by Austria and Prussia, who subsequently fought the Austro-Prussian War (1866), after which they were absorbed by Prussia.

A plebiscite in 1920 resulted in northern Schleswig being returned to Denmark.

SCINDE (1852-54)

Stamp-issuing status: inactive; Stamps issued: 3.

A district on the lower Indus River, bordering on the Arabian Sea. Scinde is now part of Pakistan.

The Scinde was occupied by Great Britain in 1850 and separate stamps were used until their replacement by the first Indian issue in 1854.

SCUTARI (1909-11, 1915-20)

Stamp-issuing status: inactive.

A seaport in northern Albania. The Italian post office in Scutari used 10 overprinted Italian stamps from 1909-11 and during the World War I Italian occupation.

In December 1918, the Italians withdrew and Scutari was placed under an international commission to protect it from Serbia.

Until March 1920, various stamps were issued specifically for use in Scutari, after which time the city was placed under Albanian administration.

SEGOVIA (1937)

Stamp-issuing status: inactive.

A province of north-central Spain.

Contemporary Spanish stamps were overprinted by the National Civil Governor in October and November 1937.

SEIYUN, KATHIRI STATE OF (1942-67)

Stamp-issuing status: inactive; Stamps issued: 41.

A former British protectorate in south Arabia. The area was autonomous until its incorporation into the People's Republic of Southern Yemen.

SELANGOR (1881-)

Stamp-issuing status: active; Population: 1 million (1960 estimate); Stamps issued: more than 140; Stamps per year for last decade: 1.

Sultanate in the south Malay Peninsula. Selangor was under British protection after 1874 and joined the Federation of Malaya in 1948.

SENEGAL (1887-)

Stamp-issuing status: active; Population: 6.4 million; Stamps issued: more than 850; Issues per year for last decade: 28.

A republic on the west coast of Africa. The first French settlement began in 1626, and the area remained under either French or (temporarily) British rule.

After 1854, France used Senegal as its base for expansion in West Africa. In 1904 French West Africa was established, with its capital at Dakar, Senegal's capital. French West African stamps were used 1944-59.

In 1958, Senegal became an autonomous state within the French Union, and in 1959 it joined with the French Sudan to form the Federation of Mali. Senegal withdrew from the union in 1960, and on June 26, 1960, became independent. It retains close ties with France.

SENEGAMBIA AND NIGER (1903-06)

Stamp-issuing status: inactive; Stamps issued: 13.

A French African administrative unit (1902-04) comprising French holdings in the Senegal and Niger area.

In 1904, the area was renamed Upper Senegal and Niger, and in 1906, stamps of this new entity were released.

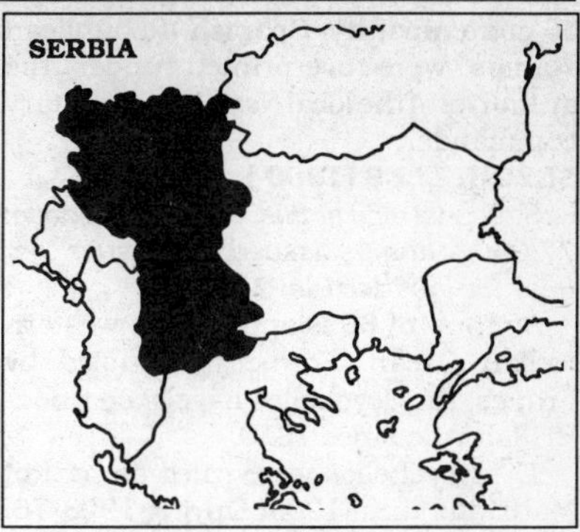

SERBIA (1866-1918, 1941-44)

Stamp-issuing status: inactive; Population: 3 million (1920 estimate); Stamps issued: 181.

A former state in the Balkans, now part of Yugoslavia. Serbia was a powerful kingdom until its conquest by the Turks in 1389.

Serbia gained autonomy in 1829 and independence in 1878. Serbia assumed leadership of the movement to unite the southern Slavs in the early 20th century, especially after the defeat of Turkey during the Balkan Wars (1912-13).

The assassination of the heir to the Austro-Hungarian crown by a Serbian nationalist in 1914 led to an Austro-Hungarian declaration of war on Serbia, which escalated into World War I.

By the end of 1915, Serbia was occupied by German, Austrian and Bulgarian forces, while the Serbian government and army retired to Corfu. Another 42 stamps were overprinted for use during this period.

With the collapse of Austria-Hungary in the autumn of 1918, Serbia became the nucleus of the Yugoslav state. The Kingdom of the Serbs, Croats and Slovenes was established on Dec. 1, 1918, under the Serbian monarchy. In 1929 the state was renamed Yugoslavia.

During 1941-44, Serbia was recreated as a German puppet state. An additional 126 stamps were issued during the war years.

SEVILLE (1936-38)

Stamp-issuing status: inactive.

A province in southern Spain.

During the Civil War, a large number

of contemporary Spanish Republican stamps were overprinted under the authority of the local Nationalist military commander.

SEYCHELLES (1890-)

Stamp-issuing status: active; Population: 77,000; Stamps issued: 6; Issues per year for last decade: 24.

A group of 86 islands in the western Indian Ocean. Formerly occupied by France, the Seychelles have been under British rule since 1810.

The Seychelles were ruled as part of Mauritius until 1903. During 1903-76, the islands were administered as a separate colony. Although the ruling party preferred to continue the Seychelles' association with Britain, sustained pressure from the Organization of African Unity and United Nations forced it to declare independence on June 29, 1976.

In 1977, the government was overthrown in a coup, and a socialist regime came to power. In 1979, opposition political parties were abolished. The U.S.S.R. has actively attempted to establish its influence in the country.

SHAN STATES (1943)

Stamp-issuing status: inactive.

During 1942-43, the Shan States of eastern Burma were separated from the puppet Burmese government established by the Japanese.

In December 1943, the Shan States were reincorporated into Burma, and their stamps were overprinted for use throughout the country.

SHANGHAI (1865-98)

Stamp-issuing status: inactive; Population: 3.49 million; Stamps issued: 192.

One of the major cities and ports of China. Shanghai was opened to European settlement in 1843. In 1864, dissatisfied with the high charges of the Chinese private postal agencies, Shanghai organized a postal system under the Municipal Council.

Agencies of the Shanghai Local Post eventually operated in 16 cities within China. In 1898 the service was integrated with those of the Chinese government.

SHANSI (1941-42)

Stamp-issuing status: inactive.

A province in northern China, west of Peking. Regular Chinese stamps were overprinted by occupying Japanese forces during World War II.

After 1945, the area was in Communist hands, using the stamps of North China (1946-50) and then of the Peking regime.

SHANTUNG (1941-42)

Stamp-issuing status: inactive.

A province of northern China, for which overprinted Chinese stamps were issued under the Japanese occupation.

SHARJAH (1963-72)

Stamp-issuing status: inactive.

A sheikdom in eastern Arabia on the Persian Gulf. One of the Trucial States under British protection from 1892-1971, Sharjah joined in the United Arab Emirates in 1971.

SIBENIK (SEBENICO) (1944)

Stamp-issuing status: inactive.

A city on the Adriatic coast of Yugoslavia. After Italy joined the Allies, the area was occupied by Croatian partisans, who overprinted Italian stamps for use in the region.

SIBERIA (1919-20)

Stamp-issuing status: inactive; Stamps issued: 10.

In November 1918, anti-Bolshevik forces in Siberia formed a moderate socialist government under Adm. Kolchak. The armies of this regime soon occupied most of Siberia and invaded European Russia. At one point, they threatened Moscow, but they were eventually routed by the Red Army in late 1919. The Red counteroffensive overthrew Kolchak in January 1920, and the Siberian state rapidly disintegrated.

SIERRA LEONE (1859-)

Stamp-issuing status: active; Population: 3.5 million; Stamps issued: more than 1,100; Issues per year for last decade: 51.

A republic in west Africa. The coastal area was occupied by Great Britain after 1791, the hinterland coming under British protection in 1896.

In 1961, Sierra Leone became independent. Long one of the most progressive of Britain's west African colonies, Sierra Leone's early political stability and economic growth have given way to coups, countercoups, rampant corruption and an economy heavily dependent on foreign aid.

SIMI (1912-32)

Stamp-issuing status: inactive; Stamps issued: 26.

One of the Dodecanese Islands in the eastern Aegean Sea. The area was obtained from Turkey by Italy in 1912, at which time Italian stamps overprinted "Simi" were issued.

These issues were superseded by the general issues for the Aegean Islands in 1919, although two sets, overprinted with the name of the island, were released in 1930 and 1932.

SINALOA (1929)

Stamp-issuing status: inactive; Stamps issued: 2.

A state of northern Mexico bordering on the Pacific Ocean. Sinaloa issued stamps briefly in 1929, during a revolution against the central government.

SINGAPORE (1948-)

Stamp-issuing status: active; Population: 2.6 million; Stamps issued: more than 525; Issues per year for last decade 23.

An island off the southern tip of the Malay Peninsula. Singapore was a British territory administered as part of the Straits Settlements from 1826 to 1942 and under Japanese occupation from 1942 to 1945.

In 1946, Singapore became a separate crown colony, joining with Malaya, Sarawak and Sabah in 1963 to form the Federation of Malaysia.

In 1965, Singapore withdrew from the federation and proclaimed itself an independent republic. Singapore has a dynamic economy and enjoys the second highest per-capita income in the Far East.

SINKIANG (1915-49)

Stamp-issuing status: inactive.

The westernmost province of China. Because the currency used in Sinkiang differed in value from that used in the rest of China, the province used overprinted Chinese issues until 1949, when the Communists assumed control.

SIRMOOR (1879-1902)

Stamp-issuing status: inactive; Population: 148,568; Stamps issued: 37.

A former feudatory state in northern India.

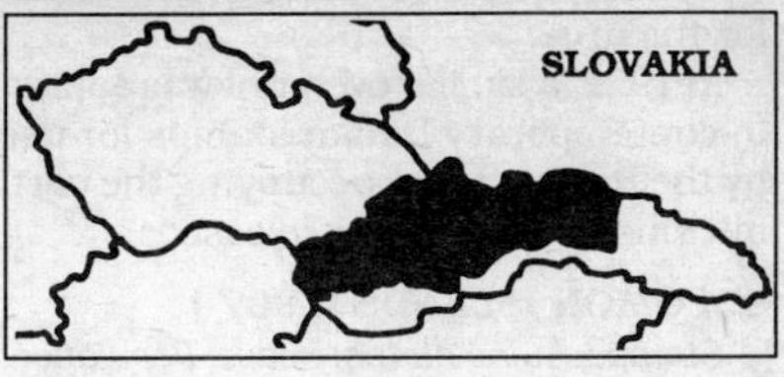

SLOVAKIA (1939-45)

Stamp-issuing status: inactive; Population: 2.5 million (1944 estimate); Stamps issued: 218.

A province in eastern Czechoslovakia. In March 1939, it declared its independence under German protection. In 1945, Slovakia was re-incorporated into Czechoslovakia.

SLOVENIA (1919-21, 1941-1945)

Stamp-issuing status: inactive; Stamps issued: 102.

A province of northwestern Yugoslavia. Slovenia was a part of Hungary until 1918, when it became part of the independent Kingdom of the Serbs, Croats and Slovenes. Slovenia issued stamps until 1921, when the first national issues were released.

During World War II, Slovenia was divided between Germany and Italy, both of which issued separate stamps for their zones. After the war, the province was re-occupied by Yugoslavia, and overprinted stamps of the German occupation (Ljubljana), Germany proper, and Hungary were used, until replaced by regular Yugoslav issues.

SMILTEN (1919)

Stamp-issuing status: inactive.

A city in Latvia. Russian stamps were surcharged by the municipal authorities for local use in 1919.

SMOLENSK (1922)

Stamp-issuing status: inactive.

A city in western Russia. Surcharged Russian stamps were issued for local use by the city authorities in 1922.

SMYRNA (1909-14, 1919)

Stamp-issuing status: inactive.

The major port of western Turkey. The Italian and Russian post offices in the city used stamps of Italy and the Russian Levant, respectively, overprinted with the name of the city.

During the Greek occupation of 1919-22, overprinted Greek stamps were issued for the area.

In 1922, a similar overprint was applied to contemporary Italian stamps for use by the Italian forces occupying the port, but this set was never released.

SOLOMON ISLANDS (1907-)

Stamp-issuing status: active; Population: 249,000; Stamps issued: more than 580; Issues per year for last decade: 23.

A group of islands in the western South Pacific. The islands were a British protectorate designated as the British Solomon Islands until 1975, when, as the group approached independence, the "British" was dropped. The Solomons became self-governing in 1976 and fully independent in 1978.

SOMALIA (1903-)

Stamp-issuing status: active; Population: 6.4 million; Stamps issued: more than 700; Issues per year for last decade: 15.

An area on the eastern coast of Africa. The colony was established as Italian Somaliland in 1905.

In 1936, it was merged with Eritrea and Ethiopia to form Italian East Africa. In 1941, the area was occupied by Great Britain, which held it until 1950, using overprinted British stamps.

In 1950, the area was returned to Italy, under a U.N. trusteeship. In 1960, the area became independent, merging with the former British Somaliland Protectorate to form the Republic of Somalia.

In 1970, the nation's name was changed to the Somali Democratic Republic.

A military coup in 1969 brought an increasingly socialistic regime to power. Relations with the U.S.S.R. strengthened, and a major Soviet naval base was established at Berbera.

Soviet-Somali relations cooled when Moscow switched its support to Ethiopia in the two nations' dispute over the Ogaden, a large eastern region of Ethiopia populated primarily by Somalis. In 1977, Soviet advisors were expelled from Somalia.

In 1978, Somali forces were expelled from the Ogaden by Ethiopian and Cuban troops. Over one million Somali refugees from the region have fled to Somalia.

SOMALI COAST (1894-1967)

Stamp-issuing status: inactive; Population: 86,000 (1967 estimate); Stamps issued: 378.

A former French African colony on the Gulf of Aden. In 1967, the colony's name was changed to the French Territory of the Afars and Issas. In 1977, the name was changed to Djibouti.

SOMALILAND PROTECTORATE (1903-60)

Stamp-issuing status: inactive; Population: 650,000 (1960 estimate); Stamps issued: 158.

A former British protectorate in eastern Africa, bordering on the Gulf of Aden. The area was occupied by Italy from 1940-41.

On June 26, 1960, the territory became independent as part of the Somali Republic.

SOPRON (1956-57)

Stamp-issuing status: inactive.

A town in western Hungary. During the 1956 anti-Communist uprising, contemporary Hungarian stamps were overprinted for use in the area held by the rebels.

SOSNOWICE (1916)

Stamp-issuing status: inactive.

A city in southern Poland. Local stamps were issued by the municipal authorities during the World War I Austrian occupation.

SOUTH AFRICA (1910-)

Stamp-issuing status: active; Population: 32 million; Stamps issued: more than 670; Issues per year for last decade: 19.

Republic occupying the southernmost portion of Africa. In 1910, the British colonies of Cape of Good Hope, Natal, Transvaal and Orange River Colony united to form the Union of South Africa, a self-governing dominion within the British Commonwealth.

In 1961, the republic was established.

Since 1948, South African internal policy has been based on apartheid, a program of separate development of the races. This policy has reserved for the white minority (17.5 percent of the population) the best jobs, political control of the government, and much higher wages than those of other ethnic groups. The plan aims at the eventual creation of a large number of independent ethnic states.

Four black states (Bantustans) have been created to date: Transkei (1976); Bophuthatswana (1977); Venda (1979); and Ciskei (1981). None has received international recognition. All issue stamps that are routinely used within their borders. Some catalog editors, for political reasons, have not included them in their listings.

South Africa has been ostracized by most of the nations of the world because of apartheid. Its economic strength, however, and the economic dependence of its black African neighbors traditionally enabled the country to prosper.

Outside of the country, opposition to apartheid has increased greatly, not least in the United States, which prohibited importation of South African stamps effective Nov. 24, 1986.

SOUTH ARABIA (1959-67)

Stamp-issuing status: inactive; Population: 771,000; Stamps issued: 29.

A former federation of British territories in southwestern Arabia. South Arabia became independent in 1967 as the People's Republic of Southern Yemen.

SOUTH AUSTRALIA (1855-1913)

Stamp-issuing status: inactive; Population: 360,000 (1901 estimate); Stamps issued: 241.

A state of Australia, occupying the south-central part of the continent. South Australia was a British colony from 1836 to 1901, when it joined with five other colonies to form the Commonwealth of Australia.

SOUTH BULGARIA (1885-86)

Stamp-issuing status: inactive; Stamps issued: 40.

The former province of Eastern Rumelia in the southeast Balkans. In September 1885, a coup overthrew the nominally Turkish administration and established South Bulgaria, uniting with Bulgaria.

Bulgarian stamps replaced those of South Bulgaria in 1886.

SOUTH CHINA (1949-50)

Stamp-issuing status: inactive.

The Communist South China Liberation Area included the provinces of Kwangtung and Kwangsi. Regional issues were used after the occupation of Canton.

SOUTH GEORGIA (1963-79)

Stamp-issuing status: inactive; Population: 25 (1975 estimate); Stamps issued: 67.

An island in the South Atlantic Ocean. In 1962, when neighboring areas were detached from the Falkland Islands to become the British Antarctic Territory, South Georgia remained a Falklands' dependency.

SOUTH GEORGIA AND SOUTH SANDWICH ISLANDS (1986-)

Stamp-issuing status: active; Population: 500 (1987); Stamps issued: more than 20.

Two groups of islands in the extreme south Atlantic Ocean, South Georgia is about 875 miles east southeast of the Falkland Islands and about 1,000 miles equidistant from Cape Horn and the tip of the Antarctic Peninsula. The even more remote and southerly South Sandwich Islands are uninhabited.

The last remaining component of the Falkland Islands Dependencies, South Georgia and the South Sandwich Islands assumed its new title in 1985 and issued stamps beginning the following year.

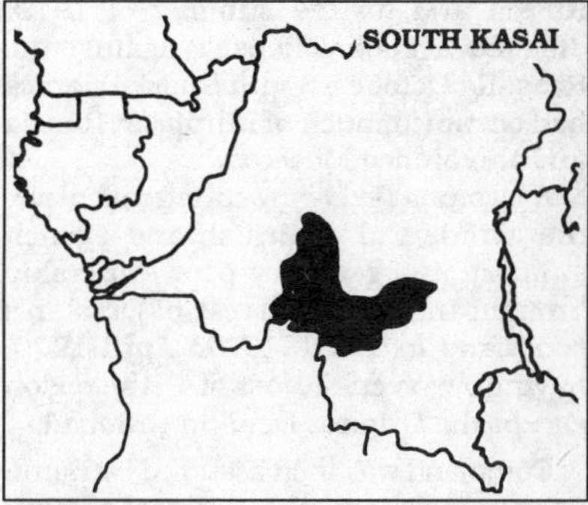

SOUTH KASAI (1961)

Stamp-issuing status: inactive; Stamps issued: 30.

A district of Zaire that declared itself autonomous after the Congo became independent from Belgium. This revolt was subsequently suppressed by the Belgian Congo central government.

SOUTH MOLUCCAS (1950)

Stamp-issuing status: inactive.

A group of islands in the Indonesian archipelago, west of New Guinea.

During 1950, the South Moluccas revolted against the Indonesian central government and overprinted 17 Dutch Indies and Indonesian stamps "Republik

Maluku Selatan." These stamps were apparently placed into local use.

The main island, Amboina, was occupied by Indonesian troops in November 1950, although Moluccan resistance continued in the outer islands until 1955.

During 1951-54, a long series of South Moluccan issues were marketed in the U.S., but there is no evidence that these were ever actually used in the areas under Moluccan control.

Some 35,000 South Moluccans emigrated to the Netherlands, and among this group nationalist sentiments still run high.

SOUTH RUSSIA (1919-21)

Stamp-issuing status: inactive; Stamps issued: 52.

In October 1918, the Volunteer Army, composed primarily of veterans of the Russian Imperial Army, was formed under the command of Gen. Denikin. Denikin soon assumed leadership of almost all of the anti-Bolshevik elements in southern Russia and, in the summer of 1919, directed a major offensive against the Reds. By October, South Russian forces had occupied much of European Russia and threatened Moscow.

A vigorous Red Army counteroffensive, the withdrawal of British and French support, and generally poor leadership brought the rapid collapse of Denikin's command in late 1919. In April 1920, having overseen the loss of all the region except the Crimea, Denikin resigned.

Command was then assumed by Baron Peter Wrangel, probably the most effective of the White Russian leaders. Wrangel's administration of the Russian territories reflected an understanding of the economic goals of the revolution. Unfortunately, his superiors kept him from assuming a leadership position that equaled his talents, until the White Russian cause had been lost by less able leaders.

Wrangel consolidated the Volunteer Army and held the Crimea until November 1920, when the army and its dependents were evacuated. The remnants of the South Russian forces temporarily settled in a number of refugee camps in Turkey and the Balkans, and a large number of Russian, Ukrainian and South Russian stamps were overprinted and surcharged for use in the camps. These issues were used until the camps were shut down in June 1921.

SOUTHERN NIGERIA (1901-14)

Stamp-issuing status: inactive; Population: 8.5 million (1912 estimate); Stamps issued: 56.

A former administrative unit comprised of British holdings in southern Nigeria. In 1914, it was merged with Northern Nigeria to form the Colony and Protectorate of Nigeria.

SOUTHERN RHODESIA (1924-53, 1964-65)

Stamp-issuing status: inactive; Population: 4 million (1964 estimate); Stamps issued: 113.

A former British colony in southeastern Africa. Administered as part of Rhodesia until 1923, Southern Rhodesia was ruled as a separate colony from 1923 to 1953.

The territory was part of the Federation of Rhodesia and Nyasaland from 1953 to 1964, and again became a separate colony from 1964 to 1965.

In 1965, the controlling white minority declared Southern Rhodesia independent of Great Britain.

SOUTH-WEST AFRICA (NAMIBIA) (1923-)

Stamp-issuing status: active; Population: 1.18 million; Stamps issued: more than 475; Issues per year for last decade: 18.

A territory in southwestern Africa. South-West Africa was a German colony until 1915, when it was occupied by the Union of South Africa.

It has since been administered by South Africa, originally under a mandate from the League of Nations.

In 1968, the U.N. General Assembly, in response to demands by 36 African states, created a council to administer the region, which was renamed Namibia. South Africa refused to transfer control, and in 1970, South Africa's action was condemned by the U.N. Security Council.

A 1977 pre-independence referendum (in which only whites could vote) was rejected by black nationalist groups, and the Marxist group, SWAPO, began a guerrilla war against South Africa.

Stamps of South-West Africa were

included in the prohibition against importing South African stamps into the United States that came into effect Nov. 24, 1986.

SOUTHWEST CHINA (1949-50)

Stamp-issuing status: inactive.

The Communist Southwest China Liberation Area included the provinces of Kweichow, Szechwan, Yunnan, Sikang and Tibet.

SPAIN (1850-)

Stamp-issuing status: active; Population: 38.2 million; Stamps issued: more than 2,900; Issues per year for last decade: 48.

A kingdom in southwestern Europe, occupying the greater part of the Iberian Peninsula. Part of the Roman Empire from the second century B.C. until the fourth century A.D., Spain was subsequently overrun by Germanic tribes, which formed the Kingdom of the Visigoths (West Goths) until 711.

The Arabs invaded Spain in that year, soon occupying all of the peninsula except a few Christian enclaves in the north.

During the Middle Ages, Spain was reconquered by the Christians, who gradually pushed the Arabs south in a series of wars lasting from the 9th century until 1492, when the Arab stronghold of Granada fell.

During this period, the states of Aragon and Castile came to include most of modern Spain, and the marriage of Ferdinand of Aragon and Isabella of Castile brought the union of the two states and the beginning of modern Spain.

Spain's conquest of Granada in 1492, and the discovery of America by Columbus in the same year, brought Spain rapidly into the position of a great power.

During the 16th century, Spain built a vast American empire and dominated western European affairs. Spanish power peaked c. 1580, when the Spanish king became king of Portugal as well, bringing that nation's empire under Spanish rule.

The rise of the Netherlands, which overthrew Spanish rule in the late 16th century, along with the growing power of Britain on the seas and France on the Continent, marked the beginning of a long decline for Spain. Although she continued to rule a huge American empire, by 1700 Spain had become a second-class power.

During the Napoleonic Wars, Spain was conquered by France, and Napoleon's brother, Joseph, was placed on the Spanish throne. Spain's colonies refused to accept Joseph's rule and proclaimed their allegiance to the legitimate monarch, Ferdinand VII. Because of this instability, Spain's American colonies were, in effect, self-governing for most of two decades.

With Ferdinand's restoration in 1815, Spain attempted to regain control of her American colonies. Unwilling to return to their subservient status, the colonies revolted, and by the mid-1820s, Spanish rule had been overthrown on the American mainland. Lacking the wealth of her empire, Spain was thereafter a cipher in European affairs.

In 1898-99, Spain was defeated by the U.S. in the Spanish-American War, losing her last American (Cuba and Puerto Rico) and Pacific (the Philippines and Guam) colonies.

In 1931, the monarchy was ousted by a leftist republican movement, which instituted many liberal reforms but was unable to restore order in the country.

On July 18, 1936, a conservative army officer, Francisco Franco Bahamonde, led a mutiny against the regime in Morocco, beginning the Spanish Civil War (1936-39). Franco was supported by Germany and Italy, while the Republicans were supported by the U.S.S.R.

The Spanish Civil War was in effect a dress rehearsal for World War II. The efficacy of modern weapons, the emphasis upon aircraft as a primary combat tool, and the principle of total war (against civilian as well as military personnel) were tested here.

After a bloody war in which one million died, the Nationalists defeated the Republicans, and Franco assumed complete control of the country.

During World War II, Spain remained neutral, much to the disgust and frustration of Franco's German and Italian allies. Despite this, in 1946, because of the regime's close fascist associations, Spain was expelled from the United Nations. It was re-admitted in 1955.

In 1947, Franco declared Spain a

monarchy and provided for his succession by an heir to the Bourbon dynasty, overthrown by the Republicans in 1931. Upon his death in November 1975, Prince Juan Carlos assumed the crown.

Juan Carlos immediately dissolved the harsher institutions of the Franco regime, and in June 1976, free elections brought moderates and democratic socialists to power.

A right-wing coup in February 1981 failed, when the army remained loyal to the government.

SPAIN — CARLIST GOVERNMENT (1873-75)

Stamp-issuing status: inactive; Stamps issued: 7.

In 1833, King Ferdinand VII abrogated the Salic Law (requiring succession through the male line), so that his daughter, Isabella, could succeed him on the Spanish throne. Ferdinand's brother, Don Carlos, who would otherwise have assumed the throne, refused to accept this, and upon Ferdinand's death in 1834 pressed his claim. This brought the First Carlist War of 1834-39.

In 1872, Don Carlos' grandson, also named Don Carlos, re-asserted his family's claim and soon controlled large areas in northern Spain. The establishment of a republican regime in Madrid in 1873 brought many Spanish monarchists into his camp.

In December 1875, the Spanish monarchy was restored, and the Carlists rapidly lost ground. By February 1876, the Carlist movement had collapsed completely.

SPAIN — CIVIL WAR MUNICIPAL ISSUES (1936-37)

Stamp-issuing status: inactive.

During the Spanish Civil War, many cities and districts on both sides issued provisional overprints on Spanish postage and fiscal issues.

These were used as propaganda, as controls to distinguish regular stocks of stamps from looted stocks, and as profit-making philatelic productions.

Among those overprints legitimately used are those of Burgos, Cadiz, the Canary Islands, Malaga, San Sebastian, Santa Cruz de Tenerife and Seville.

SPANISH GUINEA (1902-60)

Stamp-issuing status: inactive; Population: 210,000 (1959 estimate); Stamps issued: 446.

Former Spanish colony in western Africa, bordering on the Gulf of Guinea. The territory is comprised of Rio Muni, Fernando Po (after 1909), and Elobey, Annobon and Corisco (after 1909).

Fernando Po and Rio Muni were separated in 1960, reuniting in 1968 to form the independent Republic of Equatorial Guinea.

SPANISH MOROCCO (1903-56)

Stamp-issuing status: inactive; Population: 1 million (1955 estimate); Stamps issued: 523.

The northern portion of Morocco, administered by Spain until 1956, when it was merged into the independent Kingdom of Morocco.

SPANISH SAHARA (SPANISH WESTERN SAHARA) (1924-76)

Stamp-issuing status: inactive; Population: 76,000 (1975 estimate); Stamps issued: 322.

A former Spanish possession in northwestern Africa, comprising Cape Juby, La Aguera and Rio de Oro. A large (100,000 square mile), sparsely populated (12,793 in 1960) area, the Spanish Sahara is mostly desert and was of little interest to outsiders until the discovery of rich phosphate deposits.

From the 1960s, Morocco, Mauritania and Algeria all pressed claims to the area. In November 1975, thousands of unarmed Moroccans crossed into the territory (the "Green March"), and in February 1976, Spain withdrew from the colony. The Spanish Sahara was divided between Morocco and Mauritania, although a nationalist group, Polisario, declared the area independent and, with Algerian support, continues to wage a guerrilla war against Morocco and Mauritania.

In 1980, Mauritania made peace with Polisario and gave up its portion of the area to Morocco. Fighting between Polisario and Morocco continues.

SPANISH WEST AFRICA (1949-51)

Stamp-issuing status: inactive; Population: 95,000 (1951 estimate); Stamps issued: 26.

The former administrative unit comprising the Spanish colonies of Ifni, Spanish Sahara and southern Morocco.

SPASSK (1920-22)

Stamp-issuing status: inactive.

A city in central Russia. Russian stamps were overprinted with new values by the local authorities.

SRI LANKA (1972-)

Stamp-issuing status: active; Population: 16.3 million (1985); Stamps issued: more than 375; Issues per year for last decade: 33.

The name of Ceylon was officially changed to Sri Lanka on May 22, 1972.

STAMPALIA (1912-32)

Stamp-issuing status: inactive; Stamps issued (total): 26.

The westernmost of the Dodecanese Islands in the eastern Aegean Sea. Now the Greek island of Astipalaia.

Stampalia was obtained from Turkey by Italy in 1912, at which time 10 Italian stamps overprinted "Stampalia" were issued, with an additional surcharge added in 1916.

The island's stamps were superseded by those of the Aegean Islands in 1929, although two sets totaling 15 stamps were overprinted for use in Stampalia in 1930 and 1932.

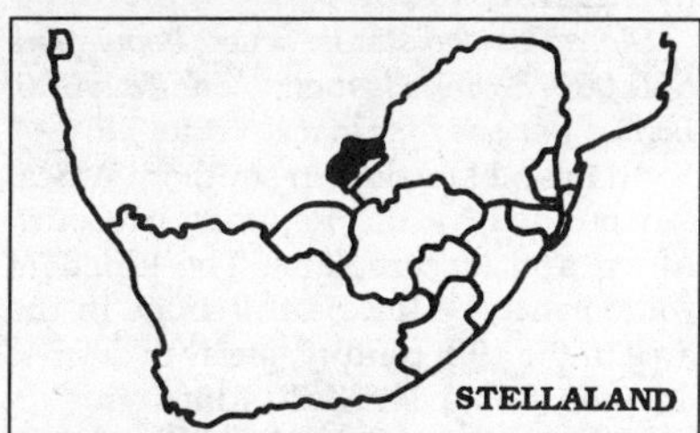

STELLALAND (1884-85)

Stamp-issuing status: inactive; Stamps issued: 6.

A short-lived Boer republic in southern Africa. The republic was suppressed by Great Britain in 1885 and was incorporated into British Bechuanaland.

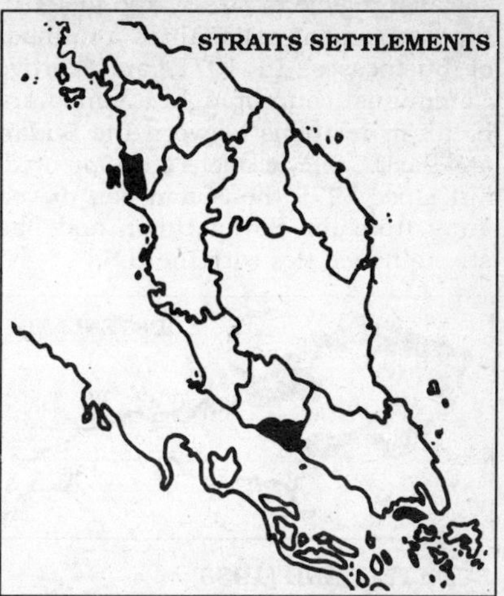

STRAITS SETTLEMENTS (1867-1946)

Stamp-issuing status: inactive; Population: 1.44 million (estimate); Stamps issued: 270.

Former British colony in Malaya, comprising Singapore, Penang, Province Wellesley and Malacca, along with the dependencies of the Cocos (Keeling) Islands, Christmas Island and Labuan.

Prior to 1867, unoverprinted British Indian stamps were in use. The colony was occupied by Japan in 1942-45 and dissolved in 1946.

SUDAN (1897-)

Stamp-issuing status: active; Population: 21.4 million; Stamps issued: more than 400; Issues per year for last decade: 6.

A republic in northeastern Africa, south of Egypt. Under Egyptian control from 1820 to 1885, the Sudan was united under native control after the Mahdi led a religious war against foreigners from 1881 to 1885.

In 1898, the area was reconquered by the British, and an Anglo-Egyptian condominium was established. In 1954, the Sudan became self-governing and, on Jan. 1, 1956, became an independent republic.

Since its independence, Sudan has fought a prolonged civil war in the southern third of the country, where the predominantly black, pagan population seeks independence from the Arab, Moslem north.

In 1969, a military coup brought a socialist regime to power, and in 1970, the government nationalized a number of businesses. In 1971, an abortive Communist coup brought a temporary break in relations between the Sudan and the U.S.S.R. Relations later improved, but since 1975 the Sudan has moved away from the Soviet Union and has strengthened ties with the U.S.

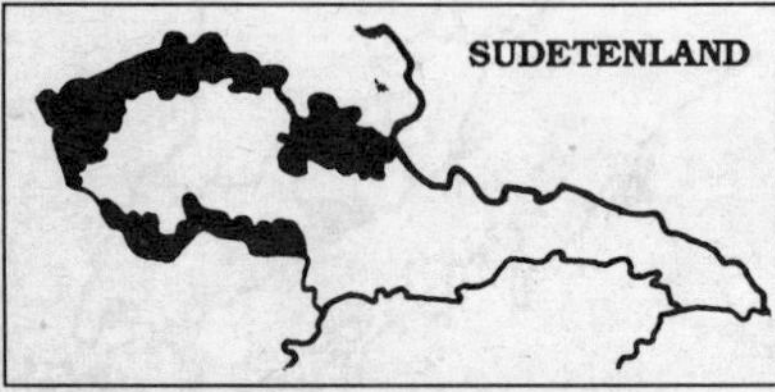

SUDETENLAND (1938)

Stamp-issuing status: inactive.

The western border area of Czechoslovakia in which the majority of the population is German-speaking. After the Munich Agreement of Sept. 21, 1938, transferring the region to Germany, local Nazis seized control, pending formal German annexation on Oct. 1.

A host of Czechoslovakian stamps overprinted "Wir sind frei" (We are free) were used during this brief period in Asch, Karlsbad, Konstantinsbad, Niklasdorf, Reichenberg-Maffersdorf, Mahrisch-Ostran and Ramburg.

SUEZ CANAL (1868)

Stamp-issuing status: inactive.

During 1859-69, the Compagnie Universelle du Canal Maritime de Suez constructed the Suez Canal in Egypt, linking the Mediterranean and Red seas.

Until 1867, the company transported mail between Port Said and Suez for free. The company then decided charges for this service, and in July 1868, special stamps were issued.

The stamps were not popular and were withdrawn from sale Aug. 16, 1868. They were demonetized Aug. 31, and the service was taken over by the Egyptian government.

SUNGEI UJONG (1878-95)

Stamp-issuing status: inactive; Stamps issued: 32.

Former Federated Malay State under British protection. The territory was incorporated into Negri Sembilan in 1895.

SUPEH (1941-42)

Stamp-issuing status: inactive.

A province of central China, for which overprinted Chinese stamps were issued during the Japanese occupation.

SURINAM (1873-)

Stamp-issuing status: active; Population: 375,000; Stamps issued: more than 1,200; Issues per year for last decade: 42.

A state in northern South America. Disputed by Great Britain, France and the Netherlands during the 17th-18th centuries, Surinam became a Dutch possession after 1815.

In 1954, Surinam, along with the Netherlands Antilles, became an integral part of the Kingdom of the Netherlands.

In 1975, it became fully independent at the initiative of the Netherlands. Some 40 percent of Surinam's population (mostly East Indians) emigrated to the Netherlands in the period immediately prior to independence.

SWAHILILAND (WITU) (1889)

Stamp-issuing status: inactive; Stamps issued: 96.

Until the late 19th century, the Sultan of Zanzibar controlled much of the coast of East Africa. Germany secured concessions from the sultan in the area around Lamu, Kenya, which in 1890 were ceded to Britain as part of the settlement for the British transfer of Heligoland to Germany. Prior to this (July-August 1889) the German postal agent at Lamu printed and issued stamps for use in the region.

SWAZILAND (1889-)

Stamp-issuing status: active; Population: 560,000; Stamps issued: more than 500; Issues per year for last decade: 25.

An inland kingdom in southern Africa, surrounded by the Republic of South Africa and Mozambique. The kingdom was formed by the Bantu tribes in the area in the 19th century, partly in defense against the warlike Zulu Kingdom.

In 1881, Great Britain and the South African Republic (Transvaal) guaranteed Swaziland's independence. During 1894-99, the state was under the protection of the Transvaal and, after 1902, came under British administration.

In 1963, it was recognized as a British

protectorate and, on Sept. 6, 1968, became independent.

Swaziland is an absolute monarchy. Its fertile lands and abundant mineral resources have made significant economic growth possible. It is closely linked with South Africa, and a handful of South African whites dominate the economy.

SWEDEN (1855-)

Stamp-issuing status: active; Population: 8.4 million; Stamps issued: more than 1,830; Issues per year for last decade: 48.

Constitutional monarchy in northern Europe, occupying the eastern portion of the Scandinavian Peninsula. Militaristic expansion in the 17th century made the Baltic Sea a Swedish lake, but after 1709, a series of defeats stripped Sweden of most of her empire.

In 1813, Sweden joined in the war against Napoleon, receiving Norway (independent 1905) as compensation.

Sweden has since maintained a policy of armed neutrality and has devoted her energies to social and industrial development.

Although long under a socialist government, some 91 percent of the economy is privately owned. Swedish social programs are extensive, although in recent years the high cost of maintaining them has encouraged the growth of a black market of goods and services unreported to the tax collector.

SWITZERLAND (1850-)

Stamp-issuing status: active; Population: 6.5 million; Stamps issued: 1,400; Issues per year for last decade: 27.

A land-locked federation in central Europe, situated between France, Germany, Austria and Italy. The country has three official languages: German, French and Italian.

The nucleus of modern Switzerland appeared in the late 13th century, and in 1648, the Confederation became independent. Switzerland has not been involved in a foreign war since 1515 and, learning the lesson of Napoleon's seizure of the country, has since 1815 maintained armed neutrality.

Switzerland has no military alliances and does not belong to the United Nations, although it participates in a number of U.N. programs and has U.N offices in Geneva. In recent years, there has been some pressure within the Swiss government to join the organization officially.

The stability of Switzerland and of the Swiss franc has made the country one of the world's banking centers.

SYRIA (1919-)

Stamp-issuing status: active; Population: 10.5 million; Stamps issued: more than 1,950; Issues per year for last decade: 34.

A republic in western Asia, bordering on the Mediterranean Sea.

Under Turkish control after 1516, Syria was occupied by the Allies late in World War II. British and French forces occupied the coastal areas, while the interior was taken by an Arab Army, led by T.E. Lawrence ("Lawrence of Arabia") and Faisal, son of King Hussein of the Hejaz.

Lawrence and Faisal established an independent government, which claimed authority over Lebanon, Jordan, Palestine and Iraq, as well as Syria. This regime was recognized by a Syrian congress, but France soon overthrew the government and occupied the country.

Faisal was compensated by being made king of Iraq, which his family ruled until 1958.

In 1922, France assumed formal control of Syria under a League of Nations mandate. In 1941, a republic government was established, and the country became independent, although French troops remained until 1946.

Syria was united with Egypt during 1958-61. Since 1963, it has been ruled by the Baathist party, a socialist, pan-Arab group.

Syria is one of the "front-line" Arab states opposing Israel and is now the chief occupation force in Lebanon (with which Syria was then united). It has received massive military aid from the Soviet Union, as well as annual subsidies from the oil-rich Arab states. It has consistently taken a hard line against Israel, although in recent years there has been some rapprochement with the West.

SZECHWAN (1933-36)

Stamp-issuing status: inactive.

A province in southern China. For a time, surcharged Chinese issues were used in the province because of the devaluation of the local currency.

SZEGED (1919)

Stamp-issuing status: inactive.

A city in southern Hungary. Between May and November 1919, Szeged was the seat of the anti-Bolshevik Hungarian National Government, under Admiral Horthy. The occupying French forces prevented Horthy from attacking the Bolsheviks, but after the fall of the regime, the Nationalists occupied Budapest and established the National Republic.

In June 1919, the Horthy government overprinted 49 Hungarian issues for use in the area under its authority.

- T -

TAHITI (1882-93, 1903, 1915)

Stamp-issuing status: inactive; Stamps issued: 59.

An island in the South Pacific. A former French colony, Tahiti merged into French Polynesia in 1893. Except for the issues of 1903 and 1915, stamps of French Polynesia have been in use since 1893.

TAIWAN (FORMOSA) (1886-95, 1945-50)

Stamp-issuing status: active; Population: 19.7 million; Stamps issued: more than 1,650; Issues per year for last decade: 53.

Island off the coast of China, in the west Pacific Ocean. Formosa was a Chinese province until 1895, when it was ceded to Japan.

Local Chinese inhabitants objected and proclaimed an independent republic, which was soon suppressed by Japanese forces.

In 1945, it was re-occupied by China and, in 1949, became the last stronghold of Nationalist resistance to the Communists.

The Republic of China on Taiwan has continued to operate independently since that time.

TAMMERFORS (1866-81)

Stamp-issuing status: inactive.

A city in west-central Finland. Several issues were made by the local postmaster for use within his district.

TANGANYIKA (1921-35, 1961-64)

Stamp-issuing status: inactive; Population: 9.5 million (1962 estimate); Stamps issued: 87.

The major portion of the former German East Africa colony, placed under British administration after World War I.

A part of Kenya, Uganda and Tanganyika after 1935, it became independent on Dec. 9, 1961. In 1964, it merged with Zanzibar to become the United Republic of Tanganyika and Zanzibar, renamed Tanzania in 1965.

TANGIER (1927-57)

Stamp-issuing status: inactive.

In 1923, Great Britain, France and Spain declared Tangier, in northern Morocco, an international zone.

Stamps of French Morocco and Spanish Morocco, as well as special British, French and Spanish issues for Tangier, were used.

In 1957, the city was annexed by Morocco.

TANZANIA (1965-)

Stamp-issuing status: active; Population: 22.4 million; Stamps issued: more than 400; Issues per year for last decade: 28.

A republic in southeastern Africa, bordering on the Indian Ocean. The territory formed with the union of Tanganyika and Zanzibar in 1964 as the United Republic of Tanganyika and Zanzibar.

In October 1965, the name was changed to the United Republic of Tanzania.

Tanzania has maintained socialist policies at home and a neutral policy in its foreign affairs. Its relations with its two northern neighbors, Kenya and Uganda, have been strained. During 1978-79, clashes occurred with Uganda, culminating in a successful Tanzanian invasion, which overthrew Ugandan dictator Idi Amin.

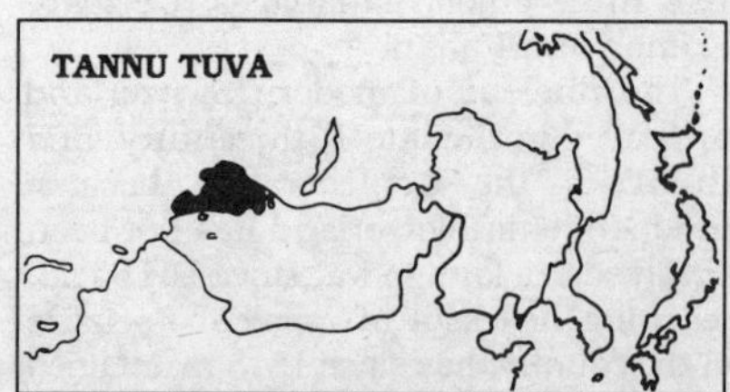

TANNU TUVA (1926-34)

Stamp-issuing status: inactive; Population: 65,000 (estimate); Stamps issued:

38.

An area in northern Asia between Mongolia and Siberia. Long disputed between Russia and China, the district was established in 1926 as an independent republic under Soviet protection.

In 1946, it was absorbed into the Soviet Union.

TASMANIA (VAN DIEMAN'S LAND) (1853-1913)

Stamp-issuing status: inactive; Population: 172,000 (1901 estimate); Stamps issued: 117.

Island off the southeastern coast of Australia. A dependency of the British colony of New South Wales from 1803 to 1825, the island became the colony of Van Dieman's Land in 1825.

In 1856, the name of the colony was changed to Tasmania. In 1901, Tasmania joined in the Commonwealth of Australia.

TELSIAI (TELSCHEN) (1941)

Stamp-issuing status: inactive.

A city in northwestern Lithuania. A total of 25 different overprinted Russian stamps were issued by the German military commander of the area during July and August 1941.

TEMESVAR (1919)

Stamp-issuing status: inactive.

A district of the Banat, occupied by Serbia after World War I. After the Serbian evacuation, Romanian forces occupied the area, and Temesvar was subsequently annexed by Serbia.

Both Serbian and Romanian forces overprinted a total of 16 Hungarian stamps for use in the area.

TERUEL (1937)

Stamp-issuing status: inactive.

A province in northeastern Spain. Overprinted Spanish stamps were issued in 1937 by the local Nationalist authorities.

TETE (1913-14)

Stamp-issuing status: inactive; Population: 367,000 (estimate); Stamps issued: 40.

Formerly a district of Zambezia in the colony of Portuguese East Africa, Tete now is part of western Mozambique.

TETUAN (1908-09)

Stamp-issuing status: inactive.

A city in northern Morocco, formerly part of Spanish Morocco. The city name was handstamped on 15 Spanish and Spanish Offices in Morocco stamps for use there in 1908.

THAILAND (SIAM) (1883-)

Stamp-issuing status: active; Population: 51 million; Stamps issued: more than 1,250; Issues per year for last decade: 36.

A kingdom in southeast Asia. After 1350, Thailand was the dominant power in the Malaya-Indo-China region.

European encroachments in the 19th century reduced this power, although Thailand, alone among the native states of the region, was able to maintain its independence.

An ally of Japan during World War II, Thailand was able to re-occupy some of its lost territory. These were given up when, in 1945, the Thai government repudiated its declaration of war against Great Britain and the U.S.

After World War II, Thailand aligned itself with the West. During the Vietnamese War, Thai troops were active in South Vietnam (until 1972) and in Laos (until 1974). Since that time, it has been under increasing pressure from Laos and Cambodia, which support Communist guerrillas within Thailand.

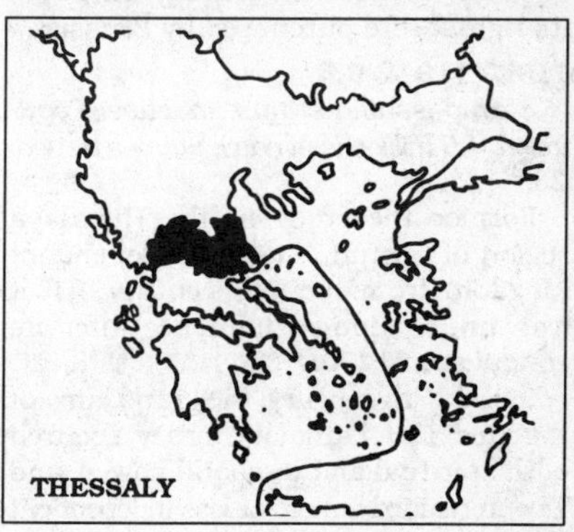

THESSALY (1898)

Stamp-issuing status: inactive.

During the Turko-Greek War of 1898, a set of five octagonal stamps was issued for use by the Turkish forces in Thessaly.

THRACE (1913-20)

Stamp-issuing status: inactive; Stamps issued: 128.

A district in the southeastern Balkans, bordering on the Aegean and Black Seas.

Under Turkish rule from the 14th century, the western portion of Thrace was occupied by Bulgaria in 1912. In 1913, an autonomous Moslem regime briefly ousted the Bulgarians. During its ephemeral existence, this regime issued lithographed stamps, as well as overprints on Turkish, Greek and Bulgarian issues.

In 1913 western Thrace was incorporated into Bulgaria, using regular Bulgarian issues. In October 1918, this area was taken from Bulgaria by the Allies, who overprinted Bulgarian stamps for use in the zone. In May 1920, western Thrace was mandated to Greece, and in August, Greece annexed the territory.

Eastern Thrace remained in Turkish hands until 1918, when it, too, was occupied by the Allies. Like the western portion of the province, it was turned over to Greece in 1920. After the Greek defeat in the Graeco-Turkish War (1922), it was returned to Turkey.

THURN AND TAXIS (1852-67)

Stamp-issuing status: inactive; Stamps issued: 54.

A princely house that maintained a postal monopoly in central Europe from the 16th century until 1806.

After 1815, it operated postal services in parts of western Germany. In 1867, its rights were purchased by Prussia.

TIBET (1912-65)

Stamp-issuing status: inactive; Population: 1.5 million (estimate); Stamps issued: 23.

Former theocracy in the Himalaya region of central Asia. An independent kingdom from the 7th century, Tibet was under Mongol influence after its conquest in 1270.

In the 17th century, the grand lama of the Red Hat Lamaistic order secured both spiritual and temporal power, and Tibet remained a more or less independent state under the grand lamas until 1904, after which British influence was strong.

During 1910-12, a pro-Chinese regime was in power, but Chinese troops were withdrawn following the 1912 Revolution, and Tibet again became independent.

In 1950, eastern Tibet was seized by China, and in 1953, a communist government was installed in Tibet itself, supplanting the theocratic regime of the Dalai Lama.

In 1956, a Tibetan revolt within China spread to Tibet, resulting in the dissolution of the Tibetan government in 1959. Although the uprising was crushed ruthlessly (charges of genocide were made against the Chinese in 1961), periodic uprisings have broken out as recently as 1976.

TIENTSIN (1900-22)

Stamp-issuing status: inactive.

A diagonal "China" handstamp was added to German stamps to furnish a seven-value issue for use in the German post office in Tientsin in 1900.

City in northern China. The Italian post offices in Tientsin used 32 Italian stamps overprinted with the name of the city in 1917-21.

TIFLIS (1857)

Stamp-issuing status: inactive.

The capital city of Georgia (U.S.S.R.). In 1857, the Russian viceroy of the area issued a stamp for local use.

TIMOR (1885-1975)

Stamp-issuing status: inactive; Population: 660,000 (1976 estimate); Stamps issued: 451.

An island in the Malay Archipelago. Divided between the Dutch and Portuguese since the 17th century, Timor was formally partitioned in 1919.

After the liberal Portuguese revolution in 1974, the Portuguese portion of Timor declared itself independent of Portugal, but was soon disputed by internal factions.

Indonesia restored order in Timor, which remains under de facto Indonesian control.

TLACOTALPAN (1856)

Stamp-issuing status: inactive.

A village in the state of Veracruz in eastern Mexico. A single extremely scarce 1/2-real handstamped issue was produced there in 1856.

TOBAGO (1879-96)

Stamp-issuing status: inactive; Population: 25,358 (1889 estimate); Stamps issued: 31.

An island in the West Indies, north of Trinidad. In 1889, Tobago was united with Trinidad to form the colony of Trinidad and Tobago.

TOGO (1897-)

Stamp-issuing status: active; Population: 3.06 million (estimate 1986); Stamps issued: more than 2,000; Issues per year during last decade: 72.

A republic in West Africa, bordering on the Gulf of Guinea. Togo was a German protectorate until 1914, when it was occupied by Anglo-French forces.

After World War I, the territory was divided between Britain and France, under League of Nations mandate. The British portion subsequently became part of Ghana, while the French zone became the present republic (1958).

Togo became fully independent in 1960. Its stamp issues since that time have been voluminous, including a host of colorful stamps and souvenir sheets on every conceivable topic.

Togo has been ruled as a military dictatorship since 1967. Although the government is repressive, the political stability that it provides has made possible steady economic progress.

TOKELAU ISLANDS (1948-)

Stamp-issuing status: active; Population: 1,600; Stamps issued: more than 125; Issues per year for last decade: 10.

A group of islands in the Pacific Ocean, north of Samoa. Attached to the Gilbert and Ellice Islands, Tokelau Islands were placed under Western Samoan administration in 1926.

On Jan. 1, 1949, they became a dependency of New Zealand.

TOMSK (1920)

Stamp-issuing status: inactive.

A city in western Siberia. During the Russian Civil War, the local authorities issued a surcharged Russian stamp for use in the area.

TONGA (1886-)

Stamp-issuing status: active; Population: 98,689 (1987 estimate); Stamps issued: more than 1,225; Issues per year during last decade: 45.

A group of islands in the South Pacific Ocean, south of Samoa. United during the mid-19th century, Tonga came under British protection in 1900.

On June 4, 1970, Tonga again became fully independent.

Tonga's economy has traditionally depended on copra and bananas. The discovery of offshore oil in the 1970s and government efforts to develop tourism bode well for the country's economic future.

From the late 1960s to the early '80s, Tonga issued a host of unconventional stamps, including garish self-adhesive and foil productions embossed and die-cut into many unusual shapes. Beginning in about 1981, however, Tonga returned to more traditional and conservative stamp-issuing policies.

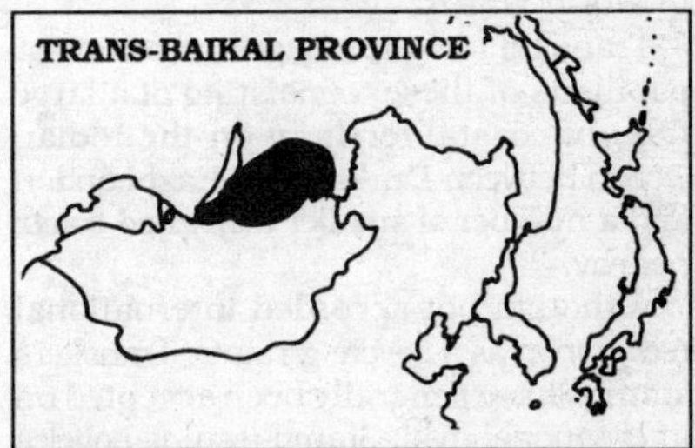

TRANSBAIKAL PROVINCE (1920)

Stamp-issuing status: inactive.

Shortly after the fall of the Kolchak regime in January 1920, a local warlord in eastern Siberia, the Ataman Semenov, proclaimed himself ruler of Siberia. Four Russian stamps were surcharged for use in his short-lived domain. He maintained control of the area around Chita and Lake Baikal until October, when his government was overthrown by partisans of the Far Eastern Republic. Semenov fled to Mongolia.

TRANSCAUCASIAN FEDERATED REPUBLICS (1923-24)

Stamp-issuing status: inactive; Population: 5.9 million (1923 estimate); Stamps issued: 31.

A former Soviet administrative district in the Caucasus, comprising Armenia, Azerbaijan and Georgia.

In 1917, a short-lived independent Transcaucasian Republic was proclaimed, but this state soon fell to invading German,

Turkish and British forces.

After considerable turmoil, the area was occupied by Soviet forces in 1922. In that year, the Transcaucasian Soviet Federated Socialist Republic was proclaimed. In the following year, it joined the U.S.S.R.

In 1936, this unit was dissolved, and its three component states were separated.

TRANSKEI (1976-)

Stamp-issuing status: active; Stamps issued to 1984: more than 150; Issues per year 1976-84: 20.

One of South Africa's so-called Bantustans or Bantu homelands, a scattering of nominally semi-autonomous states for otherwise disenfranchised black South Africans located on the sites of reserves set up under the policies of the white-run apartheid government prior to World War II.

Transkei is the largest and most populous of these, consisting of a large tract of coastal territory on the Indian Ocean between Durban and East London and a number of smaller disjointed tracts nearby.

Although not accorded international recognition as a sovereign state, Transkei's stamps have generally been accepted on international mail. Stamp-issuing policies have been conservative.

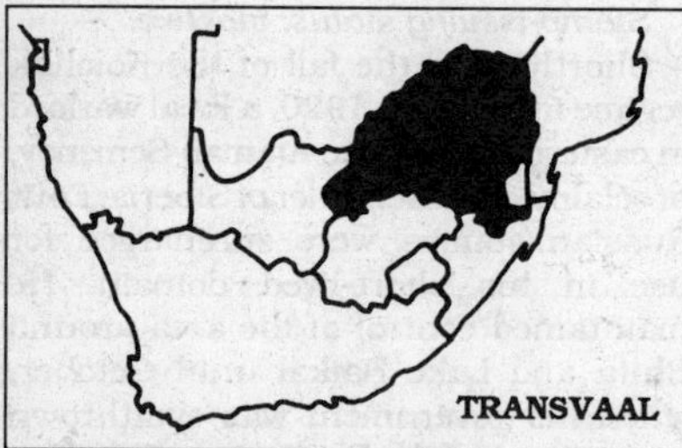

TRANSVAAL (1870-1910)

Stamp-issuing status: inactive; Population: 1.26 million (1904 estimate); Stamps issued: 294.

Former Boer republic (South African Republic) and British colony in southern Africa; now a province of the Republic of South Africa.

Boer settlements north of the Cape Colony were recognized as the independent South African Republic in 1852, but during 1877-82, British forces occupied the area.

In 1881, the Transvaal again became independent, but increasing tension with the British led to the Boer War of 1899-1902, after which the country became a British colony.

In 1910, the Transvaal joined with Natal, Cape Colony and the Orange River Colony to form the Union of South Africa.

TRANSYLVANIA (1919)

Stamp-issuing status: inactive.

A principality annexed from the Turks by Hungary in the 18th century, Transylvania was occupied and absorbed by Romania after World War I. Two issues of a distinctive (and frequently counterfeited) round overprint were applied to a total of 122 Hungarian stamps for use during 1919.

During 1940-44, it was re-occupied by Hungary, finally being returned to Romania after World War II.

TRAVANCORE (1888-1949)

Stamp-issuing status: inactive; Population: 6.1 million (1941 estimate); Stamps issued: 110.

A former feudatory state in southern India. In 1949, it merged with Cochin to form Travancore-Cochin, which issued stamps for use in the new territory.

TRAVANCORE-COCHIN (1949-51)

Stamp-issuing status: inactive: Population: 7.5 million; Stamps issued: 46.

The United State of Travancore-Cochin was formed on July 1, 1949, by the merger of Travancore and Cochin, along with the formerly British-held towns of Tangasseri and Anjengo. Indian stamps have been used since April 1, 1951.

TREBIZONDE (1909-14)

Stamp-issuing status: inactive.

A Turkish port on the Black Sea. The Russian post office in the city used 10 stamps of the Russian Levant overprinted "Trebizonde" after 1909.

TRENGGANU (1910-)

Stamp-issuing status: active; Population: 302,171 (1960 estimate); Stamps issued: more than 125; Issues per year during last decade: 1.

Former non-federated Malay state under Siamese influence until a British protectorate was established in 1909. Trengganu joined the Federation of Malaya in 1948.

TRIESTE (1947-54)

Stamp-issuing status: inactive; Population: 263,000 (1954 estimate); Stamps issued: 471.

A former Italian territory at the northern end of the Adriatic Sea. After World War II, it was occupied by Allied forces and, in 1954, was partitioned between Italy (the northern portion of the seaport of Trieste) and Yugoslavia (the southern section).

These two zones, A and B respectively, issued stamps during 1947-54, while Trieste was a free territory — zone A being under Allied administration, while zone B was administered by Yugoslavia.

TRINIDAD (1851-1913)

Stamp-issuing status; inactive; Population: 387,000 (1889 estimate); Stamps issued: 130.

An island in the Caribbean, off the coast of Venezuela. Taken from Spain by Great Britain in 1797, Trinidad was united with Tobago in 1889 to form the colony of Trinidad and Tobago.

TRINIDAD AND TOBAGO (1913-)

Stamp-issuing status: active; Population: 1.2 million; Stamps issued: more than 450; Issues per year for last decade: 19.

Two islands in the Caribbean, off the coast of Venezuela. The two British colonies were united in 1889, Tobago becoming a ward of the united colony in 1899.

From 1958-1962, the colony was a member of the West Indies Federation, becoming independent in August 1962.

Trinidad has long been an oil-refining center and has begun exploiting recently discovered oil reserves of its own. It is one of the most prosperous of the Caribbean states.

TRIPOLITANIA (1923-35, 1948-50)

Stamp-issuing status: inactive; Population: 570,716 (1921); Stamps issued: 153.

Former Italian colony in North Africa. Tripolitania was occupied from Turkey in 1912 and merged with Cyrenaica in 1934 to form the colony of Libia.

During World War II, Libia was occupied by Anglo-French forces, and Tripolitania was occupied by the British until 1950, when it was incorporated into the independent Kingdom of Libya.

TRISTAN DA CUNHA (1952-)

Stamp-issuing status: active; Population: 260; Stamps issued: more than 420; Issues per year for last decade: 19.

A group of islands in the mid-South Atlantic Ocean. A British possession since 1816, Tristan da Cunha became a dependency of the colony of St. Helena in 1936.

TRUCIAL STATES (1961-63)

Stamp-issuing status: inactive; Population: 86,000; Stamps issued: 11.

A group of Arab sheikdoms — Abu Dhabi, Ajman, Dubai, Fujeira, Manama, Ras al Khaima, Sharjah and Kalba, and Umm al Qiwain — in eastern Arabia, bordering on the Persian Gulf.

These states were under British protection from 1892-1971, joining to form the United Arab Emirates in 1971. In June 1963, Trucial States issues were replaced by those of the individual states, which, in turn, were superseded by those of the U.A.E. in 1972.

TUNISIA (1888-)

Stamp-issuing status: active; Population: 7.4 million (1986); Stamps issued: more than 1,050; Issues per year for last decade: 22.

Republic in North Africa. Tunisia was under Turkish rule from 1574 until 1881, when it became a French protectorate.

After World War II, nationalist feeling increased, and in 1955, France granted Tunisia internal autonomy. In March 1956, Tunisia became independent.

Tunisia has maintained a moderate, generally pro-Western policy since it became independent. Since the 1960s, it has urged a policy of negotiation with Israel.

In 1974, Tunisia and Libya tentatively agreed to merge, but Tunisia soon withdrew from the agreement. Relations between the two countries have been strained. In 1979, a Libyan-backed invasion of Tunisia from Algeria was thwarted.

TURKEY (1863-)

Stamp-issuing status: active; Population: 51.8 million (1986 estimate); Stamps issued: more than 2,450; Issues per year for last decade: 36.

A republic in southeastern Europe and western Asia.

The area now occupied by Turkey was the center of a number of ancient civilizations, and it remained the center of the Eastern Roman Empire for nearly a thousand years after the fall of Rome itself. During most of this period, the empire was the dominant power of the region.

The empire, weakened by the inroads of Crusaders who found it easier to ransack Christian lands than to fight infields, rapidly lost ground in the 13th and 14th centuries. The Ottoman Turks conquered the outlying provinces, and in 1453 they occupied Constantinople, which became their capital and the center of their own empire.

During the next century, the Turks conquered southeastern Europe, North Africa and much of the Middle East. At its apex (1550-1683), the Turkish Empire stretched from the borders of Poland and the Russian steppes to the Sahara, and from Algeria to Arabia.

From the late 17th century on, the Turkish Empire became increasingly weak and poorly administered, and its military power declined rapidly. During the 19th century, the territorial integrity of the state was maintained only because the European powers could not agree upon the division of the spoils.

In a series of generally unsuccessful wars during 1878-1913, most of Turkey's outlying provinces became independent or were lost to its more powerful neighbors.

In 1914, the Turks joined the Central Powers. Their defeat cost Turkey most of its remaining territory, and by 1919 only Asia Minor remained. At that point, it became apparent that the Allies intended to dismember Turkey altogether. In reaction to this threat, a nationalist Turkish government was formed in Ankara in 1920, with Mustafa Kemal as president.

The Nationalists defeated the Greeks, whom they expelled from Western Asia Minor and Eastern Thrace and compelled the Allies to withdraw from the Dardanelles and Cilicia. The Treaty of Lausanne (1923) confirmed Turkish independence and established its borders along roughly ethnic lines.

Kemel established the republic and launched an ambitious program of social reform and industrialization.

Turkey remained neutral during most of World War II, declaring war on the Axis in February 1945. Since that time, it has been aligned with the West, although tension with Greece, a fellow NATO member, over the status of Cyprus, has at times threatened to estrange Turkey from its Western allies.

TURKISH REPUBLIC OF NORTHERN CYPRUS (1974-)

Stamp-issuing status: active; Stamps issued: more than 200; Issues per year for last decade: 16.

The northern and northeastern 40 percent of the Mediterranean island of Cyprus, occupied by Turkey following its 1974 invasion. A buffer zone manned by United Nations peacekeeping forces separates it from the predominantly Greek southern portion of the island.

Stamps were issued even prior to the invasion, though an independent Turkish Republic of Northern Cyprus was only proclaimed in November 1983. Although its legitimacy is not recognized by other countries, its stamps have been regularly accepted as valid on international mail.

TURKS ISLANDS (1867-1900)

Stamp-issuing status: inactive; Population: 2,000 (1894 estimate); Stamps issued: 58.

A group of islands in the West Indies, south of the Bahamas. In 1848, along with the Caicos Islands, they were transferred from Bahamian to Jamaican administration, first as a separate colony (1848-73) and later as a dependency of Jamaica (1873-1959).

Stamps inscribed "Turks and Caicos Islands" replaced those inscribed "Turks Islands" in 1900.

TURKS AND CAICOS ISLANDS (1900-)

Stamp-issuing status: active; Population: 8,000; Stamps issued: more than 750; Issues per year for last decade: 45.

Two groups of islands in the West Indies, south of the Bahamas. Ruled by Great Britain from the Bahamas after the early 18th century, the Turks and Caicos were separated as a colony in 1848 and became a dependency of Jamaica in 1873.

In 1959, they again became a separate British colony.

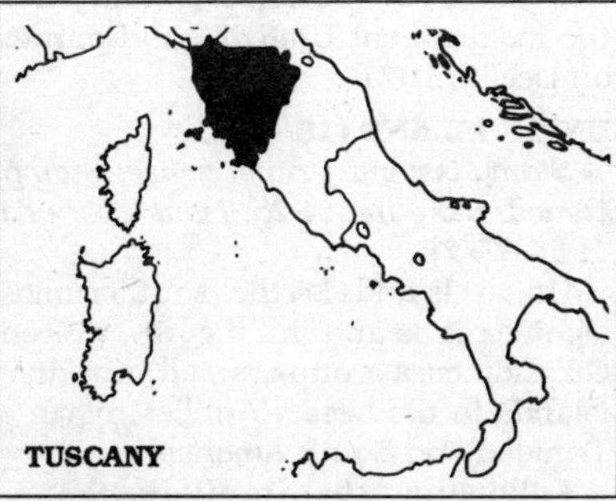

TUSCANY (1851-60)

Stamp-issuing status: inactive; Population: 2.89 million; Stamps issued: 24.

A former grand duchy in west-central Italy. In 1859, the duke was deposed, and in 1860, Tuscany was united with Sardinia.

TUVALU (1976-)

Stamp-issuing status: active; Population: 8,200; Stamps issued: more than 500 (including subsidiary islands: more than 1,500); Issues per year for last decade: 45 (140).

The nine islands previously comprising the Ellice Islands, Tuvalu is located in the central South Pacific south of Kiribati, north of Fiji and northeast of Australia. The islands chose independence from the Gilbert and Ellice Islands in a 1974 referendum, Tuvalu's first stamps appearing at the beginning of 1976.

In the early 1980s, Tuvalu stepped up what had been a moderate stamp-issuing program, reaching a climax in 1984-88 with the release of about 100 stamps by each of the component islands of Funafuti, Nanumaga, Nanumea, Niutao, Nui, Nukufetau, Nukulaelae and Vaitupu. Only Niulakita, population 74, lacked its own issues, most of which displayed popular topics largely unrelated to the islands. There are now signs that Tuvalu is considering a return to more conservative policies.

TWO SICILIES (1858-62)

Stamp-issuing status: inactive; Stamps issued: 26.

Former kingdom comprising southern Italy and Sicily. First created by the Normans in the 11th century, the kingdom passed through various hands until the Bourbon dynasty was overthrown by Garibaldi in 1860.

The area was united with Sardinia in 1860, and Italian stamps have been used since 1862.

- U -

UBANGI-SHARI (1915-37)

Stamp-issuing status: inactive; Population: 833,916; Stamps issued: 109.

Former French colony in central Africa. Occupied by France during 1887-98, Ubangi-Shari was established as a colony in 1904. In 1910, it joined Gabon, the Middle Congo and Chad to form French Equatorial Africa. From 1936 to 1960, French Equatorial African stamps were used.

In 1958, Ubangi-Shari became the autonomous Central African Republic. It became fully independent in 1960.

UDINE (1918)

Stamp-issuing status: inactive.

A city in northeastern Italy, occupied by Austrian forces during World War I. During this period, the municipal authorities issued a stamp for local use.

UGANDA (1895-1902, 1962-)

Stamp-issuing status: active; Population: 14.3 million; Stamps issued: more than 550; Issues per year for last decade: 38.

An independent state in East Africa. Formerly a British protectorate, Uganda became independent in 1962.

In 1971, Gen. Idi Amin seized control of the government. His administration was erratic and blood-thirsty. Some 45,000 East Indians were expelled in 1972, disrupting the economy, since much of the commerce had been in their hands. In 1973, the U.S. broke relations with Uganda, and most Western nations suspended aid, which was replaced by Soviet and Libyan support.

During the next few years, some 300,000 Ugandans were killed, all opponents or suspected opponents of the regime. This reign of terror, along with generally poor government administration, reduced the Ugandan economy to a shambles.

In March 1979, after a period of increasing tension, Uganda was invaded by a Tanzanian force, supported by Ugandan exiles. In April, Amin was forced to flee the country, and found asylum in Libya, one of the few nations with whom he had remained on friendly terms.

A provisional government was established to administer the country and to normalize Ugandan affairs. The government since has been unstable, and the economic and social structures remain in chaos. Anarchy and ruthless government repression are again becoming the norm.

UKRAINE (1918-23, 1941-43)

Stamp-issuing status: inactive; Population: 32 million (1933 estimate); Stamps issued: 51.

A large district in southwestern Russia, now a republic within the Soviet Union.

Under Russian rule since the 18th century, the Ukraine declared its independence in 1917. After several years of warfare, the Bolsheviks finally occupied the Ukraine in 1920, establishing a Soviet Republic, which was absorbed into the Soviet Union in 1923.

While there are only 38 stamps displaying the Ukraine's distinctive trident overprint from this era, the trident's themselves offer an almost endless variety for specialists. During World War II, the Ukraine was occupied by Germany, and overprinted German stamps were used in the area.

UMM AL QIWAIN (1964-72)

Stamp-issuing status: inactive; Population: 5,700; Stamps issued: 70.

A sheikdom in the Trucial States in eastern Arabia. Under British protection from 1892-1971, Umm al Qiwain joined the independent United Arab Emirates on Dec. 2, 1971.

UNION ISLAND (1984-)

Stamp-issuing status: active; Stamps issued: more than 225; Issues per year 1984-87: 76.

Union Island is the southernmost significant island in the St. Vincent Grenadines, a group of small subsidiary islands in the Lesser Antilles, north of Trinidad and South America.

Following the proliferation of Grenadines of St. Vincent issues that began in the early 1970s, stamps began to be issued for Union Island in 1984.

UNITED ARAB EMIRATES (1972-)

Stamp-issuing status: active; Population: 1.3 million; Stamps issued: more than 200; Issues per year for last decade: 13.

A union of sheikdoms in eastern Arabia. Formed Dec. 2, 1971, by Abu Dhabi, Ajman, Dubai, Fujeira, Sharjah and Umm al Qiwain.

Ras al Khaima joined the U.A.E. in February 1972. In August 1972, general U.A.E. issues superseded those of the individual states.

This region was long extremely poor, but in recent years the exploitation of large petroleum reserves, with the staggering increase in petroleum prices, has given the U.A.E. one of the highest per capita gross national products in the world.

UNITED NATIONS (1951-)

Stamp-issuing status: active; Stamps issued: more than 800; Issues per year for last decade: 40.

The United Nations is an organization for the maintenance of international security and peace. Established in 1945, the U.N. now includes virtually every sovereign nation in the world.

U.N. stamps are used on all mail handled at U.N. post offices in New York, Geneva, and Vienna. Separate issues are released for the use of the Geneva and Vienna offices.

UNITED STATES OF AMERICA (1847-)

Stamp-issuing status: active; Population: 239.4 million; Stamps issued: more than 2,600; Issues per year for last decade: 67.

Republic occupying the central portion of North America, along with Alaska, Hawaii and a large number of island possessions in the Caribbean Sea and the Pacific Ocean.

The U.S. was formed from the union of the 13 British mainland North American colonies south of Canada in 1783, after an eight-year war against Great Britain.

During 1803-53, the U.S. expanded rapidly westward, increasing its territory through conquest, purchase and negotiation.

Alaska was purchased from Russia in 1867, and in 1898, Hawaii was annexed, at the request of its inhabitants. In the following year, Puerto Rico, Guam and the Philippines were acquired from Spain, following the short Spanish-American War.

The U.S. long avoided involvement in foreign affairs, except in the Western Hemisphere, where U.S. interest was concentrated. In 1917, the U.S. entered World War I and played an instrumental role in the defeat of the Central Powers. Following the war, it reverted to its isolationalist policy.

During the first two years of World War II, the U.S. resisted involvement, although its sympathies were strongly with the Allies, to whom it supplied economic aid. The Japanese attack on the major U.S. Pacific naval base at Pearl Harbor forced the country into the war. Again, the U.S. played the decisive part in defeating Germany and its allies.

Following World War II, the U.S. realized that it could not avoid international problems by ignoring them and embarked on a policy of active involvement in the regions where its interests were paramount.

U.S. economic aid sparked the European postwar economic boom, and its administration of Japan saw the rapid expansion of Japanese industry.

U.S. stamps were first issued in 1847, although a number of local postmasters had been issuing provisional stamps since 1845. U.S. issues have been used in many nations throughout the world, reflecting, in most cases, the presence of American troops. Most U.S. possessions use U.S. stamps.

UNITED STATES POST OFFICE IN CHINA (1919-22)

Stamp-issuing status: inactive.

From 1867-1922, the U.S. maintained a post office in Shanghai, China. During 1867-1919, unoverprinted U.S. stamps were used, and during 1919-22, a total of 18 surcharged issues were used. This post office was closed on Dec. 31, 1922.

UNITED STATES — POSTMASTERS' PROVISIONALS (1845-47)

In 1845, the postmaster of New York City began using postage stamps for mail handled by his office. Other postmasters' provisionals appeared during the next two years.

In 1847, the U.S. Post Office, convinced of the desirability of utilizing postage stamps, began issuing stamps for nationwide use. These general issues replaced the provisionals.

Postmasters' provisionals were used by Alexandria, Va.; Annapolis, Md. (envelope); Baltimore, Md. (both stamps and postal stationery); Boscawen, N.H.; Brattleboro, Vt.; Lockport, N.Y.; Millbury, Mass.; New Haven, Conn. (postal stationery); New York, N.Y.; Providence, R.I.; and St. Louis, Mo.

During 1846, the New York provisionals were used experimentally on New York-bound mail from Boston, Albany and Washington.

UPPER SILESIA (1920-22)

Stamp-issuing status: inactive; Stamps issued: 44.

A former German territory on the Polish border. A plebiscite in 1920 was indecisive, and in 1922 the League of Nations partitioned the district between Germany and Poland.

After World War II, the German portion of the area was annexed by Poland.

UPPER VOLTA (1920-32, 1959-)

Stamp-issuing status: inactive; Population: 6.7 million (1984 estimate); Stamps issued: 1,010; Issues per year for last decade: 45.

A republic in West Africa, north of Ghana. A French colony from 1919-32, Upper Volta was subsequently divided between the French Sudan, Ivory Coast and Niger.

In 1947, it was reconstituted within French West Africa, and in 1958, was established as a republic within the French community.

In 1960, Upper Volta became independent.

URUGUAY (1856-)

Stamp-issuing status: active; Population: 2.94 million (1985 estimate); Stamps issued: more than 1,550; Issues per year for last decade: 34.

A republic in South America, on the Atlantic coast between Brazil and Argentina. Under Spanish rule until 1810, associated with La Plata from 1810-16, and conquered by Brazil in 1816, Uruguay finally became independent in 1827.

Uruguay's history during the 19th century was one of anarchy and civil war, with occasional armed intervention by Argentina and Brazil.

After 1900, a stable government enabled the country to make considerable economic and social progress. The rise of radical terrorism by the leftist "Tupamaros" during the 1960s, however, disrupted the country and brought a rightist military takeover in 1973.

- V -

VADUZ (1918)

Stamp-issuing status: inactive.

The capital of Liechtenstein. During World War I, the Austrian War Office disrupted the ordinary postal system, necessitating the issuance of a provisional stamp in Vaduz.

This stamp was valid for local use and for transmittal to Sevelen, Switzerland.

VAITUPU (1984-)

Stamp-issuing status: active; Stamps issued: more than 100; Issues per year 1984-87: 36.

One of nine small islands in the Tuvalu Islands, formerly the Ellice Island group in the Gilbert and Ellice Islands. The island chain is located east of the Solomon Islands and north of Fiji in the southeastern central Pacific Ocean.

Like the other Tuvalu Islands, Vaitupu issued a flurry of stamps depicting such diverse subjects as cars, locomotives, cricket players and the British Royal Family in the mid-1980s.

VALENCIENNES (1914)

Stamp-issuing status: inactive.

A city in northern France, near the Belgian border. Soon after the city's occupation by German forces at the beginning of World War I, the Chamber of Commerce issued a stamp for local use. This stamp was in use from Sept. 3 to Oct. 30, 1914.

VALONA (1909-11, 1914-18)

Stamp-issuing status: inactive.

Albanian seaport. The Italian post office used eight overprinted Italian stamps from 1909-11.

In October 1914, Moslem revolutionaries issued a series of stamps, used briefly before Valona was occupied by Italian troops.

During the Italian occupation, two surcharged Italian stamps were again used in the city.

VANUATU (1980-)

Stamp-issuing status: active; Population: 137,000 (1984 estimate); Stamps issued: more than 200; Issues per year since 1980: 31.

A Y-shaped chain of volcanic southwestern Pacific islands about 250 miles northeast of New Caledonia, southeast of the Solomon Islands.

These islands were administered as the joint Anglo-French condominium of the New Hebrides from 1906 until 1980, when independence was granted to the new republic of Vanuatu. Bilingual stamps were introduced in 1980.

VATICAN CITY (1929-)

Stamp-issuing status: active; Population: 1,000; Stamps issued: more than 900; Issues per year for last decade: 29.

A tiny (108.7 acres) enclave in Rome, the Vatican City is the sole remnant of the once-extensive Papal state in Italy.

During 1870-1929, the Papacy and Italy disputed sovereignty, but the Lateran Pact of 1929 restored normal relations, with temporal authority of the Pope recognized in the Vatican City, which became an independent state, subject to certain limitations.

VEGLIA (KRK) (1920)

Stamp-issuing status: inactive.

An island off the northwestern coast of Yugoslavia. During d'Annunzio's occupation of Fiume, regular Fiume issues were overprinted for Veglia.

VENDA (1979-)

Stamp-issuing status: active; Stamps issued to 1983: more than 80; Issues per year 1979-83: 20.

One of South Africa's so-called Bantustans or Bantu homelands, a scattering of nominally semi-autonomous states for otherwise disenfranchised black South Africans located on the sites of reserves set up under the policies of the white-run apartheid government prior to World War II.

Venda is the most northerly of these, located in the northern portion of what was Transvaal, near the border with Zimbabwe and Mozambique.

Although not accorded international recognition as a sovereign state, Venda's stamps have generally been accepted on international mail. Stamp-issuing policies have been conservative.

VENEZIA GIULIA (1918-19, 1945-47)

Stamp-issuing status: inactive; Stamps issued (total): 71.

Former Austrian territory at the northern end of the Adriatic Sea, including the port of Trieste.

The area was occupied by Italy after World War I, during which time 40 overprinted Austrian stamps were used. After World War II, the area was occupied by the Allies, and 31 overprinted Italian stamps were issued from 1945 to 1947 (Trieste zone A).

Yugoslavia occupied part of the territory (zone B), issuing stamps for use there.

VENEZIA TRIDENTINA (1918-19)

Stamp-issuing status: inactive.

A territory in northern Italy, also known as Trentino. The area was occupied by Italy from Austria after World War I, at which time 21 overprinted Austrian stamps were used.

VENEZUELA (1859-)

Stamp-issuing status: active; Population: 18.3 million; Stamps issued: more than 2,475; Issues per year for last decade: 23.

Republic on the northern coast of South America.

Under Spanish rule after 1546, Venezuela expelled the Spanish after a bloody 10-year civil war (1811-21). It at first formed part of Bolivar's Great Colombia, separating from that union in 1830.

Venezuela's history during the 19th century was marked by a succession of military dictatorships and chronic internal disorder.

During 1907-45, Venezuela saw significant economic growth, and in 1945, democratic government was established. Several military coups followed, but since 1959 Venezuela's governments have been progressive and democratically elected.

One of the founding members of OPEC, Venezuela had benefitted enormously from the massive increases in oil prices during the 1970s. Oil revenues are funding major economic expansion and public-works projects.

VICTORIA (1850-1913)

Stamp-issuing status: inactive; Population: 1.2 million (1901 estimate); Stamps

issued: 272.

A state in southeastern Australia. Detached from New South Wales in 1851, Victoria joined the Commonwealth of Australia in 1901.

VICTORIA LAND (1911)

Stamp-issuing status: inactive.

A region of Antarctica. In 1911-12, Robert Falcon Scott organized his ill-fated South Pole Expedition, and two New Zealand stamps were overprinted "Victoria Land" for use by the expedition members.

Scott and four members of his party reached the South Pole on Jan. 18, 1912, but died on the return trip to their base.

VIETNAM (1945-54)

Stamp-issuing status: inactive; Population: 22.6 million (1949 estimate); Stamps issued: 43.

Country in Southeast Asia, occupying the eastern half of the Indo-Chinese Peninsula.

Vietnam comprises Annam, Tonkin and Cochin China, which have been under Chinese control or influence for most of their history since 111 B.C.

In 1854, France began to extend its control in the area, which was completed by 1884. During World War II, Vietnam was occupied by the Japanese, who supported the regime of the Emperor Bao Dai of Annam.

The Vietminh League, a union of nationalists aiming for an independent Vietnam, grew up in opposition to the Japanese, and in 1945, deposed Bao Dai, declaring Vietnamese independence.

During 1946-54, France fought the Vietminh, hoping to preserve their Indo-Chinese Empire. In July 1949, the State of Vietnam was established under Bao Dai, in association with the French Union.

The defeat of France by the Vietminh forces, which had come under complete Communist control, brought the partition of the country in 1954.

The northern half became the Communist Democratic Republic of Vietnam, and in the following year, the southern portion became the Republic of Vietnam.

VIETNAM, DEMOCRATIC REPUBLIC OF (NORTH VIETNAM) (1954-)

Stamp-issuing status: active; Stamps issued: more than 1,700; Issues per year (1975-85): 80.

A Communist people's republic occupying the northern half of Vietnam.

The Democratic Republic of Vietnam was established in 1954, after the defeat of French forces by the nationalist Vietminh. The North continued to support the Communist Vietcong in the South against the South Vietnamese regime, increasing its aid after 1959.

In 1964, North Vietnamese troops began to fight in the South, bringing the U.S. actively into the war.

During 1965-69, the war was largely a stalemate, with neither side able to achieve any permanent success. Growing domestic opposition to the U.S. involvement in the war brought a cease-fire in January 1973, after which U.S. forces were withdrawn, and U.S. aid to the South was reduced.

In early 1975, a renewed Communist offensive brought about the rapid collapse of the South Vietnamese regime, and a Communist government was installed in the South.

In 1976, the two countries were merged into the Socialist Republic of Vietnam.

Since its 1975 victory, Vietnam has exercised control of Laos and, in 1978-79, established a client regime in Kampuchea, where scattered Khmer Rouge resistance continues. A Chinese invasion of Vietnam in February 1979, brought heavy fighting but did not escalate into a full-blown war.

Since the Communist victory, millions of South Vietnamese have been forcibly resettled in the countryside, and hundreds of thousands have fled the South.

Importation of stamps from Vietnam was legally prohibited as of April 30, 1975.

VIETNAM, REPUBLIC OF (SOUTH VIETNAM) (1955-75)

Stamp-issuing status: inactive; Population: 16.5 million (1975 estimate); Stamps issued: 517.

After the loss of the northern half of Vietnam to the Communists in 1954, the southern portion of the country withdrew from the French Union and deposed its ruler, Bao Dai. On Oct. 26, 1955, the Republic of Vietnam was established.

After 1956, fighting with the Communists continued, the southern Communist Vietcong being supported and supplied by North Vietnam. The U.S. supported the South with aid and, after June 1965, with troops.

After 1969, because of growing opposition to involvement among Americans, the U.S. began to reduce its involvement, and in January 1973, a cease-fire between the U.S., North Vietnam and the Vietcong provided for the withdrawal of U.S. forces.

The U.S. reduced aid to the South, weakening that regime's position, so that in early 1975, a North Vietnamese invasion, in violation of the cease-fire, quickly brought the South Vietnamese collapse.

A Provisional Revolutionary Government, under North Vietnamese direction, assumed control of the South in May 1975. Importation of stamps from Vietnam was legally prohibited as of April 30, 1975.

VILNIUS (1941)

Stamp-issuing status: inactive.

A city in Lithuania. Vilnius was occupied by German forces from 1941 to 1944. During the early stage of the occupation, nine overprinted Russian stamps were used.

VITORIA (1937)

Stamp-issuing status: inactive.

The capital of the province of Alava in northern Spain. The Nationalist authorities overprinted contemporary Spanish stamps for use in the area in April 1937.

VRYBURG (1899-1900)

Stamp-issuing status: inactive; Stamps issued (total): 8.

A town of British Bechuanaland, occupied by the Boers in November 1899 and re-occupied by the British in May 1900. Both forces overprinted one another's stamps for use in the town.

- W -

WADHWAN (1888-c. 1895)

Stamp-issuing status: inactive; Population: 44,259; Stamps issued: 3.

A former feudatory state in western India.

WALLIS AND FUTUNA ISLANDS (1920-)

Stamp-issuing status: active; Population: 13,100; Stamps issued: more than 560; Issues per year for last decade: 24.

Two archipelagos in the South Pacific Ocean, under French protection since 1888.

WARSAW (1915)

Stamp-issuing status: inactive.

The capital of Poland. During World War I, 14 stamps were issued or surcharged by the Warsaw Citizens Committee under the authority of the German military commander.

A number of World War II German occupation of Poland issues were overprinted and two new designs were issued during the 1944 Warsaw Uprising. These are scarce, desirable and often forged.

WARWISZKI (1923)

Stamp-issuing status: inactive.

A city in northeastern Poland. Formerly part of Lithuania, the city was occupied by Polish forces in 1923, at which time Polish stamps were overprinted for local use.

WENDEN (LIVONIA) (1862-1902)

Stamp-issuing status: inactive; Stamps issued: 12.

A former district of the Russian province of Livonia that issued stamps until 1902, when Russian stamps replaced those of Wenden. The area was divided between Latvia and Estonia in 1918.

WESTERN AUSTRALIA (1854-1913)

Stamp-issuing status: inactive; Population: 190,000 (1912 estimate); Stamps issued: 101.

A large state of western Australia. Formerly a separate colony, Western Australia joined in forming the Commonwealth of Australia in January 1901.

WESTERN HUNGARY (LAJTABANAT) (1921)

Stamp-issuing status: inactive.

Following World War I, the Allies assigned the formerly Hungarian province of Burgenland to Austria because of its proximity to Vienna and its predominantly German population. Hungarian irregulars were in occupation of the province, however, and refused to evacuate.

Through Italian mediation, a plebiscite was held in December 1921. The district around Odenburg (Sopron) was awarded to Hungary and the rest of the province to Austria.

During the Hungarian occupation, overprinted Hungarian stamps and a locally produced set were in use.

WESTERN UKRAINE (1918-19)

Stamp-issuing status: inactive; Stamps issued: 99.

A briefly independent state in central Europe. Formed in October 1918 from the Austro-Hungarian territories of central and eastern Galicia and Bukovina in an attempt to unite the region with the Ukraine.

In November 1918, Romania occupied Bukovina, and in January 1919, the balance of the Western Ukraine united with the Ukrainian National Republic. In July 1919, the area was occupied by Poland, which, in turn, lost it to the U.S.S.R.

WEST IRIAN (1962-70)

Stamp-issuing status: inactive; Population: 923,440 (1973 estimate); Stamps issued: 73.

Formerly Netherlands New Guinea. Under U.N. administration from 1962 to 1963, West Irian was placed under Indonesian administration on May 1, 1963.

WILAYAH PERSEKUTUAN (1979-)

Stamp-issuing status: active; Population: 937,875; Stamps issued: 21; Issues per year 1979-86: 3.

Federal territories (as distinct from the states) of Malaysia, comprising the capital, Kuala Lumpur, since 1974, and the island of Labuan beginning in 1984.

Issues for use in these territories, but uninscribed as such, were produced in 1979 and 1983-84. The first purpose-inscribed stamps did not appear until late 1986.

WILKOMIR (UKMERGE) (1941)

Stamp-issuing status: inactive.

A city in central Lithuania. During the early months of the German occupation during World War II, five different overprinted Russian stamps were used in the area.

WOSNESSENSK (1942)

Stamp-issuing status: inactive.

A city in the southern Ukraine. During World War II, a provisional issue of two stamps was made by the German military commander.

WRANGEL ISSUES (1902-21)

Stamp-issuing status: inactive; Stamps issued: 359.

The last major White Russian (anti-Soviet) commander during the Russian Civil War, Baron Peter Wrangel, was forced to evacuate his forces and followers to refugee camps in Turkey and the Balkans in 1920.

Stamps of Russia, Russian Offices in Turkey, South Russia and the Ukraine were overprinted for use in these camps.

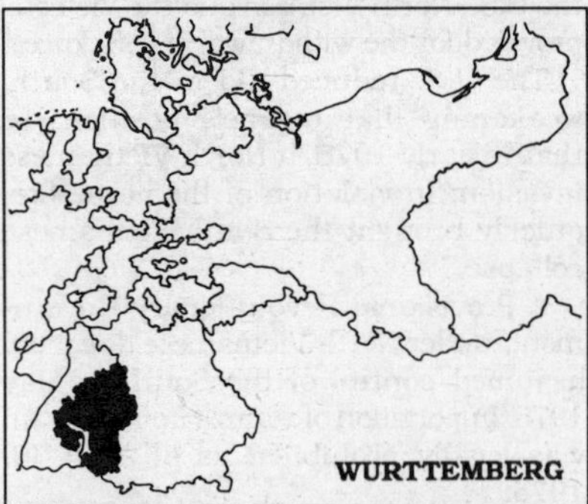

WURTTEMBERG (1851-1923)

Stamp-issuing status: inactive; Population 2.58 million; Stamps issued: 246.

Former kingdom in southern Germany. Wurttemberg joined the German Empire in 1870. Its regular issues were replaced by those of Germany in 1902, although its official issues continued in use until 1923.

- Y -

YEMEN (1926-)

Stamp-issuing status: active; Stamps issued: more than 1,400; Issues per year during last decade: 21.

An ancient state in southwest Arabia. Under Turkish suzerainty until 1918, Yemen became independent after Turkey's defeat in World War I.

During 1958-61, Yemen was loosely affiliated with Egypt in the United Arab States. In 1962, a military coup ousted the imam, and a pro-Egyptian republic was established.

Royalist resistance continued in the interior until 1969, during which time both sides issued a vast number of stamps, most aimed strictly at stamp collectors.

In April 1970, an agreement between the Yemen Arab Republic and Saudi Arabia introduced royalists into the Y.A.R. government, ending the existence of the Mutawakelite Kingdom. At about the same time, the country's stamp-issuing policy settled back to normal.

YEMEN (PEOPLE'S DEMOCRATIC REPUBLIC) (1968-)

Stamp-issuing status: active.

A republic in southwest Arabia, south of the Yemen Arab Republic. Established in 1967, when the Federation of South Arabia became independent from Great Britain.

The area was originally named the People's Republic of Southern Yemen; the current name was adopted in 1970.

South Yemen has maintained close ties with the U.S.S.R. It has supported Marxist guerrillas in northern Yemen and in Oman. A number of Cuban troops are stationed in the country. In 1978, South Yemeni troops aided Ethiopian and Cuban forces against the rebels in Eritrea. In July 1978, Egypt, the Yemen Arab Republic and Saudi Arabia suspended relations with South Yemen, following a coup that brought the most radical elements of the region to power.

YUCATAN (1924)

Stamp-issuing status: inactive; Stamps issued: 6.

A state in southeastern Mexico. Yucatan was the center of a revolt against the central government from 1923 to 1924.

YUGOSLAVIA (1918-)

Stamp-issuing status: active; Population: 23 million; Stamps issued: more than 2,600; Issues per year for last decade: 52.

A state in south Europe, bordering the Adriatic Sea. Yugoslavia was formed on Dec. 1, 1918, from the union of Serbia, Bosnia and Herzegovina, Croatia, Dalmatia, Montenegro and Slovenia, as the Kingdom of the Serbs, Croats and Slovenes.

In 1925, the name Yugoslavia was adopted. During World War II, Yugoslavia was occupied by the Axis, with a number of German and Italian puppet states being created, while the balance of its territory was annexed by its neighbors.

Resistance groups were active during the war. In late 1944, German forces were driven from the country, and a people's republic was proclaimed.

The Communist postwar regime, under the late Josip Broz Tito, broke with Moscow in 1948 and has since maintained its independence from the U.S.S.R.

Many Yugoslavs work in western Europe, and trade with both western and eastern Europe is active.

Separatism remains a major threat to the nation, and since Tito's death in 1980, leadership has been rotated among members of each republic and autonomous province.

YUGOSLAVIAN OFFICES ABROAD (1943-44)

Stamp-issuing status: inactive.

During World War II, 14 stamps and a souvenir sheet were issued by the Yugoslav government in exile in London. These issues were valid for use aboard Yugoslav vessels fighting against the Axis powers.

YUNNAN (1926-35)

Stamp-issuing status: inactive.

A province of southwestern China. Regular Chinese stamps were overprinted for use within the province due to a difference in exchange rates between Yunnan and the rest of the country.

- Z -

ZAIRE (1971-)

Stamp-issuing status: active; Population: 32 million (1987 estimate); Stamps issued: more than 500; Issues per year during last decade: 38.

The Congo Democratic Republic, formerly the Belgian Congo, adopted the name Zaire in November 1971.

After a turbulent first decade of independence, the relative political stability of the 1970s enabled the government to improve the economic condition of Zaire.

In 1977 and 1978, Cuban-trained Shaban (Katangan) exiles invaded Zaire from Angola. These invasions were defeated with assistance from Morocco, France, Belgium, Egypt and the United States.

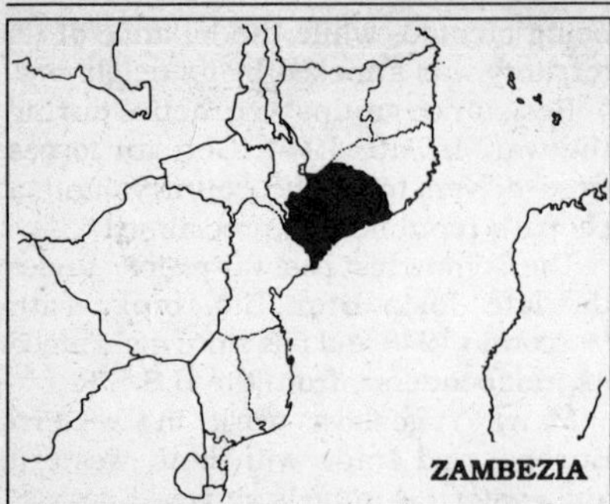

ZAMBEZIA (1894-1917)

Stamp-issuing status: inactive; Stamps issued: 102.

A former district of Mozambique, in southeast Africa. In 1913, Zambezia was divided into two districts, Quelimane and Tete, which briefly issued their own stamps, until these were replaced by those of Mozambique.

ZAMBIA (1964-)

Stamp-issuing status: active; Population: 7 million (1986); Stamps issued: more than 440; Issues per year for last decade: 25.

A republic in southern Africa. Formerly the British protectorate of Northern Rhodesia, Zambia became independent on Oct. 24, 1964.

ZANTE (1941, 1943-44)

Stamp-issuing status: inactive.

One of the Ionian Islands off the western coast of Greece. Zante was occupied by Italy in 1941, and locally overprinted Greek stamps were used for a time. During 1943-44, three overprinted issues of the Italian Ionian Islands were used under the German authorities, who occupied the island following Italy's surrender to the Allies.

ZANZIBAR (1895-1968)

Stamp-issuing status: inactive; Population: 355,000 (1967 estimate); Stamps issued: 393.

A group of islands off the coast of Tanganyika in East Africa. An important trading center, Zanzibar was occupied at various times by the Portuguese and Arabs, the latter establishing a powerful state in East Africa when the sultan of Muscat moved his capital to Zanzibar.

In 1885, the sultanate's mainland possessions were divided between Germany, Great Britain and Italy. In 1890, the islands were placed under British protection.

On Dec. 10, 1963, Zanzibar became independent, and in January 1964, the sultan was deposed. The new regime ousted British and Americans and slaughtered thousands of Arab residents. In April 1964, Zanzibar joined with Tanganyika to form the United Republic of Tanganyika and Zanzibar, renamed Tanzania in 1965.

ZARA (ZADAR) (1943)

Stamp-issuing status: inactive; Stamps issued: 47.

A province on the eastern coast of the Adriatic. Taken from Austria by Italy after World War I, it was occupied by Germany in 1943, at which time Italian issues were overprinted by the German authorities.

After World War II, the area became part of Yugoslavia.

ZARAGOZA (1937)

Stamp-issuing status: inactive.

A province of northern Spain. The Nationalist authorities overprinted contemporary Spanish issues for use in Zaragoza in 1937.

Through the late 1940s, a number of large, colorful charity stamps were issued in Zaragoza. Although inscribed "Sin Valor Postal" ("Without postal value"), these are often mistaken for postage stamps.

ZARASAI (ZARGRAD) (1941)

Stamp-issuing status: inactive.

A city in Lithuania. During the early months of the city's occupation during World War II, the German military commander issued overprints on seven different Russian stamps for use in the area.

ZARKI (1918)

Stamp-issuing status: inactive.

A city in southern Poland. Local issues were made by the municipal authorities under the auspices of the German military command.

ZAWIERCIE (1916)

Stamp-issuing status: inactive.

A city in southern Poland. Two local issues were made by the municipal authorities under the auspices of the German military command.

ZELAYA (BLUEFIELDS) (1904-12)

Stamp-issuing status: inactive; Stamps issued: 131.

A province of Nicaragua on the eastern coast. For a time, the use of silver currency along the coast, while paper currency was used in the rest of the country, necessitated separate stamp issues for the area.

ZIL ELWANNYEN SESEL (1980-)

Stamp-issuing status: active; Population: 3,000; Stamps issued: more than 160; Issues per year 1980-88: 20.

An isolated group of 25 islands north of Malagasy and the Comoro Islands, west of Seychelles and Mauritius, off the east coast of Africa.

The islands were formerly part of the British Indian Ocean Territories (1968-76) and then the Seychelles. Issues purportedly for use in these so-called Seychelles outer islands appeared in 1980. The names inscribed on its stamps have seen several variations, including Zil Eloigne Sesel (1980-82) and Zil Elwagne Sesel (1982-84).

ZIMBABWE (1980-)

Stamp-issuing status: active; Population: 8.8 million (1987); Stamps issued: more than 150; Issues per year 1980-87: 21.

In May 1979, Rhodesia was officially renamed Zimbabwe Rhodesia, a combination of the African and European names of the country. In 1979, after six years of bitter civil war, the white regime in Salisbury and the black nationalist factions reached a compromise, resulting in a relatively peaceful transition to majority rule in early 1980.

ZULIA (1891)

Stamp-issuing status: inactive.

A state in northwestern Venezuela, surrounding Lake Maracaibo. In 1891, the state authorities issued two stamps, valid for inland postage, which were in use for three months.

ZULULAND (1888-98)

Stamp-issuing status: inactive; Population: 230,000 (1896 estimate); Stamps issued: 24.

An area of southeastern Africa, which was united into a native kingdom under the Zulu tribe in the 19th century.

Conquered by Great Britain in 1887, Zululand was incorporated into Natal in 1898.

ZURICH (1843-50)

Stamp-issuing status: inactive; Stamps issued: 5.

A canton of Switzerland that issued a number of stamps prior to the release of general Swiss issues in 1850.

Country Name Cross-Index

Over the years, and especially since the breakup of the European colonial empires since the 1960s, many nations have adopted new names. Below is a short list of some of the changes that most often confuse stamp collectors.

IS	WAS
Aruba	Part of Netherlands Antilles
Bangladesh	East Pakistan
Belize	British Honduras
Benin	Dahomey
Botswana	Bechuanaland Protectorate
British Antarctic Territories	Part of Falkland Islands Dependencies
Burkina Faso	Upper Volta
Burundi	Urundi
Cambodia	Khmer Republic (1971-75) Democratic Kampuchea (1975-79)
Colombia	Grenadine Confederation (1858-61) United States of New Grenada (1861) United States of Colombia (1861-85)
Djibouti Republic	Somali Coast (1902-67) French Territory of the Afars and Issas (1967-77)
Equatorial Guinea	Fernando Po and Rio Muni (Spanish Guinea)
Ghana	Gold Coast
Guinea	French Guinea
Guinea-Bissau	Portuguese Guinea
Guyana	British Guiana
Indonesia	Netherlands Indies
Iran	Persia
Iraq	Mesopotamia
Israel	Palestine
Jordan	Trans-Jordan
Kenya	British East Africa
Kiribati	Gilbert Islands
Lesotho	Basutoland
Malagasy Republic	Madagascar
Malawi	British Central Africa (1891-1907) Nyasaland (1907-64)
Malaysia	Malaya and Sarawak and Sabah (North Borneo)
Mali	French Sudan
Melaka	Malacca
Micronesia, Palau	Caroline Islands
Pulau Penang	Penang
Rwanda	Ruanda
Sabali	North Borneo
Somalia	Italian Somalia and British Somliland Protectorate
South Georgia and South Sandwich Islands	Part of Falkland Islands Dependencies

IS	WAS
Sri Lanka	Ceylon
Tanzania	Tanganyika and Zanzibar
Thailand	Siam
Tuvalu	Ellice Islands
United Arab Emirates	Trucial States
Vanuatu	New Hebrides
West Irian	Netherlands New Guinea
Yemen People's Democratic Republic	Aden (1937-65) South Arabia (1965-67) People's Republic of Southern Yemen (1967-71)
Zaire	Congo Free State (1885-1908) Belgian Congo (1908-60) Congo Democratic Republic (1960-71)
Zambia	Northern Rhodesia
Zil Elwannyen Sesel	British Indian Ocean Territory (previously part of Seychelles)
Zimbabwe	Southern Rhodesia (1924-65) Rhodesia (1965-80)

Post Codes of the World

The post codes systems used by the countries of the world may vary in content. The codes may include all numbers, or a combination of numbers and letters. The placement in the address also will change depending on the requirements in each country. Many countries use post codes to standardize addresses so that the mail can be handled by mechanized or automated sorting equipment.

Many postal administrations have created symbols or slogans for publicity purposes for their post codes. These are intended to make the public familiar with the codes. The emblems also serve as a continuous reminder to add the code to the address. In the United States, Mr. ZIP is credited with making the public aware of the five-digit ZIP Code and the successful 97-percent use rate.

Some countries may use a code for the country name, such as A for Austria or IS for Iceland. This country code, established for the Road Traffic Convention, is not necessary for the delivery of the mail.

On Nov. 3, 1961, the Federal German Post Office became the first administration to introduce post codes. The United States put its ZIP Code into use on July 1, 1963.

The general accepted practice is to capitalize the destination country name in the address. The specimen address given is for postal administration headquarters in each country where a post code is recorded.

Name of Country	Code's Nature and Position	Specimen Address for Mail Addressed to Country	Code's First Day of Use and Symbol
Algeria	5 digits on left of city	Monsieur John Doe 4 Blvd. Salah Bouakouir 16000 Algiers ALGERIA	1972
Argentina	4 digits on left of city	Senor John Doe Sarmiento 151, Room 306 100 Buenos Aires ARGENTINA	Nov. 1, 1975 stylized dove
Australia	4 digits after city and region	Mr. John Doe Post Office Box 302 Carlton South, Victoria 3053 AUSTRALIA	July 1, 1967 arrow
Austria	4 digits before city	Herrn John Doe Post Office Box 8 1011 Vienna AUSTRIA	Jan. 1, 1966 postal fox
Bangladesh	Dash, then 4 digits after city	Mr. John Doe Post Office Dhaka-1000 BANGLADESH	unknown
Belgium	4 digits before city	Monsieur John Doe Organizations of Posts 1000 Brussels BELGIUM	Dec. 15, 1969 Slogan: "Use the Routing Numbers"
Bermuda	3 digits after city, dash between 1st and 2nd digits	Mr. John Doe Post Office Hamilton 1-11 BERMUDA	March 1, 1973
Brazil	5 digits before city, period between 1st and 2nd digits, followed by dash	Senor John Doe SBN-Conjunto 3-Bloco A 70.002-Brasilia DF BRAZIL	June 1, 1971 shooting carrier

Name of Country	Code's Nature and Position	Specimen Address for Mail Addressed to Country	Code's First Day of Use and Symbol
Bulgaria	4 digits before city	Mr. John Doe 44 Rue Dencoglou 1000 Sofia BULGARIA	Jan. 1, 1975 handstamp
Burma	5 digits after city	Mr. John Doe 43 Bo Aung Gyaw St. Rangoon 11181 BURMA	Feb. 12, 1980
Canada	Combination of 6 digits and letters with space between 3rd and 4th. Put on last line	Mr. John Doe Canada Post Corp. Ottawa, Ontario CANADA K1A OB1	April 1, 1971 Slogan: "Postal C O D E Postal"
China	6 digits before city	Mr. John Doe Post Office Box 100804 Beijing PEOPLE'S REPUBLIC OF CHINA	July 1, 1980 (tests before this date)
Czechoslovakia	5 digits before city with space between 3rd and 4th	Mr. John Doe Olsanska 5 125 02 Prague 3 CZECHOSLOVAKIA	Jan. 1, 1983
Denmark	4 digits before city	Mr. John Doe Vesterbrogade 67 1530 Copenhagen V DENMARK	Sept. 20, 1967 postal bee
Faroe Islands	3 or 4 digits before city	Mr. John Doe Postal Administration 159 Torshavn FAROE ISLANDS	unknown
Finland	5 digits before city	Mr. John Doe Postal Box 654 00101 Helsinki FINLAND	Jan. 1, 1971 small postman
France	5 digits before city	Monsieur John Doe 34, Rue de Vaugirard 75700 Paris FRANCE	Oct. 1965: test 1972: nationwide carrier with pansy
French Guiana	5 digits before city	Monsieur John Doe Rue Fiedmond 97308 Cayenne FRENCH GUIANA	1972
East Germany	4 digits before city, but zeros at end can be omitted	Herrn John Doe Mauerstrasse 69-75 1066 Berlin GERMAN DEMOCRATIC REPUBLIC	Jan. 1, 1965 postwoman
West Germany	4 digits before city, but zeros at end can be omitted	Herrn John Doe Adenauerallee 81 5300 Bonn 1 FEDERAL REPUBLIC OF GERMANY	Nov. 3, 1961 forget-me-not
Great Britain	7 letters and digits after city with space before last 3 items	Mr. John Doe 33 Grosvenor Place London SW1X 1PX GREAT BRITAIN	1966: test 1972: nationwide
Greece	5 digits before city	Mr. John Doe Hellenic Posts 10188 Athens GREECE	unknown

Name of Country	Code's Nature and Position	Specimen Address for Mail Addressed to Country	Code's First Day of Use and Symbol
Guadelope	5 digits before city with space 3rd and 4th digits	Monsieur John Doe Posts & Telecommunications 97 109 Basse Terre GUADELOUPE	1972
Hungary	4 digits after country name. Put on last line	Mr. John Doe Posts & Telecommunications Budapest, HUNGARY 1540	Jan. 1, 1973 crow
Iceland	3 digits before city	Mr. John Doe Smaraslot 9 210 GARDABAE ICELAND	March 30, 1977 postman
India	Dash, then 6 digits after city	Mr. John Doe Parliament Street New Delhi-110001 INDIA	Aug. 15, 1972 Slogan: "Use PIN Code" (Postal Index Number Code)
Indonesia	5 digits after city	Mr. John Doe 37 Jalan Kebon Sirih Jakarta 10340 INDONESIA	unknown
Iran	5 digits before city	Mr. John Doe Post Office Box 111 14154 Tehran IRAN	unknown
Israel	5 digits before city, space between 2nd and 3rd digits	Mr. John Doe 23 Rue Yafo 91 999 Jerusalem ISRAEL	Aug. 15, 1980
Italy	5 digits before city	Signor John Doe Viale America No. 201 00144 Rome ITALY	June 1, 1967 postman
Japan	5 digits before country, dash between 3rd and 4th digits. First 3 digits only for main post offices	Mr. John Doe 3-2 Kasumigaseki 1 chome Tokyo 100-01 JAPAN	July 1, 1968 postman
Korea, South	5 digits after city, dash between 3rd and 4th digits. First 3 digits only for main post offices	Mr. John Doe Ministry of Communications Seoul 110-01 KOREA	July 1, 1970 postmen
Lesotho	3 digits after city	Mr. John Doe P.O. Box 413 Maseru 100 LESOTHO	Nov. 1, 1977
Liechtenstein	4 digits before city	Mr. John Doe Principality of Liechtenstein 9490 Vaduz LIECHTENSTEIN	June 26, 1964
Luxembourg	4 digits before city	Mr. John Doe 2020 Luxembourg LUXEMBOURG	July 7, 1980
Malaysia	4 digits after city with dash between 2nd and 3rd digits	Mr. John Doe Postal Services Kuala Lumpur 50-60 MALAYSIA	Oct. 25, 1972 Slogan: "Please the Post Code"

Name of Country	Code's Nature and Position	Specimen Address for Mail Addressed to Country	Code's First Day of Use and Symbol
Maldives	4 digits after city with space between 2nd and 3rd digits	Mr. John Doe Marine Drive Male 20 20 MALDIVES	unknown
Marshall Islands	5 digits after country	Mr. John Doe P.O. Box 890 Majuro MARSHALL ISLANDS 96960	July 1, 1963
Martinique	5 digits before city	Monsieur John Doe Posts & Telecommunications 97262 Fort de France MARTINIQUE	1972
Mexico	5 digits before city followed by dash	Senor John Doe San Antonio Abad 130 06820-Mexico, D.F. MEXICO	April 20, 1981 dove
Micronesia	5 digits after country	Mr. John Doe Post Office Ponape FEDERATED STATES OF MICRONESIA 96941	July 1, 1963
Monaco	5 digits before country	Monsieur John Doe 2, Avenue St-Michael 98930 MONACO	1972
Nepal	4 digits after country	Mr. John Doe Postal Services Kathmandu NEPAL 7110	1973: 6 digits April 13, 1977: changed to 4 digits
Netherlands	4 digits and 2 letters before city with space between	Mr. John Doe Postal Box 3000 2500 GA The Hague NETHERLANDS	March 1, 1978 smiling face
Norway	4 digits before city	Mr. John Doe Post Office Box 1181 0107 Oslo 1 NORWAY	March 18, 1968
Pakistan	5 digits after city with dash	Mr. John Doe Post Office Islamabad-44000 PAKISTAN	unknown
Palau	5 digits after country	Mr. John Doe Post Office Koror REPUBLIC OF PALAU 96940	July 1, 1963
Philippines	Letter with dash, then 3 digits after city	Mr. John Doe Liwasang Bonifacia Manila D-406 PHILIPPINES	Jan. 1, 1968
Poland	5 digits before city with dash between 2nd and 3rd digits	Mr. John Doe Place Malachowskiego 2 00-930 Warsaw POLAND	Jan. 1, 1973 stylized bird
Portugal	4 digits before city	Mr. John Doe Rue Conde Redondo 79 1192 Lisbon PORTUGAL	Jan. 1, 1979

Name of Country	Code's Nature and Position	Specimen Address for Mail Addressed to Country	Code's First Day of Use and Symbol
Reunion	5 digits before city	Monsieur John Doe Posts & Telecommunications 97495 Saint Denis REUNION	1972
Romania	4 digits before city, 5 digits before capital	Mr. John Doe Boulevard Dinicu Golescu No. 38 77113 Bucharest ROMANIA	Feb. 1, 1975
St. Pierre and Miquelon	5 digits before city	Monsieur John Doe Posts & Telecommunications 97500 St. Pierre ST. PIERRE & MIQUELON	1972
San Marino	5 digits before country	Signor John Doe Casella Postale 1 47031 SAN MARINO	June 1, 1967
Singapore	4 digits after city	Mr. John Doe 31 Exeter Road Singapore 0923 SINGAPORE	unknown
South Africa	4 digits before city	Mr. John Doe Private Bag X505 0001 Pretoria REPUBLIC OF SOUTH AFRICA	Oct. 6, 1973 elephant
Spain	5 digits before city	Senor John Doe Posts and Telgraphs 28070 Madrid SPAIN	July 16, 1982
Sweden	5 digits before city with space between 3rd and 4th digits	Mr. John Doe Post Office 105 00 Stockholm SWEDEN	March 19, 1968 pencil
Switzerland	4 digits before city	Herrn John Doe Posts and Telegraphs 3030 Bern SWITZERLAND	June 26, 1964
Taiwan	5 digits after city	Mr. John Doe Directorate of Posts Taipei 10605 TAIWAN	unknown
Thailand	5 digits after city	Mr. John Doe Communications Authority Bangkok 10400 THAILAND	Feb. 25, 1982 postman
Tunisia	4 digits before city	Mr. John Doe Post Office 1030 Tunis TUNISIA	March 20, 1980
Turkey	5 digits before city	Mr. John Doe Department of Posts 06101 Ankara TURKEY	unknown
United States of America	5 digits after state	Mr. John Doe 475 L'Enfant Plaza Washington, D.C. 20260	July 1, 1963 Mr. ZIP
Union of Soviet Socialist Republics	6 digits after city	Mr. John Doe 7, Rue Gorki Moscow 103375 UNION OF SOVIET SOCIALIST REPUBLICS	Jan. 1, 1971

Name of Country	Code's Nature and Position	Specimen Address for Mail Addressed to Country	Code's First Day of Use and Symbol
Vatican City	5 digits before city	Signor John Doe Administration of Posts 00120 Vatican City VATICAN	June 1, 1967
Venezuela	4 digits with dash and letter after city	Senor John Doe Apartado 4080 Caracas 1010-A VENEZUELA	unknown
Vietnam	5 digits after country	Mr. John Doe Pac Bo Hoa An Cao Lan VIETNAM 22494	unknown
Yugoslavia	5 digits before city	Mr. John Doe Palmoticeva 2 11001 Belgrade YUGOSLAVIA	Jan. 1, 1971

Universal Postal Union

The Universal Postal Union is a representative body that regulates international mail. Currently, 170 countries belong to the UPU.

The UPU's main objective is to unite the world into a single postal district so that no barrier, either physical or political, obstructs the delivery of the mails. Secondary goals include the standardization of weights and mailing rates.

It is difficult to imagine what communications would be like without the UPU. Before the founding of the UPU in 1874, each country's postal administration had its own system of weights and rates. Few postal administrations had agreements with others pertaining to such matters. There were more than 1,200 different postal rates.

Postal services between countries were haphazard at best and nearly impossible in most cases. The creation of the UPU enabled standardization of rates and weights and other policies. Today it is possible to mail postal materials to almost any location in the world, utilizing the services of the UPU.

As early as 1841, a German economist, J. Von Herrfeldt, proposed an international postal union. Nothing tangible came from his proposal, but his ideas may have influenced later postal officials.

At least two organizations served as forerunners to the UPU. In 1851, a British organization, the International and Colonial Postage Association, contracted with 20 foreign countries to apply similar rules to domestic and international mails. Twenty-seven countries agreed to the association's goals at the International Statistical Congress in 1853.

In 1863, Montgomery Blair, Postmaster General of the United States, initiated a meeting of 15 European and American countries in Paris. This group produced a non-binding contract that outlined an organization of postal unions. Basically, the idea of the UPU was created at this meeting. However, a truly international postal organization still did not exist.

Heinrich von Stephan, director general of post of the Confederation of Northern Germany, is known as the father of the UPU. At his proposal, representatives of 22 states met in Bern, Switzerland, during 1874.

The countries were: Austria, Belgium, Denmark, Egypt, France, Germany, Great Britain, Greece, Hungary, Italy, Luxembourg, the Netherlands, Norway, Portugal, Romania, Russia, Serbia, Spain, Sweden, Switzerland, Turkey and the United States.

The representatives drafted the treaty that resulted in the formation of the General Postal Union. The treaty came into force on July 1, 1875 (Jan. 1, 1876, for France). In 1878, the General Postal Union was renamed the Universal Postal Union.

On July 1, 1948, the UPU officially became a member of the United Nations' systems of organizations.

Any country, whether a U.N. member or not, can apply to belong to the UPU. A country that does not belong to the United Nations is admitted if the request is approved by at least two-thirds of the Union's member countries.

Mainland China was admitted to the United Nations in 1971. At the same time, Taiwan was expelled. The member countries of the UPU were consulted in April 1972 on how the United Nations' actions regarding the two Chinas would affect Taiwan's standing in the UPU.

It was decided that representatives of the government of Mainland China would be the sole representatives of China in the UPU.

UPU Regulations

The acts of the Union include a constitution, general regulations, a convention and detailed regulations.

The constitution is the basic act of the UPU. It sets forth the Union's aims and lays down precise rules concerning its structure. The conditions governing the application of the constitution are specified in the general regulations.

The convention contains certain common rules applicable to the international postal services and the provisions governing letter-post services. The detailed regulations supplement the convention.

Letter-post items include letters, aerogrammes, postcards, printed matter, literature in raised relief for the blind, and small packets. The convention fixes the rates, the maximum and minimum weight and size limits and the conditions of acceptance for these items.

The acts of the union are reviewed and revised every five years in a congress. Representatives of member nations attend these congresses.

The UPU, its rules and regulations have influenced and affected stamp and postal history collectors in a variety of ways.

Some of the effects began with the 1874 congress in Bern. At the congress, rates were reduced and simplified. The basic letter rate was set at 25 French gold centimes per 15 grams, with variations ranging from 20c to 32c permitted. The U.S. equivalent of 25c was 5¢. The U.S. 5¢ blue Zachary Taylor stamp was released in June 1875 to pay the new rate to UPU member countries.

Covers sent between member countries also soon reflected the new lower rates. Likewise, other rates set by the UPU throughout the years have been represented on stamps and covers.

At the 1874 congress, it was agreed that stamps should be used to prepay mail sent between countries. Non-prepaid mail would be charged twice the regular rate. This ruling resulted in virtually all international mail being prepaid by postage stamps.

The UPU also provided for the free forwarding of letters between member countries in most cases. For this reason, UPU covers are seldom found with combination franking; that is, with postage stamps of two or more countries.

Uniform colors for stamps to be used on international mail were agreed on at the fifth UPU congress held in 1897 in Washington, D.C. The purpose of uniform colors was to allow for easy recognition of fully paid international mail.

The colors selected were based on a survey of stamp colors then used by member nations. The colors were: dark blue for the international letter rate; red for the international postcard rate; and green for international printed matter.

The United States changed the colors of its stamps to fit into this arrangement in 1898.

Member nations liberally interpreted the color agreement. For example, an international letter-rate stamp may have a blue border with other colors in the main design. The policy was eliminated at the 13th UPU congress held in Brussels, Belgium, in 1953.

Another subject discussed at the 1897 congress was a universal postage stamp that would be valid for postage in all member countries. The purpose of the universal stamp would be to prepay return postage for correspondents in foreign countries and as a convenience for mailing remittances abroad. The idea was defeated due to the fluctuation in currency in the different countries.

Although the universal stamp proposal was defeated in 1897, the 1906 UPU congress in Rome created the International Reply Coupon, by which the sender can furnish return postage to someone in another country. The effective date of the IRC was Oct. 1, 1907.

Individual countries order IRCs from the UPU headquarters in Bern, Switzerland. In the United States, IRCs are sold at post offices. One IRC can be exchanged at a post office for a stamp paying the surface mail rate. Two or more IRCs are required for airmail rates.

Also at the 1906 congress, a free franking privilege was given to prisoners of war, and provisions were made for picture postcards to be handled the same as ordinary postal cards.

The UPU leaves matters relating to domestic stamps to the individual countries. Each country is free to choose the themes for its stamps, the face values, the number of stamps per set and the number of issues per year.

There have been a few exceptions.

The requirement that stamps intended for international mail should bear a face value or denomination was enacted at the 1897 congress in Washington, D.C. At the 1906 congress, it was decided that the denominations should be in Arabic figures. Because of these regulations, the United States non-denominated stamps, such as the E stamp, are limited to domestic use.

At the 1924 congress in Stockholm, Sweden, a provision was introduced requiring that "postage stamps and franking machine impressions shall, as far as possible, bear the name of the country of origin in Roman letters." The words "as far as possible" were deleted at the 1964 congress in Vienna, Austria.

Great Britain does not observe this provision. Instead, the effigy of the sovereign is used to denote that a stamp is from Great Britain.

The UPU has recommended that postal administrations issue square, rectangular or triangular stamps. This is merely a recommendation, not a regulation.

Guildelines regarding the size of stamps were passed at the 1979 congress in Rio de Janerio, Brazil. The guidelines basically say that a stamp's vertical and horizontal dimensions should be no smaller than 15 millimeters (approximately 1/2 inch) and no larger than 50mm (approximately 2 inches).

The UPU also has suggested that countries include the year date on their stamps. This is merely a suggestion and not binding.

The purpose of including year dates is to help collectors sort their stamps.

The suggestion came from a meeting of UPU officials with representatives of the International Federation of Philately (FIP), the International Federation of Stamp Dealers' Associations (IFSDA) and the International Association of Stamp Catalogue Publishers (ASCAT) in 1983.

Many countries now include the year date on their stamps. The United States does not.

Despite the fact that the UPU does not interfere in what stamps a country issues, it has made a few broad suggestions regarding the themes of stamps.

For example, a recommendation made at the 1979 congress in Rio de Janeiro stated: "Postal administrations should choose, when issuing postage stamps, subjects likely to contribute to mutual understanding among peoples, to the dissemination of culture and, generally speaking, to strenthening the bonds of international friendship."

In addition, the International Bureau of the UPU passes on to member nations requests from the United Nations or its specialized agencies regarding the issuance of commemorative stamps. For example, a 1984 UPU circular asked members to issue stamps in 1985 devoted to International Youth Year.

Regarding one aspect of the future of international mail and postal history, the UPU already has extensively studied the wider use of electronic mails in the international postal service.

The UPU also plays a role in stamp verification. It receives every stamp of all denominations and types used in the territory of each member nation. It is required to distribute these stamps to all other member nations.

UPU as a Topic

Several cancels, stamps and other philatelic items have honored the UPU and its congresses.

The first special cancellation for a UPU congress was used in Vienna, Austria, in 1891. The 1897 congress in Washington, D.C., was commemorated with a special Washington postmark. In addition, 125 sets of stamps and stationery were overprinted for presentation to the delegates.

In 1900, an extraordinary congress was held in Bern for the 25th anniversary of the UPU. For this occasion, Switzerland issued the world's first commemoratives honoring the UPU (Scott 98-103).

In 1920, Spain issued the first stamps to actually mark a UPU congress (Scott 318-30). Since then, the host country has issued stamps for each congress.

On June 17, 1947, Lebanon became the first country, other than a host nation, to release stamps honoring a UPU congress (Scott C129-34).

In 1957, the Swiss postal administration began issuing official stamps for use from the International Bureau of the UPU in Bern.

UPU Organization

The congress, the Executive Council, Consultative Council for Postal Studies and the International Bureau are the main bodies of the UPU.

The congress, which is composed of representatives of member countries, is the supreme authority of the union. In principle, the congress is convened every five years.

The main function of the congress is to study and revise the acts of the union.

The Executive Council (EC) comprises 40 members elected by congress with due regard for equitable geographic distribution. It meets every year at the UPU headquarters in Bern.

The EC ensures the continuity of the UPU's work. It coordinates and supervises UPU activities between congresses. The EC also studies administrative, legislative and legal problems of interest to the postal service, draws up proposals and makes recommendations to the congress.

The Consultative Council for Postal Studies (CCPS) includes 35 members elected by congress for the period between congresses. In principle, the CCPS meets annually at UPU headquarters.

The CCPS is responsible for organizing studies of major technical, operational and economical problems affecting postal administrations in UPU member countries.

The UPU's central office, known as the International Bureau (IB), is located in Bern. The IB coordinates, publishes and disseminates information about the international postal service.

The IB considers requests for amendments to the acts of the union, gives notice of changes adopted and takes part in the preparation of the work of the congress. At the request of the parties concerned, the IB also gives opinions on disputes.

Restricted Postal Unions

The UPU authorizes its members to establish restricted postal unions at a regional level. The aim of these unions is to improve reciprocal relations between member countries and to find solutions to postal problems of a continental, regional or sub-regional nature.

The UPU requires that these unions do not introduce provisions that are less favorable for the public than those laid down in the UPU acts.

The UPU currently maintains relations with the eight restricted unions, including the Postal Union of the Americas and Spain of which the United States Postal Service is a member.

Congresses

Nineteen congresses have been held by the UPU since its organization. The 20th congress is scheduled for 1989. The following list provides a thumbnail sketch and principal business of each of the congresses.

1. Bern, Switzerland, Sept. 15 - Oct. 9, 1874. Treaty concerning the creation of a General Postal Union. Number of countries represented, 22; number of participants, 42.

2. Paris, France, May 2 - June 4, 1878. Insured letters and money orders. Number of countries represented, 37; number of participants, 63; number of proposals, 413.

3. Lisbon, Portugal, Feb. 4 - March 21, 1885. Postal cards, collection of bills. Number of countries represented, 48; number of participants, 84; number of proposals, 818.

4. Vienna, Austria, May 20 - July 4, 1891. Insured parcels, subscriptions to newspapers, Cash-on-Delivery (COD). Number of countries represented, 49; number of participants, 99; number of proposals, 553.

5. Washington, D.C., May 5 - June 15, 1897. Number of countries represented, 56; number of participants, 103; number of proposals, 653.

6. Rome, Italy, April 7 - May 26, 1906. Reply coupons. Number of countries represented, 63; number of participants, 133; number of proposals, 798.

7. Madrid, Spain, Oct. 1 - Nov. 30, 1920. Gold franc becomes base currency, provisions concerning postal identity cards included in convention, transfers. Number of countries represented, 69; number of participants, 171; number of proposals, 2,248.

8. Stockholm, Sweden, July 4 - Aug. 28, 1924. Fiftieth anniversary of UPU. Number of countries represented, 78; number of participants, 182; number of proposals, 1,501.

9. London, England, May 10 - June 28, 1929. Small packets, airmail

provisions. Number of countries represented, 85; number of participants, 179; number of proposals, 1,895.

10. Cairo, Egypt, Feb. 1 - March 20, 1934. Postal travelers' checks. Number of countries represented, 81; number of participants, 153; number of proposals, 1,666.

11. Buenos Aires, Argentina, April 1 - May 23, 1939. Number of countries represented, 81; number of participants, 174; number of proposals, 1,108.

12. Paris, France, May 7 - July 5, 1947. U.N.-UPU Agreement, Executive and Liaison Committee. Number of countries represented, 79; number of participants, 291; number of proposals, 821.

13. Brussels, Belgium, May 14 - July 11, 1952. Extension to literature for the blind of the exception from postal charges granted to prisoners of war. Number of countries represented, 91; number of participants, 283; number of proposals, 1,712.

14. Ottawa, Canada, Aug. 14 - Oct. 3, 1957. Consultative Committee for Postal Studies, savings. Number of countries represented, 96; number of participants, 290; number of proposals, 1,288.

15. Vienna, Austria, May 29 - July 11, 1964. Constitution, technical cooperation. Number of countries represented, 122; number of participants, 520; number of proposals, 1,244.

16. Tokyo, Japan, Oct. 1 - Nov. 14, 1969. Possibility of compensating very high inward handling charges. Number of countries represented, 133; number of participants, 528; number of proposals, 1,156.

17. Lausanne, Switzerland, May 22 - July 4, 1974. UPU centenary. Number of countries represented, 141; number of participants, 714; number of proposals, 1,035.

18. Rio de Janeiro, Brazil, Sept. 12-Oct. 22, 1979. Revision of Acts of Union; incorporation into Universal Postal Convention of Insured Letters Agreement. Number of countries represented, 143; number of participants, 824; number of proposals, 1,351.

19. Hamburg, West Germany, June 18-July 27, 1984. Declaration of Hamburg, stresses UPU's role in strengthening the international postal service and in improving the standard and speed of international mail circulation. Number of countries represented, approximately 145; number of participants, approximately 917; number of proposals, approximately 850.

20. Washington, D.C., Nov. 13-Dec. 14, 1989.

Director General

Adwaldo Cardoso Botto de Barros of Brazil is director-general of the International Bureau and secretary-general of the UPU. He was named to that post during the conference at Hamburg, West Germany, to take office Jan. 1, 1985.

Felix Ciceron of France is deputy director-general.

Member Countries

As of Jan. 1, 1989, the membership of the UPU had increased to a total of 170.

The following list constitutes the membership of the Universal Postal Union as of January 1989. The date of current membership is shown in brackets.

Afghanistan (April 1928)
Albania (March 1922)
Algeria (1964)
Angola (1977)
Argentina (April 1878)
Australia (October 1907)
Austria (1946)
Bahamas (1974)
Bahrain (1973)
Bangladesh (February 1973)
Barbados (November 1967)
Belgium (July 1875)
Belize (October 1982)
Benin (April 1961)
Bhutan (March 1969)
Bolivia (April 1886)
Botswana (January 1968)
Brazil (July 1877)
Brunei (January 1985)
Bulgaria (July 1879)
Burkina Faso (March 1963)
Burma (October 1949)
Burundi (May 1969)
Byelorussian S.S.R. (May 1947)
Cameroon (July 1960)
Canada (July 1878)
Cape Verde (1976)

Central African Republic (December 1961)
Chad (June 1961)
Chile (April 1881)
China (March 1914)
Colombia (July 1881)
Comoros (1976)
Congo (July 1961)
Costa Rica (January 1883)
Cuba (October 1902)
Cyprus (November 1961)
Czechoslovakia (May 1920)
Denmark (July 1875)
Djibouti (1979)
Dominica (1979)
Dominican Republic (October 1880)
Ecuador (July 1880)
Egypt (July 1875)
Equatorial Guinea (July 1970)
Ethiopia (1945)
Fiji (June 1971)
Finland (February 1918)
France (July 1875)
Gabon (July 1961)
Gambia (October 1974)
Germany, East (1974)
Germany, West (1955)
Ghana (October 1957)
Great Britain (July 1875)
British Overseas Territories (various)
Greece (July 1875)
Grenada (1979)
Guatemala (August 1881)
Guinea (May 1959)
Guinea-Bissau (1974)
Guyana (March 1967)
Haiti (July 1881)
Honduras (April 1879)
Hungary (July 1875)
Iceland (November 1919)
India (July 1876)
Indonesia (1951)
Iran (September 1877)
Iraq (April 1929)
Ireland (September 1923)
Israel (December 1949)
Italy (July 1875)
Ivory Coast (March 1961)
Jamaica (August 1963)
Japan (June 1877, dropped in 1948, restored 1949)
Jordan (May 1947)
Kampuchea (Khmer) (December 1951)
Kenya (October 1964)
Kiribati (August 1984)
Korea, North (June 1974)
Korea, South (1949)
Kuwait (February 1960)
Laos (May 1952)
Lebanon (May 1946)
Lesotho (September 1967)
Liberia (April 1879)
Libya (June 1952)
Liechtenstein (April 1962)
Luxembourg (July 1875)
Malagasy Republic (November 1961)
Malawi (October 1966)
Malaysia (January 1958)
Maldives (August 1967)
Mali (April 1961)
Malta (May 1965)
Mauritania (March 1967)
Mauritius (August 1969)
Mexico (April 1879)
Monaco (October 1955)
Mongolia (August 1963)
Morocco (October 1956)
Mozambique (1979)
Nauru (April 1969)
Nepal (October 1956)
Netherlands (July 1875)
Netherland Antilles and Aruba (December 1954)
New Zealand (October 1907)
Nicaragua (May 1882)
Niger (June 1961)
Nigeria (July 1961)
Norway (July 1875)
Oman, Sultanate of (August 1971)
Pakistan (November 1947)
Panama (June 1904)
Papua New Guinea (1976)
Paraguay (July 1881)
Peru (April 1879)
Philippines (January 1922)
Poland (May 1919)
Portugal (July 1875)
Qatar (January 1969)
Romania (July 1875)
Rwanda (April 1963)
St. Kitts and Nevis (January 1988)
St. Lucia (1980)
St. Vincent & Grenadines (1981)
St. Thomas & Prince Islands (August 1977)
Salvador (April 1879)
San Marino (July 1915)
Saudi Arabia (January 1927)
Senegal (June 1961)

Seychelles (1979)
Sierre Leone (January 1962)
Singapore (January 1966)
Solomon Islands (May 1984)
Somalia (July 1960)
Spain (July 1875)
Sri Lanka (July 1949)
Sudan (July 1956)
Surinam (1976)
Swaziland (November 1969)
Sweden (July 1875)
Switzerland (July 1875)
Syria (May 1946)
Tanzania (March 1963)
Thailand (July 1885)
Togo (March 1962)
Tonga (January 1972)
Trinidad and Tobago (June 1963)
Tunisia (November 1956)
Turkey (July 1875)
Tuvalu (February 1981)
Uganda (February 1964)
Ukrainian S.S.R. (May 1947)
Union of Soviet Socialist Republics (As Russia July 1875)
United Arab Emirates (March 1973)
United States of America (July 1875)
Uruguay (July 1880)
Vanuatu (July 1982)
Vatican City (June 1929)
Venezuela (January 1880)
Vietnam (October 1951)
Western Samoa (August 1989)
Yemen Arab Republic (January 1930)
Yemen (People's Democratic Republic) (June 1968)
Yugoslavia (December 1921)
Zaire (July 1960)
Zambia (March 1967)
Zimbabwe (April 1980)

Postal History Societies By State

The following is a list of postal history societies by state. Also included is the society's publication.

Alaska

Alaska Collectors Club, 2337 Giant Oaks Drive, Pittsburgh, Pa. 15241; *The Alaskan Philatelist*, bimonthly.

Arizona

Arizona-New Mexico Postal History Society, 370 Deer Pass Drive, Sedona, Ariz. 86336; *The Roadrunner*, quarterly.

California

Western Cover Society, 1615 Rose St., Berkeley, Calif. 94703; *Western Express*, quarterly.

Colorado

Colorado Postal History Society, 1025 Monroe St., Denver, Colo. 80206; *Colorado Postal Historian*, quarterly.

Connecticut

Postal History Society of Connecticut, Box 276, Bloomfield, Conn. 06002; *The Journal of the Postal History Society of Connecticut*, quarterly.

Georgia

Georgia Postal History Society, Box 262, Griffin, Ga. 30244; *Georgia Postal History Society Bulletin*, irregular.

Hawaii

Hawaiian Philatelic Society, Box 10115, Honolulu, Hawaii 96816-0115; newsletter.

Illinois

Illinois Postal History Society, Box 1129, Waukegan, Ill. 60085; *Illinois Postal Historian*, quarterly.

Indiana

Indiana Postal History Society, 9635 E. Randall St., Columbus, Ind. 47201; newsletter.

Iowa

Iowa Postal History Society, 1298 29th St. N.E., Cedar Rapids, Iowa 52402; *Iowa Postal History Society Bulletin*, quarterly.

Maryland

Maryland Postal History Society, Box 13430, Baltimore, Md. 21203; untitled publication each year for BALPEX, also quarterly newsletter.

Massachusetts

Massachusetts Postal Research Society, Robert S. Borden, Box 202, North Abington, Mass. 02351; *The Massachusetts Spy*, bimonthly.

Michigan

Peninsular State Philatelic Society, Richard G. Ebach, 2265 Linda St., Saginaw, Mich. 48603; *Peninsular Philatelist*, quarterly, with occasional postal history articles; the PSPS is not a postal history society but does serve as a contact for postal history collectors.

Minnesota

Minnesota Postal History Society, Henry L. Lieske, 55 Idaho Ave. N., Golden Valley, Minn. 55427; newsletter.

Montana

Postcard/Paper Club, Tom Mulvaney, Box 814, East Helena, Mont. 59635; *Postcard/Paper Club Newsletter*, biannual.

Nevada

Nevada Postal History Study Group, Ted Gruber, Box 13408, Las Vegas, Nev. 89112; articles published in *La Posta*.

New Hampshire

New Hampshire Postal History Society, 38 Pleasant St., Somersworth, N.H. 03878; *Granite Posts*, quarterly.

New Jersey

New Jersey Postal History Society, 28 Briar Lane, Basking Ridge, N.J. 07920; *NJPH*, bimonthly.

New Mexico

See Arizona.

New York

Long Island Postal History Society, 97-10 71st Ave., Forest Hills, N.Y. 11375; *Long Island Postal Historian*, quarterly.

North Carolina

North Carolina Postal History Society, 602 Pearson Circle, New Bern, N.C. 28560; *The Journal of the North Carolina Postal History Society*, quarterly.

North Dakota

North Dakota Postal History Society, Box 280, Maddock, N.D. 58348; *Dakota Collector*, quarterly.

Ohio

Ohio Postal History Society, Box 441, Worthington, Ohio 43085; *Ohio Postal History Journal*, quarterly.

Oregon

Oregon Postal History Society, 201 Lowell St., Klamath Falls, Ore. 97601; *Oregon Postal History Journal*, quarterly.

Pennsylvania

Pennsylvania Postal History Society, 329 Milne St., Philadelphia, Pa. 19144; *Pennsylvania Postal Historian*, quarterly.

Rhode Island

Rhode Island Philatelic Society, Box 9385, Providence, R.I. 02940; *RI Phil Newsletter*, bimonthly.

South Carolina

South Carolina Study Group, Bob Stets, Box 142, Walterboro, S.C. 29488; no publication.

South Dakota

Occasional articles in *Dakota Collector*; see North Dakota.

Texas

The Texas Postal History Society, 5825 Caldwell, Waco, Texas 76710; *The Texas Postal History Society Bulletin*, quarterly.

Vermont

Vermont Philatelic Society, Oak Terrace Apartments, No. 10C, Colchester, Vt. 05446; *The Vermont Philatelist*, quarterly.

Virginia

Virginia Postal History Society, 2703 Dellrose Ave., Richmond, Va. 23228; *Way Markings*, quarterly.

Wisconsin

Wisconsin Postal History Society, N95 W32259 County Line Road, Hartland, Wis. 53029; *Badger Postal History*, quarterly.

Wyoming

Alan Patera, Box 2093, Lake Grove, Ore. 97035; *The Wyoming Collector*, quarterly.

Regional societies

Western Cover Society, 1615 Rose St., Berkeley, Calif. 94703; *Western Express*, quarterly.

Confederate Stamp Alliance, Box 14, Manitowoc, Wis. 54220; *The Confederate Philatelist*, bimonthly.

Private postal history journals

The Heliograph, Western Postal History Museum, Box 40725, Tucson, Ariz. 85717; quarterly.

La Posta, Box 135, Lake Oswego, Ore. 97034; bimonthly.

P.S.: A Quarterly Journal of Postal History, Box 175, Wyantskill, N.Y. 12198, quarterly.

Postal History U.S.A., 430 Ivy Ave., Crete, Neb. 68333, quarterly.

Note: In most cases, the addresses given are for the secretary of the society. Other addresses are for a contact person or for a newsletter editor.

Number Ones of the World

This listing includes the stamps listed as No. 1 for each country of the world as listed in the *Scott Postage Stamp Catalogue.*

Country	Issue date	Denomination
Abu Dhabi	March 30, 1964	5 naye paise bright yellow green
Aden	April 1, 1937	1/2 anna light green
Afganistan	1871	1 shahi black
Aguera, La	1920	1 centimos blue green
Aitutaki	1903	1/2 penny green
Ajman	June 20, 1964	1 naye paise multicolor
Alaouites	1925	10 centimes violet brown
Albania	June 1913	2 1/2 paras ocher
Alderney	June 14, 1983	1 penny multicolor
Alesandretta	1938	10 centimes violet brown
Algeria	1924	1 centimes dark gray
Allenstein	1920	5 pfennig green
Alwar	1877	1/2 anna ultramarine
Andorra	1928	2 centimos carmine rose
Andorra, French	1931	1 centimes red brown
Angola	1870	5 reis black
Angra	1892	5 reis yellow
Anguilla	Sept. 4, 1967	1/2¢ brown
Anjouan	1892	1 centimos blue
Annam and Tonkin	1888	1 centimes brown
Antigua	1862	6 pence blue green
Argentina	May 1, 1858	5 centavos red
Armenia	1919	60 kopecks light orange
Ascension	1922	1/2 penny green and black
Australia	1913	1/2 penny yellow green
Austria	1850	1 kreuzer yellow
Azerbaijan	1919	10 kopecks multicolor
Azores	1868	5 reis black
Baden	1851	1 kreuzer dark buff
Bahamas	1859	1 penny dull lake
Bahrain	Aug. 10, 1933	3 pies gray
Bamra	1888	1/2 anna yellow
Bangladesh	July 29, 1971	10 paisas red, dark purple and light brown
Barbados	1852	1/2 penny deep green
Barbuda	July 13, 1922	1/2 penny green
Barwani	April 1921	1/2 anna Prussian blue
Basutoland	Dec. 1, 1933	1/2 penny emerald
Batum	1919	5 kopecks green
Bavaria	1849	1 kreuzer black
Bechuanaland	1886	4 pence blue
Belgian Congo	1886	5 centimes green
Belgium	1849	10 centimes brown
Benin	1892	1 centimes bluish
Bergedorf	1861	1/2 schilling pale blue
Bermuda	1865	1 penny dull rose
Bhopal	1876	1/2 anna black
Bhor	1879	1/2 anna carmine
Bhutan	Oct. 10, 1962	2 chetrum red and gray
Bolivia	1867	5 centavos blue green
Bosnia and Herzegovina	1879	1/2 novcica black
Botswana	Sept. 30, 1966	2 1/2¢ multicolor
Brazil	Aug. 1, 1843	30 reis black
Bremen	1855	3 grote blue

Country	Issue date	Denomination
British Antarctic Territory	Feb. 1, 1963	1/2 penny dark blue
British Central Africa	1891	1 penny black
British Columbia and Vancouver Island	1860	2 1/2 pence dull rose
British East Africa	1890	1/2 anna lilac
British Guiana	1850	2¢ pale rose
British Honduras	1866	1 penny blue
British Indian Ocean Territory	Jan. 17, 1968	5¢ multicolor
Brunei	1906	1¢ violet and black
Bundi	1894	1/2 anna slate
Burma	April 1, 1937	3 pies slate
Burundi	July 1, 1962	25 centimes dark green and dull orange
Bushire	Aug. 15, 1915	1 chahis green and orange
Bussahir	1895	1/2 anna pink
Bulgaria	June 1, 1879	5 centimes black and yellow
Cambodia	1951	10¢ dark blue green
Cameroon	1897	3 pfennig green
Canada	1851	3 pence red
Canal Zone	1904	2 centavos rose
Cape of Good Hope	Sept. 1, 1953	1 penny red
Cape Verde	1877	5 reis black
Caroline Islands	1900	3 pfennig dark brown
Castellorizo	1920	1 centimes gray
Cayman Islands	1900	1/2 penny green
Central Africa	1959	15 franc multicolor
Central Lithuania	1920	25 fennigi red
Ceylon	1857	1 penny blue
Chad	1922	1 centimes red and violet
Chamba	1886	1/2 anna green
Charkhari	1894	1 anna green
Chile	1853	5 centavos brown red
China	1878	1 candareen green
Christmas Island	Oct. 15, 1958	2¢ yellow orange
Cochin	1892	1/2 anna yellow
Cocos Islands	June 11, 1963	3 pence dark red brown
Colombia	1859	2 1/2 centavos green
Conferderate States of America	1861	5¢ green
Cook Islands	1892	1 penny black
Costa Rica	1863	1/2 reis blue
Crete	1898	20 paras blue
Crete	1898	20 paras violet
Croatia	April 12, 1941	50 paras orange
Cuba	1855	1/2 peso blue green
Cyprus	1880	1/2 penny rose
Cyrenaica	1923	1 centesimi olive green and brown orange
Czechoslovakia	1918	3 haleru red violet
Dahomey	1899	1 centimes lilac blue
Dalmatia	May 1, 1919	1 corona brown and green
Danish West Indies	1856	3¢ dark carmine
Danzig	1920	5 pfennig green
Denmark	1851	2 rigsbank daler blue
Dhar	1897	1/2 pies red
Dominica	1874	1 penny violet
Dominican Republic	1865	1/2 reales rose
Dubai	June 15, 1963	1 naye paise dull blue and carmine rose

Country	Issue date	Denomination
Duttia	1893	1/2 anna orange red
East Africa and Uganda Protectorates	1903	1/2 annas gray green
Eastern Rumelia	1880	1/2 paras yellow green
Eastern Silesia	1920	1 heller dark brown
Ecuador	1865	1 reales ultramarine
Egypt	Jan. 1, 1866	5 paras slate green
Elobey, Annobon and Corisco	1903	1/4 centimos carmine
Epirus	Feb. 1914	1 lepta black and blue
Equatorial Guinea	Oct. 12, 1968	1 peseta multicolor
Eritrea	1892	1 centesimi bronze green
Estonia	1918	5 kopecks pale red
Ethopia	1894	1/4 guerche green
Falkland Islands	1878	1 penny claret
Faridkot	1879	1 folus ultramarine
Faroe Islands	Jan. 1919	2 ore green
Federated States of Micronesia	July 12, 1984	20¢ multicolor
Fernando Po	1868	20 centimos brown
Fiji	1870	1 penny pink
Finland	1856	5 kopecks blue
Fiume	Dec. 2, 1918	10 filler brown orange
France	1849	10 centimes bister
French Congo	1891	5 centimes lilac blue
French Equatorial Africa	1936	1 centimes brown violet
French Guiana	Dec. 1886	5 centimes brown
French Guinea	1892	1 centimes lilac blue
French India	1892	1 centimes lilac blue
French Morocco	1891	5 centimes green
French Polynesia	1892	1 centimes lilac blue
French Southern and Antarctic Territories	April 25, 1956	50 centimes multicolor
French Sudan	1894	1 centimes lilac blue
French West Africa	1943	1 1/2 franc dark violet
Fujeira	Sept. 22, 1964	1 naye paise multicolor
Funchal	1892	5 reis yellow
Gabon	1886	5 centimes red
Gambia	Jan. 1869	4 pence pale brown
German East Africa	1893	2 pesa brown
German New Guinea	1897	3 pfennig brown
German South-West Africa	1897	3 pfennig dark brown
Germany	1872	1/4 groschen violet
Ghana	March 6, 1957	2 pence rose red
Gibraltar	Jan. 1, 1886	1/2 penny green
Gilbert and Ellice Islands	Jan. 1, 1911	1/2 penny green
Gold Coast	July 1875	1 penny blue
Grand Comoro	1897	1 centimes lilac blue
Great Britain	May 6, 1840	1 penny black
Greece	1861	1 lepta chocolate
Greenland	1938	1 ore olive black
Grenada	1861	1 penny green
Griqualand West	1874	1 penny blue
Guadeloupe	1884	20 centimes brown
Guatemala	March 1, 1871	1 centavos ocher
Guernsey	Oct. 1, 1969	1 penny multicolor
Guyana	May 26, 1966	2¢ dark green
Gwalior	1885	1/2 anna green
Haiti	1881	1 centimes vermilion
Hamburg	1859	1/2 schilling black

Country	Issue date	Denomination
Hanover	1850	1 groschen gray blue
Hatay	1939	10 santims deep orange
Hawaii	1851	2¢ blue
Heligoland	1867	1/2 schilling blue green and rose
Honduras	1866	2 reales green
Hong Kong	Dec. 8, 1862	2¢ pale brown
Horta	1892	5 reis yellow
Hungary	1871	2 kreuzer orange
Hyderabad (Deccan)	1869	1/2 anna brown
Iceland	1873	2 skillings ultramarine
Idar	1939	1/2 anna light green
Ifni	1941	1 centimos green
India	1854	1/2 annas red
Indo-China	1889	5¢ deep violet
Indore	1889	1/2 anna orange
Inhambane	July 1, 1895	5 reis black
Ionian Islands	1859	1/2 penny orange
Iran	1868	1 shahis dull violet
Iraq	1923	1/2 annas olive green
Ireland	Feb. 17, 1922	1/2 penny green
Isle of Man	July 5, 1973	1/2 penny multicolor
Israel	May 16, 1948	3 mils orange
Italian Colonies	July 11, 1932	10 centesimi gray black
Italian East Africa	Feb. 7, 1938	2 centesimi red orange
Ivory Coast	1892	1 centimes lilac blue
Jaipur	1904	1/2 anna ultramarine
Jamaica	1860	1 penny blue
Jammu and Kashmir	1866	1/2 anna gray black
Japan	April 20, 1871	48 mon brown
Jasdan	1942	1 anna green
Jersey	Oct. 1, 1969	1/2 penny multicolor
Jhalawar	1887	1 pies yellow green
Jind	1885	1/2 anna green
Johore	1876	2¢ brown
Jordan	Nov. 1920	1 milliemes dark brown
Jugoslavia	1918	3 heller olive green
Karelia	1922	5 pennia dark gray
Kathiri State of Seiyun	1942	1/2 anna dark green
Kedah	1912	1¢ green and black
Kelantan	1911	1¢ gray green
Kenya	Dec. 12, 1963	5¢ blue, buff and dark brown
Kenya, Uganda & Tanzania	1921	1¢ black
Kiauchau	1900	5 pfennig carmine
Kionga	May 29, 1916	1/2 centavos blue
Kishangarh	1899	1 anna green
Korea	1884	5 mon rose
Kuwait	1923	1/2 annas green
Labuan	May 1879	2¢ green
Laos	1951	10¢ dark green and emerald
Las Bela	1897	1/2 anna white
Latakia	1931	10 centimes red violet
Latvia	Dec. 18, 1918	5 kapeikas carmine
Lebanon	1924	10 centimes violet brown
Leeward Islands	1890	1/2 penny lilac and green
Lesotho	Oct. 4, 1966	2 1/2¢ red brown, red and black
Liberia	1860	6¢ red
Libya	1912	1 centesimi brown

Country	Issue date	Denomination
Liechtenstein	1912	5 heller yellow green
Lithuania	Dec. 27, 1918	10 skatiku black
Lourenco Marques	1895	5 reis yellow
Lubeck	1859	1/2 schilling gray lilac
Luxembourg	Sept. 15, 1852	10 centimes gray black
Macao	1884	5 reis black
Madagascar (British)	1884	1 penny violet
Madagascar	1889	5 centimes lavendar
Madeira	Jan. 1, 1868	20 reis bister
Malacca	Dec. 1, 1948	10¢ purple
Malawi	July 6, 1964	3 pence dark gray and light orange
Malaya	1900	1¢ lilac and green
Malaysia	Sept. 16, 1963	10¢ violet and yellow
Maldive Islands	Sept. 9, 1906	2¢ orange brown
Mali	Nov. 7, 1959	25 franc multicolor
Malta	1860	1/2 penny buff
Manchukuo	July 26, 1932	1/2 fen gray brown
Marienwerder	1920	5 pfennig green
Marshall Islands	1897	3 pfennig green
Martinique	1886	5 centimes green
Mauritania	1906	1¢ slate
Mauritius	1847	1 penny orange
Mecklenburg-Schwerin	1856	1/4 schilling red
Mecklenburg-Strelitz	1864	1/4 silbergroschen orange
Memel	Aug. 1, 1920	5 pfennig green
Mexico	1856	1/2 reales blue
Middle Congo	1907	1 centime olive gray and brown
Modena	1852	5 centesimi green
Moheli	1906	1 centimes lilac blue
Monaco	1885	1 centimes olive green
Mongolia	1924	1 buff, gray and brown
Montenegro	1874	2 novcic yellow
Montserrat	1876	1 penny red
Morocco	1956	5 franc bright blue and indigo
Mozambique	1877	5 reis black
Mozambique Company	1892	5 reis black
Nabha	1885	1/2 anna green
Nandgaon	1892	1/2 anna blue
Natal	1857	3 pence rose
Nauru	1916	1/2 penny green
Negri Sembilan	1891	2¢ rose
Nepal	1881	1 anna ultramarine
Netherlands	1852	5¢ light blue
Netherlands Antilles	1873	2 1/4¢ green
Netherlands Indies	1870	1¢ slate green
Netherlands New Guinea	1950	1¢ slate blue
Nevis	1861	1 penny lake rose
New Britain	Oct. 17, 1914	1 penny brown
New Brunswick	1851	3 pence red
New Caledonia	1859	10 centimes black
New Guinea	1925	1/2 penny orange
New Hebrides	1908	1/2 penny gray green
New Hebrides	1908	5 centimes green
New South Wales	1850	1 penny red
New Zealand	July 18, 1855	1 penny dull carmine
Newfoundland	1857	1 penny brown violet
Nicaragua	Dec. 2, 1962	2 centavos dark blue

Country	Issue date	Denomination
Niger	1921	1 centimes brown violet and violet
Niger Coast Protectorate	1892	1/2 penny vermilion
Nigeria	1914	1/2 penny green
Niue	1902	1 penny carmine
Norfolk Island	June 10, 1947	1/2 penny deep orange
North Borneo	1883	2¢ brown
North German Confederation	1868	1/4 groschen red lilac
North Ingermanland	1920	5 pennia green
Northern Nigeria	Feb. 1914	1/2 penny lilac and green
Northern Rhodesia	1925	1/2 penny dark green
Norway	1855	4 skilling blue
Nossi-be	1889	25 centimes lavender
Nova Scotia	1851	1 penny red brown
Nowanuggur	1877	1 dokra dull blue
Nyasaland Protectorate	July 22, 1908	1 shilling black
Nyassa	1898	5 reis yellow
Obock	1892	1 centimes lilac blue
Oldenburg	1852	1 groschen blue
Oltre Giuba	July 29, 1925	1 centesimi brown
Oman	Nov. 20, 1944	3 pence slate
Orange River Colony	1868	1/2 penny red brown
Orchha	1913	1/2 anna ultramarine
Pahang	1889	2¢ rose
Pakistan	1947	3 pence slate
Palau	March 10, 1983	20¢ multicolor
Palestine	1918	1 piastre deep blue
Panama	1878	5 centavos gray green
Papua New Guinea	1901	1/2 penny yellow green
Paraguay	Aug. 1, 1870	1 reales rose
Parma	1852	5 centesimi yellow
Patiala	1884	1/2 anna green
Penang	Dec. 1, 1948	10¢ purple
Penrhyn Island	1902	1/2 penny green
People's Republic of China	Oct. 8, 1949	30 yuan blue
Perak	1878	2¢ brown
Perlis	Dec. 1, 1948	10¢ purple
Peru	Dec. 1, 1857	1 reales blue
Philippines	1854	5 cuartos orange
Pitcairn Islands	1940	1/2 penny blue green and orange
Poland	1860	10 kopecks blue and rose
Ponta Delgada	1892	5 reis yellow
Poonch	1876	6 pies red
Portugal	1853	5 reis orange brown
Portuguese Africa	April 1, 1898	2 1/2 reis blue green
Portuguese Congo	Aug. 5, 1894	5 reis yellow
Portuguese Guinea	1881	5 reis black
Portuguese India	Oct. 1, 1871	10 reis black
Prince Edward Island	Jan. 1, 1861	2 pence dull rose
Prussia	1850	4 pfennig yellow green
Puerto Rico	1873	25 centimes gray
Qatar	April 1, 1957	1 naye paise light brown
Quatiti State of Shirh and Mukalla	1942	1/2 anna dark green
Queensland	Nov. 1, 1860	1 penny deep rose
Quelimane	1913	1/4 centavos blue green
Rajasthan	1948	1/2 anna deep green
Rajpeepla	1880	1 piastre ultramarine

Country	Issue date	Denomination
Ras Al Khaima	Dec. 21, 1964	5 naye paise brown and black
Reunion	1852	15 centimes blue
Rhodesia	1890	1/2 penny black and vermilion
Rio de Oro	1905	1 centimo blue green
Rio Muni	1960	25 centimos dark violet blue
Romagna	1859	1/2 bajocchi straw
Roman States	1852	1/2 bajocchi gray blue
Romania	July 1858	27 parale rose
Rouad, Ile	Jan. 12, 1916	5 centimes green
Ruanda-Urundi	1924	6 centimes orange yellow
Russia	Dec. 10, 1857	10 kopecks brown and blue
Rwanda	July 1, 1962	10 centimes brown and gray green
Ryukyu Islands	1948	5 sen magenta
Saar	Jan. 30, 1920	2 pfennig gray
Sabah	July 1, 1964	1¢ red brown and green
St. Christopher	1870	1 penny dull rose
St. Helena	Jan. 1856	6 pence blue
St. Kitts	June 23, 1980	5¢ multicolor
St. Kitts-Nevis	1903	1/2 penny green and violet
St. Lucia	Dec. 18, 1860	1 penny rose red
St. Pierre and Miquelon	1885	5 centimes vermilion
St. Thomas and Prince Islands	1869	5 reis black
St. Vincent	1861	1 penny rose red
Ste. Marie de Madagascar	1894	1 centimes lilac blue
Salvador, El	1867	1/2 reales blue
Samoa	1877	1 penny blue
Samoa	1877	1 penny blue
San Marino	1877	2 centesimi green
Sarawak	March 1, 1869	3¢ brown
Sardinia	1851	5 centesimi gray black
Saudi Arabia	1916	1/4 piaster green
Saxony	1850	3 pfennigs green
Schleswig	Jan. 25, 1920	2 1/2 pfennig gray
Schleswig-Holstein	1850	1 schilling dull blue and greenish blue
Selangor	1878	2¢ brown
Senegal	1887	5 centimes red
Senegambia and Niger	1903	1 centimes lilac blue
Serbia	1866	1 paras dark green
Seychelles	1890	2¢ green and rose
Shanghai	1865	2 candareen black
Sharjah and Dependencies	July 10, 1963	1 naye paise light blue green and pink
Siberia	1919	35 kopecks dull green
Sierra Leone	1859	6 pence dull violet
Singapore	1948	1¢ black
Sirmoor	1879	1 piastre green
Solomon Islands	Feb. 14, 1907	1/2 penny ultramarine
Somali Coast	1894	5 centimes green and red
Somalia	Oct. 1903	1 besas brown
Somaliland Protectorate	1903	1/2 annas light green
Soruth	1864	1 anna bluish
South Africa	1913	1/2 penny green
South Arabia	Nov. 25, 1963	15¢ black and red
South Australia	1855	1 penny dark green
South Georgia	July 10, 1963	1/2 penny dull red
South Russia	1918	25 kopecks dull orange yellow
South-West Africa	Jan. 2, 1923	1/2 penny green

Country	Issue date	Denomination
Southern Nigeria	1901	1/2 penny yellow green and black
Southern Rhodesia	1924	1/2 penny dark green
Spain	Jan. 1, 1850	6 cuartos black
Spanish Guinea	1902	5 centimos dark green
Spanish Morocco	1903	1/4 centimos bister brown
Spanish Sahara	1924	5 centimos blue green
Spanish West Africa	June 5, 1949	4 pesetas gray green
Stellaland	Feb. 1, 1884	1 penny red
Straits Settlements	Sept. 1, 1867	1 1/2¢ blue
Sudan	March 1, 1897	1 milliemes brown
Surinam	1873	1¢ lilac green
Swaziland	1889	1/2 penny gray
Sweden	1855	3 skilling banco blue green
Switzerland	1850	2 1/2 rappen black and red
Switzerland-Basel	1845	2 1/2 rappen black, crimson and blue
Switzerland-Geneva	1843	10 centimes yellow green
Switzerland-Zurich	1843	4 rappen black
Syria	Nov. 21, 1919	1 milliemes gray
Tahiti	1882	25 centimes dark violet and orange
Tannu Tuva	1926	1 kopecks red
Tanzania	July 7, 1964	20¢ black and emerald
Tasmania	Nov. 1, 1853	1 penny blue
Tete	1913	1/4 centavos blue green
Thailand	1883	1 solot carmine
Thrace	1913	10 lepta rose
Thurn and Taxis	1852	1/4 groschen red brown
Tibet	1912	1/6 trangka green
Timor	1885	5 reis black
Tobago	1879	1 penny rose
Togo	1897	3 pfennig green
Tokelau	June 22, 1948	1/2 penny red brown and rose lilac
Tonga	1886	1 penny carmine rose
Transcaucasian Federated Republics	1923	10 kopecks dark blue
Transvaal	1869	1 penny brown lake
Travancore	1888	1 cash ultramarine
Travancore-Cochin	July 1, 1949	2 pies violet black
Trengganu	1910	1¢ gray green
Trieste	1947	25¢ bright blue green
Trinidad	1851	1 penny brick red
Trinidad and Tobago	1913	1/2 penny green
Tripolitania	Oct. 24, 1923	20 centesimi olive green and brown orange
Tristan da Cunha	Jan. 1, 1952	1/2 penny purple
Trucial States	Jan. 7, 1961	5 naye paise emerald
Tunsia	July 1, 1888	1 centimes blue
Turkey	1863	20 paras yellow
Turkey in Asia	1920	3 piastre red lilac
Turks and Caicos Islands	1900	1/2 penny green
Turks Islands	1867	1 penny rose
Tuscany	1851	1 quattrini black
Tuvalu	Jan. 1, 1976	1¢ multicolor
Two Sicilies	1858	1/2 grana pale lake
Ubangi-Shari	1915	2 centimes violet and brown
Uganda	1895	5 cowries black
Ukraine	1918	3 1/2 rubles black and gray
United Arab Emirates	Aug. 1972	5 fils multicolor

Country	Issue date	Denomination
United Nations	1951	1¢ magenta
United States	July 1, 1847	1¢ red brown
Upper Senegal and Niger	1906	1 centimes slate
Upper Silesia	Feb. 20, 1920	2 1/2 pfennig slate
Upper Volta	1920	1 centimes brown violet and violet
Uruguay	Oct. 1, 1956	60 centavos blue
Vatican City	Aug. 1, 1929	5 centesimi dark brown and pink
Venezuela	Jan. 1, 1859	1/2 real yellow
Victoria	1850	1 penny dull red
Vietnam	Aug. 16, 1951	10¢ olive green
Virgin Islands	1866	1 penny green
Wallis and Futuna Islands	1920	1 centimes green
West Irian	1962	1¢ vermilion and yellow
Western Australia	1854	1 penny black
Western Ukraine	1918	5 shagiv dull red
Wurttemberg	1851	1 kreuzer buff
Yemen	1926	2 1/2 bogaches black
Yemen, People's Democratic Republic	April 1, 1968	5 fils blue
Zambezia	1894	5 reis yellow
Zambia	Oct. 24, 1964	3 pence blue brown and green
Zanzibar	1895	1/2 anna green
Zuzuland	1888	1/2 penny vermilion

Number Ones By Date

May 6, 1840	Great Britain 1 penny black
1843	Switzerland-Geneva centimes yellow green
1843	Switzerland-Zurich 4 rappen black
Aug. 1, 1843	Brazil 30 reis black
1845	Switzerland-Basel 2 1/2 rappen black, crimson and blue
1847	Mauritius 1 penny orange
July 1, 1847	United States 1¢ red brown
1849	Bavaria 1 kreuzer black
1849	Belgium 10 centimes brown
1849	France 10 centimes bister
1850	Austria 1 kreuzer yellow
1850	British Guiana 2¢ pale rose
1850	Hanover 1 groschen gray blue
1850	New South Wales 1 penny red
1850	Prussia 4 pfennig yellow green
1850	Saxony 3 pfennig green
1850	Schleswig-Holstein 1 schilling dull blue and greenish blue
1850	Switzerland 2 1/2 rappen black and red
1850	Victoria 1 penny dull red
Jan. 1, 1850	Spain 6 cuartos black
1851	Baden 1 kreuzer dark buff
1851	Canada 3 pence red
1851	Denmark 2 rigsbank daler blue
1851	Hawaii 2¢ blue
1851	New Brunswick 3 pence red
1851	Nova Scotia 1 penny red brown
1851	Sardinia 5 centesimi gray black
1851	Trinidad 1 penny brick red
1851	Tuscany 1 quattrini black
1851	Wurttemberg 1 kreuzer buff
1852	Barbados 1/2 penny deep green

1852	Modena 5 centesimi green
1852	Netherlands 5¢ light blue
1852	Oldenburg 1 groschen blue
1852	Parma 5 centesimi yellow
1852	Reunion 15 centimes blue
1852	Roman States 1/2 bajocchi gray blue
1852	Thurn and Taxis 1/4 groschen red brown
Sept. 15, 1852	Luxembourg 10 centimes gray black
1853	Chile 5 centavos brown red
1853	Portugal 5 reis orange brown
Nov. 1, 1853	Tasmania 1 penny blue
1854	India 1/2 annas red
1854	Philippines 5 cuartos orange
1854	Western Australia 1 penny black
1855	Bremen 3 grote blue
1855	Cuba 1/2 peso blue green
1855	Norway 4 skilling blue
1855	South Australia 1 penny dark green
1855	Sweden 3 skilling banco blue green
July 18, 1855	New Zealand 1 penny dull carmine
1856	Danish West Indies 3¢ dark carmine
1856	Finland 5 kopecks blue
1856	Mecklenburg-Schwerin 1/4 schilling red
1856	Mexico 1/2 real blue
Jan. 1856	St. Helena 6 pence blue
1857	Ceylon 1 penny blue
1857	Natal 3 pence rose
1857	Newfoundland 1 penny brown violet
Dec. 1, 1857	Peru 1 real blue
Dec. 10, 1857	Russia 10 kopecks brown and blue
1858	Two Sicilies 1/2 grana pale lake
May 1, 1858	Argentina 5 centavos red
July 1858	Romania 27 parale rose
1859	Bahamas 1 penny dull lake
1859	Central Africa 15 francs multicolor
1859	Colombia 2 1/2 centavos green
1859	Hamburg 1/2 schilling black
1859	Ionian Islands 1/2 penny orange
1859	Lubeck 1/2 schilling gray lilac
1859	New Caledonia 10 centimes black
1859	Sierra Leone 6 pence dull violet
Jan. 1, 1859	Venezuela 1/2 reales yellow
1860	British Columbia and Vancouver Island 2 1/2 pence dull rose
1860	Jamaica 1 penny blue
1860	Liberia 6¢ red
1860	Malta 1/2 penny buff
1860	Poland 10 kopecks blue and rose
Nov. 1, 1860	Queensland 1 penny deep rose
Dec. 18, 1860	St. Lucia 1 penny rose red
1861	Bergedorf 1/2 schillings pale blue
1861	Conferderate States of America 5¢ green
1861	Greece 1 lepta chocolate
1861	Grenada 1 penny green
1861	Nevis 1 penny lake rose
1861	St. Vincent 1 penny rose red
Jan. 1, 1861	Prince Edward Island 2 pence dull rose
1862	Antigua 6 pence blue green
Dec. 8, 1862	Hong Kong 2¢ pale brown
1863	Costa Rica 1/2 reis blue
1863	Turkey 20 paras yellow
1864	Mecklenburg-Strelitz 1/4 silbergroschen orange
1864	Soruth 1 anna bluish

1865	Bermuda 1 penny dull rose
1865	Dominican Republic 1/2 reales rose
1865	Ecuador 1 reales ultramarine
1865	Shanghai 2 candareen black
1866	British Honduras 1 penny blue
1866	Honduras 2 reales green
1866	Jammu and Kashmir 1/2 anna gray black
1866	Serbia 1 paras dark green
1866	Virgin Islands 1 penny green
Jan. 1, 1866	Egypt 5 paras slate green
1867	Bolivia 5 centavos blue green
1905	Rio De Oro 1 centimo blue green
1867	Heligoland 1/2 schilling blue green and rose
1867	El Salvador 1/2 reales blue
1867	Turks Islands 1 penny rose
Sept. 1,1867	Straits Settlements 1 1/2¢ blue
1868	Azores 5 reis black
1868	Fernando Po 20 centimos brown
1868	Iran 1 shahis dull violet
1868	North German Confederation 1/4 groschen red lilac
1868	Orange River Colony 1/2 penny red brown
Jan. 1, 1868	Madeira 20 reis bister
1869	Hyderabad (Deccan) 1/2 anna brown
1869	St. Thomas and Prince Islands 5 reis black
1869	Transvaal 1 penny brown lake
Jan. 1869	Gambia 4 pence pale brown
March 1, 1869	Sarawak 3¢ brown
1870	Angola 5 reis black
1870	Fiji 1 penny pink
1870	Netherlands Indies 1¢ slate green
1870	St. Christopher 1 penny dull rose
Aug. 1, 1870	Paraguay 1 reales rose
1871	Afganistan 1 shahi black
1871	Hungary 2 kreuzer orange
March 1, 1871	Guatemala 1 centavos ocher
April 20, 1871	Japan 48 mon brown
Oct. 1, 1871	Portuguese India 10 reis black
1872	Germany 1/4 groschen violet
1873	Iceland 2 skillings ultramarine
1873	Netherlands Antilles 2. 25¢ green
1873	Puerto Rico 25 centimes gray
1873	Surinam 1¢ lilac green
1874	Dominica 1 penny violet
1874	Griqualand West 1 penny blue
1874	Montenegro 2 novcic yellow
July 1875	Gold Coast 1 penny blue
1876	Bhopal 1/2 anna black
1876	Johore 2¢ brown
1876	Montserrat 1 penny red
1876	Poonch 6 pies red
1877	Alwar 1/2 anna ultramarine
1877	Cape Verde 5 reis black
1877	Mozambique 5 reis black
1877	Nowanuggur 1 dokra dull blue
1877	Samoa 1 penny blue
1877	San Marino 2 centesimi green
1878	China 1 candareen green
1878	Falkland Islands 1 penny claret
1878	Panama 5 centavos gray green
1878	Perak 2¢ brown
1878	Selangor 2¢ brown
1879	Bhor 1/2 anna carmine

1879	Bosnia and Herzegovina 1/2 novcica black
1879	Faridkot 1 folus ultramarine
1879	Sirmoor 1 piastre green
1879	Tobago 1 penny rose
May 1879	Labuan 2¢ green
June 1, 1879	Bulgaria 5 centimes black and yellow
1880	Cyprus 1/2 penny rose
1880	Eastern Rumelia 1/2 paras yellow green
1880	Rajpeepla 1 Piastre ultramarine
1881	Haiti 1 centimes vermilion
1881	Nepal 1 anna ultramarine
1881	Portuguese Guinea 5 reis black
1882	Tahiti 25 centimes dark violet and orange
1883	North Borneo 2¢ brown
1883	Thailand 1 solot carmine
1884	Guadeloupe 20 centimes brown
1884	Korea 5 mon rose
1884	Macao 5 reis black
1884	Madagascar 1 penny violet
1884	Patiala 1/2 anna green
Feb. 1, 1884	Stellaland 1 penny red
1885	Gwalior 1/2 anna green
1885	Jind 1/2 anna green
1885	Monaco 1 centimes olive green
1885	Nabha 1/2 anna green
1885	St. Pierre and Miquelon 5 centimes vermilion
1885	Timor 5 reis black
1886	Bechuanaland 4 pence blue
1886	Belgian Congo 5 centimes green
1886	Chamba 1/2 anna green
1886	Gabon 5 centimes red
1886	Martinique 5 centimes green
1886	Tonga 1 penny carmine rose
Jan. 1, 1886	Gibraltar 1/2 pence green
Dec. 1886	French Guiana 5 centimes brown
1887	Jhalawar 1 pies yellow green
1887	Senegal 5 centimes red
1888	Annam and Tonkin 1 centimes brown
1888	Bamra 1/2 anna yellow
1888	Zuzuland 1/2 pence vermilion
1888	Travancore 1 cash ultramarine
July 1, 1888	Tunsia 1 centimes blue
1889	Indo-China 5¢ deep violet
1889	Indore 1/2 anna orange
1889	Madagascar 5 centimes lavendar
1889	Nossi-be 25 centimes lavender
1889	Pahang 2¢ rose
1889	Swaziland 1/2 pence gray
1890	British East Africa 1/2 anna lilac
1890	Leeward Islands 1/2 pence lilac and green
1890	Rhodesia 1/2 pence black and vermilion
1890	Seychelles 2¢ green and rose
1891	British Central Africa 1 penny black
1891	French Congo 5 centimes lilac blue
1891	French Morocco 5 centimes green
1891	Negri Sembilan 2¢ rose
1892	Angra 5 reis yellow
1892	Anjouan 1 centimos blue
1892	Benin 1 centimes bluish
1892	Cochin 1/2 anna yellow
1892	Cook Islands 1 penny black
1892	Eritrea 1 centesimi bronze green

1892	French Guinea 1 centimes lilac blue
1892	French India 1 centimes lilac blue
1892	French Polynesia 1 centimes lilac blue
1892	Funchal 5 reis yellow
1892	Horta 5 reis yellow
1892	Ivory Coast 1 centimes lilac blue
1892	Mozambique Company 5 reis black
1892	Nandgaon 1/2 anna blue
1892	Niger Coast Protectorate 1/2 penny vermilion
1892	Obock 1 centimes lilac blue
1892	Ponta Delgada 5 reis yellow
1893	Duttia 1/2 anna orange red
1893	German East Africa 2 pesa brown
1894	Bundi 1/2 anna slate
1894	Charkhari 1 anna green
1894	Ethopia 1/4 guerche green
1894	French Sudan 1 centimes lilac blue
1894	Somali Coast 5 centimes green and red
1894	Ste. Marie de Madagascar 1 centimes lilac blue
1894	Zambezia 5 reis yellow
Aug. 5, 1894	Portuguese Congo 5 reis yellow
1895	Bussahir 1/2 anna pink
1895	Lourenco Marques 5 reis yellow
1895	Uganda 5 cowries black
1895	Zanzibar 1/2 anna green
July 1, 1895	Inhambane 5 reis black
1897	Cameroon 3 pfennig green
1897	Dhar 1/2 pies red
1897	German New Guinea 3 pfennig brown
1897	German South-West Africa 3 pfennig dark brown
1897	Grand Comoro 1 centimes lilac blue
1897	Las Bela 1/2 anna white
1897	Marshall Islands 3 pfennig green
1897	Togo 3 pfennig green
March 1, 1897	Sudan 1 milliemes brown
1898	Crete 20 paras blue
1898	Nyassa 5 reis yellow
April 1, 1898	Portuguese Africa 2 1/2 reis blue green
1899	Dahomey 1 centimes lilac blue
1899	Kishangarh 1 anna green
1900	Caroline Islands 3 pfennig dark brown
1900	Cayman Islands 1/2 pence green
1900	Kiauchau 5 pfennig carmine
1900	Malaya 1¢ lilac and green
1900	Turks and Caicos Islands 1/2 pence green
1901	Papua New Guinea 1/2 pence yellow green
1901	Southern Nigeria 1/2 pence yellow green and black
1902	Niue 1 penny carmine
1902	Penrhyn Island 1/2 pence green
1902	Spanish Guinea 5 centimos dark green
1903	Aitutaki 1/2 pence green
1903	East Africa and Uganda Protectorates 1/2 annas gray green
1903	Elobey, Annobon and Corisco 1/4 centimos carmine
1903	Senegambia and Niger 1 centimes lilac blue
1903	Somaliland Protectorate 1/2 annas light green
1903	Spanish Morocco 1/4 centimos bister brown
1903	St. Kitts-Nevis 1/2 pence green and violet
Oct. 1903	Somalia 1 besas brown
1904	Canal Zone 2 centavos rose
1904	Jaipur 1/2 anna ultramarine
1905	Rio De Oro 1 centimos blue green
1906	Brunei 1¢ violet and black

1906	Mauritania 1¢ slate
1906	Moheli 1 centimes lilac blue
1906	Upper Senegal and Niger 1 centimes slate
Sept. 9, 1906	Maldive Islands 2¢ orange brown
1907	Middle Congo 1 centimes olive gray and brown
Feb. 14, 1907	Solomon Islands 1/2 pence ultramarine
1908	New Hebrides 1/2 pence gray green
1908	New Hebrides 5 centimes green
July 22, 1908	Nyasaland Protectorate 1 shilling black
1910	Trengganu 1¢ gray green
1911	Kelantan 1¢ gray green
Jan. 1, 1911	Gilbert and Ellice Islands 1/2 pence green
1912	Kedah 1¢ green and black
1912	Libya 1 centesimi brown
1912	Liechtenstein 5 heller yellow green
1912	Tibet 1/6 Trangka green
1913	Australia 1/2 pence yellow green
1913	Orchha 1/2 anna ultramarine
1913	Quelimane 1/4 centavos blue green
1913	South Africa 1/2 pence green
1913	Tete 1/4 centavos blue green
1913	Thrace 10 lepta rose
1913	Trinidad and Tobago 1/2 pence green
June 1913	Albania 2 1/2 paras ocher
1914	Nigeria 1/2 pence green
Feb. 1914	Epirus 1 lepta black and blue
Feb. 1914	Northern Nigeria 1/2 pence lilac and green
Oct. 17, 1914	New Britain 1 penny brown
1915	Ubangi-Shari 2 centimes violet and brown
Aug. 15, 1915	Bushire 1 chahis green and orange
1916	Nauru 1/2 pence green
1916	Saudi Arabia 1/4 piaster green
Jan. 12, 1916	Ile Rouad 5 centimes green
May 29, 1916	Kionga 1/2 centavos blue
1918	Czechoslovakia 3 haleru red violet
1918	Estonia 5 kopecks pale red
1918	Jugoslavia 3 heller olive green
1918	Palestine 1 piastre deep blue
1918	South Russia 25 kopecks dull orange yellow
1918	Ukraine 3 1/2 rubles black and gray
1918	Western Ukraine 5 shagiv dull red
Dec. 2, 1918	Fiume 10 filler brown orange
Dec. 18, 1918	Latvia 5 kapeikas carmine
Dec. 27, 1918	Lithuania 10 skatiku black
1919	Armenia 60 kopecks light orange
1919	Azerbaijan 10 kopecks multicolor
1919	Batum 5 kopecks green
1919	Siberia 35 kopecks dull green
Jan. 1919	Faroe Islands 2 ore green
May 1, 1919	Dalmatia 1 corona brown and green
Nov. 21, 1919	Syria 1 milliemes gray
1920	Aguera, La 1 centimos blue green
1920	Allenstein 5 pfennig green
1920	Castellorizo 1 centimes gray
1920	Central Lithuania 25 fennigi red
1920	Danzig 5 pfennig green
1920	Eastern Silesia 1 heller dark brown
1920	Marienwerder 5 pfennig green
1920	North Ingermanland 5 pennia green
1920	Turkey in Asia 3 piastre red lilac
1920	Upper Volta 1 centimes brown violet and violet
1920	Wallis and Futuna Islands 1 centimes green

Jan. 25, 1920	Schleswig 2 1/2 pfennig gray
Jan. 30, 1920	Saar 2 pfennig gray
Feb. 20, 1920	Upper Silesia 2 1/2 pfennig slate
Aug. 1, 1920	Memel 5 pfennig green
Nov. 1920	Jordan 1 milliemes dark brown
1921	Kenya, Uganda, Tanzania 1¢ black
1921	Niger 1 centimes brown violet and violet
April 1921	Barwani 1/2 anna Prussian blue
1922	Ascension 1/2 pence green and black
1922	Chad 1 centimes red and violet
1922	Karelia 5 pennia dark gray
Feb. 17, 1922	Ireland 1/2 pence green
July 13, 1922	Barbuda 1/2 pence green
1923	Cyrenaica 1 centesimi olive green and brown orange
1923	Iraq 1/2 annas olive green
1923	Kuwait 1/2 annas green
1923	Transcaucasian Federated Republics 10 kopecks dark blue
Jan. 2, 1923	South-West Africa 1/2 pence green
Oct. 24, 1923	Tripolitania 20 centesimi olive green and brown orange
1924	Algeria 1 centimes dark gray
1924	Lebanon 10 centimes violet brown
1924	Mongolia 1¢ buff, gray and brown
1924	Ruanda-Urundi 6 centimes orange yellow
1924	Southern Rhodesia 1/2 pence dark green
1924	Spanish Sahara 5 centimos blue green
1925	Alaouites 10 centimes violet brown
1925	New Guinea 1/2 pence orange
1925	Northern Rhodesia 1/2 pence dark green
July 29, 1925	Oltre Giuba 1 centesimi brown
1926	Tannu Tuva 1 kopeck red
1926	Yemen 2 1/2 bogaches black
1928	Andorra 2 centimos carmine rose
Aug. 1, 1929	Vatican City 5 centesimi dark brown and Pink
1931	Andorra, French 1 centimes red brown
1931	Latakia 10 centimes red violet
July 11, 1932	Italian Colonies 10 centesimi gray black
July 26, 1932	Manchukuo 1/2 fen gray brown
Aug. 10, 1933	Bahrain 3 pies gray
Dec. 1, 1933	Basutoland 1/2 pence emerald
1936	French Equatorial Africa 1 centimes brown violet
April 1, 1937	Aden 1/2 anna light green
April 1, 1937	Burma 3 pies slate
1938	Alesandretta 10 centimes violet brown
1938	Greenland 1 ore olive black
Feb. 7, 1938	Italian East Africa 2 centesimi red orange
1939	Hatay 10 santims deep orange
1939	Idar 1/2 anna light green
1940	Pitcairn Islands 1/2 pence blue green and orange
1941	Ifni 1 centimos green
April 12, 1941	Croatia 50 paras orange
1942	Jasdan 1 anna green
1942	Kathiri State of Seiyun 1/2 anna dark green
1942	Quatiti State of Shirh and Mukalla 1/2 anna dark green
1943	French West Africa 1 1/2 franc dark violet
Nov. 20, 1944	Oman 3 pence slate
1947	Pakistan 3 pence slate
1947	Trieste 25¢ bright blue green
June 10, 1947	Norfolk Island 1/2 penny deep orange
1948	Rajasthan 1/2 anna deep green
1948	Ryukyu Islands 5 sen magenta
1948	Singapore 1¢ black
May 16, 1948	Israel 3 mils orange

June 22, 1948	Tokelau 1/2 pence red brown and rose lilac
Dec. 1, 1948	Malacca 10¢ purple
Dec. 1, 1948	Penang 10¢ purple
Dec. 1, 1948	Perlis 10¢ purple
June 5, 1949	Spanish West Africa 4 pesetas gray green
July 1, 1949	Travancore-Cochin 2 pies violet black
Oct. 8, 1949	People's Republic of China 30 yuan blue
1950	Netherlands New Guinea 1¢ slate blue
1951	Cambodia 10¢ dark blue green
1951	Laos 10¢ dark green and emerald
1951	United Nations 1¢ magenta
Aug. 16, 1951	Vietnam 10¢ olive green
Jan. 1, 1952	Tristan da Cunha 1/2 pence purple
Sept. 1, 1953	Cape of Good Hope 1 penny red
1956	Morocco 5 francs bright blue and indigo
April 25, 1956	French Southern and Antarctic Territories 50 centimes multicolor
Oct. 1, 1956	Uruguay 60 centavos blue
March 6, 1957	Ghana 2 pence rose red
April 1, 1957	Qatar 1 naye paise light brown
Oct. 15, 1958	Christmas Island 2¢ yellow orange
1959	Romagna 1/2 bajocchi straw
Nov. 7, 1959	Mali 25 franc multicolor
1960	Rio Muni 25 centimos dark violet blue
Jan. 7, 1961	Trucial States 5 naye paise emerald
1962	West Irian 1¢ vermilion and yellow
July 1, 1962	Burundi 25 centimes dark green and dull orange
July 1, 1962	Rwanda 10 centimes brown and gray green
Oct. 10, 1962	Bhutan 2 chetrum red and gray
Dec. 2, 1962	Nicaragua 2 centavos dark blue
Feb. 1, 1963	British Antarctic Territory 1/2 pence dark blue
June 11, 1963	Cocos Islands 3 pence dark red brown
June 15, 1963	Dubai 1 naye paise dull blue and carmine rose
July 10, 1963	Sharjah and Dependencies 1 naye paise light blue green and pink
July 10, 1963	South Georgia 1/2 pence dull red
Sept. 16, 1963	Malaysia 10¢ violet and yellow
Nov. 25, 1963	South Arabia 15¢ black and red
Dec. 12, 1963	Kenya 5¢ blue, buff and dark brown
March 30, 1964	Abu Dhabi 5 naye paise bright yellow green
June 20, 1964	Ajman 1 naye paise multicolor
July 1, 1964	Sabah 1¢ red brown and green
July 6, 1964	Malawi 3 pence dark gray and light orange
July 7, 1964	Tanzania 20¢ black and emerald
Sept. 22, 1964	Fujeira 1 naye paise multicolor
Oct. 24, 1964	Zambia 3 pence blue brown and green
Dec. 21, 1964	Ras Al Khaima 5 naye paise brown and black
May 26, 1966	Guyana 2¢ dark green
Sept. 30, 1966	Botswana 2 1/2¢ multicolor
Oct. 4, 1966	Lesotho 2 1/2¢ red brown, red and black
Sept. 4, 1967	Anguilla 1/2¢ brown
Jan. 17, 1968	British Indian Ocean Territory 5¢ multicolor
April 1, 1968	Yemen, People's Democratic Republic 5 fils blue
Oct. 12, 1968	Equatorial Guinea 1 peseta multicolor
Oct. 1, 1969	Guernsey 1 penny multicolor
Oct. 1, 1969	Jersey 1/2 penny multicolor
July 29, 1971	Bangladesh 10 paisas red, dark purple and light brown
Aug. 1972	United Arab Emirates 5 fils multicolor
July 5, 1973	Isle of Man 1/2 penny multicolor
Jan. 1, 1976	Tuvalu 1¢ multicolor
June 23, 1980	St. Kitts 5¢ multicolor
March 10, 1983	Palau 20¢ multicolor
June 14, 1983	Alderney 1 penny multicolor
July 12, 1984	Federated States of Micronesia 20¢ multicolor

Chapter 2

U.S. Postal Service

Significant Dates in U.S. Postal History

1639: General Court of Massachusetts designates Richard Fairbanks' tavern in Boston as collection point for overseas mail.
1673: Boston Post Road named for the postal system begun there the same year.
1690: The first paper mill in the United States is opened by William Rittenhouse in Philadelphia, Pa.
1692: British Crown issues a grant to Thomas Neale to set up and maintain a post office in the Colonies for a term of 21 years.
1753: Benjamin Franklin appointed joint postmaster general for the Colonies under the British.
1756: Handstamped postal markings introduced in New York.
1766: Repeal of the unpopular stamp act.
1774: Baltimore journalist William Goddard establishes a private postal system to compete with that of the British.
1775: Benjamin Franklin named first postmaster general under the Continental Congress.
1782: Congress of the confederation guarantees mail service as a symbol of freedom, decreeing that private letters cannot be opened.
1789: Samuel Osgood named first postmaster general under U.S. Constitution.
1794: First letter carriers appear on the streets of some American cities.
1799: Government-owned coach service begins. First route between Philadelphia and New York City opened.
1800: Martha Washington becomes first president's wife to have franking privilege.
1813: Congress declares all steamship lines to be post routes.
1817: Machine-made paper is produced in the United States by Thomas Gilpin, at Brandywine Creek in Delaware.
1825: Dead Letter Office is established in Washington, D.C.
1828: Postmaster general becomes presidential cabinet post.
1842: Adhesive postage introduced in the United States by the City Despatch Post of New York City.
1845: Star Route contractor system created.
1847: First adhesive postage stamps issued by the United States.
1853: Parsons Paper Co. of Holyoke, Mass., began first large-scale production of paper in the United States.
1853: Stamped, embossed envelopes first produced in the United States.
1855: Registered mail introduced.
1856: Pre-payment of mail becomes obligatory.
1857: First perforated U.S. postage stamps produced.
1858: Street letter boxes debut.
1860: Pony Express service inaugurated.
1861: Pony Express service discontinued.
1861: Confederate postage stamps released.
1862: First U.S. revenue stamps released.
1862: Experimental traveling post office attempted.
1863: Free city mail delivery service starts in 49 cities.
1863: Uniform letter rates — regardless of distance — enacted by Congress.
1863: Scott publishes first catalog for stamp collectors.
1864: Railway post office introduced.
1867: International money orders first offered.
1869: First U.S. pictorial issues released.
1872: Post Office Department becomes an executive department of government.
1873: U.S. postal cards are first

introduced.
1873: First U.S. postal card issued.
1874: Universal Postal Union founded (originally the General Postal Union).
1879: Domestic mail divided into four classes.
1879: Postage due stamps first produced for use in the United States.
1885: Special delivery introduced.
1886: American Philatelic Society founded.
1887: *American Philatelist* first published by APS.
1887: International parcel post inaugurated.
1893: The Columbian series becomes the first U.S. commemoratives.
1893: First privately printed postcards for use with adhesive stamps permitted.
1893: Pneumatic tube mail service begins in Philadelphia, Pa.
1894: Bureau of Engraving and Printing takes over production of U.S. stamps.
1894: Society of Philatelic Americans founded.
1894: Guidelines with arrows at both ends begin as standard practice on flat-plate stamp production.
1896: Rural free delivery enacted by Congress.
1898: Privately printed postcards designated "Private Mailing Cards" permitted.
1900: Free mail delivery is extended to 796 offices with 15,322 letter carriers.
1900: First U.S. booklet stamps produced.
1901: Number of U.S. post offices peaks at 76,945.
1907: American National Red Cross produces first U.S. Christmas Seals.
1908: Government-produced coil stamps introduced.
1911: Postal savings initiated.
1912: Village mail delivery introduced.
1913: Parcel post service begun, includes COD and insurance rates.
1915: Rotary press printing introduced for stamp production.
1918: Airmail service inaugurated between New York City and Washington, D.C.
1918: Inverted 24¢ airmail Jenny produced.
1920: First cross-country airmail flight — New York to San Francisco — occurs.
1920: Metered postage introduced.
1921: Government philatelic agency founded — first like it in the world.
1922: USPOD policy governing first-day dates and cities established.
1923: George W. Linn creates first commercial cacheted first-day cover.
1925: The 1 1/2¢ Harding stamp becomes the first U.S. fractional denomination stamp.
1925: Special handling services are introduced.
1926: First souvenir sheet to be released by USPOD (White Plains).
1928: *Linn's Stamp News* founded.
1930: Zeppelin service stamps issued for limited time.
1932: First-class postage rises from 2¢ to 3¢.
1934: Ding Darling designs first U.S. duck stamp.
1934: First American Philatelic Congress held.
1935: Transpacific airmail service started.
1937: First official first-day-of-issue cancellation.
1939: Transatlantic airmail service started.
1941: Highway post office rolls into operation.
1942: "V" mail service in use.
1942: Revenue stamps placed on sale to collectors.
1943: Postal delivery zone system introduced.
1945: First U.S. mail sorting machine introduced.
1947: Helicopter airmail service begins in Los Angeles, Calif.
1948: Air parcel post system begins.
1953: Post office begins flying regular first-class mail between certain cities.
1955: Certified mail service begins.
1957: Giori press printing introduced for printing multicolor intaglio stamps.
1958: First-class postage rises from 3¢ to 4¢.
1959: First official Missile Mail dispatched from submarine to mainland, in Florida.
1962: USPOD intentionally reprints large quantities of the 4¢ Dag Hammarskjold color invert to destroy its value.
1962: First U.S. Christmas stamps released.
1963: First-class postage rises from 4¢

to 5¢.
1963: ZIP Code introduced.
1963: First U.S. phosphor-coated stamps produced.
1964: The first U.S. se-tenant stamps were released as that year's Christmas issue.
1964: First 24-hour self-service post office in use.
1966: Postal savings terminated.
1968: First-class postage rises from 5¢ to 6¢.
1968: $1 Airlift stamp released for use on parcels to overseas servicemen.
1968: Huck multicolor press introduced for stamp production.
1969: First postage stamp canceled on the moon by Apollo 11 mission.
1970: MAILGRAM (combination letter-telegram) introduced.
1970: Postal Reorganization Act signed into law.
1970: Experimental Express Mail service begun.
1971: U.S. Postal Service begins; postmaster general eliminated from cabinet.
1971: Star routes become highway contract routes. First-class mail rates rise from 6¢ to 8¢.
1974: Highway post offices terminated.
1974: First satellite transmission of MAILGRAMS.
1974: First-class mail rates rise from 8¢ to 10¢.
1974: First self-adhesive U.S. stamp released.
1975: First non-denominated U.S. stamps are released as year's Christmas stamps.
1975: First-class mail rates rise from 10¢ to 13¢.
1976: Post office class categories eliminated.
1977: Airmail abolished as a separate domestic rate category.
1977: Express Mail becomes permanent new class of service.
1977: Railway post office's final run, June 30.
1978: U.S. Postal Service begins copyrighting postage stamps and other philatelic products.
1978: First-class mail rates rise from 13¢ to 15¢.
1979: New envelope dimension standards go into effect.
1980: INTELPOST service introduced.
1981: First-class postage rises from 15¢ to 18¢.
1981: The first plate number coil stamps appear on 18¢ Flag issue.
1981: First-class postage rises from 18¢ to 20¢.
1982: E-COM service inaugurated.
1983: Express Mail one-day service flies onto the scene with $9.35 stamp.
1985: First-class postage rises from 20¢ to 22¢.
1985: Highest denomination postage stamp ($10.75) is released for Express Mail service.
1985: Postage due stamps discontinued and withdrawn from sale.
1987: Experimental stamp released on phosphor-coated paper.
1988: First-class postage rises from 22¢ to 25¢.

Post Office Development and Growth

Statistical Background

The following tables, taken from various editions of the "Annual Report of the Postmaster General" and "Comprehensive Statement on Postal Operations (January 1982)," demonstrate the development of the U.S. post office since the establishment of the nation's Constitution. While the provision of a vast sea of numbers sometimes tends to obscure what was happening on the grass-roots level, there is a great deal to be learned from such mundane facts as the number of post offices and the number of postal pieces in any given year.

Generally, one can see the growth and expansion of postal communications. For the first two years of service, there were only 75 post offices; by 1900 there were more than 76,000. The amount of mail matter carried has reached mind-boggling proportions.

There is also the other side of the story. The number of post offices is now much reduced from the turn of the century, due to such factors as the introduction of the Rural Free Delivery system, and the current drive to reduce postal costs. The number of pieces carried decreased during the Depression, and the last few years also show some examples of slackening off, possibly in response to rising rates and improving alternatives.

Statistical tables can be important sources of useful data, but they must be read with a critical eye and reference to supplementary information.

Post Office Development and Growth for Fiscal Years 1789-1846 (pre-stamp period)

Year	Number of post offices	Income[3]	Expenses[3]	Dead letters received	Amount from dead letters[17]
1789	75	[1]$7,510	[1]$7,560		
1790	75	37,935	32,140		
1791	89	46,294	36,697		
1792	195	67,443	54,530		
1793	209	104,746	72,039		
1794	450	128,947	89,972		
1795	453	160,620	117,893		
1796	468	195,066	131,571		
1797	554	213,998	150,114		
1798	639	232,977	179,084		
1799	677	264,846	188,037		
1800	903	280,804	213,994		
1801	1,025	320,442	255,151		
1802	1,114	327,044	281,916		
1803	1,258	351,822	322,364		
1804	1,405	389,449	337,502		
1805	1,558	421,373	377,367		
1806	1,710	446,105	417,233		
1807	1,848	478,762	453,885		
1808	1,944	460,564	462,828		
1809	2,012	506,633	498,012		
1810	2,300	551,684	495,969		
1811	2,403	587,246	499,098		
1812	2,610	649,208	540,165		
1813	2,708	703,154	631,011		
1814	2,670	730,270	727,126		
1815	3,000	1,043,065	748,121		
1816	3,260	961,782	804,022		
1817	3,459	1,002,973	916,515		
1818	3,618	1,130,235	1,035,832		
1819	4,000	1,204,737	1,117,861		
1820	4,500	1,111,927	1,160,926		
1821	4,650	1,059,087	1,165,481		
1822	4,709	1,117,490	1,167,572		
1823	4,043	1,130,115	1,156,995		
1824	5,182	1,197,758	1,188,019		
1825	5,677	1,306,525	1,229,043		
1826	6,150	1,447,703	1,366,712		
1827	7,300	1,524,633	1,469,959		
1828	7,530	1,659,915	1,689,945		
1829	8,004	1,707,418	1,782,132		
1830	8,450	1,850,583	1,932,708	[12]380,000	
1831	8,686	1,997,811	1,936,122	500,000	
1832	9,205	2,258,570	2,266,171		
1833	10,127	2,617,011	2,930,414		
1834	10,693	2,823,749	2,910,605		
1835	10,770	2,993,556	2,757,350		
1836	11,091	3,408,323	2,841,766		
1837	11,767	4,101,703	3,288,319	900,000	
1838	12,519	4,238,733	4,430,662		[13]12,060
1839	12,780	4,484,657	4,636,536		
1840	13,468	4,543,522	4,718,236		
1841	13,778	4,407,726	4,499,687		
1842	13,733	4,546,850	4,627,717		
1843	13,814	4,296,225	4,374,754		2,668
1844	14,103	4,237,288	4,298,513		20
1845	14,183	4,289,842	4,320,732		1,192
1846	14,601	3,487,199	4,076,037		1,824

See footnotes at end of tables.

Post Office Development and Growth for Fiscal Years 1847-1917

Year	Number of post offices	Income[3]	Expenses[3]	Postage stamps issued[4]	Stamped envelopes[5] & wrappers[6]	Postal cards issued[6]
1847	15,146	$3,880,309	$3,979,542			
1848	16,159	4,555,211	4,326,850	860,380		
1849	16,749	4,705,176	4,479,049	955,727		
1850	18,417	5,499,985	5,212,953	1,540,545		
1851	19,796	6,410,601	6,278,402	1,246,548		
1852	20,901	5,184,526	7,108,459	54,136,319		
1853	22,320	5,240,725	7,982,757	56,344,006	5,000,000	
1854	23,548	6,255,586	8,577,424	56,330,000	21,384,100	
1855	24,410	6,642,136	9,968,342	72,977,300	23,451,725	
1856	25,565	6,920,822	10,405,286	126,045,210	33,764,050	
1857	26,586	7,353,952	11,508,058	154,729,465	33,033,400	
1858	27,977	7,486,793	12,722,470	176,761,835	30,971,375	
1859	28,539	7,968,484	15,754,093	192,201,920	30,280,300	
1860	28,498	8,518,067	14,874,601	216,370,660	29,280,025	
1861	28,586	8,349,296	13,606,759	211,788,518	[6]26,027,300	
1862	28,875	8,299,821	11,125,364	251,307,105	27,234,159	
1863	29,047	11,163,790	11,314,207	338,340,385	25,548,750	
1864	28,878	12,438,254	12,644,786	334,054,610	28,218,800	
1865	28,882	14,556,159	13,694,728	387,419,455	[7]26,206,175	
1866	29,389	14,386,986	15,352,079	347,734,325	39,094,725	
1867	25,163	15,237,027	19,235,483	371,599,605	63,086,650	
1868	26,481	16,292,001	22,730,793	383,470,500	73,364,650	
1869	27,106	17,314,176	23,698,132	421,047,460	81,675,100	
1870	28,492	18,879,537	23,998,838	468,118,445	86,289,500	
1871	30,045	20,037,045	24,390,104	498,126,175	104,675,275	
1872	31,863	21,915,426	26,658,192	541,445,070	113,925,750	
1873	33,244	22,996,742	29,084,946	601,931,520	131,172,600	31,094,000
1874	34,294	26,471,072	32,126,415	632,733,420	136,418,500	91,079,000
1875	35,547	26,791,314	33,611,309	682,342,470	149,766,400	107,616,000
1876	36,383	28,644,198	33,263,488	698,799,090	165,520,250	150,815,000
1877	37,345	27,531,585	33,486,322	689,580,670	170,651,450	170,015,500
1878	38,253	29,277,517	34,165,084	742,461,940	183,500,350	200,630,000
1879	40,588	30,041,983	33,449,899	774,358,780	177,561,950	221,797,000
1880	42,989	33,315,479	36,542,804	875,681,970	207,137,000	272,550,500
1881	44,512	36,785,398	39,592,566	954,128,450	227,067,050	308,536,500
1882	46,231	41,876,410	40,482,021	1,114,560,330	256,565,450	351,498,000
1883	46,820	45,508,693	43,282,944	1,202,743,800	259,266,450	379,516,750
1884	48,434	43,325,959	47,224,560	1,459,768,460	322,232,050	362,876,750
1885	51,252	42,560,844	50,046,235	1,465,122,935	322,751,400	339,416,500
1886	53,614	43,948,423	51,004,744	1,620,784,100	354,008,100	355,648,000
1887	55,157	48,837,609	53,006,194	1,746,985,520	381,611,300	355,939,250
1888	57,376	52,695,177	56,458,315	1,867,173,140	433,635,750	381,797,500
1889	58,999	56,175,611	62,317,119	1,961,980,840	451,864,300	386,808,500
1890	62,401	60,882,098	66,259,548	2,219,737,060	513,832,950	429,515,350
1891	64,329	65,931,786	73,059,519	2,397,503,340	556,226,250	424,216,750
1892	67,119	70,930,475	76,980,846	2,543,270,210	593,684,700	511,433,500
1893	68,403	75,896,993	81,581,681	2,750,293,090	656,279,436	530,505,600
1894	69,805	75,080,479	84,994,112	2,602,278,355	571,475,218	468,499,750
1895	70,064	76,983,128	87,179,551	2,795,424,808	598,848,900	492,305,550
1896	70,360	82,499,208	90,932,670	3,025,481,467	616,040,250	524,820,140
1897	71,022	82,665,462	94,077,242	3,063,633,885	585,032,000	523,608,250
1898	73,570	89,012,618	98,053,523	3,418,458,360	606,447,000	556,380,650
1899	75,000	95,021,384	101,632,161	3,692,775,815	628,456,000	573,634,150
1900	76,688	102,353,579	107,740,268	3,998,544,564	707,555,000	587,815,250
1901	76,945	111,631,193	115,554,921	4,239,273,696	772,839,000	659,614,800
1902	75,924	121,848,047	124,785,697	4,621,285,723	853,128,000	547,204,090
1903	74,169	134,224,443	138,784,488	5,270,549,115	948,654,000	770,657,950
1904	71,131	143,582,624	152,362,117	5,330,886,845	1,020,255,250	702,907,450
1905	68,131	152,826,585	167,399,169	5,751,017,915	1,074,918,000	728,285,100
1906	65,600	167,932,783	178,449,779	6,284,450,495	1,230,287,750	798,917,850
1907	62,658	183,585,006	190,238,288	7,061,036,615	1,418,840,250	805,568,700
1908	60,704	191,478,663	208,351,886	7,651,400,405	1,266,002,559	809,426,750
1909	60,144	203,562,383	221,004,103	8,731,875,393	1,509,626,246	926,478,900
1910	59,580	224,128,658	229,977,225	9,067,164,886	1,506,861,598	726,441,000
1911	59,237	237,879,824	237,648,927	10,046,068,728	1,690,775,385	975,138,748
1912	58,729	246,744,016	248,525,450	9,929,173,748	1,684,624,161	909,411,045
1913	58,020	266,619,526	262,067,541	10,812,507,736	1,724,730,140	946,861,679
1914	56,810	287,934,565	283,543,769	11,112,254,281	1,864,713,929	962,072,326
1915	56,380	287,248,165	298,546,026	11,226,386,415	1,793,764,296	975,542,228
1916	55,935	312,057,689	306,204,033	11,671,842,200	1,853,791,461	1,047,894,800
1917	55,414	329,726,116	319,838,718	12,451,522,117	2,161,108,013	1,112,337,760

Post Office Development and Growth for Fiscal Years 1847-1917

Reg., cert., insured & c.o.d. mail[15]	Dead letters received	Amount from dead letters[17]	POs issuing money orders[14]	Mail of all kinds handled[16]	Year
	1,800,000	$ 187		124,173,000	1847
		1,296			1848
	2,100,000	99			1849
		1,748			1850
	2,750,000	1,675			1851
		8,265			1852
		1,384			1853
		4,346			1854
		4,976			1855
[9]620,332		8,383			1856
717,537		6,756			1857
562,903		3,410			1858
501,059	2,500,000	3,134			1859
500,774	2,000,000	3,803			1860
386,113	2,550,000				1861
302,987	2,282,018	1,052			1862
372,893	2,550,416				1863
259,798	3,508,825				1864
282,533	4,368,087	5,222	419		1865
275,103	5,198,605	18,393	766		1866
249,075	4,306,508	17,485	1,224		1867
	4,162,144	30,502	1,468		1868
	3,952,862	8,818	1,466		1869
	4,152,460	8,023	1,694		1870
	4,194,748	10,596	2,076		1871
	4,241,374	7,299	2,452		1872
	4,402,348	6,208	2,775		1873
	4,601,773	8,721	3,069		1874
	3,628,808	9,180	3,404		1875
4,007,817	3,542,494	9,889	3,401		1876
4,348,127	3,288,290	4,945	3,697		1877
4,898,804	3,186,805	8,937	4,143		1878
5,429,022	2,996,513	3,323	4,512		1879
6,996,513	3,057,141	6,506	4,829		1880
8,338,918	3,233,621	6,584	5,163		1881
9,627,922	4,160,554	7,657	5,491		1882
10,594,716	4,379,398	12,279	5,927		1883
11,246,545	4,564,451	9,619	6,310		1884
11,043,256	4,710,240	12,097	7,056		1885
11,648,227	4,791,698	8,858	7,357	3,747,000,000	1886
12,524,421	5,335,363	10,976	7,853	3,495,100,000	1887
13,677,169	6,217,876	10,535	8,241	3,576,100,000	1888
14,061,866	6,206,893	12,103	8,727	3,860,200,000	1889
14,947,081	6,517,556	12,050	9,382	4,005,408,000	1890
15,047,602	6,829,460	13,860	10,070	4,369,900,000	1891
15,260,094	6,780,980	15,929	12,069	4,776,575,000	1892
15,561,410	7,131,027	13,895	18,434	5,021,841,000	1893
15,050,554	7,101,044	14,940	19,262	4,919,090,000	1894
14,428,081	6,319,873	12,219	19,691	5,134,281,000	1895
15,106,336	6,253,363	11,957	18,825	5,693,719,000	1896
14,559,083	5,976,960	11,454	20,031	5,781,002,000	1897
15,600,220	6,295,853	10,527	22,388	6,214,447,000	1898
16,086,022	6,885,983	13,115	26,784	6,576,310,000	1899
18,422,649	7,536,158	14,465	29,649	7,129,990,000	1900
20,814,501	8,507,257	15,605	30,529	7,424,390,000	1901
22,831,400	9,300,351	18,459	31,680	8,085,447,000	1902
25,951,178	10,153,528	20,961	34,547	8,867,467,000	1903
28,213,870	10,923,239	22,210	35,094	9,502,460,000	1904
30,200,177	10,973,361	23,787	36,832	10,187,506,000	1905
34,165,484	11,663,377	24,090	37,444	11,361,091,000	1906
38,255,649	13,005,255	26,056	37,572	12,255,666,000	1907
40,151,797	13,145,172	36,644	43,313	13,364,069,000	1908
40,539,545	11,997,325	28,913	50,043	14,004,577,000	1909
42,053,574	12,545,133	30,783	51,791	14,850,103,000	1910
42,766,459	13,614,416	32,854	51,809	16,900,552,000	1911
42,235,600	13,268,199	33,122	52,815	17,588,659,000	1912
[10]43,489,172	13,214,346	31,143	54,594	18,567,445,000	1913
[11]56,397,194	12,082,342	39,077	55,949		1914
60,042,590	10,781,927	38,514	55,670		1915
70,473,197	10,839,890	45,856	56,026		1916
84,117,774	13,614,927	57,938	56,170		1917

Post Office Development and Growth for Fiscal Years 1918-1988

Year	Number of post offices	Income[3]	Expenses[3]	Postage stamps issued[4]	Stamped envelopes[5] & wrappers[6]	Postal cards issued[6]
1918	54,347	$[2]388,975,962	$324,833,728	13,065,784,862	1,819,307,148	707,111,300
1919	53,084	[2]436,239,126	362,497,636	15,020,470,168	1,844,884,905	456,924,490
1920	52,641	437,150,212	454,322,609	13,212,790,033	2,350,073,359	986,156,087
1921	52,168	463,491,275	620,993,674	13,869,934,907	2,738,934,489	1,081,206,536
1922	51,950	484,853,541	545,644,209	14,261,948,813	2,364,372,708	1,111,124,439
1923	51,613	532,827,925	556,850,966	15,478,095,130	2,721,475,103	1,253,195,951
1924	51,266	572,948,778	587,376,916	15,954,475,462	2,964,464,261	1,293,184,528
1925	50,957	599,591,478	639,281,648	17,386,555,506	2,997,177,406	1,497,366,700
1926	50,601	659,819,801	679,704,053	16,333,410,317	3,001,858,230	1,668,240,506
1927	50,266	683,121,989	714,577,492	15,999,701,194	3,145,946,376	1,834,456,466
1928	49,944	693,633,921	725,699,766	16,676,492,729	3,201,458,891	1,872,040,126
1929	49,482	696,947,578	782,343,648	16,917,274,874	3,228,586,578	1,783,897,145
1930	49,063	705,484,098	803,667,219	16,268,856,071	3,164,127,424	1,643,212,150
1931	48,733	656,463,383	802,484,840	15,559,164,487	2,847,439,346	1,531,245,650
1932	48,159	588,171,923	793,684,323	14,650,970,133	2,384,792,755	1,334,753,100
1933	47,641	587,631,364	699,887,186	11,917,442,423	1,644,993,351	1,389,523,602
1934	46,506	586,733,166	630,732,934	12,525,716,839	1,580,819,713	1,590,257,450
1935	45,686	630,795,302	696,503,235	13,610,497,410	1,617,677,432	1,754,030,250
1936	45,230	665,343,356	753,616,212	13,835,399,920	1,647,890,978	1,917,793,442
1937	44,877	726,201,110	772,743,145	15,108,639,409	1,663,818,025	2,226,153,250
1938	44,586	728,634,051	772,307,506	14,912,092,916	1,643,815,325	2,186,720,600
1939	44,327	745,955,075	784,549,842	15,073,795,772	1,605,075,706	2,170,572,250
1940	44,024	766,948,627	807,629,180	16,381,427,297	1,649,548,500	2,256,519,650
1941	43,739	812,827,735	836,858,580	16,381,321,410	1,645,254,500	2,400,188,380
1942	43,358	859,817,491	873,950,372	19,492,121,339	1,676,573,172	2,370,061,600
1943	42,654	966,227,288	952,529,098	19,123,977,153	1,797,400,250	2,316,989,950
1944	42,161	1,112,877,174	1,068,986,872	19,106,171,157	1,902,312,750	1,912,990,100
1945	41,792	1,314,240,132	1,145,002,246	20,239,986,294	2,064,773,000	2,282,280,350
1946	41,751	1,224,572,173	1,353,654,000	19,180,426,775	1,815,915,500	2,477,853,770
1947	41,760	1,299,141,041	1,504,799,000	19,542,256,985	1,996,449,500	2,951,299,600
1948	41,695	1,410,971,284	1,687,805,000	20,432,059,035	2,117,572,750	3,656,590,675
1949	41,607	1,571,851,202	2,149,322,000	21,047,376,040	2,219,743,500	3,468,718,950
1950	41,464	1,677,486,967	2,222,949,000	20,647,164,914	2,052,155,500	3,872,300,900
1951	41,193	1,776,816,354	2,341,399,000	21,521,806,685	2,004,568,500	4,183,748,200
1952	40,919	1,947,316,280	2,666,860,000	22,067,082,690	2,274,659,750	2,984,123,500
1953	40,609	2,091,714,112	2,742,126,000	22,960,961,855	2,338,622,250	2,330,921,050
1954	39,405	[3]2,268,516,717	[3]2,667,664,000	22,219,068,245	2,265,309,250	2,360,534,150
1955	38,316	2,349,476,528	2,712,150,214	23,105,454,370	2,189,520,750	2,515,392,025
1956	37,515	2,419,353,664	2,883,305,122	23,722,488,960	2,571,416,250	2,911,276,350
1957	37,012	2,496,614,310	3,044,438,004	24,257,859,530	1,966,335,500	2,046,515,000
1958	36,308	2,550,220,791	3,440,810,346	22,879,828,252	2,040,211,000	2,375,065,000
1959	35,750	3,035,231,808	3,640,368,053	27,980,885,070	2,228,812,720	2,969,055,000
1960	35,238	3,276,588,433	3,873,952,908	23,773,570,200	2,005,442,000	1,773,090,000
1961	34,955	3,423,058,716	4,249,413,744	23,001,808,400	2,021,031,500	1,653,595,000
1962	34,797	3,557,040,595	4,331,617,483	25,405,928,600	1,789,414,500	1,463,665,000
1963	34,498	[3]3,879,127,992	[3]4,698,527,911	31,669,175,000	2,344,716,750	2,487,038,000
1964	34,040	4,276,123,326	4,927,824,958	24,692,325,800	1,928,981,500	1,563,165,000
1965	33,624	4,483,389,833	5,275,839,877	22,691,105,600	1,670,725,500	1,092,380,000
1966	33,121	4,784,186,482	5,726,522,930	23,503,958,800	1,627,788,500	1,289,000,000
1967	32,626	5,101,982,384	6,249,026,677	26,320,986,420	1,512,996,000	1,011,675,000
1968	32,260	5,660,111,244	6,680,971,666	34,667,494,050	1,853,426,500	1,431,310,500
1969	32,064	6,255,883,348	7,278,849,508	27,383,826,600	1,374,121,000	846,695,000
1970	32,002	6,472,737,791	7,982,551,936	26,182,562,000	1,368,097,500	830,649,500
1971	31,947	8,751,484,000	8,955,264,000			
1972	31,686	9,245,388,000	9,522,378,000			
1973	31,385	9,716,405,000	9,818,306,000			
1974	31,000	10,761,456,000	11,298,036,000			
1975	30,754	11,552,328,000	12,578,429,000			
1976	30,521	12,843,714,000	13,922,736,000			
1977	30,521	14,709,939,000	15,310,169,000			
1978	30,518	15,854,566,000	16,219,619,000			
1979	30,449	17,825,629,000	17,529,303,000			
1980	30,326	19,253,000,000	19,559,000,000			
1981	30,242	20,898,000,000	21,486,000,000			
1982	30,155	23,627,793,000	21,369,139,000			
1983	29,990	24,699,399,000	24,083,073,000			
1984	29,750	26,474,705,000	26,357,353,000			
1985	29,557	28,955,721,000	29,207,201,000			
1986	29,344	31,021,203,000	30,716,595,000			
1987	29,319	32,297,000,000	32,519,700,000			
1988	29,203	35,522,306,000	36,119,186,000			

Post Office Development and Growth for Fiscal Years 1918-1988

Reg., cert., insured & c.o.d. mail[15]	Dead letters received	Amount from dead letters[17]	POs issuing money orders[14]	Mail of all kinds handled[16]	Year
109,070,762	14,451,953	$71,709	55,668		1918
149,754,951	22,982,604	199,222	54,826		1919
192,397,014	19,353,413	226,962	54,395		1920
220,856,945	19,683,259	223,621	54,183		1921
238,736,406	16,586,419	183,965	54,201		1922
269,840,470	19,238,548	143,993	54,181	23,054,832,000	1923
286,755,587	21,618,168	176,340	54,195		1924
294,174,647	21,332,232	223,197	54,269		1925
271,871,648	24,056,928	184,489	55,589	25,483,529,000	1926
266,283,318	25,854,845	149,116	54,616	26,686,556,000	1927
265,584,415	23,649,044	146,322	54,803	26,837,005,000	1928
270,577,460	23,079,619	128,932	54,357	27,951,548,000	1929
266,356,558	22,685,940	147,280	54,161	27,887,823,000	1930
233,384,741	19,957,684	122,992	55,040	26,544,352,000	1931
192,580,879	17,210,588	93,603	55,081	24,306,744,000	1932
150,737,943	10,708,353	89,389	56,106	19,868,456,000	1933
149,535,527	11,466,622	88,391	53,803	20,625,827,000	1934
154,950,349	12,567,130	87,310	53,106	22,331,752,000	1935
170,571,613	12,328,618	118,979	51,610	23,571,315,000	1936
176,302,102	13,802,638	103,722	51,304	25,801,279,000	1937
168,216,454	13,700,683	105,045	51,119	26,041,979,000	1938
169,866,593	13,226,456	96,452	50,956	26,444,846,000	1939
168,145,205	13,028,111	95,696	50,705	27,749,467,000	1940
173,827,676	13,744,889	100,701	50,745	29,235,791,000	1941
205,706,286	14,990,943	133,193	51,900	30,117,633,000	1942
297,581,386	15,437,258	220,705	53,694	32,818,262,000	1943
297,455,473	15,469,045	308,798	53,915	34,930,685,000	1944
279,530,763	14,144,856	351,162	53,435	37,912,067,000	1945
278,800,771	18,676,852	456,148	48,510	36,318,158,000	1946
310,456,030	18,184,742	476,690	48,344	37,427,706,000	1947
338,638,938	18,100,456	507,152	48,406	40,280,374,000	1948
364,807,636	18,142,721	465,442	49,239	43,555,108,000	1949
347,667,006	18,922,309	397,107	49,269	45,063,737,000	1950
348,592,983	22,935,365	443,304	48,318	46,908,410,000	1951
342,631,183	22,797,455	464,397	49,599	49,905,875,000	1952
331,151,247	23,174,794	429,583	48,482	50,948,156,000	1953
316,578,914	20,043,201	379,851	47,153	52,213,170,000	1954
310,310,171	20,625,463	421,573	47,789	55,233,564,000	1955
305,244,988	21,088,494	365,312	46,561	56,441,216,000	1956
302,986,760	23,808,568	439,614	45,222	59,077,633,000	1957
262,153,838	24,054,103	551,372	44,804	60,129,911,000	1958
270,403,560	21,487,114	514,459	44,615	61,247,220,000	1959
270,867,819	21,969,725	560,979	44,600	63,674,604,000	1960
267,349,907	21,822,853	613,307	44,764	64,932,859,000	1961
269,707,097	22,300,117	673,531	44,953	66,493,190,000	1962
271,987,671	23,547,406	680,293	44,845	67,852,738,000	1963
274,962,977	22,744,417	748,784	44,684	69,676,477,000	1964
273,352,431	24,893,349	779,255	44,586	71,873,166,000	1965
274,124,608	27,332,964	770,814	44,333	75,607,302,000	1966
280,368,237	30,415,977	904,571	44,150	78,366,572,000	1967
285,009,957	32,774,881	935,390	43,431	79,516,731,000	1968
260,901,000	36,363,344	1,095,254	43,220	82,004,501,000	1969
240,143,000	37,422,610	1,089,110	43,112	84,881,833,000	1970
258,730,000			42,287	86,983,000,000	1971
259,886,000			42,254	87,156,084,000	1972
254,023,000			41,434	89,683,439,000	1973
250,524,000			40,914	90,098,108,000	1974
252,373,000			40,546	89,265,979,000	1975
257,721,000			40,392	89,767,903,000	1976
242,910,000			40,322	92,223,912,000	1977
226,165,000			39,870	96,913,154,000	1978
206,910,000			39,733	99,828,883,000	1979
216,138,000			39,486	106,311,062,000	1980
218,373,000			39,457	110,130,400,000	1981
270,375,000				114,049,210,000	1982
225,773,000				119,381,419,000	1983
237,767,000				131,544,620,000	1984
236,215,000				140,097,956,000	1985
249,888,000				147,376,000,000	1986
263,440,000				153,931,000,000	1987
259,463,000				160,491,000,000	1988

[1]For 3 months only.
[2]Revenues for 1918 and 1919 include $44,500,000 and $71,392,000, respectively, war-tax revenue accruing from increased postage.
[3]Basis of reporting changed. Reporting on accrued cost basis beginning in 1963.
[4]Postage stamps first issued under act of March 3, 1847, and placed on sale at New York, N.Y., July 1, 1847.
[5]Stamped envelopes first issued June 1853 under act of Aug. 31, 1852.
[6]Newspaper wrappers first issued under act of Feb. 27, 1861, not made after Oct. 9, 1934.
[7]Special-request envelopes first issued in 1865.
[8]Postal cards first issued May 1, 1873, under act of June 8, 1872.
[9]Letters first registered July 1, 1855, under act of March 3, 1855.
[10]Insurance service inaugurated Jan. 1, 1913, under act of Congress, Aug. 24, 1912.
[11]C.o.d. service inaugurated July 1, 1913, under act of Congress, Aug. 24, 1912.
[12]Letters returned to writers.
[13]Aggregate accumulation from 1789 to 1838.
[14]Indicates number of post offices, stations and branches. Money-order system went into operation Nov. 1, 1864, under act of Congress of May 17, 1864.
[15]Indicates number of pieces of mail in domestic system given the noted services. Certified mail introduced June 6, 1955.
[16]Beginning 1968 volume based on new probability sample data; not comparable with previous years.
[17]Includes both dead letters and parcels.

U.S. Postmasters General

Following is a listing of postmasters general of the United States and the authorities under whom they served. Dates of entry into service and home states also are noted.

Benjamin Franklin, Pennsylvania
July 26, 1775
Continental Congress

Richard Bache, Pennsylvania
Nov. 7, 1776
Continental Congress

Ebenezer Hazard, New York
Jan. 28, 1782
Continental Congress

Samuel Osgood, Massachusetts
Sept. 26, 1789
George Washington

Timothy Pickering, Pennsylvania
Aug. 12, 1791
George Washington

Joseph Habersham, Georgia
Feb. 25, 1795
George Washington

Gideon Granger, Connecticut
Nov. 28, 1801
Thomas Jefferson

Return J. Meigs Jr., Ohio
April 11, 1814
James Madison

John McLean, Ohio
July 1, 1823
James Monroe

William T. Barry, Kentucky
April 6, 1829
Andrew Jackson

Amos Kendall, Kentucky
May 1, 1835
Andrew Jackson

John M. Niles, Connecticut
May 26, 1840
Martin Van Buren

Francis Granger, New York
March 8, 1841
William Henry Harrison
and John Tyler

Charles A. Wickliffe, Kentucky
Oct. 13, 1841
John Tyler

Cave Johnson, Tennessee
March 7, 1845
James K. Polk

Jacob Collamer, Vermont
March 8, 1849
Zachary Taylor

Nathan K. Hall, New York
July 23, 1850
Millard Fillmore

Samuel D. Hubbard, Connecticut
Sept. 14, 1852
Millard Fillmore

James Campbell, Pennsylvania
March 8, 1853
Franklin Pierce

Aaron V. Brown, Tennessee
March 7, 1857
James Buchanan

Joseph Holt, Kentucky
March 14, 1859
James Buchanan

Horatio King, Maine
Feb. 12, 1861
Abraham Lincoln

Montgomery Blair, District of Columbia
March 9, 1861
Abraham Lincoln

William Dennison, Ohio
Oct. 1, 1864
Abraham Lincoln
and Andrew Johnson

Alexander W. Randall, Wisconsin
July 25, 1866
Andrew Johnson

John A.J. Creswell, Maryland
March 6, 1869
Ulysses S. Grant

James W. Marshall, New Jersey
July 7, 1874
Ulysses S. Grant

Marshall Jewell, Connecticut
Sept. 1, 1874
Ulysses S. Grant

James N. Tyner, Indiana
July 13, 1876
Ulysses S. Grant

David McK. Key, Tennessee
March 13, 1877
Rutherford B. Hayes

Horace Maynard, Tennessee
Aug. 25, 1880
Rutherford B. Hayes

Thomas L. James, New York
March 8, 1881
James A. Garfield
and Chester A. Arthur

Timothy O. Howe, Wisconsin
Jan. 5, 1882
Chester A. Arthur

Walter Q. Gresham, Indiana
April 11, 1883
Chester A. Arthur

Frank Hatton, Iowa
Oct. 14, 1884
Chester A. Arthur

William F. Vilas, Wisconsin
March 7, 1885
Grover Cleveland

Don M. Dickinson, Michigan
Jan. 17, 1888
Grover Cleveland

John Wanamaker, Pennsylvania
March 6, 1889
Benjamin Harrison

Wilson S. Bissell, New York
March 7, 1893
Grover Cleveland

William L. Wilson, West Virginia
April 4, 1895
Grover Cleveland

James A. Gary, Maryland
March 6, 1897
William McKinley

Charles Emory Smith, Pennsylvania
April 22, 1893
William McKinley
and Theodore Roosevelt

Henry C. Payne, Wisconsin
Jan. 15, 1902
Theodore Roosevelt

Robert J. Wynne, Pennsylvania
Oct. 10, 1904
Theodore Roosevelt

George B. Cortelyou, New York
March 7, 1905
Theodore Roosevelt

George van L. Meyer, Massachusetts
March 4, 1907
Theodore Roosevelt

Frank H. Hitchcock, Massachusetts
March 6, 1909
William Taft

Albert S. Burleson, Texas
March 5, 1913
Woodrow Wilson

Will H. Hayes, Indiana
March 5, 1921
Warren G. Harding

Hubert Work, Colorado
March 4, 1922
Warren G. Harding

Harry S. New, Indiana
March 4, 1923
Calvin Coolidge

Walter F. Brown, Ohio
March 6, 1929
Herbert Hoover

James A. Farley, New York
March 4, 1933
Franklin D. Roosevelt

Frank C. Walker, Pennsylvania
Sept. 11, 1940
Franklin D. Roosevelt

Robert E. Hannegan, Missouri
July 1, 1945
Franklin D. Roosevelt
and Harry S. Truman

Jesse M. Donaldson, Illinois
Dec. 16, 1947
Harry S. Truman

Arthur E. Summerfield, Michigan
Jan. 21, 1953
Dwight D. Eisenhower

J. Edward Day, California
Jan. 21, 1961
John F. Kennedy

John A. Gronouski, Wisconsin
Sept. 30, 1963
John F. Kennedy
and Lyndon B. Johnson

Lawrence F. O'Brien, Massachusetts
Nov. 3, 1965
Lyndon B. Johnson

W. Marvin Watson, Texas
April 26, 1968
Lyndon B. Johnson

Winton M. Blount, Alabama
Jan. 22, 1969
Richard M. Nixon

E.T. Klassen, Massachusetts
Dec. 7, 1971
Richard M. Nixon
and Gerald Ford, USPS

Benjamin F. Bailar, Illinois
Feb. 15, 1975
Gerald Ford
and Jimmy Carter

William F. Bolger, Connecticut
March 15, 1978
Jimmy Carter
and Ronald Reagan

Paul N. Carlin, Illinois
Jan. 1, 1985
Ronald Reagan

Albert V. Casey, Texas
Jan. 6, 1986
Ronald Reagan

Preston R. Tisch, New York
Aug. 17, 1986
Ronald Reagan

Anthony M. Frank, California
March 1, 1988
Ronald Reagan

USPS Organization

Stamps Division

Stamp collectors are strongly affected by the policies of the Stamps Division, Office of Customer Programs, USPS. This division is part of the responsibility of the assistant postmaster general for philatelic and retail services. It is here that projects involving the production and distribution of philatelic materials, the encouragement of prospective collectors, and the development of USPS philatelic communications are handled.

The current director of the USPS' office of stamps and philatelic marketing is W.L. "Pete" Davidson. Davidson's office handles both the Stamps Division and the Philatelic Sales Division.

The director of the Stamps Division, which handles stamp production and distribution, is Don McDowell.

The director of the philatelic marketing branch of the Stamps Division is Mary Margaret Grant.

Other contacts result from USPS participation in various exhibitions, and from Stamp Support Branch publicity releases dealing with newly available stamps and other items. Constructive comments and proposals are always encouraged by mail.

New collectors are approached through two annual advertising campaigns featuring recent U.S. issues. These are the spring and fall philatelic promotions. New young collectors are approached through the Benjamin Franklin Stamp Club school program utilizing philatelic materials.

The Stamp Support Branch is involved in the selection of topics and designs for new U.S. emissions, and handles questions dealing with these matters. First-day cover and plate number inquiries are other frequent topics of Stamp Support Branch mail. The director of the Stamp Support Branch is Dickey Rustin.

Stamp Support Branch correspondence should be addressed to USPS Headquarters, Room 5670, 475 L'Enfant Plaza SW, Washington, D.C. 20260-6753.

Philatelic Sales Division

The Philatelic Sales Division, headed by Robert Brown, provides over-the-counter and mail-order service for selected stamped paper stock and specialty items.

This division oversees the operation of 420 philatelic centers and all mail orders.

Processing of mail orders takes place at the USPS facility in Merrifield, Va. Fulfillment of these orders is done at the USPS limestone caves in Kansas City, Mo. All operations will be moved from Merrifield to Kansas City in 1990.

The Philatelic Sales Division is also responsible for the processing of all U.S. first-day covers, first-day ceremony programs and souvenir pages. A list of materials currently available may be obtained from the USPS Philatelic Sales Division, Washington, D.C. 20265-9997.

Postal Inspection Service

The following information on security and law enforcement relating to the U.S. Postal Service is excerpted from the "Postal Inspection Service Law Enforcement Report," March-April 1976, and has been updated.

The publication is designed to inform interested persons regarding actual cases handled by the service. Further information on the work of the Postal Inspection Service may be obtained from the offices listed in this section. The report reads as follows:

Under Public Law 91-375, August 12, 1970, more commonly known as the Postal Reorganization Act, the Postal Inspection Service . . . was delegated responsibility for the protection of the mails, enforcement of postal laws, installation and personnel security, postal inspections, and internal audits.

The Service is headed by the Chief Postal Inspector, who directs the execution of policies, regulations, and procedures governing all investigations, including presentation of evidence to the Department of Justice and U.S. Attorneys in investigations of a criminal nature.

The Chief Postal Inspector now performs

collateral duties and responsibilities as the Agency's Inspector General. Thus, in addition to the investigative law enforcement, internal audit and security services to the public, the Chief Postal Inspector as Inspector General, is responsible for promoting the economy and efficiency of Postal Service programs and reducing the incidence of fraud, waste and abuse.

Statutory authority has been granted Postal Inspectors to serve subpoenas and warrants, and make arrests, by the provisions of Title 18, U.S.C., Section 3061. It should be emphasized, however, that these powers are only exercised in the enforcement of laws regarding property of the United States in the custody of the Postal Service, the use of the mails, and other postal offenses.

Generally, the responsibilities of the Inspection Service fall into three main categories. (The first is) the enforcement of postal laws and some 85 federal statutes through the investigation and apprehension of persons committing crimes against the Postal Service.

(Also), the protection of personnel, mail, postal funds and property through a wide variety of physical and personnel security procedures and the presence of a uniformed Security Force.

(Finally), the internal audit of all Postal Service financial and non-financial operations.

About 67 percent of the investigative time of the Inspection Service is spent on criminal investigations. Nearly 25 percent of investigative time is devoted to the audit program, with the remainder to personnel, physical security and administrative investigations.

To perform this work, the Inspection Service has approximately 5,600 people of whom 1,700 are Inspectors and 180 are Special Investigators who assist in criminal investigations. These people are located in major cities throughout the United States . . .

The newest category of Inspection Service personnel is the Security Police Officer. There are presently some 2,600 of these men and women located at postal installations throughout the country . . .

Historically, the role of the Inspection Service concentrated primarily on the investigation and apprehension of criminals, but this approach (has) had to be broadened to include a greater emphasis on the protection of the mail . . . employees, and facilities, through the prevention of postal crimes.

This decision resulted in the implementation of various new programs designed to strengthen . . . overall security given the more than 90 billion letters and parcels which move through the mail stream each year.

Addresses of Postal Inspectors

CENTRAL REGION

Regional Chief Postal Inspector
Main Post Office Building
Chicago, Ill. 60607-5401
312-765-4605

Chicago Division
U.S. Post Office Building
Canal & Van Buren Streets
Chicago, Ill. 60669-2201
312-765-4500

Denver Division
Main Post Office Building
1823 Stout Street, Room 339
Denver, Colo. 80202-2597
303-297-6220

Des Moines Division
Box 566
Des Moines, Iowa 50302-0566
515-253-9060

Detroit Division
GMF Box 119
Detroit, Mich. 48232-3201
313-226-8184

Indianapolis Division
3750 Guion Road, Suite 300
Indianapolis, Ind. 46222-1669
317-923-1601

Kansas City Division
3101 Broadway, Suite 850
Kansas City, Mo. 64111-2416
816-932-0400

Milwaukee Division
Box 788
Milwaukee, Wis. 53201-0788
414-291-2475

St. Louis Division
200 S. Hanley Road, 10th Floor
St. Louis, Mo. 63199-2201
314-854-4760

St. Paul Division
U.S. Post Office & Customhouse
Box 64558
St. Paul, Minn. 55164-2201
612-293-3200

EASTERN REGION

Regional Chief Postal Inspector
Box 3000
Bala Cynwyd, Pa. 19004-3609
215-668-4784

Baltimore Division
Box 1856
Baltimore, Md. 21203-1856
301-347-4380

Harrisburg Division
Box 3535
Harrisburg, Pa. 17105-3535
717-257-2330

Cincinnati Division
120 West 5th Street, Suite 600
Cincinnati, Ohio 45202-2713
513-684-5700

Charlotte Division
2901 I-85 South, GMF
Charlotte, N.C. 28228-3000
704-393-4470

Philadelphia Division
Box 7500
Philadelphia, Pa. 19101-9000
215-895-8450

Pittsburgh Division
1001 California Avenue
Pittsburgh, Pa. 15290-9000
412-359-7900

Richmond Division
Box 25009
Richmond, Va. 23260-5009
804-775-6267

Washington Division
Box 96096
Washington, D.C. 20066-6096
202-636-2339

Cleveland Division
Box 5726
Cleveland, Ohio 44101-0726
215-443-4000

NORTHEAST REGION

Regional Chief Postal Inspector
Northeast Region
Gateway 2 Center, 8th Floor
South Newark, N.J. 07175-0001
201-621-5500

Hartford Division
Box 2169
Hartford, Conn. 06145-2169
203-646-6060

San Juan Division
Box 3667
San Juan, Puerto Rico 00936-9614
809-753-2856

Boston Division
Box 2217
Boston, Mass. 02205-2217
617-654-5825

Newark Division
Box 509
Newark, N.J. 07101-5901
201-596-5450

New York Division
Box 555
James A. Farley Building
GPO
New York, N.Y. 10116-0555
212-330-3844

Buffalo Division
685 Ellicott Square Bldg.
Buffalo, N.Y. 14203-2545
716-856-3674

SOUTHERN REGION

Regional Chief Postal Inspector
1407 Union Avenue, 10th Floor
Memphis, Tenn. 38161-0001
901-722-7700

Birmingham Division
Box 2767
Birmingham, Ala. 35202-2767
205-521-0270

Houston Division
Box 1276
Houston, Texas 77251-1276
713-236-7000

New Orleans Division
Box 51690
New Orleans, La. 70151-1690
504-589-1200

Tampa Division
Box 22526
Tampa, Fla. 33622-2526
813-228-2481

Miami Division
Box 520772
Miami, Fla. 33152-0772
305-591-0379

Atlanta Division
Main Post Office
Box 16489
Atlanta, Ga. 30321-0489
404-765-7369

Ft. Worth Division
Box 162929
Ft. Worth, Texas 76161-2929
817-885-1111

Memphis Division
Box 3180
Memphis, Tenn. 38173-0180
901-576-2077

WESTERN REGION

Regional Chief Postal Inspector
850 Cherry Avenue, 5th Floor
San Bruno, Calif. 94096-0100
415-742-4411

Phoenix Division
Box 20666
Phoenix, Ariz. 85036-0666
602-223-3660

San Diego Division
Box 2110
San Diego, Calif. 92112-2110
619-233-0610

Portland Division
921 S.W. Washington, Suite 790
Portland, Ore. 97205-2896
503-294-2263

Oakland Division
7717 Edgewater Drive, Suite 202
Oakland, Calif. 94621-3013
415-636-2600

Los Angeles Division
Box 2000
Pasadena, Calif. 91102-2000
818-405-1200

San Francisco Division
Box 882000
San Francisco, Calif. 94188-2000
415-550-5602

Seattle Division
Box 400
Seattle, Wash. 98111-4000
206-442-6300

Chapter 3

U.S. Postage Stamps

U.S. postage stamps were first introduced in 1847, with the release of the 5¢ Franklin stamp, Scott No. 1. Shortly after that time, U.S. postage stamps became a highly sought-after collectible, with many avid followers.

Many early collectors, as well as modern-day collectors, had little knowledge about those pieces of paper they saved.

There is a great deal of history connected with each U.S. stamp issue. This includes, of course, the history behind the stamp's subject, whether person or event, as well as the history being made at the time of the stamp's release. In some cases, the latter directly affects a stamp issue — either making the stamp possible or altering original plans.

Much of this type of history has been presented by many sources over the years and fills volumes with interesting facts. This much is obvious stamp history.

A stamp's history, however, also includes a wealth of information about the stamp itself. The most obvious of this information is the catalog number, description of the stamp and its denomination.

In addition to these basics, there are many other facts about any given stamp. In some cases, these production-related facts help determine a stamp's value.

These include first-day information. In what city was a stamp issued? How many first-day covers were canceled? What date or dates are acceptable as a first day?

Other, more technical information includes printing and production data. How many of a given stamp were printed? Who designed the stamp and, if applicable, who engraved the design?

The following section provides most of this information currently available to collectors. Much of this data was gleaned from many different sources — some of which contradict others. Some bits of important information also have been completely lost to collectors over the years.

Although quite informative, these tables are not yet complete. We anticipate this section will continue to grow and become even more useful as our editors continue to gather other sources for additional information. Corrections and updates to these tables are welcomed.

Scott number	Denom.	Design	First day of issue	Printer	First-day city	First-day quantities	Designer	Engraver
1	5¢	Benjamin Franklin	July 1, 1847	Rawdon, Wright, Hatch	New York, N.Y.		J.P. Major	A.B. Durant
2	10¢	George Washington	July 1, 1847	Rawdon, Wright, Hatch	New York, N.Y.		J.P. Major	A.B. Durant
3	5¢	Benjamin Franklin	1875	BEP				Charles K. Burt
4	10¢	George Washington	1875	BEP				Charles K. Burt
5	1¢	Benjamin Franklin	July 1, 1851	Toppan, Carpenter, Casilear			Edward Purcell	Joseph Pease
6	1¢	Benjamin Franklin	April 19, 1857	Toppan, Carpenter			Edward Purcell	Joseph Pease
7	1¢	Benjamin Franklin	July 1, 1851	Toppan, Carpenter			Edward Purcell	Joseph Pease
8	1¢	Benjamin Franklin	April 1857	Toppan, Carpenter			Edward Purcell	Joseph Pease
8A	1¢	Benjamin Franklin	unknown	Toppan, Carpenter			Edward Purcell	Joseph Pease
9	1¢	Benjamin Franklin	June 8, 1852	Toppan, Carpenter			Edward Purcell	Joseph Pease
10	3¢	George Washington	July 1, 1851	Toppan, Carpenter			Edward Purcell	Joseph Pease
11	3¢	George Washington	unknown	Toppan, Carpenter			Edward Purcell	Joseph Pease
12	5¢	Thomas Jefferson	March 24, 1856	Toppan, Carpenter			Edward Purcell	Joseph Pease
13	10¢	George Washington	May 12, 1855	Toppan, Carpenter			Edward Purcell	Joseph Pease
14	10¢	George Washington	unknown	Toppan, Carpenter			Edward Purcell	Joseph Pease
15	10¢	George Washington	unknown	Toppan, Carpenter			Edward Purcell	Joseph Pease
16	10¢	George Washington	unknown	Toppan, Carpenter			Edward Purcell	Joseph Pease
17	12¢	George Washington	July 1, 1851	Toppan, Carpenter			Edward Purcell	Joseph Pease
18	1¢	Benjamin Franklin	Jan. 25, 1861	Toppan, Carpenter			Edward Purcell	Joseph Pease
19	1¢	Benjamin Franklin	July 26, 1857	Toppan, Carpenter			Edward Purcell	Joseph Pease
20	1¢	Benjamin Franklin	July 25, 1857	Toppan, Carpenter			Edward Purcell	Joseph Pease
21	1¢	Benjamin Franklin	July 26, 1857	Toppan, Carpenter			Edward Purcell	Joseph Pease
23	1¢	Benjamin Franklin	July 25, 1857	Toppan, Carpenter			Edward Purcell	Joseph Pease
24	1¢	Benjamin Franklin	Nov. 17, 1857	Toppan, Carpenter	Castleton, Va.		Edward Purcell	Joseph Pease
25	3¢	George Washington	Feb. 28, 1857	Toppan, Carpenter			Edward Purcell	Joseph Pease
26	3¢	George Washington	1857	Toppan, Carpenter			Edward Purcell	Joseph Pease
26a	3¢	George Washington	July 11, 1857	Toppan, Carpenter			Edward Purcell	Joseph Pease
27	5¢	Thomas Jefferson	Oct. 6, 1858	Toppan, Carpenter			Edward Purcell	Joseph Pease
28	5¢	Thomas Jefferson	Aug. 23, 1857	Toppan, Carpenter			Edward Purcell	Joseph Pease
28A	5¢	Thomas Jefferson	March 31, 1858	Toppan, Carpenter			Edward Purcell	Joseph Pease
29	5¢	Thomas Jefferson	July 4, 1859	Toppan, Carpenter			Edward Purcell	Joseph Pease

Scott number	Denom.	Design	First day of issue	Printer	First-day city	First-day quantities	Designer	Engraver
30	5¢	Thomas Jefferson	May 8, 1861	Toppan, Carpenter			Edward Purcell	Joseph Pease
30A	5¢	Thomas Jefferson	March 4, 1860	Toppan, Carpenter			Edward Purcell	Joseph Pease
31	10¢	George Washington	July 27, 1857	Toppan, Carpenter			Edward Purcell	Joseph Pease
32	10¢	George Washington	July 27, 1857	Toppan, Carpenter	Lancaster, Pa.		Edward Purcell	Joseph Pease
33	10¢	George Washington	July 27, 1857	Toppan, Carpenter			Edward Purcell	Joseph Pease
34	10¢	George Washington	July 27, 1857	Toppan, Carpenter			Edward Purcell	Joseph Pease
35	10¢	George Washington	May 9, 1859	Toppan, Carpenter			Edward Purcell	Joseph Pease
36	12¢	George Washington	July 30, 1857	Toppan, Carpenter	New York, N.Y.		Edward Purcell	Joseph Pease
37	24¢	George Washington	1860	Toppan, Carpenter			Edward Purcell	Joseph Pease
38	30¢	Benjamin Franklin	Aug. 8, 1860	Toppan, Carpenter			Edward Purcell	Joseph Pease
39	90¢	George Washington	1860	Toppan, Carpenter			Edward Purcell	Joseph Pease
40	1¢	Benjamin Franklin	1875	CBNC			Edward Purcell	Joseph Pease
41	3¢	George Washington	1875	CBNC			Edward Purcell	Joseph Pease
42	5¢	Thomas Jefferson	1875	CBNC			Edward Purcell	Joseph Pease
43	10¢	George Washington	1875	CBNC			Edward Purcell	Joseph Pease
44	12¢	George Washington	1875	CBNC			Edward Purcell	Joseph Pease
45	24¢	George Washington	1875	CBNC			Edward Purcell	Joseph Pease
46	30¢	Benjamin Franklin	1875	CBNC			Edward Purcell	Joseph Pease
47	90¢	George Washington	1875	CBNC			Edward Purcell	Joseph Pease
55	1¢	Benjamin Franklin	1861	NBNC			Edward Purcell	
56	3¢	George Washington	1861	NBNC			Edward Purcell	Joseph Pease
57	5¢	Thomas Jefferson	1861	NBNC			Edward Purcell	Joseph Pease
58	10¢	George Washington	1861	NBNC			Edward Purcell	Joseph Pease
59	12¢	George Washington	1861	NBNC			Edward Purcell	Joseph Pease
60	24¢	George Washington	1861	NBNC			James Macdonough	William Marshall
61	30¢	Benjamin Franklin	1861	NBNC			James Macdonough	Joseph Pease
62	90¢	George Washington	1861	NBNC			James Macdonough	Joseph Pease
62B	10¢	George Washington	Sept. 17, 1861	NBNC			Edward Purcell	Joseph Pease
63	1¢	Benjamin Franklin	Aug. 17, 1861	NBNC			James Macdonough	Joseph Pease
64	3¢	George Washington	unknown	NBNC			James Macdonough	Joseph Ourdan
65	3¢	George Washington	1861	NBNC			James Macdonough	Joseph Ourdan
66	3¢	George Washington	unknown	NBNC			James Macdonough	Joseph Ourdan
67	5¢	Thomas Jefferson	Aug. 19, 1861	NBNC			James Macdonough	William Marshall
68	10¢	George Washington	Aug. 20, 1861	NBNC			James Macdonough	William Marshall

Scott number	Denom.	Design	First day of issue	Printer	First-day city	First-day quantities	Designer	Engraver
69	12¢	George Washington	August 1861	NBNC			James Macdonough	William Marshall
70	24¢	George Washington	Jan. 7, 1862	NBNC			James Macdonough	William Marshall
71	30¢	Benjamin Franklin	Aug. 20, 1861	NBNC	New London, Conn.		James Macdonough	Joseph Pease
72	90¢	George Washington	August 1861	NBNC			James Macdonough	Joseph Pease
73	2¢	Andrew Jackson	July 6, 1863	NBNC			James Macdonough	Joseph Ourdan
74	3¢	George Washington	unknown	NBNC			James Macdonough	Joseph Ourdan
75	5¢	Thomas Jefferson	Jan. 2, 1862	NBNC			James Macdonough	William Marshall
76	5¢	Thomas Jefferson	Feb. 3, 1863	NBNC			James Macdonough	William Marshall
77	15¢	Abraham Lincoln	1866	NBNC	Chicago, Ill.		James Macdonough	Joseph Ourdan
78	24¢	George Washington	Feb. 20, 1863	NBNC			James Macdonough	William Marshall
79	3¢	George Washington	1867	NBNC			James Macdonough	Joseph Ourdan
80	5¢	Thomas Jefferson	1867	NBNC			James Macdonough	William Marshall
81	30¢	Benjamin Franklin	1867	NBNC			James Macdonough	Joseph Pease
82	3¢	George Washington	1867	NBNC			James Macdonough	Joseph Ourdan
83	3¢	George Washington	1867	NBNC			James Macdonough	Joseph Ourdan
84	2¢	Andrew Jackson	1867	NBNC			James Macdonough	Joseph Ourdan
85	3¢	George Washington	1867	NBNC			James Macdonough	Joseph Ourdan
85A	1¢	Benjamin Franklin	1867	NBNC			James Macdonough	Joseph Pease
85B	2¢	Andrew Jackson	1867	NBNC			James Macdonough	Joseph Ourdan
85C	3¢	George Washington	1867	NBNC			James Macdonough	Joseph Ourdan
85D	10¢	George Washington	1867	NBNC			James Macdonough	William Marshall
85E	12¢	George Washington	1867	NBNC			James Macdonough	William Marshall
85F	15¢	Abraham Lincoln	1867	NBNC			James Macdonough	Joseph Ourdan
86	1¢	Benjamin Franklin	1867	NBNC			James Macdonough	Joseph Pease
87	2¢	Andrew Jackson	1867	NBNC			James Macdonough	Joseph Ourdan
88	3¢	George Washington	1867	NBNC			James Macdonough	Joseph Ourdan
89	10¢	George Washington	1867	NBNC			James Macdonough	William Marshall
90	12¢	George Washington	1867	NBNC			James Macdonough	William Marshall
91	15¢	Abraham Lincoln	1867	NBNC			James Macdonough	Joseph Ourdan
92	1¢	Benjamin Franklin	1867	NBNC			James Macdonough	Joseph Pease
93	2¢	Andrew Jackson	1867	NBNC			James Macdonough	Joseph Ourdan
94	3¢	George Washington	1867	NBNC			James Macdonough	Joseph Ourdan
95	5¢	Thomas Jefferson	1867	NBNC			James Macdonough	William Marshall
96	10¢	George Washington	1867	NBNC			James Macdonough	William Marshall

Scott number	Denom.	Design	First day of issue	Printer	First-day city	First-day quantities	Designer	Engraver
97	12¢	George Washington	1867	NBNC			James Macdonough	William Marshall
98	15¢	Abraham Lincoln	1867	NBNC			James Macdonough	Joseph Ourdan
99	24¢	George Washington	1867	NBNC			James Macdonough	William Marshall
100	30¢	Benjamin Franklin	1867	NBNC			James Macdonough	Joseph Pease
101	90¢	George Washington	1867	NBNC			James Macdonough	Joseph Pease
102	1¢	Benjamin Franklin	1875	NBNC			James Macdonough	Joseph Pease
103	2¢	Andrew Jackson	1875	NBNC			James Macdonough	Joseph Ourdan
104	3¢	George Washington	1875	NBNC			James Macdonough	Joseph Ourdan
105	5¢	Thomas Jefferson	1875	NBNC			James Macdonough	William Marshall
106	10¢	George Washington	1875	NBNC			James Macdonough	William Marshall
107	12¢	George Washington	1875	NBNC			James Macdonough	William Marshall
108	15¢	Abraham Lincoln	1875	NBNC			James Macdonough	Joseph Ourdan
109	24¢	George Washington	1875	NBNC			James Macdonough	William Marshall
110	30¢	Benjamin Franklin	1875	NBNC			James Macdonough	Joseph Pease
111	90¢	George Washington	1875	NBNC			James Macdonough	Joseph Pease
112	1¢	Benjamin Franklin	March 27, 1869	NBNC			E. Pitcher	Joseph Pease
113	2¢	Post Horse, Rider	March 27, 1869	NBNC			James Macdonough	Christian Rost
114	3¢	Locomotive	March 27, 1869	NBNC			James Macdonough	Christian Rost
115	6¢	George Washington	1869	NBNC			E. Pitcher	William Marshall
116	10¢	Shield and Eagle	April 1, 1869	NBNC			James Macdonough	Douglas Ronaldson
117	12¢	SS *Adriatic*	April 5, 1869	NBNC			James Macdonough	James Smillie
118	15¢	Landing of Columbus	April 2, 1869	NBNC			E. Pitcher	James Smillie
119	15¢	Landing of Columbus	1869	NBNC			E. Pircher	James Smillie
120	24¢	Declaration of Independence	April 7, 1869	NBNC			E. Pitcher	James Smillie
121	30¢	Shield, Eagle and Flags	May 15, 1869	NBNC			E. Pitcher	Joseph Ourdan
122	90¢	Abraham Lincoln	May 10, 1869	NBNC			E. Pitcher	James Ourdan
123	1¢	Benjamin Franklin	1875	NBNC			E. Pitcher	Joseph Pease
124	2¢	Post Horse, Rider	1875	NBNC			E. Pitcher	Christian Rost
125	3¢	Locomotive	1875	NBNC			James Macdonough	Christian Rost
126	6¢	George Washington	1875	NBNC			E. Pitcher	William Marshall
127	10¢	Shield and Eagle	1875	NBNC			James Macdonough	Douglas Ronaldson
128	12¢	SS *Adriatic*	1875	NBNC			James Macdonough	James Smillie

Scott number	Denom.	Design	First day of issue	Printer	First-day city	First-day quantities	Designer	Engraver
129	15¢	Landing of Columbus	1875	NBNC			E. Pitcher	James Smillie
130	24¢	Declaration of Independence	1875	NBNC			E. Pitcher	James Smillie
131	30¢	Shield, Eagle and Flags	1875	NBNC			James Macdonough	Douglas Ronaldson
132	90¢	Abraham Lincoln	1875	NBNC			E. Pitcher	Joseph Ourdan
133	1¢	Benjamin Franklin	1880	NBNC			E. Pitcher	Joseph Pease
134	1¢	Benjamin Franklin	April 1870	NBNC			Butler Packard	Joseph Pease
135	2¢	Andrew Jackson	April 1870	NBNC			Butler Packard	Lewis Delnoce
136	3¢	George Washington	April 12, 1870	NBNC			Butler Packard	Joseph Ourdan
137	6¢	Abraham Lincoln	April 1870	NBNC			Butler Packard	Joseph Ourdan
138	7¢	E.M. Stanton	April 1870	NBNC			Butler Packard	Joseph Ourdan
139	10¢	Thomas Jefferson	April 1870	NBNC			Butler Packard	Lewis Delnoce
140	12¢	Henry Clay	April 18, 1870	NBNC			Butler Packard	Lewis Delnoce
141	15¢	Daniel Webster	April 1870	NBNC			Butler Packard	Joseph Ourdan
142	24¢	Gen. Winfield Scott	1870	NBNC			Butler Packard	Joseph Ourdan
143	30¢	Alexander Hamilton	April 1870	NBNC			Butler Packard	Joseph Ourdan
144	90¢	Commodore Perry	April 12, 1870	NBNC			Butler Packard	Lewis Delnoce
145	1¢	Benjamin Franklin	April 1870	NBNC			Butler Packard	Joseph Pease
146	2¢	Andrew Jackson	April 1870	NBNC			Butler Packard	Lewis Delnoce
147	3¢	George Washington	March 13, 1870	NBNC			Butler Packard	Joseph Ourdan
148	6¢	Abraham Lincoln	April 1870	NBNC			Butler Packard	Joseph Ourdan
149	7¢	E.M. Stanton	March 1871	NBNC			Butler Packard	Joseph Ourdan
150	10¢	Thomas Jefferson	April 1870	NBNC			Butler Packard	Lewis Delnoce
151	12¢	Henry Clay	April 1870	NBNC			Butler Packard	Lewis Delnoce
152	15¢	Daniel Webster	April 1870	NBNC			Butler Packard	Joseph Ourdan
153	24¢	Gen. Winfield Scott	April 1870	NBNC			Butler Packard	Joseph Ourdan
154	30¢	Alexander Hamilton	April 1870	NBNC			Butler Packard	Joseph Ourdan
155	90¢	Commodore Perry	April 1870	NBNC			Butler Packard	Lewis Delnoce
156	1¢	Benjamin Franklin	July 1873	CBNC			Butler Packard	Joseph Pease
157	2¢	Andrew Jackson	July 1873	CBNC			Butler Packard	Lewis Delnoce
158	3¢	George Washington	July 1873	CBNC			Butler Packard	Joseph Ourdan
159	6¢	Abraham Lincoln	July 1873	CBNC			Butler Packard	Joseph Ourdan
160	7¢	E.M. Stanton	July 1873	CBNC			Butler Packard	Joseph Ourdan

Scott number	Denom.	Design	First day of issue	Printer	First-day city	First-day quantities	Designer	Engraver
161	10¢	Thomas Jefferson	July 1873	CBNC			Butler Packard	Lewis Delnoce
162	12¢	Henry Clay	July 1873	CBNC			Butler Packard	Lewis Delnoce
163	15¢	Daniel Webster	July 1873	CBNC			Butler Packard	Joseph Ourdan
165	30¢	Alexander Hamilton	July 1873	CBNC			Butler Packard	Joseph Ourdan
166	90¢	Commodore Perry	July 1873	CBNC			Butler Packard	Lewis Delnoce
167	1¢	Benjamin Franklin	1875	CBNC			Butler Packard	Joseph Pease
168	2¢	Andrew Jackson	1875	CBNC			Butler Packard	Lewis Delnoce
169	3¢	George Washington	1875	CBNC			Butler Packard	Joseph Ourdan
170	6¢	Abraham Lincoln	1875	CBNC			Butler Packard	Joseph Ourdan
171	7¢	E.M. Stanton	1875	CBNC			Butler Packard	Joseph Ourdan
172	10¢	Thomas Jefferson	1875	CBNC			Butler Packard	Lewis Delnoce
173	12¢	Henry Clay	1875	CBNC			Butler Packard	Lewis Delnoce
174	15¢	Daniel Webster	1875	CBNC			Butler Packard	Joseph Ourdan
175	24¢	Gen. Winfield Scott	1875	CBNC			Butler Packard	Joseph Ourdan
176	30¢	Alexander Hamilton	1875	CNBC			Butler Packard	Joseph Ourdan
177	90¢	Commodore Perry	1875	CBNC			Butler Packard	Lewis Delnoce
178	2¢	Andrew Jackson	June 1875	CBNC			Butler Packard	Lewis Delnoce
179	5¢	Zachary Taylor	June 1875	CBNC			Butler Packard	Charles Skinner
180	2¢	Andrew Jackson	1875	CBNC			Butler Packard	Lewis Delnoce
181	5¢	Zachary Taylor	1875	CBNC			Butler Packard	Charles Skinner
182	1¢	Benjamin Franklin	1879	ABNC			Butler Packard	Joseph Pease
183	2¢	Andrew Jackson	1879	ABNC			Butler Packard	Lewis Delnoce
184	3¢	George Washington	1879	ABNC			Butler Packard	Joseph Ourdan
185	5¢	Zachary Taylor	1879	ABNC			Butler Packard	Charles Skinner
186	6¢	Abraham Lincoln	1879	ABNC			Butler Packard	Joseph Ourdan
187	10¢	Thomas Jefferson	1879	ABNC			Butler Packard	Lewis Delnoce
188	10¢	Thomas Jefferson	1879	ABNC			Butler Packard	Lewis Delnoce
189	15¢	Daniel Webster	1879	ABNC			Butler Packard	Joseph Ourdan
190	30¢	Alexander Hamilton	1879	ABNC			Butler Packard	Joseph Ourdan
191	90¢	Commodore Perry	1879	ABNC			Butler Packard	Lewis Delnoce
192	1¢	Benjamin Franklin	1880	ABNC			Butler Packard	Joseph Pease
193	2¢	Andrew Jackson	1880	ABNC			Butler Packard	Lewis Delnoce
194	3¢	George Washington	1880	ABNC			Butler Packard	Joseph Ourdan
195	6¢	Abraham Lincoln	1880	ABNC			Butler Packard	Joseph Ourdan

Scott number	Denom.	Design	First day of issue	Printer	First-day city	First-day quantities	Designer	Engraver
196	7¢	E.M. Stanton	1880	ABNC			Butler Packard	Joseph Ourdan
197	10¢	Thomas Jefferson	1880	ABNC			Butler Packard	Lewis Delnoce
198	12¢	Henry Clay	1880	ABNC			Butler Packard	Lewis Delnoce
199	15¢	Daniel Webster	1880	ABNC			Butler Packard	Joseph Ourdan
200	24¢	Gen. Winfield Scott	1880	ABNC			Butler Packard	Joseph Ourdan
201	30¢	Alexander Hamilton	1880	ABNC			Butler Packard	Joseph Ourdan
202	90¢	Commodore Perry	1880	ABNC			Butler Packard	Lewis Delnoce
203	2¢	Andrew Jackson	1880	ABNC			Butler Packard	Lewis Delnoce
204	5¢	Zachary Taylor	1880	ABNC			Butler Packard	Charles Skinner
205	5¢	James A. Garfield	April 10, 1882	ABNC			Thomas Morris, Sr.	Charles Skinner
205C	5¢	James A. Garfield	1882	ABNC			Thomas Morris, Sr.	Charles Skinner
206	1¢	Benjamin Franklin	August 1881	ABNC			Butler Packard	Joseph Pease
207	3¢	George Washington	July 16, 1881	ABNC			Butler Packard	Joseph Pease
208	6¢	Abraham Lincoln	June 1882	ABNC			Butler Packard	Joseph Ourdan
209	10¢	Thomas Jefferson	April 1882	ABNC			Butler Packard	Lewis Delnoce
210	2¢	George Washington	Oct. 1, 1883	ABNC	any city		Thomas Morris, Sr.	Alfred Jones
211	4¢	Andrew Jackson	Oct. 1, 1883	ABNC	any city		Thomas Morris, Sr.	Alfred Jones
211B	2¢	George Washington	1883	ABNC			Thomas Morris, Sr.	Alfred Jones
211D	4¢	Andrew Jackson	1883	ABNC			Thomas Morris, Sr.	Alfred Jones
212	1¢	Benjamin Franklin	June 1887	ABNC			Thomas Morris, Sr.	Alfred Jones
213	2¢	George Washington	Sept. 10, 1887	ABNC			Thomas Morris, Sr.	Alfred Jones
214	3¢	George Washington	Oct. 3, 1887	ABNC			Butler Packard	Joseph Ourdan
215	4¢	Andrew Jackson	November 1888	ABNC			Thomas Morris, Sr.	Alfred Jones
216	5¢	James A. Garfield	February 1880	ABNC			Thomas Morris, Sr.	Charles Skinner
217	30¢	Alexander Hamilton	January 1888	ABNC			Butler Packard	Joseph Ourdan
218	90¢	Commodore Perry	February 1888	ABNC			Butler Packard	Lewis Delnoce
219	1¢	Benjamin Franklin	Feb. 22, 1890	ABNC			Thomas Morris, Sr.	Edward Stiemle
219D	2¢	George Washington	Feb. 22, 1890	ABNC	any city		Thomas Morris, Sr.	Charles Skinner
220	2¢	George Washington	Feb. 22, 1890	ABNC			Thomas Morris, Sr.	Charles Skinner
221	3¢	Andrew Jackson	Feb. 22, 1890	ABNC			Thomas Morris, Sr.	Charles Skinner
222	4¢	Abraham Lincoln	June 2, 1890	ABNC			Thomas Morris, Sr.	Alfred Jones
223	5¢	Ulysses S. Grant	June 2, 1890	ABNC			Thomas Morris, Sr.	Charles Skinner
224	6¢	James A. Garfield	Feb. 22, 1890	ABNC			Thomas Morris, Sr.	Charles Skinner
225	8¢	William T. Sherman	March 21, 1893	ABNC			Thomas Morris, Sr.	Charles Skinner

Scott number	Denom.	Design	First day of issue	Printer	First-day city	First-day quantities	Designer	Engraver
226	10¢	Daniel Webster	Feb. 22, 1890	ABNC			Thomas Morris	Charles Skinner
227	15¢	Henry Clay	Feb. 22, 1890	ABNC			Thomas Morris	Charles Skinner
228	30¢	Thomas Jefferson	Feb. 22, 1890	ABNC			Thomas Morris	Alfred Jones
229	90¢	Commodore Perry	Feb. 22, 1890	ABNC			Thomas Morris	Edward Stiemle
230	1¢	Columbus in Sight of Land	Jan. 1, 1893	ABNC	Boston, Mass.		Alfred Major	Alfred Jones
231	2¢	Landing of Columbus	Jan. 1, 1893	ABNC	Boston, Mass.		Alfred Major	Alfred Jones
232	3¢	Santa Maria	Jan. 1, 1893	ABNC	Boston, Mass.		Alfred Major	Robert Savage
233	4¢	Fleet of Columbus	Jan. 1, 1893	ABNC	Boston, Mass.		Alfred Major	Charles Skinner
234	5¢	Columbus Soliciting Aid from Queen Isabella	Jan. 1, 1893	ABNC	Boston, Mass.		Alfred Major	Charles Skinner
234	6¢	Columbus Welcomed at Barcelona	Jan. 1, 1893	ABNC	Boston, Mass.		Alfred Major	Robert Savage
236	8¢	Columbus Restored to Favor	March 1893	ABNC	Boston, Mass.		Alfred Major	Charles Skinner
237	10¢	Columbus Presenting Natives	Jan. 1, 1893	ABNC	Arlington Heights, Mass.		Alfred Major	Robert Savage
238	15¢	Columbus Announcing His Discovery	Jan. 2, 1893	ABNC			Alfred Major	Charles Skinner
239	30¢	Columbus at La Rabida	Jan. 2, 1893	ABNC			Alfred Major	Alfred Jones
240	50¢	Recall of Columbus	Jan. 2, 1893	ABNC			Alfred Major	Robert Savage
241	$1	Queen Isabella Pledging Her Jewels	Jan. 2, 1893	ABNC			Alfred Major	Charles Skinner
242	$2	Columbus in Chains	Jan. 2, 1893	ABNC	any city		Alfred Major	Robert Savage
243	$3	Columbus Describing His Third Voyage	Jan. 2, 1893	ABNC			Alfred Major	Alfred Jones
244	$4	Queen Isabella & Columbus	Jan. 2, 1893	ABNC			Alfred Major	Alfred Jones
245	$5	Christopher Columbus	Jan. 2, 1893	ABNC			Alfred Major	Alfred Jones
246	1¢	Benjamin Franklin	October 1894	BEP			Thomas Morris	Edward Stiemle
247	1¢	Benjamin Franklin	1894	BEP			Thomas Morris	Edward Stiemle
248	2¢	George Washington	October 1894				Thomas Morris	Charles Skinner
249	2¢	George Washington	Oct. 1, 1894	BEP			Thomas Morris	Charles Skinner
250	2¢	George Washington	1894	BEP			Thomas Morris	Charles Skinner

Scott number	Denom.	Design	First day of issue	Printer	First-day city	First-day quantities	Designer	Engraver
251	2¢	George Washington	1894	BEP			Thomas Morris	Charles Skinner
252	2¢	George Washington	1894	BEP			Thomas Morris	Charles Skinner
253	3¢	Andrew Jackson	September 1894	BEP			Thomas Morris	Charles Skinner
254	4¢	Abraham Lincoln	September 1894	BEP			Thomas Morris	Alfred Jones
255	5¢	Ulysses S. Grant	September 1894	BEP			Thomas Morris	Charles Skinner
256	6¢	James A. Garfield	July 1894	BEP			Thomas Morris	Charles Skinner
257	8¢	William T. Sherman	March 1895	BEP			Thomas Morris	Charles Skinner
258	10¢	Daniel Webster	September 1894	BEP			Thomas Morris	Charles Skinner
259	15¢	Henry Clay	October 1894	BEP			Thomas Morris	Charles Skinner
260	50¢	Thomas Jefferson	November 1894	BEP			Thomas Morris	Alfred Jones
261	$1	Oliver Perry	November 1894	BEP			Thomas Morris	Edward Stiemle
262	$2	James Madison	December 1894	BEP			Thomas Morris	George Smillie
263	$5	John Marshall	December 1894	BEP			Thomas Morris	William Phillips
264	1¢	Benjamin Franklin	March 1895	BEP			Thomas Morris	Edward Stiemle
265	2¢	George Washington	May 1895	BEP			Thomas Morris	Charles Skinner
266	2¢	George Washington	1895	BEP			Thomas Morris	Charles Skinner
267	2¢	George Washington	1895	BEP			Thomas Morris	Charles Skinner
268	3¢	Andrew Jackson	October 1895	BEP			Thomas Morris	Charles Skinner
269	4¢	Abraham Lincoln	June 1895	BEP			Thomas Morris	Alfred Jones
270	5¢	Ulysses S. Grant	June 11, 1895	BEP			Thomas Morris	Charles Skinner
271	6¢	James A. Garfield	August 1895	BEP			Thomas Morris	Charles Skinner
272	8¢	William T. Sherman	July 1895	BEP			Thomas Morris	Charles Skinner
273	10¢	Daniel Webster	June 1895	BEP			Thomas Morris	Charles Skinner
274	15¢	Henry Clay	September 1895	BEP			Thomas Morris	Charles Skinner
275	50¢	Thomas Jefferson	November 1895	BEP			Thomas Morris	Alfred Jones
276	$1	Oliver Perry	August 1895	BEP			Thomas Morris	Edward Stiemle
276A	$1	Oliver Perry	August 1895	BEP			Thomas Morris	Edward Stiemle
277	$2	James Madison	August 1895	BEP			Thomas Morris	George Smillie
278	$5	John Marshall	August 1895	BEP			Thomas Morris	William Phillips
279	1¢	Benjamin Franklin	Jan. 25,1898	BEP			Thomas Morris	Edward Stiemle
279B	2¢	George Washington	1898	BEP	New York, N.Y.		Thomas Morris	Charles Skinner
280	4¢	Abraham Lincoln	October 1898	BEP			Thomas Morris	Alfred Jones
281	5¢	Ulysses S. Grant	March 1898	BEP			Thomas Morris	Charles Skinner
282	6¢	James A. Garfield	December 1898	BEP			Thomas Morris	Charles Skinner

Scott number	Denom.	Design	First day of issue	Printer	First-day city	First-day quantities	Designer	Engraver
282C	10¢	Daniel Webster	November 1898	BEP			Thomas Morris	Charles Skinner
283	10¢	Daniel Webster	1898	BEP			Thomas Morris	Charles Skinner
284	15¢	Henry Clay	November 1898	BEP			Thomas Morris	Charles Skinner
285	1¢	Jacques Marquette on the Mississippi	June 17, 1898	BEP	Washington, D.C.		R.O. Smith	George Smillie
286	2¢	Farming in the West	June 17, 1898	BEP	Pittsburgh, Pa.		R.O. Smith	Marcus Baldwin
287	4¢	Indian Hunting Buffalo	June 17, 1898	BEP			R.O. Smith	George Smillie
288	5¢	John Charles Fremont on the Rocky Mountains	June 17, 1898	BEP	Washington, D.C.		R.O. Smith	Marcus Baldwin
289	8¢	Troops Guarding Wagon Train	June 17, 1898	BEP	Washington, D.C.		R.O. Smith	Robert Ponickau
290	10¢	Hardships of Emigration	June 17, 1898	BEP			R.O. Smith	Marcus Baldwin
291	50¢	Western Mining Prospector	June 17, 1898	BEP	Washington, D.C.		R.O. Smith	George Smillie
292	$1	Western Cattle in Storm	June 17, 1898	BEP			R.O. Smith	Marcus Baldwin
293	$2	Mississippi River Bridge at St Louis	June 17, 1898	BEP	Washington, D.C.		R.O. Smith	Marcus Baldwin
294	1¢	Fast Lake Navigation (Steamship *City of Alpena*)	May 1, 1901	BEP	Buffalo, N.Y.		R.O. Smith	George Smillie
295	2¢	Empire State Express	May 1, 1901	BEP	Buffalo, N.Y.		R.O. Smith	Marcus Baldwin
296	4¢	Electric Automobile in Washington	May 1, 1901	BEP	Buffalo, N.Y.		R.O. Smith	
297	5¢	Bridge at Niagara Falls	May 1, 1901	BEP	Buffalo, N.Y.		R.O. Smith	
298	8¢	Canal Locks at Sault Ste. Marie	May 1, 1901	BEP	Buffalo, N.Y.		R.O. Smith	
299	10¢	Fast Ocean Navigation (Steamship *St. Paul*)	May 1, 1901	BEP	Buffalo, N.Y.		R.O. Smith	
300	1¢	Benjamin Franklin	Feb. 3, 1903	BEP			R.O. Smith	M.W. Dodson
301	2¢	George Washington	Jan. 17, 1903	BEP			R.O. Smith	George Smillie
302	3¢	Andrew Jackson	February 1903	BEP			R.O. Smith	George Smillie
303	4¢	Ulysses S. Grant	February 1903	BEP			R.O. Smith	George Smillie
304	5¢	Abraham Lincoln	January 1903	BEP			R.O. Smith	George Smillie
305	6¢	James A. Garfield	February 1903	BEP			R.O. Smith	Marcus Baldwin

Scott number	Denom.	Design	First day of issue	Printer	First-day city	First-day quantities	Designer	Engraver
306	8¢	Martha Washington	December 1902	BEP			R.O. Smith	George Smillie
307	10¢	Daniel Webster	February 1903	BEP			R.O. Smith	Marcus Baldwin
308	13¢	Benjamin Harrison	Nov. 18, 1902	BEP			R.O. Smith	Marcus Baldwin
309	15¢	Henry Clay	May 27, 1903	BEP			R.O. Smith	
310	50¢	Thomas Jefferson	March 23, 1903	BEP			R.O. Smith	George Smillie
311	$1	David G. Farragut	June 5, 1903	BEP			R.O. Smith	
312	$2	James Madison	June 5, 1903	BEP			R.O. Smith	George Smillie
313	$5	John Marshall	June 5, 1903	BEP			R.O. Smith	George Smillie
319	2¢	Washington Shield	Nov. 12, 1903	BEP				George Smillie
323	1¢	Robert R. Livingston	April 30, 1904	BEP			C.A. Huston	Marcus Baldwin
324	2¢	Thomas Jefferson	April 30, 1904	BEP	Moline, Ill.		C.A. Huston	George Smillie
325	3¢	James Monroe	April 30, 1904	BEP			C.A. Huston	George Smillie
326	5¢	William McKinley	April 30, 1904	BEP			C.A. Huston	George Smillie
327	10¢	Map of Louisiana Purchase	April 30, 1904	BEP			C.A. Huston	Robert Ponicau
328	1¢	Capt. John Smith	April 26, 1907	BEP	Fortress Monroe, Va.		C.A. Huston	Marcus Baldwin
329	2¢	Founding of Jamestown	April 26, 1907	BEP	Norfolk, Va.		Marcus Baldwin	Robert Ponicau
330	5¢	Pocahontas	April 26, 1907	BEP	Norfolk, Va.		C.A. Huston	George Smillie
331	1¢	Benjamin Franklin	December 1908	BEP			C.A. Huston	Marcus Baldwin
332	2¢	George Washington	November 1908	BEP				
333	3¢	George Washington	December 1908	BEP				
334	4¢	George Washington	December 1908	BEP				
335	5¢	George Washington	December 1908	BEP				
336	6¢	George Washington	December 1908	BEP				
337	8¢	George Washington	December 1908	BEP				
338	10¢	George Washington	January 1909	BEP				
339	13¢	George Washington	January 1909	BEP				
340	15¢	George Washington	January 1909	BEP				
341	50¢	George Washington	Jan. 13, 1909	BEP				
342	$1	George Washington	Jan. 29, 1909	BEP				
343	1¢	Benjamin Franklin	December 1908	BEP				
344	2¢	George Washington	Dec. 10, 1908	BEP				
345	3¢	George Washington	March 3, 1909	BEP				

Scott number	Denom.	Design	First day of issue	Printer	First-day city	First-day quantities	Designer	Engraver
346	4¢	George Washington	Feb. 25, 1909	BEP				
347	5¢	George Washington	Feb. 25, 1909	BEP				
348	1¢	Benjamin Franklin	Dec. 29, 1908	BEP				
349	2¢	George Washington	January 1909	BEP				
350	4¢	George Washington	Aug. 15, 1910	BEP				
351	5¢	George Washington	January 1909	BEP				
352	1¢	Benjamin Franklin	January 1909	BEP				
353	2¢	George Washington	Jan. 12, 1909	BEP				
354	4¢	George Washington	Feb. 23, 1909	BEP				
355	5¢	George Washington	Feb. 23, 1909	BEP				
356	10¢	George Washington	Jan. 7, 1909	BEP				
357	1¢	Benjamin Franklin	Feb. 16, 1909	BEP				
358	2¢	George Washington	Feb. 16, 1909	BEP				
359	3¢	George Washington	1909	BEP				
360	4¢	George Washington	1909					
361	5¢	George Washington	1909	BEP				
362	6¢	George Washington	1909	BEP				
363	8¢	George Washington	1909	BEP				
364	10¢	George Washington	1909	BEP				
365	13¢	George Washington	1909	BEP				
366	15¢	George Washington	1909	BEP				
367	2¢	Abraham Lincoln	Feb. 12, 1909				C.A. Huston	Marcus Baldwin
367	2¢	Abraham Lincoln	Feb. 12, 1909	BEP			C.A. Huston	Marcus Baldwin
368	2¢	Abraham Lincoln	Feb. 12, 1909	BEP	Canton, Ohio		C.A. Huston	Marcus Baldwin
369	2¢	Abraham Lincoln	February 1909	BEP			C.A. Huston	Marcus Baldwin
370	2¢	William H. Seward	June 1, 1909		Modesto, Calif.		C.A. Huston	Marcus Baldwin
372	2¢	Henry Hudson's *Half Moon* and Fulton's *Clermont*	Sept. 25, 1909		Boston, Mass.		Marcus Baldwin	Marcus Baldwin
373	2¢	Hudson's *Half Moon* and Fulton's *Clermont*	Sept. 25, 1909	BEP			Marcus Baldwin	Marcus Baldwin
374	1¢	Benjamin Franklin	Nov. 23, 1910	BEP				
375	2¢	George Washington	Nov. 23, 1910	BEP				
376	2¢	George Washington	Nov. 23, 1909	BEP				

Scott number	Denom.	Design	First day of issue	Printer	First-day city	First-day quantities	Designer	Engraver
377	4¢	George Washington	Jan. 20, 1911	BEP				
378	5¢	George Washington	Jan. 25, 1911	BEP				
379	6¢	George Washington	Jan. 25, 1911	BEP				
380	8¢	George Washington	Feb. 8, 1911	BEP				
381	10¢	George Washington	Jan. 24, 1911	BEP				
382	15¢	George Washington	March 1, 1911	BEP				
383	1¢	Benjamin Franklin	Jan. 3, 1911	BEP				
384	2¢	George Washington	Jan. 3, 1911	BEP				
385	1¢	Benjamin Franklin	Nov. 1, 1910	BEP				
386	2¢	George Washington	Nov. 1, 1910	BEP				
387	1¢	Benjamin Franklin	Jan. 11, 1910	BEP				
388	2¢	George Washington	Nov. 1, 1910	BEP				
389	3¢	George Washington	Jan. 24, 1911	BEP				
390	1¢	Benjamin Franklin	Dec. 12, 1910	BEP				
391	2¢	George Washington	Dec. 23, 1910	BEP				
392	1¢	Benjamin Franklin	Dec. 12, 1910	BEP				
393	2¢	George Washington	Dec. 16, 1910	BEP				
394	3¢	George Washington	Sept. 18, 1911	BEP				
395	4¢	George Washington	April 15, 1912	BEP				
396	5¢	George Washington	March 1913	BEP				
397	1¢	Vasco Nunez de Balboa	Jan. 1, 1913	BEP	San Francisco		C.A. Huston	J. Eissler
398	2¢	Pedro Miguel Locks, Panama Canal	January 1913	BEP	San Francisco		C.A. Huston	Marcus Baldwin
399	5¢	Golden Gate	Jan. 1, 1913	BEP	San Francisco		C.A. Huston	L.C. Schofield
400	10¢	Discovery of San Francisco Bay	Jan. 1, 1913	BEP	San Francisco		From Painting	Marcus Baldwin
401	1¢	Benjamin Franklin	December 1914	BEP				
402	2¢	George Washington	February 1915	BEP				
403	5¢	George Washington	February 1915	BEP				
404	10¢	George Washington	July 1915	BEP				
405	1¢	George Washington	February 1912	BEP				
406	2¢	George Washington	February 1912	BEP				
407	7¢	George Washington	April 1914	BEP				
408	1¢	George Washington	March 1912	BEP				

Scott number	Denom.	Design	First day of issue	Printer	First-day city	First-day quantities	Designer	Engraver
409	2¢	George Washington	February 1912	BEP				
410	1¢	George Washington	March 1912	BEP				
411	2¢	George Washington	March 1912	BEP				
412	1¢	George Washington	March 18, 1912	BEP				
413	2¢	George Washington	February 1912	BEP				
414	8¢	Benjamin Franklin	Feb 12, 1912	BEP				
415	9¢	Benjamin Franklin	April 1914	BEP				
416	10¢	Benjamin Franklin	Jan. 11, 1912	BEP				
417	12¢	Benjamin Franklin	April 1914	BEP				
418	15¢	Benjamin Franklin	Feb. 12, 1914	BEP				
419	20¢	Benjamin Franklin	April 1914	BEP				
420	30¢	Benjamin Franklin	April 1914	BEP				
421	50¢	Benjamin Franklin	April 29, 1914	BEP				
422	50¢	Benjamin Franklin	Feb. 12, 1912	BEP				
423	$1	Benjamin Franklin	Feb. 12, 1912	BEP				
424	1¢	George Washington	Sept. 5, 1914	BEP				
425	2¢	George Washington	Sept. 5, 1914	BEP				
426	3¢	George Washington	Sept. 18, 1914	BEP				
427	4¢	George Washington	Sept. 7, 1914	BEP				
428	5¢	George Washington	Sept. 14, 1914	BEP				
429	6¢	George Washington	Sept. 28, 1914	BEP				
430	7¢	George Washington	Sept. 10, 1914	BEP				
431	8¢	Benjamin Franklin	Sept. 26, 1914	BEP				
432	9¢	Benjamin Franklin	Oct. 6, 1914	BEP				
433	10¢	Benjamin Franklin	Sept. 9, 1914	BEP				
434	11¢	Benjamin Franklin	Aug. 11, 1915	BEP				
435	12¢	Benjamin Franklin	Sept. 10, 1914	BEP				
437	15¢	Benjamin Franklin	Sept. 16, 1914	BEP				
438	20¢	Benjamin Franklin	Sept. 19, 1914	BEP				
439	30¢	Benjamin Franklin	Sept. 19, 1914	BEP				
440	50¢	Benjamin Franklin	Dec. 10, 1915	BEP				
441	1¢	George Washington	Nov. 14, 1914	BEP				
442	2¢	George Washington	July 22, 1914	BEP				
443	1¢	George Washington	May 29, 1914	BEP				

Scott number	Denom.	Design	First day of issue	Printer	First-day city	First-day quantities	Designer	Engraver
445	3¢	George Washington	Dec. 18, 1914	BEP				
446	4¢	George Washington	Oct. 2, 1914	BEP				
447	5¢	George Washington	July 30, 1914	BEP				
448	1¢	George Washington	Dec. 12, 1915	BEP				
449	2¢	George Washington	Dec. 5, 1915	BEP				
450	2¢	George Washington	February 1916	BEP				
452	1¢	George Washington	Nov. 11, 1914	BEP				
453	2¢	George Washington	July 3, 1914	BEP				
454	2¢	George Washington	June 1915	BEP				
455	2¢	George Washington	December 1915	BEP				
456	3¢	George Washington	Feb. 2, 1916	BEP				
457	4¢	George Washington	Feb. 18, 1916	BEP				
458	5¢	George Washington	March 9, 1916	BEP				
459	2¢	George Washington	June 30, 1914	BEP				
460	$1	Benjamin Franklin	Feb. 8, 1915	BEP				
461	2¢	George Washington	June 17, 1918	BEP				
462	1¢	George Washington	Sept. 27, 1916	BEP				
463	2¢	George Washington	Sept. 25, 1916	BEP				
464	3¢	George Washington	Nov. 11, 1916	BEP				
465	4¢	George Washington	Oct. 7, 1916	BEP				
466	5¢	George Washington	Oct. 17, 1916	BEP				
467	5¢	George Washington	March 7, 1917	BEP				
468	6¢	George Washington	Oct. 10, 1916	BEP				
469	7¢	George Washington	Oct. 10, 1916	BEP				
470	8¢	Benjamin Franklin	Nov. 13, 1916	BEP				
471	9¢	Benjamin Franklin	Nov. 16, 1916	BEP				
472	10¢	Benjamin Franklin	Oct. 17, 1916	BEP				
473	11¢	Benjamin Franklin	Nov. 16, 1916	BEP				
474	12¢	Benjamin Franklin	Oct. 10, 1916	BEP				
475	15¢	Benjamin Franklin	Nov. 16, 1916	BEP				
476	20¢	Benjamin Franklin	Dec. 5, 1916	BEP				
476A	30¢	Benjamin Franklin	1916,	BEP				
477	50¢	Benjamin Franklin	March 2, 1917	BEP				
478	$1	Benjamin Franklin	Dec. 22, 1916	BEP				

Scott number	Denom.	Design	First day of issue	Printer	First-day city	First-day quantities	Designer	Engraver
479	$2	James Madison	March 22, 1917	BEP				
480	$5	John Marshall	March 22, 1917	BEP				
481	1¢	George Washington	November 1916	BEP				
482	2¢	George Washington	Dec. 8, 1916	BEP				
482A	2¢	George Washington	1916	BEP				
483	3¢	George Washington	Oct. 13, 1917	BEP				
484	3¢	George Washington	1917	BEP				
485	5¢	George Washington	March 1917	BEP				
486	1¢	George Washington	January 1918	BEP				
487	2¢	George Washington	Nov. 15, 1916	BEP				
488	2¢	George Washington	1919	BEP				
489	3¢	George Washington	Oct. 10, 1917	BEP				
490	1¢	George Washington	Nov. 17, 1916	BEP				
491	2¢	George Washington	Nov. 17, 1916	BEP				
492	2¢	George Washington	1916	BEP				
493	3¢	George Washington	July 23, 1917	BEP				
494	3¢	George Washington	Feb. 4, 1918	BEP				
495	4¢	George Washington	April 15, 1917	BEP				
496	5¢	George Washington	Feb. 15, 1916	BEP				
497	10¢	George Washington	Jan. 31, 1922	BEP	Washington, D.C.			
498	1¢	George Washington	March, 1917	BEP				
499	2¢	George Washington	March, 1917	BEP				
500	2¢	George Washington	1917	BEP				
501	3¢	George Washington	March 1917	BEP				
502	3¢	George Washington	1917	BEP				
503	4¢	George Washington	March 1917	BEP				
504	5¢	George Washington	March 1917	BEP				
505	5¢	George Washington	March 23, 1917	BEP				
506	6¢	George Washington	March 1917	BEP				
507	7¢	George Washington	March 1917	BEP				
508	8¢	Benjamin Franklin	March 1917	BEP				
509	9¢	Benjamin Franklin	March 1917	BEP				
510	10¢	Benjamin Franklin	March 1917	BEP				
511	11¢	Benjamin Franklin	May 1917	BEP				

Scott number	Denom.	Design	First day of issue	Printer	First-day city	First-day quantities	Designer	Engraver
512	12¢	Benjamin Franklin	May 1917	BEP				
513	13¢	Benjamin Franklin	Jan. 10, 1919	BEP				
514	15¢	Benjamin Franklin	May 1917	BEP				
515	20¢	Benjamin Franklin	May 1917	BEP				
516	30¢	Benjamin Franklin	May 1917	BEP				
517	50¢	Benjamin Franklin	May 1917	BEP				
518	$1	Benjamin Franklin	May 1917	BEP				
519	2¢	George Washington	Oct. 10, 1917	BEP				
520	$1	Benjamin Franklin	August 1918	BEP				
521	$5	Benjamin Franklin	August 1918	BEP				
525	1¢	George Washington	December 1918	BEP				
526	2¢	George Washington	March 15, 1920	BEP				
527	2¢	George Washington	March 20, 1920	BEP				
528	2¢	George Washington	May 4, 1920	BEP				
528A	2¢	George Washington	June 24, 1920	BEP				
528B	2¢	George Washington	Nov. 3, 1920	BEP				
529	3¢	George Washington	March 1918	BEP				
530	3¢	George Washington	June 30, 1918	BEP				
531	1¢	George Washington	January 1919	BEP				
532	2¢	George Washington	March 1919	BEP				
533	2¢	George Washington	May 1920	BEP				
534	2¢	George Washington	May 1920	BEP				
534A	2¢	George Washington	July 1920	BEP				
534B	2¢	George Washington	December 1920	BEP				
535	3¢	George Washington	1918	BEP				
536	1¢	George Washington	August 1919	BEP				
537	3¢	"Victory" and Flags of Allies	March 3, 1919	BEP			C.A. Huston	Marcus Baldwin
538	1¢	George Washington	June 1919	BEP				
539	2¢	George Washington	1919	BEP				
540	2¢	George Washington	June 14, 1919	BEP				
541	3¢	George Washington	June 1919	BEP				
542	1¢	George Washington	May 26, 1920	BEP				
543	1¢	George Washington	May 1921	BEP				

Scott number	Denom.	Design	First day of issue	Printer	First-day city	First-day quantities	Designer	Engraver
544	1¢	George Washington	1923	BEP				
545	1¢	George Washington	May 1921	BEP				
546	2¢	George Washington	May 1921	BEP				
547	$2	Benjamin Franklin	Nov. 1, 1920	BEP				
548	1¢	The *Mayflower*	Dec. 21, 1920	BEP				
549	2¢	Landing of the Pilgrims	Dec. 21, 1920	BEP	Washington, D.C.			
550	5¢	Signing of the Compact	Dec. 21, 1920	BEP	Washington, D.C.			
551	1¢	Nathan Hale	April 4, 1925	BEP				
552	1¢	Benjamin Franklin	Jan. 17, 1923	BEP				
553	1 1/2¢	Warren G. Harding	March 19, 1925	BEP				
554	2¢	George Washington	Jan. 15, 1923	BEP				
555	3¢	Abraham Lincoln	Feb. 12, 1923	BEP				
556	4¢	Martha Washington	Jan. 15, 1923	BEP				
557	5¢	Theodore Roosevelt	Oct. 27, 1922	BEP				
558	6¢	James Garfield	Nov. 20, 1922	BEP				
559	7¢	William McKinley	May 1, 1923	BEP				
560	8¢	Ulysses S. Grant	May 1, 1923	BEP				
561	9¢	Thomas Jefferson	Jan. 15, 1923	BEP				
562	10¢	James Monroe	Jan. 15, 1923	BEP				
563	11¢	Rutherford B. Hayes	Oct. 4, 1922	BEP				
564	12¢	Grover Cleveland	May 20, 1923	BEP				
565	14¢	American Indian	May 1, 1923	BEP				
566	15¢	Statue of Liberty	Nov. 11, 1922	BEP				
567	20¢	Golden Gate	May 1, 1923	BEP				
568	25¢	Niagara Falls	Nov. 11, 1922	BEP				
569	30¢	Buffalo	March 20, 1923	BEP				
570	50¢	Arlington Amphitheater	Nov. 11, 1923	BEP				
571	$1	Lincoln Memorial	Feb. 12, 1923	BEP				
572	$2	United States Capitol	March 20, 1923	BEP				
573	$5	Head of Freedom Statue, Capitol Dome	March 20, 1923	BEP				
610	2¢	Warren G. Harding	Sept. 1, 1923	BEP				
614	1¢	Ship *Nieu Nederland*	May 1, 1924	BEP				
615	2¢	Balloons Landing at	May 1, 1924	BEP				

Scott number	Denom.	Design	First day of issue	Printer	First-day city	First-day quantities	Designer	Engraver
		Fort Orange						
616	5¢	Jan Ribault Monument at Mayport, Fla.	May 1, 1924	BEP				
617	1¢	Washington at Cambridge	April 4, 1925	BEP				
618	2¢	"Birth of Liberty" by Henry Sandham	April 4, 1925	BEP				
619	5¢	"The Minute Man" by Daniel Chester French	April 4, 1925	BEP				
620	2¢	Sloop *Restaurationen*	May 18, 1925	BEP				
621	5¢	Viking Ship	May 18, 1925	BEP				
622	13¢	Benjamin Harrison	Jan. 11, 1926	BEP				
623	17¢	Woodrow Wilson	Dec. 28, 1925	BEP				
627	2¢	Liberty Bell	May 10, 1926	BEP				
628	5¢	Statue of John Ericsson	May 29, 1926	BEP				
629	2¢	Alexander Hamilton's Battery	Oct. 18, 1926	BEP				
643	2¢	Green Mountain Boy	Aug. 3, 1927	BEP				
644	2¢	Surrender of Gen. Burgoyne	Aug. 3, 1927	BEP				
645	2¢	Washington at Prayer	May 26, 1928	BEP				
646	2¢	Molly Pitcher Overprint	Oct. 20, 1928	BEP				
647	2¢	Hawaii Overprint	Aug. 13, 1928	BEP				
648	5¢	Hawaii Overprint	Aug. 13, 1928	BEP				
649	2¢	Wright Airplane	Dec. 12, 1928	BEP				
650	5¢	Globe and Airplane	Dec. 12, 1928	BEP				
651	2¢	Surrender of Fort Sackville	Feb. 25, 1929	BEP				
654	2¢	Edison's First Lamp	June 5, 1929	BEP				
657	2¢	Maj. Gen. John Sullivan	June 17, 1929	BEP				
658	1¢	Kansas Overprint	May 1, 1929	BEP				
659	2¢	Kansas Overprint	May 1, 1929	BEP				
660	2¢	Kansas Overprint	May 1, 1929	BEP				

Scott number	Denom.	Design	First day of issue	Printer	First-day city	First-day quantities	Designer	Engraver
661	3¢	Kansas Overprint	May 1, 1929	BEP				
662	4¢	Kansas Overprint	May 1, 1929	BEP				
663	5¢	Kansas Overprint	May 1, 1929	BEP				
664	6¢	Kansas Overprint	May 1, 1929	BEP				
665	7¢	Kansas Overprint	May 1, 1929	BEP				
666	8¢	Kansas Overprint	May 1, 1929	BEP				
667	9¢	Kansas Overprint	May 1, 1929	BEP				
668	10¢	Kansas Overprint	May 1, 1929	BEP				
669	10¢	Nebraska Overprint	May 1, 1929	BEP				
670	2¢	Nebraska Overprint	May 1, 1929	BEP				
671	2¢	Nebraska Overprint	May 1, 1929	BEP				
672	3¢	Nebraska Overprint	May 1, 1929	BEP				
673	4¢	Nebraska Overprint	May 1, 1929	BEP				
674	5¢	Nebraska Overprint	May 1, 1929	BEP				
675	6¢	Nebraska Overprint	May 1, 1929	BEP				
676	7¢	Nebraska Overprint	May 1, 1929	BEP				
677	8¢	Nebraska Overprint	May 1, 1929	BEP				
678	9¢	Nebraska Overprint	May 1, 1929	BEP				
679	10¢	Nebraska Overprint	May 1, 1929	BEP				
680	2¢	Gen. Wayne Memorial	Sept. 14, 1929	BEP				
681	2¢	Lock No. 5 Monongahela River	Oct. 19, 1929	BEP				
682	2¢	Massachusetts Bay Colony Seal	April 8, 1930	BEP				
683	2¢	Gov. Joseph West and Chief Shadoo	April 10, 1930	BEP				
684	2¢	Warren G. Harding	Dec. 1, 1930	BEP				
685	4¢	William H. Taft	June 4, 1930	BEP				
686	2¢	Statue of Col. George Washington	July 9, 1930	BEP				
687	2¢	General von Steuben	Sept. 17, 1929	BEP				
690	2¢	General Casimir Pulaski	Jan. 16, 1931	BEP				
702	2¢	"The Greatest Mother"	May 21, 1931	BEP				
703	2¢	Rochambeau, Washing-	Oct. 19, 1931	BEP				

Scott number	Denom.	Design	First day of issue	Printer	First-day city	First-day quantities	Designer	Engraver
		ton, de Grasse						
704	1¢	Washington by Charles Wilson Peale, 1777	Jan. 1, 1932	BEP				
705	1¢	Washington from Houdon Bust	Jan. 1, 1932	BEP				
706	2¢	Washington by Charles Wilson Peale, 1772	Jan. 1, 1932	BEP				
707	2¢	Washington by Gilbert Stuart, 1796	Jan. 1, 1932	BEP				
708	3¢	Washington by Charles Wilson Peale, 1777	Jan. 1, 1932	BEP				
709	4¢	Washington by Charles Peale Polk	Jan. 1, 1932	BEP				
710	5¢	Washington by Charles Wilson Peale, 1795	Jan. 1, 1932	BEP				
711	6¢	Washington by John Trumbull, 1792	Jan. 1, 1932	BEP				
712	7¢	Washington by John Trumbull, 1780	Jan. 1, 1932	BEP				
713	8¢	Washington by Charles B.J.F. Saint-Memin	Jan. 1, 1932	BEP				
714	9¢	Washington by W. Williams, 1794	Jan. 1, 1932	BEP				
715	10¢	Washington by Gilbert Stuart, 1795	Jan. 1, 1932	BEP				
716	2¢	Ski Jumper	Jan. 25, 1932	BEP				
717	2¢	Boy and Girl Planting Tree	April 22, 1932	BEP				
718	3¢	Runner at Starting Mark	June 15, 1932	BEP				

Scott number	Denom.	Design	First day of issue	Printer	First-day city	First-day quantities	Designer	Engraver
719	5¢	Myron's Doscobolus	June 15, 1932	BEP				
720	3¢	Washington by Gilbert Stuart	June 16, 1932	BEP				
724	3¢	William Penn	Oct. 24, 1932	BEP				
725	3¢	Daniel Webster	Oct. 24, 1932	BEP				
726	3¢	Gen. James E. Oglethorpe	Feb. 12, 1932	BEP	Savannah, Ga.	200,000	C.A. Huston	J. Eissler
727	3¢	Washington's Headquarters at Newburgh, N.Y.	April 19, 1933	BEP	Newburgh, N.Y.	349,571	A.R. Meissner	L.S. Schofield
728	1¢	Restoration of Fort Dearborn	May 25, 1933	BEP	Chicago, Ill.	232,251	V.S. McCloskey, Jr.	L.S. Schofield
729	3¢	Federal Building	May 25, 1933	BEP	Chicago, Ill.	232,251	V.S. McCloskey, Jr.	J. Eissler
730	1¢	Restoration of Fort Dearborn	Aug. 25, 1933	BEP	Chicago, Ill.	65,218	V.S. McCloskey, Jr.	L.S. Schofield
731	3¢	Federal Building	Aug. 25, 1933	BEP	Chicago, Ill.	65,218	V.S. McCloskey, Jr.	J. Eissler
732	3¢	Group of Workers	Aug. 15, 1933	BEP	Washington, D.C.	65,000	V.S. McCloskey, Jr.	L.S. Schofield
733		Map of the World (on van der Grinten's Projection)	Oct. 9, 1933	BEP			V.S. McCloskey, Jr.	J.C. Benzing
734	5¢	Statue of Gen. Tadeusz Kosciuszko	Oct. 13, 1933	BEP	Multiple	124,000	V.S. McCloskey, Jr.	Alfred Jones
735	3¢	Type of Byrd Issue	Feb. 10, 1934	BEP	New York, N.Y.	450,715	V.S. McCloskey, Jr.	J.C. Benzing
736	3¢	*The Ark* and *The Dove*	March 23, 1933	BEP	St. Mary's City	148,785	A.R. Meissner	J.C. Benzing
737	3¢	Adaptation of Whistler's Portrait of His Mother	May 2, 1933	BEP	any city		V.S. McCloskey, Jr.	J.C. Benzing
738	3¢	Whistler's Mother	May 2, 1934	BEP			V.S. McCloskey, Jr.	J.C. Benzing
739	3¢	Nicolet's Landing	July 7, 1934	BEP	Green Bay, Wis.	130,000	V.S. McCloskey, Jr.	C.T. Arlt
740	1¢	El Capitan, Yosemite (California)	July 16, 1934	BEP	Yosemite, Calif.	60,000	V.S. McCloskey, Jr.	J.C. Benzing
741	2¢	View of Grand Canyon (Arizona)	July 24, 1934	BEP	Grand Canyon, Ariz.	75,000	V.S. McCloskey, Jr.	J.C. Benzing
742	3¢	Mt. Rainier and Mirror Lake	Aug. 3, 1934	BEP	Longmire, Wash.	64,500	V.S. McCloskey, Jr.	L.S. Schofield

Scott number	Denom.	Design	First day of issue	Printer	First-day city	First-day quantities	Designer	Engraver
		(Washington)						
743	4¢	Cliff Palace, Mesa Verde Park (Colorado)	Sept. 25, 1934	BEP	Mesa Verde, Colo.	51,882	V.S. McCloskey, Jr.	C.T. Arlt
744	5¢	Old Faithful, Yellowstone (Wyoming)	July 30, 1934	BEP	Yellowstone, Wyo.	87,000	V.S. McCloskey, Jr.	C.T. Arlt
745	6¢	Crater Lake (Oregon)	Sept. 5, 1934	BEP	Carter Lake, Ore.	45,282	V.S. McCloskey, Jr.	L.S. Schofield
746	7¢	Great Head, Acadia Parka (Maine)	Oct. 2, 1934	BEP	Bar Harbor, Maine	51,312	V.S. McCloskey, Jr.	J.C. Benzing
747	8¢	Great White Throne, Zion Park (Utah)	Sept. 18, 1934	BEP	Zion, Utah	43,605	V.S. McCloskey, Jr.	C.T. Arlt
748	9¢	Mt. Rockwell (Mt. Sinopah) and Two Medicine Lake Glacier	Aug. 27, 1934	BEP	Glacier Park, Mont.	52,626	V.S. McCloskey, Jr.	C.T. Arlt
749	10¢	Great Smoky Mountains (North Carolina)	Oct. 8, 1934	BEP	Sevierville, Tenn.	39,000	Esther Richards	L.S. Schofield
750	3¢	Mt. Rainier and Mirror Lake	Aug. 28, 1933	BEP	Atlantic City, N.J.	40,000	V.S. McCloskey, Jr.	J.C. Benzing
751	1¢	El Capitan, Yosemite	Oct. 10, 1934	BEP	Omaha, Neb.	125,000	V.S. McCloskey, Jr.	J.C. Benzing
752	3¢	Washington's Headquarters	March 15, 1935	BEP			A.R. Meissner	L.S. Schofield
753	3¢	Byrd Issue	March 15, 1935	BEP			V.S. McCloskey, Jr.	J.C. Benzing
754	3¢	Whistler's Mother	March 15, 1935	BEP			V.S. McCloskey, Jr.	J.C. Benzing
755	3¢	Nicolet's Landing	March 15, 1935	BEP			V.S. McCloskey, Jr.	C.T. Arlt
756	1¢	El Capitan, Yosemite	March 15, 1935	BEP			V.S. McCloskey, Jr.	J.C. Benzing
757	2¢	View of Grand Canyon	March 15, 1935	BEP			V.S. McCloskey, Jr.	L.S. Schofield
758	3¢	Mt. Rainier and Mirror Lake	March 15, 1935	BEP			V.S. McCloskey, Jr.	J.C. Benzing
759	4¢	Cliff Palace, Mesa Verde	March 15, 1935	BEP			V.S. McCloskey, Jr.	C.T. Arlt
760	5¢	Old Faithful, Yellowstone	March 15, 1935	BEP			V.S. McCloskey, Jr.	C.T. Arlt
761	6¢	Crater Lake	March 15, 1935	BEP			V.S. McCloskey, Jr.	L.S. Schofield
762	7¢	Great Head, Acadia Park	March 15, 1935	BEP			V.S. McCloskey, Jr.	J.C. Benzing
763	8¢	Great White Throne, Zion Park	March 15, 1935	BEP			V.S. McCloskey, Jr.	C.T. Arlt

Scott number	Denom.	Design	First day of issue	Printer	First-day city	First-day quantities	Designer	Engraver
764	9¢	Mt. Rockwell, Two Medicine Lake	March 15, 1935	BEP			V.S. McCloskey, Jr.	C.T. Arlt
765	10¢	Great Smoky Mountains	March 15, 1935	BEP			Esther Richards	L.S. Schofield
766	1¢	Fort Dearborn	March 15, 1935	BEP			V.S. McCloskey, Jr.	L.S. Schofield
767	3¢	Federal Building	March 15, 1935	BEP			V.S. McCloskey, Jr.	J. Eissler
768	3¢	Byrd Issue	March 15, 1935	BEP			V.S. McCloskey, Jr.	J.C. Benzing
769	1¢	El Capitan	March 15, 1935	BEP			V.S. McCloskey, Jr.	J.C. Benzing
770	3¢	Mt. Rainier and Mirror Lake	March 15, 1935	BEP			V.S. McCloskey, Jr.	J.C. Benzing
771	16¢	Great Seal of the United States	March 15, 1935	BEP			V.S. McCloskey, Jr.	J. Eissler
772	3¢	The Charter Oak	April 26, 1935	BEP	Hartford, Conn.	217,800	V.S. McCloskey, Jr.	J.C. Benzing
773	3¢	View of San Diego Exposition	May 29, 1935	BEP	San Diego, Calif.	214,042	A.R. Meissner	C.T. Arlt
774	3¢	Boulder Dam (Hoover Dam)	Sept. 30, 1935	BEP	Boulder City, Nev.	166,180	V.S. McCloskey, Jr.	C.T. Arlt
775	3¢	Michigan State Seal	Nov. 1, 1935	BEP	Lansing, Mich.	176,962	A.R. Meissner	L.C. Kauffmann
776	3¢	Sam Houston, Stephen Austin and the Alamo	March 2, 1936	BEP	Gonsales, Texas	319,150	A.R. Meissner	C.T. Arlt
777	3¢	Statue of Roger Williams	May 4, 1936	BEP	Providence, R.I.	245,400	A.R. Meissner	C.T. Arlt
778	3¢	Connecticut, California, Michigan and Texas	May 9, 1936	BEP	New York, N.Y.	297,194		
782	3¢	Arkansas Post, Old and New State Houses	June 15, 1936	BEP	Little Rock, Ark.	376,693	A.R. Meissner	C.T. Arlt
783	3¢	Map of Oregon Territory	July 14, 1936	BEP	Multiple	400,000	A.R. Meissner	C.T. Arlt
784	3¢	Susan B. Anthony	Aug. 20, 1936	BEP		178,500	V.S. McCloskey, Jr.	C.T. Arlt
785	1¢	Washington, Nathanael Greene and Mt. Vernon	Dec. 15, 1936	BEP		390,749	William Schrage	M.D. Fenton
786	2¢	Maj. Gen. Andrew Jackson, Gen. Winfield Scott and the Hermitage	Jan. 15, 1937	BEP		292,570	William Schrage	J. Eissler
787	3¢	Gens. William Sherman, Ulysses S. Grant and	Feb. 18, 1937	BEP		320,888	V.S. McCloskey, Jr.	F. Pauling

Scott number	Denom.	Design	First day of issue	Printer	First-day city	First-day quantities	Designer	Engraver
		Philip Sheridan						
788	4¢	Gens. Robert E. Lee, "Stonewall" Jackson and Stratford Hall	March 23, 1937	BEP		331,000	William Schrage	L.C. Kauffmann
789	5¢	West Point	May 26, 1937	BEP	West Point, N.Y.	160,000	L.E. Schick	C.T. Arlt
790	1¢	John Paul Jones and John Barry	Dec. 15, 1936	BEP		390,749	A.R. Meissner	C.T. Arlt
791	2¢	Stephen Decatur and Thomas MacDonough	Feb. 15, 1937	BEP		292,570	A.R. Meissner	J. Eissler
792	3¢	Adms. David Farragut and David Porter	Feb. 18, 1937	BEP		320,888	A.R. Meissner	L.C. Kauffmann
793	4¢	Adms. Sampson, Dewey and Schley	May 26, 1937	BEP		331,000	A.R. Meissner	J. Eissler
794	5¢	Seal of U.S. Naval Academy and Naval Cadets	May 26, 1937	BEP	Annapolis, Md.	202,806	A.R. Meissner	F. Pauling
795	3¢	Manasseh Cutler, Rufus Putnam and Map of Northwest Territory	July 13, 1937	BEP	Annapolis, Md.	130,531	A.R. Meissner	L.C. Kauffmann
796	5¢	Virginia Dare and Parents	Aug. 18, 1937	BEP	Marietta, Ohio	226,730	William Schrage	C.T. Arlt
797	10¢	Great Smoky Mountains	Aug. 26, 1937	BEP	Asheville, N.C.	164,215	William Schrage	C.T. Arlt
798	3¢	Adoption of the Constitution	Sept. 17, 1937	BEP	Philadelphia, Pa.	281,478	A.R. Meissner	J. Eissler
799	3¢	Statue of Kamehameha I, Honolulu	Oct. 18, 1937	BEP	Honolulu, Hawaii	320,334	A.R. Meissner	C. Chalmers
800	3¢	Mt. McKinley	Nov. 12, 1937	BEP	Juneau, Alaska	230,370	V.S. McCloskey, Jr.	C.T. Arlt
801	3¢	LaFortaleza, San Juan	Nov. 25, 1937	BEP	San Juan, P.R.	244,054	William Schrage	J. Eissler
802	3¢	Charlotte Amalie Harbor, St. Thomas	Dec. 15, 1937	BEP	Charlotte Amalie, Virgin Islands	225,469	V.S. McCloskey, Jr.	C.T. Arlt
803	1¢	Benjamin Franklin	May 19, 1938	BEP	Philadelphia, Pa.	224,901	William Schrage	J. Eissler
804	1¢	George Washington	April 25, 1938	BEP	Philadelphia, Pa.	124,037	Elaine Rawlinson	J. Eissler
805	2¢	Martha Washington	May 5, 1938	BEP	Philadelphia, Pa.	128,339	William Schrage	L.C. Kauffmann
806	2¢	John Adams	June 3, 1938	BEP	Philadelphia, Pa.	127,806	William Schrage	C.A. Brooks

Scott number	Denom.	Design	First day of issue	Printer	First-day city	First-day quantities	Designer	Engraver
807	3¢	Thomas Jefferson	June 16, 1938	BEP	Philadelphia, Pa.	118,097	William Schrage	C.T. Arlt
808	4¢	James Madison	July 1, 1938	BEP	Philadelphia, Pa.	118,765	William Schrage	L.C. Kauffmann
809	5¢	The White House	July 11, 1938	BEP	Philadelphia, Pa.	118,820	William Schrage	J.R. Lowe
810	5¢	James Monroe	July 21, 1938	BEP	Philadelphia, Pa	98,282	R.L. Miller, Jr.	J. Eissler
811	6¢	John Quincy Adams	July 28, 1938	BEP	Philadelphia, Pa.	97,428	William Schrage	F. Pauling
812	7¢	Andrew Jackson	Aug. 4, 1938	BEP	Philadelphia, Pa.	98,414	William Schrage	C.A. Brooks
813	8¢	Martin Van Buren	Aug. 11, 1938	BEP	Philadelphia, Pa.	94,857	William Schrage	C.A. Brooks
814	9¢	William H. Harrison	Aug. 18, 1938	BEP	Philadelphia, Pa.	91,229	William Schrage	C.A. Brooks
815	10¢	John Tyler	Sept. 2, 1938	BEP	Philadelphia, Pa.	83,707	William Schrage	C.T. Arlt
816	11¢	James K. Polk	Sept. 8, 1938	BEP	Philadelphia, Pa.	63,966	R.L. Miller, Jr.	L.C. Kauffman
817	12¢	Zachary Taylor	Sept. 14, 1938	BEP	Philadelphia, Pa.	62,935	William Schrage	J. Eissler
818	13¢	Millard Filmore	Sept. 22, 1938	BEP	Philadelphia, Pa.	58,965	William Schrage	F. Pauling
819	14¢	Franklin Pierce	Oct. 6, 1938	BEP	Philadelphia, Pa.	49,819	William Schrage	L.C. Kauffmann
820	15¢	James Buchanan	Oct. 13, 1938	BEP	Philadelphia, Pa.	52,209	R.L. Miller, Jr.	C.A. Brooks
821	16¢	Abraham Lincoln	Oct. 20, 1938	BEP	Philadelphia, Pa.	59,566	William Schrage	C.T. Arlt
822	17¢	Andrew Johnson	Oct. 27, 1938	BEP	Philadelphia, Pa.	55,024	William Schrage	L.C. Kauffmann
823	2¢	Ulysses S. Grant	Nov. 3, 1938	BEP	Philadelphia, Pa.	53,124	William Roach	C.A. Brooks
824	2¢	Rutherford B. Hayes	Nov. 10, 1938	BEP	Philadelphia, Pa.	54,124	R.L. Miller, Jr.	C.A. Brooks
825	20¢	James A. Garfield	Nov. 10, 1938	BEP	Philadelphia, Pa.	51,971	William Roach	C.A. Brooks
826	21¢	Chester A. Arthur	Nov. 22, 1938	BEP	Philadelphia, Pa.	44,367	V.S. McCloskey, Jr.	W.O. Marks
827	22¢	Grover Cleveland	Nov. 22, 1938	BEP	Philadelphia, Pa.	44,358	V.S. McCloskey, Jr.	M.D. Fenton
828	24¢	Benjamin Harrison	Dec. 2, 1938	BEP	Philadelphia, Pa.	46,592	V.S. McCloskey, Jr.	C.A. Brooks
829	25¢	William McKinley	Dec. 2, 1938	BEP	Philadelphia, Pa.	45,691	V.S. McCloskey, Jr.	J.R. Lowe
830	30¢	Theodore Roosevelt	Dec. 8, 1938	BEP	Philadelphia, Pa.	43,528	William Roach	J.R. Lowe
831	50¢	William Howard Taft	Dec. 8, 1938	BEP	Philadelphia, Pa.	41,984	William Roach	H. R. Rollins
832	$1	Woodrow Wilson	Aug. 29, 1938	BEP	Philadelphia, Pa.	24,618	V.S. McCloskey, Jr.	L.C. Kauffmann
833	$2	Warren G. Harding	Sept. 29, 1938	BEP	Philadelphia, Pa.	19,895	V.S. McCloskey, Jr.	F. Pauling
834	$5	Calvin Coolidge	Nov. 17, 1938	BEP	Philadelphia, Pa.	15,615	V.S. McCloskey, Jr.	J. Eissler
835	3¢	Old Courthouse, Williamsburg, Va.	June 21, 1938	BEP	Philadelphia, Pa.	232,873	V.S. McCloskey, Jr.	M.D. Fenton
836	3¢	Landing of First Swedish and Finnish Settlers in America	June 27, 1938	BEP	Wilmington, Del.	225,617	A.R. Meissner	C.T. Arlt
837	3¢	Colonization of the West	July 15, 1938	BEP	Marietta, Ohio	180,170	R.L. Miller, Jr.	C.T. Arlt

Scott number	Denom.	Design	First day of issue	Printer	First-day city	First-day quantities	Designer	Engraver
838	3¢	Old Capitol, Iowa City	Aug. 24, 1938	BEP	Des Moines, Iowa	209,860	A.R. Meissner	C.T. Arlt
839	1¢	George Washington	Jan. 20, 1939	BEP			Elaine Rawlinson	J. Eissler
840	2¢	Martha Washington	Jan. 20, 1939	BEP			William Schrage	L.C. Kauffmann
841	2¢	John Adams	Jan. 20, 1939	BEP			William Schrage	C.A. Brooks
842	3¢	Thomas Jefferson	Jan. 20, 1939	BEP			William Schrage	C.T. Arlt
843	4¢	James Madison	Jan. 20, 1939	BEP			William Schrage	L.C. Kauffman
844	5¢	The White House	Jan. 20, 1939	BEP			William Schrage	J.R. Lowe
845	5¢	James Monroe	Jan. 20, 1939	BEP			R.L. Miller, Jr.	J. Eissler
846	6¢	John Quincy Adams	Jan. 20, 1939	BEP			William Schrage	F. Pauling
847	10¢	John Tyler	Jan. 20, 1939	BEP			William Schrage	C.T. Arlt
848	1¢	George Washington	Jan. 27, 1939	BEP			Elaine Rawlinson	J. Eissler
849	2¢	Martha Washington	Jan. 27, 1939	BEP			William Schrage	L.C. Kauffmann
850	2¢	John Adams	Jan. 27, 1939	BEP			William Schrage	C.A. Brooks
851	3¢	Thomas Jefferson	Jan. 27, 1939	BEP			William Schrage	C.T. Arlt
852	3¢	Tower of the Sun	Feb. 18, 1939	BEP	San Franscisco	352,165	William Roach	C.A. Brooks
853	3¢	Trylon and Perisphere	April 1, 1939	BEP	New York, N.Y.	585,565	C. Dale Badgeley	E.M. Weeks
854	3¢	Washington Taking Oath of Office	April 30, 1939	BEP	New York, N.Y.	395,644	A. R. Meissner	J. Eissler
855	3¢	Sandlot Baseball Game	June 12, 1939	BEP	Cooperstown, N.Y.	389,199	William Roach	C.A. Brooks
856	3¢	Theodore Roosevelt, Gen. George Goethals, Ship in Gaillard Cut	Aug. 15, 1939	BEP	*USS Charleston*, Canal Zone	230,974	William Roach	W.O. Marks
857	3¢	Stephen Daye Press	Sept. 25, 1939	BEP	New York, N.Y.	292,270	William K. Schrage	C.T. Arlt
858	3¢	Map of North and South Dakota, Montana and Washington	Nov. 2, 1939	BEP	Bismarck, N.D.	292,535	A. R. Meissner	M.D. Fenton
859	1¢	Washington Irving	Jan. 29, 1940	BEP	Tarrytown, N.Y.	170,969	William Roach	C.T. Arlt
860	2¢	James Fenimore Cooper	Feb. 5, 1940	BEP	Cooperstown, N.Y.	154,836	William Roach	C.T. Arlt
861	3¢	Ralph Waldo Emerson	Feb. 5, 1940	BEP	Boston, Mass.	185,148	William Roach	C.T. Arlt
862	5¢	Louisa May Alcott	Feb. 5, 1940	BEP	Concord, Mass.	134,325	William Roach	C.T. Arlt
863	10¢	Samuel L. Clemens (Mark Twain)	Feb. 13, 1940	BEP	Hannibal, Mo.	150,492	William Roach	C.T. Arlt
864	1¢	Henry Wadsworth Longfellow	Feb. 16, 1940	BEP	Portland, Me.	160,508	William Roach	C.A. Brooks

Scott number	Denom.	Design	First day of issue	Printer	First-day city	First-day quantities	Designer	Engraver
865	2¢	John Greenleaf Whittier	Feb. 16, 1940	BEP	Haverhill, Mass.	148,423	William Roach	C.A. Brooks
866	3¢	James Russell Lowell	Feb. 20, 1940	BEP	Cambridge, Mass.	148,735	William Roach	C.A. Brooks
867	5¢	Walt Whitman	Feb. 24, 1940	BEP	Camden, N.J.	134,185	William Roach	C.A. Brooks
868	10¢	James Witcomb Riley	Feb. 24, 1940	BEP	Greenfield, Ind.	131,760	William Roach	C.A. Brooks
869	1¢	Horace Mann	March 14, 1940	BEP	Boston, Mass.	186,854	William Roach	C.T. Arlt
870	2¢	Mark Hopkins	March 14, 1940	BEP	Williamstown, Mass.	140,286	William Roach	C.T. Arlt
871	3¢	Charles W. Eliot	March 28, 1940	BEP	Cambridge, Mass.	155,708	William Roach	C.T. Arlt
872	5¢	Frances E. Willard	March 28, 1940	BEP	Evanston, Ill.	140,483	William Roach	C.T. Arlt
873	10¢	Booker T. Washington	April 7, 1940	BEP	Tuskegee Institute, Ala.	163,507	William Roach	C.T. Arlt
874	1¢	John James Audubon	April 8, 1940	BEP	St. Francisville, La.	144,123	William Roach	J.T. Vail
875	2¢	Dr. Crawford W. Long	April 8, 1940	BEP	Jefferson, Ga.	158,128	William Roach	J.T. Vail
876	3¢	Luther Burbank	April 17, 1940	BEP	Santa Rosa, Cal.	147,033	William Roach	J.T. Vail
877	5¢	Dr. Walter Reed	April 17, 1940	BEP	Washington, D.C.	154,464	William Roach	J.T. Vail
878	10¢	Jane Addams	April 26, 1940	BEP	Chicago, Ill.	132,375	William Roach	J.T. Vail
879	1¢	Stephen Collins Foster	May 3, 1940	BEP	Bardstown, Ky	183,461	William Roach	C.T. Arlt
880	2¢	John Philip Sousa	May 3, 1940	BEP	Washington, D.C.	131,422	William Roach	C.T. Arlt
881	3¢	Victor Herbert	May 13, 1940	BEP	New York, N.Y.	168,200	William Roach	C.T. Arlt
882	5¢	Edward A. MacDowell	May 13, 1940	BEP	Peterborough, N.H.	135,155	William Roach	C.T. Arlt
883	10¢	Ethelbert Nevin	June 10, 1940	BEP	Pittsburgh, Pa.	121,951	William Roach	C.T. Arlt
884	1¢	Gilbert Charles Stuart	Sept. 5, 1940	BEP	Naragansett, R.I.	131,965	William Roach	C.T. Arlt
885	2¢	James A. McNeill Whistler	Sept. 16, 1940	BEP	Lowell, Mass.	130,962	William Roach	C.T. Arlt
886	3¢	Augustus Saint-Gaudens	Sept. 16, 1940	BEP	New York, N.Y.	138,200	William Roach	C.T. Arlt
887	5¢	Daniel Chester French	Sept. 16, 1940	BEP	Stockbridge, Mass.	124,608	William Roach	C.T. Arlt
888	10¢	Frederic Remington	Sept. 30, 1940	BEP	Canton, N.Y.	116,219	William Roach	C.T. Arlt
889	1¢	Eli Whitney	Oct. 7, 1940	BEP	Savannah, Ga.	140,868	William Roach	C.A. Brooks
890	2¢	Samuel F.B. Morse	Oct. 7, 1940	BEP	New York, N.Y.	135,388	William Roach	C.A. Brooks
891	3¢	Cyrus Hall McCormick	Oct. 14, 1940	BEP	Lexington, Va.	137,415	William Roach	C.A. Brooks
892	5¢	Elias Howe	Oct. 14, 1940	BEP	Spencer, Mass.	126,334	William Roach	C.A. Brooks
893	10¢	Alexander Graham Bell	Oct. 28, 1940	BEP	Boston, Mass.	125,372	William Roach	C.A. Brooks

Scott number	Denom.	Design	First day of issue	Printer	First-day city	First-day quantities	Designer	Engraver
894	3¢	Pony Express Rider	April 3, 1940	BEP	St. Joseph, Mo.	355,438	William Roach	C.A. Brooks
895	3¢	The Three Graces (Botticelli)	April 14, 1940	BEP		182,401	William Roach	C.T. Arlt
896	3¢	Idaho State Capitol	July 3, 1940	BEP	Boise, Idaho	182,401	William Schrage	J.R. Lowe
897	3¢	Wyoming State Seal	July 10, 1940	BEP	Cheyenne, Wyo.	156,709	A.R. Meissner	C.A. Brooks
898	3¢	Coronado and His Captains by Gerald Cassidy	Sept. 7, 1940	BEP	Albuquerque, N.M.	161,012	V.S. McCloskey, Jr.	C.A. Brooks
899	1¢	Statue of Liberty	Oct. 16, 1940	BEP		450,083	William Roach	C.T. Arlt
900	2¢	90-millimeter Anti-Aircraft Gun	Oct. 16, 1940	BEP		450,083	William Roach	H.R. Rollins
901	3¢	Torch of Enlightenment	Oct. 16, 1940	BEP		450,083	William Roach	J.R. Lowe
902	3¢	Emancipation Monument; Lincoln and Kneeling Slave	Oct. 20, 1940	BEP	World's Fair, N.Y.	156,146	William Roach	C.T. Arlt
903	3¢	State Capitol, Montpelier	March 4, 1941	BEP	Montpelier, Vt.	182,423	Alvin R. Meissner	C.T. Arlt
904	3¢	Daniel Boone and Three Frontiersmen	June 1, 1941	BEP	Frankfort, Ky.	155,730	William Roach	C.A. Brooks
905	3¢	American Eagle	July 4, 1942	BEP		191,168	Mark O'Dea	J.S. Edmondson
906	5¢	Map of China, Lincoln and Sun Yat-sen	July 7, 1942	BEP	Denver, Colo.	168,746	William Roach	L.C. Kauffmann
907	2¢	Allegory of Victory	Jan. 14, 1943	BEP		178,865	Leon Helguera	C.A. Brooks
908	1¢	Liberty Holding the Torch of Freedom and Enlightenment	Feb. 12, 1943	BEP		193,800	Paul Manship	C.T. Arlt
909	5¢	Flag of Poland	June 22, 1943	ABNC	Chicago, Ill.	224,172		
910	5¢	Flag of Czechoslovakia	July 12, 1943	ABNC		145,112		
911	5¢	Flag of Norway	July 27, 1943	ABNC		130,054		
912	5¢	Flag of Luxembourg	Aug. 10, 1943	ABNC		166,367		
913	5¢	Flag of Netherlands	Aug. 24, 1943	ABNC		148,763		
914	5¢	Flag of Belgium	Sept. 14, 1943	ABNC		154,220		
915	5¢	Flag of France	Sept. 28, 1943	ABNC		163,478		
916	5¢	Flag of Greece	Oct. 12, 1943	ABNC		166,553		

Scott number	Denom.	Design	First day of issue	Printer	First-day city	First-day quantities	Designer	Engraver
917	5¢	Flag of Yugoslavia	Oct. 26, 1943	ABNC		161,835		
918	5¢	Flag of Albania	Nov. 9, 1943	ABNC		162,275		
919	5¢	Flag of Austria	Nov. 23, 1943	ABNC		172,285		
920	5¢	Flag of Denmark	Dec. 7, 1943	ABNC		173,784		
921	5¢	Flag of Korea	Nov. 2, 1943	ABNC		192,860		
922	3¢	Golden Spike Ceremony	May 10, 1944	BEP	Ogden, Utah	447,324	William Roach	C.T. Arlt
923	3¢	*Savannah*	May 22, 1944	BEP	Kings Point, N.Y.	333,796	V.S. McCloskey, Jr.	C.A. Brooks
924	3¢	Telegraph Wires and Morse's First Transmitted Words	May 24, 1944	BEP	Washington, D.C.	278,387	V.S. McCloskey, Jr.	C.T. Arlt
925	3¢	Aerial View of Corregidor, Manila Bay	Sept. 27, 1944	BEP		214,865	William Roach	C.A. Brooks
926	3¢	Motion Picture Showing for the Armed Forces in South Pacific	Oct. 31, 1944	BEP	Hollywood, Calif.	367133	William Roach	C.T. Arlt
927	3¢	State Seal, Gates of St. Augustine and Capitol at Tallahassee	March 3, 1945	BEP	Tallahassee, Fla.	228,435	William Roach	C.A. Brooks
928	5¢	"Toward United Nations, April 25, 1945"	April 25, 1945	BEP	San Francisco	417,450	V.S. McCloskey, Jr.	C.A. Brooks
929	3¢	Marines Raising Flag on Iwo Jima	July 11, 1945	BEP		391,650	V.S. McCloskey, Jr.	C.A. Brooks
930	1¢	Roosevelt and Hyde Park Residence	July 26, 1945	BEP	Hyde Park, N.Y.	390,219	V.S. McCloskey, Jr.	C.A. Brooks
931	2¢	Roosevelt and the "Little White House" at Warm Springs	Aug. 24, 1945	BEP	Warm Springs, Ga.	426,142	William Roach	C.A. Brooks
932	3¢	Roosevelt and White House	June 27, 1945	BEP		391,650		
933	5¢	Roosevelt, Map of Western Hemisphere and Four Freedoms	Jan. 30, 1948	BEP		466,766	V.S. McCloskey, Jr.	C.A. Brooks
934	3¢	U.S. Troops Passing Arch of Triumph, Paris	Sept. 28, 1945	BEP		392,300	William Roach	C.A. Brooks

Scott number	Denom.	Design	First day of issue	Printer	First-day city	First-day quantities	Designer	Engraver
935	3¢	U.S. Sailors	Oct. 27, 1945	BEP	Annapolis, Md.	460,352	V.S. McCloskey, Jr.	M.D. Fenton
936	3¢	Coast Guard Landing Craft and Supply Ship	Nov. 10, 1945	BEP	New York, N.Y.	405,280	Ken Riley	E.R. Grove
937	3¢	Alfred E. Smith	Nov. 26, 1944	BEP	New York, N.Y.	424,950	V.S. McCloskey, Jr.	C.T. Arlt
938	3¢	Flags of U.S. and State of Texas	Dec. 29, 1945	BEP	Austin, Texas	397,860	James B. Winn	E.R. Grove
939	3¢	Liberty Ship Unloading Cargo	Feb. 26, 1940	BEP		432,141	V.S. McCloskey, Jr.	M.D. Fenton
940	3¢	Honorable Discharge Emblem	May 9, 1940	BEP		492,786	V.S. McCloskey, Jr.	E.R. Grove
941	3¢	Andrew Jackson, John Sevier and State Capitol, Nashville	June 1, 1946	BEP	Nashville, Tenn.	463,512	V.S. McCloskey, Jr.	C.A. Brooks
942	3¢	Iowa State Flag and Map	Aug. 3, 1946	BEP	Iowa City, Iowa	517,505	V.S. McCloskey, Jr.	M.D. Fenton
943	3¢	Smithsonian Institution	Aug. 10, 1946	BEP		402,448	William Roach	E.R. Grove
944	3¢	"Capture of Santa Fe" by Kenneth Chapman	Oct. 16, 1946	BEP	Santa Fe, N.M.	384,300	William Roach	C.T. Arlt
945	3¢	Thomas Edison	Feb. 11, 1947	BEP	Milan, Ohio	632,473	William Roach	C.T. Arlt
946	3¢	Joseph Pulitzer and Statue of Liberty	April 10, 1947	BEP	New York, N.Y.	580,870	V.S. McCloskey, Jr.	V.S. McCloskey
947	3¢	Washington and Franklin, Early and Modern Mail Vehicles	May 17, 1947	BEP	New York, N.Y.	712,873	Leon Helguera	M.D. Fenton
948	15¢	Washington and Franklin	May 19, 1947	BEP	New York, N.Y.	502,175	R. L. Miller, Jr.	C.A. Brooks
949	3¢	"The Doctor" by Luke Fildes	June 9, 1947	BEP	Atlantic City, N.J.	508,016	C.R. Chickering	C.A. Brooks
950	3¢	Pioneers Entering the Valley of the Great Salt Lake	July 24, 1947	BEP	Salt Lake City, Utah	456,416	C.R. Chickering	M.D. Fenton
951	3¢	Naval Architect's Drawing of Frigate Constitution	Oct. 21, 1947	BEP	Boston, Mass.	683,416	Andrew H. Hepburn	M.D. Fenton
952	3¢	Great White Heron and	Dec. 5, 1947	BEP	Florida City, Fla..	466,647	Robert I. Miller, Jr.	A.W. Dintaman

Scott number	Denom.	Design	First day of issue	Printer	First-day city	First-day quantities	Designer	Engraver
		Map of Florida						
953	3¢	Dr. George Washington Carver	Jan. 5, 1948	BEP	Tuskegee Institute, Alabama	402,179	William Roach	E.R. Grove
954	3¢	Sutter's Mill, Coloma,	Jan. 24, 1948	BEP	Coloma, Calif.	526,154	C.R. Chickering	M.D. Fenton
955	3¢	Map, Seal of Mississippi Territory and Gov. Winthrop Sargent	April 7, 1948	BEP	Natchez, Miss.	434,804	William Schrage	M.D. Fenton
956	3¢	Four Chaplains and Sinking *SS Dorchester*	May 28, 1948	BEP	Washington, D.C.	459,070	C.R. Chickering	M.D. Fenton
957	3¢	Map on Scroll and State Capitol of Wisconsin	May 29, 1948	BEP	Madison, Wis.	470,280	V.S. McCloskey, Jr.	R.M. Bower
958	5¢	Swedish Pioneer with Covered Wagon Moving Westward	June 4, 1948	BEP	Chicago, Ill.	364,318	C.R. Chickering	C.T. Arlt
959	3¢	Elizabeth Stanton, Carrie Chapman Catt and Lucretia Mott	July 19, 1948	BEP	Seneca Falls, N.Y.	401,923	V.S. McCloskey, Jr.	C.T. Arlt
960	3¢	William Allen White	July 31, 1948	BEP	Emporia, Kan.	385,648	William Roach	C.A. Brooks
961	3¢	Niagara Railway Suspension Bridge	Aug. 2, 1948	BEP	Niagara Falls, N.Y.	406,467	Leon Helguera	G.A. Gundersen
962	3¢	Francis Scott Key and American Flags of 1814 and 1948	Aug. 9, 1948	BEP	Frederick, Md.	505,930	V.S. McCloskey, Jr.	R.M. Bower
963	3¢	Girl and Boy Carrying Books	Aug. 11, 1948	BEP	Washington, D.C.	347,070	V.S. McCloskey, Jr.	M.D. Fenton
964	3¢	John McLoughlin, Jason Lee and Wagon on Oregon Trail	Aug. 14, 1948	BEP	Oregon City, Ore.	365,898	C.R. Chickering	C.T. Arlt
965	3¢	Chief Justice Harlan Stone	Aug. 25, 1948	BEP	Chesterfield, N.H.	362,170	C.R. Chickering	C.T. Arlt
966	3¢	Observatory, Palomar Mountain, Calif.	Aug. 30, 1948	BEP	Palomar Mountain, Calif.	401,365	V.S. McCloskey, Jr.	G.A. Gundersen
967	3¢	Clara Barton and	Sept. 7, 1948	BEP	Oxford, Mass.	362,000	C.R. Chickering	C.A. Brooks

Scott number	Denom.	Design	First day of issue	Printer	First-day city	First-day quantities	Designer	Engraver
		Red Cross						
968	3¢	Light Brahma Rooster	Sept. 9, 1948	BEP	New Haven, Conn.	475,000	C.R. Chickering	M.D. Fenton
969	3¢	Star and Palm Frond	Sept. 21, 1948	BEP	Washington, D.C.	386,064	C.R. Chickering	A.W. Dintaman
970	3¢	Fort Kearney Pioneer Group	Sept. 22, 1948	BEP	Minden, Neb.	429,633	William Roach	G.A. Gundersen
971	3¢	Peter Stuyvesant, Early and Modern Fire Engines	Oct. 4, 1948	BEP	Dover, Del.	399,630	William Roach	R.M. Bower
972	3¢	Map of Indian Territory and Seals of Five Tribes	Oct. 15, 1948	BEP	Muskogee, Okla.	459,528	R. L. Miller	C.A. Brooks
973	3¢	Statue of Capt. William O. (Bucky) O'Neill by Solon Borglum	Oct. 27, 1948	BEP	Prescott, Ariz.	399,198	V.S. McCloskey, Jr.	C.T. Arlt
974	3¢	Juliette Gordon Low and Girl Scout Emblem	Oct. 29, 1948	BEP	Savannah, Ga.	476,573	William K. Schrage	G.A. Gundersen
975	3¢	Will Rogers	Nov. 4, 1948	BEP	Claremore, Okla.	450,350	C.R. Chickering	M.D. Fenton
976	3¢	Fort Bliss and Rocket Firing	Nov. 5, 1948	BEP	El Paso, Texas	421,000	C.R. Chickering	C.A. Brooks
977	3¢	Moina Michael and Poppy Plant	Nov. 9, 1948	BEP	Athens, Ga.	374,090	V.S. McCloskey, Jr.	C.A. Brooks
978	3¢	Lincoln and Quotation from Gettysburg Address	Nov. 19, 1948	BEP	Gettysburg, Pa.	511,990	C.R. Chickering	R.M. Bower
979	3¢	Torch and Emblem of American Turners	Nov. 20, 1948	BEP	Cincinnati, Ohio	434,090	Alvin R. Meissner	A.W. Dintman
980	3¢	Joel Chandler Harris	Dec. 9, 1948	BEP	Eatonton, Ga.	426,199	William Roach	R.M. Bower
981	3¢	Pioneer and Red River Oxcart	March 3, 1949	BEP	St. Paul, Minn.	458,750	C.R. Chickering	C.A. Brooks
982	3¢	Washington, Robert E. Lee and University Building, Lexington, Va.	April 12, 1949	BEP	Lexington, Va.	447,910	V.S. McCloskey, Jr.	E.R. Grove
983	3¢	Puerto Rican Farmer Holding Cogwheel and	April 27, 1949	BEP	San Juan, P.R.	390,416	C.R. Chickering	G.A. Gundersen

Scott number	Denom.	Design	First day of issue	Printer	First-day city	First-day quantities	Designer	Engraver
		Ballot Box						
984	3¢	James Stoddert's 1718 Map of Regions About Annapolis	May 23, 1949	BEP	Annapolis, Md.	441,802	C.R. Chickering	G.A. Gundersen
985	3¢	Union Soldier G.A.R. Veteran of 1949	Aug. 29, 1949	BEP	Indianapolis, Ind.	471,696	C.R. Chickering	C.A. Brooks
986	3¢	Edgar Allan Poe	Oct. 7, 1949	BEP	Richmond, Va.	371,020	William Roach	R.M. Bower
987	3¢	Coin, Symbolizing Banking Services	Jan. 3, 1950	BEP	Saratoga Springs, N.Y.	388,622	C.R. Chickering	G.A. Gundersen
988	3¢	Samuel Gompers	Feb. 27, 1950	BEP	Washington, D.C.	332,023	V.S. McCloskey, Jr.	C.A. Brooks
989	3¢	Statue of Freedom on Capitol Dome	April 20, 1950	BEP	Washington, D.C.	371,743	V.S. McCloskey, Jr.	C.A. Brooks
990	3¢	Executive Mansion	June 12, 1950	BEP	Washington, D.C.	376,789	William Schrage	M.D. Fenton
991	3¢	Supreme Court Building	Aug. 2, 1950	BEP	Washington, D.C.	324,007	C.R. Chickering	G.A. Gundersen
992	3¢	United State Capitol	Nov. 22, 1950	BEP	Washington, D.C.	352,215	R.L. Miller	C.T. Arlt
993	3¢	"Casey" Jones and Locomotive of 1900 and 1950	April 29, 1950	BEP	Jackson, Tenn.	420,830	C.R. Chickering	C.A. Brooks
994	3¢	Kansas City Skyline 1950 and Westport Landing 1850	June 3, 1950	BEP	Kansas City, Mo.	405,390	V.S. McCloskey, Jr.	R.M. Bower
995	3¢	Three Boys, Statue of Liberty and Scout Badge	June 30, 1950	BEP	Valley Forge, Pa.	622,972	C.R. Chickering	C.A. Brooks
996	3¢	Gov. William Henry Harrison and First Indiana Capitol in Vincennes	July 4, 1950	BEP	Vincennes, Ind.	359,643	C.R. Chickering	G.A. Gundersen
997	3¢	Gold Miner, Pioneers and SS *Oregon*	Sept. 9, 1950	BEP	Sacramento, Calif.	391,919	V.S. McCloskey, Jr.	M.D. Fenton
998	3¢	Confederate Soldier and United Confederate Veteran	May 30, 1951	BEP	Norfolk, Va.	374,235	C.R. Chickering	C.A. Brooks
999	3¢	Carson Valley circa 1851	July 14, 1951	BEP	Genoa, Nev.	336,890	C.R. Chickering	C.A. Brooks
1000	3¢	Detroit Skyline,	July 24, 1951	BEP	Detroit, Mich.	323,094	V.S. McCloskey, Jr.	C.A. Brooks

Scott number	Denom.	Design	First day of issue	Printer	First-day city	First-day quantities	Designer	Engraver
		Cadillac Landing						
1001	3¢	Colorado Capitol, Mount of the Holy Cross, Combine and Bronco Buster	Aug. 1, 1951	BEP	Minturn, Colo.	311,568	William Schrage	G.A. Gundersen
1002	3¢	American Chemical Society Emblem and Symbols of Chemistry	Sept. 4, 1951	BEP	New York, N.Y.	436,419	C.R. Chickering	H.F. Fichter
1003	3¢	Washington Evacuating Army, Fulton Ferry House	Dec. 10, 1951	BEP	Brooklyn, N.Y.	420,000	C.R. Chickering	C.A. Brooks
1004	3¢	Betsy Ross Showing Flag to Washington, Robert Morris and George Ross	Jan. 2, 1953	BEP	Philadelphia, Pa.	314,312	V.S. McCloskey, Jr.	C.A. Brooks
1005	3¢	Farm, 4-H Club Emblem, Boy and Girl	Jan. 15, 1952	BEP	Springfield, Ohio	383,290	C.R. Chickering	M.D. Fenton
1006	3¢	Charter and Three Stages of Rail Transportation	Feb. 28, 1952	BEP	Baltimore, Md.	441,600	C.R. Chickering	C.A. Brooks
1007	3¢	School Girls and Safety Patrolman Autos of 1902 and 1952	March 4, 1952	BEP	Chicago, Ill.	520,123	C.R. Chickering	R.M. Bower
1008	3¢	Torch of Liberty and Globe	April 4, 1952	BEP	Washington, D.C.	313,518	C.R. Chickering	A.W. Dintaman
1009	3¢	Spillway, Grand Coulee Dam	May 15, 1952	BEP	Grand Coulee, Wash.	341,680	C.R. Chickering	H.F. Fichter
1010	3¢	Marquis de Lafayette, Flags, Cannon and Landing Party	June 13, 1952	BEP	Georgetown, S.C.	349,102	V.S. McCloskey, Jr.	C.A. Brooks
1011	3¢	Sculptured Heads on Mt. Rushmore	Aug. 11, 1952	BEP	Keystone, N.D.	337,027	William Schrage	M.D. Fenton
1012	3¢	George Washington Bridge and Covered	Sept. 6, 1952	BEP	Chicago, Ill.	318,483	V.S. McCloskey, Jr.	M.D. Fenton

Scott number	Denom.	Design	First day of issue	Printer	First-day city	First-day quantities	Designer	Engraver
		Bridge of 1850s						
1013	3¢	Women of the Marine Corps, Army, Navy and Air Force	Sept. 11, 1952	BEP	Washington, D.C.	308,062	William Schrage	C.A. Brooks
1014	3¢	Gutenberg Showing Proof to the Elector of Mainz	Sept. 30, 1952	BEP	Washington, D.C.	387,078	V.S. McCloskey, Jr.	A.W. Dintaman
1015	3¢	Newspaper Boy, Torch and Group of Homes	Oct. 4, 1952	BEP	Philadelphia, Pa.	626,000	C.R. Chickering	R.M. Bower
1016	3¢	Globe, Sun and Red Cross	Nov. 21, 1952	BEP	New York, N.Y.	439,252	V.S. McCloskey, Jr.	C.A. Brooks
1017	3¢	National Guardsman, Amphibious Landing and Disaster Service	Feb. 23, 1953	BEP	Washington, D.C.	387,618	C.R. Chickering	H.F. Fichter
1018	3¢	Ohio Map, State Seal and Buckeye Leaf	March 2, 1953	BEP	Chillicothe, Ohio	407,983	V.S. McCloskey, Jr.	M.D. Fenton
1019	3¢	Medallion, Pioneers and Washington Scene	March 2, 1953	BEP	Olympia, Wash.	344,047	C.R. Chickering	R.M. Bower
1020	3¢	James Monroe, Robert Livingston and Marquis Francois de Barbe-Marbois	April 30, 1953	BEP	St. Louis, Mo.	425,600	William Schrage	C.A. Brooks
1021	5¢	Commodore Matthew C. Perry and First Anchorage off Tokyo Bay	July 14, 1953	BEP	Washington, D.C.	320,541	C.R. Chickering	C.A. Brooks
1022	3¢	Selection of Frieze, Supreme Court Room	Aug. 24, 1953	BEP	Boston, Mass.	410,036	William Schrage	C.A. Brooks
1023	3¢	Home of Theodore Roosevelt	Sept. 14, 1953	BEP	Oyster Bay, N.Y.	379,750	William Schrage	R.M. Bower
1024	3¢	Agricultural Scene and Future Farmer	Oct. 13, 1953	BEP	Kansas City, Mo.	424,193	R.L. Miller	A.W. Dintaman
1025	3¢	Truck, Farm and Distant City	Oct. 27, 1953	BEP	Los Angeles, Calif.	875,021	William Schrage	C.A. Brooks

Scott number	Denom.	Design	First day of issue	Printer	First-day city	First-day quantities	Designer	Engraver
1026	3¢	Gen. George S. Patton, Jr. and Tanks in Action	Nov. 11, 1953	BEP	Fort Knox, Ky.	342,600	William Schrage	M.D. Fenton
1027	3¢	Dutch Ship in New Amsterdam Harbor	Nov. 20, 1953	BEP	New York, N.Y.	387,914	C.R. Chickering	R.M. Bower
1028	3¢	Map and Pioneer Group	Dec. 30, 1953	BEP	Tuscon, Ariz.	363,250	C.R. Chickering	A.W. Dintaman
1029	3¢	Low Memorial Library, Columbia University	Jan. 4, 1954	BEP	New York, N.Y.	550,745	V.S. McCloskey, Jr.	C.A. Brooks
1030	1¢	Benjamin Franklin	Oct. 20, 1955	BEP	Washington, D.C.	223,122	C.R. Chickering	C.A. Brooks
1031	1¢	George Washington	Aug. 26, 1954	BEP	Chicago, Ill.	272,581	C.R. Chickering	R.M. Bower
1031A	1¢	Palace of the Governors, Santa Fe	June 17, 1960	BEP	Santa Fe, N.M.	501,848	Tyler Dingee	M.D. Fenton
1032	2¢	Mount Vernon	Feb. 22, 1956	BEP	Mount Vernon, Va.	270,109	William Schrage	C.A. Brooks
1033	2¢	Thomas Jefferson	Sept. 15, 1954	BEP	San Francisco	307,300	C.R. Chickering	C.A. Brooks
1034	3¢	Bunker Hill Monument Massachusetts Flag of 1776	June 17, 1959	BEP	Boston, Mass.	315,060	R. L. Miller	A.W. Dintaman
1035	3¢	Statue of Liberty	June 24, 1954	BEP	Albany, N.Y.	340,001	C.R. Chickering	C.A. Brooks
1036	4¢	Abraham Lincoln	Nov. 19, 1954	BEP	New York, N.Y.	374,064	C.R. Chickering	R.M. Bower
1037	5¢	The Hermitage, Home of Andrew Jackson, near Nashville	March 16, 1959	BEP	Hermitage, Tenn.	320,000	C.R. Chickering	M.D. Fenton
1038	5¢	James Monroe	Dec. 2, 1954	BEP	Fredericksburg, Va.	255,650	C.R. Chickering	A.W. Dintaman
1039	6¢	Theodore Roosevelt	Nov. 18, 1954	BEP	New York, N.Y.	257,551	C.R. Chickering	M.D. Fenton
1040	7¢	Woodrow Wilson	Feb. 10, 1956	BEP	Staunton, Va.	200,111	C.R. Chickering	R.M. Bower
1041	8¢	Statue of Liberty	April 9, 1954	BEP	Washington, D.C.	340,077	C.R. Chickering	R.M. Bower
1042	8¢	Statue of Liberty	March 22, 1958	BEP	Cleveland, Ohio	223,899	C.R. Chickering	R.M. Bower
1042A	8¢	John J. Pershing	Nov. 17, 1961	BEP	New York, N.Y.	321,031	R. J. Jones	M.D. Fenton
1043	9¢	The Alamo, San Antonio	June 14, 1961	BEP	San Antonio, Texas	207,086		
1044	10¢	Independence Hall	July 4, 1956	BEP	Philadelphia, Pa.	220,930	C.R. Chickering	C.A. Brooks
1044A	11¢	Statue of Liberty	June 15, 1961	BEP	Washington, D.C.	238,905	William Schrage	M.D. Fenton
1045	12¢	Benjamin Harrison	June 6, 1959	BEP	Oxford, Ohio	225,869	V.S. McCloskey, Jr.	R.M. Bower
1046	15¢	John Jay	Dec. 12, 1956	BEP	Washington, D.C.	205,680	C.R. Chickering	A.W. Dintaman
1047	20¢	Monticello	April 13, 1956	BEP	Charlottesville, Va.	147,860	William Schrage	C.A. Brooks

Scott number	Denom.	Design	First day of issue	Printer	First-day city	First-day quantities	Designer	Engraver
1048	25¢	Paul Revere	April 18, 1958	BEP	Boston, Mass.	196,530	V.S. McCloskey, Jr.	R.M. Bower
1049	30¢	Robert E. Lee	Sept. 21, 1955	BEP	Norfolk, Va.	120,166	C.R. Chickering	M.D. Fenton
1050	40¢	John Marshall	Sept. 24, 1955	BEP	Richmond, Va.	113,972	C.R. Chickering	R.M. Bower
1051	50¢	Susan B. Anthony	Aug. 25, 1955	BEP	Louisville, Ky.	110,220	C.R. Chickering	C.A. Brooks
1052	$1	Patrick Henry	Oct. 7, 1955	BEP	Joplin, Mo.	80,191	C.R. Chickering	C.A. Brooks
1053	$5	Alexander Hamilton	March 19, 1956	BEP	Patterson, N.J.	34,272	C.R. Chickering	C.A. Brooks
1054	1¢	George Washington	Oct. 8, 1954	BEP	Baltimore, Md.	196,318	C.R. Chickering	R.M. Bower
1054A	1¢	Palace of Governors, Santa Fe	June 17, 1960	BEP	Santa Fe, N.M.	501,848	Tyler Dingee	M.D. Fenton
1055	2¢	Thomas Jefferson	Oct. 22, 1954	BEP	St. Louis, Mo.	162,050	C.R. Chickering	C.A. Brooks
1056	3¢	Bunker Hill Monument and Massachusetts Flag of 1776	Sept. 9, 1959	BEP	Los Angeles, Calif.	198,680	R. L. Miller	A.W. Dintaman
1057	3¢	Statue of Liberty	July 20, 1954	BEP	Washington, D.C.	137,139	C.R. Chickering	R.M. Bower
1058	4¢	Abraham Lincoln	July 31, 1958	BEP	Mandan, N.D.	184,079	C.R. Chickering	R.M. Bower
1059	5¢	The Hermitage, Home of Andrew Jackson near Nashville	May 1, 1959	BEP	Denver, Colo.	202,454	C.R. Chickering	M.D. Fenton
1059A	25¢	Paul Revere	Feb. 25, 1965	BEP	Wheaton, Md.	184,954	V.S. McCloskey, Jr.	R.M. Bower
1060	3¢	"The Sower," Mitchell Pass and Scotts Bluff	May 7, 1954	BEP	Nebraska City, Neb.	401,015	C.R. Chickering	C.A. Brooks
1061	3¢	Wheat Field and Pioneer Wagon Train	May 31, 1954	BEP	Fort Leavenworth, Kan.	349,145	C.R. Chickering	R.M. Bower
1062	3¢	George Eastman	July 12, 1954	BEP	Rochester, N.Y.	630,448	William Schrage	C.A. Brooks
1063	3¢	Meriwether Lewis, William Clark and Sacagawea Landing on Missouri	July 28, 1954	BEP	Sioux City, Iowa	371,557	C.R. Chickering	C.A. Brooks
1064	3¢	Charles Wilson Peale in His Museum, Self-portrait	Feb. 15, 1955	BEP	Philadelphia, Pa.	307,040	V.S. McCloskey, Jr.	C.A. Brooks
1065	3¢	Open Book and	Feb. 12, 1955	BEP	East Lansing, Mich.	419,241	William Schrage	A.W. Dintaman

Scott number	Denom.	Design	First day of issue	Printer	First-day city	First-day quantities	Designer	Engraver
		Symbols of Subjects Taught						
1066	3¢	Torch, Globe and Rotary Emblem	Feb. 23, 1955	BEP	Chicago, Ill.	350,625	C.R. Chickering	R.M. Bower
1067	3¢	Marine, Coast Guard, Army, Navy and Air Force Personnel	May 21, 1955	BEP	Washington, D.C.	300,436	C.R. Chickering	C.A. Brooks
1068	3¢	Great Stone Face	June 21, 1955	BEP	Franconia, N.H.	330,630	William Schrage	R.M. Bower
1069	3¢	Map of Great Lakes and Two Steamers	June 28, 1955	BEP	Sainte Marie, Mich.	316,616	C.R. Chickering	C.A. Brooks
1070	3¢	Atomic Energy Encircling the Hemispheres	July 28, 1955	BEP	Washington, D.C.	351,940	George R. Cox	R.M. Bower
1071	3¢	Map of Fort Ticonderoga, Ethan Allen and Artillery	Sept. 18, 1955	BEP	Fort Ticonderoga, N.Y.	342,946	Enrico Arno	C.A. Brooks
1072	3¢	Andrew W. Mellon	Dec. 20, 1955	BEP	Washington, D.C.	278,897	V.S. McCloskey, Jr.	R.M. Bower
1073	3¢	"Franklin Taking Electricity from the Sky" by Benjamin West	Feb. 17, 1955	BEP	Philadelphia, Pa.	351,260	C.R. Chickering	C.A. Brooks
1074	3¢	Log Cabin	April 5, 1956	BEP	Booker T. Washington Birthplace Va.	272,659	C.R. Chickering	M.D. Fenton
1075	11¢	Fifth International Philatelic Exhibition	April 28, 1956	BEP	New York, N.Y.	429,327	V.S. McCloskey, Jr.	
1076	3¢	New York Coliseum and Columbus Monument	April 30, 1956	BEP	New York, N.Y.	526,090		M.D. Fenton
1077	3¢	Wild Turkey	May 5, 1956	BEP	Fond du Lac, Wis.	292,121	Robert W. Hines	C.A. Brooks
1078	3¢	Pronghorn Antelope	June 22, 1956	BEP	Gunnison, Colo.	294,731	Robert W. Hines	M.D. Fenton
1079	3¢	King Salmon	Nov. 9, 1956	BEP	Seattle, Wash.	346,800	Robert W. Hines	M.D. Fenton
1080	3¢	Harvey Washington Wiley	June 27, 1956	BEP	Washington, D.C.	411,761	Robert L. Miller	C.A. Brooks
1081	3¢	President Buchanan's Home, Lancaster, Pa.	Aug. 5, 1956	BEP	Lancaster, Pa.	340,450	V.S. McCloskey, Jr.	C.A. Brooks

Scott number	Denom.	Design	First day of issue	Printer	First-day city	First-day quantities	Designer	Engraver
1082	3¢	Mosaic, AFL-CIO Headquarters	Sept. 3, 1956	BEP	Camden, N.J.	338,450	V.S. McCloskey, Jr.	R.M. Bower
1083	3¢	Nassau Hall, Princeton, N.J.	Sept. 22, 1956	BEP	Princeton, N.J.	350,756	V.S. McCloskey, Jr.	R.M. Bower
1084	3¢	Devil's Tower National Monument	Sept. 24, 1956	BEP	Devil's Tower, Wyo.	285,090	C.R. Chickering	A.W. Dintaman
1085	3¢	Children of the World	Dec. 15, 1956	BEP	Washington, D.C.	305,125	Ronald Dias	C.A. Brooks
1086	3¢	Alexander Hamilton and Federal Hall	Jan. 11, 1957	BEP	New York, N.Y.	305,117	William K. Schrage	R.M. Bower
1087	3¢	Allegory	Jan. 15, 1956	BEP	Washington, D.C.	307,630	C.R. Chickering	C.A. Brooks
1088	3¢	Flag of Coast, Geodetic Survey and Ships at Sea	Feb. 11, 1957	BEP	Seattle, Wash.	309,931	Harold E. MacEwen	M.D. Fenton
1089	3¢	Corinthian Capital and Mushroom Type Head and Shaft	Feb. 23, 1956	BEP	New York, N.Y.	368,840	Robert J. Schultz	R.M. Bower
1090	3¢	American Eagle and Pouring Ladle	May 22, 1957	BEP	New York, N.Y.	473,284	Anthony Petruccelli	R.M. Bower
1091	3¢	Aircraft Carrier and Jamestown Festival Emblem	June 10, 1957	BEP	*USS Saratoga*, Norfolk, Va.	365,933	Richard A. Genders	R.M. Bower
1092	3¢	Map of Oklahoma, Arrow and Atom Diagram	June 14, 1957	BEP	Oklahoma City, Okla.	327,172	William K. Schrage	M.D. Fenton
1093	3¢	Teacher and Pupils	July 1, 1957	BEP	Philadelphia, Pa.	357,986	C.R. Chickering	C.A. Brooks
1094	4¢	"Old Glory"	July 4, 1957	BEP	Washington, D.C	523,879	V.S. McCloskey, Jr.	C.A. Brooks
1095	3¢	"Virgina of Sagadahock" and Seal of Maine	Aug. 15, 1957	BEP	Bath, Maine	347,432	Ervine Metzel	R.M. Bower
1096	8¢	Ramon Magaysay	Aug. 31, 1957	BEP	Washington, D.C	334,558	Arnold Copeland	C.A. Brooks
1097	3¢	Marquis de Lafayette	Sept. 6, 1957	BEP	Easton, Pa.	698,277	Ervine Metzl	C.A. Brooks
1098	3¢	Whooping Cranes	Nov. 22, 1957	BEP	New York, N.Y.	778,287	Robert W. Hines	R.M. Bower
1099	3¢	Bible, Hat and Quill Pen	Dec. 27, 1957	BEP	Flushing, N.Y.	357,770	Robert Geissmann	R.M. Bower
1100	3¢	Bountiful Earth	March 15, 1958	BEP	Ithaca, N.Y.	451,292	Denver Gillen	C.A. Brooks

Scott number	Denom.	Design	First day of issue	Printer	First-day city	First-day quantities	Designer	Engraver
1104	3¢	U.S. Pavillion at Brussels Exhibition	April 17, 1958	BEP	Detroit, Mich.	428,073	Bradbury Thompson	C.A. Brooks
1105	3¢	James Monroe	April 28, 1958	BEP	Montross, Va.	326,988	Frank P. Conley	C.A. Brooks
1106	3¢	Minnesota Lakes and Pines	May 11, 1958	BEP	St. Paul, Minn.	475,552	Homer Hill	M.D. Fenton
1107	3¢	Solar Disc and Hands from Michelangelo's "Creation of Adam"	May 31, 1958	BEP	Chicago, Ill.	397,000	Ervine Metzl	R.M. Bower
1108	3¢	Gunston Hall Virginia	June 12, 1958	BEP	Lorton, Va.	349,801	Rene Clarke	M.D. Fenton
1109	3¢	Mackinac Bridge	June 25, 1958	BEP	Mackinac Bridge, Mich.	445,605	Arnold Copeland	R.M. Bower
1110	4¢	Simon Bolivar	July 24, 1958	BEP	Washington, D.C.	708,777	Arnold Copeland	C.A. Brooks
1111	8¢	Simon Bolivar	July 24, 1958	BEP	Washington, D.C.	708,777	Arnold Copeland	C.A. Brooks
1112	4¢	Neptune, Globe and Mermaid	Aug. 15, 1958	BEP	New York, N.Y.	365,072	George Giusti	C.A. Brooks
1113	1¢	Lincoln by George Healy	Feb. 12, 1959	BEP	Hodgenville, Ky.	379,862	Ervine Metzl	R.M. Bower
1114	3¢	Lincoln by Gutzon Borglum	Feb. 27, 1959	BEP	New York, N.Y.	437,737	Ervine Metzl	A.W. Dintaman
1115	4¢	Lincoln and Stephen Douglas Debating	Aug. 27, 1958	BEP	Freeport, Ill.	373,063	Ervine Metzl	M.D. Fenton
1116	4¢	Daniel Chester French Statue of Lincoln as drawn by Fritz Busse	May 30, 1959	BEP	Washington, D.C.	894,887	Ervine Metzl	C.A. Brooks
1117	4¢	Lajos Kossuth	Sept. 19, 1958	BEP	Washington, D.C.	722,188	Arnold Copeland	R.M. Bower
1118	8¢	Lajos Kossuth	Sept. 19, 1958	BEP	Washington, D.C.	722,188	Arnold Copeland	R.M. Bower
1119	4¢	Early Press and Hand Holding Quill	Sept. 22, 1958	BEP	Columbia, Mo.	411,752	Lester Beall	R.M. Bower
1120	4¢	Mail Coach and Map of Southwest U.S.	Oct. 10, 1958	BEP	San Francisco	352,760	William H. Buckley	C.A. Brooks
1121	4¢	Noah Webster	Oct. 16, 1958	BEP	West Hartford, Conn.	364,608	C.R. Chickering	A.W. Dintaman
1122	4¢	Forest Scene	Oct. 27, 1958	BEP	Tucson, Ariz.	405,959	Rudolph Wendelin	C.A. Brooks
1123	3¢	British Capture of Fort Duquesne, 1758;	Nov. 25, 1958	BEP	Pittsburgh, Pa.	421,764	William H. Buckley	C.A. Brooks

Scott number	Denom.	Design	First day of issue	Printer	First-day city	First-day quantities	Designer	Engraver
		Gen. Forbes and Washington						
1124	4¢	Covered Wagon and Mount Hood, Oregon	Feb. 14, 1959	BEP	Astoria, Ore.	452,764	Robert Hallock	C.A. Brooks
1125	4¢	Jose de San Martin	Feb. 25, 1959	BEP	Washington, D.C.	910,208	Arnold Copeland	M.D. Fenton
1126	8¢	Jose de San Martin	Feb. 25, 1959	BEP	Washington, D.C.	910,208	Arnold Copeland	M.D. Fenton
1127	4¢	NATO Emblem	April 1, 1959	BEP	Washington, D.C.	361,040	Stevan Dohanos	Reuben Barrick
1128	4¢	North Pole, Dog Sled and "Nautilus"	April 6, 1959	BEP	Cresson, Pa.	397,770	George Samerjan	C.A. Brooks
1129	4¢	Globe and Laurel	April 20, 1959	BEP	Washington, D.C.	503,618	Robert Baker	M.D. Fenton
1130	3¢	Henry Comstock at Mount Davidson Site	June 8, 1959	BEP	Virginia City, Nev.	337,233	Robert L. Miller	C.A. Brooks
1131	4¢	Great Lakes, Maple Leaf and Eagle Emblem	June 26, 1959	BEP	Massena, N.Y.	543,211	Arnold Copeland	R.M. Bower
1132	4¢	U.S. Flag 1959	July 4, 1959	BEP	Auburn, N.Y.	523,773	Stevan Dohanos	C.A. Brooks
1133	4¢	Modern Farm	Aug. 26, 1959	BEP	Rapid City, S.D.	400,613	Walter Hortens	R.M. Bower
1134	4¢	Oil Derrick	Aug. 27, 1959	BEP	Titusville, Pa.	801,859	Robert Foster	A.W. Dintaman
1135	4¢	Children	Sept. 14, 1959	BEP	New York, N.Y.	649,813	Charles H. Carter	M.D. Fenton
1136	4¢	Ernst Reuter	Sept. 29, 1959	BEP	Washington, D.C.	1,207,933	Arnold Copeland	R.M. Bower
1137	8¢	Ernst Reuter	Sept. 29, 1959	BEP	Washington, D.C.	1,207,933	Arnold Copeland	R.M. Bower
1138	4¢	Dr. Ephriam McDowell	Dec. 3, 1959	BEP	Danville, Ky.	344,603	C.R. Chickering	C.A. Brooks
1139	4¢	Quotation from Washington's Farewell Address	Feb. 20, 1960	BEP	Mount Vernon, Va.	438,335	Frank Conley	
1140	4¢	Benjamin Franklin Quotation	March 31, 1960	BEP	Philadelphia, Pa.	497,913	Frank Conley	R.J. Jones
1141	4¢	Thomas Jefferson Quotation	May 18, 1960	BEP	Charlottesville, Va.	454,904	Frank Conley	R.J. Jones
1142	4¢	Francis Scott Key Quotation	Sept. 14, 1960	BEP	Baltimore, Md.	501,129	Frank Conley	R.J. Jones
1143	4¢	Abraham Lincoln Quotation	Nov. 19, 1960	BEP	New York, N.Y.	467,780	Frank Conley	R.J. Jones
1144	4¢	Patrick Henry Quotation	Jan. 11, 1960	BEP	Richmond, Va.	415,252	Frank Conley	R.J. Jones
1145	4¢	Boy Scout Giving	Feb. 8, 1960	BEP	Washington, D.C.	1,419,955	Norman Rockwell	C.A. Brooks

Scott number	Denom.	Design	First day of issue	Printer	First-day city	First-day quantities	Designer	Engraver
		Scout Sign						
1146	4¢	Olympic Rings and Snowflake	Feb. 18, 1960	BEP	Olympic Valley, Calif.	516,456	Ervine Metzl	
1147	4¢	Thomas G. Masaryk	March 7, 1960	BEP	Washington, D.C.	1,710,726	Arnold Copeland	R.M. Bower
1148	8¢	Thomas G. Masaryk	March 7, 1960	BEP	Washington, D.C.	1,710,726	Arnold Copeland	R.M. Bower
1149	4¢	Family Walking Toward New Life	April 7, 1960	BEP	Washington, D.C.	413,298	Ervine Metzl	C.A. Brooks
1150	4¢	Water: From Watershed to Consumer	April 18, 1960	BEP	Washington, D.C.	648,988	Elmo White	C.A. Brooks
1151	4¢	SEATO Emblem	May 31, 1960	BEP	Washington, D.C.	514,926	John Maass	R.M. Bower
1152	4¢	Mother and Daughter	June 2, 1960	BEP	Washington, D.C.	830,385	Robert Sivard	C.A. Brooks
1153	4¢	U.S. Flag, 1960	July 4, 1960	BEP	Honolulu, Hawaii	820,900	Stevan Dohanos	C.A. Brooks
1154	4¢	Pony Express Rider	July 19, 1960	BEP	Sacramento, Calif.	520,223	Harold von Schmidt	R.M. Bower
1155	4¢	Man in Wheelchair Operating Drill Press	Aug. 28, 1960	BEP	New York, N.Y.	439,638	Carl Bobertz	A.W. Dintaman
1156	4¢	World Forestry Congress Seal	Aug. 29, 1960	BEP	Seattle, Wash.	350,848	C.R. Chickering	R.M. Bower
1157	4¢	Independence Bell	Sept. 16, 1960	BEP	Los Angeles, Calif.	360,297	Leon Helguera	C.A. Brooks
1158	4¢	Washington Monument and Cherry Blossoms	Sept. 28, 1960	BEP	Washington, D.C.	545,150	Gyo Fujikawa	M.D. Fenton
1159	4¢	Ignacy Jan Paderewski	Oct. 8, 1960	BEP	Washington, D.C.	1,057,438	Arnold Copeland	R.M. Bower
1160	4¢	Ignacy Jan Paderewski	Oct. 8, 1960	BEP	Washington, D.C.	1,057,438	Arnold Copeland	R.M. Bower
1161	4¢	Robert A. Taft	Oct. 16, 1960	BEP	Cincinnati, Ohio	312,116	William K. Schrage	C.A. Brooks
1162	5¢	Globe and Steering Wheel with Tractor, Car and Truck	Oct. 15, 1960	BEP	Detroit, Mich.	380,116	Arnold Copeland	M.D. Fenton
1163	4¢	Profile of Boy	Oct. 18, 1960	BEP	New York, N.Y.	435,009	C.R. Coiner	M.D. Fenton
1164	4¢	Architect's Sketch of New Post Office, Providence, R.I.	Oct. 20, 1960	BEP	Providence, R.I.	458,237	Arnold Copeland	C.A. Brooks
1165	4¢	Baron Gustaf Mannerheim	Oct. 26, 1960	BEP	Washington, D.C.	1,168,770	Arnold Copeland	R.M. Bower
1166	8¢	Baron Gustaf Mannerheim	Oct. 26, 1960	BEP	Washington, D.C	1,168,770	Arnold Copeland	R.M. Bower

Scott number	Denom.	Design	First day of issue	Printer	First-day city	First-day quantities	Designer	Engraver
1167	4¢	Camp Fire Girls Emblem	Nov. 1, 1960	BEP	New York, N.Y.	324,944	H. Edward Oliver	R.M. Bower
1168	4¢	Giuseppe Garibaldi	Nov. 2, 1960	BEP	Washington, D.C.	1,001,490	Arnold Copeland	M.D. Fenton
1169	8¢	Giuseppe Garibaldi	Nov. 2, 1960	BEP	Washington, D.C.	1,001,490	Arnold Copeland	M.D. Fenton
1170	4¢	Walter F. George	Nov. 5, 1960	BEP	New York, N.Y.	318,180	William K. Schrage	C.A. Brooks
1171	4¢	Andrew Carnegie	Nov. 25, 1960	BEP	New York, N.Y.	318,180	C.R. Chickering	C.A. Brooks
1172	4¢	John Foster Dulles	Dec. 6, 1960	BEP	Washington, D.C.	400,055	William K. Schrage	R.M. Bower
1173	4¢	Radio Waves Connecting Echo I and Earth	Dec. 15, 1960	BEP	Washington, D.C.	583,747	Ervine Metzl	C.A. Brooks
1174	4¢	Mahatma Gandhi	Jan. 26, 1961	BEP	Washington, D.C.	1,013,515	Arnold Copeland	C.A. Brooks
1175	8¢	Mahatma Gandhi	Jan. 26, 1961	BEP	Washington, D.C.	1,013,515	Arnold Copeland	C.A. Brooks
1176	4¢	The Trail Boss and Modern Range	Feb. 2, 1961	BEP	Salt Lake City, Utah	357,101	Rudolph Wendelin	M.D. Fenton
1177	4¢	Horace Greeley	Feb. 3, 1961	BEP	Chappaqua, N.Y.	359,205	C.R. Chickering	R.M. Bower
1178	4¢	Sea Coast Gun of 1861, Fort Sumter	April 12, 1961	BEP	Charleston, S.C.	602,599	C.R. Chickering	A.W. Dintaman
1179	4¢	Rifleman at Battle of Shiloh, 1862	April 7, 1962	BEP	Shiloh, Tenn.	526,062	Noel Sickles	M.D. Fenton
1180	5¢	Blue and Gray at Gettysburg, 1863	July 1, 1963	BEP	Gettysburg, Pa.	600,205	Roy Gjertson	A.W. Dintaman
1181	4¢	Battle of Wilderness, 1864	May 5, 1964	BEP	Fredricksburg, Va.	450,904	B.H. Christenson	A.W. Dintaman
1182	5¢	Appomattox, 1865	April 9, 1965	BEP	Appomattox, Va.	653,121	Leonard Fellman	A.W. Dintaman
1183	4¢	Sunflower, Pioneer Couple and Stockade	May 10, 1961	BEP	Council Grove, Kan.	480,561	C.R. Chickering	R.M. Bower
1184	4¢	Senator George W. Norris and Norris Dam	July 11, 1961	BEP	Washington, D.C.	482,875	C.R. Chickering	M.D. Fenton
1185	4¢	Navy's First Plane (Curtiss A-1 of 1911) and Naval Air Wings	Aug. 20, 1961	BEP	San Diego, Calif.	416,391	John Maass	R.M. Bower
1186	4¢	Scales of Justice, Factory, Worker and Family	Sept. 4, 1961	BEP	Milwaukee, Wis.	410,236	Norman Todhunter	C.A. Brooks
1187	4¢	"The Smoke Signal" by	Oct. 4, 1961	BEP	Washington, D.C.	723,443	C.R. Chickering	R.M. Bower

Scott number	Denom.	Design	First day of issue	Printer	First-day city	First-day quantities	Designer	Engraver
		Frederic Remington						
1188	4¢	Sun Yat-sen	Oct. 10, 1961	BEP	Washington, D.C.	463,900	C.R. Chickering	M.D. Fenton
1189	4¢	Basketball	Nov. 6, 1961	BEP	Springfield, Mass.	479,917	C.R. Chickering	M.D. Fenton
1190	4¢	Student Nurse Lighting Candle	Dec. 28, 1961	BEP	Washington, D.C.	964,005	Alfred C. Parker	R.M. Bower
1191	4¢	Shiprock, New Mexico	Feb. 6, 1962	BEP	Santa Fe, N.M.	365,330	Robert J. Jones	R.M. Bower
1192	4¢	Giant Saguaro Cactus	Feb. 14, 1962	BEP	Phoenix, Ariz.	508,216	Jimmie E. Ihms	A.W. Dintaman
1193	4¢	"Friendship 7" Capsule and Globe	Feb. 20, 1962	BEP	Cape Canaveral, Fla.	3,000,000	C.R. Chickering	R.M. Bower
1194	4¢	Great Seal of U.S. and WHO Symbol	March 30, 1962	BEP	Washington, D.C.	554,175	C.R. Chickering	R.M. Bower
1195	4¢	Charles Evans Hughes	April 11, 1962	BEP	Washington, D.C.	544,424	C.R. Chickering	R.M. Bower
1196	4¢	"Space Needle" and Monorail	April 25, 1962	BEP	Seattle, Wash.	771,856	John Maass	C.A. Brooks
1197	4¢	Riverboat on the Mississippi	April 30, 1962	BEP	New Orleans, La.	436,681	Norman Todhunter	A.W. Dintaman
1198	4¢	Sod Hut and Settlers	May 20, 1962	BEP	Beatrice, Neb.	487,450	C.R. Chickering	M.D. Fenton
1199	4¢	Senior Girl Scout and Flag	July 24, 1962	BEP	Burlington, Vt.	634,347	Ward Brackett	M.D. Fenton
1200	4¢	Brien McMahon and Atomic Symbol	July 28, 1962	BEP	Norwalk, Conn.	384,419	V.S. McCloskey, Jr.	R.M. Bower
1201	4¢	Machinist Handing Micrometer to Apprentice	Aug. 31, 1962	BEP	Washington, D.C.	1,003,548	Robert Geissmann	R.M. Bower
1202	4¢	Sam Rayburn and Capitol	Sept. 16, 1962	BEP	Bonham, Texas	401,042	Robert L. Miller	C.A. Brooks
1203	4¢	U.N. Headquarters and and Dag Hammarskjold	Oct. 23, 1962	BEP	New York, N.Y.	500,683	Herbert M. Sanborn	C.A. Brooks
1204	4¢	U.N. Headquarters and Dag Hammarksjold	Nov. 16, 1962	BEP	Washington, D.C.	75,000	Herbert M. Sanborn	C.A. Brooks
1205	4¢	Wreath and Candles	Nov. 1, 1962	BEP	Pittsburgh, Pa.	491,312	Jim Crawford	R.M. Bower
1206	4¢	Map of U.S. and Lamp	Nov. 14, 1962	BEP	Washington, D.C.	627,347	Henry K. Bencsath	M.D. Fenton
1207	4¢	"Breezing Up" by Winslow Homer	Dec. 15, 1962	BEP	Gloucester, Mass.	498,866	V.S. McCloskey, Jr.	C.A. Brooks

Scott number	Denom.	Design	First day of issue	Printer	First-day city	First-day quantities	Designer	Engraver
1208	5¢	Flag over White House	Jan. 9, 1963	BEP	Washington, D.C.	696,185	Robert J. Jones	R.M. Bower
1209	1¢	Andrew Jackson	March 22, 1963	BEP	New York, N.Y.	392,363	William K. Schrage	R.M. Bower
1213	5¢	George Washington	Nov. 23, 1962	BEP	New York, N.Y.	360,531	William K. Schrage	C.A. Brooks
1225	1¢	Andrew Jackson	May 31, 1963	BEP	Chicago, Ill.	238,952	William K. Schrage	R.M. Bower
1229	5¢	George Washington	Nov. 23, 1962	BEP	New York, N.Y.	184,627	William K. Schrage	C.A. Brooks
1230	4¢	First Page of Carolina Charter	April 6, 1961	BEP	Edenton, N.C.	426,200	Robert L. Miller	R.M. Bower
1231	5¢	Wheat	June 4, 1963	BEP	Washington, D.C.	624,342	Stevan Dohanos	A.W. Dintaman
1232	4¢	Map of West Virginia and State Capitol	June 20, 1963	BEP	Wheeling, W.Va.	413,389	Dwight Mutchler	C.A. Brooks
1233	5¢	Severed Chain	Aug. 16, 1963	BEP	Chicago, Ill.	494,886	Georg Olden	
1234	5¢	Alliance for Progress Emblem	Aug. 17, 1963	BEP	Washington, D.C.	528,095	William K. Schrage	M.D. Fenton
1235	5¢	Cordell Hull	Oct. 5, 1963	BEP	Carthage, Tenn.	391,631	Robert J. Jones	C.A. Brooks
1236	5¢	Eleanor Roosevelt	Oct. 11, 1963	BEP	Washington, D.C.	860,155	Robert L. Miller	C.A. Brooks
1237	5¢	"The Universe"	Oct. 14, 1963	BEP	Washington, D.C.	504,503	Antonio Frasconi	A.W. Dintaman
1238	5¢	Letter Carrier, 1863	Oct. 26, 1963	BEP	Washington, D.C.	544,806	Norman Rockwell	C.A. Brooks
1239	5¢	Cuban Refugees on SS *Morning Light* and Red Cross Flag	Oct. 29, 1963	BEP	Washington, D.C.	557,678	V.S. McCloskey, Jr.	R.M. Bower
1240	5¢	National Christmas Tree and White House	Nov. 1, 1963	BEP	Santa Claus, Ind.	458,619	Lily Spandorf	R.M. Bower
1241	5¢	"Columbia Jays" by John James Audubon	Dec. 7, 1963	BEP	Henderson, Ky.	518,855	Robert L. Miller	M.D. Fenton
1242	5¢	Sam Houston	Jan. 10, 1964	BEP	Houston, Texas	487,986	Tom Lea	A.W. Dintaman
1243	5¢	"Jerked Down" by Charles M. Russell	March 19, 1963	BEP	Great Falls, Mont.	487,986	William K. Schrage	C.A. Brooks
1244	5¢	Mall with Unisphere and "Rocket Thrower" by Donald De Lue	April 22, 1964	BEP	World's Fair, N.Y.	1,656,346	Robert J. Jones	A.W. Dintaman
1245	5¢	John Muir and Redwood Forest	April 29, 1964	BEP	Martinez, Calif.	446,925	Rudolph Wendelin	M.D. Fenton
1246	5¢	John F. Kennedy and Eternal Flame	May 29, 1964	BEP	Boston, Mass.	2,003,096	Raymond Loewy	M.D. Fenton

Scott number	Denom.	Design	First day of issue	Printer	First-day city	First-day quantities	Designer	Engraver
1247	5¢	Philip Carteret Landing at Elizabethtown, and Map of New Jersey	June 15, 1964	BEP	Elizabeth, N.J.	526,879	Douglas Allen	A.W. Dintaman
1248	5¢	Virginia City and Map of Nevada	July 22, 1964	BEP	Carson City, Nev.	584,973	William K. Schrage	M.D. Fenton
1249	5¢	Flag	Aug. 1, 1964	BEP	Washington, D.C.	533,439	V.S. McCloskey, Jr.	R.M. Bower
1250	5¢	William Shakespeare	Aug. 14, 1964	BEP	Stratford, Conn.	524,053	Douglas Gorsline	C.A. Brooks
1251	5¢	Drs. William and Charles Mayo	Sept. 11, 1964	BEP	Rochester, Minn.	674,846	R.J. Jones	M.D. Fenton
1252	5¢	Lute, Horn, Laurel, Oak and Music Scores	Oct. 15, 1964	BEP	New York, N.Y.	466,107	Bradbury Thompson	C.A. Brooks
1253	5¢	Farm Scene Sampler	Oct. 26, 1964	BEP	Honolulu, Hawaii	435,392	Norman Todhunter	R.M. Bower
1254	5¢	Holly	Nov. 9, 1964	BEP	Bethlehem, Pa.	794,900	Thomas F. Naegele	M.D. Fenton
1255	5¢	Mistletoe	Nov. 9, 1964	BEP	Bethlehem, Pa.	794,900	Thomas F. Naegele	M.D. Fenton
1256	5¢	Poinsettia	Nov. 9, 1964	BEP	Bethlehem, Pa.	794,900	Thomas F. Naegele	M.D. Fenton
1257	5¢	Sprig of Conifer	Nov. 9, 1964	BEP	Bethlehem, Pa.	794,900	Thomas F. Naegele	M.D. Fenton
1258	5¢	Verrazano-Narrows Bridge and Map of New York Bay	Nov. 21, 1964	BEP	Staten Island, N.Y.	619,780	Robert Miller	C.A. Brooks
1259	5¢	Abstract Design by Stuart Davis	Dec. 2, 1964	BEP	Washington, D.C.	588,046		R.M. Bower
1260	5¢	Radio Waves and Dial	Dec. 15, 1964	BEP	Anchorage, Alaska	452,255	Emil J. Willett	C.A. Brooks
1261	5¢	Gen. Andrew Jackson and Sesquicentennial Medal	Feb. 8, 1965	BEP	New Orleans, La.	466,029	Robert J. Jones	C.A. Brooks
1262	5¢	Discus Thrower	Feb. 15, 1965	BEP	Washington, D.C.	864,848	Norman Todhunter	A.W. Dintaman
1263	5¢	Microscope and Stethoscope	April 1, 1964	BEP	Washington, D.C.	744,485	Stevan Dohanos	J.S. Creamer, Jr.
1264	5¢	Winston Churchill	May 13, 1965	BEP	Fulton, Mo.	773,580	Richard Hurd	C.A. Brooks
1265	5¢	Procession of Barons and King John's Crown	June 15, 1965	BEP	Jamestown, Va.	479,065	Brook Temple	A.W. Dintaman
1266	5¢	International Coopera-tion Year Emblem	June 26, 1965	BEP	San Francisco,	402,925	Herbert M. Sanborn	C.A. Brooks
1267	5¢	Salvation Army Cen-	July 2, 1965	BEP	New York, N.Y.	634,228	Sam Marsh	G.A. Payne

Scott number	Denom.	Design	First day of issue	Printer	First-day city	First-day quantities	Designer	Engraver
		tenary						
1268	5¢	Dante after a 16th-century painting	July 17, 1965	BEP	San Francisco	424,893	Douglas Gorsline	A.W. Dintaman
1269	5¢	Herbert Hoover	Aug. 10, 1965	BEP	West Branch, Iowa	698,182	Norman Todhunter	C.A. Brooks
1270	5¢	Robert Fulton and the *Clermont*	Aug. 19, 1965	BEP	Clermont, N.Y.	550,330	John Maass	C.A. Brooks
1271	5¢	Spanish Explorer, Royal Flag of Spain and Ships	Aug. 28, 1965	BEP	St. Augustine, Fla.	465,000	Brook Temple	A.W. Dintaman
1272	5¢	Traffic Signal	Sept. 3, 1965	BEP	Baltimore, Md.	527,075	Richard F. Hurd	J.S. Creamer, Jr.
1273	5¢	Elizabeth Clarke Copley	Sept. 17, 1965	BEP	Washington, D.C.	613,484	John Carter Brown	C.A. Brooks
1274	5¢	Galt Projection World Map and Sine Wave	Oct. 6, 1965	BEP	Washington, D.C.	332,818	Thomas F. Naegele	A.W. Dintaman
1275	5¢	Adlai E. Stevenson	Oct. 23, 1965	BEP	Bloomington, Ill.	755,656	George Samerjan	C.A. Brooks
1276	5¢	Angel with Trumpet, 1840 Weather Vane	Nov. 2, 1965	BEP	Sliver Bell, Ariz.	705,039	Robert Jones	C.A. Brooks
1278	1¢	Thomas Jefferson	Jan. 12, 1968	BEP	Jeffersonville, Ind.	655,680	Robert Geissmann	E.R. Felver
1279	1 1/4¢	Albert Gallatin	Jan. 30, 1967	BEP	Gallatin, Mo.	439,010	P. Amarantides	E.R. Felver
1280	2¢	Frank Lloyd Wright and Guggenheim Museum, New York	June 8, 1966	BEP	Spring Green, Wis.	460,427	P. Amarantides	A.W. Dintaman
1281	3¢	Francis Parkman	Sept. 16, 1967	BEP	Boston, Mass.	518,355	Bill Hyde	E.R. Felver
1282	4¢	Abraham Lincoln	Nov. 19, 1965	BEP	New York, N.Y.	445,629	Bill Hyde	J.S. Creamer, Jr.
1283	5¢	George Washington	Feb. 22, 1966	BEP	Washington, D.C.	525,372	Bill Hyde	C.A. Brooks
1283B	5¢	George Washington	Nov. 17, 1967	BEP	New York, N.Y.	328,983	Stevan Dohanos	J.S. Creamer, Jr.
1284	6¢	Franklin D. Roosevelt	Jan. 29, 1966	BEP	Hyde Park, N.Y.	448,631	Richard L. Clark	J.S. Creamer, Jr.
1285	8¢	Albert Einstein	March 14, 1966	BEP	Princeton, N.J.	366,803	Frank Sebastiano	A.W. Dintaman
1286	10¢	Andrew Jackson	March 15, 1967	BEP	Hermitage, Tenn.	255,945	Lester Beall	A.W. Dintaman
1286A	12¢	Henry Ford and 1909 Model T	July 30, 1968	BEP	Greenfield Village, Mich.	342,850	Norman Todhunter	E.R. Felver
1287	13¢	John F. Kennedy	May 29, 1967	BEP	Brookline, Mass	391,195	Stevan Dohanos	A.W. Dintaman
1288	15¢	Oliver Wendell Holmes	March 8, 1968	BEP	Washington, D.C.	322,970	Richard F. Hurd	J.S. Creamer, Jr.

Scott number	Denom.	Design	First day of issue	Printer	First-day city	First-day quantities	Designer	Engraver
1288B	15¢	Oliver Wendell Holmes	June 14, 1978	BEP	Boston, Mass.	387,119	Richard F. Hurd	J.S. Creamer, Jr.
1289	20¢	George Catlett Marshall	Oct. 24, 1967	BEP	Lexington, Va.	221,206	Robert Geissmann	A.W. Dintaman
1290	25¢	Fredrick Douglass	Feb. 14, 1967	BEP	Washington, D.C.	213,730	W.D. Richard	A.W. Dintaman
1291	30¢	John Dewey	Oct. 21, 1968	BEP	Burlington, Vt.	162,790	Richard L. Clark	E.P. Archer
1292	40¢	Thomas Paine	Feb. 29, 1969	BEP	Philadelphia, Pa.	157,947	Robert Geissmann	A.W. Dintaman
1293	50¢	Lucy Stone	Aug. 13, 1968	BEP	Dorchester, Mass.	140,4010	Mark English	E.R. Felver
1294	$1	Eugene O'Neil	Oct. 16, 1967	BEP	New London, Conn.	103,102	Norman Todhunter	A.W. Dintaman
1295	$5	John Bassett Moore	Dec. 3, 1966	BEP	Smyrna, Del.	41,130	Tom Laufer	A.W. Dintaman
1297	3¢	Francis Parkman	Nov. 4, 1975	BEP	Pendleton, Ore.	166,798	Bill Hyde	E.R. Felver
1298	6¢	Franklin D. Roosevelt	Dec. 28, 1967	BEP	Washington, D.C.	312,330	Richard L. Clark	J.S. Creamer, Jr.
1299	1¢	Thomas Jefferson	Jan. 12, 1968	BEP	Jeffersonville, Ind.		Robert Geissmann	E.R. Felver
1303	4¢	Abraham Lincoln	May 28, 1966	BEP	Springfield, Ill.	322,563	Bill Hyde	J.S. Creamer, Jr.
1304	5¢	George Washington	Sept. 8, 1966	BEP	Cincinnati, Ohio	245,400	Bill Hyde	C.A. Brooks
1304C	5¢	George Washington	1981	BEP			Stevan Dohanos	C.A. Brooks
1305	6¢	Franklin D. Roosevelt	Feb. 28, 1968	BEP	Washington, D.C.	317,199	Richard L. Clark	H. F. Sharpless
1305C	$1	Eugene O'Neil	Jan. 12, 1978	BEP	Hempstead, N.Y.	121,217	Norman Todhunter	A.W. Dintaman
1305E	15¢	Oliver Wendell Holmes	June 14, 1978	BEP	Boston, Mass.		Richard Hurd	J.S. Creamer, Jr.
1306	5¢	Migratory Birds Canada-U.S. Border	March 16, 1966	BEP	Pittsburgh, Pa.	555,485	Burt E. Pringle	J.S. Creamer, Jr.
1307	5¢	Mongrel	April 9, 1966	BEP	New York, N.Y.	524,420	Norman Todhunter	C.A. Brooks
1308	5¢	Sesquicentennial Seal; Map of Indiana with 19 Stars and Old Capitol	April 16, 1966	BEP	Corydon, Ind.	575,557	Paul A. Wehr	J.S. Creamer, Jr.
1309	5¢	Clown	May 2, 1966	BEP	Delavan, Wis.	754,076	Edward Klauck	C.A. Brooks
1310	5¢	Stamped Cover	May 21, 1966	BEP	Washington, D.C.	637,802	Thomas F. Naegele	H.F. Sharpless
1311	5¢	Stamped Cover, Capitol and Washington Monument in Background	May 23, 1966	BEP	Washington, D.C.	700,882	Brook Temple	H.F. Sharpless
1312	5¢	"Freedom" Checking "Tyranny"	July 1, 1966	BEP	Miami Beach, Fla.	562,920	Herbert L. Block	J.S. Creamer, Jr.
1313	5¢	Polish Eagle and Cross	July 30, 1966	BEP	Washington, D.C.	715,603	E.D. Lewandowski	J.S. Creamer, Jr.

Scott number	Denom.	Design	First day of issue	Printer	First-day city	First-day quantities	Designer	Engraver
1314	5¢	National Park Service Emblem	Aug. 25, 1966	BEP	Yellowstone National Park	528,170	T.H. Geismar	J.S. Creamer, Jr.
1315	5¢	Combat Marine, 1966; Frogman; WWII Flier; WWI "Devil Dog" and Marine	Aug. 29, 1966	BEP	Washington, D.C.	585,923	Stella Grafakos	C.A. Brooks
1316	5¢	Women of 1890 and 1966	Sept. 12, 1966	BEP	New York, N.Y.	383,334	J.S. Creamer, Jr.	J.S. Creamer, Jr.
1317	5¢	Johnny Appleseed	Sept. 24, 1966	BEP	Leominster, Mass.	794,610	Robert Bode	A.W. Dintaman
1318	5¢	Jefferson Memorial, Tidal Basin and Cherry Blossoms	Oct. 5, 1966	BEP	Washington, D.C.	564,440	Gyo Fujikawa	C.A. Brooks
1319	5¢	Map of Central U.S. with Great River Road	Oct. 21, 1966	BEP	Baton Rouge, La.	330,933	Herbert Bayer	J.S. Creamer, Jr.
1320	5¢	Statue of Liberty and "Old Glory"	Oct. 26, 1966	BEP	Sioux City, Iowa	444,421	Stevan Dohanos	E.R. Felver
1321	5¢	"Madonna and Child" by Hans Memling	Jan. 1, 1966	BEP	Christmas, Mich.	537,650	Howard C. Mildner	E.R. Felver
1322	5¢	"The Boating Party" by Mary Cassatt	Nov. 17, 1966	BEP	Washington, D.C.	593,389	Robert J. Jones	C.A. Brooks
1323	5¢	Grange Poster, 1870	April 17, 1967	BEP	Washington, D.C.	603,460	Lee Pavao	E.R. Felver
1324	5¢	Canadian Landscape	May 25, 1967	BEP	Montreal, Canada	711,795	Ivan Chermayeff	E.R. Felver
1325	5¢	Stern of Early Canal Boat	July 4, 1967	BEP	Rome, N.Y.	784,795	George Samerjan	
1326	5¢	Peace Dove	July 5, 1967	BEP	Chicago, Ill.	393,197	Bradbury Thompson	J.S. Creamer, Jr.
1327	5¢	Henry David Thoreau	July 12, 1967	BEP	Concord, Mass.	696,789	Leonard Baskin	J.S. Creamer, Jr.
1328	5¢	Hereford Steer and Ear of Corn	July 29, 1967	BEP	Lincoln, Neb.	1,146,957	Julian K. Billings	J.S. Creamer, Jr.
1329	5¢	Radio Transmission Tower and Waves	Aug. 1, 1967	BEP	Washington, D.C.	455,190	George Olden	
1330	5¢	Davy Crockett and Scrub Pine	Aug. 17, 1967	BEP	San Antonio, Texas	462,291	Robert Bode	E.R. Felver
1331	5¢	Space Walking Astronaut	Sept. 29, 1967	BEP	Kennedy Space Center, Fla.	667,267	Paul Calle	J.S. Creamer, Jr.

Scott number	Denom.	Design	First day of issue	Printer	First-day city	First-day quantities	Designer	Engraver
1332	5¢	Gemini 4 Capsule	Sept. 29, 1967	BEP	Kennedy Space Center, Fla.	667,267	Paul Calle	J.S. Creamer, Jr.
1333	5¢	View of Model City	Oct. 2, 1967	BEP	Washington, D.C.	389,009	Francis Ferguson	J. F. Sharpless
1334	5¢	Finnish Coat of Arms	Oct. 6, 1967	BEP	Finland, Minn.	408,532	Bradbury Thompson	E.R. Felver
1335	5¢	"The Biglin Brothers Racing" by Thomas Eakins	Nov. 2, 1967	Photogravure & Color Co.	Washington, D.C.	684,054		
1336	5¢	"Madonna and Child" by Hans Memling	Nov. 6, 1967	BEP	Bethlehem, Ga.	462,118	Howard Mildner	E.R. Felver
1337	5¢	Magnolia	Dec. 11, 1967	BEP	Natchez, Miss.	379,612	Andrew Bucci	J.S. Creamer, Jr.
1338	6¢	Flag and White House	Jan. 24, 1968	BEP	Washington, D.C.	412,120	Stevan Dohanos	E.P. Archer
1338A	6¢	Flag and White House	May 30, 1969	BEP	Chicago, Ill.	248,434	Stevan Dohanos	E.P. Archer
1338D	6¢	Flag and White House	Aug. 7, 1970	BEP	Washington, D.C.	365,280	Stevan Dohanos	E.P. Archer
1338F	8¢	Flag and White House	May 10, 1971	BEP	Washington, D.C.	235,543	Stevan Dohanos	E.P. Archer
1338G	8¢	Flag and White House	May 10, 1971	BEP	Washington, D.C.	235,543	Stevan Dohanos	E.P. Archer
1339	6¢	Farm Building and Field of Ripening Grain	Feb. 12, 1968	BEP	Shawneetown, Ill.	761,640	George Barford	J.S. Creamer, Jr.
1340	6¢	Map of North and South America and Lines Converging on San Antonio	March 30, 1968	BEP	San Antonio, Texas	469,909	Louis Macouillard	E.R. Felver
1341	$1	Eagle Holding Pennant	April 4, 1968	BEP	Seattle, Wash.	105,088	Stevan Dohanos	E.P. Archer
1342	6¢	Girls and Boys	May 1, 1968	BEP	Chicago, Ill.	354,711	Edward Vebell	E.P. Archer
1343	6¢	Policeman and Boy	May 17, 1968	BEP	Washington, D.C.	407,081	Ward Brackett	J.S. Creamer, Jr.
1344	6¢	Eagle and Weather Vane	June 27, 1968	BEP		355,685	Norman Todhunter	A.W. Dintaman
1345	6¢	Ft. Moultrie, 1776 Flag	July 4, 1968	BEP	Pittsburgh, Pa.	2,924,962	R.J. Jones	R.G. Culin
1346	6¢	Ft. McHenry Flag, 1795-1818	July 4, 1968	BEP	Pittsburgh, Pa.	2,924,962	R.J. Jones	R.G. Culin
1347	6¢	Washington's Cruisers Flag, 1775	July 4, 1968	BEP	Pittsburgh, Pa.	2,924,962	R.J. Jones	R.G. Culin
1348	6¢	Bennington Flag, 1777	July 4, 1968	BEP	Pittsburgh, Pa.	2,924,962	R.J. Jones	R.G. Culin
1349	6¢	Rhode Island Flag, 1775	July 4, 1968	BEP	Pittsburgh, Pa.	2,924,962	R.J. Jones	R.G. Culin
1350	6¢	First Stars and Stripes, 1777	July 4, 1968	BEP	Pittsburgh, Pa.	2,924,962	R.J. Jones	R.G. Culin

Scott number	Denom.	Design	First day of issue	Printer	First-day city	First-day quantities	Designer	Engraver
1351	6¢	Bunker Hill Flag, 1775	July 4, 1968	BEP	Pittsburgh, Pa.	2,924,962	R.J. Jones	R.G. Culin
1352	6¢	Grand Union Flag, 1776	July 4, 1968	BEP	Pittsburgh, Pa.	2,924,962	R.J. Jones	R.G. Culin
1353	6¢	Philadelphia Light Horse Flag, 1775	July 4, 1968	BEP	Pittsburgh, Pa.	2,924,962	R.J. Jones	R.G. Culin
1354	6¢	First Navy Jack, 1775	July 4, 1968	BEP	Pittsburgh, Pa.	2,924,962	R.J. Jones	R.G. Culin
1355	6¢	Walt Disney and Children of the World	Sept. 11, 1968	Achrovure Division of Union-Camp	Marceline, Mo.	499,505	C. Robert Moore	
1356	6¢	Father Marquette and Louis Jolliet Exploring the Mississippi	Sept. 20, 1968	BEP	Sault Ste. Marie, Mich.	379,710	Stanley W. Galli	E.P. Archer
1357	6¢	Pennsylvania Rifle, Powder Horn, Tomahawk, Pipe and Knife	Sept. 26, 1968	BEP	Frankfort, Ky.	333,440	Louis Macouillard	J.S. Creamer, Jr.
1358	6¢	Ship's Wheel, Power Transmission Tower and Barge	Oct. 1, 1968	BEP	Little Rock, Ark.	358,025	Dean Ellis	E.P. Archer
1359	6¢	Leif Erikson	Oct. 9, 1968	BEP	Seattle, Wash.	376,565	Kurt Weiner	E.P. Archer
1360	6¢	Racing for Homesteads in Cherokee Strip, 1893	Oct. 15, 1968	BEP	Ponca, Okla.	339,330	Norman Todhunter	J.S. Creamer, Jr.
1361	6¢	Detail from "The Battle of Bunker's Hill" by John Trumbull	Oct. 18, 1968	BEP	New Haven, Conn.	378,285	Robert J. Jones	J.S. Creamer, Jr.
1362	6¢	Wood Ducks	Oct. 24, 1968	BEP	Cleveland, Ohio	349,719	Stanley W. Galli	E.P. Archer
1363	6¢	Angel Gabriel from "The Annunciation" by Jan van Eyck	Nov. 1, 1968	BEP	Washington, D.C.	739,055	Robert J. Jones	E.R. Felver
1364	6¢	Chief Joseph by Cyrenius Hall	Nov. 4, 1968	BEP	Washington, D.C.	415,964	Robert J. Jones	E.R. Felver
1365	6¢	Capitol, Azaleas and Tulips	Jan. 16, 1969	BEP	Washington, D.C.	1,094,184	W.D. Richard	E.R. Felver
1366	6¢	Washington Monument, Potomac River and	Jan. 16, 1969	BEP	Washington, D.C.	1,094,184	W.D. Richard	E.R. Felver

Scott number	Denom.	Design	First day of issue	Printer	First-day city	First-day quantities	Designer	Engraver
		Daffodils						
1367	6¢	Poppies and Lupines along Highway	Jan. 16, 1969	BEP	Washington, D.C.	1,084,184	W.D. Richard	E.R. Felver
1368	6¢	Blooming Crabapples Lining Avenue	Jan. 16, 1969	BEP	Washington, D.C.	1,094,184	W.D. Richard	E.R. Felver
1369	6¢	Eagle from Great Seal	March 15, 1969	BEP	Washington, D.C.	632,035	Robert Hallock	J.S. Creamer, Jr.
1370	6¢	"July Fourth" by Grandma Moses	May 1, 1969	BEP	Washington, D.C.	367,880	Robert J. Jones	J.S. Creamer, Jr.
1371	6¢	Moon Surface and Earth	May 5, 1969	BEP	Houston, Texas	908,634	Leonard E. Buckley	E.R. Felver
1372	6¢	William Christopher Handy	May 17, 1969	BEP	Memphis, Tenn.	398,216	Bernice Kochan	E.P. Archer
1373	6¢	Carmel Mission Belfry	July 16, 1969	BEP	San Diego, Calif.	530,210	Leonard Buckley	J.S. Creamer, Jr.
1374	6¢	Major Powell Exploring Colorado River, 1869	Aug. 1, 1969	BEP	Page, Ariz.	434,433	Rudolph Wendelin	J.S. Creamer, Jr.
1375	6¢	Camelia and Yellow-shafted Flicker	Aug. 2, 1969	BEP	Huntsville, Ala.	485,801	Bernice Kochan	E.P. Archer
1376	6¢	Douglas Fir	Aug. 23, 1969	BEP	Seattle, Wash.	737,935	Stanley Galli	E.P. Archer
1377	6¢	Lady's Slipper	Aug. 23, 1968	BEP	Seattle, Wash.	737,935	Stanley Galli	E.P. Archer
1378	6¢	Ocotillo	Aug. 23, 1969	BEP	Seattle, Wash	737,935	Stanley Galli	E.P. Archer
1379	6¢	Franklinia	Aug. 23, 1969	BEP	Seattle, Wash.	737,935	Stanley Galli	E.P. Archer
1380	6¢	Daniel Webster and Dartmouth Hall	Sept. 22, 1969	BEP	Hanover, N.H.	416,327	J.R. Scotford, Jr.	E.P. Archer
1381	6¢	Batter	Sept. 24, 1969	BEP	Cincinnati, Ohio	414,942	Alex Ross	J.S. Creamer, Jr.
1382	6¢	Football Player and Coach	Sept. 26, 1969	BEP	New Brunswick, N.J.	414,860	Robert Peak	E.P. Archer
1383	6¢	Dwight D. Eisenhower	Oct. 14, 1969	BEP	Abilene, Kan.	1,009,560	Robert J. Jones	E.R. Felver
1384	6¢	Winter Sunday in Norway, Maine	Nov. 3, 1969	BEP	Christmas, Fla.	555,500	Stevan Dohanos	E.P. Archer
1385	6¢	Cured Child	Nov. 20, 1969	BEP	Columbus, Ohio	342,676	Mark English	E.P. Archer
1386	6¢	"Old Models" by William M. Harnett	Dec. 3, 1969	BEP	Boston, Mass.	408,860	Robert J. Jones	E.R. Felver
1387	6¢	American Bald Eagle	May 6, 1970	BEP	New York, N.Y.	834,260	Walter Richards	E.P. Archer
1388	6¢	African Elephant Herd	May 6, 1970	BEP	New York, N.Y.	834,260	Dean Ellis	A.W. Dintaman
1389	6¢	Tlingit Chief and	May 6, 1969	BEP	New York, N.Y.	834,260	Paul Rabut	J.S. Creamer, Jr.

Scott number	Denom.	Design	First day of issue	Printer	First-day city	First-day quantities	Designer	Engraver
		Ceremonial Canoe						
1390	6¢	Brontosaurus, Stegosaurus and Allosaurus from Jurassic Period	May 6, 1970	BEP	New York, N.Y.	834,260	Robert J. Jones	E.R. Felver
1391	6¢	"The Lighthouse at Two Harbors, Maine," by Edward Hopper	July 9, 1970	BEP	Portland, Maine	472,165	Stevan Dohanos	E.R. Felver
1392	6¢	American Buffalo	July 20, 1970	BEP	Custer, S.D.	309,418	Robert Lougheed	A.W. Dintaman
1393	6¢	Dwight D. Eisenhower	Aug. 6, 1970	BEP	Washington, D.C.	823,540	Robert Geissman	A.W. Dintaman
1393D	7¢	Benjamin Franklin	Oct. 20, 1970	BEP	Philadelphia, Pa.	309,276	Robert Geissman	
1394	8¢	Dwight D. Eisenhower	May 10, 1971	BEP	Washington, D.C.	813,947	Robert Geissman	E.P. Archer
1395	8¢	Dwight D. Eisenhower	May 10, 1970	BEP	Washington, D.C.	813,540	Robert Geissman	E.P. Archer
1396	8¢	U.S. Postal Service Emblem	July 1, 1971	BEP	any city	16,300,000	Raymond Loewy/ William Smith, Inc.	
1397	14¢	Fiorello H. LaGuardia	April 24, 1972	BEP	New York, N.Y.	180,114	Robert Geissman	
1398	16¢	Ernest Taylor Pyle	May 7, 1971	BEP	Washington, D.C.	444,410	Robert Geissman	E.P. Archer
1399	18¢	Dr. Elizabeth Blackwell	Jan. 23, 1974	BEP	Geneva, N.Y.	217,938	Robert Geissman	E.P. Archer
1400	21¢	Amadeo P. Giannini	June 27, 1973	BEP	San Mateo, Calif.	282,520	Robert Geissman	A.W. Dintaman
1401	6¢	Dwight D. Eisenhower	Aug. 6, 1970	BEP	Washington, D.C.		Robert Geissman	A.W. Dintaman
1402	8¢	Dwight D. Eisenhower	May 10, 1971	BEP	Washington, D.C.		Robert Geissman	A.W. Dintaman
1405	6¢	Edgar Lee Masters	Aug. 22, 1970	BEP	Petersburg, Ill.	372,804	Fred Otnes	E.P. Archer
1406	6¢	Suffragettes, 1929 and Woman Voter, 1970	Aug. 26, 1970	BEP	Adams, Mass.	508,142	Ward Brackett	J.S. Creamer, Jr.
1407	6¢	Symbols of South Carolina	Sept. 12, 1970	BEP	Charleston, S.C.	533,000	George Samerjan	E.P. Archer
1408	6¢	Robert E. Lee, Jefferson Davis and "Stonewall" Jackson	Sept. 19, 1970	BEP	Stone Mountain, Ga.	558,546	Robert Hallock	E.R. Felver
1409	6¢	Fort Snelling, Keelboat and Tepees	Oct. 17, 1970	BEP	Fort Snelling, Minn.	497,611	David K. Stone	E.P. Archer
1410	6¢	Globe and Wheat	Oct. 28, 1970	BEP	San Clemente, Calif.	1,033,147	Arnold Copeland	
1411	6¢	Globe and City	Oct. 28, 1970	BEP	San Clemente,	1,033,147	Arnold Copeland	

Scott number	Denom.	Design	First day of issue	Printer	First-day city	First-day quantities	Designer	Engraver
					Calif.			
1412	6¢	Globe and Bluegill	Oct. 28, 1970	BEP	San Clemente, Calif.	1,033,147	Arnold Copeland	
1413	6¢	Globe and Seagull	Oct. 28, 1970	Guilford Gravure	San Clemente, Calif.	1,033,147	Arnold Copeland	
1414	6¢	Nativity by Lorenzo Lotto	Nov. 5, 1970	BEP	Washington, D.C.	2,014,450	Howard C. Mildner	
1415	6¢	Tin and Cast-iron Locomotive	Nov. 5, 1970	Guilford Gravure	Washington, D.C.	2,014,450	Stevan Dohanos	
1416	6¢	Toy Horse on Wheels	Nov. 5, 1970	Guilford Gravure	Washington, D.C.	2,014,450	Stevan Dohanos	
1417	6¢	Mechanical Tricycle	Nov. 5, 1970	Guilford Gravure	Washington, D.C.	2,014,450	Stevan Dohanos	
1418	6¢	Doll Carriage	Nov. 5, 1970	Guilford Gravure	Washington, D.C.	2,014,450	Stevan Dohanos	
1419	6¢	"U.N." and U.N. Emblem	Nov. 20, 1970	BEP	New York, N.Y.	474,070	Arnold Copeland	A. Saavedra
1420	6¢	Mayflower and Pilgrims	Nov. 21, 1970	BEP	Plymouth, Mass.	629,850	Mark English	J.S. Creamer, Jr.
1421	6¢	Disabled American Veterans Emblem	Nov. 24, 1970	BEP	Cincinnati, Ohio	813,027	Stevan Dohanos	A.W. Dintaman
1422	6¢	POW and MIA	Nov. 24, 1970	BEP	Cincinnati, Ohio	813,027	Stevan Dohanos	A.W. Dintaman
1423	6¢	Ewe and Lamb	Jan. 19, 1970	BEP	Las Vegas, Nev.	379,911	Dean Ellis	E.R. Felver
1424	6¢	Gen. Douglas MacArthur	Jan. 26, 1971	BEP	Norfolk, Va.	720,035	Paul Calle	A.W. Dintaman
1425	6¢	"Giving Blood Saves Lives"	March 12, 1971	BEP	New York, N.Y.	644,497	Howard Munce	E.P. Archer
1426	8¢	"Independence and the Opening of the West" by Thomas Hart Benton	May 8, 1971	BEP	Independence, Mo.	551,000	Bradbury Thompson	
1427	8¢	Trout	June 12, 1971	BEP	Avery Island, La.	679,483	Stanley W. Galli	
1428	8¢	Alligator	June 12, 1971	BEP	Avery Island, La.	679,483	Stanley W. Galli	
1429	8¢	Polar Bear and Cubs	June 12, 1971	BEP	Avery Island, La.	679,483	Stanley W. Galli	
1430	8¢	California Condor	June 12, 1971	BEP	Avery Island, La.	679,483	Stanley W. Galli	
1431	8¢	Map of Antarctica	June 23, 1971	BEP	Washington, D.C.	419,200	Howard Koslow	E.P. Archer
1432	8¢	Bicentennial Commission Emblem	July 4, 1971	BEP	Washington, D.C.	434,930	Chermayeff & Geismar	H.F. Sharpless

Scott number	Denom.	Design	First day of issue	Printer	First-day city	First-day quantities	Designer	Engraver
1433	8¢	The Wake of the Ferry by John Sloan	Aug. 2, 1971	BEP	Lock Haven, Pa.	482,265	Bradbury Thompson	J.S. Creamer, Jr.
1434	8¢	Earth, Sun and Landing Craft on Moon	Aug. 2, 1971	BEP	Kennedy Space Center, Fla.	2,739,204	Robert McCall	J.S. Creamer, Jr.
1435	8¢	Lunar Rover and Astronauts	Aug. 2, 1971	BEP	Kennedy Space Center, Fla.	2,739,204	Robert McCall	J.S. Creamer, Jr.
1436	8¢	Emily Dickinson	Aug. 28, 1971	BEP	Amherst, Mass.	498,180	Bernard Fuchs	A.W. Dintaman
1437	8¢	Sentry Box, Morro Castle, San Juan	Sept. 12, 1971	BEP	San Juan, P.R.	501,668	Walter Brooks	J.S. Creamer, Jr.
1438	8¢	Young Woman Drug Addict	Oct. 4, 1971	BEP	Dallas, Texas	425,330	Miggs Burroughs	
1439	8¢	Hands Reaching for CARE	Oct. 27, 1971	BEP	New York, N.Y.	402,121	Soren Noring	
1440	8¢	Decatur House, Washington, D.C.	Oct. 29, 1971	BEP	San Diego, Calif.	783,242	Melbourne Brindle	A.W. Dintaman
1441	8¢	Whaling Ship, *Charles W. Morgan*, Mystic, Conn.	Oct. 29, 1970	BEP	San Diego, Calif.	783,242	Melbourne Brindle	E.P. Archer
1442	8¢	Cable Car, San Francisco	Oct. 29, 1971	BEP	San Diego, Calif.	783,242	Melbourne Brindle	E.P. Archer
1443	8¢	San Xavier de Bac Mission Tucson, Ariz.	Oct. 29, 1971	BEP	San Diego, Calif.	783,242	Melbourne Brindle	J.S. Creamer, Jr.
1444	8¢	Adoration of the Shepards, by Giorgione	Nov. 10, 1971	BEP	Washington, D.C.	348,038	Bradbury Thompson	
1445	8¢	"Partridge in a Pear Tree"	Nov. 10, 1971	BEP	Washington, D.C.	348,038	Jamie Wyeth	
1446	8¢	Sidney Lanier	Feb. 3, 1972	BEP	Macon, Ga.	394,800	William A. Smith	E.P. Archer
1447	8¢	Peace Corps Poster	Feb. 11, 1972	BEP	Washington, D.C.	453,660	Bradbury Thompson	
1448	2¢	Cape Hatteras National Seashore	April 5, 1972	BEP	Hatteras, N.C.	505,697	W.D. Richard	J.S. Creamer, Jr.
1449	2¢	Cape Hatteras National Seashore	April 5, 1972	BEP	Hatteras, N.C.	505,697	W.D. Richard	J.S. Creamer, Jr.
1450	2¢	Cape Hatteras	April 5, 1972	BEP	Hatteras, N.C.	505,697	W.D. Richard	J.S. Creamer, Jr.

Scott number	Denom.	Design	First day of issue	Printer	First-day city	First-day quantities	Designer	Engraver
		National Seashore						
1451	2¢	Cape Hatteras National Seashore	April 5, 1972	BEP	Hatteras, N.C.	505,697	W.D. Richard	J.S. Creamer, Jr.
1452	6¢	Wolf Trap Farm, Va.	June 26, 1972	BEP	Vienna, Va.	403,396	Howard Koslow	A.W. Dintaman
1453	8¢	Old Faithful, Yellowstone	March 1, 1972	BEP	Yellowstone National Park	847,500	Robert Handville	E.P. Archer
1454	15¢	Mt. McKinley	July 28, 1972	BEP	Mt. McKinley National Park	491,456	James Barkley	J.S. Creamer, Jr.
1455	8¢	Family Planning	March 18, 1972	BEP	New York, N.Y.	691,385		J.S. Creamer, Jr.
1456	8¢	Glass Blower	July 4, 1972	BEP	Williamsburg, Va.	1,914,976	L.E. Fisher	E.P. Archer
1457	8¢	Silversmith	July 4, 1972	BEP	Williamsburg, Va.	1,914,976	L.E. Fisher	E.P. Archer
1458	8¢	Wigmaker	July 4, 1972	BEP	Williamsburg, Va.	1,914,976	L.E. Fisher	E.P. Archer
1459	8¢	Hatter	July 4, 1972	BEP	Williamsburg, Va.	1,914,976	L.E. Fisher	E.P. Archer
1460	6¢	Bicycling and Olympic Rings	Aug. 17, 1972	BEP	Washington, D.C.	971,536	Lance Wyman	
1461	8¢	Bobsledding and Olympic Rings	Aug. 17, 1972	BEP	Washington, D.C.	971,536	Lance Wyman	
1462	15¢	Running and Olympic Rings	Aug. 17, 1972	BEP	Washington, D.C.	971,536	Lance Wyman	
1463	8¢	Blackboard	Sept. 15, 1972	BEP	San Francisco	523,454	A.S. Congdon II	
1464	8¢	Fur Seals	Sept. 20, 1972	BEP	Warm Springs, Ore.	733,778	Stanley W. Galli	E.P. Archer
1465	8¢	Cardinal	Sept. 20, 1972	BEP	Warm Springs, Ore.	733,778	Stanley W. Galli	J.S. Creamer, Jr.
1466	8¢	Brown Pelican	Sept. 20, 1972	BEP	Warm Springs, Ore.	733,778	Stanley W. Galli	A.W. Dintaman
1467	8¢	Bighorn Sheep	Sept. 20, 1972	BEP	Warm Springs, Ore.	733,778	Stanley W. Galli	A.W. Dintaman
1468	8¢	Rural Post Office	Sept. 27, 1972	BEP	Chicago, Ill.	759,666	Robert Lambdin	
1469	8¢	Man's Quest for Health	Oct. 9, 1972	BEP	Miami, Fla.	607,160	V. Jack Ruther	
1470	8¢	Tom Sawyer by Norman Rockwell	Oct. 13, 1972	BEP	Hannibal, Mo.	459,013	Bradbury Thompson	J.S. Creamer, Jr.
1471	8¢	Angels from "Mary Queen of Heaven"	Nov. 9, 1972	BEP	Washington, D.C.	713,821	Bradbury Thompson	
1472	8¢	Santa Claus	Nov. 9, 1972	BEP	Washington, D.C.	713,821	Stevan Dohanos	
1474	8¢	U.S. No. 1 Magnifying Glass	Jan. 17, 1972	BEP	New York, N.Y.	434,680	Frank E. Livia	E.P. Archer
1475	8¢	"Love" by Robert Indiana	Jan. 26, 1973	BEP	Philadelphia, Pa.	422,492	Robert Indiana	

Scott number	Denom.	Design	First day of issue	Printer	First-day city	First-day quantities	Designer	Engraver
1476	8¢	Printer and Patriots Examining Pamphlet	Feb. 16, 1973	BEP	Portland, Ore.	431,784	William Smith	J.S. Creamer, Jr.
1477	8¢	Posting Broadsides	April 13, 1973	BEP	Atlantic City, N.J.	423,437	William Smith	E.P. Archer
1478	8¢	Postrider	June 22, 1973	BEP	Rochester, N.Y.	586,850	William Smith	J.S. Creamer, Jr.
1479	8¢	Drummer	Sept. 28, 1973	BEP	New Orleans, La.	522,427	William Smith	E.P. Archer
1480	8¢	British Merchantman	July 4, 1973	BEP	Boston, Mass.	897,870	William Smith	A.W. Dintaman
1481	8¢	British Three-master	July 4, 1973	BEP	Boston, Mass.	897,870	William Smith	A.W. Dintaman
1482	8¢	Boats and Ship's Hull	July 4, 1973	BEP	Boston, Mass.	897,870	William Smith	A.W. Dintaman
1483	8¢	Boat and Dock	July 4, 1973	BEP	Boston, Mass.	897,870	William Smith	A.W. Dintaman
1484	8¢	Gershwin, Sportin' Life, Porgy and Bess	Feb. 28, 1973	BEP	Beverly Hills, Calif.	448,814	Mark English	
1485	8¢	Robinson Jeffers, Man and Children of Carmel with Burro	Aug. 13, 1973	BEP	Carmel, Calif.	394,261	Mark English	
1486	8¢	Henry Ossawa Tanner, Palette and Rainbow	Sept. 10, 1973	BEP	Pittsburgh, Pa.	424,065	Mark English	
1487	8¢	Willa Cather, Pioneer Family and Covered Wagon	Oct. 20, 1973	BEP	Red Cloud, Neb.	435,785	Mark English	
1488	8¢	Nicolaus Copernicus	April 23, 1973	BEP	Boston, Mass.	1,205,212	Alvin Eisenman	A.W. Dintaman
1489	8¢	Stamp Counter	April 30, 1973	BEP	Boston, Mass.	1,205,212	Edward Vebell	
1490	8¢	Mail Collection	April 30, 1973	BEP	Boston, Mass.	1,205,212	Edward Vebell	
1491	8¢	Letter Facing on Conveyor Belt	April 30, 1973	BEP	Boston, Mass.	1,205,212	Edward Vebell	
1492	8¢	Parcel Post Sorting	April 30, 1973	BEP	Boston, Mass.	1,205,212	Edward Vebell	
1493	8¢	Mail Canceling	April 30, 1973	BEP	Boston, Mass.	1,205,212	Edward Vebell	
1494	8¢	Manual Letter Routing	April 30, 1973	BEP	Boston, Mass.	1,205,212	Edward Vebell	
1495	8¢	Electronic Letter Routing	April 30, 1973	BEP	Boston, Mass.	1,205,212	Edward Vebell	
1496	8¢	Loading Mail on Truck	April 30, 1973	BEP	Boston, Mass.	1,205,212	Edward Vebell	
1497	8¢	Mailman	April 30, 1973	BEP	Boston, Mass.	1,205,212	Edward Vebell	
1498	8¢	Rural Mail Delivery	April 30, 1973	BEP	Boston, Mass.	1,205,212	Edward Vebell	
1499	8¢	Harry S. Truman	May 8, 1973	BEP	Independence, Mo.	938,636	Bradbury Thompson	J.S. Creamer, Jr.
1500	6¢	Marconi's Spark Coil	July 10, 1973	BEP	New York, N.Y.	1,197,700	Walter and	A.W. Dintaman

Scott number	Denom.	Design	First day of issue	Printer	First-day city	First-day quantities	Designer	Engraver
		and Spark Gap					Naiad Eins	
1501	8¢	Transistors and Printed Circuit Board	July 10, 1973	BEP	New York, N.Y.	1,197,700	Walter and Naiad Eins	E.P. Archer
1502	15¢	Microphone, Speaker, Vacuum Tube and TV Camera Tube	July 10, 1973	BEP	New York, N.Y.	1,197,700	Walter and Naiad Eins	T.R. Hipschen
1503	8¢	Lyndon B. Johnson	Aug. 27, 1973	BEP	Austin, Texas	710,490	Bradbury Thompson	
1504	8¢	Angus and Longhorn Cattle	Oct. 5, 1973	BEP	St. Joseph, Mo.	521,427	Frank Waslick	J.S. Creamer, Jr.
1505	10¢	Chautauqua Tent and Buggies	Aug. 6, 1974	BEP	Chautauqua, N.Y.	411,105	John Falter	A.W. Dintaman
1506	10¢	Wheat Fields and Train	Aug. 16, 1973	BEP	Hillsboro, Kan.	468,280	John Falter	
1507	8¢	"Small Cowper Madonna" by Raphael	Nov. 7, 1973	BEP	Washington, D.C.	807,468	Bradbury Thompson	
1508	8¢	Christmas Tree in Needlepoint	Nov. 7, 1973	BEP	Washington, D.C.	807,468	Dolli Tingle	
1509	10¢	50-Star and 13-Star Flag	Dec. 8, 1973	BEP	San Francisco	341,528	Ren Wicks	E.P. Archer
1510	10¢	Jefferson Memorial and Signature	Dec. 14, 1973	BEP	Washington, D.C.	686,300	Dean Ellis	R.G. Culin, Sr.
1511	10¢	Mail Transport	Jan. 4, 1974	BEP	Washington, D.C.	335,220	Randall McDougall	
1512	6¢	Liberty Bell	Oct. 1, 1974	BEP	Washington, D.C.	221,141	Frank Lionetti	John Wallace
1519	10¢	50-Star and 13-Star Flag	Dec. 8, 1973	BEP	San Francisco		Ren Wicks	E.P. Archer
1520	10¢	Jefferson Memorial and Signature	Dec. 14, 1973	BEP	Washington, D.C.	686,300	Dean Ellis	R.G. Colin
1525	10¢	Emblem and Initials of Veterans of Foreign Wars	March 11, 1974	BEP	Washington, D.C.	543,598	Robert Hallock	H.F. Sharpless
1526	10¢	Robert Frost	March 26, 1974	BEP	Derry, N.H.	500,425	Paul Calle	A.W. Dintaman
1527	10¢	"Cosmic Jumper" and "Smiling Sage"	April 18, 1974	BEP	Spokane, Wash.	565,548	Peter Max	
1528	10¢	Horses Rounding Turn	May 4, 1974	BEP	Louisville, Ky.	623,983	Henry Koehler	
1529	10¢	Skylab	May 14, 1974	BEP	Houston, Texas	927,326	Robert T. McCall	J.S. Creamer, Jr.

Scott number	Denom.	Design	First day of issue	Printer	First-day city	First-day quantities	Designer	Engraver
1530	10¢	Michelangelo from "School of Athens" by Raphael, 1509	June 6, 1974	BEP	Washington, D.C.	1,374,765	Bradbury Thompson	
1531	10¢	"Five Feminine Virtues" by Hokusai, c. 1811	June 6, 1974	BEP	Washington, D.C.	1,374,765	Bradbury Thompson	
1532	10¢	"Old Scraps" by John Fredrick Peto, 1894	June 6, 1974	BEP	Washington, D.C.	1,374,765	Bradbury Thompson	
1533	10¢	"The Lovely Reader" by J.E. Liotard, 1746	June 6, 1974	BEP	Washington, D.C.	1,374,765	Bradbury Thompson	
1534	10¢	"Lady Writing Letter" by Gerard Terborch, 1654	June 6, 1974	BEP	Washington, D.C.	1,374,765	Bradbury Thompson	
1535	10¢	Inkwell and Quill, from "Boy with a Top" by Jean-Baptiste Simeon Chardi	June 6, 1974	BEP	Washington, D.C.	1,374,765	Bradbury Thompson	
1536	10¢	"Mrs. John Douglas" by Thomas Gainsborough	June 6, 1974	BEP	Washington, D.C.	1,374,765	Bradbury Thompson	
1537	10¢	"Don Antonio Noriega" by Francisco de Goya	June 6, 1974	BEP	Washington, D.C.	1,374,765	Bradbury Thompson	
1538	10¢	Petrified Wood	June 13, 1974	BEP	Lincoln, Neb.	856,368	Leonard F. Buckley	A.W. Dintaman
1539	10¢	Tourmaline	June 13, 1974	BEP	Lincoln, Neb.	856,368	Leonard F. Buckley	J.S. Creamer, Jr.
1540	10¢	Amethyst	June 13, 1974	BEP	Lincoln, Neb.	856,368	Leonard F. Buckley	E.P. Archer
1541	10¢	Rhodochrosite	June 13, 1974	BEP	Lincoln, Neb.	856,368	Leonard F. Buckley	T.R. Hipschen
1542	10¢	Covered Wagons at Fort Harrod	June 15, 1974	BEP	Harrodsburg, Ky.	478,239	David K. Stone	J.S. Creamer, Jr.
1543	10¢	Carpenters' Hall	July 4, 1974	BEP	Philadelphia, Pa.	2,124,957	Frank P. Conley	E.P. Archer
1544	10¢	"We ask but for peace . . ."	July 4, 1974	BEP	Philadelphia, Pa.	2,124,957	Frank P. Conley	E.P. Archer
1545	10¢	"Deriving their just powers . . ."	July 4, 1974	BEP	Philadelphia, Pa.	2,124,957	Frank P. Conley	E.P. Archer
1546	10¢	Independence Hall	July 4, 1974	BEP	Philadelphia, Pa.	2,124,957	Frank P. Conley	E.P. Archer
1547	10¢	Molecules and Drops	Sept. 23, 1974	BEP	Detroit, Mich.	587,210	Robert W. Bode	H.F. Sharpless

Scott number	Denom.	Design	First day of issue	Printer	First-day city	First-day quantities	Designer	Engraver
		of Gasoline and Oil						
1548	10¢	Headless Horseman and Ichabod Crane	Oct. 10, 1974	BEP	Tarrytown, N.Y.	514,836	Leonard E. Fisher	J.S. Wallace
1549	10¢	Retarded Child	Oct. 12, 1974	BEP	Arlington, Texas	412,882	Paul Calle	J.S. Creamer, Jr.
1550	10¢	Angel	Oct. 23, 1974	BEP	New York, N.Y.	634,990	Bradbury Thompson	
1551	10¢	"The Road-Winter" by Currier and Ives	Oct. 23, 1974	BEP	New York, N.Y.	634,990	Stevan Dohanos	
1552	10¢	Dove Weather Vane atop Mount Vernon	Nov. 15, 1974	BEP	New York, N.Y.	477,410	Don Hedin	
1553	10¢	Benjamin West, Self-portrait	Feb. 10, 1975	BEP	Swathmore, Pa.	465,017	Bradbury Thompson	
1554	10¢	Paul Laurence Dunbar	May 1, 1974	BEP	Dayton, Ohio	397,347	Walter D. Richards	
1555	10¢	David Lewelyn Griffith	May 27, 1975	BEP	Beverly Hills, Calif.	424,167	Fred Otnes	E.P. Archer
1556	10¢	Pioneer 10 Passing Jupiter	Feb. 28, 1975	BEP	Mountain View, Calif.	594,896	Robert McCall	E.P. Archer
1557	10¢	Mariner 10, Venus and Mercury	April 4, 1975	BEP	Pasadena, Calif.	563,636	Roy Gjertson	J.S. Wallace
1558	10¢	"Labor and Management"	March 13, 1975	BEP	Washington, D.C.	412,329	Robert Hallock	
1559	8¢	Sybil Ludington	March 25, 1975	BEP	Carmel, N.Y.	394,550	Neil Boyle	
1560	10¢	Salem Poor	March 25, 1975	BEP	Cambridge, Mass.	415,565	Neil Boyle	
1561	10¢	Haym Salomon	March 25, 1975	BEP	Chicago, Ill.	442,630	Neil Boyle	
1562	18¢	Peter Francisco	Feb. 25, 1975	BEP	Greensboro, N.C.	415,000	Neil Boyle	
1563	10¢	"Birth of Liberty" by Henry Sandham	April 19, 1975	BEP	Lexington, Mass.	975,020	Bradbury Thompson	
1564	10¢	Battle of Bunker Hill by John Trumbull	June 17, 1975	BEP	Charlestown, Mass.	557,130	Bradbury Thompson	
1565	10¢	Soldier with Flintlock Musket, Uniform Button	July 4, 1975	BEP	Washington, D.C.	1,134,831	Edward Vebell	
1566	10¢	Soldier with Grappling Hook, First Navy Jacket, 1775	July 4, 1975	BEP	Washington, D.C.	1,134,831	Edward Vebell	
1567	10¢	Marine with Musket,	July 4, 1975	BEP	Washington, D.C.	1,134,831	Edward Vebell	

Scott number	Denom.	Design	First day of issue	Printer	First-day city	First-day quantities	Designer	Engraver
		Full-rigged Ship						
1568	10¢	Militiaman with Musket and Powder Horn	July 4, 1974	BEP	Washington, D.C.	1,134,831	Edward Vebell	
1569	10¢	Apollo and Soyuz after Link-up, and Earth	July 15, 1975	BEP	Kennedy Space Center, Fla.	1,427,046	Robert McCall	
1570	10¢	Spacecraft before Link-up, Earth and Project Emblem	July 15, 1975	BEP	Kennedy Space Center, Fla.	1,427,046	Anatoly M. Aksamit	
1571	10¢	Worldwide Equality For Women	Aug. 26, 1975	BEP	Seneca Falls, N.Y.	476,769	Miriam Schottland	
1572	10¢	Stagecoach and Trailer Truck	Sept. 3, 1975	BEP	Philadelphia, Pa.	969,999	James L. Womer	
1573	10¢	Old and New Locomotives	Sept. 3, 1975	BEP	Philadelphia, Pa.	969,999	James L. Womer	
1574	10¢	Early Mail Plane and Jet	Sept. 3, 1975	BEP	Philadelphia, Pa.	969,999	James L. Womer	
1575	10¢	Satellite for Transmission of Mailgrams	Sept. 3, 1975	BEP	Philadelphia, Pa.	969,999	James L. Womer	
1576	10¢	Law Book, Gavel, Olive Branch and Globe	Sept. 29, 1975	BEP	Washington, D.C.	386,736	Melbourne Brindle	
1577	10¢	Engine-Turning and Coins	Oct. 6, 1975	BEP	New York, N.Y.	555,580	V.J. Ruther	J.S. Wallace
1578	10¢	Engine-Turning and Coins	Oct. 6, 1975	BEP	New York, N.Y.	555,580	V.J. Ruther	J.S. Wallace
1579	10¢	"Madonna and Child" by Domenico Ghirlandaio	Oct. 14, 1975	BEP	Washington, D.C.	730,079	Stevan Dohanos	
1580	10¢	Christmas Card by Louis Prang, 1878	Oct. 14, 1975	BEP	Washington, D.C.	730,079	Stevan Dohanos	
1581	1¢	Inkwell and Quill	Dec. 8, 1977	BEP	St. Louis, Mo.	530,033	Kramer, Miller Lomden and Glassman	A. Saavedra
1582	2¢	Speaker's Stand	Dec. 8, 1977	BEP	St. Louis, Mo.	530,033	V.J. Ruther	J.S. Creamer, Jr.
1583	3¢	Early Ballot Box	Dec. 8, 1977	BEP			Clarence Holbert	J. L. Goodbody

Scott number	Denom.	Design	First day of issue	Printer	First-day city	First-day quantities	Designer	Engraver
1584	4¢	Books, Bookmark, Eyeglasses	Dec. 8, 1977	BEP	St. Louis, Mo.	530,033	V.J. Ruther	J. L. Goodbody
1590	9¢	Dome of Capitol	March 11, 1977	BEP	New York, N.Y.		Walter Brooks	K. Kipperman
1591	9¢	Dome of Capitol	Nov. 24, 1975	BEP	Washington, D.C.	190,117	Walter Brooks	K. Kipperman
1592	10¢	Contemplation of Justice by J.E. Fraser	Nov. 17, 1977	BEP	New York, N.Y.	359,050	Walter Brooks	K. Kipperman
1593	11¢	Early American Printing Press	Nov. 13, 1977	BEP	Philadelphia, Pa.	217,755		
1594	12¢	Torch, Statue of Liberty	April 8, 1981	BEP	Dallas, Texas	280,930		
1595	13¢	Liberty Bell	Oct. 31, 1975	BEP	Cleveland, Ohio	256,734		
1596	13¢	Eagle and Shield	Dec. 1, 1975	BEP	Juneau, Alaska	418,272		
1597	15¢	Fort McKenry Flag	June 30, 1978	BEP	Baltimore, Md.	315,359	V.J. Ruther	T.R. Hipschen
1598	15¢	Fort McHenry Flag	June 30, 1978	BEP	Baltimore, Md.	315,359	V.J. Ruther	T.R. Hipschen
1599	16¢	Head, Statue of Liberty	March 31, 1978	BEP	New York, N.Y.	376,338		
1603	24¢	Old North Church	Nov. 14, 1975	BEP	Boston, Mass.	208,973		
1604	28¢	Fort Nisqually	Aug. 11, 1978	BEP	Tacoma, Wash.	159,639	James Schleyer	J.S. Creamer, Jr.
1605	29¢	Sandy Hook Lighthouse, N.J.	April 14, 1978	BEP	Atlantic City, N.J.	193,476		
1606	30¢	Morris Township School No. 2, Devils Lake	Aug. 27, 1979	BEP	Devils Lake, N.D.	186,882		
1608	50¢	Iron "Betty" Lamp, Plymouth Colony, 17th-18th Centuries	Sept. 11, 1979	BEP	San Juan, P.R.	159,540		
1610	$1	Rush Lamp and Candle Holder	July 2, 1979	BEP	San Francisco	255,575		
1611	$2	Kerosene Table Lamp	Nov. 16, 1978	BEP	New York, N.Y.	173,596	James Schleyer	J.S. Creamer, Jr.
1612	$5	Railroad Conductor's Lantern, c. 1850	Aug. 23, 1979	BEP	Boston, Mass.	129,192		
1613	3¢	Six-string Guitar	Oct. 25, 1979	BEP	Shreveport, La.	230,403	George Mercer	
1614	8¢	Saxhorns	Nov. 20, 1976	BEP	New York, N.Y.	285,290	Susan Robb	
1615	8¢	Drum	April 23, 1976	BEP	Miami, Fla.	192,270	Bernard Glassman	
1615C	8¢	Steinway Grand Piano, 1857	July 13, 1978	BEP	Interlochen, Mich.	200,392	V.J. Ruther	G.M. Chaconas
1616	9¢	Dome of Capitol	March 5, 1976	BEP	Milwaukee, Wis.	128,171	Walter Brooks	K. Kipperman

Scott number	Denom.	Design	First day of issue	Printer	First-day city	First-day quantities	Designer	Engraver
1617	10¢	Contemplation of Justice by J.E. Fraser	March 5, 1976	BEP	Tampa, Fla.	184,954		
1618	13¢	Liberty Bell	Nov. 25, 1975	BEP	Allentown, Pa.	320,387	Bernard Glassman	E.P. Archer
1618C	15¢	Fort McHenry Flag	June 30, 1978	BEP	Boston, Mass.		V.J. Ruther	T.R. Hipschen
1619	16¢	Head, Statue of Liberty	March 31, 1978	BEP	New York, N.Y.	376,338		
1622	13¢	13-Star Flag Over Independence Hall	Nov. 15, 1975	BEP	Philadelphia, Pa.	362,959	Melbourne Brindle	
1623	13¢	Flag Over Capitol	March 11, 1977	BEP	New York, N.Y.	242,208	Esther Porter	
1625	13¢	13-Star Flag Over Independence Hall	Nov. 15, 1975	BEP	Philadelphia, Pa.	362,959	Esther Porter	
1629	13¢	Drummer Boy	Jan. 1, 1976	BEP	Pasadena, Calif.	1,013,067	Vincent E. Hoffman	G.M. Chaconas
1630	13¢	Old Drummer	Jan. 1, 1976	BEP	Pasadena, Calif.	1,013,067	Vincent E. Hoffman	G.M. Chaconas
1631	13¢	Fifer	Jan. 1, 1976	BEP	Pasadena, Calif.	1,013,067	Vincent E. Hoffman	G.M. Chaconas
1632	13¢	"Interphil 76"	Jan. 17, 1976	BEP	Philadelphia, Pa.	519,902	T.W. McCaffrey	A. Saavedra
1633	13¢	Flag of Deleware	Feb. 23, 1976	BEP	Washington, D.C.		Walt Reed	
1634	13¢	Flag of Pennsylvania	Feb. 23, 1976	BEP	Washington, D.C.		Walt Reed	
1635	13¢	Flag of New Jersey	Feb. 23, 1976	BEP	Washington, D.C.		Walt Reed	
1636	13¢	Flag of Georgia	Feb. 23, 1976	BEP	Washington, D.C.		Walt Reed	
1637	13¢	Flag of Connecticut	Feb. 23, 1976	BEP	Washington, D.C.		Walt Reed	
1638	13¢	Flag of Massachusetts	Feb. 23, 1976	BEP	Washington, D.C.		Walt Reed	
1639	13¢	Flag of Maryland	Feb. 23, 1976	BEP	Washington, D.C.		Walt Reed	
1640	13¢	Flag of South Carolina	Feb. 23, 1976	BEP	Washington, D.C.		Walt Reed	
1641	13¢	Flag of New Hampshire	Feb. 23, 1976	BEP	Washington, D.C.		Walt Reed	
1642	13¢	Flag of Virginia	Feb. 23, 1976	BEP	Washington, D.C.		Walt Reed	
1643	13¢	Flag of New York	Feb. 23, 1976	BEP	Washington, D.C.		Walt Reed	
1644	13¢	Flag of North Carolina	Feb. 23, 1976	BEP	Washington, D.C.		Walt Reed	
1645	13¢	Flag of Rhode Island	Feb. 23, 1976	BEP	Washington, D.C.		Walt Reed	
1646	13¢	Flag of Vermont	Feb. 23, 1976	BEP	Washington, D.C.		Walt Reed	
1647	13¢	Flag of Kentucky	Feb. 23, 1976	BEP	Washington, D.C.		Walt Reed	
1648	13¢	Flag of Tennessee	Feb. 23, 1976	BEP	Washington, D.C.		Walt Reed	
1649	13¢	Flag of Ohio	Feb. 23, 1976	BEP	Washington, D.C.		Walt Reed	
1650	13¢	Flag of Louisiana	Feb. 23, 1976	BEP	Washington, D.C.		Walt Reed	
1651	13¢	Flag of Indiana	Feb. 23, 1976	BEP	Washington, D.C.		Walt Reed	
1652	13¢	Flag of Mississippi	Feb. 23, 1976	BEP	Washington, D.C.		Walt Reed	

Scott number	Denom.	Design	First day of issue	Printer	First-day city	First-day quantities	Designer	Engraver
1653	13¢	Flag of Illinois	Feb. 23, 1976	BEP	Washington, D.C.		Walt Reed	
1654	13¢	Flag of Alabama	Feb. 23, 1976	BEP	Washington, D.C.		Walt Reed	
1655	13¢	Flag of Maine	Feb. 23, 1976	BEP	Washington, D.C.		Walt Reed	
1656	13¢	Flag of Missouri	Feb. 23, 1976	BEP	Washington, D.C.		Walt Reed	
1657	13¢	Flag of Arkansas	Feb. 23, 1976	BEP	Washington, D.C.		Walt Reed	
1658	13¢	Flag of Michigan	Feb. 23, 1976	BEP	Washington, D.C.		Walt Reed	
1659	13¢	Flag of Florida	Feb. 23, 1976	BEP	Washington, D.C.		Walt Reed	
1660	13¢	Flag of Texas	Feb. 23, 1976	BEP	Washington, D.C.		Walt Reed	
1661	13¢	Flag of Iowa	Feb. 23, 1976	BEP	Washington, D.C.		Walt Reed	
1662	13¢	Flag of Wisconsin	Feb. 23, 1976	BEP	Washington, D.C.		Walt Reed	
1663	13¢	Flag of California	Feb. 23, 1976	BEP	Washington, D.C.		Walt Reed	
1664	13¢	Flag of Minnesota	Feb. 23, 1976	BEP	Washington, D.C.		Walt Reed	
1665	13¢	Flag of Oregon	Feb. 23, 1976	BEP	Washington, D.C.		Walt Reed	
1666	13¢	Flag of Kansas	Feb. 23, 1976	BEP	Washington, D.C.		Walt Reed	
1667	13¢	Flag of West Virginia	Feb. 23, 1976	BEP	Washington, D.C.		Walt Reed	
1668	13¢	Flag of Nevada	Feb. 23, 1976	BEP	Washington, D.C.		Walt Reed	
1669	13¢	Flag of Nebraska	Feb. 23, 1976	BEP	Washington, D.C.		Walt Reed	
1670	13¢	Flag of Colorado	Feb. 23, 1976	BEP	Washington, D.C.		Walt Reed	
1671	13¢	Flag of North Dakota	Feb. 23, 1976	BEP	Washington, D.C.		Walt Reed	
1672	13¢	Flag of South Dakota	Feb. 23, 1976	BEP	Washington, D.C.		Walt Reed	
1673	13¢	Flag of Montana	Feb. 23, 1976	BEP	Washington, D.C.		Walt Reed	
1674	13¢	Flag of Washington	Feb. 23, 1976	BEP	Washington, D.C.		Walt Reed	
1675	13¢	Flag of Idaho	Feb. 23, 1976	BEP	Washington, D.C.		Walt Reed	
1676	13¢	Flag of Wyoming	Feb. 23, 1976	BEP	Washington, D.C.		Walt Reed	
1677	13¢	Flag of Utah	Feb. 23, 1976	BEP	Washington, D.C.		Walt Reed	
1678	13¢	Flag of Oklahoma	Feb. 23, 1976	BEP	Washington, D.C.		Walt Reed	
1679	13¢	Flag of New Mexico	Feb. 23, 1976	BEP	Washington, D.C.		Walt Reed	
1680	13¢	Flag of Arizona	Feb. 23, 1976	BEP	Washington, D.C.		Walt Reed	
1681	13¢	Flag of Alaska	Feb. 23, 1976	BEP	Washington, D.C.		Walt Reed	
1682	13¢	Flag of Hawaii	Feb. 23, 1976	BEP	Washington, D.C.		Walt Reed	
1683	13¢	Ford-Pullman Monoplane and Laird Swallow Biplane	March 19, 1976	BEP	Chicago, Ill.	631,555	Robert E. Cunningham	
1684	13¢	Bell's Telephone	March 10, 1976	BEP	Boston, Mass.	662,215	George Tscherny	J.S. Wallace, Jr.

Scott number	Denom.	Design	First day of issue	Printer	First-day city	First-day quantities	Designer	Engraver
		Patent Application, 1876						
1685	13¢	Various Flasks, Separatory Funnel, Computer Tape	April 6, 1976	BEP	New York, N.Y.	557,600	Ken Davies	
1686	13¢	Surrender of Cornwallis at Yorktown by John Trumbull	May 23, 1976	BEP	Philadelphia, Pa.	879,890	Vincent E. Hoffman	R.G. Culin
1687	18¢	Declaration of Independence by John Trumbull	May 29, 1976	BEP	Philadelphia, Pa.	879,890	Vincent E. Hoffman	R.G. Culin
1688	24¢	Washington Crossing the Delaware by Emmanuel Leutze/ Eastman Johnson	May 29, 1976	BEP	Philadelphia, Pa.	879,890	Vincent E. Hoffman	R.G. Culin
1689	31¢	Washington Reviewing the Army at Valley Forge by William T. Trego	May 29, 1976	BEP	Philadelphia, Pa.	879,890	Vincent E. Hoffman	R.G. Culin
1690	13¢	Franklin and Map of North America	June 1, 1976	BEP	Philadelphia, Pa.	588,740	Bernard Reilander	J.S. Creamer, Jr.
1691	13¢	Signing of the Declaration of Independence	July 4, 1976	BEP	Philadelphia, Pa.	2,093,880	Vincent E. Hoffman	
1692	13¢	Signing of the Declaration of Independence	July 4, 1976	BEP	Philadelphia, Pa.	2,093,880	Vincent E. Hoffman	
1693	13¢	Signing of the Declaration of Independence	July 4, 1976	BEP	Philadelphia, Pa.	2,093,880	Vincent E. Hoffman	
1694	13¢	Signing of the Declaration of Independence	July 4, 1976	BEP	Philadelphia, Pa.	2,093,880	Vincent E. Hoffman	
1695	13¢	Olympic Games Diving	July 16, 1976	BEP	Lake Placid, N.Y.	1,140,189	Donald Moss	

Scott number	Denom.	Design	First day of issue	Printer	First-day city	First-day quantities	Designer	Engraver
1696	13¢	Olympic Games Skiing	July 16, 1976	BEP	Lake Placid, N.Y.	1,140,189	Donald Moss	
1697	13¢	Olympic Games Running	July 16, 1976	BEP	Lake Placid, N.Y.	1,140,189	Donald Moss	
1698	13¢	Olympic Games Skating	July 16, 1976	BEP	Lake Placid, N.Y.	1,140,189	Donald Moss	
1699	13¢	Clara Maass and Newark German Hospital Pin	Aug. 18, 1976	BEP	Belleville, N.J.	646,506	Paul Calle	
1700	13¢	Adolph S. Ochs	Sept. 18, 1976	BEP	New York, N.Y.	582,580	Bradbury Thompson	
1701	13¢	"Nativity" by John Singleton Copley	Oct. 27, 1976	BEP	Boston, Mass.	540,050	Bradbury Thompson	
1702	13¢	"Winter Pastime" by Nathaniel Currier	Oct. 27, 1976	BEP	Boston, Mass.	181,410	Stevan Dohanos	
1703	13¢	"Winter Pastime" by Nathaniel Currier	Oct. 27, 1976	BEP	Boston, Mass.	330,450	Stevan Dohanos	
1704	13¢	Washington, Nassau Hall, Hessian Prisoners and 13-Star Flag by Peale	Jan. 3, 1977	BEP	Princeton, N.J.	695,335	Bradbury Thompson	
1705	13¢	Tin Foil Phonograph	March 23, 1977	BEP	Washington, D.C.	632,216	Walter and Naiad Einsel	
1706	13¢	Zia Pot	April 13, 1977	BEP	Santa Fe, N.M.	1,194,554	Ford Ruthling	
1707	13¢	San Ildefonso Pot	April 13, 1977	BEP	Santa Fe, N.M.	1,194,554	Ford Ruthling	
1708	13¢	Hopi Pot	April 13, 1977	BEP	Santa Fe, N.M.	1,194,554	Ford Ruthling	
1709	13¢	Acoma Pot	April 13, 1977	BEP	Santa Fe, N.M.	1,194,554	Ford Ruthling	
1710	13¢	Spirit of St. Louis	May 20, 1977	BEP	Roosevelt Sta., N.Y.	3,985,989	Robert E. Cunningham	
1711	13¢	Columbine and Rocky Mountains	May 21, 1977	BEP	Denver, Colo.	510,880	V. Jack Ruther	
1712	13¢	Swallowtail Butterfly	June 6, 1977	BEP	Indianapolis, Ind.	1,218,568	Stanley Galli	
1713	13¢	Checkerspot Butterfly	June 6, 1977	BEP	Indianapolis, Ind.	1,218,568	Stanley Galli	
1714	13¢	Dogface Butterfly	June 6, 1977	BEP	Indianapolis, Ind.	1,218,568	Stanley Galli	
1715	13¢	Orange Tip Butterfly	June 6, 1977	BEP	Indianapolis, Ind.	1,218,568	Stanley Galli	
1716	13¢	Marquis de Lafayette	June 13, 1977	BEP	Charleston, S.C.	514,506	Bradbury Thompson	
1717	13¢	Seamstress	July 4, 1977	BEP	Cincinnati, Ohio	1,263,568	Leonard E. Fisher	
1718	13¢	Blacksmith	July 4, 1977	BEP	Cincinnati, Ohio	1,263,568	Leonard E. Fisher	

Scott number	Denom.	Design	First day of issue	Printer	First-day city	First-day quantities	Designer	Engraver
1719	13¢	Wheelwright	July 4, 1977	BEP	Cincinnati, Ohio	1,263,568	Leonard E. Fisher	
1720	13¢	Leatherworker	July 4, 1977	BEP	Cincinnati, Ohio	1,263,568	Leonard E. Fisher	
1721	12¢	Peace Bridge and Dove	Aug. 4, 1977	BEP	Buffalo, N.Y.	512,995	Bernard Brussel-Smith	
1722	13¢	Herkimer at Oriskany by Fredrick Yohn	Aug. 6, 1977	BEP	Utica, N.Y.	605,906	Bradbury Thompson	
1723	13¢	Energy Conservation	Oct. 20, 1977	BEP	Washington, D.C.	410,299	T.W. McCaffrey	
1724	13¢	Energy Development	Oct. 20, 1977	BEP	Washington, D.C.	410,299	T.W. McCaffrey	
1725	13¢	Farm Houses, Alta California	Sept. 9, 1977	BEP	San Jose, Calif.	709,457	Earl Thollander	
1726	13¢	Members of Continental Congress in Conference	Sept. 30, 1977	BEP	York, Pa.	605,455	David Blossom	T.R. Hipschen
1727	13¢	Movie Projector and Phonograph	Oct. 6, 1977	BEP	Hollywood, Calif.	570,195	Walter Einsel	A. Saavedra
1728	13¢	"Surrender of Burgoyne" by John Trumbull	Oct. 7, 1977	BEP	Schuylerville, N.Y.	557,529	Bradbury Thompson	
1729	13¢	Washington at Valley Forge	Oct. 21, 1977	BEP	Valley Forge, Pa.	583,139	Stevan Dohanos	
1730	13¢	Rural Mailbox	Oct. 21, 1977	BEP	Omaha, Neb.	675,786	Don Tingle	
1731	13¢	Carl Sandburg by William A. Smith	Jan. 6, 1978	BEP	Galesburg, Ill.	493,826	William A. Smith	
1732	13¢	Capt. Cook by Nathaniel Dance	Jan. 20, 1978	BEP	Honolulu, Hawaii	1,496,659		
1733	13¢	*Resolution* and *Discovery* by John Webber	Jan. 20, 1978	BEP	Honolulu, Hawaii	1,496,659		
1734	13¢	Indian Head Penny	Jan. 11, 1978	BEP	Kansas City, Mo.	512,426		
1735	15¢	Eagle	May 22, 1978	BEP	Memphis, Tenn.	689,049		
1736	15¢	Eagle	May 22, 1978	BEP	Shreveport, La.	445,003		
1737	15¢	Red Masterpiece Medallion Roses	July 11, 1978	BEP	Memphis, Tenn.	689,049		
1738	15¢	Windmill	Feb. 7, 1980	BEP	Lubock, Texas	708,411	Ronald Sharpe	
1739	15¢	Windmill	Feb. 7, 1980	BEP	Lubock, Texas	708,411	Ronald Sharpe	
1740	15¢	Windmill	Feb. 7, 1980	BEP	Lubock, Texas	708,411	Ronald Sharpe	
1741	15¢	Windmill	Feb. 7, 1980	BEP	Lubock, Texas	708,411	Ronald Sharpe	

Scott number	Denom.	Design	First day of issue	Printer	First-day city	First-day quantities	Designer	Engraver
1742	15¢	Windmill	Feb. 7, 1980	BEP	Lubock, Texas	708,411	Ronald Sharpe	
1743	15¢	Eagle	May 22, 1978	BEP	Memphis, Tenn.	689,049		
1744	13¢	Harriet Tubman and Cart Carrying Slaves	Feb. 1, 1978	BEP	Washington, D.C.	493,495	Jerry Pinkney	
1745	13¢	Quilt	March 8, 1978	BEP	Charleston, W.Va.	1,081,827	Christopher Pullman	
1746	13¢	Quilt	March 8, 1978	BEP	Charleston, W.Va.	1,081,827	Christopher Pullman	
1747	13¢	Quilt	March 8, 1978	BEP	Charleston, W.Va.	1,081,827	Christopher Pullman	
1748	13¢	Quilt	March 8, 1978	BEP	Charleston, W.Va.	1,081,827	Christopher Pullman	
1749	13¢	Ballet	April 26, 1978	BEP	New York, N.Y.	1,626,493	John Hill	
1750	13¢	Theater	April 26, 1978	BEP	New York, N.Y.	1,626,493	John Hill	
1751	13¢	Folk Dance	April 26, 1978	BEP	New York, N.Y.	1,626,493	John Hill	
1752	13¢	Modern Dance	April 26, 1978	BEP	New York, N.Y.	1,626,493	John Hill	
1753	13¢	King Louis XVI and Benjamin Franklin	May 4, 1978	BEP	York, Pa.	705,240	Bradbury Thompson	
1754	13¢	Dr. Papnicolaou, His Signature and Microscope	May 13, 1978	BEP	Washington, D.C.	535,584	Paul Calle	
1755	13¢	Jimmie Rodgers with Guitar, Brakeman's Cap and Locomotive	May 24, 1978	BEP	Meridian, Miss.	599,287	Jim Sharpe	
1756	15¢	George M. Cohan, "Yankee Doodle Dandy" and Stars	July 3, 1978	BEP	Providence, R.I.	740,750	Jim Sharpe	
1757	13¢	Wildlife from Canadian-United States Border	June 10, 1978	BEP	Toronto, Canada	1,994,067	Stanley Galli	
1758	15¢	Camera, Lens, Color Filters, Adapter Ring, Studio Light Bulb and Album	June 26, 1978	BEP	Las Vegas, Nev.	684,987	Ben Somoroff	
1759	15¢	Viking 1 Lander Scooping Soil on Mars	July 20, 1978	BEP	Hampton, Va.	805,987	Robert McCall	E.P. Archer
1760	15¢	Great Gray Owl	Aug. 26, 1978	BEP	Fairbanks, Alaska	1,690,474	Frank H. Waslick	J.S. Creamer, Jr.

Scott number	Denom.	Design	First day of issue	Printer	First-day city	First-day quantities	Designer	Engraver
1761	15¢	Saw-whet Owl	Aug. 26, 1978	BEP	Fairbanks, Alaska	1,690,474	Frank J. Waslick	J.S. Creamer, Jr.
1762	15¢	Barred Owl	Aug. 26, 1978	BEP	Fairbanks, Alaska	1,690,474	Frank J. Waslick	J.S. Creamer, Jr.
1763	15¢	Great Horned Owl	Aug. 26, 1978	BEP	Fairbanks, Alaska	1,690,474	Frank J. Waslick	J.S. Creamer, Jr.
1764	15¢	Giant Sequoia	Oct. 9, 1978	BEP	Hot Springs National Park, Ark.	1,139,100	Walter D. Richards	
1765	15¢	White Pine	Oct. 9, 1978	BEP	Hot Springs National Park,Ark.	1,139,100	Walter D. Richards	
1766	15¢	White Oak	Oct. 9, 1978	BEP	Hot Springs National Park, Ark.	1,139,100	Walter D. Richards	
1767	15¢	Gray Birch	Oct. 9, 1978	BEP	Hot Springs National Park, Ark.	1,139,100	Walter D. Richards	
1768	15¢	"Madonna and Child with Cherubim" by Andrea Dell Tobbia	Oct. 18, 1978	BEP	Washington, D.C.	533,064	Bradbury Thompson	
1769	15¢	Child on Hobby Horse and Christmas Tree	Oct. 18, 1978	BEP	Holly, Mich.	603,008	Dolli Tingle	
1770	15¢	Robert F. Kennedy	Jan. 12, 1979	BEP	Washington, D.C.	624,582	Stanley Tretick	T.R. Hipschen
1771	15¢	Martin Luther King, Jr. and Civil Rights Marchers	Jan. 13, 1979	BEP	Atlanta, Ga.	726,149	Jerry Pinkney	
1772	15¢	Children of Different Races	Feb. 15, 1979	BEP	Philadelphia, Pa.	716,149	Paul Calle	J.S. Creamer, Jr.
1773	15¢	John Steinbeck	Feb. 27, 1979	BEP	Salinas, Calif.	709,073	Bradbury Thompson	T.R. Hipschen
1774	15¢	Albert Einstein	March 4, 1979	BEP	Princeton, N.J.	641,423	Bradbury Thompson	J.S. Wallace, Jr.
1775	15¢	Coffeepot	March 19, 1979	BEP	Lancaster, Pa.	1,581,962	Bradbury Thompson	
1776	15¢	Tea Caddy	April 19, 1979	BEP	Lancaster, Pa.	1,581,962	Bradbury Thompson	
1777	15¢	Sugar Bowl	April 19, 1979	BEP	Lancaster, Pa.	1,581,962	Bradbury Thompson	
1778	15¢	Coffeepot	April 19, 1979	BEP	Lancaster, Pa.	1,581,962	Bradbury Thompson	
1779	15¢	Virginia Rotunda by Thomas Jefferson	June 4, 1979	BEP	Kansas City, Mo.	1,219,258	Walter D. Richards	
1780	15¢	Baltimore Cathedral by Benjamin Latrobe	June 4, 1979	BEP	Kansas City, Mo.	1,219,258	Walter D. Richards	
1781	15¢	Boston State House by Charles Bulfinch	June 4, 1979	BEP	Kansas City, Mo.	1,219,258	Walter D. Richards	

Scott number	Denom.	Design	First day of issue	Printer	First-day city	First-day quantities	Designer	Engraver
1782	15¢	Philadelphia Exchange by William Strickland	June 4, 1979	BEP	Kansas City, Mo.	1,219,258	Walter D. Richards	
1783	15¢	Persistent Trillium	June 7, 1979	BEP	Milwaukee, Wis.	1,436,268	Frank J. Waslick	
1784	15¢	Hawaiian Wild Broadbeak	June 7, 1979	BEP	Milwaukee, Wis.	1,436,268	Frank J. Waslick	
1785	15¢	Contra Costa Wallflower	June 7, 1979	BEP	Milwaukee, Wis.	1,436,268	Frank J. Waslick	
1786	15¢	Antioch Dunes Evening Primrose	June 7, 1979	BEP	Milwaukee, Wis.	1,436,268	Frank J. Waslick	
1787	15¢	German Shepherd Leading Man	June 15, 1979	BEP	Morristown, N.J.	588,826	Joseph Csatari	
1788	15¢	Child Holding Winner's Medal	Aug. 9, 1979	BEP	Brockport, N.Y.	651,344	Jeff Cornell	
1789	15¢	John Paul Jones by Charles Wilson Peale	Sept. 23, 1979	BEP	Annapolis, Md.	587,018	Bradbury Thompson	
1790	10¢	Decathlon, Javelin	Sept. 5, 1979	BEP	Olympia, Wash.	305,122	Robert M. Cunningham	
1791	15¢	Running	Sept. 28, 1979	BEP	Los Angeles, Calif.	1,561,366	Robert M. Cunningham	
1792	15¢	Swimming	Sept. 28, 1979	BEP	Los Angeles, Calif.	1,561,366	Robert M. Cunningham	
1793	15¢	Rowing	Sept. 28, 1979	BEP	Los Angeles, Calif.	1,561,366	Robert M. Cunningham	
1794	15¢	Equestrian	Sept. 28, 1979	BEP	Los Angeles, Calif.	1,561,366	Robert M. Cunningham	
1795	15¢	Speed Skating	Feb. 1, 1980	BEP	Lake Placid, N.Y.	1,166,302	Robert M. Cunningham	
1796	15¢	Downhill Skiing	Feb. 1, 1980	BEP	Lake Placid, N.Y.	1,166,302	Robert M. Cunningham	
1797	15¢	Ski Jump	Feb. 1, 1980	BEP	Lake Placid, N.Y.	1,166,302	Robert M. Cunningham	
1798	15¢	Hockey Goaltender	Feb. 1, 1980	BEP	Lake Placid, N.Y.	1,166,302	Robert M. Cunningham	
1799	15¢	"Virgin and Child" by Gerard David	Oct. 18, 1979	BEP	Washington, D.C.	686,990	Bradbury Thompson	
1800	15¢	Santa Claus, Christmas Tree Ornament	Oct. 18, 1979	BEP	North Pole, Alaska	511,829	Eskil Ohlsson	
1801	15¢	Will Rogers	Nov. 4, 1979	BEP	Claremore, Okla.	1,643,151	Jim Sharpe	
1802	15¢	Ribbon for Vietnam Service Medal	Nov. 11, 1979	BEP	Washington, D.C.	445,934	Stevan Dohanos	
1803	15¢	W.C. Fields	Jan. 29, 1980	BEP	Beverly Hills, Calif.	633,303	Jim Sharpe	
1804	15¢	Benjamin Banneker	Feb. 15, 1980	BEP	Annapolis, Md.	647,126	Jerry Pinkney	
1805	15¢	Letters Preserve Memories	Feb. 15, 1980	BEP	Washington, D.C.	1,083,360	Randall McDougall	

Scott number	Denom.	Design	First day of issue	Printer	First-day city	First-day quantities	Designer	Engraver
1806	15¢	P.S. Write Soon	Feb. 25, 1980	BEP	Washington, D.C.	1,083,360	Randall McDougall	
1807	15¢	Letters Lift Spirits	Feb. 25, 1980	BEP	Washington, D.C.	1,083,360	Randall McDougall	
1808	15¢	P.S. Write Soon	Feb. 25, 1980	BEP	Washington, D.C.	1,083,360	Randall McDougall	
1809	15¢	Letters Shape Opinions	Feb. 25, 1980	BEP	Washington, D.C.	1,083,360	Randall McDougall	
1810	15¢	P.S. Write Soon	Feb. 25, 1980	BEP	Washington, D.C.	1,083,360	Randall McDougall	
1811	1¢	Inkwell and Quill	March 6, 1980	BEP	New York, N.Y.	262,921	Kramer, Miller, Lomden and Glassman	A. Saavedra
1813	4¢	Weaver Violins	June 23, 1980	BEP	Williamsburg, Pa.	716,988	George Mercer	G.M. Chaconas
1816	12¢	Torch, Statue of Liberty	April 8, 1981	BEP	Dallas, Texas			
1818	18¢	Eagle	March 15, 1981	BEP	San Francisco	511,688		
1819	18¢	Eagle	March 15, 1981	BEP	San Francisco	511,688		
1820	18¢	Eagle	March 15, 1981	BEP	San Francisco	511,688		
1821	15¢	Frances Perkins	April 10, 1980	BEP	Washington, D.C.	678,966	F.R. Petrie	T.R. Hipschen
1822	15¢	Dolley Madison	May 20, 1980	BEP	Washington, D.C.	331,048	Esther Porter	J.S. Creamer, Jr.
1823	15¢	Emily Bissell	May 31, 1980	BEP	Wilmington, Del.	649,509	Stevan Dohanos	J.S. Creamer, Jr.
1824	15¢	Helen Keller and Anne Sullivan	June 27, 1980	BEP	Tuscombia, Ala.	713,061	Paul Calle	T.R. Hipschen
1825	15¢	Veterans Administration Emblem	July 21, 1980	BEP	Washington, D.C.	634,101	Malcolm Grear	
1826	15¢	Gen. Bernardo de Galvez	July 23, 1980	BEP	New Orleans, La.	658,061	Roy H. Andersen	T.R. Hipschen
1827	15¢	Brain Coral, Beaugregory Fish	Sept. 26, 1980	BEP	Charlotte Amalie, Virgin Islands	1,195,126	Chuck Ripper	
1828	15¢	Elkhorn Coral, Porkfish	Aug. 26, 1980	BEP	Charlotte Amalie, Virgin Islands	1,195,126	Chuck Ripper	
1829	15¢	Chalice Coral, Moorish Idol	Aug. 26, 1980	BEP	Charlotte Amalie, Virgin Islands	1,195,126	Chuck Ripper	
1830	15¢	Finger Coral, Sabertooth Blenny	Aug. 26, 1980	BEP	Charlotte Amalie, Virgin Islands	1,195,126	Chuck Ripper	
1831	15¢	American Bald Eagle	Sept. 1, 1980	BEP	Washington, D.C.	759,973	Peter Cocci	
1832	15¢	Edith Wharton	Sept. 5, 1980	BEP	New Haven, Conn.	633,917	Bradbury Thompson	T.R. Hipschen
1833	15¢	"Homage to the Square: Glow" by Joseph Albers	Sept. 12, 1980	BEP	Washington, D.C.	672,592	Bradbury Thompson	

Scott number	Denom.	Design	First day of issue	Printer	First-day city	First-day quantities	Designer	Engraver
1834	15¢	Heiltsuk, Bella Bella Tribe	Sept. 25, 1980	BEP	Spokane, Wash.	2,195,136	Bradbury Thompson	
1835	15¢	Chilkat Tlingit Tribe	Sept. 25, 1980	BEP	Spokane, Wash.	2,195,136	Bradbury Thompson	
1836	15¢	Tlingit Tribe Mask	Sept. 25, 1980	BEP	Spokane, Wash.	2,195,136	Bradbury Thompson	
1837	15¢	Bella Coola Tribe Mask	Sept. 25, 1980	BEP	Spokane, Wash.	2,195,136	Bradbury Thompson	
1838	15¢	Smithsonian	Oct. 9, 1980	BEP	New York, N.Y.	2,164,721	Walter D. Richards	
1839	15¢	Trinity Church	Oct. 9, 1980	BEP	New York, N.Y.	2,164,721	Walter D. Richards	
1840	15¢	Penn Academy	Oct. 9, 1980	BEP	New York, N.Y.	2,164,721	Walter D. Richards	
1841	15¢	Lyndhurst	Oct. 9, 1980	BEP	New York, N.Y.	2,164,721	Walter D. Richards	
1842	15¢	Madonna and Child	Oct. 31, 1980	BEP	Washington, D.C.	718,614	Esther Porter	
1843	15¢	Wreath and Toys	Oct. 31, 1980	BEP	Christmas, Mich.	755,108	Bob Timberlake	
1844	1¢	Dorothea Dix	Sept. 23, 1983	BEP	Hampden, Maine	164,140	Bernie Fuchs	G.M. Chaconas
1845	2¢	Igor Stravinsky	Nov. 18, 1982	BEP	New York, N.Y.	501,719	Burt Silverman	
1846	3¢	Henry Clay	July 13, 1983	BEP	Washington, D.C.	204,320	Ward Brackett	J.S. Creamer, Jr.
1847	4¢	Carl Schurz	June 3, 1983	BEP	Watertown, Wis.	165,010	Richard Sparks	T.R. Hipschen
1848	5¢	Pearl Buck	June 25, 1983	BEP	Hillsboro, W.Va.	231,852	Paul Calle	T.R. Hipschen
1849	6¢	Walter Lippmann	Sept. 19, 1985	BEP	Minneapolis, Minn.	371,990	Dennis Lyall	T.R. Hipschen
1850	7¢	Abraham Baldwin	Jan. 25, 1985	BEP	Athens, Ga.	402,285	Richard Sparks	K. Kipperman
1851	8¢	Henry Knox	July 25, 1985	BEP	Thomaston, Maine	315,937	Arthur Lidov	J.S. Wallace
1852	9¢	Sylvanus Thayer	June 7, 1985	BEP	Braintree, Mass.	345,649	Robert A. Andersen	K. Kipperman
1853	10¢	Richard Russell	May 31, 1984	BEP	Winder, Ga.	183,581	Richard Sparks	K. Kipperman
1854	11¢	Alden Partridge	Feb. 12, 1985	BEP	Northfield, Vt.	442,311	Robert A. Andersen	J.S. Wallace
1855	13¢	Crazy Horse	Jan. 15, 1982	BEP	Crazy Horse, S.D.		Brad Holland	
1856	14¢	Sinclair Lewis	March 21, 1985	BEP	Sauk Centre, Minn.	308,612	Bradbury Thompson	T.R. Hipschen
1857	17¢	Rachel Carson	May 28, 1981	BEP	Springdale, Pa.	273,686	Ward Brackett	
1858	18¢	George Mason	May 7, 1981	BEP	Gunston Hall, Va.	461,937	Richard Sparks	
1859	19¢	Sequoyah	Dec. 27, 1980	BEP	Tahlequah, Okla.	241,325	Roy H. Andersen	
1860	20¢	Ralph Bunche	Jan. 12, 1982	BEP	New York, N.Y.		Jim Sharpe	
1861	20¢	Thomas Gallaudet	June 10, 1983	BEP	West Hartford, Conn.	261,336	Christopher Calle	G.M. Chaconas
1862	20¢	Harry Truman	Jan. 26, 1984	BEP	Washington, D.C.	267,631	Dennis Lyall	T.R. Hipschen
1863	22¢	John H. Audubon	April 23, 1985	BEP	New York, N.Y.	516,249	Christopher Calle	T.R. Hipschen
1864	30¢	Frank C. Laubach	Sept. 2, 1984	BEP	Benton, Pa.	118,974	Richard Sparks	G. Chaconas
1865	35¢	Charles R. Drew	June 3, 1981	BEP	Washington, D.C.	383,882	Nathan Jones	

Scott number	Denom.	Design	First day of issue	Printer	First-day city	First-day quantities	Designer	Engraver
1866	37¢	Robert Millikan	Jan. 26, 1982	BEP	Pasadena, Calif.		Christopher Calle	
1867	39¢	Grenville Clark	May 20, 1985	BEP	Hanover, N.H.	297,797	Roy H. Andersen	G. Chaconas
1868	40¢	Lillian M. Gilbreth	Feb. 24, 1984	BEP	Montclair, N.J.	110,588	Ward Brackett	K. Kipperman
1869	50¢	Chester W. Nimitz	Feb. 22, 1985	BEP	Fredericksburg, Texas	376,166	Christopher Calle	T.R. Hipschen
1874	15¢	Everett Dirksen	Jan. 4, 1981	BEP	Pekin, Ill.	665,755	Ron Adair	
1875	15¢	Whitney Moore Young, Jr.	Jan. 30, 1981	BEP	New York, N.Y.	963,870	Jerry Pinkney	
1876	18¢	Rose	April 23, 1981	BEP	Fort Valley, Ga.	1,966,599	Lowell Nesbitt	
1877	18¢	Camellia	April 23, 1981	BEP	Fort Valley, Ga.	1,966,599	Lowell Nesbitt	
1878	18¢	Dahalia	April 23, 1981	BEP	Fort Valley, Ga.	1,966,599	Lowell Nesbitt	
1879	18¢	Lily	April 23, 1981	BEP	Fort Valley, Ga.	1,966,599	Lowell Nesbitt	
1880	18¢	Bighorn	May 14, 1981	BEP	Boise, Idaho		Jim Brandenburg	T.R. Hipschen
1881	18¢	Puma	May 14, 1981	BEP	Boise, Idaho		Jim Brandenburg	T.R. Hipschen
1882	18¢	Harbor Seal	May 14, 1981	BEP	Boise, Idaho		Jim Brandenburg	T.R. Hipschen
1883	18¢	Bison	May 14, 1981	BEP	Boise, Idaho		Jim Brandenburg	T.R. Hipschen
1884	18¢	Brown Bear	May 14, 1981	BEP	Boise, Idaho		Jim Brandenburg	T.R. Hipschen
1885	18¢	Polar Bear	May 14, 1981	BEP	Boise, Idaho		Jim Brandenburg	T.R. Hipschen
1886	18¢	Elk	May 14, 1981	BEP	Boise, Idaho		Jim Brandenburg	T.R. Hipschen
1887	18¢	Moose	May 14, 1981	BEP	Boise, Idaho		Jim Brandenburg	T.R. Hipschen
1888	18¢	White-tailed deer	May 14, 1981	BEP	Boise, Idaho		Jim Brandenburg	T.R. Hipschen
1889	18¢	Pronghorn	May 14, 1981	BEP	Boise, Idaho		Jim Brandenburg	T.R. Hipschen
1890	18¢	Flag, "For Amber Waves of Grain"	April 24, 1981	BEP	Portland, Maine	691,526	Peter Cocci	T.R. Hipschen
1891	18¢	Flag, "From Sea to Shining Sea"	April 24, 1981	BEP	Portland, Maine	691,526	Peter Cocci	T.R. Hipschen
1892	6¢	13-Star Flag	April 24, 1981	BEP	Portland, Maine	691,526	Peter Cocci	T.R. Hipschen
1893	18¢	Flag, "For Purple Mountain Majesty"	April 24, 1981	BEP	Portland, Maine	691,526	Peter Cocci	T.R. Hipschen
1894	20¢	Flag Over Supreme Court	Dec. 17, 1981	BEP	Washington, D.C.	598,169	Dean Ellis	E.P. Archer
1895	20¢	Flag Over Supreme Court	Dec. 17, 1981	BEP	Washington, D.C.	598,169	Dean Ellis	E.P. Archer
1896	20¢	Flag Over Supreme	Dec. 17, 1981	BEP	Washington, D.C.	185,543	Dean Ellis	E.P. Archer

Scott number	Denom.	Design	First day of issue	Printer	First-day city	First-day quantities	Designer	Engraver
1897	1¢	Court Omnibus	Aug. 19, 1983	BEP	Arlington, Va.	109,946	David Stone	G.M. Chaconas
1897A	2¢	Locomotive	May 29, 1982	BEP	Chicago, Ill.	290,020	David Stone	
1898	3¢	Handcar	March 25, 1983	BEP	Rochester, N.Y.	77,900	Walter Brooks	E.P. Archer
1898A	4¢	Stagecoach	Aug. 19, 1982	BEP	Milwaukee, Wis.	152,940	Jim Schleyer	
1899	5¢	Motorcycle	Oct. 10, 1983	BEP	San Francisco	188,240	Walter Brooks	K. Kipperman
1900	5¢	Sleigh	March 21, 1983	BEP	Memphis, Tenn.	141,979	Walter Brooks	E.P. Archer
1901	6¢	Bicycle	Feb. 17, 1982	BEP	Wheeling, W.Va.	814,419	David Stone	
1902	7¢	Baby Buggy	April 7, 1984	BEP	San Diego, Calif.		Jim Schleyer	K. Kipperman
1903	9¢	Mail Wagon	Dec. 15, 1981	BEP	Shreveport, La.	199,645	Jim Schleyer	G.M. Chaconas
1904	11¢	Hansom Cab	March 26, 1982	BEP	Chattanooga, Tenn.		David Stone	
1905	11¢	Railroad Caboose	Feb. 3, 1984	BEP	Chicago, Ill.	172,753	Jim Schleyer	J.S. Creamer, Jr.
1906	17¢	Electric Auto	June 25, 1981	BEP	Greenfield Village, Mich.	239,458	Chuck Jaquays	
1907	18¢	Surrey	May 18, 1981	BEP	Notch, Mo.	207,801	David Stone	
1908	20¢	Fire Pumper	Dec. 10, 1981	BEP	Alexandria, Va.	304,668	Jim Schleyer	K. Kipperman
1909	$9.35	Eagle and Moon	Aug. 12, 1983	BEP	Kennedy Space Center, Fla.	77,858		
1910	18¢	Nurse and Baby American Red Cross Centenary	May 1, 1981	BEP	Washington, D.C.	874,972	Joseph Csatari	
1911	18¢	Savings and Loan Sesquicentennial	May 8, 1981	BEP	Chicago, Ill.	740,910	Don Hedin	
1912	18¢	Exploring the Moon	May 21, 1981	BEP	Kennedy Space Center, Fla.	7,027,910	Robert McCall	
1913	18¢	Columbia Space Shuttle	May 21, 1981	BEP	Kennedy Space Center, Fla.	7,027,910	Robert McCall	
1914	18¢	Columbia Space Shuttle	May 21, 1981	BEP	Kennedy Space Center, Fla.	7,027,910	Robert McCall	
1915	18¢	Skylab	May 21, 1981	BEP	Kennedy Space Center, Fla.	7,027,910	Robert McCall	
1916	18¢	Pioneer II	May 21, 1981	BEP	Kennedy Space Center, Fla.	7,027,910	Robert McCall	
1917	18¢	Columbia Space Shuttle	May 21, 1981	BEP	Kennedy Space	7,027,910	Robert McCall	

Scott number	Denom.	Design	First day of issue	Printer	First-day city	First-day quantities	Designer	Engraver
					Center, Fla.			
1918	18¢	Columbia Space Shuttle	May 21, 1981	BEP	Kennedy Space Center, Fla.	7,027,910	Robert McCall	
1919	18¢	Space Telescope	May 21, 1981	BEP	Kennedy Space Center, Fla.	7,027,910	Robert McCall	
1920	18¢	Joseph Wharton	June 18, 1981	BEP	Philadelphia, Pa..	713,096	Rudolph de Harak	
1921	18¢	Great Blue Heron	June 26, 1981	BEP	Reno, Nev.	2,327,609	Chuck Ripper	
1922	18¢	Badger	June 26, 1981	BEP	Reno, Nev.	2,327,609	Chuck Ripper	
1923	18¢	Grizzly Bear	June 26, 1981	BEP	Reno, Nev.	2,327,609	Chuck Ripper	
1924	18¢	Ruffed Grouse	June 26, 1981	BEP	Reno, Nev.	2,327,609	Chuck Ripper	
1925	18¢	Man Using Microscope	June 29, 1981	BEP	Milford, Mich.	714,244	Martha Perske	
1926	18¢	Edna St. Vincent Millay	July 10, 1981	BEP	Austerlitz, N.Y.	725,978	Glenora C. Richards	
1927	18¢	Alcoholism	Aug. 19, 1981	BEP	Washington, D.C.	874,972	John Boyd	
1928	18¢	New York University Library by Stanford White	Aug. 28, 1981	BEP	New York, N.Y.	1,998,208	Walter D. Richards	
1929	18¢	Biltmore House by Richard Morris	Aug. 28, 1981	BEP	New York, N.Y.	1,998,208	Walter D. Richards	
1930	18¢	Palace of the Arts by Bernard Maybeck	Aug. 28, 1981	BEP	New York, N.Y.	1,998,208	Walter D. Richards	
1931	18¢	National Farmer's Bank by Louis Sullivan	June 28, 1981	BEP	New York, N.Y.	1,998,208	Walter D. Richards	
1932	18¢	Mildred Didrikson Zaharias	Sept. 22, 1981	BEP	Pinehurst, N.C.	1,231,543	Richard Gangel	
1933	18¢	Robert Tyre Jones	Sept. 22, 1981	BEP	Pinehurst, N.C.	1,231,543	Richard Gangel	
1934	18¢	Coming Through the Rye by Frederic Remington	Oct. 9, 1981	BEP	Oklahoma City, Okla.	1,367,099	Paul Calle	
1935	18¢	James Hoban Irish-American Architect of the White House	Oct. 13, 1981	BEP	Washington, D.C.	635,012	Ron Mercer	
1936	20¢	James Hoban Irish-American Architect of the White House	Oct. 13, 1981	BEP	Washington, D.C.	635,012	Ron Mercer	
1937	18¢	Battle of Yorktown	Oct. 16, 1981	BEP	Yorktown, Va.	1,098,278	Cal Sacks	

Scott number	Denom.	Design	First day of issue	Printer	First-day city	First-day quantities	Designer	Engraver
1938	18¢	Battle of the Virginia Capes	Oct. 16, 1981	BEP	Yorktown, Pa.	1,098,278	Cal Sacks	
1939	20¢	Madonna and Child by Botticelli	Oct. 28, 1981	BEP	Chicago, Ill.	481,395	Bradbury Thompson	
1940	20¢	Felt Bear on Sleigh	Oct. 28, 1981	BEP	Christmas Valley, Ore.	517,898	Naiad Einsel	
1941	20¢	John Hanson, First President of the Continental Congress	Nov. 5, 1981	BEP	Frederick, Md.	605,616	Ron Adair	
1942	20¢	Barrel Cactus	Dec. 11, 1981	BEP	Tucson, Ariz.	1,770,187	Frank J. Waslick	J.S. Creamer, Jr.
1943	20¢	Agave	Dec. 11, 1981	BEP	Tucson, Ariz.	1,770,187	Frank J. Waslick	J.S. Creamer, Jr.
1944	20¢	Beavertail Cactus	Dec. 11, 1981	BEP	Tucson, Ariz.	1,770,187	Frank J. Waslick	J.S. Creamer, Jr.
1945	20¢	Saguaro	Dec. 11, 1981	BEP	Tucson, Ariz.	1,770,187	Frank J. Waslick	J.S. Creamer, Jr.
1946	20¢	Eagle	Oct. 11, 1981	BEP	Memphis, Tenn.	304,404	Bradbury Thompson	
1947	20¢	Eagle	Oct. 11, 1981	BEP	Memphis, Tenn.	304,404	Bradbury Thompson	
1948	20¢	Eagle	Oct. 11, 1981	BEP	Memphis, Tenn.	304,404	Bradbury Thompson	
1949	20¢	Rocky Mountain Bighorn	Jan. 8, 1981	BEP	Bighorn, Mont.			
1950	20¢	Franklin D. Roosevelt	Jan. 30, 1982	BEP	Hyde Park, N.Y.		Clarence Holbert	
1951	20¢	LOVE	Feb. 1, 1982	BEP	Boston, Mass.	325,727	Mary Faulconer	
1952	20¢	George Washington	Feb. 22, 1982	BEP	Vernon, Va.		Mark English	
1953	20¢	Alabama State Bird and Flower	April 14, 1982	BEP	Washington, D.C.		Arthur and Alan Singe	
1954	20¢	Alaska State Bird and Flower	April 14, 1981	BEP	Washington, D.C.		Arthur and Alan Singe	
1955	20¢	Arizona State Bird and Flower	April 14, 1981	BEP	Washington, D.C.		Arthur and Alan Singe	
1956	20¢	Arkansas State Bird and Flower	April 14, 1982	BEP	Washington, D.C.		Arthur and Alan Singe	
1957	20¢	California State Bird and Flower	April 14, 1982	BEP	Washington, D.C.		Arthur and Alan Singe	
1958	20¢	Colorado State Bird and Flower	April 14, 1982	BEP	Washington, D.C.		Arthur and Alan Singe	
1959	20¢	Connecticut State Bird	April 14, 1982	BEP	Washington, D.C.		Arthur and Alan Singe	

Scott number	Denom.	Design	First day of issue	Printer	First-day city	First-day quantities	Designer	Engraver
		and Flower						
1960	20¢	Delaware State Bird and Flower	April 14, 1982	BEP	Washington, D.C.		Arthur and Alan Singe	
1961	20¢	Florida State Bird and Flower	April 14, 1982	BEP	Washington, D.C.		Arthur and Alan Singe	
1962	20¢	Georgia State Bird and Flower	April 14, 1982	BEP	Washington, D.C.		Arthur and Alan Singe	
1963	20¢	Hawaii State Bird and Flower	April 14, 1982	BEP	Washington, D.C.		Arthur and Alan Singe	
1964	20¢	Idaho State Bird and Flower	April 14, 1982	BEP	Washington, D.C.		Arthur and Alan Singe	
1965	20¢	Illinois State Bird and Flower	April 14, 1982	BEP	Washington, D.C.		Arthur and Alan Singe	
1966	20¢	Indiana State Bird and Flower	April 14, 1982	BEP	Washington, D.C.		Arthur and Alan Singe	
1967	20¢	Iowa State Bird and Flower	April 14, 1982	BEP	Washington, D.C.		Arthur and Alan Singe	
1968	20¢	Kansas State Bird and Flower	April 14, 1982	BEP	Washington, D.C.		Arthur and Alan Singe	
1969	20¢	Kentucky State Bird and Flower	April 14, 1982	BEP	Washington, D.C.		Arthur and Alan Singe	
1970	20¢	Louisiana State Bird and Flower	April 14, 1982	BEP	Washington, D.C.		Arthur and Alan Singe	
1971	20¢	Maine State Bird and Flower	April 14, 1982	BEP	Washington, D.C.		Arthur and Alan Singe	
1972	20¢	Maryland State Bird and Flower	April 14, 1982	BEP	Washington, D.C.		Arthur and Alan Singe	
1973	20¢	Massachusetts State Bird and Flower	April 14, 1982	BEP	Washington, D.C.		Arthur and Alan Singe	
1974	20¢	Michigan State Bird and Flower	April 14, 1982	BEP	Washington, D.C.		Arthur and Alan Singe	
1975	20¢	Minnesota State Bird and Flower	April 14, 1982	BEP	Washington, D.C.		Arthur and Alan Singe	
1976	20¢	Mississippi State	April 14, 1982	BEP	Washington, D.C.		Arthur and Alan Singe	

Scott number	Denom.	Design	First day of issue	Printer	First-day city	First-day quantities	Designer	Engraver
		Bird and Flower						
1977	20¢	Missouri State Bird and Flower	April 14, 1982	BEP	Washington, D.C.		Arthur and Alan Singe	
1978	20¢	Montana State Bird and Flower	April 14, 1982	BEP	Washington, D.C.		Arthur and Alan Singe	
1979	20¢	Nebraska State Bird and Flower	April 14, 1982	BEP	Washington, D.C.		Arthur and Alan Singe	
1980	20¢	Nevada State Bird and Flower	April 14, 1982	BEP	Washington, D.C.		Arthur and Alan Singe	
1981	20¢	New Hampshire State Bird and Flower	April 14, 1982	BEP	Washington, D.C.		Arthur and Alan Singe	
1982	20¢	New Jersey State Bird and Flower	April 14, 1982	BEP	Washington, D.C.		Arthur and Alan Singe	
1983	20¢	New Mexico State Bird and Flower	April 14, 1982	BEP	Washington, D.C.		Arthur and Alan Singe	
1984	20¢	New York State Bird and Flower	April 14, 1982	BEP	Washington, D.C.		Arthur and Alan Singe	
1985	20¢	North Carolina State Bird and Flower	April 14, 1982	BEP	Washington, D.C.		Arthur and Alan Singe	
1986	20¢	North Dakota State Bird and Flower	April 14, 1982	BEP	Washington, D.C.		Arthur and Alan Singe	
1987	20¢	Ohio State Bird and Flower	April 14, 1982	BEP	Washington, D.C.		Arthur and Alan Singe	
1988	20¢	Oklahoma State Bird and Flower	April 14, 1982	BEP	Washington, D.C.		Arthur and Alan Singe	
1989	20¢	Oregon State Bird and Flower	April 14, 1982	BEP	Washington, D.C.		Arthur and Alan Singe	
1990	20¢	Pennsylvania State Bird and Flower	April 14, 1982	BEP	Washington, D.C.		Arthur and Alan Singe	
1991	20¢	Rhode Island State Bird and Flower	April 14, 1982	BEP	Washington, D.C.		Arthur and Alan Singe	
1992	20¢	South Carolina State Bird and Flower	April 14, 1982	BEP	Washington, D.C.		Arthur and Alan Singe	
1993	20¢	South Dakota State	April 14, 1982	BEP	Washington, D.C.		Arthur and Alan Singe	

Scott number	Denom.	Design	First day of issue	Printer	First-day city	First-day quantities	Designer	Engraver
		Bird and Flower						
1994	20¢	Tennessee State Bird and Flower	April 14, 1982	BEP	Washington, D.C.		Arthur and Alan Singe	
1995	20¢	Texas State Bird and Flower	April 14, 1982	BEP	Washington, D.C.		Arthur and Alan Singe	
1996	20¢	Utah State Bird and Flower	April 14, 1982	BEP	Washington, D.C.		Arthur and Alan Singe	
1997	20¢	Vermont State Bird and Flower	April 14, 1982	BEP	Washington, D.C.		Arthur and Alan Singe	
1998	20¢	Virginia State Bird and Flower	April 14, 1982	BEP	Washington, D.C.		Arthur and Alan Singe	
1999	20¢	Washington State Bird and Flower	April 14, 1982	BEP	Washington, D.C.		Arthur and Alan Singe	
2000	20¢	West Virginia State Bird and Flower	April 14, 1982	BEP	Washington, D.C.		Arthur and Alan Singe	
2001	20¢	Wisconsin State Bird and Flower	April 14, 1982	BEP	Washington, D.C.		Arthur and Alan Singe	
2002	20¢	Wyoming State Bird and Flower	April 14, 1982	BEP	Washington, D.C.		Arthur and Alan Singe	
2003	20¢	U.S.-The Netherlands	April 20, 1982	BEP	Washington, D.C.		Heleen T. Wybrand-i-Raue	
2004	20¢	Library of Congress	April 21, 1982	BEP	Washington, D.C.		Bradbury Thompson	
2005	20¢	Consumer Education	April 27, 1982	BEP	Washington, D.C.		John Boyd	
2006	20¢	Solar Energy	April 29, 1982	BEP	Knoxville, Tenn.		Charles Harper	
2007	20¢	Synthetic Fuels	April 29, 1982	BEP	Knoxville, Tenn.		Charles Harper	
2008	20¢	Breeder Reactor	April 29, 1982	BEP	Knoxville, Tenn.		Charles Harper	
2009	20¢	Fossil Fuels	April 29, 1982	BEP	Knoxville, Tenn.		Charles Harper	
2010	20¢	Horatio Alger	April 30, 1982	BEP	Willow Grove, Pa.		Robert Hallock	
2011	20¢	Aging	May 21, 1982	BEP	Sun City, Calif.	510,677	Paul Calle	
2012	20¢	John, Lionel and Ethel Barrymore	June 8, 1982	BEP	New York, N.Y.		Jim Sharpe	
2013	20¢	Dr. Mary Walker	June 10, 1982	BEP	Oswego, N.Y.		Glenora Richards	
2014	20¢	International Peace Garden	June 30, 1982	BEP	Dunseith, N.D.			
2015	20¢	America's Libraries,	July 13, 1982	BEP	Philadelphia, Pa.		Bradbury Thompson	

Scott number	Denom.	Design	First day of issue	Printer	First-day city	First-day quantities	Designer	Engraver
		Alphabet						
2016	20¢	Jackie Robinson	Aug. 2, 1982	BEP	Cooperstown, N.Y.		Jerry Pinkney	
2017	20¢	Oldest Existing Synagogue Building in the U.S.	Aug. 22, 1982	BEP	Newport, R.I.	517,264	Donald Moss	
2018	20¢	Wolf Trap Farm Park	Sept. 1, 1982	BEP	Vienna, Va.	704,361	Richard Schlecht	
2019	20¢	Frank Lloyd Wright, Falling Water, Pa.	Sept. 30, 1982	BEP	Washington, D.C.	1,552,567	Walter D. Richards	
2020	20¢	Miles van der Rohe, Illinois Institute of Technology	Sept. 30, 1982	BEP	Washington, D.C.	1,552,567	Walter D. Richards	
2021	20¢	Walter Gropius, Gropius House, Lincoln Mass.	Sept. 30, 1982	BEP	Washington, D.C.	1,552,567	Walter D. Richards	
2022	20¢	Erro Saajimen, Dulles Airport, Washington, D.C.	Sept. 30, 1982	BEP	Washington, D.C.	1,552,567	Walter D. Richards	
2023	20¢	St. Francis of Assisi	Oct. 7, 1982	ABNC	San Francisco, Calif.	530,275	Ned Sidler	
2024	20¢	Ponce de Leon	Oct. 12, 1982	BEP	San Juan, P.R.	530,275	Richard Schlecht	
2025	20¢	Dog and Cat	Nov. 3, 1982	BEP	Danvers, Mass.	239,219		
2026	20¢	Madonna with Child	Oct. 28, 1982	BEP	Washington, D.C.	462,982		
2027	20¢	Children Sledding	Oct. 28, 1982	PBE	Snow, Okla.	676,950		
2028	20¢	Children Building Snowman	Oct. 28, 1982	BEP	Snow, Okla.	676,950		
2029	20¢	Children Skating	Oct. 28, 1982	BEP	Snow, Okla.	676,950		
2030	20¢	Children Decorating Christmas Tree	Oct. 28, 1982	BEP	Snow, Okla.	676,950		
2031	20¢	Science and Industry	Jan. 19, 1983	BEP	Chicago, Ill.	526,693	Saul Bass	R.G. Culin
2032	20¢	Balloon *Intrepid*	March 31, 1982	BEP	Albuquerque, N.M.	989,305	David Meltzer	
2033	20¢	Balloon *Explorer II*	March 31, 1982	BEP	Albuquerque, N.M.	989,305	David Meltzer	
2034	20¢	Balloons	March 31, 1982	BEP	Albuquerque, N.M.	989,305	David Meltzer	
2035	20¢	Balloons	March 31, 1982	BEP	Albuquerque, N.M.	989,305	David Meltzer	
2036	20¢	Benjamin Franklin,	March 24, 1983	BEP	Philadelphia, Pa.	526,373	Czeslaw Slania	Czeslaw Slania

Scott number	Denom.	Design	First day of issue	Printer	First-day city	First-day quantities	Designer	Engraver
		U.S.-Sweden Relations						
2037	20¢	CCC Workers in the Woods	April 5, 1983	BEP	Luray, Va.	438,824	David K. Stone	
2038	20¢	Joseph Priestley	April 13, 1983	ABNC	Northumberland, Pa.	673,266	Dennis Lyall	
2039	20¢	Volunteer Lend a Hand, Hands	April 20, 1983	BEP	Washington, D.C.	574,708	Paul Calle	K. Kipperman
2040	20¢	Sailing Ship *Concord* 1683	April 29, 1983	BEP	Germantown, Pa.	611,109	Richard Schlecht	T.R. Hipschen
2041	20¢	Brooklyn Bridge	May 5, 1983	BEP	Brooklyn, N.Y.	815,085	Howard Koslow	E.P. Archer
2042	20¢	Norris Hydroelectric Dam	May 18, 1983	BEP	Knoxville, Tenn.	837,588	Howard Koslow	Gary Slaght
2043	20¢	Runners, Electro-cardiograph Tracing	May 14, 1983	BEP	Houston, Texas	501,336	Donald Moss	
2044	20¢	Scott Joplin	June 9, 1983	BEP	Sedalia, Mo.	472,667	Jerry Pinkney	
2045	20¢	Medal of Honor	June 7, 1983	BEP	Washington, D.C.	1,623,995	Dennis J. Hom	T.J. Bakos
2046	20¢	Babe Ruth	July 6, 1983	BEP	Chicago, Ill.	1,277,907	Richard Gangel	J.S. Wallace
2047	20¢	Nathaniel Hawthorne	July 8, 1983	BEP	Salem, Mass.	442,793	Bradbury Thompson	
2048	20¢	Discus	July 28, 1983	BEP	South Bend, Ind.	909,332	Bob Peake	
2049	20¢	High Jump	July 28, 1983	BEP	South Bend, Ind.	909,332	Bob Peake	
2050	20¢	Archery	July 28, 1983	BEP	South Bend, Ind.	909,332	Bob Peake	
2051	20¢	Boxing	July 28, 1983	BEP	South Bend, Ind.	909,332	Bob Peake	
2052	20¢	Signing of the Treaty of Paris	Sept. 2, 1983	BEP	Washington, D.C.	651,208	David Blossom	
2053	20¢	Civil Service Centenary	Sept. 9, 1983	BEP	Washington, D.C.	422,206	MDB Communications	
2054	20¢	Metropolitan Opera Entrances	Sept. 14, 1983	BEP	New York, N.Y.	807,609	Ken Davies	J.S. Creamer, Jr.
2055	20¢	Charles Steinmetz and Curve on Graph	Sept. 21, 1983	BEP	Washington, D.C.	1,006,516	Dennis Lyall	T.R. Hipschen
2056	20¢	Edwin Armstrong and Frequency Modulator	Sept. 21, 1983	BEP	Washington, D.C.	1,006,516	Dennis Lyall	T.R. Hipschen
2057	20¢	Nikola Tesla and Induction Motor	Sept. 21, 1983	BEP	Washington, D.C.	1,006,516	Dennis Lyall	K. Kipperman
2058	20¢	Philo T. Fransworth and	Sept. 21, 1983	BEP	Washington, D.C.	1,006,516	Dennis Lyall	K. Kipperman

Scott number	Denom.	Design	First day of issue	Printer	First-day city	First-day quantities	Designer	Engraver
		First Television Camera						
2059	20¢	Streetcar in New York	Oct. 8, 1983	BEP	Kennebunkport, Maine	1,116,909	Richard Leech	
2060	20¢	Streetcar in Montgomery, Ala.	Oct. 8, 1983	BEP	Kennebunkport, Maine	1,116,909	Richard Leech	
2061	20¢	Streetcar in Sulpher Rock, Ark.	Oct. 8, 1983	BEP	Kennebunkport, Maine	1,116,909	Richard Leech	
2062	20¢	Streetcar in New Orleans	Oct. 8, 1983	BEP	Kennebunkport, Maine	1,116,909	Richard Leech	
2063	20¢	Madonna by Raphael	Oct. 28, 1983	BEP	Washington, D.C.	361,874	Bradbury Thompson	
2064	20¢	Santa Claus	Oct. 28, 1983	BEP	Santa Clause, Ind.	388,749	John Berkey	
2065	20¢	Martin Luther	Nov. 11, 1983	ABNC	Washington, D.C.	473,777	Bradbury Thompson	
2066	20¢	Caribou and Alaska Pipeline	Jan. 3, 1984	ABNC	Fairbanks, Ark.	816,591	Bill Bond	
2067	20¢	Ice Dancing	Jan. 2, 1984	BEP	Lake Placid, N.Y.	1,245,807	Bob Peak	
2068	20¢	Alpine Skiing	Jan. 2, 1984	BEP	Lake Placid, N.Y.	1,245,807	Bob Peak	
2069	20¢	Nordic Skiing	Jan. 2, 1984	BEP	Lake Placid, N.Y.	1,245,807	Bob Peak	
2070	20¢	Hockey	Jan. 2, 1984	BEP	Lake Placid, N.Y.	1,245,807	Bob Peak	
2071	20¢	Pillar, Dollar Sign, FDIC 50th Anniversary	Jan. 12, 1984	BEP	Washington, D.C.	536,329	Michael David Brown	
2072	20¢	LOVE	Jan. 31, 1984	BEP	Washington, D.C.	327,727	Bradbury Thompson	Dennis Brown
2073	20¢	Carter G. Woodson	Feb. 1, 1984	ABNC	Washington, D.C.	387,583	Jerry Pinkney	
2074	20¢	Hand holding flower	Feb. 6, 1984	BEP	Denver, Colo.	426,101	Michael David Brown	
2075	20¢	Dollar Sign and Coin, Credit Unions	Feb. 10, 1984	BEP	Salem, Mass.	523,583	Michael David Brown	
2076	20¢	Wild Pink Orchid	March 5, 1984	BEP	Miami, Fla.	1,063,237	Manabu Saito	
2077	20¢	Yellow Lady's Slipper Orchid	March 5, 1984	BEP	Miami, Fla.	1,063,237	Manabu Saito	
2078	20¢	Spreading Pogonia Orchid	March 5, 1984	BEP	Miami, Fla.	1,063,237	Manabu Saito	
2079	20¢	Pacific Calypso Orchid	March 5, 1984	BEP	Miami, Fla.	1,063,237	Manabu Saito	
2080	20¢	Eastern Polynesian Canoe, Golden Plover, Mauna Loa Volcano	March 12, 1984	BEP	Honolulu, Hawaii	546,930	Herb Kane	

Scott number	Denom.	Design	First day of issue	Printer	First-day city	First-day quantities	Designer	Engraver
2081	20¢	Abraham Lincoln, George Washington, National Archives	April 16, 1984	BEP	Washington, D.C.	414,415	Michael David Brown	
2082	20¢	Diving	May 4, 1984	BEP	Los Angeles, Calif.	1,172,313	Bob Peak	
2083	20¢	Long Jump	May 4, 1984	BEP	Los Angeles, Calif.	1,172,313	Bob Peak	
2084	20¢	Wrestling	May 4, 1984	BEP	Los Angeles, Calif.	1,172,313	Bob Peak	
2085	20¢	Kayak	May 4, 1984	BEP	Los Angeles, Calif.	1,172,313	Bob Peak	
2086	20¢	Bayou Wildlife	May 11, 1984	BEP	New Orleans, LA	467,408	Chuck Ripper	
2087	20¢	Lab Equipment	May 17, 1984	ABNC	New York, N.Y.	845,007	Tyler Smith	
2088	20¢	Douglas Fairbanks	May 23, 1984	BEP	Denver, Colo.	547,134	Jim Sharpe	G. Chaconas
2089	20¢	Jim Thorpe	May 24, 1984	BEP	Shawnee, Okla.	568,544	Richard Gangel	T.R. Hipschen
2090	20¢	John McCormack	June 6, 1984	BEP	Boston, Mass.	464,117	Jim Sharpe	
2091	20¢	Aerial View of St. Lawrence Seaway	June 26, 1984	ABNC	Massena, N.Y.	550,173	Ernst Barenscher	
2092	20¢	"Mallards Dropping In" by Jay N. Darling	July 2, 1984	BEP	Des Moines, Iowa	549,388	Donald M. McDowell	J.S. Wallace
2093	20¢	Sailship "The Elizabeth"	July 13, 1984	ABNC	Manteo, N.C.	443,725	Charles Lundgren	
2094	20¢	Herman Melville	Aug. 1, 1984	BEP	Bedford, Mass.	378,293	Bradbury Thompson	T.R. Hipschen
2095	20¢	Horace Moses	Aug. 6, 1984	BEP	Bloomington, Ind.	459,386	Dennis Lyall	T.R. Hipschen
2096	20¢	Smokey the Bear	Aug. 13, 1984	BEP	Capitan, N.M.	506,833	Rudolph Wendelin	
2097	20¢	Roberto Clemente	Aug. 17, 1984	BEP	Carolina, P.R.	547,387	Juan Lopez-Bonilla	
2098	20¢	Beagle and Boston Terrier	Sept. 7, 1984	BEP	New York, N.Y.	1,157,373	Roy Andersen	
2099	20¢	Chesapeake Bay Retriever and Cocker Spaniel	Sept. 7, 1984	BEP	New York, N.Y.	1,157,373	Roy Andersen	
2100	20¢	Alaskan Malamute and Collie	Sept. 7, 1984	BEP	New York, N.Y.	1,157,373	Roy Andersen	
2101	20¢	Black and Tan Coonhound and American Foxhound	Sept. 7, 1984	BEP	New York, N.Y.	1,157,373	Roy Andersen	
2102	20¢	McGruff the Crime Dog	Sept. 26, 1984	ABNC	Washington, D.C.	427,564	Randall McDougall	
2103	20¢	Hispanic Americans	Oct. 31, 1984	BEP	Washington, D.C.	416,796	Robert McCall	
2104	20¢	Stick Figures	Oct. 1, 1984	BEP	Shaker Heights,	400,659	Molly LaRue	Gary Slaght

Scott number	Denom.	Design	First day of issue	Printer	First-day city	First-day quantities	Designer	Engraver
					Ohio			
2105	20¢	Eleanor Roosevelt	Oct. 11, 1984	BEP	Hyde Park, N.Y.	479,919	Bradbury Thompson	T.R. Hipschen
2106	20¢	Abraham Lincoln Reading to Son Tad	Oct. 16, 1984	BEP	Washington, D.C.	447,559	Bradbury Thompson	T.R. Hipschen
2107	20¢	Madonna and Child by Fra Filippo Lippi	Oct. 30, 1984	BEP	Washington, D.C.	386,385	Bradbury Thompson	
2108	20¢	Santa Claus	Oct. 30, 1984	BEP	Jamaica, N.Y.	430,843	Danny LaBoccetta	
2109	20¢	Vietnam Memorial and Visitors	Nov. 10, 1984	BEP	Washington, D.C.	434,489	Paul Calle	J.S. Creamer, Jr.
2110	22¢	Jerome Kern	Jan. 23, 1985	ABNC	New York, N.Y.	503,855	Jim Sharpe	
2111	22¢	"D" Eagle	Feb. 1, 1985	BEP	Los Angeles, Calif.	513,027	Bradbury Thompson	
2112	22¢	"D" Eagle	Feb. 1, 1985	BEP	Los Angeles, Calif.		Bradbury Thompson	
2113	22¢	"D" Eagle	Feb. 1, 1985	BEP	Los Angeles, Calif.	513,027	Bradbury Thompson	
2114	22¢	Flag Over Capitol Dome	March 29, 1985	BEP	Washington, D.C.	268,161	Frank Waslick	T.R. Hipschen
2115	22¢	Flag Over Capitol Dome	March 29, 1985	BEP	Washington, D.C.	268,161	Frank Waslick	T.R. Hipschen
2116	22¢	Flag Over Capitol Dome	March 29, 1985	BEP	Washington, D.C.	234,318	Frank Waslick	T.R. Hipschen
2117	22¢	Frilled Dogwinkle	April 4, 1985	BEP	Boston, Mass.	234,318	Pete Cocci	T.R. Hipschen
2118	22¢	Reticulated Helmet	April 4, 1985	BEP	Boston, Mass.	234,318	Pete Cocci	G. Chaconas
2119	22¢	New England Neptune	April 4, 1985	BEP	Boston, Mass.	234,318	Pete Cocci	J.S. Creamer, Jr.
2120	22¢	Calico Scallop	April 4, 1985	BEP	Boston, Mass.	234,318	Pete Cocci	J.S. Wallace
2121	22¢	Lightning Whelk	April 4, 1985	BEP	Boston, Mass.	234,318	Pete Cocci	T.R. Hipschen
2122	$10.75	Eagle and Half Moon	April 29, 1985	BEP	San Francisco, Calif.	93,154	Young & Rubicam	
2123	3¢	School Bus	June 8, 1985	BEP	Arlington, Va.	131,480	Lou Nolan	K. Kipperman
2125	5¢	Buckboard	June 21, 1985	BEP	Reno, Nev.		William H. Bond	G. Chaconas
2127	6¢	Tricycle	May 6, 1985	BEP	Childs, Md.	151,494	James Schleyer	K. Kippermman
2128	8¢	Ambulance	June 21, 1985	BEP	Reno, Nev.		James Schleyer	G. Chaconas
2129	9¢	Tow Truck	Jan. 24, 1987	BEP	Tucson, Ariz.	224,285	William H. Bond	E.P. Archer
2130	10¢	Oil Wagon	April 18, 1985	BEP	Oil Center, N.M.		James Schleyer	E.P. Archer
2131	11¢	Stutz Super Bearcat	June 11, 1985	BEP	Baton Rouge, LA	135,037	Ken Dallison	T.R. Hipschen
2132	12¢	Stanley Streamer	April 2, 1985	BEP	Kingfield, Maine	173,998	Ken Dallison	G. Chaconas

Scott number	Denom.	Design	First day of issue	Printer	First-day city	First-day quantities	Designer	Engraver
2133	13¢	Pushcart	April 18, 1985	BEP	Oil Center, N.M.		James Schleyer	G. Chaconas
2134	14¢	Iceboat	March 23, 1985	BEP	Rochester, N.Y.	324,710	William H. Bond	G. Chaconas
2135	17¢	Dog Sled	Aug. 20, 1986	BEP	Anchorage, Ark.		Lou Nolan	E.P. Archer
2136	25¢	Bread Wagon	Nov. 22, 1986	BEP	Virginia Beach, Va.	151,950	William H. Bond	E.P. Archer
2137	22¢	Mary McLeod Bethune	March 5, 1985	ABNC	Washington, D.C.	413,244	James Pinkney	
2138	22¢	Broadbill Duck Decoy	March 22, 1985	ABNC	Shelburne, Vt.	932,249	Stevan Dohanos	
2139	22¢	Mallard Duck Decoy	March 22, 1985	ABNC	Shelburne, Vt.	932,249	Stevan Dohanos	
2140	22¢	Canvasback Duck Decoy	March 22, 1985	ABNC	Shelburne, Vt.	932,249	Stevan Dohanos	
2141	22¢	Redhead Duck Decoy	March 22, 1985	ABNC	Shelburne, Vt.	932,249	Stevan Dohanos	
2142	22¢	Ice Skater Special Olympic Emblem Skier	March 25, 1985	BEP	Park City, Utah	253,074	Jeff Carnell	
2143	22¢	Love	April 17, 1985	BEP	Hollywood, Calif.	283,072	Corita Kent	
2144	22¢	REA Power Line, Farmland	May 11, 1985	BEP	Madison, S.D.	472,895	Gary Slaght	
2145	22¢	U.S. No. 13, Ameripex 86	May 25, 1985	BEP	Rosemont, Ill.	457,038	Richard D. Sheaff	G. Chaconas
2146	22¢	Abigail Adams	June 14, 9185	BEP	Quincy, Mass.	491,026	Bart Forbes	
2147	22¢	Fredric Auguste Bartholdi, Statue of Liberty	July 18, 1985	BEP	New York, N.Y.	594,896	Howard Paine	
2149	18¢	George Washington and Washington Monument	Nov. 6, 1985	BEP	Washington, D.C.	376,238	Thomas Szumowski	
2150	21¢	Sealed Envelopes	Oct. 22, 1985	BEP	Washington, D.C.	119,941	Richard Sheaff	
2152	22¢	American Troops Marching in Korea	July 26, 1985	BEP	Washington, D.C.	391,754	Richard Sheaff	T.R. Hipschen
2153	22¢	Men, Women, Children, Corinthian Columns	Aug. 14, 1985	ABNC	Baltimore, Md.	265,143	Robert Brangwynne	
2154	22¢	Battle of Marne, France	Aug. 26, 1985	BEP	Milwaukee, Wis.		Richard Sheaff	Czeslaw Slania
2155	22¢	Quarter Horse	Sept. 25, 1985	BEP	Lexington, Ky.	1,135,368	Roy Andersen	
2156	22¢	Morgan Horse	Sept. 25, 1985	BEP	Lexington, Ky.	1,135,368	Roy Andersen	
2157	22¢	Saddlebred Horse	Sept. 25, 1985	BEP	Lexington, Ky.	1,135,368	Roy Andersen	
2158	22¢	Appaloosa Horse	Sept. 25, 1985	BEP	Lexington, Ky.	1,135,368	Roy Andersen	
2159	22¢	Quill Pen, Apple, Spectacles, Penmanship	Oct. 1, 1985	ABNC	Boston, Mass.	356,030	Uldis Purins	

Scott number	Denom.	Design	First day of issue	Printer	First-day city	First-day quantities	Designer	Engraver
		Quiz						
2160	22¢	YMCA Youth Camping	Oct. 7, 1985	ABNC	Chicago, Ill.	1,202,541	Dennis Luzak	
2161	22¢	Boy Scouts' 75th Anniversary	Oct. 7, 1985	ABNC	Chicago, Ill.	1,202,541	Dennis Luzak	
2162	22¢	Big Brothers and Sisters Federation 40th Anniversary	Oct. 7, 1985	ABNC	Chicago, Ill.	1,202,541	Dennis Luzak	
2163	22¢	Camp Fire, Inc., 75th Anniversary	Oct. 7, 1985	ABNC	Chicago, Ill.	1,202,541	Dennis Luzak	
2164	22¢	Youths and Elderly Suffering from Malnutrition	Oct. 15, 1985	ABNC	Washington, D.C.	299,485	Jerry Pinkney	
2165	22¢	Genoa Madonna, Enameled Terra-Cotta by Luca Della Robbia	Oct. 30, 1985	BEP	Detroit, Mich.		Bradbury Thompson	
2166	22¢	Poinsettia Plants	Oct. 30, 1985	BEP	Nazareth, Mich.	524,929	James Dean	
2167	22¢	Old State House, Little Rock Ark.	Jan. 3, 1986	ABNC	Little Rock, Ark.	364,729	Roger Carlisle	
2168	1¢	Margaret Mitchell	June 30, 1986	BEP	Atlanta, Ga.	316,764	Ron Adair	G. Chaconas
2169	2¢	Mary Lyon	Feb. 28, 1987	BEP	South Hadley, Mass.	349,831	Ron Adair	J.S. Creamer, Jr.
2170	3¢	Paul Dudley White	Sept. 15, 1986	BEP	Washington, D.C.		Christopher Calle	J.S. Creamer, Jr.
2171	4¢	Father Flanagan	July 14, 1986	BEP	Boys Town, Neb.	367,883	Christopher Calle	T.R. Hipschen
2172	5¢	Hugo L. Black	Feb. 27, 1986	BEP	Washington, D.C.	303,012	Christopher Calle	K. Kipperman
2176	10¢	Red Cloud	Aug. 15, 1987	BEP	Red Cloud, Neb.	300,472	Robert Andersen	J.S. Creamer, Jr.
2177	14¢	Julia Ward Howe	Feb. 12, 1987	BEP	Boston, Mass.	454,829	Ward Brackett	J.S. Creamer, Jr.
2178	15¢	Buffalo Bill Cody	June 6, 1988	BEP	Cody, Wyo.		Jack Rosenthal	
2179	17¢	Belva Ann Lockwood	June 18, 1986	BEP	Middleport, N.Y.	249,215	Christopher Calle	J.S. Creamer, Jr.
2180	21¢	Chester Carlson	Oct. 21, 1988	BEP	Rochester, N.Y.		Susan Sanford	
2182	23¢	Mary Cassatt	Nov. 4, 1988	BEP	Philadelphia, Pa.		Dennis Lyall	
2183	25¢	Jack London	Jan. 11, 1986	BEP	Glen Ellen, Calif.	358,686	Richard Sparks	T.R. Hipschen
2188	45¢	Harvey Cushing	June 17, 1988	BEP	Cleveland, Ohio		Bradbury Thompson	
2191	56¢	John Harvard	Sept. 3, 1986	BEP	Boston, Mass.		Robert Andersen	T.R. Hipschen

Scott number	Denom.	Design	First day of issue	Printer	First-day city	First-day quantities	Designer	Engraver
2192	65¢	H.H. "Hap" Arnold	Nov. 5, 1988	BEP	Gladwyne, Pa.		Christopher Calle	
2194	$1	Bernard Revel	Sept. 23, 1986	BEP	New York, N.Y.		Tom Broad	K. Kipperman
2195	$2	William Jennings Bryan	March 19, 1986	BEP	Salem, Ill.	123,430	Tom Broad	K. Kipperman
2196	$5	Bret Harte	Aug. 25, 1987	BEP	Twain Harte, Calif.	111,431	Arthur Lidov	T.R. Hipschen
2197	25¢	Jack London	May 3, 1988	BEP	State College, Pa.	675,924	Richard Sparks	
2198	22¢	Handstamped Cover, Philatelic Memorabilia	Jan. 23, 1986	BEP	State College, Pa.	675,924	Richard Sheaff	J.S. Creamer, Jr.
2199	22¢	Boy Examining Stamp Collection	Jan. 23, 1986	BEP	State College, Pa.	675,924	Richard Sheaff	K. Kipperman
2200	22¢	No. 386 Under Magnifying Glass, Sweden Nos. 268, 271	Jan. 23, 1986	BEP	State College, Pa.	675,924	Richard Sheaff	Lars Sjooblom
2201	22¢	1986 Presidents Miniature Sheet	Jan. 23, 1986	BEP	State College, Pa.	675,924	Richard Sheaff	T.R. Hipschen
2202	22¢	Love and Puppy	Jan. 30, 1986	BEP	New York, N.Y.		Saul Mandel	
2203	22¢	Sojourner Truth	Feb. 4, 1986	BEP	New Paltz, N.Y.	342,985	Jerry Pinkney	
2204	22¢	Texas Flag and Silver Spur	March , 1986	ABNC	San Antonio, Texas	380,450	Don Adair	
2205	22¢	Muskellunge	March 21, 1986	BEP	Seattle, Wash.	988,184	Chuck Ripper	
2206	22¢	Atlantic Cod	March 21, 1986	BEP	Seattle, Wash.	988,184	Chuck Ripper	
2207	22¢	Largemouth Bass	March 21, 1986	BEP	Seattle, Wash.	988,184	Chuck Ripper	
2208	22¢	Bluefin Tuna	March 21, 1986	BEP	Seattle, Wash.	988,184	Chuck Ripper	
2209	22¢	Catfish	March 21, 1986	BEP	Seattle, Wash.	988,184	Chuck Ripper	
2210	22¢	Public Hospitals	April 11, 1986	ABNC	New York, N.Y.	403,665	Uldis Purins	
2211	22¢	Edward Kennedy, "Duke" Ellington	April 29, 1986	ABNC	New York, N.Y.	397,894	Jim Sharpe	
2216	22¢	Nine Presidents of the U.S.	May 22, 1986	BEP	Chicago, Ill.	9,009,599	Jerry Dadds	T.R. Hipschen
2217	22¢	Nine Presidents of the U.S.	May 22, 1986	BEP	Chicago, Ill.	9,009,599	Jerry Dadds	J.S. Wallace
2218	22¢	Nine Presidents of the U.S.	May 22, 1986	BEP	Chicago, Ill.	9,009,599	Jerry Dadds	J.S. Wallace
2219	22¢	Eight Presidents of the U.S.	May 22, 1986	BEP	Chicago, Ill.	9,009,599	Jerry Dadds	G. Chaconas

Scott number	Denom.	Design	First day of issue	Printer	First-day city	First-day quantities	Designer	Engraver
		and the White House						
2220	22¢	Elisha Kent Kane	May 28, 1986	ABNC	North Pole, Ark.	760,999	Dennis Lyall	
2221	22¢	Adolphus W. Greely	May 28, 1986	ABNC	North Pole, Ark.	760,999	Dennis Lyall	
2222	22¢	Vilhjalmur Stefansson	May 28, 1986	ABNC	North Pole, Ark.	760,999	Dennis Lyall	
2223	22¢	Robert E. Peary, Matthew Henson	May 28, 1986	ABNC	North Pole, Ark.	760,999	Dennis Lyall	
2224	22¢	Statue of Liberty	July 4, 1986	BEP	New York, N.Y.	1,540,308	Howard Paine	Claude Jumelet
2225	1¢	Omnibus	Nov. 26, 1986	BEP	Washington, D.C.	57,845	David Stone	G. Chaconas
2226	2¢	Locomotive	March 6, 1987	BEP	Milwaukee, Wis.	169,484	David Stone	G. Chaconas
2228	4¢	Stage Coach	August 1986	BEP			James Schleyer	K. Kipperman
2231	8¢	Ambulance	Aug. 29, 1986	BEP			James Schleyer	G. Chaconas
2235	22¢	Navajo Blanket	Sept. 4, 1986	BEP	Window Rock, Ariz.	1,102,520	Derry Noyes	
2236	22¢	Navajo Blanket	Sept. 4, 1986	BEP	Window Rock, Ariz.	1,102,520	Derry Noyes	
2237	22¢	Navajo Blanket	Sept. 4, 1986	BEP	Window Rock, Ariz.	1,102,520	Derry Noyes	
2238	22¢	Navajo Blanket	Sept. 4, 1986	BEP	Window Rock, Ariz.	1,102,520	Derry Noyes	
2239	22¢	T. S. Eloit	Sept. 26, 1986	BEP	St. Louis, Mo.	304,764	Bradbury Thompson	T.R. Hipschen
2240	22¢	Woodcarving, Highlander Figure	Oct. 1, 1986	ABNC	Washington, D.C.	629,399	Bradbury Thompson	
2241	22¢	Woodcarving, Ship Figurehead	Oct. 1, 1986	ABNC	Washington, D.C.	629,399	Bradbury Thompson	
2242	22¢	Woodcarving. National Figure	Oct. 1, 1986	ABNC	Washington, D.C.	629,399	Bradbury Thompson	
2243	22¢	Woodcarving, Cigar-Store Figure	Oct. 1, 1986	ABNC	Washington, D.C.	629,399	Bradbury Thompson	
2244	22¢	Madonna by Perugino	Oct. 24, 1986	BEP	Washington, D.C.	467,999	Dolli Tingle	
2245	22¢	Village Scene	Oct. 24, 1986	BEP	Snow Hivll, Md.	504,851	Bradbury Thompson	
2246	22¢	White Pine	Jan. 26, 1987	BEP	Lansing, Mich.	379,117	Robert Wilbert	
2247	22¢	Runner in Full Stride	Jan. 29, 1987	BEP	Indianapolis, Ind.	344,731	Lon Busch	
2248	22¢	Love	Jan. 30, 1987	BEP	San Francisco, Calif.	333,329	John Alcorn	

Scott number	Denom.	Design	First day of issue	Printer	First-day city	First-day quantities	Designer	Engraver
2249	22¢	Jean Baptiste Pointe du Sable	Feb. 20, 1987	BEP	Chicago, Ill.	313,054	Thomas Blackshear	
2250	22¢	Enrico Caruso	Feb. 27, 1987	BEP	New York, N.Y.	389,834	Jim Sharpe	
2251	22¢	Fourteen Achievement Badges	March 12, 1987	BEP	Washington, D.C.	556,391	Richard Sheaff	E.P. Archer
2252	3¢	Conestoga Wagon	Feb. 29, 1988	BEP	Conestoga, Pa.		Richard Schlect	
2253	5¢	Milk Wagon	Sept. 25, 1987	BEP	Indianapolis, Ind.	162,571	Lou Nolan	G. Chaconas
2254	5¢	Elevator	Sept. 16, 1988	BEP	New York, N.Y.		Lou Nolan	
2255	8¢	Carreta	Aug. 30, 1988	BEP	San Jose, Calif.		Richard Schlect	
2256	8¢	Wheel Chair	Aug. 12, 1988	BEP	Tucson, Ariz.		Christopher Calle	
2257	10¢	Canal Boat	March 11, 1987	BEP	Buffalo, N.Y.	171,952	William H. Bond	E.P. Archer
2258	13¢	Patrol Wagon	Oct. 29, 1988	BEP	Anaheim, Calif.		Richard Schlect	
2259	13¢	Coal Car	July 19, 1988	BEP	Pittsburgh, Pa.		Richard Schlect	
2260	15¢	Tugboat	July 12, 1988	BEP	Long Beach, Calif.		Richard Schlect	
2261	17¢	Popcorn Wagon	July 7, 1988	BEP	Chicago, Ill.		Lou Nolan	
2262	18¢	Racing Car	Sept. 25, 1987	BEP	Indianapolis, Ind.		Tom Broad	G. Chaconas
2263	20¢	Cable Car	Sept. 28, 1988	BEP	San Francisco, Calif.		Dan Romano	
2264	21¢	Fire Engine	Sept. 28, 1988	BEP	San Angelo, Texas		Christopher Calle	
2265	21¢	Railroad Mail Car	Aug. 16, 1988	BEP	Santa Fe, N.M.		David Stone	
2266	24¢	Tandem Bicycle	Oct. 26, 1988	BEP	Redmond, Wash.		Christopher Calle	
2267	22¢	Congratulations!	April 20, 1987	BEP	Atlanta, Ga.	1,588,129	Oren Sherman	
2268	22¢	Get Well!	April 20, 1987	BEP	Atlanta, Ga.	1,588,129	Oren Sherman	
2269	22¢	Thank You!	April 20, 1987	BEP	Atlanta, Ga.	1,588,129	Oren Sherman	
2270	22¢	Love You, Dad!	April 20, 1987	BEP	Atlanta, Ga.	1,588,129	Oren Sherman	
2271	22¢	Best Wishes!	April 20, 1987	BEP	Atlanta, Ga.	1,588,129	Oren Sherman	
2272	22¢	Happy Birthday	April 20, 1987	BEP	Atlanta, Ga.	1,588,129	Oren Sherman	
2273	22¢	Love You, Mother!	April 20, 1987	BEP	Atlanta, Ga.	1,588,129	Oren Sherman	
2274	22¢	Keep in Touch!	April 20, 1987	BEP	Atlanta, Ga.	1,588,129	Oren Sherman	
2275	22¢	Six Profiles	April 28, 1987	BEP	Washington, D.C.	556,391	Jerry Pinkney	K. Kipperman
2276	22¢	Flag and Fire Works	May 9, 1987	BEP	Denver, Colo.		Peter Cocci	
2277	(25¢)	"E," Earth	March 22, 1987	BEP	Washington, D.C.		Robert McCall	
2278	25¢	Flag and Clouds	May 6, 1988	BEP	Boxborough, Mass.		Peter Cocci	
2279	(25¢)	"E," Earth	March 22, 1988	BEP	Washington, D.C.		Robert McCall	
2280	25¢	Flag and Yosemite	May 20, 1988	BEP	Yosemite, Calif.		Peter Cocci	

Scott number	Denom.	Design	First day of issue	Printer	First-day city	First-day quantities	Designer	Engraver
2281	25¢	Honey Bee	Sept. 2, 1988	BEP	Omaha, Neb.		Chuck Ripper	
2282	(25¢)	"E," Earth	March 22, 1988	BEP	Washington, D.C.		Robert McCall	
2283	25¢	Pheasant	April 29, 1988	BEP	Rapid City, S.D.		Chuck Ripper	
2284	25¢	Blue Jay	May 28, 1988	BEP	Arlington, Va.		Chuck Ripper	
2285	25¢	Owl	May 28, 1988	BEP	Arlington, Va.		Chuck Ripper	
2285A	25¢	Flag and Clouds	July 5, 1988	BEP	Washington, D.C.		Peter Cocci	
2286	22¢	Barn Swallow	June 13, 1988	BEP	Toronto, Canada		Chuck Ripper	
2287	22¢	Monarch Butterfly	June 13, 1988	BEP	Toronto, Canada		Chuck Ripper	
2288	22¢	Bighorn Sheep	June 13, 1988	BEP	Toronto, Canada		Chuck Ripper	
2289	22¢	Broad-tailed Hummingbird	June 13, 1988	BEP	Toronto, Canada		Chuck Ripper	
2290	22¢	Cottontail	June 13, 1988	BEP	Toronto, Canada		Chuck Ripper	
2291	22¢	Ospery	June 13, 1988	BEP	Toronto, Canada		Chuck Ripper	
2292	22¢	Mountain Lion	June 13, 1988	BEP	Toronto, Canada		Chuck Ripper	
2293	22¢	Luna Moth	June 13, 1988	BEP	Toronto, Canada		Chuck Ripper	
2294	22¢	Mule Deer	June 13, 1988	BEP	Toronto, Canada		Chuck Ripper	
2295	22¢	Grey Squirrel	June 13, 1988	BEP	Toronto, Canada		Chuck Ripper	
2296	22¢	Armadillo	June 13, 1988	BEP	Toronto, Canada		Chuck Ripper	
2297	22¢	Eastern Chipmunk	June 13, 1988	BEP	Toronto, Canada		Chuck Ripper	
2298	22¢	Moose	June 13, 1988	BEP	Toronto, Canada		Chuck Ripper	
2299	22¢	Black Bear	June 13, 1988	BEP	Toronto, Canada		Chuck Ripper	
2300	22¢	Tiger Swallowtail	June 13, 1988	BEP	Toronto, Canada		Chuck Ripper	
2301	22¢	Bobwhite	June 13, 1988	BEP	Toronto, Canada		Chuck Ripper	
2302	22¢	Ringtail	June 13, 1988	BEP	Toronto, Canada		Chuck Ripper	
2303	22¢	Red-winged Blackbird	June 13, 1988	BEP	Toronto, Canada		Chuck Ripper	
2304	22¢	American Lobster	June 13, 1988	BEP	Toronto, Canada		Chuck Ripper	
2305	22¢	Black-tailed Jack Rabbit	June 13, 1988	BEP	Toronto, Canada		Chuck Ripper	
2306	22¢	Scarlet Tanager	June 13, 1988	BEP	Toronto, Canada		Chuck Ripper	
2307	22¢	Woodchuck	June 13, 1988	BEP	Toronto, Canada		Chuck Ripper	
2308	22¢	Roseate Spoonbill	June 13, 1988	BEP	Toronto, Canada		Chuck Ripper	
2309	22¢	Bald Eagle	June 13, 1988	BEP	Toronto, Canada		Chuck Ripper	
2310	22¢	Alaskan Brown Bear	June 13, 1988	BEP	Toronto, Canada		Chuck Ripper	
2311	22¢	Iiwi	June 13, 1988	BEP	Toronto, Canada		Chuck Ripper	
2312	22¢	Badger	June 13, 1988	BEP	Toronto, Canada		Chuck Ripper	

Scott number	Denom.	Design	First day of issue	Printer	First-day city	First-day quantities	Designer	Engraver
2313	22¢	Pronghorn	June 13, 1988	BEP	Toronto, Canada		Chuck Ripper	
2314	22¢	River Otter	June 13, 1988	BEP	Toronto, Canada		Chuck Ripper	
2315	22¢	Ladybug	June 13, 1988	BEP	Toronto, Canada		Chuck Ripper	
2316	22¢	Beaver	June 13, 1988	BEP	Toronto, Canada		Chuck Ripper	
2317	22¢	White-tailed Deer	June 13, 1988	BEP	Toronto, Canada		Chuck Ripper	
2318	22¢	Blue Jay	June 13, 1988	BEP	Toronto, Canada		Chuck Ripper	
2319	22¢	Pika	June 13, 1988	BEP	Toronto, Canada		Chuck Ripper	
2320	22¢	Bison	June 13, 1988	BEP	Toronto, Canada		Chuck Ripper	
2321	22¢	Snowy Egret	June 13, 1988	BEP	Toronto, Canada		Chuck Ripper	
2322	22¢	Gray Wolf	June 13, 1988	BEP	Toronto, Canada		Chuck Ripper	
2323	22¢	Mountain Goat	June 13, 1988	BEP	Toronto, Canada		Chuck Ripper	
2324	22¢	Deer Mouse	June 13, 1988	BEP	Toronto, Canada		Chuck Ripper	
2325	22¢	Black-tailed Pairie Dog	June 13, 1988	BEP	Toronto, Canada		Chuck Ripper	
2326	22¢	Box Turtle	June 13, 1988	BEP	Toronto, Canada		Chuck Ripper	
2327	22¢	Wolverine	June 13, 1988	BEP	Toronto, Canada		Chuck Ripper	
2328	22¢	American Elk	June 13, 1988	BEP	Toronto, Canada		Chuck Ripper	
2329	22¢	California Sea Lion	June 13, 1988	BEP	Toronto, Canada		Chuck Ripper	
2330	22¢	Mockingbird	June 13, 1988	BEP	Toronto, Canada		Chuck Ripper	
2331	22¢	Racoon	June 13, 1988	BEP	Toronto, Canada		Chuck Ripper	
2332	22¢	Bobcat	June 13, 1988	BEP	Toronto, Canada		Chuck Ripper	
2333	22¢	Black-footed Ferret	June 13, 1988	BEP	Toronto, Canada		Chuck Ripper	
2334	22¢	Canada Goose	June 13, 1988	BEP	Toronto, Canada		Chuck Ripper	
2335	22¢	Red Fox	June 13, 1988	BEP	Toronto, Canada		Chuck Ripper	
2336	22¢	Delaware State Seal, People, Ship	July 4, 1987	BEP	Dover, Del.	505,770	Richard Sheaff	R.G. Culin
2337	22¢	Independence Hall	Aug. 27, 1988	BEP	Harrisburg, Pa.	367,184	Richard D. Sheaff	
2338	22¢	Colonial Farmer	Sept. 11, 1987	BEP	Trenton, N.J.	432,899	Jim Lamb	
2339	22¢	White Oak Tree	Jan. 6, 1988	BEP	Atlanta, Ga.		Greg Harlin	
2340	22¢	Sailing Ship	Jan. 9, 1988	BEP	Hartford, Conn.		Christopher Calle	
2341	22¢	Boston Street Scene	Feb. 5, 1988	BEP	Boston, Mass.			
2342	22¢	Sailing Ship	Feb. 15, 1988	BEP	Annapolis, Md.		Stephen Hustuedt	
2343	25¢	Palm Trees	May 21, 1988	ABNC	Columbia, S.C.		Bob Timberlake	
2344	22¢	Stone Face	June 21, 1988	ABNC	Concord, N.H.		Thomas Szumowski	
2345	25¢	Williamsburg, Va.	June 25, 1988	BEP	Williamsburg, Va.		Pierre Mion	

Scott number	Denom.	Design	First day of issue	Printer	First-day city	First-day quantities	Designer	Engraver
2346	25¢	New York Street Scene	July 23, 1988	BEP	Albany, N.Y.		Bradbury Thompson	
2349	22¢	Arabesque, Dar Batha Palace Door	July 17, 1987	BEP	Washington, D.C.	372,814	Howard Paine	R.G. Culin
2350	22¢	William Cuthbert Faulkner	Aug. 3, 1987	BEP	Oxford, Miss.	480,024	Bradbury Thompson	T.R. Hipschen
2351	22¢	Lacemaking	Aug. 14, 1988	BEP	Ypsilanti, Mich.		Libby Thiel	E.P. Archer
2352	22¢	Lacemaking	Aug. 14, 1988	BEP	Ypsilanti, Mich.		Libby Thiel	J.S. Wallace
2353	22¢	Lacemaking	Aug. 14, 1988	BEP	Ypsilanti, Mich.		Libby Thiel	G. Chaconas
2354	22¢	Lacemaking	Aug. 14, 1988	BEP	Ypsilanti, Mich.		Libby Thiel	T.R. Hipschen
2355	22¢	Excerpts from the Preamble of the Constitution	Aug. 28, 1987	BEP	Washington, D.C.	1,008,799	Bradbury Thompson	
2356	22¢	Excerpts from the Preamble of the Constitution	Aug. 28, 1987	BEP	Washington, D.C.	1,008,799	Bradbury Thompson	
2357	22¢	Excerpts from the Preamble of the Constitution	Aug. 28, 1987	BEP	Washington, D.C.	1,008,799	Bradbury Thompson	
2358	22¢	Excerpts from the Preamble of the Constitution	Aug. 28, 1987	BEP	Washington, D.C.	1,008,799	Bradbury Thompson	
2359	22¢	Excerpts from the Preamble of the Constitution	Aug. 28, 1987	BEP	Washington, D.C.	1,008,799	Bradbury Thompson	
2360	22¢	Hand, Quill Pen and Constitution	Sept. 17, 1987	BEP	Philadelphia, Pa.	719,975	Howard Koslow	R.G. Culin
2361	22¢	Pen Point and Ledger Sheet	Sept. 21, 1987	BEP	New York, N.Y.	362,099	Lou Nolan	
2362	22¢	Stourbridge Lion Locomotive	Oct. 1, 1987	BEP	Baltimore, Md.	976,694	Richard Leech	R.G. Culin
2363	22¢	Best Friend of Charleston Locomotive	Oct. 1, 1987	BEP	Baltimore, Md.	976,694	Richard Leech	R.G. Culin
2364	22¢	John Bull Locomotive	Oct. 1, 1987	BEP	Baltimore, Md.	976,694	Richard Leech	R.G. Culin
2365	22¢	Brother Jonathan	Oct. 1, 1987	BEP	Baltimore, Md.	976,694	Richard Leech	R.G. Culin

Scott number	Denom.	Design	First day of issue	Printer	First-day city	First-day quantities	Designer	Engraver
		Locomotive						
2366	22¢	Gowan & Marx Locomotive	Oct. 1, 1987	BEP	Baltimore, Md.	976,694	Richard Leech	R.G. Culin
2367	22¢	Moroni Madonna	Oct. 23, 1987	BEP	Washington, D.C.	320,406	Bradbury Thompson	
2368	22¢	Christmas Ornaments	Oct. 23, 1987	BEP	Anaheim, Calif.	375,858	Jim Dean	
2369	22¢	Skiing	Jan. 10, 1988	ABNC	Anchorage, Ark.		Bart Forbes	
2370	22¢	Caricature of an Australian Koala and an American Bald Eagle	Feb. 26, 1988	BEP	Washington, D.C.		Roland Harvey	
2371	22¢	James Weldon Johnson	Feb. 2, 1988	ABNC	Nashville, Tenn.		Thomas Blackshear	
2372	22¢	Siamese and Exotic Shorthair Cats	Feb. 5, 1988	ABNC	New York, N.Y.		John Dawson	
2373	22¢	Abyssinian and Himalayan	Feb. 5, 1988	ABNC	New York, N.Y.		John Dawson	
2374	22¢	Maine Coon and Burmese Cats	Feb. 5, 1988	ABNC	New York, N.Y.		John Dawson	
2375	22¢	American Shorthair and Persian	Feb. 5, 1988	ABNC	New York, N.Y.		John Dawson	
2376	22¢	Knute Rockne	March 9, 1988	BEP	Notre Dame, Ind.		Peter Cocci	
2377	25¢	Francis Ouimet	June 13, 1988	ABNC	Brookline, Mass.		M. Gregory Rudd	
2378	25¢	Rose and Love	July 4, 1988	BEP	Pasadena, Calif.		Richard Sheaff	
2379	45¢	Rose and Love	July 4, 1988	BEP	Shreveport, La.		Richard Sheaff	
2380	25¢	Gymnastic Rings	Aug. 19, 1988	BEP	Colorado Springs, Colo.		Bart Forbes	
2381	25¢	Locomobile	Aug. 25, 1988	BEP	Detroit, Mich.		Ken Dallison	
2382	25¢	1929 Pierce Arrow	Aug. 25, 1988	BEP	Detroit, Mich.		Ken Dallison	
2383	25¢	1931 Cord	Aug. 25, 1988	BEP	Detroit, Mich.		Ken Dallison	
2384	25¢	1932 Packard	Aug. 25, 1988	BEP	Detroit, Mich.		Ken Dallison	
2385	25¢	1935 Duesenberg	Aug. 25, 1988	BEP	Detroit, Mich.		Ken Dallison	
2386	25¢	Nathaniel Palmer	Sept. 14, 1988	ABNC	Washington, D.C.		Dennis Lyall	
2387	25¢	Lt. Charles Wilkes	Sept. 14, 1988	ABNC	Washington, D.C.		Dennis Lyall	
2388	25¢	Richard E. Bird	Sept. 14, 1988	ABNC	Washington, D.C.		Dennis Lyall	
2389	25¢	Lincoln Ellsworth	Sept. 14, 1988	ABNC	Washington, D.C.		Dennis Lyall	
2390	25¢	Folk Art - Deer	Oct. 1, 1988	BEP	Sandusky, Ohio		Paul Calle	

Scott number	Denom.	Design	First day of issue	Printer	First-day city	First-day quantities	Designer	Engraver
2391	25¢	Folk Art - Horse	Oct. 1, 1988	BEP	Sandusky, Ohio		Paul Calle	
2392	25¢	Folk Art - Camel	Oct. 1, 1988	BEP	Sandusky, Ohio		Paul Calle	
2393	25¢	Folk Art - Goat	Oct. 1, 1988	BEP	Sandusky, Ohio		Paul Calle	
2394	$8.75	Eagle and Moon	Oct. 4, 1988	BEP	Terre Haute, Ind.		Ned Seidler	
2395	25¢	Love You	Oct. 22, 1988	BEP	King of Prussia, Pa.		Harry Zelenko	
2396	25¢	Happy Birthday	Oct. 22, 1988	BEP	King of Prussia, Pa.		Harry Zelenko	
2397	25¢	Thinking of You	Oct. 22, 1988	BEP	King of Prussia, Pa.		Harry Zelenko	
2398	25¢	Best Wishes	Oct. 22, 1988	BEP	King of Prussia, Pa.		Harry Zelenko	
2399	25¢	Madonna and Child by Botticelli	Oct. 20, 1988	BEP	Washington, D.C.		Bradbury Thompson	
2400	25¢	One-horse Open Sleigh and Village Scene	Oct. 20, 1988	BEP	Berlin, N.H.		Joan Landis	

Quantities Issued for U.S. Stamps

The following are listings of quantities issued of U.S. stamps. These listings include all 19th-century stamps, all U.S. commemoratives and airmail stamps. Not included are 20th-century definitives. To the best of our knowledge, no complete listing of quantities issued has been prepared for 20th-century definitives. We hope that someone will meet the challenge to delve through the plate reports of the Bureau of Engraving and Printing to produce such a listing.

Quantities Issued for 19th-Century U.S. Stamps

Scott number	Quantity
1	3,700,000
2	865,000
3	4,779
4	3,883
5	29,040
6	not available
7	not available
8	215,000
8A	not available
9	not available
10	50,000,000
11	312,000,000
12	150,000
13	500,000
14	2,325,000
15	2,000,000
16	200,000
17	2,500,000
18	not available
19	not available
20	not available
21	not available
22	not available
23	not available
24	not available
25	38,750,000
26	620,000,000
27	135,000
28	270,000
29	825,000
30 & 30A	570,000
31	not available
32	not available
33	not available
34	not available
35	not available
36	5,800,000
37	750,000
38	357,000
39	29,000
40	3,846

Scott number	Quantity
41	479
42	878
43	516
44	489
45	479
46	480
47	454
62B	500,000
63	138,000,000
64	100,000
65	1,782,000,000
66	not available
67	175,000
68	27,300,000
69	7,314,000
70	400,000
71	3,300,000
72	388,700
73	256,566,000
74	not available
75	1,000,000
76	6,500,000
77	2,139,300
78	9,620,000
79	50,000
80	2,000
81	2,000
82	not available
83	300,000
84	200,000
85	500,000
85A	1,000
85B	500,000
85C	100,000
85D	2,000
85E	100,000
85F	not available
86	3,000,000
87	25,000,000
88	80,000,000
89	1,500,000
90	1,000,000
91	500,000
92	7,000,000
93	50,000,000

Scott number	Quantity
94	225,000,000
95	680,000
96	3,500,000
97	2,600,000
98	2,000,000
99	200,000
100	280,000
101	30,000
102	3,195
103	979
104	465
105	672
106	451
107	389
108	397
109	346
110	346
111	317
112	16,605,000
113	83,643,450
114	386,814,750
115	4,882,650
116	3,299,550
117	3,012,700
118	1,298,840
119	140,000
120	235,250
121	254,010
122	47,360
123 & 133	8,252
124	4,755
125	1,406
126	2,226
127	1,947
128	1,584
129	1,981
130	2,091
131	1,535
132	1,356
134	5,000,000
135	10,000,000
136	50,000,000
137	400,000
138	120,000
139	80,000
140	10,000
141	80,000
142	2,000
143	20,000
144	28,000
145	140,000,000
146	250,000,000
147	1,200,000,000
148	27,600,000
149	2,825,000
150	10,920,000
151	3,890,000
152	5,500,000
153	1,148,000
154	893,000

Scott number	Quantity
155	185,000
156	780,000,000
157	112,500,000
158	2,610,000,000
159	47,000,000
160	2,500,000
161	30,000,000
162	2,915,000
163	5,500,000
164	not available
165	2,050,000
166	197,000
167 & 192	388
168 & 193	416
169 & 194	267
170 & 195	185
171 & 196	473
172 & 197	180
173 & 198	282
174 & 199	169
175 & 200	286
176 & 201	179
177 & 202	170
178	279,000,000
179	38,000,000
180 & 203	917
181 & 204	317
182	590,000,000
183	440,000,000
184	1,335,000,000
185	42,000,000
186	23,650,000
187	16,000,000
188	22,000,000
189	14,750,000
190	4,000,000
191	215,000
205	167,351,000
205C	not available
206	3,372,279,000
207	1,482,380,900
208	11,360,800
209	146,500,000
210	4,320,000,000
211	78,500,000
211B	2,000
211D	2,000
212	1,325,000,000
213	3,580,000,000
214	15,000,000
215	24,500,000
216	85,000,000
217	915,000
218	135,000
219	2,206,093,450
219D	100,000,000
220	6,244,719,500
221	46,877,250
222	66,759,475
223	152,236,530

Scott number	Quantity	Scott number	Quantity
224	9,253,400	261	26,284
225	12,087,800	261A	8,762
226	70,591,710	262	10,027
227	5,548,710	263	6,251
228	1,735,018	264	1,971,338,063
229	219,721	265	300,000,000
230	440,195,550	266	125,000,000
231	1,464,588,750	267	7,475,000,000
232	11,501,250	268	203,057,170
233	19,181,550	269	78,167,836
234	35,248,250	270	123,775,455
235	4,707,550	271	20,712,875
236	10,656,550	272	96,217,820
237	16,516,950	273	59,983,007
238	1,576,950	274	7,013,612
239	617,250	275	1,065,390
240	243,750	276	192,449
241	55,050	276A	63,803
242	45,550	277	31,720
243	24,713	278	26,965
244	22,993	279	5,216,159,932
245	21,844	279B	12,000,000,000
246	100,000,000	280	153,499,379
247	305,000,000	281	279,622,170
248	40,000,000	282	46,457,540
249	100,000,000	282C	42,000,000
250	910,000,000	283	65,000,000
251	100,000,000	284	15,993,313
252	80,000,000	285	70,993,400
253	20,214,300	286	159,720,800
254	16,718,150	287	4,924,500
255	30,688,840	288	7,694,180
256	5,120,800	289	2,927,200
257	2,426,100	290	4,629,760
258	12,263,180	291	530,400
259	1,583,920	292	56,900
260	175,330	293	56,200

Quantities Issued for U.S. Commemoratives

Scott number	Quantity
230	449,195,550
231	1,464,588,750
232	11,501,250
233	19,181,550
234	35,248,250
235	4,707,550
236	10,656,550
237	16,516,950
238	1,576,950
239	617,250
240	243,750
241	55,050
242	45,550
243	27,650
244	26,350
245	27,350
285	70,993,400
286	159,720,800
287	4,924,500
288	7,694,180
289	2,927,200
290	4,629,760
291	530,400
292	56,900
293	56,200
294	91,401,500
295	209,759,700
296	5,737,100
297	7,201,300
298	4,921,700
299	5,043,700
323	79,779,200
324	192,732,400
325	4,542,600
326	6,926,700
327	4,011,200
328	77,728,794
329	149,497,994
330	7,980,594
367	148,387,191
368	1,273,900
369	637,000
370	152,887,311
371	525,400
372	72,634,631
373	216,480
397 & 401	334,796,926
398 & 402	503,713,086
399 & 403	29,088,726
400 & 404	16,968,365
537	99,585,200
548	137,978,207
549	196,037,327
550	11,321,607
610	1,459,487,085
611	770,000

Scott number	Quantity
612	99,950,300
614	51,378,023
615	77,753,423
616	5,659,023
617	15,615,000
618	26,596,600
619	5,348,800
620	9,104,983
621	1,900,983
627	307,731,900
628	20,280,500
629	40,639,485
630 (sheet of 25)	107,398
643	39,974,900
644	25,628,450
645	101,330,328
646	9,779,896
647	5,519,897
648	1,459,897
649	51,342,273
650	10,319,700
651	16,684,674
654	31,679,200
655	210,119,474
656	133,530,000
657	51,451,880
658	13,390,000
659	8,240,000
660	87,410,000
661	2,540,000
662	2,290,000
663	2,700,000
664	1,450,000
665	1,320,000
666	1,530,000
667	1,130,000
668	2,860,000
669	8,220,000
670	8,990,000
671	73,220,000
672	2,110,000
673	1,600,000
674	1,860,000
675	980,000
676	850,000
677	1,480,000
678	530,000
679	1,890,000
680	29,338,274
681	32,680,900
682	74,000,774
683	25,215,574
688	25,609,470
689	66,487,000
690	96,559,400
702	99,074,600
703	25,006,400
704	87,969,700
705	1,265,555,100
706	304,926,800

Scott number	Quantity
707	4,222,198,300
708	456,198,500
709	151,201,300
710	170,565,100
711	111,739,400
712	83,257,400
713	96,506,100
714	75,709,200
715	147,216,000
716	51,102,800
717	100,869,300
718	168,885,300
719	52,376,100
724	49,949,000
725	49,538,500
726	61,719,200
727	73,382,400
728	348,266,800
729	480,239,300
730 (sheet of 25)	456,704
730a	11,417,600
731 (sheet of 25)	441,172
731a	11,029,300
732	1,978,707,300
733	5,735,944
734	45,137,700
735 (sheet of 6)	811,404
735a	4,868,424
736	46,258,300
737	193,239,100
738	15,432,200
739	64,525,400
740	84,896,350
741	74,400,200
742	95,089,000
743	19,178,650
744	30,980,100
745	16,923,350
746	15,988,250
747	15,288,700
748	17,472,600
749	18,874,300
750 (sheet of 6)	511,391
750a	3,068,346
751 (sheet of 6)	793,551
751a	4,761,306
752	3,274,556
753	2,040,760
754	2,389,288
755	2,294,948
756	3,217,636
757	2,746,640
758	2,168,088
759	1,822,684
760	1,724,576
761	1,647,696
762	1,682,948
763	1,638,644
764	1,625,224
765	1,644,900

Scott number	Quantity
766 (pane of 25)	98,712
766a	2,467,800
767 (pane of 25)	85,914
767a	2,147,850
768 (pane of 6)	267,200
768a	1,603,200
769 (pane of 6)	279,960
769a	1,679,760
770 (pane of 6)	215,920
770a	1,295,520
771	1,370,560
772	70,726,800
773	100,839,600
774	73,610,650
775	75,823,900
776	124,324,500
777	67,127,650
778 (sheet of 4)	2,809,039
778a	2,809,039
778b	2,809,039
778c	2,809,039
778d	2,809,039
782	72,992,650
783	74,407,450
784	269,522,200
785	105,196,150
786	93,848,500
787	87,741,150
788	35,794,150
789	36,839,250
790	104,773,450
791	92,054,550
792	93,291,650
793	34,552,950
794	36,819,050
795	84,825,250
796	25,040,400
797	5,277,445
798	99,882,300
799	78,454,450
800	77,004,200
801	81,292,450
802	76,474,550
835	73,043,650
836	58,564,368
837	65,939,500
838	47,064,300
852	114,439,600
853	101,699,550
854	72,764,550
855	81,269,600
856	67,813,350
857	71,394,750
858	66,835,000
859	56,348,320
860	53,177,110
861	53,260,270
862	22,104,950
863	13,201,270
864	51,603,580

Scott number	Quantity
865	52,100,510
866	51,666,580
867	22,207,780
868	11,835,530
869	52,471,160
870	52,366,440
871	51,636,270
872	20,729,030
873	14,125,580
874	59,409,000
875	57,888,600
876	58,273,180
877	23,779,000
878	15,112,580
879	57,322,790
880	58,281,580
881	56,398,790
882	21,147,000
883	13,328,000
884	54,389,510
885	53,636,580
886	55,313,230
887	21,720,580
888	13,600,580
889	47,599,580
890	53,766,510
891	54,193,580
892	20,264,580
893	13,726,580
894	46,497,400
895	47,700,000
896	50,618,150
897	50,034,400
898	60,943,700
902	44,389,550
903	54,574,550
904	63,558,400
906	21,272,800
907	1,671,564,200
908	1,227,334,200
909	19,999,646
910	19,999,646
911	19,999,646
912	19,999,646
913	19,999,646
914	19,999,646
915	19,999,646
916	14,999,646
917	14,999,646
918	14,999,646
919	14,999,646
920	14,999,646
921	14,999,646
922	61,303,000
923	61,001,450
924	60,605,000
925	50,129,350
926	53,479,400
927	61,617,350
928	75,500,000

Scott number	Quantity
929	137,321,000
930	128,140,000
931	67,255,000
932	133,870,000
933	76,455,400
934	128,357,750
935	138,863,000
936	111,616,700
937	308,587,700
938	170,640,000
939	135,927,000
940	260,339,100
941	132,274,500
942	132,430,000
943	139,209,500
944	114,684,450
945	156,540,510
946	120,452,600
947	127,104,300
948	10,299,600
949	132,902,000
950	131,968,000
951	131,488,000
952	122,362,000
953	121,548,000
954	131,109,500
955	122,650,500
956	121,953,500
957	115,250,000
958	64,198,500
959	117,642,500
960	77,649,600
961	113,474,500
962	120,868,500
963	77,800,500
964	52,214,000
965	53,958,100
966	61,120,010
967	57,823,000
968	52,975,000
969	77,149,000
970	58,332,000
971	56,228,000
972	57,832,000
973	53,875,000
974	63,834,000
975	67,162,200
976	64,561,000
977	64,079,500
978	63,388,000
979	62,285,000
980	57,492,610
981	99,190,000
982	104,790,000
983	108,805,000
984	107,340,000
985	117,020,000
986	122,633,000
987	130,960,000
988	128,478,000

Scott number	Quantity
989	132,090,000
990	130,050,000
991	131,350,000
992	129,980,000
993	122,315,000
994	122,170,000
995	131,635,000
996	121,860,000
997	121,120,000
998	119,120,000
999	112,125,000
1000	114,140,000
1001	114,490,000
1002	117,200,000
1003	116,130,000
1004	116,175,000
1005	115,945,000
1006	112,540,000
1007	117,415,000
1008	2,899,580,000
1009	114,540,000
1010	113,135,000
1011	116,255,000
1012	113,860,000
1013	124,260,000
1014	115,735,000
1015	115,430,000
1016	136,220,000
1017	114,894,600
1018	118,706,000
1019	114,190,000
1020	113,990,000
1021	89,289,600
1022	114,865,000
1023	115,780,000
1024	115,244,600
1025	123,709,600
1026	114,789,600
1027	115,759,600
1028	116,134,600
1029	118,540,000
1060	115,810,000
1061	113,603,700
1062	128,002,000
1063	116,078,150
1064	116,139,800
1065	120,484,800
1066	53,854,750
1067	176,075,000
1068	125,944,400
1069	122,284,600
1070	133,638,850
1071	118,664,600
1072	112,434,000
1073	129,384,550
1074	121,184,600
1075	2,900,731
1076	119,784,200
1077	123,159,400
1078	123,138,800
1079	109,275,000
1080	112,932,200
1081	125,475,000
1082	117,855,000
1083	122,100,000
1084	118,180,000
1085	100,975,000
1086	115,299,450
1087	186,949,627
1088	115,235,000
1089	106,647,500
1090	112,010,000
1091	118,470,000
1092	102,230,000
1093	102,410,000
1094	84,054,400
1095	126,266,000
1096	39,489,600
1097	122,990,000
1098	174,372,800
1099	114,365,000
1100	122,765,200
1104	113,660,200
1105	120,196,580
1106	120,805,200
1107	125,815,200
1108	108,415,200
1109	107,195,200
1110	115,745,280
1111	39,743,640
1112	114,570,200
1113	120,400,200
1114	91,160,200
1115	114,860,200
1116	126,500,000
1117	120,561,280
1118	44,064,576
1119	118,390,200
1120	125,770,200
1121	114,114,280
1122	156,600,200
1123	124,200,200
1124	120,740,200
1125	133,623,280
1126	45,569,088
1127	122,493,280
1128	131,260,200
1129	47,125,200
1130	123,105,000
1131	126,105,050
1132	209,170,000
1133	120,835,000
1134	115,715,000
1135	118,445,000
1136	111,685,000
1137	43,099,200
1138	115,444,000
1139	126,470,000
1140	124,560,000
1141	115,455,000

Scott number	Quantity	Scott number	Quantity
1142	122,060,000	1202	120,715,000
1143	120,540,000	1203	121,440,000
1144	113,075,000	1204	40,270,000
1145	139,325,000	1205	861,970,000
1146	124,445,000	1206	120,035,000
1147	113,792,000	1207	117,870,000
1148	44,215,200	1230	129,945,000
1149	113,195,000	1231	135,620,000
1150	121,805,000	1232	137,540,000
1151	115,353,000	1233	132,435,000
1152	111,080,000	1234	135,520,000
1153	153,025,000	1235	131,420,000
1154	119,665,000	1236	133,170,000
1155	117,855,000	1237	130,195,000
1156	118,185,000	1238	128,450,000
1157	112,260,000	1239	118,665,000
1158	125,010,000	1240	1,291,250,000
1159	119,798,000	1241	175,175,000
1160	42,696,000	1242	125,995,000
1161	106,610,000	1243	128,025,000
1162	109,695,000	1244	145,700,000
1163	123,690,000	1245	120,310,000
1164	123,970,000	1246	511,750,000
1165	124,796,000	1247	123,845,000
1166	42,076,800	1248	122,825,000
1167	116,210,000	1249	453,090,000
1168	126,252,000	1250	123,245,000
1169	42,746,400	1251	123,355,000
1170	124,117,000	1252	126,970,000
1171	119,840,000	1253	121,250,000
1172	117,187,000	1254-1257	1,407,760,000
1173	124,390,000	1258	120,005,000
1174	112,966,000	1259	125,800,000
1175	41,644,200	1260	122,230,000
1176	110,850,000	1261	115,695,000
1177	98,616,000	1262	115,095,000
1178	101,125,000	1263	119,560,000
1179	124,865,000	1264	125,180,000
1180	79,905,000	1265	120,135,000
1181	125,410,000	1266	115,405,000
1182	112,845,000	1267	115,855,000
1183	106,210,000	1268	115,340,000
1184	110,810,000	1269	114,840,000
1185	116,995,000	1270	116,140,000
1186	121,015,000	1271	116,900,000
1187	111,600,000	1272	114,085,000
1188	110,620,000	1273	114,880,000
1189	109,110,000	1274	26,995,000
1190	145,350,000	1275	128,495,000
1191	112,870,000	1276	1,139,930,000
1192	121,820,000	1306	116,835,000
1193	289,240,000	1307	117,470,000
1194	120,155,000	1308	123,770,000
1195	124,595,000	1309	131,270,000
1196	147,310,000	1310	122,285,000
1197	118,690,000	1311	14,680,000
1198	122,730,000	1312	114,160,000
1199	126,515,000	1313	128,475,000
1200	130,960,000	1314	119,535,000
1201	120,055,000	1315	125,110,000

Scott number	Quantity
1316	114,853,200
1317	124,290,000
1318	128,460,000
1319	127,585,000
1320	115,875,000
1321	1,173,547,420
1322	114,015,000
1323	121,105,000
1324	132,045,000
1325	118,780,000
1326	121,985,000
1327	111,850,000
1328	117,225,000
1329	111,515,000
1330	114,270,000
1331-1332	120,865,000
1333	110,675,000
1334	110,670,000
1335	113,825,000
1336	1,208,700,000
1337	113,330,000
1339	141,350,000
1340	144,345,000
1342	147,120,000
1343	130,125,000
1344	158,700,000
1345-1354	228,040,000
1355	153,015,000
1356	132,560,000
1357	130,385,000
1358	132,265,000
1359	128,710,000
1360	124,775,000
1361	128,295,000
1362	142,245,000
1363	1,410,580,000
1364	125,100,000
1365-1368	192,570,000
1369	148,770,000
1370	139,475,000
1371	187,165,000
1372	125,555,000
1373	144,425,000
1374	135,875,000
1375	151,110,000
1376-1379	159,195,000
1380	129,540,000
1381	130,925,000
1382	139,055,000
1383	150,611,200
1384	1,709,795,000
1385	127,545,000
1386	145,788,800
1387-1390	201,794,200
1391	171,850,000
1392	142,205,000
1405	137,660,000
1406	135,125,000
1407	135,895,000
1408	132,675,000

Scott number	Quantity
1409	134,795,000
1410-1413	161,600,000
1414-1414a	683,730,000
1415-1418, 1415a-1418a	489,255,000
1419	127,610,000
1420	129,785,000
1421-1422	134,380,000
1423	136,305,000
1424	134,840,000
1425	130,975,000
1426	161,235,000
1427-1430	175,679,600
1431	138,700,000
1432	138,165,000
1433	152,125,000
1434-1435	176,295,000
1436	142,845,000
1437	148,755,000
1438	139,080,000
1439	130,755,000
1440-1443	170,208,000
1444	1,074,350,000
1445	979,540,000
1446	137,355,000
1447	150,400,000
1448-1451	172,730,000
1452	104,090,000
1453	164,096,000
1454	53,920,000
1455	153,025,000
1456-1459	201,890,000
1460	67,335,000
1461	179,675,000
1462	46,340,000
1463	180,155,000
1464-1467	198,364,800
1468	185,490,000
1469	162,335,000
1470	162,789,950
1471	1,003,475,000
1472	1,017,025,000
1473	165,895,000
1474	166,508,000
1475	320,055,000
1476	166,005,000
1477	163,050,000
1478	159,005,000
1479	147,295,000
1480-1483	196,275,000
1484	139,152,000
1485	128,048,000
1486	146,008,000
1487	139,608,000
1488	159,475,000
1489-1498	486,020,000
1499	157,052,800
1500	53,005,000
1501	159,775,000
1502	39,005,000
1503	152,624,000

Scott number	Quantity
1504	145,840,000
1505	151,335,000
1506	141,085,000
1507	885,160,000
1508	939,835,000
1525	143,930,000
1526	145,235,000
1527	13,5052,000
1528	156,750,000
1529	164,670,000
1530-1537	190,156,800
1538-1541	167,212,800
1542	156,265,000
1543-1546	195,585,000
1547	148,850,000
1548	157,270,000
1549	150,245,000
1550	835,180,000
1551	882,520,000
1552	213,155,000
1553	156,995,000
1554	146,365,000
1555	148,805,000
1556	173,685,000
1557	158,600,000
1558	153,355,000
1559	63,205,000
1560	157,865,000
1561	166,810,000
1562	44,825,000
1563	144,028,000
1564	139,928,000
1565-1568	179,855,000
1569-1570	161,863,200
1571	145,640,000
1572-1575	168,655,000
1576	146,615,000
1577-1578	146,196,000
1579	739,430,000
1580	878,690,000
1629-1631	219,455,000
1632	157,825,000
1633-1682	436,005,000
1683	159,915,000
1684	156,960,000
1685	158,470,000
1686	1,990,000
1687	1,983,000
1688	1,953,000
1689	1,903,000
1690	164,890,000
1691-1694	208,035,000
1695-1698	185,715,000
1699	130,592,000
1700	158,332,800
1701	809,955,000
1702-1703	963,370,000
1704	150,328,000
1705	176,830,000
1706-1709	195,976,000

Scott number	Quantity
1710	208,820,000
1711	192,250,000
1712-1715	219,830,000
1716	159,852,000
1717-1720	188,310,000
1721	163,625,000
1722	156,296,000
1723-1724	158,676,000
1725	154,495,000
1726	168,050,000
1727	156,810,000
1728	153,736,000
1729	882,260,000
1730	921,530,000
1731	156,560,000
1732-1733	202,155,000
1744	156,525,000
1745-1748	165,182,400
1749-1752	157,598,400
1753	102,856,000
1754	152,270,000
1755	94,600,000
1756	151,570,000
1757	15,170,400
1758	161,228,000
1759	158,880,000
1760-1763	186,550,000
1764-1767	168,136,000
1768	963,120,000
1769	916,800,000
1770	159,297,600
1771	166,435,000
1772	162,535,000
1773	155,000,000
1774	157,310,000
1775-1778	174,096,000
1779-1782	164,793,600
1783-1786	163,055,000
1787	161,860,000
1788	165,775,000
1789	160,000,000
1790	67,195,000
1791-1794	186,905,000
1795-1798	208,295,000
1799	873,710,000
1800	931,880,000
1801	161,290,000
1802	172,740,000
1803	168,995,000
1804	160,000,000
1805-1810	232,134,000
1821	163,510,000
1822	256,620,000
1823	95,695,000
1824	153,975,000
1825	160,000,000
1826	103,850,000
1827-1830	204,715,000
1831	166,545,000
1832	163,310,000

Scott number	Quantity	Scott number	Quantity
1833	160,000,000	2047	110,925,000
1834-1837	152,404,000	2048-2051	395,424,000
1838-1841	152,420,000	2052	104,340,000
1842	692,500,000	2053	114,725,000
1843	718,715,000	2054	112,525,000
1874	160,155,000	2055-2058	193,055,000
1875	159,505,000	2059-2062	207,725,000
1876-1879	210,633,000	2063	715,975,000
1910	165,175,000	2064	848,525,000
1911	107,240,000	2065	165,000,000
1912-1919	337,819,000	2066	120,000,000
1920	99,420,000	2067-2070	319,675,000
1921-1924	178,930,000	2071	103,975,000
1925	100,265,000	2072	554,675,000
1926	99,615,000	2073	120,000,000
1927	97,535,000	2074	106,975,000
1928-1931	167,308,000	2075	107,325,000
1932	101,625,000	2076-2079	306,912,000
1933	99,170,000	2080	120,000,000
1934	101,155,000	2081	108,000,000
1935	101,200,000	2082-2085	313,350,000
1936	167,360,000	2086	130,320,000
1937-1938	162,420,000	2087	120,000,000
1939	597,720,000	2088	117,050,000
1940	792,600,000	2089	115,725,000
1941	167,130,000	2090	116,600,000
1942-1945	191,560,000	2091	120,000,000
1950	163,939,200	2092	123,575,000
1952	180,700,000	2093	120,000,000
1953-2002	666,950,000	2094	117,125,000
2003	109,245,000	2095	117,225,000
2004	112,535,000	2096	95,525,000
2006-2009	124,640,000	2097	119,125,000
2010	107,605,000	2098-2101	216,260,000
2011	173,160,000	2102	120,000,000
2012	107,285,000	2103	108,140,000
2013	109,040,000	2104	117,625,000
2014	183,270,000	2105	112,896,000
2015	169,495,000	2106	116,500,000
2016	164,235,000	2107	751,300,000
2017	110,130,000	2108	786,225,000
2018	110,995,000	2109	105,300,000
2019-2022	165,340,000	2110	124,500,000
2023	174,180,000	2137	120,000,000
2024	110,261,000	2138-2141	300,000,000
2026	703,295,000	2142	120,580,000
2027-2030	788,880,000	2143	729,700,000
2031	118,555,000	2144	124,750,000
2032-2035	226,128,000	2145	203,496,000
2036	118,225,000	2146	126,325,000
2037	114,290,000	2147	130,000,000
2038	165,000,000	2152	119,975,000
2039	120,430,000	2153	120,000,000
2040	117,025,000	2154	119,975,000
2041	181,700,000	2155-2158	147,940,000
2042	114,250,000	2159	120,000,000
2043	111,775,000	2160-2163	130,000,000
2044	115,200,000	2164	120,000,000
2045	108,820,000	2165	759,200,000
2046	184,950,000	2166	757,600,000

Scott number	Quantity
2198-2201	67,996,800
2202	947,450,000
2203	130,000,000
2204	136,500,000
2205-2209	219,990,000
2210	130,000,000
2211	130,000,000
2216	5,825,050
2217	5,825,050
2218	5,825,050
2219	5,825,050
2220-2223	130,000,000
2224	220,725,000
2235-2238	240,525,000
2239	131,700,000
2240-2243	240,000,000
2244	690,100,000
2245	882,150,000
2246	167,430,000
2247	166,555,000
2248	811,560,000
2249	142,905,000
2250	130,000,000
2251	149,980,000
2267-74	610,425,000
2275	156,995,000
2286-2335	645,975,000
2336	166,725,000
2337	186,575,000
2338	184,325,000
2339	165,845,000

Scott number	Quantity
2340	155,170,000
2341	102,100,000
2342	103,325,000
2343	162,045,000
2344	153,295,000
2345	160,245,000
2346	183,290,000
2349	157,475,000
2350	156,225,000
2351-2354	163,980,000
2355-2359	584,340,000
2360	168,995,000
2361	163,120,000
2362-2366	394,776,000
2367	4,650,000
2368	4,650,000
2369	158,870,000
2370	145,560,000
2371	97,300,000
2372-2375	158,556,000
2376	97,300,000
2377	153,045,000
2378	841,240,000
2379	169,765,000
2380	157,215,000
2381-2385	32,667,900
2386-2389	162,142,500
2390-2393	305,015,000
2395-2398	1,932,000
2399	821,285,000
2400	1,030,850,000

Airmail Stamps' Quantities Issued

Scott number	Quantity
C1	3,395,854
C2	3,793,887
C3	2,134,888
C4	6,414,576
C5	5,309,275
C6	5,285,775
C7	42,092,800
C8	15,597,307
C9	17,616,350
C10	20,379,179
C11	106,887,675
C12	97,641,200
C13	93,536
C14	72,428
C15	61,296
C16	57,340,050
C17	76,648,803
C18	324,070
C19	302,205,100
C20	10,205,400
C21	12,794,600
C22	9,285,300
C23	349,946,500
C24	19,768,150
C25	4,746,527,700
C26	1,744,878,650
C27	67,117,400
C28	78,434,800
C29	42,359,850
C30	59,880,850
C31	11,160,600
C32	864,753,100
C33	971,903,700
C34	207,976,550
C35	756,186,350
C36	132,956,100
C37	33,244,500
C38	38,449,100
C39	5,070,095,200
C40	75,085,000
C41	260,307,500
C42	21,061,300
C43	36,613,100
C44	16,217,100
C45	80,405,000
C46	18,876,800
C47	78,415,000
C48	50,483,977
C49	63,185,000
C50	72,480,000
C51	1,326,960,000
C52	157,035,000
C53	90,055,200
C54	79,290,000
C55	84,815,000
C56	38,770,000
C57	39,960,000
C58	98,160,000
C59	unknown
C60	1,289,460,000
C61	87,140,000
C62	unknown
C63	unknown
C64	unknown
C65	unknown
C66	42,245,000
C67	unknown
C68	63,890,000
C69	62,255,000
C70	55,710,000
C71	*50,000,000
C72	unknown
C73	unknown
C74	*60,000,000
C75	unknown
C76	152,364,800
C77	unknown
C78	unknown
C79	unknown
C80	unknown
C81	unknown
C82	unknown
C83	unknown
C84	78,210,000
C85	96,240,000
C86	58,705,000
C87	unknown
C88	unknown
C89	unknown
C90	unknown
C91-C92	unknown
C93-C94	unknown
C95-C96	unknown
C97	unknown
C98	unknown
C99	unknown
C100	unknown
C101-C104	*165,000,000
C105-C108	*165,000,000
C109-C112	*175,000,000
C113	98,600,000
C114	110,475,000
C115	167,625,000
C116	45,700,000
C117	22,975,000
C118	201,150,000
C119	111,550,000

* Quantity ordered printed

U.S. Stamp Series

United States stamp series go back to this country's first stamp issues, the 1847 5¢ Franklin and 10¢ Washington, Scott numbers 1 and 2.

Most U.S. stamp series through the Washington-Franklin definitives of the early 20th century are well-documented, with most major types and collectible varieties well-known.

Since the 1922 definitive series, however, there is a serious shortfall of readily accessible documentation of our country's stamps. In many cases, information about some stamps has not yet been published.

Catalog listings for stamps produced during the past 60 years have become sparser and less complete. Major varieties are often overlooked by specialized catalog editors.

In addition, technological advances in the production of U.S. stamps during the past six decades have created a number of collectible varieties that previously had no precedent. These include certain types of perforation differences and the addition of phosphorescent tagging.

Many definitive and commemorative stamp series during this time period are affected by these factors and boast several different types for any given stamp design.

Many recent major U.S. varieties are not yet listing in the Scott U.S. Specialized catalog. In many instances, collectors have no access to necessary information regarding these stamps. Most of these unlisted varieties are major production types that are easily discernible to the collector.

This section is devoted to listing all commemorative and definitive U.S. stamp series from 1922 to the present. Listed in each table are all known collectible types found for each stamp.

The criteria for listing as a collectible variety here is whether a type is easily identifiable on both mint and used single stamps.

For this reason, certain gum types, hi-brite papers and other varieties that can only be determined or proven on mint or on used stamps are not listed here.

Each table in this section is organized primarily according to denomination. Catalog numbers (if applicable) are secondary. Other pertinent information about each stamp, including date of issue, format, design description, perforation gauge, press information and tagging, is presented when necessary or desirable.

Corrections and additions to the information presented here, much of it for the first time, are welcomed.

1922 Definitives

Denom.	Scott number	Date of issue	Format	Description	Perforations	Press
1/2¢	551	4/4/25	sheet	Nathan Hale	11	flat
1/2¢	653	5/25/29	sheet	Nathan Hale	11x10 1/2	rotary
1¢	552	1/17/23	sheet	Benjamin Franklin	11	flat
1¢	552a	8/11/23	booklet	Benjamin Franklin	11	flat
1¢	575	3/20/23	sheet	Benjamin Franklin	imperf	flat
1¢	578	———	sheet (coil waste)	Benjamin Franklin	11x10	rotary
1¢	581	4/21/23	sheet	Benjamin Franklin	10	rotary
1¢	594	———	sheet (coil waste)	Benjamin Franklin	11	rotary
1¢	596	———	sheet (coil waste)	Benjamin Franklin	10	rotary
1¢	597	7/18/23	sideways coil	Benjamin Franklin	10 vertical	rotary
1¢	604	7/19/24	endwise coil	Benjamin Franklin	10 horizontal	rotary
1¢	632	6/10/27	sheet	Benjamin Franklin	11x10 1/2	rotary
1¢	632a	11/2/27	booklet	Benjamin Franklin	11x10 1/2	rotary
1¢	658	5/1/29	sheet	Benjamin Franklin (Kans. overprint)	11x10 1/2	rotary
1¢	669	5/1/29	sheet	Benjamin Franklin (Neb. overprint)	11x10 1/2	rotary
1 1/2¢	553	3/19/25	sheet	Warren G. Harding	11	flat
1 1/2¢	576	4/4/25	sheet	Warren G. Harding	imperf	flat
1 1/2¢	582	3/19/25	sheet	Warren G. Harding	10	rotary
1 1/2¢	598	3/19/25	coil	Warren G. Harding	10 vertical	rotary
1 1/2¢	605	5/9/25	coil	Warren G. Harding	10 horizontal	rotary
1 1/2¢	631	8/27/26	sheet	Warren G. Harding	11	rotary
1 1/2¢	633	5/17/27	sheet	Warren G. Harding	11x10 1/2	rotary
1 1/2¢	659	5/1/29	sheet	Warren G. Harding (Kans. overprint)	11x10 1/2	rotary
1 1/2¢	670	5/1/29	sheet	Warren G. Harding (Neb. overprint)	11x10 1/2	rotary
1 1/2	684	12/1/30	sheet	Warren G. Harding	11x10 1/2	rotary
1 1/2	686	12/1/30	coil	Warren G. Harding	10 vertical	rotary
2¢	554	2/15/23	sheet	George Washington	11	flat
2¢	554c	2/10/23	booklet	George Washington	11	flat
2¢	554d	———	sheet	George Washington	10x11 (perf 10 top or bottom)	flat
2¢	577	———	sheet	George Washington	imperf	flat
2¢	579	———	sheet (coil waste)	George Washington	11x10	rotary
2¢	583	4/14/24	sheet	George Washington	10	rotary
2¢	583a	8/27/26	booklet	George Washington	10	rotary
2¢	595	———	sheet (coil waste)	George Washington	11	rotary
2¢	599	Jan. '23	coil type I	George Washington	10 vertical	rotary
2¢	599A	March '29	coil type II	George Washington	10 vertical	rotary
2¢	606	12/31/25	coil	George Washington	10 horizontal	rotary
2¢	634	12/10/26	sheet type I	George Washington	11x10 1/2	rotary
2¢	634A	Dec. '28	sheet type II	George Washington	11x10 1/2	rotary

1922 Definitives (continued)

Denom.	Scott number	Date of issue	Format	Description	Perforations	Press
2¢	634b	——	carmine lake, sheet type I	George Washington	11x10 1/2	rotary
2¢	634d	2/25/27	booklet	George Washington	11x10 1/2	rotary
2¢	646	10/20/28	sheet (Molly Pitcher overprint)	George Washington	11x10 1/2	rotary
2¢	647	8/13/28	sheet (Hawaii overprint)	George Washington	11x10 1/2	rotary
2¢	660	5/1/29	sheet (Kans. overprint)	George Washington	11x10 1/2	rotary
2¢	671	5/1/29	sheet (Kans. overprint)	George Washington	11x10 1/2	rotary
2¢	610	9/1/23	sheet	Warren G. Harding	11	flat
2¢	611	11/15/23	sheet	Warren G. Harding	imperf	flat
2¢	612	9/12/23	sheet	Warren G. Harding	10	rotary
2¢	613	——	sheet	Warren G. Harding	11	rotary
3¢	555	2/12/23	sheet	Abraham Lincoln	11	flat
3¢	584	8/1/25	sheet	Abraham Lincoln	10	rotary
3¢	600	5/10/24	coil	Abraham Lincoln	10 vertical	rotary
3¢	635	2/3/27	sheet	Abraham Lincoln	11x10 1/2	rotary
3¢	635a	2/7/34	sheet (re-issue)	Abraham Lincoln	11x10 1/2	rotary
3¢	661	5/1/29	sheet (Kans. overprint)	Abraham Lincoln	11x10 1/2	rotary
3¢	672	5/1/29	sheet (Neb. overprint)	Abraham Lincoln	11x10 1/2	rotary
4¢	556	1/15/23	sheet	Martha Washington	11	flat
4¢	556b	——	sheet	Martha Washington	10x11 (perf 10 top or bottom)	flat
4¢	585	March '25	sheet	Martha Washington	11x10	rotary
4¢	601	8/5/23	coil	Martha Washington	10 vertical	rotary
4¢	636	5/17/27	sheet	Martha Washington	11x10 1/2	rotary
4¢	662	5/1/29	sheet	Martha Washington (Kans. overprint)	11x10 1/2	rotary
4¢	673	5/1/29	sheet	Martha Washington (Neb. overprint)	11x10 1/2	rotary
4¢	685	6/4/30	sheet	William Taft	11x10 1/2	rotary
4¢	687	9/18/30	coil	William Taft	10 vertical	rotary
5¢	557	10/27/22	sheet	Theodore Roosevelt	11	flat
5¢	557c	——	sheet	Theodore Roosevelt	10x11 (perf 10 top or bottom)	flat
5¢	586	12/24	sheet	Theodore Roosevelt	10	rotary
5¢	602	3/5/24	coil	Theodore Roosevelt	10 vertical	rotary
5¢	637	3/24/27	sheet	Theodore Roosevelt	11x10 1/2	rotary
5¢	648	8/13/28	sheet	Theodore Roosevelt (Hawaii overprint)	11x10 1/2	rotary
5¢	663	5/1/29	sheet	Theodore Roosevelt (Kans. overprint)	11x10 1/2	rotary
5¢	674	5/1/29	sheet	Theodore Roosevelt (Neb. overprint)	11x10 1/2	rotary

1922 Definitives (continued)

Denom.	Scott number	Date of issue	Format	Description	Perforations	Press
6¢	558	11/20/22	sheet	James Garfield	11	flat
6¢	587	March '25	sheet	James Garfield	10	rotary
6¢	638	7/27/27	sheet	James Garfield	11x10 1/2	rotary
6¢	664	5/1/29	sheet	James Garfield	11x10 1/2	rotary
6¢	675	5/1/29	sheet	James Garfield	11x10 1/2	rotary
6¢	723	8/18/32	coil	James Garfield	10 vertical	rotary
7¢	559	5/1/23	sheet	William McKinley	11	flat
7¢	588	5/29/26	sheet	William McKinley	10	rotary
7¢	639	3/24/27	sheet	William McKinley	11x10 1/2	rotary
7¢	665	5/1/29	sheet	William McKinley (Kans. overprint)	11x10 1/2	rotary
7¢	676	5/1/29	sheet	William McKinley (Neb. overprint)	11x10 1/2	rotary
8¢	560	5/1/23	sheet	Ulysses S. Grant	11	flat
8¢	589	5/29/26	sheet	Ulysses S. Grant	10	rotary
8¢	640	6/10/27	sheet	Ulysses S. Grant	11x10 1/2	rotary
8¢	666	5/1/29	sheet	Ulysses S. Grant (Kans. overprint)	11x10 1/2	rotary
8¢	677	5/1/29	sheet	Ulysses S. Grant (Neb. overprint)	11x10 1/2	rotary
9¢	561	1/15/23	sheet	Thomas Jefferson	11	flat
9¢	590	5/29/26	sheet	Thomas Jefferson	10	rotary
9¢	641	5/17/27	sheet	Thomas Jefferson	11x10 1/2	rotary
9¢	667	5/1/29	sheet	Thomas Jefferson (Kans. overprint)	11x10 1/2	rotary
9¢	678	5/1/29	sheet	Thomas Jefferson (Neb. overprint)	11x10 1/2	rotary
10¢	562	1/15/23	sheet	James Monroe	11	flat
10¢	562c	———	sheet	James Monroe	10x11 (perf 10 top or bottom)	flat
10¢	591	6/8/25	sheet	James Monroe	10	rotary
10¢	603	12/1/24	coil	James Monroe	10 vertical	rotary
10¢	642	2/3/27	sheet	James Monroe	11x10 1/2	rotary
10¢	668	5/1/29	sheet	James Monroe (Kans. overprint)	11x10 1/2	rotary
10¢	679	5/1/29	sheet	James Monroe (Neb. overprint)	11x10 1/2	rotary
11¢	563	10/4/22	sheet	Rutherford B. Hayes	11	flat
11¢	692	9/4/31	sheet	Rutherford B. Hayes	11x10 1/2	rotary
12¢	564	3/20/23	sheet	Grover Cleveland	11	flat
12¢	693	8/25/31	sheet	Grover Cleveland	11x10 1/2	rotary
13¢	622	1/11/26	sheet	Benjamin Harrison	11	flat
13¢	694	9/4/31	sheet	Benjamin Harrison	11x10 1/2	rotary
14¢	565	5/1/23	sheet	Hollow Horn Bear	11	flat
14¢	695	9/8/31	sheet	Hollow Horn Bear	11x10 1/2	rotary
15¢	566	11/11/22	sheet	Statue of Liberty	11	flat
15¢	696	8/27/31	sheet	Statue of Liberty	11x10 1/2	rotary
17¢	623	12/28/25	sheet	Woodrow Wilson	11	flat
17¢	697	7/25/31	sheet	Woodrow Wilson	10 1/2x11	rotary
20¢	567	5/1/23	sheet	Golden Gate	11	flat
20¢	698	9/8/31	sheet	Golden Gate	10 1/2x11	rotary
25¢	568	11/11/22	sheet	Niagara Falls	11	flat
•25¢	568	———	sheet	Niagara Falls	11x10 (10 on one side)	flat
25¢	699	7/25/31	sheet	Niagara Falls	10 1/2x11	rotary
30¢	569	3/20/23	sheet	Bison	11	flat
30¢	700	9/8/31	sheet	Bison	10 1/2x11	rotary
50¢	570	11/11/22	sheet	Arlington	11	flat

1922 Definitives (continued)

Denom.	Scott number	Date of issue	Format	Description	Perforations	Press
				Amphitheater		
50¢	701	9/4/31	sheet	Arlington Amphitheater	10 1/2x11	rotary
$1	571	2/12/23	sheet	Lincoln Memorial	11	flat
$2	572	3/20/23	sheet	U.S. Capitol	11	flat
$5	573	3/20/23	sheet	Head of Freedom Statue	11	flat

Canal Zone stamps have not been added because they were created for use abroad and were not valid in the United States.

The Molly Pitcher, Hawaii, Kansas and Nebraska overprinted stamps have been added because they were created from 1922 definitive series stamps.

*Perforation error — Perf 10 appears on only one side of the stamp, usually top or bottom.

Scott 578-79 and 594-95 were created from coil waste and released in sheets of 70 or 100 stamps.

Plate varieties and color shades are not listed in this table, except Scott 635a, a re-issue. It is a brighter violet than 635.

1940 Famous Americans

Denom.	Scott number	Date of Issue	Description	Profession
1¢	859	1/29/40	Washington Irving	author
1¢	864	2/16/40	Henry Wadsworth Longfellow	poet
1¢	869	3/14/40	Horace Mann	educator
1¢	874	4/8/40	John James Audubon	scientist
1¢	879	5/3/40	Stephen Collins Foster	composer
1¢	884	9/5/40	Gilbert Charles Stuart	artist
1¢	889	10/7/40	Eli Whitney	inventor
2¢	860	1/29/40	James Fenimore Cooper	author
2¢	865	2/16/40	John Greenleaf Whittier	poet
2¢	870	3/14/40	Mark Hopkins	educator
2¢	875	4/8/40	Dr. Crawford W. Long	scientist
2¢	880	5/3/40	John Philip Sousa	composer
2¢	884	9/5/40	James A. McNeill Whistler	artist
2¢	889	10/7/40	Samuel F.B. Morse	inventor
3¢	861	2/5/40	Ralph Waldo Emerson	author
3¢	866	2/26/40	James Russell Lowell	poet
3¢	871	3/28/40	Charles W. Eliot	educator
3¢	876	4/17/40	Luther Burbank	scientist
3¢	881	5/13/40	Victor Herbert	composer
3¢	886	9/16/40	Agustus Saint-Gaudens	artist
3¢	891	10/14/40	Cyrus Hall McCormick	inventor
3¢	945	2/11/47	Thomas Edison	inventor
3¢	953	1/5/48	George Washington Carver	scientist
3¢	960	7/31/48	William A. White	author
3¢	965	8/24/48	Harlan F. Stone	chief justice
3¢	975	11/4/48	Will Rogers	humorist
3¢	980	12/9/48	Joel Chandler Harris	author
3¢	986	10/7/49	Edgar Allen Poe	poet
3¢	988	1/27/50	Samuel Gompers	labor leader
5¢	862	2/5/40	Louisa May Alcott	author
5¢	867	2/26/40	Walt Whitman	poet
5¢	872	3/28/40	Frances E. Willard	educator
5¢	877	4/17/40	Dr. Walter Reed	scientist
5¢	882	5/13/40	Edward A. MacDowell	composer

1940 Famous Americans (continued)

Denom.	Scott number	Date of Issue	Description	Profession
5¢	887	9/16/40	Daniel Chester French	artist
5¢	892	10/14/40	Elias Howe	inventor
10¢	863	2/13/40	Samuel L. Clemens (Mark Twain)	author
10¢	868	2/24/40	James Witcomb Riley	poet
10¢	873	4/7/40	Booker T. Washington	educator
10¢	878	4/26/40	Jane Addams	scientist
10¢	883	6/10/40	Ethelbert Nevin	composer
10¢	888	9/30/40	Frederic Remington	artist
10¢	893	11/28/40	Alexander Graham Bell	inventor

Famous Americans Type

Denom.	Scott number	Date of Issue	Description	Profession
3¢	1062	7/12/54	George Eastman	inventor/industrialist
3¢	1072	12/20/55	Andrew Mellon	financier
4¢	1120	10/16/58	Noah Webster	lexicographer/author
4¢	1138	12/3/59	Ephraim McDowell	surgeon
4¢	1161	10/10/60	Robert A. Taft	politician
4¢	1170	11/5/60	Walter F. George	politician
4¢	1171	11/25/60	Andrew Carnegie	industrialist/ philanthropist
4¢	1172	12/6/60	John F. Dulles	secretary of state
4¢	1177	2/3/61	Horace Greeley	publisher/editor

1954 Liberty series

Denom.	Scott number	Date of issue	Description	Format	Printing	Tagging
1/2¢	1030	10/20/55	Benjamin Franklin	sheet	wet	no
1/2¢	——	——	" "	sheet	dry	no
1¢	1031	8/26/54	George Washington	sheet	wet	no
1¢	——		" "	sheet	dry	no
1¢	1054	10/8/54	" "	coil	wet	no
1¢	——	——	" "	coil	dry	no
1 1/4¢	1031A	6/17/60	Palace of the Governors	sheet	dry	no
1 1/4¢	1054A	6/17/60	" "	vert. coil	dry	no
1 1/2¢	1032	2/22/56	Mount Vernon	sheet	dry	no
2¢	1033	9/15/54	Thomas Jefferson	sheet	dry	no
2¢	1055	10/22/54	" "	coil	wet	no
2¢	——	——	" "	coil	dry	no
2¢	1055a	5/6/68	" "	coil	dry	yes
2 1/2¢	1034	6/17/57	Bunker Hill sheet	dry		no
2 1/2¢	1056	9/9/59	" "	coil	dry	no
3¢	1035	6/24/54	Statue of Liberty	sheet	wet	no
3¢	——	——	" "	sheet	dry	no
3¢	1035b	7/6/66	" "	sheet	dry	yes
3¢	1035a	6/30/54	" "	booklet	wet	no
3¢	——	——	" "	booklet	dry	no
3¢	1057	7/20/54	" "	coil	wet	no
3¢	——	——	" "	coil	dry	no

1954 Liberty Series (continued)

Denom.	Scott number	Date of issue	Description	Format	Printing	Tagging
3¢	1057b	Oct. '66 EKU 12/29/66	" "	coil	dry	yes
4¢	1036	11/19/54	Abraham Lincoln	sheet	wet	no
4¢	——	——	" "	sheet	dry	no
4¢	1036b	11/2/63	" "	sheet	dry	yes
4¢	1036a	7/31/58	" "	booklet	dry	no
4¢	——	——	" "	coil	wet*	no
4¢	1058	7/31/58	" "	coil	dry	no
4 1/2¢	1037	3/16/59	The Hermitage	sheet	dry	no
4 1/2¢	1059	5/1/59	" "	vert. coil	dry	no
5¢	1038	12/2/54	James Monroe	sheet	dry	no
6¢	1039	11/18/55	Theodore Roosevelt	sheet	wet	no
6¢	——	——	" "	sheet	dry	no
7¢	1040	1/10/56	Woodrow Wilson	sheet	dry	no
8¢	1041	4/9/54	Statue of Liberty	sheet	flat and rotary	no
8¢	1042	3/22/58	" "	sheet	Giori (redrawn)	no
8¢	1042A	11/17/61	John J. Pershing	sheet	dry	no
9¢	1043	6/14/56	The Alamo	sheet	dry	no
10¢	1044	7/4/56	Independence Hall	sheet	dry	no
10¢	1044b	7/6/66	" "	sheet	dry	yes
11¢	1044A	6/15/61	Statue of Liberty	sheet	dry	no
11¢	1044Ac	1/11/67	" "	sheet	dry	yes
12¢	1045	6/6/59	Benjamin Harrison	sheet	dry	no
12¢	1045a	4/20/68	" "	sheet	dry	yes
15¢	1046	12/12/58	John Jay	sheet	dry	no
15¢	1046a	7/6/66	" "	sheet	dry	yes
20¢	1047	4/13/56	Monticello	sheet	dry	no
25¢	1048	4/18/58	Paul Revere sheet		dry	no
25¢	1059A	2/25/65	" "	coil	dry	no
25¢	1059Ab	4/3/73	" "	coil	dry	yes
30¢	1049	9/21/55	Robert E. Lee	sheet	wet	no
30¢	——	——	" "	sheet	dry	no
40¢	1050	9/24/55	John Marshall	sheet	wet	no
40¢	——	——	" "	sheet	dry	no
50¢	1051	8/25/55	Susan B. Anthony	sheet	wet	no
50¢	——	——	" "	sheet	dry	no
$1	1052	10/7/55	Patrick Henry	sheet	wet	no
$1	——	——	" "	sheet	dry	no
$5	1053	3/19/56	Alexander Hamilton	sheet	dry	no

EKU — Earliest Known Use

* The 4¢ wet-printed Lincoln coil is known only as a Bureau precancel.

The release dates for the dry-printed varieties are not given here because although the press information is available, actual release dates may have been later.

In addition to the stamps listed here, a commemorative souvenir sheet was issued by the U.S. Post Office Dept. for the Fifth International Philatelic Exhibition (FIPEX) on April 28, 1956. It bears the designs of the 3¢ and 8¢ values of the 1954 Liberty series.

Shiny and dull gum varieties exist for several values in this series. They have not been listed here as major varieties.This listing shows only major varieties that are easily distinguishable on a mint or used single stamp.

Liberty Perf Varieties Caused by Equipment Changes

Perforations	**Wet printing**	**Dry printing**
Large holes	1¢, 2¢, 3¢, 4¢	1¢, 1 1/4¢, 2¢, 2 1/2¢, 3¢, 4¢, 4 1/2¢ 7¢ blue airmail
Small holes	None	1¢, 1 1/4¢, 2¢, 2 1/2¢, 3¢, 4¢, 4 1/2¢, 25¢ red and blue 7¢ airmails

U.S. Christmas Stamps

Denom.	**Scott Number**	**Date of Issue**	**Description**	**Tagging**
4¢	1205	11/1/62	Christmas Wreath	none
5¢	1240	11/1/63	National Christmas Tree	none
5¢	1240a	11/2/63	" "	overall
5¢	1254-57	11/9/64	Se-tenant block plants	none
5¢	1254a-57a	11/10/64	" "	overall
5¢	1276	11/2/65	Angel With Trumpet Weather Vane	none
5¢	1276a	11/15/65	" "	overall
5¢	1321	11/1/65	Madonna and Child	none
5¢	1321a	11/2/66	" "	overall
5¢	1336	11/6/67	Madonna and Child	overall
6¢	1363	11/1/68	Angel Gabriel	block
6¢	1363a	11/2/68	" "	none
6¢	1384	11/3/69	Winter Sunday	block
6¢	1384a	11/4/69	" " precanceled Atlanta in black	block
6¢	1384a	11/4/69	" " precanceled Atlanta in green	block
6¢	1384a	11/4/69	" " precanceled Baltimore	block
6¢	1384a	11/4/69	" " precanceled Memphis	block
6¢	1384a	11/4/69	" " precanceled New Haven	block
6¢	1414	11/5/70	Lorenzo Lotto Nativity	overall
6¢	1414	11/27/70	" " reprint	overall
6¢	1414a	11/5/70	" " precanceled	overall
6¢	1414a	11/27/70	" " reprint	overall
6¢	1415-18	11/5/70	Christmas Toys	overall
6¢	1415a-18a	11/5/70	Christmas Toys precanceled	overall
8¢	1444	11/10/71	Adoration of the Shepherds	overall
8¢	1445	11/10/71	Partridge in a Pear Tree	overall
8¢	1471	11/9/72	Angels	overall
8¢	1472	11/9/72	Santa Claus	overall
8¢	1507	11/7/73	Raphael Madonna	bar
8¢	1508	11/7/73	Needlepoint Christmas Tree	bar
10¢	1550	10/23/74	Angel Altarpiece	overall
10¢	1551	10/23/74	The Road — Winter	overall
10¢	1552	11/15/74	Dove Weather Vane self adhesive	none
10¢ (non-denom.)	1579	10/14/75	Madonna	block
10¢	1580	10/14/75	Prang Christmas Card	block
10¢	1580	——	" " L-perforated	block
10¢	1580b	——	" " EE-perforated 10 1/2 by 11	block
13¢	1701	10/27/76	Copley's Nativity	block
13¢	1702	10/27/76	Currier's Winter Pastime	overall
13¢	1703	10/27/76	" "	block
13¢	1729	10/21/77	Washington at Valley Forge	block
13¢	1730	10/21/76	Rural Mailbox	block
15¢	1768	10/18/78	Madonna and Child	block

U.S. Christmas Stamps (continued)

Denom.	Scott Number	Date of Issue	Description	Tagging
15¢	1769	10/18/78	Hobby Horse	block
15¢	1799	10/18/79	Virgin and Child	block
15¢	1800	10/18/79	Santa Tree Ornament	block
15¢	1842	10/31/80	Madonna and Child	block
15¢	1843	10/31/80	Wreath and Toys	block
20¢ (non-denom.)	1939	10/28/81	Madonna and Child	block
20¢ (non-denom.)	1940	10/28/81	Teddy Bear on Sleigh	block
20¢	2027-30	10/28/82	Children at Play	block
20¢	2026	10/28/82	Madonna and Child	block
13¢	2025	11/3/82	Kitten and Puppy	block
20¢	2063	10/28/83	Madonna and Child	block
20¢	2064	10/28/83	Santa Claus	block
20¢	2107	10/30/84	Madonna and Child	block
20¢	2108	10/30/84	Santa Drawn by Child	block
22¢	2165	10/30/85	Terra-cotta Madonna	block
22¢	2166	10/30/85	Poinsettia	block
22¢	2244	10/24/86	Madonna and Child	block
22¢	2245	10/24/86	Village Scene	block
22¢	2367	10/23/87	Madonna	overall
22¢	2368	10/23/87	Christmas Ornaments	block
25¢	2399	10/20/88	Madonna and Child	block
25¢	2400	10/20/88	Snow Scene	overall

1938 Presidential Definitive Series

Denom.	Scott number	Date of issue	Description	Format
1/2¢	803	5/19/38	Benjamin Franklin	sheet
1¢	804	4/25/38	George Washington	sheet
1¢	804b	1/27/39	" "	booklet
1¢	839	1/20/39	" "	coil
1¢	848	1/27/39	" "	vert. coil
1 1/2¢	805	5/5/38	Martha Washington	sheet
1 1/2¢	849	1/27/29	" "	coil
2¢	806	6/3/38	John Adams	sheet
2¢	806b	1/27/29	" "	booklet
2¢	841	1/20/39	" "	coil
2¢	850	1/27/39	" "	vert. coil
3¢	807	6/16/38	Thomas Jefferson	sheet
3¢	807a	1/27/39	" "	booklet
3¢	842	1/20/39	" "	coil
3¢	851	1/27/39	" "	vert. coil
4¢	808	7/1/38	James Madison	sheet
4¢	843	1/20/39	" "	coil
4 1/2¢	809	7/11/38	White House	sheet
4 1/2¢	844	1/20/39	" "	coil
5¢	810	7/21/38	James Monroe	sheet
5¢	845	1/20/39	" "	coil
6¢	811	7/28/38	John Q. Adams	sheet
6¢	846	1/20/39	" "	coil
7¢	812	8/4/38	Andrew Jackson	sheet
8¢	813	8/1/38	Martin Van Buren	sheet
9¢	814	8/18/38	William H. Harrison	sheet
10¢	815	9/2/38	John Tyler	sheet
10¢	847	1/20/39	" "	coil
11¢	816	9/8/38	James K. Polk	sheet

1938 Presidential Definitive Series (continued)

Denom.	Scott number	Date of issue	Description	Format
12¢	817	9/14/38	Zachary Taylor	sheet
13¢	818	9/22/38	Millard Fillmore	sheet
14¢	819	10/6/38	Franklin Pierce	sheet
15¢	820	10/13/38	James Buchanan	sheet
16¢	821	10/20/38	Abraham Lincoln	sheet
17¢	822	10/27/38	Andrew Johnson	sheet
18¢	823	11/3/38	Ulysses S. Grant	sheet
19¢	824	11/10/38	Rutherford B. Hayes	sheet
20¢	825	11/10/38	James Garfield	sheet
21¢	826	11/22/38	Chester A. Arthur	sheet
22¢	827	11/22/38	Grover Cleveland	sheet
24¢	828	12/2/38	Benjamin Harrison	sheet
25¢	829	12/2/38	William McKinley	sheet
30¢	830	12/8/38	Theodore Roosevelt	sheet
50¢	831	12/8/38	William H. Taft	sheet
$1	832	8/29/38	Woodrow Wilson	sheet
$1	832b	1951	" " Watermarked USIR by error	sheet
$1	832c	8/31/54	400-subject flat plate dry printing whiter, thicker paper red-violet and black	sheet
$2	833	9/29/38	Warren G. Harding	sheet
$5	834	11/17/38	Calvin Coolidge	sheet

There are many different color varieties of the above stamps, as well as the electric-eye printings. These have not been listed here except for the dry-printed $1 Wilson because it is a different type of printing and paper.

Prominent Americans

Denom.	Scott number	Date of issue	Description	Format	Identifying features	Tagging
1¢	1278	1/12/68	Thomas Jefferson	sheet	———	yes
1¢	1278c	———	Thomas Jefferson	sheet	Bureau precancel	no
1¢	1278a	1/12/86	Thomas Jefferson	booklet	———	yes
1¢	1299	1/12/68	Thomas Jefferson	coil	———	yes
1¢	1299a	1/12/68	Thomas Jefferson	coil	Bureau precancel	no
1 1/4¢	1279	1/30/67	Albert Gallatin	sheet	———	no
2¢	1280	6/8/66	Frank Lloyd Wright	sheet	———	yes
2¢	1280b	———	Frank Lloyd Wright	sheet	Bureau precancel	no
2¢	1280a	1/8/68	Frank Lloyd Wright	booklet	———	yes
3¢	1281	9/16/67	Francis Parkman	sheet	———	yes
3¢	1281a	———	Francis Parkman	sheet	Bureau precancel	no
3¢	1297	11/4/75	Francis Parkman	coil	———	yes
3¢	1297b	———	Francis Parkman	coil	Bureau precancel	no
3¢	1297b	———	Francis Parkman	coil	double line, no city	no
3¢	1297b	———	Francis Parkman	coil	car-rt sort overprint	no
4¢	1282	11/19/65	Abraham Lincoln	sheet	———	no
4¢	1282a	———	Abraham Lincoln	sheet	———	yes

Prominent Americans (continued)

Denom.	Scott number	Date of issue	Description	Format	Identifying features	Tagging
4¢	1282a	——	Abraham Lincoln	sheet	Bureau precancel	yes
4¢	1303	5/28/66	Abraham Lincoln	coil	——	yes
4¢	1303a	——	Abraham Lincoln	coil	Bureau precancel	no
5¢	1283	2/22/66	George Washington	sheet	——	no
5¢	1283	——	George Washington	sheet	Bureau precancel	no
5¢	1283a	2/23/66	George Washington	sheet	——	yes
5¢	1283B	11/17/67	George Washington	sheet	re-engraved, clean-shaven	yes
5¢	1283Bd	——	George Washington	sheet	re-engraved, Bureau precancel	no
5¢	1304	9/8/66	George Washington	coil	——	yes
5¢	1304a	——	George Washington	coil	Bureau precancel	no
5¢	1304c	1981	George Washington	coil	re-engraved	yes
6¢	1284	1/29/66	Franklin D. Roosevelt	sheet	——	no
6¢	1284	——	Franklin D. Roosevelt	sheet	Bureau precancel	no
6¢	1284a	12/29/66	Franklin D. Roosevelt	sheet	——	yes
6¢	1284b	12/28/67	Franklin D. Roosevelt	booklet	——	yes
6¢	1298	12/28/67	Franklin D. Roosevelt	endwise coil	——	yes
6¢	1305	2/28/68	Franklin D. Roosevelt	sidewise coil	——	yes
6¢	1305	——	Franklin D. Roosevelt	sidewise coil	Bureau precancel	no
8¢	1285	3/14/66	Albert Einstein	sheet	——	no
8¢	1285	——	Albert Einstein	sheet	Bureau precancel	no
8¢	1285a	7/6/66	Albert Einstein	sheet	——	yes
10¢	1286	3/15/67	Andrew Jackson	sheet	——	yes
10¢	1286b	——	Andrew Jackson	sheet	Bureau precancel	no
12¢	1286A	7/30/68	Henry Ford	sheet	——	yes
12¢	1286Ab	——	Henry Ford	sheet	Bureau precancel	no
13¢	1287	5/29/67	John F. Kennedy	sheet	——	yes
13¢	1287a	——	John F. Kennedy	sheet	Bureau precancel	no
15¢	1288	3/8/68	Oliver W. Holmes	sheet	type I	yes
15¢	1288a	——	Oliver W. Holmes	sheet	Bureau precancel type I	no
15¢	1288a	——	Oliver W. Holmes	sheet	Bureau precancel type I, no city	no
15¢	1288d	——	Oliver W. Holmes	sheet	type II	yes
15¢	1288B	6/14/78	Oliver W. Holmes	booklet	redrawn	yes
15¢	1305E	6/14/78	Oliver W. Holmes	coil	type I	yes
15¢	1305Ef	——	Oliver W. Holmes	coil	Bureau precancel type I	no
15¢	1305Ei	——	Oliver W. Holmes	coil	Bureau precancel	yes

Prominent Americans (continued)

Denom.	Scott number	Date of issue	Description	Format	Identifying features	Tagging
20¢	1289	10/24/67	George Marshall	sheet	type II ———	no
20¢	1289	———	George Marshall	sheet	Bureau precancel	no
20¢	1289	———	George Marshall	sheet	Bureau precancel, no city	no
20¢	1289a	4/3/73	George Marshall	sheet	———	yes
25¢	1290	2/14/67	Frederick Douglass	sheet	———	no
25¢	1290	———	Frederick Douglass	sheet	Bureau precancel	no
25¢	1290a	4/3/73	Frederick Douglass	sheet	———	yes
30¢	1291	10/21/68	John Dewey	sheet	———	no
30¢	1291	———	John Dewey	sheet	Bureau precancel	no
30¢	1291a	4/3/73	John Dewey	sheet	———	yes
40¢	1292	1/29/68	Thomas Paine	sheet	———	no
40¢	1292	———	Thomas Paine	sheet	Bureau precancel	no
40¢	1292a	4/3/73	Thomas Paine	sheet	———	yes
50¢	1293	8/13/68	Lucy Stone	sheet	———	no
50¢	1293	———	Lucy Stone	sheet	Bureau precancel	no
50¢	1293a	4/3/73	Lucy Stone	sheet	———	yes
$1	1294	10/16/67	Eugene O'Neill	sheet	———	no
$1	1294	———	Eugene O'Neill	sheet	Bureau precancel	no
$1	1294a	4/3/73	Eugene O'Neill	sheet	———	yes
$1	1305c	1/12/73	Eugene O'Neill	coil	———	yes
$5	1295	12/3/66	John Bassett Moore	sheet	———	no
$5	1295a	4/3/73	John Bassett Moore	sheet	———	yes

American Folklore

Denom.	Scott number	Date of issue	Description	Designer	Tagging
5¢	1317	9/24/66	Johnny Appleseed	Robert Bode	no
5¢	1317a	9/26/66	Johnny Appleseed	Robert Bode	yes (overall)
5¢	1330	8/17/67	Davy Crockett	Robert Bode	yes (overall)
6¢	1357	9/26/68	Daniel Boone	Louis MacOvillard	yes (overall)
6¢	1370	5/1/69	Grandma Moses	Robert J. Jones	yes
8¢	1470	10/13/72	Tom Sawyer	Bradbury Thompson	yes
10¢	1548	10/10/74	Headless Horseman	Leonard E. Fisher	yes

U.S. Love Stamps

Denom.	Scott number	Date of issue	Description	Designer
8¢	1475	1/26/73	Stacked "Love"	Robert Indiana
20¢	1951	2/1/82	Flowered "Love"	Mary Faulconer
20¢	1951a	———	same perf 11	same
20¢	2071	1/12/84	Love with hearts	Bradbury Thompson
22¢	2143	4/17/85	Painted Love	Corita Kent
22¢	2202	1/30/86	Puppy love	Saul Mandel

U.S. Love Stamps (continued)

Denom.	Scott number	Date of issue	Description	Designer
22¢	2248	1/30/87	Graphic heart	John Alcorn
25¢	2378	7/4/88	Love rose	Richard Sheaff
45¢	2379	8/8/88	Love roses	Richard Sheaff
25¢	to come	to come	Love Birds	Jayne Hertco

American Folk Art Series

Denom.	Scott number	Date of issue	Description	Designer	Printing
13¢	1706-09	4/13/77	Pueblo Indian Pottery	Ford Ruthling	photogravure
13¢	1745-48	3/8/78	Quilts	Christopher Pullman	photogravure
15¢	1775-78	4/19/79	Pennsylvania Toleware	Bradbury Thompson	photogravure
15¢	1834-37	9/25/80	Pacific North West Indian Masks	Bradbury Thompson	photogravure
22¢	2138-41	3/22/85	Duck Decoys	Stevan Dohanos	photogravure
22¢	2235-38	9/4/86	Navajo Art	Derry Noyes	photogravure
22¢	2240-43	10/1/86	Woodcarved Figurines	Bradbury Thompson	photogravure
22¢	2351-54	8/14/87	Lacemaking	Libby Thiel	offset/intaglio
25¢	2390-93	10/1/88	Carousel Animals	Paul Calle	offset/intaglio
25¢	to come	1990	Indian Headdresses	to come	to come

Americana Series

Denom.	Scott number	Date of issue	Description	Format	Identifying features	Tagging
1¢	1581	12/8/77	Inkwell and Quill	sheet	———	yes
1¢	1581a	———	Inkwell and Quill	sheet	city, Bureau precancel	no
1¢	1811	3/6/80	Inkwell and Quill	coil	———	yes
2¢	1582	12/8/77	Speaker's Stand	sheet	greenish paper	yes
2¢	1582	———	Speaker's Stand	sheet	yellow paper	yes
2¢	1582b	1981	Speaker's Stand	sheet	cream paper	yes
2¢	1582a	———	Speaker's Stand	sheet	city, Bureau precancel	no
3¢	1584	12/8/77	Ballot Box	sheet	———	yes
3¢	1584a	———	Ballot Box	sheet	no city, Bureau precancel	no
3.1¢	1613	10/25/79	Guitar	coil	———	yes
3.1¢	1613a	———	Guitar	coil	no city, Bureau precancel	no
3.5¢	1813	6/23/80	Violins	coil	———	yes
3.5¢	1813a	———	Violins	coil	no city, Bureau precancel	no
4¢	1585	12/8/77	Books, Glasses	sheet	———	yes
4¢	1585a	———	Books, Glasses	sheet	no city, Bureau precancel	no
7.7¢	1614	11/20/76	Saxhorns	coil	yellowish paper	yes
7.7¢	1614	———	Saxhorns	coil	whitish paper	yes
7.7¢	1614a	———	Saxhorns	coil	city, Bureau precancel	no
7.9¢	1615	4/23/76	Drum	coil	———	yes

Americana Series (continued)

Denom.	Scott number	Date of issue	Description	Format	Identifying features	Tagging
7.9¢	1615a	——	Drum	coil	city, Bureau precancel	no
7.9¢	1615a	——	Drum	coil	Car-rt-sort overprint	no
8.4¢	1615c	7/13/78	Piano	coil	——	yes
8.4¢	1615cd	——	Piano	coil	city, Bureau precancel	no
8.4¢	1615cd	——	Piano	coil	no city, Bureau precancel	no
9¢	1590	3/11/77	Capitol	booklet	perf 11x10 1/2 whitish paper	yes
9¢	1590a	3/11/77	Capitol	booklet	perf 10, whitish paper	yes
9¢	1591	11/24/75	Capitol	sheet	gray paper	yes
9¢	1591a	——	Capitol	sheet	no city, gray paper Bureau precancel	no
9¢	1616	3/5/76	Capitol	coil	grayish paper	yes
9¢	1616b	——	Capitol	coil	city, Bureau precancel	no
9¢	1616b	——	Capitol	coil	no city, Bureau precancel	no
9¢	1616b	——	Capitol	coil	presort first class overprint-wide space	no
9¢	1616b	——	Capitol	coil	presort first class overprint-narrow space	no
10¢	1592	11/17/77	Contemplation of Justice	sheet	——	yes
10¢	1592a	——	Contemplation of Justice	sheet	Chicago Bureau precancel	no
10¢	1617	11/4/77	Contemplation of Justice	coil	——	yes
10¢	1617a	——	Contemplation of Justice	coil	city name, Bureau precancel	no
10¢	1617a	——	Contemplation of Justice	coil	no city, Bureau precancel	no
11¢	1593	11/13/75	Printing Press	sheet	——	yes
12¢	1594	4/8/81	Torch	sheet	——	yes
12¢	1816	4/8/81	Torch	coil	——	yes
12¢	1816a	——	Torch	coil	no city, brownish with Bureau precancel	no
12¢	1816a	——	Torch	coil	red-brown with presort overprint	no
13¢	1595	10/31/75	Liberty Bell	booklet	——	yes
13¢	1618	11/25/75	Liberty Bell	coil	——	yes
13¢	1618a	——	Liberty Bell	coil	city name, Bureau precancel	no
13¢	1618a	——	Liberty Bell	coil	no city, Bureau precancel	no
13¢	1618a	——	Liberty Bell	coil	presort overprint wide spacing	no
13¢	1618a	——	Liberty Bell	coil	presort overprint narrow spacing	no
13¢	1596	12/1/75	Eagle and Shield	sheet	perf 11 1/4, perfect perfs	yes
13¢	1596	——	Eagle and Shield	sheet	perf 11, line perfs	yes

Americana Series (continued)

Denom.	Scott number	Date of issue	Description	Format	Identifying features	Tagging
13¢	1596	——	Eagle and Shield	sheet	city name, Bureau precancel	yes
13¢	1596	——	Eagle and Shield	sheet	no city, Bureau precancel	yes
13¢	1622	11/15/75	Flag Over Independence Hall	sheet	perf 11x10 1/2 bottom margins	yes
13¢	1622c	1981	Flag Over Independence Hall	sheet	perf 11, side margins	yes
13¢	1625	11/15/75	Flag Over Independence Hall	coil	——	yes
13¢	1623	3/11/77	Flag Over Capitol	booklet	perf 11x10 1/2	yes
13¢	1623b	3/11/77	Flag Over Capitol	booklet	perf 10	yes
15¢	1597	6/30/78	Fort McHenry Flag	sheet	perf 10	yes
15¢	1598	6/30/78	Fort McHenry Flag	booklet	perf 11x10 1/2	yes
15¢	1618c	6/30/78	Fort McHenry Flag	coil	——	yes
16¢	1599	3/31/78	Liberty	sheet	——	yes
16¢	1619	3/31/78	Liberty	coil	overall tagging, Cottrell, bluish tinge, joint lines	yes
16¢	1619	3/31/78	Liberty	coil	Huck, white paper no lines, block tagging	yes
24¢	1603	11/14/75	Old North Church	sheet	——	yes
28¢	1604	8/11/78	Fort Nisqually	sheet	——	yes
29¢	1605	4/14/78	Lighthouse	sheet	——	yes
30¢	1606	8/27/79	Schoolhouse	sheet	——	yes
30¢	1606	——	Schoolhouse	sheet	no city precancel	yes
50¢	1608	9/11/79	Iron Betty Lamp	sheet	——	yes
50¢	1608	——	Iron Betty Lamp	sheet	no city, 11.5mm bar space	yes
50¢	1608	——	Iron Betty Lamp	sheet	no city, 10.5mm bar space	yes
$1	1610	7/2/79	Candleholder	sheet	——	yes
$1	1610	——	Candleholder	sheet	no city, 11.25mm bar space	yes
$1	1610	——	Candleholder	sheet	no city, 10.5mm bar space	yes
$2	1611	11/16/78	Kerosene Lamp	sheet	——	yes
$5	1612	8/23/79	Conductor's Lantern	sheet	——	yes

Literary Arts Series

Denom.	Scott number	Date of issue	Description	Designer	Printing
13¢	1731	1/6/78	Carl Sandburg	William A. Smith	intaglio
15¢	1773	2/27/79	John Steinbeck	Bradbury Thompson	intaglio
15¢	1832	9/5/80	Edith Wharton	Bradbury Thompson	intaglio
18¢	1926	7/10/81	Edna St. Vincent Millay	Glenora Case Richards	photogravure
20¢	2010	4/30/82	Horatio Algers	Robert Hallock	intaglio
20¢	2047	7/8/83	Nathaniel Hawthorne	Bradbury Thompson	photogravure
20¢	2094	8/1/84	Herman Melville	Bradbury Thompson	intaglio
22¢	2239	9/26/86	T.S. Eliot	Bradbury Thompson	intaglio
22¢	2350	8/3//87	William Faulkner	Bradbury Thompson	intaglio
25¢	to come	7/21/89	Ernest Hemingway	M. Gregory Rudd	photogravure
25¢	to come	1990	Marianne Moore	to come	to come

Black Heritage Series

Denom.	Scott number	Date of issue	Description	Designer
13¢	1744	2/1/78	Harriet Tubman	Jerry Pinkney
15¢	1771	1/13/79	Martin Luther King	Jerry Pinkney
15¢	1804	2/15/80	Benjamin Banneker	Jerry Pinkney
15¢	1875	1/30/81	Whitney Moore Young	Jerry Pinkney
20¢	2016	8/2/82	Jackie Robinson	Jerry Pinkney
20¢	2044	6/9/83	Scott Joplin	Jerry Pinkney
20¢	2073	2/1/84	Carter G. Woodson	Jerry Pinkney
22¢	2137	3/5/85	Mary McLeod Bethune	Jerry Pinkney
22¢	2203	2/4/86	Sojourner Truth	Jerry Pinkney
22¢	2249	2/20/87	Jean Baptiste Pointe du Sable	Thomas Blackshear
22¢	2371	2/2/88	James W. Johnson	Thomas Blackshear
25¢	2402	2/3/89	A. Philip Randolph	Thomas Blackshear
25¢	—	1990	Ida B. Wells	—

U.S. Non-denominated Definitives

A guide to the five non-denominated contingency definitives issued by the United States Postal Service

Denom.	Indicator	Date of Issue	Date of Rate Increase
15¢	A	May 22, 1978	May 29, 1978
18¢	B	March 15, 1981	March 22, 1981
20¢	C	Oct. 11, 1981	Nov. 1, 1981
22¢	D	Feb. 1, 1985	Feb. 17, 1985
25¢	E	March 22, 1988	April 3, 1988

Performing Arts Series

Denom.	Scott number	Date of issue	Description	Designer	Printing
13¢	1755	5/24/78	Jimmie Rodgers	Jim Sharpe	photogravure
15¢	1756	7/3/78	George M. Cohan	Jim Sharpe	photogravure
15¢	1801	11/4/79	Will Rogers	Jim Sharpe	photogravure
15¢	1803	1/29/80	W.C. Fields	Jim Sharpe	photogravure
20¢	2012	6/8/82	The Barrymores	Jim Sharpe	photogravure
20¢	2088	5/23/84	Douglas Fairbanks	Jim Sharpe	photogravure
20¢	2090	6/6/84	John McCormack	Jim Sharpe, Ron Mercer (Ireland)	photogravure
22¢	2110	1/23/85	Jerome Kern	Jim Sharpe	photogravure
22¢	2211	4/29/87	Duke Ellington	Jim Sharpe	photogravure
22¢	2250	2/27/87	Enrico Caruso	Jim Sharpe	photogravure
25¢	2411	3/25/89	Arturo Toscanini	Jim Sharpe	photogravure

American Architecture Series

Denom.	Scott number	Date of issue	Designer	Printing
15¢	1779-82	6/4/79	Walter D. Richards	intaglio
15¢	1838-41	10/9/80	Walter D. Richards	intaglio
18¢	1928-31	8/28/81	Walter D. Richards	intaglio
20¢	2019-22	9/30/82	Walter D. Richards	intaglio

Great Americans Series

Denom.	Scott number	Date of issue	Description	Tagging	Perfs	Designer
1¢	1844	9/23/83	Dorothea Dix	block	(11 1/4) perfect	Bernie Fuchs
1¢	——	———	Dorothea Dix	block	(10 3/4) line	Bernie Fuchs
1¢	2168	6/30/86	Margaret Mitchell	block	perfect	Ron Adair
2¢	1845	11/18/82	Igor Stravinsky	overall	line	Burt Silverman
2¢	2169	2/28/87	Mary Lyon	block	perfect	Ron Adair
3¢	1846	7/13/83	Henry Clay	overall	line	Ward Brackett
3¢	2170	9/15/86	Paul Dudley White	block	perfect	Chris Calle
4¢	1847	6/3/83	Carl Shurz	overall	line	Richard Sparks
4¢	2171	7/14/86	Father Flanagan	block	perfect	Chris Calle
5¢	1848	6/25/83	Pearl S. Buck	overall	line	Paul Calle
5¢	2172	2/27/86	Hugo Black	block	perfect	Chris Calle
6¢	1849	9/19/85	Walter Lippmann	block	line	Dennis Lyall
7¢	1850	1/25/85	Abraham Baldwin	block	line	Richard Sparks
8¢	1851	7/25/85	Henry Knox	overall	line	Arthur Lidov
9¢	1852	6/7/85	Sylvanus Thayer	block	line	Robert Anderson
10¢	1853	5/31/84	Richard Russell	block	line	Richard Sparks
10¢	2176	8/15/87	Red Cloud	block	perfect	Robert Anderson
11¢	1854	2/12/85	Alden Partridge	overall	line	Robert Anderson
13¢	1855	1/15/82	Crazy Horse	overall	line	Brad Holland
14¢	1856	3/21/85	Sinclair Lewis	block	line	Bradbury Thompson
14¢	2177	2/12/87	Julia Ward Howe	block	perfect	Ward Brackett
15¢	2178	6/6/88	Buffalo Bill	block	perfect	Jack Rosenthal
17¢	1857	5/28/81	Rachel Carson	overall	line	Ward Brackett
17¢	2179	6/18/86	Belva Ann Lockwood	block	perfect	Chris Calle
18¢	1858	5/7/81	George Mason	overall	line	Richard Sparks
19¢	1859	12/27/80	Sequoyah	overall	line	Roy Andersen
20¢	1860	1/12/82	Ralph Bunche	overall	line	Jim Sharpe
20¢	1861	6/10/83	Thomas Gallaudet	overall	line	Dennis Lyall
20¢	1862	1/26/84	Harry S. Truman	block	(10 3/4) line	Chris Calle
20¢	——	Aug. '88	Harry S. Truman	block	(11 1/4) perfect	Chris Calle
21¢	2180	10/21/88	Chester Carlson	block	perfect	Susan Sanford
22¢	1863	4/23/85	John J. Audubon	block	(10 3/4) line	Chris Calle
22¢	——	1987	John J. Audubon	block	(11 1/4) perfect	Chris Calle
23¢	2182	11/4/88	Mary Cassatt	block	perfect	Dennis Lyall
25¢	2183	1/11/86	Jack London sheet	block	(11 1/4) perfect	Richard Sparks
25¢	2183a	5/3/88	Jack London booklet	block	(11 1/4) perfect	Richard Sparks
25¢	2197	5/3/88	Jack London	block	(10x9 3/4) perfect	Richard Sparks
28¢	to come	9/14/89	Sitting Bull	to come	to come	to come
30¢	1864	9/2/84	Frank Laubach	block	(10 3/4) line	Richard Sparks
30¢	——	1987	Frank Laubach	block	(11 3/4) perfect	Richard Sparks
35¢	1865	6/3/81	Charles Drew	overall	line	Nathan Jones
37¢	1866	1/26/82	Robert Millikan	overall	line	Chris Calle
39¢	1867	5/20/85	Grenville Clark	block	(10 3/4) line	Roy Andersen
39¢	——	1987	Grenville Clark	block	(11 1/4) perfect	Roy Andersen
40¢	1868	2/24/84	Lillian Gilbreth	block	(10 3/4)	Ward Brackett

Great Americans Series (continued)

Denom.	Scott number	Date of issue	Description	Tagging	Perfs	Designer
40¢	—	1987	Lillian Gilbreth	block	line (11 3/4) perfect	Ward Brackett
45¢	2188	6/17/88	Dr. Harvey Cushing	block	perfect	Bradbury Thompson
50¢	1869	2/22/85	Chester Nimitz	overall	line	Chris Calle
50¢	—	8/25/86	Chester Nimitz	block	(11 1/4) perfect	Chris Calle
56¢	2191	9/3/86	John Harvard	block	perfect	Robert Anderson
65¢	2192	11/5/88	Hap Arnold	block	perfect	Chris Calle
$1	2194	9/23/86	Bernard Revel	block	perfect	Tom Broad
$1	2194A	6/7/89	Johns Hopkins	block	perfect	Bradbury Thompson
$2	2195	3/19/86	William Jennings Bryan	block	perfect	Tom Broad
$5	2196	8/25/87	Bret Harte	block	perfect	Arthur Lidov

Great Americans Series Perforation Varieties

	L perforator (perf approx. 10 3/4)	**Eureka perforator (perf approx. 11 1/4)**
1¢ Dix	floating plate numbers, small tagging block	bull's-eye on-line perforator, large tagging block
22¢ Audubon	floating plate numbers, small tagging block	fixed plate number positions, large tagging block
30¢ Laubach	floating plate numbers, small tagging block	fixed plate number positions, large tagging block
40¢ Gilbreth	floating plate numbers, small tagging block	fixed plate number positions, large tagging block
50¢ Nimitz	fixed plates, I-8 press overall tagging	fixed plates, A press, block tagging

All stamps listed above were printed on the A press, except the early version of the 50¢ Nimitz stamp.

Transportation Coils

Denom.	Scott number	Date of issue	Description	Press	Tagging
1¢	1897	8/19/83	Omnibus	Cottrell	Overall
1¢	2225	11/26/86	Omnibus (re-engraved)	B	Block
2¢	1897A	5/20/82	Locomotive	Cottrell	Overall
2¢	2226	3/6/87	Locomotive	B	Block
3¢	1898	3/25/83	Handcar	Cottrell	Overall
3¢	2252	2/29/88	Conestoga Wagon	B	Block
3.4¢	2123	6/8/85	School Bus	Cottrell	Overall
3.4¢	2123a	6/8/85	School Bus precancel	Cottrell	None
4¢	1898A	8/19/82	Stagecoach	Cottrell	Overall

Transportation Coils (continued)

Denom.	Scott number	Date of issue	Description	Press	Tagging
4¢	1898Ab	8/19/82	Stagecoach precancel	Cottrell	None
4¢	2228	8/15/86*	Stagecoach (re-engraved)	B	Block
4.9¢	2124	6/21/85	Buckboard	Cottrell	Overall
4.9¢	2124a	6/21/85	Buckboard precancel	Cottrell	None
5¢	1899	10/10/83	Motorcycle	Cottrell	Overall
5¢	2253	9/25/87	Milk Wagon	B	Block
5.2¢	1900	3/21/83	Sleigh	Cottrell	Overall
5.2¢	1900a	3/21/83	Sleigh precancel	Cottrell	None
5.3¢	2254	9/16/88	Elevator service inscribed	B	None
5.5¢	2125	11/1/86	Star Route Truck	B	Block
5.5¢	2125a	11/1/86	Star Route Truck service inscribed	B	None
5.9¢	1901	2/17/82	Bicycle	Cottrell	Overall
5.9¢	1901a	2/17/82	Bicycle precancel	Cottrell	None
6¢	2126	5/6/85	Tricycle	B	Block
6¢	2126a	5/6/85	Tricycle precancel	B	None
7.1¢	2127	2/6/87	Tractor	B	Block
7.1¢	2127a	2/6/87	Tractor service inscribed	B	None
7.1¢	2127a	5/26/89	Tractor service inscribed ZIP+4	B	None
7.4¢	1902	4/7/84	Baby Buggy	B	Block
7.4¢	1902a	4/7/84	Baby Buggy precancel	B	None
7.6¢	2255	8/30/88	Carreta service inscribed	B	None
8.3¢	2128	6/21/85	Ambulance	Cottrell	Overall

Transportation Coils (continued)

Denom.	Scott number	Date of issue	Description	Press	Tagging
8.3¢	2128a	6/21/85	Ambulance precancel	Cottrell	None
8.3¢	2231	8/29/86	Ambulance adapted precancel	B	None
8.4¢	2256	8/12/88	Wheel chair service inscribed	B, C or D	None**
8.5¢	2129	1/24/87	Tow Truck	B	Block
8.5¢	2129a	1/24/87	Tow Truck precancel	B	None
9.3¢	1903	12/15/81	Mail Wagon	Cottrell	Overall
9.3¢	1903a	12/15/81	Mail Wagon precancel	Cottrell	None
10¢	2257	4/11/87	Canal Boat	B	Block
10.1¢	2130	4/18/85	Oil Wagon	B	Block
10.1¢	2130a	4/18/85	Oil Wagon black overprint	B	None
10.1¢	—	6/27/88	Oil Wagon red overprint	B	None
10.9¢	1904	3/26/82	Hansom Cab	Cottrell	Overall
10.9¢	1904a	3/26/82	Hansom Cab precancel	Cottrell	None
11¢	1905	2/3/84	Caboose	B	Block
11¢	1905a	2/3/84	Caboose precancel	B	None
11¢	2131	6/11/85	Stutz Bearcat	Cottrell	Overall
12¢	2132	4/2/85	Stanley Steamer	Cottrell	Overall
12¢	2132a	4/2/85	Stanley Steamer precancel	Cottrell	None
12¢	—	9/3/87*	Stanley Steamer adapted precancel	B	None
12.5¢	2133	4/18/85	Pushcart	B	Block
12.5¢	2133a	4/18/85	Pushcart precancel	B	None
13¢	2258	10/29/88	Police Patrol Wagon service inscribed	B	None
13.2¢	2259	7/19/88	Railroad Coal Car service inscribed	B	None

Transportation Coils (continued)

Denom.	Scott number	Date of issue	Description	Press	Tagging
14¢	2134	3/23/85	Iceboat	Cottrell	Overall
14¢	—	9/30/86*	Iceboat adapted	B	Block
15¢	2260	7/12/88	Tugboat	B	Block
16.7¢	2261	7/7/88	Popcorn Wagon service inscribed	B	None
17¢	1906	6/25/81	Electric Auto	Cottrell	Overall
17¢	1906a	6/25/81	Electric Auto precancel	Cottrell	None
17¢	2135	8/20/86	Dog Sled	B	Block
17.5¢	2262	9/25/87	Marmon Wasp	B	Block
17.5¢	2262a	9/25/87	Marmon Wasp service inscribed	B	None
18¢	1907	5/18/81	Surrey	Cottrell	Overall
20¢	1908	12/10/81	Fire Pumper	Cottrell	Overall
20¢	2263	10/28/88	Cable Car	B	Block
20.5¢	2264	9/28/88	Fire Engine service inscribed	B	None
21¢	2265	8/16/88	Railroad Mail Car service inscribed	B, C or D	None**
24.1¢	2266	10/26/88	Tandem bicycle service inscribed	B	None
25¢	2136	11/22/86	Bread Wagon	B	Overall

*Earliest date of use
**The C and D presses are used interchangeably.

Sports Series

Denom.	Scott number	Date of issue	Description	Designer	Printing
18¢	1932	9/22/81	Babe Zaharias	Richard Gangel	intaglio
18¢	1933	9/22/81	Bobby Jones	Richard Gangel	intaglio
20¢	2046	7/6/83	Babe Ruth	Richard Gangel	intaglio
20¢	2089	5/24/84	Jim Thorpe	Richard Gangel	intaglio
20¢	2097	8/17/84	Roberto Clemente	Juan Lopez Bonilla	photogravure
22¢	2376	3/9/88	Knute Rockne	Peter Cocci and Thomas Hipschen	offset/intaglio
25¢	2377	6/13/88	Francis Ouimet	M. Gregory Rudd	photogravure
25¢	2417	6/10/89	Lou Gehrig	Bart Forbes	photogravure
25¢	to come	1990	Jesse Owens	to come	to come

Constitution Bicentennial Series

Denom.	Scott number	Date of issue	Description	Designer	Printing
22¢	2336	4/4/87	Delaware Statehood	Richard Sheaff	photogravure
22¢	2337	8/26/87	Pennsylvania Statehood	Richard Sheaff	photogravure
22¢	2338	9/11/87	New Jersey Statehood	Jim Lamb	photogravure
22¢	2339	1/6/88	Georgia Statehood	Greg Harlin	photogravure
22¢	2340	1/9/88	Connecticut Statehood	Chris Calle	offset/intaglio
22¢	2341	2/6/88	Massachusetts Statehood	Richard Sheaff	intaglio
22¢	2342	2/15/88	Maryland Statehood	Stephen Hustuedt	offset/intaglio
22¢	2343	5/23/88	South Carolina Statehood	Bob Timberlake	photogravure
22¢	2344	6/21/88	New Hampshire Statehood	Thomas Szumowski	photogravure
22¢	2345	6/25/88	Virginia Statehood	Pierre Mion	offset/intaglio
22¢	2346	7/23/88	New York Statehood	Bradbury Thompson	offset/intaglio
22¢	2355-59	8/28/87	Drafting of the Constitution	Bradbury Thompson	photogravure
22¢	2360	9/17/87	Signing of the Constitution	Howard Koslow	offset/intaglio
25¢	2412	4/4/89	House of Representatives	Howard Koslow	offset/intaglio
25¢	2413	4/6/89	Senate	Howard Koslow	offset/intaglio
25¢	2414	4/16/89	Executive Branch	Howard Kowlow	offset/intaglio
25¢	to come	8/22/89	North Carolina Statehood	to come	to come
25¢	to come	9/25/89	Drafting of Bill of Rights	to come	to come
—	——	1990	Rhode Island Statehood	to come	to come
—	to come	1990	Judicial Branch	Howard Koslow	to come

Pioneers in Aviation Stamp Series

Scott number	Date of issue	Description	Designer	Printing
C91-92	9/23/78	31¢ Wright Brothers	Ken Dallison	offset/intaglio
C93-94	3/29/79	21¢ Octave Chanute	Ken Dallison	offset/intaglio
C95-96	11/20/79	25¢ Wiley Post	Ken Dallison	offset/intaglio
C99	12/30/80	28¢ Blanche Stuart Scott	Paul Calle	photogravure
C100	12/30/80	35¢ Glenn Curtiss	Ken Dallison	photogravure
C113	2/13/85	33¢ Alfred Verville	Ken Dallison	photogravure
C114	2/13/85	39¢ Lawrence & Elmer Sperry	Howard Koslow	photogravure
C118	5/14/88	45¢ Samuel Langley	Ken Dallison	offset/intaglio
C119	6/23/88	36¢ Igor Sikorsky	Ren Wicks	gravure/intaglio

1983 Official Mail Series

Denom.	Scott number	Date of Issue	Format	Printing	Designer
1¢	0127	1/12/85	sheet	intaglio	Bradbury Thompson
1¢	0143	7/5/89	sheet	offset	" "
4¢	0128	1/12/85	sheet	intaglio	" "
13¢	0129	1/12/85	sheet	intaglio	" "
14¢(D)	0138	2/4/85	sheet	intaglio	" "
14¢	0129A	5/15/85	sheet	intaglio	" "
15¢	0138A	6/11/88	coil	offset	" "
17¢	0130	1/12/85	sheet	intaglio	" "
20¢	0135	1/12/85	coil	intaglio	" "
20¢	0138B	5/19/88	coil	offset	" "
22¢(D)	0139	2/4/85	coil	intaglio	" "
22¢	0136	5/15/85	coil	intaglio	" "

1983 Official Mail Series (continued)

Denom.	Scott number	Date of Issue	Format	Printing	Designer
25¢(E)	0140	3/22/88	coil	offset	" "
25¢	0141	6/11/88	coil	offset	" "
$1	0132	1/12/85	sheet	intaglio	" "
$5	0133	1/12/85	sheet	intaglio	" "

Joint Issues

Year	Date	Issue	Scott number	Country	Scott number	Design data
1959	June 26	St. Lawrence Seaway	1131	Canada	387	similar
1960	Sept. 16	Mexican Independence	1157			similar design, different formats
	Sept. 15	Mexican Independence		Mexico	910	Mexico had added values and designs.
1965	Aug. 28	Settlement of Florida	1271	Spain	1312	similar
1975	July 15	Apollo-Soyuz	1569-70	Russia	4339-40	similar (Russia has additional values and designs.)
1976	June 1	U.S. Independence	1690	Canada	691	similar
1977	Aug. 4	Peace Bridge	1721	Canada	737	completely different
1980	Oct. 13	Philip Mazzei	C98			
	Oct. 18	Philip Mazzei		Italy	1439	completely different
1981	Oct. 13	James Hoban	1935, 1936			
	Sept. 29	James Hoban		Ireland	504	similar
1982	April 20	Diplomatic Recognition	2003	Netherlands	640-41	similar
1983	Mar. 24	Treaty of Amity and Commerce	2036	Sweden	1453	similar
1983	April 29	German Immigration	2040			
	May 5	German Immigration		West Germany	1397	similar
1983	Sept. 2	Treaty of Paris	2052	France	1899	completely different
1984	June 6	John McCormack	2090	Ireland	594	similar
1984	June 26	St. Lawrence Seaway	2091	Canada	1015	different vignette and size
1986	Jan. 23	Stamp Collecting booklet	2198-2201	Sweden	1585-88	only one of four stamps is similar
1986	May 24	Francis Vigo postal card	UX111	Italy		similar
1986	July 4	Statue of Liberty	2224	France	2014	similar
1987	July 17	Diplomatic Relations with Morocco	2349	Morocco		similar
1988	Jan. 26	Australia Bicentennial	2370	Australia		similar

Joint Issues (continued)

Year	Date	Issue	Scott number	Country	Scott number	Design data
1989	July 14	French Revolution Bicentennial	to come	France	to come	France created triptych from original concept.

Note: A United States stamp issued in 1965 for the 20th anniversary of the United Nations was similar to the design of the U.N. stamp. This stamp was not a joint issue but rather was part of an omnibus series issued by several countries.

Look-alike Stamps That Differ in Design Size and Catalog Value

Scott No.	Stamp description	Press	Dimensions	1990 Scott used value
462	1¢ perf. 10 Washington	F	18 1/2-19 x 22mm	.15
543	1¢ perf. 10 Washington	R	19 x 22 1/2mm	.06
498	1¢ perf. 11 Washington	F	18 1/2-19 x 22mm	.05
544	1¢ perf. 11 Washington	R	19 x 22 1/2mm	$2,400
545	1¢ perf. 11 Washington	R	19 1/2-20 x 22mm	$45
552	1¢ perf. 11 Franklin	F	18 1/2-19 x 22mm	.05
594	1¢ perf. 11 Franklin	R	19 3/4 x 22 1/4mm	$3,500
596	1¢ perf. 11 Franklin	R	19 1/4 x 22 3/4mm	$13,500
554	2¢ perf. 11 Washington	F	18 1/2-19 x 22mm	.05
595	2¢ perf. 11 Washington	R	19 3/4 x 22 1/4mm	$225
610	2¢ perf. 11 Harding	F	19 1/4 x 22 1/4mm	.10
613	2¢ perf. 11 Harding	R	19 1/4 x 22 3/4mm	$13,500

F = flat-plate press
R = rotary press

Modern U.S. Stamp Issues Perforated on More Than One Type of Equipment

Year	Description	Scott	Perforation Equipment	Perforation Measurement
1975	10¢ Prang Christmas	1580	Andreotti in-line (bull's eye)	11.2 x 11.2
	10¢ Prang Christmas	1580	L-perforator (imperfect)	10.9 x 10.9
	10¢ Prang Christmas	1580b	Electric Eye (EE) (imperfect)	10.5 x 11.3
1975	13¢ Eagle & Shield	1596	Andreotti in-line (bull's-eye)	11.2 x 11.2
	13¢ Eagle & Shield	1596	L-perforator (imperfect)	10.9 x 10.9
1977	9¢ Capitol Dome & 13¢ Flag Over Capitol booklet	1590 & 1623	Goebel in-line (bull's-eye)	11 x 10 1/2
	9¢ Capitol Dome & 13¢ Flag Over Capitol booklet	1590a & 1623b	Goebel in-line (bull's-eye)	10 x 10
1975	13¢ Flag Over Independence Hall	1622	Huck in-line (bull's-eye)	10.9 x 10.6
1981	13¢ Flag Over Independence Hall	1622c	A-press in-line (bull's-eye)	11.2 x 11.2
1977	13¢ Colorado Statehood	1711	L-perforator (imperfect)	10.9 x 10.9
	13¢ Colorado Statehood	1711	Andreotti in-line (bull's-eye)	11.2 x 11.2
1978	(15¢) A-series sheet	1735	Andreotti in-line (bull's-eye)	11.2 x 11.2
	(15¢) A-series sheet	1735	L-perforator (imperfect)	10.9 x 10.9
1979	15¢ John Paul Jones	1789	L-perforator (imperfect)	11 x 12 (2nd)
	15¢ John Paul Jones	1789a	L-perforator (imperfect)	11 x 11 (3rd)

Modern U.S. Stamp Issues Perforated on More Than One Type of Equipment (continued)

Year	Description	Scott	Perforation Equipment	Perforation Measurement
	15¢ John Paul Jones	1789b	L-perforator (imperfect)	12 x 12 (Orig)
1980	15¢ Winter Olympics	1795-98	EE (imperfect)	11.3 x 10.5
	15¢ Winter Olympics	1795-98a	Andreotti in-line (bull's-eye)	11.2 x 11.2
1983	1¢ Dorothea Dix	1844	A-press in-line (bull's-eye)	11.2 x 11.2
	1¢ Dorothea Dix	1844	L-perforator	10.9 x 10.9
1984	20¢ Truman	1862	L-perforator (imperfect)	10.9 x 10.9
1988	20¢ Truman	1862	Eureka, off-press (bull's-eye)	11.2 x 11.2
1985	22¢ John J. Audubon	1863	L-perforator (imperfect)	10.9 x 10.9
	22¢ John J. Audubon	1863	Eureka, off-press (bull's-eye)	11.2 x 11.2
1984	30¢ Laubach	1864	L-perforator (imperfect)	10.9 x 10.9
	30¢ Laubach	1864	Eureka, off-press (bull's-eye)	11.2 x 11.2
1985	39¢ Grenville Clark	1867	L-perforator (imperfect)	10.9 x 10.9
	39¢ Grenville Clark	1867	Eureka, off-press (bull's-eye)	11.2 x 11.2
1984	40¢ Lillian Gilbreth	1868	L-perforator (imperfect)	10.9 x 10.9
	40¢ Lillian Gilbreth	1868	Eureka, off-press (bull's-eye)	11.2 x 11.2
1985	50¢ Chester Nimitz	1869	L-perforator (imperfect)	10.9 x 10.9
	50¢ Chester Nimitz	1869	Eureka, off-press (bull's-eye)	11.2 x 11.2
1981	20¢ Flag Over Supreme Court	1894	A-press in-line (bull's-eye)	11.2 x 11.2
	20¢ Flag Over Supreme Court	1894	L-perforator (imperfect)	10.9 x 10.9
1982	20¢ Love	1951	EE (imperfect)	11.3 x 10.5
	20¢ Love	1951a	Andreotti in-line (bull's-eye)	11.2 x 11.2
1982	20¢ Birds & Flowers	1953-2002c	EE (imperfect)	10.5 x 11.3
	20¢ Birds & Flower	1953-2002b	Andreotti in-line (bull's-eye)	11.2 x 11.2
1988	25¢ Jack London ($1.50 & $3 booklets)	2197	Goebel in-line (bull's-eye)	10.0 x 9.75
	25¢ Jack London ($5 booklet)	2183a	Eureka, off-press (bull's-eye)	11.2 x 11.2
1980	40¢ Mazzei	C98	Andreotti in-line (bull's-eye)	11.2 x 11.2
	40¢ Mazzei	C98a	EE (imperfect)	10.5 x 11.3
1983	40¢ Summer Olympics	C105-8	Andreotti in-line (bull's-eye)	11.2 x 11.2
	40¢ Summer Olympics	C105d-8d	L-perforator (imperfect)	10.9 x 10.9

*This chart compiles information covering differences between look-alike products found in some 30 different articles from several sources. No claim can be made that the chart is either complete or totally accurate. Numbers are given according to the Scott 1989 U.S. Specialized catalog.

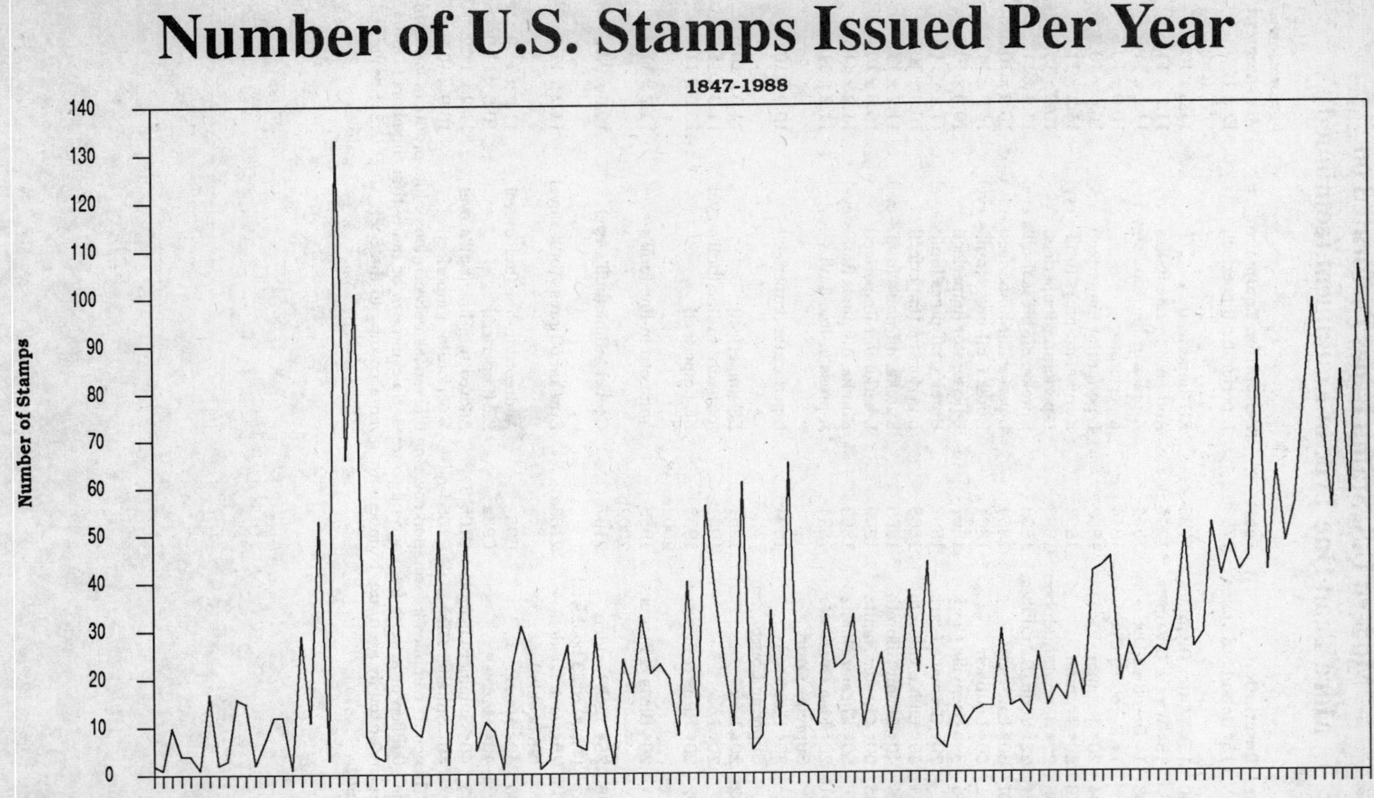

This graph reflects the number of stamps issued by the United States from 1847 to 1988. The quantities issued each year appear on page 319.

Number of U.S. Stamps Issued Per Year

Year	Number of Stamps	Year	Number of Stamps	Year	Number of Stamps	Year	Number of Stamps
1847	2	1887	51	1923	34	1956	24
1852	1	1888	5	1924	10	1957	16
1853	10	1890	11	1925	65	1958	42
1854	4	1891	9	1926	15	1959	43
1855	4	1892	1	1927	14	1960	45
1856	1	1893	23	1928	10	1961	19
1857	17	1894	31	1929	33	1962	27
1858	2	1895	25	1930	22	1963	22
1859	3	1896	1	1931	24	1964	24
1860	16	1897	3	1932	33	1965	26
1861	15	1898	20	1933	10	1966	25
1862	2	1899	27	1934	19	1967	32
1863	7	1901	6	1935	25	1968	50
1864	12	1902	5	1936	8	1969	26
1865	12	1903	29	1937	18	1970	29
1866	1	1904	11	1938	38	1971	52
1867	29	1906	2	1939	21	1972	41
1869	11	1907	24	1940	44	1973	48
1870	53	1908	17	1941	7	1974	42
1871	3	1909	33	1942	5	1975	45
1873	133	1910	21	1943	14	1976	88
1874	66	1911	23	1944	10	1977	42
1875	101	1912	20	1945	13	1978	64
1876	8	1913	8	1946	14	1979	48
1877	4	1914	40	1947	14	1980	56
1878	3	1915	12	1948	30	1981	80
1879	51	1916	56	1949	14	1982	99
1880	17	1917	37	1950	15	1983	74
1881	10	1918	22	1951	12	1984	55
1882	8	1919	10	1952	25	1985	84
1883	17	1920	61	1953	14	1986	58
1884	51	1921	5	1954	18	1987	106
1885	2	1922	8	1955	15	1988	92
1886	23						

Plate Numbers on U.S. Coil Stamps

Plate Number Coil stamps known to exist in collector hands. Square indicates a plate number reported only in precanceled condition. Circle indicates number reported precanceled and unprecanceled. List updated July 20, 1989.

Transportation coils

Scott	Denom.	Plate numbers						
1897	1¢	1	2	3	4	5	6	
2225	1¢	1	2					
1897A	2¢	2	3	4	6	8	10	
2226	2¢	1						
1898	3¢	1	2	3	4			
2252	3¢	1						
2123	3.4¢	(1)	(2)					
1898A	4¢	1	2	(3)	(4)	(5)	(6)	
2228	4¢	1						
2124	4.9¢	[1]	[2]	(3)	(4)	[5]	[6]	
1899	5¢	1	2	3	4			
2253	5¢	1						
1900	5.2¢	(1)	(2)	(3)	[4]	(5)	[6]	
2254	5.3¢	[1]						
2125	5.5¢	(1)	[2]					
1901	5.9¢	(3)	(4)	[5]	[6]			
2126	6¢	(1)	[2]					
2127	7.1¢	(1)						
2127a	7.1¢	(1)						
1902	7.4¢	(2)						
2255	7.6¢	[1]	[2]					
2128	8.3¢	(1)	(2)	[3]	[4]			
2231	8.3¢	[1]	[2]					
2256	8.4¢	[1]	[2]					
2129	8.5¢	(1)	[2]					
1903	9.3¢	(1)	(2)	(3)	(4)	(5)	(6)	[8]
2257	10¢	1						
2130	10.1¢	(1)	[2]					
To come	10.1¢	[2]	[3]					
1904	10.9¢	(1)	(2)	[3]	[4]			
1905	11¢	(1)						
2131	11¢	1	2	3	4			
2132	12¢	(1)	(2)					
To come	12¢	[1]						
2133	12.5¢	(1)	(2)					
2258	13¢	[1]						
2259	13.2¢	[1]						
2134	14¢	1	2	3	4			
To come	14¢	2						
2260	15¢	1						
2261	16.7¢	[1]						
1906	17¢	(1)	(2)	(3)	(4)	(5)	(6)	(7)
2135	17¢	2						
2262	17.5¢	(1)						
1907	18¢	1-18						
1908	20¢	1-16						
2263	20¢	1	2					
2264	20.5¢	[1]						
2265	21¢	[1]	[2]					
2266	24.1¢	[1]						
2136	25¢	1-5						

Flags

Scott	Denom.	Plate numbers		
1891	18¢	1-7		
1895	20¢	1-6	8-13	(14)
2115	22¢	1-8	10-22	T1
2280	25¢	1-5	7-9	
Phos-phored	25¢	5-9		

Others

Scott	Denom.	Plate numbers				
2005	20¢	1	2	3	4	
2112	D	1	2			
2279	E	1111	1211	1222	2222	
2149	18¢	1112	[11121]	3333	[33333]	[43444]
2150	21.1¢	(111111)	(111121)			
2281	25¢	1	2			
0135	20¢	1				

U.S. Stamp Nicknames

A nickname, according to the dictionary, is "a descriptive name given instead of, or in addition to, the one belonging to a person, place or thing."

The following is a listing of many of the nicknames used in the collecting of U.S. stamps.

Alexandria Blue Boy refers to the unique 5¢ postmaster's provisional issued at Alexandria, Va., which was used on a cover that contained a love letter telling the recipient to "burn this letter," which, thankfully, the recipient did not. It is listed in the Scott catalog as 1X2 and as "unique."

August Issues is the nickname given to the group of stamps listed as 55-62 in the Scott catalog. These stamps bear the notation "not regularly issued" next to their listing. They were originally meant to be essays produced by the Continental Bank Note Co., as part of the company's bid to produce U.S. stamps.

Baby Zepp refers to airmail issue Scott C18, picturing the *Graf Zeppelin* visiting the Chicago World's Fair in 1933. The adjective "baby" refers to the fact that the value of the stamp is considerably less than the Zepps (see below), Scott C13-15.

Bank Notes is the nickname given to the 19th-century stamps produced by the Continental Bank Note Co., National Bank Note Co. and the American Bank Note Co. on contract to the U.S. Post Office.

Black Jack is the nickname given to a 19th-century issue that features a portrait of Andrew Jackson and is printed in black. The portrait, which appears on several different stamps, is listed in the Scott catalog as design A32, and as stamp numbers 73, 84, 85B, 87 and 93.

Blue Papers is a nickname that tends to confuse many collectors. It refers to a number of stamps printed in 1908 on experimental paper that had a much higher degree of rag content than most normal paper used for printing stamps. Actually, the paper tends to look more gray than blue.

Broken Circle is a term used to describe a number of different stamps that contain printing varieties in which a circle appearing on the stamp is somehow defective. These issues include Scott 616, the 5¢ Hugenot-Walloon; 704, the 1/2¢ Washington; and 1460, the 6¢ Olympic, which is said to have a "broken ring" for the same reason.

Broken Hat describes a minor printing variety of the 2¢ 1893 Columbian commemorative in which Columbus' hat appears to have a piece missing.

Buggy Whip refers to a plate crack that appears on some copies of the 4.9¢ Transportation coil series stamp. The vertical crack shows up where a whip would be stored on a buckboard.

Bureau Issues are those stamps produced by the Bureau of Engraving and Printing, starting in 1894. Different definitive series are nicknamed numerically as bureau issues, e.g., first bureaus, second bureaus, etc.

Caps is the name given to some interesting plate varieties of the 2¢ 1890 American Bank Note issues, in which tiny white spots on top of the numeral "2" are found. The copies found with this variety are worth a premium, although the regular versions are still worth but a few pennies.

Columbians is the nickname given to the U.S. set of commemorative issues, all but one of which were issued on Jan. 1 and 2, 1893, to honor the World Columbian Exposition held in Chicago.

Day's Folly refers to Scott 1204, an intentionally produced inverted issue of Scott 1203, a memorial stamp in honor Dag Hammarskjold. Shortly after an error pane of 50 of these stamps turned up at a post office window, Postmaster General Edward Day ordered the printing of 40 million of them, so as not to create a valuable error stamp. The original pane of 50 was donated to the American Philatelic Society.

Farley's Follies refer to Scott 753-771, which were 935 intentionally-produced imperforate reprints of stamps the USPOD had issued during 1933 and 1934. They were reprinted to overcome the objections of the public, who decried the fact that the Postmaster General James A. Farley had given imperforate copies of these issues, which he had removed from the printing presses prior to their completion, to relatives and government officials.

Flags refer to a series of 13 stamps picturing the flags of countries overrun by the Germans during World War II (Scott 909-921). "Flags" is also a nickname used to refer to machine cancellations in the shape of a flag.

Hemingway Find refers to a find of 105 St. Louis Bear postmaster's provisionals on cover in a banking firm in 1912. At first discarded and sold as "paper waste," and then salvaged, the covers were eventually sold by Harmer's auction for tens of thousands of dollars in 1948. Hemingway was the name of the paper scrap company.

Inverted Jenny is the nickname given to Scott C3a, the famous 1918 airmail stamp on which the airplane was printed upside down as a result of a printing error.

Kicking Mule is the name used to refer to a series of 19th-century hand cancellations, used in a number of cities. The cancellations depict a mule with hind legs kicking up in the air.

Merry Widow refers to Scott E7, the 10¢ Special Delivery stamp featuring Mercury's helmet. At the time it was issued, there was a hit New York show playing called *The Merry Widow*, which featured ladies' hats that looked like the helmet pictured on the stamp.

Orangeburg Coil refers to Scott 389, a 3¢ Washington Head coil stamp with a different perforation gauge than the other 3¢ coils. This gauge was used by one company for a very short time in 1911. The Orangeburg coil is one of the rarest 20th-century coil stamps and got its nickname from the city in which it was used.

Prairie Dog refers to a printing flaw on Scott 650, the 5¢ Aeronautics stamp. This tiny plate flaw resembles a prairie dog taking a ride on the airplane depicted on the stamp. This flaw is restricted to one stamp on sheets produced from plate 19658.

Prexies is the nickname for the series of definitive stamps issued in 1938 that picture all of the deceased presidents (through the date of issuance) in chronological order from lowest value to highest value in the series. They are also referred to as the "presidentials."

Speedies is the name given to Special Delivery stamps, and comes from the nickname given by postal workers to special delivery mail. *The Speedy* is the name of the book written by Henry M. Gobie on the history of U.S. Special Delivery service.

Wedding Band refers to Scott 38, the airmail stamp honoring the 50th anniversary of New York City as a five-borough entity. The band around the five boroughs looks like a wedding ring.

W-F Heads is the nickname or abbreviation associated with "Washington-Franklin Heads," the series of look-alike definitives picturing the portraits of George Washington and Benjamin Franklin. The stamps were issued between 1908 and 1922.

Zepps refer to Scott C13, C14 and C15, a series of three high-value airmail stamps issued in 1930 for prepaying postage rates for mail carried aboard the *Graf Zeppelin*. They were issued on April 19 and withdrawn from sale on June 30. This short sales period partly accounts for the Zepps' relative scarcity.

ZIP Code is the abbreviation and nickname for "Zone Improvement Plan," the five digit suffix program introduced in 1962 to speed the sorting of mail.

Chapter 4

Citizens' Stamp Advisory Committee

History and Purpose

The purpose of the U.S. Citizens' Stamp Advisory Committee is, officially, to "provide the Postal Service with breadth of judgment and depth of experience in various areas which influence subject matter, character and beauty of postage stamps."

The 15 members are selected to reflect a wide range of educational, geographic and professional backgrounds, with the graphic arts, philately, history and education well represented. Members are appointed by and serve at the pleasure of the postmaster general.

The committee has two separate but related functions. It recommends the subject matter for stamp issues, and also develops and recommends stamp designs.

In both areas, as its name indicates, the committee is merely advisory. Although nearly all committee recommendations are accepted, the sole responsibility for U.S. postage stamps lies with the postmaster general. The final decisions on both subject and design are his.

Some subjects recommended by the committee are not approved; some subjects not recommended by the committee are approved by the postmaster general. Occasionally the committee is notified that the postmaster general has decided to issue a stamp on a subject never brought before the committee. In that case, the committee proceeds with its second function, developing a suitable design.

Committee recommendations are sent to the postmaster general shortly after each meeting by the manager of the Stamp Support Branch, formerly the Stamp Information Branch, which is responsible for Postal Service liaison with the committee. The postmaster general's decisions, recommendations or statements of policy are reported back to the committee, usually at the opening of the next meeting.

There have been changes in the committee's areas of responsibility in recent years. Originally it dealt only with commemorative stamps in sheet form, perhaps 13 issues a year. The responsibility has been extended to cover all stamps — regulars, airmails, coils, and booklets, as well as postal cards and aerogrammes.

There also have been changes of emphasis in the committee's work. One change has been a continuing effort to gain enough lead time to permit the best possible art and printing. The goal is three years. There will always be a few stamps that must be issued on a rush schedule, but this is no longer true of the bulk of the stamp program. In early 1989, programs for 1990 and 1991 had been closed, programs through 1995 had been pretty well blocked out, and subjects were assigned as far ahead as the year 2000.

Another change has been an increasing emphasis on the work of subcommittees. Every request that reaches the Postal Service is considered by the CSAC, if only briefly. A new subject is held for further action or referred to a subcommittee if a single member shows an interest in it.

The subcommittees represent a variety of areas — topicals, Great Americans, Performing Arts, Literary Arts, Christmas, music, medicine, Black Heritage and subjects with anniversary dates like the Constitution bicentennial, the Columbus quincentenary or World War II. The subcommittees are headed by chairmen with special qualifications or interest in the subjects covered. Subcommittee reports provide an informed basis for full committee discussions.

Subject Matter

There is no lack of subject matter for the committee to consider. The Postal Service receives 20,000 to 30,000 letters with some 1,500 to 2,000 different stamp-subject requests each year. The number of commemoratives has not increased much over the years, but in a rate change year the number of issues may reach the seventies, with the total of different stamp designs required well above that.

The goal is to select the most interesting, important or educational of the available subjects. Decisions are made with all users of the Postal Service in mind, not just stamp collectors. Marketing is important. Colorful topical subjects of the kind that repeatedly lead *Linn's Stamp News*' annual stamp popularity polls are not pushed out of the program because something else seems more important.

Design Development

When a subject is approved, it is assigned to one of the committee's five design coordinators, who are professional graphic designers under contract with the Postal Service. The artist asked to design the stamp is selected because of his known work in the desired field — wildlife, horses, cats, ships or portraits, for example. The design coordinator briefs the aritst on the special requirements for stamp art and the committee's suggestions for the particular subject. For new artists, a visit to the Bureau of Engraving and Printing may be arranged for a thorough briefing on reproduction requirements.

The artist is placed under contract with the Postal Service. Payment is $750 for three different "concepts" or preliminary art visualizations, rough sketches for the committee's consideration. If one of the concept sketches is approved, the contract is revised to a total of $3,000 for the finished art. For multiple pieces, the price is $3,000 each for two, $2,500 each for three or four, and $2,000 each for five to 10, or any larger number.

The best designs from an artistic or graphics point of view are worthless if they cannot be printed satisfactorily as a stamp on the presses of the BEP or other private contract printers. For a number of years, a Reproduction Subcommittee of the Citizens' Stamp Advisory Committee met at the Bureau the day before CSAC meetings to preview all stamp art. The subcommittee helped coordinate the artistic creativity of the designer with the necessities of production by one of the Bureau's presses — intaglio or recess engraving (one, two or three colors), process full-color gravure, or a combination of offset and intaglio, since offset alone is not considered a security method of printing.

Meeting with the subcommittee were the design coordinators and responsible postal and Bureau officials. When problems were found, the art was returned to the design coordinators with suggestions for the artists.

In the summer of 1985, after Postmaster General Paul C. Carlin had given his Advisory Committee a "charter of excellence" involving a considerable expansion of its duties and responsibilities, the committee approved a plan for a Quality Assurance Subcommittee to be headed by a new vice chairman of the full CSAC.

The four-member committee met for the first time in October 1985. Meetings are now held the day before the full committee meeting. In the morning, the Quality Subcommittee meets alone, sees the new art, and discusses its quality and suitablity for the subject. The design coordinators and representatives of the BEP and the American Bank Note Company meet separately to consider technical production problems. All of the design coordinators meet with the Quality Subcommittee after lunch.

Designs are presented to the full committee by the design coordinator who supervised the work of the artist. The coordinators, as contract employees of the Postal Service, have no committee vote. Some striking designs are given immediate approval. Others are sent back to the artist with suggestions for revision, or they are rejected outright. If necessary, a new artist is selected.

Compensation

Members of the committee who are officials or employees of other government agencies, such as the BEP or the National Gallery of Art, receive no compensation for their committee work. Members appointed from the private sector are entitled to a fee of $214 a day. Those from outside the Washington area are provided with travel requests for air transportation and actual travel expenses for food and lodging.

History and Membership

The idea of an advisory committee to improve U.S. stamp design developed in the 1930s and 1940s. Foreign countries were beginning to issue colorful stamps in modern graphic designs, and both stamp collectors and artists were asking why the United States could not have colorful stamps. Harry L. Lindquist, publisher of *Stamps* magazine and friend of many New York artists, provided a bridge between stamp collectors and artists.

In 1941, Paul Berdanier, a New York advertising agency art director, formed a Committee of Volunteer Artists in an effort to improve stamp art. Members included W.A. Dwiggins, Clarence Hornung, Gordon Grant, Robert Fawcett, Gustav Jensen, Fred Cooper, Stanley Crane, Warren Chappell, Sam March, Lucien Berhnard, Walter Dorwin Teague, and later Paul Manship and Leon Helguera.

In 1942, through Lindquist's contacts with the Post Office Department, the committee was given an opportunity to design a United Nations for Victory commemorative. After an informal competition, postal officials selected a "United Nations" sketch by Helguera and a plaster cast by Manship on a "Four Freedoms" theme. Characteristically, both designs were modified extensively without consulting the artists.

The next decade has been described as the lowest point in U.S. stamp design. Stamp art was assembled at the Bureau of Engraving and Printing from bits and pieces provided by stamp sponsors and approved by postal officials with little knowledge or appreciation of art. But with the inauguration of President Eisenhower in 1953, a new element entered the picture.

The Republicans had promised to get government out of areas that could be better handled by private industry. Postmaster General Arthur E. Summerfield decided to make a start with stamps.

The Commission of Fine Arts, which had been actively supervising commemorative coin design, indicated an interest in stamps, much to the consternation of postal officials, who didn't want another agency looking over their shoulders. The political implications made stamp subjects and designs difficult enough. But in 1955 the commission, the National Academy of Design and the Post Office Department, agreed to set up a committee of artists to advise on stamp design.

It was a distinguished group — Norman Kent, Fritz Eichenberg and Anthony de Francisci with Thomas Maitland Cleland, Paul Manship and Edward A. Wilson as alternates. But there was considerable foot-dragging in the Post Office Department. No formal meeting was ever held, and apparently the artists were consulted informally only once or twice.

Summerfield Committee

The situation changed abruptly in 1957 when L. Rohe Walter, Summerfield's special assistant for public information, suddenly realized the public relations potential of an effective stamp program and arranged to have the Division of Philately, which had been under Finance, placed under his control.

Walter checked the files, asked advice, and killed several birds with one stone by forming his own seven-member Citizens' Stamp Advisory Committee — three stamp collectors, three artists and an official of the U.S. Information Agency to coordinate stamps with the government's then-extensive foreign propaganda activities.

Members of the Summerfield committee were:

ABBOTT WASHBURN, Washington, D.C. (March 1957-January 1961).

Washburn, deputy director of the U.S. Information Agency, technically was an alternate for the director, Arthur Larson. **ROBERT SIVARD** and **C. ROBERT PAYNE** at times attended meetings as alternates for Washburn.

H.L. LINDQUIST, New York, New York (March 1957-January 1961). Lindquist, named as chairman of the National Federation of Stamp Clubs, had been active in President Eisenhower's People to People program.

FRANKLIN R. BRUNS JR., Takoma Park, Maryland (March-November 1957). Bruns was named curator of the Smithsonian Institution's Division of Philately and Postal History. He resigned from the committee upon accepting appointment as director of the Post Office Department's Division of Philately, but served as the committee's ex-officio chairman.

SOL GLASS, Baltimore, Maryland (March 1957-January 1961). Glass, a department store official, was president of the Bureau Issues Association.

ARNOLD COPELAND, Fairfield, Connecticut (March 1957-January 1961). Copeland was president of Westport Artists, Inc., Westport, Connecticut. He was director of visual planning for the Kudner advertising agency in New York.

ERVINE METZL, New York, New York (March 1957-January 1961). Metzl, president of the Society of Illustrators, was by far the strongest force on the committee for improvement of stamp design.

WILLIAM H. BUCKLEY, New York, New York (March 1957-January 1961). Buckley was president of the Art Directors Club of New York. He was art director for Benton and Bowles, Inc.

ROBERT E. FELLERS, Washington, D.C. (August 1957-January 1961). Fellers was a member ex-officio after his retirement as director of the Post Office Department's Division of Philately.

BERNARD DAVIS, Philadelphia, Pennsylvania (December 1957-January 1961). Davis, who succeeded Bruns on the committee, was founder and director of the National Philatelic Museum in Philadelphia and chairman of the Stamp Committee of President Eisenhower's People to People program.

DONALD R. McLEOD, Chevy Chase, Maryland (April 1958-January 1961). McLeod was named ex-officio as superintendent of the Engraving Division, Bureau of Engraving and Printing.

The committee, with Metzl leading the way, did succeed in improving stamp designs considerably, but fought without success to increase color flexibility through use of photogravure and lithography as well as recess engraving.

Committee members, ex-officio members and alternates were presented the Post Office Department's Benjamin Franklin Service Award by Postmaster General Summerfield at the committee's final meeting on December 15, 1961.

Day Committe

The inauguration of President Kennedy in 1961 and his selection of J. Edward Day as his postmaster general brought some sharp changes of direction. James F. Kelleher took over the supervision of philatelic policy, and Day named a new Citizens' Stamp Advisory Committee conspicuously lacking the U.S. Information Agency representative.

Members of Postmaster General Day's committee were:

BRUCE CATTON, Bethesda, Maryland (April 1961-February 1963). Catton, a historian noted for his works on the Civil War and editor of *American Heritage* magazine, was named to provide sound historic judgment within the committee.

JOHN WALKER, Washington, D.C. (April 1961-January 1969). One of the world's leading art gallery directors, Walker brought with him not only art judgment but the resources of the National Gallery. J. **CARTER BROWN**, his deputy, served frequently as his alternate.

NORMAN TODHUNTER, New York, New York (April 1961-January 1969). Todhunter, an art director with the J. Walter Thompson advertising agency in New York, was the strong art figure on the committee with a coherent stamp design policy. He fought for, and eventually won, greater flexibility in color printing.

JOHN MAASS, Philadelphia, Pennsylvania (April 1961-February 1965). Maass, visual presentation director for the City of Philadelphia, like Todhunter served as an art director in the development of many stamps.

DONALD R. McLEOD, Chevy Chase, Maryland (April 1961-February 1965). McLeod, who as superintendent of the Engraving Division at the Bureau had served ex-officio on the former committee, was named a regular member of this one.

GEORGE W. BRETT, Washington, D.C. (April 1961-August 1963). Brett, a geologist with the U.S. Geological Survey, was vice president (later president, chairman and chairman emeritus) of the Bureau Issues Association and an authority on U.S. stamp production.

DAVID LIDMAN, New York, New York (April 1961-January 1969). Lidman, chief makeup editor and stamp columnist for the *New York Times*, was president of the American Philatelic Congress and a director of the American Philatelic Society. Lidman was named chairman of the committee in May 1962, following the resignation of Franklin Bruns as director of the Division of Philately, a post in which he had been serving ex-officio as chairman.

DR. JAMES J. MATEJKA JR., Chicago, Illinois (April 1961-August 1963, and February 1965-January 1969). Dr. Matejka was an active philatelist and co-founder of Chicago's COMPEX show.

ROBERT W. BAUGHMAN, Liberal, Kansas (April 1961-August 1963). A wealthy wheat farmer and stamp collector, vice president (later president) of the Society of Philatelic Americans.

ROGER KENT, San Francisco, California (April 1961-January 1969). Kent was an attorney, stamp collector, and chairman of the California Democratic Central Committee.

WILLIAM N. POSNER, Rochester, New York (April 1961-March 1967). Certified public accountant, topical collector, and chairman of the Democratic County Committee in Monroe County, New York.

STANLEY H. FRYCZYNSKI JR., Bayonne, New Jersey (April 1962-August 1963). A funeral director active in New Jersey politics and president of the American First Day Cover Society.

CATHERINE DRINKER BOWEN, Philadelphia, Pennsylvania (February 1963-August 1963). A historian named to replace Bruce Catton, who had resigned.

Gronouski Committee

Postmaster General Day resigned in August 1963, and his Stamp Advisory Committee went out of existence. His successor was John A. Gronouski, who selected as his special assistant for public information and philately a young newspaperman, Ira Kapenstein. A new committee was not named until February 1964 when Lidman, Walker, Todhunter, Maass, McLeod, Kent and Posner were re-appointed.

In February 1965, Dr. Matejka was re-appointed to the committee, and there were three other changes.

REUBEN K. BARRICK, Arlington, Virginia (February 1965-January 1969). Chief of the Office of Designing, Engraving and Development at the Bureau of Engraving and Printing, replaced Donald McLeod, who had retired.

WALTER KARWIEC, Chicago, Illinois (February 1965-March 1966). An editorial cartoonist for the *Polish Daily News* in Chicago, replaced John Maass, who had resigned because of ill health.

ROGER L. STEVENS, Washington, D.C. (February 1965-January 1969). Stevens, special assistant to the president on the arts and chairman of the John F. Kennedy Center for the Performing Arts, was added.

O'Brien Committee

When Lawrence F. O'Brien replaced John Gronouski as postmaster general in November 1965, he asked members of the committee to continue to serve, and also retained Ira Kapenstein, who quickly became his right-hand man in many areas.

In March 1966, O'Brien made three new appointments.

STEVAN DOHANOS, Westport, Connecticut (March 1966-January 1969). An artist, illustrator and designer of a number of stamps, Dohonos was added in place of Krawiec and immediately began serving as an art director, working with other artists assigned to design stamps. Although his term, like that of the rest of the committee, expired in January 1969, he served continuously until his designation as a non-voting design coordinator in January 1978.

ANDREW WYETH, Chadds Ford, Pennsylvania (March 1966-March 1967). One of the best known and most popular of American painters. He resigned at the end of his one-year appointment.

KURT WIENER, Washington, D.C. (March 1966-January 1969). Wiener, owner of H.K. Press in Washington, lithographers of art gallery and museum publications, brought a needed background in modern printing techniques to the committee.

In March 1967, with the departure of Wyeth and Posner, O'Brien named two new members.

BELMONT FARIES, Clifton, Virginia (March 1967-January 1969). News editor of the *Washington Star*, stamp columnist and editor.

DR. ELSIE M. LEWIS, Washington, D.C. (March 1967-January 1969). Dr. Lewis, acting head of the Department of History at Howard University in Washington, provided a needed professional background in American history.

Watson Committee

In April 1968, Marvin Watson, President Johnson's special assistant and appointments secretary, was named postmaster general replacing O'Brien, who had resigned to direct Robert Kennedy's campaign for the presidency. Watson named Bill McSweeny his special assistant for public information and philately and asked O'Brien's Stamp Advisory Committee to continue. He did make three additions during a little more than nine months in office.

DR. JOHN P. ROCHE, Washington, D.C. (June 1968-January 1969). A special consultant to President Johnson on leave from Brandeis University, where he had been professor of history and politics.

MRS. ALBERT D. LASKER, New York, New York (July 1968-January 1969). Philanthropist in many medical fields who had been interested in the Beautification of America program sponsored by Lady Bird Johnson.

WILBUR J. COHEN, Silver Spring, Maryland (November 1968-January 1969). Secretary of Health, Education and Welfare and a stamp collector.

Blount Committee

With the inauguration of President Nixon, his postmaster general, Winton M. Blount, asked for the resignations of the Citizens' Stamp Advisory Committee. Four members, chairman David Lidman, Norman Todhunter, John Walker and Roger Kent, had served continuously since 1961.

Blount named James M. Henderson as his special assistant for public information and philately, and Virginia Brizendine, director of the Division of Philately, was persuaded to remain for a few months to aid in the transition. In July 1969, Blount announced his new Citizens' Stamp Advisory Committee.

STEVAN DOHANOS, Westport, Connecticut (July 1969-January 1978). Dohanos, the only member of the old committee re-appointed, had carried on the stamp artwork of the department during the interim. He was named chairman of the new committee.

J. CARTER BROWN, Washington, D.C. (July 1969-January 1978). Newly appointed director of the National Gallery of Art. He had served as an alternate for John Walker from 1961-1969. **JOHN BULLARD** and **HOWARD ADAMS** served as his alternates.

JAMES A. CONLON, Burke, Virginia (July 1969-July 1977). Director of the Bureau of Engraving and Printing. **KENNETH DeHART** and **EDWARD FELVER** served as his alternates.

BRADBURY THOMPSON, Riverside, Connecticut (July 1969-January 1978). One of the country's most distinguished designers and an authority on typography who had been responsible for several postage stamps. Along with Stevan Dohanos he was named a non-voting design coordinator in January 1978.

JAMES B. WYETH, Chadds Ford, Pennsylvania (July 1969-January 1978). Son of Andrew Wyeth and an outstanding young artist. (He was then 23.)

MRS. PAUL MELLON, Upperville, Virginia (July 1969-October 1973). Philanthropist and art patroness.

WALTER G. MacPEEK, North Brunswick, New Jersey (July 1969-died January 21, 1973.) Retired Boy Scout official and stamp editor of *Boys' Life* magazine

COLONEL RANDLE B.. TRUETT, Arlington, Virginia (July 1969-September 1975). Historian for the National Park Service, lecturer and philatelist.

FRED W. SPEERS, Escondido, California (July 1969-died Aug. 30, 1971). Savings and loan official and philatelist.

EDWIN A. MORRIS, Greensboro, North Carolina (July 1969-June 1971). Business executive and clothing manufacturer.

MRS. IKE KAMPMANN JR., (later Mrs. Holt Atherton), San Antonio, Texas (October 1969-June 1971).

New Blount Committee

In October 1971, Postmaster General Blount, shortly before resigning, named a new Citizens' Stamp Advisory Committee for the Postal Service, re-appointing all of the old members except Fred Speers, Edwin Morris, and Mrs. Kampmann, and adding five new members.

WILLIAM DOUGLAS ARANT, Birmingham, Alabama (October 1971-September 1975). A past president of the Alabama Bar Association.

FRANKLIN R. BRUNS JR., Takoma Park, Maryland (October 1971-March 1979). Bruns, who had served on the first Stamp Advisory Committee in 1957 and then had been ex-officio chairman as director of the Division of Philately from 1957 to 1962, returned as curator of the Smithsonian Institution's Division of Postal History. He died March 24, 1979.

EMERSON CLARK, Burbank, California (October 1971-January 1984). An aeronautical engineer with Lockheed Aircraft Corporation, chairman of the American Philatelic Society's recruiting program and later APS president.

BELMONT FARIES, Clifton, Virginia (October 1971 —). Newspaperman, stamp columnist and editor who had previously, served from March 1967 through January 1969.

ROBERT OSTERHOFF, Rochester, New York (October 1971-September 1975). Founder and executive secretary of the Junior Philatelic Society of America, then 24.

Bailar Committee

Postmaster General Elmer T. Klassen continued the Blount committee, but his successor, Benjamin F. Bailar, made several changes in September 1975. Belmont Faries was designated chairman, and Stevan Donhanos and Bradbury Thompson design coordinators with responsibility for stamp art. Colonel Truett, Douglas Arant and Robert Osterhoff were dropped, and six new members named.

ERNEST BORGNINE, Beverly Hills, California (September 1975-January 1984). Movie and television actor and stamp collector.

JAMES J. MATEJKA JR., Chicago, Illinois (September 1975-January 1978). Dr. Matejka, prominent Midwest philatelist, had served twice on earlier committees, April 1961 to August 1963 and February 1965 to January 1969.

DR. VIRGINIA NOELKE, San Angelo, Texas (September 1975 —). Professor of history, Angelo State University.

JOHN SAWYER III, Chicago, Illinois (September 1975 —). Educator, marketing manager for Education Systems Corporation, former superintendent of school districts in Illinois and Texas.

JOHN THOMAS, New York, New York (September 1975-July 1981). Well-known stamp collector long active in the American Topical Association. He resigned because of illness in July 1981 and died January 6, 1982.

DR. DOROTHY WORCESTER, Somers, Connecticut (September 1975-October 1979). Design specialist, director of consumer research for the Milton Bradley Company.

Bolger Committee

In January 1978, Postmaster General William F. Bolger re-appointed Faries, Bruns, Clark, Borgnine, Noelke, Sawyer, Thomas and Worcester. Wyeth, who had been too busy with his art career to attend meetings, and Dr. Matejka, who had a conflicting assignment, were dropped. Carter Brown declined re-appointment because of pressures of his duties at the National Gallery of Art. Conlon had not been replaced after his retirement as director of the Bureau of Engraving and Printing, but the Bureau was represented by his successors as director, Seymour Berry and Harry

Clements, with technical advice of Edward R. Felver and Leonard F. Buckley. Dohanos and Thompson continued to serve as design coordinators, but without a committee vote.

The changes left the committee rather short of voting members, and in October 1979, Postmaster General Bolger reorganized it with six re-appointments and 10 new members.

Chairman Belmont Faries, Ernest Borgnine, Emerson Clark, Dr. Virginia Noelke, John Sawyer and John Thomas were re-appointed. New members were:

THEODORIC C. (TED) BLAND, Kansas City, Mo. (August 1979-November 1984). Retired district manager postmaster at Kansas City, and stamp collector, Bland joined the committee in August 1979, filling the vacancy left by the death of Franklin Bruns. His appointment was announced with that of the other new members in October.

HARRY CLEMENTS, Washington, D.C. (October 1979-December 1983). Director of the Bureau of Engraving and Printing. He had represented the Bureau at committee meetings since his appointment as director in January 1979.

WILBUR J. COHEN, Austin, Texas (October 1979-June 1987). Former Secretary of Health, Education and Welfare and a stamp collector. He had been a member of the committee from November 1968 to January 1969.

RAUL GANDARA, Santurce, Puerto Rico (October 1979-November 1984). Retired fire chief of Puerto Rico and stamp collector.

DR. C. DOUGLAS LEWIS, Washington, D.C. (October 1979 —). Curator of sculpture, National Gallery of Art. Appointed vice chairman in June 1985.

EDWARD MALLEK, Honolulu, Hawaii (October 1979-December 1985). Retired businessman and stamp collector.

JAMES A. MICHENER, St. Michaels, Maryland (October 1979-December 1986). Novelist, historian and stamp collector. Accepted appointment with the understanding that he would not be able to attend meetings immediately. Became an active member in January 1981.

MARY ANN OWENS, Brooklyn, New York (October 1979 —). Accredited international stamp show judge, officer of the American Topical Association and topical stamp collector.

HOWARD E. PAINE, Washington, D.C. (October, 1979-May 1981). Art director of *National Geographic* magazine, expert in graphics, printing and typography and stamp collector. Named design coordinator succeeding Stevan Dohanos, who gave up the assignment to devote full time to his painting.

CLAIRE WILBUR, New York, New York (October 1979). Film producer and topical stamp collector. She did not serve.

Two new members were named to the committee in 1981:

DERRY NOYES, Washington, D.C. (May 1981-July 1983). Illustrator and designer, head of her own graphics firm, Derry Noyes Graphics. She filled the vacancy left by Howard Paine's acceptance of the design coordinator post.

DR. JOHN WEAVER, Rancho Palos Verdes, California (September, 1981-December 1985). Geographer and educator, president emeritus of the University of Wisconsin System and professor of geography at the University of Southern California. Filled the vacancy left by the resignation of John Thomas.

One new member was announced early in 1982:

JERRY PINKNEY, Croton-on-Hudson, New York (March 1982 —). Well-known artist and graphic illustrator, designer of all stamps in the Black Heritage series through the Sojourner Truth issue of 1986.

Three new members joined the committee in 1983.

ROBERT J. LEUVER, Arlington, Virginia (January 1983-March 1988). Director of the Bureau of Engraving and Printing, who resigned to become executive director of the American Numismatic Association.

CLINTON T. ANDREWS, Anchorage, Alaska (January 1983-March 1987). Managing editor and editorial page editor of the *Anchorage Times*. Andrews died March 7, 1987.

JUDGE EDWARD A. BEARD, Bethesda, Maryland (May 1983-March 1987). Retired judge of the Superior

Court of the District of Columbia. Died March 17, 1987.

In July 1983, Derry Noyes left the committee to join Bradbury Thompson and Howard Paine as a design coordinator. Richard D. Sheaff, owner of Sheaff Design, Inc. of Chestnut Hill, Massachusetts, a well-known stamp collector, was added to the design staff at the same time, bringing it to four.

Postmaster General Bolger added three members to the committee early in 1984, bringing the total to 18:

RICHARD (DIGGER) PHELPS, Notre Dame, Indiana (March 1984 —). Head basketball coach at Notre Dame University and a stamp collector.

NORMA J. NIEHOFF, New York, New York (March 1984-December 1985). A vice president of Dreyfus Service Corporation and a stamp collector.

JOHN R. FOXWORTH JR., West Bloomfield, Michigan (March 1984 —). An executive with General Motors Corporation and a past president of the American Philatelic Society and the Council of Philatelic Organizations (COPO).

Carlin Committee

On Jan. 1, 1985, Paul N. Carlin became postmaster general, succeeding William F. Bolger, who retired December 31, 1984. Postmaster General Carlin appointed two new members to the committee, effective Feb. 1, to fill vacancies left by the departure in November of Raul Gandara and Theodore C. Bland.

WILLIAM D. DUNLAP, Minneapolis, Minnesota (February 1985). Chief executive officer of Campbellithun advertising agency there. He attended no meetings and was dropped. Dunlap had been special assistant to the postmaster general for special projects in the last year of the old Post Office Department, an assignment that included supervision of the stamp program.

ANN DeWITT HARVEY, Sudbury, Massachusetts (February 1985 —). Artist and graphic design specialist, owner of Screen Designs in Sudbury.

Carlin made a third appointment, effective April 1, to provide representation for the West:

JACK ROSENTHAL, Casper, Wyoming (April, 1985 —). Television broadcasting executive and expert in classic U.S. stamps.

When the Advisory Committee reorganized itself in response to Postmaster General Carlin's "challenge for excellence," it reduced its authorized membership from 18 to 15. Three members, Norma Niehoff, Edward Mallek and Dr. John Weaver, left the committee in December 1985.

Tisch Committee

James Dean of Annandale, Virginia, artist and graphic designer, was added to the design coordinator staff in November 1986, bringing it to five.

In April 1987, Postmaster General Preston R. Tisch appointed three members to the committee to replace James Michener, who had resigned because of other commitments, and Clinton T. Andrews and Judge Edward A. Beard, who had died the previous month:

RICHARD COYNE, Palo Alto, California (April 1987 —). Founder, editor and publisher of Communication Arts, a graphics arts journal.

BEATRICE RIVAS SANCHEZ, Kansas City, Missouri (April 1987 —). Art administrator printmaker and president of the Kansas City Art Institute.

STEVEN HELLER, New York, New York (April 1987-October 1988). Art director of the *New York Times Book Review* and editor of the journal of the American Institute of Graphic Arts. He did not become an active member of the committee and resigned in October 1988.

Frank Committee

GEORGE STEVENS JR., (April 1988 —). Film producer and director and co-chairman of the board of directors of the American Film Institute. Appointed to the committee by Postmaster General Anthony M. Frank.

Liaison

Postal Service liaison with the Citizens' Stamp Advisory Committee is through its Stamp Information Branch.

Because of the administrative burden associated with the large number of stamp-subject suggestions each year, the Postal Service does not encourage direct correspondence with members of the committee but will forward presentations.

The address is Citizens' Stamp Advisory Committee, c/o Stamp Support Branch, U.S. Postal Service, Washington, D.C. 20260-6753.

Formal requests for issuance of a stamp should be sent to The Postmaster General, U.S. Postal Service, Washington, D.C. 20260-0010.

Postal Service and Citizens' Stamp Advisory Committee Stamp Subject Criteria

The U.S. Postal Service and the members of the Citizens' Stamp Advisory Committee have set certain basic criteria used in determining the eligibility of subjects for commemoration on U.S. stamps and stationery. These criteria first were formulated in 1957 and have been refined and expanded gradually since then.

Following are the 11 major areas now guiding commemorative subject selection:

1. It is a general policy that U.S. postage stamps and stationery primarily will feature American or American-related subjects.

2. No living person shall be honored on U.S. postage.

3. Commemorative stamps or postal stationery items honoring individuals usually will be issued on, or in conjunction with, significant anniversaries of their birth, but no postal item will be issued sooner than 10 years after the individual's death. The only exception to the 10-year rule is the issuance of stamps honoring deceased U.S. presidents. They may be honored with a memorial stamp on the first birth anniversary following death.

4. Events of historical significance shall be considered for commemoration only on anniversaries in multiples of 50 years.

5. Only events and themes of widespread national appeal and significance will be considered for commemoration. Events or themes of local or regional significance may be recognized by a philatelic or special cancellation, which may be arranged through the local postmaster.

6. Stamps or stationery items shall not be issued to honor fraternal, political, sectarian or service organizations that exist primarily to solicit and/or distribute funds; commercial enterprises; or specific products.

7. Stamps or stationery items shall not be issued to honor cities, towns, municipalities, counties, primary or secondary schools, hospitals, libraries, or similar institutions. Due to the limitations placed on annual postal programs and the vast number of such locales, organizations and institutions in existence, it would be difficult to single out any one for commemoration.

8. Requests for observance of statehood anniversaries will be considered for commemorative postage stamps only at intervals of 50 years from the date of the state's first entry into the Union. Requests for observance of other state-related or regional anniversaries will be considered only as subjects for postal stationery, and again only at intervals of 50 years from the date of the event.

9. Stamps or stationery items shall not be issued to honor religious institutions or individuals whose principal achievements are associated with religious undertakings or beliefs.

10. Stamps or postal stationery items with added values, referred to as semi-postals, shall not be issued. Due to the vast number of worthy fund-raising organizations in existence, it would be difficult to single out specific ones to receive such revenue. There also is a strong U.S. tradition for private fund-raising for charities, and the administrative costs involved in accounting for sales would tend to negate the revenue derived.

11. Requests for commemoration of significant anniversaries of universities and other institutions of higher education shall be considered only in regard to Historic Preservation series postal cards featuring an appropriate building on the campus.

Ideas for stamp subjects that meet the criteria may be addressed to the Citizens' Stamp Advisory Committee, Stamp Information Branch, U.S. Postal Service, Washington, D.C. 20260-6352. Subjects should be submitted at least three years in advance of the proposed date of issue to allow sufficient time for design and production, if the proposal is approved.

Reproduction of Postage Stamps

Designs of postage stamps issued after Jan. 1, 1978, are copyrighted and may not be reproduced except under license granted by the U.S. Postal Service. Earlier designs are in the public domain and may be reproduced without permission for philatelic, educational, historical and newsworthy purposes. When reproducing any designs, those protected by copyright or those in the public domain, it is necessary to comply with Title 18, U.S. Code, Section 504 as amended. This statute provides that uncanceled stamps, when reproduced in actual colors, must be depicted less than 75 percent or more than 150 percent of actual size in any linear dimension.

U.S. Stamp Popularity Polls

Starting with the United States stamp issues of 1948, *Linn's Stamp News* each year has conducted a readers' survey to determine the most popular, worst, and least necessary stamp emissions of the previous year. In the earlier polls, only two categories were used, Best and Worst. Over the years, many changes have been made until, starting in 1979, readers voted in six different categories.

In the earlier polls, participants voted for first place, second place, and sometimes third place in the categories offered. The following tabulation lists the first, second and third (if used) choices in that order.

1948

BEST — Lincoln's Gettysburg Address commemorative; Rough Riders commemorative.

WORST — American Turners Society centennial commemorative; Fort Kearney commemorative.

1948 3¢ Gettysburg Address

1949

BEST — Universal Postal Union 25¢ airmail commemorative; Annapolis Tercentenary comemorative; Washington and Lee commemorative.

WORST — Edgar Allan Poe Famous American issue; Puerto Rico Gubernatorial Election commemorative.

1949 25¢ UPU Airmail

1950

BEST — Freedom stamp, one of four in National Capital Sesquicentennial series; Legislative stamp from the same series.
WORST — Railroad Engineers of America (Casey Jones) commemorative; California Statehood commemorative.
LEAST NECESSARY — American Bankers Association commemorative; Samuel Gompers Famous American issue.

1950 3¢ Freedom

1951

BEST — Nevada commemorative; Landing of Cadillac commemorative.
WORST — Colorado Statehood commemorative; United Confederate Veterans

commemorative.
LEAST NECESSARY — Battle of Brooklyn commemorative.
APPROPRIATE DESIGN — American Chemical Society commemorative.

1951 3¢ Nevada

1952

BEST — International Red Cross commemorative; Airmail stamp in denomination of 80¢.

WORST — Mount Rushmore National Memorial commemorative; North Atlantic Treaty Organization commemorative.

LEAST NECESSARY — Baltimore and Ohio Railroad Charter commemorative.

APPROPRIATE DESIGN — International Red Cross commemorative.

1952 3¢ International Red Cross

1953

BEST — 300th Anniversary of New York City commemorative; Commodore Matthew Calbraith Perry commemorative.

WORST — Trucking Industry commemorative; Ohio Statehood Sesquicentennial commemorative.

LEAST NECESSARY — Trucking Industry commemorative.

APPROPRIATE DESIGN — Sagamore Hill commemorative.

1953 3¢ New York City

1954

BEST — Lewis and Clark commemorative; Statue of Liberty 8¢ issue.
WORST — Nebraska Territorial commemorative; Kansas Territorial commemorative.
LEAST NECESSARY — Airmail 4¢ issue.
APPROPRIATE DESIGN — Special Delivery issue.

1954 3¢ Lewis and Clark

1955

BEST — Rotary International commemorative; Atoms for Peace commemorative.
WORST — Fort Ticonderoga commemorative; Land Grant Colleges commemorative.
LEAST NECESSARY — Andrew W. Mellon Famous American issue.

1955 8¢ Rotary International

1956

BEST — Wildlife Conservation showing

pronghorn antelope; Wheatland commemorative.

WORST — Pure Food and Drug Laws commemorative; Nassau Hall commemorative.

LEAST NECESSARY — Pure Food and Drug Laws commemorative.

BEST DESIGN (not considering color) — Wheatland commemorative.

1956 3¢ Wildlife Conservation

1957

BEST — American Flag commemorative; Wildlife Conservation issue showing whooping crane.

WORST — Polio commemorative; Oklahoma Statehood commemorative.

LEAST NECESSARY — Shipbuilding commemorative.

BEST DESIGN (not considering color) — Flushing Remonstrance commemorative.

1957 4¢ American Flag

1958

BEST — Forest Conservation issue; Mackinac Bridge commemorative.

WORST — Gardening/Horticulture commemorative; Journalism/ Freedom of the Press commemorative.

LEAST NECESSARY — Gardening/ Horticulture commemorative.

1958 4¢ Forest Conservation

1959

BEST — 49-star American Flag commemorative; St. Lawrence Seaway Opening commemorative.

WORST — Dental Health commemorative; Balloon Jupiter commemorative.

LEAST NECESSARY — Dr. Ephraim McDowell commemorative in Famous American issue.

1959 4¢ 49-star American Flag

1960

BEST — United States-Japan commemorative; Pony Express 4¢ commemorative.

WORST — World Refugee Year commemorative; Boys Clubs of America commemorative.

LEAST NECESSARY — American Woman commemorative.

1960 4¢ United States-Japan

1961

BEST — Frederic Remington commemorative; Range Conservation commemorative.

WORST — Nursing commemorative; Naismith/Basketball commemorative.

LEAST NECESSARY — Naismith/Basketball commemorative.

1961 4¢ Frederic Remington

1962

BEST — Winslow Homer commemorative; New Mexico Statehood commemorative.

WORST — Apprenticeship commemorative; Battle of Shiloh commemorative.

LEAST NECESSARY — Apprenticeship commemorative.

1962 4¢ Winslow Homer

1963

BEST — John James Audubon commemorative; City Mail Delivery commemorative.

WORST — Emancipation Proclamation commemorative; Science commemorative.

LEAST NECESSARY — Science commemorative.

1963 5¢ Audubon

1964

BEST — Homemakers commemorative; Charles M. Russell American Painting commemorative.

WORST — Fine Arts commemorative; Amateur Radio Operators commemorative.

LEAST NECESSARY — Fine Arts commemorative.

1965

BEST — Copley American Painting commemorative; Adlai Stevenson Memorial issue.

WORST — Salvation Army commemorative; Traffic Safety commemorative.

LEAST NECESSARY — Dante Alighieri commemorative; Physical Fitness/Sokol commemorative.

1965 5¢ Copley American Painting

1966 5¢ Beautification of America

1967 5¢ Space

1966

BEST — Beautification of America commemorative; Christmas issue.

WORST — Great River Road commemorative; Humane Treatment of Animals commemorative.

LEAST NECESSARY — Great River Road commemorative.

1967

BEST — Twin Space commemorative pair; Christmas issue.

WORST — Henry David Thoreau commemorative; Canada Centennial commemorative.

LEAST NECESSARY — Urban Planning commemorative.

1968

BEST — Waterfowl Conservation commemorative showing ducks in flight; American Indian commemorative showing Chief Joseph.

WORST — Support our Youth commemorative; Leif Erikson commemorative.

LEAST NECESSARY — Arkansas River Navigation commemorative.

1968 6¢ Waterfowl Conservation

1969

BEST — First Man on the Moon airmail commemorative; Apollo 8 commemorative.

WORST — W.C. Handy commemorative; Professional Baseball commemorative.

LEAST NECESSARY — W.C. Handy commemorative; Dartmouth College Case/Daniel Webster commemorative.

1970

BEST — Maine Statehood commemorative; Natural History issue.

WORST — Wildlife Conservation issue; South Carolina commemorative.

1969 10¢ First Man on the Moon

1970 6¢ Maine Statehood

LEAST NECESSARY — Christmas Toys block.

1971

MOST POPULAR — Wildlife Conservation issue; Space Achievement Decade issue.

WORST — Blood Donor issue; American Revolution Bicentennial issue.

LEAST NECESSARY — American Wool Industry issue; Christmas Partridge issue.

1972

MOST POPULAR — Wildlife Conservation block; Cape Hatteras block.

WORST — Osteopathic Medicine issue; Parent Teachers Association issue.

LEAST NECESSARY — Osteopathic Medicine issue; Family Planning issue.

1973

MOST POPULAR — Boston Tea Party block; Love issue.

WORST — Love issue; Postal Service Employees issue.

LEAST NECESSARY — Postal Service Employees issue; Love issue.

1974

MOST POPULAR — Mineral Heritage block of four; Skylab issue; Universal Postal Union stamps.

WORST — Preserve the Environment issue; Zip Code issue; Energy Conservation issue.

LEAST NECESSARY — Horse Racing issue; Universal Postal Union stamps; Zip Code issue.

1975

MOST POPULAR — Apollo-Soyuz pair; Banking and Commerce issue, two designs; U.S. Military Services (uniforms) four designs.

WORST — Collective Bargaining issue; International Women's Year issue; Contributors to the Cause, four designs.

1971 8¢ Wildlife Conservation

1972 8¢ Wildlife Conservation

1973 8¢ Boston Tea Party

LEAST NECESSARY — Collective Bargaining issue; International Women's Year issue; D.W. Griffith issue.

1976

MOST POPULAR — State Flags issue, 50 different designs; Bicentennial souvenir sheets, four designs; Spirit of '76 triptych.
WORST — A.S. Ochs issue; Telephone Centennial issue; Interphil '76 issue.
LEAST NECESSARY — A.S. Ochs issue; Bicentennial souvenir sheets, four designs; Chemistry issue.

1977

MOST POPULAR — Butterflies block; Pueblo Pottery block; Lindbergh Transatlantic Flight.
BEST DESIGN — Pueblo Pottery block; Butterflies block, Colorado Statehood Centennial.
WORST — Energy pair; Talking Pictures; Peace Bridge.
LEAST NECESSARY — Energy pair; Talking Pictures; Butterflies block.

1978

MOST POPULAR — American Owls block; CAPEX souvenir sheet; American Trees block.
BEST DESIGN — American Trees block;

1974 10¢ Mineral Heritage

1975 10¢ Apollo-Soyuz

CAPEX souvenir sheet; American Owls block.

LEAST POPULAR — Harriet Tubman; American Quilts block; Carl Sandburg.

LEAST NECESSARY — CAPEX souvenir sheet; American Quilts blocks; Photography.

1979

MOST POPULAR — Endangered Flowers block; Summer 1980 Olympics block; Pennsylvania Toleware block.

BEST DESIGN — American Architecture block; Endangered Flowers block; Pennsylvania Toleware block.

MOST IMPORTANT — Vietnam Veterans (regular); International Year of the Child; Summer 1980 Olympics.

LEAST POPULAR — Dr. Martin Luther King; Robert F. Kennedy; Santa Claus (Christmas).

WORST DESIGN — Dr. Martin Luther King; Santa Claus (Christmas); Robert F. Kennedy.

LEAST NECESSARY — Robert F. Kennedy; Pennsylvania Toleware block; Dr. Martin Luther King.

1980

MOST POPULAR — Coral Reefs block; Winter Olympics block; Letter Writing strip of six.

LEAST POPULAR — W.C. Fields; American Education; Edith Wharton.

1976 13¢ State Flags

1977 13¢ Butterflies

1978 15¢ American Owls

BEST DESIGN — Coral Reefs block; American Architecture block; Northwest Indian Masks block.

WORST DESIGN — American Education; Veterans Administration; Edith Wharton.

1979 15¢ Endangered Flowers

1980 15¢ Coral Reefs

MOST IMPORTANT — Winter Olympics block; Helen Keller/Anne Sullivan;

American Architecture block.
LEAST NECESSARY — W.C. Fields; Frances Perkins; Edith Wharton.

1982 20¢ State Birds and Flowers

1981

MOST POPULAR — Space Achievements, block of eight; Desert Plants, block of four; Wildlife Habitats, block of four.
LEAST POPULAR — Professional Management; Savings and Loans; Whitney Moore Young.
BEST DESIGN — Desert Plants block; Space Achievements block; Wildlife Habitats block.
WORST DESIGN — Professional Management; Savings and Loans; Space Achievements.

MOST IMPORTANT — Space Achievements block; International Year of Disabled Persons; Wildlife Habitats block.

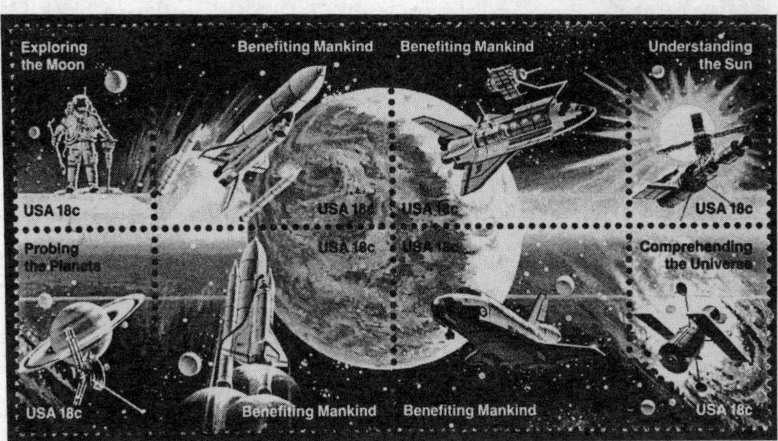

1981 15¢ Space Achievements

LEAST NECESSARY — Professional Management; Savings and Loans; James Hoban 18¢.

1982

MOST POPULAR — State Birds and Flowers pane of 50 (Scott 1953-2002).
LEAST POPULAR — Netherlands (Scott 2003)
BEST DESIGN — State Birds and Flowers pane of 50 (Scott 1953-2002)
WORST DESIGN — Netherlands (Scott 2003)
MOST IMPORTANT — George Washington (Scott 1952)
LEAST NECESSARY — Wolf Trap Farm (Scott 2018)

1983

Commemoratives

MOST POPULAR — Balloons block (Scott 2032-35)
LEAST POPULAR — Civil Service (Scott 2053)
BEST DESIGN — Balloons block (Scott 2032-35)
WORST DESIGN — Civil Service (Scott 2053)
MOST IMPORTANT — Medal of Honor (Scott 2045)
LEAST NECESSARY — Martin Luther (Scott 2065)

Definitives

MOST POPULAR — Eagle & Moon booklet

(Scott 1909)
LEAST POPULAR — Dorothea Dix (Scott 1844)
BETS DESIGN — Eagle & Moon booklet (Scott 1909)
WORST DESIGN — Dorothea Dix (Scott 1844)
MOST IMPORTANT — Eagle & Moon booklet (Scott 1909)
LEAST NECESSARY — Eagle & Moon booklet (Scott 1909)

Postal Stationery

MOST POPULAR — Yachting postal card (Scott UX100)
LEAST POPULAR — Non-profit envelope (Scott U604)
BEST DESIGN — Yachting postal card (Scott UX100)
WORST DESIGN — Non-profit envelope (Scott U604)
MOST IMPORTANT — Paralyzed Veterans envelope (Scott U605)
LEAST NECESSARY — Non-profit envelope (Scott U604)

1984

FAVORITE STAMP — Dogs block (Scott 2098-2101)

Commemoratives

BEST DESIGN — Dogs block (Scott 2098-2101)
WORST DESIGN — Family Unity (Scott 2104)
MOST IMPORTANT — Vietnam Veterans Memorial (Scott 2109)
LEAST NECESSARY — Hispanic Americans (Scott 2103)

Definitives

BEST DESIGN — Harry Truman (Scott 1862)
WORST DESIGN — Richard Russell (Scott 1853)
MOST IMPORTANT — Harry Truman (Scott 1862)
LEAST NECESSARY — Baby Buggy coil (Scott 1902)

Postal stationery

BEST DESIGN — Maryland postal card (Scott UX101)
WORST DESIGN — Small Business envelope (Scott U606)
MOST IMPORTANT — Torch postal card (Scott UX102)
LEAST NECESSARY — Small Business envelope (Scott U606)

1985

FAVORITE STAMP — Horses block (Scott 2155-58)

Commemoratives

BEST DESIGN — Horses block (Scott 2155-58)
WORST DESIGN — Love (Scott 2143)
MOST IMPORTANT — Help End Hunger (Scott 2164)
LEAST NECESSARY — Junipero Serra (Scott C116)

Definitives

BEST DESIGN — Seashells booklet (Scott 2117-21)
WORST DESIGN — Letters (Scott 2150)
MOST IMPORTANT — Flag booklet (Scott 2116)
LEAST NECESSARY — Postage due (Scott J104)

Postal stationery

BEST DESIGN — China Clipper card (Scott UXC22)

1983 20¢ Balloons

1984 20¢ Dogs

1985 22¢ Horses

WORST DESIGN — George Wythe card (Scott UX107)
MOST IMPORTANT — Bison envelope (Scott U608)
LEAST NECESSARY — D envelope (Scott U607)

1986

FAVORITE STAMP — Stamp Collecting booklet

Commemoratives

BEST DESIGN — Stamp Collecting booklet
WORST DESIGN — Public Hospitals
MOST IMPORTANT — Statue of Liberty
LEAST NECESSARY — Public Hospitals

Definitives

BEST DESIGN — Jack London

WORST DESIGN — Belva Lockwood
MOST IMPORTANT — Father Flanagan
LEAST NECESSARY — Omnibus (re-engraved)

Postal stationery

BEST DESIGN — AMERIPEX postal card
WORST DESIGN — Stamp Collecting postal card
MOST IMPORTANT — National Guard postal card
LEAST NECESSARY — Francis Vigo postal card

1987

FAVORITE STAMP — American Wildlife

Commemoratives

BEST DESIGN — American Wildlife
WORST DESIGN — Pan American Games
MOST IMPORTANT — Signing of the Constitution
LEAST IMPORTANT — Special Occasions booklet

Definitives

BEST DESIGN — Flag With Fireworks
WORST DESIGN — Julia Ward Howe
MOST IMPORTANT — Flag With Fireworks
LEAST NECESSARY — Bret Harte

Postal stationery

BEST DESIGN — Take Pride in America postal card
WORST DESIGN — Official mail envelope
MOST IMPORTANT — Constitutional Convention postal card
LEAST IMPORTANT — Official mail envelope

1988

FAVORITE STAMP — Carousel Animals

1986 22¢ Stamp Collecting

1987 22¢ American Wildlife

1988 25¢ Carousel Animals

WORST STAMP — Special Occasions booklet

Commemoratives

BEST DESIGN — Carousel Animals

LEAST NECESSARY — Special Occasions booklet

Definitives

BEST DESIGN — 25¢ Flag Over Yosemite coil

LEAST NECESSARY — 23¢ Mary Cassatt sheet

Postal stationery

BEST DESIGN — 15¢ America the Beautiful postal card

LEAST NECESSARY — 25¢ Snowflake envelope

Chapter 5

U.S. Stamp Printing Bureau of Engraving and Printing

Although the role of the Bureau of Engraving and Printing in supplying this nation's needs for postage stamps may have post-dated the Civil War by some years, the fact is that the BEP, which came into existence on Aug. 29, 1862, was an indirect consequence of that conflict.

Primarily the result of the self-confidence, courage, ingenuity, and patriotism of one man — Spencer Morton Clark — it is, as well, the result of the foresight of President Lincoln's first Secretary of the Treasury, Salmon P. Chase— his confidence in Clark's ability and recognition of his accomplishments.

At the time of the firing on Fort Sumter and the president's call for volunteers to quell the rebellion, the nation was already on the fringe of bankruptcy and scarcely in a position to finance a war.

It was this, along with other war matters, that prompted the president to call Congress into special session on July 4, 1861. During this session, Secretary Chase recommended to Congress both a system of taxation and one of floating loans. His scheme for borrowing included the issuance of non-interest-bearing notes that would circulate as money.

Although there was doubt in the minds of many that the government had the constitutional authority to issue paper money, Congress adopted the Chase plan in the Act of July 17, 1861, and as a result, the first government-issued paper money came into being.

These notes, because of certain provisions of their issuance, became popularly known as "demand notes." These were produced by the New York bank note companies — American Bank Note Co. and National Bank Note Co. — under contract with the government.

One of the provisions of the new law specified that the authorized securities should be "signed by the First or Second Comptroller, or the Register of the Treasury and countersigned by such other officer or officers as the Secretary of the Treasury may designate."

The impracticability of such a procedure soon became evident. If the designated officers were to perform duties other than sign their names to securities, they would have to be relieved of that task.

Corrective action was soon forthcoming, and on Aug. 5, 1861, just 19 days after enactment of the original legislation, President Lincoln signed a bill that changed the signature requirements to those of the Treasurer of the United States and Register of the Treasury.

The new legislation also provided that the secretary might designate other personnel to sign the notes for these officers, and ultimately 70 clerks were assigned to the loan branch of the secretary's office for this purpose. These persons signed their own names to the notes.

With such a variety of signatures on notes, security was less than desired. Spencer Clark, the chief clerk of the Bureau of Construction in the department and acting engineer in charge of that bureau, suggested to Secretary Chase that the notes be imprinted with the facsimile signatures of the required officers.

As additional evidence of lawful issue,

he also proposed that the notes be imprinted with a copy of the Treasury seal and further suggested this processing be done in the Treasury building.

The secretary approved Clark's proposal, and Congress gave its approval with legislation adopted Feb. 25, 1862. Clark was instructed to design a seal for use on the notes and to procure the necessary machinery for the imprinting.

Thus the Treasury began its first actual work in connection with the printing of currency, which was eventually to lead to the printing of the nation's postage stamps. Specifically, the beginning date was Aug. 29, 1862, with Clark having one male assistant and four female operatives.

Secretary Chase was so pleased with Clark's machines that he asked him to investigate the possibilities relating to the printing of securities issued by the government.

Clark's investigation determined the government was paying substantial prices to the bank note companies for printing notes. He told the secretary he could produce the work in the department for a "a comparatively small outlay, at a great saving of cost in the issues."

While the date of the first printing in the department is in question, it is known that in July 1862 Charles Neale, a plate printer, was brought into the department as a clerk in anticipation of authority to print currency at the Treasury.

On Oct. 11, 1862, he was appointed to superintend the plate-printing operation and was assigned the task of securing presses, ink and paper, and recruiting workmen.

One of the first products produced by the Bureau was fractional currency. These were the miniature notes issued by the government in place of coins during the Civil War and for some years afterwards.

It was the circulation of a variety of items intended as substitute coins that in Secretary Chase's words, "created a manifest necessity for a fractional currency authorized by the National Government."

He proposed alternative remedies: one, reduce the weight of small coins; the other, use revenue or postage stamps in place of coins. Congress preferred the latter and by an act approved July 17, 1862, provided that postage or other U.S. stamps be receivable in payments due to the government. The same act made the use of any items intended to circulate as money in amounts of less than $1 unlawful.

Realizing that the glue on stamps would make them inconvenient for the purpose, the secretary requested the postmaster general to supply stocks without adhesive.

The suggestion resulted in an arrangement by the Post Office Department with private bank note companies for printing small notes, comprising in their design reproductions of postage stamps. These were printed in denominations of 5¢, 10¢, 25¢ and 50¢.

Although the legend appearing on the reverse of these notes implies they were issued under the Act of July 17, 1862, that act does not make any mention of postage currency whatsoever.

The same desperate need for Civil War financing, which indirectly led to the creation of the component that eventually grew into the Bureau of Engraving and Printing, resulted in the formation of the U.S. Internal Revenue system

Until that time, the government had relied almost exclusively on tariffs and other customs taxes for its income. An act of July 1, 1862, authorized the president to appoint a commissioner of internal revenue, who was given authority to assess, levy, and collect taxes and provide stamps "for expressing and denoting the several stamp duties" imposed by the legislation.

This act became the basis of the present internal revenue system, as far as items taxed and organizations to collect revenues are concerned. Along with other taxing requirements, it provided for stamp taxes on medicines, perfumes, cosmetics, playing cards and certain commercial papers.

First Revenue Stamps

Although the bulk of the printing of the first U.S. revenue stamps was assigned to private bank note firms, the Bureau was printing beer and cigar stamps as early as 1867, with the next few years seeing an increase in the number of revenue stamps printed and processed by the Bureau.

The annual report of the chief for fiscal year 1870 indicated deliveries of 31 million stamps embracing distilled spirits, beer, tobacco, custom cigars, and special tax stamps. By 1873, deliveries had risen to over 244 million stamps and the categories broadly extended.

By 1875, most of the work had reverted to private bank note companies, since their bids for producing a variety of stamps were fewer than those of the Bureau, which continued to print only the custom cigar and special tax stamps.

An act appropriating funds for government expenses for fiscal year 1877 required that internal revenue stamps be printed in the Bureau, provided the cost did not exceed that paid under existing contracts to private bank note companies.

However, the secretary of the treasury felt the Bureau would be unable to compete with the private firms, and it was not until the following year, under a new secretary, that the Bureau resumed manufacture of almost all the internal revenue items.

Since that time, the Bureau has figured prominently in the production of revenue stamps, although the commissioner has had a prerogative in the placement of stamp orders as these stamps have been needed.

Aside from the staggering amount of revenue stamps manufactured in the Bureau, a further significance of these items derives from the part they played in the introduction of improved machines and processes employed by the Bureau.

The tremendous stamp requirements not only contributed to the introduction of power plate printing presses in 1878, but spurred the improvements made to this type of equipment during the period of its original use by the Bureau.

The need for additional revenue items was also responsible for the extended use of typographic printing made in 1890 and of offset printing made in 1914.

Early Stamp Production

Although the U.S. postal system dates back to 1782 and the first general issue of postage stamps was introduced in 1847, it was not until July 1, 1894, that the Bureau took over the production of these stamps.

Prior to that date, there had been only two exceptions to the general procedure followed by the Post Office Department in obtaining its stamps from private bank note companies. The particular reasons why the services of the Bureau were employed in these two instances remains unexplained.

In January 1875, William M. Ireland, acting third assistant postmaster general, advised the Bureau by letter that the Post Office Department was "making preparations to sell to stamp collectors and others, specimens of all postage stamps ever issued under its auspices."

The letter noted that plates existed for all the several issues except those for the first issue of 1847. The Bureau was instructed to re-engrave the plates for the 5¢ and 10¢ stamps and, from these plates, prepare 10,000 of each denomination. There were 11,450 specimens of the 5¢ value and 10,000 of the 10¢ denomination delivered to the Post Office Department.

Strictly speaking, these items produced by the Bureau cannot be regarded as reprints of the original issue. The earlier stamps had been demonetized in 1861, soon after the outbreak of the Civil War. Furthermore, the Bureau prints were specifically declared invalid as postage stamps.

It is interesting to note that in 1947 the Bureau was again called upon to reproduce the original designs in connection with the production of a souvenir sheet commemorating the centenary of U.S. postage stamps.

Another request was received by the Bureau from the Post Office Department on May 20, 1875. It called for the preparation of a die for a new 5¢ ordinary postage stamp. The item was required by the revised foreign letter rate agreed upon by the member countries of the General Postal Union in convention at Bern, Switzerland, in 1874.

This new rate was to become effective July 1, 1875, but the treaty agreement was not ratified until May 3, 1875. This short interval between the time of ratification and the effective date may account for the Bureau being asked to assist in this instance.

The die was prepared from a portrait of Zachary Taylor, already on hand, and engraved with a border of style compatible with that of the ordinary series of postage stamps then current.

The feasibility and propriety of assigning the printing of postage stamps to the Bureau had long been debated. Legislative authority for having the work done at the Bureau on a qualified basis had been included in the appropriation act for the Post Office Department in 1879.

Although the act passed in 1881 repealed the 1879 proviso in full, there was deemed to be no legal impediment to the manufacture of postage stamps by the Bureau.

This fact was borne out by specifications issued by the Post Office Department in 1885, 1889 and 1893 for printing the stamps on a four-year contract basis.

Each expressly stipulated that, should the secretary of the treasury submit bids or estimates found to be more advantageous to the government than those submitted by private contractors, the postmaster general reserves the right to award the contracts to the Bureau.

There were three private bidders for supplying stamps under the 1893 request, while a proposal to do the work was also submitted by the chief of the Bureau, with approval of the secretary of the treasury. The latter bid was almost $7,000 less than the lowest bid from a private contractor.

When the Bureau's proposal was made public, there was a loud and strong protest voiced by the private contractors. In addition to arguing that the Bureau had no legal authority to perform the service, they contended the agency had not submitted its offer in accordance with terms outlined in the Post Office Department's advertisement for bids.

Submitted to the Department of Justice for review, the latter held there was no legal impediment involved, and the contract was awarded to the Bureau on Feb. 21, 1894.

In April 1894, the Post Office Department turned over to the Bureau dies, rolls and plates of the then current stamps. No further use was made of the plates except for some of the newspaper and periodical stamp plates. Most of the dies for the regular issues, however, were employed in the manufacture of new plates after being altered to distinguish the Bureau printings.

Since that date, most postage stamps supplied to the Post Office Department and its successor, the U.S. Postal Service, have come from the Bureau of Engraving and Printing.

Printing Problems

As might have been expected, the Bureau was not without its trials and tribulations in getting the postage stamp operations under way.

One of the most vexing problems encountered involved the gumming of stamps. While past experience had provided the Bureau the basics for actually printing the stamps, when awarded the contract, it had no gumming machines.

Heretofore such stampwork as had been produced in the Bureau had been gummed by hand, but with the great volume of postage stamps needed, such a procedure would have been totally inadequate.

Since gumming equipment was not manufactured on a commercial basis, it was impossible to purchase the needed machinery. Furthermore, the private bank note firm that previously produced the stamps would not make its equipment available or divulge its mode of operations.

It thus became incumbent upon the Bureau to develop its own machines. Working only upon the recollections of an employee who had previously been in the service of a private contractor and who had operated the equipment, the Bureau was able to accomplish the task.

The first stamps printed by the Bureau were placed on sale by the Post Office Department on July 18, 1894. They were the 6¢ reddish brown regular issue and followed by the 4¢ denomination, which was issued on Sept. 11.

By the end of the first year of operation, the Bureau had printed and delivered more than 21 million sheets of stamps for the Post Office Department, embracing 13 denominations of regular postage, as well as miscellaneous values of special delivery, postage due, and newspaper and periodical stamps.

With the termination of the Spanish-American War in 1898, the Bureau found itself involved in still another philatelic operation. Under the terms of the peace treaty, Guam, the Philippine Islands, and Puerto Rico were ceded to the United States, while Cuba was relinquished to the United States in trust for the Cuban people.

Initially, these territories were administered by military governments under the jurisdiction of the U.S. War Department, except Guam, which was placed under the charge of the Navy Department. The Bureau was called upon to supply the postage stamps used in these territories.

Originally, all four areas were furnished regular U.S. postage stamps overprinted with the name of the respective territory in which the stamps were to be used.

In 1906, the U.S. postage stamps overprinted "Philippines" were replaced by a special issue peculiar to the Islands. The Bureau continued to produce Philippine postage stamps until the Islands took on the status of an independent republic on July 4, 1946. The last stamps so produced were the three denominations of identical design commemorating Philippine independence.

The practice of furnishing regular U.S. postage stamps overprinted "Cuba" was short-lived. In 1899, at the request of the U.S. Post Office Department, the Bureau designed and printed an issue of stamps, comprising 1-centavo, 2c, 3c, 5c and 10c ordinary values and a 10c special delivery stamp especially for use there.

Although the U.S. military administration of the island ceased in May 1902, the Bureau continued to furnish the stamps for the Republic of Cuba until fiscal year 1905.

With the establishment of regular mail service under the jurisdiction of the U.S. Post Office on Guam and Puerto Rico, overprinted stamps for these islands were not required after 1900. Since that time, regular U.S. postage stamps have been used on the two islands.

Vending Machines

In this day, when it seems coin-operated vending machines have but recently become standard equipment in factories, offices, places of amusement, etc., it may come as a bit of a surprise to hear that a variety of such machines were being marketed in the early 1880s.

With the turn of the 20th century bringing a tremendous increase in the uses to which equipment of this type was being put, it was not long before dispensing machine manufacturers began to look to the sale of stamps as a new use for their products.

At the time, postage stamp printing was confined to individual sheet form. To obtain stocks for stamp dispensing, it was necessary for either the machine manufacturer or the private user to attach a given number of sheets of stamps, one to another, cut the rows of stamps into strips, and then wind the strips into coils. A tedious task to say the least.

To add to the user's woes, the sheets had already been perforated for separating the stamps by hand, and work so perforated often proved too fragile for dispensers. The solution lay in making imperforate sheets available to be produced into coils privately.

Imperforate sheets for this purpose were distributed on an experimental basis in 1906 and, by 1908, were available at post offices as a regular stock item.

In the meantime, the Bureau had been experimenting in processing stamps into coil form. The first fruits of this experimental work were issued in February 1908.

These coils were produced from regular sheets of 400 stamps, perforated horizontally and cut into strips of 20. The strips were then pasted together to form coils of 500 or 1,000 stamps each. It was not long before the Bureau developed a machine for preparing coils, which materially reduced processing costs.

In 1910, an improved model was developed that cut the pasted stream of horizontally or vertically perforated sheets of 400 stamps into strips, trimmed the margins, and wound the strips into coils in one operation.

Through the use of this machine, the Bureau was able to produce the stamp coils at a much lower cost, and the improved production rates, in turn, were reflected in the service charges made by the Post Office Department for coiled stamps.

It was fortunate that steps had been taken to develop this type of equipment. Without it, the Bureau would have been hard-pressed to meet the unprecedented orders for stamps in coil form that were received beginning in mid-1958.

A major factor in this regard was the decision of the Post Office Department to inaugurate an intensive drive to popularize coiled stamps with special emphasis placed on a new 100-stamp printed web down to finished products of precisely 100, 500, or 3,000 stamps.

It was the ever increasing demand for stamps in coil form that prompted the third assistant postmaster general in 1909 to recommend that steps be taken to find a method of printing postage stamps that would enable the Post Office Department to provide improved service and keep abreast of demands.

Inasmuch as up to this time all postage stamps had been printed in sheet form, it was felt the solution lay in the development of a press for printing stamps in a continuous roll form.

Working on this theory, Benjamin F. Stickney, the Bureau's mechanical expert and designer, developed plans for a rotary press that would wet the paper stock, print the stamps, gum and dry them, and perforate the work, while in web form.

Since the Bureau lacked funds to finance construction of such a machine, the Post Office Department was approached on the matter.

Stickney Press

So promising were Stickney's ideas that in 1910 the postmaster general authorized the expenditure of $5,600 for the construction of an experimental machine in accordance with the plans, from money appropriated to the Post Office Department for expenses incidental to investigating and testing mechanical and labor-saving devices.

The confidence expressed by the Post Office Department in financing the construction of an experimental press in accordance with Stickney's plans was well-placed. Although several years were spent in the development under Bureau supervision, by the spring of 1914, the press was ready to be put into production.

The first stamps produced on the rotary press were the 2¢ ordinary variety of the 1911 series. This rotary-printed stamp was first issued on June 30, 1914. As additional presses were acquired, the production of other denominations of coiled postage and revenue stamps was assigned to the machines.

For a time there were problems to be overcome, but by July 1, 1926, all ordinary postage stamps of 10¢ denomination and under were being produced on the rotary presses. With the gradual increases in the quantities ordered, stamps of the higher denominations, with the exception of the $1, $2, and $5 values, were transferred from the flatbed to the rotary press in 1931. The last of the Stickney presses was decommissioned in March 1962.

Offset-Lithographic Printing

It was an emergency situation during World War I and the years immediately following that resulted in the first printing of U.S. postage stamps by the offset method.

In the early part of 1918, the Bureau receive a shipment of barytes (a substance used in the manufacture of printing inks) that was to bring about this temporary innovation in the production of U.S. postage stamps.

While the samples selected from this lot for test purposes passed the basic requirements for the item, it later was discovered that a large quantity of the total supplied was below standard. The inks manufactured with that portion contained coarse particles that caused the intaglio printing plates to wear rapidly.

Against a normal life expectancy of from six to eight weeks, plates in some cases were wearing out in 10 days.

The coarse barytes had been used in the manufacture of the purple ink employed in the printing of the 3¢ regular stamp. Requirements for this denomination were running about 25 million stamps per day, largely because of the increase in the domestic letter rate from 2¢ to 3¢ in November 1917.

As stocks became rapidly depleted, the Bureau director requested and received permission from the Post Office Department to resort to the offset method of printing on an interim basis.

Previously, the Bureau had experimented with offset printing of postage stamps in connection with its efforts to manufacture stamps suitable for use in dispensing machines. Based on the findings of these tests, it was known an acceptable stamp could be produced by the offset method.

The necessary offset plates were hastily prepared, and printing commenced on March 12, 1918, with the first delivery of offset-printed stamps made 10 days later.

About the same time, it was observed that the plates for printing the 1¢ ordinary stamp were also wearing rapidly, and permission was obtained to print stocks of that denomination on offset presses.

The third time in which U.S. postage stamps were printed in their entirety by the offset method occurred in March 1920. Ironically, it was shortly after the first-class domestic postal rate was reduced to its prewar level. At that time it was the printing of 2¢ stamps that necessitated the same treatment, and as before, it was poor quality barytes that caused the trouble.

Problems of Perforation

From the very beginning of the Bureau's takeover of postage stamp production in 1894, it was plagued by the excessive amount of spoilage occurring during the perforation operation. The same problem had been experienced by the private bank note companies that produced the stamps prior to that time.

The wetting and drying of the paper, essential to the plate printing method of producing stamps, as well as the gumming of the printed sheets, caused the work to expand and contract. Inasmuch as these physical changes were not uniform throughout a sheet, it was difficult to perforate stamps without punching into the printed areas.

So long as postage stamps were produced in single sheet form, the situation could be controlled to some extent by manually adjusting the perforating equipment to allow for variances that occurred.

The printing of stamps in web form on the Stickney presses was another thing. The changeling conditions were cumulative, and it was not unusual that there would be a variance in size and stamp location between the first and last sheets from the same roll.

There were other contributing factors to the variations that occurred in the stamps printed in rolls, such as temperature, atmospheric conditions and water absorption characteristics of the paper.

Experimentation with the perforating of printed rolls of postage stamps by means of electronic controls was begun by the Bureau in 1930. This resulted in development of primary equipment that was designed and built for part manual and part electronic control.

Further improvements were made and a pilot machine constructed that reduced the need for manual corrections to a minimum. First delivery, comprising some nine million stamps perforated on this machine, was shipped in February 1935.

As a result of further extensive experimentation, a production machine was developed by Bureau personnel, incorporating more advanced mechanical and electrical controls. It was put into operation by 1939, and two years later, five improved production models were purchased and installed. Over the years, further refinements in the equipment have been made.

World War II Issues

With World War II approaching a victorious conclusion, the War Department, in mid-1943, placed with the Bureau an order for the production of a special issue of postage stamps to go along as a companion issue for military currency to be used in countries being occupied by U.S. troops.

The initial order, for stamps to be used in Italy, was printed at the Bureau by the offset process in 400-subject sheets, each subject being the exact size of the ordinary U.S. postage stamp. The paper used was a pre-gummed, unwatermarked, white sulphite stock.

Orders were subsequently received and processed by the Bureau for additional quantities of Allied Military Italian postage stamps and for furnishing supplemental French, Committee French, Allied Military German, and supplemental Austrian postage stamps.

In 1943, a decision was made by the Post Office Department to issue a series of postage stamps honoring those nations that had fallen victim to the Axis Powers during the second world war. It was proposed that these stamps carry a reproduction of the flags of the respective countries in true colors.

With the Bureau lacking suitable equipment for the satisfactory and expeditious production of stamps in multicolor, it became necessary to subcontract the work to a private firm. Thus, for the first time since 1894, an issue of U.S. postage stamps was printed outside the Bureau.

The designing and printing of these stamps was handled by the American Bank Note Co. of New York, with 13 stamps issued, honoring Albania, Austria, Belgium, Czechoslovakia, Denmark, France, Greece, Korea, Luxembourg, the Netherlands, Norway, Poland, and Yugoslavia.

A representative of the Bureau was stationed at the printing plant for the duration of the contract. Borders for the stamps were the same for all of the series and were printed from engraved plates. The central designs for each stamp — a reproduction, in appropriate colors, of the flag of the particular country — was produced by the offset letterpress.

Figures released by the Post Office show slightly fewer than 20 million stamps issued for each of Poland, Czechoslovakia, Norway, Luxembourg, the Netherlands, Belgium, and France, and slightly fewer than 15 million stamps issued for Greece, Yugoslavia, Albania, Austria, Denmark and Korea.

Subsequent years have seen a number of additional stamps printed outside the Bureau under private contract. The first cases were where equipment for gravure printing was available and before the Bureau's own gravure equipment was installed.

The Eakins American Painting commemorative of 1967 was printed by Photogravure and Color Co. of Moonachie, N.J. It was the first U.S. stamp to be printed by the gravure method. the following year, the Walt Disney commemorative was printed in the plant of the Achrovure Division of Union Camp Corp., at Englewood, N.J.

In 1970, the Bureau entered into a contract with Guilford Gravure, Inc., Guilford, Conn., for the lease of their plant and equipment for the printing of the Anti-Pollution commemorative issue and the Christmas stamps on that firm's Andreotti Rotogravure press.

In anticipation of the Bureau's installation of its new Andreotti equipment — then on order — crews from the Bureau of Engraving and Printing manned the equipment, using ungummed rolls of paper for the printing order. These rolls were then returned to the Bureau for gumming on the Cottrell press and perforating.

In more recent years, starting in 1979, a number of gravure printed issues have been produced each year by private contractors under a policy of the U.S. Postal Service. This policy may be extended even further shortly.

Multicolor Problems

The Bureau's role in the production of multicolor postage stamps is a "johnny-come-lately" story when the overall picture is viewed. This is not to say there was not an interest along this line, but rather, the ever-increasing demands upon existing facilities forestalled and delayed the development of suitable printing equipment.

Although the first bicolor postage stamp was issued by the Post Office Department in 1869, it was to be another 30 years before another set of postage stamps —the first by the Bureau — was to appear.

It was originally planned that the Trans-Mississippi "Omaha" Exposition issue of stamps in 1898 — the first set of commemorative stamps issued by the Bureau — would be produced in bicolor. However, because of the outbreak of the Spanish-American War in April of that year, and the subsequent heavy demands for the Bureau's service in the production of war revenue items, the idea was abandoned.

The commemorative stamps issued in connection with the Pan-American Exposition held in Buffalo, N.Y., in 1901 were the first bicolor stamps produced by the Bureau. The six denominations comprising this series were printed with distinctive borders, each of a different color, with the vignettes, or central subjects, in black.

There were other two-color stamps printed during the intervening years, of which the 24¢ airmail issue of 1918 is probably the most well-known. This fame can be attributed to a quirk of fate, but one that could happen with the printing process in use at that time for the production of the multicolor stamps.

Similar to the bicolor stamps in the Pan-American issue, this issue had a separately printed central subject of a mail plane in flight, printed in blue. Inadvertently, a sheet of these stamps was printed with the plane flying upside down.

The error went undetected through a number of examinations, and it was only after the sheet of stamps was sold at a post office window that the purchaser realized he had an oddity.

During the post-World War II years, marked by a tremendous advancement in the field of graphic arts, many countries issued varieties of multicolor stamps printed by typographic, lithographic, or gravure methods.

Recognizing this growing interest in multicolor stamps, the Bureau undertook extensive exploration into the potential of these processes for the printing of U.S. postage stamps. It was felt, however, that the resultant printed impressions were considerably inferior in quality to intaglio-printed work.

This factor, coupled with the knowledge that the equipment employed in the processes was readily available on the open market and thus could be easily secured by counterfeiters, prompted rejection of the use of the more common printing methods.

It was during the period of evaluation of two intaglio sheetfed rotary presses in 1955-56 for the dry-printing of currency, that one of the machines showed extensive potential for multicolor printing.

In view of the growing demand for more colorful postage stamps, it was decided at the conclusion of the currency tests late in 1956 to acquire this press for further experimentation in connection with the production of stamps.

Initial expectations concerning this machine were soon justified, and it was used to produce the 4¢ American Flag stamp issued on July 4, 1957. This was the first time the flag had been reproduced in full color on a U.S. postage stamp, a step that drew wide acclaim.

Philatelic 'Firsts'

In February 1962, the Bureau teamed up with the Post Office Department in a project that was to mark another "first" in the nation's stamp history.

Shortly after Astronaut Alan Shepard became America's first space pioneer, Post Office Department officials conceived the idea of a special postage stamp as a suitable tribute to the nation's space exploration efforts.

With officials of the National Aeronautics and Space Administration and the Bureau, the department worked out a proposal for issuing a commemorative stamp simultaneously with the completion of the first orbital flight by an American astronaut.

In light of the fact that the flight might be unsuccessful, it was decided to withhold any advance notice relating to the stamp. The stamp itself was produced under strict security precautions.

Describing the security procedures followed in connection with the production of the stamp, the Bureau in its official "History" notes the "log of the activities relating to the printing and processing of this item would read like a cloak-and-dagger drama."

Instead of the usual formal written orders and receipts between the Post Office Department and the Bureau, in this instance all instructions were given verbally, and the proposed designs, models, and die proofs were transmitted by hand-to-hand operations.

Ostensibly, the Bureau's designer of the stamp took annual leave from his job, but actually went into seclusion at his home studio to design the item. The engraver who did the lettering performed his work on weekends when no one else was in the shop.

The picture engraver, supposedly on vacation, came in at night to engrave the central subject for the new stamp. The printing plates were made when the manufacturing division was supposedly closed.

When the plates were ready to go to press, the multicolor pressroom was completely sealed off from the rest of the plant and declared "off limits" except for persons directly concerned.

When production of the stamps was completed, they were removed, over a weekend, to the packaging and shipping area, where they were stored in a newly finished vault.

On weekends, the stamps were dispatched from the Bureau to the registry section of the Washington city post office for shipment throughout the country. In the meantime, postal inspectors at 301 points across the nation were alerted to receive unidentified sealed packages from Washington, to be kept unopened awaiting further instructions.

Two philatelic canceling machines were shipped by the Post Office Department from Detroit to Jacksonville, Fla., with instructions that these be held for postal equipment technicians.

While this was going on, the Post Office Department ordered one million unmarked envelopes, ostensibly for headquarters' supplies, but in reality to be processed as "first-day covers" — souvenir day-of-issue cancellations marking the momentous achievement at Cape Canaveral.

Project Mercury stamps were affixed to the envelopes by employees of the department's philatelic section, working behind locked doors at night and over the weekend.

A large number of the stamped envelopes were transported to Cape Canaveral, and the canceling machines were ordered to be delivered to a National Aeronautics and Space Administration official there. Everything was ready for release of the new stamp.

At 3:30 p.m. Feb. 20, 1962, the moment that Astronaut John Glenn was retrieved from the ocean and his flight pronounced a success, postal inspectors throughout the country were instructed to open the sealed cartons and release the contents for sale. Immediately, cancellation was begun of the first-day covers.

For the first time in American history, a stamp went on sale all over the nation at the exact hour of the event it commemorated, with no advance "leak" that it was forthcoming.

The Bureau and Post Office Department teamed up for another philatelic first on the occasion of the release of the postage stamp saluting the first landing of man on the moon, on July 20, 1969.

On that occasion, when the first postal astronauts started for the moon, they carried with them an engraved master die, reduced in weight, from which the printing plates to produce the stamp were later made.

The master die went to the lunar surface in the module. A die proof on the now famous moon letter was canceled aboard the capsule with the first space postmark, the ring die, containing the words "Moon Landing, U.S.A. — July 20, 1969."

Production Equipment

It has been noted how the development of the Stickney press during the early years of the 20th century virtually revolutionized procedures for the printing of postage stamps, moving production from sheetfed to rotary webfed equipment.

Through these years of Bureau service, various improvements were made in the Stickney press. With demand for postage stamps steadily increasing each year, especially in the World War II period, the need for new high-speed equipment became more and more evident.

In 1948 two of the old stalwart Stickney presses were taken out of regular production and installed in the Bureau's engineering facility for study leading to the design of new production equipment.

Through application of the data obtained from that study, specifications were prepared for a high-speed intaglio web press that was delivered in 1950.

This equipment, the forerunner of the Cottrell press, was specially manufactured by the Huck Co. of New York City to Bureau specifications. It became popularly dubbed by Bureau of Engraving and Printing personnel as "The Huck Press."

Essentially intended for experimental use, with a few additional perfections, it was found suitable for regular production work. The press was used for the printing of the 3¢ International Red Cross commemorative of 1952.

That stamp had the honor of being the first bicolor U.S. postage stamp produced in web sheet form.

Further developmental work conducted with the equipment to achieve maximum operational efficiency and economy culminated in the decision to purchase in 1955 five electronically actuated webfed presses of similar, but improved design.

These were manufactured to Bureau specifications by the Cottrell Co. of Westerly, R.I., and were first used in the printing of the 3¢ ordinary issue of 1954.

While the basic operation principles of the equipment were the same as those of the Stickney press, the new machines were much larger in size with a speed and production approximately triple that of the old machines.

These presses, equipped with a typographic attachment for precanceling stamps when required, produced about 60 percent of all U.S. stamps issued in 1981, having been employed in the printing of numerous single-color ordinary and commemorative stamps.

An early morning fire at the Bureau's annex building on March 5, 1982, destroyed two of the BEP's four remaining Cottrell presses and damaged the others.

The 2:45 a.m. blaze was caused by a spontaneous flareup of dust and ink in the pressroom's exhaust ducts.

The two less severely affected presses were put back in service within about 72 hours, while the other pair were declared a total loss. The loss of the two presses actually represented little more than their early retirement. As it was, the Bureau had planned to phase two of its aged Cottrells out of service in May 1982 anyway. The two remaining Cottrell presses were subsequently retired at the close of the day shift on Nov. 20, 1985. A partial replacement, the C press, a three-color intaglio press that can print coil and book stamps from rolls of paper, began operation during mid-1982. The C press, if necessary, could also produce sheet-format stamps, regulars and commemoratives. Actually, what has been done has been to use the intaglio portion of the A press to pick up most of the sheet-format jobs formerly produced on the Cottrells.

First Giori Equipment

In connection with its responsibility for the production of all U.S. paper money, the Bureau had long sought means of overcoming the difficulties associated with printing currency from engraved plates using premoistened paper.

Finally in 1954, investigation developed to the extent that printing by the dry intaglio method was deemed feasible. Two companies that felt they had equipment suitable for the purpose offered their machines to the Bureau for evaluation.

During the ensuing two-year trial period, one of the presses, a product of the Giori organization, showed extensive potential for multicolor printing.

As noted earlier, the success of these tests led to the decision to acquire the press for further experimentation, with the result that this machine was used to produce the 4¢ American Flag stamp issued in 1957.

The various stamps produced on this press were so well-received that the Bureau purchased another of these machines in 1959. An even larger machine was acquired in 1963. These were all sheetfed rotary presses.

Andreotti Press

In 1969, the Post Office Department requested the Bureau to undertake the printing of aerogrammes. Heretofore, these items had been produced by the Government Printing Office, which had to release the job because that agency was not prepared to make equipment changes required by a contemplated design change of the item.

As a consequence, it became incumbent upon the Bureau to acquire the necessary printing equipment for the task. The Bureau's decision to proceed was in part prompted by the fact that the work would be produced by the gravure method, and the availability to the Bureau of such equipment for analysis in the production of postage stamps would be of inestimable help in the Bureau's search to improve its capabilities for the production of multicolor stamp issues.

The gravure process is particularly well-suited for printed reproductions of full color artwork and designs. It is also especially useful for the high-fidelity reproduction of paintings popularly used for commemorative stamp designs.

Accordingly, the Bureau solicited bids for a rotogravure press, and a contract was awarded to the Miehle Company of Chicago, Ill., for a seven-color machine. The design and construction of this press were undertaken for the American firm by Andreotti S.P.A. of Ceprano, Italy.

This machine, installed in 1970-71, is approximately 110 feet long and weighs 62 tons. It consists essentially of an unwind rollstand, seven printing units (with provision for an eighth), an extended dryer, and provisions for either sheeting or rewinding.

In addition, this unit can print on both sides of the web of paper on the same pass through the press. This feature was used in the production of the Postal Service Employees issue of 1973 and the quartet of stamps honoring the Contributors to the Cause, issued in 1975.

Although the press was not originally equipped for perforating, this feature was added later. Later still, the in-line perforating was phased out with the introduction of the new Eureka separate perforating machines.

The first postage stamp printed on this press was the 8¢ Missouri Statehood commemorative issue of 1971.

Web 3-Color Intaglio 'B' Press

This press, procured in 1973, has been used in the production of coil and booklet stamps. Specially designed and supplied to the BEP by the Giori organization, it was built by Koenig and Bauer of Wurzbur, West Germany. It can perform one- to three-color intaglio printing, tagging and precanceling, as required.

The press initiated an innovation in Bureau intaglio press equipment with the introduction of a continuous-surface printing base. For example, the printing base supplies an engraved, concentric, seamless, cylindrical surface containing 936 coil-size stamps (18 across and 52 around) without a break. The printing cylinder numbers thus repeat every 52 stamps, or every revolution. Since the printing base is tapered on the inside, it is termed a sleeve.

Because there are no seams in the printing surface, "line pairs" have become a thing of the past as related to this equipment. While the press is intended primarily to produce coil stamps, it has also been used in the printing of book stamps.

In production, a pregummed paper web is fed into the press from an automatic roll unwind unit. This passes through the three-color intaglio printing unit, then through a precanceling unit (when applicable), through a phosphor tagging unit and finally to an automatic rewind unit. After each printing operation, the web passes through a drying oven.

Printing inks are applied to the engraved printing bases by way of one to three "cut-out" rollers. Raised portions of the cut-out rollers receive ink from the ink fountains and selectively deposit it on predetermined locations on the printing base as it revolves. After all of the inks have been applied to the base, it continues to revolve toward the wiping system.

The wiping system consists of a wiper roller and a tank containing a cleaning solution, brushes, and a scraper blade. The upper portion of the wiper roller is in constant contact with the printing base, while the lower portion is partially immersed in the cleaning solution. The wiper roller is cleaned as it rotates in the bath.

The wiper roller, as cleaned, rotates in a direction opposite to that of the printing base but without overly disturbing the ink in the engravings. The printing operation then takes place by exerting great pressure on the stamp paper as it passes between the printing base and a fiber impression cylinder. The transferred ink print is then set in passing through drying units. When phosphorescent ink has been applied in a subsequent operation it is also set by an appropriate unit.

This press became operational in November 1975, producing the 13¢ Flag Over Independence Hall coil stamp. The regular operating speed is 300 feet per minute, providing a production capacity of 18 to 20 million stamps per eight-hour shift.

Web 8-Color Gravure Intaglio 'A' Press

Another piece of stamp printing equipment acquired by the Bureau in 1973 is an intaglio color press also supplied by the Giori organization and built by Koenig and Bauer of Wurzburg, West Germany. This press includes five gravure units supplied by Andreotti of Italy.

It is capable of producing postage stamps in eight colors (five by gravure and three by intaglio). In the beginning, it incorporated additional features required by the Bureau, including perforating, sheeting, and tagging. Since then, perforating and sheeting on the press have been discontinued. An interesting feature is that the gravure and intaglio units can be operated separately or in tandem.

A pregummed paper web is fed into the press from an automatic roll unwind unit. The paper then passes through an oven, which conditions it, then through the five gravure units, the three-color intaglio unit and a perfecting overprint unit, when applicable.

In the beginning, the paper also passed through a phosphor tagging unit, a perforating unit, and finally to a sheeter. However, as already mentioned, perforating has been discontinued and a rewind roll stand has been incorporated. The perforating was discontinued in favor of perforating on separate equipment, the Eureka off-line machines. This also made the rewind roll stand necessary.

This press can produce sheet, book, or coil stamps from a roll of paper. After each printing operation, the ink is set by appropriate drying units. If phosphorescent tagging ink has been applied, it is set by a separate curing unit.

The gravure printing cylinders comprise photoengraved copper to which a chromium surface has been added. When the press is in operation, the printing cylinder turns in an ink fountain where the image-forming cells are filled with ink. A doctor blade then wipes excess ink from the surface of the cylinder prior to its coming into contact with the paper web. The paper draws the ink out of the cells under pressure contact, a transfer facilitated through electrostatic-assist equipment. The fifth gravure unit has the capability to print either the obverse or the reverse of the paper web.

The following section of the press with the intaglio printing base provides an engraved concentric, seamless printing surface termed a sleeve. Printing from this three-color intaglio unit is performed in the same manner as already described for the "B" press

The subsequent perfecting overprint unit prints from raised rubber plates and has the capability of printing on both sides of the web in one pass through the press. This is accomplished by using two plate cylinders, which, after being inked, transfer the image to respective blanket cylinders. The paper web is passed between the two blanket cylinders, thus printing the obverse and reverse simultaneously, if required. The two blanket cylinders act as the impression cylinder for each other.

This press was designed to produce sheet stamps, but can produce coil or book types. The intaglio printing base originally contained an image area large enough to accommodate 460 subjects of commemorative-size stamps, 10 subjects across and 46 subjects around (920 subjects of regular-size stamps). The gravure cylinder units at first contained one-half the image area of the intaglio form and so accommodated 230 commemorative-size subjects. Delivered sheets, however, were in standard 200-subject or 400-subject sizes.

The cylinder numbers, in view of the cylinder sizes and the two-to-one ratio between the gravure cylinder circumference and the intaglio printing base circumference caused the numbers to be in different positions on the sheets with each succeeding print, termed "floating." This was changed in 1986 so that instead of 920-subject production from the intaglio printing bases, it became 800 subjects. The gravure units were made to agree with the companion Andreottis, or 400 subjects for regular issues. This allowed the production of the usual standard 50-subject and 100-subject-size panes with the numbers in the corners. The change was especially made to provide printed rolls that could be readily handled by the new Eureka off-line perforators.

Initial production from the A press occurred in late 1976 with the printing of part of the 1976 skating-scene Christmas stamp.

Booklet-Forming Machines

Among the newer pieces of equipment installed in the Bureau of Engraving and Printing for the production of U.S. postage stamps are the booklet-forming machines manufactured by Goebel of West Germany.

The first unit was installed in the summer of 1976, followed by two others later in the year. A total of six machines were operational by the end of 1977.

While the basic part of these machines is similar to those supplied by Goebel to a number of other countries for the vending of postage stamps in booklet form, the machines at the Bureau incorporate a number of technical improvements designed by the BEP.

A change incorporated in the units for the Bureau is the capability of perforating the stamps as they pass through the machines. This was a separate operation relative to earlier machines manufactured by Goebel.

The U.S. machines are used to assemble both vending machine booklets and those for over-the-counter sales in post offices. Many different arrangements can be produced. The machines can bind from one to several unfolded panes, folded panes, or a combination of the two. An examined roll of stamps as it comes from a book printing press feeds the machines. The roll is then slit into strips as appropriate, perforated, and moved into the binding assembly area, where the strip(s) are enclosed in a hardcover, sliced into individual booklets, folded, counted, and delivered.

What eventually becomes a cover for the booklets starts from a roll of stiff stock that has been printed on another press, or that may, alternatively, have passed through an offset-litho and flexographic printing unit on the booklet-forming machine. The unit is capable of printing on both sides of the cover stock and in two colors on one side, and one color on the other. The cover is subsequently "scored" and the stamp panes attached by moistening the selvage edge. Prior to this, a "cohesive" has been applied to an outer edge of the cover. This serves to keep the booklet closed until all the stamps have been removed.

The average production rate of a Goebel booklet-forming machine is about 15,000 booklets per hour, but this will vary, depending on the number of stamps enclosed, or more specifically the number of panes.

Intagliocolor '8' Press

The Intagliocolor "8" press is a four-plate, three-color Giori, sheetfed, high-speed intaglio printing press. It produces up to 9,000 sheets per hour and is capable of printing in three colors simultaneously from each plate.

The press can feed and deliver individual loads comprising up to 10,000 sheets each. These loads are deposited into one of two delivery elevators at the end of the press. The press continues to print during the removal of a load since the sheets for the following load are switched to the second delivery elevator.

Various sizes and types of paper stock, including pregummed postage stamp paper, can be used on this press in a variety of subject sizes.

Ink rollers are plastic-covered and are sectioned on a pantograph capable of routing five areas of these rollers at one time. This routing of each ink roller permits precise placement of the ink into the areas of the engraving designated for the colors applied to the printing plate. A maximum of three ink rollers can apply a like number of colors.

Two wipers remove ink from the surface of the plates. The first wiping utilizes a plastic roller prewiper that simultaneously removes ink from the surface of the plates and compresses ink into the engraved lines. No solvent or water solution is used with this dry wiping unit.

The second wiping utilizes a water-wipe system using a plastic roller that turns in a water-based cleaning solution. This plastic wiper removes all of the remaining ink from the surface of the plates prior to the printing process.

The Interphil stamp of 1976 was the first stamp produced on this press.

Many other stamps have since been produced on this or similar presses that are also used for currency. However, there has been no stamp production on these since 1985, as the Bureau has gone to all-web production and these are sheetfed presses. The original I-8 press has also been scrapped.

Web Three-Color Intaglio 'C' Press

This press is an improvement over the "B" press and does many of the same things. Procured in 1982 from Goebel of West Germany, it was first used in producing the 20¢ Flag Over the Supreme Court coil in mid-1982. It is a very productive press. It handles paper roll-to-roll but has no in-line perforating or sheeting capability. It does add phosphor tagging or precanceling.

The web width on the "C" press is greater than on the "B" press, resulting in the ability to print 20 stamps across the web as compared to 18 on "B." This synchronizes production with the Goebel coilers, which produce 20 coils at a time. It has also permitted the return to the definitive-size stamp in the over-the-counter books without any adverse impact on printing production.

The press prints at 350 to 400 feet per minute and is presently used to print either book or coil stamps. While this keeps the press busy, it can also produce single-color or multicolor regular or commemorative sheet stamps. The sleeve, which comprises the printing base, also permits a "Cottrell" format that would provide sheet stamps with a margin on all four sides of the final USPS pane.

Coil Production

The Bureau of Engraving and Printing is currently producing coils by two different setups. The oldest method, initiated in the late 1950s, utilizes 18-subject-width plates (across the web) and equipment developed by the Huck Co. This equipment includes four examining machines that accept the printed rolls as they come from the "B" press. Once examined, they are passed onto any one of four perforating-slitting-coiling machines, which turn out either 500-subject or 3,000-subject coils. These are then individually wrapped in polyester by subsequent machinery.

The other setup was started in 1982 with production from the "C" press and the use of 20-subject-width printing bases. The subsidiary equipment was supplied by Goebel and comprises four examining machines again, two perforating-slitting-coiling machines and two packing machines. The packing machines box the coils in individual transparent plastic box segments that are jointly formed together in the making. Individual boxes can then be readily separated by post office counter clerks from the original 50-coil units, called subpacks.

Web 6-Color Offset 3-Color Intaglio 'D' Press

This is another Goebel press, obtained in 1984, and it went into production starting in April 1984 on the 20¢ Smokey the Bear commemorative. It combines six offset-lithographic units with a three-color intaglio unit. It also has phosphor tagging capability.

Normal running speed is considered to be about 350 feet a minute. It will produce commemorative stamps primarily, though it is similar to the "C" press except for the offset units. Thus, it can be used to print coil and booklet issues as well as Cottrell-format sheets.

The press handles paper in a roll-to-roll manner, and it does not have an in-line perforator or sheeter. Fully utilized, it takes six offset-lithographic plates (one for each unit) and one intaglio sleeve subject to one to three-ink reception. Both the "C" and "D" presses are up-to-the minute with electronic controls and the latest in driers. The "D" press uses wet offset but can be changed to dry offset.

The addition of this press has eliminated the necessity of double and triple press runs previously required in connection with combination offset-litho and intaglio printings. The latter had involved utilizing presses such as the I-8 type of press.

New Perforators

Five new perforators, produced by the Eureka Security Printing Co. of Jessup, Pa., were added, starting in 1985. These are webfed stroke-type "perfect-corner" machines built for sheet work. They are consequently a bit different in operation from the Goebel stroke perforators that are used for booklet and coil work.

Each of the machines perforates web segments of 200-subject commemoratives and 400-subject regulars in two strokes (two panes of 50- or 100-subjects side by side at a time) and are rated at 300 strokes a minute. Sheeting-out is performed at the delivery end.

By obtaining special male and female platens, other perforating arrangements can be performed, examples being the Presidential sheetlets produced for Ameripex in 1986, and the $5 regular of 1987.

The addition of these perforators has meant that in a span of roughly 10 years, the BEP has changed from all rotary-action perforators to stroke types for the majority of their product.

Six-Color Web Offset-Litho Presses

Two of these presses, procured in 1980, are available. Called Optiforma presses by their builder, Goebel of West Germany, each is a six-color web offset press capable of running roll to roll and roll to sheet. They will print any of the sheet, book or coil formats currently used in the Bureau. They run at speeds of 1,000 feet per minute during roll-to-roll operation. During roll-to-sheet operation their top speed is 600 feet per minute. The sheeters and rewind stands are of the quick-change type.

The six offset units are individual tower units that have replacements of various repeat lengths to accommodate all formats. The presses have in-line slot perforator and marginal hole punch capabilities. The unwind and rewinds are completely automatic for continuous running ability. Wet and/or dry offset can be run.

The Bureau has produced the 39¢ Graphics aerogramme, part of the 25¢ Bee stamp and a number of stamp booklet covers on these presses, as well as many in-house printing jobs. They have also been used to print official stamps such as the "E" coil and the 15¢, 20¢ and 25¢ Official coils issued in 1988.

Either 450- or 500-subject plates (18x25 or 20x25) have been used in coil production.

Design Center

Dedicated in January 1987, a special design center has been setup in the Bureau of Engraving and Printing. It involved a cost of $2.6 million and was primarily supplied by equipment from Hell Graphic Systems, West Germany. The center comprises a pre-press electronic system, allowing designers to manipulate artwork by computer, handling changes in colors, shapes, location, and sizes in short order. Data can be stored and negatives produced for offset-litho and gravure printing. The setup allows changes to be made and considered in seconds where formerly it could take weeks.

American Bank Note Company

The early history of postage stamp printing in the United States finds a number of firms figuring in the production process covering approximately 50 years before the Bureau of Engraving and Printing took over printing stamps for the Post Office Department.

Prior to 1845, when uniform rates for postage were set by an act of Congress, postmasters accepted letters for delivery either by receiving payment in advance, in which case they marked "Paid" on the wrapper, or by noting on the wrapper the amount of the established fee the recipient was to pay.

The Act of 1845 authorized postmasters to use stamps to indicate prepaid postage and to arrange for the manufacture of stamps until such time as the Post Office Department could do so for the postal system as a whole.

In New York City, Postmaster Robert H. Morris turned to the firm of Rawdon, Wright and Hatch to produce stamps for use by his post office. This same firm in 1842 had manufactured stamps — precursors of postage stamps — for a private message-carrying company in New York.

These first stamps issued for New York City were later to become known as the New York postmaster's provisionals. Two years later, in 1847, this same firm was to produce the first U.S. postage stamps.

It is interesting to note that the firm, its identification now increased to Rawdon, Wright, Hatch and Edson, established another milestone in postage stamp history when it executed an order for three denominations for the Canadian Post Office in 1849.

Another predecessor of the present American Bank Note Co., Toppan, Carpenter, Casilear and Co., obtained the contract for the printing of U.S. postage stamps in 1851. Originally scheduled to run through 1856, this contract was later extended four additional years.

In 1861, the National Bank Note Co., a new firm, having been organized only two years earlier, was awarded the contract for the printing of the new series of postage stamps. The change in contractors apparently was made on the basis of designs submitted. With the outbreak of the Civil War, a change in design was felt imperative by government officials.

Still another new company was to enter the postage stamp printing field when the postmaster general awarded the contract in early 1873 to the Continental Bank Note Co.

This firm had entered the bank note and security business in January 1863, at a time when the volume of business, especially in bank notes, increased tremendously as a result of the war.

It is of interest that eventual entrance of the American Bank Note Co. into the field, just as well as its eventual departure as the printer of U.S. postage stamps, came directly as a result of the creation of the government's Bureau of Engraving and Printing.

The Bureau was organized during the decade following the Civil War, and in 1877 an act of Congress provided that all U.S. notes and securities should be printed by the Bureau.

The three bank note printing companies (American, National and Continental) that had been printing these items had no alternatives other than to face the facts. With the U.S. note business gone, there was enough business left for one major company, but not for three.

In December 1878, the three firms agreed to a consolidation, with the American Bank Note Co. the surviving unit. The offices of National and Continental were closed.

Lester G. Brookman in his book, *U.S. Postage Stamps of the 19th Century*, noted that after the American Bank Note Co. took over the Continental Bank Note Co. on Feb. 4, 1879, the stamp contract held by Continental apparently was assumed by American and fulfilled by that firm.

ABNC was to continue to hold the printing contract for U.S. postage stamps through 1893.

The contract was again up for bids that year. The chief of the Bureau of Engraving and Printing of the Treasury Department, with the approval of the secretary of the treasury, entered a bid for the work under a clause in the official specifications issued to bidders.

The Bureau's figures were substantially below those submitted by other bidders. This, coupled with the convenience of having the work done in Washington, where nearly all other securities of the government were then being printed, resulted in the work being awarded to the Bureau.

American Bank Note Co.'s final contribution to this period of U.S. postage stamp production was the famous Columbian issue of 15 stamps produced in 1893 in connection with the Columbian Exposition in Chicago, marking the 400th anniversary of the discovery of America by Christopher Columbus.

This set of stamps, long recognized as the hallmark of U.S. postage, was the last printed by a private concern for the U.S. government in the 19th century. Until recently, most issues of postage stamps since 1894 have been printed by the Bureau in Washington.

American Bank Note Co. was to figure in one of these exceptions, when the Bureau offered it a subcontract for the printing of the 1943-44 Overrun Countries issue, 13 different designs picturing the flag of each country in its true colors. The Bureau had no press capable of printing the multicolor flags. ABNC printed 195 million of the stamps with intaglio frames and offset multicolor flags for 54¢ per thousand.

ABNC also had a role in production of the first two gravure stamps issued by the United States. It perforated both the 1967 Biglin Brothers Racing issue printed by the Photogravure and Color Co. of Moonachie, N.J., and the 1968 Walt Disney commemorative printed by the Achrovure Division of the Union-Camp Corp., Englewood, N.J.

The 1979-80 Contract

In 1978 the Postal Service became concerned about its escalating stamp production costs — up 90 percent in three years. In fiscal 1973 the average cost of stamps of all kinds printed by the Bureau was 85¢ per thousand. In fiscal 1977 it was $1.65 per thousand.

Postal officials decided to try a relatively small test of outside printing. They asked for bids on four multicolor gravure commemorative issues, a total of 640 million stamps. ABNC, despite its long record as a stamp printer, had no gravure capability. It arranged a joint venture with J.W. Ferguson & Sons of Richmond, Va. Ferguson had webfed Champlain presses capable of printing up to eight colors and was experienced in high volume printing for such products as Coca Cola, Seven Up and Campbell's Soup.

The joint venture won the contract with a bid of $1.97 per thousand. This was broken down as $1.95 for the first stamp, $1.91 for the second, $1.97 for the third and $2.05 for the fourth, well below Bureau charges for the most recent stamps meeting the contract specifications — the Jimmie Rodgers issue at $2.26 and the George M. Cohan stamp at $2.40.

The outside contract at such a sharp reduction in price was a shock to the Bureau officials and employees alike. The 640 million stamps were only a little more than 1 percent of expected stamp needs for the two-year period. But if a commercial press could print stamps of equal quality for less, the Bureau faced possible loss of much or all of its stamp printing.

Operating efficiencies were quickly found. For the Martin Luther King stamp issued in January 1979, the cost was $1.65 per thousand, well below the contract price. It was a little higher, $1.70, for the Special Olympics issue.

Averaging the Bureau's actual cost figures for three comparable stamps and its estimated cost of the fourth produced by ABNC gives a figure of $1.80 compared with ABNC's $1.97, or 17¢ less per thousand.

The Bureau, which must break even but does not need to make a profit, had proved it could beat any commercial price if it wanted to.

The ABNC stamps produced under the 1979-80 contract were the John Paul Jones stamp of 1979 and the Benjamin Banneker, Veterans Administration and American Education (Learning Never Ends) issues of 1980.

From the beginning, production of the ABNC stamps was supervised by Richard C. Sennett, working initially as vice president of a small ABNC subsidiary firm, for a time as an ABNC vice president and later with his own firm, Sennett Enterprises, Inc., or Senprise for short, as an independent ABNC subcontractor.

The models for the first four stamps were prepared by Joseph Daley of Roto-Cylinder in Palmyra, N.J., which made the gravure press cylinders. All models since have been the work of Sennett. Roto-Cylinder later became the Engraving Division of Armotek, its parent firm. The stamps were printed on the Fergusson presses and shipped in sheets of 200 to the ABNC facility in the Bronx for perforating, cutting into panes of 50, packaging and distribution. When the New York plant was closed in 1986, the processing was transferred to an ABNC plant in Chicago.

The net result of the first contract, Postmaster General William F. Bolger indicated, was that the Postal Service was very well satisfied with Bureau costs and service, but was not going to put all its eggs in one basket.

Bureau Director Harry Clements agreed that an occasional outside contract was a good idea, since it would give Postal Service managers assurance that they were getting quality stamps from the Bureau at a competitive price and also would help keep the Bureau competitive.

The 1982-83 Contract

By early 1982, with Bureau prices up to a $2.25 to $2.30 range for gravure stamps, the Postal Service asked for bids on three commemoratives, one in 1982 and two in 1983. The joint venture of American Bank Note Co. and J.W. Fergusson & Sons again was the low bidder at $912,450 for three issues of 165 million stamps each, an average price of $1.84 per thousand stamps. This was even lower than the $1.97 average of its previous contract. The individual stamps were priced at $1.78 per thousand for the first, $1.85 for the second and $1.90 for the third.

Stamps printed under this contract were the Francis of Assisi issue of 1982 and the Joseph Priestley and Martin Luther commemoratives of 1983.

The 1984-86 Contract

Late in 1983 ABNC was the sole bidder on a contract to print five to eight gravure commemorative stamps in each of the next three years. That would be 15 to 24 stamps with an option for as many as nine more. The contract price was $2.15 a thousand for 1984, $2.32 for 1985 and $2.44 for 1986.

This time J.W. Fergusson & Sons was not a partner in a joint venture, but ABNC had made arrangements to use leased Fergusson presses and crews.

Seven stamps were printed in 1984 — the Alaska Statehood, Carter G. Woodson, Hawaii Statehood, Health Research, St. Lawrence Seaway, Roanoke Voyages, and Crime Prevention.

Seven also was the total for 1985 — Jerome Kern, Mary McLeod Bethune, Duck Decoys, Social Security Act, Public Education, Youth block of four and Help End Hunger.

For the third year of the contract, the total was eight stamps — Arkansas Statehood, Sojourner Truth, Texas Statehood, Public Hospitals, Duke Ellington, Polar Explorers, Wood Carvings and Enrico Caruso, the last actually issued in February 1987.

The 1987-91 Contracts

In August 1986 the Postal Service gave notice of a different approach to outside stamp printing intended to encourage bids from firms that might lack equipment needed for immediate production — two overlapping contracts to print a total of 30 commemorative stamps through calendar year 1991. The first would cover deliveries of six stamps in 1987 and 1988 and three in 1989, the second deliveries of three in

1989 and six in 1990 and 1991. In 1988 the contract was revised to provide a minimum of seven issues a year.

The Postal Service solicitation reserved the right not to award either contract if it would cost more than the Bureau's projections for the five years.

American Bank Note Co. was low bidder on both contracts. For 1987 and 1988 the contract price was $2.05 per thousand, for 1989 $2.07, and for 1990 and 1991, $2.25. These are well below the prices in the previous contract, $2.15 a thousand in 1984, $2.32 in 1985 and $2.44 in 1986.

American Bank Note Co. actually printed two 1987 stamps under the contract — Pennsylvania Statehood and New Jersey Statehood. Its 1988 issues were Georgia Statehood, Winter Olympics, James Weldon Johnson, Cats, South Carolina, Francis Ouimet, New Hampshire and the Antarctic Explorers block of four.

In addition, ABNC produced the Pheasant and Special Occasions booklets under a separate contract. Another 1988 contract provided for press testing and evaluation for some 20 varieties of coated stamp paper.

With multiple-year contracts to print a substantial share of the Postal Service's gravure stamps beginning in 1984, Sennett Enterprises was in a position to make capital investment in conjunction with Armotek in state-of-the-art equipment, including laser scanners and computer editing of designs.

The firm also has installed scanning and electronic editing equipment in its Fairfax, Va., office. With it, stamp design art can be scanned and edited using Scitex software programs. It is then electronically transmitted to Armotek Engraving Division at Palmyra for final high-resolution adjustment of the copy to be used in engraving gravure press cylinders.

Changes can be made at either end and transmitted to the other location as digital information on a dedicated telephone line. A four-color printer with 300 dots-per-inch (dpi) output can provide a print in a few minutes, making it possible to review requested changes almost immediately, and make a quick and confident judgment on their desirability.

Errors, Freaks and Oddities

Nothing makes a stamp collector's head turn so fast as an obvious error in an issued stamp. Many of the hobby's true blue chips are errors from the early days: the United States 1869 inverts on the 15¢, 24¢ and 30¢ values, Spain's 1851 2-real value in a 6-real blue sheet, and New South Wales stamps of the 1850s and '60s on paper with the wrong watermark, to name a few.

Most stamps of this era had relatively small printings compared to today. In addition, they were used with little thought given to looking for or saving errors, or misprints of lesser significance. Most of the varieties that have been found were used, and they exist in very small quantities. Incidentally, this is a good reason to keep your eyes open; there is always a possibility that classic errors still can be found in old albums or accumulations.

In the early days of stamp collecting, collectors gathered "EFOs" — Errors, Freaks and Oddities — to dress up their traditional collections. Many modern-day collectors continue to collect EFOs in that fashion. Now, however, a recent upswing in collecting and studying EFOs forms its own specialty area. Modern-day specialization has been fostered by the greatly increased awareness of and search for EFO material. This search is often rewarded because of the increasing complexity of modern production equipment. This complexity results in many minor varieties and errors in greater quantities than in the past.

Terms and Definitions

The lack of commonly accepted definitions of EFO categories has been an impediment to the growth of EFO collecting. Since they were without clear sense of what the "E," "F" and "O" stood for, collectors in large numbers found the area complex and difficult. It was difficult to understand how EFO values were set, so collectors merely kept what they came across. They rarely sought out EFO material unless it was listed in the catalog. Catalog listing is, of course, reserved for errors. And catalog-listed errors get space in albums. Thus, recognized errors tend to be worth more money because collectors like to fill those spaces. Without catalog listing, the freaks and oddities tended to wallow in a confusing maze of conflicting opinion and widely varying prices.

Recent work by the EFO Collectors' Club has brought some much needed order. A *Listing of Existing Errors, Freaks and Oddities According to Group* has been published by the club; it has been updated and revised for publication here. While not all catalogs recognize all of the following error designations, the list has been generally accepted within the EFO collecting fraternity.

Errors

1. Perforations entirely missing between stamps on one or more sides.

2. Perforations entirely missing between stamp and margin, if margin is of normal dimension for the issue.

3. Perforations of the wrong gauge applied on one or more sides, either through use of defective equipment or improper use of normal equipment.

4. Perforations inverted on souvenir sheets.

5. Perforations shifted so far that interpane gutter is within the perforated area of a stamp, or perforations intended to separate panes are within a printed pane with a full stamp width on either side.

6. Perforations fully doubled or tripled.

7. Pair of full stamps with interpane gutter between (either the result of a miscut or foldover).

8. Fully missing color, missing tagging or missing embossing.

9. Inverted design element, tagging or embossing.

10. Wrong color ink used.

11. Wrong plate used with correct color ink.

12. Wrong value stamp or other wrong elements, such as dates or letters appearing on some stamps of a sheet

but not others.

13. Colors reversed.

14. Stamp(s) inverted in a sheet of normal stamps.

15. Entire color(s) leading to a completed stamp, or the completed stamp, printed on reverse.

16. Full offset from paper misfeeds.

17. Double-printed double print.

18. Missing overprint, surcharge or precancel.

19. Wide overprint/surcharge/precancel settings that result from misplacement relative to interpane gutters.

20. Wide/narrow overprint/surcharge/precancel settings that result from plate setup or repair.

21. Missing, misspelled or inverted elements in overprint/surcharge/precancel that result from plate setup or repair.

22. Overprint/surcharge doubled due to double printing.

23. Overprint/surcharge fully printed on back of stamp.

24. Overprint/surcharge where none was intended.

25. A full plate number, when it is not intended to appear on the final product, as a result of paper folds or miscuts on souvenir sheets, coils, booklets, or a reverse imprint on sheet stamps.

26. Plate number totally missing from its proper location.

27. Stamps unintentionally printed on paper watermarked for another issue, or stamps not watermarked that should have been.

28. Stamps unintentionally printed sideways or inverted, vis-a-vis the watermark.

29. Watermark varieties tracing to an imperfection in the dandy roll.

30. Stamps printed on the wrong paper.

31. Inverted format on aerogrammes.

32. Multiple impressions of stationery indicia.

33. Reversed "inside out" envelope postal stationery.

34. Albino embossed stationery.

35. Fully missing, or wholly doubled or tripled grills.

36. Paper holes created in the papermaking process.

37. Gum missing from a whole stamp.

Note: The great majority of inverted non-Bureau precancels are normal and result from lack of interest in placement.

Freaks

1. Perforations entirely missing between stamp and margin, if margin is of lesser length than normal.

2. Perforations shifted into design on sheet stamps, coils, booklet panes and souvenir sheets, either horizontally, vertically, diagonally or combinations thereof (showing multiple stamps or stamps and gutter markings).

3. Gutter snipes, with less than a full width stamp on one side.

4. Wide and narrow perforator settings.

5. Perforations missing less than a full stamp width or height.

6. Perforations blind (impressed, but not pressed through), or irregular perf holes from chipped or bent pins.

7. Printers' waste (by definition, "unlawfully salvaged").

8. Overinking or underinking.

9. Partially missing color or tagging.

10. Misregistration of colors.

11. Foldovers, foldunders or creases creating crazy perfs.

12. Preprinting interior paper creases.

13. Doctor blade lines.

14. Stripper marks.

15. Double paper.

16. Paper repairs.

17. Minor shades of color differences.

18. Partial stamp printed on reverse.

19. Solvent-on-printing-plate varieties.

20. Partial offset from paper misfeed, and offsets from a flatplate printed sheet being laid atop another sheet.

21. Unintentionally misplaced indicia or postal stationery.

22. "Kiss," or double print.

23. Phantom plate numbers.

24. Partially missing overprints and surcharges.

25. Wide/narrow overprint/surcharge/precancel settings that result from misoperation of the devices involved.

26. Unprinted areas on stamps, resulting from foreign matter (for example, string, paper) on plate or sheet.

27. Partially unprinted areas on stamps, resulting from operation of the press (for example, scooped ink, dry ink wells).

28. Miscut coils, booklet panes, souvenir

sheets, and sheets that show parts of adjoining stamps or sheet markings.

29. Split watermarks.

30. Watermark varieties tracing to operation of the watermarking process (for example, partially missing).

31. Ink flaws and extra ink resulting from the printing process (for example, splatters, litho doughnuts).

32. Giori press ink bleeds.

33. Huck press joint-line ink.

34. Ink smears, fingerprints.

35. Part or all of overprint or surcharge misregistered on stamp or on each other.

36. Overprint or surcharge doubled due to an accidental second strike ("kiss") while sheet is in the press.

37. Overprint/surcharge partially printed on back of stamp.

38. Unusual gum skips, or gum partially missing.

39. Partial grill varieties.

40. Stamp paper that has changed color in production process (for example, in drying process).

41. Rejection markings, indicating printer's waste to be destroyed.

Oddities

1. Plate varieties (for example, double transfers, layout lines, position dots).

2. Design errors and ghosts.

3. Intentionally created (altered) varieties made after release (for example, color changelings, attempts to create higher value stamps).

4. Rotary coil end strips, flatplate coil paste-ups.

5. Stamps printed on the edge of watermarked paper showing edge/margin markings.

6. Reconstruction of sheets showing a total background picture.

7. Essays, proofs and specimens.

8. Private perfs.

9. Unusual local overprints.

10. Experimental perforations and roulettes (for example, diamond shape, alternating size).

11. Non-standard paper (other than error instances) used for printing stamps or postal stationery.

12. Inappropriate design elements or watermark design.

13. Cinderellas of non-existent countries.

14. Bisects.

15. Cancels that change the design.

16. Cancellation and meter varieties: missing, inverted, misspellings or substitutions of numbers.

17. Spacing and sheet layout varieties.

18. Errors in cachets (factual, spelling, etc.).

19. Pre-first-day-of-issue cancels.

20. Intentionally created errors.

21. Intentionally produced gutter pairs.

22. British wing margins.

23. Provisional overprints.

24. Stamps printed on reverse of maps, currency, and other items.

25. Stamps that have had designs, ads or other data printed on reverse side.

26. "T" cancels on stamps, denoting postage due use.

27. Different perforations on stamps of the same design, resulting from random use of different pieces of available equipment, or equipment altered or repaired with no concern for resulting material.

How does a collector go about segregating these? Certain underlying principles determine why stamp or stationery defects are assigned under one or another group. Errors, for instance, are usually total: no perforations, no color, full stamps on either side of an intersheet gutter.

Freaks generally are defined to be a lesser degree of production problem, problems that are partial, and those not exactly repeatable. Paper creases, misperforations and partially missing colors are examples of these.

Oddities, as a class, include unusual issuances (for example, stamps printed on the backs of maps), usages (bisects), variations stemming from the stamp design through preproduction process (for example, essays and plate varieties), and cancel/meter varieties. They may be normal for what they are, but they are not often found because of their odd nature.

Any one of these variations, or a group of them, can be collected as a specialty; a collector might also try to get an example of each. Some collectors will restrict their EFOs to one country, or even one major issue within a country.

Others simply accumulate and enjoy anything they come across, saving them in no particular reasoned order. The method is really up to you.

Not all errors are found in catalogs. Missing gum, for instance, can be reproduced without detection. It should also be noted that some material in the freak or oddity classes is far more spectacular than many true errors. Yet, because they are of a lesser level of importance, and the examples vary from item to item, they can't be considered real errors.

Still, whether catalog listed or not, all of it is collectible. This is in stark contrast to most other fields of human endeavor; imperfections are usually shunned by the public. Why are they sought in stamp collecting? The reasons are based in the production process.

The people who design and produce postage stamps have historically looked upon their products with pride. Some have shown more pride than others, but the aim has been almost universally uniform: the perfection of the final product. Considerable craftsmanship has gone into production processes. To the maximum possible degree, uniformity of final product was sought to assure maximum protection against counterfeiting. Inspection to weed out unacceptable variations from the normal (printers waste) has been brought to a high state of technology.

Hampering perfection is the fact that every printing operation has printer's waste as a byproduct. The more complex the machinery, the more printer's waste is created. The printer's objective is twofold: to minimize it as a cost factor, and to detect and destroy it as a security measure. On the whole, security printers do an exceptional job of accomplishing both objectives. Consider that the United States Bureau of Engraving and Printing produced 38 billon stamps in fiscal year 1983. Not only were their costs competitive with private sector firms (who cannot even print the same range of stamp products), but the percentage of waste that slipped through quality control is a very small portion of 1 percent.

On only one issue — the 20¢ Flag Over the Supreme Court — has there been any appreciable number of imperforate errors released. Other errors and varieties have been found in only small quantities, and most are of a minor nature.

However, it is every collector's dream to walk into a post office and buy a major error over the counter, just as W.T. Robey did in 1918 when he bought the only sheet of inverted 24¢ airmails at a Washington, D.C., post office. It is not likely that this will happen to any of us, but it is possible. It is wise to check carefully any stamps before using them. Sad stories are told of people breaking up sheets of missing colors and using half of them before noticing the error. Another unfortunate is the patron who returns to a post office, belligerently thrusts a partial roll of imperf coils at a clerk, and says: "Give me some stamps that I don't have to tear apart!"

Should you be a lucky EFO finder, keep these things in mind:

It is extremely unlikely that the U.S. Postal Service will order more errors produced to match yours, as they did with the Dag Hammerskjold stamp in 1962. The Postal Service was harshly criticized by collectors for that fiasco, and it has not done so since, despite many opportunities. This means that you can announce your find at once if you wish.

If you announce your find and get it verified as a genuine error, you may wish to put it on the market. Should many more of the same errors come to light, selling early will likely get you a better price. Buyers and sellers will not yet know of the find. If you sell early and few others subsequently are found, the price you get will likely be lower than what turns out to be a relatively scarce error might command later on.

You might do well to discuss your find and its marketability with one or more of the several firms (auctioneers and/or mail-approval dealers) who advertise as specialists in EFO collecting. Then make your decision.

The pricing of EFO material is based on the law of supply (how many examples are out there) and demand (how many want what you have), just as in any other area of stamp collecting. EFO demand, however, is affected by many factors. The principal one is how many people collect the basic stamp. U.S. stamps are widely collected, and airmail stamps seem to hold a special fascination for many people. Thus, the 24¢ inverted Curtiss Jenny (Scott C3a) is an extremely expensive stamp, even though equally significant and scarcer errors from countries that are not as popular are relatively inexpensive.

Another contributor to demand is the visual attractiveness or the "flashiness factor" of the EFO item. The C3a is obvious at first glance. A missing black or green color is equally noticeable. If the missing color is yellow or gray, or even the luminescent tagging, the price is probably going to be considerably less. The stamp simply will not be as widely sought.

A third important demand consideration is knowledge of and about the EFO. If no one knows that a particular item exists, no one will want it. The C3a is known to nearly every collector of U.S. stamps. It has a history in which we can involve ourselves: the lucky find, the preservation of it from the government's attempt to retrieve it, its highly publicized thefts and recoveries and its fantastic price rises. Compare this to the perforated 10 top and bottom errors of the Washington-Franklin heads of 1918-1922. Despite catalog listing, few American collectors realize they exist; fewer still seek them out. The result is that with fewer than a dozen examples known of these perforation errors (compared to 100 inverted Jennies), their price is less than one-hundredth of the C3a.

Final consideration is that EFO collectors seem to prefer mint to used material. Even though some errors are extremely rare in any condition, there are those who shun used examples.

Literature

Several excellent books discuss production processes in depth, and explain the ways in which EFOs are created. Probably the finest is *Fundamentals of Philately* by L.N. and M. Williams. This book is out of print, but a revision is in process. Watch for details to be announced by the American Philatelic Society.

A helpful book for collectors of U.S. EFOs is Dr. Stanley B. Segal's *Errors, Freaks and Oddities on U.S. Stamps, Question Marks In Philately*, published by the Bureau Issues Association, 4630 Greylock, Boulder, Colo. 80301.

If you need references to literature on specific countries or issues, it is suggested that you consult with one of the many philatelic literature dealers who advertise in the philatelic press, the APS Research Library (Box 8338, State College, Pa. 16801) or the EFO Collectors Club, Box 1125, Falls Church, Va. 22041.

Where to Look

Everywhere and anywhere there are stamps, a diamond in the rough may be hiding. If you're lucky, you will make the discovery and not have to pay any premium. The first source is, of course, the post office. Look carefully at your purchases. Look hard for the minor varieties: ink splatters, plate cracks, missing perforation(s), offsets on the back, etc. While not expensive, they are fun to collect. Keep a sharp eye as you look through mixtures, old albums, dealers stocks, the envelopes from 20-year-old correspondence, and even your incoming mail. The key is to consciously remember what you are looking for.

If you have specific wants and are willing to pay for them, more than 75 dealers and auctioneers feature EFO material as part of their business. Watch the ads in the philatelic press.

Finally, look for collectors with similar interests at your local clubs, or in other groups to which you belong. Let it be known that you're an "EFOer," and other EFO collectors who have stored a few away may offer some to you.

Chapter 6

U.S. Postal Rates

1692-1899

(For more detailed information on early rates, consult the American Stampless Cover Catalog.)

— COLONIAL RATES —

Effective Date		
1692	Single-Sheet Letter Rates:	
	Not more than 80 miles	4-4 1/2 pence
	Philadelphia, Pa. to Conn., Md. and Va.	9 pence
	New York to Boston, Mass., Md. and Va.	12 pence
	Boston, Mass. to N.J. and Philadelphia, Pa.	15 pence
	Boston, Mass. to Md. and Va.	24 pence
1710	Single-Sheet Letter Rates:	
	Less than 60 miles	4 pence
	60-100 miles	6 pence
	Boston, Mass. to Conn. and Maine	9 pence
	Boston, Mass. to New York	1 shilling
	New York to Charleston, S.C.	1 sh. 6 pence
	Philadelphia, Pa. to Boston, Mass.	1 sh. 9 pence
	New York to London, England (packet boat)	1 shilling
	Rates were doubled and tripled for two and three lettersheets, respectively. One full-rate amount was added for each quarter-ounce weight after one ounce.	
1765 (Oct. 10)	Single-Sheet Letter Rates:	
	From one port to any other American port	4 pence
	Less than 60 miles (inland)	4 pence
	60-100 miles (inland)	6 pence
	An additional 2 pence was added to each additional 100-mile distance beyond the 6 pence rate. An additional 2 pence was added to the inland rate for each incoming private ship letter to any place beyond port of entry.	

— AMERICAN CONTINENTAL CONGRESS AND CONFEDERATION RATES —

1774	Single-Sheet Letter Rates:	
	Less than 60 miles	5 1/4 pence
	60-100 miles	8 pence
	100-200 miles	10 1/2 pence
	200-300 miles	1 sh. 1 penny (13 pence)
1775 (July 26)	The American Continental Congress established a general post office with rates "20% less than those appointed by act of parliament of 1765."	
1775 (Sept. 30)	The July 26 resolution was suspended. The 1765 British single-page letter rates were adopted, but were expressed only in terms of pennyweights (dwt) and grains (gr) of silver. (24 gr = 1 dwt)	
	Less than 60 miles	1 dwt, 8 gr
	60-100 miles	2 dwt
	To each additional 100 miles or fraction, or on each incoming ship letter, 16 gr was added to the inland rate.	
1777 (Oct. 17)	1775 rates were increased by 50% by Congress.	
1779 (April 16)	1777 rates were doubled by Congress.	
1779 (Dec. 28)	The 1775 rates were multipled by 20 times by Congress.	
1780 (May 5)	The 1775 rates were multipled by 40 times by Congress.	

1780 (Dec. 12)	Rates payable in specie (coin) were reduced to 1/2 of the rates of 1765 and 1775 (Sept. 30).
1781 (Feb. 24)	Postage was increased to double the 1775 (Sept. 30) rates.
1781 (Oct. 19)	Ordinance by Congress re-enacted the rates of 1775 (Sept. 30) estimating 1 pennyweight (1 dwt) at five-ninetieths (one eighteenth) of a Spanish silver dollar (Piece of eight reales), which was equivalent to the previous 3 pence sterling for 1 pennyweight, as the Spanish silver dollar had a standard value of 4 shillings 6 pence (54 pence) sterling.
1782 (Jan. 1)	The Sept. 30 1775 rates were restored.
1788	Congress by Resolution of Oct. 20, 1787, reduced the rates of 1782 effective April 5, 1788, "as nearly 25 percentum as will consist with the mode of calculating pennyweight and grains of silver, in order to reduce them to the currencies of the several states," as follows:

Miles Inland	**Single**
To 60	1 dwt
60 to 100	1 dwt, 8 gr
100 to 200	2 dwt
200 to 300	2 dwt, 16 gr
300 to 400	3 dwt
400 to 500	3 dwt, 8 gr
Each Ship Letter:	
Add to Inland	**Postage at Port**
16 gr	(16 gr)

— STATEHOOD PERIOD —

1792 (June 1)	Single-Page Letters:	
	Not over 30 miles	6¢
	30 to 60 miles	8¢
	60 to 100 miles	10¢
	100 to 150 miles	12 1/2¢
	150 to 200 miles	15¢
	200 to 250 miles	17¢
	250 to 350 miles	20¢
	350 to 450 miles	22¢
	Over 450 miles	25¢
	Letters weighing 1 ounce, 4 times single rate; for each additional ounce, add 4 times single rate.	
	By U.S. Government Packet Boat, to, from or intra-U.S., 8¢ per sheet.	
	By private ship (provided for receipt of such letters only) to or intra-U.S., 4¢ each, when delivered at port of arrival; 4¢ each plus regular postage if further forwarded through the mail.	
	Newspapers, 1¢ each for 100 miles; 1 1/2¢ each over 100 miles.	

(1st Constitutional newspaper act)

1794 (June 1)	Re-enacts rates of 1792, plus additions:	
	Local (drop) letters	1¢
	Way letters were assessed 2¢ each, plus regular postage	
1799 (probably March 2)	Single-page letters:	
	Not over 40 miles	8¢
	40 to 90 miles	10¢
	90 to 150 miles	12 1/2¢
	150 to 300 miles	17¢
	300 to 500 miles	20¢
	Over 500 miles	25¢
	6¢ was added to every letter carried by boat, plus an additional 2¢ if delivered anywhere beyond port of entry.	
1810 (April 30)	1799 rates re-enacted, plus addition	
	Local (drop) letters	1¢
1815 (Feb. 1)	All rates increased by 50% (distance rates only)	
1816 (March 31)	1799 and 1810 rates restored.	

1816 (May 1)	Single-page letters:		
	Not over 30 miles		6¢
	30 to 80 miles		10¢
	80 to 150 miles		12 1/2¢
	150 to 400 miles		18 1/2¢
	Over 400 miles		25¢
1825 (May 1)	1816 rates re-enacted, with changes:		
	150-400 miles		18 3/4¢
	Local (drop) letters		1¢
	Way Mail		1¢
	By private ship (First act providing for sending such letters from or intra-U.S., 1¢ each. Act of March 2, 1799, still applied to such letters received.)		
1845 (July 1)	Half-ounce letters		
		Prepaid	**Collect**
	Under 300 miles, per 1/2 oz.	5¢	5¢
	Over 300 miles, per 1/2 oz.	10¢	10¢
	Drop letters	2¢	
	Carrier fee	2¢	
	Circulars	2¢ per sheet	
1847 (July 1)	Postage stamp use authorized		
	Unsealed circulars		
	1 oz. or less	3¢	
1847-48	East, to or from Havana (Cuba) per 1/2 oz.	12 1/2¢	12 1/2¢
	East, to or from Chagres (Panama) per 1/2 oz.	20¢	20¢
	East, to or from Panama, across Isthmus, per 1/2 oz.	30¢	30¢
	To or from Astoria (Ore.) or Pacific Coast, per 1/2 oz.	40¢	40¢
	Along Pacific Coast, per 1/2 oz.	12 1/2¢	12 1/2¢
1849 (March 3)	Any letter weighing more than one ounce but less than two was charged double rate. Two additional rates (10¢) were charged for each additional ounce or fraction thereof.		
1851 (July 1)		**Prepaid**	**Collect**
	Up to 3,000 miles, per 1/2 oz.	3¢	5¢
	Over 3,000 miles, per 1/2 oz.	6¢	10¢
	Drop letters	1¢	
	Unsealed circulars:		
	1 oz. or less up to 500 miles	1¢	
	Over 500 miles to 1,500 miles	2¢	
	Over 1,500 miles to 2,500 miles	3¢	
	Over 2,500 miles to 3,500 miles	4¢	
	Over 3,500 miles	5¢	
	Advertised letters 1¢ each, plus regular postage		
	Printed matter		**Prepaid with stamps or doubled**
	Up to 500 miles		1¢ per ounce
	501 to 1,500 miles		2¢ per ounce
	1,501 to 2,500 miles		3¢ per ounce
	2,501 to 3,500 miles		4¢ per ounce
	Over 3,500 miles		5¢ per ounce
1852 (Oct. 1)	Unsealed circulars (Provided for stamped envelopes)		
	3 oz. or less anywhere in U.S.		1¢
	Each additional ounce		1¢
	(Double charge if collect)		

1855 (April 1)	Prepayment of postage made compulsory	
	Not over 3,000 miles, per 1/2 oz.	3¢
	Over 3,000 miles, per 1/2 oz.	10¢
	Drop letters	1¢
1860 (April 3)	Drop letters (carrier)	1¢
	Carrier fee	1¢
1861 (Feb. 27)	Returned dead letters charge full postage.	
	Private shipletters to or intra-U.S. charged 5¢ for delivery at port of entry, plus additional 2¢ if delivered beyond (plus regular postage)	
	Postage from any point east of the Rocky Mountains to any state or territory on the Pacific Coast and vice-versa was set at 10¢ prepaid per half-ounce.	
	Letters by soldiers in the service to be carried without prepayment of postage. Postage was paid by recipient.	
1863 (July 1)	Distance differential of postage eliminated pre-payment per half-ounce	
	Any distance (domestic)	3¢
	Drop letters	2¢
	Printed matter, per 3 circulars	2¢
	Private ship letters were sent at double letter rates.	
1883 (Oct. 1)	Letter rate reduced one-third	
	All parts of United States, per 1/2 oz.	2¢
1885 (July 1)	Weight increased to 1 oz.	
	All parts of United States, per 1 oz.	2¢
1896 (Oct. 1)	Rural free delivery started	
1917 (Nov. 2)	War emergency	
	All parts of United States, per 1 oz.	3¢

Selected U.S. Domestic Mail Rates: 1900-1967

	in effect 1-1-00	11-2-17	7-1-19	4-15-25	7-1-28	7-6-32	7-1-33	3-26-44	1-1-52	7-1-52	8-1-58	1-1-59	7-1-60	1-7-63	1-1-64	1-1-65
First-class																
Letter rates:																
Single rate*	2/2/1	3/2/2	2/2/1	—	—	3/3/1	3/2/1	3/3/1	3/3/2	—	4/4/3	—	—	5/5/4	—	—
Postal/postcard rates:																
Single rate	1	2	1	1/2**	1	—	—	—	2	—	3	—	—	4	—	—
Third-class (bulk)***																
Commercial mailings:																
basic sort	None	—	—	—	1	—	—	—	—	1.5	—	2	2.5	2.625	2.75	2.875
Non-profit mailings:																
basic sort	None	—	—	—	1	—	—	—	—	—	—	—	1.25	—	—	—

* For many years, first-class was divided into three categories: non-local; local at carrier offices; and local at non-carrier offices

** The higher rate is for private postcards

*** Prior to July 1, 1952, there was no separate rate for non-profit bulk mailings

Selected U.S. Domestic Mail Rates: 1968 to 1979

	1-7-68	7-1-69	5-16-71	3-12-72	7-6-72	3-2-74	7-6-74	9-14-75	12-31-75	7-6-76	7-18-76	7-6-77	5-29-78	7-6-78	1-28-79	7-6-79
First-class																
Letter rates:																
Single rate																
1st ounce	6	—	8	—	—	10	—	—	13	—	—	—	15	—	—	—
Addn'l. ounces	6	—	8	—	—	10	—	9	11	—	—	—	13	—	—	—
Bulk rate																
ZIP+4 unsorted	None	—	—	—	—	—	—	—	—	—	—	—	—	—	—	
basic sort (3 or 5 digit)	None	—	—	—	—	—	—	—	—	12	—	—	13	—	—	—
basic sort, ZIP+4	None	—	—	—	—	—	—	—	—	—	—	—	—	—	—	—
carrier route sort	None	—	—	—	—	—	—	—	—	—	—	—	—	—	—	—
Postcard rates:																
Single rate	5	—	6	—	—	8	—	7	9	—	—	—	10	—	—	—
Bulk rate																
ZIP+4 unsorted	None	—	—	—	—	—	—	—	—	—	—	—	—	—	—	—
basic sort	None	—	—	—	—	—	—	—	—	8	—	—	9	—	—	—
basic sort, ZIP+4	None	—	—	—	—	—	—	—	—	—	—	—	—	—	—	—
carrier route sort	None	—	—	—	—	—	—	—	—	—	—	—	—	—	—	—
Third-class (bulk)																
Commercial mailings:																
basic sort	3.6	3.8/4*	4/4.2	5	4.8/5	6.1/6.3	—	—	7.7/7.9	—	7.5/7.7	—	8.4	—	—	—
5-digit sort	None	—	—	—	—	—	—	—	—	—	—	—	—	—	—	—
carrier route sort	None	—	—	—	—	—	—	—	—	—	—	—	—	—	6.9	—
Non-profit mailings:																
basic sort	1.4	1.6	1.7	—	—	—	1.8	—	—	1.9	2	2.1	2.4	2.7	—	3.1
5-digit sort	None	—	—	—	—	—	—	—	—	—	—	—	—	—	—	—
carrier route sort	None	—	—	—	—	—	—	—	—	—	—	—	—	—	—	—

* Lower rate applies to first 250,000 in a calendar year.

Selected U.S. Domestic Mail Rates: 1980 to date

	4-23-80	7-6-80	3-22-81	7-6-81	11-1-81	1-10-82	7-28-82	1-9-83	5-22-83	10-9-83	2-17-85	1-1-86	3-9-86	4-20-86	4-3-88
First-class															
Letter rates:															
Single rate															
1st ounce	—	—	18	—	20	—	—	—	—	—	22	—	—	—	25
Addn'l. ounces	—	—	17	—	—	—	—	—	—	—	—	—	—	—	20
Bulk rate															
ZIP+4 unsorted	—	—	—	—	—	—	—	—	—	19.1	21.1	—	—	—	24.1
basic sort (3 or 5 digit)	—	—	15	—	17	—	—	—	—	—	18	—	—	—	21
basic sort, ZIP+4	—	—	—	—	—	—	—	—	—	16.5	17.5	—	—	—	20.5
carrier route sort	—	—	14	—	16	—	—	—	—	—	17	—	—	—	19.5
Postcard rates:															
Single rate	—	—	12	—	13	—	—	—	—	—	14	—	—	—	15
Bulk rate															
ZIP+4 unsorted	—	—	—	—	—	—	—	—	—	12.1	13.1	—	—	—	14.1
basic sort	—	—	11	—	12	—	—	—	—	—	—	—	—	—	13
basic sort, ZIP+4	—	—	—	—	—	—	—	—	—	11.5	—	—	—	—	12.5
carrier route sort	—	—	10	—	11	—	—	—	—	—	—	—	—	—	11.5
Third-class (bulk)															
Commercial mailings:															
basic sort	—	—	10.4	—	10.9	—	—	—	11	—	12.5	—	—	—	16.7
5-digit sort	—	—	8.8	—	9.3	—	—	—	—	—	10.1	—	—	—	13.2
carrier route sort	6.7	—	6.4	—	7.9	—	—	—	7.4	—	8.3	—	—	—	10.1
Non-profit mailings:															
basic sort	—	3.5	—	3.8	—	5.9	4.9	5.2	—	—	6	7.4	8.7	8.5	8.4
5-digit sort	—	—	3.3	2.9	—	5	4	4.3	—	—	4.9	6.3	7.2	7.1	7.6
carrier route sort	3	3.2	3.1	1.9	—	4	3	3.3	—	—	3.4	4.8	5.7	5.5	5.3

U.S. Domestic Postal Rates

First Class

The single-piece rates are applied to each letter or piece of first-class mail according to its weight.

All first-class mail weighing 12 ounces or less, except postal and postcards: 25¢ for the first ounce or fraction of an ounce; 20¢ for each additional ounce or fraction of an ounce.

Single postal cards sold by the post office: 15¢ each. Double postal cards sold by the post office: 30¢ (15¢ each half). Single postcards: 15¢ each. Double postcards (reply portion of double postcard does not have to bear postage when originally mailed): 30¢ (15¢ each half).

Business reply — rates vary to requirement, consult post office.

Second Class

Second-class mail includes newspapers and periodical publications with second-class mail privileges.

Third Class

Third-class mail includes circulars, books, catalogs and other printed matter, merchandise, seeds, cuttings, bulbs, roots, scions and plants, weighing less than 16 ounces.

Discount Rates

A widely varied schedule of discount rates exist for certain classes of U.S. mail. Most notable are the special bulk rate discounts for large or multiple-piece mailings, and the different presort and ZIP+4 rates, which provide for varying discounts from applicable postage rates. The carrier-route presort allows for the biggest presort discount rate. With the different requirements and rate schedules involved for all these classifications, consultation with the local post office is recommended for any mailers who might qualify for these discounts. Most of these discounts require certain minimum mailing requirements, and qualified non-profit organizations are often given discounts beyond even the regular discounted rates.

Priority Mail (Heavy Pieces)

Priority mail provides first-class service for heavy items (over 12 ounces), those that would otherwise go parcel post. It is primarily for heavy items that must go at the first-class rate, or for parcels needing expedited service.

Local zone is within the delivery limits of the local post office; Zone 1 is within the same sectional center; Zone 2 is up to 150 miles; Zone 3, to 300 miles; Zone 4, to 600 miles; Zone 5, to 1,000 miles; Zone 6, to 1,400 miles; Zone 7, to 1,800 miles; and Zone 8, beyond 1,800 miles. The zone mileage figures are approximate. The official zone chart furnished by a post office shows the complete zone structure from that office.

Priority Mail

Weight — over 12 oz. but not exceeding (pounds)	Local 1, 2 & 3	Zone 4	Zone 5	Zone 6	Zone 7	Zone 8
1	$2.40	$2.40	$2.40	$2.40	$2.40	$2.40
1.5	2.40	2.40	2.40	2.40	2.40	2.40
2	2.74	3.16	3.45	3.74	3.96	4.32
3	2.74	3.16	3.45	3.74	3.96	4.32
4	3.18	3.75	4.13	4.53	4.92	5.33
5	3.61	4.32	4.86	5.27	5.81	6.37
6	4.15	5.08	5.71	6.31	6.91	7.66
7	4.58	5.66	6.39	7.09	7.80	8.67
8	5.00	6.23	7.07	7.87	8.68	9.68
9	5.43	6.81	7.76	8.66	9.57	10.69
10	5.85	7.39	8.44	9.44	10.45	11.70
11	6.27	7.97	9.12	10.22	11.33	12.71

Priority Mail (continued)

Weight — over 12 oz. but not exceeding (pounds)	Local 1, 2 & 3	Zone 4	Zone 5	Zone 6	Zone 7	Zone 8
12	6.70	8.55	9.81	11.01	12.22	13.72
13	7.12	9.12	10.49	11.79	13.10	14.73
14	7.55	9.70	11.17	12.57	13.99	15.74
15	7.97	10.28	11.86	13.36	14.87	16.75
16	8.39	10.86	12.54	14.14	15.75	17.75
17	8.82	11.44	13.22	14.92	16.64	18.76
18	9.24	12.01	13.90	15.70	17.52	19.77
19	9.67	12.59	14.59	16.49	18.41	20.78
20	10.09	13.17	15.27	17.27	19.29	21.79
21	10.51	13.75	15.95	18.05	20.17	22.80
22	10.94	14.33	16.64	18.84	21.06	23.81
23	11.36	14.90	17.32	19.62	21.94	24.82
24	11.79	15.48	18.00	20.40	22.83	25.83
25	12.21	16.06	18.69	21.19	23.71	26.84
26	12.63	16.64	19.37	21.97	24.59	27.84
27	13.06	17.22	20.05	22.75	25.48	28.85
28	13.48	17.79	20.73	23.53	26.36	29.86
29	13.91	18.37	21.42	24.32	27.25	30.87
30	14.33	18.95	22.10	25.10	28.13	31.88
31	14.75	19.53	22.78	25.88	29.01	32.89
32	15.18	20.11	23.47	26.67	29.90	33.90
33	15.60	20.68	24.15	27.45	30.78	34.91
34	16.03	21.26	24.83	28.23	31.67	35.92
35	16.45	21.84	25.52	29.02	32.55	36.93
36	16.87	22.42	26.20	29.80	33.43	37.93
37	17.30	23.00	26.88	30.58	34.32	38.94
38	17.72	23.57	27.56	31.36	35.20	39.95
39	18.15	24.15	28.25	32.15	36.09	40.96
40	18.57	24.73	28.93	32.93	36.97	41.97
41	18.99	25.31	29.61	33.71	37.85	42.98
42	19.42	25.89	30.30	34.50	38.74	43.99
43	19.84	26.46	30.98	35.28	39.62	45.00
44	20.27	27.04	31.66	36.06	40.51	46.01
45	20.69	27.62	32.35	36.85	41.39	47.02
46	21.11	28.20	33.03	37.63	42.27	48.02
47	21.54	28.78	33.71	38.41	43.16	49.03
48	21.96	29.35	34.39	39.19	44.04	50.04
49	22.39	29.93	35.08	39.98	44.93	51.05
50	22.81	30.51	35.76	40.76	45.81	52.06
51	23.23	31.09	36.44	41.54	46.69	53.07
52	23.66	31.67	37.13	42.33	47.58	54.08
53	24.08	32.24	37.81	43.11	48.46	55.09
54	24.51	32.82	38.49	43.89	49.35	56.10
55	24.93	33.40	39.18	44.68	50.23	57.11
56	25.35	33.98	39.86	45.46	51.11	58.11
57	25.78	34.56	40.54	46.24	52.00	59.12
58	26.20	35.13	41.22	47.02	52.88	60.13
59	26.63	35.71	41.91	47.81	53.77	61.14
60	27.05	36.29	42.59	48.59	54.65	62.15
61	27.47	36.87	43.27	49.37	55.53	63.16
62	27.90	37.45	43.96	50.16	56.42	64.17
63	28.32	38.02	44.64	50.94	57.30	65.18
64	28.75	38.60	45.32	51.72	58.19	66.19
65	29.17	39.18	46.01	52.51	59.07	67.20
66	29.59	39.76	46.69	53.29	59.95	68.20
67	30.02	40.34	47.37	54.07	60.84	69.21
68	30.44	40.91	48.05	54.85	61.72	70.22

Priority Mail (continued)

Weight — over 12 oz. but not exceeding (pounds)	Local 1, 2 & 3	Zone 4	Zone 5	Zone 6	Zone 7	Zone 8
69	30.87	41.49	48.74	55.64	62.61	71.23
70	31.29	42.07	49.42	56.42	63.49	72.24

Exception: Parcels weighing less than 15 pounds, measuring over 84 inches in length and girth combined, are chargeable with a minimum rate equal to that for a 15 pound parcel for the zone to which addressed.

Fourth-Class (Parcel Post) Rates

(See Priority Mail for zone boundaries.)

Weight 1 pound and not exceeding (pounds)	Zones 1 & 2	Zone 3	Zone 4	Zone 5	Zone 6	Zone 7	Zone 8
2	$1.69	$1.81	$1.97	$2.24	$2.35	$2.35	$2.35
3	1.78	1.95	2.20	2.59	2.98	3.42	4.25
4	1.86	2.10	2.42	2.94	3.46	4.05	5.25
5	1.95	2.24	2.65	3.29	3.94	4.67	6.25
6	2.04	2.39	2.87	3.64	4.43	5.30	7.34
7	2.12	2.53	3.10	4.00	4.91	5.92	8.30
8	2.21	2.68	3.32	4.35	5.39	6.55	9.26
9	2.30	2.82	3.55	4.70	5.87	7.17	10.22
10	2.38	2.97	3.78	5.05	6.35	7.79	11.18
11	2.47	3.11	4.00	5.40	6.83	8.42	12.14
12	2.56	3.25	4.22	5.75	7.30	9.03	13.09
13	2.64	3.40	4.44	6.10	7.78	9.65	14.03
14	2.69	3.48	4.56	6.27	8.02	9.96	14.50
15	2.75	3.55	4.67	6.44	8.24	10.24	14.94
16	2.79	3.63	4.78	6.60	8.45	10.52	15.35
17	2.84	3.70	4.88	6.75	8.66	10.77	15.74
18	2.89	3.76	4.98	6.90	8.85	11.02	16.11
19	2.93	3.83	5.07	7.03	9.03	11.25	16.45
20	2.98	3.89	5.16	7.16	9.20	11.47	16.79
21	3.02	3.95	5.25	7.29	9.37	11.68	17.10
22	3.06	4.01	5.33	7.41	9.53	11.88	17.41
23	3.10	4.07	5.41	7.53	9.68	12.08	17.70
24	3.14	4.12	5.49	7.64	9.83	12.26	17.97
25	3.18	4.18	5.56	7.75	9.97	12.44	18.24
26	3.22	4.23	5.64	7.85	10.11	12.62	18.50
27	3.26	4.28	5.71	7.96	10.24	12.79	18.75
28	3.29	4.33	5.78	8.05	10.37	12.95	18.99
29	3.33	4.38	5.85	8.15	10.50	13.11	19.23
30	3.37	4.43	5.91	8.25	10.62	13.26	19.45
31	3.40	4.48	5.98	8.34	10.74	13.41	19.67
32	3.44	4.53	6.04	8.43	10.85	13.56	19.89
33	3.47	4.58	6.10	8.51	10.97	13.70	20.10
34	3.51	4.62	6.16	8.60	11.08	13.83	20.30
35	3.54	4.67	6.22	8.68	11.18	13.97	20.50

Exception: Parcels weighing less than 15 pounds, measuring over 84 inches but not exceeding 100 inches in length and girth combined, are chargeable with a minimum rate equal to that for a 15 pound parcel for the zone to which addressed. Special lower rates exist for items such as books, bound printed matter, manuscripts, library items, items mailed in bulk or presorted, and other materials. The local post office should be consulted for such rates and requirements.

International Mail

International mail includes letters, letter packages, printed matter, small packages of merchandise and samples, and parcel post destined for foreign countries. APO (Army Post Office) and FPO (Fleet Post Office) mail is not considered international mail.

Below is a listing of international postal rates, including surface and air rates.

NOTE: Letter-class mail to Mexico receives first-class service in the United States and airmail service in Mexico at rates equal to domestic U.S. rates. The first-class rate to Canada is 30¢, 21¢ for postcards.

Surface Rates

Mexico (see note in introduction): 25¢ first ounce; 20¢ each additional ounce or fraction through 12 ounces; eight-zone priority rates for heavier weights. Weight limit is 4 pounds to all countries.

Countries other than Canada and Mexico, 1 ounce, 40¢; 23¢ per ounce for each additional ounce up to 8 ounces; over 8 ounces to 1 pound, $3.80; over 1 to 1 1/2 pounds, $5.20; over 1 1/2 to 2 pounds, $6.60; and $1 for each additional 1/2 up to 4 pound limit.

Air Rates

All countries other than Canada and Mexico, 45¢ per half ounce up to and including two ounces, 42¢ each additional half ounce or fraction.

Postcard rates to Mexico is the same as U.S. domestic rates. To Canada, the rate is 21¢. To other countries, the surface rate is 28¢, while the air rate is 36¢ per card. Size limits are: 6 by 4 1/2 inches maximum; 5 1/2 by 3 1/2 inches minimum. Double reply cards are not useable outside domestic application.

Aerogrammes, or self-contained airmail lettersheets (in which enclosures are not permitted), are 39¢.

Express Mail International Service (EMS) offers high-speed mail service to many countries. The Custom Designed Service provides delivery on a fixed schedule that is tailored to the need of the customer from any location in the United States. The On-Demand Service provides delivery when shipments cannot be made on a regular basis.

Express Mail International Service includes merchandise and document reconstruction insurance at no additional charge and provides an Express Mail Corporate Account option. Unlike domestic Express Mail, there is no service guarantee for International Express Mail. Weight limit is generally 33 or 44 pounds. See Individual Country Listings for service availability.

Following is a more complete country listing, with parcel post data as well.

Country	Express Mail Service Available	Max. Wt. for Parcel Post (Air & Surface)	Parcel Post Insurance Available
Afghanistan	No	44	No
Albania	No	44	No
Algeria	No	44	$500
Andorra	No	44	$500
Angola	No	22	No
Anguilla	No	22	$500
Antigua (Barbuda)	No	22	$60
Argentina	Yes	44	$500
Aruba (Neth. Antilles)	No	44	$500
Ascension	No	44	$160
Australia	Yes	44	$500
Austria	Yes	44	$500
Azores	Yes	44	$500
Bahamas	Yes	22	$500*
Bahrain	Yes	22	No
Bangladesh	Yes	22	$500
Barbados	Yes	44	$205
Belgium	Yes	44	$500
Belize	No	44	$500
Benin (Dahomey)	No	44	No
Bermuda	Yes	44	$410
Bhutan	No	22	$410
Bolivia	No	44	No
Botswana	No	22	$500
Brazil	Yes	44	No
British Virgin Is.	No	44	$155
Brunei	No	22	No
Bulgaria	No	44	$500
Burkina Faso	Yes	44	No
Burma	No	22	$500*
Burundi	No	44	$500
Cameroon	No	44	$450
Canada	Yes	66	$500
Cape Verde	No	22	$410
Cayman (Leeward Islands)	Yes	44	No
Central African Rep.	No	44	No
Chad	Yes	44	$410
Chile	Yes	22	No
China, People's Rep. of	Yes	44	$410
China, Rep. of (see Taiwan)			
Colombia	Yes	44	No
Comoros	No	44	No
Congo (People's Rep.)	No	44	$500
Corsica	Yes	44	$500
Costa Rica	No	44	No

Country	Express Mail Service Available	Max. Wt. for Parcel Post (Air & Surface)	Parcel Post Insurance Available
Cuba	No	No	No
Cyprus	Yes	44	$500
Czechoslovakia	No	33	$500
Denmark	Yes	44	$500
Djibouti	Yes	44	$500
Dominica	No	22	No
Dominican	No	44	No
*East Timor	No	0	No
Ecuador	No	44	—
Egypt	Yes	44	$500
El Salvador	No	44	No
Equatorial Guinea	No	44	No
Estonia (U.S.S.R.)	No	22	$410
Ethiopia	No	44	$410
Falkland Islands	No	44	$155
Faroe Islands	Yes	44	$500
Fiji	No	22	$500
Finland	Yes	44	$500
France	Yes	44	$500
French Guiana	No	44	$500
French Polynesia	No	44	$500
Gabon	No	44	No
Gambia	No	22	$500
German Democratic Rep.	No	44	$500
Germany, Federal Rep.	Yes	44	$500
Ghana	No	22	$500
Gibraltar	No	44	$80
Great Britain[1]	Yes	44	$1200
Greece	Yes	44	$500
Greenland	No	44	$500
Grenada and Grenadines	No	22	$100
Guadeloupe		44	$500
Guatemala	No	44	No
Guinea	Yes	44	$500
Guinea Bissau	No	22	$21
Guyana	Yes	22	$85
Haiti	No	44	No
Honduras	No	44	No
Hong Kong	Yes	22	$500
Hungary	Yes	44	$500
Iceland	Yes	44	$500
India	Yes	44	$500*
Indonesia	Yes	22	No
Iran	No	44	$500
Iraq	No	44	$500*
Ireland (Eire)	Yes	22	$1000*
Israel	Yes	33	No
Italy	Yes	44	$500
Ivory Coast[1]	Yes	44	$500
Jamaica	No	22	No
Japan	Yes	22	$500
Jordan	Yes	44	No
Kenya	No	22	$455
Kiribati	No	44	No
Korea, Dem. People's Rep.	No	0	—
Korea, Rep. of	Yes	22	$500
Kuwait	Yes	44	$500
Laos	No	44	No
Latvia (U.S.S.R.)	No	22	$410
*Lebanon	No	11	No
Lesotho	No	22	No
Liberia	No	22	$410
Libya	No	44	No
Liechtenstein	No	44	$500
Lithuania (U.S.S.R.)	No	22	$410
Luxembourg	Yes	44	$500
Macao	Yes	44	$410
Madeira Islands	Yes	22	$500
Malagasy Republic.	No	44	$500
Malawi	No	22	$160
Malaysia	Yes	22	$410
Maldives, Rep. of	No	22	No
Mali	Yes	44	$500
Malta	No	22	No
Martinique	No	44	$500
Mauritania	No	44	$500
Mauritius	No	22	No
Mexico (rate is per oz.)	Yes	44	No
Monaco (France)	Yes	44	$500
Mongolia People's Rep.	No	0	No
Montserrat	No	44	$500
Morocco	Yes	44	$500
Mozambique	No	22	No
Nauru	No	22	$205
Nepal	No	44	No
Netherlands	Yes	44	$500
Netherlands Antilles	Yes	44	$500
New Caledonia	No	44	$500
New Zealand	Yes	22	$500
Nicaragua	No	44	$410
Niger	Yes	44	$410
Nigeria	Yes	22	$190
Norway	Yes	44	$500
Oman	Yes	22	$500
Pakistan	Yes	22	$500
Panama	Yes	44	No
Papua New Guinea	No	44	$500
Paraguay	No	44	No
Peru	No	44	No
Philippines	No	44	$205
Pitcairn Islands	No	22	No
Poland	No	44	$410
Portugal	Yes	44	$500
Qatar	Yes	44	$500
Reunion	No	44	$500
Romania	No	44	$410
Rwanda	Yes	44	No
Nevis-St. Christopher	No	44	$70
St. Helena	No	44	$160
St. Lucia	No	44	$100
St. Pierre and Miquelon	No	44	$500
St. Thomas & Prince Is.	No	44	$410
St. Vincent and Grenadines	No	22	$125
San Marino (Italy)	No	44	$500
Saudi Arabia	Yes	22	No
Senegal	Yes	44	$500

Country	Express Mail Service Available	Max. Wt. for Parcel Post (Air & Surface)	Parcel Post Insurance Available
Seychelles	No	22	No
Sierra Leone	No	44	$185
Singapore	Yes	22	$500
Solomon Islands	No	44	No
Somalia	No	44	$410
South Africa (Rep.)	Yes	44	No
Spain	Yes	44	$410
Sri Lanka	No	44	$95
Sudan	No	44	$80
Surinam(e)	No	44	$100
Swaziland	Yes	44	$500
Sweden	Yes	44	$500
Switzerland	Yes	44	$500
Syria	No	44	$500
Taiwan	Yes	44	$500
Tanzania	Yes	22	$490
Thailand	Yes	44	$125
Togo	No	44	$500
Tonga	No	22	No
Trinidad and Tobago	No	22	$500
Tristan da Cunha	No	22	No
Tunisia	Yes	44	$500
Turkey	Yes	44	$500
Turks & Caicos Is.	No	22	No
Tuvalu (Ellice Is.)	No	44	No
Uganda	No	22	$75
U.S.S.R.	Yes	22	$410
United Arab Emirates	Yes	44	$500
Uruguay	Yes	44	No
Vanuatu	No	44	No
Vatican City	No	44	$410
Venezuela	Yes	44	No
Vietnam, Soc. Rep. of	No	0	No
Wallis	No	22	$500
Western Samoa	No	22	$500
Yemen Arab Rep.	No	22	No
Yemen People's Democratic Rep.	No	44	$500
Yugoslavia	No	22	$500
Zaire	No	44	No
Zambia	No	44	$250
Zimbabwe	Yes	44	$500

*Restrictions apply. Consult postmaster.

[1] Consult postmaster for insurance fees over $500.

REGISTRATION is available to practically all countries. The fee is $3.25. Maximum indemnity payable is $25.20. To Canada only, payment of the $3.25 fee will provide indemnity for loss up to $100, and payment of a $3.55 fee will provide indemnity up to $200. Consult post office for further details.

INTERNATIONAL REPLY COUPONS are available at all post offices and are handy to use for small payments. One reply coupon will repay a single rate surface letter from any country.

PAYMENTS to overseas nations may be made by international postal money order or by banker's draft. The international money orders (not acceptable in some nations) are available from many post offices. Banker's drafts are available through most commercial banks. Generally personal checks are not acceptable to Mints and Central Banks.

Check your post office occasionally to update this chart. These rates are accurate as of June 1989; postal rates are subject to occasional change, and additional restrictions on mail matter are applied by certain nations from time to time.

Chapter 7

U.S. Postal Regulations

Philatelic Guidelines

The United States Postal Service is sometimes restricted as to what it can do in providing special services for stamp collectors. Guidelines to be followed by postal personnel are detailed in the U.S. Postal Service *Domestic Mail Manual*, as well as other guides, such as the *Postal Operations Manual* and the *Postal Bulletin*. Those sections of the manual are reproduced in part as follows, with slight variations being made to eliminate unnecessary repetition and sections dealing with Postal Service internal affairs, accounting, etc. These are the postal regulations that most directly affect philately and the mailing public.

Section 160: Philately

161 POLICY

161.1 There is a single national policy governing the release, sale and discontinuance of postage stamps and postal stationery. The policy is established by the Philatelic and Retail Services Department, USPS Headquarters, Washington, D.C. 20260-6700.

161.2 The policy governing stamps and philatelic products shall be administered by the Office of Stamps and Philatelic Marketing.

161.3 Uniform application of policies provides a high degree of integrity to the entire program, and all post offices, postal employees and contractors shall comply with the policies set forth in this subchapter. The Postal Service will avoid the creation of philatelic rarities.

162 PURPOSE AND SELECTION OF COMMEMORATIVE STAMPS, POSTAL STATIONERY AND PHILATELIC PRODUCTS

162.1 Purpose. Commemorative stamps and postal stationery (postal cards, embossed stamped envelopes and aerogrammes) explain the cultural and historical heritage of the United States. They describe our nation's achievements, portray the natural wonders of our country, instill pride in America, and focus attention on worthy causes, issues and interests which are of national concern. The Postal Service encourages the widespread use of these stamps and stationery items to promote our national ideals, progress and heritage. Commemorative stamps are not intended to replace regular stamps of the same class, but are provided upon request when available.

162.2 Selection. Subjects for commemorative postage stamps and postal stationery may be proposed by the public through correspondence to the Citizens' Stamp Advisory Committee. The committee, which is composed of individuals from outside the Postal Service appointed by the postmaster general, reviews suggestions and makes recommendations for commemorative stamps and postal stationery to the postmaster general, who makes the final selections. Because the committee works far in advance of actual stamp issuance, all proposals should be submitted at least two years prior to the desired issuance date. All suggestions should be forwarded to the Citizens' Stamp Advisory Committee, U.S. Postal Service, c/o Stamp Support Branch, 475 L'Enfant Plaza SW, Washington, D.C. 20260-6352.

162.3 Philatelic Products. Philatelic products are produced and sold to expand interest in the hobby of stamp collecting by demonstrating both the fun and the informative value of stamps.

163 DISTRIBUTION AND SALE OF STAMPS, POSTAL STATIONERY AND PHILATELIC PRODUCTS

163.1 Distribution

.11 All post offices receive initial supplies of new issue commemorative stamps without requisition. Philatelic products such as Mint Sets, Stamp Collecting Kits, etc., are distributed automatically to Stamp Distribution Post

Offices.

.12 Stamp Distribution Offices (SDOs) shall:

a. Establish a program for the distribution of new philatelic products and the replenishment of existing philatelic products to associate post offices.

b. Ensure that less-than-bulk quantities of stamps are supplied to all post offices so they can be placed on sale in accordance with instructions issued in the *Postal Bulletin*.

163.3 Retail Sales

.31 General. Stamps, postal stationery and philatelic products are sold at various types of postal retail facilities which are described in this part. Most of these facilities have regular stamp windows or have been designated as Stamp Collecting Centers. Stamp Collecting Centers sell the current commemorative stamps and philatelic products. Other post offices provide specialized philatelic services and sell the full range of stamps and philatelic products offered by the Postal Service. These facilities, as well as the Philatelic Sales Division, are referred to collectively as philatelic outlets.

.32 Philatelic Centers. Philatelic centers are retail selling areas of self-contained facilities separate from the lobby window positions. Some philatelic outlets are referred to as Postiques. (Postique is a registered trademark of the U.S. Postal Service.) They display and sell all current stamps and related philatelic products. The stamps and postal stationery stock offered for sale includes commemorative stamps, definitive and regular issue stamps, coils, postage due stamps, airmail and special delivery stamps, booklets and booklet panes, packets of stamped, embossed envelopes, postal cards, and message reply cards and aerogrammes. The Philatelic Sales Division is a Philatelic Center.

.33 Dedicated Philatelic Windows. A Dedicated Philatelic Window is a lobby window designated to sell stamps and related philatelic products only. No other postal services are available at Dedicated Philatelic Windows, which are to be identified so that customers desiring normal postal services are directed to other windows. The same items sold at Philatelic Centers are also sold at Dedicated Philatelic Windows.

.34 Temporary Philatelic Stations

.341 Purpose of Participation. Post offices establish special temporary stations to provide philatelic services, and to sell commemorative stamps and philatelic products. These stations may include specially constructed counters or mobile retail units. They are most frequently located at stamp shows, philatelic exhibitions, stamp dedications, state fairs, conventions, parades or at other locations or activities of significant public or philatelic interest.

.342 Requests for Participation. Requests for Postal Service participation at such events should be made by the sponsors or organizers to the local postmaster for initial action. Only requests for first day of issue or other special support, which must come from the national level, should be directed to the Stamp Support Branch. All first day ceremonies are conducted under the direction of the Stamp Support Branch. The payment of fees for space may not be authorized below the headquarters level. Once a postmaster has agreed to participate in an exhibition, a unilateral withdrawal from such a commitment may not be made without the approval of the Philatelic Marketing Division based upon a showing of good cause.

.343 Authorization. Temporary philatelic stations may be authorized by the postmaster. Postmasters are authorized to participate at events where admission fees are charged by the sponsor, but in these cases the same cancellation used at the event must be available on request to those not attending the event.

.344 Ceremonies. Postmasters and other local officials are encouraged to participate in opening ceremonies for stamp exhibitions or other stamp ceremonies arranged by philatelic groups, whether or not a temporary philatelic station has been authorized.

.345 Announcement and Publicity

a. Posters.

(1) An announcement of temporary philatelic station and any show cancellation must be posted on the main post office lobby bulletin board and may be

posted in other post offices within a 10-mile radius of the event so that collectors will be advised of the USPS' participation. In case of larger shows the posting may occur throughout the sectional center.

(2) Posters should be placed on display at least 15 days before the event but in no case more than 30 days before the event.

(3) All announcements must emphasize the temporary philatelic station. The announcement should mention the name of the stamp show, pictorial or standard cancellation (if any), the dates and hours open to the public, and the location. Promotional material for the show itself must not be incorporated.

b. Press Releases. The postmaster should also announce through press releases to local newspapers the planned establishment of this station. The post office, however, must not distribute free flyers to homes, sell or distribute tickets, exchange ticket coupons, or authorize the use of post office facilities for direct show promotion.

.346 Arrangements

a. General. Postmasters should insure that detailed planning begins well in advance of the show so that participation brings credit to the USPS and provides a wide range of stamps and philatelic products to collectors. Particular attention should be taken in selecting sales personnel who are knowledgeable about stamp collecting and who have retail experience. All clerks should be fully trained in philatelic sales and cancellation policies.

b. Stamp Stock.

(1) The postmaster should secure a wide range of philatelic products and current postage, using the Philatelic Sales Division stock list (Form 3300) as a guide. Consideration should be given to prepackaging sets of regular issues or postage dues for sale to collectors. No stamp which has been withdrawn from sale by the Philatelic Sales Division may be sold by any philatelic station. Withdrawals are noted in the *Postal Bulletin*.

(2) Postmasters should requisition philatelic stock not already available in their post office from the Regional Accountable Paper Depository on Form 17, Stamp Requisition, indicating the quantity required and that it is for a stamp show. For stamp shows, stamps with a denomination higher than $1 may be requisitioned in plate blocks of four as noted in 163.2

(3) At the conclusion of the show, excess philatelic stock, including remainders from commemorative sheets, should be sold at the regular windows for postage purposes.

c. Philatelic Products. Postmasters should display and sell philatelic products such as Commemorative Mint Sets, the "Postal Sevice Guide to U.S. Stamps" and Stamp Collecting Kits.

d. Sales Restrictions. The sales policies regarding plate number blocks, marginal markings and line markings on coil stamps are described in 163.532 and .533.

e. Security and Facilities. Postmasters should insure that sufficient security for the stamp stock is provided at the show site and that all other facilities are adequate.

f. Appearance. Postmasters should insure that the appearance of the temporary philatelic station brings credit to the Postal Service by utilizing attractive signs and having space for satisfactory service. The hours that the station is open should be posted.

g. Prompt Service. At those exhibitions where a large number of collectors are expected, postmasters should consider utilizing a speedy line or customer numbers which can be distributed and announced so that customers will not have to wait to make their purchases.

h. Cancellation Service.

(1) Cancellation service should be provided separately from stamp sales. A sufficient number of clerks should be available to provide speedy service.

(2) Clerks should be trained in advance how to provide handstamped postmarks of philatelic quality. Refer to 164.3 for cancellation regulations.

163.4 Mail Order Sales

.41 The Philatelic Sales Division services mail orders for postage stamps of selected quality and other philatelic items. Customers may obtain an order form listing items available by writing to the Philatelic Sales Division, U.S. Postal Service, Washington, D.C. 20265-9998.

.42 Post offices may not fill mail orders for stamps and other philatelic items other than mail orders under the Stamps by Mail program and orders for local precancels.

.43 Customers must furnish a self-addressed, stamped envelope for return of precanceled stamps.

.44 Postmasters may not order precancel devices solely to satisfy collector demands.

.45 Philatelic Centers and Dedicated Philatelic Windows may accept and fill mail orders for special cacheted envelopes with cancellations authorized under 165.1. This section shall not affect procedures outlined in 164.83 for purchase of newly issued stamps by cover services from the first day of issue post office.

163.5 Sales Policies

.51 New Issues. Only the post office or offices designated as the official first day of issue office(s) shall sell a new item on the first day of sale. New issues shall be placed on sale at all other offices on the day after the first day of sale.

.52 Regular Stamp Windows and Stamp Collecting Centers

.521 Commemorative Stamps

a. It is the Postal Service's intent that all commemorative stamps be sold and none destroyed.

b. Offices shall place commemorative stamps on regular sale, holding aside only enough for the local philatelic demand. All supplies should be sold within 60 days after being placed on sale. After 60 days, clerks should sell all remaining commemorative stamps to customers in place of other sheet stamps.

c. Commemorative stamps of local interest may remain on sale for a longer period but in no case after the date of withdrawal from sale announced in the *Postal Bulletin*.

.522 Plate Number Blocks/Marginal Markings (All Stamps)

a. Definition. Plate number blocks are the stamps located on one corner of a pane of stamps with a plate number or numbers printed on the margin (selvage). Plate number blocks may include as few as four stamps where a single number appears, or as many as 20 where multiple floating numbers and other marginal markings, such as Mr. ZIP and notice of Copyright appear.

b. Setting Aside Plate Number Blocks. Clerks shall break panes of stamps for regular sale purposes, as follows:

(1) First tear stamps from the edge of the panes farthest from the plate number or marginal markings in order to preserve the plate block for collectors.

(2) Set aside quantities of plate blocks or marginal markings as panes are broken during regular sales transactions, but do not set them aside in advance.

c. Minimum Purchase Requirements and Sales Limitations.

(1) When the clerk has a broken pane of stamps from which the plate block or other marginal marking has been sold, and when no plate block or other marginal marking has been set aside, the following minimum purchases must be made by a customer desiring the plate block or other marginal marking:

Denomination	Minimum Purchase
$0.01 to $0.50	Full marginal strip of stamps (two rows deep having all marginal markings)
$0.51 to $0.99	Half marginal strip
$1 to $5	Block of 4 stamps

Exception: There are no minimum purchase requirements when a clerk has: (a) only full panes of the requested stamp in stock, or (b) a broken pane that contains the plate block or other marginal marking.

(2) There are limitations to sales as follows: Each customer for whom a pane has been broken is limited to one marginal strip (1¢-50¢); a half marginal strip (51¢-99¢); or a block of four stamps ($1-$5) for each stamp subject, per day. It is necessary to place a limit on individual sales of plate blocks and other marginal markings so that the stamp stock available at post office windows may accommodate as many collectors as possible each day. Customers requesting more than the maximum permissible purchase in denominations of the first-class rate and below, should be asked to inquire on another day. Customers requesting more than the maximum permissible purchase

in denominations higher than the first-class rate should be asked to inquire on another day, or should be referred to the Philatelic Sales Division.

d. Return of Unsold Stamp Stock. Broken panes of stamps without marginal strips and which exceed clerk requirements for regular stamp sales or use on parcel post, should be returned to the main stamp stock. To return stock, the clerk shall complete Form 17 in accordance with section 552 of Handbook F-1. The returned stock must be redistributed in the following priority: (1) to fulfill Stamps by Mail requests; (2) to be utilized in locally prepared stamp packages for vending machines; and (3) to be sold at other regular stamp windows. After 30 days, any stock remaining unsold at regular stamp windows is returned (using Form 17) to the main stamp stock and handled in accordance with the F-1, 450.

e. Exceptions to Sales Policies. The Office of Stamps and Philatelic Marketing may establish exceptions to the sales policies on selected stamp issues. Exceptions are announced in the *Postal Bulletin.*

.523 Coiled Stamps. These offices may not open and break coils of stamps.

Exception: Coils of new issue stamps may be opened and sold in less than full coil quantities, subject to the following limitations:

a. Sales of new issue coiled stamps in less than full coils are restricted to a one-month period beginning with the authorized first day of sale for each particular stamp issue.

b. These sales are further restricted to a single stamp window at each location designated by the postmaster to conduct such sales.

c. Coiled stamps of fractional denomination must be sold in multiples that reach full-cent amounts.

d. Stamps remaining in partial coils after expiration of the sales period will be used for general postage if practical.

.524 Precanceled Stamps. There is no limitation on the sale to collectors of sheet stamps or full coils of each of the precanceled denominations available. Purchases may be made in person or by mail by non-permit holders for collection purposes only. Mail order requests must be accompanied by stamped, self-addressed envelopes for the return of the stamps purchased by the collector. Precanceled stamp policy is described in detail in 143.

.53 Philatelic Outlets

.531 Commemorative Stamps. These offices may keep an issue on sale until a notice of its removal from sales at the Philatelic Sales Division is published in the Postal Bulletin.

.532 Plate Number Blocks/Marginal Markings (All Stamps). The sales and disposition policies described in 163.522 apply except as follows:

a. Clerks may sell each customer one matched-set of four marginal strips for any stamp in stock.

b. There are no limitations on the sale of plate blocks of stamps having denominations from $1 to $5.

c. The Philatelic Sales Division mail order section may, however, sell any quantity of marginal strips of stamps of issues having a face value above the first-class letter rate. For issues having a face value at or below the first-class letter rate, marginal strips will be sold only when full panes are ordered.

.533 Coiled Stamps. These offices may open coils of stamps as requested, except that coils having fractional denominations can only be sold in multiples that reach full-cent amounts. To guarantee receipt of "line pairs" or "line markings" on coils, the following minimum purchases are required:

a. Bulk rate denominations (when fractional) — minimum of 30 stamps;

b. $1 — minimum of six stamps;

c. All other denominations — minimum of 25 stamps. Note: A "line marking" is the vertical line of color appearing at intervals of 25 stamps made by the joint or seam where printing plates meet on a rotary press. The "line pair" consists of the two coil stamps on either side of the "line marking." Line markings may not be visible on all coils.

.534 Precanceled Stamps. The sales policy described in 163.524 applies except that coils of precanceled stamps may be opened for the sale of individual stamps to collectors.

.535 Stamp Credit (Accountability). Philatelic outlets should maintain a good working level of stamp stock, postal stationery and philatelic products to meet the needs of collectors and encourage philatelic interest. Therefore, postmasters may maintain a postage stock of up to $125,000 for each philatelic outlet at their office. This stock may be in excess of normal authorized stock limits. (This does not apply to the Philatelic Sales Division).

.536 Inventory of Available Items. Updated lists (Form 3300) of items available at the Philatelic Sales Division will be furnished periodically to philatelic outlets to guide them in maintaining a current inventory for collectors. All listed stamps shall be maintained by permanent philatelic outlets unless sold out and not available by requisition.

.537 Stamp Packets. Stamps withdrawn from sale which are incorporated in philatelic products such as Mint Sets or Collecting Kits may be sold by philatelic windows, postal stores, stamp collecting centers, and the Philatelic Sales Division.

163.6 Stamp Withdrawals. Notices concerning stamp withdrawals are published in the Postal Bulletin and give effective dates for removing stamps from sale. On the effective withdrawal date, philatelic outlets must immediately return their supply of the withdrawn stamp to the main stamp stock, using a Form 17. The stock must then be redistributed to regular stamp windows for sale for a period of 30 days.

164 CANCELLATIONS FOR PHILATELIC PURPOSES

164.1 Definition and Policy

.11 A postmark is a postal cancellation which contains the post office name, state, ZIP Code and month, day and year the canceling post office accepted custody of the material except as provided in 164.71 and 164.74. Other postal markings are made by validators, obliterators or special purpose cancelers.

.12 The Postal Service shall endeavor to make all unusual postmarking services widely known to collectors through advance national publicity so as to avoid such postmarks being available only to small groups of people.

.13 It is the policy of the Postal Service to prohibit backdating of mail except:

a. When postal operating requirements and public demand necessitate that cancellation commence prior to and continue after date contained in the postmark;

b. When replacements are being made of damaged, defective, or missing cancellations or covers; or

c. When all requirements for cancellations were met by customers and cancellations were not applied because of errors of postal personnel.

d. When specifically authorized in writing by the General Manager, Philatelic Sales Division.

164.2 Philatelic Postmarking

.21 General. Postmarking for philatelic purposes is provided at the request of collectors or cover servicers for postmarking outside ordinary mail processing. This service requires special procedures and arrangements so that other postal operations and services are not interferred with or disrupted. It may involve handstamping requested either on a hand back or mail back basis and may entail the holding of mail for cancellation. Before this specialized service can be provided, all its conditions must be met. As a free service, it is limited to transactions with fewer than 50 envelopes or other items. For 50 or more envelopes or other items, advance approval of the Stamps Division is required before service can be provided.

.22 Cooperation With Collectors

a. Employees should strive to furnish clear and legible postmarks to stamp collectors by insuring that cancellation machines and handstamp devices are properly inked. Postal employees shall give special attention to mail bearing an endorsement that is of philatelic value or to requests for light cancellations and should avoid canceling stamps by pen or illegible smudging; however, stamps must be canceled sufficiently to protect postal revenue.

b. The Postal Service cannot provide special attention to a philatelic cover if it has been routinely entered into the mailstream by the sender.

c. Postmarking devices may be used only under the supervision of authorized postal personnel.

d. All handstamped postmarks shall be made with black ink unless the customer specifically indicates a preference for the color otherwise in use.

e. Employees should exercise care in handling all philatelic covers to assure that they are not damaged in mail handling. These covers are generally identifiable by a design printed on the left side of the envelope.

f. Postal employees should assure that philatelic covers are not overcanceled, backstamped, marked "received this date" or otherwise defaced on front or back, used as a top piece in a bundle for destination package for labeling purposes; or bent, folded, mutilated or damaged by rubber bands.

.23 Hand Back and Mail Back Service. Postmarks rather than other obliterations should be used to provide the following services whenever they are available:

a. Hand Back Service.

(1) Post offices shall honor requests for hand back cancellation service where a customer personally presents an addressed or unaddressed envelope, postal card or other item described in 164.73 to a postal clerk for cancellation with the current day's postmark and immediate return or hand back to the customer.

(2) The envelope, card or other item does not enter the mailstream. All such materials must bear uncanceled postage at the applicable first-class rate.

(3) So that service to other customers is not disrupted, there is a limit of 50 cancellations which can be provided for any single customer.

(4) This service may be provided for special die hub or regular machine cancellations only when the particular cancellation machine is readily accessible to the postal clerk, where the providing of such service will not interfere with other sales or mail processing operations and will not inconvenience other customers.

b. "Mail Back" Service. "Mail back" service refers to that service authorized by the Philatelic Sales Division for stamp dealers and cover servicers which permits envelopes, cards or other items submitted for cancellation to be returned in bulk through the mail. Conditions of service are further described in 164.83. This form of "mail back" service must be approved in writing in advance by the Philatelic Sales Division. Mail back service shall not be provided for special die hub or machine cancellations.

164.3 Permissible Cancellation Devices

.31 Handstamped Cancellations for Collectors. The following postmark devices may be used to provide handstamped cancellations for collectors:

a. Standard cancellation with killer bars (Item 550).

b. Circular cancellation without killer bars.

c. First day of issue cancellation at post office where an item is first issued.

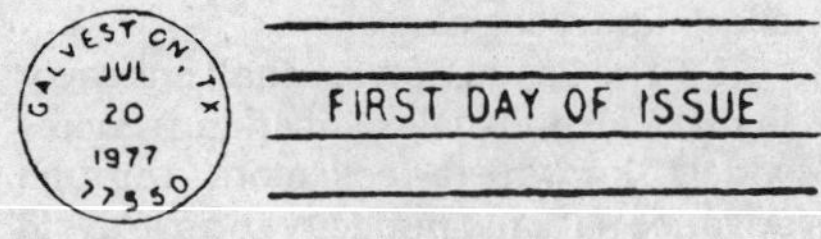

d. Bull's-eye cancellation.

e. Pictorial cancellation subject to conditions set forth in 164.42.

.32 Obliterators. The following devices are obliterators and may be used for philatelic purposes in cases where none of the postmarks or postmarking devices described in 164.31 are available:

a. Validator stamp (also known as a registry stamp or round dater — Item 570).

b. Parcel post canceler (Item 502).

c. Rubber oval stamp (Item 0-681).

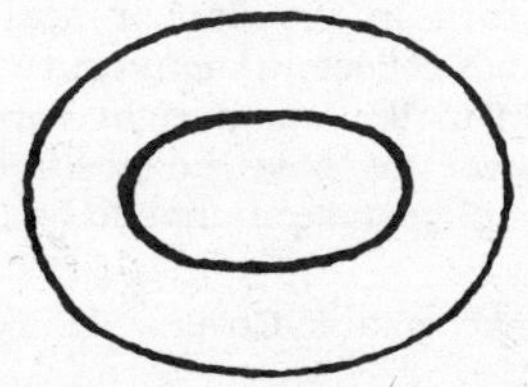

d. Receiving or dating stamp (Item 552).

164.4 Types of Postmarks or Cancellations

.41 First Day of Issue. These cancellations are provided by the post office when a philatelic issue is first placed on sale and are dated to show that day. They include both machine and hand-stamp cancellations. The words "First Day of Issue" appear in the killer bars. Requests for first day cancellations must be postmarked no later than the date specified in the *Postal Bulletin* to qualify for service. Bull's-eye cancellations are used when the conventional first day of issue postmark will not cancel all the unused stamps on an item presented for postmarking.

.42 Pictorial Cancellations. These cancellations are authorized to be used only at temporary philatelic stations and at other philatelic outlets. They shall not be used at regular stamp windows for special local celebrations. Cancellations used are generally handstamps except when volume requires the use of a machine cancellation. They may be used only during the operation of the temporary philatelic station. Requests for such cancellations must be at the post office offering the service no later than the date of the cancellation to qualify for service. A station may be authorized only one pictorial cancellation during its operation at an event. Different cancellations for each day of an event are authorized only for international philatelic exhibitions recognized by the Office of Stamps and Philatelic Marketing and held in the United States.

.43 Special Die Hub Cancellations. Special die hub cancellations contain words relating to an event. These cancellations are applied by machine to live mail. Hand back service may be provided only as described in 164.23a. Mail back (return in bulk) service shall not be provided, but cancellation can be provided on addressed envelopes or postal cards which are delivered to the addressee or addressees through mail delivery. Cancellations of philatelic quality are often not possible.

.44 Standard Cancellations. Circular handstamped cancellations with or without killer bars may be provided upon request at post offices, stations and branches. They are available every day the office is open for business. No slogan or pictorial material may be included. Mail requests for these cancellations must be at the post office offering the service on the date of the cancellation to qualify for service.

.45 Flight Cancellations. Refer to 164.6. These cancellations are made by regular cancellation equipment or by handstamp depending on volume.

.46 Regular Machine Cancellations. Post offices may not machine cancel mail with the regular postmark when the envelopes are unaddressed or when the customer requests hand back service except as described in 164.23a. Mail back (return in bulk) service shall not be provided, but cancellations can be provided on addressed envelopes or postal cards which are delivered to the addressee or addressees through mail delivery.

164.5 First Day of Issue

.51 First Day Sale. A particular post office or postal facility is usually designated to have the exclusive sale of a new issue on the day it is issued. No other postal facility may begin general sale of the new issue until the following day. For purposes of this section, the word issue shall mean postage stamp, stamp booklet, or booklet pane, postal card, stamped envelope or aerogramme.

.52 Notification. New stamps and other philatelic issues are announced by notices displayed in post office lobbies, in the *Postal Bulletin* and through news releases distributed to the press and philatelic periodicals.

.53 First Day Covers

a. Definition. A first day cover is an envelope, postcard, or other item of reasonable dimension bearing a new stamp or booklet pane or a new postal card, a new stamped envelope or a new aerogramme canceled with a die reading First Day of Issue and showing place and date of first-day sale.

b. Procedures. Customers who want first-day cancellations of new stamps have two options:

(1) Buy stamps at local post offices and affix them to their own envelopes. Mail the stamped envelopes to the postmaster at the city of issuance for cancellation. Preferential service is accorded covers on which collectors have affixed their own stamps.

(2) Submit envelopes with proper remittance to cover the cost of the stamps desired. The Postal Service will affix and cancel the stamps except as indicated in d. of this section. Remittance should be made by money order or cashier's, certified or personal check made payable to the U.S. Postal Service. Orders containing personal checks will be held until the checks have cleared. Cash will not be accepted, nor will postage stamps or foreign coins and currency; any orders containing such remittance will be returned unserviced. All covers must bear addresses to the right side of the envelope and at least 5/8 of an inch up from the bottom of the envelope. Requests must be postmarked no later than the date specified in the announcement to qualify for cancellation service. Covers must not be returned in outer envelopes even when furnished by collectors because to do so impedes operating efficiency.

c. Requirements. Envelopes submitted by collectors must be of ordinary letter size and must be properly addressed. Collectors should place a filler of postal card thickness in each envelope, and either turn in the flap or seal it. If applicable, collectors should put a pencil notation in the upper right corner of each cover to show the position and number of postage stamps to be placed there.

d. Unacceptable Covers. The issuing

post office shall not provide cancellation service on covers submitted through the mail which are unaddressed, or bear stamps issued after the issue date and before the submittal cut-off date, or bear previously canceled stamps, nor may the post office provide hand back service on any items presented after the first day of issuance. These restrictions can be waived only by written authorization of the Stamps Division.

e. Bulk Orders. The post office servicing first-day covers shall not accept from any one customer more than 50 envelopes requiring that stamps be affixed. When more than 50 envelopes are submitted, they must be returned unserviced to the customer, with a statement that service will be provided upon resubmittal of stamped envelopes of 50 or fewer envelopes. Care must be taken to prevent customers from avoiding this rule by placing multiple smaller orders. Customers desiring cancellations on more than 50 covers must buy and affix their own stamps to their envelopes.

f. Handstamped Cancellations. Handstamped cancellations will be applied at the first-day ceremony location, at the main office windows of the first day post office, and on covers which cannot be fully canceled by postal cancellation machines. In all other cases, machine cancellations will be supplied, except as provided in 164.83.

g. Hand Back Service. Hand back service for first day cancellations is limited to the first day of issue. Material to be canceled must be presented to the main office window of the first day post office.

h. Mail Orders for Mint Stamps. The first day post office may not accept mail order requests for uncanceled stamps from customers outside their service area, except for cover servicers as provided in 164.83a.

i. Cancellation Deadlines. Deadlines for submitting less than 50 covers for first day of issue cancellations are established by the Stamp Support Branch. Cancellations deadlines for submitting bulk orders (more than 50 covers) are established by the General Manager, Philatelic Sales Division. Any exceptions to the deadline dates must be specifically authorized by the General Manager, Philatelic Sales Division.

.54 Unofficial First Day Covers. Stamps acquired at the first day post office may be canceled at any post office. Envelopes containing new stamps canceled on the first day of sale at a post office other than the issuing office are known as "unofficial first day covers."

164.6 Flight Covers

.61 Definition. The Postal Service authorizes special cachet and cancellation services for mail carried on inaugural flights and other aviation events of national interest. Flight covers generally bear official USPS cachets, the postmark of the city of origin and the backstamped postmark of the city of destination.

.62 Authorization. The Stamps Division may authorize cachet and cancellation service for:

a. All stop points on a new airmail route;

b. New stop points on an existing route; and

c. Other aviation events of national interest.

Notices authorizing official cachets and cancellation services are published in the *Postal Bulletin.* This service will not be authorized for new aircraft used on an existing airmail route. Backstamped postmarks may be authorized where international airmail service is inaugurated to a stop point in the United States when the postal administration of the country of the flight's origin officially requests that the U.S. Postal Service provide philatelic treatment to mail carried on the flight.

.63 Preparation of Covers. Collectors must pre-address each cover to the right of the envelope and at least 5/8 of an inch from the bottom of the envelope. Each envelope must bear postage at the applicable airmail rate. Each envelope should include a uniform enclosure of the approximate weight of a postal card to assure a good impression. A clear space, 2 1/2 inches by 2 1/2 inches, on the lower portion of the envelope and to the left of the address must be allowed for the cachet. An additional 1 1/2 inches to the left of the innermost stamp must be provided to permit a clear postmark.

.64 Submittal of Covers. Collectors should send the envelopes for inaugural cachets under cover and endorsed "Flight Covers" to the post office or airport mail facility applying the cachet and postmark. A request to hold covers for the inaugural service should be enclosed, indicating the directional service and cachet desired.

.65 Compliance With Collectors' Requests

a. Direction Specified. Post offices should comply with requests for dispatch in a particular direction to the greatest extent practicable unless otherwise specified by the Stamps Division. No directional service will be accorded for events of national aviation interest.

b. Direction Not Specified. In the absence of specific requests, post offices should dispatch covers on the actual first flight, regardless of direction.

c. Incomplete Instructions. If the collector's request is not clear, post offices should dispatch covers in accordance with the judgment of the dispatching office.

d. Color of Ink Used for the Cachet. The Stamp Support Branch will determine the color of ink to be used on the cachet at each stop point. Requests from collectors for other ink colors must not be honored.

e. Position of Cachet. Post offices should apply cachets legibly and neatly to the left side of the address side of the cover.

.66 When Cachets Must Not Be Applied. Cachets must not be applied to:

a. Covers for immediate return to sender. All covers must be dispatched on the flight.

b. Covers bearing a previous official or unofficial cachet.

c. Covers lacking sufficient clear space for application of cachet without obscuring the address.

d. Aerogrammes and postal cards.

e. Double postal or postcards intended for return reply purposes.

f. Covers received after the flight.

g. Covers on which postage is not fully prepaid.

h. Covers containing previously canceled postage stamps.

i. Anything other than a flight cover.

.67 Backstamping. All inaugural covers will be backstamped with machine or hand cancellation devices at the destination post office. Postage stamps are not required for the second cancellation. Requests for additional or special backstamping must not be honored.

.68 Delay of Flight. If, after postmarking of covers has begun, the flight is canceled or the scheduled date of departure is delayed to a subsequent date, the postmark dates already stamped on the flight covers will not be changed, replacement covers will not be issued, nor will any liability be accepted.

164.7 When and Where Philatelic Postmarking May Be Done

.71 Date and Place of Postmarking

a. Postmarking provided for philatelic purposes may commence prior to the actual date of the cancellation requested and may continue after that date when demand, processing capability, or other requirements of the Postal Service dictate. Under no circumstances may any postmarked materials be released before the date of the cancellation.

b. The Regional Director, Marketing and Communications, may determine that local processing capability requires that philatelic cancellation services be performed at an office other than the post office whose cancellation is used; in these cases, however, all materials to be postmarked must be received at or deposited in the post office whose cancellation is being used, or at an office designated by the Regional Director of Marketing and Communications or the Philatelic Sales Division.

.72 Preparation Requirements. Postcards, postal cards and envelopes submitted through the mail must bear postage at the applicable rate and complete addresses, except as provided in 164.83d. Materials submitted for handback service need not be addressed.

.73 Special Materials on Which Cancellations Are Requested. The materials described in this section may be canceled as indicated. Photographs, postcards or other materials having a glossy-coated, or hard calendered surface, or any material that does not readily accept ink, are submitted for cancellation at the customer's risk. The U.S. Postal Service is not responsible for smudged cancels or offsetting in this type of work.

a. Plain Cards, Slips of Paper, and Blank Envelopes. Postal employees may not place postmarks for customers on plain slips of paper, plain cards or blank envelopes which do not bear unused postage in an amount equaling or exceeding the first-class rate.

b. Picture Postcards (Maximum Cards). Picture postcards with the stamp placed on the face of the card rather than on the address side are known as maximum cards. Postmasters may cancel these cards and hand them back to the person presenting them.

c. Posters, Portfolios and Other Memorabilia. These items with the stamps placed thereon may be canceled when presented in person for hand back service. Submittal and return through the mail is not permitted.

d. Already Canceled Stamps/Multiple Cancellations. Items bearing previously canceled stamps and postmarks are acceptable for additional cancellations when uncanceled first-class postage is affixed to receive the subsequent cancellation. Such material may be submitted and returned through the mail. When fewer than 50 items are submitted for the subsequent cancellation, they must all be addressed and must be returned to the addressee as individual pieces and not in outer envelopes. Return under separate cover is allowed only as specified in 164.82. First day of issue cancellations may not be provided on a hand back basis after the first day of issuance. Mint stamps to cover the first-class rate must be affixed for each cancellation.

e. Currency. Currency bearing unused postage stamps of first-class value or items bearing currency with stamps affixed or adjacent thereto may be canceled when presented in person for hand back service. Submittal and return through the mail is not permitted. The Postal Service does not accept responsibility for currency in its possession in conjunction with philatelic services.

f. Backs of Envelopes. Post offices may cancel unused stamps when they are affixed to the reverse side of envelopes bearing already-canceled stamps. This service is available only for envelopes presented for hand back service. They may not be returned through the mail, even when outer envelopes are provided. Such a cancellation denotes only that the item was presented to the post office for postmarking on that date; it does not denote that the envelope was carried by the Postal Service and should be differentiated from flight covers described in 164.6. This type of cover may be presented, for instance, in situations re-enacting Pony Express routes, promoting special airline flights, balloon ascents, and the like, on which covers are carried outside the mail service.

g. Foreign Postage Stamps. Unused foreign postage stamps may be canceled with a U.S. Postal Service postmark only when unused U.S. postage of the appropriate rate is canceled with the same stroke.

.74 Holding the Mail

a. Post offices may hold mail to comply with customers' requests that the mail be postmarked on a specified date. Post offices may not, however, hold mail for an event where the date of occurrence is not certain or where it is subject to change or for cancellation on a day when the office will be closed, except as authorized by the Philatelic Sales Division. In these latter instances, the envelopes submitted should be returned unserviced in an outer envelope to the customer with a short note explaining why the requested service cannot be performed.

b. There will be a limit of 50 covers per customer which can be held for cancellation. Except on first day covers where customers have affixed their own stamps, quantities above this number must receive the prior written authorization of the Stamps Division. The Stamps Division may also authorize the holding of mail for events of nationwide interest.

.75 Damaged or Missing Covers

a. Requests for replacement of first day cancellations, pictorial cancellations, and standard cancellations may be accepted at the appropriate post office for a period of 60 days from the date of issuance for first day covers, or 30 days from the date of cancellation for pictorial and standard cancellations.

b. Replacement cancellations will be made for poor quality of cancellation, damage to the envelope, or other similar defects. Replacements will not be made, however, in cases where envelopes were marked on the back by letter sorting machine code numbers as they moved through the mail system.

c. The customer must return the unsatisfactory cover or covers to the appropriate post office for replacement.

d. Replacement covers must be returned to the customer in a penalty envelope so that a stale postmark does not appear in the mailstream.

e. Damaged covers should be disposed of in accordance with Handbook F-1, Post Office Accounting Procedures.

f. The Postal Service will not replace missing or unsatisfactory standard machine cancellations, special die hub cancellations, or flight cancellations, as these cancellations are made in the course of live mail processing.

g. All claims for non-receipt of other covers submitted for servicing by the Postal Service must be sent to the appropriate post office no later than 60 days from the date of postmark or from the date cancellations were last applied. Claims for replacement cancellations filed after this time will not be honored and will be returned to the customer with a short explanation as to why the request cannot be honored.

h. The Postal Service is not responsible for damage or loss of cacheted covers or of other items of value.

.76 Special Requests. Requests for cancellations at postal facilities that normally do not cancel mail must be made in writing to the Field Director, Marketing and Communications at least 60 days in advance to permit regional authorization and appropriate national publicity. These requirements also apply to requests for cancellations at offices which are inaccessible to the public or to requests for cancellations at any offices on dates when mail is not normally canceled (i.e., Sundays and holidays). Cover servicers, as described in 164.8, must submit their requests for cancellations to the Philatelic Sales Division.

.77 Military Post Offices. Military post offices, including APOs and FPOs, may handstamp covers both on a handback basis and on mail order requests in conformance with all policies and in accordance with all conditions and procedures herein stated, except that:

a. The postal chief at each such installation may establish the maximum number of covers individual collectors or dealers may submit;

b. Military post offices may not establish temporary philatelic stations or provide pictorial cancellations.

164.8 Cover Servicers and Dealers

.81 General. In order to more efficiently provide philatelic services, the Postal Service is clarifying its regulations on cover services dealers to specify that their submissions must be of 50 or more identical pieces. Smaller quantity orders can be handled better through the centralized first day cover process.

.82 Definition. Cover servicers and dealers include those individuals, groups or commercial enterprises that submit 50 or more envelopes or other items for identical cancellations, whether presented in one or more packages, and request return in bulk.

.83 Mailback Service

a. Written authorization must be obtained from the Philatelic Sales Division for more than 50 rubber composition cancellations. Copies of authorizations will be sent to the Postmaster and appropriate Division office. Postmasters will be requested to complete a Cancellation Confirmation information sheet and return it to the Philatelic Sales Division which will bill the cover servicers or dealer for the cancellation charge. A service charge as indicated in 164.83 is established by the Philatelic Sales Division for rubber composition cancellations.

b. Mailback service, or return under cover in bulk, is available to dealers only when return postage, registration if desired, and all other applicable fees such as special handling and special delivery are remitted to the postmaster at the place of postmarking. Such requests which do not include such payment will be held until the proper amount is received. In the event of overpayment by the cover servicer, the amount in excess of postage and fees required shall be returned separately in mint postage stamps. If the refund is $10 or more, it must be sent under registered mail.

c. Mailback service is generally permitted on first-day-of-issue, pictorial, or standard cancellations requested on the following materials: envelopes, postal cards, maximum cards and posters, portfolios, or other memorabilia. The Postal Service will not accept covers for first-day-of-issue cancellation which bear a stamp issued after the date of the postmark but before the expiration date for submittal.

d. Unless the cover servicer has received Headquarters' written approval for cancellation service, the envelopes will be returned to the cover servicer, unserviced, with a letter stating that advance approval from the Philatelic Sales Division must be obtained before the request can be honored.

e. Mailback service with overwrapping for cover servicers and dealers submitting 50 or more addressed covers will be subject to a service charge established by the Philatelic Sales Division. This service charge must be paid by check or money order before the mailing will be processed.

f. Cover servicers and dealers wishing to use a protective overwrapping provided by the United States Postal Service for mailing first day covers must have a signed agreement on file with the Philatelic Sales Division. This agreement specifies guidelines that must be met by the cover servicer or dealer in order to protect the United States Postal Service revenue.

.84 Conditions of Service

a. First Day of Issue Cancellations. Customers recognized as first day cover servicers will be permitted, though not required, to purchase mint stamps by mail from the first day post office or from the Philatelic Sales Division on the date of issuance. Metal die-hub cancellations will be provided to dealers free of charge only when stamp-affixed envelopes are submitted. All stamped envelopes must be returned for servicing within the prescribed time limit. Rubber composition cancellations will be provided subject to a service charge established by the Philatelic Sales Division.

b. Pictorial Cancellations. These rubber composition cancellations are provided subject to approval by and a service charge established by the Philatelic Sales Division, except for exhibition or convention sponsors as indicated in 164.95.

c. Special Die Hub Machine Cancellations. All envelopes must be addressed. They will be canceled free of charge on any quantity of envelopes submitted, but may not be returned in bulk.

d. Standard Cancellations. These rubber composition cancellations may be applied on unaddressed covers and returned in bulk only when authorized by the Philatelic Sales Division. Orders are subject to a service charge established by the Philatelic Sales Division.

e. Flight Cancellations. These covers must be addressed, and service is subject to approval by the Stamp Support Branch. A service fee is charged when hand-stamped cancellations are requested.

164.9 Cancellation Services at Temporary Philatelic Stations

.91 Approval. Postmasters may request authority from the Field Director, Marketing and Communications, to provide cancellation service at temporary philatelic stations. Only the standard circular cancellation shall be provided, unless the sponsors or organizers apply to the postmaster for use of a pictorial cancellation at least 10 weeks prior to the event. The sponsors or organizers must also propose a design and finished artwork for a pictorial cancellation. The cancellation service and design require the approval of the postmaster and the Field Director, Marketing and Communications.

.92 Requirements. All cancellations must carry the name of the exhibition or event, followed by the word station or sta, the city, state and ZIP Code, and the month, day and year. Pictorial cancellations that endorse the ideals, policies, programs, products, campaigns, or candidates of religious, anti-religious, commercial, political, fraternal, trade, labor, public interest, or special interest organizations will not be approved. However, cancellations may be approved that recognize events such as meetings or conventions sponsored by or involving such organizations, providing their designs do not include words, symbols, or illustrations referring to ideals, policies, programs, products, campaigns, or candidates. If there is doubt as to whether a proposed cancellation meets these requirements, the manager, Stamp Support Branch, USPS headquarters, should be consulted before granting approval. Overall dimensions must not exceed 4 inches horizontally and 2 inches vertically.

.93 Publicity. The Field Director, Marketing and Communications, must submit a reproducible copy of the pictorial cancellation (actual size) to the Stamp Support Branch so that appropriate national publicity can be arranged. The use of standard cancellations at temporary philatelic stations must also be reported. All reports should include the dates the temporary philatelic stations will be open. Reports and copies of pictorial cancellations shall be submitted the first of each month for those cancellations authorized two months later (e.g., January 1 for March authorization; February 1 for April, etc.).

.94 Equipment. Pictorial and standard cancellations shall be applied by rubber handstamps purchased by the region. If more than 100,000 pieces of mail are anticipated, the region may apply to the Stamps Division at least 60 days in advance for purchase of a metal die for machine cancellation. These cancellations may only be provided for the duration of the temporary philatelic station.

.95 Service Limitations. Except for the exhibition or convention sponsor, handstamping as a free service will be limited to a maximum of 50 covers for any single individual or group. The sponsor may obtain any reasonable amount of hand backs free of service charge for its members, and special folders or programs prepared by the sponsor may be canceled and made available upon the opening of the show. Individuals or groups requiring more than 50 handstamped cancellations may obtain this service only by paying a special fee. Written application for this service must be made in advance to and authorized by the Philatelic Sales Division.

.96 Use and Return of Equipment. Philatelic cancellation handstamps, like other canceling devices, may be used only under the supervision of authorized postal personnel and must be returned by the postmaster to the Field Director, Marketing and Communications, 65 days after close of the exhibition or convention, by which time all replacement requests will have been handled. The Field Director, Marketing and Communications, shall destroy the cancellation device upon receipt.

165 SPECIAL PHILATELIC SERVICES, PRODUCTS AND PROGRAMS

165.1 Postal Cacheted Envelopes. Postal Service produced cachets or cacheted envelopes are permitted only for first flights and for major postal or aviation events, such as the opening of a new Philatelic Center or Dedicated Philatelic Window. All such cachets or cacheted envelopes must be approved by the appropriate regional and headquarters organizations, and their approval must be communicated to the Stamp Support Branch at least two months prior to the event so that national publicity of their availability can be arranged.

165.2 Presentations. The postmaster general, the assistant postmaster general, Philatelic and Retail Services Department, and the General Manager, Stamps Division, and the Manager, Stamp Support Branch, are authorized to approve the use of canceled and uncanceled U.S. postage stamps, postal stationery and other philatelic products for information and official postal business purposes and as official presentations of the U.S. Postal Service. All such presentations shall be approved in writing by one of the three authorized officials with a statement indicating the intended use. These presentations shall not be used as postage and will be restricted to those instances when the best interests of the Postal Service will be served.

165.3 Autographs. Postal employees have the prerogative to accept or refuse requests for autographs. Employees should exercise fairness in handling such requests. Nothing of value may be accepted or requested in exchange for autographs.

166 COPYRIGHT OF PHILATELIC DESIGNS

166.1 Policy. The designs of postage stamps, stamped envelopes, postal cards, aerogrammes, souvenir cards and other philatelic items issued on or after Jan. 1, 1978, have been copyrighted by the U.S. Postal Service in accordance with Title 17, United States Code.

166.2 Permission for Use. The use of illustrations of the designs covered by such copyrights is permitted as follows:

a. In editorial matter in newspapers, magazines, journals, books, philatelic catalogs and philatelic albums.

b. In advertising matter, circulars or price lists for the sale of the postal items illustrated.

c. In advertising matter, circulars or price lists for the sale of newspapers, magazines, journals, books, philatelic catalogs and philatelic albums containing illustrations of philatelic designs.

d. In motion picture films, microfilms, slides or electronic tape for projection upon a screen or for use in telecasting. No print or other reproduction from such films, slides or tapes shall be made except for the uses permitted in 166.2a, b and c.

166.3 Reproduction of Designs. Illustrations permitted by 166.2a, b and c may be in color or in black and white and may depict philatelic items as uncanceled or canceled. When depicting uncanceled items in color, illustrations must be less than 75 percent or more than 150 percent, in linear dimension, of the size of the design of the philatelic items as issued. Color illustrations of canceled philatelic items and black and white illustrations of uncanceled or canceled philatelic items may be in any size.

166.4 Requests for Licenses. The U.S. Postal Service may grant licenses for the use of illustrations of its copyright designs outside the scope of the above permission. Requests for such licenses should be addressed to the chairman, Intellectual Property Rights Board, Office of Procurement, U.S. Postal Service, Washington, D.C. 20260-6234.

Section 170: Special Cancellations

171 AUTHORIZATION

171.1 Description. Special cancellations are machine cancellations in which a slogan or message publicizing an event is engraved on a die hub and used to cancel mail. They may be used only in post offices which have 190 or more revenue units and cancel a significant volume of mail. The special cancellations described in this section are not of philatelic quality.

Other types of cancellations are:

a. First day of issue cancellations authorized by the Stamps Division in accordance with 164.5.

b. Handstamped cancellations for collectors described in 164.3.

c. Pictorial cancellations authorized by the Stamps Division in accordance with 164.42.

d. Postal message cancellations are used to convey official postal messages or slogans and are authorized in accordance with 175.

171.2 Purpose. Special cancellations are authorized when the scheduled event to be observed is:

a. For a national purpose for which Congress has made an appropriation, or

b. Of general public interest and importance and is to endure for a definite period of time and is not to be conducted for private gain or profit.

171.3 Prohibitions. Special cancellations are not authorized for:

a. Events of interest primarily to a particular local group.

b. Fraternal, political, religious, service, commercial or trade organizations.

c. Campaigns or events promoting the sale or use of private products or services.

d. Idea or slogan promotions not directly connected with an event of general public interest and importance.

e. Post office anniversaries.

f. Recruitment programs.

g. Events which occur during a period when all canceling machines in the post office have already been scheduled for the use of other special cancellation die hubs.

171.4 Periods of Use. Special cancellations may not be used longer than 6 months. Special cancellations that are approved on an annual basis are limited to one 60-day period annually.

172 REVOCATION

Permission to use any special cancellation may be curtailed or revoked when it is necessary to use special postmarking dies for Postal Service purposes.

173 REQUIREMENTS FOR OBTAINING SPECIAL CANCELLATION DIE HUBS

173.1 Application

.11 The application, for a purpose described in 171.2, must be submitted in writing to the postmaster at the post office where the special cancellation is to be used.

.12 The application must be submitted by the sponsor at least four months before the date the special cancellation is to be used.

.13 The application must provide the following information:

a. Complete description and schedule of the event to be observed, including evidence that it is not being conducted for private gain or profit.

b. Wording of the proposed cancellation:

(1) Space available for the wording is shown in the illustration below. Wording is limited to 3 lines of not more than 20 letters, numbers, or spaces each. Do not use illustrations or designs, as in most circumstances, such designs are not easily reproduced on a die hub. The wording must directly reflect the event to be commemorated.

ONANCOCK, VIRGINIA

300TH ANNIVERSARY

1680–1980

(2) Wording on a special cancellation must be standardized and approved by the sponsor's national headquarters when the sponsor is an affiliate or local chapter of a national organization. Standardized requests for national events must be forwarded to the Office of Classification and Rates Administration, USPS Headquarters, Washington, D.C. 20260-5360.

c. Name and telephone number of the post office where the cancellation is to be used.

d. Period of use desired.

e. Number of die hubs required.

f. Name, address and phone number of the sponsor who will be billed for the cost of manufacturing the die hubs.

g. The application described in this section should be in the form of a letter from the sponsor to the postmaster, giving all of the information required.

.14 A request must be submitted for reuse of recurring annual cancellations three months prior to the date the sponsor desires the cancellation to be used again. In the case of national cancellations, a single request from the national sponsor is sufficient.

173.2 Referral by Postmaster

.21 Forward the application to your designated mail classification center (see subchapter 130) as soon as it is received. Enclose the information described in 173.22 and 173.23.

.22 Furnish the name of the manufacturer and the model number of the canceling machine on which the special die hub will be used. If the machine is a Model Flier, Model M, or Model G, the correct die hub part number must be stated. The part number for Model Flier and Model M machines is 1535 for a hub that uses a round base ring die, and 1535 G for a hub that uses a square base ring die. The part number for a Model G machine is 218A for a hub that uses a round base ring die, and 218E for a hub that uses a square base ring die. A part number is not required for other machines.

.23 State the effect the approval would have on the use of special cancellations already approved for that office.

173.3 Approval and Disapproval. The sponsor is informed through the postmaster of the approval or denial of the application. If approved, the Division Manager, Mailing Requirements, arranges for the manufacture of the die hub and instructs the postmaster on its use by memorandum or Form 3617, Order For Special Canceling Machine Die Hubs. If the request is not approved, the postmaster is advised by the Division

Manager, Mailing Requirements, of the decision and the reason.

173.4 Cost. The sponsor must pay the cost of manufacturing the special cancellation die hub and any cost incurred in adapting canceling machines for its use or for installing the hub. The approximate cost of a die hub can be obtained from the Division Manager, Mailing Requirements. The organization or person assuming the cost of manufacturing the die hub will be billed by the manufacturer.

174 DISPOSITION

174.1 After Use. Used die hubs may not be given to sponsors or transferred to another post office. Used die hubs not retained for future use must be sent for disposal to Mail Equipment Shops, 2135 5th St. NE, Washington, D.C. 20260-6224.

174.2 Special Request. A request from the sponsor that a special cancellation die hub be retained for an appropriate purpose, such as placement in a museum, library, historical site, or other suitable use may be approved by the Office of Classification and Rates Administration.

174.3 Replacement. When a special cancellation die hub must be replaced, the local sponsor must be notified immediately so that they may, if they desire, apply for a replacement through the local postmaster. The sponsor must pay for replacement die hubs.

175 POSTAL MESSAGE CANCELLATIONS

175.1 Purpose. Postal message cancellation die hubs are normally used to convey official Postal Service messages or slogans. They may be used as long as the slogan or message remains timely, or as long as the Regional Director, Mail Processing, considers necessary.

175.2 Authorization

.21 Application. Heads of postal installations having 190 or more revenue units, who require postal message die hubs, should submit the requests on Form 4636, Requisition for Postmarking Dies and Engraved Station Die Hubs. Send Form 4636 to the regional director, Mail Processing, accompanied by a letter explaining the intended use and duration.

.22 Approval. Approved requests for postal message cancellations should be forwarded to the installation's area supply center. Requests for die hubs to be used on Mark II or M-36 Facer Cancellers should be sent to the Western Area Supply Center, Topeka, Kan. 66624-9998.

176.1 Postage. Mailers requesting that their mail be canceled with a special cancellation must affix first-class postage to the mail. The mail must bear a complete address. Stamps issued by foreign countries may not be placed on the mail.

176.2 Prohibitions

.21 Holding the Mail. Mail must not be held to comply with a customer's request that the mail be postmarked with a special cancellation on a particular date.

.22 Backdating. Backdating of mail to comply with customer's requests is prohibited. No exceptions to the above policy will be granted unless specifically authorized in writing by the General Manager, Philatelic Sales Division.

.23 Returns. Mail bearing the special cancellation must not be enclosed in another envelope for return, even if the customer provides a postage paid envelope for return (see 164.43).

.24 Replacements. Replacement of damaged envelopes canceled with a special cancellation is prohibited.

Available Postage and Regulations Affecting Collectors

Section 140: Postage

141 STAMPED ENVELOPES, POSTAL CARDS, AEROGRAMMES

141. 1 Plain Stamped Envelopes

.11 Envelopes Available at Post Offices. Denominations available depend on current postage rates.

.12 Sales at Post Offices. Only sizes 6 3/4 and 10 regular are sold in less than full box lots. Boxes contain 500 envelopes.

.13 Nonprofit Envelopes. Only nonprofit organizations and political committees that have obtained authorizations to mail at the special bulk third-class rates (see 623) may purchase nonprofit envelopes. Sales are made in full box lots only, except at philatelic outlets (see 141.15). Nonprofit envelopes are precanceled.

.14 Window Envelopes.

.141 Sale. Window envelopes are sold in full box lots only, except at philatelic outlets (see 141.15).

.142 Standard Window Sizes. Standard windows are 1 1/8 inches high and 4 3/4 inches wide and are located 1/2 inch from the bottom of the envelope. In size 6 3/4, the window is located 7/8 inch from the left edge; in size 10 it is 3/4 inch from the left edge. On double window envelopes, the second window (designed for a return address) is located 1/2 inch from the top and left edges, and measures 3/4 inch high and 2 1/2 inches wide

.143 Other Window Sizes. Other window sizes and locations occasionally may be produced. Window sizes cannot exceed 1 1/2 inches high and 5 inches wide; window location cannot be nearer than 3/8 inch to any edge of the envelope, and must conform to general Postal Service mail addressing guidelines.

.15 Envelope Sales at Philatelic Outlets. Window and nonprofit stamped envelopes may be sold at philatelic outlets in less than full box lots of 500. The selling price of a single window or nonprofit stamped envelope will be the price listed for each appropriate size and type on the current issue of Form 3300, *Philatelic Catalog*. Philatelic outlets will not sell full box lots of window and nonprofit stamped envelopes.

.16 Envelope Dimensions

.161 Regular Sizes. Dimensions may vary 1/16 inch, as follows:

a. Size 6 3/4 — 3 5/8 by 6 1/2 inches

b. Size 10 — 4 1/8 by 9 1/4 inches

.162 Intermediate Sizes. Intermediate sizes are those between 6 3/4 and 10 (as determined by surface area in square inches). Guidelines include:

a. Length: No greater than 9 1/2 inches nor less than 6 1/2 inches;

b. Height: No greater than 5 inches nor less than 3 5/8 inches;

c. Surface Area: No greater than 39 square inches; and

d. Length divided by height: Between 1.3 and 2.5, inclusive.

.16 Private Printing of Return Addresses. Stamped envelopes may be privately printed in any style, provided at least 3 1/2 inches of clear space is left at the right end of the address side of the envelope.

141.2 Printed Stamped Envelopes (Special-Request)

.21 Printed Stamped Envelopes Available By Mail Order. Denominations available depend on current postage rates.

.22 How to Order Printed Stamped Envelopes. Printed stamped envelopes are available only by direct mail order from the U.S. Stamped Envelope Agency, Williamsburg, Pa. 16693-0500. Customers prepare Form 3203, Printed Stamped Envelopes Order, and mail it with the proper remittance to the Stamped Envelope Agency. Payment must be made by check or money order for the full cost of the sizes, types and quantities of envelopes ordered. Postal employees will assist customers in completing and mailing the order form as necessary. If a customer wants to pay for an order with cash, issue a no-fee money order and send it with Form 3203 to the Stamped Envelope Agency.

.23 Style of Printing Return Addresses

.231 All lines of the return address will be printed in capitals and lowercase letters with flush left margin, using 8-point Helvetica type, as shown in this sample.

.232 Sample Style of Printing:

Mr. and Mrs. John Doe	*(bold sanserif)*
475 L'Enfant Plaza, SW Washington, DC 20260-9998	*(light sanserif)*

.24 Required Printing

.241 Local Address. The printed address must include the local address. The adequacy of the address, to insure return of undeliverable mail, will be determined by the postmaster. Any one of the following may be used:

a. Street address.

b. Post office box number.

c. Rural route number and box number.

d. Name of building and room number, including street address.

e. A street address and a post office box number may be shown in the return address. When both addresses are shown, mail will be returned to the address indicated in the line immediately preceding the city, state and ZIP Code. The ZIP Code must be that of the delivery unit serving the address shown in the line immediately preceding the city and state.

.242 Name of Post Office. The printed return address must include the name of the post office or branch post office, state and ZIP Code.

.25 Optional Printing

.251 Name

a. The name may be that of an individual, firm, corporation, institution, association or society. It may include the name and title of an officer of the concern (as John Doe, Treasurer, Washington Educational Association) and such titles as M.D., D.D.S., Rev., and LL.D.

b. Descriptive words, such as druggist, attorney at law, esquire, or C.P.A. are not considered titles, but represent business or professional names, which may also be printed. Such descriptive words are printed subject to the conditions set forth in 141.252.

c. The name of a branch or department of a business may be printed only when necessary to insure return of undeliverable mail; i.e., when other branches or departments are located at the same post office address.

.252 Advertising

a. A brief statement or descriptive phrase devoted to advertising may be printed either following the name or on one or two separate lines. There may not be more than two such lines devoted to permissible advertising and these two lines should appear between the name (or main line) and the local address.

b. An individual or organization engaged in business, professional, educational, social, cultural, charitable, political or other endeavors may advertise. The advertisement may describe the nature of the business of the individual or organization, or refer to the goods, services or works provided by the individual or organization.

c. Statements or descriptive phrases which describe the nature of a business and contain a reference to the quality of the goods or services produced, such as Best Tires in Town or Complete Insurance, will be permitted.

d. Nothing will be printed which would make the envelope nonmailable under 18 U.S.C. 1463, which prohibits the mailing of indecent matter on wrappers or envelopes.

.253 Phone Numbers. The phone number of any individual or group may be printed on the envelope and must appear immediately preceding the local address.

.254 Postal Instructions. Only the postal instructions in this section may be included as part of the printed return address. The request to return endorsement in 141.254a shall appear above the name and address. All other postal endorsements shall appear below the line with the city, state and ZIP Code. A combination of endorsements may be used:

a. Request to Return. A request to return undelivered mail after a specified number of days (not less than 3 and not more than 30) may be printed. If a return request is included on envelopes to be mailed at third-class rates, those pieces must bear an authorized endorsement that incorporates the words Return Postage Guaranteed (see Exhibits 159.151c through e). Sample printing:

After 5 Days, Return to

b. Address Correction. By use of the endorsement Address Correction Requested or incorporation of those words into another endorsement authorized by Exhibits 159.151a, or c through f, a request for address correction service may be printed on pieces of Express, first-, or third-class mail. (Address correction service is provided automatically for second-class mail.) The new address of the addressee, or the reason why the piece is undeliverable, will be furnished the mailer upon payment of the applicable fee (see 215, Exhibit 310i, or 612.2, as appropriate to the specific class of mail). Sample Printing:

Address Correction Requested

Note: On a mailpiece, this endorsement must be printed in at least 8-point type.

e. Forwarding Third-Class Mail. As provided by 691, a request may be made to forward third-class mail by printing on each piece an authorized endorsement that incorporates the words "Forwarding and Return Postage Guaranteed" (see Exhibits 159.151c through e). Sample printing:

Forwarding and Return Postage Guaranteed

Note: On a mailpiece, this endorsement must be printed in at least 8-point type.

.26 Other Requirements

a. No line of either required or optional printing may exceed 47 characters and spaces.

b. The total number of lines of required and optional printing may not exceed seven.

c. The last two lines of printing shall be reserved for the street address or P.O. box number where mail is to be delivered, and the city, state and ZIP Code.

.27 Nonstandard Printing. No printing other than that permitted by 141.24, 141.25 and 141.26 is allowed on printed envelopes unless approved by the Stamps Division. Requests for nonstandard printing will be considered on orders of one million or more identical envelopes and should be addressed to the General Manager, Stamps Division, U.S. Postal Service, Washington, D.C. 20260-6751. The decision of the Stamps Division, based on production requirements and the acceptability of the requested printing, will be final.

.28 Rejected Envelopes. Printed stamped envelopes may be rejected by the customer because of defective manufacture, mistakes in printing, denomination, size, etc. Postage value only will be refunded if it is the purchaser's mistake. Full invoice value will be refunded if the Postal Service is at fault.

.29 Refund or Replacement of Rejected Envelopes

.291 Refunds

a. Purchase Error. Postage value only may be refunded. Such a refund may be made at a post office or by returning the envelopes to the Stamped Envelope Agency. Refunds at post offices will be processed according to 147.24 and 147.26. Rejected envelopes for which a refund has been made will be disposed of in the same manner as unused meter stamps as provided in 147.272a (4).

b. Postal Service Error. Refunds for the total cost of the envelopes must be made by the Stamped Envelope Agency. The envelopes must be returned to the Agency with an explanation of the error.

Note: Only customers whose names appear in the return address, or their representatives, may submit rejected printed stamped envelopes for a refund.

.292 Replacement

a. When the error is the fault of the Postal Service, the customer may request that the envelopes be replaced. Return the envelopes to the Stamped Envelope Agency with an explanation of the errors and sufficient information to provide a corrected replacement order.

b. When the error resulted from erroneous information provided on the original order, the customer must remit the manufacturing fee for the replacement order. That fee is the difference between the full selling price of the envelopes and the postage value.

c. The customer must enclose a message with the returned order citing the reason the envelopes are rejected and whether a replacement or refund is desired.

.293 Returning Envelopes. Post offices will assist customers in returning rejected envelopes to the Stamped Envelope Agency under the above conditions. Provide the customer with a penalty label for returning the envelopes.

141.3 Postal Cards Available. Denominations available depend on current postage rates.

Note: All domestic postal cards are precanceled. Postal cards in sheets for use in printing must be cut to regulation size, 3 1/2 by 5 1/2 inches, so that the stamp appears in the upper right corner. Cases of sheet postal cards may be broken for sale. Return addresses are not printed on postal cards by the Postal Service.

141.4 Aerogrammes. Denomination depends on current aerogramme rate.

142 ADHESIVE STAMPS

142.1 Availability and Use

.11 Types. Denominations range from 1¢ to $5, with some values available in coil or booklet form.

.12 Use. Affix stamps firmly in the

upper right corner of the address side of the mail cover. Any stamp partly concealed by an overlapping stamp may not be counted as postage. Postal employees (other than rural carriers as prescribed in 156.41) are not required to affix stamps to mail.

.13 Perforating. Postage and special delivery stamps may be perforated with an identifying mark if the holes do not exceed 1/32 of an inch in diameter and if the space taken by the mark is not larger than 1/2 inch square.

.14 Reuse Prohibited. Reuse of stamps with intent to cause loss to the government or the Postal Service is punishable by fine and imprisonment.

142.2 Purchase

.21 Acceptable Form of Payment. Foreign or mutilated money is not acceptable. When the post office cannot make change, the exact amount of the purchase must be paid. Checks are acceptable for all postal supplies and services, except money orders, provided they conform to the Postal Service check acceptance policy. A charge of at least $10 will be levied against a customer whose check is returned by the bank as uncollectible. Where state law permits a charge higher than $10, the postmaster must charge the higher amount. Written notice will be given to the customer that the check was returned by the bank as uncollectible and that the charge plus the amount of the returned check must be promptly remitted. The customer must use a money order or certified check if the amount due is sent by mail.

.22 Purchase Receipts. If the customer wants a receipt for purchases and has prepared the receipt in advance, the postal employee will stamp it upon payment. If the customer has not prepared but wants a receipt for purchases, Form 1096, Cash Receipt, will be used for postage and other services for which verification of payment is not already provided. The postal employee will fill in the total amount of the purchase and will stamp the form upon payment.

.23 Postage Due. Postage due must be paid in cash. Postage due stamps may not be used for paying postage.

142.3 Validity of Stamps. All postage stamps issued by the United States since 1860 are good for postage from any point in the United States or from any other place where the United States domestic mail service operates. The following are not good for postage:

.311 Airmail postage stamps may be used to pay regular postage and fees for special services.

.312 Unprecanceled bulk rate and nonprofit rate stamps may be used to pay regular postage and fees for special services, providing the mailpiece is endorsed above the address and below the postage to indicate the appropriate class of the mailpiece and, if applicable, the special service desired. The total postage affixed must at least equal the postage charge for the class of the mailpiece and, if applicable, the proper fee for the special service desired.

142.32 Stamps which are not valid. The following are not valid for postage:

a. Mutilated or defaced stamps.

b. Stamps cut from stamped envelopes, aerogrammes, or postal cards.

c. Stamps covered or coated in such manner that the canceling or defacing marks cannot be imprinted directly on the stamps.

d. Nonpostage stamps (migratory bird hunting and conservation stamps, U.S. saving and thrift stamps, etc).

e. Postage due, special delivery, special handling and certified mail stamps.

f. United Nations stamps, except on mail deposited at United Nations, New York.

g. Stamps of other countries.

h. Stamps on which any unauthorized design, message, or other marking has been overprinted.

142.4 Unlawful Use of Stamps

.41 By Postal Employees. It is unlawful for postal employees entrusted with the sale or custody of postage stamps to:

a. Use stamps in payment of debts or purchase of saleable items.

b. Sell stamps except for cash.

c. Sell stamps for more or less than face value.

.42 Counterfeit Stamps. Counterfeit stamps will be confiscated and sent to the postal inspector in charge of the division in which the post office is located.

A receipt identifying the stamps will be given to persons from whom counterfeit stamps are confiscated.

142.5 Reproduction of Stamps

.51 Postmasters may not give opinions to the public concerning the reproduction of foreign or domestic postage stamps.

.52 Persons desiring information concerning reproductions of domestic stamps issued before January 1, 1978, or of any foreign stamps should address their inquiries to the Office of the Director, U.S. Secret Service, Treasury Department, Washington, D.C. 20226-0008.

.53 Persons desiring information concerning reproductions of domestic postage stamps issued after January 1, 1978, should first review the general reproduction permission provision set out in 166. Any further inquiries should be addressed to the chairman, Intellectual Property Rights Board, Office of Procurement, USPS headquarters, Washington, D.C. 20260-6234.

142.6 Imitations of Stamps and Official Markings

.61 Postage Stamps. Matter bearing imitations of postage stamps, in adhesive or printed form, or private seals or stickers which are like a postage stamp in form and design, shall not be accepted for mailing.

.62 Official Markings and Designs. Matter bearing decorative markings and designs, in adhesive or printed form, which imitate the markings and designs used to identify official postal services shall not be accepted for mailing. See Exhibit 142.62, prohibited imitations.

.63 Permissible Seals and Stickers. Seals or stickers that do not imitate postage stamps by having such characteristics as words, numerals, or other markings which indicate a value may be attached to other than the address side of mail.

143 PRECANCELED STAMPS

143.1 General

.11 Definition. Precanceling means the cancellation of adhesive postage stamps, stamped envelopes, or postal cards in advance of mailing. Precanceling may be done either by the Postal Service or by the mailer under a postal permit. Since postage due stamps are not accepted as payment of postage in advance of mailing, they are not precanceled. Precanceled commemorative stamps are not made available because commemorative stamps are sold for only a limited time.

.12 Methods of Precanceling

.121 Precanceling By the Mailer. Mailers who meet the requirements of 143.2 may precancel adhesive stamps, postal cards and stamped envelopes by using a mailer's precancel postmark. Postal cards are precanceled at the time of printing and do not require a mailer's precancel postmark unless desired by the mailer.

.122 Precanceling By Postal Service

a. All Post Offices. All post offices are authorized to requisition precanceled stamps and stamped envelopes in quantities as described in Handbook F-1, 420.

b. Local Precanceling. Post offices which have precanceling devices, such as an electroplate or handstamps, may continue to use such equipment to precancel limited quantities of stamps upon request by customers. Requests for large quantities of precanceled stamps are to be filled by requisitioning precanceled stamps, rather than by performing a more costly local precanceling service.

.14 Mailing Permit Required

a. Customers who desire to prepay mailings by using stamps and stamped envelopes precanceled by the Postal Service must complete Form 3620, Permit to Use Precanceled Stamps for Government Precanceled Stamped Envelopes Application, and file the form at the post office where the precanceled mailings will be deposited.

b. The postmaster will approve or disapprove the application. If approved, he will issue the permit on Form 3620 to the applicant. Each permit must be dated and numbered consecutively beginning with No. 1 for the first permit issued at the post office.

.15 Place of Mailing. Mail bearing precanceled postage must be presented to authorized postal employees at weigh units, window units, or detached mail units of the post office where the permit is held. Deposit of mail bearing precanceled postage in street collection boxes is not permitted.

.16 Revocation of Mailer's Permit

.161 Permits may be revoked if used in operating any scheme or enterprise of an unlawful character, or for the purpose of purchasing or acquiring stamps or mailer's precancel postmarks for other than mailing purposes, or for any noncompliance with the format requirement or the instructions on the permit (Form 3620).

.162 The postmaster at the post office that issued the permit will notify the permit holder by letter, stating that the permit is to be canceled, and giving the reason for cancellation. The permit holder is allowed 10 days to file a written statement showing why the permit should not be revoked.

.163 When no answer is filed, the postmaster will cancel the permit. If an answer is filed, the postmaster will forward the answer, along with a statement of the facts, to the MSC manager/postmaster, who will determine whether the permit should continue in effect. Notice of decision will be given the permit holder through the postmaster.

.17 Precanceling Techniques. The Postal Service uses three techniques to precancel stamps. See 143.171, 143.172, and 143.173.

.171 Stamps Precanceled by Bars Only

a. Endorsement. Stamps requisitioned with a precancel imprint will have one highly visible line across their faces. Except for stamps precanceled locally, the precancel imprint no longer will bear parallel lines and types showing the post office of mailing or its two-letter state abbreviation (see 143.172).

b. Illustrations. (See Exhibit 143.171b).

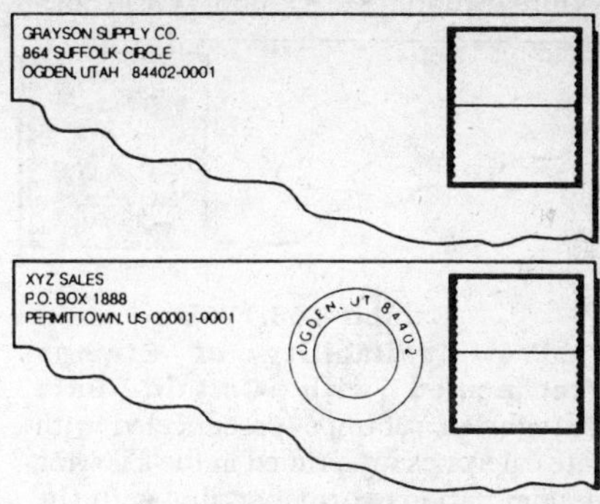

Exhibit 143.171b

.172 Stamps Precanceled with City and State

a. Endorsement stamps precanceled by post offices must have two highly visible parallel lines across the face of each stamp. The name of the post office of mailing and its two-letter state abbreviation must appear between the two parallel lines. Permanent black ink must be used.

b. Illustration. (See Exhibit 143.172b).

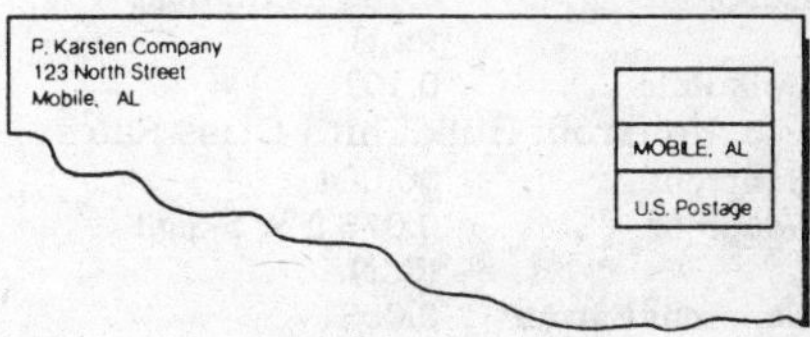

Exhibit 143.172b

.173 Stamps Precanceled with Rate Designations

a. Endorsement. Precanceled stamps can be requisitioned with the rate category preprinted as the precancellation device. See 143.174. Precancellation is accomplished by the printed legend as opposed to the legend and parallel horizontal lines as in the past. These stamps are intended for use on matter mailed as part of a qualifying mailing of the rate category shown on the stamps. Mailpieces bearing a rate category precancellation legend must include the return address. If the return address is not within the delivery area of the post office of mailing, the mailer must place a cancellation endorsement on the piece or submit information to the post office shown in the return address as required by 143.177.

Illustration. (See Exhibit 143.173b).

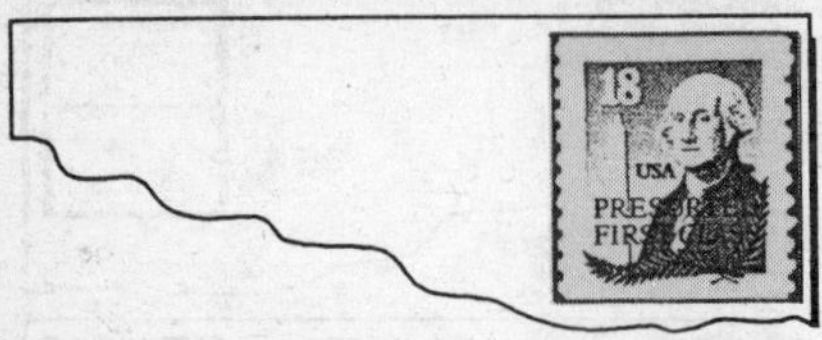

Exhibit 143.173b

.174 Availability of Stamps Precanceled with Certain Rate Categories. Stamps precanceled with rate categories are printed in the following denominations corresponding with the third unit of postage for the categories below.

a. Discounted First-Class Rates:

Rate Category Printed on Stamps	Stamp Denomination
ZIP+4	$0.241
Presorted First-Class	0.21
ZIP+4	0.205
Presorted First-Class	0.13 (For Cards Only)

b. Regular Bulk Third-Class Rates:

Bulk Rate	$0.167
Bulk Rate	0.132 (For 5-digit Rate)
Bulk Rate	0.101

c. Nonprofit Bulk Third-Class Rates:

Nonprofit	$0.084
Nonprofit	0.076 (For 5-digit Rate)
Nonprofit Carrier Route Sort	0.053

.175 Other Uses of Stamps Precanceled with Rate Category.

Stamps precanceled with rate category (143.174) may be used to pay single piece rated postage on mail provided the mail is endorsed to show the proper class such as FIRST-CLASS MAIL or THIRD-CLASS MAIL. The endorsement must be placed immediately below the postage.

.176 Overprinting. If precanceled postage on a single piece is over $1, the precanceled stamps must be overprinted or handstamped in black ink, by the mailer with the mailer's initials and the numerical abbreviations of the month and year for use; for example: "A.B. Co. 9-78." Precanceled stamps overprinted in this way are acceptable on mail during the month shown, and through the 10th of the following month.

.177 Return Address. In all instances, mailpieces bearing any precancel imprint must include a complete domestic return address. If the return address is not within the delivery area of the post office of mailing, the mailer must either place a cancellation endorsement to the left of the postage showing city, two-letter state abbreviation, and ZIP Code where mailed, or submit, at the time of mailing, a duplicate of the mailing statement and a sample mailpiece, both in an envelope stamped and addressed to the postmaster at the post office shown in the return address.

.18 Requisitioning Stamps

.181 Small Quantities Precanceled by Handstamp. Small quantities of regular-issue stamps may be precanceled by handstamp designed to precancel 10 stamps at each impression.

.182 Ordering Precanceled Adhesive Stamps and Stamped Envelopes. Post offices must requisition precanceled adhesive stamps and stamped envelopes in the same manner as other adhesive stamps and stamped envelopes.

143.2 Mailer's Precancel Postmark

.21 Application

a. Applications to use a mailer's precancel postmark on adhesive stamps, postal cards, and stamped envelopes must be filed on Form 3620, Permits to Use Precanceled Stamps or Government Precanceled Stamped Envelopes Application, at the post office where mailings will be made.

b. A "specimen mailpiece" bearing the proposed mailer's precanceled postmark must accompany the application.

c. The post office will forward the application and specimen mailpiece to the MSC Manager, Mailing Requirements, for final review.

.22 Approval

.221 The MSC manager/postmaster will appove or disapprove the application. The application and specimen mailpiece will be returned to the postmaster.

.222 The post office will date each approved application upon receipt from the MSC, and number the permits consecutively beginning with No. 1 for the first mailer's precancel postmark permit issued at the post office.

.223 A permit to use precanceled stamps or envelopes will be issued on Form 3620 and endorsed to indicate that it is for a "Mailer's Precancel Postmark."

.23 Format

.231 Upon approval by the MSC manager/postmaster, mailers may use a precancel postmark on adhesive postage stamps, postal cards, and stamped envelopes. The precanceling imprint must include:

a. The city, state and 5-digit ZIP Code of the post office where the precancel permit is held and the mailings will be deposited.

b. The date of mailing (if First-Class Mail).

c. The permit number, preceded by the words "Mailer's Postmark," and sufficient cancellation lines to fully deface the postage.

d. In lieu of printing the city, state and 5-digit ZIP Code of the post office where the precancel permit is held, the precanceling imprint may show the endorsement "Mailed from ZIP Code," followed by the 5-digit ZIP Code assigned to the postmaster at the office of mailing.

Note: Only the postmaster's ZIP Code listed in Publication 65, National Five-Digit ZIP Code and Post Office Directory, may be printed in the permit imprint.

.232 The permit number must not be obscured. Black ink must be used for cancellation and must provide adequate indelibility and sufficient contrast to prevent reuse of the stamp.

.233 Mailers are authorized to use either design shown under Format A for their precanceled postmark. See Exhibit 143.233, Format A.

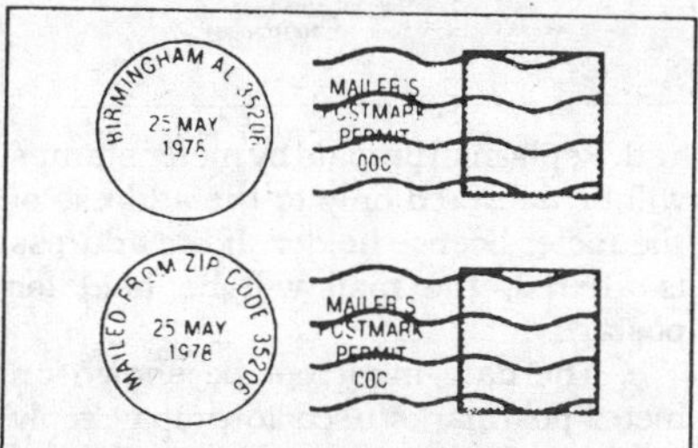

Exhibit 143.233, Format A

.234 Format B may be used by mailers who presently have the die. New dies should not be made for Format B. See Exhibit 143.234, Format B.

.235 No other format of a mailer's precancel postmark may be authorized.

Exhibit 143.234, Format B

.24 Revocation of Mailer's Permit

.241 Permits may be revoked if used in operating any scheme or enterprise of an unlawful character, or for the purpose of purchasing or acquiring stamps for other than mailing purposes, including resale, or for any noncompliance with the format requirements or the instructions on the Precancel Permit (Form 3620).

.242 The postmaster at the post office which issued the permit will notify the permit holder by letter, stating that the permit is to be canceled, and giving the reason for cancellation. The permit holder is allowed 10 days to file a written statement showing why the permit should not be revoked.

.243 When no answer is filed, the postmaster will cancel the permit. If an answer is filed, the postmaster will forward the answer, along with a statement of the facts, to the MSC manager/postmaster, who will determine whether the permit shall be continued in effect. Notice of decision will be given the permit holder through the postmaster.

143.3 Philatelic Sales

.31 Nonpermit Holders

Stamp collectors may buy precanceled postage for philatelic purposes, that include collecting and exchanging philatelic items. However, collectors may not mail matter bearing precanceled postage if they do not have a permit to use precanceled postage at the post office where the mail is presented.

.311 There is no limitation on the sale to collectors of sheet stamps or full coils of stamps of each of the precanceled denominations available at a post office. Purchases may be made in person or by mail by nonpermit holders for collection purposes only. Complete rolls of precanceled coil stamps may not be broken for philatelic sales except at authorized philatelic outlets. Instructions for selling plate blocks are in 163.5.

.312 Precanceled stamps are available at post offices which have them on hand or have a handstamp for precanceling purposes. Post offices may not acquire a precancel handstamp solely to meet philatelic demand. Precancellations may be applied only to regular-issue stamps, not commemoratives, and only to those denominations which see legitimate use by local mailers. The creation of philatelic oddities, or the precanceling of issues or denominations which would not otherwise see legitimate mail use, is not permitted. Handstamps, once acquired, may be retained by post offices to fill requests from philatelists.

.313 Postmasters will comply with requests for imprints of a precanceling device on their own stamp stock, but not for imprints on blank sheets of paper or on stamps submitted by a collector or other individual. Care should be exercised when precanceling stamps for collectors to ensure legible and well-centered impressions. Permanent ink must be used for precanceling.

.314 Each mail order must be accompanied with a stamped, self-addressed envelope for use in returning the stamps to the purchaser.

.32 Permit Holders. Collectors who have a permit to mail matter bearing precanceled postage at the post office where their mail is presented may buy precanceled postage for philatelic purposes or for the purpose of paying postage. Precanceled stamps may be purchased for the purpose of paying postage or for philatelic purposes. Permit holders may not sell unused precanceled stamps obtained under their permit.

.14 Prohibition. Precanceled postage stamps may not be used on matter mailed in boxes, cases, bags, or other containers designed to be reused for mailing purposes.

144 POSTAGE METERS AND METER STAMPS

144.1 Postage Meters

.11 Use of Meter Stamps

.111 Postage may be paid by printing meter stamps with a postage meter on any class of mail. Metered mail is entitled to all privileges and subject to all conditions applying to the various classes of mail.

.112 Meter stamps may be used to prepay reply postage on (1) Express Mail shipments up to a maximum of five pounds; (2) First-class postcards, letters and flats up to a maximum of 11 ounces; (30) Single-piece fourth-class; (4) Library rate mail.

a. Meter stamps must be printed directly on the envelope, postcard or label that bears the return address of the meter license holder in an amount sufficient to prepay the appropriate postage in full.

b. Only meter-stamped, return address labels may be used on single-piece, special fourth-class rate, or library-rate mail, and these labels must adhere in such a manner so they will not come off in one piece.

c. Any photographic, mechanical or electronic process, or any combination of such processes, other than handwriting, typewriting, or handstamping, may be used to prepare the address side of reply mail prepaid by meter stamps. The address side must be prepared both as to style and content in the following form without the addition of any matter other than a return address, except facing identification marks (FIMs) or bar codes:

(Meter stamp to be placed here)

NO POSTAGE STAMP NECESSARY
POSTAGE HAS BEEN PREPAID BY

John Doe Company
123 Tremont Street
New York, NY 10010-0001

d. Reply mail prepaid by meter stamps will be delivered only to the address of the meter license holder. If the address is altered, the mail will be held for postage.

e. The date must not be shown on meter postmarks used to prepay reply postage

.113 Postage meter stamps for zero

postage shall not be affixed to items delivered by other carriers since this would give the impression of Postal Service delivery.

.12 Description of Meters. Postage meters are made to print single, several, or all denominations of postage. They contain in one sealed unit the printing die or dies and two recording counters. One adds and keeps a total of all postage printed by the meter. The other subtracts and shows the balance of postage remaining in the meter, after the use of which it will lock. From time to time, mailers take the meter to the post office to have this counter set for additional postage, which is added to the balance remaining. Payment must be made for each additional setting.

.13 Meter Manufacturers. Postage meters may be leased from authorized manufacturers who are held responsible by the Postal Service for the control, operation, maintenance and replacement, when necessary, of meters manufactured by them. The following manufacturers are presently authorized to lease meters to mailers:

POSTALIA, INC., 1423 Centre Circle Drive, Downers Grove, Ill. 60515-1087.

Friden Alcatel, 30955 Huntwood, Hayward, Calif. 94544-7005.

Pitney Bowes, Inc., Walter H. Wheeler Jr. Dr., Stamford, Conn. 06926-0001.

Rockaway Corporation, doing business as INTERNATIONAL MAILING SYSTEMS, (a division of Better Packages, Inc.), 19 Forest Parkway, Shelton, Conn. 06484-0903.

.14 Possession No one, other than the manufacturer, is authorized to have possession of a postage meter without both a valid postage meter license and a rental agreement with the meter manufacturer. Anyone who fails to satisfy both requirements must surrender the meter to the manufacturer upon request.

144.2 Meter License

.21 Application. A customer may obtain a license to use a postage meter by submitting Form 3601-A, *Application for a Postage Meter License* (or a form supplied by the manufacturer containing the same information and format), to the post office where his metered mail will be deposited. No fee is charged. On approval, the postmaster will issue a license. By submitting an application a customer agrees that the license will be immediately revoked and the meter immediately removed if the meter is used in operating any fraudulent scheme or enterprise of an unlawful character.

.22 Responsibilities of Licensee

.221 After a meter has been delivered to a licensee, he must keep it in his custody until returned to the authorized manufacturer or to the post office. A customer may not have a meter in his possession unless it has been checked into service by the Postal Service. Avoiding the payment of postage through tampering with or misusing a meter is punishable by law.

.222 Although licensees are not required to maintain a Form 3602-A, Daily Record of Meter Register Readings, they are encouraged to do so, as use of this form will hasten the discovery of meter malfunctions. If at any time the sum of the two figures does not equal the total entered in the Form 3602-A at the last setting, the meter should be taken immediately to the post office, station, or branch where it was set or last examined. If desired, the post office will provide Form 3602-A when the meter is initially checked into service. Additional copies will be provided as the forms are filed.

.223 The meters in the custody of the licensee and his records relating to meter transactions or latest Form 3603, Receipt for Postage Meter Settings, must be immediately available for examination and audit by the Postal Service or meter manufacturer, upon request (see 144.962).

.224 If a meter is not reset within a 6-month period, it must be presented together with related Forms 3602-A, or latest Form 3603, for examination at the post office, station, or branch where it is regularly set. (For CMR meters, see 144.383 and 144.976.)

.225 If the meter's printing or recording mechanism is in any way faulty, it shall be immediately taken to the post office, station or branch where it is regularly set or examined to be checked out of service. The faulty meter must not be used under any circumstances.

.226 A licensee must notify the licensing post office whenever the name, address or phone number on Form 3601-A changes.

.23 Revocation

.231 A license will be revoked if a meter is used in operating any scheme or enterprise of an unlawful character, for nonuse during any consecutive 12 months, or for any failure of the licensee to comply with the regulations governing the use of postage meters.

.232 The meter license holder will be notified by the postmaster if the license is to be revoked and the reasons for revocation. Form 3604, Nonuse of Mailing Permit or Meter License, may be used if revocation for nonuse is being considered.

144.4 Meter Stamps

.41 Designs. The types, sizes, and styles of meter stamps are fixed when meters are approved by the Postal Service for manufacture. Only approved designs may be used.

a. General Examples:

b. Official Mail:

.42 Legibility. Meter stamps must be legible and not overlap. Illegible or overlapping meter stamps will not be counted in determining postage paid.

.43 Fluorescent Ink. The use of fluorescent ink is mandatory for postage imprints on letter-size metered mail. Failure to use fluorescent ink may result in the revocation of the meter license. Letter-size mail is defined as being from 5 inches to 11 1/2 inches long, 3 1/2 inches to 6 1/8 inches wide, and .007 inches to .25 inches thick.

.44 Meter Stamps on Tape. When meter stamps are printed on tape, only tape approved by the Postal Service may be used.

.45 Position. Meter stamps must be printed or stuck in the upper right corner of the envelope, address label, or tag.

.46 Content. Meter stamps must show the city and state designation of the licensing post office, meter number and amount of postage for all classes of mail. Upon approval of the licensing post office, meter indicia may contain the name and state designation of its local classified branch, which sets the meter. This authorization does not apply to classified stations or contract stations or branches. As an alternative, the ZIP Code designation may be shown in the meter postmark instead of the city/state designation. When this occurs, the words Mailed From ZIP Code must appear in place of the city designation and the mailer's delivery address ZIP Code in place of the state. When it is necessary to print multidenomination meter stamps on more than one tape, the circle showing the post office must appear on each tape.

.47 Date of Mailing

.471 Dates shown in the meter postmark of any type or kind of mail must be the actual date of deposit, except when the mailing piece is deposited after the last scheduled collection of the day. When deposit is made after the last scheduled collection of the day, mailers are encouraged but not required to use the date of the next scheduled collection. When a .00 postage meter impression is used to correct the date of metered mail, the date in that impression shall be considered to be the actual date of deposit.

.472 The month, day and year must be shown in the meter postmark on all first-class mail, and on all registered, certified, insured, COD, special delivery and special handling mail, whether the postmark is printed directly on the mailing piece or on a separate tape. The exception to this is prepaid reply postage.

.473 The month and year must be shown on meter postmarks printed on a separate tape for second-, third-, and fourth-class pieces. The day may be omitted. Mailing pieces postmarked on a separate tape with only the month and year may be accepted during the month shown and through the third day of the following month when, in the judgment of the postmaster, the mailing was unavoidably delayed prior to its deposit with the Postal Service.

.474 The date (day, month or year) is not required to be shown on meter postmarks printed directly on a third-, or fourth-class mailing piece.

.475 The date must not be shown on meter postmarks used to prepay reply postage in accordance with 144.112.

.48 Hour of Mailing. The hour of mailing may be shown only on first-class or special delivery mail, and then only when it is mailed in time to be dispatched at the hour shown.

.49 Ad Plates

.491 Advertising matter, slogans, return addresses and the postal markings specified in 144.492 may be printed with the meter stamps within space limitations. Licensees must obtain the plates for the printing of this matter from authorized meter manufacturers to assure suitable quality and content in accordance with the requirements of the Postal Service. Ad plate messages should be clearly distinguished by the inclusion of the name of the mailer or words such as "Mailers Message." The ad plate must not be obscene, defamatory of any particular person or group, or deceptive, nor shall it advocate unlawful action.

.492 Postal markings related to the class or category of mail, such as First-Class, Presorted First-Class, Priority Mail, ZIP+4 Presort, ZIP+4 presort, ZIP+4 Barcoded, Third-Class, Blk Rt., Nonprofit Org., Carrier Route Presort, Basic ZIP+4, 5-digit ZIP+4, Fourth-Class, Fourth-Class Bulk Rates, Special Fourth-Class Rate, Presorted Special Fourth-Class Rate, Bound Printed Matter, and Library Rate are permissible. If a postal marking is to appear in the ad plate area, no other matter is to be printed. The marking must fill the entire ad plate area to the extent practicable. All words must be in bold, capital letters which are at least 1/4 of an inch in height or 18-point type and legible at two feet. Exceptions for small ad plates that will not accommodate any of the above markings will not be considered.

145 Permit Imprints (Mail Without Affixed Postage)

145.1 General

.11 Definition. Mailers may be authorized to mail material without affixing postage if payment of postage is made at the time of mailing from an advance deposit account established with the Postal Service for that purpose. Each piece of mail sent by a mailer under this method of payment must bear a permit imprint to indicate that postage has been paid. This method of payment may be used to pay special service fees as well as postage.

.12 Application. A permit to use permit imprints and pay postage in cash at the time of mailing may be obtained by submitting Form 3601, Application to Mail Without Affixing Postage Stamps, with a fee of $60, to the post office where mailings will be made. The postmaster will give the applicant a receipt for the fee on Form 3544. There is no other fee for the use of permit imprints so long as the permit remains active. Note: The applicant must also pay an annual bulk mailing fee if matter will be mailed at Presort First-Class rates, Third-Class Bulk Mail rates, or Presorted Special Fourth-Class rates. (See Exhibits 310, D through H, 341, 612.1, 641 and 712.1).

.13 Revocation

.131 The permit will be revoked if used in operating any unlawful scheme or enterprise, for nonuse during any 12-month period, or for any noncompliance with the regulations governing the use of permit imprints.

.132 The permit holder will be notified by the postmaster if the permit is to be revoked and the reasons for revocation. Form 3604, Nonuse of Mailing Permit or Meter License, may be used if revocation is for nonuse.

.133 The permit holder may appeal the revocation to the postmaster. If no written statement of objection is filed by the permit holder within 10 days, the postmaster will cancel the permit.

.134 If revocation is because of nonuse and the permit holder indicates that he will resume mailings within a 90-day period, the permit will be continued for a period not to exceed 90 days.

.135 If the postmaster does not grant the appeal, he must notify the customer.

.136 The permit holder may appeal the initial decision to the Field Division General Manager/Postmaster or the Rates and Classification Center (if the initial decision was made at the division level). The appeal must be submitted in writing to the postmaster, who will forward the appeal to the appropriate division or center.

145.2 Preparation of Permit Imprints.

.21 General. Embossed or unembossed permit imprints may be made by printing press, handstamp, lithography, mimeograph, multigraph, address plate or similar device. They may not be typewritten or hand-drawn. The content of the imprint must be in accordance with 145.3 and the format in accordance with 145.4. No other forms of imprints may be used. The imprint must be legible and must be of a color that contrasts sufficiently with the paper and the imprint's background to make the imprint readable. A different color may be used to highlight the background of a permit imprint.

.22 Placement of Permit Imprints. On letter-sized mailpieces, the entire imprint must be placed either (1) in the upper right corner of the address side of each letter-sized piece, aligned parallel with the length of the piece, or (2) in the upper right corner of an address label if it is aligned parallel with the length of the label. The placement of the imprint on the address label should not interfere with the Optical Character Reader (OCR) read area, and the placement of the address label on the mailpiece should not interfere with the "Barcode Clear Zone." See Exhibit 122.33. On flat-sized mailpieces, it is recommended that the entire imprint be placed in the upper right corner of the address area, aligned parallel with the orientation of the address. The position (but not the format) of the imprint on fourth-class bound printed matter may be varied so that automatic data processing equipment may be used to simultaneously print the address, imprint, and other postal information.

.23 Bulk Third-Class Mail Bearing References to Expedited Handling or Delivery. With the exception of postcard-size mail and imprints placed on address labels, permit imprints on bulk third-class mail bearing references to expedited handling or delivery (such as PRIORITY, EXPRESS, OVERNIGHT, et cetera) must be prepared as follows:

a. Mailers must display the words Bulk Rate or Nonprofit Org more prominently than any other words used in the permit imprint.

b. Mailers must leave a clear space of not less than 3/8 of an inch around the entire permit imprint.

145.3 Content of Permit Imprints

.31 First-Class Mail. Permit imprints must show city and state; First-Class Mail, or Priority, or Priority Mail; U.S. Postage Paid; and permit number. They may show the mailing date, amount of postage paid or the number of ounces for which postage is paid. (See 145.41a-145.41e). The ZIP Code of the permit holder may be shown immediately following the name of the state or in a separate inscription reading ZIP Code 00000 when it is possible to include the ZIP Code without creating uncertainty as to the permit holder's correct address or permit number. Instead of printing the city and state of mailing in the permit imprint, mailers may print the endorsement Mailed From ZIP Code, followed by the 5-digit ZIP Code assigned to the postmaster at the office of mailing. The permit imprint indicia may also include the markings required by 362.

Note: Only the Postmaster's ZIP Code listed in Publication 65, National 5-digit ZIP Code and Post Office Directory, may be printed on the permit imprint.

.32 Second-Class Mail. There is no permit imprint for second-class mail. Second-class publications mailed by publishers or news agents must be prepared with the second-class imprint and other markings as prescribed in 453.2 and 455. The second-class imprint is not a permit imprint. Copies of second-class publications not mailed by publishers or news agents or otherwise not eligible for the publisher's second-class rates in 411.2 and/or 411.3 must be mailed at applicable rates other than second-class (Express Mail, or First-, Third-, or Fourth-Class). (See 411.4).

.33 Third- and Fourth-Class Mail. Third- and Fourth-Class Mail permit imprints must contain the same information as required in First-Class Mail imprints, except the date and the words "First-Class," or "Priority," or "Priority Mail," must be omitted. Permit indicia may include the amount of postage paid, weight of piece, and markings required by 662, 725.1, or 760.

.34 Mail With Special Services. Permit mail with special services paid by permit must show first-class mail, if first-class mail; if first-class mail, U.S. postage and fees paid; city and state; and permit number. The company's name may be shown in place of the city and permit number in accordance with 145.35.

.35 Company Permit Imprints for Any Class of Mail

.351 Availability. The city, state, and permit number may be omitted if the permit holder has permits at two or more post offices, and if the exact name of the company or individual holding the permits is shown in the permit imprint.

.352 Return Address

a. When a company permit imprint is used, the mailing piece must bear a complete domestic return address as described in 122.15, located in the upper left corner of the address side as recommended by 122.31.

b. On unendorsed bulk third-class

MAILGRAM
Postage Charges
PAID
Western Union

b. Formats for Official Mail (First-Class)

FIRST-CLASS MAIL
POSTAGE & FEES PAID
Agency Name
Permit No. G-__

PRESORTED
FIRST-CLASS MAIL
POSTAGE & FEES PAID
Agency Name
Permit No. G-__

FIRST-CLASS
CARRIER ROUTE PRESORT
POSTAGE & FEES PAID
Agency Name
Permit No. G-__

ZIP + 4
POSTAGE & FEES PAID
Agency Name
Permit No. G-__

ZIP + 4 PRESORT
POSTAGE & FEES PAID
Agency Name
Permit No. G-__

c. Formats for Official Mail (Third-Class)

THIRD-CLASS MAIL
POSTAGE & FEES PAID
Agency Name
Permit No. G-__

BULK RATE
POSTAGE & FEES PAID
Agency Name
Permit No. G-__

BULK RATE
CARRIER ROUTE PRESORT
POSTAGE & FEES PAID
Agency Name
Permit No. G-__

d. Formats for Official Mail (Fourth-Class)

FOURTH-CLASS MAIL
POSTAGE & FEES PAID
Agency Name
Permit No. G-__

SPECIAL FOURTH-CLASS RATE
POSTAGE & FEES PAID
Agency Name
Permit No. G-__

PRESORTED
SPECIAL FOURTH-CLASS RATE
POSTAGE & FEES PAID
Agency Name
Permit No. G-__

BOUND PRINTED MATTER
POSTAGE & FEES PAID
Agency Name
Permit No. G-__

BULK RATE
BOUND PRINTED MATTER
POSTAGE & FEES PAID
Agency Name
Permit No. G-__

mail, the return address may appear below the permit imprint.

.353 Records. For one year, the permit holder must maintain, and make available for review upon the request of postal officials, the following records for each mailing bearing a company permit imprint.

a. The post office at which the mailing was made;

b. The date(s) of mailing;

c. The total weight of the mailing;

d. The weight of a single piece;

e. The total number of pieces mailed;

f. The amount of postage paid; and

g. A sample of the mailing piece.

145.4 Format of Permit Imprints

.41 Permit imprints for other than official mail or Mailgrams must be prepared in one of the following formats. Any of the formats may be used to display the information prescribed by 145.3.

.42 Permit imprints for Mailgrams and official mail must be prepared in one of the formats shown in Exhibits 145.42a-145.42d.

a. First-Class Mail

b. Second-, Third-, and Fourth-Class Mail (Date and First-Class Mail Omitted)

c. Bulk Third-Class Mail

d. Special Rates for Authorized Organizations Only

e. Official Mail (First-Class)

f. Official Mail (Fourth-Class) (Date and First-Class Mail Omitted)

145.5 Mailings With Permit Imprints

.51 Minimum Quantity. Permit imprint mailings must consist of a minimum of 200 pieces or 50 pounds, except as provided in 145.52. Minimum quantities of mail necessary to mail at the nonpresort ZIP+4 rate, or at any of the First-Class presort rates, the Fourth-Class zone bulk rate, and the special Fourth-Class presort rate and the bulk pound printed matter rates are higher.

.52 Exceptions to Minimum Quantities. A mailing consisting of less than the required minimum will be accepted by the Postal Service if one of the following requirements is met:

a. First-Class Mail. An occasional mailing for a mailer whose total daily mailings are not much more than 200 pieces but who, to cooperate with the post office, presents a portion of his mailings early in the day.

b. All Classes of Mail. A large mailing which extends over two or more consecutive days and the last deposit, made to complete the mailing, is less than the minimum. Note: In order to be considered an exception, the mailer must include an explanation on the Form 3602, Statement of Mailing With Permit Imprints.

145.6 Use of Permit Imprints

.61 General. Permit imprints indicate that the postage for matter on which they appear has been paid under the permit imprint system. Therefore, imprints must not ordinarily appear on matter which has not had postage so paid thereon (as, for example, matter which is circulated as an enclosure with other matter either by mail or by means other than mail).

a. See 136.312 for combination mailings containing enclosures which may have postage paid by permit imprint.

b. Permit imprints may appear on address labels, wrappers, envelopes, and other containers, and on complete mailing pieces, which have not had postage paid thereon under the permit imprint system provided it would be impracticable to omit the permit imprint (e.g. when envelopes are shipped from a printer to a permit imprint permit holder).

.62 Place of Acceptance. Permit imprint matter will be accepted for mailing only at the post office shown in the permit imprint except: (a) when company permit imprints are used as provided for by 145.35 or (b) when arrangements for acceptance at other post offices are made under the provisions of 145.8.

146 Prepayment and Postage Due

146.1 Postage Payment

.11 Prepayment Required. Postage on all mail must be fully prepaid at the time of mailing, with the following exceptions:

a. Business reply mail, or metered reply mail handled as business reply mail, (see 917)

b. Federal Government and free mail, (see 137)

c. Certain mail for the blind, (see 135)

d. Mail sent by members of the Armed

Forces, (see 134)

e. Keys and identification devices returned to owners, (see 610)

.12 Mailable Matter Not Bearing Postage Found in the Mail

.121 Matter of any class, including that for which special services are indicated (see 911.262 for registered mail), received at either the office of mailing or office of address without any postage (see 146.4), will be endorsed returned for postage and returned to the sender without an attempt at delivery. If no return address is shown, or if the delivery and return address are identical, or if it is determined that the delivery address and the return address, while different, are actually for the same person or organization, the piece will be disposed of in accordance with 159.4.

.122 Metered reply mail, which is prepared in accordance with 144.112, for the mailer's inadvertent failure to imprint a meter stamp on the envelope, will be treated as business reply mail (see 917), and will be delivered upon payment of postage and business reply fee of $.40 per piece.

.123 Except as provided in 146.123a or b, mailable matter not bearing postage (including but not limited to parcels, newspapers and magazines, books, and records) intended for delivery by a private delivery company but found in collection boxes or other receptacles designated for the deposit of mail by the public or in any facilities or mail processing operations of the Postal Service, will be returned as promptly as possible to the sender postage due, and not delivered to the addressee or returned to the private delivery company. Address correction service or forwarding service will not be provided. Postage due, rated according to 146.222c, will be determined by computing postage due from the point at which the unpaid mailable matter entered the mail to the sender's location. However, when the entry point of the unpaid mailable matter is unknown, postage due will be computed from the point where it was first found in the mail to the sender's location.

a. If the sender cannot be identified or if mailable matter is refused by sender, the procedures in 159.5 will be followed.

b. Promptly notify the private delivery company to pick up the matter by the close of the company's next workday, if it appears that mailable matter was:

(1) Erroneously delivered to a post office by a private delivery company.

(2) Deposited in a Postal Service collection box or receptacle by a private delivery company's customer in error.

.13 Insufficient Prepayment

.131 Mail of any class, including that for which special services are indicated, except Express Mail (see 286), registered mail (see 911.262), non-standard first-class mail (see 353.4), and non-standard single-piece third-class mail (see 652.4), received at either the office of mailing or office of address without sufficient postage will be:

a. Marked to show the total deficiency of postage and fees.

b. Dispatched promptly to the addressee by means of the regular or special service indicated.

c. Delivered to addressee on payment of the charges marked on the mail. Note: When quantity mailings of 10 or more pieces are received at the office of mailing without sufficient postage, the mailer will be notified, without charge, preferably by telephone, in order that the postage charges may be adjusted before the mail is dispatched.

.132 When the addressee refuses to pay the deficient postage, or when the mail is undeliverable for any other reason, it will be handled as follows:

a. First-class mail bearing a return address will be returned to the sender and, after payment by the sender of the deficient postage, will be delivered.

b. Mail other than first-class bearing a return address will be returned to the sender and delivered on payment by the sender of the total of the deficient postage, the forwarding postage, if any, and the return postage.

c. All mail that does not bear a return address will be disposed of in accordance with 159.

.133 The methods for handling insufficiently prepaid and/or undeliverable Express Mail shipments are covered in 273.42. Express Mail shipments are never endorsed "Postage Due" and collection of deficient postage is never attempted from the addressee.

.14 Postage on Mail Insufficiently Prepaid. Postage stamps affixed to mail are canceled when the mail is first received in the post office. Postage stamps or meter stamps originally affixed to insufficiently prepaid mail will, when the mail is again presented for mailing, be accepted in payment of postage to the amount of their face value.

.15 Parcels Containing Written Matter. At the office of address, parcels subject to postage due will be handled as follows:

a. Postage due at the first-class rate will be charged on parcels consisting mainly of first-class matter.

b. Postage due will be charged for parcels in which a minor portion of the contents is nonpermissible written matter:

Difference between First-Class rate and rate paid	Postage-Due Charge
$0.01-$0.25	Full amount
0.26-1.00	$0.25
1.01 or more	1.00

146.2 Mailable Matter Not Bearing Postage Found In or On Private Mail Receptacles

.21 Penalty. Whoever knowingly and willfully deposits any mailable matter such as statements of account, circulars, sale bills, or other like matter, on which no postage has been paid, in any letterbox established, approved or accepted by the postmaster general for the receipt or delivery of mail matter on any route with intent to avoid payment of lawful postage thereon, shall for each such offense be fined not more than $300.

.22 Collection of Postage

.221 General. Except as permitted in 156.58, any mailable matter not bearing postage found in, upon, attached to, supported by, or hung from, the private mail receptacles described in 151.1, is subject to the payment of the same postage as would be paid if carried by mail. For mailable matter not bearing postage found in the mail, see 146.12.

.222 Distribution to less than complete route. When there is a distribution of pieces to some, but not all, addresses on a route, they will be handled as follows:

a. Each piece will be taken to the delivery unit.

b. The date and approximate time of finding will be recorded on the piece. If the address where the piece is found is different from the address, if any, on the label, the address where found will be recorded, as well as the approximate time and date.

c. Postage on each piece found will be computed as follows:

(1) First-Class Matter. First-class rates will be applied to matter which would require first-class postage if mailed.

(2) Second-Class Publications, Books, Records, Circulars, Catalogs and Merchandise. If the piece weighs less than 16 ounces, either the single-piece third-class rate or the applicable fourth-class rate, whichever is lower, will be applied (see 611.12). If the piece weighs 16 ounces or more, the applicable fourth-class rate will be applied.

.223 Distribution to all or substantially all addresses on a route. If there is a distribution of identical pieces to all or substantially all addresses on a route, only two copies, each dated, initialed and marked with the address where found, will be taken to the office along with a written notation of the total number of identical pieces observed on the route. The postmaster must prepare a memorandum showing the details to support the claim of postage, which will be computed in accordance with 146.222c.

.224 Request for payment

a. If there is reason to believe that a private delivery firm or an individual within the delivery area of the post office is responsible for the delivery, the local postmaster will notify the firm or individual as promptly as possible concerning the number of pieces and the amount of postage due. The applicable provisions of this manual will be explained. If the firm or individual receiving a request for postage offers objection that these regulations have not been applied properly in the particular case, the facts will be investigated before any action is taken. If, within five days after receiving a request for the postage, or within five days after receiving a renewed request following investigation of an objection, the firm or individual agrees to pay the postage due, payment will be accepted and the articles will be delivered to the addressees. The firm or individual paying the postage may choose to redeliver the pieces rather than have the Postal Service deliver them. Receipt for payment will be handled in accordance with 146.224c. If the pieces are found to have been removed improperly, they will be delivered without postage charge.

b. If the firm or individual responsible for delivery is not known or if the firm presented with a request fails to pay the postage, the pieces will be returned as promptly as possible to the publisher or manufacturer, postage due, with each piece endorsed to show that the articles were found in or on the addressee's mailbox without postage. If a publisher or manufacturer provides the name and telephone number of a person to contact about pieces found in mailboxes and orally or in writing guarantees payment of postage, the pieces will not be returned but will be redelivered promptly to the addressees. If the pieces are refused by the publisher or manufacturer or if the publisher or manufacturer is unknown, the procedures in 159.5 will be followed.

c. An equivalent amount of postage due stamps affixed to a sheet of paper and properly canceled as a receipt for money collected will be given the person or firm paying postage. If payment is in the form of uncanceled stamps or meter stamps, they will be affixed to a sheet, canceled and returned as a receipt for payment. No other receipt will be issued.

.23 Report to Other Office. If the person or firm or distributor responsible for the impermissible use of the private mail receptacles is located within the area served by another post office, a sample piece will be sent with a report of the facts to the postmaster at that location with request that he take action in accordance with 146.22.

.24 Repeated Violations. If the person or firm or distributor responsible for the impermissible use of the private mail receptacles continues the impermissible use after having been notified that the use is impermissible, the postmaster will submit a sample piece and report of the facts (see 146.22) to the postal inspector in charge.

146.3 Collection of Postage Due

.31 Collected On Delivery. Customers must pay for postage due mail in cash only, prior to delivery to them. However, postage on quantity mailings found in private mail boxes will be collected as provided in 146.22.

.32 Use of Postage Stamps, Permit Imprints or Customer Meter Strips. Postage stamps, permit imprints, and customer meter strips may not be used for payment of postage due, except by Government agencies as provided by 137.265b.

.34 Advance Deposit. If postage due collections amount to approximately $10 or more every 60 days, payment may be made by advance deposits of money.

146.4 When Not Collected. When it is apparent from the impression of a cancellation that a postage stamp has been wholly or partially lost, the piece must be handled, in the absence of contrary evidence, as if correct postage had been paid for the class and weight of the piece. Handle registered mail requiring additional postage in accordance with 911.26.

147 EXCHANGES AND REFUNDS

147.1 Exchanges of Stamps

.11 Unserviceable Stamps

.111 Post Office Mistake. Mistakes in selling damaged, defective, or otherwise unserviceable stamps may be corrected by the post office by exchanging stamps at full value.

.112 Damaged in Customer's Possession. Stamps which are damaged or otherwise become unusable for postage because of humidity, moisture, or other causes while in a customer's possession may be exchanged at full value only for an equal number of stamps of the same denomination. Unserviceable stamps accepted from customers under these conditions must be those which have been on sale at post offices within 12 months preceding the transaction. Quantities of the same denomination in excess of $10 must be returned in the same configuration as when purchased: i.e., sheets, coils, booklets. Each such transaction is further limited to stamps with a total value of $100 or less from each customer.

.113 Determining Quantities. The stamps presented for exchange must be in substantially whole condition, with the denomination evident. If customers return partially stuck-together coils of stamps and the stamps cannot be counted, postmasters may accept the customer's estimate of the number of stamps remaining in the coil and give equal quantities in exchange.

.114 Appeal. Customers denied an exchange for damaged stamps may appeal the postmaster's decision to the Consumer Advocate. U.S. Postal Service, Washington, D.C. 20260-6720.

.12 Purchaser's Mistake. Mistakes made by purchaser in buying adhesive stamps of the wrong denomination or stamped envelopes or postal cards of the wrong kind, size, or denomination may be corrected by exchanging stamps at full value. Only full panes of stamps, coils of stamps in the original sealed wrappers, full boxes of stamped envelopes, or original sealed packs of postal cards may be exchanged.

Any customer exchanging $250 or more of such stock must furnish proof of identity (driver's license, military I.D., or other valid identification) and must present the stock in exchange to the postal unit at which his or her mail is delivered. This will allow the clerk exchanging the stock to validate the customer's address. A record of each transaction of $250 or more will be made, showing name of customer, type of I.D., business firm, address, amount, and denominations exchanged. Any suspicious circumstances should be reported immediately to the local inspector or inspector-in-charge.

.13 Unserviceable Postal Stationery and Unused Precanceled Stamps. Unserviceable and spoiled stamped envelopes or postal cards, if uncanceled, and unused precanceled stamps and postal cards, will be exchanged for other postage-stamped paper as follows:

a. Stamped envelopes (mutilated no more than is necessary to remove contents), for postage value plus value of postage added as a result of rate increase or for additional service.

b. Unmutilated aerogrammes (airletter sheets), for postage value less 1¢ for each aerogramme redeemed.

c. Unmutilated single and double postal cards, for 85 percent of postage value plus full value of postage added as a result of rate increase or for additional service.

(1) Either half of a double postal card may be redeemed if the double card has been printed and cut for use as single cards.

(2) Unused double postal cards printed for reply purposes should not be separated; however, if they have been separated in error, and the purchaser presents both halves, the cards may be redeemed.

(3) Reply halves of double postal cards that have been returned to sender outside of the mails are not redeemable by the original purchaser even though the reply half received no postal service.

d. Sheet postal cards spoiled in the process of cutting to size, for 85 percent of postage value plus full value of postage added as a result of rate increase or for additional service, if all cut sections are submitted.

e. Stamps affixed to commercial envelopes and postcards, for 90 percent of postage value. Envelopes and postcards must be in a substantially whole condition and in lots of at least 50 of the same denomination and value.

f. Unused precanceled stamps in full coils or in full sheets redeemed from precanceled permit holders, for 90 percent of postage value.

Note: Stamped envelopes or aerogrammes (airletter sheets) with a printed return address and postal cards with any printed matter of the purchaser, may be exchanged only by the purchaser. If there is no purchaser's printing, they may be exchanged by any responsible person. When redemption cannot be made at time of presentation, the postmaster will furnish a receipt on Form 3210 for uncanceled, unserviceable, or spoiled envelopes or postal cards, or for unused, precanceled stamps left in his custody.

.14 Conversion of Postage Stamps to Other Forms of Postage

.141 General. Mailers may submit postage stamps for conversion to a meter setting or advance deposit for permit imprint mailings under the conditions set forth in 147.142 through 147.146. A conversion charge of 10 percent of the face value of the stamps or $250, whichever is greater, will be deducted when the stamps are converted. No part of any amount applied to a meter setting or trust account from the conversion of postage stamps will be later refundable in cash, or by other means.

.142 Where to Apply. All requests to convert postage stamps to meter or permit imprint postage must be sent to the general manager, Stamps Division, U.S. Postal Service, Washington, D.C. 20260-6351. The general manager, Stamps Division, will forward a copy of the request to the inspector-in-charge of the division in which the requester's post office is located.

.143 What May be Converted. Only full panes of stamps, or coils of stamps in the original sealed wrappers, will be accepted for conversion. Commemorative stamps issued no earlier than one year prior to the date of the request for conversion or issues of regular stamps which have not been officially withdrawn from sale at the Philatelic Sales Branch will be accepted under these conditions.

.144 Conversion Rate. The amount of postage applied to a meter setting or permit imprint trust account through conversion will be the lesser of the full face value of the stamps submitted minus 10 percent, or full face value minus $250.

.145 Submittal of Request. The customer must submit a letter to the general manager, Stamps Division, requesting conversion of the stamps to meter or permit imprint postage. The letter must include the name, denomination, quantity and value of postage stamps for which conversion is requested, and name of the post office where the stamps were purchased. Evidence of purchase for the stamps must also be included with the request.

.146 Approval. The general manager, Stamps Division, will review the request and may ask the mailer to submit additional records to support the information in the request. The general manager, Stamps Division, will approve or deny the request. If the conversion is authorized, the postmaster will be advised of the proper procedures for accepting the postage stamps and making the required accounting entries. The general manager, Stamps Division, will determine the post office which has the capabilities to destroy the postage stamps. The credit will be applied to the post office where the mailer has his meter set or deposits his permit imprint mail.

.15 Non-exchangeable. The following are non-exchangeable:

a. Adhesive stamps, unless mistakes were made in purchasing, stamps were defective, or stamps were affixed to commercial envelopes and postcards, or as provided in 147.14.

b. Stamps cut from postal cards, stamped envelopes, or aerogrammes (airletter sheets).

c. Parts and pieces of postal cards.

d. Postal cards, stamped envelopes and aerogrammes received for reply purposes.

e. Mutilated and defaced stamps.

147.2 Refunds

.21 Justification

.211 When postage and special or retail service fees have been paid and no service is rendered, or when the amount collected was in excess of the lawful rate, a refund may be made:

a. Refunds for postage and fees paid by stamps, permit imprints, or meter impressions, unused meter impressions, and unused units set in meters are handled according to 147.24.

b. Refunds for retail services and fees not paid by means of stamps, permit imprint, or meter impressions are handled according to 147.26.

.212 The Postal Service is assumed to be at fault and no service is rendered in cases involving returned articles improperly accepted in both domestic and international services because of excess size or weight.

.213 Mailers who customarily weigh

and rate their mail are expected to be familiar with basic requirements and the Postal Service is not considered to be at fault when these mailers are required to withdraw articles from the mail prior to dispatch.

.214 See 147.222 and 147.25 for special provisions for refunding the postage value of unused meter stamps.

.215 A postage refund may be provided the sender for first-class, third-class single piece, and fourth-class mail torn or defaced during processing by the Postal Service to such extent that identification of addressee or intended delivery point cannot be made. This applies only when the failure to process and/or deliver is the fault of the Postal Service. Where possible, the damaged item will be returned with the postage refund.

.216 Postmasters will grant or deny requests for refunds in accordance with the provisions of 147.2. Guidance is available from the RCC in difficult cases.

.22 Amount Allowable

.221 Refund of 100 Percent Will Be Made:

a. When the Postal Service is at fault.

b. For the excess when postage or fees have been paid in excess of the lawful rate.

c. When service to the country of destination has been suspended.

d. When postage is fire-scarred while in the custody of the Postal Service, including fire in letterbox, and the mail is returned to sender without service.

e. When special delivery stamps are erroneously used in payment of postage, and the mail is returned to the sender without service.

f. When fees are paid for special delivery, special handling and certified mail, and the article fails to receive the special service for which the fee has been paid.

g. When surcharges are erroneously collected on domestic registered mail, or collected in excess of the proper amount, or represented by stamps affixed to matter not actually accepted for registration.

h. For fees paid for return receipts or for restricted delivery when the failure to furnish the return receipt or its equivalent, or erroneous delivery, or non-delivery, is due to the fault or negligence of the Postal Service.

i. For annual bulk mailing fee when no bulk mailings of third-class matter are made during the year for which the annual fee has been paid.

j. When customs clearance and delivery fees are erroneously collected.

k. When fees are paid for registry or insurance service on mail addressed to a country to which such services are not available, unless claim for indemnity is made.

l. When Express Mail is not delivered according to the terms of the service standards as delineated in 222.2, 222.3, 224.4 and 230.

.222 A partial refund shall be made:

a. When complete and legible unused meter stamps are submitted within one year from the dates appearing in the stamps. See 147.25.

b. When the face value of the stamps does not exceed $250, refunds of 90 percent will be made.

c. When the face value of the stamps exceeds $250, refunds will be made for the face value of the stamps less $10 per hour for the actual man-hours required to process the refund, with a minimum charge of $25 deducted from the amount of the refund.

d. The employee processing the refund will enter the following endorsement on the reverse of Form 3533, Application and Voucher for Refund of Postage and Fees:

I certify that (number) hours were required to process this refund. The certifying and witnessing employees will both sign this certification.

.223 When mail is returned at the request of the sender or for a reason not the fault of the Postal Service, any difference between the amount paid and the appropriate surface rate chargeable from mailing office to interception point and return will be refunded.

.23 Unallowable Refunds. No refund will be made:

a. For an application fee to use permit imprints.

b. For registered, insured and COD fees after the mail has been accepted by the post office even though it is later withdrawn from the mailing post office.

c. For unused adhesive stamps (see 147.11 and 147.12).

d. For adhesive stamps affixed to unmailed matter.

.24 Application for Postage Refund

.241 Customers who wish to request a refund must submit an application on Form 3533, Application and Voucher for Refund of Postage and Fees, to the postmaster together with the envelope or wrapper, or the portion thereof having names and addresses of sender and addressee, canceled postage and postal markings, or other evidence of payment of the amount of postage and fees for which refund is desired. An adverse decision by the postmaster may be appealed through the postmaster to the appropriate General Manager, RCC.

.242 Requests for refunds for optional-procedure mailings must be submitted to the General Manager, Rates and Classifications Center.

.25 Meters and Meter Stamps

.251 Postage Adjustments. The postage value of unused units set in a meter surrendered to the post office to be checked out of service may be refunded or, if desired, an equivalent amount will be transferred to another meter used by the same license holder. If the meter is withdrawn from service because of faulty mechanical operation, a final postage adjustment or refund may be withheld pending report of the meter manufacturer of the cause of faulty operation. If the meter is damaged by fire, a refund or transfer of postage will be made only if the registers are legible, or can be reconstructed by the meter manufacturer.

148 REVENUE DEFICIENCY

148.1 General. The term revenue deficiency refers to insufficient payment by a mailer or other postal customer of postage, fees, or box rent. For example, a deficiency may result from an incorrect setting of a postage meter by a post office employee; from an impermissible enclosure included in a second-class publication; or from sending mail matter at a rate lower than the specified rate. Revenue deficiencies are usually disclosed during the course of a postal inspector's audit or local financial examination. The postmaster renders the initial ruling to the customer. The ruling cites the amount of the deficiency and the circumstances involved.

148.2 Appeal of Ruling. A mailer may appeal any ruling assessing a revenue deficiency by filing an appeal within 15 days of its receipt, to the General Manager, Rates and Classification Center, for the post office of mailing. If the deficiency was assessed initially by the General Manager, Rates and Classifications Center, the mailer may appeal the ruling, within 15 days of its receipt, by filing a written appeal to the Director, Office of Classification and Rates Administration, Washington, D.C. 20260-5360. The mailer may be asked to furnish additional information or documents to support the appeal. Failure to furnish information or documents within 30 days of such a request will be grounds for denying an appeal. A final agency decision will be made as soon as practicable after receipt of the appeal and any necessary supporting documents.

149 INDEMNITY CLAIMS

149.1 Special Services With Indemnity Provisions

Indemnity claims may be filed for insured, COD, registered, or Express Mail. (See the International Mail Manual for international insured and registered mail indemnity claims. See 149.5 for Express Mail provisions.)

149.2 General Instructions for Filing Claims on Insured, COD, and Registered Mail

.21 Who May File. A claim for complete loss (wrapper and contents) of an insured article may be filed by the mailer or addressee. A claim for complete loss (wrapper and contents) of a COD or registered article may only be filed by the mailer. All claims for complete loss of contents, partial loss, or damage may be filed by the mailer or addressee.

.22 When to File

.221 General. Indemnity claims must be filed within one year from the date the article was mailed. Follow-up claims (duplicates, inquiries, etc.) must be filed no sooner than 45 days, nor later than six months from the date the original claim was filed. All appeals concerning

Postal Service claim decisions must be filed within three months of the original decision on the claim.

.222 Loss Claims

a. Insured and COD. The mailer may not file a claim until 30 days after the date of mailing for insured articles and 45 days after the date of mailing for COD articles. This includes articles sent as Express Mail COD shipments. Exceptions: Claims for loss must not be submitted until 45 days after the date of mailing for parcels sent by first-class (including priority), SAM or PAL mail, and until 75 days after the date of mailing for parcels sent by surface ocean transportation between:

(1) The contiguous 48 states and any state, territory or possession of the United States located outside the contiguous 48 states (including any location or unit having an APO or FPO designation as part of the address).

(2) Any state, territory or possession of the United States located outside the contiguous 48 states and any other state, territory or possession of the United States located outside the contiguous 48 states (including any location or unit having an APO or FPO designation as part of the address).

b. Registered. The customer may not file a claim involving loss until 15 days after the date of mailing in the case of domestic mail, or articles addressed to or mailed from an APO or FPO.

.223 Complete or Partial Loss of Contents. Damage or Rifling Claims. Claims for complete or partial loss of contents, damage, or alleged rifling must be filed immediately.

.23 Copies of Delivery Records. Customers may obtain copies of delivery records on numbered insured, COD, registered, and Express Mail shipments by sending a request to the post office of address. The request must include all mailing information such as article number, date mailed, names and addresses of mailer and addressee, and type of mailing (insured, COD, etc.). The fee is $5 for each copy of the delivery record requested and must be sent with the request.

.24 Required Information

.241 Evidence of Insurance, COD, or Registration

The customer must submit evidence that the article was an insured, COD or registered mailing. Acceptable evidence includes either:

a. The original mailing receipt issued at the time of mailing (reproduced copies are not acceptable); or

b. The wrapper, which must have the names and addresses of both the mailer and addressee and the appropriate mail endorsement indicating Postal Service handling as insured, COD, or registered mail. Note: Indemnity may be limited to $50 for insured; $10 for COD mail and $100 for registered mail if only the wrapper is submitted as evidence.

.242 Evidence of Value. The customer must submit evidence of value for all claims. All statements must be dated and signed by the maker. Acceptable evidence includes:

a. Sales receipt.

b. Invoice.

c. Statement of value from a reputable dealer.

d. Catalog value of a similar article.

e. Statement describing the article lost or damaged, including where purchased, date, amount and whether the article was new or used. If handmade, the price of material used and labor must be stated. The items must be described in sufficient detail for the Postal Data Center (PDC) to determine that the value claimed is accurate.

f. Paid repair bills, estimates of repair costs, or appraisals may be used instead of estimates of value in the case of claims for partial damage. When there is a possibility that the cost of repair exceeds actual value, other evidence of value may be required.

g. Statement of costs for duplication and premium for surety bond when the claim is for loss of securities or certificates of stock.

.25 Payable and Non-payable Claims

.251 Payable Claims. Subject to 149.252, insurance for loss or damage to registered, insured, or COD mail within the amount covered by the fee paid is payable for:

a. Lost articles based on their actual value at the time and place of mailing. Depreciation is deducted for used items.

b. Cost of repairing a damaged article or replacing a totally damaged article, not exceeding actual value of the article.

c. Remittance due on a COD parcel for which no remittance has been received by the mailer.

d. Death of bees, crickets or baby poultry due to physical damage to the package or delay for which the Postal Service is responsible. In the absence of definite evidence showing responsibility for death of bees, crickets or baby poultry, the Postal Service will be presumed to be at fault if 10 percent or more are dead on delivery, and indemnity will be paid for all dead bees, crickets or poultry; otherwise the Postal Service will not be presumed to be at fault (see 149.252k, 149.2521 and 124.63).

e. Costs incurred in duplicating or obtaining documents, or their original cost if they cannot be duplicated. These costs include:

(1) Cost of duplicating service.

(2) Notary fees.

(3) Bonding fees for replacement of stock or bond certificates.

(4) Reasonable attorney's fees, if actually required to replace the lost or damaged documents.

(5) Other direct and necessary expenses or costs, as determined by the Postal Service.

f. The extra cost of gift wrapping if the gift wrapped article was enclosed in another container for handling in the mail.

g. Cost of outer container if specially designed and constructed for goods sent.

h. The established fair market value of stamps and coins having philatelic or numismatic value, as determined by a recognized dealer of stamps or coins.

i. Federal, state or city sales tax paid on articles which are lost or totally damaged.

j. Postage (not fee) paid for sending damaged articles for repair. The Postal Service must be used for this purpose. Other reasonable transportation charges may be included if postal service is not available.

k. Photographic film and negatives will be compensated for only at the cost of the film stock. No indemnity will be paid for the content of the film, nor for the photographer's time and expenses in taking the photographs.

.252 Non-payable Claims. Payment will not be made in excess of the actual value of the article, or in excess of the maximum amount covered by the fee paid. Indemnity will not be paid in the following situations:

a. The article was not rightfully in the mail. This includes parcels and COD articles sent to addressees without their consent for purposes of sale or on approval.

b. The claim is filed more than one year from the date the article was mailed; the duplicate claim or inquiry is not initiated within six months of the original claim filing date; or the appeal of the Postal Service decision is not filed within three months of the date of the original decision.

c. Evidence of insurance coverage has not been presented.

d. Loss, rifling, or damage occurred after delivery by the Postal Service.

e. The claim is based on sentimental loss rather than actual value.

f. The claim is for replacement value, and such value exceeds the actual value at the time and place of mailing.

g. The loss resulted from delay of the mail.

h. The claim is for consequential loss rather than for the article itself.

i. The contents froze, melted, spoiled or deteriorated.

j. The damage consisted of abrasion, scarring, or scraping of suitcases, handbags and similar articles which were not properly wrapped for protection.

k. The death of baby poultry was due to shipment to points where delivery could not be made within 72 hours from the time of hatching.

l. The death of honeybees, crickets and harmless live animals was not the fault of the Postal Service (see 124.63).

m. A failure on the part of the second party (the addressee if the claim is filed by the mailer, or the mailer if the claim is filed by the addressee) to fully cooperate in the completion of the claim.

n. The article is so fragile as to prevent its safe carriage in the mails, regardless of packaging.

o. Personal compensation for time required to replace lost documents.

p. Damaged articles, mailing container and packaging were not submitted to the Postal Service for inspection.

q. The claim was submitted after the article had been transported outside of the mails by other carriers or by private conveyance.

r. The damage was caused by shock, transportation environment, or x-ray, and no evidence of damage to the mailing container exists.

s. The container and packaging were not submitted to the Postal Service for inspection on a partial or complete loss of contents claim.

t. The mail article or part or all of its contents were officially seized while in the military postal system overseas.

.26 Replacement Shipments. If a replacement shipment has been sent to a customer to replace the original article(s) lost, Replacement shipment must be indicated on the claim and a copy of the invoice evidencing the replacement must be attached to the claim form.

.27 Estimates, Appraisals and Depreciation

.271 If necessary, the article may be returned to the customer by the Postal Service so he may obtain an appraisal or estimate. Postal Service personnel must give and take receipts for damaged articles on Form 3831, Receipt for Articles Damaged in Mails. Important: The condition of the article must be noted on the receipt.

.272 The Postal Service depreciates a used article either lost or damaged based on the life expectancy of the article.

.28 Processing Claims

.281 Post Offices, Classified Stations and Branches

Post offices, classified stations and branches will:

a. Accept and process registered, insured and COD claims upon the presentation of the required information.

b. Assist customers in preparation of claim form.

c. Complete post office portion of the claim.

d. Route completed forms in accordance with the type of claim being processed.

.282 St. Louis PDC/Office of Mail Classification. The St. Louis PDC (or the Office of Classification and Rates Administration, USPS headquarters, at its discretion), will adjudicate and pay or disallow all claims.

.283 Appeals. Appeals are filed with the director of the St. Louis PDC. If the director of the PDC sustains the denial, the appeal may be forwarded to the director, Office of Classification and Rates Administration, USPS headquarters, for a final review and adjudication (see 149.81).

Insured and COD Claims

.31 How to File

.311 Required Forms. A customer may file a claim at any post office, classified branch, or station. Form 3812, Request for Payment of Domestic Postal Insurance, dated August 1977 or later, must be used to request payment for the loss or damage of insured mail. A claim has not been filed until a completed Form 3812 has been accepted by the Postal Service. The form is a four-part snap out set which includes two copies of Form 1510-A, Inquiry for the Loss or Rifling of Mail Matter, and one copy of Form 3841, Post Office Record of Claim. Do not complete a separate Form 1510 or Form 3841 for insured or COD claims.

.312 Evidence of Loss or Damage

a. Complete Loss Claims Filed by the Mailer. All mailers filing claims for complete loss of insured mail must provide proof that a loss has actually occurred before post offices will accept a claim for indemnity. This proof may be supplied by any one of the following methods:

(1) The mailer may obtain a claim form, Form 3812, Request For Payment of Domestic Postal Insurance, from any post office. The mailer must then complete the claim form and mail it to the addressee. Postal Service personnel will not mail the claim form for the mailer, but assistance in completing the form will be provided upon request. The addressee must complete Items 15 and 19 on the claim form and return it to the mailer. If the addressee has signed the claim form

and indicated the article was not received 30 days or more after the date of mailing, the mailer may then take the claim form, along with the original mailing receipt, to a post office and file the claim.

(2) If the mailer is unable to obtain the cooperation of the addressee in signing Form 3812 for numbered insured articles or, if he prefers, the mailer may send a check or money order for $5 to the post office of address and request a copy of the delivery record, provided 30 days or more have elapsed since the date of mailing. Such requests for delivery records must contain the date the article was mailed, the insurance number and the complete name and address of the mailer and addressee (see 149.23).

(3) If the mailer receives a notice from the post office of address that a delivery record is not on file, the mailer may take this notice and original mailing receipt to any post office and file a claim for loss. Post offices accepting such claims must attach a copy of the notice from the addressee post office to the Form 3812 claim set and send them to the St. Louis PDC for adjudication.

(4) If the mailer has written and signed documentation (such as a letter dated at least 30 days after the date of mailing) from the addressee stating the addressee did not receive the article, the mailer may take this documentation to a post office, along with the original mailing receipt, and file a claim. The Postal Service employee must attach this documentation, or a copy of it, to the claim form.

b. Complete Loss Claims Filed By The Addressee. An addressee may file a claim for the loss of an insured article if the addressee presents the following to the post office accepting the claim:

(1) The original mailing receipt. Copies of original mailing receipts are not acceptable.

(2) A Form 3812 that has been signed by the mailer and on which the mailer has designated the payee.

(3) Evidence of value.

Note: If the addressee does not have all of the above information, only the mailer will be allowed to file a claim for loss of an insured article.

c. Complete or Partial Loss of Contents. For complete or partial loss of contents claims, the container and packaging must be presented to the Postal Service for inspection when the claim is filed. Exception: The claimant may submit a Form 673, Report of Rifled Article, or a Form 3760, Parcel Search Request (which was received from the Postal Service), to file a claim.

d. Damage Claims. For damage claims, the article with the mailing container and packaging must be presented to the Postal Service for inspection at the time the claim is filed.

.32 Disposition of Damaged Article. (See 149.6.)

149.4 Registered Mail Claims

.41 Claim Filing Instructions

.411 Required Forms. Except for articles registered in conjunction with merchandise return service, a customer may file a claim at any post office, classified station or branch. Claims for articles registered in conjunction with merchandise return service may only be filed by the merchandise return permit holder and the claims must be filed only at the post office where the merchandise return permit is held. Form 565, Registered Mail Application For Indemnity/ Inquiry (May 1982 or later) must be used to file a claim for loss or damage of registered mail that was insured by the Postal Service. Do not complete a separate Form 1510-B or 3841-A for registered claims. A claim has not been filed until a completed Form 565 has been received by the Postal Service.

.42 Disposition of Damaged Article. (See 149.6.)

149.5 Express Mail Claims

.51 How to File

.511 Who May File. Claims for complete loss may be filed only by the mailer. Claims for damage or partial loss may be filed by either the mailer or the addressee. (See 295 and 296.)

.512 Required Forms. Claims for loss or damage filed by the mailer must be filed on Form 5690, Express Mail Application For Indemnity. A claim has not been filed until a completed Form 5690 has been accepted by the Postal Service.

.513 When to File

a. Loss Claims. All claims for loss may be filed no earlier than seven days following the date of mailing, 45 days after the date of mailing for articles with COD service. All claims must be filed not later than 90 days from the date of mailing.

b. Damage Claims. Claims for damage or partial loss should be filed immediately, but must be filed no later than 60 days from the date of mailing. Claims filed by the addressee must be returned to the post office of mailing for signature by the mailer, designation of the payee by the mailer, and inclusion of the customer receipt copy of the mailing label.

.514 Required Information

a. General. The mailer or addressee must present the damaged article and packaging at the post office when the claim is filed. The mailer must also provide the customer receipt copy of the mailing label at the time the claim is filed, or when the claim is returned from the post office of address for signature by the mailer. The customer receipt copy of the mailing label must be attached to the claim form at the time the claim is filed (see 296). If the article was sent Express Mail COD, the mailer must also provide the original COD receipt.

b. Merchandise and Document Reconstruction. In the event claims are required for both merchandise insurance and document reconstruction insurance on the same shipment, two Forms 5690 must be completed and processed. Complete documentation must be attached to each claim form, supporting the type of loss or damage claimed. The two claims must be submitted together.

.52 Disposition of Damaged Article. (See 149.6.)

.53 Adjudication. The St. Louis PDC (or the Office of Classification and Rates Administration, USPS headquarters, at its discretion) will adjudicate and pay or disallow all Express Mail claims.

149.6 Disposition of Damaged Articles

For a completely damaged article that will have little or no salvage value (such as smashed glassware), allow the customer to retain the article if he or she so desires; otherwise destroy it. If the completely damaged insured, COD or Express Mail article will have salvage value, retain it for 90 days, then forward it to your dead parcel branch (see 159.561b) on the next weekly dispatch. Use Form 3831, Receipt For Article(s) Damaged in Mails. If the customer's claim is denied, the article must be returned upon request. For registered mail damage claims, the article and the packaging must be retained and protected at the post office until released by notification from the St. Louis PDC.

149.7 Payment Conditions, Recovery of Articles, and Reimbursement

.71 Payment Conditions

.711 Insufficient Fee. If, through established error by the Postal Service, a fee was charged which was less than that required to cover the amount of insurance coverage requested at the time of mailing, the mailer may be permitted to pay the deficiency in fee. Indemnity may be paid within the limit fixed for the higher fee. This only applies to the insurance fee when the article is insured. An additional fee may not be paid to register an article previously insured or to increase the indemnity on the registered article.

.712 Loss or Total Damage. If the insured, registered or COD article was lost or the entire contents totally damaged, the payment will include an additional amount for the postage (not fee) paid by the mailer.

.713 Mailer and Addressee Claim Insurance. If both mailer and addressee claim insurance, they should decide between themselves who should receive payment. If no agreement is reached, payment will be made to the mailer, if a payment is due.

.714 Incompetent or Deceased Payee. If the payee is incompetent or deceased, payment will be made to the legal representative. If there is no legal representative, payment will be made to such relative or representative of the payee as is entitled to receive the amount due, in accordance with applicable state laws.

.72 Disposition of Recovered Article. When a lost registered, insured, COD or Express Mail article is recovered, the payee may accept the article and reimburse the Postal Service for the full amount paid if the article is undamaged, or for such other amount as may be determined by the director, Office of Classification and Rates Administration, USPS headquarters, if the article is damaged, has depreciated in value, or the contents are not intact.

.73 Reimbursements

.731 Reimbursement Tendered. If reimbursement is tendered representing an overpayment, erroneous or improper indemnity claim payment, or a voluntary indemnity refund, postal personnel will accept it and issue a receipt. Send all reimbursements to the St. Louis PDC, with all claim identifying information. Personal checks, money orders, or other negotiable instruments should be made payable to the Postal Service. If the instrument is made payable to the postmaster, he must sign his name and restrictively endorse it "pay to postal service" and remit as above. Do not mark any entry in the cashbook.

.732 Reimbursement Not Tendered. When an overpayment, erroneous or improper indemnity claim payment is disclosed and repayment is not tendered, report it to the director, St. Louis PDC, by memorandum, so it may be placed under accounts receivable control by the PDC.

149.8 Appeals and Postal Service Authority

.81 Appeals. All appeals of Postal Service claim decisions must be filed within three months of the date of the original decision. Appeals must be sent to: Postal Data Center, P.O. Box 80140, St. Louis, Mo. 63180-9140.

.82 Postal Service Authority. The requirements established in 149 may be waived in favor of the customer when the director, Office of Classification and Rates Administration, USPS headquarters, determines it is in the best interest of the Postal Service.

Duck and Savings Stamps

942 Nonpostal Stamps

942.1 Migratory Bird Hunting and Conservation Stamps

.11 Purpose. Migratory bird hunting and conservation stamps are required by federal law to hunt migratory birds, such as ducks, geese, etc. Post offices act as agents of the Federal Government in selling these stamps to provide a convenient location for purchasing them.

.12 Where Sold. Migratory bird hunting and conservation stamps are sold at all post offices in CAGs A-G, and at certain designated offices in CAGs K and L where there is a demand for them. A current migratory bird poster will be displayed in the lobby.

.13 Price. Migratory bird hunting and conservation stamps cost $10 each.

.14 Instructions on Administration of Hunting Laws. Postal employees will not instruct purchasers of migratory bird hunting and conservation stamps on matters relating to administration of hunting laws. Inquiries should be directed to the Fish and Wildlife Service, Washington, D.C. 20240-001, or local game wardens.

.15 Redemption from Public. Blocks composed of two or more attached unused stamps, sold on consignment to any person but not resold, may be redeemed at any time on or before the last day of the stamp year. Stamps validated by signature or stamps which appear to have been removed from a hunting license or identification card will not be accepted.

.16 Accounting for Stamps. Receipt to evidence payment must not be issued if stamps are not available. Money from sales must be treated as postal funds. Refunds must be made from postal funds, and redeemed stock must be treated as nonsalable.

.2 United States Savings Stamps. Post offices no longer redeem U.S. savings stamps posted in albums, previously acceptable as postal funds. Refer holders to a Federal Reserve Bank or branch, or advise holders to mail albums at their own risk to the Bureau of Public Debt, Parkersburg, W.Va. 26106-1328.

Mail Classification and Rates

The *Domestic Mail Manual* provides detailed instructions for the proper classification of mail matter, and the computation of postage rates. Familiarity with the regulations can often avoid repacking and needless expense.

The information given here is current through March 19, 1989. Additional changes in some rates may occur, and postal patrons should watch for further announcements.

First Class

First-class mail consists of mailable postal cards, postcards, most matter wholly or partially in writing or typewriting (except authorized additions to second-, third-, and fourth-class mail and acceptable written or typewritten matter listed in the manual), matter closed against inspection, bills and statements of account, and matter having the character of actual and personal correspondence.

Postal Cards: A postal card is a card supplied by the Postal Service with a postage stamp printed or impressed on it, for the transmission of messages. A double-reply postal card consists of two attached cards, one of which may be detached by the receiver and returned by mail as a reply. Each card has a printed impressed postage stamp of the first-class postcard rate.

Postcards: Postcards are privately printed mailing cards for the transmission of messages. A double postcard consists of two attached postcards, one of which may be detached by the receiver and returned by mail as a reply. Each card is subject to the first-class card rate. However, postage need not be paid on the reply portion until it is detached and mailed as a reply. The paper or card stock used for single and double postcards may be of any light color that does not prevent legible addresses and postmarks from being placed thereon. Brilliant colors must not be used. Single postcards and each part of double postcards must conform to the following specifications to qualify for mailing at the card rate:

a. Postcards may not be smaller than 3 1/2 by 5 inches or larger than the size fixed by the Convention of the Universal Postal Union in effect (currently 4 1/4 by 6 inches).

b. Postcards must be rectangular in shape, and of approximately the same form, quality and weight as postal cards.

c. A postcard must be made of an unfolded and uncreased piece of paper or card stock of approximately the quality and weight of a postal card. The thickness must be uniform and not less than 0.007 of an inch thick.

Standards: The following minimum size standards apply to first-class mail:

a. All mailing pieces must be at least 0.007 of an inch thick.

b. All mailing pieces that are 1/4 of an inch thick or less must be: rectangular in shape; at least 3 1/2 inches high; and at least 5 inches long.

NOTE: First-class mailing pieces that do not meet the minimum size standards are prohibited from the mails.

To insure prompt and efficient processing of first-class mail, it is recommended that all envelopes, cards and self-mailers have an aspect ratio of width (height) to length between 1 to 1.3 and 1 to 2.5 inclusive, and be sealed or secured on all four edges so that they can be handled by machines.

Size Limits: First-class mail weighing one ounce or less is non-standard if it exceeds any of the following size limits:

a. Its length exceeds 11 1/2 inches, or

b. Its height exceed 6 1/8 inches, or

c. Its thickness exceeds 1/4 of an inch, or

d. Its aspect ratio (length divided by height) does not fall between 1 to 1.3 and 1 to 2.5 inclusive.

Non-standard mail often results in delays or damage to mail because it does not lend itself to machine processing. For this reason, mailers are encouraged to avoid mailing non-standard first-class mail. A surcharge of 10¢ is assessed on each piece of non-standard first-class mail.

Second Class

Second-class mail matter includes printed publications issued at least four times annually, at regular intervals. The purpose must be the dissemination of information, and there must be a legitimate subscribers list. The publication must be issued from a "known office of publication," and second-class original entry authorization must be obtained at the post office serving the known office of publication.

Publications not entitled to second-class rates include those primarily for advertising purposes, and those circulated free or at a nominal charge. Some exceptions are made for special groups.

A special classification, with finite qualifications and requirements, exists for "controlled circulation" publications, restricted to use by qualified mailers, and subject to its own schedule of rates and fees.

Special application must be made for permission to use second-class rates.

Third Class

The *Domestic Mail Manual* defines third-class matter as material that is "not mailed or required to be mailed as first-class mail; not entered as second-class mail; and less than 16 ounces in weight."

This includes circulars sent in identical terms to several persons, and printed matter weighing less than 16 ounces.

There is a rate for single pieces, and also a bulk rate covering mailings of identical pieces weighing not less than 50 pounds, or encompassing at least 200 pieces; only the size and weight must be the same to qualify as "identical."

The same size standards and restrictions apply to third-class mail as those previously outlined for first-class mail, with the exception of keys and identification devices sent through the mail.

Special rates are authorized for certain types of organizations.

Fourth Class

Fourth-class mail consists of mailable matter not mailed or required to be mailed as first-class mail; weighing 16 ounces or more (except special or library rate fourth-class); and not entered as second-class mail (except as specifically provided for transient rate matter).

A zone system based upon the distance between the point of mailing and the destination is used in computing rates. Special rates are provided for catalogs and similar advertising matter, books and similar educational materials, and materials mailed by libraries.

There are specific size and weight limits for fourth-class matter. Parcels mailed between first-class offices are limited to 40 pounds or a total of 84 inches in length and girth combined; parcels mailed under other circumstances are limited to 70 pounds or a combined measurement of 100 inches.

The larger limits are enforced for rural and star routes; military post offices and those in Alaska, Hawaii, Puerto Rico, and the Trust Territory of the Pacific Islands; official mail; and specified materials including educational items and library mailings.

The regulations specify what may be enclosed with fourth-class mailings.

Express Mail

This is a type of "guaranteed" rapid delivery system between major U.S. cities, with a widely varied rate schedule. At least one form of Express Mail guarantees articles received by 5 p.m. (or other deadline time as established by any individual office) at a postal facility offering Express Mail service will be delivered by 3 p.m. the next day or the shipment can be picked up as early as 10 a.m. the next business day. Rates include insurance, shipment receipt, and record of delivery at the destination post office. Express Mail service is available for any mailable articles up to 70 lbs. The Postal Service will refund, upon application to originating office, the postage for any Express Mail shipments not meeting the service standard except for those delayed by strike or work stoppage.

The program now includes a 100 percent refund of postage and fees if shipment is not delivered within 25 hours; use of official mail indicia for government agencies; and liability insurance.

There are four major types of Express Mail services: (1) Customer designed

Service — a courier-type service custom tailored to the users' requirements for specific pick-up and delivery times; (2) International service — offers overnight and second-day delivery to different countries with which reciprocal Express Mail service has been arranged; (3) Next day service — is an overnight system for delivery of shipments mailed at selected post offices; and (4) Same day airport service — offers dispatch on the next available flight between designated airport mail facilities. The Postal Service maintains the full rate and weight limitation tables. For further information, contact your local post office.

Special Handling

For preferential handling in dispatch and transportation of third- and fourth-class mail, the special handling service is provided. This service does not provide special delivery. The fee for pieces up to and including 10 pounds in weight is $1.55, and for more than 10 pounds, $2.25. The fees are in addition to the postage fees incurred.

Special Delivery

Special delivery means an item of mail is delivered as soon as practicable after it arrives at the addressee's post office. It virtually assures delivery on the day received at the post office but generally does not speed up the transportation time to that point from the origin. The special delivery fee is in addition to the regular postage. The basic first-class fee for a piece not weighing more than 2 pounds is $5.35, over two pounds and less than 10, $5.75. Pieces weighing more than 10 pounds are charged $7.25. All other classes of mail are charged $5.65, $6.50 and $8.10, respectively.

Money Orders

Postal money orders provide for sending money through the mail safely with money notes rather than cash. Fees are 75¢ for domestic money orders up to $35; and $1 for money orders from $35.01 to the $700 maximum. They may be purchased and redeemed at any post office. Domestic U.S. money orders are authorized for payment in U.S. and Canadian post offices and banks.

International money orders can be purchased in amounts up to $700 at all larger first-class post offices. Maximum limit may be lower to some countries. Such money orders are available to countries that accept such orders by mutual or intermediary agreements.

Insurance Fees

Third-class and fourth-class mail may be insured for protection against loss or damage. Also, first-class mail that contains third- or fourth-class matter may be insured, and should be endorsed "Third-" or "Fourth-Class Mail Enclosed," along with the first-class or priority mail endorsement. Liability for insured mail is limited to $500, and the fee schedule is as follows:

Liability	Fee
$0.01 to $50	$0.70
$50.01 to $100	$1.50
$100.01 to $150	$1.90
$150.01 to $200	$2.20
$200.01 to $300	$3.15
$300.01 to $400	$4.30
$400.01 to $500	$5.00

Certified Mail

Certified mail service provides for a record of delivery to be maintained by the post office from which delivered. The carrier delivering the item obtains a signature from the addressee on a receipt form that is kept for two years. The charge for certified mail is 85¢. It is primarily for first-class items that have no money value; there is no insurance feature.

Certified mail may be deposited in a collection box if the mailer has attached a "certified mail" sticker and appropriate postage and fees.

Registered Mail

Domestic first-class or priority mail may be registered with indemnity limit of $25,000. It is offered for the protection of valuable papers, stamps, jewelry and other items of value. Registered mail provides for a receipt to the customer at the time of mailing and a post office record of the mailing.

Registered mail is accounted for by number from time of mailing to delivery and is transported separately from other mail under lock. The registry fees, in addition to first-class postage, are scaled according to declared value of mail. Minimum fee is $4.50; the full fee schedule may be obtained at any post office. Registered mail may not be deposited in collection boxes because a receipt must be issued at point of mailing.

Additional Services

COD Mail — First-class, third-class and fourth-class mail may be sent COD, which provides the post office to Collect On Delivery the price of the item delivered and return payment to sender by money order. The fee schedule for this service varies according to the value to be collected, as well as the value for which an item is insured. Liability does not exceed $500. Payment and fee schedules are available from the local post office. A combination of registration and COD is also available, with various combined fees.

Return Receipt — Return receipts furnish the mailer with evidence of delivery, and are obtainable for mail that is sent COD, is minimally insured, or that is registered or certified. If requested at the time of mailing, the fee is $1 for a receipt showing signature and date of delivery, or $1.35 for a receipt showing signature, date and place of delivery. If requested after mailing, the fee is $5.

Restricted Delivery — Restricted delivery is a service by which a mailer may direct that delivery be made only to the addressee or to an agent for the addressee when specifically authorized in writing by the addressee to receive his or her mail, and may be obtained for COD mail, insured mail, registered or certified mail. In addition to postage and other fees, the restricted delivery fee is $2.

Chapter 8

U.S. First Days

United States Stamps

Day by Day

With the launching of a new regular postage series late in 1922 the United States Post Office Department established a policy of issuing new stamps on specific dates and at places appropriate to their subjects. This policy, which has been continued by the U.S. Postal Service, brought the first-day cover into the philatelic picture, adding a new facet to the avocation of stamp collecting.

Since this policy was implemented Oct. 4, 1922 with an 11¢ stamp (Scott 563) featuring the portrait of Rutherford B. Hayes, released at Fremont, Ohio, to mark the birth centenary of this former president, more than 2,000 varieties of U.S. stamps have made their debut on 336 different days of the year. The only dates since late 1922 when one or more varieties of U.S. stamps haven't had first days are:

January 7, 21, 22, 28, 31
February 9, 19, 21
March 17, 27
April 15
May 12
September 13
October 3, 25
November 8, 27, 28
December 4, 13, 14, 16, 18, 19, 22, 23, 24, 25, 26

Because holiday mailings tax the facilities of the United States Postal Service during December, the USPS tries to avoid releasing new stamps during that month. Consequently, December has more "stampless" days than any of the other months of the year.

The following "day-by-day" listing of first days covers only adhesive postage stamps issued since Oct. 4, 1922. A good many earlier U.S. stamps are known to have made their first appearances on specific dates (a fact usually established by postmarks), but it seems appropriate to limit this listing to those adhesives for which an "official" date of issue exists as a result of a postal service policy.

The listing, by months and Scott catalog numbers (shown in parentheses), through 1988, follows:

January

1. Washington Bicentennial series (704-15) 1932
   13¢ (three) Spirit of 1776 (1629-31) 1976
2. 3¢ Betsy Ross (1004) 1952
   26¢ Mount Rushmore airpost (C88) 1974
   25¢, 31¢ International airmail (C89-C90) 1976
3. 3¢ American Banker's Association (987) 1950
   7¢ Alaska Statehood (C53) 1959
   13¢ Washington at Princeton (1704) 1977
   20¢ Alaska Statehood (2065) 1984
   22¢ Arkansas Statehood (2167) 1986
4. 3¢ Columbia University (1029) 1954
   10¢ ZIP Code (1511) 1974
   15¢ Everett M. Dirksen (1874) 1981
5. 3¢ George Washington Carver (953) 1948
   10¢ Star Runway airmail, sheet and coil (C72-C73) 1968
6. 4¢ New Mexico Statehood (1191) 1962
   13¢ Carl Sandburg (1731) 1978
   20¢ Winter Olympics block (2067-70) 1984
   22¢ Georgia Statehood (2339) 1988
7. Not a first day to date
8. 5¢ Battle of New Orleans (1261) 1965
   20¢ Bighorn booklet (1949) 1982
9. 5¢ American Flag (1208) 1963
   22¢ Connecticut (2340) 1988
10. 7¢ Woodrow Wilson (1040) 1956
    5¢ Sam Houston (1242) 1964
    22¢ Winter Olympics (2369) 1988
11. 13¢ Benjamin Harrison (622) 1926
    4¢ Patrick Henry Credo (1144) 1961
    3¢ Alexander Hamilton (1086) 1967

18¢ Statue of Liberty airmail (C87) 1974
13¢ Indian Head Cent (1734) 1978
25¢ Jack London, sheet (2183) 1986
12. 1¢ Thomas Jefferson (1278) 1968
15¢ Robert F. Kennedy (1770) 1979
20¢ Ralph Bunche (1860) 1982
1¢-$5 Official Mail (O127-35) 1983
20¢ FDIC (2071) 1984
13. 15¢ Statue of Liberty airmail (C63) 1961
15¢ Martin Luther King Jr. (1771) 1979
14. 2¢ Allied Nations (907) 1943
15. 2¢ George Washington (554) 1923
4¢ Martha Washington (556) 1923
9¢ Thomas Jefferson (561) 1923
10¢ James Monroe (562) 1923
2¢ Army (786), 2¢ Navy (791) 1937
5¢ DC-4 Skymaster airmail (C37) 1948
3¢ 4-H Clubs (1005) 1952
3¢ Pennsylvania Academy (1064) 1955
3¢ Polio (1087) 1957
13¢ Crazy Horse (1855) 1982
16. 1¢ Benjamin Franklin (552) 1923
2¢ General Pulaski (690) 1931
6¢ Beautification (1365-68) 1969
17. 2¢ Washington coil, sidewise (599) 1923
3¢ Benjamin Franklin (1073) 1956
13¢ INTERPHIL '76 (1632) 1976
18. 6¢ DC-4 Skymaster airmail (C39) 1949
19. 6¢ America's Wool (1423) 1971
20¢ Science and Industry (2031) 1983
20. Presidential coils, sidewise (839-47) 1939
4¢ George Washington Credo (1139) 1960
13¢ (two) Capt. Cook (1732, 1732a, 1733) 1978
21. Not a first day to date
22. Not a first day to date
23. 18¢ Dr. Elizabeth Blackwell (1399) 1974
22¢ Jerome Kern (2110) 1985
22¢ Stamp Collecting booklet (2198-2201) 1986
24. 3¢ California Gold Discovery (954) 1948
8.5¢ Tow Truck (2129) 1987
25. 20¢ Map and Planes airmail (C9) 1927
2¢ Lake Placid Olympics (716) 1932
7¢ Abraham Baldwin (1850) 1985
26. 4¢, 8¢ Mahatma Gandhi, Champion of Liberty (1174-75) 1961
6¢ Douglas MacArthur (1424) 1971
8¢ Love (1475) 1973
37¢ Robert Millikan (1866) 1982
20¢ Harry S. Truman (1862) 1984
22¢ Michigan Statehood (2246) 1987
22¢ Australia Bicentennial (2370) 1988
27. Presidential coils, endwise (848-51) 1939
3¢ Samuel Gompers (988) 1950
28. Not a first day to date
29. 1¢ Washington Irving (859) 1940
2¢ James Fenimore Cooper (860) 1940
6¢ Franklin D. Roosevelt (1284) 1966
40¢ General George Marshall (1292) 1968
15¢ W.C. Fields (1803) 1980
22¢ Pan-American Games (2247) 1987
30. 5¢ Franklin D. Roosevelt (933) 1946
1 1/4¢ Albert Gallatin (1279) 1967
15¢ Whitney Moore Young (1875) 1981
20¢ Franklin Roosevelt (1950) 1982
22¢ Love (2202) 1986
22¢ Love (2248) 1987
31. 20¢ Love (2072) 1984

February

1. 13¢ Harriet Tubman (1744) 1978
15¢ (four) Winter Olympics (1795-98) 1980
20¢ Love (1951) 1982
20¢ Carter G. Woodson (2073) 1984
22¢ D-series sheet, coil & booklet (2111-13) 1985
2. 4¢ Range Conservation (1176) 1961
22¢ James Weldon Johnson (2371) 1988
3. 3¢ Lincoln, rotary (635) 1927
10¢ James Monroe, rotary (642) 1927
4¢ Horace Greeley (1177) 1961
8¢ Sidney Lanier (1446) 1972
11¢ Caboose (1905) 1984
4. 22¢ Sojourner Truth (2203) 1986
14¢ D Official (O138) 1985
22¢ Cats (2372-75) 1988
5. 3¢ Ralph Waldo Emerson (861) 1940
5¢ Louisa M. Alcott (862) 1940
6. 20¢ Soil to Water Conservation (2074) 1984

7.1¢ Tractor (2127) 1987
22¢ Massachusetts Statehood (2341) 1988
7. 15¢ (five) Windmills (1738-42) 1980
8. 4¢ Boy Scout Jubilee (1145) 1960
9. Not a first day to date
10. 5¢ Winged Globe airmail (C12) 1930
National Stamp Exhibition souvenir sheet of six 3¢ Byrd (735) 1934
16¢ Airmail Special Delivery bicolor (CE2) 1936
8¢ Pamphleteer (1476) 1973
10¢ Benjamin West (1553) 1975
20¢ Credit Union (2075) 1984
11. 3¢ Thomas Edison (945) 1947
3¢ Coast & Geodetic Survey (1088) 1957
8¢ Peace Corps (1447) 1972
12. 3¢ Abraham Lincoln (555) 1923
$1 Lincoln Memorial (571) 1923
3¢ Gen. Oglethorpe (726) 1933
1¢ Four Freedoms (908) 1943
3¢ Land Grant Colleges (1065) 1955
1¢ Lincoln Centennial (1113) 1959
6¢ Illinois Statehood (1339) 1968
14¢ Julia Ward Howe (2177) 1977
11¢ Alden Partridge (1854) 1985
13. 10¢ Map and Planes airmail (C7) 1926
10¢ Samuel Clemens (863) 1940
33¢ Alfred Verville airmail (C113) 1985
39¢ Sperry (C114) 1985
14. 4¢ Oregon Statehood Centennial (1124) 1959
4¢ Arizona Statehood (1192) 1962
25¢ Frederick Douglass (1290) 1967
15. 20¢, 50¢ China Clipper airmail (C21-C22) 1937
5¢ Physical Fitness (1262) 1965
15¢ International Year of the Child (1772) 1979
15¢ Benjamin Banneker (1804) 1980
44¢ Transpacific airmail (C115) 1985
22¢ Maryland (2342) 1988
16. 1¢ James Wadsworth Longfellow (864) 1940
2¢ John Greenleaf Whittier (865) 1940
17. 5.9¢ Bicycle (1901) 1982
18. 3¢ Army (787), 3¢ Navy (792) 1937
3¢ San Francisco Exposition (852) 1939
4¢ Winter Olympics (1146) 1960
19. Not a first day to date
20. 3¢ James Russell Lowell (866) 1940
5¢ Walt Whitman (867) 1940
4¢ Project Mercury (1193) 1962
22¢ Jean Baptiste Pointe du Sable (2249) 1987
21. Not a first day to date
22. 1 1/2¢ Mount Vernon (1032) 1956
5¢ George Washington (1283) 1966
20¢ George Washington (1952) 1982
50¢ Chester Nimitz (1869) 1985
23. 3¢ National Guard (1017) 1953
8¢ Rotary International (1066) 1955
3¢ Architects (1089) 1957
13¢ (50) State Flags (1633-82) 1976
24. 10¢ James Whitcomb Riley (868) 1940
40¢ Lillian Gilbreth (1868) 1984
25. 2¢ George Rogers Clark (651) 1929
4¢, 8¢ San Martin Champion of Liberty (1125-26) 1959
15¢ (six) National Letter Writing (1805-10) 1980
26. 3¢ Merchant Marine (939) 1946
27. 3¢ Lincoln Sesquicentennial (1114) 1959
15¢ John Steinbeck (1773) 1979
5¢ Hugo Black (2172) 1985
22¢ Enrico Caruso (2250) 1987
28. 3¢ B.&O. Railroad (1006) 1952
8¢ George Gershwin (1484) 1973
10¢ Pioneer Jupiter (1556) 1975
2¢ Mary Lyon (2169) 1987
29. 3¢ Conestoga Wagon (2252) 1988

March

1. 8¢ Yellowstone Park Centenary (1453) 1972
2. 3¢ Texas Centennial (776) 1936
3¢ Ohio Sesquicentennial (1018) 1953
3¢ Washington Territory (1019) 1953
22¢ Republic of Texas (2204) 1986
3. 3¢ Florida Statehood (927) 1945
3¢ Minnesota Territory (981) 1949
4. 5¢ Roosevelt coil, sidewise (602) 1924
3¢ Vermont Sesquicentennial (903) 1941
3¢ American Automobile Association (1007) 1952
15¢ Albert Einstein (1774) 1979
22¢ Mary McLeod Bethune (2137)
5. 5¢ Theodore Roosevelt (602) 1924
9¢ Americana coil (1616) 1976
20¢ Orchid block (2076-79) 1984
6. 1¢ Americana coil (1811) 1980
2¢ Re-engraved Locomotive (2226) 1987

7. 4¢, 8¢ Masaryk Champion of Liberty (1147-48) 1960
8. 15¢ Justice Oliver Wendell Holmes (1288) 1968
   13¢ (four) American Quilts (1745-48) 1978
9. 22¢ Knute Rockne (2376) 1988
10. 13¢ Telephone Centenary (1683) 1976
11. 10¢ Veterans of Foreign Wars (1525) 1974
   13¢ (seven), 9¢ (one) booklet pane (1590 9¢, 1623, 1623a) 1977
12. 6¢ Blood Donors (1425) 1971
   20¢ Hawaii Statehood (2080) 1984
   22¢ Girl Scouts (2251) 1987
13. 10¢ Collective Bargaining (1558) 1975
14. 1¢ Horace Mann, 2¢ Mark Hopkins (869-70) 1940
   8¢ Albert Einstein (1285) 1966
15. Farley Special Printings (752-71) 1935
   3¢ Gardening/Horticulture (1100) 1958
   10¢ Andrew Jackson (1286) 1967
   6¢ American Legion (1369) 1969
   "B" (18¢) sheet, coil, booklet (1818-20) 1981
16. 4 1/2¢ The Hermitage (1037) 1959
   5¢ Migratory Bird Treaty (1306) 1966
17. Not a first day to date
18. 8¢ Family Planning (1455) 1972
19. 1 1/2¢ Harding, profile (553) 1925
   1 1/2¢ Harding, perf 10 rotary (582) 1925
   1 1/2¢ Harding coil, sidewise (598) 1925
   5¢ Charles M. Russell (1243) 1964
   13¢ Commercial Aviation (1684) 1976
   $2 William Jennings Bryan (2195) 1986
20. 12¢ Grover Cleveland (564) 1923
   30¢ Buffalo (569) 1923
   $2 U.S. Capitol (572) 1923
   $5 Head of Freedom Statue (573) 1923
   1¢ Franklin, imperf (575) 1923
21. 8¢ Tri-motored Plane airmail (C26) 1944
   5.2¢ Sleigh (1900) 1983
   14¢ Sinclair Lewis (1856) 1985
   22¢ Fish booklet (2205-09) 1986
22. 8¢ Statue of Liberty (1042) 1958
   1¢ Andrew Jackson (1209) 1963
   22¢ Decoys (2138-41) 1985
   25¢ E-Series sheet coil & booklet (2277, 2279, 2282) 1988
   25¢ E-Series official (O140) 1988
23. 3¢ Maryland Tercentenary (736) 1934
   4¢ Army (788), 4¢ Navy (793) 1937
   13¢ Sound Recording (1705) 1977
   14¢ Iceboat (2134) 1985
24. 5¢ Roosevelt, perf 11 by 10 1/2 (637) 1927
   7¢ McKinley, perf 11 by 10 1/2 (639) 1927
   20¢ U.S.-Sweden (2036) 1983
25. 8¢, 10¢, 10¢, 18¢ Contributors to the Cause series (1559-62) 1975
   22¢ Winter Special Olympics (2142) 1985
26. 5¢ DC-4 Skymaster airmail (C33) 1947
   80¢ Diamond Head airmail (C46) 1952
   10¢ Robert Frost (1526) 1974
   10.9¢ Hansom Cab (1904) 1982
27. Not a first day to date
28. 3¢ Charles Eliot (871) 1940
   5¢ Frances E. Willard (872) 1940
29. 25¢ (two) Octave Chanute airmail (C93-C94) 1979
   22¢ Flag over Capitol sheet, coil and booklet (2114-16) 1985
   44¢ New Sweden airmail (C117) 1988
30. 4¢ Malaria Eradication (1194) 1962
   8¢ Alaska Statehood (C70) 1967
   6¢ Hemisfair (1340) 1968
31. 4¢ Benjamin Franklin Credo (1140) 1960
   16¢ Americana (Liberty) regular and coil (1599, 1619) 1978
   20¢ Balloons (2032-35) 1983

April

1. 3¢ New York World's Fair (853) 1939
   4¢ North Atlantic Treaty (1127) 1959
   5¢ Crusade Against Cancer (1263) 1965
2. 13¢ booklet pane, "Stamp Collecting" label (1595d) 1976
   12¢ Stanley Steamer (2132) 1985
3. 3¢ Pony Express (894) 1940
4. 1/2¢ Nathan Hale, flat plate (551) 1925
   1 1/2¢ Harding, imperf (576) 1925
   4¢ Martha Washington, perf 10 rotary (585) 1925
   5¢ Roosevelt, perf 10 rotary (586) 1925
   6¢ Garfield, perf 10 rotary (587) 1925
   1¢, 2¢, 5¢ Lexington-Concord series (617-19) 1925

3¢ North Atlantic Treaty Organization (1008) 1952
$1 Airlift (1341) 1968
10¢ Mariner 10 (1557) 1975
22¢ Shells booklet (2117-21) 1985

5. 3¢ Booker T. Washington (1074) 1956
2¢ Cape Hatteras block (1448-51) 1972
20¢ Civilian Conservation Corps (2037) 1983
6. 4¢ Arctic Exploration (1128) 1959
5¢ Carolina Charter (1230) 1963
13¢ Chemistry (1685) 1976
7. 10¢ Booker T. Washington (873) 1940
3¢ Mississippi Territory (955) 1948
4¢ World Refugee Year (1149) 1960
4¢ Shiloh (1179) 1962
7.4¢ Baby Buggy (1902) 1984
8. 2¢ Massachusetts Bay Colony (682) 1930
1¢ John James Audubon (874) 1940
2¢ Dr. Crawford W. Long (875) 1940
12¢ Americana sheet (1594), coil (1816) 1981
40¢ Summer Olympics (C105-08) 1983
9. 8¢ Statue of Liberty, flat plate (1041) 1954
5¢ Appomattox (1182) 1965
5¢ Humane Treatment of Animals (1307) 1966
10. 2¢ Carolina-Charleston (683) 1930
3¢ Joseph Pulitzer (946) 1947
15¢ Frances Perkins (1821) 1980
11. 15¢ Special Delivery (E13) 1925
4¢ Charles Evans Hughes (1195) 1962
22¢ Public Hospitals (2210) 1986
10¢ Canal Boat (2257) 1987
12. 3¢ Washington & Lee University (982) 1949
4¢ Fort Sumter (1178) 1961
13. 20¢ Monticello (1047) 1956
8¢ Posting a Broadside (1477) 1973
13¢ (four) Pueblo Indian Pottery (1706-09) 1977
20¢ Joseph Priestley (2038) 1983
14. 3¢ Pan American Union (895) 1940
29¢ Americana (Lighthouse) (1605) 1978
20¢ (50) State Birds & Flowers (1953-2002) 1982
15. Not a first day to date
16. 5¢ Indiana Statehood (1308) 1966
20¢ National Archives (2081) 1984
17. 3¢ Luther Burbank (876) 1940
5¢ Dr. Walter Reed (877) 1940
3¢ Brussels Fair (1104) 1958
5¢ National Grange (1323) 1967
22¢ Love (2143) 1985
18. 25¢ Paul Revere (1048) 1958
4¢ Water Conservation (1150) 1960
10¢ EXPO '74 (1527) 1974
10.1¢ Oil Wagon (2130) 1985
12.5¢ Push Cart (2133) 1985
19. 65¢, $1.30, $2.60 Graf Zeppelin airmail (C13-C15) 1930
3¢ Newburgh Peace (727) 1933
10¢ Lexington-Concord (1563) 1975
15¢ (four) Pennsylvania Toleware (1775-78) 1979
20. 3¢ Statue of Freedom (989) 1950
8¢ World Trade (1129) 1959
20¢ U.S.-Netherlands (2003) 1982
20¢ Volunteerism (2039) 1983
20¢ Special Occasions (2267-74) 1987
21. 20¢ Library of Congress (2004) 1982
22. 2¢ Arbor Day (717) 1932
25¢ Abraham Lincoln airmail (C59) 1960
5¢ New York World's Fair (1244) 1964
23. 8¢ Copernicus (1488) 1973
7.9¢ bulk rate coil (1615) 1976
18¢ (four) Flowers (1876-79) 1981
22¢ John Audubon (1863) 1985
24. 14¢ Fiorello LaGuardia (1397) 1972
18¢ Flag sheet, coil booklet (1890-93) 1981
25. 1¢ Presidential (Washington) (804) 1938
5¢ United Nations Conference (928) 1945
4¢ Seattle World's Fair (1196) 1962
26. 3¢ Charter Oak (772) 1935
10¢ Jane Addams (878) 1940
20¢ Columbia Jays airmail (C71) 1967
13¢ (four) American Dance (1749-52) 1978
27. 3¢ Puerto Rico Election (983) 1949
20¢ Consumer Education (2005) 1982
28. FIPEX souvenir sheet (1075) 1956
3¢ James Monroe (1105) 1958
22¢ United Way (2275) 1987
29. 3¢ Railroad Engineers (993) 1950
5¢ John Muir (1245) 1964
20¢ Worlds Fair (2006-09) 1982
20¢ U.S.-Germany (2040) 1983

$10.75 Express Mail booklet (2122) 1985
22¢ Duke Ellington (2211) 1986
25¢ Pheasant booklet (2283) 1988
30. 3¢ Washington Inauguration (854) 1939
3¢ Louisiana Purchase (1020) 1953
3¢ FIPEX commemorative (1076) 1956
4¢ Louisiana Statehood (1197) 1962
8¢ Postal People (1489-98) 1973
20¢ Horatio Alger (2010) 1982

May

1. 7¢ William McKinley (559) 1923
8¢ Ulysses S. Grant (560) 1923
14¢ American Indian (565) 1923
20¢ Golden Gate (567) 1923
1¢, 2¢, 5¢ Huguenot-Walloon series (614-16) 1924
State overprints (658-79) 1929
6¢ Support Our Youth (1342) 1968
6¢ Grandma Moses (1370) 1969
10¢ Paul Laurence Dunbar (1554) 1975
18¢ Red Cross (1910) 1981
2. 3¢ Mother's Day (737-38) 1934
5¢ American Circus (1309) 1966
3. 1¢ Stephen Foster (879) 1940
2¢ John Philip Sousa (880) 1940
15¢ Montgomery Blair (C66) 1963
11¢ City of Refuge (C84) 1972
25¢ Jack London booklet 1988
4. 3¢ Rhode Island Tercentenary (777) 1936
10¢ Horse Racing (1528) 1974
13¢ French Alliance (1753) 1978
20¢ Summer Olympics block (2082-85) 1984
5. 1 1/2¢ Martha Washington (805) 1938
3¢ Wild Turkey (1077) 1956
5¢ Battle of the Wilderness (1181) 1964
6¢ Apollo 8 (1371) 1969
20¢ Brooklyn Bridge (2041) 1983
6. 6¢ (four) Natural History (1387-90) 1970
6¢ Tricycle (2126) 1985
25¢ Flag With Cloud sheet (2278) 1988
7. 3¢ Nebraska Territory (1060) 1954
16¢ Ernie Pyle (1398) 1971
11¢ Jetliner sheet and coil (C78, C82) 1971
18¢ George Mason (1858) 1981
8. 8¢ Missouri Statehood (1426) 1971
8¢ Harry Truman Memorial (1499) 1973
18¢ Savings and Loans (1911) 1981
9. 1 1/2¢ Harding coil, endwise (605) 1925
3¢ (four) TIPEX souvenir sheet (778) 1936
3¢ Honorable Discharge Emblem (940) 1946
22¢ Flag With Fireworks sheet (2276) 1987
10. 3¢ Lincoln coil, sidewise (600) 1924
2¢ Sesquicentennial Exposition (627) 1926
3¢ Transcontinental Railroad (922) 1944
4¢ Kansas Statehood (1183) 1961
60¢ Special Delivery (E23) 1971
11. 6¢ Alexandria Bicentennial (C40) 1949
3¢ Minnesota Statehood (1106) 1958
20¢ Louisiana World Exposition (2086) 1984
22¢ Royal Electrification (2144) 1985
12. Not a first day to date
13. 3¢ Victor Herbert (881) 1940
5¢ Edward McDowell (882) 1940
5¢ Winston Churchill (1264) 1965
13¢ Dr. Papanicolau (1754) 1978
14. 6¢ Eagle airmail (C23) 1938
10¢ Skylab (1529) 1974
18¢ (ten) Wildlife booklet (1880-89) 1981
20¢ Physical Fitness (2043) 1983
45¢ Samuel Langley airmail (C118) 1988
15. 3¢ Grand Coulee Dam (1009) 1952
10¢ Airmail 50th Anniversary (C74) 1968
9¢ Delta Wing Plane airmail (C77) 1971
14¢ Official Mail (O129A) 1985
22¢ Official Mail coil (O136) 1985
16. 30¢ Transatlantic airmail (C24) 1939
17. 1 1/2¢ Harding, rotary (633) 1927
4¢ Martha Washington (636) 1927
9¢ Thomas Jefferson (641) 1927
3¢ Stamp Centenary (947) 1947
6¢ Law and Order (1343) 1968
6¢ W.C. Handy (1372) 1969
20¢ Health Research (2087) 1984
18. 2¢, 5¢, Norse-American series (620-21) 1925

4¢ Thomas Jefferson Credo (1141) 1960
18¢ Surrey coil (1906) 1981
18¢ Surrey (1907) 1981
20¢ Tennessee Valley Authority (2042) 1983

19. 1/2¢ Presidential (Franklin) (803) 1938
5¢, 10¢ CIPEX souvenir sheet (948) 1947
20¢ Official Mail coil (O138B) 1988

20. 4¢ Homestead Act Centennial (1198) 1962
13¢ Solo Transatlantic Flight (1710) 1977
15¢ Dolley Madison (1822) 1980
2¢ Locomotive (1897A) 1982
39¢ Grenville Clark (1867) 1985
25¢ Flag Over Yosemite (2280) 1988

21. 2¢ Red Cross (702) 1931
3¢ Air Force Reserve (1067) 1955
5¢ SIPEX (1310) 1966
21¢ Airmail (C81) 1971
13¢ Colorado Statehood (1711) 1977
18¢ (eight) Space Achievements (1912-19) 1981
20¢ Aging Together (2011) 1982

22. 3¢ Steamship (923) 1944
3¢ Steel Industry (1090) 1957
"A" (15¢) regular and coil (1735-42) 1978
22¢ Presidential souvenir sheets (2216-2219a-i) 1986

23. 3¢ Annapolis Tercentenary (984) 1949
5¢ SIPEX souvenir sheet (1311) 1966
20¢ Douglas Fairbanks (2088) 1984
22¢ Flag Over Capitol testing coil (2115b) 1987
25¢ South Carolina (2343) 1988

24. 3¢ Telegraph Centenary (924) 1944
13¢ Jimmie Rodgers (1755) 1978
20¢ Jim Thorpe (2089) 1984

25. 1/2¢ Nathan Hale, rotary (653) 1929
1¢, 3¢ Century of Progress (728-29) 1933
5¢ Canada Centenary (1324) 1967
22¢ Ameripex (2145) 1985

26. 2¢ Valley Forge (645) 1928
10¢ Lindbergh airmail, booklet (C10a) 1928
5¢ Army (789), 5¢ Navy (794) 1937

27. 10¢ David Wark Griffith (1555) 1975

28. 3¢ Four Chaplains (956) 1948
17¢ Rachel Carson (1849) 1981
17¢ Rachel Carson (1857) 1981
22¢ Arctic Explorers (2220-23) 1986
25¢ Owl & Grosbeak (2284-85) 1988

29. 7¢ McKinley, perf 10 rotary (588) 1926
8¢ Grant, perf 10 rotary (589) 1926
9¢ Thomas Jefferson (590) 1926
5¢ John Ericsson (628) 1926
3¢ San Diego Exposition (773) 1935
3¢ Wisconsin Centennial (957) 1948
6¢ Powered Flight 50th Anniversary (C47) 1953
5¢ John F. Kennedy Memorial (1246) 1964
13¢ John F. Kennedy (1287) 1967
13¢, 18¢, 24¢, 31¢ INTERPHIL '76 souvenir sheets (1686-89) 1976

30. 3¢ Confederate Veterans (998) 1951
4¢ Lincoln Sesquicentennial (1116) 1959

31. 3¢ Kansas Territory (1061) 1954
3¢ Geophysical Year (1107) 1958
4¢ SEATO (1151) 1960
15¢ Emily Bissell (1823) 1980
10¢ Richard Russell (1853) 1984

June

1. 3¢ Kentucky Statehood (904) 1942
3¢ Tennessee Statehood (941) 1946
13¢ Benjamin Franklin (1690) 1976
20¢ Flag booklet (1896a) 1982

2. 4¢ American Woman (1152) 1960

3. 2¢ Presidential (Adams) (806) 1938
3¢ Kansas City Centennial (994) 1950
35¢ Charles Drew (1859) 1981
4¢ Carl Schurz (1847) 1983
35¢ Charles Drew (1865) 1981

4. 4¢ William Howard Taft (685) 1930
5¢ Swedish Pioneers (958) 1948
5¢ Food for Peace (1231) 1963
15¢ (four) American Architecture (1779-82) 1979

5. 2¢ Edison's First Light (654) 1929
15¢ Certified Mail (FA1) 1955

6. 12¢ Benjamin Harrison (1045) 1959
10¢ (eight) Universal Postal Union Centenary (1530-37) 1974
13¢ (four) Butterflies (1712-15) 1977
20¢ John McCormack (2090) 1984
15¢ Buffalo Bill (2178) 1988

7. 15¢ (four) Endangered Flowers (1783-86) 1979
20¢ Medal of Honor (2045) 1983
9¢ Sylvanus Thayer (1852) 1985

8. 10¢ James Monroe, perf 10 rotary

(591) 1925
4¢ Silver Centennial (1130) 1959
2¢ Frank Lloyd Wright (1280) 1966
20¢ The Barrymores (2012) 1982
3.4¢ Schoolbus (2123) 1985

9. 3¢ Doctors (949) 1947
20¢ Scott Joplin (2044) 1983

10. 1¢ Benjamin Franklin, rotary (632) 1927
8¢ U.S. Grant, rotary (640) 1927
10¢ Ethelbert Nevin (883) 1940
3¢ Naval Review (1091) 1957
10¢ Liberty Bell airmail (C57) 1960
13¢ (six) CAPEX sheet (1757a-h) 1978
20¢ Mike Walker (2013) 1982
20¢ Thomas Gallaudet (1861) 1983
17¢ Postage Due (O104) 1985

11. 2¢ Edison's Light, rotary (655) 1929
2¢ Edison's Light, coil (656) 1929
11¢ Stutz Bearcat (2131) 1985
15¢ & 25¢ Official Mail coils (O138A and O141) 1988

12. 3¢ Baseball (855) 1939
3¢ Executive Mansion (990) 1950
3¢ Gunston Hall (1108) 1958
8¢ Wildlife Conservation (1427-30) 1971

13. 3¢ Marquis de Lafayette (1010) 1952
10¢ Mineral Heritage (1538-41) 1974
13¢ Lafayette (1716) 1977
22¢ Wildlife (2286-2335) 1987
25¢ Francis Ouimet (2377) 1988

14. 9¢ The Alamo (1043) 1956
3¢ Oklahoma Statehood (1092) 1957
22¢ Abigail Adams (2146) 1985

15. 3¢, 5¢ Olympic Games (718-19) 1932
3¢ Arkansas Centennial (782) 1936
11¢ Statue of Liberty, Giori (1044A) 1961
5¢ New Jersey Tercentenary (1247) 1964
5¢ Magna Carta (1265) 1965
10¢ Kentucky Settlement (1542) 1974
15¢ Seeing Eye Dogs (1787) 1979

16. 3¢ Washington, portrait by Stuart (720) 1932
3¢ Presidential (Jefferson) (807) 1938

17. 2¢ Sullivan Expedition (657) 1929
2 1/2¢ Bunker Hill Monument (1034) 1959
1 1/4¢ Palace of Governors (1031A) 1960
10¢ Battle of Bunker Hill (1564) 1975
28¢ Summer Olympics airmail (C108-04) 1983
45¢ Harvey Cushing (2188) 1988

18. 10¢ Charles Lindbergh's Flight (C10) 1927
18¢ Professional Management (1920) 1981
17¢ Belva Ann Lockwood (2179) 1986

19. Bicolored Postage Due series (J88-J101) 1959

20. 5¢ West Virginia Statehood (1232) 1963

21. 3¢ Constitution Ratification (835) 1938
3¢ New Hampshire (1068) 1955
4.9¢ Buckboard (2124) 1985
8.3¢ Ambulance (2128) 1985
25¢ New Hampshire (2344) 1988

22. 5¢ Poland Flag (909) 1943
3¢ Antelope (1078) 1956
8¢ Post Rider (1478) 1973

23. 8¢ Antarctic Treaty (1431) 1971
36¢ Igor Sikorsky airmail (C119) 1988

24. 3¢ Washington, vertical coil (721) 1932
3¢ Statue of Liberty (1035) 1954

25. 6¢ Transport Plane (C25) 1941
3¢ Mackinac Bridge (1109) 1958
17¢ Electric Auto (1905) 1981
17¢ Electric Auto (1906) 1981
5¢ Pearl Buck (1848) 1983
25¢ Virginia (2345) 1988

26. 4¢ St. Lawrence Seaway (1131) 1959
5¢ International Cooperation Year (1266) 1965
6¢ Wolf Trap Farm (1452) 1972
15¢ Photography (1758) 1978
18¢ (four) Wildlife Habitats (1921-24) 1981
20¢ St. Lawrence Seaway (2091) 1984

27. 3¢ Swedish-Finnish Tercentenary (836) 1938
3¢ Franklin Roosevelt Memorial (932) 1945
3¢ Dr. Harvey Wiley (1080) 1956
6¢ Register and Vote (1344) 1968
21¢ Amadeo Giannini (1400) 1973
15¢ Helen Keller and Anne Sullivan (1824) 1980

28. 3¢ Soo Locks (1069) 1955
15¢ Statue of Liberty airmail (C62) 1961

29. 18¢ Disabled Persons (1925) 1981

30. 3¢ Boy Scout Jamboree (995) 1950
15¢ Americana (Flag) regular (two) and coil (1597, 1598, 1618C) 1978
20¢ Peace Garden (2014) 1982
1¢ Margaret Mitchell (2168) 1986

July

1. 6¢ Winged Globe (C19) 1934
4¢ Presidential (Madison) (808) 1938
3¢ Teachers of America (1093) 1957
5¢ Gettysburg (1180) 1963
5¢ Bill of Rights (1312) 1966
8¢ U.S. Postal Service Emblem (1396) 1971
2. 5¢ Salvation Army (1267) 1965
$1 Americana (Rush Lamp) (1610) 1979
20¢ Waterfowl Preservation (2092) 1984
3. 3¢ Idaho Statehood (896) 1940
15¢ George M. Cohan (1756) 1978
4. 3¢ Win the War (905) 1942
3¢ Indiana Territory (996) 1950
10¢ Independence Hall (1044) 1956
4¢ 48-star Flag (1094) 1957
4¢ 49-star Flag (1132) 1959
4¢ 50-star Flag (1153) 1960
5¢ Erie Canal (1325) 1967
6¢ Historic Flags (1345-54) 1968
8¢ Bicentennial Commission Emblem (1432) 1971
8¢ Colonial Craftsmen (1456-59) 1972
8¢ Boston Tea Party (1480-83) 1973
10¢ Continental Congress (1543-46) 1974
10¢ Revolutionary Uniforms (1565-68) 1975
13¢ (four) Declaration of Independence (1691-94) 1976
13¢ (four) Skilled Hands for Independence (1717-20) 1977
22¢ Statue of Liberty (2224) 1986
22¢ Delaware Statehood (2336) 1987
25¢ Love (2378) 1988
5. 5¢ Search for Peace (1326) 1967
25¢ Flag With Clouds booklet (2285A) 1988
6. 20¢ Babe Ruth (2046) 1983
7. 3¢ Wisconsin Tercentenary (739) 1934
5¢ Chinese Resistance (906) 1942
16.7¢ Popcorn Wagon (2261) 1988
8. 20¢ Nathaniel Hawthorne (2047) 1983
9. 2¢ Braddock's Field (688) 1930
6¢ Maine Statehood (1391) 1970
10. 3¢ Wyoming Statehood (897) 1940
6¢, 8¢, 15¢, 11¢ Progress in Electronics (1500-02, C86) 1973
18¢ Edna St. Vincent Millay (1926) 1981
11. 4 1/2¢ Presidential (White House) (809) 1938
3¢ Marine Corps (929) 1945
4¢ Senator George Norris (1184) 1961
15¢ Roses (booklet) (1738) 1978
12. 10¢ Special Delivery (E12) 1922
5¢ Czechoslovakia Flag (910) 1943
3¢ George Eastman (1062) 1954
6¢ Bald Eagle airmail (C67) 1963
5¢ Henry Thoreau (1327) 1967
15¢ Tugboat (2250) 1988
13. 3¢ Northwest Ordinance Sesquicentennial (795) 1937
17¢ Statue of Liberty airmail (C80) 1971
8.4¢ coil (1615C) 1978
20¢ America's Libraries (2015) 1982
3¢ Henry Clay (1846) 1983
20¢ Roanoke Voyages (2093) 1984
14. 3¢ Oregon Territory (783) 1936
3¢ Nevada Settlement (999) 1951
5¢ Opening of Japan (1021) 1953
4¢ Father Flanagan (2171) 1986
15. 3¢ Northwest Territory (837) 1938
10¢ Apollo-Soyuz (1569-70) 1975
16. 1¢ Yosemite National Park (740) 1934
6¢ California Settlement (1373) 1969
13¢ (four) Olympic Games block (1695-98) 1976
17. 5¢ Dante Alighieri (1268) 1965
22¢ Morocco (2349) 1987
18. 1¢ Franklin, coil sidewise (597) 1923
22¢ Bartholdi (2147) 1985
19. 1¢ Franklin coil, endwisc (604) 1924
3¢ Progress of Women (959) 1948
4¢ Pony Express Centennial (1154) 1960
13.2¢ Coal Car (2259) 1988
20. 6¢ Wildlife Conservation (1392) 1970
15¢ Viking Mission to Mars (1759) 1978
21. 5¢ Presidential (Monroe) (810) 1938
15¢ Veterans Administration (1825) 1980
22. 5¢ Nevada Statehood (1248) 1964
23. 15¢ Gen. Bernardo de Galvez (1826) 1980
25¢ New York (2346) 1988
24. 2¢ Grand Canyon (741) 1934

3¢ Utah Settlement (950) 1947
3¢ Cadillac's Landing (1000) 1951
4¢, 8¢, Simon Bolivar, Champion of Liberty (1110-11) 1958
4¢ Girl Scouts (1199) 1962
8¢ Amelia Earhart (C68) 1963

25. 5¢ Beacon airmail (C11) 1928
17¢ Woodrow Wilson, rotary (697) 1931
25¢ Niagara Falls, rotary (699) 1931
8¢ Henry Knox (1851) 1985

26. 1¢ Franklin Roosevelt Memorial (930) 1945
22¢ Korean Veterans (2152) 1985

27. 6¢ James Garfield, rotary (638) 1927
5¢ Norway Flag (911) 1943

28. 6¢ Presidential (John Q. Adams) (811) 1938
3¢ Lewis and Clark (1063) 1954
3¢ Atoms for Peace (1070) 1955
4¢ Brian McMahon (1200) 1962
15¢ Mount McKinley (1454) 1972
20¢ Summer Olympics (2048-51) 1983

29. 5¢ Nebraska Statehood (1328) 1967

30. 5¢ Yellowstone National Park (744) 1934
25¢ Bay Bridge airmail (C36) 1947
5¢ Poland Millennium (1313) 1966

31. 3¢ William Allen White (960) 1948
5¢ New York City 50th anniversary (C38) 1948
5¢ Eagle in Flight airmail (C50) 1958
7¢ Jet Airliner sheet and coil (C51-C52) 1958

August

1. 3¢ Lincoln, perf 10 rotary (584) 1925
3¢ Colorado Statehood (1001) 1951
6¢ Air Force (C49) 1957
8¢ "Tagged" airmail (C64a) 1963
5¢ Register and Vote (1249) 1964
5¢ Voice of America (1329) 1967
6¢ John Wesley Powell (1374) 1969
20¢ Herman Melville (2094) 1984

2. 3¢ U.S.-Canada Friendship (961) 1948
3¢ Supreme Court Building (991) 1950
6¢ Alabama Statehood (1375) 1969
8¢ John Sloan (1433) 1971
8¢ Space Achievement Decade (1434-35) 1971
20¢ Jackie Robinson (2016) 1982

3. 2¢ Vermont Sesquicentennial (643) 1927
2¢ Burgoyne Campaign (644) 1927
3¢ Mount Rainier (742) 1934
3¢ Iowa Statehood (942) 1946
22¢ William Faulkner (2350) 1987

4. 7¢ Presidential (Jackson) (812) 1938
13¢ Peace Bridge (1721) 1977

5. 4¢ Martha Washington coil, sidewise (601) 1923
3¢ Wheatland (1081) 1956

6. 6¢ Dwight D. Eisenhower (1393) 1970
10¢ Chautauqua (1505) 1974
13¢ Herkimer at Oriskany (1722) 1977
20¢ Horace Moses (2095) 1984

7. 6¢ Flag Over White House, Huck press (1338D) 1970

8. 45¢ Love (2379) 1988

9. 3¢ Francis Scott Key (962) 1948
15¢ Special Olympics (1788) 1979

10. 5¢ Luxembourg Flag (912) 1943
3¢ Smithsonian Institution (943) 1946
5¢ Herbert Hoover (1269) 1965

11. 8¢ Presidential (Van Buren) (813) 1938
3¢ Youth Month (963) 1948
3¢ Mount Rushmore (1011) 1952
28¢ Americana (Fort Nisqually) (1604) 1978

12. 7¢ Airmail, red (C60) 1960
8.4¢ Wheelchair (2256) 1988

13. 2¢, 5¢ Hawaii Sesquicentennial (647-48) 1928
15¢ Special Delivery (E16) 1931
50¢ Lucy Stone (1293) 1968
8¢ Robinson Jeffers (1485) 1973
20¢ Smokey The Bear (2096) 1984

14. 3¢ Oregon Statehood (964) 1948
5¢ Shakespeare (1250) 1964
22¢ Social Security (2153) 1985
22¢ Lacemaking (2351-54) 1987

15. 8¢ Airmail (C4) 1923
3¢ NRA (732) 1933
3¢ Panama Canal (856) 1939
10¢ Airmail (C27) 1941
3¢ Shipbuilding (1095) 1957
4¢ Atlantic Cable (1112) 1958
4¢ Re-engraved Stagecoach (2228) 1986
10¢ Red Cloud (2176) 1987

16. 5¢ Emancipation Proclamation (1233) 1963
10¢ Kansas Winter Wheat (1506) 1974

21¢ Mail Car (2265) 1988
17. 16¢ Airmail (C5) 1923
7¢ Balloon Jupiter (C54) 1959
5¢ Alliance for Progress (1234) 1963
5¢ Davy Crockett (1330) 1967
20¢ Roberto Clemente (2097) 1984
6¢, 8¢, 15¢ Olympic Games (1460-62), 11¢ (C85) 1972
18. 6¢ James Garfield (723) 1932
5¢ Virginia Dare (796) 1937
9¢ Presidential (W.H. Harrison) (814) 1938
13¢ Clara Maass (1699) 1976
19. 5¢ Winged Globe airmail (C16) 1931
15¢ Airmail (C28) 1941
5¢ Robert Fulton (1270) 1965
18¢ Alcoholism (1927) 1981
1¢ Omnibus (1897) 1983
4¢ Stage Coach (1898) 1983
25¢ Summer Olympics (2380) 1988
20. 15¢ New York Skyline airmail (C35) 1947
4¢ Naval Aviation (1185) 1961
17¢ Dog Sled (2135) 1986
21. 24¢ Biplane airmail (C6) 1923
7¢ Hawaii Statehood (C55) 1959
22. 6¢ Edgar Lee Masters (1405) 1970
20¢ Touro Synagogue (2017) 1982
44¢ Junipero Serra airmail (C116) 1985
23. 6¢ Botanical Congress (1376-79) 1969
$5 Americana (Railroad conductor's lantern) (1612) 1979
24. 3¢ Iowa Territory (838) 1938
5¢ Netherlands Flag (913) 1943
2¢ Franklin Roosevelt Memorial (931) 1945
3¢ American Bar Association (1022) 1953
25. 12¢ Cleveland, rotary (693) 1931
1¢, 3¢ APS souvenir sheets (730-31) 1933
3¢ Justice Harlan F. Stone (965) 1948
6¢ DC-4 Skymaster, coil, airmail (C41) 1949
50¢ Patrick Henry (1051) 1955
5¢ National Park Service Emblem (1314) 1966
$5 Bret Harte (2196) 1987
25¢ Classic Cars (2381-85) 1988
26. 3¢ Susan B. Anthony (784) 1936
10¢ SPA souvenir sheet (797) 1937
1¢ Washington (1031) 1954
4¢ Soil Conservation (1133) 1959
6¢ Woman Suffrage (1406) 1970
10¢ International Women's Year (1571) 1975
15¢ (four) American Owls (1760-63) 1978
15¢ (four) Coral Reefs (1827-30) 1980
22¢ WWI Veteran (2154) 1985
22¢ Pennsylvania (2337) 1987
27. 1 1/2¢ Harding, imperf, rotary (631) 1926
15¢ Statue of Liberty, rotary (696) 1931
9¢ Zion National Park (748) 1934
20¢ Airmail (C29) 1941
4¢ Lincoln-Douglas Debates (1115) 1958
4¢ Petroleum Industry (1134) 1959
10¢ Pan American Games (C56) 1959
8¢ Lyndon B. Johnson Memorial (1503) 1973
28. 3¢ APS souvenir sheet (750) 1934
4¢ Hire the Handicapped (1155) 1960
5¢ Florida Settlement (1271) 1965
8¢ Emily Dickinson (1436) 1971
18¢ (four) Architecture (1928-31) 1981
22¢ Drafting of the Constitution (2355-59) 1987
29. 3¢ Grand Army of the Republic (985) 1949
4¢ World Forestry Congress (1156) 1960
5¢ Marine Corps Reserve (1315) 1966
8.3¢ Re-engraved Ambulance (2231) 1986
30. 16¢ Airmail Special Delivery (CE1) 1934
10¢ Pan American Union Building airmail (C34) 1947
7.6¢ Carreta (2255) 1988
3¢ Mount Palomar Observatory (966) 1948
31. $1 Wilson, dry printing (832c) 1954
8¢ Magsaysay, Champion of Liberty (1096) 1957
4¢ Apprenticeship (1201) 1962

September

1. 2¢ Warren G. Harding Memorial (610) 1923
15¢ Organized Labor (1831) 1980
20¢ Wolf Trap Farm Park (2018) 1982
2. 10¢ Presidential (Tyler) (815) 1938
20¢ Treaty of Paris (2052) 1983
30¢ Frank Laubach (1864) 1984

56¢ John Harraro (2191) 1986
25¢ Honeybee (2281) 1988
3. 4¢ Eagle In Flight airmail (C48) 1954
3¢ Labor Day (1082) 1956
30¢ Special Delivery (E21) 1957
5¢ Traffic Safety (1272) 1965
10¢ (four) Postal Service Bicentennial (1572-75) 1975
4. 11¢ Hays, rotary (692) 1931
13¢ Benjamin Harrison, rotary (694) 1931
50¢ Arlington Amphitheater, rotary (701) 1931
3¢ American Chemical Society (1002) 1951
4¢ Workmen's Compensation (1186) 1961
22¢ Navajo Blankets (2235-38) 1986
5. 6¢ Crater Lake (745) 1934
1¢ Gilbert Stuart (884) 1940
2¢ James Whistler (885) 1940
10¢ Summer Olympics (1790) 1979
15¢ Edith Wharton (1832) 1980
6. 3¢ Engineering Centennial (1012) 1952
3¢ Lafayette Bicentenary (1097) 1957
7. 3¢ Coronado Expedition (898) 1940
3¢ Clara Barton (967) 1948
20¢ Dogs block (2098-2101) 1984
8. 14¢ American Indian, rotary (695) 1931
20¢ Golden Gate, rotary (698) 1931
30¢ Buffalo, rotary (700) 1931
9. 3¢ Poultry Industry (968) 1948
3¢ California Statehood (997) 1950
10¢ Moon Landing (C76) 1969
20¢ Civil Service (2053) 1983
10. 8¢ Henry O. Tanner (1486) 1973
11. 3¢ Service Women (1013) 1952
5¢ Doctors Mayo (1251) 1964
6¢ Walt Disney (1355) 1968
50¢ Americana (Iron "Betty" lamp) (1608) 1979
22¢ New Jersey (2338) 1987
12. 2¢ Harding, rotary (612) 1923
5¢ Women's Clubs (1316) 1966
6¢ South Carolina (1407) 1970
8¢ San Juan, Puerto Rico (1437) 1971
15¢ American Education (1833) 1980
13. Not a first day to date
14. 2¢ Battle of Fallen Timbers (680) 1929
12¢ Presidential (Taylor) (817) 1938
5¢ Belgium Flag (914) 1943
3¢ Sagamore Hill (1023) 1953
4¢ Dental Health (1135) 1959
4¢ Francis Scott Key Credo (1142) 1960
20¢ Metropolitan Opera (2054) 1983
25¢ Antarctic Explorers (2386-89) 1988
15. 2¢ Thomas Jefferson (1033) 1954
8¢ Parent-Teacher Associations (1463) 1972
3¢ Paul Dudley White (2170) 1986
16. 3¢ Augustus Saint-Gaudens (886) 1940
5¢ Daniel Chester French (887) 1940
4¢ Mexican Independence (1157) 1960
4¢ Sam Rayburn (1202) 1962
3¢ Francis Parkman (1281) 1967
5.3¢ Elevator (2254) 1988
17. 2¢ General Von Steuben (689) 1930
3¢ Constitution Sesquicentennial (798) 1937
5¢ John Singleton Copley (1273) 1965
22¢ Signing of the Constitution (2360) 1987
18. 15¢ Map airmail (C8) 1926
8¢ Zion National Park (747) 1934
3¢ Fort Ticonderoga (1071) 1955
13¢ Adolf Ochs (1700) 1976
19. 4¢, 8¢ Kossuth Champion of Liberty (1117-18) 1958
6¢ Stone Mountain Memorial (1408) 1970
6¢ Walter Lippmann (1849) 1985
20. 6¢ Father Marquette (1356) 1968
8¢ (four) Wildlife Conservation (1464-67) 1972
8¢ Willa Cather (1487) 1973
21. 3¢ Gold Star Mothers (969) 1948
30¢ Robert E. Lee (1049) 1955
20¢ American Inventors (2055-58) 1983
22¢ CPA (2361) 1987
22. 13¢ Presidential (Fillmore) (818) 1938
3¢ Fort Kearny (970) 1948
3¢ Nassau Hall (1083) 1956
4¢ Freedom of the Press (1119) 1958
6¢ Dartmouth College Case (1380) 1969
18¢ Babe Didrikson Zaharias (1932) 1981
18¢ Bobby Jones (1933) 1981
23. 10¢ Energy Conservation (1547) 1974

31¢ (two) Wright Brothers (C91-C92) 1978
15¢ John Paul Jones (1789) 1979
1¢ Dorothea Dix (1844) 1983
$1 Bernard Revel (2194) 1986

24. 40¢ John Marshall (1050) 1955
3¢ Devil's Tower (1084) 1956
5¢ Johnny Appleseed (1317) 1966
6¢ Professional Baseball (1381) 1969

25. 4¢ Mesa Verde National Park (743) 1934
3¢ Printing Tercentenary (857) 1939
30¢ Twin Motor Transport airmail (C30) 1941
5¢ DC-4 Skymaster airmail (C32) 1946
15¢ (four) Northwest Indian Masks (1834-37) 1980
22¢ Horses (2155-58) 1985
5¢ Milk Wagon (2253) 1987
17.5¢ Marmon Wasp (2262) 1987

26. 8¢ Winged Globe airmail (C17) 1932
6¢ Daniel Boone (1357) 1968
6¢ Intercollegiate Football (1382) 1969
22¢ T.S. Eliot (2239) 1986
20¢ Crime Prevention (2102) 1987

27. 3¢ Corregidor (925) 1944
8¢ Mail Order Business (1468) 1972

28. 5¢ French Flag (915) 1943
3¢ U.S. Army (934) 1945
4¢ U.S.-Japan Treaty (1158) 1960
8¢ Drummer (1479) 1973
15¢ (four) Summer Olympics (1791-94) 1979
20.5¢ Fire Engine (2264) 1988

29. $2 Presidential (Harding) (833) 1938
4¢, 8¢ Reuter, Champion of Liberty (1136-37) 1959
5¢ (two) Space Walk (1331-32) 1967
10¢ Peace Through Law (1576) 1975

30. 3¢ Boulder Dam (774) 1935
10¢ Frederic Remington (888) 1940
3¢ Gutenberg Bible (1014) 1952
20¢ Architecture (2019-22) 1982

October

1. 6¢ Arkansas River Navigation (1358) 1968
6.3¢ Bulk rate coil (1518) 1974
20¢ Family Unity (2104) 1984
22¢ Public Education (2159) 1985
22¢ Woodcarving (2240-43) 1986
22¢ Locomotives (2362-66) 1987
25¢ Carousel Animals (2390-93) 1988

2. 50¢ Graf Zeppelin airmail (C18) 1933
7¢ Acadia National Park (746) 1934
5¢ Urban Planning (1333) 1967

3. Not a first day to date

4. 11¢ Rutherford B. Hayes (563) 1922
3¢ Volunteer Firemen (971) 1948
3¢ Newspaper Boys (1015) 1952
4¢ Frederic Remington (1187) 1961
8¢ Drug Abuse (1438) 1971
$8.75 Express Mail (2394) 1988

5. 5¢ Cordell Hull (1235) 1963
8¢ Dr. Robert Goddard (C69) 1964
5¢ Beautification of America (1318) 1966
8¢ Angus Cattle (1504) 1973

6. 14¢ Presidential (Pierce) (819) 1938
11¢ International Telecommunication Union (1274) 1965
5¢ Finland Independence (1334) 1967
10¢ (two) Banking and Commerce (1577-78) 1975

7. 1¢ Eli Whitney (889) 1940
2¢ Samuel F.B. Morse (890) 1940
3¢ Edgar Allen Poe (986) 1949
15¢ UPU 75th anniversary (C43) 1949
$1 Patrick Henry (1052) 1955
20¢ St. Francis of Assisi (2023) 1982
22¢ International Youth Year (2160-63) 1985

8. 10¢ Great Smoky Mountains (749) 1934
4¢, 8¢ Paderewski Champion of Liberty (1159-60) 1960
20¢ Streetcars (2059-62) 1983

9. 3¢ Byrd Antarctic Expedition (733) 1933
6¢ Leif Erickson (1359) 1968
8¢ Osteopathic Medicine (1469) 1972
15¢ (four) American Trees (1764-67) 1978
15¢ (four) Architecture (1838-41) 1980
18¢ Coming Through the Rye (1934) 1981

10. 1¢ Trans-Mississippi Exhibition souvenir sheet (751) 1934
4¢ Overland Mail (1120) 1958
4¢ Senator Robert Taft (1161) 1960
4¢ Republic of China (1188) 1961
10¢ Legend of Sleepy Hollow (1548) 1974
5¢ Motorcycle (1899) 1983

11. 5¢ Eleanor Roosevelt (1236) 1963
"C" (20¢) sheet, coil, booklet (1946-48) 1981
20¢ Eleanor Roosevelt (2105) 1984

12. 3¢ Washington, horizontal coil (722) 1932
    5¢ Greek Flag (916) 1943
    10¢ Retarded Children (1549) 1974
    20¢ Ponce de Leon (2024) 1982
13. 5¢ Kosciuszko (734) 1933
    15¢ Presidential (Buchanan) (820) 1938
    3¢ Future Farmers (1024) 1953
    8¢ Tom Sawyer (1470) 1972
    40¢ airmail Philip Mazzei (C98) 1980
    18¢, 20¢ James Hoban (1935-36) 1981
14. 3¢ Cyrus McCormick (891) 1940
    5¢ Elias Howe (892) 1940
    5¢ Science (1237) 1963
    6¢ Dwight Eisenhower Memorial (1383) 1969
    10¢ (two) Christmas (1579-80) 1975
15. 5¢ American Music (1252) 1944
    3¢ Indian Centennial (972) 1948
    4¢ Wheels of Freedom (1162) 1960
    6¢ Cherokee Strip (1360) 1968
    22¢ Help End Hunger (2164) 1985
16. 1¢, 2¢, 3¢ National Defense (899-901) 1940
    3¢ Kearney Expedition (944) 1946
    4¢ Noah Webster (1121) 1958
    $1 Eugene O'Neill (1294) 1967
    18¢ (two) Yorktown/Virginia Capes (1937-38) 1981
    20¢ Nation of Readers (2106) 1984
17. 1¢ Franklin, perf 10 rotary (581) 1923
    6¢ Fort Snelling (1409) 1970
18. 2¢ Battle of White Plains (629) 1926
    2¢ White Plains Souvenir Sheet (630) 1926
    3¢ Hawaii Territorial (799) 1937
    4¢ Boys' Clubs of America (1163) 1960
    6¢ John Trumbull (1361) 1968
    15¢ (two) Christmas (1768-69) 1978
    15¢ (two) Christmas (1799-1800) 1979
19. 2¢ Ohio River Canalization (681) 1929
    2¢ Yorktown Sesquicentennial (703) 1931
20. 2¢ Molly Pitcher (646) 1928
    16¢ Presidential (Lincoln) (821) 1938
    3¢ 13th Amendment (902) 1940
    1/2¢ Benjamin Franklin (1030) 1955
    4¢ Automated Post Office (1164) 1960
    25¢ Traditional and Contemporary Christmas (2399-2400) 1988
21. 3¢ Old Ironsides (951) 1947
    5¢ Great River Road (1319) 1966
    30¢ John Dewey (1291) 1968
    21¢ Chester Carlson (2180) 1988
22. 7¢ Airmail coil, red (C61) 1960
    21.1¢ Letters (2150) 1985
    25¢ Special Occasions (2395-98) 1988
23. 4¢ Dag Hammarskjold Memorial (1203) 1962
    5¢ Adlai Stevenson Memorial (1275) 1965
    10¢ Christmas (1550-51) 1974
    22¢ Traditional and Contemporary Christmas (2367-2378) 1987
24. 3¢ William Penn (724) 1932
    3¢ Daniel Webster (725) 1932
    20¢ George C. Marshall (1289) 1967
    6¢ Wildlife Conservation (1362) 1968
    22¢ Traditional and Contemporary Christmas (2244-45) 1986
25. Not a first day to date
26. 5¢ Yugoslavia Flag (917) 1943
    4¢, 8¢ Mannerheim, Champion of Liberty (1165-66) 1960
    5¢ City Mail Delivery (1238) 1963
    5¢ Homemakers (1253) 1964
    5¢ Savings Bonds/Servicemen (1320) 1966
    24.1¢ Tandem Bike (2266) 1988
27. 5¢ Theodore Roosevelt (557) 1922
    17¢ Presidential (A. Johnson) (822) 1938
    3¢ U.S. Navy (935) 1945
    3¢ Rough Riders (973) 1948
    3¢ Trucking Industry (1025) 1953
    4¢ Forest Conservation (1122) 1958
    8¢ CARE Anniversary (1439) 1971
    13¢ (two) Christmas (1701-02) 1976
28. 10¢ Alexander Graham Bell (893) 1940
    6¢ Anti-Pollution (1410-13) 1970
    20¢ (two) Christmas (1939-40) 1981
    20¢ Traditional and Contemporary Christmas (2026-30) 1982
    20¢ Traditional (2063) and Contemporary (2064) Christmas 1983
    20¢ Cable Car (2263) 1988
29. 50¢ Airmail (C31) 1941
    3¢ Juliette Lowe (974) 1948
    5¢ Red Cross Centennial (1239) 1963
    8¢ Historic Preservation (1440-43) 1971

13¢ Patrol Wagon (2258) 1988
30. 13¢, 17¢ Special Delivery (E17-E18) 1944
20¢ Traditional and Contemporary Christmas (2107-2108) 1984
31. 3¢ Motion Pictures (926) 1944
13¢ Liberty Bell (1595) 1975
15¢ (two) Christmas (1842-43) 1980
20¢ Hispanic Americans (2103) 1984

November

1. 3¢ Michigan Centenary (775) 1935
4¢ Camp Fire Girls (1167) 1960
4¢ Christmas (1205) 1962
5¢ Christmas (1240) 1963
5¢ Christmas (1321) 1966
6¢ Christmas (1363) 1968
31¢ Summer Olympics (airmail) (C97) 1979
5.5¢ Star Route Truck (2125) 1985
2. 3¢ Four States (858) 1939
5¢ Korea Flag (921) 1944
4¢, 8¢ Garibaldi, Champion of Liberty (1168-69) 1960
5¢ Christmas (1276) 1965
5¢ Thomas Eakins (1335) 1967
3. 6¢ Christmas (1384) 1969
13¢ Puppy and Kitten (2025) 1982
4. 3¢ Will Rogers (975) 1948
6¢ Chief Joseph (1364) 1968
3¢ Parkman, coil (1297) 1975
15¢ Will Rogers (1801) 1979
35¢ Summer Olympic (C109-12) 1983
23¢ Mary Cassatt (2182) 1988
5. 3¢ Fort Bliss (976) 1948
4¢ Walter George Memorial (1170) 1960
6¢ Christmas (1414-18) 1970
20¢ John Hanson (1941) 1981
65¢ Hap Arnold (2192) 1988
6. 4¢ Basketball (1189) 1961
5¢ Christmas (1336) 1967
18¢ Washington and Monument (2149) 1985
7. 8¢ Christmas (1507-08) 1973
8. Not a first day to date
9. 5¢ Albania Flag (918) 1943
3¢ Moina Michael (977) 1948
3¢ King Salmon (1079) 1956
5¢ Christmas (1254-57) 1964
8¢ Christmas (1471-72) 1972
10. 19¢ Presidential (Hayes) (824) 1938
20¢ Presidential (Garfield) (825) 1938
3¢ Coast Guard (936) 1945
8¢ Christmas (1444-45) 1971
8¢ Pharmacy (1473) 1972
20¢ Vietnam Veteran's Memorial (2109) 1984
11. 15¢ Statue of Liberty (566) 1922
25¢ Niagara Falls (568) 1922
50¢ Lincoln Memorial (570) 1922
3¢ General George S. Patton (1026) 1953
15¢ Vietnam Veterans (1802) 1979
20¢ Martin Luther (2065) 1983
12. 3¢ Alaska Territory (800) 1937
13. 11¢ Freedom of the Press (1593) 1975
14. 4¢ Higher Education (1206) 1962
24¢ Old North Church (1603) 1975
15. 2¢ Harding, imperf (611) 1923
10¢ Christmas, self-stick (1552) 1974
13¢ Flag and Independence Hall (1622) 1975
13¢ Flag, coil (1625) 1975
16. 4¢ Hammarskjold, special printing (1204) 1962
17. $5 Presidential (Coolidge) (834) 1938
8¢ John J. Pershing (1042A) 1961
5¢ Mary Cassatt (1322) 1966
5¢ Washington, redrawn (1283B) 1967
8¢ Stamp Collecting (1474) 1972
20¢ Flag two pane booklet (1896b) 1983
18. 10¢ UPU 75th Anniversary (C42) 1949
6¢ Theodore Roosevelt (1039) 1955
2¢ Igor Stravinsky (1845) 1982
19. 3¢ Gettysburg Address (978) 1948
4¢ Abraham Lincoln (1036) 1954
4¢ Lincoln Credo (1143) 1960
20. 6¢ James Garfield (558) 1922
3¢ American Turners (979) 1948
3¢ New York City (1027) 1953
15¢ Statue of Liberty airmail (C58) 1959
6¢ Hope for Crippled (1385) 1969
6¢ United Nations Anniversary (1419) 1970
7.7¢ coil, (1614) 1976
25¢ (two) Wiley Post (airmail) (C95-C96) 1979
21. 3¢ International Red Cross (1016) 1952
5¢ Verrazano Narrows Bridge (1258) 1964
6¢ Landing of Pilgrims (1420) 1970
22. 25¢ China Clipper airmail (C20) 1935
3¢ U.S. Capitol (992) 1950
3¢ Wildlife Conservation (1098) 1957

20¢ USA and Jet airmail (C75) 1968
25¢ Bread Wagon (2136) 1986
23. 5¢ Austria Flag (919) 1943
5¢ Washington (1213) 1962
24. 6¢ Disabled American Veterans (1421) 1970
6¢ Honoring U.S. Servicemen (1422) 1970
9¢ Freedom to Assemble (1591) 1975
25. 3¢ Puerto Rico Territory (801) 1937
4¢ Fort Duquesne (1123) 1958
4¢ Andrew Carnegie (1171) 1960
13¢ Liberty Bell, coil (1618) 1975
26. 3¢ Alfred E. Smith (937) 1945
1¢ Re-engraved Omnibus (2225) 1986
27. Not a first day to date
28. Not a first day to date
29. 10¢ Special Delivery (E15) 1927
30. 25¢ UPU 75th Anniversary (C44) 1949
22¢ Flag With Fireworks booklet (2276a) 1987

December

1. 10¢ Monroe coil, sidewise (603) 1924
1 1/2¢ Harding, full-face (684) 1930
1 1/2¢ Harding coil, full-face (686) 1930
13¢ American Eagle and Shield (1596) 1975
2. 24¢ Presidential (B. Harrison) (828) 1938
25¢ Presidential (McKinley) (829) 1938
5¢ James Monroe (1038) 1954
5¢ Fine Arts (1259) 1964
3. 4¢ Dr. Ephraim McDowell (1138) 1959
$5 John Bassett Moore (1295) 1966
6¢ William Harnett (1386) 1969
4. Not a first day to date
5. 3¢ Everglades National Park (952) 1947
8¢ Airmail, sheet and coil (C64-C65) 1962
6. 4¢ John Foster Dulles (1172) 1960
7. 5¢ Denmark Flag (920) 1943
5¢ John James Audubon (1241) 1963
8. 30¢ Presidential (T. Roosevelt) (830) 1938
50¢ Presidential (W.H. Taft) (831) 1938
9. 3¢ Joel Chandler Harris (980) 1948
10. 2¢ Washington, rotary (634) 1926
3¢ Battle of Brooklyn (1003) 1951
20¢ Fire Pumper (1907) 1981
20¢ Fire Pumper (1908) 1981
11. 5¢ Mississippi Statehood (1337) 1967
20¢ (four) Desert Plants (1942-45) 1981
12. 2¢, 5¢ Aeronautics Conference (649-50) 1928
13. Not a first day to date
14. Not a first day to date
15. 1¢ Army (785), 1¢ Navy (790) 1936
3¢ Virgin Islands (802) 1937
3¢ Children's Issue (1085) 1956
4¢ Echo I (1173) 1960
4¢ Winslow Homer (1207) 1962
5¢ Amateur Radio (1260) 1964
9.3¢ Mail Wagon (1900) 1981
9.3¢ Mail Wagon (1903) 1981
16. Not a first day to date
17. 6¢ Wright Brothers (C45) 1949
20¢ Flag Over Supreme Court, sheet, coil, booklet (1894-96) 1981
18. Not a first day to date
19. Not a first day to date
20. 3¢ George Eastman (1072) 1955
21. 1¢, 2¢, 5¢ Pilgrim Tercentenary series (548-50) 1920
22. Not a first day to date
23. Not a first day to date
24. Not a first day to date
25. Not a first day to date
26. Not a first day to date
27. 3¢ Religious Freedom (1099) 1957
13¢ airmail, coil (C83) 1973
19¢ Sequoyah (1859) 1980
28. 17¢ Woodrow Wilson (623) 1925
4¢ Nurses of America (1190) 1961
29. 3¢ Texas Statehood (938) 1945
30. 3¢ Gadsden Purchase (1028) 1953
28¢ Blanche Stuart Scott airmail (C99) 1980
35¢ Glenn Curtiss airmail (C100) 1980
31. 2¢ Washington coil, endwise (606) 1923

Chapter 9

State Duck Stamps

The following are addresses for ordering state duck stamps from the states currently issuing them. Some non-current state duck stamps from previous years are also available from some states.

Alabama, Accounting Section, Duck Stamp, Department of Conservation and Natural Resources, 64 N. Union, Montgomery, Ala. 36130.

Alaska, Department of Revenue, Licensing Section, 1111 W. 8th St., Room 108, Juneau, Alaska 99801.

Arizona, Game and Fish Department, 2222 W. Greenway Road, Phoenix, Ariz. 85023.

Arkansas, Game and Fish Commission, 2 Natural Resources Drive, Little Rock, Ark. 72205.

California, Department of Fish and Game, 3211 S St., Sacramento, Calif. 95816.

Colorado has no current waterfowl stamps.

Connecticut has not issued waterfowl stamps.

Delaware, Division of Fish and Wildlife, 89 King's Highway, Box 1401, Dover, Del. 19903.

Florida, Game and Fresh Water Fish Commission, Farris Bryant Building, 620 S. Meridian, Room 204, Tallahassee, Fla. 32399-1600.

Georgia, Department of Natural Resources, Game and Fish Division, Suite 1362, Floyd Towers East, 205 Butler St. S.E., Atlanta, Ga. 30334.

Hawaii has not issued waterfowl stamps.

Idaho, Collector Stamps, Idaho Department of Fish and Game, Box 25, Boise, Idaho 83707.

Illinois, Department of Conservation, License and Permit Section, 524 S. Second St., Lincoln Tower Plaza, Springfield, Ill. 62701-1787.

Indiana, Department of Natural Resources, Division of Fish and Wildlife, State Office Building, Room 607, Indianapolis, Ind. 46204.

Iowa, Department of Natural Resources, Wallace State Office Building, Des Moines, Iowa 50319.

Kansas, Department of Wildlife and Parks, Rural Route 2, Box 54A, Pratt, Kan. 67124.

Kentucky, Department of Fish and Wildlife Resources, Division of Fiscal Control, 1 Game Farm Road, Frankfort, Ky. 40601.

Louisiana, Duck Stamp, Wildlife and Fisheries, 400 Royal St., New Orleans, La. 70130.

Maine, Department of Inland Fisheries and Wildlife, 284 State St., State House Station 41, Augusta, Maine 04333.

Maryland, Department of Natural Resources, Licensing and Consumer Services, 580 Taylor Ave., Box 1869, Annapolis, Md. 21404.

Massachusetts, Division of Fisheries and Game, Leverett Saltonstall Building, Government Center, 100 Cambridge St., Room 1902, Boston, Mass. 02202.

Michigan, Department of Natural Resources, License Control, Box 30181, Lansing, Mich. 48909.

Minnesota, Department of Natural Resources, Box 26, St. Paul, Minn. 55155.

Mississippi, Game and Fish Commission, Department of Wildlife Conservation, License Department, Box 451, Jackson, Miss. 39205-0451.

Missouri, Department of Conservation, Fiscal Section, Box 180, Jefferson City, Mo. 65102.

Montana, Fish and Game Commission, 1420 E. Sixth Ave., Helena, Mont. 59620.

Nebraska has not issued waterfowl stamps.

Nevada, Department of Wildlife, Attn: License Office, Box 10678, Reno, Nev. 89520.

New Hampshire, Fish and Game Department, 2 Hazen Drive, Concord, N.H. 03301.

New Jersey, Division of Fish, Game and Wildlife, Waterfowl Stamp, CN 400, Trenton, N.J. 08625.

New Mexico has not issued waterfowl stamps.

New York, Division of Fish and Wildlife, License and Promotional Sales Unit, 50 Wolf Road, Room 111, Albany, N.Y. 12233.

North Carolina, Wildlife Resources Commission, 512 N. Salisbury St., Raleigh, N.C. 27611.

North Dakota, Game and Fish Department, 100 N. Bismarck Expressway, Bismarck, N.D. 58501.

Ohio, Division of Wildlife, Survey and Inventory Section, 1500 Dublin Road, Columbus, Ohio 43215.

Oklahoma, Department of Wildlife Conservation, 1801 N. Lincoln, Box 53465, Oklahoma City, Okla. 73152.

Oregon, Department of Fish and Wildlife, Box 59, Portland, Ore. 97207.

Pennsylvania, Game Commission, 2001 Elmerton Ave., Harrisburg, Pa. 17110-9797.

Rhode Island, Division of Fish and Wildlife, Oliver Stedman Government Center, 4808 Tower Hill Road, Wakefield, R.I. 02879.

South Carolina, Wildlife and Marine Resources Department, Rembert C. Dennis Building, Box 167, Columbia, S.C. 29202.

South Dakota, Game, Fish and Parks, License Division, 412 W. Missouri, Pierre, S.D. 57501.

Tennessee, Department of Wildlife Resources, Information and Education Division, Box 40747, Nashville, Tenn. 37204.

Texas, Parks and Wildlife Department, License Office, 4200 Smith School Road, Austin, Tex. 78744.

Utah, Natural Resources, Wildlife Resources, 1596 W. North Temple, Salt Lake City, Utah 84116.

Vermont, Agency of Natural Resources, 103 S. Main St., 10 South, Waterbury, Vt. 05676.

Virginia, Duck Stamp, Box 11104, Richmond, Va. 23230.

Washington, Department of Wildlife, 600 N. Capitol Way, Olympia, Wash. 98504.

West Virginia, Department of Natural Resources, Waterfowl Stamp Program, Box 67, Elkins, W.Va. 26241.

Wisconsin, Department of Natural Resources, Box 7924, Madison, Wis. 53707.

Wyoming has no current waterfowl stamp. The state does issue a conservation stamp. Only Wyoming's 1985 conservation stamp pictures waterfowl.

Chapter 10

Souvenir Cards

Official Issues

Souvenir cards have been issued for many years with reproductions of stamps and philatelic engravings, but it is only since 1968 that such cards have been issued on a regular basis from official sources. The two major U.S. issuing agencies that now provide philatelic souvenir cards are the Bureau of Engraving and Printing and the United States Postal Service.

Souvenir cards are not actual stamps; therefore, they have no postal value. In recent years, however, they have become increasingly valuable to the collector. This is due mainly to the limited availability of such cards, especially the older issues. Originally, the cards were either given away to patrons of the stamp shows at which they were issued, or sold by the issuing agency for about $1.

The Bureau cards are generally issued for U.S. stamp and coin shows, while the U.S. Postal Service cards are issued for foreign international exhibitions. Since 1987, some BEP cards contain die imprints of actual U.S. stamps. These are extremely desirable to some collectors.

Because these cards usually are available for only a limited amount, they are mostly in the hands of collectors and potential collectors. Therefore, the value of such souvenir cards, no longer available from the issuing agency, is now determined by the collectors who deal with them.

The following sections list all the souvenir cards that have been issued according to issuing agency, along with a brief history, description and production information when available. Production details for many of the cards issued in the 1980s are not available.

Bureau of Engraving and Printing

The Bureau of Engraving and Printing has officially produced souvenir cards in honor of special stamp (and coin) shows since 1969. All these cards have been released for shows and events in the United States, and contain engraved reproductions of various U.S. stamp and currency issues.

In December 1975, the BEP changed its policy concerning the sale of souvenir cards. As of the first of that month, the Bureau would supply cards for only 90 days after the issue date. Before December 1975, there had been no time limit. Also on this date, back issues of remaining cards were offered for the last time (until Jan. 15, 1976), and then all remaining cards were destroyed.

BEP now sells souvenir cards until Dec. 31 following the Fiscal Year of issuance (for example, cards issued between Oct. 1, 1988, and Sept. 30, 1989, will be on sale until Dec. 31, 1989), unless sold out earlier. The current prices of BEP souvenir cards: mint $4 ($5.50 by mail), post office canceled $4.25 ($5.75 by mail). There is a 50¢ discount per card if 10 of the same item are ordered. Orders may be mailed to Bureau of Engraving and Printing, Mail Order Sales, Room 602-11A, 14th and C Streets, S.W., Washington, D.C. 20228.

Orders for souvenir cards more than two weeks before the release date will not be accepted.

Following is a list of all BEP souvenir cards issued, a description of each card and how it was produced, and the number of cards issued and sold. Number sold, based on final figures from the BEP, should represent an accurate number of cards in circulation. Also included are two earlier issues by Bureau union members that served as forerunners to the Bureau cards, though they were not official issues. All cards measure 8 1/2 by 10 1/2 inches, except where noted. Most of the different-sized cards have been released since 1980.

March 13, 1954, Postage Stamp Design Exhibition, National Philatelic Museum, Philadelphia, Pa.

Card of four single-color engravings of buildings in Washington, D.C.: the Washington Monument (pale green), National Gallery of Art (lavender), Washington Cathedral (reddish orange) and U.S. Capitol (black). Inscription: "Souvenir sheet designed, engraved and printed by members, Bureau, Engraving and Printing. Reissued by popular request."

The original engravings were created by the Bank Note Engravers Guild in 1946 for the convention catalog of the International Plate Printers, Die-Stampers and Engravers Union of North America. The design was used again for a 1951 convention, using different colors. The originals were in a single color, but were re-engraved for multicolor in a 1965 souvenir program. Gallery, designer Robert L. Miller, picture engraver Carl T. Arlt, letter engraver Axel W. Christensen; Capitol, designer Robert L. Miller, picture engraver Charles A. Brooks, letter engravers George L. Huber and John S. Edmondson; Cathedral, designer William K. Schrage, picture engraver Edward R. Grove, letter engraver Charles A. Smith, ornamental borders Richard M. Bower; Monument, designer Victor S. McCloskey Jr., picture engraver Matthew D. Fenton, ornamental engraver Arthur W. Dintaman, letter engraver John S. Edmondson. These scenes re-appeared on future cards.

May 21-30, 1966, SIPEX, Sixth International Philatelic Exhibition, Washington, D.C.

Card of three multicolored views of Washington, same as the above card without the monument. Inscribed: "Designed, Engraved, and Printed by Union Members of Bureau of Engraving and Printing."

Quantity issued: 4,000. Size: 7 by 9 inches.

July 16-20, 1969, SANDIPEX, 200th anniversary of settlement of California, San Diego, Calif.

Card of three multicolored views of Washington, same as the above card (Capitol, Art Gallery, Cathedral). This was the first official souvenir card released by the Bureau of Engraving and Printing. Collectors may also recall that a 6¢ postage stamp, Carmel Mission Belfry, designed by Leonard Buckley and Howard C. Mildner, also was issued for the California bicentennial.

Quantity sold: 10,706.

Aug. 12-16, 1969, 78th annual convention of the American Numismatic Association, Philadelphia, Pa.

The large American Eagle on this card is a reproduction of the die designed and engraved by craftsmen of the Continental Bank Note Company for use on various U.S. securities. This eagle is flanked by smaller eagles from the engravings used on the $10 U.S. notes of series 1869, 1875, 1878 and 1880. According to the legend on the card, the large American Eagle design notes were dubbed "Jackass Notes," because "over the years many fanciful explanations have been proffered concerning the engraver's intent in executing the design. None has any real basis in fact. The resemblance of the eagle, in inverted position, to the lowly donkey's head is purely illusionary."

Quantity issued: 12,400. Quantity sold: 12,347.

Size: 6 by 9 inches.

Oct. 2-12, 1969, Fresno Numismatic Society District Fair, Fresno, Calif.

City of Washington scenes similar to SANDIPEX card (Art Gallery, Capitol, Cathedral). See first three entries in this section.

Card production: Giori multicolor intaglio vignettes, flatbed typographic text.

Quantity issued: 3,804. Quantity sold: 3,798.

Nov. 21-23, 1969, American Stamp Dealers' Association National Postage Stamp Show, New York, N.Y.

Block of four from engraved vignette of design of first U.S. special delivery stamp produced by BEP in blue color of this issuance.

Basic design of vignette had been used in production of all issuances of the 10¢ special delivery stamp by the American Bank Note Co. (in blue and orange) prior to the printing of postage stamps by the BEP in 1894, which modified the vignette to distinguish it from the American Bank Note issues. The original ABNC designer was Thomas F. Morris Sr.

Card production: die-stamped vignettes, flatbed typographic text.

Quantity issued: 14,969. Quantity sold: 14,964.

March 20-22, 1970, International Stamp Exhibition (INTERPEX), New York, N.Y.

Vignettes of four U.S. stamps with New York City subjects, printed in original colors: 3¢ ordinary 1954 Statue of Liberty (designer Charles R. Chickering); 3¢ 300th Anniversary of New York City commemorative, 1953 (designer Charles R. Chickering); 15¢ 1947 airmail (designers Victor S. McCloskey Jr. and Leon Helguera); 5¢ 1948 Golden Anniversary of New York City airmail (designer Victor S. McCloskey Jr.).

Card designed by Howard Mildner. Production: die-stamped vignette, flatbed typographic text.

Quantity issued: 12,463. Quantity sold: 12,454.

May 29-31, 1970, Combined Philatelic Exhibition of Chicagoland (COMPEX), Chicago, Ill.

Vignettes from original engraving used for 50¢ Graf Zeppelin airmail stamp, 1933, in a block of four in green color of original stamp (designer Victor S. McCloskey Jr.).

Production: die-stamped vignettes, flatbed typographic text.

Quantity issued: 27,344. Quantity sold: 27,336.

Aug. 18-22, 1970, 79th annual convention of the American Numismatic Association, St. Louis, Mo.

Collage in original colors of portions of various securities from original dies used in their production by the BEP to exemplify arts and skills of high-quality engraving and intaglio-printed reproductions.

Card designed by Leonard Buckley. Production: die-stamped vignette, flatbed typographic text and Treasury Department Seal (with collage).

Quantity issued: 12,017. Quantity sold: 12,013.

Nov. 5-8, 1970, 84th annual convention, American Philatelic Society (HAPEX), Honolulu, Hawaii.

Vignettes from engravings used in design of three stamps related to Hawaiian history: 7¢ 1959 Hawaii Statehood commemorative airmail (designer Joseph Feher); 3¢ 1937 Hawaii Territorial series (designer A.R. Meissner); 80¢ 1952 airmail (designer Victor S. McCloskey Jr.).

Card designed by Howard Mildner. Production: die-stamped vignettes, flatbed typographic text.

Quantity issued: 30,249. Quantity sold: 30,235.

March 12-14, 1971, 13th International Stamp Exhibition (INTERPEX), New York, N.Y.

Block of four of vignette of original engravings of 4¢ 1962 Project Mercury commemorative in colors of original (designer Charles R. Chickering); text superimposed over background beige tint of enlargements of subsequent issues with astronautical themes: 5¢ 1967 Space Twins commemorative, 6¢ 1969 Apollo 8 commemorative, and 10¢ 1969 First Man on the Moon commemorative airmail.

Card data: Giori multicolor intaglio vignettes, offset surface background tints, flatbed typographic text.

Quantity issued: 80,946. Quantity sold: 80,904.

April 23-25, 1971, 12th annual National Western Philatelic Exposition (WESTPEX), San Francisco, Calif.

Vignettes from engravings of four commemorative issues related to California history, each in color of original: 3¢ 1950 California Statehood (designer Victor S. McCloskey Jr.); 1¢ 1934 Yosemite National Park (designer Victor S. McCloskey Jr.); 3¢ 1948 Mount Palomar Observatory (designer Victor S. McCloskey Jr.); 3¢ 1939 Golden Gate International Exposition (designer William A. Roach).

Card designed by Howard Mildner. Production: die-stamped vignettes, flatbed typographic text.

Quantity issued: 48,228. Quantity sold: 48,199.

May 21-23, 1971, National Philatelic Exhibition (NAPEX), Washington, D.C.

Vignettes of stamps representative of the three branches of U.S. Government from 150th anniversary of National Capital series, 1950, in colors of originals: 3¢ Judicial, the U.S. Supreme Court Building (designer Charles R. Chickering); 3¢ Executive, the White House (designer William K. Schrage); 3¢ Legislative, the Capitol (designer Robert L. Miller).

Card designed by Howard C. Mildner. Production: die-stamped vignettes, flatbed typographic text.

Quantity issued: 44,478. Quantity sold: 44,429.

Aug. 10-14, 1971, 80th Anniversary Convention of the American Numismatic Association, Washington, D.C.

Face of the $1 silver certificate, series 1896, designed by Will H. Low, New York City artist, and printed from a plate prepared from original master die.

Production: rotary sheetfed intaglio vignette, flatbed typographic text.

Quantity issued: 54,721. Quantity sold: 54,694.

Aug. 26-29, 1971, joint 85th annual convention of the American Philatelic Society and 75th annual Texas Philatelic Association (TEXANEX), San Antonio, Texas.

Vignettes of stamps concerned with Texas history: 9¢ 1956 ordinary, the Alamo (designer Charles R. Chickering); 5¢ 1964 Sam Houston commemorative (designer Tom Lee); 3¢ 1945 Texas Statehood (designer James B. Winn).

Card designed by Howard C. Mildner. Production: die-stamped vignettes, flatbed typographic text.

Quantity issued: 68,215. Quantity sold: 68,131.

Nov. 19-21, 1971, 23rd ASDA National Postage Stamp Show, New York, N.Y.

Reproduction, in color, of vignettes of original engravings for 1930 Graf Zeppelin airmail, 65¢, $1.30 and $2.60 (designers A.R. Meissner and C.A. Huston).

Production: die-stamped vignettes, flatbed typographic text.

Quantity issued: 94,625. Quantity sold: 94,563.

Nov. 26-Dec. 1, 1971, 75th anniversary of the Collectors Club, New York, N.Y. (ANPHILEX).

Simulations of basic designs of first U.S. stamps, 1847, reproduced from engravings of basic designs prepared for souvenir sheet issued in 1947 for centennial of U.S. postage stamps, and printed in colors similar to original stamps. Souvenir sheet: designer Robert L. Miller Jr.; portrait of Franklin 5¢ stamp, Charles A. Brooks; portrait of Washington 10¢ stamp, Carl T. Arlt.

The 1947 sheet design was based on Post Office Department layout, the die proofs of the 1847 stamps having been supplied by Centenary International Philatelic Exhibition Committee.

Card production: die-stamped vignettes, flatbed typographic text.

Quantity issued: 80,148. Quantity sold: 80,110.

March 17-19, 1972, 14th International Stamp Exhibition (INTERPEX), New York, N.Y.

Block of four reproduction of vignette of 4¢ 1960 Echo I Communications for Peace commemorative (designer Ervine Metzl); text over blue tint background of four other stamps depicting space-related subjects: 1948 Centennial of Fort Bliss, army center for rocket and guided missile research; 1964 Dr. Robert H. Goddard airmail commemorative; 1971 twin 8¢ Space Achievement commemorative.

Card production: die-stamped vignette, offset surface-printed background tint and text.

Quantity issued: 110,257. Quantity sold: 79,646.

April 6-9, 1972, New Orleans Philatelic Exposition (NOPEX), New Orleans, La.

Block of four of vignette of 3¢ 1953 Louisiana Purchase commemorative of sculpture theme of Louisiana Purchase Exposition, St. Louis, 1904 (designer William K. Schrage). Text over blue tint background of enlarged reproductions of the five stamps of the 1904 Louisiana Purchase commemorative series.

Card production: die-stamped vignette, offset surface-printed background tint and text.

Quantity issued: 65,067. Quantity sold: 60,518.

Aug. 15-19, 1972, 81st anniversary convention of the American Numismatic Association, New Orleans, La.

Reproduction of face of $2 silver certificate, series 1896, printed from plate specially produced from original master die. Design, "Science Presenting Steam and Electricity to Commerce and Manufacture," by Edwin H. Blashfield, 19th-century allegorical painter.

Card production: rotary sheetfed intaglio vignette, flatbed typographic text.

Quantity issued: 74,172. Quantity sold: 69,078.

Oct. 20-22, 1972, combined 78th annual convention of the Society of Philatelic Americans and 33rd national exhibition of Associated Stamp Clubs of Southeast Pennsylvania and Delaware (SEPAD), Philadelphia, Pa.

Reproduction of block of four Independence Hall ordinary 10¢ 1956 (designer Charles R. Chickering).

Card production: die-stamped vignette, offset surface-printed text.

Quantity issued: 87,285. Quantity sold: 53,722.

Nov. 17-19, 1972, 24th ASDA National Postage Stamp Show, New York, N.Y.

Reproduction of four portraits of 10¢ 1940 Famous Americans series: composer Ethelbert Nevin, author Samuel L. Clemens (Mark Twain), poet James Whitcomb Riley, artist Frederic Remington (designer William L. Roach).

Card production: die-stamped vignettes, offset surface text.

Quantity issued: 77,153. Quantity sold: 64,161.

Nov. 24-26, 1972, Stamp Expo, San Francisco, Calif.

Block of four of vignette of 25¢ 1947 airmail (designer William K. Schrage).

Card production: die-stamped vignette, offset surface text.

Quantity issued: 82,838. Quantity sold: 53,220.

March 9-11, 1973, 15th International Stamp Exhibition (INTERPEX), New York, N.Y.

Block of four of vignette of 3¢ 1948 Centennial of Fort Bliss (designer Charles R. Chickering).

Card production: die-stamped vignette, offset surface text and tint.

Quantity issued: 88,541. Quantity sold: 49,911.

May 25-27, 1973, Combined Philatelic Exhibition of Chicagoland (COMPEX), Chicago, Ill.

Block of four of vignette of $5 1893 Columbian Exposition series (designer Alfred Sarony Major), medallion profile of Columbus, copied from 50¢ silver coin of Chicago World's Columbian Exposition. Block, in black of original stamp, framed by border of green, flanked at left by enlargement of vignette entitled "Columbus in his Study," printed in green.

Card designed by Esther Porter. Production: die-stamped vignette, offset surface tint and text.

Quantity issued: 50,459. Quantity sold: 49,038.

Aug. 23-27, 1973, 82nd anniversary convention of the American Numismatic Association, Boston, Mass.

Reproduction of face of $5 silver certificate, series 1896, printed from a plate specially produced from original master die. Design, "America," executed by Walter Shirlaw, illustrator and banknote engraver.

Card production: rotary sheetfed intaglio vignette, offset surface text.

Quantity issued: 49,544. Quantity sold: 49,530.

Sept. 14-16, 1973, joint 25th anniversary National Philatelic Exhibition (NAPEX) and 50th anniversary convention of American Air Mail Society, Washington, D.C.

Reproduction in block of four of engraved frame and vignette on 24¢ 1918 airmail (designer C.A. Huston), denomination and postal data eliminated. Flanked on right by portrayal of airplane "Jenny" used to carry mail on first route, 1918, Washington-Philadelphia-New York.

Card designed by Peter Cocci. Production: die-stamped vignette, offset surface tint and text.

Quantity issued: 42,276. Quantity sold: 41,492.

Nov. 16-18, 1973, 25th ASDA National Postage Stamp Show, New York, N.Y.

Block of four of vignette of 1¢ 1943 Four Freedoms stamp (designer Paul Manship) in upper right corner flanked at left by reproductions of the 4¢ 1960-1961 American Credo stamps (designer Frank Conley).

Card production: die-stamped vignette,

offset surface tint and text.

Quantity issued: 52,449. Quantity sold: 42,761.

Dec. 7-9, 1973, Stamp Expo-North, San Francisco, Calif.

Block of four of vignette used for 25¢ 1935 Trans-Pacific airmail (designer A.R. Meissner).

Card production: die-stamped vignette, offset surface text.

Quantity issued: 70,487. Quantity sold: 35,098.

March 8-10, 1974, 75th anniversary of Milwaukee Philatelic Society, Milwaukee, Wis.

Block of four of vignette used on 15¢ 1949 Universal Postal Union airmail commemorative (designer C.R. Chickering), flanked at left by artist's rendition of monument at Bern, Switzerland, symbol of the UPU.

Card production: die-stamped vignette, offset surface tint and text.

Quantity issued: 42,992. Quantity sold: 34,742.

Aug. 13-17, 1974, 83rd anniversary convention of the American Numismatic Association, Bal Harbour, Fla.

Reproduction of proposed "Agriculture and Forestry" obverse of $10 silver certificate, 1897 "Educational" series, which never appeared on the note (designer Walter Shirlaw).

Card production: rotary sheetfed intaglio vignette, offset surface text.

Quantity issued: 41,591. Quantity sold: 41,591.

May 9-11, 1975, National Philatelic Exhibition of Washington, D.C. (NAPEX).

Block of four of vignette from original engraving for 3¢ 1932 Washington Bicentennial commemorative (designer C.A. Huston), from a painting by Charles Willson Peale.

Card production: die-stamped vignette, offset surface text and background tint (artist's conception, Washington taking command).

Quantity issued: 67,500. Quantity sold: 26,313.

Aug. 15, 1975, International Women's Year.

Brochure with removable souvenir card. Reproduction of series 1886 $1 silver certificate portrait of Martha Washington (painting by Jalabert, designer Thomas F. Morris); 5¢ 1940 Frances E. Willard commemorative (Washington, D.C., Public Library photograph by Perry Pictures); 3¢ 1948 commemorative of 100 years of progress for American women depicting Elizabeth Stanton, Carrie C. Catt and Lucretia Mott (designer Victor S. McCloskey Jr.); 10¢ 1940 Jane Addams commemorative (photograph by Moffett, Chicago; designer William A. Roach).

Card production: rotary sheetfed intaglio vignettes, offset surface text and tint.

Quantity issued: 28,039. Quantity sold: 28,022.

Aug. 19-24, 1975, 84th anniversary convention of the American Numismatic Association, Los Angeles, Calif.

Reproduction of engraving on reverse of 1896 $1 silver certificate, designed and executed by Thomas F. Morris, with portraits of Martha (1878) and George Washington (1867).

Card production: rotary sheetfed intaglio vignette, offset surface text.

Quantity issued: 54,981. Quantity sold: 45,593.

Nov. 21-23, 1975, ASDA National Postage Stamp Show, New York, N.Y.

Block of four of vignette of 3¢ 1951 Battle of Brooklyn commemorative (designer C.R. Chickering). Flanked on right by engraving of Washington as Army colonel by Lorenzo J. Hatch, from a painting by John Trumbull.

Card production: die-stamped vignette, offset surface text and logos.

Quantity issued: 34,370. Quantity sold: 33,411.

May 29-June 6, 1976, INTERPHIL '76, International Philatelic Exhibition, Philadelphia, Pa.

Reproduction of block of four of vignette of 1869 24¢ Declaration of Independence stamp; flanked on right by an engraving of Thomas Jefferson and on the left by an engraving of the reading of the Declaration of Independence from Independence Hall, Philadelphia, Pa.

Card production: engraved vignettes, offset surface-printed text and logo, printed on cream certificate deed paper. Size: 6 1/4 by 9 inches.

Quantity sold: 44,864.

May 29-June 6, 1976, INTERPHIL '76 — Special souvenir card prepared by the Bureau of Engraving and Printing for the American Revolution Bicentennial Administration for insertion in the INTERPHIL '76 souvenir catalog.

The BEP produced a special souvenir "card" on cream-colored paper stock for the ARBA for insertion in the special 6- by 9-inch INTERPHIL '76 catalog. A total of 9,230 six-subject sheets, or 55,380 souvenir cards, were produced, with total catalog production around 50,000. Remaining cards were destroyed, while catalogs were still available for some time afterwards from the American Philatelic Society.

The cards are perforated about 1/4 inch from the bound edge of the catalog for removal. Featured is a reproduction of the 10¢ Independence Hall (series 1954-61) definitive (designer C.R. Chickering), as well as an enlarged vignette of the obverse of the $100 currency note (Independence Hall).

Final quantity sold is unknown; there are no reports of how many, if any, of the catalogs finally were destroyed.

May 30-Sept. 6, 1976, Bicentennial Exposition on Science and Technology, Kennedy Space Center, Cape Canaveral, Fla.

Reproduction of two engravings: a 1949 engraving by Charles Brooks, modeled by Charles Chickering, depicting the first flight of the Wright brothers at Kitty Hawk, and a 1967 engraving by Edward Felver depicting man's first walk in space.

Card production: engraved vignettes, offset surface text and logo.

Quantity sold: 27,795.

June 11-13, 1976, Stamp Expo '76 Bicentennial, Los Angeles, Calif.

Third in Bicentennial series from BEP (following ASDA '76 and INTERPHIL '76). On the right are four flags from the 1968 6¢ Historic Flag series (designers Robert J. Jones, Leonard C. Buckley and Howard C. Mildner), in this order, top to bottom: 1775 Bunker Hill, 1776 Grand Union, 1776 Fort Moultrie, 1777 Bennington.

On the left is an engraved vignette of a Continental soldier and long rifle, backed by a replica of the first U.S. "Stars and Stripes."

Card production: engraved vignettes, offset surface text and logo.

Quantity sold: 24,323.

Aug. 24-29, 1976, 85th anniversary convention of the American Numismatic Association, New York, N.Y.

Card complementing previous issues on the Educational series of currency. Reproduction of the back of the 1896 $2 silver certificate (the face appeared on the 1972 ANA card), picturing Robert Fulton and Samuel F.B. Morse, with portraits probably engraved by Lorenzo Hatch. The note was designed and executed by Thomas F. Morris. Also included are the ANA and Bicentennial logos.

Card production: engraved currency reproduction, offset surface text and logos.

Quantity sold: 38,636.

March 4-6, 1977, MILCOPEX '77, Milwaukee, Wis.

Reproduction of 1933 3¢ Byrd Antarctic Expedition II issue (designer V.S. McCloskey Jr.); 1959 4¢ Arctic Explorations issue (designer George Samerjar); and working model of dog team and sled from 1959 4¢ Arctic Explorations issue.

Card production: engraved vignettes, offset surface text and logo.

Quantity sold: 24,686.

May 20-22, ROMPEX '77, Denver, Colo.

Reproduction of block of four of the 1951 3¢ Colorado issue (designer William K. Schrage), plus a background rendition of Colorado scenery, executed by a BEP artist.

Card production: engraved vignettes, offset surface text and logo.

Quantity sold: 23,287.

Aug. 23-28, 1977, 86th anniversary convention of the American Numismatic Association, Atlanta, Ga.

Reproduction of the obverse of the $5 silver certificate, series 1899, engraved by G.F.C. Smillie from a model adapted from an 1872 photograph of Running Antelope by Alexander Gardner.

Card production: engraved currency reproduction, offset surface text and logo.

Quantity sold: 56,806.

Sept. 2-5, 1977, PURIPEX '77, San Juan, Puerto Rico.

Reproduction of a block of four of the 3¢ 1937 Puerto Rico Territorial issue, showing La Fortaleza (designers William Schrage and William Roach), plus an enlarged background impression of the "San Juan Gate" from the same 1937 3¢ Puerto Rico issue.

Card production: engraved vignettes, offset surface text and logos.

Quantity sold: 23,056

Nov. 16-20, 1977, ASDA National Postage Stamp Show, New York, N.Y.

Reproduction of block of four of the vignette of the 1949 6¢ Wright Brothers commemorative airmail issue (modified stamp design by Gary Chaconas); view of Kitty Hawk Memorial modeled by Charles R. Chickering based on illustration from a 1947 *National Geographic* magazine; stock die engraved by Richard Bowery; card modeled by Clarence Holbert.

Card production: engraved vignettes, offset text and illustration.

Quantity sold: 28,272.

June 2-4, 1978, International Paper Money Show, Memphis, Tenn.

Reproduction of the vignette of the reverse of the $10 National Bank Note (Act of 1863), vignette used again on the reverse of the $500 Federal Reserve Note, series 1918. Vignette engraved in 1869 by Frederick Girsch from a painting by W.H. Powell, which hangs in the U.S. Capitol Rotunda, depicting the discovery of the Mississippi.

Card production: engraved vignette, offset text.

Quantity sold: 28,004.

June 23-25, 1978, CENJEX '78, Freehold, N.J.

Reproduction of block of four of the vignette of the 1936 1¢ Army issue depicting Gen. Washington, Gen. Greene and Mount Vernon (designer William K. Schrage); also reproduced are enlarged reproductions of other U.S. stamps, including the 1928 2¢ Molly Pitcher, 1930 2¢ Gen. Von Steuben, 1929 2¢ Battle of Fallen Timbers, 1957 3¢ Alexander Hamilton, and 1977 13¢ Lafayette.

Card production: engraved vignettes, offset text and illustrations.

Quantity sold: 23,493.

July 4, 1979, private card produced by the International Plate Printers, Die Stampers and Engravers Union of North America.

On this date, with the permission of the BEP, the union members donated their time and effort (using BEP equipment by special permission) to produce a special souvenir card that reproduces "Miss Liberty Rising from the Capitol," an engraving by George F.C. Smillie, originally used on the reverse of Liberty Loan bonds, 1927-42 (modified to show clouds rather than the Capitol dome). Sale of this unofficial, privately produced 8- by 11-inch souvenir card was to benefit the widow of Ed Snipes, former president of the BEP plate printers union. The text describes the engraving process.

Card production: fully engraved.

Quantity issued: 2,500. Quantity sold: 2,500.

Feb. 15-17, 1980, ANA '80, American Numismatic Association mid-year convention, Albuquerque, N.M.

Reproduction of the reverse of the $5 Silver Certificate, series 1896, designed by Thomas F. Morris, portraits engraved by Lorenzo Hatch, central symbolic design (head and wings) engraved by George F.C. Smillie. Card completes the BEP Education series of currency reproductions for numismatic events.

Card production: engraved vignette, offset text, (8x10).

Quantity sold: 24,500 (estimate).

June 6-8, 1980, International Paper Money Show, Memphis, Tenn.

Reproduction of the face of the $10 U.S. note, series 1901, known as the "Buffalo Bill." Lewis and Clark portraits engraved by G.F.C. Smillie; bison engraved by Marcus W. Baldwin, designed by Ostrander Smith based on a Charles R. Knight wash drawing.

Card production: engraved vignette, offset text, (8x10).

Quantity issued: 25,000 (estimate).

July 4-6, 1980, NAPEX, National Philatelic Exhibition of Washington, Bethesda, Md.

Reproduction of block of four of the

U.S. 1923 $5 definitive featuring the head of the Freedom statue on the Capitol dome, designed by C.A. Huston and engraved by J. Eissler, H.I. Earle, E.M. Weeks and E. Hass. Card modeled by Clarence Holbert.

Card production: engraved vignettes, offset text, (6x8).

Quantitiy issued: 25,000 (estimate).

Sept. 8, 1980, BEP Visitors Center, Washington, D.C.

Reproduction of a simulated postage stamp, showing progressive color proofs of multicolor stamp production in various stages. The design shows an eagle in flight, and the word "Freedom."

Card production: intaglio and offset.

Quantity issued: 50,000 (initial order, estimate).

Sept. 25-28, 1980, ASDA Stamp Festival, New York, N.Y.

Reproduction of a block of four of the 1948 U.S. 3¢ Francis Scott Key commemorative (designer Victor S. McCloskey Jr.).

Card production: intaglio and offset, (6x8).

Quantity issued: 25,000 (estimate).

March 20-22, 1981, STAMP EXPO '81 (South), Anaheim, Calif.

Reproduction of a block of four of the 1967 U.S. 13¢ Kennedy definitive (designer Stevan Dohanos, based on a photograph by Jacques Lowe).

Card production: intaglio and offset, (6x8).

Quantity issued: 25,000 (estimate).

April 22, 1981, BEP Visitors Center, Washington, D.C.

Numismatically oriented card to complement 1980 philatelic Visitors Center souvenir card. Includes illustrations of the art of currency engraving. Available Indefinitely.

Card production: intaglio and offset, (5 1/2x7 1/2).

Quantity issued: 50,000 (initial order, estimate).

June 19-21, 1981, MEMPHIS '81, Memphis, Tenn.

Reproduction of the face of the $20 gold certificate, series 1905. Canceled cards include 18¢ Flag stamp and first-day Visitors Center cancel.

Card production: intaglio and offset, (8x10).

Quantity issued: 25,000 (estimate).

July 28-Aug. 2, 1981, ANA '81, American Numismatic Association convention, New Orleans, La.

Reproduction of the "Silver Dollar" back of the $5 silver certificate, series 1886. Canceled cards include 18¢ Flag stamp and first-day Visitors Center cancel.

Card production: intaglio and offset.

Quantity issued: 25,000 (estimate).

March 5-7, 1982, MILCOPEX '82, Milwaukee, Wis.

Reproduction of a modified block of four of the 1959 Ernst Reuter commemorative, part of the U.S. Champion of Liberty series at the time. Canceled cards include 20¢ Flag stamp and first-day Visitors Center cancel.

Card production: intaglio and offset.

Quantity issued: 25,000 (estimate).

June 18, 1982, International Paper Money Show, June 18-20, Memphis, Tenn.

Card reproduces "Brown Back" $100 note of the First National Bank of Nashville from the Second Charter Period. Canceled cards are franked with 20¢ Flag stamp and June 18 Visitors Center cancel.

Aug. 17, 1982, American Numismatic Association Convention, Aug. 17-22, Boston, Mass.

Card reproduces obverse and reverse of the Great Seal of the United States in honor of its 200th anniversary. Canceled cards have Aug. 17 Visitors Center cancel.

Oct. 12, 1982, ESPAMER '82, Oct. 12-17, San Juan, Puerto Rico.

Card reproduces a block of four of the $4 1893 Columbian issue, plus drawing symbolizing the discovery of Puerto Rico. Canceled cards have Oct. 12 Visitors Center cancel.

Jan. 5, 1983, FUN '83, Florida United Numismatists, Jan. 5-8, Orlando, Fla.

Card reproduces the reverse of the $100 "Coin" note, series 1890. Canceled cards have Jan. 5 Visitors Center cancel.

June 17, 1983, TEXANEX-TOPEX '83, June 17-19, San Antonio, Texas.

Card reproduces Texas flag stamp from 1976 State Flags sheet and 1936 3¢ Texas Centennial issue. Canceled cards have June 17 Visitors Center cancel.

Aug. 16, 1983, ANA '83, Aug. 16-21,

San Diego, Calif.

Card reproduces series 1915 $20 Federal Reserve Bank Note. Canceled cards have June 17 Visitors Center cancel.

Oct. 21, 1983, Philatelic Show '83, Oct. 21-23, Boston, Mass.

Card reproduces two U.S. 1932 Summer Olympic commemoratives. Canceled cards have Oct. 21 Visitors Center cancel.

Nov. 17, 1983, National Postage Stamp Show, Nov. 17-20, New York, N.Y.

Card reproduces block of four 1940 Victor Herbert stamps (Famous Americans series). Canceled cards havc Nov. 17 Visitors Center cancel.

Jan. 4, 1984, FUN '84, Jan. 4-7, Tampa, Fla. (Florida United Numismatists).

Card reproduces series 1880 $1 U.S. Note reverse. Canceled cards are franked with 20¢ Flag stamp and Jan. 4 Visitors Center cancel.

April 27, 1984, Stamp Expo '84 South, April 27-29, Los Angeles, Calif.

Card reproduces block of four 1979 Summer Olympics stamps and Olympic torch. Canceled cards are franked with 28¢ Summer Olympic airmail stamp and April 27 Visitors Center cancel.

April 27, 1984, ESPANA '84, April 27-May 6, Madrid, Spain.

Card reproduces block of four U.S. stamps ($1 Columbian) and vignette commemorating Christopher Columbus' voyage to the New World. Canceled cards are franked with 20¢ Flag Over Supreme Court stamp and April 27 Visitors Center cancel.

May 25, 1984, COMPEX '84, May 25-27, Rosemont, Ill.

Card reproduces block of four of the 1¢ Century of Progress value showing Fort Dearborn, along with a map of the Northwest during the 1760-1836 period. Canceled cards are franked with 20¢ Flag Over Supreme Court stamp and May 25 Visitors Center cancel.

June 15, 1984, International Paper Money Show, June 15-17, Memphis, Tenn.

One numismatically oriented card picturing a $10,000 series 1878 U.S. note. Canceled cards are franked with 20¢ Flag Over Supreme Court stamp with hand cancel.

Nov. 15, 1984, American Stamp Dealers' Association (ASDA) show, New York City, Nov. 15-18.

Card shows block of four of the U.S. 1972 8¢ Tom Sawyer commemorative and a vignette of the riverboat *Mississippi*. Canceled cards are franked with 20¢ Flag Over Supreme Court definitive.

Jan. 31, 1985, Long Beach Numismatic and Philatelic Exposition, Long Beach Calif., Jan. 31-Feb. 3.

Card shows the U.S. 1948 3¢ California Gold Rush stamp and a series 1865 $20 gold certificate. Canceled cards are franked with 20¢ Flag Over Supreme Court definitive.

March 1, 1985, MILCOPEX, Milwaukee, Wis., March 1-3.

Card shows block of four of U.S. 1940 Famous Americans stamp honoring composer and conductor John Philip Sousa, along with musical notation of *The Stars and Stripes Forever.* Canceled cards are franked with 20¢ John McCormack commemorative.

April 18, 1985, International Coin Club show, El Paso, Texas, April 18-21.

Numismatic-oriented card. Reproduces reverse of 1902 $50 bank note. Canceled cards are franked with 22¢ Flag Over Capitol definitive.

May 17, 1985, Pacific Northwest Numismatic Association convention, Seattle, Wash., May 17-19.

Numismatic Association convention, Seattle, Wash., May 17-19. Numismatic-oriented card. Reproduces reverse of a 1914 $50 Federal Reserve note. Canceled cards are franked with 22¢ Flag Over Capitol definitie.

June 7, 1985, National Philatelic Exhibition (NAPEX), Arlington, Va., June 7-9.

Card shows a block of four 1982 U.S. International Peace Garden commemoratives and vignette of U.S. and Canadian flags joined by outstretched hands. Canceled cards are franked with 22¢ Flag Over Capitol definitive.

June 14, 1985, International Paper Money Show, Memphis, Tenn., June 14-16.

Numismatic-oriented card reproduces

reverse of 1898 $10,000 United States note. Canceled cards are franked with 22¢ Flag Over Capitol definitive.

Aug. 20, 1985, American Numismatic Association convention, Baltimore, Md., Aug. 20-25.

Numismatic-oriented design features reverse of 1882 $500 gold certificate. Canceled cards are franked with Capitol stamp.

Nov. 14, 1985, International Paper Money Show, Cherry Hill, N.J., Nov. 14-17.

Numismatic-oriented card showing face of 1882 $10 National Bank Note. Canceled cards have 22¢ definitive.

Jan. 2, 1986, Florida United Numismatists convention, Tampa, Fla., Jan. 2-5.

Numismatic-oriented card featuring face of 1890 $100 treasury note. Canceled cards are franked with 22¢ stamp.

Feb. 19, 1986, American Numismatic Association convention, Salt Lake City, Utah, Feb. 19-23.

Numismatic-oriented card shows reverse of 1901 $10 U.S. note. Canceled cards have a 22¢ stamp.

March 21, 1986, Garfield Perry Stamp Club March Party, Cleveland, Ohio, March 21-23.

Card reproduces a block of four 1902 8¢ Martha Washington definitive stamps. Canceled cards are franked with 22¢ Flag Over Capitol stamp.

May 22, 1986, AMERIPEX '86, Rosemont, Ill., May 22-June 1.

Card pictures a family working on its stamp collection, plus reproduces the U.S. 1¢ Franklin issue of 1870, 20¢ Treaty of Paris and 8¢ Stamp Collecting stamps. Canceled cards are franked with 22¢ AMERIPEX stamp.

June 20, 1986, International Paper Money Show, Memphis, Tenn., June 20-22.

Design reproduces the back of a second issue series 1902 $5 National Currency note of the Third Charter period (numismatic theme). The vignette on the note depicts the landing of the Pilgrims. Canceled cards are franked with 22¢ Flag Over Capitol stamp.

Aug. 5, 1986, American Numismatic Association convention, Milwaukee, Wis., Aug. 5-9.

Design reproduces the face of a second issue 5¢ fractional currency note (numismatic theme). Canceled cards are franked with a 22¢ Flag Over Capitol stamp.

Sept. 5, 1986, HOUPEX, Houston, Texas, Sept. 5-7.

Three 1954 Statue of Liberty stamps in Liberty series. Canceled cards are franked with 22¢ Statue of Liberty stamp.

Oct. 2, 1986, LOBEX, Long Beach, Calif., Oct. 2-5.

Block of four 50¢ 1898 U.S. Western Mining Prospector stamps, face of $10 gold certificate. Canceled cards are franked with 22¢ Statue of Liberty stamp.

Nov. 13, 1986, National World and Paper Money Convention, St. Louis, Mo., Nov. 13-16.

Numismatic theme. Features offset mintage of fractional currency. Canceled cards have 22¢ stamp.

Dec. 11, 1986, Dallas Coin and Stamp Exposition, Dallas, Texas, Dec. 11-14.

Block of four stamps marking the 300th anniversary of the landing of the Pilgrims, $10,000 Federal Reserve Note. Canceled cards have 22¢ stamp.

Jan. 7, 1987, Florida United Numismatists show, Orlando, Fla., Jan. 7-10.

Numismatic theme pictures face of 1874 $1 United States note. Canceled cards are franked with 22¢ stamp.

Feb. 27, 1987, American Numismatic Association Mid-winter Convention, Charlotte, N.C., Feb. 27-March 1.

Numismatic theme. Features $500,000,000 coupon treasury note.

June 19, 1987, International Paper Money Show, Memphis, Tenn., June 19-21.

Design reproduces the back of a $20 gold certificate, series 1922 (numismatic theme). The certificate features the great seal of the United States. Canceled cards are franked with 22¢ Liberty stamp.

Aug. 26, 1987, American Numismatic Association convention, Atlanta, Ga., Aug. 26-30.

Numismatic theme. Design features back of $2 silver certificate, 1886 series. Canceled cards have 22¢ stamp.

Sept. 18, 1987, Great Eastern Numis-

matic Association, Cherry Hill, N.J., Sept. 18-20.

Numismatic theme. Design features back of $10 gold certificate, 1907 series. Canceled cards have 22¢ stamp.

Oct. 16, 1987, Stamp Exhibition of Southern California (SESCAL), Los Angeles, Calif., Oct. 16-18.

Design features a die imprint of the 1937 Signing of the Constitution stamp. Canceled cards have 22¢ stamp.

Nov. 12, 1987, Hawaii State Numismatic Association, Honolulu, Hawaii, Nov. 12-15.

Numismatic theme. Design features face of $5 silver certificate, 1923 series, known as the Lincoln porthole note, and a die imprint of the 1937 Hawaii Territorial stamp. Canceled cards have 22¢ stamp.

Jan. 7, 1988, Florida United Numismatists Convention (FUN), Lake Buena Vista, Fla., Jan. 7-10, 1988.

Design features the fifth issue 50¢ fractional currency note featuring a bust of William H. Crawford, secretary of both the War and Treasury departments (1815-1825). Canceled cards have 22¢ stamp.

March 11, 1988, American Numismatic Association mid-winter convention, Little Rock, Ark., March 11-13, 1988.

Design features face of $10,000 gold certificate, series 1882, with portrait of Andrew Jackson. Canceled cards have 22¢ stamp.

June 24, 1988, International Paper Money Show (IPMS), Memphis, Tenn., June 24-26, 1988.

Design features the reverse of a series 1899 $5 silver certificate. Canceled cards have 25¢ stamp.

July 20, 1988, American Numismatic Association national convention, Cincinnati, Ohio, July 20-24, 1988.

Design features reverse of a series 1918 $2 Federal Reserve Bank Note — a vignette of a 1914 period battleship. Canceled cards have 25¢ stamp.

Aug. 25, 1988, American Philatelic Society (Stampshow), Detroit, Mich., Aug. 25-28, 1988.

Design features die imprint of 1938 stamp honoring the 150th anniversary of the ratification of the Constitution. Canceled cards have 25¢ stamp.

Oct. 6, 1988, Illinois Numismatic Association (ILNA), Chicago, Ill., Oct. 6-9, 1988.

Design features the reverse of a series 1915 $10 Federal Reserve bank note. Canceled cards have 25¢ stamp.

Nov. 18, 1988, MIDAPHIL '88, Kansas City, Mo., Nov. 18-20, 1988.

Design features die imprint of 1926 2¢ Liberty Bell stamp celebrating the United States sesquicentennial. Card also has intaglio reproduction of a riverboat engraving. Canceled cards have 25¢ stamp.

Jan. 5, 1989, Florida United Numismatists (FUN), Orlando, Fla., Jan. 5-8, 1989.

Design features the face of an 1891 $50 Treasury note. Canceled cards have 25¢ stamp.

March 3, 1989, American Numismatic Association (ANA) Mid-Winter show, Colorado Springs, Colo., March 3-5, 1989.

Design features the reverse side of a series 1878 $5,000 legal tender note. Canceled cards have 25¢ stamp.

April 28, 1989, International Coin Club of El Paso, Texas, April 28-30, 1989.

Design features the reverse side of a series 1918 $5,000 Federal Reserve note. Canceled cards have 25¢ stamp.

June 23, 1989, International Paper Money Show (IPMS), Memphis, Tenn., June 23-25, 1989.

Design features the face of a series 1907 Treasury note. Canceled cards have 25¢ stamp.

Aug. 9, 1989, American Numismatic Association (ANA), Pittsburgh, Pa., Aug. 9-13, 1989.

Design features the reverse side of a series 1891 $1,000 silver certificate. Canceled cards have 25¢ stamp.

Aug. 24, 1989, American Philatelic Society (Stampshow 89), Anaheim, Calif., Aug. 24-27.

Design features a die imprint of 1923 series 14¢ stamp picturing Chief Hollow Horn Bear, plus related intaglio print.

United States Postal Service

Souvenir cards have been issued by the United States Postal Service and its predecessor, the U.S. Post Office Department, since 1960. They are generally issued for international stamp shows outside the United States or for special purposes of a domestic nature.

The actual forerunner of the U.S. souvenir card was a 1938 issue by the U.S. Post Office Department in conjunction with the Philatelic Truck, which toured the U.S. from 1939 to 1941. The card was 3 by 4 1/2 inches, showing the White House on blue and white paper. Over 750,000 copies were printed and distributed nationwide, and the last copies were printed on ungummed stock after the gummed issues began to appear affixed in unwanted places, apparently due to the original recipients throughout the country.

Current records and information provide more figures regarding the quantity of those souvenir cards issued. Officially, 187,000 gummed cards and 579,500 ungummed cards were issued. These figures probably approximate the number in public circulation more closely than they they represent the number actually issued.

All cards after these two pictorial forerunners measure 6 by 8 inches, and the cards issued for foreign exhibitions were generally distributed free to patrons at those foreign international exhibitions. The mint price for cards in the United States was $1 until 1976, when the price increased to $1.25 per mint card. As of 1989, the price was about $2 for mint cards. Canceled cards were also offered, starting in 1976, franked with U.S. postage and canceled with the special USPS show cancellation for the event being noted. Canceled cards are generally priced at the cost of mint cards, plus the cost of the stamps used in franking. Mail orders are subject to a $10 minimum order requirement, plus a 50¢ handling charge per order. Orders may be mailed to Philatelic Sales Division, U.S. Postal Service, Washington, D.C. 20265.

Although there are no specific time limits imposed on USPS souvenir card orders, most cards are removed from sale within approximately one year from the date of issuance. Some may remain on sale longer, and others may be withdrawn sooner, especially if stocks become depleted. USPS policy on future issues may change.

March 26-April 5, 1960, First International Philatelic Congress, Barcelona, Spain.

Reproduction of vignette of 1893 2¢ Columbian issue, Landing of Columbus, printed in black, from the painting by Vanderlyn in the Rotunda of the U.S. Capitol.

Quantity sold: 10,391.

Nov. 1-9, 1968, EFIMEX, International Philatelic Exhibition, Mexico City, Mexico.

Reproduction of $1 1898 Trans-Mississippi (Cattle in Storm) issue (designer R. Ostrander Smith); after a John A. MacWhirter painting, "The Vanguard."

Quantity sold: 50,000 (estimate).

Sept. 18-26, 1970, PHILYMPIA, London International Stamp Exhibition, London, England.

Reproductions of Pilgrim Tercentenary issue of 1920: the Mayflower (1¢), the Landing of the Pilgrims (2¢) and the Signing of the Mayflower Compact (5¢); designer C.A. Huston, original sketches (2¢ and 5¢) by Edwin White.

Quantity sold: 75,000 (estimate).

Nov. 6-14, 1971, EXFILIMA, Third Inter-American Philatelic Exhibition, Lima, Peru.

Reproduction of three stamps: the 1958 Simon Bolivar and the 1959 Jose de San Martin commemoratives of the Champion of Liberty U.S. issues, modeler William K. Schrage, designers Arnold Copeland, Ervine Metzl and William H. Buckley; and the 1936-37 10-centavo Inca Courier issue of Peru.

Quantity sold: 50,000 (estimate).

June 24-July 9, 1972, BELGICA, Brussels International Philatelic Exhibition, Brussels, Belgium.

Reproduction of 1943 5¢ Belgian Flag of Overrun Countries series, designed and engraved by the American Bank Note Co.; 1953 3¢ Gen. George S. Patton Jr. commemorative, designer William A. Schrage; and 1958 3¢ Brussels Universal and International Exhibition commemorative, modeler V.S. McCloskey Jr., designer Bradbury Thompson.

Quantity sold: 167,119.

Aug. 18, 1972, OLYMPIA Philatelie Munchen, Munich, Germany.

Reproduction of Olympic emblem and 1972 Olympic issue of four stamps: 6¢, bicyling; 8¢, bobsledding; 15¢, running; and 11¢ airmail, skiing; designer Lance Wyman.

Quantity sold: 139,031.

Aug. 26-Sept. 2, 1972, EXFILBRA, Fourth Inter-American Philatelic Exhibition, Rio de Janeiro, Brazil.

Reproduction of U.S. 1930 $1.30 Graf Zeppelin issue, designers C.A. Hall and A.R. Meissner; and two 1929 Brazil airmail issues: the 200-reis Santos-Dumont Airship, and the 300r Augusto Severo Airship "Pax."

Quantity sold: 118,904.

Aug. 28-30, 1972, National Postal Forum, Washington, D.C.

Reproduction of block of four of 1971 8¢ USPS emblem regular issue, designer Raymond Loewy-William Smith, Inc., modeler Ronald C. Sharpe.

Quantity sold: 114,000.

April 30, 1973, Special issue souvenir card to U.S. Postal Service employees for "Postal People Day."

The USPS issued a special 11- by 14-inch souvenir card to all postal employees; the card was distributed free, and was not available to the general public. Card reproduces the 10 8¢ 1973 Postal People stamps, designed by Edward Vebell, and the inscriptions imprinted on the backs.

May 11-20, 1973, IBRA, International Philatelic Exhibition, Munich, Germany.

Reproduction of the official show emblem, and 1930 65¢ U.S. Graf Zeppelin issue, designers C.A. Hall and A.R. Meissner.

Quantity sold: 133,292.

July 4-7, 1973, APEX, International Airmail Exposition, Manchester, England.

Reproduction of 1918 24¢ U.S. airmail error, with inverted illustration of the Curtiss Jenny airplane, designer C.A. Huston; the 1927 Newfoundland 60¢ De Pinedo airmail issue; and the 1925 Honduras 25¢ airmail surcharge.

Quantity sold: 115,932.

Aug. 19-Sept. 2, 1973, POLSKA, World Philatelic Exhibition in Poznan, Poland.

Reproduction of three stamps honoring Nicolaus Copernicus: 1973 8¢ U.S. commemorative, designed by Alvin Eisenman from an 18th-century engraving; and two 1972 Polish issues, of 1-zloty and 1.50zl values.

Quantity sold: 156,536.

Feb. 3-6, 1974, National Hobby Industry Trade Show, Chicago, Ill.

Reproduction of block of four of 1972 Colonial Craftsmen from Bicentennial series, designed by Leonard Everett Fisher, flanked on left by enlarged views of silversmith and glassblower vignettes.

Quantity sold: 93,994.

June 7-16, 1974, INTERNABA, International Stamp Exhibition, Basel, Switzerland.

Reproduction of eight 1974 10¢ stamps commemorating the centennial of the Universal Postal Union, above four-language message from Postmaster General E.T. Klassen, honoring UPU centennial and the Swiss Philatelic Societies.

The eight stamps were designed by Bradbury Thompson from the following paintings: Hokusai's "Five Feminine Virtues;" John Fredrick Peto's "Old Scraps;" Jean-Etienne Liotard's "The Lovely Reader;" Gerard Terborch's "Lady Writing Letter;" Thomas Gainsborough's portrait of Mrs. John Douglas; Francisco de Goya's portrait of Don Antonio Noriega; Raphael's Michelangelo from "School of Athens;" and Jean-Baptiste Simeon Chardin's inkwell and quill from "Boy with a Top."

Quantity sold: 65,000.

Sept. 21-29, 1974, STOCKHOLMIA, International Philatelic Exhibition, Stockholm, Sweden.

Reproduction of 1938 3¢ U.S. Swedish-Finnish Tercentenary issue, designer A.R. Meissner, from painting "Landing of the First Swedish and Finnish Settlers in America," by Stanley M. Arthurs; 1946 10-ore Swedish re-engraved regular issue of King Gustaf V, from the 1939 10o regular issue; and the 1967 45o King Gustav VI Adolf issue on his 85th birthday.

Quantity sold: 75,500.

Oct. 26-Nov. 3, 1974, EXFILMEX, Inter-American Philatelic Exposition, Mexico City, Mexico.

Reproduction of 1960 commemorative of the 150th anniversary of Mexican independence, one from both countries of the joint U.S.-Mexican issue, designers Leon Helguera and C.R. Chickering; U.S. 4¢ value and English inscriptions, Mexican 30-centavo value and Spanish inscription.

Quantity sold: 75,000.

April 4-13, 1975, ESPANA, World Stamp Exhibition, Madrid, Spain.

Reproduction of 4¢ 1893 U.S. Columbian issue of the fleet of Columbus, from a Spanish engraving of the ships Nina, Pinta and Santa Maria; and the 5¢ 1965 Florida Quadricentennial commemorative joint issue with Spain (3-peseta value), designer Brook Temple.

Quantity sold: 106,765.

June 6-16, 1975, ARPHILA Exhibition, Paris, France.

Reproduction of three stamps commemorating art: 1965 French issue, Raoul Dufy's "The Red Violin;" U.S. 1961 4¢ issue of Frederic Remington's "The Smoke Signal," designer C.R. Chickering; and 1962 4¢ issue of Winslow Homer's "Breezing Up," designer V.S. McCloskey Jr. Beneath the stamps is a two-language message from Postmaster General Benjamin Franklin Bailar.

Quantity sold: 79,932.

April 1-4, 1976, WERABA '76, Third International Space Stamp Exhibition, Zurich, Switzerland.

Reproduction of se-tenant pair, 1971 8¢ U.S. Space Achievement issue, designer Robert McCall. Canceled card franked with 10¢ 1975 Apollo-Soyuz se-tenant pair (20¢ total postage).

Quantity sold: 79,000.

May 30-Sept. 6, 1976, Bicentennial Exposition on Science and Technology, Kennedy Space Center, Fla.

Reproduction of 1969 10¢ airmail Moon Landing stamp, designer Paul Calle. Canceled card franked with 1975 10¢ Pioneer and 1975 10¢ Mariner stamps (20¢ total postage).

Quantity sold: 108,983.

July 26, 1976, Colorado Centennial (Aug. 1), U.S. Bicentennial commemorative card.

Reproduction of 1898 5¢ Trans-Mississippi issue, "Fremont on Rocky Mountains" (designer Raymond Ostrander Smith, from J.W. Orr illustration); 1934 4¢ Mesa Verde National Park issue (designer V.S. McCloskey Jr.); 1976 13¢ Colorado State Flag from 50 State Flags issue (designer Walt Reed, modeler Peter Cocci). Canceled card franked with 1976 13¢ Franklin stamp.

Quantity sold: 84,833.

Aug. 20-29, 1976, HAFNIA '76, Copenhagen, Denmark.

Marks the 125th anniversary of Denmark's first postage stamp, reproduced on the card, along with the 1851 1¢ Franklin stamp, designer Edward Purcell (questionable designation). Canceled card franked with 1976 13¢ Franklin stamp.

Quantity sold: 85,558.

Oct. 14-24, 1976, ITALIA '76, Milan, Italy.

Reproduces 1951 Italian stamp honoring Christopher Columbus and 1952 Italian stamp noting Leonardo da Vinci, plus the 1960 U.S. 4¢ Champion of Liberty issue in honor of Guiseppe Garibaldi, designers Arnold Copeland, Ervine Metzl and William H. Buckley. Canceled card franked with 1976 13¢ Franklin stamp.

Quantity sold: 86,854.

Oct. 30-31, 1976, NORDPOSTA '76, Hamburg, Germany.

Reproductions of 1959 10pfennig+5pf German stamp marking the centenary of Hamburg stamps, 50pf+25pf 1966 German stamp honoring Gen. (Baron) Friedrich Wilhelm von Steuben, designer A.R. Meissner. Canceled card franked with 1976 13¢ Clara Maass stamp.

Quantity sold: 82,652.

May 26-June 5, AMPHILEX '77, Amsterdam, The Netherlands.

Reproductions of two Netherlands definitives depicting Queen Wilhelmina (1894 5¢ issue and 1947 25¢ issue) and the U.S. 1953 3¢ New York commemorative, designer C.R. Chickering. Canceled card franked with 1977 13¢ Lindbergh Flight stamp.

Quantity sold: 87,973.

Aug. 28-Sept. 4, 1977, SAN MARINO '77, Republic of San Marino.

Reproduction of the first-issue 1877 San Marino 2-centesimi stamp and the first two U.S. stamps, the 5¢ Franklin and 10¢ Washington of 1847. U.S. stamp reproductions taken from new engravings closely matching the originals (not the official reprints); 5¢ Franklin reproduction vignette engraver Edward P. Archer, lettering engraver Robert G. Culin; 10¢ vignette engraver John S. Wallace Jr., lettering engraver James L. Goodbody. Card designed and modeled by Peter Cocci. Canceled card franked with 1977 13¢ Lafayette stamp.

Quantity issued: 75,000 (estimate).

March 20-29, 1978, ROCPEX '78, Taipei, Taiwan, Republic of China.

Reproduction of block of four 1977 13¢ Pueblo Pottery stamps (denominations removed), designed by Ford Ruthling, and two values ($1 and $8) from the second Porcelain series of the Republic of China, 1973. Canceled cards were not officially prepared; sold mint only.

Quantity issued: 75,000 (estimate).

May 20-25, 1978, NAPOSTA '78, Frankfurt am Main, Federal Republic of Germany.

Reproduction of the 70-pfennig German stamp of 1976 honoring Carl Schurz and the U.S. Bicentennial, and the 3¢ Lincoln and 11¢ Hayes issues of the U.S. 1922-25 definitive series. Canceled card franked with 1975 13¢ Eagle and Shield definitive.

Quantity issued: 75,000 (estimate).

Sept. 15-23, 1979, BRASILIANA '79, Rio de Janeiro, Brazil.

Reproduction of 1973 20-centavo stamp honoring Alberto Santos-Dumont and the 1978 31¢ U.S. airmail se-tenant pair honoring the Wright Brothers, designed by Ken Dallison. Canceled card franked with 1978 Wright Brothers airmail pair (two 31¢ stamps).

Quantity issued: 75,000 (estimate).

Nov. 2-4, 1979, JAPEX '79, Tokyo, Japan.

Reproduction of the 15-yen Japan EXPO '70 stamp (first issue) and the 1960 4¢ U.S. issue honoring ties between the United States and Japan, designed by Gyo Fujikawa. Canceled card franked with 1978 15¢ Fort McHenry Flag definitive.

Quantity issued: 75,000 (estimate).

May 6-14, 1980, LONDON 1980, London, England.

Reproduction (enlarged) of the 1907 2¢ U.S. commemorative honoring Jamestown, designed by M.W. Baldwin. Canceled cards not officially prepared; sold mint only.

Quantity issued: 80,000 (estimate).

June 13-22, 1980, NORWEX '80, Oslo, Norway.

Reproduction of the 1975 Norwegian 1.25-krone American Emigration Sesquicentennial issue and the U.S. 2¢ and 5¢ Norse-American stamps, designed by C.A. Huston. Canceled cards franked with 1980 15¢ Winter Olympics commemorative.

Quantity issued: 80,000 (estimate).

Nov. 15-19, 1980, ESSEN '80, Essen, Federal Republic of Germany.

Reproduction of a 1954 West German stamp noting the 500th anniversary of printing by movable type, and a U.S. 1952 3¢ stamp with the same theme (designer V.S. McCloskey Jr.). Canceled cards have the 15¢ Albert Einstein commemorative affixed.

Quantity issued: 80,000 (estimate).

May 22-31, 1981, WIPA '81, Vienna, Austria.

Reproduction of a 1967 Austrian stamp marking the 125th anniversary of the Vienna Philharmonic Orchestra, and a 1964 U.S. 5¢ commemorative for American Music (designer Bradbury Thompson). Canceled cards have the 18¢ Flag stamp affixed.

Quantity issued: 80,000 (estimate).

Oct. 1-31, 1981, National Stamp Collecting Month.

Reproduction of the $5 Columbian commemorative from the United States in 1893, plus the U.S. 18¢ Space Achievements stamp picturing the Space Shuttle "Columbia" from the eight-design se-tenant issue of 1981 (single design showing landing approach only). Canceled cards have the 18¢ Flag coil stamp affixed.

Quantity issued: 100,000 (estimate).

Oct. 9-18, 1981, PHILATOKYO '81,

Tokyo, Japan.

Reproduction of 1963 Japanese stamp noting letter writing, plus U.S. 1974 Universal Postal Union commemorative depicting letter writing (single Hokusai design only from eight-design set, designed by Bradbury Thompson). Canceled cards have a pair of the 15¢ Letter Writing se-tenant stamps affixed.

Quantity issued: 80,000 (estimate).

Nov. 7-9, 1981, NORDPOSTA '81, Hamburg, Federal Republic of Germany.

Reproduction of a German semipostal with a ship theme, plus the 1944 U.S. 3¢ Steamship issue (designer V.S. McCloskey Jr.). Canceled cards have the non-denominated "C" stamp (20¢) affixed.

Quantity issued: 80,000 (estimate).

May 20-24, 1982, CANADA '82, Toronto, Ontario, Canada.

Reproductions of the 1859 Canada Beaver issue and the 1869 U.S. Eagle and Shield pictorial issue. Canceled cards franked with 20¢ Flag definitive.

Quantity issued: 80,000 (estimate).

June 11-21, 1982, PHILEXFRANCE '82, Paris, France.

Reproductions of the 1976 French American Bicentennial commemorative and the 1978 U.S. French Alliance commemorative. Canceled cards franked with a se-tenant pair of the 18¢ Battles of Yorktown-Virginia Capes commemoratives.

Quantity issued: 80,000 (estimate).

Oct. 1, 1982, National Stamp Collecting Month, Oct. 1-31.

Card reproduces U.S. 24¢ airmail invert. Canceled cards are franked with a 35¢ Glenn Curtiss airmail stamp and special cancel.

Oct. 12, 1982, ESPAMER '82, Oct. 12-17, San Juan, Puerto Rico.

Card reproduces new Ponce de Leon commemorative and two previous U.S. issues with a Puerto Rico theme. Canceled cards franked with 20¢ Ponce de Leon stamp and show first-day cancel.

March 24, 1983, Sweden joint issue.

Card marking joint commemorative between Sweden and United States for the bicentennial of trade relations between the two countries.

May 5, 1983, German joint issue.

Card marking joint commemorative between the Federal Republic of Germany and United States for the 300th anniversary of German immigration to the United States.

May 21, 1983, TEMBAL '83, May 21-29, Basel, Switzerland.

Card reproduces 1845 2 1/2-rappen Swiss Basel Dove stamp and 1967 U.S. 20¢ Columbia Jays airmail stamps. Canceled cards are franked with 20¢ Birds & Flowers stamp and show first-day cancel.

July 29, 1983, BRASILIANA '83, July 29-Aug. 7, Rio de Janeiro, Brazil.

Card reproduces 1843 Brazil 30-reis Bull's-Eye first issue and 1847 U.S. George Washington first issue. Canceled cards are franked with 20¢ 1982 Washington commemorative and show first-day cancel.

Aug. 4, 1983, BANGKOK '83, Aug. 4-13, Bangkok, Thailand.

Card reproduces first 1883 Thai King Chulalongkorn stamp and 1883 U.S. Washington Bank Note stamp. Canceled cards are franked with 20¢ 1982 Washington commemorative and show first-day cancel.

Aug. 19, 1983, International Philatelic Memento Card, Aug. 19.

Special card designed primarily for use by USPS foreign agents at international stamp shows they attend on behalf of the Postal Service. These should be considered only marginally as souvenir cards. Card reproduces U.S. 1970 6¢ Bald Eagle commemorative. Canceled cards are franked with 20¢ Flag stamp and Washington, D.C., cancel.

Oct. 1, 1983, National Stamp Collecting Month, Oct. 1-31.

Card reproduces $2 1898 U.S. Trans-Mississippi stamp. Canceled cards are franked with 20¢ stamp and Oct. 1 cancel.

April 27, 1984, ESPANA, April 27-May 6, Madrid, Spain.

Card reproduces the 1930 Spanish 40-centimo tribute to Christopher Columbus and the U.S. 1893 Columbian Exposition 4¢ value. Canceled cards are franked with 20¢ Flag stamp and show cancel.

June 19, 1984, HAMBURG, June 19-26, Hamburg, West Germany.

Card marks the 19th Universal Postal

Union Congress and features reproductions of the 1949 West German stamp honoring Heinrich von Stephan and the 1963 U.S. Montgomery Blair airmail stamp. Canceled cards are franked with Concord commemorative and show cancel.

June 26, 1984, St. Lawrence Seaway 25th Anniversary.

Card reproduces the 1959 U.S. and Canadian stamps marking the opening of the seaway. Canceled cards are franked with 1984 U.S. St. Lawrence Seaway commemorative canceled on first day; and with both 1984 U.S. and Canadian Seaway commemoratives, each bearing the first-day cancel of the respective country.

Sept. 21, 1984, AUSIPEX '84, Sept. 21-30, Melbourne, Australia.

Card reproduces U.S. 1898 10¢ Trans-Mississippi and Western Australian 1854 1-penny Swan River Settlement stamps. Canceled cards are franked with 20¢ Flag Over Supreme Court definitive and show first-day cancel.

Oct. 1, 1984, National Stamp Collecting Month, Oct. 1-31.

Card reproduces 20¢ Family Unity commemorative. Canceled cards are franked with 20¢ Family Unity stamp and National Stamp Collecting Month pictorial cancel.

Oct. 22, 1984, PHILAKOREA '84, Oct. 22-31, Seoul, Korea.

Card reproduces 1975 Korean stamp showing Mount Sorak National Park and the 1934 United States stamp depicting the Grand Canyon National Park. Canceled cards are franked with the 20¢ Hawaiian Statehood commemorative and PHILAKOREA cancel.

Feb. 26, 1985, International Philatelic Memento Card.

Special card designed primarily for use by USPS foreign agents at international stamp shows they attend for the Postal Service. These should be considered only marginally as souvenir cards. Card reproduces U.S. 1847 10¢ George Washington stamp. Canceled cards are franked with non-denominated D stamp and Washington, D.C. cancel.

March 18, 1985, OLYMPHILEX, Lausanne, Switzerland, March 18-24.

Card, which honors the International Olympic Committee, reproduces the 1983 U.S. 40¢ Olympic airmail stamp (male gymnast) and 1984 Swiss 80-centime stamp commemorating the home of the IOC. Canceled cards exist.

May 14, 1985, ISRAPHIL, Tel Aviv, Israel, May 14-22.

Card reproduces the U.S. 1922 15¢ Statue of Liberty stamp and Israeli 1950 22 prutot showing a symbolic struggle for free immigration. Canceled cards are franked with Flag Over Capitol definitive and ISRAPHIL cancel.

July 5, 1985, ARGENTINA '85, Buenos Aires, Argentina, July 5-14.

Card reproduces the 1978 U.S. 15¢ Rose booklet stamp and 1960 Argentinean 1-peso+1p Passionflower semipostal. Canceled cards are franked with Flag Over Capitol definitive and ARGENTINA '85 cancel.

Sept. 11, 1985, MOPHILA '85, Hamburg, West Germany, Sept. 11-15.

Card reproduces U.S. 1901 4¢ Trans-Mississippi and West German 1982 50-pfennig+25pf stamps showing autos. Canceled cards are franked with two 11¢ Stutz Bearcat coils and MOPHILA cancel.

Oct. 25, 1985, ITALIA, Rome, Italy, Oct. 25-Nov. 3.

Card reproduces U.S. 1958 3¢ International Geophysical Year commemorative and 1961 Italian 500-lira Michelangelo stamp. Canceled cards are franked with 22¢ AMERIPEX commemorative and ITALIA cancel.

Feb. 21, 1986, International Philatelic Memento Card.

Card reproduces the U.S. 1974 Statue of Liberty airmail. Canceled cards are franked with 22¢ Frederic August Bartholdi commemorative and New York City cancel.

Aug. 28, 1986, STOCKHOLMIA '86, Stockholm, Sweden, Aug. 28-Sept. 7.

Card reproduces U.S. 1869 2¢ and 1936 Swedish stamps, both showing a post rider. Canceled cards are franked with U.S. Flag stamp and STOCKHOLMIA cancel.

June 13, 1987, CAPEX '87, Toronto, Ontario, Canada, June 13-21.

Card reproduces U.S. 1923 30¢ Bison

and 1981 Canadian Vancouver Island Marmot stamps. Canceled cards are franked with a randomly selected U.S. Wildlife stamp and USPS CAPEX '87 cancel.

Oct. 16, 1987, HAFNIA '87, Copenhagen, Denmark, Oct. 16-25.

Card reproduces the 10¢ Pan American stamp with value omitted and a 1976 Danish semipostal stamp (Scott B52) that also features a ship. The canceled card bears a 22¢ Flag with Fireworks stamp and is canceled with the HAFNIA '87 imprint.

Nov. 13, 1987, MONTE CARLO, Exposition Philatelique, Monaco, Nov. 13-17.

Card reproduces U.S. Scott 2287 Monarch butterfly and Scott 2300 Tiger Swallowtail without denominations. Also reproduced is a 3.40-franc Butterfly stamp of Monaco. Canceled cards are franked with a randomly selected U.S. Wildlife stamp canceled with exposition imprint.

June 1, 1988, FINLANDIA '88, Helsinki, Finland, June 1-12.

Card reproduces 1938 U.S. Swedish-Finnish Tercentenary stamp and Finnish version of 1988 New Sweden joint issue. Canceled cards are franked with a 44¢ U.S. New Sweden stamp and canceled.

July 7, 1989, PHILEXFRANCE 89. Paris, France, July 7-17.

Card reproduces French triptych honoring the bicentennial of the French Revolution and features a die imprint of the U.S. version. Canceled cards are franked with either a 25¢ Flag With Clouds stamp or 45¢ airmail stamp.

Chapter 11

Linn's U.S. Stamp Market Index

Linn's U.S. Stamp Market Index is a measurement of the United States stamp market, based on a representative sample of U.S. stamps in the condition in which they are most often bought and sold. It includes used and unused 19th-century singles; unused, original gum and mint, never-hinged 20th-century singles; unused, original gum and mint, never-hinged airmail singles; and one coil line pair. Most are tracked in fine-to-very-fine condition.

The specific items included in the index are: Scott 1 used with four margins; Scott 11, 68, 73, 77, 113, 119 and 179 used, fine-to-very-fine; Scott 207, 224, 233, 239, 280, 288, 292, 299, 306, 339, 523, 573, C1, C3, C6, C13-15 unused, original gum, fine-to-very-fine; and Scott 230, 285, 325, 328, 372, 374, 400A, 548-50, 617-19, 630, 704-15, 730-31, 859-93, 909-21, 1075, C7-9, C18, C25-31, C46, C57, C61 line pair and C66 mint, never-hinged, fine-to-very-fine.

Values have been computed from a January 1970 base figure of 100. This system is the same sort of system used to create the Consumer Price Index.

For the years shown here, the Stamp Market Index charts a pattern of rise, boom, bust and partial recovery in the U.S. stamp market.

During 1970-77, retail prices showed steady double-digit annual growth. With an average increase of 17.32 percent per year, values more than tripled between the beginning of 1970 and the end of 1977.

During 1978, the index rose 46.84 percent, followed by a 50.17-percent jump in 1979. The pace slowed dramatically during 1980 and 1981. These years saw meager increases of 7.91 percent and 2.64 percent, respectively.

The Stamp Market Index peaked in June 1981, when stamp prices broke the 900 barrier — nine times their level in January 1970. The market slipped slightly in July 1981 but held steady through the rest of that year.

The bust developed during 1982. Price levels in December of that year were 24.76 percent below those of the year before. This decline in prices slowed but continued during 1983-86. Stamp prices reached their lowest ebb of the 1980s in October 1986, at 438.47.

Since then, prices have slowly stabilized and steadily risen. The final Stamp Market Index point recorded on the accompanying chart, a June 1989 measurement of

482.12, represents a 10-percent rebound from the low point of the post-boom downturn in stamp prices.

It is significant to note that the Stamp Market Index does not include price measurements for U.S. stamps in very-fine grade or higher, for U.S. plate number coils or for U.S. postal history — three areas in U.S. collecting that have grown vigorously throughout the 1980s.

Linn's U.S. Stamp Market Index

Year	Jan.	Feb.	March	April	May	June	July	Aug.	Sept.	Oct.	Nov.	Dec.
1970	100.00	100.07	104.72	106.70	107.76	113.09	115.63	118.20	120.97	119.94	122.13	121.64
1971	128.94	127.94	132.93	132.04	134.62	135.82	138.06	136.82	138.62	140.08	144.43	147.69
1972	151.02	167.08	157.60	159.45	161.86	159.31	164.02	168.12	168.10	174.42	177.09	173.57
1973	177.94	179.89	182.86	184.37	184.82	185.06	186.41	186.67	189.80	192.61	195.64	196.70
1974	202.76	202.84	208.38	210.90	211.91	214.64	220.77	221.18	224.20	233.06	236.63	236.63
1975	238.43	238.65	239.68	239.34	244.80	247.84	249.41	251.37	257.95	264.45	272.26	269.57
1976	274.00	276.93	280.68	290.64	301.64	301.83	302.61	304.17	305.58	307.08	312.33	313.47
1977	322.50	325.63	337.28	341.49	340.58	340.75	342.78	348.07	350.94	352.97	363.73	364.99
1978	376.20	380.40	409.71	437.41	457.51	487.35	497.52	506.62	515.70	534.71	539.03	535.95
1979	527.97	541.37	567.37	590.41	653.14	706.45	711.22	710.93	701.37	719.77	761.09	804.86
1980	812.39	837.12	806.82	817.89	824.01	854.75	863.47	890.43	853.15	885.33	882.56	868.49
1981	863.51	866.65	872.48	871.14	881.44	900.46	866.53	894.77	884.28	878.24	877.96	886.35
1982	822.11	790.77	781.91	723.93	722.62	720.10	727.47	724.97	735.52	695.82	652.85	666.91
1983	643.32	598.78	618.92	628.28	630.31	602.80	615.00	605.71	618.80	592.96	581.21	598.12
1984	599.94	599.36	579.92	568.57	564.50	550.79	546.58	531.77	523.54	503.30	507.95	502.82
1985	497.72	509.02	514.55	522.79	523.03	529.86	531.65	529.13	529.79	530.86	528.19	519.21
1986	507.07	498.23	504.42	489.50	492.03	494.11	471.26	462.87	455.17	438.37	440.32	449.99
1987	452.49	453.31	458.80	472.05	480.68	486.67	487.46	487.32	489.22	491.93	492.25	493.50
1988	490.13	486.77	483.21	491.93	492.39	194.12	496.07	497.25	497.86	498.05	496.53	495.85
1989	496.70	495.63	492.75	488.48	487.97							

Chapter 12

Law and Philately

The object of this chapter is to highlight the legal ramifications of various policies and practices relevant to stamp collectors, exhibitors and dealers.

Unordered Stamps or Other Philatelic Merchandise

The problem of consumers in the United States receiving merchandise in the mail they did not want and did not request became so annoying during the 1960s that the Congress of the United States decided to specifically legislate against the mailing of practically all types of unordered goods. The law concerning this matter appeared as Section 3009 of the Postal Reorganization Act, enacted Aug. 12, 1970 (39 USC 3009).

According to the act, there are only two kinds of merchandise that can be sent legally through the mails to a person without his consent or agreement:

1. Free samples that are clearly and plainly marked as such.

2. Merchandise mailed by a charitable organization asking for contributions.

In either of the above cases, the consumer can consider the merchandise as a gift if he likes. In all other instances, it is illegal to send merchandise to anyone unless he has previously requested it.

If a person receives unordered merchandise of any kind, he can take it as a gift. He does not have to pay for it, and it is illegal for the individual or firm sending it to him to dun him for it or send him a bill.

If anyone experiences difficulty with unordered merchandise or is tormented with statements demanding payment for such, he should contact the Federal Trade Commission, 6th Street and Pennsylvania Avenue, Washington, D.C. 20580, or the nearest FTC field office. Field offices of the Federal Trade Commission are located in nearly all of the major cities in the United States.

Following the federal government's lead, a number of states have enacted similar legislation forbidding the offer of merchandise to residents of their state which was "not actually ordered or requested by the recipient" (Art.83, Sec.21A, Annotated Code of Maryland).

CONCLUSION: Anyone receiving unrequested approvals or any other unordered philatelic merchandise may simply keep it as a gift. There is no liability to pay for it nor any responsibility to return it.

Possession of Counterfeit Postage Stamps

The question has been posed as to whether it is unlawful under the various statutory provisions and court decisions of the United States to retain in one's possession, knowingly or unknowingly, a counterfeit stamp when its owner has no intent whatsoever to dispose of it.

In 1976 a veritable storm of controversy developed in the philatelic press over this question. The legal office of the United States Secret Service, a division of the Treasury Department charged with enforcing violations of any federal statute dealing with securities or obligations, foreign or domestic, has consistently maintained that its agents are entitled to pick up any counterfeit stamps held by private individuals or firms regardless of the intent of the collector as to its usage.

However, a number of private attorneys, collectors themselves, after studying the various provisions of the federal criminal statutes dealing with U.S. and foreign financial obligations and securities (postage and revenue stamps are defined in the statutes as falling within this terminology) have apparently come to the opposite conclusion based on the fact that these statutory provisions indicate there must be "criminal intent," i.e., an intention to victimize or defraud someone in the usage of a counterfeit stamp.

Without such criminal intent, suggest most philatelic attorneys, mere possession of a counterfeit stamp does not violate any provision of law, and such stamp may be retained for reference or collecting purposes.

More recently, known forgeries of United States and foreign postage stamps described as such have been displayed in stamp exhibits and offered in public auctions without reported incident.

The major statutory provisions generally cited are as follows: Title 18, United States Code, Sections 8, 15, 471, 472, 478, 480, 501, 502.

Those sections, especially Section 501, kept philately from being included in the Hobby Protection Act, Public Law 93-167, 93rd Congress, H.R. 5777, Nov. 29, 1973. The Hobby Protection Act is an act to require that reproductions and imitations of coins and political items be marked as copies with the date of manufacture.

The Senate and the House of Representatives felt that the sections mentioned provided ample protection for the hobby of philately.

Those sections are reprinted herewith from the United States Code:

Sec. 8. Obligation or other security of the United States defined.

The term "obligation or other security of the United States" includes all bonds, certificates of indebtedness, national bank currency, Federal Reserve notes, Federal Reserve bank notes, coupons, United States notes, Treasury notes, gold certificates, silver certificates, fractional notes, certificates of deposit, bills, checks, or drafts for money, drawn by or upon authorized officers of the United States, stamps and other representatives of value, of whatever denomination, issued under any Act of Congress, and canceled United States stamps. (June 25, 1948, ch. 645, 62 Stat. 685.)

Sec. 15. Obligation or other security of foreign government defined.

The term "obligation or other security of any foreign government" includes, but is not limited to, uncanceled stamps, whether or not demonetized. (Added Pub. L. 85-921, Title 3, Sept. 2, 1958, 72 Stat. 1771.)

Sec. 471. Obligations or securities of United States.

Whoever, with intent to defraud, falsely makes, forges, counterfeits, or alters any obligation or other security of the United States, shall be fined not more than $5,000 or imprisoned not more than fifteen years, or both. (June 25, 1948, ch. 645, 62 Stat. 705.)

Sec. 472. Uttering counterfeit obligations or securities.

Whoever, with intent to defraud, passes, utters, publishes, or sells, or attempts to pass, utter, publish, or sell, or with like intent brings into the United States or keeps in possession or conceals any falsely made, forged, counterfeited, or altered obligation or other security of the United States, shall be fined not more than $5,000 or imprisoned not more than fifteen years, or both. (June 25, 1948, ch. 645, 62 Stat. 705.)

Sec. 478. Foreign obligations or securities.

Whoever, within the United States, with intent to defraud, falsely makes, alters, forges, or counterfeits any bond, certificate, obligation, or other security of any foreign government, purporting to be or in imitation of any such security issued under the authority of such foreign government, or any treasury note, bill, or promise to pay, lawfully issued by such foreign government and intended to circulate as money, shall be fined not more than $5,000 or imprisoned not more than five years, or both. (June 25, 1948, ch. 645, 62 Stat. 707.)

Sec. 480. Possessing counterfeit foreign obligations or securities.

Whoever, within the United States, knowingly and with intent to defraud, possesses or delivers any false, forged, or counterfeit bond, certificate, obligation, security, treasury note, bill, promise to pay, bank note, or bill issued by a bank or corporation of any foreign country, shall be fined not more than $1,000 or imprisoned not more than one year, or both. (June 25, 1948, ch. 645, 62 Stat. 707.)

Sec. 501. Postage stamps and postal cards.

Whoever forges or counterfeits any

postage stamp, or any stamp printed upon any stamped envelope, or postal card, or any die, plate, or engraving therefor; or

Whoever makes or prints, or knowingly uses or sells, or possesses with intent to use or sell, any such forged or counterfeited postage stamp, stamped envelope, postal card, die, plate, or engraving; or

Whoever makes, or knowingly uses or sells, or possesses with intent to use or sell, any paper bearing the watermark of any stamped envelope, or postal card, or any fraudulent imitation thereof; or

Whoever makes or prints or authorizes to be made or printed, any postage stamp, stamped envelope, or postal card, of the kind authorized and provided by the Post Office Department, without the special authority and direction of said department; or

Whoever after such postage stamp, stamped envelope, or postal card has been printed, with intent to defraud, delivers the same to any person not authorized by an instrument in writing, duly executed under the hand of the Postmaster General and the seal of the Post Office Department, to receive it —

Shall be fined not more than $500 or imprisoned not more than five years, or both. (June 25, 1948, ch. 645, 62 Stat. 713.)

Sec. 502. Postage and revenue stamps of foreign governments.

Whoever forges, or counterfeits, or knowingly utters or uses any forged or counterfeit postage stamp or revenue stamp of any foreign government, shall be fined not more than $500 or imprisoned not more than five years, or both. (June 25, 1948, ch. 645, 62 Stat. 713.)

CONCLUSION: What few tangential court decisions there have been on this subject, where counterfeit obligations or securities have been seized, such as currency or foreign stamps, would appear to be against the government's position, since without any showing of criminal intent to defraud, the items seized have generally been ordered returned to the owners.

A contrary decision would, at the very least, seem to be unrealistic and impractical, since most expertizing foundations make considerable use of counterfeit items for comparative purposes in determining whether a submitted stamp is genuine or not.

Reproduction and Duplication of U.S. Stamp Designs

In 1974 a controversy developed between the U.S. Postal Service on the one hand and certain dealers, dealers' organizations and stamp exhibitions on the other, as to whether a private commercial enterprise or stamp exhibition is free to reproduce U.S. postage stamps in souvenir card form or otherwise without the permission of the Postal Service.

A number of dealers and stamp exhibitions have issued souvenir cards in this manner in the past, and the Postal Service apparently has no intention to make its position retroactive, nor does its current position have anything to do with the counterfeiting provisions referred to earlier in this chapter.

Purely and simply the Postal Service believes it has the right to license the reproduction of U.S. stamp designs for future commercial use on a paid basis, citing as its authority the legal claim of copyright as set forth in the Act of Jan. 27, 1938, c. 10, 52 Stat. 6. Section 1 of

"That the Postmaster General shall prepare, in such form and at such times as he shall deem advisable, and, upon his request, the Public Printer shall print as a public document to be sold by the Superintendent of Documents, illustrations in black and white of postage stamps of the United States, together with such descriptive, historical, and philatelic information with regard to such stamps as the Postmaster General may deem suitable:

"Provided, that notwithstanding the provisions of Section 52 of the Act of Jan. 12, 1895 (U.S.C., 1934 edition, Title 44, Sec. 58), stereotype or electrotype plates, or duplicates thereof used in the publications authorized to be printed by this section shall not be sold or otherwise disposed of but shall remain the property of the United States:

"And provided further, that notwithstanding the provisions of Section 7 of the Copyright Act of March 4, 1909 (U.S.C., 1934 edition, Title 17, Sec. 7), or any other provision of law, copyright may be secured by the Postmaster General on behalf of the United States in the whole or any part of the publication authorized by this section."

Based on the foregoing statutory provision and the legal history of the Act, the Postal Service is of the opinion it may legally prevent the reproduction or duplication of its stamp designs or license them for such purposes on a fee-paid basis, and apparently would be willing to liberally license such usage with the view to bringing in further revenue to the Postal Service since stamp designs, like delivery of the mail, are, in its opinion, services paid for with the public's funds.

CONCLUSION: This controversy has not been resolved and will probably take serious negotiation or suit in an appropriate federal court to decide.

N.B. — The Postal Service also claims trademark and service rights in distinctive words and phrases that appear as a part of most postage stamp designs, such as "U.S. Mail," "U.S. Postage," "U.S. Airmail," "Certified Mail," etc.

Treasury Department Dictum Regarding Stamp Reproduction

Reprinted here are applicable sections of the law that provide guidance for reproduction of U.S. and foreign postage stamps in souvenir card formats. Briefly, the law does not allow private citizens the right to produce U.S. security items except under restrictions that are spelled out here.

The use of illustrations and motion picture films and slides of postage and revenue stamps is detailed by the Secret Service of the Treasury Department in a facts sheet.

The facts sheet notes that the Treasury Department sponsored legislation to liberalize and clarify laws relating to the use of illustrations and films of paper money, postage and revenue stamps, checks, bonds and other obligations of the United States and foreign governments.

This legislation was passed by Congress and approved by the president on Sept. 2, 1958 (Public Law 85-921, 85th Congress), and was further amended on June 20, 1968, to permit reproductions of postage stamps in color under certain conditions (Public Law 90-353, 90th Congress).

The facts sheet includes the following information:

United States Postage Stamps

Black and White Illustrations: Canceled and uncanceled United States postage stamps may be illustrated in any size in black and white in articles, books, journals, newspapers, or albums for philatelic educational, historical, and newsworthy purposes.

No individual facsimiles of United States postage stamps are permitted. No individual photographs are permitted, except glossy prints necessary to reproduce the illustrations in publications.

Colored Illustrations: Canceled and uncanceled United States postage stamps may be illustrated in color in articles, books, journals, newspapers or albums for philatelic, educational, historical and newsworthy purposes. Illustrations in color of uncanceled United States postage stamps must be of a size less than three-fourths or more than one and one-half, in linear dimension of each part of the stamps illustrated. Colored illustrations of canceled United States postage stamps may be in any size. The canceled stamps illustrated must bear an official cancellation mark, i.e., the stamps must have been used for postage.

Foreign Postage Stamps

Black and White Illustrations: Black and white illustrations of uncanceled foreign postage stamps in any size are permitted for philatelic, educational, historical, and newsworthy purposes in articles, books, journals, newspapers, and albums. Black and white illustrations of canceled foreign postage stamps are permissible in any size and for any purpose.

As in the case of United States stamps, no individual facsimiles or photographs of foreign postage stamps are permitted, except glossy prints necessary to reproduce the illustrations in publications.

Colored Illustrations: Uncanceled foreign postage stamps may be illustrated in color in articles, books, journals, newspapers or albums for philatelic, educational, historical and newsworthy purposes, provided such illustrations are of a size less than three-fourths or more than one and one-half in linear dimension of each part of the stamp illustrated. Colored illustrations of canceled foreign postage stamps are permissible in any size and for any purpose. The canceled foreign postage stamps illustrated must bear an official cancellation mark, i.e., the stamps must have been used for postage.

Motion-Picture Films and Slides of United States and Foreign Postage Stamps: Motion picture films and slides of United States and foreign postage stamps in black and white or in color for projection upon a screen or for use in telecasting are permissible, but not for advertising purposes except philatelic advertising.

Advertising

Printed Illustrations: Black and white illustrations in any size of canceled and uncanceled U.S. and foreign postage stamps are permitted in philatelic advertising of legitimate dealers in stamps or publishers of or dealers in philatelic articles, books, journals, newspapers, or albums.

Colored illustrations of canceled U.S. and foreign postage stamps may be used for philatelic advertising in any size. Uncanceled U.S. and foreign postage stamps may be illustrated in color for philatelic advertising, provided such illustrations are of a size less than three-fourths or more than one and one-half in linear dimension of each part of the stamps illustrated.

Films: The use of reproductions of canceled and uncanceled U.S. and foreign postage stamps in films for philatelic advertising purposes is permissible.

U.S. and Foreign Revenue Stamps

Printed Illustrations of U.S. Revenue Stamps: Printed illustrations of U.S. revenue stamps are permitted under the same conditions and for the same purposes as illustrations of U.S. postage stamps, except that colored illustrations of U.S. revenue stamps are not permitted.

Printed Illustrations of Foreign Revenue Stamps: Printed illustrations of foreign revenue stamps are permitted on the same conditions and for the same purposes as illustrations of foreign postage stamps. Colored illustrations, but only of canceled foreign revenue stamps, are permissible.

Motion-Picture Films and Slides of Revenue Stamps: Films of U.S. and foreign revenue stamps are permissible in the same manner as films of U.S. and foreign postage stamps.

Destruction of Plates and Negatives

The plates and negatives, including glossy prints, of paper money, postage stamps and revenue stamps, bonds, and other obligations and securities of the U.S. and foreign governments, used in printing the illustrations in publications must be destroyed after their final use for the purpose for which they were made.

No prints or enlargements from motion-picture films or slides of paper money, postage or revenue stamps, bonds, or other obligations are permitted, except prints may be made from such films or slides for the purpose of reproducing illustrations in publications, provided there is compliance with all other restrictions relating to the use of such illustrations.

Excerpts From Applicable Statutes

. . . Title 18, U.S. Code, Section 474 - whoever prints, photographs, or in any other manner makes or executes, any engraving, photograph, print, or impression in the likeness of any . . . obligation or other security of the United States, or any part thereof, or sells, any such engraving, photograph, print or impression, except to the United States, or brings into the United States, any such engraving, photograph, print, or impression, except by direction of some proper officer of the United States; . . . Shall be fined not more than $5,000 or imprisoned not more than fifteen years, or both.

. . . Title 18, U.S. Code, Section 475 - whoever designs, engraves, prints, makes, or executes, or utters, issues, distributes, circulates or uses any business or professional card, notice, placard, handbill, or advertisement in the likeness or similitude of any obligation or security of the United States issued under or authorized by any Act of Congress or writes, prints or otherwise impresses upon or attaches to any such instrument; obligation, or security, or any coin of the United States, any business or professional card, notice, or advertisement, or any notice or advertisement whatever, shall be fined not more than $500.

. . . Title 18, U.S. Code, Section 8 - The term obligation or other security of the United States includes all bonds, certificates of indebtedness, national bank currency, Federal Reserve notes, Federal Reserve bank notes, coupons, United States notes, Treasury notes, gold certificates, silver certificates, fractional notes, certificates of deposit, bills, checks, or drafts for money, drawn by or upon authorized officers of the United States, stamps and other representatives of value, of whatever denomination, issued under any Act of Congress, and canceled United States stamps.

. . . Title 18, U.S. Code, Section 15 - The term obligation or other security of any foreign government includes, but is not limited to, uncanceled stamps, whether or not demonetized.

Title 18, U.S. Code, Section 504 - Notwithstanding any other provision of this chapter, the following are permitted:

(1) the printing, publishing, or importation, or the making or importation of the necessary plates for such printing or publishing, of illustrations of

(A) postage stamps of the United States,

(B) revenue stamps of the United States,

(C) any other obligation or other security of the United States, and

(D) postage stamps, revenue stamps, notes, bonds, and any other obligation or other security of any foreign government, bank, or corporation, for philatelic, numismatic, educational, historical, or newsworthy purposes in articles, books, journals, newspapers, or albums (but not for advertising purposes, except illustrations of stamps, and paper money in philatelic or numismatic articles, books, journals, newspapers, or albums). Illustrations permitted by the foregoing provisions of this section shall be made in accordance with the following conditions:

(i) all illustrations shall be in black and white, except that illustrations of postage stamps issued by the United States or by any foreign government may be color;

(ii) all illustrations (including illustrations of uncanceled postage stamps in color) shall be of a size less than three-fourths or more than one and one-half, in linear dimension, or each part of any matter so illustrated which is covered by sub-paragraph (A), (B), (C), or (D) of this paragraph, except that black and white illustrations of postage stamps issued by the United States may be in the exact linear dimension in which the stamps were issued; and

(iii) the negatives and plates used in making the illustrations shall be destroyed after their final use in accordance with this section.

(2) the making or importation, but not for advertising purposes except philatelic advertising, of motion-picture films, microfilms, or slides, for projection upon a screen or for use in telecasting, of postage and revenue stamps and other obligations and securities of the United States, and postage and revenue stamps, notes, bonds, and other obligations or securities of any foreign government, bank, or corporation. No prints or other reproductions shall be made from such films or slides, except for the purpose of paragraph (1), without the permission of the Secretary of the Treasury.

Importation of Stamps and Covers into the United States

Until recently it had generally been assumed that postage and revenue stamps, as well as postal stationery, imported into the United States were free of customs duties under the well-known provisions of Sec. 274.40 of the Tariff Schedules of the United States, which read as follows:

"Postage and revenue stamps, cancelled or not cancelled, and government stamped envelopes and postal cards bearing no printing other than the official imprint thereon . . . Free."

However, the Customs Service has ruled that first-day covers issued by a foreign government, i.e., "official" first-day covers, may continue to be imported free of duty, but that first-day covers produced by private commercial individuals or firms are subject to duty under the appropriate provisions for certain printed matter.

Apparently the reasoning in this case is two-fold: 1) one government does not tax the officially issued documentation of another under the usages of international courtesy; and, probably even more important, 2) that the officially issued covers are usually much cheaper than the privately issued ones, costing only a penny or two over the face value of the stamp, whereas the cacheted privately issued cover tends to be considerably more expensive, making the entire product into a manufactured paper article.

CONCLUSION: Privately produced cacheted foreign first-day covers may be treated as manufactured paper articles for purposes of assessing customs duty.

Privately Overprinted Postage Stamps

On May 20, 1977, the United States Postal Service issued a 13¢ commemorative postage stamp to mark the 50th anniversary of Col. Charles Lindbergh's historic transatlantic flight from New York to Paris. At the time of the issuance of the stamp, considerable dissatisfaction was expressed by the philatelic public to the effect that not enough descriptive language appears on the stamp to indicate to the present generation the reason for its commemorative issuance; the wording "50th Anniversary Solo Transatlantic Flight," in miniscule type, being considered insufficient to recognize Col. Lindbergh's tremendous historic achievement, and that more explicit wording should have appeared on the stamp.

To remedy this situation, an enterprising Florida dealer purchased a larger number of sheets of this stamp and added two lines of larger print— "SPIRIT OF ST. LOUIS" in the upper left corner and "CHARLES A. LINDBERGH" underneath the airplane, making the stamp more attractive and more appealing to the stamp collector.

The dealer then sent in his advertisement to the philatelic press offering to sell the "retouched" stamps as mint singles and on cover. His advertisement was rejected because of concern that tampering with an issue of the United States Government might contravene some provisions of Federal law.

Inquiry made by legal counsel on behalf of the dealer in this regard resulted in the following reply from the Postal Service:

This replies to your letter of March 7, 1978, asking on behalf of a client whether it would be unlawful to overprint and sell to collectors the 13¢ U.S. postage stamp commemorating the fiftieth anniversary of the first "Solo Transatlantic (airplane) Flight." The stamp as issued depicts a single propeller airplane flying in the sky over the ocean and the rising (or setting) sun in the background; the only written information on the official stamp design consists of the origin country and postage amount marking ("USA-13¢") required by the Universal Postal Convention, and the brief and relatively inconspicuous legend: "50th Anniversary Solo Transatlantic Flight." The proposed overprinting would consist of the following additional words, in larger print than the original legend: "SPIRIT OF ST. LOUIS" and "CHARLES A. LINDBERGH."

The Postal Service's basic legal authority with respect to postage stamps is to "provide and sell" them, 39 U.S.C. 404(3) (1970), renumbered as 39 U.S.C. 404(a)(3), Pub. L. No. 94-421, September 24, 1976, sec. 9(a), 90 Stat. 1310. We have therefore maintained that "postage stamps when purchased by the public become the property of the purchaser." 9 Op. Solic. P.O. Dep't No. 544 at 646 (1944). In the absence of any applicable legal prohibition, therefore, your client may do what he pleases to or with any postage stamps he lawfully purchases.

Since the proposed overprinting would not be in the form of an official postmark, the overprinting would not appear to raise any questions under 18 U.S.C. 503 (1976).

A further letter addressed to the Legal Counsel of the United States Secret Service with regard to the possibility of violating the prohibition in the counterfeiting laws against impressing notices on postage stamps, 18 U.S.C. 8, 475 (1976), or any other provisions resulted in a somewhat similar reply to the effect that "if the overprinting process does not involve the reproduction of any United States stamp, but the overprint is placed on genuine stamps, there would appear to be no legal objection to your client's proposed plan."

In view of the foregoing, the advertisement was placed in the philatelic press and a quantity of mint stamps and covers sold and distributed. The above statement of the Postal Service that the dealer could do what he pleases with the altered stamps included, of course, the obvious fact that they could be validly used as postage even though they might confuse a few sharp-eyed postal clerks.

In this connection, the Postal Service had some later thoughts and decided to issue an amendment to Sec. 142.3 of the Domestic Mail Manual (clause "h"). For the benefit of collectors and dealers, that section of the Manual is set forth in its present entirety as follows:

142.3 Validity of Stamps. All postage stamps issued by the United States since 1860 are good for postage from any point in the United States or from any other place where the United States domestic mail service operates.

Airmail postage stamps may be used to pay regular postage and fees for special services.

Unprecanceled bulk rate and nonprofit rate stamps may be used to pay regular postage and fees for special services, providing the mailpiece is endorsed above the address and below the postage to indicate the appropriate class of the mailpiece and, if applicable, the special service desired. The total postage affixed must at least equal the postage charge for the class of the mailpiece and, if applicable, the proper fee for the special service desired.

The following are not good for postage:

a. Mutilated or defaced stamps.

b. Stamps cut from stamped envelopes, aerogrammes or postal cards.

c. Stamps covered or coated in such a manner that the canceling or defacing marks cannot be imprinted directly on the stamps.

d. Non-postage stamps (migratory-bird hunting and conservation stamps, U.S. saving and thrift stamps, etc.)

e. Postage due, special delivery, special handling and certified mail stamps.

f. United Nations stamps, except on mail deposited at United Nations, N.Y.

g. Stamps of other countries.

h. Stamps on which any unauthorized design, message or other marking has been overprinted.

(39 U.S.C. 401(2), 404(a)(2), 404(a)(4), 410(a)).

This rule amends postal regulations so as to make invalid for use as postage any postage stamps on which any unauthorized design, message or other marking has been overprinted. The need for this regulation was suggested by inquiries by Postal Service customers with regard to the validity as postage of overprinted stamps.

Under present regulations stamps that are mutilated or defaced (i.e., canceled) are considered invalid. The term "unauthorized design, message, or marking" in the final rule is intended to exclude from invalidation authorized markings, such as precanceled stamps and precanceled postmarks under Secs. 143.1 and 143.3 of the *Domestic Mail Manual*.

On September 8, 1978, the Postal Service published for comment its proposal to revise the regulations as described above. (43 FR39593). The Postal Service received eight letters of comment referring to this proposal, which were divided between those in favor (5), those opposed (1), and those discussing other postal matters (2).

The argument against the proposal was to the effect that stamps individualized through overmarking or overprinting were "in the best American tradition of Freedom of Speech and should not be banned or unduly controlled." The prohibition which was proposed, however, was not an absolute prohibition against the marking or printing of private messages on postage stamps, or against the communication of private messages through the mails.

The rule would leave undisturbed the general rule that "postage stamps when purchased by the public become the property of the purchaser," 9 Op.Solic. P.O. Dep't No. 544 at 646(1944), under which a purchaser of postage stamps may generally mark or overprint his property as he pleases.* Nor would the rule interfere with businesses that overprint stamps with non-commercial messages, and re-sell the overprinted stamp at a profit to collectors of such articles who do not intend to use the stamps as postage.

The prohibition in the regulation is limited only to private markings on stamps to be used for postage, or the attached selvage area beyond the perforations, on which private markings or overprintings may interfere with postal operations in which the prompt and unimpeded recognition of genuine mint postage stamps is necessary. Since the proposal would do just that and nothing more, it would not be an undue restraint of commercial or other speech.

***There is a statutory prohibition against impressing commercial messages on postage stamps and other U.S. Government obligations or securities. 18 U.S.C. 8;475(1978). Enforcement responsibility for this prohibition is vested principally in the U.S. Secret Service. 18 U.S.C.3056(1978). This regulation appears to be intended to prevent advertising falsely implying U.S. Government sponsorship of private products or services.**

CONCLUSION: Dealers may overprint genuine United States postage stamps and sell them as "philatelic souvenirs," but such stamps will no longer be valid for postage.

Private Express Statutes

I. United States Code Excerpts From Title 18

CHAPTER 83. POSTAL SERVICE

Sec. 1693. Carriage of mail generally

Whoever, being concerned in carrying the mail, collects, receives, or carries any letter or packet, contrary to law, shall be fined not more than $50 or imprisoned more than 30 days, or both.

Sec. 1694. Carriage of matter out of mail over post routes

Whoever, having charge or control of any conveyance operating by land, air or water, which regularly performs trips at stated periods on any post route, or from one place to another between which the mail is regularly carried, carries, otherwise than in the mail, any letters or packets, except such as relate to some part of the cargo of such conveyance, or to the current business of the carrier, or to some article carried at the same time by the same conveyance, shall, except as otherwise provided by law, be fined not more than $50.

Sec. 1695. Carriage of matter out of mail on vessels

Whoever carries any letter or packet on board any vessel which carries the mail, otherwise than in such mail, shall, except as otherwise provided by law, be fined not more than $50 or imprisoned not more than 30 days, or both.

Sec. 1696. Private express for letters and packets

(a) Whoever establishes any private express for the conveyance of letters or packets, or in any manner causes or provides for the conveyance of the same by regular trips or at stated periods over any post route which is or may be established by law, or from any city, town, or place to any other city, town, or place, between which the mail is regularly carried, shall be fined not more than $500 or imprisoned not more than 6 months, or both.

This section shall not prohibit any person from receiving and delivering to the nearest post office, postal car, or other authorized depository for mail matter any mail matter properly stamped.

(b) Whoever transmits by private express or other unlawful means, or delivers to any agent thereof, or deposits at any appointed place, for the purpose of being so transmitted any letter or packet, shall be fined not more than $50.

(c) This chapter shall not prohibit the conveyance or transmission of letters or packets by private hands without compensation, or by special messenger employed for the particular occasion only. Whenever more than 25 such letters or packets are conveyed or transmitted by such special messenger, the requirements of section 601 of title 39, shall be observed as to each piece.

Sec. 1697. Transportation of persons acting as private express

Whoever, having charge or control of any conveyance operating by land, air, or water, knowingly conveys or knowingly permits the conveyance of any person acting or employed as a private express for the conveyance of letters or packets, and actually in possession of the same for the purpose of conveying them contrary to law, shall be fined not more than $150.

Sec. 1698. Prompt delivery of mail from vessel

Whoever, having charge or control of any vessel passing between ports or places in the United States, and arriving at any such port or place where there is a post office, fails to deliver to the postmaster or at the post office, within 3 hours after his arrival, if in the daytime, and if at night, within 2 hours after the next sunrise, all letters and packages brought by him or within his power or control and not relating to the cargo, addressed to or destined for such port or place, shall be fined not more than $150.

For each letter or package so delivered he shall receive 2¢ unless the same is carried under contract.

Sec. 1699. Certification of delivery

from vessel

No vessel arriving within a port or collection district of the United States shall be allowed to make entry or break bulk until all letters on board are delivered to the nearest post office, except where waybilled for discharge at other ports in the United States at which the vessel is scheduled to call and the Postal Service does not determine that unreasonable delay in the mails will occur, and the master or other person having charge or control thereof has signed and sworn to the following declaration before the collector or other proper customs officer:

I, A.B., master —, of the —, arriving from —, and now lying in the port of —, do solemnly swear (or affirm) that I have to the best of my knowledge and belief delivered to the post office at — every letter and every bag, packet, or parcel of letters on board the said vessel during her last voyage, or in my possession or under my power or control, except where waybilled for discharge at other ports in the United States at which the said vessel is scheduled to call and which the Postal Service has not determined will be unreasonably delayed by remaining on board the said vessel for delivery at such ports.

Whoever, being the master or other person having charge or control of such vessel, breaks bulk before he has arranged for such delivery or onward carriage, shall be fined not more than $100.

Sec. 1725. Postage unpaid on deposited mail matter

Whoever knowingly and willfully deposits any mailable matter such as statements of accounts, circulars, sale bills, or other like matter, on which no postage has been paid, in any letterbox established, approved, or accepted by the Postal Service for the receipt or delivery of mail matter on any mail route with intent to avoid payment of lawful postage thereon, shall for each such offense be fined not more than $300.

Note: Sec. 1725 is not regarded as a Private Express Statute; however, its provisions may be relevant to Private Express violations.

Excerpts From Title 39

CHAPTER 6. PRIVATE CARRIAGE OF LETTERS

Sec. 601. Letters carried out of the mail

(a) A letter may be carried out of the mails when:

(1) it is enclosed in an envelope;

(2) the amount of postage which would have been charged on the letter if it had been sent by mail is paid by stamps, or postage meter stamps, on the envelope;

(3) the envelope is properly addressed;

(4) the envelope is so sealed that the letter cannot be taken from it without defacing the envelope;

(5) any stamps on the envelope are canceled in ink by the sender; and

(6) the date of the letter, of its transmission or receipt by the carrier is endorsed on the envelope in ink.

(b) The Postal Service may suspend the operation of any part of this section upon any mail route where the public interest requires the suspension.

Sec. 602. Foreign letters out of the mails

(a) Except as provided in section 601 of this title, the master of a vessel departing from the United States for foreign ports may not receive on board or transport any letter which originated in the United States that:

(1) has not been regularly received from a United States post office; or

(2) does not relate to the cargo of the vessel.

(b) The officer of the port empowered to grant clearances shall require from the master of such a vessel, as a condition of clearance, an oath that he does not have under his care or control, and will not receive or transport, any letter contrary to the provisions of this section.

(c) Except as provided in section 1699 of title 18, the master of a vessel arriving at a port of the United States carrying letters not regularly in the mails shall deposit them in the post office at the port of arrival.

Sec. 603. Searches authorized

The Postal Service may authorize any officer or employee of the Postal Service to make searches for mail matter transported in violation of law. When the authorized officer has reason to believe that mailable matter transported contrary to law may be found therein, he may open and search any:

(1) vehicle passing, or having lately passed, from a place at which there is a post office of the United States;

(2) article being, or having lately been, in the vehicle; or

(3) store or office, other than a dwelling house, used or occupied by a common carrier or transportation company, in which an article may be contained.

Sec. 604. Seizing and detaining letters

An officer or employee of the Postal Service performing duties related to the inspection of postal matters, a customs officer, or United States marshal or his deputy, may seize at any time, letters and bags, packets, or parcels containing letters which are being carried contrary to law on board any vessel or on any post road. The officer or employee who makes the seizure shall convey the articles seized to the nearest post office, or, by direction of the Postal Service or the Secretary of the Treasury, he may detain them until 2 months after the final determination of all suits and proceedings which may be brought within 6 months after the seizure against any person for sending or carrying the letters.

Sec. 605. Searching vessels for letters

An officer or employee of the Postal Service performing duties related to the inspection of postal matters, when instructed by the Postal Service to make examinations and seizures, and any customs officer without special instructions shall search vessels for letters which may be on board, or which may have been conveyed contrary to law.

Sec. 606. Disposition of seized mail

Every package or parcel seized by an officer or employee of the Postal Service performing duties related to the inspection of postal matters, a customs officer, or United States marshal or his deputies, in which a letter is unlawfully concealed, shall be forfeited to the United States. The same proceedings may be used to enforce forfeitures as are authorized in respect of goods, wares, and merchandise forfeited for violation of the revenue laws. Laws for the benefit and protection of customs officers making seizures for violating revenue laws apply to officers and employees making seizures for violating the postal laws.

Questions Answered on Private Express Statutes

Effective Oct. 20, 1974, the Postal Service adopted revised regulations to implement the Private Express Statutes. Adoption of the regulations was preceded by studies of relevant legal and economic factors, and also by the publication of two Notices of Proposed Rulemaking that afforded the public opportunity to provide the Postal Service with views and comments.

The text of the new regulations was published in the Sept. 16, 1974, issue of the *Federal Register*, 39 F.R. 33211-33213. (An omission of a word was added to section 310.1 (a)(7)(vii) in the October 8, 1974, issue of the *Federal Register*, 39 F.R. 36114.)

Private carriage of intra-company letters is permitted only if postage is paid or if the carriage is by regular bona fide employees of the company. See Question and Answer IV.

Checks are not letters when traveling from, to, or between financial institutions. See Question and Answer VI. In other cases, checks are considered letters under the new regulations.

The questions and answers that follow are general guidelines but do not constitute an authoritative statement of the governing regulations. The Postal Service's regulations published in the *Federal Register* provide an authoritative source for guidance in this area. Answers to specific questions may be obtained by writing to the Assistant General Counsel, Opinions Division, Law Department, U.S. Postal Service, Washington, D.C. 20260.

Q. I. What are the Private Express Statutes?

A. A group of Federal statutes giving the Postal Service the exclusive right, with certain limited exceptions, to carry letters for others. The statutes are based upon the provision in the U.S. Constitution that empowers Congress "to establish Post Offices and post roads."

Q. II. What is a "letter" for purposes of the Private Express Statutes?

A. A "letter," as defined by Postal Service regulations, is a "message" directed to a specific person or address and recorded in or on a tangible object. The word "message" is defined as any information or intelligence that can be recorded by means that include, but are not limited to, written or printed characters, drawings, holes, or magnetic recordings, etc. The phrase "tangible objects" is defined as including, but as not limited to, paper (sheets or cards), recording discs, and magnetic tapes.

Q. III. What is the basic purpose of the Private Express Statutes?

A. To protect that portion of the Postal Service's revenues that is derived from the transportation of letters for others. This protection is needed to provide a secure economic foundation so that the Postal Service can render service throughout the country, irrespective of the "loss" or "gain" from its operations in any specific area.

Q. IV. What, basically, do the Private Express Statutes require?

A. The Statutes require, in general, that "letters" may be transported for others only by the Postal Service; alternatively, if means other than the Postal Service are used, the applicable postage must, generally, be paid. The basic prohibition is against a person's carrying letters for another person without payment of postage, i.e., operating in competition with the Postal Service. Therefore, an individual may transport his own letters, and a company may transport its own letters (but not those of a parent, subsidiary, or affiliated firm), if it uses its own regular salaried bona fide employees (not contractors or casual employees) to do so, even though postage is not paid.

Q. V. Are intra-company letters covered by the Private Express Statutes?

A. Yes, but see IV.

Q. VI. Are any "messages" not treated as letters?

A. Yes. For example, telegrams, newspapers and periodicals are not letters. In addition, checks, drafts and certain other financial instruments, securities, and title and insurance policies are not letters when shipped to, from or between financial institutions. As to checks and drafts, financial institutions are defined as banks, savings banks, savings and loan institutions, credit unions, and their offices, affiliates, and facilities. As to other instruments, financial institutions are defined as institutions that perform functions involving the bulk generation, clearance, and transfer to such instruments.

A special situation exists with respect to data-processing materials. The Postal Service has exercised its authority to suspend the operation of the Private Express Statutes so as to allow any person to carry such materials for others, outside the mails and without payment of postage, if certain conditions are met. The transmission must be completed within 12 hours after leaving the sender, or by noon of the addressee's next business day, and the data processing must commence within 36 hours after receipt at the data-processing center.

Persons wishing to transport data-processing materials (for others) under the suspension, must file certain information with the Postal Service. The necessary forms may be obtained from the Private Express Liaison Officer, Customer Services Department, U.S. Postal Service, Washington, D.C. 20260.

Q. VII. Did mailers have a voice in establishing the Postal Service's Private Express regulations?

A. Yes. The Postal Service informed mailers and the public and its new regulations were published in the *Federal Register* on July 2, 1973, and again on Jan. 31, 1974. All views and arguments were reviewed and evaluated. The present regulations of the Postal Service were adopted only after this process was completed.

Q. VIII. Are earlier regulations or issuances of the Postal Service on the Private Express Statutes now obsolete?

A. To the extent that they are contrary to the regulations published in the Sept. 16 and Oct. 8, 1974 issues of the *Federal*

Register, any opinions, regulations, or publications of the Postal Service (including POD Publication 111, "Restrictions on Transportation of Letters," Fifth Edition, July 1967, republished June, 1973) should no longer be used as the basis for decisions or actions by mailers or others.

Q. IX. In those situations in which the Private Express Statutes and regulations permit the carriage of letters without the payment of postage, can such letters be placed into, or attached to, or hung from letter boxes or other receptacles for the receipt or deposit of mail?

A. No.

Q. X. How can I obtain additional information about the Private Express Statutes?

A. Write to the Assistant General Counsel, Opinions Division, U.S. Postal Service, Washington, D.C. 20260. If you want information about the applicability of the Private Express Statutes to a specific situation, submit a complete statement of the facts and, if possible, examples of the materials in question. The Assistant General Counsel, Opinions Division, will render advice and will also furnish copies of the Private Express regulations that the Postal Service adopted, effective Oct. 20, 1974.

Stamp Embargoes

Stamps from certain countries are subject to import restrictions in the United States as the result of general trade embargoes against those countries. The embargoes generally prohibit the importation of goods, including stamps, from the affected countries, as well as the buying and selling of such goods brought illegally into the United States.

The prohibitions include used and unused stamps as well as stamps from the embargoed countries purchased or imported from any foreign country.

The embargoed countries, along with the effective dates of the restrictions are:

North Korea, Dec. 17, 1950
Cuba, Feb. 7, 1962
North Vietnam, May 5, 1964
Kampuchea (Cambodia), April 17, 1975
South Vietnam, April 30, 1975
Libya, Jan. 7, 1986
Nicaragua, May 6, 1986
South Africa, Nov. 24, 1986
Iran, Oct. 29, 1987

The restrictions for South Africa also apply to South-West Africa (Namibia) and the homelands of Bophuthatswana, Ciskei, Transkei and Venda. The U.S. government does not recognize South Africa's claim to South-West Africa, nor does it recognize the homelands.

The Nicaragua embargo was set to expire May 1988 but was extended on April 25, 1988.

The effective embargo date for each country is important because stamps issued before that date are not included in the embargo. In other words, it is legal to buy and sell any Libyan stamps issued before Jan. 7, 1986. However, it is illegal to import these items directly from Libya.

The embargoes were enacted for political or diplomatic reasons. They are enforced by the Office of Foreign Assets Control of the Department of the Treasury.

The intent of the embargoes is to cause economic hardship to nations with whose policies the U.S. government disagrees by denying access to the U.S. market for their goods. These goods only incidentally include postage stamps and philatelic materials.

The trade restrictions were imposed under a variety of acts, including the Trading With the Enemy Act of 1917, the International Emergency Economic Powers Act of 1977, the International Security and Development Cooperation Act of 1985 and the Comprehensive Anti-Apartheid Act of 1986 (South Africa, South-West Africa and the homelands only).

It is not illegal to have stamps from embargoed countries in the United States if the stamps were brought in legally.

The embargoes do not in any way limit the exchange of mail between the United States and the affected areas. Thus, any stamps from an embargoed country may enter the United States on mail from that country.

In the course of personal travel to an embargoed country, visitors may bring back a certain dollar-value amount of goods for personal use, including stamps. This amount ranges from $100 to $400 for the embargoed countries.

Merchandise, including stamps, brought into the United States under those provisions, may not be sold or traded commerically under any circumstances. Such commerical use of imported goods from these countries would subject the traveler to criminal penalties.

A spokesman for the Department of the Treasury's Office of Foreign Assets Control reported that the trade restrictions with South Africa also limit what products cannot be brought back in the course of personal travel.

Banned South African items include products from any goverment-owned company. INTERSAPA, the philatelic agency of the South African government, would probably qualify as a government-owned company.

Stamps from embargoed countries also can be purchased in packets, provided that the packets are made up of predominantly used stamps and that the number and value of the embargoed stamps does not exceed 10 percent of the total number of stamps or 10 percent of the total value of the packet. This exception to the embargo does not apply if any of the stamps have in any way been segregated from any other stamps in the packet.

The packets can be obtained directly or indirectly from embargoed countries. They can be purchased abroad or imported in accordance with the aforementioned provisions.

The trade restrictions allow for licenses for the purchase or importation of certain goods, including stamps. However, licenses are granted only where satisfactory documentary proof is submitted that the stamps have not been in the prohibited countries on or after the effective date of the embargo. Also, there must be proof that there has been no financial interest of nationals of these countries therein since that date.

Persons desiring to obtain such licenses have found it extremely difficult to obtain proof sufficient to satisfy licensing standards.

The maximum penalty for importing embargoed stamps is a fine of up to $50,000 and up to 10 years in a federal prison. The maximum penalties are not as stringent for some of the countries.

An amendment to the Omnibus Trade Bill signed into law by President Reagan on Aug. 23, 1988, has significantly changed the terms of the embargo policy. It is not certain whether this amendment applies to stamps.

The amendent, which was introduced by Rep. Howard L. Berman (D.-Calif.), reads in part, "The authority granted to the President in this sub-section does not include the authority to regulate or prohibit, directly or indirectly, the importation from any country, or the exportation to any country, whether commerical or otherwise, of publications, films, posters, phonograph records, photographs, microfilms, microfiche, tapes or other informational materials . . ."

Stamps are not specifically mentioned in the amendment. However, a broad interpretation of the amendment could be construed to include them. The law would probably need to be tested in court to determine whether the amendment would apply to stamps.

Chapter 13

Worldwide Postal Agencies

Most countries maintain an agency or bureau through which they sell their recent and current postal issues direct to collectors or dealers. These issues can include mint or canceled-to-order stamps, first-day covers, postal stationery, postmarks and other items.

Each agency has its own set of regulations governing ordering instructions, acceptable methods of payment and deadlines for ordering. Many bureaus and agencies offer standing-order accounts. A minimum deposit is usually required to open such an account.

Therefore, interested collectors should write to the desired agency to find out individual requirements and procedures.

Some countries do not sell their postal paper in small amounts direct to collectors. Rather they sell stamps and other items only in large quantities to dealers and wholesalers. The following listing includes such information when known.

One's name and address should be printed or typed very clearly on all correspondence, especially to non-English speaking nations, in order to prevent delays or non-replies.

When sending inquiries or orders to a foreign country, it is best to use airmail. Surface mail can take several weeks to reach its destination.

Enclosure of an International Reply Coupon aids in facilitating a reply from many countries. IRCs are usually available at any post office in the United States and abroad.

The remittance of funds by personal check is always subject to collection or negotiation charges, thus reducing the actual payment value of said remittance. Collectors are advised not to send cash.

Currency exchange rates are omitted because of continual fluctuation. The latest exchange rates can be ascertained through a local banking establishment.

The following listing includes mail addresses only. The country's over-the-counter sales agency can be in a different section of the stipulated city or even in a different city altogether.

Many countries' postal administrations produce philatelic bulletins detailing recent and/or upcoming postal issues. The administrations make these announcements available to interested collectors either for a nominal fee or for free.

A listing of various agencies that represent countries in the United States follows the country listings. These agents, plus other agents that represent a country in other parts of the world, are included in the country listings.

Standard abbreviations used throughout this listing of postal agencies are as follows:

BD = Bank Deposit.
BPO = British Postal Order.
CBC = Certified Bank Check.
CDA = Certified Deposit Account.
CTO = Canceled to Order.
FDC = First Day Covers.
IBD = International Bank Draft.
IMO = International Money Order.
IRC = International Reply Coupon.
PC = Personal Check.
SODA = Standing-Order Deposit Account.
USMO = United States Money Order.
USPSMO = U.S. Postal Service Money Order.

AFGHANISTAN

Director of Posts, Philatelic Section, Kabul, Afghanistan. Details of services not provided.

AITUTAKI

Aitutaki Post Office, Aitutaki, Cook Islands, South Pacific Ocean. Deals with individual orders for mint and CTO stamps, FDCs. SODA available. SODA orders shipped postpaid; transient orders are postage extra. CBC accepted.

ALAND

Mariehamns Postkontor, Filateliservicen, PB 100, 22101 Mariehamn, Finland; or Postimerkkikeskus, Box 654, SF-00101 Helsinki, Finland. Deals with individual orders for mint stamps, FDCs, postal stationery, maximum cards, year sets, presentation packs. SODA available from Finland Stamp Agency in North America with minimum deposit of U.S. $10. Small shipping/handling fee charged. CBC, PC, USPSMO, USMO accepted by the Finland Stamp Agency in North America.

Printers: Bank of Finland Security Printing House, Frenckell Printing House.

Government Agency: Unicover World Trade Corp. (Finland Stamp Agency in North America), 1 Unicover Center, Cheyenne, Wyo. 82008-0017.

ALBANIA

Exportal, Rue 4 Shkurti, Tirana, Albania.

Deals with orders for over five sets. Details of services not provided.

Government Agency: Albania General Trading Co. Ltd., 788-90 Finchley Road, London NW11 7UR, England.

ALDERNEY

Philatelic Bureau, Postal Headquarters, Guernsey, Great Britain. Deals with individual orders for mint and CTO stamps, FDCs, inscription blocks and gutter pairs. SODA available. SODA orders shipped postpaid; 25-penny handling charge for single orders; IRCs accepted. CBC, BD, PC, IMO, IBD, USPSMO accepted. Printers: Helio Courvoisier, Switzerland; Harrison & Sons, England; Cartor, France; The House of Questa, England.

The Guernsey Post Office issues and sells stamps on behalf of Alderney.

Government Agencies: Inter-Governmental Philatelic Corp., 460 W. 34th St., New York, N.Y. 10001; Max Stern, 234 Flinders St., Melbourne, Victoria 3001, Australia; Nordfrim, DK 5450 Otterup, Denmark; Theodore Champion, 13 rue Drouot, 75009 Paris, France; Richard Borek, Box 3220, Theordor-Heuss-Strasse 7, Braunschweig, West Germany; British and Overseas Philatelic Agency, Box 80, Shibuya, Tokyo 150-91, Japan; J.A. Visser, Box 184, 3300 AD Dordrecht, Netherlands; The Stamp Arcade, Box 1532, Port Elizabeth 6000, South Africa; Maderphil, Avda de Roma, 157 6a, Barcelona 11, Spain; Frimarkshuset AB, S-793 01 Leksand, Sweden; De Rosa International, Av du Tribunal Federal 34, 1005 Lausanne, Switzerland.

ALGERIA

Receveur Principal des Postes, Alger R.P., Algeria. Deals with individual orders for mint stamps, FDCs (extra charge), special postmarks. SODA available. Orders shipped postpaid. CBC, IMO accepted.

Government Agency: Theodore Champion, 13 rue Drouot, 75009 Paris, France.

ANDORRA (French)

Service Philatelique De La Poste, 18 rue Francois Bonvin, F-75758, Paris, Cedex 15, France. Deals with individual orders for mint stamps. SODA available with the first remittance covering at least four-month purchases, plus minimum deposit of 10 to 250 francs for postage by registered mail; IRCs accepted. BD, PC (takes about six weeks), IMO, IBD, VISA, MasterCard accepted.

Printer: Government Printing Office, Perigueux. Also handles postage stamps of UNESCO, Council of Europe, all French issues, St. Pierre and Miquelon and definitives of Monaco.

ANDORRA (Spanish)

Direccion General de Correos y Telegrafos, Seccion de Filatelia, Palacio de Comunicaciones 28070, Madrid, Spain. Deals with individual orders for mint stamp sets only. No SODA available. Orders sent postage and handling extra; IRCs accepted. IMO accepted.

Printer: Spanish National Printer.

ANGOLA

Centro Filatelico de Angola, Lda., C.P. 2688, Luanda, Angola. Deals with individual orders for mint stamps, FDCs, special postmarks (agency supplies envelopes). SODA available with minimum balance required. Orders shipped postage extra. CBC, PC, IMO accepted.

ANGUILLA

The Postmaster, General Post Office, The Valley, Anguilla, West Indies. Deals with individual orders for mint and CTO stamps, FDCs, inscription blocks, aerogrammes. SODA available with minimum deposit of U.S. $15. Orders shipped postage extra; IRCs accepted. CBC, BD, IMO, IBD, USPSMO, accepted.

Printer: The House of Questa, England.

Government Agency: John Lister Ltd., 49 Shelton St., Covent Garden, London WC2, England.

ANTIGUA-BARBUDA

Philatelic Bureau, Barbuda Post Office, Codrington, Barbuda, West Indies (Via Antigua). Deals with individual orders for mint or CTO stamps, FDCs. SODA available. Orders shipped postage extra. CBC, BD accepted.

Government Agency: Inter-Governmental Philatelic Corp., 460 W. 34th St., New York, N.Y. 10001.

ARGENTINA

Seccion Filatelia, Correo Central, Local 55, 1000 Buenos Aires, Argentina. Deals with individual orders for mint stamps. No SODA available. Postage is extra. IMO, CBC accepted. Minimum order for foreign residents is U.S. $25. Also offers postmarks from Argentina's Antarctic bases.

Printer: Sociedad del Estado Casa de Moneda (Argentine State Mint).

ARUBA

Aruba Philatelic Service, Post Office, Oranjestad, Aruba. Deals with individual orders for mint and CTO stamps, FDCs. SODA available. CBC, bank notes accepted.

ASCENSION

Postmaster, Jamestown, St. Helena, South Atlantic. Deals with individual orders for mint stamps, FDCs, special postmarks (bureau or customers supply envelopes). No SODA available. Orders shipped postage extra. CBC on London bank, U.S. bank notes, BPO, IMO accepted.

Government Agencies: CAPHCO Ltd., Old Inn House, 2 Carshalton Road Sutton, Surrey SM1 4RN, England; British & Overseas Philatelic Agency Ltd., Box 80, Shibuya, Tokyo 105-91, Japan.

AUSTRALIA

Australian Philatelic Bureau, GPO Box 9988, Melbourne, Victoria 3001, Australia. Deals with individual orders for mint and CTO stamps, FDCs, stamp packs, postal stationery, maximum cards, annual collections, heritage books, special postmarks (bureau supplies pictorial envelopes for A$0.20 each, plus value of stamp). SODA available with recommended minimum deposit of U.S. $25. Orders shipped postpaid by surface, postage extra by air (two IRCs acceptable). CBC, IMO, BD, VISA, MasterCard, American Express, Diners Club accepted.

Printers: Leigh-Mardon, Melbourne; CPE Australia, Melbourne.

Also handles postal issues of the Australian Antarctic Territory.

Government Agencies: Unicover World Trade Corp. (Australian Stamp Agency in North America), 1 Unicover Center, Cheyenne, Wyo. 82008-0010 (offers SODA services to all North American collectors); Australian Stamp Bureau (Great Britain), Old Inn House, 2 Carshalton Road, Sutton, Surrey SM1 4RN, England; Australian Stamp Bureau (Austria), Holbeinstrasse 2, D-2880 Brake, West Germany; Australian Stamp Bureau (Italy), Via Orazio 22, 1-80122 Naples, Italy; Australian Stamp Bureau (Spain), Avda de Roma 157 6a, Barcelona 11, Spain; Australian Stamp Bureau (Switzerland), Av du Tribunal Federal 34, 1005 Lausanne, Switzerland.

AUSTRALIAN ANTARCTIC TERRITORY

Australian Philatelic Bureau, GPO Box 9988, Melbourne, Victoria 3001, Australia. Deals with individual orders for mint and CTO stamps, FDCs, stamp packs, special postmarks (bureau supplies pictorial envelopes for A$0.20 each, plus value of stamp). SODA available with recommended minimum deposit of U.S. $25. Orders shipped postpaid by surface, postage extra by air (two IRCs acceptable). CBC, IMO, BD, VISA, MasterCard, American Express, Diners Club accepted.

Printers: Leigh-Mardon, Melbourne;

CPE Australia, Melbourne.

Government Agencies: Unicover World Trade Corp. (Australian Stamp Agency in North America), 1 Unicover Center, Cheyenne, Wyo. 82008-0010 (offers SODA services to all North American collectors); Australian Stamp Bureau (Great Britain), Old Inn House, 2 Carshalton Road, Sutton, Surrey SM1 4RN, England; Australian Stamp Bureau (Austria and West Germany), Holbeinstrasse 2, D-2880 Brake, West Germany; Australian Stamp Bureau (Italy), Via Orazio 22, 1-80122 Naples, Italy; Australian Stamp Bureau (Spain), Avda de Roma 157 6a, Barcelona 11, Spain; Australian Stamp Bureau (Switzerland), Av du Tribunal Federal 34, 1005 Lausanne, Switzerland.

AUSTRIA

Oesterreichische Post, Briefmarkenversandstelle, A-1211 Vienna, Austria. Deals with standing and individual orders for mint and CTO stamps, FDCs (sales agency supplies envelopes). Orders shipped postage extra plus cost of the FDC and a fee for affixing stamps. CBC, IMO accepted.

Printer: Austrian State Printing Office, Vienna.

Government Agencies: Inter-Governmental Philatelic Corp., 460 W. 34th St., New York, N.Y. 10001; Austrian Philatelic Bureau, 866 Kingston Road, Toronto, Ontario, Canada M4E 1S3 (SODA available); Theodore Champion, 13 rue Drouot, 75009 Paris, France (sales in France only).

AZORES

Direccao de Relacoes Internacionais e Filatelia, Av. Casal Ribeiro, 28-6°, 1096 Lisbon Codex, Portugal. Deals with individual orders for mint stamps, FDCs (agency supplies envelopes). SODA available with minimum deposit of $15. Orders shipped postage extra. IMO, CBC, bank notes (except escudos) accepted.

Government Agencies: Interpost, Box 378, Malverne, N.Y. 11565; Georg Roll Nachfolger, Holbeinstrasse 2, Box 1346, D-2880 Brake, West Germany; J.A. Visser, Box 184, 3300 AD Dordrecht, The Netherlands.

BAHAMAS

Postmaster General, GPO, P.O. Box N8302, Nassau, Bahamas. Deals with individual orders for mint and CTO stamps, gutter pairs, FDCs, postcards/maximum cards, presentation packs. SODA available. IMO, BPO, BD, PC in sterling (United Kingdom), U.S. dollars, or Canadian dollars accepted.

Printers: Handled by CAPHCO.

Government Agencies: CAPHCO Ltd., Old Inn House, 2 Carshalton Road, Sutton, Surrey SM1 4RN, England; British & Overseas Philatelic Agency Ltd., Box 80, Shibuya, Tokyo 150-91, Japan.

BAHRAIN

Philatelic Bureau, Postal Directorate, Box 1212, State of Bahrain, Arabian Gulf. Deals with individual orders for mint stamps, FDCs, special postmarks (customer supplies envelopes). SODA available. Orders shipped postage extra. PC, BD accepted.

Printers: Harrison & Sons, England; De La Rue & Co., England; Oriental Press, Bahrain.

Government Agency: James Davis & Son, 45-47 Church St., Rickmansworth WD3 1D6, England.

BANGLADESH

Office of the Director General, Bangladesh Post Office, Dacca 1000, Bangladesh. Deals with individual orders for mint stamps and FDCs (extra charge). SODA available. BD accepted.

Government Agency: John Lister Ltd., 49 Shelton St., Covent Garden, London WC2, England.

BARBADOS

Philatelic Bureau, GPO, Bridgetown, Barbados, West Indies. Deals with individual orders for mint and CTO stamps, FDCs, postal stationery, plate number and inscription blocks. SODA available with a minimum balance of B$25 required. Orders shipped postage extra. CBC, IMO, IBD, USPSMO accepted.

Printers: The House of Questa, England; Walsall Security Printers, England; Format International Security Printers, England.

Government Agent: CAPHCO Ltd.,

Old Inn House, 2 Carshalton Road, Sutton, Surrey SM1 4RN, England.

BELGIUM

Regie des Postes, Division 1.1.4.2., Service des Collectionneurs, Centre Monnaie, 1000 Brussels, Belgium. Deals with individual orders for mint and CTO stamps, postal stationery. SODA available with minimum balance of 700 francs. Orders shipped postpaid by surface, 3fr per 5 grams for airmail. CBC, IMO accepted.

Printer: Malines Stamp Printing Office, Mechelen.

BELIZE

Belize Philatelic Bureau, Private Bag No. 1, Belize City, Belize, Central America. Deals with individual orders for mint and CTO stamps, FDCs, postmarks, postal stationery. SODA available. CBC, IMO accepted. Orders shipped postpaid.

Government Agencies: CAPHCO Ltd., Old Inn House, 2 Carshalton Road, Sutton, Surrey SM1 4RN, England.

BENIN

Office des Postes et Telecommunications, Cotonou, Republique Populaire du Benin. Deals with individual orders for mint stamps, FDCs. SODA information not provided. Orders sent postage extra. CBC accepted.

Government Agency: Theodore Champion, 13 rue Drouot, 75009 Paris, France.

BERLIN (West)

Versandstelle fur Postwertzeichen, Postfach 20 00, 1000 Berlin 12, West Germany. Deals with individual orders for mint and CTO stamps, postal stationery. SODA available. Orders shipped postage extra. IMO, BD, CBC accepted.

Printer: Federal Printing Office, Berlin.

Government Agencies: Theodore Champion, 13 rue Drouot, 75009 Paris, France (sales in France only); J.A. Visser, Box 184, 3300 AD Dordrecht, Netherlands.

BERMUDA

Bermuda Philatelic Bureau, GPO, Hamilton, HMPM, Bermuda. Deals with individual orders for mint and CTO stamps, FDCs, postal stationery, plate number blocks, postcards. SODA available with a minimum deposit of $30. Orders shipped airmail postage extra; IRCs accepted. BD, CPC, IMO IBD, American Express accepted.

Printers: The House of Questa, Harrison & Sons, Format International Security Printers, Walsall Security Printers (all England); BDT Security Printers, Ireland.

Government Agencies: CAPHCO Ltd., Old Inn House, 2 Carshalton Road, Sutton, Surrey SM1 4RN, England; Unitrade, Box 172, Toronto, Ontario Canada M5W 1B2.

BHUTAN

Dy. Director, Philatelic Bureau, GPO, Thimphu, Bhutan. Deals with individual/dealer orders for mint and CTO stamps, FDCs, postal stationery, special postmarks. SODA available with minimum deposit of U.S. $5. Orders shipped postage extra; IRCs accepted. CBC, IMO, IBD, USPSMO, USMO accepted.

Printers: The House of Questa, England; Format International Security Printers, England; Toppan Printing Press, Japan.

Government Agency: Inter-Governmental Philatelic Corp., 460 W. 34th St., New York, N.Y. 10001.

BOLIVIA

Direccion Nacional de Correos, Seccion Filatelica, La Paz, Bolivia. Details of services not provided.

BOPHUTHATSWANA

Philatelic Services and INTERSAPA, Private Bag X505, 0001 Pretoria, Republic of South Africa. Deals with individual orders for mint and CTO stamps, Framas, FDCs, postal stationery, control blocks with plate numbers, stamp sets, special postmarks (agency supplies datestamp cards), albums. SODA available with minimum deposit of SA$15. Orders shipped postpaid BD, IBD accepted.

Printer: Government Printer, Pretoria.

Stamps from Bophuthatswana are prohibited in the United States as part of a general trade embargo.

Government Agencies: South African Philatelic Agency, c/o James Davis, 45-47 Church St., Rickmansworth WD3 1DG, England; J. Ferrier, Philart, CH-1261 Gingins, Switzerland.

BOTSWANA

Department of Postal Service, Philatelic Bureau, Box 100, Gaborone, Botswana. Deals with orders for mint and CTO stamps, FDCs. Orders shipped postage extra. BD, IMO, BPO, U.S., Canadian, West German, Swiss and South African currency accepted.

Government Agencies: Inter-Governmental Philatelic Corp., 460 W. 34th St., New York, N.Y. 10001; British & Overseas Philatelic Agency, Box 80, Shibuya, Tokyo 150-91, Japan.

BRAZIL

ECT, Assessoria Filatelica, SCS, Quadra 4, Bloco A, No. 230, Edificio Apolo, 7° Andar, 70300 Brasilia, DF, Brazil. Deals with individual orders for U.S. $5 or more for mint and CTO stamps, FDCs, postal stationery, special postmarks. SODA available with minimum deposit of U.S. $15. Orders shipped postage extra. CBC, BD, IMO, IBD, USPSMO accepted.

Printer: Brazilian State Mint, Rio de Janeiro.

Government Agencies: Unicover World Trade Corp. (Brazil Stamp Agency in North America), 1 Unicover Center, Cheyenne, Wyo. 82008-0005; Georg Roll Nachfolger, Holbeinstrasse 2, Box 1346, D-2880 Brake, West Germany; Infynsa, Juan Alvarez Mendizabal, 1-6°-5, Box 8477, Madrid 8, Spain.

BRITISH ANTARCTIC TERRITORY

Postmaster for British Antarctic Territory, c/o GPO, Port Stanley, Falkland Islands. Deals with individual orders for mint stamps, FDCs, special postmarks (customer supplies envelopes). SODA available. Orders shipped postage extra plus handling fee. CBC, PC, IMO accepted.

Government Agencies: CAPHCO Ltd., Old Inn House, 2 Carshalton Road, Sutton, Surrey SM1 4RN, England; British & Overseas Philatelic Agency Ltd., Box 80, Shibuya, Tokyo 150-91, Japan.

BRITISH VIRGIN ISLANDS

The Postmaster, Philatelic Bureau, Road Town, Tortola, British Virgin Islands. Deals with individual orders for mint and CTO stamps, FDCs, plate number or inscription blocks. SODA available with minimum balance of U.S. $5 required. Orders shipped postpaid. CBC, PC, IMO, IBD, USPSMO, USMO, BPO, VISA, MasterCard, American Express, Diner's Club accepted.

Printers: Various through Inter-Governmental Philatelic Corp.

Government Agent: Inter-Governmental Philatelic Corp., 460 W. 34th St., New York, N.Y. 10001.

BRUNEI

Postal Services Department, GPO, Bandar Seri Begawan 2050, Brunei Darussalam. Deals with individual orders for mint and CTO stamps, FDCs, postal stationery, plate number blocks, postmarks (customer supplies addressed envelopes). SODA available with minimum deposit of U.S. $15. Orders shipped postage extra plus service fee; IRCs accepted. IMO (through Singapore, Malaysia), IBD, BPO accepted. Printers: Harrison & Sons, England; Secura Singapore, Singapore; Cartor, France; Security Printers, Malaysia.

Government Agencies: Inter-Governmental Philatelic Corp., 460 W. 34th St., New York, N.Y. 10001; CAPHCO Ltd., Old Inn House, 2 Carshalton Road, Sutton, Surrey SM1 4RN, England.

BULGARIA

Ministere du Transport et Communications, Service Philatelique Postal, 44 Rue Dencoglou, Sofia, Bulgaria. Details of services not provided.

BURKINA FASO

Service Philatelique, Offices des Postes et Telecommunications, Ouagodougou, Burkina Faso. Details of services not provided.

Government Agency: Theodore Champion, 13 rue Drouot, 75009 Paris, France.

BURMA

Myanma Export Import Corp., Export Division, Philatelic Section, Rangoon, Burma. Deals with individual orders for mint stamps. No information on SODA provided. Orders shipped postage extra, plus a packing charge. CBC accepted.

BURUNDI

Agence Philatelique du Burundi, Boite Postale 45, Bujumbura, Burundi. Deals with individual orders for mint stamps, FDCs. SODA available with minimum deposit. Orders shipped postage extra. CBC accepted.

CAMEROON

Principale Philatelique, Centre Philatelique PTT, Yaounde, Cameroon. Details of services not provided.

Government Agencies: Inter-Governmental Philatelic Corp., 460 W. 34th St., New York, N.Y. 10001; Theodore Champion, 13 rue Drouot, 75009 Paris, France; John Lister Ltd., 49 Shelton St., Convent Garden, London WC2, England (except in U.S.).

CANADA

National Philatelic Centre, Canada Post Corp., Antigonish, Nova Scotia, Canada B2G 2R8. Deals with individual orders for mint stamps, FDCs, postal stationery, plate number (new plate definitives only) and inscription blocks, annual collections, albums, catalogs, souvenir cards, novelties. SODA available. Orders shipped postpaid. CBC, PC (Canadian, U.S. or British), IMO (Canadian), IBD (Canadian, U.S, British), USPSMO, USMO, VISA, MasterCard accepted.

Printers: Ashton-Potter, Toronto; British American Bank Note, Ottawa; Canadian Bank Note.

Government Agency: Unicover World Trade Corp. (Canada Post Stamp Service in the United States), 1 Unicover Center, Cheyenne, Wyo. 82008-0018.

CAPE VERDE ISLANDS

Direccao dos Servicos de Correios e Telecomunicacoes, Praia, Republica de Cabo Verde. Deals with individual orders for mint stamps, FDCs, postal stationery. SODA not available. Orders shipped postage extra. IBD accepted.

Government Agency: Inter-Governmental Philatelic Corp., 460 W. 34th St., New York, N.Y. 10001.

CAYMAN ISLANDS

Postmaster General, Philatelic Bureau, GPO, George Town, Grand Cayman, Cayman Islands, British West Indies. Deals with individual orders for stamps, FDCs, postal stationery, special postmarks (customer supplies envelopes). SODA available with minimum deposit of U.S. $25. Orders shipped postage extra. IMO, USPSMO, USMO, Canada PMO, BPO, sterling bank notes, CBC accepted.

Printers: Various through CAPHCO.

Government Agencies: CAPHCO Ltd., Old Inn House, 2 Carshalton Road, Sutton, Surrey SM1 4RN, England; Theodore Champion, 13 rue Drouot, 75009 Paris, France; British & Overseas Philatelic Agency Ltd., Box 80, Shibuya, Tokyo 150-91, Japan.

CENTRAL AFRICAN REPUBLIC

Service Philatelique des PTT, Bangui, Central African Republic. Details of services not provided.

Government Agency: Theodore Champion, 13 rue Drouot, 75009 Paris France.

CHAD

Receveur General des PTT, Ndjamena, Chad. Details of services not provided.

CHILE

Empresa de Correos de Chile, Servicio Filatelico, Moneda 1155, Santiago, Chile. Deals with individual orders for two or more mint or CTO stamps, FDCs. Orders shipped postage extra; IRCs accepted. SODA available with minimum deposit of U.S. $30. CBC, PC, IMO, IBD, USPSMO, USMO, IRC accepted.

Printer: Casa de Moneda de Chile.

Government Agencies: Unicover Trade Corp., 1 Unicover Center, Cheyenne, Wyo. 82008-0020; James Davis & Son, 45-47 Church St., Rickmansworth WD3 1DG, England; Georg Roll, Holbeinstrasse 2, D-2880 Brake, West Germany; Infynsa, Juan Alvarez Mendizabal, 1-6°-5, Madrid 8, Spain.

CHINA

China National Philatelic Corp., He Ping Men, Beijing, China. Deals with orders for 100 or more sets for mint or CTO stamps, FDCs, postal stationery, special postmarks, plate number or inscription blocks. SODA available. Orders sent postpaid. CBC, IMO, IBD accepted.

Printer: Beijing Postage Stamp Printing House.

Government Agencies: Unicover World Trade Corp. (China Stamp Agency in North America), 1 Unicover Center, Cheyenne, Wyo. 82008-0003; Harry Allen, Rickmansworth, Herts. WD3 1EY, England; Philimex 58, rue du Faubourg Montmartre, 75009, Paris, France; Richard Borek, Theodor-Heuss-Strasse 7, 3330 Braunschweig, West Germany; Japan Philatelic Co. Ltd. Box 2, Shinjuku, Tokyo 160-91, Japan; Frimarkshuset AB, S-793 01, Leksand, Sweden; Philder SA, Box 68, 6830 Chiasso No. 3, Switzerland.

TAIWAN (CHINA, REPUBLIC OF)

Philatelic Department, Directorate General of Posts, Taipei 10603, Taiwan, Republic of China. Deals with individual orders for mint stamps, FDCs, special postmarks (bureau supplies envelopes). SODA available with minimum deposit of U.S. $10. Orders shipped postpaid via registered surface mail, postage extra via airmail. CBC, PC, IMO, U.S. bank notes accepted.

Printers: China Color Printing Co., Taiwan; China Engraving and Printing Works, Taiwan.

Government Agencies: World Wide Philatelic Agency, Inc., 2031 Carolina Place, Fort Mill, S.C. 29715; John Lister Ltd., 49 Shelton St., Convent Garden, London WC2, England (except in U.S.); Theodore Champion, 13 rue Drouot, 75009 Paris, France (sales in France only).

CHRISTMAS ISLAND

Philatelic Bureau, Christmas Island, Indian Ocean 6798. Deals with individual orders for mint and CTO stamps, FDCs, postal stationery, special sets, albums, special postmarks (bureau or customer supplies envelopes). SODA available. All orders shipped postpaid. Orders exceeding $100 for clients in Australia and $50 for other clients are dispatched by registered mail with clients paying appropriate fee. CBC drawn on Australian bank, IMO, Australian postal order accepted.

Government Agencies: CAPHCO Ltd., Old Inn House, 2 Carshalton Road, Sutton, Surrey SM1 4RN, England; British & Overseas Philatelic Agency Ltd., Box 80, Shibuya, Tokyo 150-91, Japan.

CISKEI

Philatelic Services and INTERSAPA, Private Bag X505, 0001 Pretoria, Republic of South Africa. Deals with individual orders for mint and CTO stamps, Framas, FDCs, postal stationery, control blocks with plate numbers, stamp sets, special postmarks (agency supplies datestamp cards), albums. SODA available with minimum deposit of SA$15. Orders shipped postpaid. BD, IBD accepted.

Printer: Government Printer, Pretoria.

Stamps from Ciskei are prohibited in the United States as part of a general trade embargo.

Government Agencies: South African Philatelic Agency, c/o James Davis & Son, 45-47 Church St., Richmansworth WD3 1DG, England; J. Ferrier, Philart-SA, CH-1261 Gingins, Switzerland.

COCOS (KEELING) ISLANDS

Philatelic Bureau, Cocos (Keeling) Islands, Indian Ocean 6799. Deals with individual orders for mint and CTO stamps, FDCs, stamp packs. SODA available. Orders shipped airmail postpaid. CBC in Australian currency, PC, BD, IMO, BPO, IRC accepted.

Government Agencies: Herrick Stamp Co., Box 219, Lawrence, N.Y. 11559.

COLOMBIA

Oficina Filatelica, Administracion Postal Nacional, Oficina 209, Edificio Murillo Toro, Bogota 1, Colombia. Deals with individual orders for mint stamps, FDCs, special postmarks (agency supplies envelopes). SODA available with minimum deposit. Orders shipped postage extra. CBC, IMO accepted.

COMORO ISLANDS

Direction Generale des PTT, Service Philatelique, Moroni, Comoro Islands. Details of services not provided.

Government Agency: Theodore Champion, 13 rue Drouot, 75009 Paris, France.

CONGO PEOPLE'S REPUBLIC

Direction Generale des PTT, Service Philatelique, Brazzaville, Congo People's Republic. Details of services not provided.

Government Agency: Theodore Champion, 13 rue Drouot, 75009 Paris, France.

COOK ISLANDS

Philatelic Bureau, Post Office, Rarotonga, Cook Islands, South Pacific. Deals with individual orders for mint stamps, FDCs. SODA available with minimum deposit required. SODA orders shipped postage extra. CBC accepted.

Printer: Heraclio Fournier, Spain.

COSTA RICA

Oficina Filatelica, Direccion Nacional de Comunicaciones, San Jose, Costa Rica. Deals with individual orders for mint stamps, FDCs. SODA available with minimum deposit of U.S. $50 ($250 for dealers). CBC, IMO accepted.

Printer: Casa Grafica, San Jose.

CUBA

COPREFIL (Empresa de Correos, Prensa y Filatelia), Apartado 1000, Havana 1, Cuba, or office in Canada, COPREFIL, 1415 Pine Ave. W, Montreal, Que., Canada H3G 1B2. Deals with individual orders for mint and CTO stamps, FDCs.

Stamps from Cuba are prohibited in the United States as part of a general trade embargo.

Government Agency: Theodore Champion, 13 rue Drouot, 75009 Paris, France (sales in France only).

CYPRUS

Philatelic Service, GPO, Nicosia, Cyprus. Deals with individual orders for mint and CTO stamps, FDCs, special postmarks. SODA available with minimum balance of C£5. Orders shipped postage extra; IRCs accepted. CBC, BD, IMO, IBD, USPSMO accepted.

Printers: Mich. A. Moatsos, Graphic Arts, Greece; Graphic Arts, Alexandros Matsoukis, Greece; Harrison & Sons, England; Helio Courvoisier, Switzerland.

Government Agencies: Inter-Governmental Philatelic Corp., 460 W. 34th St., New York, N.Y. 10001; Government Philatelic Agencies, Unitrade Associates, 127 Cartwright Ave., Toronto, Ontario, Canada M6A 1V4; Harry Allen, Rickmansworth, Herts. WD3 1EY, England; N. Larcos, Box 236, Spit Junction, NSW 2088, Australia; Theodore Champion, 13 rue Drouot, 75009 Paris, France (sales in France only); Jurgen Ehrlich, 5 Koln 41, Peter-Berchem str. 3, West Germany; Sephanos Frangoudis, Stadium 60, Athens 105 64, Greece; J.A. Visser, Box 184, 3300 AD Dordrecht, Netherlands; Frimarkshuset Agentur AB, S-793 01, Leksand, Sweden; Philart, CH-1261 Gingins, Switzerland.

CZECHOSLOVAKIA

Artia Foreign Trade Corp., Box 790, Prague 1, Czechoslovakia. Deals only with bulk orders for mint and used stamps, FDCs, postal stationery, kiloware. SODA available with minimum of 100 sets mint or used and minimum deposit of U.S. $200. CBC accepted.

Printer: Czechoslovakia State Printing Office.

DENMARK

Postens Frimaerkecenter, Vesterbrogade 67, DK 1620 Copenhagen V, Denmark. Deals with individual orders for mint stamps, FDCs, postal stationery, marginal blocks of four, annual collections. SODA available. Orders shipped postpaid. PC, IMO, bank notes accepted.

Printer: PTT Stamp Printing Office, Copenhagen.

Government Agent: Nordica Inc., Box 284, Old Bethpage, N.Y. 11804.

DJIBOUTI

Office des Postes et Telecommunications, Djibouti, Republic of Djibouti. Deals with individual orders for mint stamps, FDCs (customer supplies envelopes). Orders shipped postage extra. CBC, PC, USMO accepted.

Government Agencies: L'Agence des Timbres-poste d'Outre-Mer, 85, avenue La Bourdonnais, 75007 Paris, France (exclusive agent for first day covers); Theodore Champion, 13 rue Drouot, 75009 Paris, France.

DOMINICA

Postmaster, Stamp Order Division, GPO, Roseau, Dominica, West Indies. Deals with individual orders for mint and CTO stamps, FDCs, special postmarks. SODA available. Orders shipped postage extra; IRCs accepted. CBC, IMO, IBD, USPSMO, USMO accepted.

Printer: The House of Questa, England.

Government Agency: Inter-Governmental Philatelic Corp., 460 W. 34th St., New York, N.Y. 10001.

DOMINICAN REPUBLIC

Philatelic Section, GPO, Santo Domingo, Dominican Republic. Deals with individual orders for mint stamps, FDCs, special postmarks (customer supplies envelopes). SODA available. Orders shipped postage extra plus handling charge of 50¢ per order. CBC, IMO, USPSMO accepted.

Printers: Litografia Ferrua & Hnos., Editorial Padilla (both of Dominican Republic).

ECUADOR

Departamento Filatelico, Museo Postal del Estado, Direccion General de Correos, Correo Central, Quito, Ecuador. Details of services not provided.

Printer: National Geographic Institute.

EGYPT

Postal Organization Philatelic Office, Cairo, Arab Republic of Egypt. Deals with individual orders for mint and CTO stamps, FDCs, postal stationery, plate number or inscription blocks, special postmarks. SODA available with minimum deposit of U.S. $25, IMO, CBC, BD, PC, bank transfers (drawn on the Central Bank of Egypt, Cairo), IRC accepted.

Printer: Postal Printing House, Cairo.

EQUATORIAL GUINEA

Oficina Filatelica de la Direccion General de Correos, Malabo, Republic of Equatorial Guinea. Details of services not provided.

ETHIOPIA

Ethiopian Postal Service, Philatelic Section, Box 1112, Addis Ababa, Ethiopia. Deals with individual orders for mint stamps, FDCs. SODA available. Details of additional services not provided.

Government Agencies: Inter-Governmental Philatelic Corp., 460 W. 34th St., New York, N.Y. 10001; Les Editions Rodan, Ch. de Waterloo Stwg. 868/870, 1180 Brussels, Belgium.

FALKLAND ISLANDS

Postmaster, Philatelic Bureau, Post Office, Port Stanley, Falkland Islands. Deals with individual orders for mint and CTO stamps, FDCs, postal stationery. SODA available with minimum deposit of equivalent of £10. Orders shipped postage extra plus handling fee; IRCs accepted. CBC, PC, IMO, traveler's checks accepted. Also handles issues of the British Antarctic Territory.

Government Agencies: CAPHCO Ltd., Old Inn House, 2 Carshalton Road, Sutton, Surrey SM1 4RN, England; British & Overseas Philatelic Agency Ltd., Box 80, Shibuya, Tokyo 150-91, Japan.

FAROES

Frimerkjadeildin, FR-159 Torshavn, Faroes. Deals with individual orders for mint and CTO stamps, FDCs, special postmarks (customer supplies envelopes). SODA available with no minimum deposit. Orders shipped postpaid. Publishes a biannual magazine, which is shipped free to all customers. CBC, PC, IMO, IRC accepted.

Printers: Joh. Enschede, Netherlands; Helio Courvoisier, Switzerland; Bank of Finland.

Government Agency: Nordica Inc., Box 284, Old Bethpage, N.Y. 11804.

FIJI

Philatelic Bureau, Box 100, Suva, Fiji. Deals with individual orders for mint and CTO stamps, FDCs, postal stationery, plate number or inscription blocks, special postmarks. SODA available. Orders shipped postpaid. CBC, BD (Bank of New Zealand, Suva, Fiji), IMO, IBD, VISA, MasterCard, American Express, Diners Club accepted.

Printers: The House of Questa, England; Format International Security Printers, England; BDT International Security Printers, Ireland; Walsall Security Printers, England.

Also handles postage stamps from

Pitcairn Islands.

Government Agencies: CAPHCO Ltd., Old Inn House, 2 Carshalton Road, Sutton, Surrey SM1 4RN, England; Australia Post, GPO Box 2020S, Melbourne, Victoria 3000, Australia.

FINLAND

Posts and Telecommunications of Finland, Philatelic Center, Box 654 (Salomonkatu 1), SF-00101 Helsinki, Finland. Deals with individual orders for mint and CTO stamps, FDCs, postal stationery, plate numbers for definitives, maximum cards, year sets, presentation packs. SODA available with U.S. $10 minimum deposit for Finland Stamp Agency in North America; SODA not available from Finland. CBC, PC, IMO, USPSMO accepted.

Printers: Bank of Finland Security Printing House, Frenckell Printing House, Finland.

Also handles postage stamps of Aland.

Government Agency: Unicover World Trade Corp. (Finland Stamp Agency in North America), 1 Unicover Center, Cheyenne, Wyo. 82008-0017.

FRANCE

Service Philatelique De La Poste, 18 rue Francois Bonvin, F-75758, Paris, Cedex 15, France. Deals with individual orders for mint and CTO stamps, postal stationery. SODA available with the first remittance covering at least four-month purchases, plus minimum deposit of 50 francs for postage by registered mail. All orders shipped postage extra; IRCs accepted. BD, PC (takes about six weeks), IMO, IBD, VISA, MasterCard.

Printer: Government Printing Office, Perigueux.

Also handles postage stamps of UNESCO, Council of Europe, French Andorra, St. Pierre and Miquelon and definitives of Monaco.

Government Agent: Unicover World Trade Corp. (French Stamp Agency in North America), 1 Unicover Center, Cheyenne, Wyo. 82008-0009.

FRENCH COMMUNITY

Agence Comptable des Timbres Poste d'Outremer, 85 Avenue de la Bourdonnais, Paris 75007, France; Bureau d'Etudes des Postes et Telecommunications d'Outremer, 5 Rue Oswaldo Cruz, 75016 Paris, France. Agencies supply new issues of most existing and former French colonies. SODA available. PC, IMO accepted.

FRENCH POLYNESIA

Centre Philatelique, Papeete, Tahiti, French Polynesia. Deals with individual orders for mint and CTO stamps, FDCs, postal stationery, plate number and inscription blocks, maximum cards, special postmarks. SODA available with minimum balance of 5,000 francs. Orders shipped postpaid. CBC, BD, PC, IMO, IBD, USPSMO, USMO, IRC accepted.

Printers: Cartor, France; French Government Printing Office; Edila.

Government Agency: World Wide Philatelic Agency, 2031 Carolina Place, Fort Mill, S.C. 29715.

FRENCH SOUTHERN AND ANTARCTIC TERRITORIES

Agence Comptable des Timbres Poste d'Outremer, 85 Avenue de la Bourdonnais, Paris 75007, France; Bureau d'Etudes des Postes et Telecommunications d'Outremer, 5 Rue Oswaldo Cruz, 75016 Paris, France. Agencies supply new issues of most existing and former French colonies. Details of services not provided.

GABON

Service Philatelique, Direction Generale des PTT, Libreville, Gabon. Details of services not provided.

Government Agency: Theodore Champion, 13 rue Drouot, 75009 Paris, France.

GAMBIA

Postmaster General, GPO, Banjul, The Gambia. Details of services not provided.

Government Agent: Inter-Governmental Philatelic Corp., 460 W. 34th St., New York, N.Y. 10001.

GERMANY, EAST

VEB Philatelie Wermsdorf, Abt. Export/Import, Postfach 266, 7010 Leipzig, German Democratic Republic. Deals only with bulk orders for mint and CTO stamps, FDCs, postal stationery, special postmarks. Orders shipped postpaid within Europe; postage extra elsewhere. CBC, PC accepted.

Printer: VEB Wertpapierdruckerei, Leipzig.

GERMANY, WEST

Versandstelle fur Postwertzeichen, Sammler — Service der Post, Box 20 00, 6000 Frankfurt 1, Federal Republic of Germany. Deals with individual orders for mint and CTO stamps and postal stationery. SODA available. Orders shipped postage extra. IMO, BD, CBC accepted.

Printers: Federal Printing Office, Berlin; Graphischer Grossbetrieb A. Bagel, Dusseldorf.

Government Agencies: Interpost, Box 378, Malverne, N.Y. 11563; Theodore Champion, 13 rue Drouot, 75009 Paris, France (sales in France only); J.A. Visser, Box 184, 3300 AD Dordrecht, Netherlands.

GHANA

Philatelic Bureau, Department of Posts, Accra, Ghana. Details of services not provided.

Government Agency: Inter-Governmental Philatelic Corp., 460 W. 34th St., New York, N.Y. 10001.

GIBRALTAR

Gibraltar Post Office, Philatelic Bureau, Box 5662, Gibraltar. Deals with individual orders for mint and CTO stamps, FDCs, postal stationery, plate number and inscription blocks, special postmarks. SODA available with minimum balance of £5. Orders shipped postage extra. CBC, BD, PC, IMO, IBD accepted.

Printers: The House of Questa, England, BDT International Security Printers, England; Harrison & Sons, England, Walsall Security Printers, England; Format International Security Printers, England, Joh. Enschede & Sons, Netherlands; Helio Courvoisier, Switzerland; Cartor, France.

Government Agencies: Inter-Governmental Philatelic Corp., 460 W. 34th St., New York, N.Y. 10001 (U.S., Central and South America, Japan); Government Philatelic Agencies, Unitrade Associates, 127 Cartwright Ave., Toronto, Ontario, Canada M6A 1V4, Canada (Canada); Nordfrim, DK 5450 Otterup, Denmark (Nordic countries); Richard Borek, Theodor-Heuss-Strasse 7, 3300 Braunschweig, West Germany (Germany, West Berlin, Austria); De Rosa International, Av du Tribunal Federal 34, 1005 Lausanne, Switzerland (Italy, Switzerland); CAPHCO Ltd., Old Inn House, 2 Carshalton Road, Sutton, Surrey SM1 4RN, England (remainder of world).

GREAT BRITAIN

British Philatelic Bureau, 20 Brandon St., Edinburgh EH3 5TT, Scotland. Deals with individual orders for mint stamps, FDCs, postal stationery, plate number blocks, special postmarks. SODA available with minimum balance of £1. Orders shipped postpaid. CBC, BD, PC, IMO, IBD accepted.

Printers: Harrison & Sons Ltd., The House of Questa (both England).

Government Agencies: Interpost, Box 378, Malverne, N.Y. 11565; Max Stern, Box 997H, GPO, Melbourne, Victoria 3001, Australia; Nordrim A/C, No. 9870, Nordfyns Frimerkehandel, DK 5450 Otterup, Denmark; Thedore Champion, 13 rue Drouot, 75009 Paris, France; Georg Roll Nachfolger, Holbeinstrasse 2, Box 1346, D-2880 Brake, West Germany; British Post Office Agency, British & Overseas Philatelic Agency, Box 80, Shibuya, Tokyo 150-91, Japan; De Rosa International, Av du Tribunal Federal 34, 1005 Lausanne, Switzerland.

GREECE

Greek Post Office, Philatelic Service, 100 Aeolou St., GR-101 88, Athens, Greece. Deals with individual orders for mint and CTO stamps, FDCs. SODA available with minimum balance of 1,000 drachmae. Orders shipped postpaid. CBC, PC, IMO, IBD accepted.

Printers: Mich. A Moatsos, Graphic Arts; Graphic Arts, Alexandros Matsovkis (both Greece).

Government Agencies: Interpost, Box 378, Malverne, N.Y. 11565 (America); De Rosa International, Av du Tribunal, Federal 34, CH-1005 Lausanne, Switzerland (Europe).

GREENLAND

Kalaallit Alakkeriviat, Groenlands Postvaesen, Wilders Plads, Building O, Box 100, DK Copenhagen K, Denmark. Deals with individual orders for mint and CTO stamps, FDCs, plate number blocks, maximum cards, special postmarks. SODA with minimum balance required. Orders shipped postpaid. CBC, BD, PC, IMO, IBD, USPSMO accepted.

Printer: Danish Post Office Stamp Printing Office.

Government Agency: Nordica Inc., Box 284, Old Bethpage, N.Y. 11804.

GRENADA

Postmaster General, GPO, St. George's, Grenada, West Indies. Details of services not provided.

Government Agency: Inter-Governmental Philatelic Corp., 460 W. 34th St., New York, N.Y. 10001.

GRENADA, GRENADINES OF

Postmaster General, GPO St. George's, Grenada, West Indies. Details of services not provided.

Government Agency: Inter-Governmental Philatelic Corp., 460 W. 34th St., New York, N.Y. 10001.

GUATEMALA

Direccion General de Correos y Telegrafos, Departamento Filatelico, Guatemala, Central America. Deals with individual orders for mint stamps. SODA available. IMO, CBC, BD accepted.

GUERNSEY

Philatelic Bureau, Postal Headquarters, Guernsey, Channel Islands, Great Britain. Deals with individual orders for mint and CTO stamps, FDCs, postal stationery, plate number or inscription blocks, special postmarks. SODA available with $20 deposit. SODA orders shipped postpaid; 25 pence handling charge on one-time only orders. CBC, BD, PC, IMO, IBD, USPSMO, VISA, MasterCard, American Express and Diners Club accepted.

Printers: Cartor, France; The House of Questa, England; BDT International Security Printers, Ireland; Helio Courvoisier, Switzerland; Harrison & Sons, England; De La Rue, England; Delrieu; Waddington Security Printers, England; Format International Security Printers, England.

Also handles emissions of Alderney.

Government Agencies: Guernsey Philatelic Agency (SODA available), 460 W. 34th St., New York, N.Y. 10001; Unitrade Associates, 127 Cartwright Ave., Toronto, Ontario, Canada M6A 1V4; Max Stern, Box 997H, GPO, Melbourne, Victoria 3001, Australia; Nordfrim, Otterup DK 5450, Denmark; Theodore Champion, 13 rue Drouot, 75009 Paris, France; Richard Borek, Theodor-Heuss-Strasse 7, 3300 Braunschweig, West Germany; BOPC, Shoei Building, 1-11-3 Shiboya, Shibuya-Ku, Tokyo 150, Japan; J.A. Visser B.V., Box 184, 3300 AD Dordrecht, Netherlands; Maderphil, Avda de Roma 157, 6a, Barcelona 11, Spain; Frimarkshuset AB, S-7931, Leksand, Sweden; De Rosa International, Av. du Tribunal Federal 34, 1005 Lausanne, Switzerland; Stamp Arcade, Box 1532, Port Elisabeth 6000, South Africa.

GUINEA

Agence Philatelique, Boite Postale 814, Conakry, Republic of Guinea. Deals with individual orders for a minimum of U.S. $15.60. SODA information not provided. Orders shipped postage extra. CBC, BD accepted.

GUINEA-BISSAU

Direccao Servicos dos Correios e Telecomunicacoes e Telefones, Bissau, Guinea-Bissau. Details of services not provided.

Government Agency: D & G Philatelics Inc., Box 237, 370 Hempstead Ave., West Hempstead, N.Y. 11552.

GUYANA

Guyana Post Office Corp., Robb Street, Georgetown, Guyana. Deals with individual orders for mint and CTO stamps, FDCs, postal stationery, plate number blocks, special postmarks. SODA available with a minimum balance of $50. Orders shipped postage extra. CBC, IMO, IBD, USPSMO, USMO accepted.

Printers: Format International Security Printers, England; others by tender.

Government Agencies: Dr. E.A. Oud

Kirik, KTZ Holdings Corp., Box 359, New Jersey 08559; Compania Filatelica, Mundial (Panama) Ltd., Apartado Postal 4669, Panama 5, Panama.

HAITI

Office du Timbre, Direction General des Impots, Box 3, Port-Au-Prince, Haiti, West Indies. Details of services not provided.

HONDURAS

Departamento Filatelico, Direccion General de Correos, Tegucigalpa, D.C., Honduras, Central America. Deals with individual orders for mint stamps, FDCs, inscription blocks. SODA available with minimum balance of U.S. $20. Orders shipped by certified airmail postage extra; IRCs accepted. CBC, IMO accepted.

Printer: Centro Tecnico Tipo Litografico Nacional (CETTNA).

HONG KONG

Hong Kong Post Office, Philatelic Bureau, GPO 2, Connaught Place, Hong Kong. Deals with individual orders for mint stamps, FDCs. SODA available with minimum deposit of HK$100. Orders shipped postage extra plus handling fee. BPO, IMO accepted.

Government Agencies: Interpost, Box 378, Malverne, N.Y. 11565.

HUNGARY

Philatelia Hungarica, Box 600, Budapest 1373, Hungary. Deals only with bulk orders (dealers). Details not provided.

Government Agency: Unicover World Trade Corp. (Hungary Stamp Agency in North America), 1 Unicover Center, Cheyenne, Wyo. 82008-0011.

ICELAND

Frimerkjasalan, Postboks 1445, Reykjavik, Iceland. Deals with individual orders for mint stamps, FDCs. SODA available with minimum deposit of 500 krone. IMO, CBC accepted.

Government Agency: Nordica, Box 284, Old Bethpage, N.Y. 11804.

INDIA

Philatelic Bureau, GPO, Bombay 400001, India. Deals with individual orders (minimum order of 2 rupees) for mint stamps, FDCs. SODA available with minimum deposit of $15 required. Orders shipped postage extra plus a handling fee of 1 percent on all orders. IMO, BPO, CPC, IBD accepted.

Printer: India Security Press.

Government Agencies: Inter-Governmental Philatelic Corp., 460 W. 34th St., New York, N.Y. 10001; James Davis & Son, 45-47 Church St., Rickmansworth WD3 1DG, England; Richard Borek, Theodor-Heuss-Strasse 7, 3300 Braunschweig, West Germany; Philart, CH-1261 Gingins, Switzerland.

INDONESIA

Philatelic Subdivision, Headquarters of Postal Services J1, 34 Jalan Jakarta, Bandung, Indonesia. Deals with orders for mint stamps, FDCs, postal stationery. SODA available. Orders shipped postage extra. CBC, IMO accepted.

Printer: Perum Peruri, Indonesia.

Government Agencies: Hugo J. van Reijen, International Philatelic Agencies, Koninginneweg 133, Box 5497, Amsterdam 1007, Netherlands (Europe and Africa).

IRAN

Philatelic Bureau, General Directorate of Posts, Tehran, Iran. Deals with individual orders for mint stamps, FDCs (service fee extra). SODA available. Orders shipped every four months, postage extra; IRCs accepted. CBC, IMO, bank notes.

Printer: Government Printing Press Organization, Iran.

Stamps from Iran are prohibited in the United States as part of a general trade embargo.

IRAQ

Posts and Savings Administration, Stamp Department, Philatelic Bureau, Baghdad, Republic of Iraq. Deals with individual and bulk orders for mint stamps, FDCs, special postmarks (customer supplies envelopes). SODA available. Orders shipped postpaid, handling fee extra. CBC, IMO, bank notes accepted.

IRELAND

The Controller, Philatelic Bureau, GPO, Dublin 1, Ireland. Deals with individual orders for mint stamps, FDCs, special postmarks (customer supplies envelopes), postal stationery. SODA available. Orders shipped postage extra. CBC, BPO, IMO accepted.

Printers: Irish Government Printers and Irish Security Stamp Printing.

Government Agencies: Interpost, Box 378, Malverne, N.Y. 11565; James Davis & Son, 45-47 Church St., Rickmansworth WD3 1DG, England; Max Stern, 234 Flinders St., Box 9974, GPO Melbourne, 3001 Victoria, Australia; Andre Schittecatte, Chaussee de Waterloo 868/870, B-1180 Brussels, Belgium; Nordfrim, DK 5450 Otterup, Denmark; Theodore Champion; 13 rue Drouot, Paris 75009, France; Georg Roll Nachfolger, Holbeinstrasse 2, D-2880 Brake, West Germany; Philart, CH-1261 Gingins, Geneva, Switzerland.

ISLE OF MAN

Philatelic Bureau, Box 10M, Douglas, Isle of Man. Deals with individual orders for $10 or more for mint and CTO stamps, FDCs, postal stationery, stamp replica postcards. SODA available. Standing orders and additional orders amounting to more than £15 are supplied without handling charge. Additional orders for less than £15 are subject to handling charge of 25 pence for account holders and 30p for non-account holders. CBC, BD, PC, IMO, IBD, USPSMO, VISA, MasterCard accepted.

Printers: The House of Questa, England; Joh. Enschede, Netherlands; BDT International Security Printing, Ireland; Cartor, France.

Government Agencies: Inter-Governmental Philatelic Corp., 460 W. 34th St., New York, N.Y. 10001; CAPHCO Ltd., Old Inn House, 2 Carshalton Road, Sutton, Surrey SM1 4RN, England; Max Stern, Box 997H, GPO, Melbourne, Victoria 3001, Australia; Nordfrim, DK 5450 Otterup, Denmark; Theodore Champion, 13 rue Drouot, 75009 Paris, France (sales in France only); Richard Borek Agenturen, Theodor-Heuss-Strasse 7, 3300 Braunschweig, West Germany; British and Overseas Philatelic Agency, Box 80, Shibuya, Tokyo 150-91, Japan; J.A. Visser, Box 184, 3300 AD Dordrecht, Netherlands; Maderphil, S Avda de Roma 157, 6a, 08011 Barcelona, Spain; Frimarkshuset, S793 01, Leksand, Sweden.

ISRAEL

Postal Authority Philatelic Service, 12 Jerusalem Blvd., 61 080 Tel Aviv-Yafo, Israel. Deals with individual orders for a minimum or three units of mint stamps and/or FDCs, special postmarks (on envelopes). SODA available with minimum deposit of U.S. $60. Orders shipped postage extra. CBC, PC accepted.

Printers: Government Printer, Jerusalem; E. Lewin-Epstein Ltd, Tel Aviv.

Government Agencies: Unicover World Trade Corp. (Israel Stamp Agency in North America), 1 Unicover Center, Cheyenne, Wyo. 82008-0006; Harry Allen, Israel Philatelic Agency in Great Britain, Box 5, Rickmansworth WD3 1EY, England.

ITALY

Ufficio Principale Filatelico, Via Mario de' Fiori, 103/A, 00187 Rome, Italy. Deals with individual orders for mint stamps, FDCs, postal stationery, special postmarks (agency supplies envelopes for 200 lire each or customer supplies envelopes). SODA available. Orders shipped postage extra. IMO accepted.

Printer: State Polygraphic Institute, Rome.

IVORY COAST

Office des Postes et Telecommunications, Direction des Services Postaux, Service Philatelique, Abidjan, Ivory Coast. Deals with individual orders for mint stamps, FDCs. SODA available. Orders sent postage extra. IMO accepted.

Government Agency: Theodore Champion, 13 rue Drouot, 75009 Paris, France.

JAMAICA

Head Postmaster, Philatelic Bureau, GPO, Kingston, Jamaica. Deals with individual orders for mint stamps, FDCs. SODA available. Orders shipped postage extra. IMO, USPSMO, Canadian MO, BPO, BD, CBC accepted.

Government Agencies: CAPHCO Ltd., Old Inn House, 2 Carshalton Road, Sutton, Surrey SM1 4RN, England;

British & Overseas Philatelic Agency Ltd., Box 80, Shibuya, Tokyo 150-91, Japan.

JAPAN

Philatelic Section, CPO Box 888, Tokyo 100-91, Japan. Deals with individual orders for mint stamps, postal stationery. SODA available with a minimum deposit of 4 yen. CBC, IMO, USPSMO accepted.

Printer: Ministry of Finance Printing Bureau, Tokyo.

JERSEY

The Jersey Post Office, Philatelic Bureau, Dept. 304, Jersey, Channel Islands, via Great Britain. Deals with individual orders for mint and CTO stamps, FDCs, postal stationery, plate number and inscription blocks, presentation packs, yearbooks, special postmarks (customer supplies envelopes). SODA available with minimum deposit of U.S. $15. Orders shipped postpaid, plus handling fee (postage extra for airmail). CBC (drawn in British £ on a London bank) BD, PC, IMO, IBD (drawn in British £ on a London bank), USPSMO, USMO, American Express, VISA, Diners Club, Access accepted.

Printers: Helio Courvoisier, Switzerland; The House of Questa, England; Cartor, France; BDT International Security Printers, Ireland.

Government Agencies: Interpost, Box 378, Malverne, N.Y. 11565; CAPHCO Ltd., Old Inn House, 2 Carshalton Road, Sutton, Surrey SM1 4RN, England; Max Stern, 234 Flinders St., Melbourne, Victoria 3001, Australia; Nordfrim, DK 5450 Otterup, Denmark; Theodore Champion, 13 rue Drouot, 75009 Paris, France (sales in France only); Richard Borek, Theodor-Heusse-Strasse 7, 25/26, 3300 Braunschweig, West Germany; British and Overseas Philatelic Agency Ltd., Box 80, Shibuya, Tokyo 150-91, Japan; J.A. Visser, Box 184, 3300 AD Dordrecht, The Netherlands; Frimarkshuset AB, S-793 01 Leksand, Sweden; De Rosa International, Av du Tribunal Federal 34, CH 1005 Lausanne, Switzerland.

JORDAN, HASHEMITE KINGDOM OF

Ministry of Communications, Philatelic Section, P.O. Box 71, Amman, Jordan. Deals in complete mint sets only. SODA not available. Orders sent postage extra. CBC accepted.

KAMPUCHEA (CAMBODIA)

Agence Philatelique, Direction Generale des PTT, Phnom Penh, Kampuchea (Cambodia). No information available.

Stamps from Kampuchea are prohibited in the United States as part of a general trade embargo.

KENYA

Philatelic Bureau, Box 30368, Nairobi, Kenya. Deals with individual orders for mint and CTO stamps, FDCs, postal stationery, plate number or inscription blocks, special postmarks. SODA available. Orders sent postage extra; IRCs accepted. CBC, IMO, IBD, USPSMO accepted.

Printers: Harrison & Sons, England; Helio Courvoisier, Switzerland; The House of Questa, England; De La Rue, England; Cartor, France; Natprint, Zimbabwe.

Government Agencies: Inter-Governmental Philatelic Corp., 460 W. 34th St., New York, N.Y. 10001; CAPHCO Ltd., Old Inn House, 2 Carshalton Road, Sutton, Surrey SM1 4RN, England.

KIRIBATI

Philatelic Bureau, Box 494, Betio, Tarawa, Kiribati. Deals with individual orders for mint and CTO stamps, FDCs, postal stationery, plate number or inscription blocks, special postmarks. SODA available with A$10 balance. Orders shipped postpaid. CBC, BD, PC, IMO, IBD accepted.

Printers: The House of Questa, Format International (both England), CPE Australia.

Government Agencies: CAPHCO Ltd., Old Inn House, 2 Carshalton Road, Sutton, Surrey SM1 4RN, England; Fiji Philatelic Bureau, Box 100, Suva, Fiji.

KOREA, NORTH

Korea Stamp Corp., Pyongyang,

Democratic People's Republic of Korea. Details of services not provided.

Stamps from North Korea are prohibited in the United States as part of a general trade embargo.

KOREA, SOUTH

Korean Philatelic Center, CPO Box 5122, Seoul 100-651, Republic of Korea. Deals with individual orders for mint and CTO stamps, FDCs, postal stationery, plate number or inscription blocks, special postmarks. SODA available with minimum balance of U.S. $10. Orders shipped postage extra. CBC, BD, IMO, IBD, USPSMO, USMO, IRC accepted.

Printer: Korean Security Printing and Minting Corp.

Government Agencies: Kent Research Stamp Co., 201 Mill Road, Box 86, Hewlett, N.Y. 11557; H.L. Peng, Box 38, Mucha, Taipei, Taiwan 116, Republic of China; Goro Iizuka, Plant Kiki Co., 1-11 Izumicho, Chiyoda-ku, Tokyo, Japan; CS Philatelic Agency, 3 Coleman St. No. 04-24, Peninsula Hotel and Shopping Complex, Singapore 0617; Infynsa, Box 8486, Madrid 8, Spain.

KUWAIT

Director, Post Office Department, Philatelic Bureau, Safat Post Office, Kuwait. Deals with individual orders for mint stamps, postal stationery, FDCs (customer provides envelopes). SODA information not provided. Orders shipped postage extra. CBC, BD accepted.

LAOS

Service Philatelique des PTT, Vientiane, Laos. Details of services not provided.

LEBANON

Receveur Principal des Postes, Service Philatelique, Beirut, Lebanon. Details of services not provided.

LESOTHO

Philatelic Bureau, Private Bag No. 1, Maseru, Lesotho. Deals with individual orders for mint and CTO stamps, FDCs, cylinder blocks. SODA available. Orders shipped postpaid. CBC, IMO, IBD, bank notes accepted.

Printers: BDT International, Ireland; The House of Questa, England.

Government Agency: Inter-Governmental Philatelic Corp., 460 W. 34th St., New York, N.Y. 10001.

LIBERIA

Liberia Philatelic Agent, Ministry of Posts and Telecommunications, Monrovia, Liberia. Details of services not provided.

Government Agency: CAPHCO Ltd., Old Inn House, 2 Carshalton Road, Sutton, Surrey SM1 4RN, England.

LIBYA

Service Philatelique, Direction Generale des PTT, Tripoli, Libya. Details of services not provided.

Stamps from Libya are prohibited in the United States as part of a general trade embargo.

LIECHTENSTEIN

Official Philatelic Service, FL-9490 Vaduz, Principality of Liechtenstein. Deals with individual orders for minimum of two copies of mint stamps, FDCs, maximum cards, special postmarks (customer supplies envelopes). SODA available by advance payment. SODA orders shipped postpaid. CBC accepted.

Printers: Austrian Government Printing Office, Austria (line engraving); Helio Courvoisier, Switzerland (photogravure).

LUXEMBOURG

Direction des Postes, Office des Timbres, L-2020, Luxembourg, Grand Duchy of Luxembourg. Deals with individual orders for mint and CTO stamps, FDCs, postal stationery. SODA available. SODA orders shipped postpaid. CBC, PC (if can be cashed in Luxembourg) IMO, IBD accepted.

Printers: Helio Courvoisier, Switzerland; Austrian Government Printing Office; Swiss Postal Printing Office.

MACAO

CTT, Divisao de Filatelia, Largo do Senado, Macao. Deals with individual orders for mint stamps, FDCs. SODA available. Orders shipped postage extra. PC, cash accepted.

Government Agency: Interpost, Box 378, Malverne, N.Y. 11565.

MADEIRA

Philatelic Office, Av. Casal Ribeiro

28-6°, 1096 Lisbon Codex, Portugal. Deals with individual orders for mint stamps, FDCs (agency supplies envelopes). SODA available. Orders shipped postage extra. IMO, CBC, bank notes (except escudos) accepted.

Government Agencies: Interpost, Box 378, Malverne, N.Y. 11565; J.A. Visser, Box 184, 3300 AD Dordrecht, Netherlands.

MALAGASY REPUBLIC (Madagascar)

Service Philatelique, Direction Generale des PTT, Tananarive-RP, Malagasy Republic. Details of services not provided.

Government Agency: Theodore Champion, 13 rue Drouot, 75009 Paris, France.

MALAWI

Post Office Philatelic Bureau, Box 1000, Blantyre, Malawi. Deals with individual orders for mint and CTO stamps, postal stationery, FDCs, special postmarks (bureau supplies envelopes). SODA available. Orders shipped postpaid. CBC, BD, PC, IMO, IBD, USPS, USMO accepted.

Printers: Harrison & Sons, England; The House of Questa, England; Cartor, France; Helio Courvoisier, Switzerland.

Government Agencies: Inter-Governmental Philatelic Corp., 460 W. 34th St., New York, N.Y. 10001.

MALAYSIA

Director General of Posts, Post Office Headquarters, Kuala Lumpur, Malaysia. Details of services not provided.

Government Agencies: Inter-Governmental Philatelic Corp., 460 W. 34th St., New York, N.Y. 10001; British & Overseas Philatelic Agency, Box 80, Shibuya, Tokyo 150-91, Japan.

MALDIVES, REPUBLIC OF

Philatelic Bureau, GPO, Male, Republic of Maldives, Indian Ocean. Deals with individual orders for mint and CTO stamps, FDCs. SODA available. Orders shipped postage extra plus handling fee. Orders restricted to U.S. $20 each. CBC, IMO accepted.

Government Agency: Inter-Governmental Philatelic Corp., 460 W. 34th St., New York, N.Y. 10001.

MALI

Service Philatelique, Direction Generale des PTT, Bamako, Mali. Details of services not provided.

Government Agency: Theodore Champion, 13 rue Drouot, 75009 Paris, France.

MALTA

Philatelic Bureau, GPO, Auberge d'Italie, Valletta, Malta. Deals with individual orders for mint and CTO stamps, FDCs, postal stationery, plate number or inscription blocks, special postmarks (customer supplies envelopes). SODA available with minimum deposit of M£5 required. Handling fee charged. CBC, IMO, IBD, USPSMO accepted.

Printer: Printex Ltd.

Government Agency: Herrick Stamp Co., Box 219, Lawrence, N.Y. 11559.

MARSHALL ISLANDS

Marshall Islands Stamps & Philatelic Center, 1 Unicover Center, Cheyenne, Wyo. 82008-0021. Deals with individual orders for mint stamps, FDCs, commemorative panels. SODA not available.

Government Agency: Unicover World Trade Corp. (Stamps and Philatelic Center of the Republic of the Marshall Islands Postal Service), 1 Unicover Center, Cheyenne, Wyo. 82008-0021.

MAURITANIA

Service Philatelique, Direction Generale des PTT, P.O. Box 99, Nouakchott, Mauritania. Details of services not provided.

Government Agency: Theodore Champion, 13 rue Drouot, 75009 Paris, France.

MAURITIUS

Philatelic Bureau, GPO, Port Louis, Mauritius. Deals with individual orders for mint and CTO stamps, FDCs, postal stationery, plate number or inscription blocks, special postmarks. SODA available with minimum balance of U.S. $10. Orders shipped postage extra plus handling charge; IRCs accepted. CBC, BD, IMO, IBD accepted.

Printers: assigned by tender by CAPHCO.

Government Agent: CAPHCO Ltd., Old Inn House, 2 Carshalton Road, Sutton, Surrey SM1 4RN, England.

MEXICO

Gerencia De Servicio Filatelico, San Antonio Abad 130-7°, Piso, Col. Transito, 06820 Mexico, D.F., Mexico. Deals with individual orders for mint stamps, plate number blocks, special postmarks. SODA available with minimum balance of U.S. $50. Orders shipped postage extra. CBC, BD, PC, IMO, IBD, USPSMO accepted.

Printer: Mexican Government Stamps and Values Printing Office.

MICRONESIA

Micronesia Philatelic Center, GPO Box 7794, New York, N.Y. 10116. Deals with individual orders for mint and CTO stamps, FDCs, postal stationery, plate number or inscription blocks, commemorative cards. SODA available with minimum balance of $10. SODA orders shipped postpaid; minimum of $1 postage and handling charged on one-time orders. CBC, PC, IBD, USPSMO, USMO accepted.

Printers: The House of Questa, England; Walsall Security Printers, England.

Government Agency: Inter-Governmental Philatelic Corp., 460 W. 34th St., New York, N.Y. 10001.

MONACO

Office des Emissions de Timbres-Poste, Departement de Finances, Principality of Monaco. Deals with orders from subscribers only. No standing order is available. Subscribers receive at each issuance an order form to be returned within indicated period. Mint and CTO stamps available at face value, FDCs (plus cost of envelope). Orders shipped postpaid. Deposit accounts, PC, IMO accepted.

Printer: French Government Printing Office.

Government Agency: Unicover World Trade Corp. (Stamp Agency of the Principality of Monaco in North America), 1 Unicover Center, Cheyenne, Wyo. 82008-0016.

MONGOLIA

Directeur de Bureau des Philatelistes, P.O. Box 175, Ulan Bator, Mongolia. Details of services not provided.

MONTSERRAT

Montserrat Philatelic Bureau, GPO, Plymouth, Montserrat, West Indies. Deals with individual orders for mint and CTO stamps, FDCs, plate imprint blocks, postmarks (agency supplies envelopes with charge). SODA available. Ordering deadline is six months after issue date. Orders shipped postpaid. BPO, CBC, BD, IMO, VISA, MasterCard, Diner's Club, American Express, Access, Eurocard accepted.

Government Agency: D & G Philatelic Inc., Box 237, 370 Hempstead Ave., West Hempstead, N.Y. 11552.

MOROCCO

Ministere des PTT, Division Postale, Rabat, Morocco. Deals with individual orders for mint stamps, FDCs, special postmarks (customer supplies envelopes). SODA available. Orders shipped postage extra. CBC, IMO accepted.

Government Agency: Theodore Champion, 13 rue Drouot, 75009 Paris, France.

MOZAMBIQUE

Philatelic and Numismatic Enterprise, Box 4444, Maputo 1, Mozambique. Deals with individual orders for mint stamps (complete sets only), FDCs, special postmarks (customer supplies envelopes). SODA available. Orders shipped postage extra. CBC, bank notes accepted.

Printer: National Printers (governmental agency) of Maputo.

Government Agency: CAPHCO, Old Inn House, 2 Carshalton Road, Sutton, Surrey SM1 4RN, England.

NAURU

Executive Officer, Philatelic Bureau, Republic of Nauru, Central Pacific. Deals with individual orders for mint and CTO stamps, FDCs, postal stationery, inscription blocks, presentation packs, maximum cards, special postmarks. SODA available with minimum balance of A$5. Orders shipped postpaid. CPC (drawn on Australian bank), BD (to Bank of Nauru), IMO (in U.S. currency drawn on a bank in the United States), IBD (drawn on Bank of Nauru or any bank in Australia), U.S., British, Australian, West German, French and Swiss currency.

Printers: CPE Australia; BDT International, Ireland; The House of Questa, England; Format International Security Printers, England; and others .

Government Agency: CAPHCO Ltd., Old Inn House, 2 Carshalton Road, Sutton, Surrey SM1 4RN, England.

NEPAL

Officer-in-Charge, Nepal Philatelic Bureau, Sundhara, Kathmandu, Nepal. Deals with individual orders for mint stamps, postal stationery, FDCs, blocks, special postmarks (bureau supplies envelopes). SODA available with minimum deposit of $25. Orders shipped postage extra. CBC, BD, IMO accepted.

NETHERLANDS

Netherlands Post Office Philatelic Service, Box 30051, 9700 RN Groningen, Netherlands. Deals with individual orders for stamps. SODA available. Orders shipped postpaid, handling charge extra on small orders. Payment by IMO, certain bank notes accepted. Payment can be made directly into account through ABN Bank, 335 Madison Ave., New York, N.Y. 10017 (for U.S. customers), or ABN Bank, 61 Threadneedle St., London, England 2P2 HH (for U.K. customers).

Government Agency: World Wide Philatelic Agency, Inc., 2031 Carolina Place, Fort Mill, S.C. 29715.

NETHERLANDS ANTILLES

Philatelic Service Office, Postmaster, Willemstad, Curacao, Netherlands Antilles. Deals with individual orders for mint and CTO stamps, FDCs, postal stationery, plate blocks. SODA available. Orders shipped by airmail registered. CBC, bank notes, traveler's checks accepted.

Printer: Joh. Enschede, Netherlands.

Government Agencies: World Wide Philatelic Agency, Inc., 2031 Carolina Place, Fort Mill, S.C. 29715; International Philatelic Agencies, 1 Rohais, Box 219, St. Peter Port, Guernsey, Channel Islands, Great Britain; International Philatelic Agencies, Box 5497, Amsterdam, Netherlands.

NEVIS

Nevis Philatelic Bureau, GPO, Charlestown, Nevis, West Indies. Deals with individual orders for mint and CTO stamps, FDCs, postal stationery, plate or inscription blocks, special postmarks, PHQ cards, presentation packs. SODA available with minumum balance of U.S. $20. Orders shipped postpaid. CBC, BD, PC, IMO, IBD, USPSMO, USPS, major credit cards accepted.

Printers: The House of Questa; Format International Security Printers; Walsall Security Printers (all England).

Government Agencies: Inter-Governmental Philatelic Corp., 460 W. 34th St., New York, N.Y. 10001; CAPHCO Ltd., Old Inn House, 2 Carshalton Road, Sutton, Surrey SM1 4RN, England.

NEW CALEDONIA

Philatelic Bureau, Recette Principale des Postes, Noumea, New Caledonia. Deals with individual orders for mint and CTO stamps, FDCs, postal stationery. SODA available with minimum balance of 3,000 francs. Orders shipped postage extra; IRC accepted. CBC, IMO, IBD accepted.

Printers: French Government Printing Office, Cartor (both France); Edila.

NEW ZEALAND

Philatelic Bureau, 110 Victoria Ave., Private Bag, Wanganui, New Zealand. Deals with individual orders for mint stamps, FDCs, plate number or imprint blocks, year and presentation packs, special postmarks (bureau supplies special postcards on SODA only). SODA available. Orders shipped postage extra. CBC, IMO, BPO, VISA, MasterCard, American Express, Diner's Club accepted.

Also handles the stamps of Tokelau.

Government Agencies: Unicover World Trade Corp. (New Zealand Stamp Agency in North America), 1 Unicover, Cheyenne, Wyo. 82008-0014; British & Overseas Philatelic Agency, Box 80, Shibuya, Tokyo 150-91, Japan.

NICARAGUA

Division de Especies Postales y Filatelia, Telcor, Edificio Zacaris Guerra 7MO, Piso, Apartado 325, Managua,

Nicaragua, Central America. Deals with individual orders for mint stamps, FDCs, special postmarks (agency provides envelopes). SODA available. Orders shipped postage extra. CBC, PC, IMO accepted.

Stamps from Nicaragua are prohibited in the United States as part of a general trade embargo.

NIGER

Service Philatelique, Direction Generale des PTT, Niamey, Niger. Details of services not provided.

Government Agency: Theodore Champion, 13 rue Drouot, 75009 Paris, France.

NIGERIA

Nigerian Philatelic Service, GPO, Tinubu Street, P.M.B. 12647, Lagos, Nigeria. Deals with individual orders for mint and CTO stamps, FDCs, special postmarks (bureau or customer supply envelopes). SODA available. Orders shipped postage extra plus handling charge. BPO, IMO, British and American PC accepted.

Printer: Nigerian Security Printing and Minting Co. Ltd., Lagos.

Government Agencies: CAPHCO Ltd., Old Inn House, 2 Carshalton Road, Sutton, Surrey SM1 4RN, England; British & Overseas Philatelic Agency, Box 80, Shibuya, Tokyo 150-91, Japan.

NIUAFO'OU

The Stamp Section, Treasury Building, Nuku'alofa, Tonga. Deals with individual orders for mint and CTO stamps, FDCs, plate number or inscription blocks, postal stationery, special postmarks. SODA available. Orders shipped airmail postage extra. CBC, BD, IBD accepted.

Printer: Walsall Security Printers, England.

Government Agency: Combined Philatelic Agency, 184/186 Portland Road, London SW25 4QB, England.

NIUE

Post Office, Philatelic Bureau, Niue, Government of Niue, Alofi, Niue, South Pacific (via New Zealand). Deals with individual orders for mint stamps, FDCs, special postmarks (bureau supplies envelopes). SODA available. Orders shipped postage extra. CBC, IMO, CPO accepted.

NORFOLK ISLAND

Senior Philatelic Officer, Norfolk Island 2899, via Australia. Deals with individual orders for mint and CTO stamps, FDCs (bureau supplies envelopes). SODA available with unspecified deposit. Orders shipped postpaid. CBC, IMO accepted.

Printers: CPE Australia; Leigh-Mardon, Australia; Mercury-Walch, Australia.

Government Agencies: Inter-Governmental Philatelic Corp., 460 W. 34th St., New York, N.Y. 10001; CAPHCO Ltd., Old Inn House, 2 Carshalton Road, Sutton, Surrey SM1 4RN, England; Australian Philatelic Bureau, GPO Box 9988, Melbourne, Victoria 3001, Australia; Stirling & Co., Box 949, Christchurch, New Zealand.

NORWAY

Norwegian Post Philatelic Bureau, Box 3770, Gamlebyen, N-0135 Oslo 1, Norway. Deals with individual orders for mint and CTO stamps, FDCs, postal stationery, annual collections. SODA available. Orders shipped postpaid. CBC, PC, IMO, IBD, USPSMO, USMO, MasterCard, American Express, Diner's Card (minimum of 200 krone) accepted.

Printers: Emil Moestue; Norges Bank (both Norway).

OMAN, SULTANATE OF

Philatelic Department, Ministry of Posts, Telegraphs & Telephones, Box 3338, Ruwi, Sultanate of Oman. Deals with individual orders for mint stamps, FDCs (agency supplies envelopes). SODA available. Orders shipped postage extra plus service fee. CBC, British and U.S. currencies accepted.

Government Agencies: CAPHCO Ltd., Old Inn House, 2 Carshalton Road, Sutton, Surrey SM1 4RN, England; British & Overseas Philatelic Agency, Box 80, Shibuya, Tokyo 150-91, Japan.

PAKISTAN

Pakistan Philatelic Bureau, GPO, Karachi, Pakistan. Deals with individual orders for mint and CTO stamps, FDCs, special postmarks (customer supplies envelopes). SODA available. Orders shipped postage extra. CBC, BPO, IMO accepted. Printer: Pakistan Security Printing Corp.

Government Agency: James Davis & Son, 45-47 Church St., Rickmansworth WD3 1DG, England.

PALAU

Palau Philatelic Bureau, GPO, Box 7775, New York, N.Y. 10116. Deals with individual orders for mint stamps, FDCs, commemorative panels. SODA not available.

Government Agency: Inter-Governmental Philatelic Corp., 460 W. 34th St., New York, N.Y. 10001.

PANAMA

Direccion General de Correos y Telecomunicaciones, Departamento de Filatelia, Apartado 3421, Panama 1, Panama. Deals with individual orders for mint stamps, FDCs, special postmarks (customer supplies envelopes). SODA available. Orders shipped postage extra plus handling charge. CBC, IMO accepted.

PAPUA NEW GUINEA

Philatelic Bureau, Box 1, Boroko, Papua New Guinea. Deals with individual orders for mint stamps, FDCs, issue postmarks (bureau supplies envelopes). SODA available. Orders sent postpaid. BPO, CBC, IMO, BD, bank notes accepted.

Government Agencies: Inter-Governmental Philatelic Corp., 460 W. 34th St., New York, N.Y. 10001; D & G Philatelic Inc., Box 237, 370 Hempstead Ave., West Hempstead, N.Y. 11582; CAPHCO Ltd., Old Inn House, 2 Carshalton Road, Sutton, Surrey SM1 4RN, England; British & Overseas Philatelic Agency, Box 80, Shibuya, Tokyo 150-91, Japan.

PARAGUAY

Departamento Filatelica, Direccion General de Correos, Asuncion, Paraguay. Details of services not provided.

PENRHYN ISLAND

Penrhyn Post Office, Penrhyn, Northern Cook Islands, South Pacific Ocean. Deals with individual orders for mint and CTO stamps, FDCs. SODA available. SODA orders shipped postpaid; transient orders postage extra. CBC accepted.

PERU

Division Filatelica de la Direccion General de Correos, Jr. Conde de Superunda 170, Lima 1, Peru. Details of services not provided.

PHILIPPINES

Stamp and Philatelic Section, Postal Services Office, Liwasang Bonifacio, 1000 Manila, Philippines. Deals with individual orders for mint and CTO stamps, FDCs, airletter sheets, special postmarks. SODA available with minimum balance of U.S. $50. Orders sent postage extra; IRCs accepted. CBC, IMO, IBD, USPSMO accepted.

Printers: APO Production Unit; Amstar Co. (both Philippines).

PITCAIRN ISLANDS

Philatelic Sales Office, Pitcairn Islands Administration, British Consulate-General, Private Bag, Auckland, New Zealand. Deals with individual orders (handling charge of NZ$0.50 on orders under NZ$5) for mint and CTO stamps, FDCs. SODA available with minimum deposit of NZ$20 required. Orders shipped postpaid by surface mail; difference between surface and airmail charged for airmail; registration extra; IRCs accepted. CBC, BD, IMO, IBD, USPSMO, VISA, Bank Card and MasterCard accepted.

Printers: The House of Questa, England; Walsall Security Printers, England; BDT International Printing, Ireland.

Government Agencies: CAPHCO Ltd., Old Inn House, 2 Carshalton Road, Sutton, Surrey SM1 4RN, England; Australian Philatelic Bureau, GPO Box 9988, Melbourne, Victoria 3001, Australia; Fiji Post Philatelic Bureau, Box 100, Suva, Fiji.

POLAND

Ars Polona, Box 1001, 00-222 Warsaw, Poland. Deals only with bulk quantity orders (minimum of U.S. $20) for mint and CTO stamps, FDCs, postal stationery, special postmarks. SODA available for year sets and catalogs. Orders sent postpaid. CBC, BD, IMO, IBD, USPSMO, USMO accepted.

Printers: State Printing Works of Securities, Warsaw; Wertpapierdruckerei,

East Germany.

PORTUGAL

Direccao de Relacoes, Internacionais e Filatelia, Av. Casal Ribeiro 28-2°, 1096 Lisbon Codex, Portugal. Deals with individual orders for mint and CTO stamps, FDCs, postal stationery, topical and annual collections. SODA available with minimum balance of $15. Orders shipped postage extra; IRCs accepted. CBC, BD, IMO accepted.

Also handles the stamps of Macao.

Printers: Imprensa Nacional-Casa da Moeda, Lisbon; Casa Maia, Oporto.

Government Agencies: Interpost, Box 378, Malverne, N.Y. 11565; Unitrade Associates, 127 Cartwright Ave., Toronto, Ontario, Canada M6A 1V4; Harry Allen, Box 5, Richmansworth, Herts. WD3 1EY, England; Theodore Champion, 13 rue Drouot, 75009 Paris, France (sales in France only); Georg Roll Nachfolger, Holbeinstrasse 2, D-2880 Brake, West Germany; J.A. Visser, Box 184, 3300 AD Dordrecht, Netherlands; Frimarkshuset AB, S-793 01, Leksand, Sweden; De Rosa International, Av du Tribunal Federal 34, CH-1005 Lausanne, Switzerland; Direccao Dos Correios e Telecomunicacoes, Divisao De Filatelia, Largo Do Senado, Macao.

QATAR

Philatelic Bureau, Department of Posts, Doha, State of Qatar. Deals with individual orders for mint stamps, postal stationery, FDCs (bureau supplies envelopes). SODA available. No shipping details provided. BD, CBC accepted.

Government Agencies: Inter-Governmental Philatelic Corp., 460 W. 34th St., New York, N.Y. 10001; James Davis & Son, 45-47 Church St., Rickmansworth WD3 1DG, England.

REDONDA

Redonda Philatelic Bureau, Redonda, Antigua. Deals with individual orders for mint stamps. SODA available with minimum deposit required. Orders shipped postage extra. PC, IMO accepted.

ROMANIA

Rompresfilatelia, Calea Grivitei 64166, Bucharest, Romania. Deals with individual orders for mint stamps, kiloware, packet material, FDCs. SODA available. Orders sent postage extra; IRCs accepted. CBC, IMO, IBD accepted.

Printer: Romanian Postal Administration.

RWANDA

Direction Generale des PTT, Kigale, Rwanda, or **Agences Philateliques Gouvernementales, Chaussee de Waterloo 868/870, 1180 Brussels, Belgium.** Deals with individual orders of 10 francs or more for mint and CTO stamps, FDCs, postal stationery. SODA available with a minimum balance of U.S. $20. Orders shipped postpaid. CBC, BD, PC, IBD, USMO accepted.

Printers: Malines Stamp Printing Office, Belgium.

ST. HELENA

Postmaster, Philatelic Bureau, c/o Post Office, Jamestown, St. Helena, South Atlantic. Deals with individual orders for mint stamps, FDCs, special postmarks (bureau or customers supply envelopes). SODA available. Orders shipped postage extra, plus handling charge. CBC on London bank, BPO, IMO accepted.

Also handles stamps of Ascension and Tristan da Cunha.

Government Agencies: CAPHCO Ltd., Old Inn House, 2 Carshalton Road, Sutton, Surrey SM1 4RN, England; British & Overseas Philatelic Agency, Box 80, Shibuya, Tokyo 150-91, Japan.

ST. KITTS

The Manager, St. Kitts Philatelic Bureau, GPO, Basseterre, St. Kitts, West Indies. Deals with individual orders for mint stamps, FDCs, presentation packs, PHQ cards. SODA available. Orders shipped postpaid. PC, CBC, IMO, USPSMO, BPO accepted.

Government Agency: CAPHCO Ltd., Old Inn House, 2 Carshalton Road, Sutton, Surrey SM1 4RN, England.

ST. LUCIA

General Manager, St. Lucia Philatelic Bureau, Box 1537, Castries, St. Lucia, West Indies. Deals with individual orders for mint and CTO stamps, FDCs, postal stationery, plate number and inscription blocks, special postmarks. SODA available. Orders shipped postpaid. CBC, BD, PC, IMO, IBD, USPSMO, USMO accepted.

Printers: Harrison & Sons; The House of Questa; Format International Security Printers (all England).

Government Agencies: D & G Philatelic Inc., Box 237, 370 Hempstead Ave., West Hempstead, N.Y. 11582; CAPHCO Ltd., Old Inn House, 2 Carshalton Road, Sutton, Surrey SM1 4RN, England.

ST. PIERRE & MIQUELON

Bureau Philatelic de l'Archipel, 3 Place de l'Eglise, Box 4330, St. Pierre, F-97500, St. Pierre & Miquelon. Deals with individual orders for mint stamps, FDCs. SODA available with the first remittance covering at least three-month purchases, plus postage by registered mail. All orders shipped postage extra. CBC, IMO accepted.

Printer: French Government Printing Office, Perigueux.

ST. THOMAS & PRINCE ISLANDS

Direccao dos Correios e Telecomunicacoes, Seccao Filatelica, St. Thomas, Democratic Republic of St. Thomas and Prince Islands. Deals with individual orders for mint stamps and postal stationery. Orders sent postage extra. CBC accepted.

Government Agency: D & G Philatelic Inc., Box 237, 370 Hempstead Ave., West Hempstead, N.Y. 11582.

ST. VINCENT

St. Vincent Philatelic Services, GPO, Kingstown, St. Vincent, West Indies. Deals with individual orders for mint and CTO stamps, FDCs. SODA available. Orders shipped postpaid. PC, IMO, BD, BPO, VISA, MasterCard accepted.

Government Agencies: Inter-Governmental Philatelic Corp., 460 W. 34th St., New York, N.Y. 10001; D & G Philatelic Inc., Box 237, 370 Hempstead Ave., West Hempstead, N.Y. 11582.

ST. VINCENT, GRENADINES OF

St. Vincent Philatelic Services, GPO, Kingstown, St. Vincent, West Indies. Deals with individual orders for mint and CTO stamps, FDCs. SODA available. Orders shipped postpaid. PC, IMO, BD, BPO accepted.

Government Agency: Inter-Governmental Philatelic Corp., 460 W. 34th St., New York, N.Y. 10001.

SALVADOR

Direccion General de Correos, Departamento de Filatelia, Republic of El Salvador, Central America. Deals with individual orders for mint and CTO stamps, FDCs, special postmarks. SODA available with a minimum deposit of U.S. $50 (certified check). Orders shipped postage extra. CBC, USPSMO, USMO accepted.

Printer: Direccion de Servicos Graficos.

SAN MARINO, REPUBLIC OF

Philatelic Office, Piazza Garibaldi, 47031 Republic of San Marino. Deals with individual orders for mint stamps, FDCs, special postmarks (customer supplies envelopes). SODA available. Orders shipped postage extra. CBC, IMO accepted.

SAUDI ARABIA

Division of Posts and Telegraphs, Philatelic Section, Riyadh, Saudi Arabia. Details of services not provided.

SENEGAL

Office des Postes et Telecommunications du Senegal, Bureau Philatelique, Dakar, Senegal. Deals with individual orders for mint stamps, FDCs (bureau provides envelopes). Orders sent postage extra. CBC, IMO accepted.

Government Agency: Theodore Champion, 13 rue Drouot, 75009 Paris, France.

SEYCHELLES

Philatelic Bureau, Box 60, Victoria, Mahe, Seychelles, Indian Ocean. Deals with individual orders for mint stamps, FDCs (bureau provides envelopes). SODA available.

Government Agency: CAPHCO Ltd., Old Inn House, 2 Carshalton Road, Sutton, Surrey SM1 4RN, England.

SIERRA LEONE

Director General, Posts and Telecommunications Department, Headquarters, GPO, Freetown, Sierra Leone. Deals with individual orders for mint and CTO stamps, FDCs, postal stationery, special postmarks. SODA not available. Orders sent postage extra; IRCs excepted. CBC, BD, IMO, IBD, USPSMO, USMO accepted.

Printers: The House of Questa, England; BDT International Security Printers, Ireland; Format International Security Printers, England; Harrison & Sons, England.

Government Agency: Inter-Governmental Philatelic Corp., 460 W. 34th St., New York, N.Y. 10001.

SINGAPORE

Philatelic Bureau, Postal Services Group, Telecoms, 31 Exeter Road 25-00, Comcentre, Singapore 0923, Republic of Singapore. Deals with individual orders for mint and CTO stamps, FDCs, postal stationery, plate number or inscription blocks, special postmarks. SODA available with minimum deposit of S$30. Orders shipped postage extra; IRCs accepted. PC, IBD, BPO, travelers' checks accepted. Printers: Secura Singapore; CPE Australia; Leigh-Mardon, Australia; The House of Questa, England; Harrison & Sons, England.

Government Agencies: Inter-Governmental Philatelic Corp., 460 W. 34th St., New York, N.Y. 10001; Harry Allen, Rickmansworth, Herts. WD3 1EY, England; Max Stern, 234 Flinders St., Georg Roll Nachfolger, Holbeinstrasse 2, Box 1346, D-2880 Brake, West Germany; Port Phillip Arcade, Box 997 H, GPO, Melbourne 3001, Australia.

SOLOMON ISLANDS

Philatelic Bureau, GPO, Box G31, Honiara, Solomon Islands, South Pacific. Deals with individual orders for mint and CTO stamps, FDCs, maximum cards, presentation packs. SODA available with minimum deposit adequate for one-year supply of stamps. BD, PC, IMO, American Express accepted. Mint stamps sent airmail postage extra; FDC and CTOs shipped postpaid.

Government Agencies: CAPHCO Ltd., Old Inn House, 2 Carshalton Road, Sutton, Surrey SM1 4RN, England; Fiji Philatelic Bureau, Box 100, Suva, Fiji; British & Overseas Philatelic Agency, Box 80, Shibuya, Tokyo 150-91, Japan.

SOMALI DEMOCRATIC REPUBLIC

Philatelic Service, Ministry of Posts & Telecommunications, Mogadishu, Somali Democratic Republic. Deals with individual orders for mint stamps, FDCs, special postmarks (either agency or customer supplies envelopes). SODA available. Orders shipped postage extra. BD, IMO (United Kingdom and Italy only) accepted.

Printer: State Polygraphic Institute, Rome.

SOUTH AFRICA, REPUBLIC OF

Philatelic Services and INTERSAPA, Private Bag X505, Pretoria 0001, Republic of South Africa. Deals with individual orders for mint and CTO stamps, Framas, FDCs, postal stationery, control blocks with plate numbers, stamp sets, albums, special postmarks (agency supplies datestamp cards). SODA available with minimum deposit of $15. Orders sent postpaid. BD, IBD accepted.

Printer: Government Printer, Pretoria.

Also handles stamps of South-West Africa, Transkei, Bophuthatswana, Venda and Ciskei.

Stamps from South Africa, South-West Africa, Transkei, Bophuthatswana, Venda and Ciskei are prohibited in the United States as part of a general trade embargo.

Government Agencies: South African Philatelic Agency, c/o James Davis, 45-47 Church St., Rickmansworth WD3 1DG, England; J. Ferrier, Philart, CH-1261 Gingins, Switzerland.

SOUTH GEORGIA AND SOUTH SANDWICH ISLANDS

Manager, Philatelic Bureau, Post Office, Port Stanley, Falkland Islands. Deals with individual orders for mint and CTO stamps, FDCs, postal stationery.

SODA available with a minimum deposit of equivalent of £10. Orders shipped postage extra; IRCs accepted. CBC, PC, IMO, traveler's checks accepted.

Government Agencies: CAPHCO Ltd., Old Inn House, 2 Carshalton Road, Sutton, Surrey SM1 4RN, England; British & Overseas Philatelic Agency, Box 80, Shibuya, Tokyo 150-91, Japan.

SOUTH-WEST AFRICA

Philatelic Services and INTERSAPA, Private Bag X505, Pretoria 0001, Republic of South Africa. Deals with individual orders for mint and CTO stamps, Framas, FDCs, postal stationery, control blocks with plate numbers, stamp sets, albums, special postmarks (agency supplies datestamp cards). SODA available with minimum deposit of $15. Orders sent postpaid. BD or IBD accepted.

Printer: Government Printer, Pretoria.

Stamps from South-West Africa are prohibited in the United States as part of a general trade embargo.

Government Agencies: South African Philatelic Agency, c/o James Davis, 45-47 Church St., Rickmansworth WD3 1DG, England; J. Ferrier, Philart, CH-1261 Gingins, Switzerland.

SPAIN

Direccion General de Correos e Telegrafos, Seccion De Filatelia, Palacio de Comunicaciones, 28070 Madrid, Spain. Deals with individual orders for mint stamp sets only. No SODA available. Orders sent postage and handling extra; IRCs accepted. IMO accepted.

Printer: Spanish National Printer.

Also handles Spanish Andorra stamps.

SRI LANKA

Philatelic Bureau, Department of Posts, Fourth Floor, Ceylinco House, Colombo 1, Sri Lanka. Deals with individual orders for mint and CTO stamps, FDCs, postal stationery, plate number blocks. SODA available with minimum balance of U.S. $30. Orders shipped postage extra; IRCs accepted. CBC, IMO, IBD accepted.

Printers: Joh. Enschede, Netherlands; De La Rue, England; Harrison & Sons, England; The House of Questa, England; Format International Security Printers, England; Malaysian Security Printers; Goznak Stamp Printing Office, Soviet Union; Secura Singapore, Singapore.

Government Agencies: Inter-Governmental Philatelic Corp., 460 W. 34th St., New York, N.Y. 10001; CAPHCO Ltd., Old Inn House, 2 Carshalton Road, Sutton, Surrey SM1 4RN, England.

SUDAN

Director General, Philatelic Office, Posts and Telegraphs, Public Corp., Khartoum, Sudan. Deals with individual and bulk orders of mint stamps, FDCs, special postmarks (customers and bureau supply envelopes). SODA available. Orders shipped postage extra. CBC, BPO, U.S. and sterling bank notes and BD accepted.

SURINAM

Postal Administration, Philatelic Department, Paramaribo, Surinam. Details of services not provided.

Government Agency: World Wide Philatelic Agency, Inc., 2031 Carolina Place, Fort Mill, S.C. 29715; International Philatelic Agencies, 1 Rohais, Box 219, St. Peter Port, Guernsey, Channel Islands, Great Britain.

SWAZILAND

Swaziland Stamp Bureau, Department of Posts & Telecommunications, Box 555, Mbabane, Swaziland. Deals with individual orders for mint and CTO stamps, FDCs (private FDCs canceled for charge of 10¢ each, plus postage), control blocks, special postmarks (agency supplies envelopes), year packs, postal stationery. SODA available with minimum deposit of 20 emalangeni. Orders shipped postpaid, plus handling charge of 50¢ per order. CBC, IMO, USPSMO, BD accepted.

Government Agencies: CAPHCO Ltd., Old Inn House, 2 Carshalton Road, Sutton, Surrey SM1 4RN, England; British & Overseas Philatelic Agency, Box 80, Shibya, Tokyo, 150-91, Japan.

SWEDEN

PFA Swedish Stamps, S-1645 88, Kista, Sweden. Deals with individual orders for mint stamps, FDCs, postal stationery, maximum cards, annual sets. SODA available with $10 deposit (Sweden Stamp Agency in North America). Small shipping, handling and insurance fee charged (North American agency). CBC, PC, USPSMO, USMO accepted (North American agency).

Printer: Swedish PFA Stamp Printing House.

Government Agency: Unicover World Trade Corp. (Sweden Stamp Agency in North America), 1 Unicover Center, Cheyenne, Wyo. 82008-0008.

SWITZERLAND

Philatelic Service PTT, Zeughausgasse 19, CH-3030 Bern, Switzerland. Deals with individual orders for mint stamps, FDCs, special postmarks (agency supplies envelopes). SODA available with minimum balance of approximately 50 Swiss francs. SODA orders shipped postpaid. CBC, BD, PC, IMO, IBD, USPSMO, USMO, IRCs accepted.

Printers: Swiss Government Printing Office; Helio Courvoisier, Switzerland.

SYRIA

Etablissement des Postes et des Telecommunications, Service Philatelique, Damascus, Syrian Arab Republic. Details of services not provided.

TANZANIA

Tanzania Posts and Telecommunications, Department of Posts, Stamp Bureau, Box 2988, Dar-es-Salaam, Tanzania. Deals with individual orders for mint stamps, FDCs, special postmarks (customer supplies envelopes). SODA available. Orders shipped postage extra for mint stamps, postpaid with handling charge otherwise. CBC on London bank, U.S. bank notes, BPO, IMO accepted.

Government Agencies: Inter-Governmental Philatelic Corp., 460 W. 34th St., New York, N.Y. 10001; British & Overseas Philatelic Agency, Box 80, Shibuya, Tokyo 150-91, Japan.

THAILAND

Chief of Philatelic Promotion Section, The Communications Authority of Thailand, Chaengwattana Road, Laksi, Bangkok 10002, Thailand. Deals with individual orders for mint stamps, postal stationery, FDCs, annual collections. SODA available with minimum deposit of U.S. $20. Orders shipped postage extra. IMO, BD accepted.

TOGO

Direction Generale des Postes et Telecommunications, Direction des Services Postaux et Financiers, Lome, Togo. Deals with individual orders for mint stamps. Orders shipped postage extra. CBC, IMO accepted.

Government Agency: Inter-Governmental Philatelic Corp., 460 W. 34th St., New York, N.Y. 10001.

TOKELAU

New Zealand Post Philatelic Bureau, Private Bag, Wanganui, New Zealand. Deals with individual orders for mint stamps, FDCs, plate or imprint blocks. SODA available with minimum deposit of U.S. $5.25. Orders shipped postage extra. IMO, BD, VISA, MasterCard, Diner's Club, American Express accepted.

Government Agency: British & Overseas Philatelic Agency, Box 80, Shibuya, Tokyo 150-91, Japan.

TONGA

The Stamp Section, Treasury Building, Nuku'alofa, Tonga. Deals with individual orders for mint and CTO stamps, FDCs, plate number or inscription blocks, postal stationery, special postmarks. SODA available. Orders shipped airmail postage extra. CBC, BD, IBD accepted.

Printer: Walsall Security Printers, England.

Also handles the stamps of Niuafo'ou.

Government Agency: Combined Philatelic Agency, 184/186 Portland Road, London, SE25 4QB, England.

TRANSKEI

Philatelic Services and INTERSAPA, Private Bag X505, Pretoria 0001, Republic of South Africa. Deals with individual orders for mint and CTO stamps, Framas, FDCs, postal stationery, control blocks with plate numbers, stamp sets, albums, special postmarks (agency supplies datestamp cards). SODA available with minimum deposit of $15. Orders sent postpaid. BD, IBD accepted.

Printer: Government Printer, Pretoria.

Stamps from Transkei are prohibited in the United States as part of a general trade embargo.

Government Agencies: South African

Philatelic Agency, c/o James Davis, 45-47 Church St., Rickmansworth WD3 1DG, England; J. Ferrier, Philart, CH-1261 Gingins, Switzerland.

TRINIDAD & TOBAGO

Postmaster General, GPO, Port of Spain, Trinidad. Deals with individual orders for mint and CTO stamps, FDCs, postal stationery, plate number blocks. SODA not available. Orders shipped postage extra; IRCs accepted. CBC, IMO, IBD, USPSMO, USMO accepted.

Printers: Format International Security Printers, The House of Questa, Walsall Security Printers, all England (printing contracts handled by CAPHCO Ltd.)

Government Agency: CAPHCO Ltd., Old Inn House, 2 Carshalton Road, Sutton, Surrey SM1 4RN, England.

TRISTAN DA CUNHA

Postmaster, Jamestown, St. Helena, South Atlantic. Deals with individual orders for mint stamps, FDCs, special postmarks (bureau or customers supply envelopes). No SODA available. Orders shipped postage extra. CBC on London bank, U.S. bank notes, BPO, IMO accepted.

Government Agencies: CAPHCO Ltd., Old Inn House, 2 Carshalton Road, Sutton, Surrey SM1 4RN, England; British & Overseas Philatelic Agency, Box 80, Shibuya, Tokyo 150-91, Japan.

TUNISIA

Service Philatelique des PTT, Bureau Directeur de Tunis, Recette Principale, Tunis, Tunisia. Deals with individual orders for mint stamps, FDCs. SODA available. CBC, IMO accepted.

Government Agencies: World Wide Philatelic Agency, Inc., 2031 Carolina Place, Fort Mill, S.C. 29715; Theodore Champion, 13 rue Drouot, 75009 Paris, France.

TURKEY

PTT Filateli Servisi, P.K. 900 Ulus, TR-06045, Ankara, Turkey. Deals with individual orders for mint and CTO stamps, FDCs, postal stationery, special postmarks. SODA available with minimum balance of 5,000 Turkish liras. Orders shipped postage extra for airmail. CBC, IMO, IBD accepted.

Printers: Basin Offset, Ajans-Turk, Apa Offset (all in Turkey).

Government Agencies: Inter-Governmental Philatelic Corp., 460 W. 34th St., New York, N.Y. 10001; James Davis & Son, 45-47 Church St., Rickmansworth WD3 1D6, England; Theodore Champion, 13 Rue Drouot, 75009, Paris, France; Richard Borek, Theodor-Heuss-Strasse 7, 3300 Braunschweig, West Germany; International Philatelic Agencies, 1 Rohais, Box 219, St. Peter Port, Guernsey, Channel Islands, Great Britain; Japan Philatelic Co., Box 2, Suginami, Minami, Tokyo, Japan; Frimaerkshuset AB, S-793 01, Leksand, Sweden; De Rosa International, Av. du Tribunal Federal 34, 1005 Lausanne, Switzerland.

TURKISH REPUBLIC OF NORTHERN CYPRUS

Turkish Republic of Northern Cyprus, Directorate of Postal Department, Philatelic Branch, Lefkosa, Mersin 10, Turkey. Deals with individual orders for mint and CTO stamps, FDCs, postal stationery, special postmarks. SODA available with U.S. $5 minimum balance. Orders sent postage extra; IRCs accepted. CBC, IMO (certain countries) accepted.

Printers: Turk Tarih Kurumu Printing House, Ali Riza Baskan Guzel Sanatlar Printing House; Ajans Turk Printing House, Tezel Offset and Printing Co. (all Turkey).

TURKS & CAICOS ISLANDS

Philatelic Bureau, Grand Turk, Turks & Caicos Islands, West Indies. Deals with individual orders for mint and CTO stamps, FDCs (agency supplies multicolored envelopes). SODA available. Orders shipped postpaid. CBC, PC, IMO, USPSMO, BPO, U.S. currency accepted.

Government Agency: Inter-Governmental Philatelic Corp., 460 W. 34th St., New York, N.Y. 10001.

TUVALU

Tuvalu Philatelic Bureau, Funafuti, Tuvalu, Central Pacific. Deals with individual orders for mint and CTO stamps, FDCs, postal stationery, plate number and inscription blocks, special postmarks. SODA available. Orders shipped postpaid. CBC, BD, PC (established customers only), IMO, IBD, USPSMO, USMO accepted.

Printer: The House of Questa, England.

Government Agency: D & G Philatelic Inc., Box 237, 370 Hempstead Ave., West Hempstead, N.Y. 11552.

UGANDA

Uganda Posts and Telecommunications Corp., Department of Posts, Stamps Bureau, Box 7106, Kampala, Uganda. Deals with individual orders for mint and CTO stamps, FDCs, postal stationery, special postmarks. SODA available with minimum balance of U.S. $50. Orders shipped postage extra; IRCs accepted. CBC, BD, PC, IMO, IBD, USPSMO, USMO accepted.

Printers: Harrison & Sons, England; The House of Questa, England; other firms selected on tender basis.

Government Agency: Inter-Governmental Philatelic Corp., 460 W. 34th St., New York, N.Y. 10001.

UNION OF SOVIET SOCIALIST REPUBLICS

Sovinfilatelia, V/O Mezhdunarodnaya Kniga, Moscow 113095, ul. Dimitrova 39, U.S.S.R. Deals with individual orders for mint stamps (preferably complete year sets), FDCs (annual subscription only), postal stationery, plate number and inscription blocks. SODA available with minimum balance of $55. Orders shipped postpaid. CBC, PC, IMO, IBD, USPSMO, USMO accepted.

Printer: Goznak Stamp Printing Office.

Government Agencies: Unicover World Trade Corp. (USSR Stamp Service in North America), 1 Unicover Center, Cheyenne, Wyo. 82008-0012; Max Stern, Box 977H, GPO, Melbourne, Victoria 3001, Australia; Theodore Champion, 13 rue Drout, Paris, France; H.E. Sieger, 7073 Lorch Wurtt, Box 1160, Venusberg 32-24, West Germany; Chinar Exports PVT., 101-A. Surya Kiran, 19, Kastruba Gauchki Marg, New Delhi, 110001, India; Japan Philatelic Co., Box 2, Suginami, Minami, Tokyo, Japan; J.A. Visser, Box 184, 330 AD Doedrecht, Netherlands; Philder SA, Box 68, 6830 Chiasso, 3, Switzerland.

UNITED ARAB EMIRATES

Philatelic Bureau, General Postal Authority, Box 888, Dubai, United Arab Emirates, Arabian Gulf. Deals with individual orders for mint stamps, FDCs, special postmarks (customer supplies envelopes). SODA available. Orders shipped postpaid. CBC, IMO, U.S. and British bank notes accepted.

UNITED NATIONS

United Nations Postal Administration, Two United Nations Plaza, Room DC2-620, New York, N.Y. 10017. Deals with individual orders for mint stamps, FDCs, postal stationery, inscription blocks, special postmarks, souvenir cards, annual collections, catalogs. SODA available with minimum deposit of U.S. $35. Orders shipped postage extra plus handling charge if under U.S. $2. CBC, BD, PC, IMO, IBD, USPSMO, USMO accepted.

U.N. Postal Administration, Palais des Nations, CH-1211 Geneva 10, Switzerland. Deals with individual orders for mint and CTO stamps, FDCs, postal stationery, inscription blocks, special postmarks. SODA available. Orders shipped postage extra. CBC, BD, PC, IMO, IBD, USPSMO, USMO accepted.

U.N. Postal Administration, Vienna International Centre, A-1400 Vienna, Austria. Same details as UNPA/New York with Austrian currency applying.

Government Agencies: J. Davis & Son, 45-47 Church St., Rickmansworth WD3 1D6, England; Nordfrim, DK 5450 Otterup, Denmark; Theodore Champion, 13 rue Drouet, 75009 Paris, France; J.A. Visser, Box 184, 3300 AD, Dordrecht, Netherlands; De Rosa International, Av du Tribunal Federal 34, 1005 Lausanne, Switzerland; Maderphil, Avda de Roma, 157 6a, Barcelona 11, Spain; Frimarkshuset AB, S-793 01, Leksand, Sweden.

UNITED STATES OF AMERICA

U.S. Postal Service, Philatelic Sales Division, Washington, D.C. 20265-9997, U.S.A. Deals with individual orders for mint stamps, postal stationery, FDC programs, maximum cards, souvenir pages, commemorative panels, special sets. Stock lists available on request. Orders shipped postage extra with minimum of 50¢ handling charge and $10 minimum order level. CBC, PC, IMO, USPSMO, BPO accepted.

Printers: U.S. Bureau of Engraving and Printing, U.S. Government Printing Office, U.S. Envelope Co., American Bank Note Co. and private contractors.

Government Agencies: Harry Allen, International Philatelic Distributors, Rickmansworth Herts, WD3 1EY, England; Herman E. Sieger SA, Lorch/ Wurttemberg, West Germany; Japan Philatelic Co., Box 2, Shinjuku, Tokyo 160-91, Japan; J.A. Visser, Box 184, 3300 AD Dordrecht, The Netherlands (SODA available); De Rosa International, Av du Tribunal Federal 34, 1005 Lausanne, Switzerland.

URUGUAY

Direccion Nacional de Correos, Departamento de Filatelica, Casilla de Correo 1296, Montevideo, Uruguay. Deals with individual orders for mint stamps, FDCs, special postmarks (customer supplies envelopes). SODA available. IMO, IRC accepted.

Printer: Uruguay National Printing Office.

VANUATU

Philatelic Section, Post Office, Port-Vila, Vanuatu, South Pacific. Deals with individual orders for mint and CTO stamps, FDCs, postal stationery, plate number or inscription blocks, special postmarks. SODA available with minimum balance of U.S. $20. Orders shipped postpaid. IMO, IBD, BPO accepted.

Printers: The House of Questa, Format International Security Printers, Walsall Security Printers, Harrison & Sons (all England), Malaysian Security Printers.

Government Agency: CAPHCO Ltd., Old Inn House, 2 Carshalton Road, Sutton, Surrey SM1 4RN, England.

VATICAN CITY

Ufficio Filatelico del Governatorato, Vatican City. Deals with individual orders for mint stamps and special postmarks (customer supplies envelopes). No SODA available. Orders shipped postpaid. IMO, CBC, bank notes accepted.

VENDA

Philatelic Services and INTERSAPA, Private Bag X505, Pretoria 0001, Republic of South Africa. Deals with individual orders for mint and CTO stamps, Framas, FDCs, postal stationery, control blocks with plate numbers, stamp sets, albums, special postmarks. SODA available with minimum deposit of $15. Orders sent postpaid. BD, IBD accepted.

Printer: Government Printer, Pretoria.

Stamps from Venda are prohibited in the United States as part of a general trade embargo.

Government Agencies: South African Philatelic Agency, c/o James Davis, 45-47 Church St., Rickmansworth WD3 1DG, England; J. Ferrier, Philart, CH-1261 Gingins, Switzerland. GPO, Pretoria 0001, Republic of South Africa.

VENEZUELA

Instituto Postal Telegrafico de Venezuela, Oficina Filatelica Nacional, Apartado 4080, Caracas, 1010-A Venezuela. Deals with individual orders for mint stamps, FDCs, special covers. SODA available. IMO accepted.

Printer: Graficos Armitano.

VIETNAM

Vietnam Stamp Corp., 14 Tran Hung Dao St., Hanoi, Vietnam. Deals with individual orders for mint and CTO stamps, FDCs, inscription blocks, postal stationery, special postmarks, maximum cards, albums. SODA available with minimum balance of U.S. $100. Orders shipped postage extra. IMO, IBD accepted.

Printers: Cuban Stamp Printing Office; Vietnam Postal Stamp Printer, Ho Chi Minh City; Goznak Stamp Printing Office, Soviet Union; Hungarian Stamp Printing Office.

Stamps from Vietnam are prohibited in the United States as part of a general trade embargo.

Government Agency: Theodore Champion, 13 rue Drouot, 75009 Paris, France (sales in France only).

WALLIS & FUTUNA ISLANDS

Service des Postes et Telecommuni-

cations, Section Philatelique, B.P. 00 Mata-Utu, Futuna, Wallis & Futuna Islands, South Pacific. Deals with individual orders for mint stamps, FDCs (agency supplies envelopes), maximum cards. SODA available. Orders shipped postage extra. IMO accepted.

Government Agencies: Agence des Timbres-poste D'Outre-mer, 85 Avenue de La Bouronnais, 75 007 Paris, France; Centre Philatelique, Office des Postes et Telecommunications, Rue Euguene Porcheron, Quartier Latin, Noumea, New Caledonia; Centre Philatelique, Office Des Postes et Telecommunications, Papeete, French Polynesia.

WESTERN SAMOA

Supervisor, Philatelic Bureau, GPO, Apia, Western Samoa, South Pacific. Deals with individual orders for mint and used stamps and FDCs. SODA and special order deposit account available. Bureau also maintains mailing list for advance information on new issues. Orders of WS $1 or more are sent registered mail postpaid; others by ordinary airmail. BPO, IMO, BD, and U.S. and Australian bank notes (sent by registered mail) accepted.

Government Agencies: Crown Agents Stamp Bureau, St. Nicholas House, Sutton, Surrey SM1 1EL, England; Australia Philatelic Bureau, GPO, Box 9988, Melbourne, Victoria 3001, Australia; Fiji Philatelic Bureau, Box 100, Suva, Fiji; New Zealand Philatelic Bureau, Private Bag, Wangani, New Zealand.

YEMEN ARAB REPUBLIC

Ministry of Communications, Philatelic Bureau, GPO, Yemen Arab Republic. Deals with individual orders for mint and CTO stamps. CBC (forwarded by registered mail) accepted.

YEMEN, PEOPLE'S DEMOCRATIC REPUBLIC

Director General of Posts, Aden, People's Democratic Republic of Yemen. Deals with individual orders for mint stamps and CTO stamps, FDCs, postal stationery, plate number and inscription blocks, special postmarks. SODA available with minimum balance of U.S.$3. Orders shipped postage extra; IRCs accepted. CBC, IMO, IBD accepted.

YUGOSLAVIA

Jugomarka, Palmoticeva 2, Belgrade, Yugoslavia. Deals with individual orders for mint and CTO stamps, FDCs, plate number or inscription blocks, special postmarks. SODA available with minimum balance of U.S. $10. Orders shipped postage extra. CBC (preferred), BD, IMO, IBD, USPSMO accepted.

Printers: Belgrade Mint, Forum Printers (both Yugoslavia).

Government Agency: Unicover World Trade Corp. (Yugoslavia Stamp Service in North America), 1 Unicover Center, Cheyenne, Wyo. 82008-0004. (SODA available).

ZAIRE

National Office of Posts and Telecommunications, Box 7984, Kinshasa 1, Republic of Zaire, or Agences Philateliques Gouvernementales, Chaussee de Waterloo 868/870, 1180 Brussels, Belgium. Deals with individual orders for mint sets.

Printers: Malines Stamp Printing Office, Belgium.

ZAMBIA

Philatelic Bureau, Box 71857, Ndola, Zambia. Deals with individual orders for mint and CTO stamps, FDCs (service fee extra), postal stationery, special postmarks. SODA available with minimum balance of 100 kwacha. Orders shipped postage extra. CBC, BD, PC (local only), IMO, IBD accepted.

Printers: The House of Questa, Format International Security Printers, Harrison & Sons (all England), Cartor, France; Zimbabwe National Printing and Packaging; Helio Courvoisier, Switzerland.

Government Agencies: Inter-Governmental Philatelic Corp., 460 W. 34th St., New York, N.Y. 10001; CAPHCO Ltd., Old Inn House, 2 Carshalton Road, Sutton, Surrey SM1 4RN, England.

ZIL ELWANNYEN SESEL

Philatelic Bureau, Box 60, Victoria, Mahe, Seychelles, Indian Ocean. Deals with individual orders for mint stamps, FDCs (bureau provides envelopes). SODA available.

Government Agency: CAPHCO Ltd., Old Inn House, 2 Carshalton Road, Sutton, Surrey SM1 4RN, England.

ZIMBABWE

Posts and Telecommunication Corp., Philatelic Bureau, Box 4220, Harare, Zimbabwe. Deals with individual orders for mint and CTO stamps (complete sets only), FDCs (on or before first day), plate number or inscription blocks. SODA available with minimum balance of Z$20. Orders shipped postage extra. PC (U.S., United Kingdom and West Germany only), IBD and most Western currencies accepted.

Printer: National Printing and Packaging, Zimbabwe.

United States Agents

Seven philatelic representatives or agents located in the United States are listed along with the countries they represent.

Some of the agents do not sell stamps directly to collectors. This information is included when known.

Inter-Governmental Philatelic Corp. (IGPC), 460 W. 34th St., New York, N.Y. 10001, is a wholesale firm, selling primarily to stamp dealers with minimum purchase requirements. IGPC does not offer SODA for any of the following countries it represents:

Alderney, Antigua & Barbuda, Austria, Bhutan, Botswana, British Virgin Islands, Brunei, Cameroon, Cape Verde, Cyprus, Dominica, Ethiopia, the Gambia, Ghana, Grenada, Grenada-Grenadines, Guernsey, India, Isle of Man, Kenya, Lesotho, Malawi, Maldives, Malaysia, Micronesia, Nevis, Palau, Papua New Guinea, Qatar, Sierra Leone, Singapore, Sri Lanka, St. Vincent, St. Vincent-Grenadines, Tanzania, Togo, Turkey, Turks & Caicos Islands, Uganda, Zambia.

Herrick Stamp Co., Box 219, Lawrence, Long Island, N.Y. 11559, represents Cocos (Keeling) Islands and Malta.

Interpost, Box 378, Malverne, N.Y. 11565, represents the Azores, Greece, Great Britain , Hong Kong, Ireland, Jersey, Macao, Madeira, Portugal, West Berlin and West Germany.

Nordica Inc., Box 284, Old Bethpage, N.Y. 11804, represents Denmark, Faroes, Greenland and Iceland.

Unicover World Trade Corp., 1 Unicover Center, Cheyenne, Wyo. 82008-0001, represents: Australia, Brazil, Canada, Chile, China, France, Finland, Israel, Hungary, Marshall Islands, Monaco, New Zealand, Soviet Union, Sweden and Yugoslavia.

World Wide Philatelic Agency, 2031 Carolina Place, Fort Mill, S.C. 29715, sells only to dealers. It represents: French Polynesia, Netherlands, Netherlands Antilles, Surinam, Taiwan and Tunisia.

D & G Philatelic Inc., Box 237, 370 Hempstead Ave., West Hempstead, N.Y. 11552, sells only to dealers. It represents: Guinea-Bissau, Montserrat, Papua New Guinea, St. Lucia, St. Thomas and Prince Islands, St. Vincent and Tuvalu.

CAPHCO

CAPHCO Ltd., Old Inn House, 2 Carshalton Road, Sutton, Surrey SM1 4RN, England, handles the selling and distribution of stamps for several countries.

CAPHCO serves as philatelic representative for the following countries in the United States: Angola, Ascension Island, Bahamas, Barbados, Belize, Bermuda, British Antarctic Territory, Cayman Islands, Christmas Island, Falkland Islands, Fiji, Jamaica, Kiribati, Liberia, Mauritius, Mozambique, Nauru, Nigeria, Norfolk Island, Sultanate of Oman, Papua New Guinea, Pitcairn Is-lands, St. Helena, St. Kitts, St. Lucia, Seychelles, Solomon Islands, South Geor-gia & South Sandwich Islands, Swaziland, Trinidad & Tobago, Tristan da Cunha, Vanuatu, Western Samoa, Zambia, Zil Elwannyen Sesel.

Stamp Printers

The postage stamps of the world are produced by either individual government-owned establishments or by commercial security printing firms.

The listings of printers are based on information sent by philatelic bureaus, the printing firms and press releases from governments and their philatelic agencies regarding new stamp issues.

This is not a complete listing of printers of stamp issues, but it is as comprehensive a listing as possible of issues from 1987 to early 1989. Exceptions are noted.

Ajans-Turk, Ankara, Turkey
Turkey

American Bank Note Co., 70 Broad St., New York, N.Y. 10004
United States

Apa Offset, Turkey
Turkey

APO Production Unit, Inc., NEDA, Quezon City Complex, New Center, E. delos Santos Ave., Diliman, Quezon City, Philippines
Philippines

Argentine State Mint, (Sociedad del Estado Casa de Moneda), Av. Antartida, Argentina 1385, Buenos Aires, Argentina
Argentina

Ashton-Potter Ltd., 9010 Keele St., Concord, Ontario, Canada L4K 2N2
Canada

Aspioti-Elka Graphic Arts, 276 Vouliagmenis St., Athens, Greece
Cyprus
Greece

Austrian Government Printing Office, Oesterreichische Staatsdruckerei-Wiener, Zeitung, Rennweg 12A and 16, A-1030, Vienna, Austria
Austria
Cape Verde
Iceland
Liechtenstein
Luxembourg
Nepal
San Marino
United Nations

Bank of Algeria
Algeria

Bank of Finland Security Printing House, Finland
Aland
Algeria
Faroes
Finland
Libya
Morocco
Thailand

Basin Offset Printing House, Ankara, Turkey
Turkey

BDT International Security Printing, Ltd., Dublin, Ireland
Bahamas
Barbados
Bermuda
British Virgin Islands
Cayman Islands
Dominica
Fiji
Ghana
Gibraltar
Grenada
Grenada-Grenadines
Guernsey
Hong Kong
Isle of Man
Jamaica
Jersey
Lesotho
Malawi
Mauritius
Micronesia
Nauru
Palau
Papua New Guinea
Pitcairn Islands
St. Lucia
Seychelles
Sierra Leone
Tanzania

Beijing Postage Stamp Printing Office, Beijing, China
China

Belgrade Mint, Belgrade, Yugoslavia
Yugoslavia

Brazilian State Mint, Rio de Janeiro, Brazil
Brazil

British American Bank Note, Ottawa,

Ontario, Canada
Canada
Bulgaria State Printing Office
Bulgaria
Bureau of Engraving and Printing (a department of the U.S. Treasury), 14th & C Streets S.W., Washington, D.C. 20228
United States
Canadian Bank Note Co., Ltd.
Canada
Cartor SA, BP 141, Zone Industrielle No. 1, 61 300 L'aigle, France
Alderney
Benin
Burkina Faso
Brunei
Cameroon
Congo
Ethiopia
French Polynesia
Gabon
Gibraltar
Guernsey
Iraq
Isle of Man
Ivory Coast
Jersey
Kenya
Malagasy Republic
Mali
Malawi
Mauritania
New Caledonia
Niger
Senegal
Oman, Sultanate of
Thailand
Togo
United Arab Emirates
Wallis & Futuna
Zambia
Carvajal SA, Apartado 46, Cali, Colombia
Colombia
Costa Rica
Guatemala
Honduras
Panama
Peru
Casa Grafica, San Jose, Costa Rica
Costa Rica
Centro Tecnico Tipo Litografico Nacional (Cettna), Tegucigalpa, Honduras
Honduras
Chile State Mint (Casa De Moneda De Chile)
Chile
China Color Printing Co., 229 Pao-Chiao Road, Hsintien, Taipei, Taiwan
Taiwan
China Engraving & Printing Works, 235 An-Kang Road, Sec. 3 Hsintien, Taipei Hsien, Taiwan
Taiwan
Helio Courvoisier SA, Rue Jardiniere 149, CH-2301 La Chaux-de-Fonds, Switzerland

(This list, furnished by Helio Courvoisier SA, encompasses more than the years 1987-89. The year when Courvoisier first printed a country's stamp is noted in parentheses)

Algeria (1963)
Angola (1949)
Australia (1956)
Bahrain (1984)
Belgium (1945)
Burkina Faso (1986)
Chad (1988)
Colombia (1950)
Costa Rica (1949)
Cuba (1961)
Cyprus (1988)
Ecuador (1958)
Ethiopia (1936)
Faroes (1987)
Gibraltar (1984)
Guernsey (1970)
Guinea, Republic of (1960)
Guinea-Bissau (1948)
Haiti (1954)
Iceland (1958)
India (1948)
Iraq (1957)
Iran (1939)
Isle of Man (1973)
Ivory Coast (1988)
Jersey (1969)
Johore (1960)
Kenya (1982)
Kuwait (1962)
Liechtenstein (1933)
Libya (1961)
Luxembourg (1935)
Macao (1953)
Malagasy Republic (1968)
Malawi (1984)
Malaysia (1963)
Morocco (1964)

Mozambique (1949)
Nepal (1956)
New Zealand (1969)
Nicaragua (1955)
Oman, Sultanate of (1979)
Pakistan (1962)
Papua New Guinea (1962)
Peru (1960)
Philippines (1956)
Poland (1946)
Portugal (1945)
Qatar (1965)
Ruanda-Urundi (1952)
Rwanda (1962)
Salvador (1951)
San Marino (1971)
Senegal (1966)
Singapore (1962)
Somalia (1953)
Sri Lanka (1951)
Switzerland (1931)
Taiwan (1961)
Tunisia (1962)
Turkey (1935)
United Arab Emirates (1979)
United Nations (1961)
Venezuela (1950)
Western Samoa (1971)
Yemen
Yugoslavia (1950)
Vatican City (1989)
Zaire (1949)

CPE Australia, Melbourne, Australia
Australia
Australian Antarctic Territory
Christmas Island
Cocos (Keeling) Islands
Hong Kong
Kiribati
Nauru
New Zealand
Norfolk Island
Papua New Guinea
Singapore
Solomon Islands
Tokelau
United Nations
Western Samoa

Cuban Stamp Printing Office
Bulgaria
Cuba
Guinea-Bissau
Kampuchea
Laos
Nicaragua
Vietnam

Czechoslovakian Post Printing Office, Prague, Czechoslovakia
Czechoslovakia

Danish PFC's Stamp Printing Works, Telegrafvej 7, Box 25, DK 2750, Ballerup, Denmark
Denmark
Greenland

Thomas De La Rue and Co. Ltd., Box 10, De La Rue House, Basingstoke, Hampshire, England
Bahrain
Ethiopia
Ghana
Guernsey
Kenya
Sri Lanka
Sudan

Thomas De La Rue of Colombia
Colombia
Panama

Dirreccion de Servicios Graficos, El Salvador
El Salvador

Edila
Benin
Burkina Faso
Comoros Islands
Congo
Djibouti
French Polynesia
Ivory Coast
Malagasy Republic
Mali
Mauritania
New Caledonia
Niger
Senegal
Togo
Wallis & Futuna

Postal Printing House A.R. of Egypt, Cairo, Egypt
Egypt

Empresa Grafica Sanmarti SA, Lima, Peru
Peru

Joh. Enschede en Zonen, Klokhuisplein 5, Haarlem, Netherlands
(This list, furnished partly by Joh. Enschede en Zonen, includes more than the years 1987-89.)
Aland
Algeria
Aruba

Ethiopia
Faroes
Finland
Gibraltar
Guernsey
Hong Kong
Iceland
Isle of Man
Ivory Coast
Jamaica
Jersey
Kuwait
Netherlands
Netherlands Antilles
Oman, Sultanate of
Qatar
Sri Lanka
Surinam
Tunisia
United Nations

Litografia Ferrua y Hnos, Santo Domingo, Dominica

Dominica

Format International, Parkhouse Street, London SE5, England

Antigua & Barbuda
Bahamas
Barbados
Barbuda
Belize
Bequia
Bermuda
Bhutan
Central African Republic
Christmas Island
Congo
Dominica
Falkland Islands
Fiji
The Gambia
Ghana
Gibraltar
Grenada
Grenada-Grenadines
Guernsey
Guyana
Jamaica
Kiribati
Lesotho
Liberia
Libya
Maldive Islands
Mauritania
Mauritius
Micronesia
Nauru
Nevis
Papua New Guinea
Pitcairn Islands
Redonda
St. Kitts
St. Lucia
St. Vincent
St. Vincent-Grenadines
Seychelles
Sierra Leone
Solomon Islands
Sri Lanka
Swaziland
Tanzania
Trinidad & Tobago
Tuvalu & Islands
Uganda
Union Island
Vanuatu
Western Samoa
Zambia
Zil Elwannyen Sesel

Forum Printers, Novi Sad, Yugoslavia

Yugoslavia

Heraclio Fournier SA, Apartado 94, 01080 Vitoria, Spain

(This list, furnished partly by Heraclio Fournier, includes more than the years 1987-89.)

Aitutaki
Algeria
Bangladesh
Bhutan
British Virgin Islands
Burundi
Cook Islands
Costa Rica
Ecuador
Ethiopia
Guinea, Republic of
Haiti
Honduras
Iraq
Kenya
Kuwait
Lebanon
Liberia
Malagasy Republic
Mauritania
Morocco
New Zealand
Nicaruga
Niue
Norfolk Island

Oman, Sultanate of
Papua New Guinea
Penrhyn
Pitcairn Islands
Rwanda
St. Vincent
Senegal
Singapore
Spain
Sri Lanka
Tokelau
Tunisia
United Nations
Venezuela
Yemen Arab Republic
Zaire

French Government Printing Office, Z.I. De Boulazac, F 24017, Perigueux Cedex, France

Benin
Burkina Faso
Denmark
France
French Andorra
French Polynesia
French Southern & Antarctic Territories
Ivory Coast
Mali
Monaco
Morocco
New Caledonia
Niger
St. Pierre & Miquelon
Switzerland
Tunisia
Wallis & Futuna

Frenckell Printing House, Finland

Aland
Finland

Federal Printing Office of West Germany, Bundesdruckerei, Oranienstrasse 91, 1000 Berlin 61, West Germany

West Berlin
West Germany

Goznak Stamp Printing Office, Soviet Union

Afghanistan
Bangladesh
Congo
Ethiopia
Hungary
Iran
Jordan
Malagasy Republic
Soviet Union
Sri Lanka
Tanzania
Yemen, People's Democratic Republic

Graficas Armitano, Venezuela

Venezuela
Graficos Jorcar
Salvador

Graphischer Grossbetrieb, A. Bagel, Dusseldorf, West Germany

West Germany

Harrison & Sons (High Wycombe) Ltd., Harrison House, Coat Lane, High Wycombe, Buckinghamshire HP13 5EZ, England

Alderney
Bermuda
Bahrain
Botswana
Brunei
Burkina Faso
Congo
Cyprus
Ethiopia
Fiji
Gabon
Gibraltar
Great Britain
Guernsey
Hong Kong
Ivory Coast
Jamaica
Kenya
Kuwait
Malawi
Mauritius
Nepal
New Zealand
Norway
Oman, Sultanate of
Papua New Guinea
Qatar
St. Lucia
Senegal
Sierra Leone
Singapore
Sri Lanka
Thailand
Togo
Tristan da Cunha
Uganda
United Arab Emirates
Vanuatu
Zambia

Holders Security Press, London,

England
Tanzania

The House of Questa Ltd., Parkhouse Street, London SE5 7TP, England
Alderney
Anguilla
Antigua & Barbuda
Ascension Island
Bahamas
Barbados
Barbuda
Belize
Bermuda
Bhutan
British Antarctic Territory
British Virgin Islands
Cayman Islands
Christmas Island
Dominica
Falkland Islands
Fiji
The Gambia
Gibraltar
Great Britain
Grenada
Grenada-Grenadines
Guernsey
Isle of Man
Jersey
Kenya
Kiribati
Lesotho
Liberia
Malawi
Maldives
Marshall Islands
Micronesia
Mongolia
Montserrat
Nauru
Nevis
Niue
Palau
Pitcairn Islands
Redonda
St. Helena
St. Kitts
St. Lucia
St. Vincent
St. Vincent-Grenadines
Seychelles
Sierra Leone
Singapore
Solomon Islands
South Georgia & South Sandwich Islands
Sri Lanka
Swaziland
Tanzania
Thailand
Tokelau
Trinidad & Tobago
Tonga
Tristan da Cunha
Turks & Caicos
Tuvalu
Uganda
United Nations
Vanuatu
Western Samoa
Zambia
Zil Elwannyen Sesel

Hungarian Banknote Printing Office, Budapest, Hungary
Hungary

Imprensa Nacional-Casa de Moeda, Lisbon, Portugal
Azores
Madeira
Portugal

Impressor SA, Switzerland
Central African Republic
Guinea, Republic of
Libya
Malagasy Republic
Mauritania
Togo

India Security Press, Nashik Road, 422101, New Delhi, Maharashtra State, India
India
Nepal

The Indonesian Government Security Printing and Minting Co., (Perum Peruri), Jln. Palatehen 4, Kebayoran Baru, Jakarta, Selatan, Indonesia
Indonesia

Iran Government Printing Press Organization
Iran

Irish Security Stamp Printing Ltd.
Ireland

Israel Government Printers, Jerusalem, Israel
Israel

Italian State Polygraphic Institute, Piazza Verdi 10, 00100 Rome, Italy
Italy
San Marino
Somalia
Sri Lanka

Vatican City

Japanese Ministry of Finance Stamp Printing Bureau, 2-2, Toranomon, Minato-Ku, Tokyo 105, Japan

Japan
Sri Lanka
Thailand
United Nations

N. Kartografike

Albania

Korea Security Printing & Minting Corp., 90 Kajong-dong, Taejon, 302-350, South Korea

South Korea

Korea Stamp Corp., Pyongyang, North Korea

North Korea

Kultura Hungarian Foreign Trading Co., Box 149, 1389 Budapest 62, Hungary

Hungary
Iraq
Jordan
Peru
Yemen Arab Republic

La Papelera SA

Bolivia

Leigh-Mardon Pty. Ltd., 15-31 Keys Road, Moorabbin, Victoria 3189, Australia

(This list, furnished by Leigh-Mardon, includes more than the years 1987-89.)

Australia
Australian Antartic Territory
Bangladesh
Cocos (Keeling) Islands
Ethiopia
Hong Kong
Malaysia
New Zealand
Norfolk Island
Papua New Guinea
Singapore
Solomon Islands
Tanzania
Thailand
Tokelau

E. Lewin Epstein Ltd., Tel Aviv, Israel

Israel

Litografia y Imprenta, LFL SA, Costa Rica

Costa Rica

Litografia Maia, Oporto, Portugal

Guinea-Bissau
Macao
Madeira
Portugal

Litografia Nacional Ltda., Oporto, Portugal

Bolivia
Macao
Paraguay
Portugal

Malines Stamp Printing Office, B-2800 Mechelen, Belgium

Belgium
Rwanda
Zaire

Alexandros Matsoukis Graphic Arts, Athens, Greece

Cyprus
Greece

Mercury-Walch, (division of Davies Brothers Ltd.), Hobart, Tasmania, Australia

Australia
Norfolk Island

Mexico State Mint, Talleres De Impresion De Estampillas y Valores, Legaria No. 662, Col. Irrigacion, Mexico, D.F., Mexico

Mexico

Military Geographical Institute

Ecuador

Mich. A. Moatsos Corp., Graphic Arts, Athens, Greece

Cyprus
Greece

Emil Moestue A/S, Norway

Norway
Somalia

Mozambique National Printers of Maputo, Maputo, Mozambique

Angola
Mozambique

New Zealand Government Printing Office, Wellington, New Zealand

New Zealand
Tokelau

Nigerian Security Printing and Minting Co., Lagos, Nigeria

Nigeria

Norges Banks Seddeltykkeri, Norway

Norway

Oriental Press, Bahrain

Bahrain
Kuwait
United Arab Emirates

Pakistan Security Printing Corp.

Pakistan

Yemen, People's Democratic Republic

Paraguay State Printers, Asuncion, Paraguay

Paraguay

Poland State Securities Printing Works, Ul. Sanguszki 1, Warsaw, Poland

Poland

Printex Ltd., Mill Street, Qormi, Malta

Malta

Secura Singapore Pte. Ltd., 4th Lokyang Road, Jurong Town, Singapore 2262

Brunei
Pakistan
Singapore
Sri Lanka

Security Printers (M) Sdn. Bhd., Box 211, Petaling Jaya, Selangor, Malaysia

Brunei
Liberia
Malaysia
New Zealand
Sri Lanka
Vanuatu
Yemen, People's Democratic Republic

Security Press, Riyadh, Saudi Arabia

Saudi Arabia

South African Government Printer, Pretoria, South Africa

Bophuthatswana
Ciskei
South Africa
South-West Africa
Transkei
Venda

Spanish National Printer, Fabrica Nacional de Moneda y Timbre, Jorge Juan 106, Madrid 9, Spain

Equatorial Guinea
Spain
Spanish Andorra

PFA Swedish Stamps, S-164 88 Kista, Sweden

Finland
Iceland
Sweden
United Nations

Swiss PTT Stamp Printing Office, Bern, Switzerland

Luxembourg
Switzerland

Syrian Government Printer

Syria

Taller Nacional, Guatemala

Guatemala

Tezel Offset and Printing Co. Ltd., Lafkosa, Turkey

Turkish Republic of Northern Cyprus

Tiefdruck Schwann-Bagel, GmbH, Dusseldorf, West Germany

West Germany

Trejos SA, Costa Rica

Costa Rica
Panama

Uruguay National Printing Office, Uruguay

Uruguay

Vietnam State Printing Office, Hanoi, Vietnam

Vietnam

Walsall Security Printers Ltd., Box 26, Midland Road, Walsall, WS1 3QL, England

(This list, most of which was furnished by Walsall Security Printers, includes more than the years 1987-89).

Anguilla
Antigua & Barbuda
Ascension Island
Bahamas
Barbados
Barbuda
Belize
Bermuda
Bhutan
Botswana
British Antarctic Territory
British Virgin Islands
Brunei
Cayman Islands
Chad
Christmas Island
Dominica
Falkland Islands
Fiji
Fujeira
The Gambia
Gibraltar
Gilbert & Ellice Islands
Great Britain
Grenada
Grenada-Grenadines
Guyana
Hong Kong
Jamaica
Kenya
Kiribati
Lesotho
Liberia
Libya
Malawi

Maldive Islands
Mauritius
Micronesia
Montserrat
Nauru
Nevis
New Zealand
Nicaragua
Niuafo'ou
Norfolk Island
Papua New Guinea
Pitcairn Islands
Redonda
St. Helena
St. Kitts
St. Lucia
St. Vincent
Seychelles
Sierra Leone
Solomon Islands
South Georgia & South Sandwich Islands
Swaziland
Tanzania
Togo
Tonga
Trinidad and Tobago
Tristan Da Cunha
Turks & Caicos
Tuvalu
Uganda
Vanuatu
Western Samoa
Zil Elwannyen Sesel

VEB Wertpapierdruckerei, Leipzig, East Germany

Angola
Bulgaria
East Germany
Mongolia
Poland
Sri Lanka
United Arab Emirates

National Printing & Packaging, Harare, Zimbabwe

Botswana
Kenya
Tanzania
Zambia
Zimbabwe

Annual Stamp Totals

Michel-Rundschau, the German-language magazine produced by the publishers of the Michel catalog, records the number of new stamps and souvenir sheets issued worldwide each year. *Michel-Rundschau*'s annual survey includes definitives, commemoratives, officials, postage dues, semipostals and overprinted stamps. Souvenir sheets are counted as one unit. Individual stamps in the souvenir sheets are not counted separately. Different types of stamps, watermarks, and perforations are counted. Varieties are not counted.

The stamp-related information in the following tables is used with the permission of Schwaneberger Verlag of Munich, Germany. This information appeared in various issues of *Michel-Rundschau*.

Based on the *Michel-Rundschau* new-issue survey results, the 10 worst offenders from the preceding years are listed in the accompanying chart. The worst offenders are those countries that have issued the most stamps and souvenir sheets during a particular year.

For this list, countries are grouped with the areas they administer. For example, Grenada and the Grenada-Grenadines are listed together.

The numbers of stamps and souvenir sheets issued by United States each year also are included, along with the United States' rank for that year, even though the United States may not be one of the 10 worst offenders.

The term "unit" indicates the total of stamps and souvenir sheets from a particular country.

Population counts are based on yearly estimates from *The World Almanac and Book of Facts* published by Newspaper Enterprise Association, Inc. a Scripps-Howard division, and *The CBS News Almanac* published by Hammond Almanac Inc.

Worldwide Annual Stamp Totals

Year	Units	Stamps	Souvenir sheets
1987	9107	8344	763
1986	9509	8716	793
1985	10056	9141	915
1984	10126	9254	908
1983	8655	7830	825
1982	8679	7793	886
1981	8427	7666	761
1980	8232	7575	657
1979	7804	7185	619
1978	8028	7235	793
1977	7409	6847	562
1976	7719	7046	673
1975	7525	6970	555
1974	7098	6537	561
1973	6783	6419	364

Worst Offenders and United States

1987	Total units	Stamps	Souvenir sheets	Population
1. Guyana	356	350	6	779,000
2. Grenada and Grenada-Grenadines	284	243	41	87,000
3. Guinea	209	101	108	6,147,000
4. St. Vincent and islands	197	182	15	112,000
5. Tuvalu and islands	181	169	12	9,000
6. Antigua and Barbuda	174	154	20	86,000
7. Malagasy Republic	152	82	70	11,148,000
8. Hungary	134	120	14	10,571,000
9. Paraguay	127	118	9	4,518,000
10. Sierra Leone	122	105	17	4,318,000
12. United States	110	110	—	244,600,000

1986	Total units	Stamps	Souvenir sheets	Population
1. Tuvalu	278	245	33	8,580
2. St. Vincent and islands	272	236	36	103,000
3. Grenada and Grenada-Grenadines	259	216	43	86,000
4. Guyana	221	218	3	771,000
5. Antigua and Barbuda	171	137	34	82,000
6. Vietnam	144	134	10	61,994,000
7. Hungary	140	128	12	10,624,000
8. Malaysia	132	132	—	15,820,000
9. Central African Republic	130	90	40	2,744,000
10. Paraguay	128	115	13	4,119,000
57. United States	51	47	4	242,200,000

1985	Total units	Stamps	Souvenir sheets	Population
1. Tuvalu and islands	384	373	11	8,580
2. St. Vincent and islands	346	322	24	102,000
3. Central African Republic	259	157	102	2,664,000
4. Guyana	244	244	—	768,000
5. Guinea	230	117	113	5,597,000
6. Libya	207	139	18	3,752,000
7. Grenada and Grenada-Grenadines	187	157	30	113,000
8. Antigua and Barbuda	184	155	29	80,000
9. Hungary	148	134	14	10,644,000
10. Burkina Faso	136	105	31	6,907,000
22. United States	80	80	—	239,000,000

1984	Total units	Stamps	Souvenir sheets	Population
1. St. Vincent and islands	309	308	1	138,000
2. Libya	272	252	20	3,684,000
3. North Korea	234	213	21	19,630,000
4. Guyana	220	220	—	775,000
5. Central African Republic	214	117	97	2,585,000
6. Togo	173	117	56	2,926,000
7. Vietnam	166	157	9	59,030,000
8. Grenada and Grenada-Grenadines	146	115	31	113,000
9. Guinea	134	64	70	5,579,000
10. Hungary	128	118	10	10,681,000
44. United States	57	57	—	237,200,000

1983	Total units	Stamps	Souvenir sheets	Population
1. Chad	218	112	106	4,990,000
2. Central African Republic	196	125	71	2,512,000
3. Libya	193	175	18	3,498,000
4. Guyana	185	185	—	833,000
5. Hungary	128	112	16	10,691,000
6. Nicaragua	126	118	8	2,812,000
7. Paraguay	119	106	13	3,526,000
8. Cuba	113	106	7	9,889,000
9. Guinea	111	60	51	5,430,000
10. Vietnam	111	102	9	57,612,000
27. United States	68	68	—	235,100,000

1982	Total units	Stamps	Souvenir sheets	Population
1. North Korea	209	148	61	18,700,000
2. Chad	188	98	90	4,600,000
3. Central African Republic	178	119	59	2,400,000
4. Guyana	156	154	2	900,000
5. United States	144	144	—	232,600,000
6. St. Thomas and Prince Islands	130	68	62	100,000
7. Hungary	124	110	14	10,700,000
8. Guinea-Bissau	114	52	62	800,000
9. Libya	106	84	22	3,200,000
10. Nicaragua	106	101	5	2,600,000
11. Soviet Union	106	99	7	268,800,000

1981	Total units	Stamps	Souvenir sheets	Population
1. North Korea	213	176	37	19,900,000
2. Central African Republic	206	132	74	2,400,000
3. St. Thomas and Prince Islands	173	113	60	90,000
4. Guinea-Bissau	156	72	84	660,000
5. Paraguay	135	123	12	3,300,000
6. Togo	129	116	13	2,600,000
7. Guyana	128	128	—	850,000
8. China	115	114	1	1,004,000,000
9. Hungary	114	100	14	10,800,000
10. Soviet Union	111	106	5	268,800,000
15. United States	84	84	—	226,504,825

1980	Total units	Stamps	Souvenir sheets	Population
1. Togo	209	172	37	2,544,000
2. Panama	195	192	3	1,940,000
3. North Korea	162	128	34	19,000,000
4. Zaire	140	124	16	28,090,000
5. Hungary	126	114	12	10,710,000
6. Soviet Union	114	108	6	266,670,000
7. Cook Islands	104	90	14	18,112 (1976)
8. Libya	102	96	6	2,980,000
9. Belize	96	80	16	144,657
10. China	95	93	2	1,027,000,000
50. United States	50	50	—	226,504,825

1979	Total units	Stamps	Souvenir sheets	Population
1. North Korea	205	173	32	18,717,000
2. Comoros	171	119	52	359,000
3. Hungary	152	140	12	10,710,000
4. Togo	136	124	12	2,544,000
5. Paraguay	127	110	17	3,117,000
6. Libya	125	103	22	2,920,000
7. Bulgaria	117	99	18	8,827,000
8. Romania	108	98	10	22,057,000
9. Soviet Union	100	92	8	262,436,000
10. Liberia	96	92	4	1,788,000
63. United States	41	41	—	218,059,000

1978	Total units	Stamps	Souvenir sheets	Population
1. Comoros	329	158	171	370,000
2. Guinea-Bissau	211	92	119	540,000
3. North Korea	202	178	24	16,650,000
4. Soviet Union	136	127	9	258,930,000
5. Paraguay	134	115	19	2,890,000
6. Central African Republic	123	90	33	2,690,000
7. China	101	97	4	958,230,000
8. East Germany	101	99	2	16,760,000
9. Vietnam	100	100	—	49,260,000
10. Ghana	97	86	11	10,480,000
46. United States	48	47	1	219,500,000

1977	Total units	Stamps	Souvenir sheets	Population
1. Burundi	226	210	16	3,970,000
2. Hungary	156	144	12	10,650,000
3. Antigua and Barbuda	147	132	15	69,700
4. Togo	133	119	14	2,350,000
5. Soviet Union	124	116	8	258,700,000
6. Paraguay	115	95	20	2,800,000
7. Guinea	110	104	6	4,650,000
8. North Korea	107	100	7	16,500,000
9. Central African Republic	101	92	9	2,610,000
10. Vietnam	95	95	—	47,870,000
70. United States	35	35	—	217,700,000

1976	Total units	Stamps	Souvenir sheets	Population
1. Comoros	244	114	130	310,000
2. North Korea	210	98	12	16,250,000
3. Guinea-Bissau	191	100	91	530,000
4. Togo	146	129	17	2,280,000
5. Hungary	140	128	12	10,600,000
6. Paraguay	133	108	25	2,720,000
7. Soviet Union	131	121	10	257,900,000
8. Bulgaria	99	90	9	8,760,000
9. Burundi	96	78	18	3,860,000
10. East Germany	92	89	3	16,790,000
10. Romania	92	81	11	21,450,000
15. United States	79	75	4	216,817,000

1975	Total units	Stamps	Souvenir sheets	Population
1. Equatorial Guinea	346	280	66	310,000
2. Grenada and Grenada-Grenadines	219	196	23	119,000
3. Hungary	160	146	14	10,540,000
4. Burundi	152	144	8	3,760,000
5. Cambodia (Khmer Rouge)	138	60	78	7,890,000
6. Paraguay	135	105	30	2,650,000
7. Upper Volta	128	109	19	6,030,000
8. Togo	114	106	8	2,220,000
9. Soviet Union	113	106	7	254,380,000
10. Rwanda	100	77	23	4,200,000
70. United States	37	37	—	214,500,000

1974	Total units	Stamps	Souvenir sheets	Population
1. Equatorial Guinea	326	254	12	310,000
2. Burundi	192	166	26	3,680,000
3. Hungary	152	138	14	10,510,000
4. Antigua and Barbuda	137	122	15	70,000
5. Togo	131	116	15	2,171,000
6. Dahomey	124	83	41	3,029,000
7. Soviet Union	117	109	8	252,064,000
8. East Germany	105	103	2	17,170,000
9. Albania	102	95	7	2,420,000
10. Maldive Islands	95	84	11	120,000
61. United States	36	35	1	211,390,000

1973	Total units	Stamps	Souvenir sheets	Population
1. Equatorial Guinea	231	173	58	300,000
2. Hungary	188	170	18	10,410,000
3. Burundi	180	170	10	3,600,000
4. Rwanda	146	132	14	3,980,000
5. Paraguay	133	116	17	2,670,000
6. Togo	121	106	15	2,120,000
7. Soviet Union	112	102	10	250,900,000
8. Upper Volta	96	73	26	5,740,000
9. East Germany	94	92	2	16,980,000
10. Bulgaria	92	8	11	8,620,000
65. United States	37	37	—	211,210,000

Chapter 14

Stamp Collecting Basics

To outline all of the facets and sidelines of stamp collecting is much like trying to define outer space. Each has almost limitless boundaries. While this chapter will explore the more common philatelic pursuits, the possibilities are by no means complete. They can never be complete, because collecting stamps and related material defies full annotation.

Stamp collecting's charm is its individual, tailormade freedom to fit the desires of any collector for as much as he wishes to spend in time, money and effort. For beginning collectors, some good advice is not to take on more than they can handle comfortably in all of those areas. That maxim applies whether stamps are collected by country, by topic, by time period or within any other personal parameters.

Many years ago, it was possible to collect all the stamps of the world. A small, optimistic minority may still try to do so. But with nearly a half million stamps already issued worldwide, and with thousands more being released each year, that is an impossible dream — even for the opulent few. Great rarities and thousands of varieties now make it impractical for anyone, however wealthy, to attain world completeness.

These following guidelines may aid you in whatever your collecting choices may be.

Enjoyment: Collect what pleases you or what interests you. If you are smitten by the colorful new stamps of some offbeat island, collect them — regardless of their future worth, postal validity or philatelic prestige. If you cannot afford to obtain all that's available in your field, limit yourself to what intrigues you the most. No law says that your collection must be absolutely complete.

Many fine, award-winning collectors follow that path, collecting stamps or covers just for the fun of it. F. Burton Sellers, a prominent collector, works hard on the stamps of Haiti, Panama and United States possessions. For sideline enjoyment, he likes a topical, "wine on stamps." He delights in another collection called simply, "Cuz I Like 'Em," a potpourri of stamps with unusual cancels, odd shapes and advertisements printed on their gummed sides.

Ernst M. Cohn, who owns one of the world's top-notch collections of the Paris Balloon mail of 1870-71, can't wait for the postman to arrive. He's looking for mail properly stamped and addressed to him, but which the post office has misdirected and delayed. Cohn collects plenty of these postal "goofs" right at his front door.

The late Emerson Clark, a past president of the American Philatelic Society, specialized in the stamps of Canada and Mexico. For a philatelic dessert, he doted on something he called "Libations, Liver Pills and Loose Ends." This melange consisted of advertising covers from breweries, vintners, distilleries and liquor merchants; patent medicine stamps and covers; and such wild items as envelope ads reading, "Electric Beans For Tired People," and "Stansfield's Unshrinkable Underwear."

The message from these prominent collectors is clear: You can be serious about stamp collecting and have fun at the same time. These fine collectors are saying you may do what you please, without worrying about cataloging, organization or whether anyone else collects that way. Collecting stamps and their related material is probably the least structured hobby in the world; you can do exactly as you wish.

Common sense: Be aware of your financial limitations, and beware of unbelievable bargains and outrageous pricing. Most beginning collectors attempt too much — try for too broad a stamp spectrum. Collecting every U.S. postage stamp is now almost an impossible dream.

Counting all available varieties of U.S. stamps, only one or two complete U.S. collections are thought to exist.

Collecting stamps issued within a time span was more popular decades ago than it is now. Our grandfathers often tightened their collecting to a set period — a few years or a couple of decades. Even today, many serious stamp collectors will limit themselves to one stamp, with all of its varieties, essays, proofs and postal usages; one set of definitives or commemoratives; or just a year or two's worth of issues.

Tightening your collecting goals will allow you to become more knowledgeable about what you do collect. With that focused knowledge comes price sagacity, better selectivity and, very possibly, more enjoyment. All of that leads to another point.

Authoritative sources: Let yourself be guided by any and all reliable sources. Read avidly, seek information and assistance in your stamp searching, follow the philatelic press, and never be afraid or too proud to ask for help from fellow collectors and dealers who know your collecting field.

Join a local stamp club — or start one if none exists in your community. (See the Stamp Organizations chapter of this almanac.) When it comes to stamp collecting, camaraderie and knowledge just seem to go together.

International, national and regional societies now embrace almost every collecting phase and stamp-issuing country. Seek them out. Many societies publish data about specific collecting fields in newsletters, papers and journals. Some maintain libraries whose books are available to members. You also can find a list of these specialized groups in the Stamp Organizations chapter.

Techniques: Learn as much as you can about the stamp hobby, its tools, language and methods. Good basic catalogs will give you much of this information; their introductions often can educate you on terms, printing methods and stamp design. Read them, though they may seem complex at first. A thorough knowledge of these will help attain your collecting goals. When you realize, for example, that a tiny variance in perforations can mean the difference between a common stamp and one of great value, you will appreciate the wisdom of a quest for philatelic knowledge.

Although you have been advised to limit your collecting goals, don't apply that rule to your accumulation of knowledge. As with antique and art collecting, knowledge and discernment are the keys to common-sense approaches and the enjoyment of your hobby. With those caveats in mind, what are the major choices when it comes to collecting stamps?

Postage Stamps

Stamps are defined most simply as a government adhesive or imprinted stamp placed on a piece of mail as evidence of prepayment of postage. In effect, they are receipts for money paid for a future postal usage. (In this section's context, "stamps" will mean adhesive stamps only. The printed indicia on postal stationery will be discussed in the postal stationery section.)

Postage stamps can be collected in a multitude of styles:

Commemorative stamps are those that have only one printing. They honor a specific event, person, place, historical happening or anniversary. Commemoratives remain on sale for a limited time.

Special stamps, such as the U.S. Love and Christmas issues, are reprinted as needed, but normally stay on sale for a shorter period than definitives.

Definitive stamps are the workhorses of the Postal Service. Often called regular stamps, they can remain on sale for years and are reprinted time and again.

Airmail stamps are printed to meet airmail rates on letters and postcards, both domestic and international. They can include both definitive and commemorative types.

Newspaper stamps have been used by countries around the world to indicate postal charges paid on newspapers, journals and periodicals. (In the United States, they were used only from 1865 to 1898.)

Occupation stamps are those overprinted or altered in design by an invading force occupying another country.

Official stamps are issued for use only by a government department or its officials.

Parcel post stamps cover package and parcel rates.

Special delivery and **Express stamps** pay the extra postal fees for those special services.

Mourning stamps, either commemoratives or definitives, are issued to honor a deceased head of state or prominent person.

Provisional stamps are those sanctioned for temporary service until regular issues become available.

Registration stamps pay the fees on registered mail. If the letter is lost, a mailer's receipt provides compensation to the mailer.

Carrier stamps, issued and used both privately and officially in the United States from 1851 to 1863, were used to pay postage from and to post offices in a designated area.

Franchise stamps, issued only by foreign countries, are supplied free to individuals and organizations for franking mail.

Military stamps, also of foreign origin, are used either to frank mail of armed forces personnel, or to show that no postal fees are to be assessed against such mail.

Precanceled stamps, used primarily by bulk mailers, are canceled before they are sold (either by the Bureau of Engraving and Printing or a local printer) to facilitate faster handling of large mail lots.

Semipostal stamps have been issued by many foreign nations to raise funds for charities and special events. They normally carry two values, such as 15f+5f — one being the postage fee, the other a donation that the postal patron has no choice but to pay.

Surcharged stamps are those that have had their denomination changed by overprinting a new value on an older stamp.

Overprinted stamps have their purpose for issuance altered. This happened with the Molly Pitcher commemorative overprint printed on the U.S. 2¢ carmine definitive of 1923. The commemorative overprint was not applied until 1928. (Note: The same stamp can be both overprinted and surcharged.)

Souvenir sheets are small sheets of stamps, often bearing a commemorative legend in their selvage. They have been issued by several countries, with the first U.S. issue being the 25-stamp White Plains sheet of 1926 to honor an international stamp show. The first souvenir sheet is thought to have been issued by Luxembourg in 1906. The stamps within these sheets are valid for postage.

Special handling stamps were used in the United States to raise fourth-class mail to first-class service, and in other countries for similar or military purposes.

Meter stamps are applied or affixed to mail after being printed by special machines. These devices not only stamp mail, but also include a form of precancellation, thus speeding up post office handling. Meters are set for a selected dollar amount by taking them to the post office and paying postal fees. (One meter maker now offers resetting by phone.) Primarily used by concerns with large daily mailings, individual meter stamps can be printed in any amount of postage.

Perfins, an acronym for PERForated INitials, are stamps with holes punched to resemble numbers, letters or trademarks. They were used, here and abroad, primarily in the first half of this century by private firms to prevent employee pilferage of company postage. Many perfin collectors still punch their own stamps with initials or abbreviations today. Postal regulations say that perfining stamps within certain hole and area size limitations is a legitimate practice.

International Reply Coupons can be purchased from post offices worldwide. They are enclosed with a letter to prepay an answer from a recipient in a foreign country. The foreign addressee can exchange them for postage of his own country.

Non-Postage Stamps

Thousands of collectors also collect stamps that were not intended or valid for any postal use. Some of these are, nonetheless, official government issues. Among these non-postal stamps are:

Postage due stamps, which do not prepay or frank mail, indicate an amount due the government on an underfranked piece of delivered mail.

Revenue stamps, issued by many countries and often called "fiscals," are receipts for payment of fees or taxes. This is a broad classification. In the case of U.S. issues, they include boating, cigarette, consular service, wines and cordials, U.S. Internal Revenue, documentary, proprietary, stock transfer, playing cards, future delivery, tobacco, potato, narcotic, customs, private die proprietary, motor vehicle, distilled spirits, firearms transfer, rectification, telegraph, and hunting permit stamps to pay fees or taxes. (Great Britain and the Commonwealth members issued several stamps marked "Postage and Revenue." These served a dual purpose.) Many nations have issued revenue stamps.

Postal note stamps, issued by the United States from 1945 to 1951, supplemented money-order service by making up fractions of one dollar.

Savings stamps, issued by the U.S. Post Office Department from 1911 to 1966, were receipts for depositing amounts from 10¢ to $5 in Postal Saving or U.S. Savings Bond Accounts. (The Treasury Department also issued stamps from 1917 to 1945, redeemable for War Certificates, Defense Bonds, War Bonds, War Savings or Treasury Certificates.)

Postage currency stamps, issued by the United States from 1862 to 1876, in 5¢ to 50¢ values, helped alleviate the shortage of small coins that began early in the Civil War.

Local stamps, privately made by individuals or companies, paid fees for carrying mail to a government post office.

Cinderella stamps, broadly defined as any stamps except those issued as postage stamps or postal stationery, are said by the Cinderella Stamp Club to be "locals, telegraph stamps, revenues, bogus and phantom issues, Christmas seals, registration labels, and advertising and exhibition labels."

Post office seals, appearing in the United States in 1872, have no value or franking power. Designed to prevent tampering with registered letters, they were later used by the post office to repair damaged mail and to close mail received unsealed.

Specimen stamps, either overprinted or perforated with the word "Specimen" or its foreign equivalent, are invalid for postal use. They often were submitted by the issuing country to the Universal Postal Union. Some U.S. stamps are found with that marking in issues from 1851 to 1904.

But that's not all that is available for the stamp collector; some issues defy rigid classification. Belgium, for example, issued several stamps from 1894 to 1913 that bore a detachable label. If you wanted your mail delivered on Sunday, you tore the label off. If you did not want a Sunday delivery, you left it attached to the stamp. The Netherlands issued some odd marine insurance stamps in 1921, all of which featured a floating safe in their vignettes.

There have been stamps issued by colleges, for concentration camps, for special departments of a government, for certified mail, and for computing the volume of mail from one source. Some Czechoslovakian issues guaranteed personal delivery to the addressee. Railway stamps were used in Belgium, and emergency stamps have been authorized during a postal strike.

When it comes to choosing what to collect, the stamp list is almost endless.

Stamp Condition

Once you have decided what stamps you want to collect, another question arises: Should you save stamps that are mint (pristine issues with full original gum, just as they came from the post office); unused stamps (those that may have some of the gum missing, or have been hinged, but are uncanceled and have never seen postal use); or used stamps (those that, either on or off cover, bear an official cancellation)?

From a cost standpoint, the beginner will find it least expensive to collect used stamps, much more costly to save unused issues, and most expensive to go after mint copies. That general statement is usually, but not always, true. In a few cases, a certain used stamp may be more expensive than its mint variety, but those instances are so rare as to be almost meaningless.

Many great collections consist of used stamps only. Many collecting purists prefer the used specimens, based on the premise that stamps are created to move mail. To those collectors, a stamp without a cancel has never fulfilled its reason for existence.

Used stamps are more plentiful than mint copies. You will have more to choose from, and they are easier to find. Used stamps, especially the older varieties, are far cheaper than mint copies. As an example, take the prices on the U.S. $5 America issue of 1923. In used condition it catalogs at $12.50; in mint condition it lists at $200 and up. That's typical of the price relationship — used versus mint — on most older U.S. stamps.

For the new or young collector just trying his wings in this hobby, most used stamps will represent no great loss if his collecting interests change, or if his lack of experience causes him to damage some stamps. Youngsters, perhaps between the ages of 6 to 12, should be encouraged to save used stamps at the outset for both of those reasons.

Unused, hinged, uncanceled varieties will be easier to find than pristine mint stamps, but their prices will be far higher than used stamps. If a collector is content with the clean, unmarked face of a stamp, even though the gum on the back is partial, missing or hinged, these unused types will cost less than mint copies — sometimes far less.

Still, many stamp addicts seek nothing but the post office fresh mint copies. Beauty is one reason, but resale value may be another. Many collectors are also investors at heart. They feel that the extra cost of a mint stamp with full original gum will be more than returned when the collection is finally sold, by them or their heirs.

Mint? Unused? Used? The choice again is yours. A collector can save what he wants, but should go into collecting with his eyes open as to price differences and the resultant effect on his pocketbook.

But the total condition of a stamp embraces far more than these mint, unused or used factors. Here we come to the alphabet soup of stamp condition: S, XF, VF, F and Ave. Those letters stand for Superb, Extra Fine, Very Fine, Fine and Average — all basically referring to a stamp's centering, but taking other conditions into account as well.

A perfectly centered stamp with a hole in it should not be classified as extra fine or superb. A canceled stamp with tire tracks that obliterate the vignette could not be termed a very-fine used copy. As a rule, however, dealers and catalogs will use these terms to describe a stamp's centering only.

Superb means what it implies: The stamp vignette is exactly centered on the paper; opposite margins are equal and large.

Extra-Fine stamps have the design almost perfectly centered, with all margins nearly the equivalent of a superb copy.

Very-Fine copies will have the design fairly well-centered, but still measurably off center. All margins should be substantial, with perforations well away from the design.

Fine stamps can be those that are visibly off center, but the perforations do not cut into the design — however close they may come.

Average copies will show the perforations cutting into the design.

Another grade exists called **Poor**. These are usually fit only to be used as space fillers until a better copy may be obtained. The perfs are well into the design; the centering is awful; the stamp may be dirty and smudged. In a few rare and valuable stamps, only poor copies exist. Such is the case with the unique 1¢ magenta of British Guiana. Only in such events should poor stamps be acceptable.

Gum

One great dealer/collector once said that the most valuable thing in the world, ounce for ounce, is original stamp gum. Based on the price differences it can cause, "gum has to be worth at least $1 million a quart." He was not being facetious. Full original gum on the first few issues of the United States can send auction prices soaring to double or triple the worth of a partially gummed or hinged unused stamp. Ridiculous? A lot of collectors think so, but the condition of a stamp's gum remains a marketing, if irrational, fact of stamp life.

Gum condition is generally divided into six major classifications.

Original gum (OG): This is self-explanatory; the stamp bears all of the gum with which it was issued.

Regummed (RG): Sometime during its existence, new gum has been applied to the stamp. This greatly decreases its value. Many years ago, regumming was detectable with a high-powered microscope; examination of the perf teeth would show very minute strands of new gum extending outward. That couldn't have happened at the printer's, since stamp paper is gummed before it is perforated.

Regummers have since become so expert that they now pass that test. They regum the stamps, slipping them into perf jigs that prevent the wayward strands, or use other means to duplicate OG. In fact, regumming is now such an exact science that many collectors no longer will pay exorbitant prices for a so-called original-gum stamp. Likewise, many stamp expertizing committees no longer render a judgment on gum. For those reasons, the beginner — and even the experienced collector— may be well-advised to avoid collecting original-gum stamps. Some regummers of today are just too good.

No Gum (NG): Either the stamp was issued without gum, or the gum has been removed.

Never hinged (NH): The stamp shows no traces of ever having been hinged, and the gum is not disturbed in any manner. If the gum has been disturbed, the stamp cannot be considered as having original gum for pricing purposes.

Lightly hinged (LH): The stamp has been hinged with a peelable hinge that has been carefully removed. Only slight traces of hinging remain.

Heavily hinged (HH): Heavy remnants of a hinge may remain, or missing gum may be noted where the hinge once was. The danger here is that the stamp paper may have been thinned, in which event the stamp has a fault.

Any fault in the stamp should be noted in a dealer's price list, auction catalog or in a face-to-face sale. Faults include thins, short perfs, creases, tears, stains, ink marks, pinholes, or scrapes.

Any other unusual fault should be spelled out from dealer to customer. Some repairs, tiny tears and thins may be revealed under high magnification, ultraviolet light examination, or in watermark fluid immersions.

Stamp Care and Handling

One of the first and most important lessons a collector should learn is the use of stamp tongs. These are tweezer-like tools, especially made for stamps, without the harsh metal edges found on dime-store tweezers.

Stamps should seldom (ideally, never) be handled by fingers. Even the cleanest, driest hands may leave traces of skin oil that can stain the stamp or disturb the gum. Obviously, stamps should never be handled with wet or dirty hands. In newer issues with metallic ink, it is even possible that the ink will tarnish on contact with the skin.

Well-made stamp tongs can be had in many varieties. Spade tongs have the ends flat and thin. Professional tongs are long (5 inches to 7 inches), and have sharp pointed ends. Several versions exist between those two extremes. Whichever style you select, tongs will be a minor cost for the protection they will give your stamps from finger handling.

Soaking Stamps

Most stamps will be safe in cold water soaking to remove them from an envelope or other paper. Some inks are fugitive, however, and may run when immersed in water. Such stamps are usually indicated in standard catalogs. Even with careful handling, these issues are best left on paper, lest they be damaged.

Be careful of colored papers and some cancellation inks, particularly purple inks. These will run when immersed, often so badly that they will affect other stamps in the water bath.

Stamp lifts are available. These are miniature sweatboxes, constructed so that a water-soaked sponge lies beneath an open grillwork platform on which the stamp is placed. The moisture in the stamp lift removes the stamp from paper without having the stamp immersed in water. This may take several hours, however, and only one or two stamps usually can fit into a stamp lift. It is a slower process than using a water bath, but it is preferable when the stamp involved is of some value.

Stamps should be allowed to soak or lift until they come free of the paper. They should be removed at that point and allowed to dry. Placing them between blotter-like papers under a small weight will ensure that they dry flat and unwrinkled.

Stamps may be stored in albums, stock books, envelopes and boxes. However they are stored, they should be kept as free as possible from the ravages of excessive heat and humidity. Air conditioning and dehumidifiers help here, especially in tropical areas and during the more humid months in many U.S. locales. If stamps are kept in safe-deposit boxes, such bank locations should be air-conditioned.

Keeping stamps in unheated rooms, such as attics and garages, is unwise. Placing them near a basement furnace is courting disaster. It's also advisable to avoid, if possible, spots within a room that receive direct sunlight. Sunlight can fade stamps, and the sun's heat can soften gum, causing mint stamps to stick together.

Albums and stock books should be stored upright, so that the weight of additional albums piled on top is avoided.

Like people, stamps need to breathe once in a while. Regardless of where you store them, it is a good idea to take your albums and stock books off the shelf frequently and open them, page by page. Just a few moments of air circulation will help prevent gum and paper damage that can occur when stamps are left for weeks and months in an airless environment.

Duplicates and other loose stamps may be safely relegated to something like the proverbial cigar box, providing the containers in which they are placed have no migratory glue, grease or wax that can affect them. Storing them in glassine envelopes within boxes is a worthwhile precaution.

Keep an eye out also for possible insect infestation. The gum on stamps can be a delicacy for roaches, silverfish and all sorts of crawling, creeping insects. Many a collector has left a collection untouched and unexamined for months, only to find that moisture, sun, heat, the lack of fresh air or insects have caused irreparable havoc to his stamps. Dealers' storage of stamps is, of course, just as subject to these hazards as collector storage.

Mounting Stamps

Whether you use preprinted album pages (about 90 percent of collectors do) or plain pages, you still have to mount the stamps somehow. It matters little whether the album itself is a $100 gold-stamped, leather one or simply a good three-ring binder. So long as the pages are substantial enough for the material placed thereon, how you mount your stamps poses the same problems.

Two basic methods exist: hinges and mounts.

Many experienced collectors will tell you that the great collections of the world have usually been hinged. If you are saving used stamps, there is little reason to consider any other more expensive method. But when many of those fine collections were formed in the past, hinge-mounting was the only process available. If you are saving mint copies, you may wish to use nothing but plastic mounts.

If you hinge your stamps, be certain to use peelable stamp hinges especially made for that purpose. Never stick stamps down with their own gum, and never use any of the commercial tapes now on the market to affix stamps. Don't try to make your own hinges from paper and the commercial glues found in many stores. Most of these glues and tapes contain chemicals that react with the stamps. Good stamp hinges cost as little as one-fifth of a cent.

Using hinges, however, is not as easy as it may appear. When properly applied, they will hold your stamps in rank-and-file order, and keep them in good condition for easy removal if necessary.

Most stamp hinges sold today come pre-folded. The smaller folded portion goes as close to the top of the stamp as possible, without being visible from the stamp's face side. The larger fold holds the stamp to the page. Placing the hinge to the top of the stamp will allow you to lift it with tongs, after it has been applied to the page, to examine the back of the stamp. That's why the pieces of gummed paper are called "hinges"; they hinge the stamp so you can gently raise it without removing it from the page.

Apply the small part of the hinge to the stamp first. When you lick it — and later the larger portion that sticks to the page — do so carefully. Keep the moisture as far from the fold in the hinge as possible. Don't lick the hinge as though you were licking an ice cream cone; merely a touch of the tongue is enough to hold the stamp properly.

The biggest mistake that most collectors make is using too much moisture. The second biggest mistake is trying to remove and reposition a stamp that has already been hinged to a page. If you are not happy with the placement of a newly hinged stamp, never try to move it at once. The glue first must dry thoroughly before the stamp and hinge can be taken off the page for another attempt. You may tear the stamp if you remove it with a wet hinge. Wait for a half hour, go on to other stamps, and then come back to remove the misplaced stamp.

The development of pocket-style mounts with a transparent front, and either a clear or black backing that adheres to the page, was probably responsible for the "never-hinged" craze that exists today. Before these came along, hinging was the only way to mount. Many stamp experts and dealers are dubious about U.S. issues of the 1800s that are sold as "never-hinged." If these came from old collections, they are probably regummed.

Transparent, gum-protecting mounts come pre-cut to fit most sizes and shapes needed for stamps, covers and souvenir sheets. Showgard and Scott make them with the backs split horizontally so the stamp may be inserted and kept in place at the top and bottom. Hawid makes plastic mounts that are open on three sides; only the bottom is sealed. Other varieties also exist.

Most mount makers make their products available in long strips that can be cut to size for any unusual shapes or se-tenant combinations of stamps. These are cheaper and more flexible than the pre-cut sizes. However, they do require a razor blade and metal ruler, or a special gadget that looks like a miniature paper cutter, to slice a mount neatly and squarely.

If you are adamant about keeping the gum sides of your stamps clean and pristine, plastic mounts are the only choice. If that is of little or no importance, hinges will do the job just as well at a much cheaper cost. Plastic mounts usually sell for about 2 1/2¢ to 3¢ per stamp — much more for larger pieces.

Whichever route you take, it is wise to follow this precept: Within an album or collection of stamps, use either hinges or mounts consistently. Side by side, album pages will look peculiar if some stamps are hinged and some are mounted.

Essays and Proofs

Essays are designs for stamp vignettes, stamp borders, or both combined, that were never approved and used in the final printing of a stamp. Even though a design is finally adopted with only slight modifications, it is still an "essay." To attain the status of a proof, a proposed design, or essay, must be exactly like the issued stamp for which it was submitted.

All U.S. stamps were made by private bank note companies from 1847 to 1894. Essays and printing bids were submitted by those firms. As early as 1851, the U.S. Post Office Department established a policy of advertising for stamp proposals to be accompanied by essays, or examples of the stamps to be furnished. After the bids were opened, an Expert Committee was asked to rule on the designs, colors and paper.

Today, the procedure is usually for the Citizens' Stamp Advisory Committee to pass on a U.S. stamp subject, choose an artist or artists to design a stamp for the printing medium selected, then take the final artwork to the postmaster general for his approval.

Not always is the first assigned artist

able to render a satisfactory design. A case in point would be the 1984 Louisiana World Exposition stamp. On this occasion, the first artist submitted designs that were not acceptable. The Postal Service and CSAC turned to designer Chuck Ripper, who came up with the final stamp art on his first attempt.

Essays on older U.S. issues were made in small quantities; usually the outside printing firm kept several copies. Today, design essays are kept by the U.S. Postal Service; few, if any, ever reach the stamp trade in any format.

Early essays could take the form of vignette models mounted on a card. Around the design, the artist might draw in pencil cross-hatching, or even the suggested frame and lettering. Combinations of essays for the vignette and the frame were sometimes built into full models in the exact size of the final stamp.

Occasionally, essays are now prepared as artist's sketches. In a number of early cases, however, finished plate essays — fully gummed, perforated, and sometimes grilled — would be submitted. All such material, whether just an art sketch or final plate proof, remains an essay until the production and release of a stamp exactly like it. Then it becomes a proof.

It should be noted that reprints of stamps previously issued and sold by the Postal Service are not classified as proofs, even though such reprints may have been sold for collectors' benefit only.

When an essay was fully approved, one engraver may have done the vignette only and had proofs of his work pulled at any point. Another engraver, completing the frame and lettering, may also have had progress proofs of his work made. Two groups of proofs of one stamp were ultimately created: one for the vignette and one for the frame.

When Ripper's art for the Louisiana Expo issue was accepted, it became an "artist's proof." As engravers have copies of their work printed, these are called "progressive proofs," or "engraver's proofs." Proofs taken from a die are "die proofs"; those pulled from a plate before printing are "plate proofs." Various colors often are used in making proofs; these are "trial color proofs," but genuine design proofs nonetheless. When a proof is printed in the exact color of the stamp, it is termed a "color proof."

Although proofs are known to exist in many varied styles, those listed below are the most common:

Large die proofs were printed on paper about the size of the engraver's die block, 40 millimeters by 50mm, or larger. Margins often show the imprint, letters and numbers of the original contract printers. In the United States these large die proofs usually were printed in India paper and mounted on cards. Those with the engraver's name or an official approval designation are highly valued.

Small die proofs have extremely narrow margins, seldom larger than 3mm to 5mm in width. Approximately 300 types were printed for 85 album sets prepared by the Bureau of Engraving and Printing in 1904. These are found on a fibrous, white wove paper. Another special printing of 413 different small die proofs was made for the 1915 Panama-Pacific Exposition. These were produced on a soft, yellowish wove paper, and are extremely scarce.

Plate proofs are found on both India paper and card stock. They were made from finished plates and are excellent impressions, showing a sharpness and color far superior to the stamp themselves.

Hybrid proofs are really plate proofs of all issues prior to 1894. They have been cut to shape and pressed onto large cards to resemble the large die proofs.

Card proofs are printed on high-quality, clear white card stock, which can vary in thickness.

India paper proofs are on a thin, soft, opaque paper, which wrinkles when wet. This paper also varies in thickness and shows particles of bamboo. Strangely, India paper was developed in China in the 18th century, and is sometimes referred to as "China paper."

The U.S. Essay-Proof Society has defined a proof as "any impression, the design of which was approved for use on an issued stamp of an established government or private post, from any die, plate, stone or type, printed for the purpose of (1) examination or reference, (2) for determination of satisfactory quality of design, color, ink, or imprinted surface, or (3) for determination of the effect of cancellation or method of separation."

Scott's *Specialized Catalogue of U.S. Stamps* lists hundreds of varieties of proofs and trial color proofs from the postmasters' provisionals of New York (1845) and Providence (1846) to the 6¢ 50th Anniversary of Powered Flight airmail of May 1953. The Scott roster includes only those proofs outside of government ownership.

Up until a half century ago or more, stamp proofs were available to the stamp trade. In early days, congressmen could secure them for their constituents upon request. Thousands were distributed in this manner, creating a collecting irony of sorts: The proofs of modern U.S. stamps usually are not available, while older proofs are frequently offered for sale.

Today, proofs are retained only by the BEP and the USPS. Engravers were allowed to keep a proof for themselves long after they became unavailable for congressional requests. But those were the only copies outside of government ownership. Occasionally, a retired engraver's estate may include a proof for outside sale, but that is extremely infrequent. The last 1953 airmail proof may have come from that source.

For all practical purposes, modern U.S. proofs are now akin to a dead country that no longer issues stamps. They are no longer obtainable by anyone.

Postal Stationery

The term, "postal stationery," refers to all types of forms and stationery issued by governments for either public or official government use. The most common types collected are: stamped envelopes, lettersheets, postal cards and letter cards. Although a stamp design is usually printed, or printed and embossed on these to show that postage has been prepaid, some postal stationery does not carry such a stamp-like addition. Examples are: formula cards used before imprinted stamps were known, the change-of-address cards still used in the United States, and aerogramme forms from a few countries.

Most postal stationery pieces are collected as "entires," that is, the whole card, sheet or envelope. As collector Dr. Rodney Mott has pointed out, the French word for postal stationery is entiers, and the German term is ganzsachen — each meaning "whole covers." Postal stationery, while not precisely like a stamp, falls under the general stamp definition of "a government adhesive or imprinted stamp placed on a piece of mail as evidence of prepayment of postage."

Postal stationery was in use long before the first adhesive postage stamps of 1840. Earlier postal charges often were based on the number of sheets in a letter, and on its total weight including the cover. Since these rates were high, it became customary and cheaper to use one of the message sheets as a self-cover, with postage usually paid by the recipient.

Later, as postal service became more dependable and organized, paying the postage fee at the post office where the letter was mailed became the more common practice, resulting in the first manuscript "paid" inscriptions and eventually in stamped "paid" markings.

In 1608 the coat of arms of Venice first appeared on lettersheets. These are thought to be the first postal stationery — indeed, the first philatelic item issued by any government. Other early types were the Luxembourg 25-centime sheets of 1790; the highly colorful British newspaper stamps of 1712-1870, which were printed directly on paper supplied the government by newspaper publishers; and Australian postal stationery, which preceded the famous English Mulready envelopes of 1840 by at least two years.

Lettersheets have been used by most countries at one time or another. One side was meant for the message; the other carried the stamped indicium, instructions for use and address. In 1863 the United States issued two lettersheets with the same stamp design, but of different sizes. A large size was intended for use by soldiers of the Civil War, with a smaller sheet for ladies' correspondence. Several heavier sheets, bearing the picture of President Ulysses

Grant, were in use between 1886 and 1894. The United States discontinued franked lettersheets because sales finally almost ceased. None has been sold in the United States since.

Stamped envelopes have existed since the 17th century, first used primarily by royalty and nobility. But since paper was expensive then, and since an envelope containing a letter was assessed double postage, their use declined. When the Penny Post was introduced in Britain, the British Post Office — undaunted by the poor reception accorded the Mulready envelopes — continued to sell stamped envelopes.

In the United States, embossed stamped envelopes were first issued in 1853. They offer an interesting challenge to the collector since so many varieties exist. They vary in size, the paper is often watermarked on old varieties and always watermarked on new U.S. envelopes, different colors of paper appear in the same issue, and modern envelopes are found in "window" and windowless styles. The manner in which the flap is cut (defined by "knife" size) can vary, as well as the gumming of the flap.

Several different dies with minor variations have been used for the same envelope issue. This number of varieties runs into the thousands.

For foreign envelopes, much the same holds true. Great Britain produced a "ladies" size in 1840 that was 2 1/2 by 4 inches. Panama has made envelopes running to 4 1/8 by 9 5/8 inches. Since some foreign governments permit large postal users to bring their own envelopes to an official insignia printer, stamped envelopes can exist in an almost infinite variety of paper colors, textures, weights and sizes.

Prior to 1984, all U.S. stamped envelopes were both printed and embossed. With the 20¢ Small Business stamped envelope of 1984, the U.S. Postal Service issued one that was gravure printed only, but with the indicium and cachet designs wrapped around the edges to prevent feasible counterfeiting. That was the first non-embossed U.S. envelope in 131 years.

Postal cards along with stamped envelopes, are the most popular types of postal stationery collected. They came along some 30 years after the first envelopes were issued, although many private and unofficial postal cards were in use as early as 1777 in France. When postal cards were first suggested, their use was frowned upon by many governments since such cards would expose the writer's thoughts to the gaze of anyone who might handle it. Others, like Dr. Emmanuel Hermann of Austria, viewed them as "the poor man's telegram."

Austria issued the first official postal card on Oct. 1, 1869. Hungary soon followed, and sales rose incredibly to more than 50 million a year between the two countries. By the end of 1870, Great Britain, Finland, Switzerland and Wurttemberg joined in — to be followed by the United States in 1873. Today, some countries, such as a few African states, still do not use them.

In Australia, they have been abandoned in favor of lettersheets.

Since 1973, the United States has issued more than 180 major varieties of postal cards, including commemoratives, definitives, airmail, message and reply, and official cards. With variations in printings, indicia, colors, textures and thicknesses of card stock, U.S. and foreign postal cards can be found in endless amounts. Many countries, notably Japan, issue many more cards than the United States. For the 180-plus U.S. postal cards, the United Postal Stationery Society (see Stamp Organizations) estimates that upwards of 500 types are known.

Postal cards with a paid reply card attached began in 1872 in Wurttemberg. These double cards may have different wording on each, although the United States recently has taken to issuing identical pairs. The two cards may be hinged at the fold by perforations, roulette cuttings or merely a straight printed line. They may be attached at top, bottom or either end.

Letter cards were introduced in Belgium in 1882, and since then, many countries have used them. These are lightweight cards of double normal postal-card size, which may be folded and sealed around three sides to keep the message private. One gummed edge is perforated to allow the recipient to open the card easily. Letter cards are strictly foreign in nature; the United States has never issued them, although private stationers have made them available for use with stamps. These private issues, of course, are not postal stationery.

Aerogrammes, sometimes called air lettersheets, are issued flat, with side and top flaps gummed, and must be folded after the message has been written. The aerogramme is made of lightweight paper, frequently covered with an overlay of printing to make it opaque. It bears its own printed stamp.

Some are very highly decorated; many foreign nations even issue Christmas aerogrammes. Here in the United States, however, they are far less popular than overseas. Much of all foreign airmail goes on aerogrammes. U.S. aerogrammes were printed by the Government Printing Office until 1968. Since then, they have been printed exclusively by the Bureau of Engraving and Printing in Washington, D.C.

Wrappers are among the more exotic types of postal stationery. The United States provided these for many years after 1860. They were already stamped so that publishers could mail their newspapers easily and conveniently. The United States and most other countries have discontinued them, making collecting them difficult. In good used condition, most varieties are almost unobtainable.

Package tags are perhaps the most unique postal stationery issued by Japan since the World War II. Similar to a lettersheet, they are about the size of a baggage tag when folded. After the message is placed inside, the tag is folded and a flexible wire inserted through a reinforced hole in one end. This can be attached to a parcel, allowing both parcel and message to arrive together.

Collecting postal stationery offers several advantages over stamp collecting. It is less easily damaged than stamps, poses no gum or perf problems, is generally cheaper to acquire, and offers the collector an opportunity to collect something different and less frequently seen.

But in another way postal stationery and stamps are much alike. Each offers an almost endless variety for the beginning collector, meaning that, here again, the beginner should limit his interest and acquisitions. For information on collecting and exhibiting, contact the United Postal Stationery Society, Box 48, Redlands, Calif. 92373.

Postmarks

If you are a postal history collector, postmarks will be more important to you than the stamps themselves. Even for the collector of used stamps only, some postmarks are more desirable than others.

As an example, the 1847 10¢ Washington issue of the United States may bear a common red cancellation that makes the stamp's catalog price $2,000, while "Canada" or "Steamer 10" markings add another $1,000 to $1,250 to its value.

Hundreds of collectors save old and modern postmarks only, not really caring which stamp bears them. Postmarks thus spread over three philatelic fields: postal history, used stamps and postmark collections. Following is a description of general postmark terms that all collectors should understand:

Postmark is an all-inclusive term for any marking officially applied to a piece of mail as it passes through the mailstream. It not only includes the circle giving date and town data, but also all the extraneous markings indicating routing, directory service, postage due, censorship, registration, special delivery, forwarding, carriage by special transportation, and many others. The lines canceling the stamp to prevent its reuse comprise a postmark. Any official marking on an envelope, such as "Mail delayed. Found in supposedly empty box," is a postmark.

Datestamps are postmarks that show the date and sometimes the actual hour of mailing. The latter are from an earlier era; today's U.S. datestamps include only date, city and state information. When this date/town data is enclosed in a circle, the postmark is called a circular datestamp (CDS).

Cancellations are those portions of postmarks that mark the stamp to prevent its reuse. Prior to the advent of stamps to prepay postage, such markings only served to provide information to postal clerks as they handled the stampless envelope. After stamps came into use, cancellations became necessary to void the stamp for repeat usage.

Cancellations come in many forms: bars or wavy lines (called "killers"), ink blobs or fancy designs (called "obliterators"), and wording for special occasions (called "slogan cancels"). Even a postman's ball-point pen squiggle, placed on a stamp that escaped being canceled at the post office, is an official cancellation.

Canceled-to-order (CTO) stamps are mint issues with original gum that bear a cancellation, even though they have never been postally used. These cancels are most often applied to entire sheets of stamps as they are printed. Typically, they are small, quarter-circle marks found at the corners of stamps. Some postal administrations create these to sell them at a discount to the stamp trade. Such CTO stamps generally are not regarded as philatelically desirable.

Canceled-by-favor stamps are those canceled in a specific manner at the request of a collector. Anytime a collector asks for and receives a form of cancellation that otherwise would not have been applied to the material being mailed, it can be described as "canceled by favor." Such an item may or may not pass through the mailstream.

Obtaining current postmarks is an activity of many postmark collectors. Requests should be addressed to the postmaster of the post office from which the postmark is desired. State the type of marking wanted: either the office's regular machine cancel, with or without slogan; or the standard handstamp, with or without killer bars. Types of current U.S. postmarks are described in the section on "Postal Regulations."

At times, special pictorial handstamps are used for a short period. These are announced in advance in releases from the U.S. Postal Service, and often in the philatelic press.

To obtain the marking desired, prepare a cover by placing first-class postage in the upper right corner, approximately one-fourth inch from the edges of the envelope. Postal cards also are acceptable. Since postal regulations state that unaddressed covers may not be canceled and returned under separate cover, you must address the cover to yourself in the lower right-hand portion of the envelope or card.

Many collectors prefer to use peelable labels for this purpose. Placing a stuffer of postcard thickness in the envelope usually will ensure a cleaner, sharper postmark. Insert the prepared cover and your note of cancel request in an outer envelope stamped with first-class postage, and send it to the proper postmaster.

Topical Collecting

The topical collector is interested only in a stamp's subject matter; which country it comes from usually means little or nothing. If the chosen topic is horses on stamps, for example, the collection may include stamps from 100 countries or more that picture horses working, horses grazing, horses racing, horses and riders, horses and carriages — almost any stamp pertaining to what horses look like, do or use.

This collecting of stamps according to design subject is now one of the fastest growing segments of the hobby, but only in the past few decades has it been recognized and accepted as a legitimate element of stamp collecting. Today, this thematic style of collecting, arranging and displaying stamps is the most satisfying way of enjoying the hobby to millions throughout the world.

Topics collected are as varied as individual interests and stamp designs. They range from agriculture to zoology, animals to the zodiac, architecture to world's fairs — anything and everything that has been pictured on stamps.

It is now almost impossible to find a topical subject that someone else does not collect. At a recent annual convention of the American Topical Association, a lady approached Donald Smith, then president of the ATA. She was certain she had discovered a topic that no one else collected. "What is it?, asked Smith. "I collect stamps that show breast-feeding mothers," she answered. Smith promptly gave her the name of another collector with the same specialty.

Topical beginners face the same selective problems as regular stamp collectors. Choosing a topic that is too broad for their interests and resources is just as dangerous as choosing too many countries, or a country that is too large.

One topical collector likes mountains on stamps, but realizes that to collect them worldwide would be too exhaustive and expensive. He restricts himself to the mountains of North and South America, on whatever countries' stamp they may appear. So long as his collection is representative of his prescribed area, it would be considered complete according to ATA exhibiting guidelines.

The nature and depth of a topical collection is left up to the individual. It can include stamps, covers, postmarks, souvenir sheets, cachets, essays, proofs and postal stationery. It can be restricted to one or a few of those. The choice is the collector's.

Topical collections vary in size based on subject matter. For a subject as broad as space, thousands of pages might be needed. For one as narrow as wheelchairs on stamps, only a few pages might do.

Topics often are directly related to a collector's vocation. Doctors frequently collect medicine on stamps, musicians might go for composers or musical instruments, teachers for books, farmers for animals, and so on. All of those topics are abundant on stamps, however, and the collector often finds that he must later restrict himself to tighter portions of his chosen topic to be effective in presenting it.

Abraham Lincoln is a popular topic, especially in the United States, but he is a perfect example of a subject that may be too expensive for the average collector. Even if a Lincoln topicalist restricts himself to cataloged material of the United States, he will find Lincoln on almost 100 items that list as more than $23,000 — and that does not include grills, re-issues, color, cancellation and printing varieties. Neither does it embrace any essays or proofs . All of those would easily take a complete U.S. Lincoln topical collection to a six-figure investment.

A beginning topicalist should examine what's available in his chosen field first, then adjust his sights accordingly.

A recent poll of about 10,000 ATA members revealed these topics as the most popular in the United States: animals, medicine, space, ships, Americana, music, religion, railroads, flowers and sports. Also high on the list were art, birds, Christmas, flags, maps, Lions and Rotary stamps, scouting and Europa issues.

If the freedom and flexibility of topical collecting appeal to you, read about the American Topical Association under Stamp Organizations.

First-Day Covers

First-day covers (FDCs) are envelopes, postal cards or postcards that bear an adhesive or imprinted stamp that was officially canceled on the item's first day of postal use. Such U.S. covers are known as far back as the 1¢ and 3¢ issues of July 1, 1851. These covers bear no "first day of issue" designation and no cachets, but they are nonetheless FDCs.

For the subsequent 70 years of stamp and postal stationery issuance, such FDCs appeared more by accident than design. Many of those from the 19th century are extremely costly, ranging from $18,500 for that 1851 1¢ issue down to $2,600 for an 1893 2¢ Columbian FDC. Finally, in the early 1920s, some dealers and a few dedicated collectors intentionally set out to create first-day-canceled covers for themselves and for sale to others.

Many of these early FDC enthusiasts lived in or around Washington, D.C., where they were within easy access to the sites of most new first-day releases. C.E. Nickles, Harold F. Whittaker, H.F. Coleman and Hugh M. Southgate, all of whom lived in the Washington area, were responsible for many of these pioneer first-day items. Nickles often announced new stamp releases and advertised their FDCs in his *Washington Stamp News*. Those of the 1923 $2 Capitol and $5 America stamps now catalog at $10,000 and $14,000, respectively.

With the appearance of the July 12, 1922, 10¢ special delivery stamp, the

U.S. Post Office Department began designating an initial sale date and official site in advance for new postal products. That notice was far shorter than the advance information given today. Those Washington FDC servicers often had to scurry to prepare their covers, thus giving rise to the term, "Washington Connection," among FDC collectors of that time.

As the notices and information about new stamp issues lengthened and improved, interest in FDCs grew, leading finally to the production of printed and pictorial cachets for the covers. The cachet, or envelope design, could carry more facts about the stamp than the stamp itself. It enriched the information about the event or person portrayed on the stamp. It led to the popular cachet collecting of FDCs that now dominates the hobby.

The first commercially printed, cacheted FDC in the United States was made and sold by George Linn, founder of *Linn's Stamp News*, for the 2¢ Harding Memorial issue of Sept. 1, 1923. Its "cachet" consisted merely of a black border around a small cover with five lines of copy about Harding in the lower left corner. This tiny, simple FDC today sells at auction for approximately $500.

During the pre-cachet era of the 1920s, the spread of the new airmail service across the nation caught the public's fancy — as well as that of stamp and FDC collectors. Nickles, Phillip Ward, A.C. Roessler and Edward Worden began servicing new first-flight covers to mark the airmail's gradual spread westward from its New York-Philadelphia-Washington original sites.

Roessler built his dealer career on airmail first-flight covers, but he — like the other pioneers mentioned — continued to supply FDCs for surface mail as well. The romance and popularity of these airmail covers is credited with bringing many newcomers to the FDC hobby.

The first pictorial cachets (those with artwork rather than simply printed words) were produced by Nickles and Roessler for the 17¢ Woodrow Wilson issue of 1925. From that time on, the number of pictorial cachets grew rapidly, and their quality and complexity improved.

Today, more than 250 full-time and part-time commercial U.S. cachetmakers offer varied cachets for each and every commemorative stamp issued. Some make cachets for definitive stamps also. The number of FDC copies produced per stamp may vary from fewer than 100 to thousands per cachetmaker. Because cachets exist in so many varieties for each stamp, most FDC collectors sooner or later became specialists.

Many prefer to collect all of the cachet types produced before or after a given year. Some collect within a more restricted time period; others attempt to secure all of the cachets made by one cachetmaker. If that cachetmaker is of recent origin, this is relatively easy. To collect FDCs of an older cachetmaker may take years of searching to complete a collection. Many current cachetmakers, especially the larger ones such as Fleetwood and Artcraft, make collecting a simple chore by automatically supplying FDCs from a deposit account.

Another FDC collecting specialty is "first cachets," defined as the first one produced for an FDC by every cachetmaker. As of this writing, more than 4,000 different first cachets have been identified, and the list grows longer each year.

Handpainted cachets and silk cachets offer other specializing opportunities. Many collectors even produce their own cachets for each issue for a personal collection. If this appeals to you, the American First Day Cover Society (see "Stamp Organizations") has a do-it-yourself handbook to help beginners create their own cachet designs.

However they collect, most FDC fans prefer that the FDCs be unaddressed. These usually sell for much more than covers with a name and address, undoubtedly because collector demand for them is greater. For those collectors who make and service their own FDCs, the use of a pencil or peelable label is advised. Either can be removed when the post office returns the cover, leaving it in a pristine state.

Topicals are also found in FDC collecting. This most often takes the form of collecting all cachets produced for one stamp or a topical category of stamps. Color also can become a cachet topic. One collector saves only those cachets that have silver or gold in the cachet colors. The subdivisions and specialties are endless, and the FDC collector can easily regulate the collection's size and cost by the approach taken.

Recently, the USPS has been allowing first-day canceling of covers up to 30 days or more after the actual first-day release of the stamp.

At least part of the reason for that policy has been the tremendous growth in the demand for FDCs. FDC demand now makes it almost impossible for either a small post office or the Philatelic Sales Division in Washington, D.C., to cancel all FDCs within 24 hours.

FDC purists feel that this post-canceling practice makes these covers questionable in their FDC status. For such collectors, unofficial FDCs are the answer, but to create them takes a bit of doing. A new stamp must be purchased at the first-day-of-issue site and transported on the same day to another, perhaps nearby, post office. A regular cancel is then secured. Though it will not bear the first-day wording in the cancellation, such a cover leaves no doubt that the stamp really was canceled on the first day of its release.

Newcomers to the FDC hobby should be aware that frauds and fakery exist in FDC collecting, just as they do in almost every hobby. It is possible for a cover faker to buy an uncacheted FDC of the late 1920s for a few dollars, add a cachet to it, and then sell it for a premium by offering it as an original product of that era. As with any hobby, knowledge should be acquired before spending a great deal of money on costlier, older FDCs.

Foreign FDCs. While the U.S. Postal Service does not create its own FDCs on a regular basis, many foreign postal administrations do. These official, government-produced FDCs are offered — usually with a cachet — to collectors at the time when new stamps go on sale.

Canada is a good example of such a country. Canada Post has been supplying FDCs through its Philatelic Service for several years, with the result that private cachetmakers now have all but disappeared in Canada. In those larger foreign nations where no such government FDCs are offered, the collector usually can find private servicers.

Since foreign regulations about FDCs are ever-changing, collectors of foreign FDCs are advised to ask about such services directly from the foreign postal administrations involved. Names and addresses of these can be found under the section entitled "Worldwide Postal Administrations and Agencies."

Postal History

Postal history collecting can be succinctly described as the amassing and the study of material that shows the use of postage stamps, handstamped, manuscript and machine markings that trace pieces of mail through old or new postal systems. Such systems have existed for some 5,000 years. Postal history material may be anything from a papyrus piece from ancient Egypt to a modern-day cover that appears in your mailbox.

More than 3,500 years before Christ walked the roads of Galilee, letters composed of cuneiform characters from Egypt, Assyria and Mesopotamia were being dispatched from one place to another. More than 700 years before Christ, the Chinese were operating a mail system of sorts over the trackless expanses of the imperial Chinese empire. The University of Paris had its own postal service in the 12th century. The German Hanseatic League ran mail drops in the 13th century. Postal history material predates stamp collecting by at least 50 centuries.

Yet, the collecting of postal history — old as it is — was really an outgrowth of stamp collecting. The first collecting urges of this hobby were stirred by stamps, not tablets or envelopes. They held that nothing should be saved except clean, mint postage stamps. Stamps already canceled and defaced, including those on covers, were at first regarded as useless scraps not worth saving.

Long after the stamp hobby began, a few collectors turned their attention to the markings, cancels and envelopes that revealed exactly how postal routines operated. Once collectors made the leap from mint stamps to the collecting of postal history items, a boom developed for pre-1847 U.S. stampless covers — their rate and route markings, cancels and other postal information thereon.

Mail had existed in the United States since colonial times. A new mania arose for the postal history collectors of the 1800s: finding and understanding these covers that told of the beginnings of a U.S. postal operation. Others began searching for similar artifacts of foreign mail systems.

Unlike their fellow stamp collectors, postal historians seek more than just stamps. They are searching out and reliving the use of stamps, postmarkings and letters that tell a story of the development of postal services for a hamlet, state or nation. Such a service may have used runners, balloons, stagecoaches, the Pony Express, dogsleds, autos, wagons, dirigibles, airplanes or satellites.

If a postal historian is concentrating on a particular locale rather than a method of service, he will seek examples of mail involving the various post offices that lived, grew or died during the postal development of that area.

A postal history collector usually will not bother with first-flight or first-day covers. They are souvenirs, often created by collectors, to mark a specific event. Postal historians seek samples of fact-revealing, everyday mail — not the relics of special events.

Advertising covers are beautiful and certainly collectible, but postal history often ignores them. A collection of postmarks, flag cancels, pictorial cancels and the like may be interesting — but they are not postal history.

Many of those collections might be arranged into a postal history subject if — and only if — they were lined up to tell a story of the post in a given area, certain time period or by a certain means. Postal history is almost always chronological, even when it is the recap of a special type of service, such as registered mail.

One longtime postal history collector maintains that the physical condition of a cover is of minor consideration. She ranks condition as third in what she looks for in a postal history piece. The first and second requisites are what she describes as a "large P" and a "small h." The "P" stands for postal interest; that always come first. The cover should tell a usage story, perhaps with unusual markings, rates or routes. The little "h" stands for history. Is the cover a true historical part of that area or of a special service?

This collector recalls finding a rare Stephen Douglas free-frank cover. It illustrated her own collecting subject of free franking in Illinois. The fact that it was signed by Douglas added the "small h" historical touch that made it even more desirable.

Another postal history collector states his standards eloquently. "The covers I want are the day-in, day-out containers for missives of love, logistics, politics, friendship, philosophy and history. They were not created or recognized for any other hobby value. They are pure romance and pure postal history."

In other words, the stamp itself is of small importance — usually.

An intriguing aspect of postal history collecting is that some of the best covers are often found in a dealer's junk box. All dealers cannot realize that a Tremainsville, Ohio, cancel is really a sought-after forerunner of the Toledo post office. Not all dealers can know that an unrecognized cancellation may come from a DPO (discontinued post office) that a collector has been seeking for years.

The postal historian who knows his subject well can pick up more bargains than a stamp collector will ever run across. Some rare and outstanding pieces have been discovered in old office buildings, ancient files in basements or attics and among hand-me-down correspondence within a family.

Much material that would be disallowed in a competitive stamp exhibit is eminently desirable in a postal history showing. Says Ernst M. Cohn, an expert in postal history, "What is just collateral material in a stamp exhibit is not merely collateral in postal history. Decrees, sailing schedules and postal rate tables are wanted and allowed — but only originals. No copies, please."

As a postal history collector, you become — not just a stamp and cover collector — but something of an expert historian on your own city, county, state or a method of postal handling. It requires much knowledge of your chosen subject. Most postal history collectors have evolved from stamp collecting. Postal history has given them an entire new approach to what many consider a step up from pure stamp collecting.

Souvenir Cards

Privately made souvenir cards have been known for decades. They can be of postcard size or larger. Many bear a stamp or group of stamps. Not until 1960, however, did any official stamp-producing government entity produce what are termed "official souvenir cards." The first to do so was the U.S. Post Office Department and later, the U.S. Postal Service. The Bureau of Engraving and Printing started producing its own souvenir cards — both for the stamp and coin fields — in 1969. In 1972 the United Nations Postal Administration followed suit.

These are the only official producers of these non-postal, but highly collectible, cardboard souvenirs of stamps and stamp collecting. Private souvenir cards abound today, produced for national and regional stamp shows and bourses. Only those made by the USPOD, the USPS, and the BEP are within the scope of this chapter.

At a 1960 First International Philatelic Congress, held in Barcelona, Spain, the Post Office Department offered its so-called Barcelona souvenir card free to any show attendee who wanted one. These six-by-eight-inch cards featured the "Landing of Columbus," an engraving taken from the reverse side of an 1875 $5 National Bank Note.

They were almost totally ignored by the showgoers, even though they were free. So many were left over following the Barcelona show that the postal employee assigned to ship the USPOD's exhibit back to Washington used the cards as stuffing for the packing crates. Today, that shunned Barcelona card lists at $375 in mint condition.

Catalogs often show this card as "Number 2," listing a card produced for the Postage Stamp Design Exhibition in Philadelphia in 1954 as "Number 1." Most serious souvenir card collectors disagree, maintaining that the Philadelphia card was strictly unofficial compared to the Barcelona item.

Since the debut of its Barcelona card, the USPOD and USPS have sponsored more than 65 additional souvenir cards, but have placed a heavy emphasis on cards for foreign stamp shows. In 1987 the USPS began overprinting postal cards for these exhibitions. The BEP faces the same confusion among collectors and catalogs as the USPS. Which BEP card was first?

Catalogs may show the SIPEX 1966 card, which bore three multicolored views of Washington, D.C., and was inscribed "Sixth International Philatelic Exhibition." This card was wholly sponsored by the union printers of the Bureau, however, not by the BEP itself. For that reason, most collectors regard the SANDIPEX souvenir card honoring a 1969 San Diego stamp show as the BEP's first.

Both the USPS and BEP have been victims of occasional errors on their souvenir cards — just as with stamps. The initial printings of the USPS 1976 ITALIA card had Giuseppe Garibaldi's name spelled "Guiseppe." The BEP's NAPEX 80 card is minus the comma the BEP always puts between "Washington" and "D.C." Other historical errors, printing gremlins and even cancellation mistakes have plagued both issuing houses.

Most souvenir cards require special mounting since they are so large, usually about 8 1/2- by 10 1/2-inches. With its NAPEX 80 card, the BEP reduced its souvenir cards to 6-by-8-inches — but that wasn't to last for long. In 1984 the Bureau went back to the larger size it has always maintained for all its numismatic souvenirs.

Souvenir cards may offer collectors the chance to own official reproductions of some very rare stamps, both foreign and domestic. Usually, however, these stamps are reproduced without any denomination of value.

Those interested in learning more about these official, but non-postal cards may wish to contact the Souvenir Card Collectors Society, Box 7116, Rochester, Minn. 55903.

Stamp Albums

Most collectors house their stamps in albums. An album is one of the most important accessories used in collecting stamps. An album helps a collector organize what might be a confusing array of stamps and can serve as a basic stamp identifier.

A great variety of stamp albums exist. This chapter discusses the basic types of albums. Most albums and pages are available through stamp accessory suppliers. Check the display and classified advertising sections of a current issue of *Linn's Stamp News*.

Some albums have fixed pages that cannot be rearranged. They are usually the best albums for beginners. Once a beginning collector learns the basics of stamp collecting, he is usually ready to use a larger album with movable pages. The most basic fixed-page album is the **Scott Stamp Collecting Album**. This is part of a kit that can be thought of as a project for a beginner. The album is a 16-page, staple-bound pamphlet and includes spaces for modern stamps of the United States and Canada. The kit includes a packet of U.S. stamps, stamp hinges and *Linn's* booklet for beginners, *Stamp Collecting Made Easy*.

Another beginner's album is the **Treasury of Stamps Album**. It is a two-fold brochure of six pages. The United States Postal Service produces it each year for distribution through the Benjamin Franklin stamp clubs organized in many schools.

The following categories list stamp albums alphabetically by title. Each entry includes notes on the album's binding and arrangement. Many of the notes are from publishers' catalogs or advertisements. Not all albums were actually examined. The addresses of the album publishers or their U.S. distributors are at the end of the chapter.

Basic Worldwide Albums

Adventurer II, H.E. Harris. A softbound version of the Traveler album of H.E. Harris; bound like a book; pages are not movable and are printed on both sides; 272 pages.

The Courier Worldwide Postage Stamp Album, Harco. Bound so that pages are not movable; 68 pages printed on both sides; world map on back cover.

The Planet Earth World-Wide Postage Stamp Album, Harco. Plastic spiral bound; 200 pages printed on both sides; includes more coverage of United States and Canada than Harco's Courier Album.

Traveler Album, H.E. Harris. Looseleaf; 272 pages printed on both sides.

Basic United States Albums

The Eagle United States Postage Stamp Album, Harco. Plastic spiral bound; 70 pages printed on both sides.

Independence Album, H.E. Harris. Same content as the Harris Liberty album, except United Nations is not included; pages are printed on both sides.

Liberty Album, H.E. Harris. Includes U.S. regular issues, commemoratives, airmails, special delivery issues, postage dues, hunting permit stamps and selected cut squares; also includes pages for United Nations; pages printed on one side; separate pages and matching binders available for booklet panes, coil pairs or line pairs, U.S. possessions, postal stationery entires and plate blocks.

Minuteman Stamp Album, Scott. Two-post binder; pages printed on one side; includes regular issues, commemoratives, airmails, special delivery issues, special handling, postage dues, Offices in China, officials, parcel post, hunting permit stamps and United Nations; annual supplements.

Old Glory United States Postage Stamp Album, Harco. Looseleaf in plastic channel binder; fits standard three-ring binder, approximately 70 pages printed on both sides; annual supplements.

Pony Express Album, Scott. Similar to the Scott Minuteman album, but pages are printed on both sides; three-ring binder.

Stars & Stripes Stamp Album, Scott. Looseleaf in three-ring binder; pages printed on both sides; includes spaces for selected United States stamps of the 1960s through 1980s, with some blank spaces to mount other stamps.

Intermediate and Advanced United States Albums

See also section for single-country albums.

The All-American Stamp Album, Minkus. Standard pages printed on one side; two-post binder; Minkus catalog numbers; includes historical notes with the stamp illustrations; spaces for regular issues, commemoratives, airmails, special deliveries, parcel post issues, special handling, postage dues, selected cut squares and stationery entires, booklet panes, Confederate States and United Nations.

National Album, Scott. Standard pages printed on one side punched for rectangular-post binder; includes spaces for provisionals, regular issues, commemoratives, airmails, special deliveries, parcel post issues, certified mail, special handling, postage dues, offices abroad, newspaper stamps, carrier stamps, hunting permit stamps and Confederate States; separate pages available for plate blocks, booklet panes, postal cards, cut squares, U.S. possessions, U.S. trust territories, plate number coils, federal and state duck stamps, federal duck plate blocks, United Nations singles and postal stationery, U.N. imprint blocks and Ryukyu Islands.

PNC Album, Stamps 'n' Stuff. Pages for plate number coil strips of five; fit any three-ring binder; blank pages available.

Presidents United States Stamp Album, Harco. Looseleaf in plastic channel binder; approximately 140 pages printed on one side; pages fit standard three-ring binder; annual supplements.

United States of America Postage Stamp Album, Harco. Looseleaf, two-post album; approximately 140 pages printed on on side; annual supplements.

U.S. Plate Number Coils, Jona Enterprises. Pages for plate number coil strips of five; pages fit any three-ring binder, 65-pound paper stock; supplements available.

White Ace Historical Album for the Stamps of the United States, The Washington Press. Pages have rounded corners and are housed in three-ring binders; historical text below each stamp illustration; pages printed on one side; pages for commemoratives, definitives, airmails, American bicentennial and revolution stamps, booklet panes, panels, souvenir sheets, Bureau souvenir cards, precancels, duck stamps, Canal Zone, Confederate States.

U. S. Revenue Albums

The Aldrich Match and Medicine Revenue Stamp Album Pages, Michael Aldrich. Looseleaf, 60 pages for medicine stamps, 32 pages for match, perfume or playing card stamps; both sections available separately; three-hole punched for standard binder.

Federal Duck Stamp Album Pages, White Ace. Looseleaf, colored borders; three-hole punched; pages have rounded corners.

Harshman & Houk State Duck Stamp Album, Harshman & Houk. Looseleaf; four volumes; one page per stamp; pages in full color; textual information on artist and duck; each set of albums is numbered and signed.

Hunter Type State Duck Stamp Pages, Sam Houston Philatelics. Pages only; fit Scott rectangular-post binder.

Combination Federal and State Duck Stamp Album, Scott. Looseleaf, standard or hingless; more than 80 pages, rectangular-post binder, hingeless pages available with black or clear mounts; regular supplements. See also Scott's National album.

Scott Revenue Pages, Revenue Specialist. Standard Scott National album pages for R, RB-RL, RV, RFV, RJA, RVB, RY, PN, PS, S, TS and WS numbers; 132 pages, available with or without binders.

Stearns & Fink Federal Duck Stamp Album, Stearns and Fink. Looseleaf; two volumes; one stamp per page; pages for RW37 and up are in color; textual information on artist and duck; regular supplements.

Canada Albums

See also section for single-country albums.

Canada and Provinces Album, H.E. Harris. Two-post binder; includes regular issues, commemoratives, airmails, special deliveries, officials, and provinces.

Canada Durable Stamp Album, Harco. Looseleaf; three-ring binder; more than 150 pages printed on one-side; heavier paper stock than Harco's Unity Canada Stamp Album; annual supplements.

Canada National Stamp Album, Harco. Looseleaf, three-post binder; more than 100 pages printed on one side; coat-of-arms design at head of each page; annual supplements.

Canada Parliament Stamp Album, Harco. Looseleaf, three-post binder; more than 100 pages printed on one side; heavier paper stock than Harco's Canada National Stamp Album; parliament building design at head of each page; annual supplements.

The Constitution Canada Postage Stamp Album, Harco. Looseleaf; plastic snap binding; more than 70 pages; fits any three-ring binder; pages printed on both sides.

Dominion of Canada Stamp Album, Harco. Looseleaf; three-ring binder; more than 150 pages; Canadian map design at head of each page; annual supplements.

Master Canada Stamp Album, Scott. Two-post binder; pages printed on one side and include Scott catalog numbers and descriptive text for each stamp or set.

Unity Canada Stamp Album, Harco. Looseleaf; three-ring binder; more than 150 pages printed on one side in full color; coat-of-arms design at head of each page; annual supplements.

White Ace Canada Album Pages, The Washington Press. Three-post binder, pages printed on one side; uses Scott numbers; separate pages for regular issues, commemoratives/airmails, Newfoundland.

Intermediate and Advanced Worldwide Albums

Citation Album, H.E. Harris. Single volume, two-post binder, pages printed on both sides. Space for 85,000 stamps.

The Comprehensive World Wide Stamp Album, Minkus. Two-post binding; pages printed on both sides; United States pages include Minkus catalog numbers; spaces for more than 40,250 stamps.

International Postage Stamp Album, Scott. Two-post binders; through 1988, 23 parts housed in 33 binders; parts 1A and 1B cover 1840-1940; subsequest parts cover stamp issues for 10 years or fewer; beginning with 1978, one year's issues per part; pages printed both sides.

Olympian Stamp Album, Harco. Two volumes; looseleaf; two-post binders; more than 1,000 pages; annual supplements.

Statesman Album and **Senior Statesman**, H.E. Harris. Statesman houses 20,000 stamps; Senior Statesman houses 45,000 stamps; both are two-post with pages printed on both sides.

Standard World Stamp Album, H.E. Harris. Two volumes; two-post binders; pages printed on both sides; space for 90,000 stamps.

World Deluxe Stamp Album, Harco. Looseleaf; two-post binder; more than 360 pages printed on both sides; annual supplements.

World Senior Stamp Album, Harco. Looseleaf; two-post binder; more than 490 pages printed on both sides; annual supplements.

World Travel Stamp Album, Harco. Looseleaf; two-post binder; more than 200 pages printed on both sides; annual supplements.

Single Country Albums

Davo. Hingless or standard pages; albums are two-post; pages scored at left for flexibility; hingeless pages have mounts for individual stamps; annual supplements; pages available for most of the popularly collected countries of the world.

Ka-Be. Hingeless. Two-post, multi-ring or springback binders; pages are double-linen hinged; individual mounts for each stamp; annual supplements; pages available for most of the popularly collected countries of the world.

Lighthouse. Hingeless. Pages housed in springback binders or in post binders; post binders have a two-post base with an additional three-post retainer that inserts over the top of the pages; stamps have individual mounts; pages have large perforations at left for flexibility; annual supplements; pages available for most of the popularly collected countries of the world.

Lindner. Hingeless. Albums use an 18-ring binder; stamp illustrations are printed on one side of a page; a single clear, side-mounted tip-on with horizontal pockets holds stamps so that they can be viewed from both sides; no between-stamp vertical weld spots in pockets; annual supplements; pages available for most of the popularly collected countries of the world.

Minkus. Standard pages. Two-post binder; pages printed on one side; annual supplements.

Safe. Hingeless. Binders are 14-ring looseleaf; pages have stamp illustrations printed on one side; stamps are housed in a full-page clear interleaf and are viewable from the front and the back; interleaf has between-stamp vertical weld spots; annual supplements; pages available for most of the popularly collected countries of the world.

Scott. Standard pages. Scott Specialty Series albums have two rectangular posts; pages printed on one side; pages include Scott catalog numbers; annual supplements; pages available for most of the popularly collected countries of the world.

Stanley Gibbons. Standard pages. Single-country albums are four-ring looseleaf; pages printed on one side; single-country albums are Great Britain, Channel Islands, Isle of Man, Canada, Australia and New Zealand. The Great Britain Windsor album is three volumes in springback binders; pages printed on both sides, with stamp illustrations and Gibbons catalog text on left hand pages and space for mounting stamps on right hand pages. Gibbons hingeless albums exist for Great Britain, Guernsey, Alderney, Australia, Canada and New Zealand. Gibbons also makes the single-volume King George VI Stamp Album and the two-volume New Imperial Stamp Album for stamps of the British Commonwealth. The former covers British Commonwealth stamps issued during the reign of King George VI. The latter covers 1840 through the reign of King George V.

White-Ace, The Washington Press. Standard pages with rounded corners; decorative borders with historical text on each stamp; pages for Bahamas, Channel Islands, Faroe Islands, Ghana, Ireland, Isle of Man, Israel, Japan, Marshall Islands, Micronesia, Monaco, Netherlands, New Zealand, Palau, Roman States, Ryukyu Islands, Togo Republic, United Nations, Vatican City.

Topical Albums

The Black American Stamp Album, Austin Enterprises. Spaces for stamps from 73 countries picturing Black Americans.

Disney Collecting Kit, Brookman/Barrett & Worthen. A 112-page album available in two kits that include stamps, hinges and *Linn's Stamp Collecting Made Easy*; difference between two kits is number of stamps included.

The Disney World of Postage Stamps Album, Inter-Governmental Philatelic Corp. Looseleaf in three-ring binder; country headings with Disney design at head of pages; card-weight pages.

Pharmacy in Philately Album, American Institute of the History of Pharmacy. Looseleaf, 80 pages to fit any three-ring binder.

White-Ace Topical Pages, The Washington Press. Standard pages with rounded corners; decorative borders with historical text on each stamp; pages for British omnibus sets, Winston Churchill, Europa, International Year of the Child, Moon Landing, Pope Paul VI, Rotary International, Universal Postal Union 100th Anniversary; other pages available with borders only for most general topics.

Album Publishers or Agents

American Institute of the History of Pharmacy
425 N. Charter St.
Madison, Wis. 53706-1508

Austin Enterprises
Box 3717
Cherry Hill, N.J. 08034-0571

Benjamin Franklin Stamp Club
United States Postal Service
Washington, D.C. 20265-9994

Brookman/Barrett & Worthen
10 Chestnut Drive
Bedford, N.H. 03102-5900

Davo
Harold Cohn & Co. Inc.
3224 N. Halsted St.
Chicago, Ill. 60657

Harco
Harold Cohn & Co. Inc.
3224 N. Halsted St.
Chicago, Ill. 60657

H.E. Harris & Co. Inc.
170 West Road
Lafayette West Industrial Park
Box 7082
Portsmouth, N.H. 03801

Harshman and Houk
Richard Houk
30 Devon Hill Lane
Granite City, Ill. 62040

Jona Enterprises
Box 189
Camp Hill, Pa. 17001-0189

Inter-Governmental Philatelic Corp.
460 W. 34th St.
New York, N.Y. 10001

Ka-Be
Harry Edelman
111-37 Lefferts Blvd.
South Ozone Park, N.Y. 11420

Lighthouse Publications Inc.
274 Washington Ave.
Box 705
Hackensack, N.J. 07602-0705

Lindner Publications Inc.
Box 922
Syracuse, N.Y. 13201

Michael Aldrich
Box 13323
St. Paul, Minn. 55113

Minkus Publications
Box 1228
Fort Mill, S.C. 29715

Revenue Specialist
Box 15565
Chattanooga, Tenn. 37415

Scott Publishing Co.
Box 828
Sidney, Ohio 45365

Safe Publications Inc.
Box 263
Southampton, Pa. 18966

Sam Houston Philatelics
Box 820087
Houston, Texas 77282-0087

Stamps 'n' Stuff
2700 University, Suite 204
W. Des Moines, Iowa 50265

Stanley Gibbons
Lighthouse Publications Inc.
274 Washington Ave.
Box 705
Hackensack, N.J. 07602-0705

Stearns and Fink
Russell A. Fink Gallery
9843 Gunston Road
Box 250
Lorton, Va. 22079

The Washington Press
2 Vreeland Road
Florham Park, N.J. 07932

Stamp Condition Terms

Stamp Descriptions

Stamp descriptions in retail lists or in auctions usually use abbreviations or symbols. These abbreviations or symbols provide general information regarding a stamp's condition, centering and gum.

For example, the description "M, NH, OG, VF" means that a stamp is mint, never hinged, with original gum and with very-fine centering. Special features or faults are usually described in greater detail. Stamp characteristics referred to by these terms and abbreviations are described in the following sections: general condition, centering and gum. Symbols appear in the section: Symbols and Abbreviations Guide.

General Condition

A stamp's general condition relates to whether or not it has been used on mail.

M — MINT — A stamp that has never been postally used or hinged. It is clean and has full, undisturbed original gum, if it was issued with gum.

UNUSED — A stamp that has never been postally used. It may have been hinged or lacks gum. It may have undergone some other change since it was issued that prevents it from being called mint. These changes can include dirt on the face, fingerprints in the gum, stains or similar changes.

U — USED — A stamp that has been postally used. Used stamps usually bear a cancel and have no gum. Many catalogs, dealers and collectors do not distinguish between used stamps and canceled-to-order stamps. CTOs are canceled stamps, usually with full original gum.

Centering

Centering describes the space between a stamp's design or border and its outer edges.

S — SUPERB — The design is perfectly centered on the face of the stamp. Opposite margins are equal.

XF — EXTRA FINE — The design is nearly perfectly centered, with all margins at least three-fourths equal to what they would be on a SUPERB centered copy.

VF — VERY FINE — The design is well-centered, but noticeably off-center. All margins are at least one-half equal to what they would be on a SUPERB centered copy.

F — FINE — Perforations are not into the design, but the design is well off-center. All margins are not more than one-half equal to what they would be on a SUPERB centered copy, but the perforations do not intrude on the frame or design of the stamp.

AVE — AVERAGE — The perforations cut slightly into the frame or design of the stamp.

FAIR — The perforations are well into the design.

P — POOR — Stamps described as poor are usually space fillers. They often have other faults in addition to being way off-center. Some rare or valuable items might be only available in poor condition.

Gum

A stamp's gum characteristics refer to the absence or presence of gum, the state of the gum and the presence of stamp hinges.

OG — ORIGINAL GUM — The stamp has the gum it had when it was issued. Some stamps may be described as having partial OG.

RG — REGUMMED — New gum has been applied to the stamp, either to part of it or all of it.

NG — NO GUM — Either the stamp was issued without gum, or the gum has been removed.

NH — NEVER HINGED — A stamp that has never been hinged. The gum is not disturbed in any way. A stamp described as NH is not necessarily OG.

LH — LIGHTLY HINGED — The stamp has had a peelable hinge applied. There are only slight traces of disturbance where the hinge has been removed.

HH — HEAVILY HINGED — A hinged stamp with a large hinge remnant or many hinge remnants. A major section of gum may be missing gum where a hinge has been. If the stamp paper is thinned, the thin should be listed as a fault.

Faults

Any fault in the stamp should be listed in the description, or the buyer will expect none. These include thins, short perfs, pulled perfs, creases, tears, stains, ink marks, pinholes, or unusual wear. Other sources of faults are possible and should be listed in a stamp description.

This listing of stamp condition terms constitutes the recommendations of *Linn's*. Dealers or collectors often make modifications to this listing. These are suggested guidelines, not absolute facts. Some terms are matters of judgment: centering is a good example. These Uniform Stamp Condition Terms are presented to aid dealers and collectors in the honest and fair appraisal of the condition of a stamp or a set.

Scott Catalog Information

The following is an explanation of how Scott catalog prices are established. This information appears in each volume of the Scott catalogs. Stamp collectors should be familiar with this information before buying or selling stamps.

Catalog Value

The Scott catalog value is a retail price, what you would expect to pay for the stamp in a grade of fine-very fine. The value listed is a reference that reflects recent actual dealer selling prices.

Dealer retail price lists, public auction results, published prices in advertising, and individual solicitation of retail prices from dealers, collectors and specialty organizations have been used in establishing the values found in the catalog.

Collectors should use this catalog as a guide in their own buying and selling. The actual price you pay for a stamp may be higher or lower than the catalog value because of one or more of the following: the amount of personal service a dealer offers, increased interest in the country or topic represented by the stamp or set, whether an item is a "loss leader," part of a special sale, or otherwise is being sold for a short period of time at a lower price, or if at a public auction you are able to obtain an item inexpensively because of little interest in the item at that time.

For unused stamps, more recent issues are valued as never hinged, with the beginning point determined on a country-by-country basis. Notes to show the beginning points are prominently noted in the text of the catalog.

Grade

A stamp's grade and condition are crucial to its value. Values quoted in the Scott catalog are for stamps graded at fine-very fine and with no faults. The accompanying illustrations show an example of a fine-very fine grade between the grades immediately below and above it: fine and very fine.

FINE stamps have the design noticeably off-center on two sides. Imperforate stamps may have small margins, and earlier issues may show the design touching one edge of the stamp. Used stamps may have heavier than usual cancellations.

FINE-VERY FINE stamps may be somewhat off-center on one side, or only slightly off-center on two sides. Imperforate stamps will have two margins

at least normal size and the design will not touch the edge. *Early issues of a country may be printed in such a way that the design naturally is very close to the edges.* Used stamps will not have a cancellation that detracts from the design. This is the grade used to establish Scott catalog values.

VERY FINE stamps may be slightly off-center on one side, with the design well clear of the edge. Imperforate stamps will have three margins at least normal size. Used stamps will have light or otherwise neat cancellations.

Condition

The above definitions describe *grade*, which is centering and (for used stamps) cancellation. *Condition* refers to the soundness of the stamp, i.e., faults, repairs, and other factors influencing price.

Copies of a stamp that are of a lesser grade and/or condition trade at lower prices. Those of exceptional quality often command higher prices.

Factors that increase the value of a stamp include exceptionally wide margins, particularly fresh color, and the presence of selvage.

Factors other than faults that decrease the value of a stamp include missing gum or regumming, hinge remnant, foreign object adhering to gum, natural inclusion, or a straight edge.

Faults include a missing piece, tear, clipped perforation, pin or other hole, surface scuff, thin spot, crease, toning, oxidation or other form of color changeling, short or pulled perforation, stains or such man-made changes as reperforation or the chemical removal or lightening of a cancellation.

Scott Publishing Co. recognizes that there is no formal, enforced grading scheme for postage stamps, and that the final price you pay for a stamp or obtain for a stamp you are selling will be determined by individual agreement at the time of the transaction.

Terms and Abbreviations

Glossary of Philatelic Terms

This glossary defines those terms most frequently encountered by stamp collectors and cover collectors. Precise definitions for many philatelic terms do not exist. One collector, dealer or society may define a term in one way, while others will use the term in a slightly different way.

This glossary defines nearly 300 terms. For special uses of some of the terms listed and defined here, contact the appropriate specialist collector group. They are listed in the Organizations chapter of this almanac.

- A -

Accessories — Any of the large variety of collecting tools and aids. Accessories include hinges, mounts, stamp tongs, perforation gauges, stock books, magnifiers and philatelic literature. Stamp albums and catalogs can also be regarded as accessories.

Adhesive — A word generally referring to a stamp. An adhesive is a label affixed to an article to prepay postal fees, in contrast to a design printed directly on an article, as with postal stationery. An adhesive can also refer to a registration label or other label added to a cover.

Admirals — A nickname for three British Commonwealth definitive series, those of Canada, 1912-25 (Scott 104-34); New Zealand, 1926 (182-84); and Rhodesia, 1913-19 (119-38). These stamps depict King George V in naval uniform.

Admirals

Aerogramme — The official Universal Postal Union designation for an airletter sheet. These sheets, with gummed flaps, are written on and folded into themselves to form their own envelope and are carried at less than the letter airmail rate. No enclosures are permitted.

Aerophilately — A specialized area of collecting concentrating on stamps or covers carried by air.

Agency — 1) The extraterritorial post offices maintained at various times by governments in the territory of other governments. Examples are the post offices maintained by many European powers in the Turkish Empire until 1923. 2) An official or private organization that publicizes or sells new issues of stamps on behalf of stamp-issuing entities.

Air Labels — Air labels, or etiquettes, are standard-sized blue labels used by UPU member nations to denote airmail carriage. They are inscribed "Par Avion" (French for "By Airmail"). The text usually includes the same message in the language of the native country. Air labels also are adhesives issued by private organizations for specific, unofficial flights. See also Semiofficial.

Airmail — The carriage of mail by air. The first regular airmail service began in 1870, when mail was carried from Paris, France, then besieged by German forces, over enemy lines by balloon. The first airmail stamp was issued by Italy in 1917 (Italy Scott C1).

Albino — An uninked impression made by a printing plate. Such errors are scarce on stamps. They are more often found on postal stationery.

Album — Albums are binders, usually with pages, for the mounting and display of stamps and covers. Albums come in many sizes, styles and themes. See the Album section in this almanac.

Album Weed — In general, a forged stamp. It also refers to unusual items that resemble postage stamps but were not intended to pay postage, like publicity labels and bogus issues. *Album Weeds* is the title of a reference on forged stamps, written by the Rev. R. Brisco Earee.

Ambulante — This word means "moving" in Spanish and other Romance languages. It appears in cancellations and indicates that the item was processed by a mobile post office.

Aniline — Ink with a coal-tar base. Such inks were used in stamp printing to prevent erasure of cancellations and reuse of stamps. Aniline inks are very sensitive and may dissolve in water or other liquids or chemicals.

Approvals — Priced selections of stamps sent to collectors by mail. The collector purchases the items he chooses, returning the balance with payment for those kept.

Army Post Office (APO) — An official United States post office for use by U.S. military units abroad. An army post office or military post office is set up to distribute mail to and from military personnel. Locations are indicated by numbers only to prevent revealing personnel locations. The locations become generally known after a war is over.

Arrow — On many sheets, small arrow-like markings appear in the selvage, generally serving as guides for the cutting of the sheets into predetermined units. Some collectors save stamps or blocks displaying these marks.

Arrow Block

Art Paper — A very fine paper with a specially prepared surface that allows the controlled application of ink or pigment.

As Is — A term written in auction descriptions and spoken or written during a retail transaction. It indicates that an item or lot is sold without guarantee or return privilege. Stamps are usually sold "as is" when they are in poor condition or are possibly not genuine.

Authentication Mark — A marking, such as initials, placed on the reverse of a stamp examined and certified to be genuine by an expert. Such markings do not detract from the value of the stamps when they represent the endorsement of recognized authorities.

- B -

Backprint — Printing on the reverse of a stamp. Some countries have printed advertising or messages on the backs of stamps.

Backstamp — A postmark applied to mail by the receiving post office or by a post office handling the piece while it is in transit. Backstamps are usually on the back of a cover.

Backstamp

Bank Mixture — A high-quality mixture of stamps. It generally represents clippings from the correspondence of banks and other businesses with extensive overseas business, and thus includes a relatively high proportion of foreign stamps of high face value. See also Mission Mixture.

Bantams — The nickname of the South African definitive series of 1942-43 (Scott 90-97). Wartime economy measures required stamps of small size to conserve paper.

Batonne — A wove or laid paper with watermark-like lines deliberately added in the papermaking process and intended as a guide for handwriting.

Bicolored Stamps — Stamps printed in two colors.

Bilingual — Refers to stamps inscribed in two languages. Most Canadian stamps include both English and French text. South African stamps are sometimes in both English and Afrikaans.

Bisect — A stamp cut or perforated

Bilingual (invert)

into two parts, each half representing half the face value of the original stamp. Officially authorized bisects have often been used during temporary shortages of commonly used denominations. Unauthorized bisects appear frequently on mail from some countries in some periods. Bisects are usually collected on full cover with the stamp tied by a cancel. At times, some countries have permitted trisects or quadrisects.

Bisect (on piece)

Bishop Mark — The earliest postmark, introduced by Henry Bishop in England circa 1661. A Bishop Mark was used to indicate the month and day that a letter was received by a post office. It encouraged prompt delivery by letter carriers.

Black Jack — The nickname of the United States 2¢ black Andrew Jackson stamp, issued between 1863 and 1875.

Black Jack

Blind Perforation — Perforations that have been only lightly impressed by the perforating pins, leaving the paper intact, but cut or with a faint impression. Some stamps that appear to be imperforate really are not if they have blind perfs. Stamps with blind perfs are minor varieties carrying little, if any, price premium over normally perforated copies.

Block — A unit of four or more unsevered stamps, including at least two stamps both vertically and horizontally. Most commonly a block refers to a block of four, or a block of stamps two high and two wide.

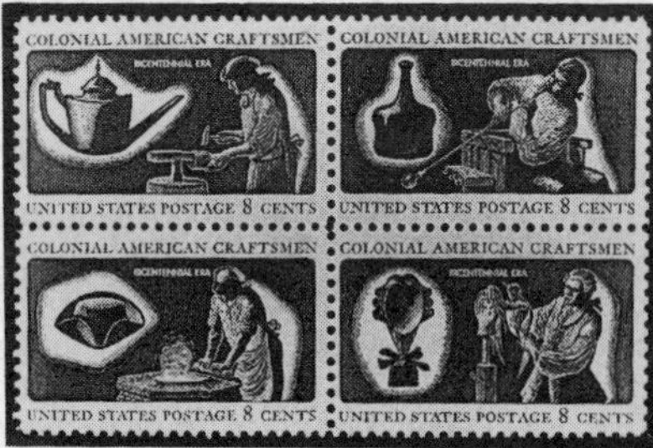

Block

Bluenose — The nickname for the Canadian 50¢ issue of 1929, picturing the schooner Bluenose, Canada Scott 158.

Bluenose

Bogus — A completely fictitious stamp-like label, created solely for sale to collectors. Bogus issues include labels for non-existent countries, non-existent values appended to regularly issued sets and issues for nations or entities without postal systems.

Bond Paper — A security paper of high quality, used to a limited extent in early stamp printing. Originally, bond was made from rags. The modern paper used for first-day covers is usually a bond quality paper.

Booklet — A unit of one or more small panes or blocks (known as booklet panes) glued, stitched or stapled together between thin card covers to form a convenient unit for mailers to purchase and carry. The first officially issued booklet was produced by Luxembourg in 1895.

Bourse — A meeting of stamp collectors and/or dealers, where stamps and covers are sold or exchanged. A bourse usually has no competitive exhibits of stamps or covers. Almost all stamp exhibits, though, do include a dealer bourse.

Bull's-Eyes — 1) The nickname for the first issue of Brazil, 1843 (Scott 1-3). The similar but smaller issues are called goat's eyes. 2) A bull's-eye cancel refers to a "socked-on-the-nose" cancel, one that is centered directly on the stamp so that the stamp shows the location and date of mailing.

Bull's-Eye (Brazil)

Bull's-Eye, socked-on-the-nose cancellation

Burelage — A design of fine, intricate lines printed on the face of security paper, either to discourage counterfeiting or to prevent the cleaning and reuse of a stamp. The burelage on some stamps is part of the stamp design.

Burele — Adjective form for burelage, meaning having a fine network of lines. Some stamps of Queensland have a burele band on the back. Also called moire.

- C -

Cachet — In French, cachet means a stamp or a seal. In cover collecting, a cachet refers to a printed or handstamped design on an envelope denoting some special feature of the cover. Cachets appear on modern first-day covers, first-flight covers and special event covers.

Canceled To Order (CTO) — Stamps are "canceled to order," usually in full sheets, by many governments. Often, the cancels are printed on the stamps at the same time that the stamp design is printed. CTO stamps are sold to stamp dealers at large discounts from face value. CTO stamps have never seen actual postal use. Most catalogs say whether they price CTO stamps or genuinely used ones. A stamp with a cancel and with full gum is likely a CTO stamp.

Cancel, Cancellation — A marking that shows a stamp has been used. Modern cancels usually include the location of the post office from which the item is mailed and the date of mailing. Some also include a section of lines, bars, text or a design that "kills" the value of the stamp. This part of a cancel is called the killer.

Cantonal Stamps — Issues of the Swiss cantons used before the release of national stamps. The cantonal issues of Basel (1845), Geneva (1843-50) and Zurich (1843-50) are among the classics of philately.

Cape Triangles — Nickname for the triangular Cape of Good Hope stamps of 1853-64, the first stamps printed in triangular format. The distinctive shape helped illiterate postal clerks distinguishing letters originating in the colony from those from other colonies.

Catalog — Comprehensive compilation of postage stamps and revenue stamps, providing descriptions and, usually, values for the items, often including stamps priced on cover.

Catalog Value — The value of a stamp as listed in a given catalog for the most common condition in which the stamp is usually collected. Some catalogs list stamps at a retail value. European catalogs call their retail catalogs "netto" catalogs. In general, a stamp's catalog value should be regarded as a target price for the stamp. Some stamps are a bargain at double their catalog value. Others may be overpriced at one quarter of their catalog value. Most catalogs have a minimum price for the most common stamps that reflects a minimum handling charge for a dealer.

Censored Mail — A cover bearing a handstamp or label indicating that the envelope has been opened and read by a censor.

Centering — The relative position of the design of a stamp in relation to its margins. Assuming that a stamp is undamaged, centering is generally a very important factor in determining condition and value.

Certified Mail — A service of most postal adminstrations that provides proof of mailing and delivery without indemnity for loss or damage.

Chalky Paper — A chalk-surfaced paper for printing stamps. Any attempt to remove the cancel on a used chalky-paper stamp will also remove the design. Immersion of such stamps in water will cause the design to lift off. Touching chalky paper with silver will leave a discernible, pencil-like mark and is a means of distinguishing chalky paper.

Changeling — A stamp whose color has been changed by contact with a chemical or sunlight.

Charity Seals — Stamp-like labels that are produced by a charity. They have no postal validity, although they are often affixed to envelopes, usually on the reverse. United States Christmas seals are an example.

Charity Seals (imperf between)

Charity Stamp (Semipostal) — A stamp sold at a higher price than its postal value. The additional charge is usually noted on the stamp and is earmarked for a special fund. The use of semipostal stamps is voluntary. Postal tax stamps are similar to semipostals, but their use is usually required for all mail being posted during a specific period.

Charity Stamp (semipostal)

Cinderella — Stamp-like label that is not a postage stamp. Cinderellas include a wide variety of stamp-like labels, seals and bogus issues.

Classic — An early issue, with a connotation of rarity, although classic stamps are not necessarily rare. A particularly scarce recent item may be referred to as a modern classic.

Cleaning (Stamps) — Soiled or stained stamps are sometimes cleaned with chemicals or by erasing. The cleaning is usually done to improve the appearance of a stamp. Sometimes it is done to make a used stamp appear unused. A cleaned stamp can also mean one from which a cancellation has been removed.

Coil — A stamp prepared in rolls for sale and use in stamp-vending and affixing machines. Coils are often imperforate on two parallel sides and bear distinctive perforations. Some are numbered on the back to distinguish them from sheet stamps.

Collateral Material — Any supportive or explanatory material relating to a given stamp or philatelic topic. The material may be either directly postal in nature (post office news releases, rate schedules, souvenir cards, promotional buttons) or non-postal (maps, photos of scenes appearing on stamps).

Combination Cover — Cover bearing the stamps of more than one country when separate postal charges are paid for transport of a cover by each country. Also stamps of the same country canceled at two different times on the same cover as a souvenir.

Commatology — Specialized collecting of postmarks. This term was invented before World War II to describe postmark collecting. It is rarely used. Usually, collectors refer to postmark collecting or marcophily.

Commemorative — A stamp issued to note a special event or anniversary. A limited quantity of these stamps is available at the post office for a limited period. See also Definitive.

Compound Perforations — Different gauge perforations on different sides of a single stamp. The sides with the different perforations are usually perpendicular.

Condition — The general state of a stamp or a cover. Condition relates to a stamp's centering, gum, perforations, freshness and color.

Controlled Mail — A system in which the mailer selects philatelically desirable issues for outgoing mail, arranges for light cancellation and secures the stamps' return by the addressee. Such controlled mail operations ensure a steady stream of collectible stamps into the trade, especially postally used examples of high face value stamps.

Copyright Block — Block of four or more United States stamps with the copyright notice marginal marking of the United States Postal Service. The copyright marking was introduced in 1978 and replaced the Mail Early marking.

Corner Card — An imprinted return address, generally in the upper left corner of an envelope, from a commercial, institutional or private source, similar to business cards or letterheads.

Counterfeit — Any stamp, cancellation or cover created for deception or imitation, intended to be used as genuine. A counterfeit stamp is designed to deceive postal authorities.

Cover — An envelope or piece of postal stationery, usually one that has been mailed. A cover also refers to folded letters that were addressed and mailed without an envelope.

Crash Cover — A cover that has been salvaged from the crash of an airplane, train, ship or other vehicle. Such covers often carry a postal marking explaining their damaged condition.

Crease — A noticeable weakening of the paper of a stamp or cover, having been caused by its being folded or bent at some point. Creases substantially lower a stamp's value. On covers, creases affect value when they go through the attached stamp or a postal marking. Stamp creases are visible in watermark fluid.

Cut Cancellation — A cancellation that cuts the stamp. Often a wedge-shaped section is cut away. On many issues, such cancellations indicate use of postage stamps as fiscals or telegraph stamps rather than as postage. Cut cancellations were used experimentally on early U.S. postage stamps to prevent re-use.

Cut Square — A postal stationery cut-out. The imprinted stamp is neatly cut from the entire envelope, wrapper or postal card in a square or rectangular piece. Collectors generally prefer to collect stationery as entire pieces rather than as cut squares. Some older stationery is only available in cut squares.

Cut Square

Cut To Shape — A non-rectangular stamp or postal stationery imprint cut to the shape of the design, rather than cut square. Cut-to-shape stamps and stationery generally have lower value than those cut square. The unique 1856 British Guiana 1¢ magenta, the world's most valuable stamp, is a cut-to-shape stamp.

Cylinder — A plate used on a modern rotary press. The plate has no seams. For United States stamps, cylinders are used to print photogravure stamps. See also Sleeve.

- D -

Dead Country — A former stamp-issuing entity that has ceased to issue its own stamps. Also, the old name of a stamp-issuing entity that has changed its name, so that the old name will no longer be used on stamps.

Definitive — Stamp issued for an indefinite period and in indefinite quantity, usually for several years or more. The United States Presidential issue of 1938 and the Transportation coil stamps are examples. Definitive stamp designs usually do not honor a specific time-dated event.

Deltiology — Picture postcard collecting.

Denomination — The face value of a stamp. It is usually printed on the stamp. Modern stamps produced for rate changes sometimes are denominated with a letter. A numerical value is assigned when the letter stamps are issued. An example of this is the U.S. E stamp, which represented the first-class rate of 25¢.

Die — The original engraving of a stamp. A transfer roller is made from a die, and printing plates are made from the transfer roller. When more than one die is used in the production of an issue, distinctive varieties are often identifiable.

Directory Markings — Postal indication of delivery attempt, stating reason for failure. Examples are "No Such Number," "Address Unknown" and "Moved."

Duck Stamp — Popular name of United States hunting permit stamp, issued for use on hunting licenses. Each annual stamp depicts waterfowl. Also, the duck stamps issued by the various states for use by hunters or for sale to collectors.

Dummy Stamp — Officially produced imitation stamp used to train employees or to test automatic stamp-dispensing machines. Dummy stamps are usually blank or carry special inscriptions, blocks or other distinguishing ornamentation. They are not valid for postage, nor are they intended to reach the hands of stamp collectors. Some do by favor of postal employees.

Duplex Cancel — A two-part postal marking comprised of a canceler and a postmark. The canceler voids the stamp so it cannot be reused. The postmark notes place and date of mailing.

Duck Stamp (plate number)

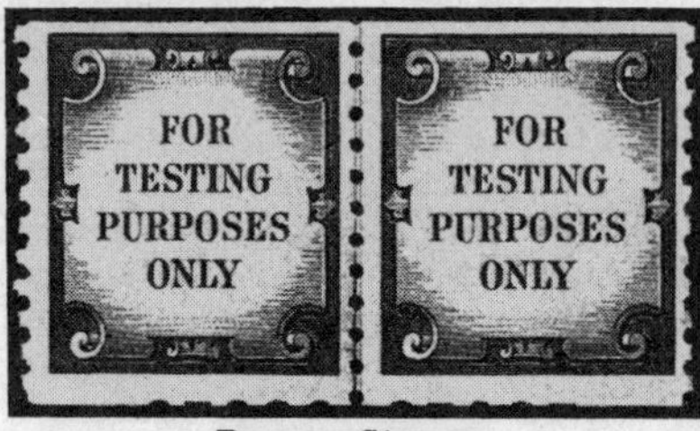

Dummy Stamps

Duplicate — An additional copy of a stamp that one already has in a collection. Beginners often consider stamps to be duplicates that really are not. They overlook perforation, watermark or color varieties.

- E -

Embossing — The process of giving relief to paper by pressing it with a die. Embossed designs are often found on postal stationery (usually on envelopes and wrappers). Occasionally stamps have been embossed.

Encased Postage Stamp — A stamp inserted into a small coin-size case with a transparent front or back. Such stamps were circulated as legal coins during periods when coins were scarce.

Entire — An intact piece of postal stationery, in contrast to a cut-out of the printed design. This term is sometimes used in reference to an intact cover or folded letter.

Error — A major mistake in the production of a stamp or postal stationery item. Printing errors include imperforate or part-perforate varieties, missing or incorrect colors and inversion or doubling of part of the design or overprint. Major errors are usually far scarcer than the normal stamps and are highly valued by collectors.

Error (invert)

Essay — The artwork of a proposed design for a stamp. Some essays are rendered photographically. Others are drawn in pencil or ink or are painted. Most essays are rejected. One becomes the essay for the accepted design.

Essay

Europa — The "United Europe" theme, celebrated on stamps of Western European nations since 1956. The original Europa stamps were issued by the nations in the European coal and steel association. Today, the European nations that are members of the postal and telecommunications association (CEPT) issue Europa stamps.

Expertization — The examination of a stamp or cover by an acknowledged expert, to determine if it is genuine. Today, an expert or expertizing body issues a signed certificate, often with an

Europa

attached photograph, attesting to the item's status.

Exploded — A stamp booklet is said to be exploded when it has been separated into its various components for purposes of display. This usually refers to booklets held together by staples. Modern glued booklets usually cannot be exploded without damaging the individual booklet panes.

- F -

Face Value — The value of a stamp as inscribed on its face, or for letter-denominated or undenominated stamps, the understood postal value of the stamp.

Facsimile — Reproduction of a genuine stamp or cover. Such items are usually made with no intent to deceive collectors or postal officials. Catalog illustrations are facsimiles.

Fake — A stamp, cover or cancel altered or concocted to appeal to a collector. In a broad sense, fakes include repairs, reperforations and regummed stamps, as well as painted-in cancels, bogus cancels or markings. Sometimes entire covers are faked.

Farley's Follies — During 1933-34, U.S. Postmaster General James A. Farley supplied a few imperforate sheets of current commemorative issues to President Franklin D. Roosevelt and other government officials. The resulting uproar from U.S. collectors forced the government to release for public sale 20 stamps in generally imperforate and ungummed condition. They are United States Scott 752-71. Numbers 752-53 are perforated.

Fast Colors — Inks resistant to fading.

Field Post Office (FPO) — A military post office operating in the field, either

Farley's Follies (imperf)

on land or at sea. See also Fleet Post Office.

Find — A new discovery, usually of something that was not thought to exist. It can be a single item or a hoard of stamps or covers.

First Day Cover (FDC) — A cover bearing a stamp tied by a cancellation showing the date of the first day of issue of that stamp.

First-Day Cover (FDC)

Fiscal — A revenue stamp or similar label denoting the payment of taxes. Fiscals are ordinarily affixed to documents and canceled by pen, canceler or mutilation. Because of their similarity to postage stamps, fiscals have occasionally been used both legally and illegally to prepay postage. See also Postal Fiscal.

Flat Plate — Printing from a flat plate, as opposed to a curved or cylindrical plate.

Flaw — A defect in a plate, causing an identifiable variety in the stamp itself.

Fleet Post Office (FPO) — An official U.S. post office for use by U.S. military naval units abroad. See also Field Post Office.

Forerunner — A stamp or postal stationery item used in a given location prior to the issuing of regular stamps for that location. Turkish stamps before 1918 canceled in Palestine are forerunners of Israeli issues. So are the various European nations' issues for use in Palestine, and the subsequent issues of the Palestine Mandate.

Forgery — A completely fraudulent reproduction of a postage stamp. There are two general types of forgeries: 1) those intended to defraud the postal authorities, see also Counterfeit; and 2) those intended to defraud the collectors, see also Bogus.

Frama — A general name used for an automatic stamp. Automatic stamps are produced individually by a machine on demand in a denomination selected by the customer. There normally is no date on the stamp, like there is on a meter strip. Also called ATM, from the German word Automatenmarken.

Frame — The outer portion of the stamp design, usually a line or a group of panels.

Frank, Franking — An indication on a cover that postage is prepaid, partially prepaid or that the letter is to be carried free of postage. Franks may be written, handstamped, imprinted or affixed. Free franking is usually limited to government correspondence or soldiers' mail. Stamps are the modern method of franking a letter.

Freak — An abnormal, usually non-repetitive occurrence in the production of stamps. Most paper folds, overinking and perforation shifts are freaks. Those abnormalities occurring regularly are called varieties or major errors.

Front — The front of a cover with most or all of the back and side panels torn away or removed. Fronts, while desirable if they bear unusual or uncommon postal markings, are less desirable than an intact cover.

Fugitive Inks — Inks that easily fade or break up in water or chemicals. To counter attempts at forgery or the removal of cancellations, many governments have used fugitive inks to print stamps.

- G -

Ghost Tagging — The appearance of a light impression in addition to the normal inked stamp impression. This is caused by misregistration of the phosphor tagging in relation to the ink. Sometimes, a plate number impression will have an entirely different number from the ink plate, giving the impression of an error: one dark (normal) number and one light (ghost) number.

Goldbeater's Skin — A thin, tough, translucent paper. The 1886 issue of Prussia was printed in reverse on Goldbeater's Skin, with the gum applied over the printing. These stamps were brittle and were virtually impossible to remove from the paper to which they were affixed.

Granite Paper — A paper with small colored fibers added when the paper is made. This paper is used as a deterrent against forgery.

Gravure — The process of creating an intaglio printing plate by photographic and chemical means, rather than by hand engraving. See also Intaglio.

Grill — A pattern of parallel lines (or dots at the points where lines would cross) forming a grid. A grill is usually: 1) the impressed breaks added to stamps as a security measure (United States issues of 1867-71 and Peru issues of 1874-79); or 2) a grill-like canceling device used on various 19th-century issues.

Gum — The mucilage applied to the backs of adhesive postage stamps, revenue stamps or envelope flaps. Gum is a concern of stamp collectors. It may crack and harm the paper of the stamp itself. It may stain or adhere to other stamps or album pages under certain climatic conditions. Many collectors are willing to pay extra for 19th- and some 20th-century stamps with intact, undisturbed original gum.

Gutter — The selvage, either unprinted or with plate numbers, advertising or accounting or control numbers, between the panes of a sheet of stamps.

Gutter

Gutter Snipe — One or more stamps to which is attached the full gutter from between panes, plus any amount of an adjoining stamp or stamps. This term is typically used in reference to U.S. stamps. Gutter snipes are freaks caused by misregistration of the cutting device or paper foldovers.

- H -

Handstamp — Cancellation or overprint applied by hand to a cover or to an adhesive .

Highway Post Office (HPO) — Portable mail-handling equipment for sorting mail in transit on highways (normally by truck). The last official U.S. HPO ran June 30, 1974.

Hinge — Stamp hinges are small, rectangular-shaped pieces of paper, usually gummed on one side, used in the mounting of stamps. Most modern hinges are peelable. Once dry, they may be easily removed from the stamp, leaving little trace of having been applied.

- I -

Imperforate — Refers to stamps without perforations or rouletting between the individual stamps in a pane. The earliest stamps were imperforate, but after about 1860, most stamps were perforated. Modern imperforates are usually errors or are produced specifically for sale to stamp collectors.

Imperforate, imperf (block, guideline)

Impression — Any stamped or embossed printing.

Imprimatur — Latin for "let it be printed." The first sheets of stamps from an approved plate, normally checked and retained in a file, prior to a final directive to begin stamp production from a plate.

India Paper — A thin, tough opaque printing paper of high quality, used primarily for striking die proofs.

Indicium — The imprint on postal stationery, as opposed to an adhesive stamp, indicating prepayment and postal validity. Plural: indicia.

Intaglio — Italian for "in recess." A form of printing in which the inked image is produced by that portion of the plate sunk below the surface. Line engraving and gravure are forms of intaglio printing.

International Reply Coupon (IRC) — Coupons issued by members of the Universal Postal Union to provide for return postage from recipients in foreign countries. IRCs are exchangeable for postage at a post office.

Invert — The term generally used to describe any error where one portion of the design is inverted in relation to the other portion(s).

- K -

Keytype — A basic design utilized for the issues of two or more postal entities, usually differing in the country name and inscription of value. Many of the earlier colonial issues of Britain, France, Spain, Germany and Portugal are keytypes.

Keytype

Kiloware — A stamp mixture, consisting of miscellaneous stamps on envelope corner paper from various sources. Kiloware is often sold by the kilogram (about 2.2 pounds).

- L -

Label — Any stamp-like adhesive that is not a postage stamp or revenue stamp.

Laid Paper — One of the two basic types of paper used in stamp printing. Laid paper is distinguished from the other type — wove paper — by the presence of thin, parallel lines visible when the paper is held to light. The lines are usually a few millimeters apart. See also Batonne.

Letterpress — Printing done directly from the inked, raised surface of the printing plate.

Line Engraving — Printing done from an intaglio plate produced from a hand-engraved die and transfer roller rather than by photographic or chemical means. See also Gravure.

Line Pair — A line between a pair of coil stamps. Stamps produced on a flatbed press have a line — from the guideline between panes. Stamps produced on a rotary press have a joint line — from the space where ink collects between the sections of curved rotary plates.

Line pair (coil)

Lithography — Printing from a flat surface with a design area that is ink-receptive. The area that is not to print is ink-repellant. The process is based on the principle that an oil-based design surface will attract oily ink.

Locals — Stamps valid within a limited area or within a limited postal system. Local post mail requires the addition of nationally or internationally valid stamps for further service. Locals have been produced both privately and officially.

- M -

Mail Early Block (ME block) — U.S. marginal marking block with the marginal selvage bearing the inscription "Mail Early (in the Day)." This first appeared on U.S. marginal selvage in 1968. It was subsequently replaced by the Copyright notice. Typically a block of four or six

Local

stamps.

Marcophily — Postmark collecting.

Margin — 1) the selvage surrounding the stamps in a sheet, often carrying inscriptions of various kinds; or 2) the unprinted area between stamps in a sheet or what is left after stamps are separated. The collectible grades of stamps are determined by the position of the design in relation to the edge of the stamp as perforated or, in the case of imperforate stamps, as cut from the sheet.

Maximaphily — Maximum card collecting.

Maximum Card — A picture postcard, a cancel, and a stamp presenting maximum concordance. The stamp is usually affixed to the picture side of the card and is tied by the cancel. Collectors of maximum cards seek to find or seek to create cards with stamp, cancel and picture in maximum agreement, or concordance. The statutes of the International Federation of Philately (FIP) give specific explanatory notes for the postage stamp, the picture postcard, the cancel, concordance of subject, concordance of place and concordance of time. (See Exhibiting chapter.)

Meter — Government permit of specified face value applied as a prepaid postmark in lieu of stamps.

Metered Mail — Mail franked by a postage meter, a device that automatically imprints the proper postal rate with a distinctive imprint in the upper right-hand area of the envelope. Meters were authorized by the UPU in 1920. They are used today by volume mailers to cut the cost of franking mail.

Miniature Sheet — A smaller-than-normal pane of stamps issued only in that form or in addition to full panes. A miniature sheet is usually without marginal markings or text saying that the sheet was issued in conjuction with or to commemorate some event. See also Souvenir Sheet.

Mint — A stamp in the same state as issued by a post office: unused, undamaged and with full original gum (if so issued with gum). Over time, handling, light and atmospheric conditions affect the mint state of stamps.

Mirror Image — Negative or reverse impression. An offset.

Mission Mixture — The lowest grade of stamp mixture, containing unsorted but primarily common, stamps on paper, as purchased from missions or other institutions. See also Bank Mixture.

Missionaries — The first stamps of Hawaii, issued in 1851-52. They are among the great classics of philately.

Mixed Perforation — See Compound Perforation.

Mixed Postage — Refers to a cover bearing the stamps of two or more stamp-issuing entities, properly used.

Mixture — A large group of stamps, understood to contain duplication. A mixture is said to be unpicked or picked. A picked mixture may have been previously gone through by a collector or dealer.

Mobile Post Office (MPO) — Portable mail-handling equipment and personnel, generally in railroad cars, trucks, streetcars or buses.

Money, Stamps As — During periods of coin shortage, stamps have circulated officially as small change. Often, stamps used in this way are printed on thin card stock, enclosed in cases of various kinds or affixed to cards. See Encased Postage Stamps.

Mounts (Stamp) — Acetate holders, clear on the front and with some sort of adhesive on the back. Mounts hold stamps with pressure and are affixed to an album page. Collectors use mounts to mount stamps or covers.

Multicolor — More than two colors.

Multiple — An unseparated unit of stamps including at least two stamps, but fewer than the number included in a full pane.

- N -

Native Paper — Crude, handmade paper produced locally, as opposed to finer, machine-made paper.

Never Hinged (NH) — A stamp without hinge marks. Usually a never-hinged stamp has original gum, but this is not always the case.

New Issue Service — A dealer service that automatically supplies subscribers with new issues of a given country, area or topic. Issues provided are determined by a pre-arranged standing order defining the quantity and types of issues.

Newspaper Stamps — Stamps issued specifically for prepayment of mailing rates for newspapers, periodicals and printed matter.

- O -

Obliteration — 1) A cancellation intended solely to deface a stamp. Also called a killer; 2) An overprint intended to deface a portion of the design of a stamp, like the face of a deposed ruler.

Obsolete — A stamp no longer available from post offices, although possibly still postally valid.

Occupation Issue — An issue released for use in territory occupied by a foreign power.

Occupation issue

Off-Center — A stamp design is not centered in relation to the edges of the stamp. Generally, off-center stamps are less desirable than stamps more nearly centered in relation to the edges. Some collectors specialize in collecting stamps that are extremely off-center.

Offices Abroad — At various times, many nations have maintained post offices in other countries, usually because of the unreliability of the local postal system. In China and the Turkish Empire, especially, many foreign nations maintained their own postal systems as part of their extraterritorial powers. Usually, special stationery and stamps were used for these offices. Most often they were overprints on the regular issues of the nations maintaining the offices.

Offices abroad (overprint)

Official — Stamp or stationery issued solely for the use of government departments and officials. Such items may or may not be available to collectors in unused condition from a post office.

Offset — 1) A printing process that transfers an inked image from a plate to a roller. The roller than applies the ink to paper; 2) The transfer of part of a stamp design or an overprint from one sheet to the back of another, before the ink has dried (also called set off). Such impressions are in reverse. They are different than stamps printed on both sides.

OHMS — Abbreviation for On His (Her) Majesty's Service. Used in perfins, overprints or franks to indicate official use in the British Commonwealth.

Omnibus Issue — An issue released by several postal entities celebrating a common theme. Omnibus issues may or may not share a keytype design.

On Paper — Stamps on paper, usually used stamps, that still bear portions of the original envelope or wrapper upon which they were used.

On Piece — A stamp on a portion of the original envelope or wrapper showing all or most of the cancel.

Original Gum (OG) — The adhesive coating on a mint or unused stamp or envelope flap applied by a postal authority or security printer, usually before the item was issued. Upon request of stamp collectors, postal authorities have at

Omnibus issue

some times offered to add gum to items first issued ungummed.

Overprint — Any printing over the original design of a stamp. An overprint that changes the value of a stamp is also called a surcharge.

Overprint

Oxidation — Darkening of the ink on certain stamps caused by contact with air or light. Some inks used in printing stamps, especially oranges, may in time turn brown or black.

- P -

Packet — 1) A pre-sorted unit of all different stamps, a common and economical way to begin a general collection; 2) a ship operating on a regular schedule and contracted by a government or post office to carry mail.

Packet Letter — A letter carried by a ship operating on a regular schedule and carrying mail by contract with a government or a post office.

Pair — Two unseparated stamps.

Pane — The unit into which a full sheet is divided before sale at post offices. The "sheets" that one normally sees at post offices are panes. Most United States full sheets are divided into four regular panes or many more booklet panes before they are shipped to post offices.

Paquebot — Cancellation indicating an item was mailed aboard a ship.

Par Avion — French for "By Air."

Parcel Post Stamps — Special stamps for payment of parcel post fees.

Part-Perforate — A stamp imperforate on one or more sides, but with at least one side perforated.

Paste-Up — The area where the ends of rolls of coiled stamps are joined with glue or tape.

Pelure Paper — A strong, thin paper occasionally used in stamp printing. Pelure paper is translucent and resembles a slightly dark, thin onion-skin paper.

Paquebot (cover, cachet)

Pen-Canceled — Stamps canceled with a pen rather than a handstamp or machine cancel. Many early stamps were routinely canceled by pen. A pen cancel may also indicate that a stamp was used as a fiscal.

Pen cancel (imperforate)

Penny Black — The black 1-penny British stamp issued May 6, 1840, bearing the portrait of Queen Victoria. It is the world's first adhesive postage stamp issued for the prepayment of postage.

Perfins — Stamps punched with "perforated initials" or designs of holes

Penny Black (imperf)

that stand for letters, numbers or symbols. Perfins are normally used by a business or government office to discourage pilferage or misuse of stamps by employees. Perfins may be either privately or officially produced.

Perfins

Perforation — The punching out of holes between stamps to make separation easy. 1) Comb perforation — Three sides of a stamp are perfed at once, with the process repeated in rows; 2) Harrow perforation — The entire sheet or unit of stamps is perforated in one operation; 3) Line perforation — Holes are punched one row at a time. Line perforations are distinguished by the uneven crossing of perforation lines and irregular corners. Comb and harrow perforations usually show alignment of holes at the corners. Some forms of perforation may be difficult to distinguish.

Perforation Gauge — A scale printed or designed on metal, plastic or cardboard to measure the number of perf holes or teeth within two centimeters.

Permit — Procedure used by businesses or post offices that imprints mailer's assigned permit number and an indication of the prepaid postage on each piece of mail. This eliminates the need to affix and cancel stamps on large mailings. The machine counts the postage used and is read periodically for accounting.

Phantasy — A bogus stamp.

Phantom Philately — The collection of bogus stamps. The name is derived from Frederick Melville's book *Phantom Philately*, one of the pioneer works on bogus issues.

Philatelic Cover — An envelope or postal card franked and mailed by a stamp collector to create a collectible object. It may or may not have carried a personal or business message. A non-philatelic cover is usually one that has carried business or personal correspondence or messages and has had its stamps applied by a non-collector. Some stamps are known only on collector-created covers. It is impossible to say whether some covers are philatelically inspired or not. See also Used and Postally Used.

Philately — The collection and study of postage stamps and postal stationery.

Phosphor — A chemical substance used in stamp production to activate machines that automatically cancel mail. The machines react to the phosphor under ultraviolet light. In 1959, Great Britain began to print phosphor lines on some of its stamps. See also Tagging.

Photogravure — A modern stamp-printing process. Plates are made photographically and chemically, rather than by hand engraving a die and transferring it to a plate. Photogravure is a form of intaglio printing. The ink in this process rests in the design depressions. The actual surface of the printing plate is wiped clean. The paper is forced into the depressions and picks up the ink, in a manner much like the line-engraved process.

Pictorial — Stamp bearing a picture of some sort, other than a portrait or coat of arms.

Plate — The basic printing unit placed on a press and used to produce stamps. Early stamps were printed from flat plates. Later curved or cylindrical plates were used. See also Cylinder and Sleeve.

Plate Block, Plate Number Block — A block of stamps from the corner or side of a pane including the selvage bearing the number(s) of the plate(s) used to print the sheet from which the pane was separated. Some stamp production methods, like booklet production, normally cut off plate numbers. In the United States, plate number blocks are collected normally as blocks of four to 20 stamps, depending on the press used to print the stamps. When each stamp in a pane is a different design, the plate block is usually collected as an entire pane.

Plating — The reconstruction of a stamp pane by collecting blocks and individual stamps representing various positions. This is possible for many older issues, but most modern issues are too uniform to make the identification of individual positions possible.

Plebiscite Issue — A stamp issue promoting a popular vote. After World War I, a number of disputed areas were placed under temporary League of Nations administration, pending plebiscites to determine which nation the populace wished to join. Special issues note the upcoming vote in several of these areas, among them Allenstein, Carinthia, Eastern Silesia, Marienwerder, Schleswig and Upper Silesia.

PNC — 1) A plate number coil stamp; 2) A philatelic-numismatic combination: a cover bearing a stamp and containing a coin, medal or token. In the latter, the coin and stamp are usually related. Often the cover is canceled on the first day of use of the coin.

Pneumatic Post — Letter distribution through pressurized air tubes. Pneumatic posts existed in many large cities in Europe, and special stamps and stationery were produced for the services.

Postage Dues — Stamps or markings indicating that insufficient postage has been affixed to the mailing piece. Postage dues are usually affixed at the office of delivery. The additional postage is collected from the addressee.

Postcard — A small card, usually with a picture on one side and a space for a written message on the other. Postcards have no imprinted stamp. See also Postal Card.

Postal Card — A government-produced postcard bearing an imprint in the upper right corner representing prepayment of postage.

Postal Fiscal — Revenue or fiscal stamps used postally.

Postal History — 1) The study of postal markings, rates and routes; 2) Anything to do with the history of the posts.

Postal Stationery — Stationery bearing imprinted stamps, as opposed to adhesive stamps. Postal stationery includes postal cards, lettercards, imprinted envelopes, wrappers, aerogrammes, telegraph cards, postal savings forms and similar government-produced items. Some early postcards had no imprinted stamp. These formular cards were sold with or without an added adhesive stamp.

Postally Used — A stamp or cover that has seen legitimate postal use, as opposed to one that has been canceled to order or favor-canceled. Postally used suggests that an item exists because it was used to carry a personal or business communication, without the sender thinking of creating an item to be collected.

Postmark — Any official postal marking. The term is usually used specifically in reference to cancellations bearing the name of a post office of origin and a mailing date.

Precancel — Stamp with a special cancellation, overprint or text allowing it to bypass normal canceling. The indication of stamps being precancels is applied by a post office before the stamps are sold. Precanceled stamps are used by volume mailers who hold a permit to use them. U.S. precancels fall into two categories: 1) Locals have the mark or text applied by a town or city post office; and 2) Bureaus have the mark or text applied by the U.S. Bureau of Engraving and Printing.

Precancel (coil)

Pre-stamp Covers — Folded letters or their outer enclosures used before the introduction of adhesive postage stamps or postal stationery.

Prexies — The nickname for the U.S. 1938-54 Presidential definitive series, Scott 803-34, 839-51.

Printer's Waste — Misprinted, misperforated or misgummed stamps designated as waste. The stamps normally are destroyed. Such material enters the philatelic market through carelessness and theft. Security printing operations often were lax near the end of a war or just after a war had ended.

Printer's waste (imperf)

Printing — The process of imprinting designs on paper from an inked surface.

Pro Juventute — Latin, meaning for the benefit of youth. Switzerland has issued Pro Juventute semipostals nearly every year since 1913.

Pro Juventute (semipostal)

Proofs — Trial impressions from a die or printing plate before actual stamp production. Proofs are made to examine a die or plate for defects and to compare the results of different inks.

Provisional — A temporary postage stamp, issued to meet postal demands until new or regular stocks of stamps can be obtained.

Proof

- R -

Railway Post Office (RPO) — Portable mail-handling equipment for sorting mail in transit on trains. The last official U.S. RPO ran June 30, 1977. See also Mobile Post Office.

Receiving Mark — A postmark or other postal marking applied by the receiving, rather than the originating, post office. See also Backstamp.

Redrawn — A stamp design that has been slightly altered yet maintains the basic design as originally issued.

Re-engraved — A stamp with an altered design made by changing a transfer roll from an original die.

Regional — Stamp sold or valid in a specific part of a stamp issuing-entity. Great Britain has issued stamps for the regions of Guernsey, Jersey, Isle of Man, Northern Ireland, Scotland and Wales. Regionals are usually sold only in a given region but are often valid for postage throughout a country.

Registered Mail — First-class mail with a numbered receipt, including a valuation of the registered item, for full or limited compensation if the mail is lost. Some countries have issued registered mail stamps. Registered mail is signed by each postal employee who handles it.

Registration Labels — Adhesive labels indicating the registry number and, usually, city of origin for registered articles sent through the mail.

Reissue — An official reprinting of a stamp from an obsolete or discontinued issue. Reissues are valid for postage. See also Reprint.

Remainders — Stocks of stamps

Registered mail stamp

remaining unsold at the time that an issue is declared obsolete by a post office. Some countries have sold remainders to the stamp trade at substantial discounts from face value. The countries often mark the stamps in some way, usually with a distinctive cancel. Uncanceled remainders usually cannot be distinguished from stamps sold over the counter before the issue was invalidated.

Repaired Stamp — A damaged stamp that has been repaired in some way to reinforce it or to make it resemble an undamaged stamp.

Replica — A reproduction of a stamp or cover. In the 19th century, replica stamps were sold as space-fillers. Replica stamps are often printed in one color in a sheet containing a number of different designs. Replicas can sometimes deceive either a postal clerk or collectors.

Reprint — A stamp printed from the original plate, after the issue has ceased to be postally valid. Official reprints are sometimes made for presentation purposes or official collections. They are often distinguishable in some way from the originals: different colors, perforations, paper or gum. Private reprints, on the other hand, are usually produced strictly for sale to collectors and often closely resemble the original stamps. Private reprints normally sell for less than original copies. Reprints are not valid for postage. See also Reissue.

Retouch — The minor repairing of a damaged plate or die, often producing a minor, but detectable, difference in the design of printed stamps.

Revenues — Stamps representing the prepayment or payment of various taxes. Revenues are affixed to official documents and to merchandise. Some stamps, including many issues of the British Commonwealth, were inscribed "Postage and Revenue" and were available for either use. Such issues are usually worth less fiscally canceled than postally used. In some cases, revenues have been used provisionally as postage stamps.

Rocket Mail — Mail flown in a rocket, even if only a short distance. Many rocket mail experiments have been conducted since 1931. Special labels, cachets or cancels usually note that mail was carried on a rocket.

'Roos — The nickname of the first Australian issue (1913). The design features a kangaroo on a map of Australia and was used as late as 1945.

'Roos

Rotary Plate — A curved or cylindrical printing plate used on a press that rotates and makes continuous impressions. Flat plates make single impressions.

Rouletting — The piercing of the paper between stamps to make their separation more convenient. No paper is actually removed from the sheet, as in perforating. Rouletting has been made by dash, sawtooth or wavy line.

Rural Free Delivery (RFD) — System for free home delivery of mail in rural areas of the United States, begun just prior to the turn of the 20th century.

Rust — A brown mold, resembling the rust in iron. Rust affects stamp paper and gum in tropical regions.

- S -

SASE — A self-addressed, stamped envelope. An unused envelope bearing address of sender and return postage. Sent to make answering easy.

Secret Marks — Reference area in a stamp's design to foil attempts at counterfeiting and to differentiate issues.

Seebeck — The nickname for various Latin American issues produced 1890-99 in contract with Nicholas Frederick Seebeck, the agent for the Hamilton Bank Note Company of New York. Seebeck agreed to provide new issues of stamps and stationery each year at no charge, in return for the right to sell remainders and reprints to collectors. The resulting furor destroyed Seebeck and blackened the philatelic reputations of the countries involved.

Selvage — The unprinted marginal paper on a sheet or pane of stamps.

Semipostal (Charity Stamp) — Stamp sold at a surcharge over postal value. The additional charge is for a special purpose. Usually recognized by the presence of two (often different) values, separated by a "+" sign, on a single stamp.

Series — A group of stamps with a similar design or theme. A series may be planned or may evolve.

Set — A unit of stamps issued for a common purpose, either at one time or over an extended period, embracing a common design or theme.

Se-tenant — French for "joined together." Two or more unseparated stamps of different designs, colors, denominations or types.

Shade — The minor variation commonly found in any basic color. Shades are usually accorded catalog status when they are very distinctive.

Sheet — A complete unit of stamps as printed. Stamps are usually printed in large sheets and are separated into two or more panes before shipment to post offices.

Ship Letter — Letter carried by private ship.

Short Set — An incomplete set of stamps, usually lacking either the high value(s) or one or more key values.

Sleeper — Stamp or other collectible item that seems to be underpriced and may have good investment potential.

Sleeve — A seamless cylindrical printing plate used in rotary intaglio printing.

Soaking — Removal of stamps from envelope paper. Most stamps may be safely soaked in water. Fugitive inks, however, will run in water, and chalky-surfaced papers will lose their designs entirely, so some knowledge of stamps is a necessity. Colored envelope paper should be soaked separately.

Souvenir Card — A philatelic card, not valid for postage, issued in conjunction with some special event.

Souvenir Sheet — A small sheet of stamps, usually including one value or a set of stamps. A souvenir sheet usually has a wide margin and a commemorative inscription.

Souvenir sheet

Space-Filler — A stamp in poor condition used to fill a space in an album until a better copy can be found.

Special Delivery — A service providing expedited delivery of mail. Also called express.

Special Handling — A U.S. service providing expeditious handling for fourth-class material.

Special Printing — Reissue of a stamp of current or recent design, often with distinctive color, paper or perforations.

Specialist — A stamp collector who intensively studies and collects the stamps and postal history of a given country or area, or who has otherwise limited his collecting field.

Specimen — Stamp or stationery item distributed to UPU members for identification purposes and to the philatelic press and trade for publicity purposes. Specimens are overprinted or punched with the word "SPECIMEN" or its equivalent, or are overprinted or punched in a way to make them different than the issued stamps. Specimens of scarce stamps tend to be less valuable than the actual stamps. Specimens of relatively common stamps are more valuable.

Specimens

Speculative Issue — A stamp or issue released primarily for sale to collectors, rather than to meet any legitimate postal need.

Splice — The repair of a break in a roll of stamp paper, or the joining of two rolls of paper for continuous printing. Stamps printed over a splice are usually removed before the normal stamps are issued.

Stamp — A postal adhesive. Initially used as a verb, meaning to imprint or impress, that is, to stamp a design.

Stampless Cover — A folded sheet or envelope carried as mail without a postage stamp. This term usually refers to covers predating the requirement that stamps be affixed to all letters (in the United States, 1856).

Stock Book — A book containing rows of pockets to hold unmounted or duplicate stamps.

Straight Edge — Flat-plate or rotary-plate stamps from the margins of panes where the sheets were cut apart. Straight-edge stamps have no perforations on one or two adjacent sides. Sometimes straight-edge stamps show a guideline.

Strip — Three or more unseparated stamps in a row, vertically or horizontally.

Surcharge — An overprint that changes or restates the denomination of a stamp.

Surcharge

Surface-Colored Paper — Paper colored on the surface only, with a white or uncolored back.

Sweatbox — A closed box containing a wet sponge-like material, over which stuck-together unused stamps are placed on a grill. Humidity softens the gum, allowing separation of stamps.

- T -

T — Abbreviation for the French "Taxe." Handstamped on a stamp, the T indicates the stamp's use as a postage due. Handstamped on a cover, it indicates that postage due has been charged. Several countries have used regular stamps with a perforated initial T as postage dues.

Tagging — Phosphor coating on stamps used to activate automatic mail-handling equipment. This may be lines, bars, letters, part of the design area or the entire stamp surface. Some stamps are issued both with and without tagging. Catalogs call them tagged or untagged.

Telegraph Stamp — Label used for the prepayment of telegraph fees. Telegraph stamps resemble postage stamps.

Telegraph stamp

Tete-Beche — French for "head to tail." Two or more unsevered stamps, one of which is inverted in relation to the other.

Tete-Beche pair

Thematic — A collection of stamps or covers relating to a specific topic. The topic is expanded by careful inquiry and is presented as a logical story. See also Topical.

Tied — A stamp is said to be tied to a cover when the cancel extends over both the stamp and the envelope paper. Stamps can also be tied by the aging of the mucilage or glue that holds them to the paper.

Tong — Tweezer-like tool used to handle stamps. Tongs prevent stamps from being soiled by dirt, oil or perspiration.

Topical — 1) Stamp or cover showing a given subject. Examples are flowers, art, birds, elephants or the Statue of Liberty. 2) The collection of stamps by the topic depicted on them, rather than by country of origin. See also Thematic.

Transit Mark — A postal marking applied by a post office between the originating and receiving post offices. It can be on the front or back of a cover, card or wrapper.

Triptych — A se-tenant strip of three related stamps, often forming one overall design.

Type — A basic design of a stamp or a set. Catalogs use type numbers or letters to save space. Catalogs show a typical design rather than every stamp with that design or a similar design.

Triptych (se-tenant)

- U -

Underprint — A fine printing underlying the design of a stamp, most often used to deter counterfeiting.

Ungummed — A stamp without gum. Ungummed stamps are either stamps issued without gum or stamps that have been stuck together and subsequently soaked apart, losing their gum in the process. Many countries in tropical climates have issued stamps without gum.

Unhinged — A stamp without hinge marks, but not necessarily with original gum.

Universal Postal Union (UPU) — An international organization formed in Bern, Switzerland, in 1874, to regulate and standardize postal usage and to facilitate the movement of mail between member nations. Today, most nations belong to the UPU. (See UPU section of this almanac.)

Unused — An uncanceled stamp that has not been used but has a hinge mark or some other disturbance that keeps it from being mint. Uncanceled stamps without gum may have been used and missed being canceled, or they may have lost their gum by accident.

Used — A stamp or stationery item that has been canceled by a postal authority to prevent its re-use on mail. In general, a used stamp is any stamp with a cancel or a precanceled stamp without gum. See also Postally Used and Philatelic Cover.

- V -

Variety — A variation from the standard form of a stamp. Varieties include watermarks, inverts, imperforates, missing colors, wrong colors and major color shifts. See also Freak.

Vignette — The central part of a stamp design, usually surrounded by a border. The vignette often shades off gradually into the surrounding area.

- W -

Want List — A list of needed stamps or covers, identified by catalog number or some other description, submitted by a collector to a dealer, usually including requirements on condition and price.

Watermark — A deliberate thinning of paper during its manufacture, to produce a semitranslucent pattern. Watermarks appear frequently in paper used in stamp printing. See also Batonne.

Wing Margin — Early British stamps from the side of a pane. British sheets printed before 1880 were perforated down the center of the gutter, producing oversized margins on one side of stamps adjacent to the gutter. Such copies are distinctive and scarcer than normal copies.

Wove Paper — A paper showing few differences in texture and thickness when held to light. In the production of wove paper, the pulp is pressed against a very fine netting, producing a virtually uniform texture. Wove paper is the most commonly used paper in stamp production.

Wrapper — A flat sheet or strip open at both ends that can be folded and sealed around a newspaper or periodical. Wrappers can have an imprinted stamp or have a stamp attached.

- Z -

Zemstvo — A local stamp issued by Russian municipal governments or zemstvos, in accordance with an imperial edict of 1870.

Zeppelin Items — The stamps issued for, or in honor of, zeppelin flights, and the cacheted covers carried on such flights.

Zeppelin

ZIP Block — U.S. marginal marking block with the selvage bearing the "Mr. ZIP" cartoon character and/or the inscription "Use ZIP Code." This first appeared on U.S. marginal selvage in 1964. Typically a ZIP block is a block of four stamps.

ZIP Code — The U.S. numerical post code used to speed and mechanize mail handling and delivery. The letters stand for Zoning Improvement Plan.

Foreign Stamp Identifier

To aid in the identification of foreign stamps, this section is designed to help identify foreign spellings, words and overprints that might indicate the origin of certain stamps. As a general rule, look for a word, first in the overprint, then in the stamp itself, that looks like a country name. If it is spelled exactly like the country in question, look to the Stamp-Issuing Entities chapter in this almanac for some historical background.

If this fails to produce results, then consult this alphabetic listing. Because of typesetting restrictions, words in foreign alphabets are not listed unless the characters closely resemble Roman characters. This generally refers to words in Greek and Russian. It also applies to certain German overprints.

By using the various sections in this almanac, you should be able to locate in any catalog most foreign stamps with identifiable English characters. For possible alternate names or country changes, consult the historical background contained in the Stamp-Issuing Entities chapter. Countries frequently may be listed under a variety of names in different catalogs.

Note that all stamps indexed here are postage stamps, as typically cataloged. Therefore, reference to tax stamps means "postal tax stamps." Reference to locals is not the usual philatelic sense of the word. As used here, a local refers to a stamp issued in local areas or internal states within larger stamp-issuing entities, such as the Indian states, Malayan states, and provisional states of some Latin American countries. In some cases, these will be true locals, while in other cases, such stamps may be postally valid within larger areas. In general, local refers to the issue of an internal state.

Reference dates are not intended to be inclusive. They are merely a guide to the period when various indexed characteristics appeared on certain stamps. In no case will indexed stamps appear before the first indicated date, but use of stamps after an included second date may be common.

- A -

A.B. on stamps of Russia: Far Eastern Republic (1923).

ABLOSUNG: local official stamps for use in Prussia (1903), Germany.

A CERTO on stamps of Peru: provisionals of Ancachs (1884), Peru.

ACORES: Azores.

AFGAN, AFGHANES: Afghanistan.

AFRICA CORREIOS: Portuguese Africa.

AFRICA OCCIDENTAL ESPANOLA: Spanish West Africa.

AFRICA ORIENTALE ITALIANA: Italian East Africa.

AFRIQUE EQUATORIALE FRANCAISE, A.E.F.: French Equatorial Africa.

AFRIQUE EQUATORIALE GABON: Gabon.

AFRIQUE OCCIDENTALE FRANCAISE: French West Africa.

AITUTAKI on stamps of Cook Islands: Aitutaki.

AITUTAKI on stamps of New Zealand: Aitutaki.

ALAOUITES on stamps of France: Alaouites.

ALAOUITES on stamps of Syria: Alaouites.

ALBANIA on stamps of Italy: offices in Turkey, Italy.

ALEXANDRIE on stamps of France: offices in Egypt, France.

ALEXANDRIE: offices in Alexandria, Egypt, France.

ALGERIE on stamps of France: Algeria.

ALGERIE: Algeria.

ALLEMAGNE DUITSCHLAND on stamps of Belgium: occupation of Germany (1919-21).

A.M.G.: Allied Military Government, appeared on various stamps throughout Europe during Allied occupation.

A.M.G. — F.T.T.: free territory of Trieste (1947-54).

A.M.G. — V.G.: Venezia Giulia, Italy (1945-47).

A.M. POST: Allied occupation, Germany (1945-46).

ANDORRA on stamps of Spain: Andorra.
ANDORRE on stamps of France: Andorra.
ANDORRE: Andorra.
ANTIOQUIA: provisionals of Antioquia (1868-1904), Colombia.
A.O. on stamps of Congo: semipostal stamps under Belgian occupation (1918), German East Africa.
A.O.F. on stamps of France: semipostal stamps (1945), French West Africa.
A.O.I. on stamps of Italy: postage due stamps (1941), Italian East Africa.
A PAYER TE BETALEN: postage due stamps, Belgium.
APURIMAC: provisionals of Apurimac (1885), Peru.
ARABIE SAODITE: Saudi Arabia.
ARCHIPEL DES COMORES: Comoro Islands.
AREQUIPA: provisionals of Arequipa (1881), Peru.
ASCENSION on stamps of St. Helena: Ascension.
A&T on stamps of French Colonies: Annam and Tonkin.
ATT., ATTS.: surcharges (1893-1908), Siam (Thailand).
AUNUS on stamps of Finland: Finnish occupation (1919), Russia.
AUR.: values, Iceland.
AUSTRALIAN ANTARCTIC TERRITORY: territorial issues, Australia.
AVISPORTO: newspaper stamps, Denmark.
AYACUCHO: provisionals of Ayacucho (1881), Peru.
AZERBAIDJAN: Azerbaijan (1919-22).

- B -

B on stamps of Straits Settlements: Bangkok (1882-85).
B.A. on stamps of Great Britain: offices in Africa.
BADEN: stamps of French occupation (1947-49), Germany.
BAGHDAD on stamps of Turkey: British occupation (1917), Mesopotamia.
BAHAWALPUR: issues of internal state (1945-49), Pakistan.
BAHRAIN on stamps of Great Britain: Bahrain (1948-60).
BAHRAIN on stamps of India: Bahrain (1933-44).
BAHT: value, Siam (Thailand).
BAJAR PORTO: postage due stamps, Indonesia.
BAMRA: locals (1888-94), India.
BANAT BACSKA on stamps of Hungary: Serbian occupation (1919), Hungary.
BANI on stamps of Germany: German occupation (1917-18), Romania.
BANI on stamps of Hungary: Romanian occupation (1919), Hungary.
BARANYA on stamps of Hungary: Serbian occupation (1919), Hungary.
BARBUDA on stamps of Leeward Islands: Barbuda (1922).
BARWANI: locals (1921-48), India.
BASEL: locals (1845), Switzerland.
BASUTOLAND on stamps of South Africa: Basutoland (1945).
BATAAN AND CORREGIDOR on stamps of the Philippines: Japanese occupation (1942), Philippines.
BATYM on stamps of Russia: Batum.
BAYERN: Bavaria.
B.C.A. on stamps of Rhodesia: British Central Africa (1891-95).
B.C.M.: British Consular Mail (1884-86), Madagascar.
B.C.O.F. JAPAN 1946: military stamps (1946-47), Australia.
BECHUANALAND on stamps of South Africa: Bechuanaland Protectorate (1945).
BECHUANALAND on stamps after 1900: Bechuanaland Protectorate.
BECHUANALAND PROTECTORATE on stamps of Cape of Good Hope (1899) or Great Britain (1897-1926): Bechuanaland Protectorate.
BELGIE: Belgium.
BELGIEN on stamps of Germany: German occupation, Belgium.
BELGIQUE: Belgium.
BELGISCH CONGO: Congo (1910-60).
BELIZE on stamps of British Honduras: Belize (1973).
BENADIR: Italian Somaliland (Somalia) (1903-26).
BENGASI on stamps of Italy: offices in Africa, Italy.
BENIN on stamps of French Colonies: Benin (1892).
BERLIN on stamps of Germany: Berlin (1948).
BESETZTES GEBIET NORDFRANKREICH on stamps of France: German occupation (1940), France.
BEYROUTH on stamps of a) France or b) Russia: offices in Turkey (Levant), a) France (1905) or b) Russia (1910).

BHOPAL: locals (1908-49), India.
BHOR: locals (1901), India.
BIAFRA on stamps of Nigeria: revolutionary forces (1968-69), Nigeria.
BIJAWAR: locals (1935-37), India.
B.I.O.T. on stamps of Seychelles: British Indian Ocean Territory (1968).
B.M.A. on stamps of Great Britain: offices in Africa (1948), Great Britain.
BMA MALAYA on stamps of Straits Settlements: Straits Settlements (1945-48).
BOCTOYHAR: offices in Turkey (1868-84), Russia.
BOfTGEBIET OB, OST (Postgebiet: old-style "S" looks like "f") on stamps of Germany: German occupation (1916-17), Lithuania.
BOGACHES, BOGCHAH, BOGSHA(S): values, Yemen.
BOHMEN UND MAHREN: Bohemia and Moravia.
BOHMEN U. MAHREN on stamps of Czechoslovakia: Bohemia and Moravia (1939).
BOLIVAR: locals (1863-1904), Colombia.
BOLLODELLA POSTA DI SICILIA: Two Sicilies (1859).
BOLLO DELLA POSTA NAPOLETANA: Two Sicilies (1958).
BOLLO POSTALE: San Marino.
BOSNA I HERCEGOVINA on stamps of Bosnia and Herzegovina: locals (1918), Yugoslavia.
BOSNIEN HERCEGOVINA: Bosnia and Herzegovina (1912-18).
BOSNIENI HERZEGOWINA: Bosnia and Herzegovina (1906-12).
BOYACA: locals (1902-04), Colombia.
BRASIL: Brazil.
BRAUNSCHWEIG: Brunswick.
BRITISH BECHUANALAND on stamps of Cape of Good Hope or Great Britain: Bechuanaland.
BRITISH BECHUANALAND: Bechuanaland.
BRITISH EAST AFRICA on stamps of British India or Zanzibar: British East Africa (1895-97).
BRITISH NEW GUINEA: Papua New Guinea (1901-05).
BRITISH OCCUPATION on stamps of Russia: Batum (1919-20).
BRITISH PROTECTORATE OIL RIVERS on stamps of Great Britain: Niger Coast Protectorate (1892-93).
BRITISH SOMALILAND on stamps of India: Somaliland Protectorate (1903).
BRITISH SOUTH AFRICA COMPANY: Rhodesia (1890-1920).
BRITISH VICE CONSULATE: Madagascar (1884-86).
BR. VIRGIN ISLANDS: Virgin Islands.
BRUNEI on stamps of Labuan: Brunei (1906).
BRUXELLES BRUSSEL: surcharge precancellation (1929), Belgium.
BUENOS AIRES: locals (1858-62), Argentina.
BUITEN BEZIT on stamps of Netherlands Indies: Netherlands Indies (1908).
BULGARIE: Bulgaria.
BUNDI: locals (1941-47), India.
BUNDI SERVICE: local official stamps (1919), India.
BUREAU INTERNATIONAL D'EDUCATION: International Bureau of Education official stamps (1944-60), Switzerland.
BUREAU INTERNATIONAL DU TRAVAIL: International Labor Bureau official stamps, Switzerland.
BURMA on stamps of India: Burma (1937).
BUSHIRE on stamps of Persia: Bushire (1915).
BUSSAHIR: locals (1895-1901), India.
BUU-CHINH: Vietnam.

- C -

CABO on stamps of Nicaragua: Cabo Gracias a Dios (1904-09), Nicaragua.
CABO JUBI on stamps of Rio de Oro: Cape Juby (1916).
CABO JUBY on stamps of Spain: Cape Juby (1919-33).
CABO JUBY on stamps of Spanish Morocco: Cape Juby (1934-48).
CABO VERDE: Cape Verde.
CADIZ: revolutionary overprint (1936), Spain.
CALCHI on stamps of Italy: Calchi, Aegean Islands (1930), Italy.
CALIMNO, CALINO on stamps of Italy: Calino, Aegean Islands, Italy.
CAMBODGE: Cambodia.
CAMEROONS U.K.T.T. on stamps of Nigeria: Cameroons (1960-61).
CAMEROUN on stamps of French Congo, Gabon or Middle Congo: Cameroun (1915-25).

CAMPECHE: provisionals (1876), Mexico.
CAMPIONE D'ITALIA: locals (1944), Italy.
CANAL ZONE on stamps of the United States or Panama: Canal Zone.
CANARIAS on stamps of Spain: Canary Islands (1936-37), Spain.
CANTON on stamps of Indo-China: offices in China (1901-23), France.
CARCHI on stamps of Italy: Calchi, Aegean Islands (1932), Italy.
CARNARO on stamps of Fiume: Fiume (1920).
CARUPANO: locals (1902), Venezuela.
CASO on stamps of Italy: Caso, Aegean Islands, Italy.
CASTELLORIZO on stamps of offices of France in Turkey: Castellorizo (1920).
CASTELLORISO on stamps of France: Castellorizo (1920).
CASTELROSSO on stamps of Italy: Castellorizo (1922-32).
CAUCA: locals (1890), Colombia.
CAVALLE: offices in Turkey, France.
CCCP: Russia.
C.CH. on stamps of French Colonies: Cochin China (1886-87).
CECHY A MORAVA: Bohemia and Moravia, Czechoslovakia.
C.E.F. on stamps of Cameroun: Cameroon Expeditionary Force (1915), Cameroons.
C.E.F. on stamps of India: China Expeditionary Force (1900-21), India.
CEFALONIA E ITACA on stamps of Greece: Italian occupation (1941), Ionian Islands.
CENT, CENTS on stamps of a) France or b) Russia: offices in China (1901-22), a) France or b) Russia.
CENTENAIRE ALGERIE: France (1929).
CENTENAIRE DU GABON: French Equatorial Africa (1938).
CENTESIMI on stamps of Austria: Austrian occupation (1918), Italy.
CENTESIMI on stamps of Bosnia and Herzegovina: postage due and special delivery, Austrian occupation (1918), Italy.
CENTESIMI DI CORONA on stamps of Italy: Italian occupation, Austria (1919) or Dalmatia (1921-22).
CENTIMES on stamps of Austria: offices in Crete (1903-07), Austria.
CENTIMES on stamps of Germany: offices in Turkey (1908), Germany.
CENTIMOS on stamps, no country name: Spain (1905).
CENTIMOS on stamps of France: French Morocco (1891-1910).
CERIGO on stamps of Greece: fraudulent overprints, Ionian Islands.
CERVANTES: official stamps (1916), Spain.
CESKOSLOVENSKA, CESKOSLOVENSKO: Czechoslovakia.
CESKO-SLOVENSKO: Slovakia (1939), Czechoslovakia.
CESKO-SLOVENSKO on a stamp with Russian characters: Carpatho-Ukraine (1939), Czechoslovakia.
CFA on stamps of France: Reunion (1945 —).
C.G.H.S. on stamps of Germany: official stamps (1920-22), Upper Silesia.
CH preceding oriental characters: Korea.
CHALA: provisionals (1884), Peru.
CHAMBRA on stamps of India: Chambra, India.
CHARKHARI: locals (1894-1945), India.
CHEMINS DE FER SPOORWEGEN: parcel post, Belgium.
CHIHUAHUA: provisionals (1872), Mexico.
CHINA on stamps of a) Germany or b) Hong Kong: offices in China, of a) Germany (1898-1913) or b) Great Britain (1917-27).
CHINE on stamps of France: offices in China (1894-1922), France.
CHRISTMAS ISLAND on stamps of Australia: Christmas Island (1958-62).
C.I.H.S. on stamps of Germany: official stamps (1920), Upper Silesia.
CILICIE on stamps of France: Cilicia (1920-21).
CILICIE on stamps of Turkey: Cilicia (1919).
CINQUANTENAIRE on stamps of French Colonies: postage due (1903), New Caledonia.
CIRENAICA on stamps of Italy: Cyrenaica.
CIRENAICA on stamps of Tripolitania: airpost (1932), Cyrenaica.
C.M.T. on stamps of Austria: Romanian occupation (1919), Western Ukraine.
CN: value, Korea.
COAMO: U.S. administration (1898), Puerto Rico.
COCHIN: locals (1892-1949), India.
CO. CI. on stamps of Yugoslavia: Ljubljana (1941), Yugoslavia.
COLIS POSTAUX: parcel post, Belgium.
COLOMBIA on stamps with map of

Panama: Panama (1887-97).
COLONIA ERITREA on stamps of Italy: Eritrea (1892-1928).
COLONIALE ITALIANE: Italian Colonies.
COLONIE ITALIANE on stamps of Italy: Italian Colonies (1932).
COLONIES DE L'EMPIRE FRANCAISE: French Colonies (1859-65).
COLONIES POSTES: French Colonies (1881-86).
COMITE FRANCAIS DE LA LIBERATION NATIONALE: semipostals (1943), French Colonies.
COMORES: Comoro Islands.
COMP A DE MOCAMBIQUE on stamps of Mozambique: Mozambique Company (1892).
COMPANHIA DE MOCAMBIQUES: Mozambique Company.
COMPANHIA DO NYASSA: Nyassa (1921-23).
COMPANIA COLOMBIANA: airpost (1920), Colombia.
COMUNE DI CAMPIONE: locals of Italian enclave in Switzerland (1944), Italy.
COMUNICACIONES: Spain (1870-99).
CONFEDERATE STATES: Confederate States (1861-65), United States.
CONFOEDERATIO HELVETICA: Switzerland.
CONGO BELGE: Congo.
CONGO FRANCAIS: French Congo.
CONGO FRANCAIS GABON: Gabon (1910).
CONGRESO DE LOS DIPUTADOS: official stamps (1896-98), Spain.
CONSEIL DE L'EUROPE: Council of Europe official stamps, France.
CONSTANTINOPLE on stamps of Russia: offices in Turkey (1909-10), Russia.
CONSTANTINOPOL on stamps of Romania: offices in Turkey (1919), Romania.
COO on stamps of Italy: Coo, Aegean Islands (1930-32), Italy.
COOK ISLANDS or **COOK IS'DS** on stamps of New Zealand: Cook Islands (1936-46).
COOK NIUE ISLANDS: Niue (1938-46).
CORDOBA: provincials (1858), Argentina.
COREAN: Korea (1884-94).
COREE: Korea (1902-03).
CORFU on stamps of Greece: Italian occupation (1941), Corfu.
CORFU on stamps of Italy: Italian occupation (1923), Corfu.
CORONA on stamps of Italy: Italian occupation, Austria (1919) or Dalmatia (1919-22).
CORREIO on stamps, no country name: Portugal (1853-65).
CORREO AEREO on stamps, no country name: Spain.
CORREO ESPANOL MARRUECOS on stamps of Spain: Spanish Morocco (1903-10).
CORREO ESPANOL TANGER: Tangier semipostals (1926), Spanish Morocco.
CORREOS ARGENTINOS: Argentina (1888-90).
CORREOS INTERIOR: Philippines (1859-63).
CORREOS MEXICO GOBIERNO REVOLUCIONARIO: Yucatan (1924), Mexico.
CORREOS NACIONALES, CORREOS NALES: Colombia (1859-86).
CORREOS Y TELEGS, CORREOS Y TELEGEOS: Spain (1879).
CORREO or **CORRESPONDENCIA URGENTE**: special delivery, Spain.
CORRIENTES: provisionals (1856-78), Argentina.
COS on stamps of Italy: Coo, Aegean Islands (1912-22), Italy.
COSTA ATLANTICA B on stamps of Nicaragua: Zelaya (1907), Nicaragua.
COSTA ATLANTICA C on stamps of Nicaragua: Cabo Gracias a Dios (1907), Nicaragua.
COSTANTINOPOLI on stamps of Italy: offices in Turkey (1909-23), Italy.
COTE D'IVOIRE: Ivory Coast.
COTE (FRANCAISE) DES SOMALIS: Somali Coast.
COUR PERMANENTE DE JUSTICE INTERNATIONALE: International Court of Justice official stamps: Netherlands.
CROISSANT ROUGE TURC: tax stamps, Turkey.
CRUZ ROJA DOMINICANA: tax stamps (1932), Dominican Republic.
CRUZ ROJA HONDURENA: tax stamps, Honduras.
CRUZ VERMELHA: Red Cross franchise stamps, Portugal.
CTOT, CTOTNHKN: Bulgaria.
CUAUTLA: provisionals (1867), Mexico.
CUBA on stamps of the United States: U.S. administration (1899), Cuba.

CUCUTA: provisionals (1904-07), Colombia.
CUERNAVACA: provisionals (1867), Mexico.
CUNDINAMARCA: locals (1870-1904), Colombia.
CURACAO: Netherlands Antilles (1873-1948).
CUZCO on stamps of Peru or Arequipa, Peru: provisionals (1882-84), Peru.
C.X.C. on stamps of Bosnia and Herzegovina: Bosnia and Herzegovina (1918), Yugoslavia.
CYPRUS on stamps of Great Britain: Cyprus (1880-81).

- D -

DAI NIPPON on stamps of Malaya or Malayan States: Japanese occupation (1942), Malaya or Malayan States.
DANMARK: Denmark.
DANSK-VESTINDIEN, DANSK-VEST-INDISKE: Danish West Indies.
DANZIG on stamps of Germany: Danzig (1920-23).
DARDANELLES on stamps of Russia: offices in Turkey (1910), Russia.
DATIA: locals (1897), India.
DBL (script characters) on stamps of Russia: Far Eastern Republic (1920).
DDR: German Democratic Republic, Germany.
DEDEAGH: offices in Turkey (1893-1903), France.
DEFICIT: postage due, Peru.
DEL GOLFO DE GUINEA: Spanish Guinea.
DEN WAISEN SIROTAM on stamps of Italy: German occupation (1944), Ljubljana, Yugoslavia.
DEUTfCHES REICH (DEUTSCHES REICH: old-style "S" looks like "f"): Germany.
DEUTfCHOfTERREICH (DEUTSCH-OSTERREICH: old-style "S" looks like "f"): Austria (1918-21).
DEUTSCHE DEMOKRATISCHE REPUBLIK: German Democratic Republic, Germany.
DEUTSCH NEU GUINEA: German New Guinea.
DEUTSCH OSTAFRIKA: German East Africa.
DEUTSCH SUDWEST AFRIKA: German Southwest Africa.
DEUTSCHE followed by **BUNDEPOST**, **FELDPOST**, **NATIONALVERSAMMLUNG**, **POfT** or **POST**: Germany.
DEUTSCHE MILITAER-VERWALTUNG MONTENEGRO on stamps of Yugoslavia: German occupation (1943), Montenegro.
DEUTSCHE POST OSTEN on stamps of Germany: German occupation (1939), Poland.
DEUTSCHES REICH(-POST): Germany.
DEUTSCHES REICH GENERAL-GOUVERNEMENT: German occupation (1941-44), Poland.
DEUTSCHLAND: Allied occupation (1945-46), Germany.
DHAR: locals (1898-1901), India.
DIEGO-SUAREZ on stamps of French Colonies: Diego-Suarez (1892-96).
DIENST on stamps of Netherlands Indies: official stamps (1911), Netherlands Indies.
DIENST SACHE: official stamps of Wurttemberg, German States, Germany.
DILIGENCIA: Uruguay (1856-57).
DINERO on stamps, no country name: Peru (1858-72).
DISTRITO on stamps of Arequipa: provisionals of Cuzco (1881-85), Peru.
DJ or **DJIBOUTI** on stamps of Obock: Somali Coast (1894-1902).
DJIBOUTI: Somali Coast.
DOLLAR on stamps of Russia: offices in China (1917), Russia.
DOPLATA: postage due, Central Lithuania or Poland.
DOPLATIT or **DOPLATNE**: postage due, Czechoslovakia.
DPRK: Korea, North (1977 —).
DRZAVA on stamps of Bosnia and Herzegovina: Bosnia and Herzegovina (1918), Yugoslavia.
DRZAVA SHS: Slovenia (1919), Yugoslavia.
DRZAVNA: Croatia (1919), Yugoslavia.
DUITSCH OOST AFRIKA BELGISCHE BEZETTING on stamps of Congo: Belgian occupation (1916-22), German East Africa.
DURAZZO on stamps of Italy: offices in Turkey (1909-16), Italy.
DUTTIA: locals (1893-1921), India.

- E -

EAAAC, EAAAE, EAAAS or similar Greek letters: Greece.
E.A.F. on stamps of Great Britain: East Africa Forces (1943-46), Great Britain.
ECUADOR on stamps of Colombia: airpost

(1928-29), Ecuador.

E E F: British occupation (1918), Palestine.

EESTI: Estonia.

EE. UU. DE C.: provisionals of Tolima (1870), Colombia.

EGEO on stamps of Italy: Aegean Islands, Italy.

EGYPTE, EGYPTIENNES: Egypt.

EINZUZIEHEN: postage due, Danzig.

EIRE: Ireland.

EJERCITO RENOVADOR: provisionals of Sinaloa (1923), Mexico.

ELfAfS (ELSASS: old-style "S" looks like "f") on stamps of Germany: German occupation (1940), France.

EL PARLAMENTO A CERVANTES: official stamps (1916), Spain.

EL SALVADOR: Salvador.

ELUA KENETA: Hawaii (1861-93).

EMP. OTTOMAN: Turkey (1876-90).

EMPIRE FRANC(AIS): France (1853-71) or French Colonies (1871-72).

ENAPIOMON: postage due, Greece.

EONIKH: tax stamps (1914), Greece.

EPMAKb: South Russia (1919).

EQUATEUR: Ecuador (1887).

E.R. on stamps with no country name: Great Britain (1952-67).

ERITREA on stamps of Great Britain: offices in Eritrea (1948-51), Great Britain.

ESCUELAS: Venezuela (1871-95).

ESPANA: Spain.

ESPANA SAHARA: Spanish Sahara.

ESPANOLA, ESPANS: Spain.

ESTADO DA INDIA: Portuguese India (1946-62).

ESTADOS UNIDOS DE NUEVA GRANADA: Colombia (1861).

EST AFRICAIN ALLEMAND on stamps of Congo: Belgian occupation (1916-22), German East Africa.

ESTERO on stamps of Italy: offices abroad (1874-85), Italy.

ETABLIS(SEMENTS FRANCAIS) DANS L'INDE: French India (1914-54).

ETABLISSEMENTS DE L'INDE: French India (1892-1907).

ETABLISSEMENTS or **ETS. (FRANCAIS) DE L'OCEANIE**: French Polynesia.

ETAT FRANCAIS: France.

ETHIOPIE, ETHIOPIENNES: Ethiopia.

ETIOPIA: Italian occupation (1936), Ethiopia.

EUPEN on stamps of Germany: Belgian occupation (1920-21), Germany.

EXPED. SCIENT.: China (1932).

EXPOSICION . . . BARCELONA: Spain (1929-30).

EXPOSITION COLONIALE INTERNATIONALE: France (1930-31).

- F -

FACTAJ on stamps of Romania: parcel post (1928), Romania.

FARIDKOT STATE on stamps of India: locals (1887-1901), India.

FDO. POO: Fernando Po (1897-99).

FEDERATED MALAY STATES: Malaya (1900-35).

FELDPOST on stamps of Germany: military stamps (1944), Germany.

FEN on stamps of Poland: locals (1918), Poland.

FEN, FN: values, Manchukuo.

FERNANDO POO: Fernando Po.

FEZZAN: French occupation (1943-51), Libya.

FIERA CAMPIONARIA TRIPOLI: Libya (1934).

FIERA DI TRIESTE on stamps of Italy: Trieste (1950-53).

FILIPINAS: Philippines.

FILLER, FT: values, Hungary.

FIUME on stamps of Hungary: Fiume (1918-19).

FLUCHTLINGSHILFE MONTENEGRO on stamps of Yugoslavia: German occupation, semipostals (1944), Montenegro.

FORCES FRANCAISES LIBRES LEVANT on stamps of Syria: French military stamps (1942), Syria.

FOROYAR: Faroe Islands.

FR. on stamps of Senegal or Mauritania: French West Africa (1943-44).

FRANC on stamps of Austria: offices in Crete (1903-04), Austria.

FRANCA on stamps of Peru: provisionals (1884), Peru.

FRANCAIS, FRANCAISE: France or French Colonies.

FRANCE D'OUTRE-MER: semipostals (1943), French Colonies.

FRANCO BOLLO: Italy or Italian States.

FRANCO MARKE: Bremen (1856-60), German States.

FRANCO SCRISOREI: Moldavia-Walachia (1862-63), Romania.

FRANQUICIA: franchise stamps (1881), Spain.

FREI DURCH ABLOSUNG: local official stamps (1903-05), Germany.

FREIMARKE: German States.

FREIFTAAT (FREISTAAT) BAYERN on stamps of Germany or Bavaria: Bavaria (1919-20), German States.

FRIMAERKE KGL POST: Denmark (1851).

FUNF GROTE: Bremen (1856-60), German States.

FURSTENTUM, FUERSTENTUM, FVERSTENTUM: Liechtenstein.

- G -

G on stamps of Cape of Good Hope: Griqualand West (1877-80).

GAB on stamps of French Colonies: Gabon (1886-89).

GABON on stamps of French Colonies: Gabon (1889).

GARCH: Saudi Arabia (1929-30).

GARZON: Tolima provisionals (1894), Colombia.

G.E.A. on stamps of East Africa and Uganda Protectorates: British occupation (1917), German East Africa.

G.E.A. on stamps of Kenya, Uganda & Tanganyika: Tanganyika (1921-22).

G ET D, G & D on stamps of Guadeloupe: Guadeloupe (1903-04).

GENERALGOUVERNEMENT: German occupation (1940-44), Poland.

GENEVE: Geneva cantonal locals (1843-49), Switzerland.

GEN.-GOUV. WARfCHAU (old-style "S" looks like "f") on stamps of Germany: German occupation (1916-17), Poland.

GEORGIE: Georgia (1919).

GEORGIENNE: Georgia (1920).

GERUSALEMME on stamps of Italy: offices in Turkey (1909-11), Italy.

GHADAMES: French occupation (1949), Libya.

GHANA on stamps of Gold Coast: Ghana (1957-65).

GIBRALTAR on stamps of Bermuda: Gibraltar (1886).

GILBERT & ELLICE PROTECTORATE on stamps of Fiji: Gilbert and Ellice Islands (1911).

GIORNALI STAMPE: newspaper stamps (1861), Sardinia, Italian States.

GOLFO DE GUINEA: Spanish Guinea (1907-49).

GORNY SLASK: unrecognized private issue, Upper Silesia.

GOVERNO MILITARE ALLEATO on stamps of Italy: Allied occupation (1943), Italy.

GOYA: Spain (1930).

G.P.E. on stamps of French Colonies: Guadeloupe (1884-91).

GRAHAM LAND on stamps of Falkland Islands: Graham Land (1944), Falkland Islands.

GRANA: Neapolitan provinces (1861), Two Sicilies, Italian States.

GRANADA: Colombia (1861).

GRANADINA: Colombia (1859-60).

GRANDE COMORE: Grand Comoro (1897-1912).

GRAND LIBAN: Lebanon (1924-27).

G.R.I. on stamps of a) German New Guinea or b) German Samoa: British administration, of a) New Britain (1914-15) or b) Samoa (1914).

G.R.I. on stamps of Marshall Islands: New Britain (1914).

GRONLAND: Greenland.

GROSSDEUTSCHES REICH: semipostals (1943-45), Germany.

GROSSDEUTSCHES REICH GENERALGOUVERNEMENT: semipostals (1943-44), German occupation, Poland.

GROSZY on stamps of Poland: surcharge (1950), Poland.

GUADALAJARA: provisionals (1867-68), Mexico.

GUADELOUPE on stamps of French Colonies: Guadeloupe (1889-91).

GUAM on stamps of United States: Guam (1899).

GUANACASTE on stamps of Costa Rica: Guanacaste locals (1885-90), Costa Rica.

GUINE: Portuguese Guinea.

GUINEA CONTINENTAL on stamps of Elobey, Annobon and Corisco: Spanish Guinea (1906).

GUINEA CONTIAL ESPANOLA: Spanish Guinea (1903-09).

GUINEA CORREOS on stamps of Spanish Guinea: fraudulent overprints (1914), Spanish Guinea.

GUINEA ECUATORIAL: Equatorial Guinea.

GUINEA ESPANOLA: Spanish Guinea (1902, 1949-60).

GUINEE: French Guinea.

GULTIG 9. ARMEE on stamps of Germany: German occupation (1918), Romania.

GUYANA on stamps of British Guiana: Guyana (1966-68).

GUYANE, GUY. FRANC. on stamps of French Colonies: French Guiana (1886-92).
GUYANE: French Guiana.
G.W. on stamps of Cape of Good Hope: Griqualand West (1877).
GWALIOR on stamps of India or British India: locals, India.

- H -

HABILITADO on stamps of Cuba: U.S. administration (1898-99), Cuba.
HADHRAMAUT: locals (1955 —), Aden.
HANG-KHONG: airmail, Vietnam.
HANNOVER: Hanover (1850-66), German States.
HASHEMITE KINGDOM: Jordan (1949 —).
HAUTE SILESIE: Upper Silesia.
HAUTE VOLTA: Upper Volta.
HAUT-SENEGAL NIGER: Upper Senegal and Niger (1914-17).
HBA on stamps of Russia: Siberia (1921).
H.E.H. THE NIZAM'S: Hyderabad locals (1927-49), India.
HEJAZ & NEJD, HEDJAZ & NEDJDE: Saudi Arabia (1929-33).
HELLAS: Greece (1966 —).
HELVETIA: Switzerland.
H.H. NAWAB SHAH (or **SULTAN**) **JAHANBEGAM**: Bhopal locals, India.
H.I.: Hawaii (1851-93).
HIRLAPJEGY: newspaper stamps (1900-22), Hungary.
HOBY: Montenegro (1874-96).
HOI HAO on stamps of Indo-China: offices in China (1901-19), France.
HOLKAR STATE: Indore locals (1886-1908), India.
HOLSTEIN: Schleswig-Holstein (1865-66), German States.
HONDA on stamps of Colombia: Tolima provisionals (1896), Colombia.
H.P. followed by Russian characters: Bulgaria.
HRVATSKA: Croatia or Croatia-Slavonia, Yugoslavia.
HRZGL: Holstein (1864), Schleswig-Holstein, German States.
HT SENEGAL-NIGER: Upper Senegal and Niger (1906-14).
HYDERABAD: locals (1946), India.

- I -

I.B.: West Irian (1970).
ICC on stamps of India: International Commission in Indo-China (1965-68), Laos and Vietnam, India.
IDAR: locals (1939-44), India.
I.E.F. on stamps of India: India Expeditionary Force military stamps (1914), India.
I.E.F. 'D' on stamps of Turkey: Mesopotamia (1919).
IERUSALEM on stamps of Russia: offices in Turkey (1909-10), Russia.
ILE ROUAD on stamps of French offices in Levant: Rouad (1916).
ILES WALLIS ET FUTUNA on stamps of New Caledonia: Wallis and Futuna Islands (1920-40).
IMPERIO COLONIAL PORTUGUES: postage due (1945), Portuguese Africa.
IMPUESTO DE GUERRA: war tax stamps (1874-98), Spain.
INDE: French India.
INDIA PORT(UGUEZA): Portuguese India (1871-86).
INDIA and Portuguese inscriptions: Portuguese India.
INDOCHINE: Indo-China.
INDONESIA REPUBLIK: Indonesia.
INDONESIA: Indonesia (1948-49), Netherlands Indies.
INDORE STATE: locals (1904-47), India.
INDUSTRIELLE KRIEGSWIRTSCHAFT: War Board of Trade official stamps (1918), Switzerland.
INHAMBANE on stamps of Mozambique: Inhambane (1895).
INKERI: North Ingermanland (1920).
INLAND on stamps with no country name: Liberia (1881).
INSELPOST on stamps of Germany: military stamps, Germany.
INSTRUCAO on stamps of Portuguese India: tax stamps (1934-35), Timor.
INSTRUCCION: Venezuela (1893-95).
INSUFFICIENTLY PREPAID: postage due (1931-33), Zanzibar.
IONIKON KPATOE: Ionian Islands (1859).
I.O.V.R.: tax stamps (1948), Romania.
IRAN: Persia (1935 —).
IRANIENNES: Persia (1935-37).
IRAQ on stamps of Turkey: Mesopotamia (1918-22).
IRIAN BARAT: West Irian (1963-68).
I.R. OFFICIAL on stamps of Great Britain: official stamps (1882-1904), Great Britain.
ISLAND: Iceland.
ISOLE ITALIANE DELL'EGEO on stamps

of Italy: Aegean Islands (1930-40), Italy.
ISOLE JONIE on stamps of Italy: Italian occupation (1941), Ionian Islands.
ISTRA: locals for Istria and the Slovene Coast (1945-46), Yugoslavia.
ITA-KARJALA: Finnish occupation (1941-43), Karelia.
ITALIA, ITALIANE, ITALIANO: Italy.
IZMIR HIMAYEI ETFAL CEMIYETI: tax stamps (1933), Turkey.

- J -

J on stamps of Peru: Yca provisionals (1884), Peru.
JAFFA on stamps of Russia: offices in Turkey (1909-10), Russia.
JAIPUR: locals (1904-49), India.
JAMHURI: Zanzibar (1964-68).
JANINA on stamps of Italy: offices in Turkey (1909-11), Italy.
JAPANESE: Japan (1876-96).
JAVA on stamps of Netherlands Indies: locals (1908), Netherlands Indies.
JEEND STATE on stamps of India: Jind locals (1885), India.
JHIND STATE on stamps of India: Jind locals (1885-1913), India.
JIND on stamps of India: locals (1913-43), India.
JOHOR with **MALAYSIA**: regional issues of Johore (1965 —), Malaysia.
JOHOR, JOHORE on stamps of Straits Settlements: regional issues of Johore (1876-91), Malaya.
JOHORE: Johore (1892-1960), Malaya.
JOURNAUX DAGBLADEN on stamps of Belgium: newspaper stamps, Belgium.
JUAN FERNANDEZ on stamps of Chile: Chile (1910).
JUBILE DE L'UNION POSTALE UNIVERSELLE: Switzerland (1900).
JUGOSLAVIA, JUGOSLAVIJA: Yugoslavia.

- K -

KAIS KON(IGL): Austria (1853-1907).
KALAYAAN NANG PILIPINAS: Japanese occupation (1943), Philippines.
KAMERUN on stamps of Germany: Cameroun (1897).
KAMERUN: Cameroun (1900-18).
KAP: values (1918-22), Latvia.
KARJALA: Karelia (1922).
KARJALA on stamps of Finland: Finnish occupation (1941-43), Karelia.
KARKI on stamps of Italy: Aegean Islands (1912-22), Italy.
KARNTEN UBfTIMMUNG (ABSTIMMUNG: old-style "A" looks like "U," "S" looks like "f") on stamps of Austria: Carinthian plebiscite (1920), Austria.
KAROLINEN: Caroline Islands.
KASAI (SOUTH KASAI) and **KATANGA**: nonrecognized states (1960-61), Congo.
KATHIRI STATE OF SEIYUN: locals (1942 —), Aden.
K.C.-NOUITA: Serbia (1866).
KEDAH: locals, Malaya, Malaysia.
(KEELING), Cocos Islands.
KELANTAN: locals, Malaya, Malaysia.
KENTTA-POSTI FALTPOST on stamps of Finland: military stamps (1943), Finland.
KENTTAPOSTIA: military stamps (1941-63), Finland.
KENYA AND UGANDA: Kenya, Uganda and Tanzania (1922-33).
KENYA UGANDA TANGANYIKA (in any order), Kenya, Uganda and Tanzania (1935-64).
KENYA UGANDA TANZANIA (in any order), Kenya, Uganda and Tanzania (1965 —).
KERASSUNDE on stamps of Russia: offices in Turkey (1909-10), Russia.
K.G.C. 19A20 on stamps of Yugoslavia: Carinthian plebiscite (1920), Yugoslavia.
K.G.L. with cents: Danish West Indies (1855-73).
K.G.L. with skillings: Denmark (1851-68).
KHMERE: Cambodia (1971 —).
KHOR FAKKAN: locals (1964 —), Sharjah and Dependencies.
KIAUTSCHOU: Kiauchau.
KIBRIS: Cyprus (1960 —).
KIBRIS CUMHURIYETI: Cyprus (1960).
KIONGA on stamps of Lourenco Marques: Kionga (1916).
KISHANGARH: locals (1904-47), India.
KISHENGARH: Kishangarh locals (1899-1904), India.
K-number-**K** on stamps of Russia: Far Eastern Republic (1920).
K 60 K on stamps of Russia: Armenia (1919).
KLAIPEDA: Lithuanian occupation (1923), Memel.
KONGELIGT: Denmark (1851).
KOP KOH: Finland (1856-66).
KORCA, KORCE(S), Albania (1914-18).

KORONA: values (1900-26), Hungary.
KOUANG-TCHEOU on stamps of Indo-China: offices in China (1906-41), France.
KPHTH: Crete (1900-10).
KRALJEVINA, KRALJEVSTVO: Yugoslavia (1921-33).
KRONE, KRONEN: values (1899-1925), Austria.
KSA: Saudi Arabia (1975 —).
K-U-K-MILITARPOST: Bosnia and Herzegovina (1912-18).
K.U.K. FELDPOST on stamps of Bosnia and Herzegovina: military stamps (1915), Austria.
K-U-K-FELDPOST: military stamps (1915-18), Austria.
K-U-K-FELDPOST with **BANI** or **LEI**: Austrian occupation (1917-18), Romania.
K-UND-K FELDPOST: military semi-postals (1918), Austria.
KUPA on stamps of Yugoslavia: Italian occupation (1941-42), Yugoslavia.
KURLAND on stamps of Germany: German occupation (1945), Latvia.
KUWAIT on stamps of India (1923-45) or Great Britain (1948-58): Kuwait.
K. WURTT. POST: Wurttemberg (1875-1900), German States.

- L -

LA AGUERA: Aguera (1920-22).
LABUAN on stamps of North Borneo: Labuan (1905-06).
LA CANEA on stamps of Italy: offices in Crete (1900-12), Italy.
LA GEORGIE: Georgia (1919).
LAIBACH: German occupation (1944-45), Ljubljana, Yugoslavia.
LAND-POST: postage due (1862), Baden, German States.
LANSA: airmail (1950), Colombia.
L.A.R.: Libyan Arab Republic (1969 —), Libya.
LAS BELA: locals (1897-1907), India.
LATTAQUIE on stamps of Syria: Latakia (1931-33).
LATVIJA, LATWIJA: Latvia.
LEI on stamps of Austria: Austrian occupation (1917-18), Romania.
LERO on stamps of Italy: Aegean Islands (1930-32), Italy.
LEROS on stamps of Italy: Aegean Islands (1912-22), Italy.
LESOTHO on stamps of Basutoland: Lesotho (1966).
LEVANT: offices in Turkey (1902-23), France.
LEVANT on stamps of a) Great Britain or b) Poland: offices in Turkey, a) Great Britain (1905-06) or b) Poland (1919-21).
LIBAN, LIBANAISE: Lebanon.
LIBAU on stamps of Germany: German occupation (1919), Latvia.
LIBIA: Libya (1912-51).
LIBYA on stamps of Cyrenaica: Libya (1951).
LIBYE: Libya.
LIETUVA, LIETUVOS: Lithuania.
LIETUVA on stamps of Russia: South District (1919), Lithuania.
LIGNES AERIENNES: military airmail (1942), Syria.
LIMA: Peru (1871-89).
LIMBAGAN on stamps of Philippines: Japanese occupation (1943), Philippines.
LIPSO on stamps of Italy: Aegean Islands (1912-32), Italy.
LIRE on stamps of Austria: Austrian occupation (1918), Italy.
LISBOA: tax stamps (1913) or franchise stamps (1903-38), Portugal.
LISSO on stamps of Italy: Aegean Islands (1930), Italy.
LITAS: values (1922-40), Lithuania.
LITWA, LITWY: Central Lithuania.
LJUBLJANSKA: German occupation (1944-45), Ljubljana, Yugoslavia.
L. MARQUES on stamps of Mozambique: Lourenco Marques (1895-97).
LMcL: Lady McLeod, private internal issue (1847), Trinidad.
LOSEN: postage due, Sweden.
LOTHRINGEN on stamps of Germany: German occupation (1940), France.
L.P. on stamps of Russia: Russian occupation (1919), Latvia.
LTSR on stamps of Lithuania: Russian occupation (1940), Lithuania.
LUBIANA on stamps of Yugoslavia: Italian occupation (1941), Ljubljana, Yugoslavia.
LUEBECK: Lubeck (1863-67), German States.
LUFTFELDPOST: military airmail (1942), Germany.
LUXEMBURG on stamps of Germany: German occupation (1940-41), Luxembourg.

- M -

MACAU: Macao.

MACAU: tax stamps, Macao.
MADAGASCAR on stamps of France: Madagascar (1895).
MADEIRA on stamps of Portugal: Madeira (1868-98).
MADRID: Spain (1920-30).
MAFEKING on stamps of Bechuanaland Protectorate or Cape of Good Hope: Cape of Good Hope (1900).
MAGYAR, MAGYAR—: Hungary.
MAGYAR NEMZETI KORMANY SZEGED on stamps of Hungary: Serbian occupation (1919), Szeged, Hungary.
MAHRA SULTANATE OF QISHN AND SOCOTRA: locals (1967), South Arabia.
MALACCA: locals, Malaya.
MALAGA on stamps of Spain: revolutionary issues (1937), Spain.
MALAGASY: Madagascar (1961 —).
MALDIVES on stamps of Ceylon: Maldive Islands (1906-09).
MALGACHE: Madagascar (1959-61).
MALMEDY on stamps of Belgium: Belgian occupation (1920-21), Germany.
MALUKU SELATAN: local or private issues (South Moluccas), Indonesia.
MANAMA: locals, Ajman.
MANIZALES: local private post, Colombia.
MARIANAS ESPANOLAS on stamps of the Philippines: Mariana Islands (1899).
MARIANEN: Mariana Islands (1899-1919).
MARIENWERDER on stamps of Germany: plebiscite (1920), Marienwerder.
MARKA: values (1919-28), Estonia.
MARKKA, MARKKAA: values, Finland.
MAROC: French Morocco or Morocco.
MAROCCO on stamps of Germany: offices in Morocco, Germany.
MAROKKO on stamps of Germany: offices in Morocco (1911), Germany.
MARRUECOS on stamps of Spain or with **ESPANOL**: Spanish Morocco.
MARRUECOS without **ESPANOL**: Northern Zone (1956-58), Morocco.
MARSHALL-INSELN: Marshall Islands.
MARTINIQUE on stamps of French Colonies: Martinique (1886-92).
MAURITANIE: Mauritania.
M.B.D. on stamps with Indian characters: Nandgaon locals (1893-95), India.
MBLEDHJA KUSHTETUESE on stamps of Albania: Italian dominion (1939), Albania.
MBRETNI(J)A: Albania.
MECKLENB.: Mecklenburg-Schwerin (1856-67), German States.
MEDELLIN: provisionals (1888-89), Antioquia, Colombia.
MEDIA ONZA: official stamps (1854-63), Spain.
MEDIO REAL: Dominican Republic (1865-79).
M.E.F. on stamps of Great Britain: Middle East Forces offices (1942-50), Great Britain.
MEJICO: Mexico (1856-64).
MELAKA: Malacca locals, Malaysia.
MEMEL on stamps of France: Memel (1920-23).
MEMEL with **KLAIPEDA**: Lithuanian occupation (1923), Memel.
MEMEL-GEBIET on stamps of Germany: Memel (1920).
METELIN on stamps of Russia: offices in Turkey (1910), Russia.
MEXICANO: Mexico.
MILITARPOST: Bosnia and Herzegovina.
MILL., MILLIEME(S) on stamps of France: offices in Egypt (1921-28), France.
M. KIR.: Hungary (1916).
MN: values (1884-95), Korea.
MOCAMBIQUE: Mozambique.
MODONES: Modena (1859), Italian States.
MONASTIR on stamps of Turkey: Turkey (1911).
MONGTSEU, MONGTZE on stamps of Indo-China: offices in China (1903-19), France.
MONT ATHOS on stamps of Russia: offices in Turkey (1909-10), Russia.
MONTE CASSINO on stamps of Poland (exile in Great Britain), Polish government in exile in Great Britain (1944), Poland.
MONTENEGRO on stamps of a) Austria or b) Yugoslavia: a) Austrian (1917-18) or b) Italian (1941-42) occupation, Montenegro.
MONTEVIDEO: Uruguay (1858-67).
MONTSERRAT on stamps of Antigua: Montserrat (1876).
MOQUEA on stamps of Peru: Moquegua provisionals (1885), Peru.
MOQUEGUA on stamps of Arequipa, Peru: provisionals (1881-85), Peru.
MOROCCO AGENCIES on stamps of Gibraltar or Great Britain: offices in Morocco, Great Britain.
MORVI STATE: locals (1931-48), India.
MOYEN CONGO: Middle Congo.

MQE on stamps of French Colonies: Martinique (1886-91).
MUSCAT & OMAN: Oman (1966-70).
M.V.i.R. on stamps of Romania or Germany: German occupation (1917-18), Romania.

- N -

NABHA on stamps of India: locals, India.
NACIONES UNIDAS: United Nations.
NANDGAM: Nandgaon locals (1891-95), India.
NAPA, NAPE: Serbia.
NAPOLETANA: Two Sicilies (1858-60), Italian States.
NA SLASK: semipostals (1921), Central Lithuania.
NATIONALER VERWALTUNGSAUSSCHUSS on stamps of Montenegro: German occupation (1943), Montenegro.
NATIONS UNIES: United Nations.
NATIONS UNIES with **HELVETIA**: official stamps, United Nations European office, Switzerland.
NAURU on stamps of Great Britain: Nauru (1916-23).
N.C.E. on stamps of French Colonies: New Caledonia (1881-93).
N.D. HRVATSKA: Croatia.
NEDERLAND: Netherlands.
NED(ERLANDSE) ANTILLEN: Netherlands Antilles (1949 —).
NED(ERLANDSCH)-INDIE: Netherlands Indies (1864-1949).
NED(ERLANDS) NIEUW GUINEA: Netherlands New Guinea (1950-62).
NEGERI SEMBILAN: Negri Sembilan locals, Malaysia.
NEGRI SEMBILAN: locals, Malaya.
NEW HEBRIDES CONDOMINIUM on stamps of Fiji: New Hebrides (1908-10).
NEZ(AVISNA) DRZ(AVA) HRVATSKA: Croatia.
N.F. on stamps of Nyasaland Protectorate: British occupation (1916), German East Africa.
NIEUW GUINEA: Netherlands New Guinea (1950-62).
NIEUWE REPUBLIEK: New Republic (1886-88).
NIPPON: Japan (1966 —).
NISIRO on stamps of Italy: Aegean Islands (1930-32), Italy.
NISIROS on stamps of Italy: Aegean Islands (1912-22), Italy.
NIUE on stamps of New Zealand: Niue.
NLLE. CALEDONIE: New Caledonia.
NO HAY ESTAMPILLAS: locals (1894-1912), Colombia.
NOPTO on stamps of Bosnia and Herzegovina: postage due (1919), Bosnia and Herzegovina: Yugoslavia.
NOPTO MAPKA: postage due, Serbia.
NORDDEUTSCHER POSTBEZIRK: North German Confederation (1868-71), German States.
NORD-DEUTSCHE-POST: North German Confederation official stamps (1870-71), German States.
NOREG: Norway.
NORFOLK ISLAND on stamps of Australia: Norfolk Island (1959).
NORGE: Norway.
NOSSI-BE on stamps of French Colonies: Nossi-Be (1891-94).
NOUVELLE CALEDONIE: New Caledonia (1905 —).
NOUVELLES HEBRIDES: French issues, New Hebrides.
NOWANUGGUR: locals (1877), India.
NOYTA: Russia.
NOYT MAPKA with foreign characters: Azerbaijan (1922-24).
NSB on stamps of French Colonies: Nossi-Be (1890-93).
N.S.W.: New South Wales.
N.W. PACIFIC ISLANDS on stamps of Australia: North West Pacific Islands.
NYASALAND: Nyasaland Protectorate.
NYASSA on stamps of Mozambique: Nyassa (1898).
N.Z.: New Zealand.

- O -

OAHA MAPKA: Finland (1866-74).
OAXACA: civil war issue (1914), Mexico.
OBOCK on stamps of French Colonies: Obock (1892).
OCCUPATION FRANCAISE on stamps of Hungary: French occupation (1919), Hungary.
OCEANIE: French Polynesia (1892-1958).
OESTERR POST with **KAIS KOENIGL**: Austria (1883-1907).
OESTERR-POST with **LIECHTENSTEIN**: Liechtenstein (1912-20).
OEUVRES DE SOLIDARITE FRANCAISE: semipostals (1943-44), French Colonies.
OFF(ENTLIG) SAK: official stamps, Norway.
OFFICIAL on stamps of Kenya and

Uganda: official stamps (1959-60), Tanganyika.

OFFISIEEL without **OFFICIAL**: official stamps, South-West Africa.

OFFISIEEL OFFICIAL: official stamps, South Africa.

OfTERREICH (OSTERREICH: old-style "S" looks like "f"): Austria.

OIL RIVERS: Niger Coast Protectorate (1892-93).

OKCA: Army of the North (1919), Russia.

OLTRE GIUBA on stamps of Italy: Oltre Giuba.

O.M.F. SYRIE on stamps of France: Syria (1920-22).

ORANGE RIVER COLONY on stamps of Cape of Good Hope: Orange River Colony (1900-02).

ORANJE VRIJ STAAT: Orange River Colony.

ORCHA POSTAGE: Orchha locals (1913-17), India.

ORCHHA STATE: locals (1939-40), India.

ORGANISATION INTERNATIONALE POUR LES REFUGIES on stamps of Switzerland: International Organization for Refugees official stamps (1950), Switzerland.

ORGANISATION METEOROLOGIQUE MONDIALE: World Meteorological Organization official stamps: Switzerland.

ORGANISATION MONDIALE DE LA SANTE: World Health Organization official stamps: Switzerland.

ORTS(-)POST: Switzerland (1850).

O.S.: official stamps (1951-52), Norway.

OSTEN on stamps of Germany: German occupation (1939), Poland.

OSTERREICH: Austria.

OSTERR(EICHISCHE) POST: Austria.

OSTLAND on stamps of Germany: German occupation (1941-43), Russia.

OTVORENIE SLOVENSKENO on stamps of Czechoslovakia: Slovakia (1939), Czechoslovakia.

OUBANGUI-CHARI(-TCHAD) on stamps of Middle Congo: Ubangi (1915-24).

O.W. OFFICIAL on stamps of Great Britain: Office of Works official stamps (1896-1902), Great Britain.

- P -

P on stamps of Straits Settlements: Perak (1878), Malaya.

P with numeral and queen's cameo, no country name: Great Britain (1971 —).

PACCHI POSTALI: parcel post, Italy, San Marino (diagonal value) or Somalia (star and crescent).

PACKHOI on stamps of Indo-China: offices in China (1903-04), France.

PAHANG: locals, Malaya, Malaysia.

PAISA: values, Nepal.

PAITA on stamps of Peru: provisionals (1884), Peru.

PAK-HOI on stamps of Indo-China: offices in China (1906-19), France.

PAKISTAN on stamps of India: Pakistan (1947-49).

PAKKE-PORTO: parcel post, Greenland.

PALESTINE on stamps of Egypt: occupation of Palestine (1948-67), Egypt.

PAPUA on stamps of British New Guinea: Papua New Guinea (1907).

PAPUA AND NEW GUINEA: Papua New Guinea (1952-71).

PARA on stamps of a) Austria b) Germany c) Russia or d) Italy: offices in Turkey, a) Austria b) Germany c) Russia or d) Italy.

PARAS on stamps of a) France b) Great Britain or c) Romania: offices in Turkey, a) France b) Great Britain or c) Romania.

PARM: Parma (1852-55), Italian States.

PARMENSI: Parma (1853-59), Italian States.

PASCO on stamps of Peru: provisionals (1884), Peru.

PATIALA on stamps of India: locals (1891-1947), India.

PATMO on stamps of Italy: Aegean Islands (1930-32), Italy.

PATMOS on stamps of Italy: Aegean Islands (1912-22), Italy.

PCOCP: Russia (1921-23).

PECHINO on stamps of Italy: offices in China (1917-19), Italy.

PEN, PENNI(A): values: Finland.

PENANG: locals, Malaya.

PENRHYN on stamps of Cook Islands: Penrhyn Island (1973 —).

PENRHYN ISLAND on stamps of New Zealand: Penrhyn Island (1902-20).

PEOPLE'S REPUBLIC OF SOUTHERN YEMEN on stamps of South Arabia: Yemen (1968).

PEOPLE'S DEMOCRATIC REPUBLIC OF YEMEN: Yemen (1971 —).

PERAK: locals, Malaya, Malaysia.

PERLIS: locals, Malaya, Malaysia.

PERSANE(S), Persia (1881-1935).

PERSEKUTUAN TANAH MELAYU:

Malaya (1957-63).
PERUANA: Peru.
PERV: Peru.
PESA on stamps of Germany: German East Africa (1893).
PFG. on stamps of Russia: German occupation (1918), Estonia.
PFENNIG: values, German States, Germany.
P.G.S. on stamps of Straits Settlements: official stamps (1890), Perak, Malaya.
PHILIPPINES on stamps of the United States: Philippines (1899-1906).
PIASTER on stamps of a) Austria or b) Germany: offices in Turkey, of a) Austria or b) Germany.
PIASTRE(S) on stamps of a) France b) Great Britain c) Italy d) Romania or e) Russia: offices in Turkey, of a) France b) Great Britain c) Italy d) Romania or e) Russia.
PIASTRE on stamps of Italy: offices in Turkey, Italy.
PILGRIM TERCENTENARY: United States (1920).
PILIPINAS: Philippines.
PINSIN(E): values: Ireland.
PISCO on stamps of Peru: provisionals (1884), Peru.
PISCOPI on stamps of Italy: Aegean Islands (1912-32), Italy.
PIURA on stamps of Peru: provisionals (1884), Peru.
PLEBISCITE OLSZTYN ALLENSTEIN on stamps of Germany: plebiscite issue (1920), Allenstein.
PLEBISCIT with **SLESVIG**: plebiscite issue (1920), Schleswig.
P.M. on stamps of Italy: military stamps (1943), regular issue during shortage (1944-45), Italy.
POCZTA (POLSKA): Poland.
POfTGEBIET: see **POSTGEBIET** and **BOfTGEBIET** (old-style "P" looks like "B," "S" looks like "f").
POHJOIS INKERI: North Ingermanland.
POLSKA: Poland.
POLYNESIE FRANCAISE: French Polynesia (1956 —).
PONCE: Puerto Rico (1898).
PORTEADO: postage due, Portugal.
PORTE DE CONDUCCION: parcel post, Peru.
PORTE DE MAR: a form of postage due for ship mail (1875), Mexico.
PORTE FRANCO with **CORREOS**: Peru (1858-72).
PORT GDANSK on stamps of Poland: offices in Danzig (1925-38), Poland.
PORT LAGOS on stamps of France: offices in Turkey (1893), France.
PORTO GAZETEI: Moldavia (1858-59), Romania.
PORTOMARKE: postage due, Bosnia and Herzegovina.
PORTO RICO on stamps of the United States: Puerto Rico (1899).
PORT SAID: offices in Egypt (1899-1928), France.
POSTA CESKOSLOVENSKA on stamps of Austria: semipostals (1919), Czechoslovakia.
POSTAGE with **CAMB AUST SIGILLUM NOV**: New South Wales (1850-51).
POSTAGE (REVENUE) with portrait of king or queen, no country name: Great Britain (1840-1967).
POSTALI: see **PACCHI POSTALI**.
POSTA ROMANA CONSTANTINOPOL on stamps of Romania: offices in Turkey (1919), Romania.
POSTAS LE NIOC: postage due, Ireland.
POSTE AERIENNE with plane on stamps of Persia: airmail (1927-29), Persia.
POSTE AERIEO with plane on stamps of Persia: airmail (1928), Persia.
POSTE ESTENSI: Modena (1852), Italian States.
POSTEK NEDEUIERGIZIANE, POSIEX-HEDEUIEEGIZIANE: Egypt (1872-79).
POSTE LOCALE: Switzerland (1849-50).
POSTES with red crescent and 1954: tax stamps (1954), Afghanistan.
POSTES OTTOMANES: Turkey (1913-22).
POSTES SERBES on stamps of France: Serbia (1916-18).
POSTGEBIET OB. OST, POfTGEBIET OB. OfT (old-style "S" looks like "f") on stamps of Germany: German occupation (1916-17), Lithuania.
POST STAMP, POST & RECEIPT or **POSTAGE** with **ANNA(S)**: Hyderabad, India.
POST ZEGEL without country name: Netherlands (1852-67).
POULS: semipostals (1952), Afghanistan.
P.P. on stamps of France: French Morocco (1903).
P.P.C. on stamps of Poland: offices in

Turkey, consular mail, Poland.
PREUSSEN: Prussia (1861-67), German States.
PRINCE FAROUK: Egypt (1929).
PRISTINA on stamps of Turkey: Turkey (1911).
PRO (PLEBISCITO) TACNA Y ARICA: plebiscite tax stamps (1925-28), Peru.
PROTECTORADO ESPANOL: Spanish Morocco.
PROTECTORATE on stamps of Bechuanaland: Bechuanaland Protectorate (1888-89).
PROTECTORAT FRANCAIS on stamps of France or French Morocco: French Morocco (1914-21).
PRO TUBERCULOSOS POBRES: tax stamps (1937-38), Spain.
PRO UNION IBEROAMERICANA: Spain (1930).
PROVISIONAL 1881-1882 on stamps of Peru: Arequipa provisionals (1881-85), Peru.
PS in intertwined script letters: Cauca locals (1882-83), Colombia.
P.S.N.C. in corners, with ship: Peru (1857).
PTO-RICO: Puerto Rico (1877-98).
PUL: values, Afghanistan.
PULAU PENANG: Penang locals, Malaysia.
PUNO on stamps of Peru or Arequipa, Peru: provisionals (1882-85), Peru.
PUTTIALLA STATE: Patiala locals (1884-90), India.
PYCCKAR NOYTA on stamps of Ukraine: offices in Turkey (1921), Russia.

- Q -

QATAR on stamps of Great Britain: Qatar (1957-60).
QARKU: Albania (1918).
QEVERRIES SE PERKOHESHME: Albania (1913).
QIND(AR), QINTAR: values, Albania.
QU'AITI STATE OF SHIHR AND MUKALLA: locals (1942-53), Aden.
QU'AITI STATE IN HADHRAMAUT: locals (1955 —), Aden.
QUAN BUU: military stamps, Vietnam.
QUELIMANE on stamps of various Portuguese colonies: Quelimane (1913).

- R -

R centered on stamps with foreign characters: Jind locals (1874-84), India.
R following numeral on stamps with foreign characters, no other English letters: Persia.
R on stamps of Colombia: registration stamps (1898), Panama.
RABAUL: German New Guinea registration label with G.R.I.: New Britain (1914).
RAJASTHAN on stamps of Jaipur or Kishangarh: locals (1949), India.
RAPPEN: values (1854-62), Switzerland.
RARNTEN, see **KARNTEN**.
RAROTONGA: Cook Islands (1919-31).
RAU on stamps of Syria: United Arab Republic (1958), Syria.
RAYON: Switzerland (1850-54).
RECARGO: war tax stamps (1898), Spain.
RECUERDO DEL I'DE FEBRERO: Honduras (1916).
REGATUL ROMANIEI on stamps of Hungary: Romanian occupation (1919), Hungary.
REGENCE DE TUNIS: Tunisia (1888-1908).
REGNO D'ITALIA on stamps of Austria: Italian occupation (1918), Austria.
REGNO D'ITALIA on stamps of Fiume: Fiume (1924).
REICH(SPOST): Germany (1872-1944).
REIS with **CORREIO**, without country name: Portugal (1853-64).
REP(UBBLICA DI) S(AN) MARINO: San Marino.
REPUB(BLICA) SOCIALE ITALIANA: Italian Social Republic (1944), Italy.
REPUBLICA DOMINICANA: Dominican Republic.
REPUBLICA INHAMBANE on stamps of various Portuguese colonies: Inhambane (1913).
REPUBLICA ORIENTAL: Uruguay (1864-66).
REPUBLICA O(RIENTAL) DEL URUGUAY: Uruguay (1866-1961).
REPUBLICA PORTUGUESA: Portugal.
REPUBLIC OF BOTSWANA on stamps of Bechuanaland Protectorate: Botswana (1966).
REPUBLIEK VAN SUID-AFRIKA: South Africa (1961-71).
REPUBLIK MALUKU SELATAN: see **MALUKU SELATAN**.
REPUBLIK INDONESIA: Indonesia.
REPUBLICA NG PILIPINAS: Japanese occupation (1944), Philippines.
REPUBLIQUE ARABE UNIE: United Arab

Republic (1958), Syria.
REPUBLIQUE CENTRAFRICAINE: Central African Republic.
REPUBLIQUE D'AZERBAIDJAN: Azerbaijan (1919-22).
REPUBLIQUE GABONAISE: Gabon (1959 —).
REPUBLIQUE ISLAMIQUE DE MAURITANIE: Mauritania (1960 —).
REPUBLIQUE RWANDAISE: Rwanda.
REPUBLIQUE TOGOLAISE: Togo (1961 —).
REPUBLIQUE TUNISIENNE: Tunisia (1957 —).
RETYMNO: Crete (1899).
REUNION on stamps of French Colonies: Reunion (1891).
R. COMMISSARIATO CIVILE on stamps of Yugoslavia: Italian occupation (1941), Ljubljana, Yugoslavia.
RF (POSTES): France.
R.H.: postage due, Haiti.
RHEINLAND-PFALZ: French occupation (1947-49), Germany.
RHODESIA on stamps of Rhodesia and Nyasaland: postage due (1965-67), Rhodesia.
RIALTAR SEALADAC NA HEIREANN on stamps of Great Britain: Ireland (1922).
RIAU on stamps of Indonesia: Riouw Archipelago (1954-60), Indonesia.
RIGSBANK SKILLING: Denmark (1851-54).
RIN, **RN**: values, Japan.
RIS on stamps of Netherlands Indies: Indonesia (1950-51).
RIZEH on stamps of Russia: offices in Turkey (1910), Russia.
RO on stamps of Turkey: Eastern Rumelia (1880).
RODI: Rhodes, Aegean Islands, Italy.
ROMAGNE: Romagna (1859-60), Italian States.
ROMANA, **ROMINA**: Romania.
ROSS DEPENDENCY: Ross Dependency (1957 —), New Zealand.
ROUMELIE ORIENTALE on stamps of Turkey: Eastern Rumelia (1880).
ROYAUME DE L'ARABIE S(A)OUDITE: Saudi Arabia.
ROYAUME DU MAROC: Morocco.
R.P.E. SHQIPERISE: Albania.
RPF with numerals on stamps of Luxembourg: German occupation (1940), Luxembourg.
RSA: South Africa (1967 —).
R.S.M.: San Marino (1949-51).
RUANDA on stamps of Congo: Belgian occupation (1916), German East Africa.
RUANDA(-)URUNDI on stamps of Congo: Ruanda-Urundi.
RUMANIEN on stamps of Germany: German occupation (1918), Romania.
RUSSISCH-POLEN, **RUſſIſCH-POLEN** (old-style "S" looks like "f") on stamps of Germany: German occupation (1915), Poland.
RWANDAISE: Rwanda.
RYUKYUS: Ryukyu Islands (1950-72).

- S -

S(ELANGOR) on stamps of Straits Settlements: Selangor (1878-91), Malaya.
S.A.: Saudi Arabia.
SAARGEBIET: Saar (1920-34).
SAARLAND: Saar (1957-59).
SAARPOST: Saar (1948).
SABAH on stamps of North Borneo: Sabah (1964).
SACHSEN: Saxony, German States.
SAHARA ESPANOL, **SAHARA OCCIDENTAL**: Spanish Sahara.
SAINT-PIERRE ET MIQUELON: St. Pierre & Miquelon.
SAINT CHRISTOPHER(-)NEVIS(-) ANGUILLA: St. Kitts-Nevis (1952-57).
SALONICCO on stamps of Italy: offices in Turkey (1909-11), Italy.
SALONIKA on stamps of Turkey: Turkey (1911).
SALONIQUE on stamps of Russia: offices in Turkey (1909-10), Russia.
SAMOA on stamps of Germany: Samoa (1900).
SAMOA without **WESTERN** on stamps of New Zealand: Samoa (1914-34).
SANDJAK D'ALEXANDRETTE: Alexandretta.
SANTANDER: provisionals (1884-1907), Colombia.
SAORSTAT EIREANN on stamps of Great Britain: Ireland (1922-23).
SAR: Syria (1961 —).
SARKARI on stamps of Soruth: Soruth official stamps, India.
SARRE on stamps of Germany: Saar (1920).
SASENO on stamps of Italy: Saseno (1923).

SAURASHTRA: Soruth locals (1929-49), India.
SCARPANTO on stamps of Italy: Aegean Islands (1912-32), Italy.
SCHLESWIG: Schleswig-Holstein (1864-65), German States.
SCINDE DISTRICT DAWK: India (1852).
SCUDO: values (1852), Roman States, Italian States.
SCUTARI DI ALBANIA on stamps of Italy: offices in Turkey (1909-16), Italy.
SEGNA TASSA or **SEGNATASSE** without country name: postage due, Italy.
SEIYUN: locals, Aden.
SEJM(-)WILNIE: Central Lithuania (1922).
SELANGOR: locals, Malaya, Malaysia.
S(E)N: values, Ryukyu Islands (1948-50) or Japan.
SENEGAL on stamps of French Colonies: Senegal (1892).
SENEGAMBIE ET NIGER: Senegambia & Niger (1903).
SERBES on stamps of France: Serbia (1916-18).
SERBIEN on stamps of a) Bosnia and Herzegovina or b) Yugoslavia: a) Austrian (1916) or b) German (1941) occupation, Serbia.
SEVILLA(-)BARCELONA: Spain (1929).
S - H in upper corners: Schleswig-Holstein (1850), German States.
SHANGHAI on stamps of United States: offices in China (1919-22), United States.
SHIHR AND MUKALLA: locals (1942-53), Aden.
SHQIP- - -, **SHQYP- - -**: Albania.
S.H.S.: Yugoslavia (1918-20).
SIEGE (OF) MAFEKING: Cape of Good Hope (1900).
SIMI on stamps of Italy: Aegean Islands (1912-32), Italy.
SINGAPORE MALAYA: Singapore (1948-59).
SIRMOOR: locals (1879-1901), India.
SIVAS on stamps of Turkey: Turkey (1930).
SLESVIG: plebiscite issue (1920), Schleswig.
SLOVENSKA, **SLOVENSKENO**, **SLOVENSKO** or **SLOVENSKY**: Slovakia (1939-44), Czechoslovakia.
SLOVENSKO-PRIMORJE: Istria (1945-46), Yugoslavia.
SLOVENI on stamps of Yugoslavia: Italian occupation (1941), Yugoslavia.
S. MARINO: San Marino.
SMIRNE on stamps of Italy: offices in Turkey (1909-22), Italy.
SMYRNE on stamps of Russia: offices in Turkey (1909-10), Russia.
S.O. 1920 on stamps of Czechoslovakia: plebiscite issue (1920), Eastern Silesia.
SOBRETASA AEREA: airmail (1929), Colombia.
SOCIEDAD-COLOMBO-ALEMANA: airmail (1920-21), Colombia.
SOCIEDADE DE GEOGRAPHIA DE LISBOA: franchise stamps (1903-38), Portugal.
SOCIETE DES NATIONS: official stamps (1922-44), League of Nations, Switzerland.
SOLDI: values (1858-65), Lombardy-Venetia, Austria.
SOLIDARITE FRANCAISE: semipostals (1943-44), French Colonies.
SOMALIA (ITALIANA) on stamps of Italy: Somalia (1922-32).
SOMALI DEMOCRATIC REPUBLIC: Somalia (1970-73).
SOMALIS: Somali Coast (1902-67).
SOMALIYA: Somalia (1973 —).
SONORA: civil war issues (1913-14), Sonora, Mexico.
SORUTH: locals (1877-1914), India.
SOUDAN on stamps of Egypt: Sudan (1897).
SOUDAN on stamps of French Colonies (1894) or Upper Senegal and Niger (1921-30): French Sudan.
SOUDAN: French Sudan.
SOURASHTRA: Soruth locals (1923-29), India.
SOUTHERN RHODESIA on stamps of Great Britain: postage due (1951 —), Southern Rhodesia.
SOUTH GEORGIA on stamps of Falkland Islands: South Georgia (1944 —), Falkland Islands.
SOUTH ORKNEYS or **SOUTH SHETLANDS** on stamps of Falkland Islands: South Orkneys or South Shetlands (1944-62), Falkland Islands.
SOUTH WEST AFRICA on stamps of South Africa: South-West Africa (1923-27).
SOWJETISCHE BESATZUNGS ZONE on stamps of Germany: Russian occupation (1948), Berlin, Germany.
SPM on stamps of French Colonies: St.

Pierre & Miquelon (1885-91).

S.Q. TRSTA-VUJA ZRACNA P: airmail (1949), Yugoslav Zone B, Trieste.

SRI LANKA: Ceylon (1972 —).

SRODKOWA with **LITWA**: Central Lithuania.

ST. without country name: values (1932-43), Thailand.

STAMPALIA on stamps of Italy: Aegean Islands (1912-32), Italy.

STATI PARM(ENSI): Parma (1852-59), Italian States.

STEMPEL with **CENTES.**: Lombardy-Venetia (1850), Austria.

STEMPEL with **KREUZER**: Austria (1850).

ST. CHRISTOPHER(-)NEVIS(-ANGUILLA): St. Kitts-Nevis (1952 —).

S. T(H)OME E PRINCIPE: St. Thomas & Prince Islands.

STOCKHOLM: Sweden (1924).

STOTHNKH: values (1911-24), Bulgaria.

ST-PIERRE M-ON on stamps of French Colonies: St. Pierre & Miquelon (1891-92).

ST. PIERRE ET MIQUELON: St. Pierre & Miquelon.

STRAITS SETTLEMENTS on stamps of Labuan: Straits Settlements (1907).

S.T. TRSTA-VUJA: Zone B (1949-51), Trieste.

S.T.T.-V.U.J.(N.)A.: Zone B, Trieste.

S(UNGEI) U(JONG) on stamps of Straits Settlements: Sungei Ujong (1878-91), Malaya.

SUBMARINO with CORREO: submarine stamps (1938), Spain.

SUID(-)AFRIKA: South Africa.

SUIDWES(-)AFRIKA: South-West Africa.

S. UJONG: Sungei Ujong (1891-94), Malaya.

SUL BOLLETTINO, SULLA RICEVUTA: parcel post, Somalia (with star and crescent) or Italy.

SULTANT D'ANJOUAN: Anjouan.

SUOMI: Finland.

SVERIGE: Sweden.

S.W.A.: South-West Africa.

SWAZIELAND: Swaziland (1889-95).

SWAZILAND on stamps of South Africa: Swaziland (1945).

SYRIAN ARAB REPUBLIC: Syria (1961 —).

SYRIE(NNE): Syria (1920-58).

SZEGED 1919 on stamps of Hungary: Szeged issue (1919), Hungary.

- T -

T on stamps a) in four corners b) with F, numeral and heraldic lion or c) of various countries: postage due, of a) Dominican Republic (1901-42) b) Belgium (1966-70) or c) country of stamp origin.

T in circle on stamps of Peru: Huacho provisionals (1884), Peru.

TACNA Y ARICA: plebiscite issue tax stamps (1925-28), Peru.

TAHITI on stamps of French Colonies or French Polynesia: Tahiti.

TAKCA: postage due (1884-99), Bulgaria.

TAKSE: postage due, Albania.

TALCA: Talca tax stamp (1942), Chile.

TANGANYIKA & ZANZIBAR: Tanzania (1964).

TANGANYIKA with **KENYA** and **UGANDA**: Kenya, Uganda and Tanzania (1935-64).

TANGER on stamps of France or French Morocco: French Morocco (1918-24).

TANGER with **CORREO(S)**: Tangier: Spanish Morocco.

TANGIER on stamps of Great Britain: offices in Morocco (1927-57), Great Britain.

TANZANIA with **KENYA** and **UGANDA**: Kenya, Uganda and Tanzania (1965 —).

TANZANIA with **ZANZIBAR** or **MUUNGANO**: Zanzibar and Tanzania (1965-68), Zanzibar.

TASSE GAZZETTE: newspaper tax stamps (1859), Modena, Italian States.

TAXA DE GUERRA on stamps with a) one or two numerals other than 0 b) two numerals beginning with 0 c) two numerals ending with 0 or d) seven numerals: 1919 war tax stamps, a) Macao b) Portuguese Africa c) Portuguese Guinea or d) Portuguese India.

TAXE on stamps of Albania: postage due (1919), Albania.

T.C. on stamps of Cochin: Travancore-Cochin locals (1950), India.

T.C.E.K.: tax stamps (1946), Turkey.

TCHAD: Chad.

TCHONGKING on stamps of Indo-China: offices in China (1903-19), France.

T.C. POSTALARI: Turkey (1931).

TE BETALEN with **A PAYER**: postage due, Belgium.

TE BETALEN with **PORT**: postage due, Netherlands, Surinam, or Netherlands Indies, Antilles or New Guinea.

TEHERAN on stamps of Persia: Persia (1902).

T.E.O. with **CILICIE** on stamps of Turkey: Cilicia (1919).

T.E.O. with **MILLIEMES** on stamps of France or French Offices in Turkey: Syria (1919).

T.E.O. on stamps of French Offices in Turkey: Syria or Cilicia (1919).

TERRES AUSTRALES ET ANTARCTIQUES FRANCAISES: French Southern and Antarctic Territories.

TERRITORIO DE IFNI on stamps of Spain: Ifni (1941-50).

TERRITOIRE DE L'ININI on stamps of French Guiana: Inini (1932-41).

TERRITOIRE DU NIGER on stamps of Upper Senegal and Niger: Niger (1921-26).

TERRITOIRE FRANCAIS DES AFARS ET DES ISSAS: Afars and Issas.

TETUAN on stamps of Spain or Spanish Offices in Morocco: Tetuan (1908), Spanish Morocco.

TETE on stamps of various Portuguese colonies: Tete (1913).

THAI(LAND): Siam (1942 —).

THAILAND with **CENT(S)**: Siamese occupation (1943-45), Malaya.

THRACE on stamps of Bulgaria: Allied occupation (1919-20), Thrace.

TIENTSIN on stamps of Italy: offices in China (1917-21), Italy.

TIMBRE IMPERIAL JOURNAUX: newspaper stamps, France.

TIMBRE POSTE on stamps of France: French Morocco (1893).

TIMBRE TAXE with **A PERCEVOIR**: postage due (1945), French Colonies.

TIMOR on stamps of Macao: Timor (1885-95).

TIMOR on stamps of Mozambique: Timor (1946).

TJENESTE with **FRIMAERKE**: official stamps (1871-1924), Denmark.

TJENESTEFRIMERKE: official stamps (1926-32), Norway.

TOGA: Tonga (1897-1949).

TOGO on stamps of Germany: Togo (1897-99).

TOGO on stamps of Gold Coast (1915-16) or Dahomey (1916-25): Togo.

TOGOLAISE: Togo (1961 —).

TOKELAU ISLANDS on stamps of New Zealand: Tokelau Islands (1966-67).

TOLIMA: provisionals (1871-1904), Colombia.

TO PAY: postage due, Great Britain.

TOSCANO: Tuscany, Italian States.

TOU: airmail (1928), Persia.

TOUVA: Tannu Tuva (1927-35).

TRAITE DE VERSAILLES on stamps of Germany: plebiscite issue (1920), Allenstein.

TRANSJORDAN: Jordan (1927-52).

TRANSPORTO PACCHI IN CONCESSIONE: parcel post authorized delivery stamps, Italy.

TRAVANCORE with **COCHIN**: Travancore-Cochin, India.

TRAVANCORE with **ANCHAL** or **ANCHEL**: Travancore or Travancore-Cochin, India.

TREBIZONDE on stamps of Russia: offices in Turkey (1909-10), Russia.

TRENGANNU: locals, Malaya, Malaysia.

TRENTINO on stamps of Austria: Italian occupation (1918), Austria.

TRIESTE on stamps of Italy: Trieste.

TRIDENTINA on stamps of Italy: Italian occupation (1918), Austria.

TRIPOLI DI BARBERIA on stamps of Italy: offices in Africa (1909-15), Italy.

TRIPOLI with **CAMPIONARIA**: Libya (1927-38).

TRIPOLITANIA on stamps of Italy: Tripolitania.

TRIPOLI MAGGIO on stamps of Libya: airmail (1934), Tripolitania.

TRISTAN DA CUNHA on stamps of St. Helena: Tristan da Cunha (1952-63).

T.TA.C.: airmail tax stamps (1931-33), Turkey.

TUMACO: Cauca provisionals (1901-12), Colombia.

TUNIS(IE): Tunisia.

TURK(IYE): Turkey.

TUVALU on stamps of Gilbert & Ellice Islands: Tuvalu (1976).

TWO PENCE without country name, under enthroned queen: Victoria (1852-54).

- U -

UAE on stamps of Abu Dhabi: United Arab Emirates (1972).

U.A. EMIRATES: United Arab Emirates.

UAPCTBO: Bulgaria (1937-44).

U.A.R. with values in a) "p" or b) "m": United Arab Republic, a) Syria (1958-61) or b) Egypt (1958-71).

U.G.: Uganda (1895).
UGANDA on stamps of British East Africa: Uganda (1902).
UGANDA with **EAST AFRICA** or **KENYA**: Kenya, Uganda and Tanzania.
UKRAINE on stamps of Germany: German occupation (1941-43), Russia.
U.K.T.T. on stamps of Nigeria: Southern Cameroons (1960-61), Cameroons.
ULTRAMAR with year (1800s): Puerto Rico (1873-76, with script overprints) or Cuba (1867-76).
ULTRAMAR with values of a) one numeral or b) two numerals: a) Macao (1911) or b) Portuguese Guinea (1919 war tax stamps).
UNEF on stamps of India: military stamps (1965), India.
UNESCO: official stamps (1961-71), U.N. Educational, Scientific and Cultural Organization, France.
U.N. FORCE (INDIA) CONGO on stamps of India: military stamps (1962), India.
UNION INTERNATIONALE DES TELECOMMUNICATIONS: official stamps, International Telecommunications Union, Switzerland.
UNION POSTALE UNIVERSELLE with **HELVETIA**: official stamps (1957-60), U.P.U. International Bureau, Switzerland.
UNTEA on stamps of Netherlands New Guinea: West Irian (1962).
UOPTO CKPNCOPN: Moldavia (1858), Romania.
UPHA TOPA: Italian occupation (1941-43), Montenegro.
URUNDI without **RUANDA** on stamps of Congo: Belgian occupation (1916), German East Africa.
U.R.I. on stamps of Yugoslavia: semi-postals without official postal value (1923), Yugoslavia.
U.S.(A.): United States.
USKUB on stamps of Turkey: Turkey (1911).

- V -

VALLEES D'ANDORRE: Andorra (1932-43).
VALONA on stamps of Italy: offices in Turkey (1909-16), Italy.
VANCOUVER ISLAND: British Columbia and Vancouver Island (1865).
VAN DIEMEN'S LAND: Tasmania (1853-69).
VATHY on stamps of France: offices in Turkey (1894-1900), France.
VATICANE, VATICANA: Vatican City.
VENEZA: Venezuela (1865-76).
VENEZIA with **GIULIA** or **TRIDENTINA** on stamps of Italy: Italian occupation (1918), Austria.
VENEZOLANA: Venezuela (1863-65).
VEREINTE NATIONEN: United Nations, Vienna (1979 —).
VIET(-)NAM with **BUU(-)CHINH**, without **CONG(-)HOA**: Vietnam (1951-56).
VIET(-)NAM CONG(-)HOA with **BUU(-) CHINH**: South Vietnam (1956-75), Vietnam.
VIET(-)NAM DAN(-)CHU CONG(-)HOA: North Vietnam, Vietnam.
VIVA ESPANA on stamps of Spain: Spain (1936-37).
VOJNA UPRAVA JUGOSLAVENSKE ARMIJE on stamps of Yugoslavia: Istria and Slovene Coast (1947), Yugoslavia.
VOM EMPFANGER EINZUZIEHEN: postage due, Danzig.
V.R. on stamps of Fiji: Fiji (1874-77).
V.R. with **TRANSVAAL** on stamps of Transvaal: Transvaal (1877-79).
V.R.I. on stamps of Transvaal: Transvaal (1900-02).
V.R. SPECIAL POST on stamps of Transvaal: Cape of Good Hope (1900).
V.U.J.(N.)A. S.T.T. on stamps of Yugoslavia: Zone B, Trieste.

- W -

WADHWAN STATE: locals (1888-89), India.
WALLIS ET FUTUNA on stamps of New Caledonia: Wallis and Futuna Islands (1920-40).
WARSZAWA: Poland (1918).
WEIHNACHTEN on stamps of Rhodes (Aegean Islands, Italy): unofficial German overprint, Aegean Islands (1944), Italy.
WENDEN(SCHEN): Wenden (1862-84), Russia.
W(EST) AUSTRALIA: Western Australia.
WESTERN SAMOA: Samoa (1935-55).
WIR SIND FREI on stamps of Czechoslovakia: German occupation (1938), unofficial, Czechoslovakia.
W(O)N: values, Korea.
WURTTEMBERG with values **PF** or **M**: French occupation (1947-49), Germany.
WURTTEMBERG with **KREUZER** or **FREIMARKE**: Wurttemberg, German States.

- X -

XAPTOEHMON: tax stamps (1917), Greece.

XEAEPA, XEJEPA: Montenegro (1902-05).

XEIMAPPA with Greek lettering: questionable postal value, Epirus.

XII FIERA CAMPIONARIA TRIPOLI: Libya (1938).

- Y -

YAR: Yemen Arab Republic (1963 —).

YCA on stamps of Peru: Yca provisionals (1884), Peru.

Y.C.P.P.: semipostals (1923), Ukraine.

YCTAB: Montenegro (1905).

YEMEN PDR: Yemen People's Democratic Republic.

Y(E)N: values, Japan, Manchukuo, Ryukyu Islands.

Y(KP.) H. P(EN) on stamps of Austria: Western Ukraine.

YKPAIHCbKA: Ukraine (1918-19).

YKSI MARKKA: Finland (1866-74).

YUNNAN(-)FOU on stamps of Indo-China: offices in China (1906-19), France.

YUNNANSEN on stamps of Indo-China: offices in France (1903-05), France.

- Z -

Z(UID) AFR(IKAANSCHE) REP(UBLIEK): Transvaal.

ZAIRE: Congo (1971 —).

ZANZIBAR on stamps of a) France or b) British East Africa or India: a) France (offices in Zanzibar, 1894-1900) or b) Zanzibar (1895-96).

ZANZIBAR with **TANZANIA**: Zanzibar (1965-68).

Z.A.R. on stamps of Cape of Good Hope: Boer occupation (1899), Cape of Good Hope.

ZEGELREGT: Transvaal (1895).

ZELAYA on stamps of Nicaragua: Zelaya (1904-11), Nicaragua.

ZENTRALER KURIERDIENST: official stamps (1956-57), German Democratic Republic, Germany.

ZONA DE OCUPATIE ROMANA: Romanian occupation (1919), Hungary.

ZONA DE PROTECTORADO ESPANOL EN MARRUECOS on stamps of Spain: Spanish Morocco (1916-25).

ZONE FRANCAISE: French occupation (1945-46), Germany.

ZRACNA POSTA: airmail, Zone B, Trieste.

ZUID(-)WEST AFRIKA on stamps of South Africa: South-West Africa (1923-25).

ZULULAND on stamps of Great Britain or Natal: Zululand (1888-94).

ZURICH: Switzerland (1843-46).

Difficult Identification

Many foreign stamps, especially those with characters from oriental languages or those in Greek or Russian, are impossible to identify by an index of English typeset characters. The most commonly encountered of these are listed, by country, in the following section, with an attempt to describe certain distinguishing characteristics. Most stamps after 1900 are readily identifiable, either by name or distinguishing characteristic.

This list is merely a general guide. It is an attempt to help collectors find some general guidance in identifying certain difficult-to-identify stamps. All references here, unless otherwise stated, are only to regular postage stamps, since many official and tax stamps, intended primarily for the use and benefit of persons within the country, often exclude the name of the issuing country. Dates, too, are only general reference points, since use of certain issues after the indicated dates is quite possible.

AFGHANISTAN, 1871-1930: circular designs, "tiger's head," mosque and Eastern characters identify certain issues.

ARMENIA, 1919-23: Socialist emblems and handstamped Russian stamps identify some issues. Issues after 1921 also have many high denominations, with numerals from 3-6 figures.

AUSTRIA, 1867-1908: KR. or KREUZER will identify values for most early issues. Newspaper stamps from this period will picture "Mercury" with winged helmet.

AZERBAIJAN, 1922-24: Russian NOYT MAPKA appears on most issues, with crescent, star, hammer and sickle. Also many large numerals, with many zeros, overprinted.

BANGLADESH, 1972: crooked tower and "20 P." value identify the one non-English issue.

BATUM, 1919-20: Russian characters, NOYTA or NOYTOBAR. Later issues overprinted "BRITISH OCCUPATION."

Bangladesh

BOSNIA AND HERZEGOVINA, 1879-1906: shield and eagle emblem.

BRAZIL, 1843-66: numerals in stylized oval, last digit "0." Values are 10, 20, 30, 60, 90, 180, 280, 300, 430 and 600.

Brazil

BULGARIA, 1879 — : most issues have the Russian NOWA, or the Russian name of Bulgaria, which begins with two characters similar to lowercase "b"s (bbATAPNR).

Bulgaria

BURMA, Japanese occupation 1942-44: peacock overprint on Burma stamps and stamps similar to Japanese stamps are typical.

CHINA, 1921-66: values in dollars and cents, as well as the sun emblem, identify many issues.

CHINA, PEOPLE'S REPUBLIC OF,

Burma

China

China (People's Republic)

1949 — : numerals followed closely by a single Chinese character identify many issues.

CRETE, 1898-99: Greek letters similar to TAXYAPOM, METAAAIK, or PEOYMNHE identify most issues.

EGYPT, 1866-1924: values in PARA or PE identify many issues.

EPIRUS, 1914-16: Greek letters similar to HNEIPOE identify most issues.

ETHIOPIA, 1894-1909: lion holding banner or king's bearded profile identify most issues.

FAR EASTERN REPUBLIC, 1920-23: script DBL overprinted on Russian stamps or NOYTOBAR MAPKA identify most issues.

FINLAND, 1891-1916: values in PEN or MARKKA with the Russian NOYTOBAR MAPKA distinguish most issues. 1891-96 stamps are generally identical with Russian stamps, except they are more "cluttered," i.e., have more dots, lines, etc., in background. Can only be distinguished by comparison or illustration.

China (Taiwan)

Far Eastern Republic

GEORGIA, 1922-23: Russian characters similar to L.L.L.R. and values of 500 or thousands identify most issues.

GREECE, 1861-1966: Greek letters similar to EAAAE identify most issues.

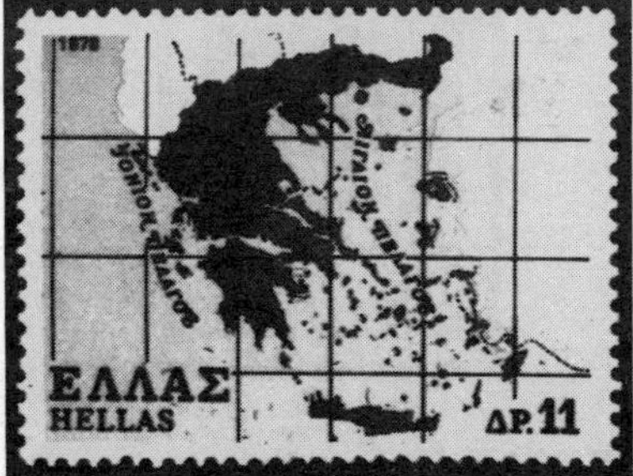

Greece

HUNGARY, 1871-72: regular issue has value KR with bearded profile, while newspaper stamps have no value and posthorn under crown of St. Stephen.

Hungary

INDIA, native states: many native states had plain stamps, generally crowded with Eastern characters. Identification is possible by illustration only.

Indian States (Bhopal)

Indian States (Idar)

Indian States (Las Bela)

ISRAEL, 1948: ancient coins and Hebrew writing identify the first Israeli issue.

Israel

JAPAN, 1871-1966: most issues through 1947 are identified by the stylized chrysanthemum, including numerous issues for other countries under Japanese occupation. After 1947, the Japanese characters for JAPAN appear, the first of which appears as a squat, angular "8."

Japan

JORDAN, 1920-27: nondescript rectangles with Arabic writing, generally subdivided into many smaller rectangles.

KOREA, 1884: a single early issue has a value of 5 Mn., plus a stylized, half-and-half-circle design in the center.

Korea

KOREA, NORTH, 1946-77: later issues include year dates beside the Oriental characters, while most issues have the four-character country name, the last character of which appears as two stacked Roman numeral "II"s, with the preceding character appearing as "O" over "T."

KOREA, SOUTH, 1946-66: similar to North Korea, with addition of CH or stylized circle, appearing as two interlocking apostrophes.

MALAYA, 1935-63, including Japanese occupation: most occupation stamps appear similar to Japanese stamps. Issues of the various Malay states, frequently inscribed MALAYA, are sometimes distinguishable only by the Eastern inscription, including issues of Kelantan, Pahang, Perak, Negri Sembilan, Selangor and Trengganu.

MANCHUKUO, 1932-45: values of FEN or FN., or stylized "snowflake" (five-pronged, star-like object with internal decorations) identifies most issues.

Manchukuo

MONGOLIA, 1924-59: Russian characters similar to "bHMAY" appear on most issues after 1950.

MONTENEGRO, 1874-1913: Russian characters similar to NOWTE, NAPA, or HOBY identify most issues.

NEPAL, 1881-1949: sun in upper right corner identifies some issues.

Nepal

PAKISTAN, 1948: issue with crescent and stars and inscription "15 AUGUST

1947."

PERSIA (IRAN), 1870-1946: lion holding sword over sun identifies many issues, while values of "D" or "R" identify others.

Persia (Iran)

PHILIPPINES, 1943-44, Japanese occupation: Japanese inscription across top beginning with characters similar to two lower-case "t"s identify most issues.

RUSSIA, 1857-1922: Russian characters similar to NOYTA, NOYTOBAR, MAPKA, P.C.O.C.P., POCCIR and PYb identify most issues. (Illustrations of slight differences and overprints are generally helpful in distinguishing such similar country issues as ARMENIA, AZERBAIJAN, FAR EASTERN REPUBLIC, BATUM, FINLAND, GEORGIA, SIBERIA, SOUTH RUSSIA, TRANSCAUCASIAN FEDERATED REPUBLICS and UKRAINE.)

Russia

RYUKYU ISLANDS, 1948-62: year dates and values in dollars and cents in addition to the Oriental characters identify most issues.

SAUDI ARABIA, 1916-29: nondescript stamps with Arabic lettering, undistinguishable without illustration.

SERBIA, 1866-1920: Russian characters similar to NOWTA or CPbNJA identify

Ryukyu Islands

Saudi Arabia

most issues.

SIBERIA, 1919-22: various handstamps on Russian stamps.

TANNU TUVA, 1926: eight-pronged wheel design identifies this issue.

Tannu Tuva

Thrace

THRACE, 1913: Greek and Arabic inscriptions on stamps of Turkey or

Transcaucasian Federated Republics

Bulgaria, as well as stamps marked "1913," identify most issues.

TRANSCAUCASIAN FEDERATED REPUBLICS, 1923: "3COCP" iden-tifies most issues, many with values of 7-8 digits.

Ukraine

TURKEY, 1863-1913: values in PARAS or crescent with starburst or script identify most issues.

UKRAINE, 1918-19: Russian char-acters similar to WATIB or YKPAIH-CbKA, or stylized facing "R"s on Russian stamps, identify most issues.

Multilingual Guide

Often the stamp collector will encounter stamps and catalogs with foreign words that may not be familiar to him. Therefore, the following section is offered to help with some of the basic philatelic terms (150), including colors, processes and directional guides that are often encountered by the average collector.

This glossary is not intended to be complete — indeed, there are too many foreign languages in the world to include even a small portion. This will provide some of the most basic terms for the stamp collector, and help with most translations that should ever arise, in five of the most frequently encountered languages: French, Spanish, Italian, German and Dutch.

Often there may be more than one translation (no more than two are included here), or there may be no exact word that corresponds to the English, so that a term close in meaning must be used instead.

Here, then, are 150 basic philatelic terms and descriptive words in English and five commonly found foreign languages. Typesetting restrictions make it impossible for this listing to include standard foreign accents, which can change the pronunciation of many vowels. Still, the basic translations and spellings are correct. For uniformity, no words are capitalized; nouns in German would typically begin with a capital letter.

ENGLISH	GERMAN	DUTCH	FRENCH	SPANISH	ITALIAN
airmail	flugpost, luftpost	luchtpost	poste aerienne	correo aereo	posta aerea
auction	versteigerung	veiling	encan, enchere	almoneda, subasta	incanto
back	ruckseitig	achterkant	verso	dorso	dorso
background	(hinter)grund	achtergrond	fond	fondo	fondo
bar	balken	balk	barre	barra	barra
bisected stamp	geteilt, halbiert	gehalveerd	timbre coupe	cortado por la mitad	frazionato
black	schwarz	zwart	noir	negro	nero
block	block	blok	bloc	bloque	blocco
blue	blau	blauw	bleu	azul	azzurro
booklet (stamps)	markenheftchen	(postzegel) boekje	carnet	cuardernillo	libretto
border	rahmen	omlijsting	cadre	marco	cornice
bottom	unten	onderkant	bas	abajo	basso
bright	lebhaft	helder	vif	vivo	vivo
broken	unterbrochen	onderbroken	interrompu	interrumpido	interrotto
brown	braun	bruin	brun	castano	bruno
canceled	gestempelt	gestempeld	annule	cancelado	annullato
cancellation	entwertung	afstempeling	obliteration	matasellado	annullo
catalog	katalog	catalogus	catalogue	catalogo	catalogo
center	mittelstuck	middenstuk	centre du timbre	centro	centro
centering	zentrierung	gecentreerd	centrage	centrado	centratura
chalky paper	kreidepapier	krijtachtig papier	papier couche	papel estucado	carta gessata
charity stamp	wohltatig-keitsmarke	weldadig-heidszegel	timbre de bienfaisance	sello de beneficenza	francobollo di beneficenza
closed	geschlossen	gesloten	ferme	cerrado	chiuso
coil	markenrolle	rol	rouleau de timbres	rollo de sellos	rotoli di francobolli
color	farbe	kleur	couleur	color	colore
commemorative	gedenkausgabe	herdenking-suitgave	commemoratif	conmemorativo	commemorativo
corner	ecke	hoek	angle	esquina	angolo
counterfeit	falschung	vervalsing	faux	falsificacion	falsificazione
cover	brief	brief	lettre	carta	lettera
cut square	ausschnitt	briefstuk	coupure	recorte	ritaglio
damaged	beschadigt	beschadigd	abime	defectuoso	difettoso
dark	dunkel	donker	fonce	oscuro	cupo, oscuro
date	datum	datum	date	fecha	data
definitive	endgultig	bepaald	definitif	definitivo	definitivo
design	entwurf, zeichnung	ontwerp	dessin	dibujo	disegno
die	urstempel, type	stempel, originele gravure	matrice	cuno	conio, matrice
double impression	doppeldruck	dubbele druk	impression double	impresion doble	impressione doppia

ENGLISH	GERMAN	DUTCH	FRENCH	SPANISH	ITALIAN
dull	trub	dof	terne	turbio	smorto
embossed	pragung	in relief	relief	relieve	rilievo
engraved	graviert, gestochen	gegraveerd	grave, gravure	grabado, caliografia	incisione, stampato
envelope	briefumschlag	envelop	enveloppe	sobre	busta
error	fehldruck, fehler	fout (druk)	erreur	error	errore
essay	essay, probedruck	proef	essai	ensayo	saggio
faulty	mangelhaft	onvolmaakt	defectueux	defectuoso	difettoso
figure	ziffer	cijfer	chiffre	cifra	cifra
first day	ersttag	eerste dag	premier jour	primer dia	primo giorno
foreign	ausland	buitenland	etranger	extranjero	estero
forerunner	vorlaufer	voorloper	precurseur	precursor	precursore
forgery	falschung	vervalsing	falsification, faux	falsificacion	falsificazione
genuine	echt	echt	authentique	autentico	autentico
glossy paper	glanzpapier	glanzend papier	papier glace	papel estucado	carta patinata
granite paper	faserpapier	papier met zijdevezels	papier melange de fils de soie	papel con filamentos	carta con fili de seta
gray	grau	grijs	gris	gris	grigio
green	grun	groen	vert	verde	verde
gum	gummi	gom	gomme	goma	gomma
gutter	zwischensteg	tussenstrook	interpanneau	pasillo	interspazio
half	halfte	de helft	moitie	mitad	meta
handstamp	handstempel	handstempel	cachet a la main	matasello de mano	timbro a mano
hinge	falz	plakker	charniere	fijasello	linguella
horizontal	liegend	horisontaal	horizontal	horizontal	coricato
imperforate	geschnitten	ongetand	non dentele	sin dentar	non dentellato
inscription	inschrift	opschrift	inscription	inscripcion	dicitura
inverted	kopfstehend	kopstaand	renverse	invertido	capovolto, invertito
issue	ausgabe	uitgave	emission	emision	emissione
laid (paper)	gestreiftes	gestreept (papier)	verge	listado	vergato
large	gross	groot	grand	grande	grosso
left	links	links	gauche	izquierdo	sinistro
letter card	kartenbrief	briefkaart	carte-lettre	carta tarjeta	carta-lettera
light	hell	licht	clair	claro	chiaro
lithography	steindruck	steendruk, lithografie	lithographie	litografia	litografia
local issue	lokalausgabe	plaatselijke uitgave	emission locale	emision local	emissione locale
margin	rand	rand	marge	borde	margine
mint	ungebraucht	ongebruikt	neuf	nuevo	nuovo
multicolored	mehrfarbig	meerkleurig	polychrome	multicolores	policromo
multiple	mehrfach	meervoudig	multiple	multiple	multiplo
narrow	eng	nauw	etroit	estrecho	stretto
not issued	unverausgabt	onuitgegeven	non emis	no emitido	non emesso
numeral	ziffer	nummer, cijfer	chiffre	cifra	numerale
occupation	besetzung	bezetting	occupation	occupacion	occupazione
official stamp	dienstmarke	dienstzegel	timbre de service	sello de servicio	francobollo servizio
offset printing	offsetdruck	offsetdruk	impression en offset	impresion offset	stampa in offset
on back	ruckseite	op de achterkant	au verso	al dorso	a tergo
orange	orange	oranje	orange	naranja	arancio
original gum	originalgummi	originele gom	gomme originale	goma original	gomma originale
overprint	aufdruck, uberdruck	opdruk	surcharge	sobrecarga	soprastampa
pair	paar	paar	paire	pareja	coppia
pale	blass	licht	pale	palido	pallido
pane	gruppe	vel	panneau	grupo	gruppo
paper	papier	papier	papier	papel	carta
parcel post	paket	pakketpost	colis-postaux	paquetes	pacchi
pen canceled	federzug-entwertung	penvernietiging	oblitere a plume	cancelado a pluma	annullato a penna
perforated	zahnung, gezahnt	getand	dentele	dentado	dentellato
photogravure	aetztiefdruck	rasterdiepdruk	heliogravure	huecograbado	fotocalcografia
piece	briefstuck	briefstuk	fragment	fragmento	frammento
pink	rosa	rose	rose	rosa	rosa
plate	platte	plaat	planche	plancha	lastra
postage due	portomarke	portzegel	timbre-taxe	sello de tasa	segnatasse
postage stamp	briefmarke	postzegel	timbre-poste	selle de correos	francobollo postale

ENGLISH	GERMAN	DUTCH	FRENCH	SPANISH	ITALIAN
postcard	postkarte	briefkaart	carte postale	tarjeta postal	carta postale
postmark	poststempel	stempel	obliteration postale	matasello	bollo
post office	postamt	postkantoor	bureau de poste	oficina postal	ufficia di posta
precancel	vorausenwertung	voorafstempeling	pre-oblitere	preobliteracion	preannullato
price	preis	prijs	prix	precio	prezzo, quotazione
printing	druck	druk	impression	impresion	stampa
proof	probe(druck)	proef	epreuve	prueba	prova
provisional	aushilfsausgabe	hulpzegel	provisoire	provisional	provvisorio
purple	purpur	purper	pourpre	purpura	porpora
rare	selten	zeldzaam	rare	raro	raro
recess printing	stichtiefdruck	diepdruk	taille douce	calcografia	calcografia
red	rot	rood	rouge	rojo	rosso
reengraving	neugravierung	nieuwe gravure	regravure	regrabado	rincisione
registration stamp	einschreibemarke	aantekenstrookje	timbre pour lettre chargee	sello de certificado	francobollo per lettere raccomandate
repaired	repariert	gerapareerd	repare	reparado	riparato
reprint	neudruck	herdruk, nadruk	reimpression	reimpresion	reimpressione
revenue stamp	stempelmarke	plakzegel	timbre fiscal	sello fiscal	francobollo fiscale
reversed	umgekehrt	omgekeerd	retourne	invertido	rovesciato
ribbed	geriffelt	geribbeld	cannele	acanalado	scanalatura
right	rechts	rechts	droite	a la derecha	destro
rotary printing	walzendruck	rotatiedruk	impression par cylindre	impresion cilindrica	stampa rotativa
rouletted	durchstochen	doorstoken	perce	picado	forato
se-tenant	zusammendruck	samenhangend	se-tenant	combinacion	combinazione
semipostal	wohltatig-keitsmarke	weldadig-heidszegel	bienfaisance	beneficencia	beneficenza
set	satz	serie	serie	serie	serie
shade	tonung, farbton	tint	nuance	tono	gradazione di colore
sheet	bogen	vel	feuille	hoja	foglio
side	seite	zijkant	cote	lado	lato
small	klein	klein	petit	pequeno	piccolo
souvenir sheet	gedenkblock	velletje	bloc commemoratif	hojita-bloque conmemorativa	foglietto com-memorativo
special delivery	eilmarke	expresse	expres	urgente	espresso
specimen	muster	specimen	specimen	muestra	saggio
strip	streifen	strook	bande	tira	striscia
surcharge	zuschlag	toeslag	surcharge	sobrecarga	soprastampa
thick	dick	dik	epais	grueso	spesso
thin	dunn	dun	mince	delgado	sottile
tinted paper	getontes papier	gekleurd papier	papier teinte	papel coloreado	carta tinto
top	oben	bovenkant	haut	arriba	alto
trial printing	druckprobe	proefdruk	epreuve essai	prueba	prova di stampa
typography	buchdruck	boekdruk	typographie	tipografia	tipografia
unused	ungebraucht	ongebruikt	neuf	nuevo	nuovo
used	gebraucht	gebruikt	oblitere	usado	usato
variety	abart	soort, varieteit	variete	variedad	varieta
vertical	senkrecht	vertikaal	vertical	vertical	verticale
watermark	wasserzeichen	watermerk	filigrane	filigrana	filigrana
white	weiss	wit	blanc	blanco	bianco
wide	weit	wijd	espace	ancho	largo
with	mit	met	avec	con	con
without gum	ohne gummi	zonder gom	sans gomme	sin goma	senza gomma
worn	abgenutzt	versleten	use	gastado	usato
wove paper	einfaches papier	velijnpapier	papier ordinaire	papel avitelado	carta unita
yellow	gelb	geel	jaune	amarillo	giallo

Foreign Currency Guide

This list gives the current names for the currency of stamp-issuing entities. This list is primarily intended to help the collector identify new stamps. Older values are not included because names of currency, value, country and territory are constantly changing. For guidance on older issues or countries, consult the section titled "Stamp-Issuing Entities."

Abbreviations included in the list are: EC for East Caribbean; CFA for the African Financial Community; CFP for the Pacific Financial Community; and NZ for New Zealand.

To better understand the following list, look at the second entry, "AITUTAKI," as an example. The major currency unit of Aitutaki is the NZ (New Zealand) dollar, which indicates that the currency of that island is tied to that of New Zealand. Unless noted as a specific type or area of currency, each currency unit will be unique to that country. In other words, entries marked simply "dollar" will not be related to other entries marked "dollar." In the Aitutaki listing, the equivalent figures indicate that one NZ dollar is equal to 100 cents.

For the most current information on exchange rates, consult banks or financial institutions or publications.

AFGHANISTAN: 1 afghani (af) = 100 pouls (p).

AITUTAKI: 1 NZ dollar ($) = 100 cents (¢).

ALAND: 1 Finnish markka (mk) = 100 pennia (p).

ALBANIA: 1 lek (l) = 100 qindarka (q).

ALDERNEY: 1 pound sterling (£) = 100 pence (p).

ALGERIA: 1 dinar (d) = 100 centimes (c).

ANDORRA (FRENCH): 1 French franc (fr) = 100 centimes (c).

ANDORRA (SPANISH): 1 Spanish peseta (pta) = 100 centimos (c).

ANGOLA: 1 kwanza (kz) = 100 lweys (1).

ANGUILLA: 1 EC dollar ($) = 100 cents (¢).

ANTIGUA & BARBUDA: 1 EC dollar ($) = 100 cents (¢).

ARGENTINA: 1 austral (a) = 100 centavos (c).

ARUBA: 1 florin (fl) = 100 cents (¢).

ASCENSION: 1 pound sterling (£) = 100 pence (p).

AUSTRALIA: 1 dollar ($) = 100 cents (¢).

AUSTRALIAN ANTARCTIC TERRITORY: 1 Australian dollar ($) = 100 cents (¢).

AUSTRIA: 1 schilling (s) = 100 groschen (g).

AZORES: 1 Portuguese escudo (esc) = 100 centavos (c).

BAHAMAS: 1 dollar ($) = 100 cents (¢).

BAHRAIN: 1 dinar (d) = 1000 fils (f).

BANGLADESH: 1 taka (t) = 100 poishas (p).

BARBADOS: 1 dollar ($) = 100 cents (¢).

BARBUDA: 1 EC dollar ($) = 100 cents (¢).

BELGIUM: 1 franc (fr) = 100 centimes (c).

BELIZE: 1 dollar ($) = 100 cents (¢).

BENIN: 1 CFA franc (fr) = 100 centimes (c).

BERLIN, WEST: 1 Deutschemark (m) = 100 pfennigs (pf).

BERMUDA: 1 dollar ($) = 100 cents (¢).

BHUTAN: 1 ngultrum (nu) = 100 chetrum (ch).

BOLIVIA: 1 peso bolivano (b) = 100 centavos (c).

BOPHUTHATSWANA: 1 South African rand (r) = 100 cents (¢).

BOTSWANA: 1 pula (p) = 100 thebe (t).

BRAZIL: 1 cruzado (cr) = 100 centavos (c).

BRITISH ANTARCTIC TERRITORY: 1 pound sterling (£) = 100 pence (p).

BRITISH VIRGIN ISLANDS: 1 U.S. dollar ($) = 100 cents (¢).

BRUNEI: 1 dollar ($) = 100 cents (¢).

BULGARIA: 1 lev (l) = 100 stotinki (st).

BURKINA FASO: 1 CFA franc (fr) = 100 centimes (c).

BURMA: 1 kyat (k) = 100 pyas (p).

BURUNDI: 1 franc (fr) = 100 centimes (c).

CAMEROON: 1 CFA franc (fr) = 100 centimes (c).

CANADA: 1 dollar ($) = 100 cents (¢).

CAPE VERDE: 1 escudo (esc) = 100 centavos (c).

CAYMAN ISLANDS: 1 dollar ($) = 100 cents (¢).
CENTRAL AFRICAN REPUBLIC: 1 CFA franc (fr) = 100 centimes (c).
CHAD: 1 CFA franc (fr) = 100 centimes (c).
CHILE: 1 peso (p) = 100 centavos (c).
CHINA: 1 yuan (y) = 100 fen (f).
TAIWAN (China, Republic of): 1 New Taiwan dollar (NT$) = 100 cents (¢).

CHRISTMAS ISLAND: 1 Australian dollar ($) = 100 cents (¢).
CISKEI: 1 South African rand (r) = 100 cents (¢).
COCOS (KEELING) ISLANDS: 1 Australian dollar ($) = 100 cents (¢).
COLOMBIA: 1 peso (p) = 100 centavos (c).
COMORO ISLANDS: 1 CFA franc (fr) = 100 centimes (c).
CONGO PEOPLE'S REPUBLIC: 1 CFA franc (fr) = 100 centimes (c).
COOK ISLANDS: 1 NZ dollar ($) = 100 cents (¢).
COSTA RICA: 1 colon (col) = 100 centimos (c).
CUBA: 1 peso (p) = 100 centavos (c).
CYPRUS: 1 pound (£) = 1000 milliemes (m).
CZECHOSLOVAKIA: 1 koruna (k) = 100 haleru (h).
DENMARK: 1 krone (kr) = 100 ore (o).
DJIBOUTI: 1 franc (fr) = 100 centimes (c).
DOMINICA: 1 EC dollar ($) = 100 cents (¢).
DOMINICAN REPUBLIC: 1 peso (p) = 100 centavos (c).
ECUADOR: 1 sucre (s) = 100 centavos (c).
EGYPT: 1 pound (£) = 1000 milliemes (m).
EQUATORIAL GUINEA: 1 CFA franc (fr) = 100 centimes (c).
ETHIOPIA: 1 birr (b) = 100 cents (¢).

FALKLAND ISLANDS: 1 pound (£) = 100 pence (p).
FAROES: 1 Danish krone (kr) = 100 ore (o).
FIJI: 1 dollar ($) = 100 cents (¢).
FINLAND: 1 markka (mk) = 100 pennia (p).
FRANCE: 1 franc (fr) = 100 centimes (c).
FRENCH POLYNESIA: 1 CFP franc (fr) = 100 centimes (c).
FRENCH SOUTHERN & ANTARCTIC TERR.: 1 French franc (fr) = 100 centimes (c).
GABON: 1 CFA franc (fr) = 100 centimes (c).
GAMBIA: 1 dalasy (dal) = 100 bututs (b).
GERMANY (East): 1 ostmark (m) = 100 pfennigs (pf).
GERMANY (West): 1 Deutschemark (m) = 100 pfennigs (pf).
GHANA: 1 cedi (c) = 100 pesewas (p).
GIBRALTAR: 1 pound (£) = 100 pence (p).
GREAT BRITAIN: 1 pound sterling (£) = 100 pence (p).
GREECE: 1 drachma (dr) = 100 lepta (l).
GREENLAND: 1 Danish krone (kr) = 100 ore (o).
GRENADA: 1 EC dollar ($) = 100 cents (¢).
GUATEMALA: 1 quetzal (q) = 100 centavos (c).
GUERNSEY: 1 pound sterling (£) = 100 pence (p).
GUINEA: 1 CFA franc (fr) = 100 centimes (c).
GUINEA-BISSAU: 1 peso (p) = 100 centavos (c).
GUYANA: 1 dollar ($) = 100 cents (¢).
HAITI: 1 gourde (g) = 100 centimes (c).
HONDURAS: 1 lempira (l) = 100 centavos (c).
HONG KONG: 1 dollar ($) = 100 cents (¢).
HUNGARY: 1 forint (ft) = 100 filler (f).
ICELAND: 1 krona (kr) = 100 aurar (a).
INDIA: 1 rupee (re) = 100 paise (p).
INDONESIA: 1 rupiah (rp) = 100 sen (s).
IRAN: 1 rial (r) = 100 dinars (d).
IRAQ: 1 dinar (d) = 1000 fils (f).
IRELAND: 1 pound (£) = 100 pence (p).
ISLE OF MAN: 1 pound sterling (£) = 100 pence (p).
ISRAEL: 1 shekel (s) = 100 agorot (a).
ITALY: 1 lira (l) = 100 centesimi (c).

IVORY COAST: 1 CFA franc (fr) = 100 centimes (c).
JAMAICA: 1 dollar ($) = 100 cents (¢).
JAPAN: 1 yen (y) = 100 sen (s).
JERSEY: 1 pound sterling (£) = 100 pence (p).
JORDAN: 1 dinar (d) = 1000 fils (f).
KAMPUCHEA: 1 riel (r) = 100 cents (¢).
KENYA: 1 shilling (/-) = 100 cents (¢).
KIRIBATI: 1 Australian dollar ($) = 100 cents (¢).

KOREA (North): 1 won (w) = 100 chon (ch).
KOREA (South): 1 won (w) = 100 chon (ch).
KUWAIT: 1 dinar (d) = 1000 fils (f).
LAOS: 1 kip (k) = 100 cents (¢).
LEBANON: 1 piaster (pi) = 100 centimes (c).
LESOTHO: 1 loti (m, from plural maloti) = 100 lisente (s from singular sente).
LIBERIA: 1 dollars ($) = 100 cents (¢).
LIBYA: 1 dinar (d) = 1000 dirhams (dh).
LIECHTENSTEIN: 1 Swiss franc (fr) = 100 rappen (rp).
LUXEMBOURG: 1 franc (fr) = 100 centimes (c).
MACAO: 1 pataca (pa) = 100 avos (a).
MADEIRA: 1 Portuguese escudo (esc) = 100 centavos (c).
MALAGASY REPUBLIC: 1 franc (fr) = 100 centimes (c).
MALAWI: 1 kwacha (k) = 100 tambalas (t).
MALAYSIA: 1 ringgit dollar ($) = 100 sen (s).
MALDIVES: 1 rufiyaa (rf) = 100 larees (l).
MALI: 1 CFA franc (fr) = 100 centimes (c).
MALTA: 1 pound (£) = 100 cents (¢).
MARSHALL ISLANDS: 1 U.S. dollar ($) = 100 cents (¢).
MAURITANIA: 1 ouguiya (um) = 5 khoums (k).
MAURITIUS: 1 rupee (re) = 100 cents (¢).
MEXICO: 1 peso (p) = 100 centavos (c).
MICRONESIA: 1 U.S. dollar ($) = 100 cents (¢).
MONACO: 1 French franc (fr) = 100 centimes (c).
MONGOLIA: 1 tugrik (t) = 100 mung (mu).
MONTSERRAT: 1 EC dollar ($) = 100 cents (¢).
MOROCCO: 1 dirham (dh) = 100 francs (fr).
MOZAMBIQUE: 1 metica (mt) = 100 centimos (c).
NAURU: 1 Australian dollar ($) = 100 cents (¢).
NEPAL: 1 rupee (re) = 100 paise (p).
NETHERLANDS: 1 gulden (g) = 100 cents (¢).
NETHERLANDS ANTILLES: 1 gulden (g) = 100 cents (¢).
NEVIS: 1 EC dollar ($) = 100 cents (¢).
NEW CALEDONIA: 1 CFP franc (fr) = 100 centimes (c).
NEW ZEALAND: 1 dollar ($) = 100 cents (¢).
NICARAGUA: 1 cordoba (cor) = 100 centavos (c).
NIGER: 1 CFA franc (fr) = 100 centimes (c).
NIGERIA: 1 naira (n) = 100 kobo (k).
NIUAFO'OU: 1 Tongan pa'anga (pa) = 100 senti (s).
NIUE: 1 NZ dollar ($) = 100 cents (¢).
NORFOLK ISLAND: 1 Australian dollar ($) = 100 cents (¢).
NORWAY: 1 krone (kr) = 100 ore (o).
OMAN (Sultanate of): 1 rial (ri) = 1000 baizas (b).
PAKISTAN: 1 rupee (re) = 100 paisa (p).
PALAU: 1 U.S. dollar ($) = 100 cents (¢).
PANAMA: 1 balboa (b) = 100 centesimos (c).
PAPUA NEW GUINEA: 1 kina (k) = 100 toea (t).
PARAGUAY: 1 guarani (g) = 100 centimos (c).
PENRHYN: 1 NZ dollar ($) = 100 cents (¢).
PERU: 1 inti (i) = 100 centavos (c).
PHILIPPINES: 1 piso (p) = 100 sentimos (s).
PITCAIRN ISLANDS: 1 NZ dollar ($) = 100 cents (¢).
POLAND: 1 zloty (zl) = 100 groszy (gr).
PORTUGAL: 1 escudo (esc) = 100 centavos (c).
QATAR: 1 riyal (ri) = 100 dirhams (d).
REDONDA: 1 dollar ($) = 100 cents (¢)
ROMANIA: 1 leu (l) = 100 bani (b).
RWANDA: 1 franc (fr) = 100 centimes (c).
ST. HELENA: 1 pound sterling (£) = 100 pence (p).
ST. KITTS: 1 EC dollar ($) = 100 cents (¢).
ST. LUCIA: 1 EC dollar ($) = 100 cents (¢).
ST. PIERRE & MIQUELON: 1 French franc (fr) = 100 centimes (c).
ST. THOMAS & PRINCE ISLAND: 1 dobra (db) = 100 centavos (c).
ST. VINCENT: 1 EC dollar ($) = 100 cents (¢).
SALVADOR: 1 colon (col) = 100 centavos (c).
SAN MARINO: 1 Italian lira (l) = 100 centesimi (c).

SAUDI ARABIA: 1 riyal (ri) = 100 halalas (h).
SENEGAL: 1 CFA franc (fr) = 100 centimes (c).
SEYCHELLES: 1 rupee (re) = 100 cents (¢).
SIERRE LEONE: 1 leone (l) = 100 cents (¢).
SINGAPORE: 1 dollar ($) = 100 cents (¢).
SOLOMON ISLANDS: 1 dollar ($) = 100 cents (¢).
SOMALIA: 1 shilling (sh) = 100 centesimos (c).
SOUTH AFRICA: 1 rand (r) = 100 cents (¢).
SOUTH GEORGIA: 1 pound (£) = 100 pence (p).
SOUTH-WEST AFRICA (NAMIBIA): 1 South African rand (r) = 100 cents (¢).
SPAIN: 1 peseta (pta) = 100 centimos (c).
SRI LANKA: 1 rupee (re) = 100 cents (¢).
SUDAN: 1 pound (£) = 100 piastres (p).
SURINAM: 1 gulden (g) = 100 cents (¢).
SWAZILAND: 1 emalangeni (e) = 100 cents (¢).
SWEDEN: 1 krona (kr) = 100 ore (o).
SWITZERLAND: 1 franc (fr) = 100 centimes (c).
SYRIA: 1 pound (£) = 100 piastres (p).
TANZANIA: 1 shilling (/-) = 100 cents (¢).
THAILAND: 1 baht (b) = 100 satang (s).
TOGO: 1 CFA franc (fr) = 100 centimes (c).
TOKELAU: 1 NZ dollar ($) = 100 cents (¢).
TONGA: 1 pa'anga (pa) = 100 seniti (s).
TRANSKEI: 1 South African rand (r) = 100 cents (¢).
TRINIDAD & TOBAGO: 1 dollar ($) = 100 cents (¢).
TRISTAN DA CUNHA: 1 pound sterling (£) = 100 pence (p).
TUNISIA: 1 dinar (d) = 1000 millimes (m).
TURKEY: 1 lira (l) = 100 kurus (k).
TURKISH REPUBLIC OF NORTHERN CYPRUS: 1 Turkish lira (l) = 100 kurus (k).
TURKS & CAICOS ISLANDS: 1 U.S. dollar ($) = 100 cents (¢).
TUVALU: 1 Australian dollar ($) = 100 cents (¢).
UGANDA: 1 shilling (/-) = 100 cents (¢).
UNION OF SOVIET SOCIALIST REPUBLICS: 1 ruble (rub) = 100 kopecks (kop).
UNITED ARAB EMIRATES: 1 dirham (d) = 100 fils (f).
UNITED NATIONS: uses U.S. currency in New York, Swiss currency in Geneva, and Austrian currency in Vienna.
UNITED STATES OF AMERICA: 1 dollar ($) = 100 cents (¢).
URUGUAY: 1 new peso (N$) = 100 centesimos (c).
VANUATU: l vatu (v) = 100 francs (fr).
VATICAN CITY: 1 Italian lira (l) = 100 centesimi (c).
VENDA: 1 South African rand (r) = 100 cents (¢).
VENEZUELA: 1 bolivar (b) = 100 centimos (c).
VIETNAM: 1 dong (d) = 100 xu.
WALLIS & FUTUNA: 1 CFP franc (fr) = 100 centimes (c).
WESTERN SAMOA: 1 tala (t) = 100 sene (s).
YEMEN ARAB REPUBLIC: 1 riyal (ri) = 100 fils (f).
YEMEN, (People's Democratic Republic): 1 dinar (d) = 1000 fils (f).
YUGOSLAVIA: 1 dinar (d) = 100 paras (p).
ZAIRE: 1 zaire (z) = 100 makuta (k).
ZAMBIA: 1 kwacha (kw) = 100 ngwee (ng).
ZIL SESEL ELWANNYEN: 1 Seychelles rupee (re) = 100 cents (¢).
ZIMBABWE: 1 dollar ($) = 100 cents (¢).

Chapter 15

Stamp Organizations

American Philatelic Society

Starting with only a few enthusiasts in the 1850s, the number of collectors of postage stamps steadily increased through the succeeding decades, and by the 1880s must have totaled 25,000 or more. Naturally, with this comparatively limited number of collectors, the avenues for purchasing and exchanging stamps and securing information about stamps were restricted to the few dealers and the diminutive stamp journals, practically all of which were published only for brief periods.

Responding to the demand of numerous collectors and local societies to form a national stamp society, 400 interested collectors indicated their willingness to assist in founding such an organization. A total of 219 sent in their proxies and each paid 25¢ for the privilege of voting by proxy.

A committee held a meeting in New York City on Sept. 13, 1886. The name, the American Philatelic Association, was adopted for the newly formed organization. The following day, John K. Tiffany, a distinguished businessman and ardent stamp collector, was elected president. He held the position for 10 years.

The first five issues of the *American Philatelist* were published in Altoona, Pa., commencing Jan. 10, 1887. A mail vote in June 1887, resulted in the *Western Philatelist* being chosen as the society's official publication.

Because of the dissension caused by this action, the membership at the second annual convention, held in Chicago, Ill., in August 1887, voted to resume publishing the *American Philatelist* as the society's official journal.

The association was first incorporated in the state of West Virginia on Nov. 2, 1891. The certificate of this incorporation appears in the Volume X, November 1896, issue of the *American Philatelist*.

On Aug. 24, 1897, at the Boston convention, authority was given the Northwestern Adjustment Co. of Minneapolis to act as an agent for the re-incorporation of the association in the state of Minnesota.

In 1897, the name of the organization was changed to the American Philatelic Society, then a few months later was changed back to the original name. Since September 1908, the name has remained unchanged as the American Philatelic Society.

The society grew steadily, and when the golden jubilee convention was held in 1936, membership stood at 4,526.

Because of the startling increase in membership and the society's expanding activities, it was considered necessary to consolidate activities in a central office and to hire full-time employees to staff it.

H. Clay Musser was appointed the first full-time secretary. He established the central office at State College, Pa., on April 1, 1945.

In 1947, the APS was elected to membership in the Federation Internationale de Philatelie (FIP) as the United States representative.

In 1958, the sales division, previously operated by J.E. Guest in Dallas, Texas, for 37 years, became one of the responsibilities of the executive secretary, who assumed the additional title of sales director. The sales division operations were moved to State College, Pa.

Col. James T. DeVoss, U.S. Army, Retired, succeeded H. Clay Musser as executive secretary and sales director upon Musser's retirement on Nov. 15, 1963.

The society was instrumental in the formation of the Federacion Inter-americana de Filatelia (FIAF) in 1966.

Daniel W. Vooys, a bank president from Canajoharie, N.Y., assumed office as president in October 1969. Under his able and imaginative leadership, the society improved its services and sought new areas in which to assist stamp collectors everywhere.

Outstanding among his accomplishments was his whole-hearted support of the effort initiated by Edward L. Willard, APS past president, to establish the American Philatelic Research Library. It was Vooys' wish that the APRL be recognized as a top-ranking library available to all stamp collectors regardless of the philatelic affiliation.

Upon the death in 1976 of James M. Chemi — who had edited *The American Philatelist* in Arizona since 1960 — the editorial offices were consolidated with the headquarters.

Chemi was succeeded as the publication's editor by Richard L. Sine, who remained in the position until 1985. Bill Welch has edited the journal since that time. The 1,000th issue of *The American Philatelist* was published in May 1984.

In the fall of 1978, Pennsylvania State University began work on a comprehensive series of correspondence courses in stamp collecting. A grant from the APS provided initial funding for the project, which is being directed by an advisory committee composed of both Penn State and APS personnel. Four courses are currently available.

A new national headquarters building was dedicated in April 1982. The building stands on a 5-acre plot at the entrance to a planned community on the outskirts of State College.

With more than 20,000 square feet of floor space, the building is asymmetric and will permit expansion in whatever direction necessary.

James T. DeVoss, after 20 years with the society, was succeeded in 1981 by Keith A. Wagner as executive director.

On Jan. 1, 1989, the APS boasted more than 56,000 members. Membership has more than doubled since 1977.

American Philatelic Research Library

The American Philatelic Research Library, located in the American Philatelic Building, is the largest public library specializing in philately in the United States. Incorporated in 1968 as the research and educational arm of the American Philatelic Society, the APRL processes requests for information and the loan of books by mail.

The library also offers researchers and browsers a wealth of philatelic materials and display racks filled with current periodicals and auction catalogs.

The APRL is the result of the long-expressed wish of thousands of collectors since the emergence of stamp collecting as a major hobby. It has been recognized for decades that a national philatelic library to serve the needs of serious philatelists, regardless of their place of residence, would be a boon to all stamp collectors and a tremendous boost to the hobby.

The need for easy access to books and articles containing information not readily available to the average collector and researcher has been apparent to many prominent stamp collectors. Some collectors have even expounded upon the theme in lectures and in articles published in the 19th and 20th centuries.

John K. Tiffany, a prominent collector of the late 19th century, an ardent advocate of the establishment of a national philatelic library and the first president of the American Philatelic Association (as the APS was then called), was instrumental in developing the lasting interest in philatelic literature that now exists.

Edward L. Willard, first president of the APRL, worked diligently for the establishment of a national philatelic library during his term as president of the APS. Finally, in 1968, Willard saw the APRL become a reality. The John K. Tiffany Library Fund and the Edward L. Willard Memorial Fund have been established to honor the contributions these two distinguished collectors made to the philatelic world. Tax-deductible donations in any amount may be made to either of these funds.

Virginia L. Horn has served as the director of library services since 1984.

Library Resources

The present library collection contains some 60,000 titles covering every aspect of stamp collecting. For beginning collectors, there are all kinds of informational handbooks, guides, dictionaries and encyclopedias. For specialist collectors, there are more than 400 worldwide handbooks, as well as periodicals and catalogs. For those beginning research in new fields of philately, there are many bibliographies and indexes.

Books, catalogs and bound periodicals can be borrowed through the mail for a small fee per book to cover the cost of postage, handling and insurance.

The materials borrowed may be kept for two weeks from the day received, and they may be renewed once for the same period. A fine is charged for each day a book is not returned according to the aforementioned rule. As many as five books may be borrowed at one time. Requests, however, can be made for more than five books with the understanding that additional books will be sent upon return of the books loaned originally.

All patrons are asked to fill out a borrower's application form before borrowing books. A borrower's application form will be sent when books are requested. Members may request the appropriate forms in advance of borrowing, so books can be sent without delay.

The appropriate fee must be sent with all book requests; books cannot be loaned on credit. Members who prefer to request books by telephone may deposit funds for future borrowing.

Members of the APS and APRL may borrow books directly from the library, while members of chapters, units, or affiliates of the APS may obtain material from the library through their chapter or affiliate representative.

All others may utilize the facilities of the library by having their local library request material for them through the interlibrary loan program.

For those patrons who are uncertain as to what may be available on a specific topic, the APRL staff can suggest books. The APRL's catalog has been computerized for easy access by the staff and visiting researchers. Computerized searches also are available by mail for a fee.

A wide variety of reference sources are available to help in answering specific questions. Reference materials, rare books and unbound periodicals cannot be circulated on loan. However, photocopies can be made of the appropriate pages of items that may be of interest. A cost per page is charged for photocopies.

APRL Membership

Any person can become a member of the APRL. The annual dues of $10 include a subscription to the library quarterly, *Philatelic Literature Review*. Membership in the APS automatically confers use of the library, but does not include a subscription to the quarterly.

The *Philatelic Literature Review* has been an authoritative and valuable source of information concerning philatelic literature for many years. Formerly published by the Philatelic Literature Association, before its merger in 1969 with the APRL, the review publishes bibliographies on special philatelic subjects and indexes for other specialized periodicals.

One of its features is the Literature Clearinghouse, where members may advertise their literature for sale or publish their want lists for needed literature. (Sample copies are available for a nominal charge.)

In September 1969, the U.S. Internal Revenue Service recognized the library as a tax-exempt institution, thus making all donations to it tax deductible. To enable collectors and friends to provide tax-deductible financial support, sustaining ($15) and contributing ($30) memberships have been established.

With these memberships, the amounts in excess of $5 are tax deductible. The names of sustaining and contributing members are published annually in the *Philatelic Literature Review*.

Additionally, life memberships ($200) are available and do not require payment of annual dues. Such contributions also qualify as tax deductible under the Internal Revenue Service regulations.

The fiscal and membership year commences Jan. 1. Dues are payable in advance and are prorated the first year of membership.

Donations of all types of philatelic literature are appreciated. Donations are acknowledged in both *The American Philatelist* and the *Philatelic Literature Review*. All literature donations also are tax deductible, which is particularly helpful in the settlement of an estate.

Many large private libraries, as well as countless individual works, already have been donated to the APRL. All such donations may be mailed to the APRL via library rate.

The libraries of the American Air Mail Society and the American Helvetia Philatelic Society, as well as the archives of the American First Day Cover Foundation, are part of the APRL's collections.

Further information is available from the APRL, Box 8338, State College, Pa. 16803.

APRL Founder Members

Ray C. Ameen
J. Oliver Amos
William T. Amos
Gordon F. Anderson
Earl P.L. Apfelbaum
Leo August
Samuel August
William H. Bauer
George Boiko
Billings E. Burlingame
Richard W. Canman
Anna M. Chemi
James M. Chemi
Sarah Mensinger
Chemi Memorial
Emerson A. Clark
Joseph M. Clary
Sylvester Colby
Donald F. Dahlquist
George R. Daley
James N. Dalton
Leslie A. Davenport
Robert L.D. Davidson
Kenneth R. de Lisle
James T. DeVoss
Dr. Harold E. Donnell
Peter G. DuPuy
George C. Dyer
Melvin T. Edmonds
Sidney Epstein
Lois M. Evans
William L. Evans
John E. Foxworth Jr.
Joe F. Frye
Marian Frye
Louis Grunin
Bernard D. Harmer
Henry E. Harris
Elizabeth H. Harrison
Horace W. Harrison
Creighton C. Hart
John T. Hastings Jr.
Bernard A. Hennig
Dolores E. Hennig
Herman Herst Jr.
Duane Hillmer
J. King Horner
Henry W. Houser
Georgia B. Hunt
Lucius Jackson
Gayle C. Jones
Lewis M. Kaufman
Arthur M. Kennedy Jr.
A. Murl Kimmel
Joseph L. Kurtzman
Maryette B. Lane
Andrew Levitt
David Lidman
Harry L. Lindquist
Lyons F. Livingston
Harold H. Longfellow
Catherine S. Lowder
Elizabeth S. Martin
George M. Martin
Robert A. Mason
Edward L. Miller
Doris H. Moran
Kendall A. Moran
James A. Morton Jr.
Edward M. Passano
Charles J. Peterson
Samuel Ray
Edward A. Richardson
Jared H. Richter
Arthur E. Ross Jr.
Arthur Salm
Harry C. Sayre III
Robert A. Scheuermann
William E. Shelton
Kelly Shryoc
J.N. Sissons

Hubert C. Skinner
Kent J. Snyder
Lauson H. Stone
Charles H. Sweeting
Alex L. ter Braake
Neil D. Thompson
Ronald J. Tomaszewski
George Trefonas
V.R. Trimmer
Daniel F. Vooys
Daniel W. Vooys
Grace E. Vooys
Lt. Col. Daniel C. Warren
Raymond H. Weill
William L. Welch
Edward L. Willard
Benjamin Wishnietsky
Marian Carne Zinsmeister
APS Writers Unit
Baltimore Philatelic Society Inc.
Chicago Philatelic Society
Crescent City Stamp Club
The Franklin Mint Corp.
Hollywood Stamp Club
Memphis Stamp Collectors Society
Mount Nittany Philatelic Society
New Haven Philatelic Society
Scott Publishing Co.
SONEX 72
Vidiforms Co. Inc.
WESTPEX

APS Accredited Judges

The following collectors and dealers (latter indicated by an asterisk) have been accredited as philatelic judges. The highest level of stamp exhibition each individual has actually served as judge is indicated in parentheses following each name — (I) International (N) National (R) Regional (L) Local. The principal area of philatelic interest is given for each accredited judge.

Many stamp exhibitions now utilize apprentice judges so that those interested might gain experience by serving with an accredited judge and thereby become sufficiently competent to meet the accreditation requirements of the APS.

Members desiring to apply for accreditation as a philatelic judge may obtain the necessary forms by writing to the chairman, Accreditation of Judges, Box 8000, State College, Pa. 16801.

Adams, James R., Indiana (N) aerophilately; postal history; U.S.; Great Britain; postal stationery; censored mail; topicals.

Adams, Jeanette Knoll, Indiana (N) postal history; postal stationery; Great Britain; British Commonwealth; Ireland; Canada; topicals; aerophilately; literature.

Allen, William C., Michigan (R) U.S.; postal history; Canada; precancels; Great Britain; Germany.

Alton, Jacquelyn S., Illinois (N) Germany; postal history.

Ball, Charles I., Ohio (N) general; postal history; postal stationery; literature.

Balough, Joseph J., Texas (N) Germany; France; U.S.; perfins; topicals; literature.

Banchik, Seymour, New York (N) Israel; U.S.; Great Britain; postal stationery.

Barker, William E., Ohio (N) postal history; U.S.; British Commonwealth; most colonial areas; Western Europe.

Barovick, Fred, New Jersey (N) general.

Bartlett, William R., Tennessee (N) U.S.; British North America; Greece; Czechoslovakia; Philippines; postal history.

Bauer, William H., Texas (I) U.S. postal history; postal stationery; Great Britain; Germany; Japan; Middle East; literature.

Beecher, Stanley H., California (N) U.S.; U.N.; Latin America; British North America.

Bize, David N. Jr., Nebraska (R) U.S.; Canada; Scandinavia; airmails; perfins; FDCs.

Blake, Paul C., California (N) India; Indochina; Laos; Cambodia; Vietnam; French Colonies; Thailand; airmail.

Blau, Fred F., Illinois (N) Palestine; Israel; Austria; Germany; U.S.; airmails.

Bobbitt, Ottis C., Texas (N) U.S.; topicals.

Boehret, Jesse D., Virginia (N) Germany and related; U.S.; maritime mail.

Boerma, Albert, Netherlands (I) Central Europe; literature; thematics.

Bohne, Werner M., Florida (I) Germany and States and colonies; Europe; U.S.; U.N.

Bomar, William J., Florida (N) U.S.; Confederacy; revenues; postal stationery.

Bowman, James W., Texas (N) U.S.; Confederates; Hawaii.

Brandeberry, R.B., Delaware (N) British Empire; Scandinavia; Netherlands and

Colonies; Switzerland; Germany.

Brooks, Anthony K., Indiana (N) Germany, Berlin; postal history; China; Europe; airmail; U.S.; worldwide military/censorship.

Brown, Harriet W., California (N) topicals; Great Britain; Canada; Monaco; France; Luxembourg; Liechtenstein; Switzerland; Japan.

Buckner, John M., Florida (I) British Empire; U.S.; Confederates; postal stationery; postal history; topicals; revenues; literature.

Clark, Douglas N., Georgia (N) U.S.; Confederacy; postal history; literature.

***Clatterbuck, W.C.**, Ohio (N) Canada; Hawaii; general.

Cohn, Ernst M., Alabama (I) Scandinavia; France; Germany; Europe; postal history; airmails; literature.

***Cole, Ezra D.**, New York (N) U.S.; British North America.

Corless, Robert D., Arizona (N) U.S.; British North America; British Colonies; general; Australasia; postal stationery.

Craig, Wallace A., California (N) Latin America; Scandinavia; postal stationery.

Cunliffe, Robert H., Pennsylvania (N) U.S.; revenues; general.

Dean, L. Wallace III, Connecticut (N) Haiti; British West Indies; U.S.; Central America; postal history.

Debo, Arno, West Germany (I) classical Europe; U.S.; South America.

de Violini, Robert, California (N) literature.

DeVoss, James T., Pennsylvania (I) U.S. Possessions; Central America; general; literature.

Dickson, Frederick S., III, Delaware (N) postal history; U.S.; thematic.

Diena, Enzo, Italy (I) Italy; Italian States; European classics.

Dillaway, Guy R., Massachusetts (N) Great Britain and Colonies; U.S.

Dixon, Michael D., Maryland (N) South America; Europe (WWI and WWII); Great Britain; Elizabeth II; postal mechanization.

Dorfman, David, Florida (N) U.S.; Cyprus; India; Israel; Palestine; Holy Land postal history.

Dormer, Edward J., Florida (N) Mexico; U.S.; British Colonies; South America; airmails.

Dougan, Charles W., Canada (N) China; Tibet; Chinese Treaty Ports; Shanghai.

Drews, Richard E., Illinois (N) U.S.; United Nations; Great Britain; Canada; Israel; Southern Europe; Nepal; Cape of Good Hope.

Dulin, Austin H., Illinois (N) Germany; Japan; topicals; U.N.; general.

***Effinger, R.C. Jr.**, Alabama (N) Germany; France; Iceland; Austria; Spain; Great Britain; Switzerland; Ryukyus.

Dunn, William S., Colorado (N) U.S.; postal history.

Elnen, Thomas E., Illinois (N) Scandinavia; British Asia and Africa; U.S.

Engstrom, Victor E., Florida (N) general; Scandinavian postal stationery; local posts.

Evans, Walter I., Missouri (N) U.S.; 19th-century classic covers of the world.

Evans-de Violini, Lois M., California (N) Japan; U.S. used in Japan and China; U.N.; literature.

Fink, Ernesto, Austria (I) Europe; Sweden; Scandinavia.

Fisher, Ingeburg L., Washington (N) topicals; Germany; postal history.

Fitz, Charles, M., New Jersey (N) topicals; Roman States; Vatican City; Israel; Ireland; Italy.

Foley, Joseph E., New Jersey (I) Ireland; British North America; British; U.S.

Follansbee, Nicholas T., California (N) Mexico; Latin America; Europe; U.S.; Far East.

Foxworth, John E. Jr., Michigan (I) U.S.; Confederates; British North America; Germany; topicals; postal stationery.

Fricks, Ernest E., New Jersey (I) postal history.

Gandara, Raul, Puerto Rico (N) Puerto Rico; Cuba; Dominican Republic; Central America; Spain; thematics; youth.

Ganz, Cheryl, Illinois (N) literature.

Ganz, P. Felix, Illinois (N) Andorra; Liechtenstein; Switzerland; U.N.; postal stationery; postal history; Arctic; Antarctic; literature.

Garabrant, L.V., New Jersey (N) topical; general; Switzerland; Ireland.

Garabrant, Melvin, New Jersey (N) France; Netherlands; topicals; general.

Garfinkel, Martin, Florida (N) Holy Land forerunners; Palestine; Israel; Zemstvos.

Goldsmith, Edward, Georgia (N) general; topicals; postal history; Spanish Antilles.

Graue, James W., Washington (N) Germany; Zeppelins; catapult mail; Gambia; literature; U.S.

Green, Nonie, Texas (N) Europe; Latin America; U.S. postal history; Canada; Thailand; airmails; postal stationery.

Greene, Inslee B., Washington (N) Australia and States; New Zealand; British America and Oceania; French Oceania; U.S.

Griffiths, John O., California (N) Great Britain and Commonwealth; Western Europe; U.S.; postal history; topicals.

Gruenebaum, Werner, Illinois (N) Germany; Austria; Hungarian navy.

Guzzio, George T., New York (I) general; topical; France; Germany; German States; U.S.

Hahn, Henry, Virginia (N) Czechoslovakia; Austria; postal history; literature.

Harris, James P., North Carolina (N) U.S.; U.N.; Confederates; British North America; literature; UPU; Great Britain.

Harris, Leo J., Minnesota (N) postal history; Latin America; Latin American airmail.

Harrison, Horace W., Maryland (N) U.S. and stampless; British America; British North America; postal history; postal stationery; literature.

Hatfield, Jack, Ohio (R) France and Colonies; British Colonies; general.

Hedley, Richard P., New York (N) Canada; British North America; British Commonwealth.

Hennig, Bernard A., Illinois (I) Germany and related; France and Colonies; Great Britain and Colonies; Russia; China; Guatemala.

Hess, Winand, California (N) Europe and Colonies; revenues; topicals.

Hooper, R. Malcolm, Connecticut (N) U.S.; precancels.

Hornung, Otto, England (N) Turkey; Holy Land; East and Central Europe; German field post in Turkey; literature.

Hotchner, John M., Virginia (N) U.S.; EFOs; 19th-century general; Italy; Russia; China; Spain; U.N.; France; literature.

Iber, Peter K., Washington, D.C. (N) Thailand; Laos; Cambodia; topicals; youth exhibits; revenues.

Illyefalvi, Kalman V., Maryland (I) British Africa; Eastern Europe; U.N.; Austria.

Ireland, Philip W., Maryland (N) China; Japan; Great Britain; British North America; Ottoman Empire and successor states.

Isaacs, Mark R., Illinois (N); Indochina; Vietnam; French Colonies; U.S. classics; military mail; independent Asia.

Jefferson, James E., California (N) U.S.; Brazil; general; literature.

Jennings, Clyde, Florida (I) U.S.; topicals.

Jersey, Stanley C., California (N) U.S.; postal history; Pacific territories; airmail 1940-75.

Johnston, Hugh W., Washington (N), topicals; inflation issues of China 1944-48 (postal history).

Jordan, Richard B., California (N) U.S. and possessions; Confederacy; British Empire; Europe and colonies; airmails; postal stationery; postal history.

Keally, James J., Pennsylvania (N) U.S.; Haiti; Canada; Europe; topicals.

Kelsey, Douglas A., Arizona (N) U.S.; British Commonwealth; aerophilately; polar; Ohio; postal history.

Kessler, Melvin M., Florida (R) U.S.; Russia and states, offices abroad; military covers; Confederates; postal history.

Kline, Roger W., New York (N) U.S.; Canada; U.N.; postal history; postal stationery.

Kraemer, James E., Canada (N) Canada; Germany; Brazil; Roman States; Vatican; Arctic; Antarctic; British colonies.

Kutz, Kenneth J., Connecticut (N) Western U.S. postal history; Canada and provinces; Australian states; New Zealand.

LaBlonde, Charles, Massachusetts (N) Switzerland; postal history.

Larsen, Paul A., Illinois (I) Germany and colonies; Denmark; British colonies; French Africa.

Leeds, David J., California (N) Latin America; West Indies; postal history; revenues.

Lievsay, John E., New York (N) 19th-century classics; U.S.; France and colonies; postal history; topicals.

Light, Theodore, Illinois (N) Asia; U.S. airmail covers.

Lloyd, Carroll L., Maryland (N) U.S.; Latin America; Greece.

Lohman, Garvin F., California (N) British

North America; Ireland; Guatemala; Costa Rica; Salvador; Sweden; Norway; Japan revenues.

Luft, Stanley J., Colorado (N) France; postal history; postal stationery; U.S.; Canada; British West Indies; Great Britain; literature; Western Europe.

Luster, Stephen, Virginia (N) topicals; postal history; U.S.; Europe.

Maisel, William H., Florida (I) U.S.; Belgium; Luxembourg; Switzerland; Netherlands; postal stationery.

Martin, Bill A., Kansas (R) U.S.

Martin, George M., Washington (N) general; U.S.; Canada; Germany; China; postal stationery; postal history; literature.

Matz, Billy, Tennessee (N) U.S.; Confederates.

Mayrisch, Lenard Jr., California (N) Central and Western Europe; postal history; Levant; Philippines; Barbados; Austria; topicals.

Mazepa, James, Illinois (N) U.S.; Mexico; Europe; airmails; postal history.

McCann, Peter P., Ohio (N) British Atlantic; British Caribbean; British Oceania; polar; Pacific Islands.

Meier, Eileen L., Virginia (N) U.N.; topicals; postal history.

Meier, Harry C., Virginia (N) postal history; Germany; U.N.; literature.

Menuz, Wayne, California (N) postal stationery; Italy and colonies; Great Britain and colonies.

Mewes, Emil W., Germany (I) Europe and colonies; postal history; literature.

Mitchell, Milton, Maryland (I) U.S.; British North America; Israel; China; Siam; Central Europe; general.

Moen, Georgia M., Washington (N) U.S.; U.N.; topicals; British Colonies.

Moll, Herbert H., Peru (I) Latin America.

Moriarty, Lawrence R., New York (N) Hungary; Fiume (Austro-Hungarian era); topicals; penalty envelopes; postal stationery.

Newman, Lowell S., New Jersey (N) U.S.; Europe; Latin America; British Empire; postal history; literature; topicals.

Nicoll, Ann de Bayley, Indiana (N) British Commonwealth; Germany; Middle East; Near East; Great Britain postal history.

Norton, George S., Massachusetts (N) U.S.; North American revenues; postal stationery; North American airmails.

Norton, Walter E., Pennsylvania (N) Lithuania; Latvia; Estonia; Klaipeda; Memel; Balkans.

Odenweller, Robert P., New Jersey (I) U.S.; British Empire; classics.

Oliver, William J., California (N) Philippines; Korea; Japan; Ryukyus.

Orton, Walter J., New York (N) U.S.; Great Britain; Newfoundland; Canada; Australia; New Zealand.

Osborn, Wilmont V., Michigan (N) U.S.; Bolivia; Germany; topicals.

Ott, Russell E., Texas (N) topicals; polar; postal history; postal stationery.

Owens, Mary Ann, New York (I) topicals; literature.

Ozment, James L., Colorado (N) U.S. and possessions; U.S. postal history; Canada; Great Britain.

Paliafito, Robert A., Arizona (I) U.S.; U.S. postal history; Italian States; Mexico.

Patterson, Curtis, Delaware (N) FDCs.

Peter, Harold E., Illinois (N) Germany and related areas; postal history; postal stationery.

Peterson, Charles J., West Germany (I) literature.

Pla, Steven A., New Mexico (N) philatelic literature; China.

Plyler, Earle F., Oklahoma (N) U.S.; France; Switzerland; British colonies.

Pomeroy, Thomas D., Oregon (R) U.S.; Canada; topicals.

Pratt, Robert H., Wisconsin (N) U.S.; Canada; St. Pierre/Miquelon; British colonies; postal history; essays and proofs.

Preston, Dickson H., Washington (N) Germany and related; airmail, zeppelin; British Commonwealth.

Rapp, William F., Nebraska (N) U.S.; Canada; Hungary; El Salvador; Portuguese colonies; postal history.

***Ray, Samuel**, California (I) general; literature; postal history; aerophilately; topicals.

Raymond, Gale J., Texas (N) British West Indies; French colonies; Pacific Islands; Tibet; Bhutan; war covers; polar.

Reed, Eugene C., Jr., New Jersey (N) U.S.; classics; postal history; aerophilately.

Rendon, Alex, New York (N) Central and South America; Europe.

Ribler, Ronald I., Virginia (N) U.S.;

Canada; British Commonwealth; Western Europe; revenues; postal history.

Riccio, Dominick J., New York (N) Czechoslovakia; Ukraine; Carpatho/Ukraine; Eastern Europe; Ireland; U.S. revenues; Ryukyus; New Hebrides.

Richardson, Martin D., Ohio (N) U.S.; postal history; local posts; revenues; airmails.

Rosen, Morris, Maryland (I) Holy Land; Israel; concentration camp and ghetto mail; German; Poland; Monaco; Olympics and sports.

Rosenberg, Howard L., Illinois (N) U.S.; Canada; Holy Land; postal history; literature.

Rosende, Roberto M., New York (I) Cuba; Spain and colonies; Portugal and colonies; Latin America; postal history.

Rowell, Milo D., California (N) Asia; British colonies; postal history; China; Ryukyus; Japan and occupations.

Ruggiero, Michael E., New York (N) Japan; Korea; China; Hong Kong; Ryukyus; Asia.

Ruthrauff, Raymond W., Sr., Pennsylvania (N) U.S.; postal history; Great Britain and colonies.

Sanford, Oliver R., California (N) Great Britain and colonies; Germany and related; Nepal; Guatemala.

Schaffling, Otto G., Connecticut (N) Germany and States; Austria; Netherlands; Hungary; Switzerland.

Schimmer, Karl H., California (N) Germany and states; France; Scandinavia; Austria; U.S.; Mexico; Central and South America.

Schumann, Stephen D., California (N) U.S.; Europe and colonies; postal history; postal stationery; literature.

Schwartz, Joseph D., California (I) U.S.; general.

Seifert, Fred F., New Mexico (N) general; British colonies; literature; postal stationery; postal history.

Sellers, F. Burton, Arizona (I) Latin America; U.S. and possessions; Canada; British North America; postal history; literature.

Selzer, Howard J., Illinois (R) Central Europe; Great Britain and colonies; postal history; Far East.

Silver, Philip, New Jersey (I) airmails; Confederates; topicals; Uruguay; U.S.

Sine, Richard L., Ohio (N) literature.

Siskin, Edward J., New Jersey (N) FDCs; U.S.; British North America; postal history.

Skavaril, Russell V., Ohio (N) U.S.; Great Britain and Commonwealth; Europe; postal history; postal stationery; topicals; literature.

Skinner, Hubert C., Louisiana (N) U.S.; postal history; Latin America; Canada; Mexico; Venezuela; Great Britain and colonies.

Smith, Donald W., Pennsylvania (N) topicals.

Spangenberg, Lorna E., California (N) topicals; Egypt; postal history of Alaska.

Steinhardt, Hans R., North Carolina (N) British Empire; Switzerland; Germany; Western Europe.

Stieber, Conrad H., California (N) Central and Western Europe; Germany and related areas.

Stillions, Clarence A., Washington, D.C., (N) British North America; Brazil; French colonies; St. Pierre/Miquelon; scouting.

Sutherland, Harry, Canada (I) Europe; North America; China.

Theimer, Ernst, New Jersey (N) Central Europe; U.S.; Europe.

Thomas, Arthur, California (N) U.S.; postal stationery; British; perfins; general.

Tinsley, W. Eugene, California (N) U.S.; British; France; postal history; Netherlands; topicals; Canada; New Zealand; Mexico.

Tobias, A.L.T., California (N) Confederates; 19th-century U.S.; Ryukyus; Bhutan; art; Europa; flight covers.

Torrey, Gordon H., Maryland (I) Europe; Russia and offices; Middle East; China; Ethiopia; Liberia; postal history.

Townsend, Norman W. Jr., Ohio (N) China and offices; People's Republic of China; Tibet; Shanghai; Hong Kong; Manuchukuo; Belgian Congo; Jamaica; aerophilately.

Trefonas, George P., Illinois (N) Greece; Turkey; Germany; France; Great Britain and colonies; airmails; Olympics.

***Van Dam, Theodore**, California (N) Spain; Germany; war covers; postal history.

van Ingen, Louise, California (N) Western Europe; South Africa; topicals; literature;

British colonies; postal stationery.

Vignola, Frank J., California (N) Asia; postal history; topicals; postal stationery.

Vogel, Hal, New Jersey (N) U.S.; Ryukyus; postal history; polar; topicals; aerophilately; literature.

Walker, W. Danforth, Maryland (N) Great Britain and Commonwealth; postal history.

Walker, Patricia Stilwell, Maryland (N) Ireland; Great Britain; postal history; literature.

Walters, Patrick A., Michigan (N) U.S.; British Commonwealth; Germany; Canada; Japan; China; aerophilately; postal history; revenues.

Warm-Griffiths, Lynne S., California (N) U.S.; Vatican; Spain; Great Britain.

Warren, Alan, Pennsylvania (N) Scandinavia; FDCs; Tibet; literature.

Washburne, Stephen S., Philadelphia (N) Portugal and colonies; postal history; Brazil; Railway Post Offices.

Welky, Robert L., Florida (N) Straits Settlements; Federated Malay States; Zemstvos; Russian local issues.

Wenz, Charles E., Arizona (N) U.S.; U.N.; Germany; Europe; postal history.

Willard, John H., Colorado (N) British Empire; Western postal history; Switzerland.

Willing, J. Richard S., California (N) Germany; German States; Heligoland; Central Europe.

Winick, Lester E., Illinois (I) literature; thematic; astrophilately; aerophilately.

Wishnietsky, Benjamin, Florida (N) U.S. and possessions; Confederates; Greece; France; postal history.

Zankel, Nathan, New Jersey (N) U.S.; Israel; Palestine and related.

Zeigler, Robert G., Indiana (N) Switzerland; U.S.; Western Europe; airmails; Great Britain and colonies; censorship; war covers.

Zielinski, Nancy B., Georgia (I) U.S. postal history; youth exhibits; literature; topicals/thematics.

Judging Seminar

The APS supports a traveling team of accredited judges to conduct judging seminars upon request of organizing committees of stamp exhibitions throughout the United States.

The judging seminars explain exhibition award levels, the difference between class shows vs. open shows, fundamental guides for exhibiting and basic qualities judges look for in an award-winning exhibit.

The chairman of the Judges Accreditation Committee will consider all requests to determine whether conducting a particular seminar is within the scope of the planning society.

Accredited judges qualified to conduct seminars who reside closest to the exhibition will be used as team members.

Interested exhibition organizing committees should direct requests to the chairman of the Judges Accreditation Committee, Box 1449, Spring, Texas 77383.

Estate Advisory Service

When the executive director is advised of an APS member's death, he will notify the family or the personal representative of the deceased member that the society is prepared to aid in the disposal of the deceased member's philatelic estate.

Upon the request of the heirs or personal representative of the deceased member, the society will suggest APS volunteer estate advisers to evaluate the philatelic estate and offer some alternatives for its disposal.

These volunteers may be dealers or collectors only, and they have promised to abide by ethical standards in offering their services.

No charge is made for this service. An evaluation is usually sufficient for estate purposes, but it is recommended that a lawyer be consulted for confirmation.

It should not be expected that the adviser will render service requiring lengthy travel or excessive time in the evaluation of the holdings or assistance to the estate without compensation. Financial arrangements should be determined before service is rendered.

It should be pointed out that there is a difference between an evaluation and an appraisal of philatelic holdings.

Members will provide evaluations at no charge. The evaluation usually consists of a perusal of the holdings with an estimate of value based on the evaluator's knowledge of the material and the current market.

On the other hand, an appraisal consists of a detailed analysis of the value of each item and entails considerable study and time. Certain qualifications must be met for an appraiser to be considered qualified by various official agencies, such as the Internal Revenue Service.

Not all APS estate advisers are qualified appraisers, and those who are should not be expected to provide this service without reasonable compensation agreed upon in advance.

Assistance to heirs of deceased members through the Estate Advisory Service is extended for a period of one year or until the estate is officially settled if earlier than one year.

This service does not extend to any non-APS member once the legal ownership of the deceased member's collection has been transferred.

All correspondence about the Estate Advisory Service may be addressed to APS headquarters.

Self-adhesive stamp album identification labels (two-tone blue, 2- by 4-inches) for APS members who may wish their heirs to utilize the Estate Advisory Service may be obtained without charge upon request to the APS Executive Director, Box 8000, State College, Pa. 16803.

A stamped-addressed envelope must be furnished — first-class postage for 1 ounce affixed for requests of one to 15 labels; first-class postage for 2 ounces for 16 to the maximum of 30 labels.

APS Expertizing Service

The American Philatelic Expertizing Service is operated in conjunction with the American Stamp Dealers' Association. More than 200 philatelic experts serve on this committee. Items for examination must be submitted on special expertizing service forms. Expertizing forms and answers to questions concerning the operation of this service may be obtained from the APS National Headquarters, Box 8000, State College, Pa. 16803.

Rules and Requirements

1. Each stamp or cover submitted for examination must be mounted or affixed to a separate form and addressed directly to the American Philatelic Expertizing Service. A coil pair, block or multiple stamps on a cover or piece shall be considered a single item. Sets of stamps will be accepted, but each stamp must be individually mounted on a separate form. Any number of forms may be included in a single package or envelope.

2. Each item must be the bona fide property of the individual submitting it for examination. The owner may assign an identification number to each item submitted.

3. The fee for a certificate of opinion, in accordance with the following schedule, must accompany each item submitted (current Scott catalog value, APS/ASDA members, non-members): $100 or less, $8, $12; $101 to $200, $10, $15; $201 to $500, $13, $20; $501 to $1,000 and all unpriced items, $15, $23; $1,001 to $1,700, $17, $25; $1,701 and over, 1 percent, 1 1/2 percent.

If it is the opinion of the committee that an item in the $1,701 and over range was misidentified when submitted, the fee will be adjusted and a refund for the difference, less expertizing and insurance expense, will be made. However, the refund will not be less than the appropriate percentage of the actual catalog value of the item or a minimum of $17 ($25 for non-members).

The fee for an uncataloged item will be the same as for an unpriced item. Stamps will not be accepted. Foreign checks, including Canadian, will not be accepted unless drawn upon a U.S. bank and payable in U.S. dollars at par.

4. One stamped, addressed No. 10 (large 9 1/2-inch) envelope must accompany each item submitted plus one small stamped, addressed envelope for each item or group of items submitted at one time. The small envelope will be used to acknowledge receipt by returning Owner's Receipt of Expertizing Service form after a number has been assigned to each item. The second envelope (No. 10) will be used to return the item submitted with the report of the opinion rendered. Unless necessary, do not use an oversized envelope as they are easily folded and frequently damage the enclosure.

No insurance against loss in the mails will be provided by the American Philatelic Expertizing Service.

5. The American Philatelic Expertizing Service reserves the right at all times to decline to examine or give an opinion on any item. Single coil stamps will not be accepted for authentication.

Imperforate varieties of stamps regularly issued perforated will not be accepted for authentication except as a joined pair or larger piece. Requests for the plate position of a stamp or overprint will not be accepted. Stamps without gum and used varieties must be thoroughly cleaned of all hinges.

6. Requests for the market or net value of an item will not be accepted, nor will an opinion as to the mint, never-hinged condition be given.

7. The decisions rendered by the American Philatelic Expertizing Service are not guarantees and are only opinions. No refunds unless no opinion is given. A minimum $4 administrative fee will be deducted from refund if item is returned without an opinion following examination.

8. Since the meanings of the terms superb, very fine, etc., are debatable, no opinion as to general condition will be given. Defects and alterations not readily apparent will be noted.

9. All reasonable care will be taken of items submitted for examination, but all items are accepted with full understanding on the part of the owner that neither the APS, the ASDA, nor members of their expertizing committees are liable for any loss or damage resulting from any cause whatsoever except for gross negligence.

Since the American Philatelic Expertizing Service is unable to obtain insurance coverage of any kind, an owner desiring coverage must carry his own insurance.

10. The APS and ASDA reserve the right to make such changes without notice to the rules and requirements as they deem necessary, but such changes will be announced as soon as possible.

11. The request for an examination constitutes an acceptance by the owner of all rules and requirements of the American Philatelic Expertizing Service.

12. No item will be accepted if the owner insists upon a deadline date for its return. Average turn-around time is 45-60 days; however, owners should allow at least 90 days before expecting a certificate.

Since items are submitted to expert committee members for their opinions by mail, unavoidable delays are often experienced.

13. Certificates remain the property of the American Philatelic Expertizing Service.

APS Insurance

Designed, administered and operated by experienced collectors, the APS Stamp Collector Insurance Plan now covers more than 12,000 APS members. Tailored to the needs of an active stamp collector, this specialized insurance coverage is available to APS members and applicants residing in the United States and Canada. (Dealer-members in the United States and Canada can be covered by a separate dealer plan available to them. Write directly to the APS Insurance Plan manager, Dan Walker, Box 157, Stevenson, Md. 21153, or call (301) 486-5500 for details.)

The APS Stamp Collector Insurance Plan charges substantially less than most other insurance companies, and in most cases the savings is more than 40 percent. More important than the savings are the other exclusive features found only in the APS-sponsored policy:

1. There is no loss-sharing (co-insurance or average) clause in the APS-sponsored policy;

2. An automatic 1 1/4 percent per month increase in the amount of insurance provides coverage for the average collector's new acquisitions and/or increases in values;

3. Newly acquired high-valued items are automatically covered up to 35 percent of the total amount of insurance or $20,000, whichever is less;

4. Individual items need not be listed unless their value exceeds $5,000 rather than the $250 (or less) required in other policies;

5. Exhibition insurance coverage is provided to participants up to $60,000 automatically at U.S. and Canadian shows

without extra charge; and

6. Shipments by a courier service, such as Federal Express or Purolator, by air express, and by registered or express mail are covered up to $60,000.

Claims paid since the plan was started in April 1966 exceed $5 million. No payment is made for a claim of less than $50, but payment is made in full for claims that exceed $50.

A detailed inventory of your stamps is not required. List your major areas of collecting interest and keep this listing to a maximum of five or six areas by logically combining similar collecting interests. For each of these listed areas all that is required is a description of the geographical area or subject; approximate period covered, such as a year range or a range of catalog numbers; the type of material such as mint, plate blocks, FDC, postal history, specialized collection, etc.; and your best estimate of replacement value.

A professional appraisal is not required. A valuation based on the average percentage of catalog value you are currently paying for stamps, or your personal estimate of the retail price of similar material to what is in your collections, is an acceptable method of estimating the replacement value of your collection.

The APS Insurance Plan manager does not want you to send him a detailed inventory, if you have one, because he does not have sufficient file space. You should keep a detailed inventory in a safe place where it will not be lost with the collection in the event of a fire, burglary, tornado, etc.

Full coverage is provided up to $50,000, even if your stamps are not protected by an approved safe or central station alarm. Coverage up to $1 million is available for all hazards not specifically excluded by the policy except for burglary and theft. With an approved safe or alarm, you can also increase your coverage for burglary and theft above $50,000.

Coverage under the APS Insurance Plan policy provides insurance against all risks of loss or damage to philatelic property, with certain named exceptions. Briefly, the types of losses that are not covered are those caused by: a) careless handling, including damage by insects, vermin, fading, etc.; b) mysterious disappearance of individual stamps unless specifically scheduled in the policy at values greater than $5,000; c) checked baggage and while in the custody of a transportation company, unless it meets one of the specifics listed in No. 6; d) theft from an unattended automobile; e) conversion and infidelity; and f) war and nuclear losses.

Coverage is written for a one-year term. About a month before the policy's expiration, you will receive a renewal premium notice continuing the coverage in force for an additional year, provided you pay the premium within the specified time.

About every four years, a revised renewal application is required. The value of all philatelic property must be disclosed on the application, including that kept in bank storage.

If you wish, you can insure for less than the full replacement value. However, experience indicates that most collectors who have suffered losses did not have sufficient insurance at the time of the loss. The value of philatelic property acquired over the years builds up much more rapidly than most collectors realize.

Loss Notice Procedure

Most claims are called into the APS Stamp Collector Insurance Plan office at the phone number listed at the beginning of this section. Losses can also be filed with Leizure Associates Inc., 508 St. Paul Place, Baltimore, Md. 21202.

Claims are handled by a claims representative who is a fellow APS member and a knowledgeable stamp collector. This claims representative will assist you in filing your claim and proof of loss.

APS Stamp Theft Committee

The services of the APS Stamp Theft Committee are not limited to APS members, but are available to all victims of stamp theft.

Members should advise victims of stamp theft in their areas to contact the APS Stamp Theft Committee and to do so promptly.

Information concerning stamp theft preventive measures may be obtained by writing the chairman of the committee and enclosing a stamped, addressed envelope.

Clippings from local newspapers concerning stamp thefts and stamp thieves are urgently solicited from all parts of the country and should be mailed to the committee. Collectors should be sure that the name of the newspaper and the date the article appeared are indicated.

All stamp collections are subject to theft. Large and valuable ones attract professional thieves. None is too small to be taken by thieves in search of money or items that can be converted into money.

Therefore, it behooves the collector to give thought to the matter and provide appropriate protection for philatelic holdings, large or small.

If your stamps should be stolen, you are advised to proceed as follows:

1. Touch nothing.

2. Call the police. Not all police officers are familiar with the hobby of stamp collecting and at the outset may not realize the significance of a stamp theft, especially if it is a large one. It may be helpful to mention to the investigating officers that major stamp thefts have been occurring all across the country, and that professional thieves are known to be engaged in stealing stamps just as they steal coins, jewelry, furs, objects of art, etc. Experience has shown that such stamp thefts are well-planned and expertly executed.

3. Notify the chairman of the APS Stamp Theft Committee, preferably by telephone. The chairman, Earl Sumner, may be reached by telephone day or night (216) 923-6811. The address of the committee is Box 293, Cuyahoga Falls, Ohio 44222.

Translation Service

The APS offers members a translation service in practically all major languages. Almost anything philatelic can be translated — letters, cancellations, inscriptions on stamps, FDC cachets, etc. Translations of one page or less are provided at no charge.

All requests for translations should be sent directly to the chairman of the APS Translation Committee, Dmytro Bykovetz Jr., 902 Stratford Ave., Melrose Park, Philadelphia, Pa. 19126.

More than one, but not more than five pages, will be translated for a charge of $1 per page after the first page. Requests for translation of more than five pages will be negotiated by the chairman with the translation committee members. The requesting member will be advised of the price before the translation is undertaken.

Postage charges on all translations must be paid by the requesting member. As a general rule, three times the postage necessary to send the translation should be enclosed to cover all forwarding and return postage requirements.

Any APS member able to translate from or to a foreign language, who is willing to serve as a member of the Translation Committee, is urged to offer his services to the committee chairman.

The translation service has proved to be reliable, and has established and cemented friendships between APS members and citizens of countries throughout the world.

APS Speakers Bureau

This list is arranged geographically, as most groups will be interested in obtaining a speaker in their own general vicinity. Addresses for the speakers listed may be found in the current membership listing. Telephone numbers may be obtained from the normal telephone company directory assistance or by inquiry to the speakers bureau chairman. The three entries under the "Requirements" heading are:

First column: One-way distance in miles beyond which the speaker expects to be reimbursed for travel expenses. Letter "A" indicates the speaker desires reimbursement for all travel expenses.

Second column: Whether speaker is willing to stay overnight if distance or meeting time requires. Letter "Y" indicates yes; "N" no.

Third column: Amount of honorarium in U.S. dollars expected by the speaker.

Many of the speakers have subjects in addition to those listed and will speak at banquets or act as masters of ceremony, as well as address stamp clubs. Although many will make shorter trips at their own expense, common courtesy indicates that they be luncheon or dinner guests when this is timely. Most speakers who have indicated a willingness to stay overnight will accept accommodations in a private home as well as in a motel or hotel.

In arranging for speakers, please observe the following:

1) All arrangements should be made directly with the speaker by the host group, not through the speakers bureau.

2) Be certain that all arrangements with respect to accommodations, expenses and honorarium are clearly understood by both parties.

3) Give speakers plenty of notice in extending speaking invitations.

4) Advise the speakers bureau of any problems that arise or suggestions for improving the listing.

All members of the American Philatelic Society willing to speak on philatelic subjects to APS chapters or other groups should request an application form from the chairman, APS Speakers Bureau, or from the APS Executive Director, Box 8000, State College, Pa. 16803.

APS Speakers Bureau

Location	Name	Requirements	Subjects
ALABAMA			
Dothan	Cohn, Ernst M.	200 Y 0	Postal History-Franco/German War 1870-71-Seminar on Philatelic Literature
ARIZONA			
Phoenix	Corless, Robert D.	200 Y 0	Australia-Canada-Ireland Postal Stationery
Sun City West	Sellers, F. Burton	100 Y 0	Haiti-APS-General
Tucson	Birkinbine II, John	100 Y 0	Confederate States-Exhibiting Methods-Arizona Territory Postal History-Buying and Selling at Auction
ARKANSAS			
Bentonville	Barasch, Alan R.	50 Y 0	Falkland Island and Dependencies-Israel-Nova Scotia
CALIFORNIA			
Campbell	Gary, Douglas L.	25 Y 0	To be arranged with program chairman
Del Mar	Hess, Winand	100 Y 0	Finland Pre-stamp Mail-Topical/Thematic Collecting and Exhibiting-German Revenues-German/German States Postal History
Los Angeles	Tobias, A.L.	200 Y 0	Petersburg, Va. CSA-U.S. Navy Transoceanic Flight Covers 1919-20
Oxnard	Evans-de Violini, Lois	50 Y 0	Japan Errors and Varieties-APS-Use of Philatelic Library for Research and Study
Salinas	Eidson, Earl L.	50 Y 0	Americana-Designer Errors
San Clemente	Hyzen, Leon	200 Y 0	24¢ 1861 Stamps and Covers
San Diego	Frank, Samuel B.	A Y 50	Embossed Revenue Stamps of Great Britain-British Stamp Act 1765-66
San Jose	Leven, Stuart H.,	100 Y 0	Sarawak Mail Routes-New Guinea-German New Guinea-N.W. Pacific Islands
	Stieber, Conrad H.	25 Y 0	Booklets of Germany-Posted 1840-1940-Mounting Stamps-Booklet Collecting
San Mateo	Adler, Sig	50 N 0	Classic Europe-German States-Italian States-First Issues of World to 1875
Sunnyvale	Burma, Benjamin H.	25 Y 0	Philatelic Nudes
West Sacramento	Oliver, William J.	100 Y 0	Philippine Airmail-Philippine/Japan Occupation-California Fishing License Stamp-Exhibiting
CONNECTICUT			
Waterbury	Rusgaitis, Victor P.	200 Y 0	Stamp Auctions-Preparing Stamps for Sale-Appraisals of Collectibles-Coins and Baseball Cards

Location	Name	Requirements	Subjects
DELAWARE			
Hockessin	Dickson, Frederick S.	50 Y 0	Cover Collecting and the Fun Beyond-Wreck of the Old 97-Exhibiting Adds Fun to Collecting-Italy Under Napoleon
DISTRICT OF COLUMBIA			
Washington	Kaufmann, Patricia	100 Y 0	Confederate Postal History-19th-Century Valentines-Bidding in Public Auctions
FLORIDA			
Atlantis	Cody, H. Graley	200 Y 0	U.S. Airmail-U.S. Philippines 1898-1946-U.S. Flags-U.S. Cancellations-Classic Precancels
Boca Raton	Herst, Herman, Jr.	50 N 0	Great Finds-Great Britain Postal History-French Balloon Post 1870-71
Coconut Creek	Shay, Arnold L.	25 Y 0	Concentration Camp Mail-Ghetto Mail-WWII Philately and Syngraphic History
Fort Lauderdale	Welky, Robert L.	50 Y 0	Worldwide Revenues-Russian Rural Posts (Zemstvos)-Straits Settlements and Malay States-Liberia
Jacksonville	Jennings, Clyde, Jr.	50 Y 0	U.S. Freaks and Oddities-Plate Number Story-U.S. Fakes and Forgeries-5¢ Blue Taylor-19th-Century U.S. Cancels/Markings-U.S. Rarities
Longwood	Bohne, Werner M.	50 Y 0	Expertizing-How to Avoid Purchasing Forgeries
New Port Richey	Garabrant, Melvin	50 Y 0	Modern France-Thematic/Topical Collecting and Exhibiting
GEORGIA			
Atlanta	Cole, Clifford C., Jr.	25 N 0	China-Japan-Macau
ILLINOIS			
Chicago	Blau, Fred F.	200 N 0	Palestine/Israel Airmails-Graf Zepp over Palestine-Polish Army in Palestine WWII-Crash Mail-Holy Land
	Gobby, Thomas J.	50 Y 0	Poznan/Posen Postal District WWII-Polish Soviet War (1919-20)-Military and Censored Mail-Polish Postal Rates/Hyperinflation
	Hennig, Bernard A.	200 Y 0	Danzig-Germany-German East Africa-Airmails-Inflation-Guatemala-Submarine WWI
Glenview	Bachenheimer, Frank	25 Y 0	Saar Postal History-Saar 1920-23-Commercial and Machine Cancels Saar 1923-35-Sears Roebuck and Mails 1896-1930
Morton Grove	Drews, Richard E.	100 Y 0	U.S. 1861-67 Issues-Please Bear With Me (Bear Thematic)-1938 Prexies and Modern Postal History

Location	Name	Requirements	Subjects
IOWA			
Rockford	Trettin, Kenneth H.	200 Y 0	Philatelic Journalism-Computers and Philately-Revenue Stamp Collecting
MARYLAND			
Bethesda	Torrey, Gordon H.	100 Y 0	Turkey Ottoman Period-Turkish Locals-Russian Offices Abroad-Iran to 1925-Allied Role in Russian Civil War 1918-21
Pikesville	Illyefalvi, Kalman V.	50 Y 0	Hungary-Union of South Africa-Postal Stationery of Union of South Africa-Exhibiting and Judging
Ruxton	Harrison, Horace W.	A Y 0	Canada Registry-Pacific Railway View Cards-Canada Postal Stationery-Canada Registered Letter Stamps-New Zealand Stamp Ads
Stevenson	Walker, W. Danforth	200 Y 0	Insurance and Security for Your Stamps-Grenada Postal History-Indian State of Barawani
MASSACHUSETTS			
Oxford	Pierce, Peter V.	50 Y 0	Revenues (Federal and State Hunting)
Weston	Dillaway, Guy R.	25 Y 25	Great Britain-Cape of Good Hope Postal History-Philatelic Exhibiting and Judging
MICHIGAN			
West Bloomfield	Foxworth, John, Jr.	200 Y 0	Topical Collecting-Citizens' Stamp Advisory Committee-APS Story-Autos and Trucks on Stamps
MISSISSIPPI			
Greenville	Goldstein, Nathan, II	50 Y 0	Printing U.S. Stamps-Electric Eye Perforating-Collecting Stamps
MISSOURI			
Webster Groves	Pope, Elizabeth	50 Y 0	Valentines-Spain-Buying and Selling at Auctions
NEBRASKA			
Crete	Rapp, William F., Jr.	200 Y 0	Hand Cancels-Nebraska Postal History-Bulgaria
NEW HAMPSHIRE			
Conway	Andrews, James C.	50 Y 0	Guatemala
NEW JERSEY			
Ridgefield Park	Schiff, Jacques, Jr.	50 Y 0	Doctored Stamps and Covers-U.S. EFOs-How to Participate in Stamp Auctions
Short Hills	Foley, Joseph E.	100 Y 0	Ireland-Cinderella Philately-APS Judging Seminar-Soldiers Story (Correspondence of Three Civil War Ohio Volunteers)
Summit	Stone, Harlan F.	50 N 0	Switzerland-Postal History Exhibiting
Westfield	Grabowski, Edward	25 Y 0	French Colonial Group Type-France: The Second Empire
NEW YORK			
Ballston Spa	Lange, John A., Jr.	50 Y 0	U.S. 3¢ 1851-57-Imperf 3¢ U.S.

Location	Name	Requirements	Subjects
			1851-57 Comparative Study by Year-U.S. 19th-Century Used-Saratoga Co. N.Y. Covers
Brooklyn	Owens, Mary Ann	25 Y 0	Thematics-Exhibiting-Judging
East Northport	Spear, Arthur H.	50 Y 0	Jamaica Stamps and Varieties-History of Messages Before 1840-Jamaica Postal History
Long Beach	Zollman, Joseph	50 Y 20	Spotlight on Judaica-Belgium on Stamps-Columnist's View of Hobby-People Places and Events on Stamps
New York	Jarrett, David L.	25 Y 0	U.S. Stampless Fancy Townmarks-U.S. Territorial Covers-Colorado Territorials
	Stollnitz, Henry S.	50 Y 0	U.S. Used Abroad-U.S. 1847 Issue-USPO Shanghai China-New York Supplementary Mail
	Weiss, Larry S.	25 Y 0	U.S. Washington-Franklin Heads-5¢ Red Errors-Unusual Washington and Franklin Heads-Identifying Washington and Franklin Heads
Staten Island	Kocheisen, Joseph	25 Y 0	Zeppelin Post-Schleswig-Holstein
Wyantskill	Harris, Robert Dalton	25 Y 0	Vienna Pneumatic Post-General Postal History of the Telegraph-Airmail Stamp Design
NORTH CAROLINA			
Kernersville	Green, Brian M.	50 Y 0	Confederate Postal History
OHIO			
Akron	Koller, Ken M.	200 Y 0	U.S. Overprints-U.S. Possessions-U.S. Specimen Stamps-U.S. Offices in China
Sidney	Sine, Richard L.	200 Y 0	Journalism-Scott Catalog
OKLAHOMA			
Tulsa	Crosby, Joe H.	200 Y 0	Importance of Philatelic Literature-Civil War Prisoners Correspondence
PENNSYLVANIA			
Boalsburg	Sente Frank L.	100 Y 0	APS Operations-Wonderful World of Revenues
	Sente, Marjory J.	200 Y 0	AFDCS Archives/Literature -Writing for the Philatelic Press
Bryn Mawr	Keally, James M., Jr.	50 Y 10	U.S. Banknote Issues-Fancy Cancels-Hawaii EFOs
Havertown	Siegel, Daniel J.	50 Y 0	Junior Philately-Estate Planning and the Collector-Fun and Philately-Exhibiting-Basic Philately-Inexpensive Philately
Johnstown	Smith, Donald W.	200 Y 0	Topical Exhibiting-ATA-Collecting Napoleon
Knoxville	Edgcomb, Cheryl B.	50 Y 0	Topical Collecting-Youth Exhibiting-Stamp Promotion-Working With Youth
Meadville	Friedberg, Richard	100 Y 0	U.S. Revenues and Classics-Auctions-Doctored Stamps

Location	Name	Requirements	Subjects
State College	DeVoss, James T.	A Y 0	APS Operations-Canal Zone-Via Panama-de Thuin Affair-Philatelic Photography
Warminster	Eggen, Dale R.	100 Y 0	Switzerland-Philatelic Literature (Country Specialized)
RHODE ISLAND			
Rumford	Gaillaguet, Raymond	100 Y 0	Bordeaux Issue of France-Franco Prussian War of 1870-Sower Issue of France-How to Mount a Collection
TENNESSEE			
Memphis	Frye, Joe F.	150 Y 0	Scandinavia-Stamp Shows-Auctions-Scandinavian Philately-Fakes and Forgeries
TEXAS			
Austin	Kerr, Allen D.	200 Y 0	Laos-British Antarctic-Cacti on Stamps-Chinese Bilingual Cancels-Tristan da Cunha
El Paso	Balough, Joseph J.	100 Y 0	Perfins-How to Put on a Show-How to Exhibit
Gainesville	Poore, Elwood	50 Y 0	Canada-U.S. Postal History-Deltiology-Philatelic Literature
San Antonio	Lande, Lester M.	25 Y 0	Preparing Albums-Exhibiting-Forgeries-Philately in Business
Spring	Bauer, William H.	100 Y 0	Colorado Postal History-Falkland Islands-Lebanon-Exhibit Preparation-Judging
VIRGINIA			
Alexandria	Scheer, Frank R.	25 Y 0	Manufacturing and Use of Steel Postmarkers-Night Mail/England's Traveling Post Office-Men/Mail in Transit-Obsolete Postal Artifacts
Falls Church	Olcheski, William J.	25 Y Neg	Putting Life in Your Stamp Club-Stamp Collecting as a Family Hobby-Stamp Writing for Fun and Money
Gloucester	Warren, Daniel	50 Y 0	Most Aspects of Great Britain Stamps and Postal History-Care and Feeding of Stamp Dealers-Collecting Latin America
Palmyra	Meier, Harry C.	100 Y 0	Germany-Exhibiting and Judging
WASHINGTON			
Yakima	Martin,George M.	50 Y 0	Postal History-U.S. Postal Cards-70 Years of Collecting-Tribulations and Joys of Collecting
WEST VIRGINIA			
Morgantown	Singer, Armand E.	25 — Neg	Nepal-Tibet-Collecting Stamps as an Investment-Himalayan Mountaineering Covers
South Charleston	MacPeek, Donald L.	200 Y 0	Venezuela Classic Stamps-Swiss WWII Military Stamps-Venezuela Escuelos Issues 1871-76-Costa Rica-Latin America EFOs and Rarities
WISCONSIN			
Green Bay	Robinson, William B.	25 N 0	Wisconsin Postal History-Philately from a Dealer's Point of View

Location	Name	Requirements	Subjects
CANADA			
Burlington, Ont.	Rowe, Kenneth	50 Y 0	Canadian Telegraphs-Forwarding Agents-Knowledge for Postal Historians
MEXICO			
Oaxaca	Freer, Phillips B.	50 Y 0	Mexico-The State of Oaxaca, Mexico-El Salvador

APS Chapters

Alabama

Birmingham Philatelic Society
Eastern Shore Stamp Collectors
Gadsden Stamp Club
Huntsville Philatelic Club
Calhoun County Stamp Club
Mobile Philatelic Society
Montgomery Area Stamp Club

Alaska

Anchorage Philatelic Society
Gastineau Philatelic Society
Northern Lights Stamp Club
Ptarmigan Stamp and Coin Society

Arizona

Flagstaff Stamp Club
Mesa Stamp Club
Arizona Society of Topical Philatelists
Kachina Chapter 25, Germany Philatelic Society
Phoenix Philatelic Association
Prescott Stamp Club
Sun City Stamp Club
Sun City West Coin and Stamp Club
Arizona Federation of Stamp Clubs
Arizona Philatelic Rangers
Tucson Stamp Club

Arkansas

Fayetteville Stamp Club
Westark Stamp Club
Mountain Home Area Stamp Club
Pinnacle Stamp Club of Arkansas
Razorback Stamp Club

California

Council of Northern California Philatelic Societies
Federated Philatelic Clubs of Southern California
Society of Southern California Philatelists
Orange County Philatelic Society
Arcadia Stamp Club
Bakersfield Stamp Club
Centennial Stamp Club
LERC Stamp Club
Peninsula Stamp Club
Monterey Peninsula Stamp Club
Diablo Valley Stamp Club
East County Stamp Club
San Pablo Pines Stamp Club
Germany Philatelic Society, Golden Gate Chapter 24
Gold Country Stamp Club
Golden Gate Stamp Club
Hi-Desert Stamp Club
Hughes El Segundo Employees Association Stamp Club
Humboldt Collectors Club
Aeronutronic Stamp Club
Fremont Stamp Club
Fresno Philatelic Society
Beckman Philatelic Society
Hemet Stamp Club
Collectors Club of Hollywood
Leisure Village Stamp and Coin Club
McDonnell Douglas Philatelic Club
Laguna Beach Stamp Club
Long Beach Stamp Club
Philatelic Society of Los Angeles
Valley Stamp Club
Saddleback Stamp Club
Scandinavia Philatelic Library of Southern California
Simi Valley Stamp Club
Solano Stamp Club
Stanislaus Stamp Club
Tamalpais Stamp Club
East Bay Collectors Club
Tri City Stamp Club
Pacific Palisades Stamp Club
Palmdale Stamp Club
Palm Springs Philatelic Society
JPL Stamp Club
Pasadena Stamp Clubs
Petaluma Philatelic Society
Poway Stamp Club
Redlands Stamp Club
TRW Stamp Club
Sequoia Stamp Club
Riverside Stamp and Coin Club
Sacramento Philatelic Society
Monterey County Stamp Club
Arrowhead Stamp Club
Philatelic "25"
San Diego County Philatelic Council
San Diego Stamp Club
BankAmerica Philatelic Society
California Collectors Club
Collectors Club of San Francisco
San Francisco Pacific Philatelic Society
San Jose Stamp Club

Philatelic Society of San Leandro
Santa Barbara Stamp Club
Santa Cruz County Stamp Club
Central Coast Stamp Club
Oakmont Philatelic Society
Sonoma County Philatelic Society
Leisure World Stamp Club
Tuolumne County Stamp Club
Stockton Stamp Club
Sun City Stamp Club
Friends of the Western Philatelic Library
LERA Stamp Club
Sunnyvale Stamp Club
Conejo Valley Philatelic Society
Torrance Stamp Club
Redwood Empire Stamp Society
Greater Valley Philatelic Society
Vallejo Stamp Club
Ventura County Philatelic Society
Glendale Stamp Club
Visalia Philatelic Society
Yuba-Sutter Philatelic Society

Colorado

Aurora Stamp Club
Boulder Stamp Club
Colorado Springs Stamp Club
Collectors' Club of Denver
Denver Germany Stamp Club
Denver Masonic Stamp Club
Denver Stamp Club
Four Corners Stamp Club
Heather Gardens Stamp Club
Northern Colorado Philatelic Society
Platte Valley Stamp Club
Rocky Mountain Philatelic Exhibitions
Rocky Mountain Stamp Club
Cherrelyn Stamp Club
Stamp Club Grand Junction
West Side Stamp Club
Arapahoe Stamp Club
Pueblo Stamp Club

Connecticut

Branford Philatelic Society
Bridgeport Philatelic Club
Brookfield Philatelic Society
Connecticut Philatelic Society
Cheshire Philatelic Society
Clinton Stamp Club
Ye Old King's Highway Stamp Club
Fairfield Philatelic Society
Manchester Philatelic Society
Meriden Stamp Club
Middletown-Portland Stamp Club
Hardware City Stamp Club
New Haven Philatelic Society
Thames Stamp Club
Norwalk Stamp Club
Farmington Valley Stamp Club
Heritage Village Stamp Club
Nutmeg Stamp Club
Waterbury Stamp Club

Delaware

Dover Stamp Club
Du Pont Stamp Club
Scandinavian Collectors Club, Chapter 13
Wilmington Stamp Club

District of Columbia

Collectors Club of Washington
Library of Congress Philatelic Club
Palisades Stamp Club
Washington Philatelic Society

Florida

Florida Federation of Stamp Clubs
Cape Coral Stamp Club
Century Stamp Club of West Palm Beach
Clearwater Stamp Club
Halifax Area Philatelic Society
Century Village East Stamp and Coin Club
Cuban Philatelic Society of America
Delray Beach Stamp Club
Florida First Coast Stamp Club
Germany Philatelic Society Chapter 23
Germany Philatelic Society Chapter 7
University City Stamp Club
Hialeah Stamp and Coin Club
Hollywood Stamp Club
Jacksonville Stamp Collectors Club
Gold Coast Stamp Club
Club Cubano Da Coleccionistas
Collier County Stamp Club
Missile Stamp Club
New Port Richey Stamp Club
Oakland Park Stamp Club
Central Florida Stamp Club
Bay County Stamp Club
Pensacola Philatelic Society
Port Charlotte Stamp Club
Port St. Lucie Stamp Club
Ridge Stamp Club
Suncoast Philatelic Society
St. Augustine YMCA Stamp Club
St. Petersburg Stamp Club
Sarasota Philatelic Club
South Miami Stamp Club

Sunrise Stamp Club
Tampa Collectors Club
Titusville-Moonport Stamp Club
Venice Stamp Club
West Florida Stamp Club
West Volusia Stamp Club
Winter Haven Stamp Club
Cresthaven Stamp and Coin Club

Georgia

Athens Philatelic Society
Atlanta Stamp Collectors Club
Greater Augusta Stamp Club
DeKalb Stamp Club
Macon Philatelic Society
Cobb County Stamp Club
Savannah Stamp Club
Stone Mountain Philatelic Society
Valdosta Stamp Club

Hawaii

Hawaiian Philatelic Society

Idaho

Boise Stamp Club
Snake River Stamp Club
Pocatello Stamp Club

Illinois

Northwest Stamp Club
Belleville-Scott AFB Stamp Club
Corn Belt Philatelic Society
Suburban Collectors' Club
Champaign-Urbana Stamp Club
Austin Philatelic Society
Beverly Hills Philatelic Society
Chicago Philatelic Society
Chicago Air Mail Society
Chicagoland Chapter, American Topical Association
Chicagoland Czechoslovak Philatelic Society
Germany Philatelic Society Chapter 5
Kankakee Valley Coin and Stamp Club
North Shore Senior Center Stamp Club
North Shore Philatelic Society
The Philaterians
Polonus Philatelic Society
Roosevelt Philatelic Society
Scandinavian Collectors Club Chapter 4
Southern Illinois Stamp Club
Spring Hill Stamp Club
Tower Stamp Club
Decatur Stamp Club
Evanston-New Trier Philatelic Society
Glen Ellyn Philatelic Club
Quad City Stamp Club
LaSalle County Stamp Club
Park Forest Stamp Club
Caterpillar Stamp Club
Peoria Philatelic Society
Tri-County Stamp Club
Rockford Stamp Club
Springfield Philatelic Society
Lake County Philatelic Society

Indiana

Madison County Bicentennial Stamp Club
Evansville Stamp Club
Anthony Wayne Stamp Society
Calumet Stamp Club
Centerville Stamp Club
Indiana Stamp Club
Northeastern Indiana Stamp Club
Northern Indiana Stamp Club
Wabash Valley Stamp Club

Iowa

Allison Stamp Club
Hawkeye Stamp Club
Cedar Valley Stamp Club
Cedar Rapids Stamp Club
Mississippi Valley Stamp Club
Oneota Stamp Club
Des Moines Philatelic Society
Iowa Women's Philatelic Society

Kansas

Cessna Stamp Club
Lawrence Stamp Club
Lindsborg Stamp Club
Flint Hills Stamp Club
Stamp Club of Leavenworth
Topeka Stamp Club
Wichita Stamp Club

Kentucky

Pennyrile Philatelic Society
Henry Clay Philatelic Society
Louisville Stamp Society
Northern Kentucky Stamp Club
Philatelic Club of Louisville
Pleasure Ridge Park Philatelic Society

Louisiana

Baton Rouge Stamp Club
Acadiana Stamp Club
Twin City Stamp Club
Crescent City Stamp Club
Red River Stamp Society

Maine

Aroostook Stamp Club
Penobscot Valley Stamp Club
Portland Stamp Club
Waterville Stamp Club
York County Stamp Club

Maryland

Annapolis Stamp Club
Baltimore Philatelic Society

Beltway Stamp Club
Chesapeake Philatelic Society
Bowie Stamp Club
Germany Philatelic Society, Chapter 16
Howard County Stamp Club
Harford County Stamp Club
Rockville-Gaithersburg Stamp Club
Goddard Space Flight Center Stamp Club
Hagerstown Stamp Club
Potomac Philatelic Society
Silver Spring Philatelic Society
Silver Hill Lions Club

Massachusetts

Amherst Stamp Club
Boston Philatelic Society
Chelmsford Stamp Club
Fall River Philatelic Society
Franklin Stamp Club
Golden Bee Stamp Club
Wachusett Philatelic Society
Lincoln Stamp Club
Samuel Osgood Stamp Club
Lynn Philatelic Society
Malden Stamp Club
Mohawk Stamp Club
New England Scandinavian Collectors Club
Nippon Stamp Club of New England
Berkshire Museum Stamp Club
Whaling City Stamp Club
Pioneer Valley Stamp Club
Stoughton Stamp Club
United Stamp Societies
William C. Stone Chapter
Waltham Stamp Club
Webster Dudley Stamp Club
Westfield Stamp Club
Worcester County Philatelic Society
Northeastern Federation of Stamp Clubs

Michigan

Peninsular State Philatelic Society
Ann Arbor Stamp Club
Birmingham Stamp Club
Dearborn Stamp Club
Collectors Club of Michigan
Detroit Philatelic Society
Michigan Stamp Club
Motor City Stamp and Cover Club
Ferndale Stamp Club
Ford Stamp Club
Greater Flint Stamp Club
Kalamazoo Stamp Club
Kent Philatelic Society
Muskegon Stamp Club
Central Michigan Philatelic Society
Floral City Stamp Club
Oak Park Stamp Club of Michigan
West Suburban Stamp Club
Pontiac Stamp Club
Saginaw Valley Stamp Society
Sault Stamp Club
Southwestern Michigan Stamp Club
Grand Traverse Stamp Club
Wolverine Stamp Club

Minnesota

Arrowhead Stamp Club
Lake Minnetonka Stamp Club
Lyon County Philatelic Society
Maplewood Stamp Club
Minnehaha Stamp Club
Minnesota Israel Philatelic Society
Twin City Philatelic Society
Rochester Stamp Club
St. Cloud Area Stamp Club
Thief River Falls Stamp Club
West Central Minnesota Stamp Club
Wild River Stamp Club

Mississippi

Gulf Coast Stamp Club
Hattiesburg Stamp Club
Rotten Bayou Stamp Club

Missouri

Columbia Philatelic Society
Kingdom Philatelic Association
Collectors Club of Kansas City
Rolla Philatelic Society
St. Joseph Stamp Collectors Club
Gladstone Philatelic Club
Greater St. Louis Stamp Club
Mound City Stamp Club
Ozark Mountain Stamp Club
St. Louis Branch No. 4

Montana

Billings Stamp Club
Gallatin Stamp Club
Garden City Stamp Club
Glacier Stamp Club
Great Falls Stamp Club

Nebraska

Central Nebraska Stamp Club
Lincoln Stamp Club
Buffalo Bill Stamp Club
Omaha Philatelic Society
West Omaha Stamp Club

Nevada

Nevada Stamp Study Society
Southern Nevada Stamp Club

New Hampshire

Great Bay Stamp Club
Greater Derry Philatelic Society

White Mountain Stamp Club
Manchester Stamp Club
Nashua Philatelic Society
Profile Stamp Club
Purgatory Stamp Club

New Jersey

North Jersey Federated Stamp Clubs
Bi-State Stamp Club
American Helvetia Philatelic Society, New Jersey Chapter
Fair Lawn Stamp Club
Molly Pitcher Stamp Club
Hamilton Township Philatelic Society
Hazlet Stamp Club
North Jersey Stamp Club
Coryell's Ferry Stamp Club
Merchantville Stamp Club
West Essex Philatelic Society
Southern New Jersey Chapter
Jockey Hollow Stamp Club
Sussex County Stamp Club
Bergen County Stamp Club
Bloomfield Philatelic Society
Cape Stamp Club
Clearbrook Stamp Club
Clifton Stamp Society
Association of Bergen County Philatelists
Pascack Stamp Club
Ocean County Stamp Club
Trenton Philatelic Society
Cuban Philatelic Society of America, New Jersey Chapter
Queen City-Warren Stamp and Cover Club
Westfield Stamp Club

New Mexico

New Mexico Philatelic Association
Alamogordo Philatelic Society
Albuquerque Philatelic Society
Los Alamos Stamp Collectors Association
Mesilla Valley Stamp Club
New Mexico Philatelic Association
Palo Duro Philatelic Society
Santa Fe Stamp Club

New York

Adirondack Stamp Club
Chai Chapter, Society of Israel Philatelists
Cheektowaga Stamp and Coin Society
Fort Stanwix Stamp Club
Harrison Stamp and Coin Club
International Stamp Club
Leatherstocking Stamp Club
Lockport Coin and Stamp Club
Federation of Central New York Philatelic Societies
Fort Orange Stamp Club
Auburn Stamp Club
Batavia-Genesee County Coin and Stamp Club
Buffalo Stamp Club
Plattsburgh Stamp Club
Riverhead Stamp Club
Roosevelt Island Philatelic Society
Sperry Stamp Club
Stamptrotters Society of Kingston
Steuben Stamp Club
Plewacki Post Stamp Society
Corning Area Stamp Club
Dansville Area Coin and Stamp Club
East Aurora Philatelic Society
Elmira Stamp Club
Northern Chautauqua Philatelic Society
Fulton Stamp Club
Finger Lakes Stamp Club
North Shore Philatelic Society
Chenango Valley Stamp Club
Allegheny Stamp Club
Ithaca Philatelic Society
Reuben E. Fenton Philatelic Society
Johnson City Stamp Club
Nassau Council Stamp Club
St. Lawrence International Stamp Club
Sullivan County Philatelic Society
Newburgh Stamp Club
Atoz Stamp Club
Niagara Frontier Stamp Club
Community Stamp Club
Oswego Stamp Club
Dutchess Philatelic Society
Putnam Philatelic Society
Kodak Stamp Club
Rochester Philatelic Association
Schenectady Stamp Club
Tri-County Stamp Club
Sodus Stamp Club
Uncle Sam Stamp Club of Troy
Wayne Stamp Club
Western Monroe Philatelic Society
Staten Island Philatelic Society
Syracuse Stamp Club
Utica Stamp Club
Jefferson County Stamp Club

North Carolina

Asheville Stamp Club
Carolinas Chapter 37, Germany Philatelic Society
Charlotte Philatelic Society
Eastern Carolina Philatelic Society
Fortnightly Collectors Club
Thermal Belt Stamp Club

Triangle Stamp Club
Cape Fear Philatelic Society
Greensboro Stamp Club
Hendersonville Stamp Club
Raleigh Stamp Club
Wilmington Philatelic Society
Winston-Salem Stamp Club

North Dakota

Fargo-Moorhead Philatelic Society

Ohio

Ashland Stamp and Coin Club
Clermont County Stamp Club
Collectors Club of Akron
Rubber City Stamp Club
Athens Stamp Club
McKinley Stamp Club
Stark County Stamp Club
Fort Hamilton Philatelic Society
Greater Cincinnati Philatelic Society
Garfield-Perry Stamp Club
Columbus Philatelic Club
Nationwide Stamp Club
Cuyahoga Falls Stamp Club
Dayton Stamp Club
Black River Stamp Club
Euclid Stamp Club
Fort Findlay Stamp Club
Medina County Stamp Club
Miami Valley Stamp Club
Sidney Stamp Club
Southwestern Stamp Club
Shaker Heights Philatelic Society
Fort Steuben Stamp Club
Tiffin Stamp Club
Stamp Collectors Club of Toledo
Warren Area Stamp Club
Wooster Stamp Club
Cuy-Lor Stamp Club
Worthington Stamp Club
Mahoning Valley Stamp Club
Zanes Trace Philatelic Society

Oklahoma

Enid Stamp Club
Lawton-Fort Sill Stamp Club
Norman Stamp Club
Washington County Philatelic Society
Muskogee Stamp Club
Oklahoma City Stamp Club
Oklahoma Philatelic Society
Southern Oklahoma Stamp Club
Tulsa Stamp Club

Oregon

Bandon Stamp Club
Greater Eugene Stamp Society
Southern Oregon Philatelic Society
Oregon Stamp Society
Salem Stamp Society
Surf 'N Sand Stamp Society
Umpqua Valley Stamp Club

Pennsylvania

Associated Stamp Clubs of Southeastern Pennsylvania and Delaware
Alle-Kiski Valley Numismatic and Philatelic Society
Allentown Philatelic Society
Ambler Stamp Club
Armstrong Activities Association Stamp Club
Bald Eagle Stamp Society
Beaver County Philatelic Society
Bethlehem Philatelic Society
Bi-State Stamp Club
Blair County Stamp Club
Blue and Gray Stamp Club
Bradford Stamp Club
Butler County Philatelic Society
Cumberland Valley Philatelic Society
Susquehanna Valley Stamp and Study Club
Westmoreland County Philatelic Society
Grove City Stamp Club
Capital City Philatelic Society
Havertown Stamp Club
Hazleton Stamp Club
Johnstown Stamp Club
Lancaster County Philatelic Society
Lebanon Stamp Collectors Club
Mount Joy Stamp Club
Educators Philatelic Society of Philadelphia
Erie Stamp Club
Frankford Arsenal Stamp Club
Germantown-Chestnut Hill Stamp Club
Greater Northeast Stamp Club
Philadelphia Chapter No. 18
Philatelic Society of Pittsburgh
Lansdowne-Upper Darby Stamp Club
North Penn Stamp Club
Pottstown Area Stamp Club
Reading Stamp Collectors Club
Spring-Ford Philatelic Society
Northeastern Pennsylvania Philatelic Society
Sharon Stamp Club
Summerset Stamp Collectors
Mount Nittany Philatelic Society
Warren County Stamp Club
Wilkinsburg Stamp Club
Wyoming Valley Stamp Club

Williamsport Stamp Club
Bux-Mont Stamp Club
White Rose Philatelic Society of York, Pa.

Rhode Island

Newport Philatelic Society
Rhode Island Philatelic Society

South Carolina

Columbia Philatelic Society
Emerald Stamp Club
Greenville Stamp Club
Spartanburg Stamp Club
Sumter Philatelic Society

South Dakota

Ringneck Stamp Club
Sioux Falls Stamp Club
Vermillion Stamp Club

Tennessee

Brentwood Philatelic Society
Chattanooga Stamp Club
Cumberland Stamp Club
West Tennessee Stamp Club
Holston Stamp Club
Knoxville Stamp Club
Memphis Stamp Collectors Society
Nashville Philatelic Society
Atomic City Stamp Club
Kentucky Lake Stamp Club

Texas

Texas Philatelic Association
Golden Spread Stamp Club
Mid-Cities Stamp Club
Austin Stamp Club
Texas A&M University Stamp Club
Sea Gull Stamp Club
Collectors Club of Dallas
Dallas Philatelic Society
El Paso Philatelic Society
Panther City Philatelic Society
Heart of Texas Stamp Club
Houston Philatelic Society
Johnson Space Center Stamp Club
Longview Stamp Club
South Plains Stamp Club
Marshall Stamp Club
Nacogdoches Stamp Club
Permian Basin Stamp Club
Port Lavaca Philatelic Society
Concho Valley Stamp Club
San Antonio Philatelic Association
Tyler Stamp Club
Wichita Falls Stamp & Coin Club

Utah

Golden Spike Stamp Club
Utah Philatelic Society

Vermont

Brattleboro Stamp Club
Chittenden County Stamp Club
Green Mountain Stamp Society
Washington County Stamp Club
Rutland County Stamp Club

Virginia

Arlington County Recreational Stamp Club
Charlottesville Stamp Club
Dan River Philatelic Society
Eastern Prince William Stamp Club
Virginia Philatelic Federation
Dolley Madison Stamp Club
Lynchburg Stamp Club
Shenandoah National Philatelic Society
Shenandoah Valley Stamp Club
Peninsula Stamp Club
Tidewater Stamp Club
Tidewater International Topics Society
Norfolk Philatelic Society
Richmond Stamp Club
Big Lick Stamp Club
Springfield Stamp Club
Ayrhill Stamp Club
Virginia Beach Stamp Club
Northern Neck Stamp Club
Williamsburg Stamp Society

Washington

Greater Eastside Stamp Society
Olympic Philatelic Society
Sno-King Stamp Club
Tri-City Stamp Club
Whidbey Island Stamp Club
Olympia Philatelic Society
Boeing Employees Stamp Club
Collectors Club of Seattle
Washington State Philatelic Society
Inland Empire Philatelic Society
Tacoma Stamp Club
Walla Walla Valley Philatelic Society
Wenatchee Valley Stamp Association
Yakima Valley Stamp Club

West Virginia

Mountain State Stamp Club
Harrison County Stamp Club
Kanawha Stamp Club
Middle Island Stamp Club
Blennerhassett Stamp Society

Wisconsin

Wisconsin Federation of Stamp Clubs
Badger Stamp Club
Baraboo Area Stamp Club
Fond du Lac Stamp Club
Germany Philatelic Society, Chapter 18

Green Bay Philatelic Society
Janesville Stamp Club
Northwoods Stamp and Coin Club
Oshkosh Philatelic Society
Polish American Stamp Club
Outagamie Philatelic Society
Walworth County Stamp Club
Kenosha Stamp and Cover Club
Manitowoc Philatelic Society
Milwaukee Philatelic Society
University of Wisconsin-Milwaukee Philatelic Society
Ripon Philatelic Society
Sheboygan Stamp Club
Central Wisconsin Stamp Club
Arrowhead Stamp Club
Waukesha County Philatelic Society
Wauwatosa Philatelic Society
Wisconsin Valley Philatelic Society

Wyoming

Cheyenne Philatelic Society
Central Wyoming Philatelic Association

Canada

Bathurst & Chaleur District Stamp Club
British Columbia Philatelic Society
Calgary Philatelic Society
Edmonton Stamp Club
Essex County Stamp Club
Hamilton Philatelic Society
Kelowna and District Stamp Club
Oakville Stamp Club
Ottawa Philatelic Society
Lakeshore Stamp Club
North Toronto Stamp Club
Nova Scotia Stamp Club
Regina Philatelic Club
St. John's Philatelic Society
St. Lawrence International Stamp Club
Societe Philatelique des Bois Francs
Societe Philatelique de Quebec
Vancouver Island Philatelic Society
Winnipeg Philatelic Society

Colombia

Club Filatelico de Bogota

Dominican Republic

Sociedad Filatelica Dominicana

Ecuador

Club Filatelico Guayaquil

England

American Stamp Club of Great Britain

Guatemala

Asociacion Filatelica de Guatemala

India

India Philatelics Stamp Collectors Association

Japan

Keystone Pacific Coin and Stamp Club
TAC Stamp Club

Mexico

Asociacion Mexicana de Filatelica

Norway

Oslo Filatelist Klubb

Panama

Isthmian Collectors Club

Puerto Rico

Puerto Rico Philatelic Society
San Juan Philatelic Circle

Saudi Arabia

Arabian Philatelic Association

APS Affiliates and Units

The APS affiliate or unit number appears in parentheses.

Americana Unit (40)
American Air Mail Society (77)
American Association of Philatelic Exhibitors (157)
American Belgian Philatelic Society (138)
American First Day Cover Society (33)
American Helvetia Philatelic Society (52)
American Philatelic Congress (139)
APS Writers Unit (30)
American Revenue Association (51)
American Society for Netherlands Philately (60)
American Society for Philatelic Pages and Panels (165)
American Society of Polar Philatelists (31)
American Topical Association (177)
Associated Collectors of El Salvador (89)
Austria Philatelic Society of New York (59)
Biology Unit (172)
Booklet Collectors Club (131)
Brazil Philatelic Association (32)
British Caribbean Philatelic Study Group (27)
British North America Philatelic Society (144)
Bullseye Cancel Collectors Club (108)
Bureau Issues Association (150)
Canal Zone Study Group (42)
Cardinal Spellman Philatelic Museum (166)
Carto-Philatelists (158)
Chemistry and Physics on Stamps Study Unit (123)
China Stamp Society (10)
Christmas Philatelic Club (74)

Christmas Seal and Charity Stamp Society (101)
Christopher Columbus Philatelic Society (124)
Cinderella Stamp Club (91)
Civil Censorship Study Group (86)
Club of Channel Islands Collectors (63)
Commonwealth International Philatelic Society (113)
Confederate Stamp Alliance (73)
COPAPHIL (142)
Croatian Philatelic Society (53)
Cuban Philatelic Society of America (173)
Eire Philatelic Association (21)
Empire State Postal History Society (28)
Errors, Freaks and Oddities Collector's Club (103)
Essay-Proof Society (159)
Ethiopian Philatelic Society (145)
Europa Study Unit (17)
Falkland Islands Philatelic Study Group (83)
Federation Quebecoise de Philatelie (169)
Fine Arts Philatelists (160)
France and Colonies Philatelic Society (45)
Franklin D. Roosevelt Philatelic Society (69)
Germany Philatelic Society (48)
Graphics Philately Association (133)
Great Britain Overprints Society (72)
Haitian Philatelic Society (81)
Hawaiian Philatelic Society (136)
Hellenic Philatelic Society of America (120)
Illinois Postal History Society (112)
India Study Circle (111)
International Churchill Society (49)
International Federation of Postcard Dealers (174)
International Philippine Philatelic Society (54)
International Society for Japanese Philately (58)
International Society for Portuguese Philately (35)
International Society of Guatemala Collectors (36)
International Society of Worldwide Stamp Collectors (151)
Iowa Postal History Society (168)
Italian American Stamp Club (175)
Italy and Colonies Study Circle (Great Britain) (132)
Italy and Colonies Study Circle (United States) (140)
JAPOS Study Group (68)
Junior Philatelists of America (26)
Korea Stamp Society (113)
Latin American Philatelic Society (104)
Law Enforcement Study Unit (146)
Liberian Philatelic Society (176)
Lions International Stamp Club (153)
Local Post Collectors Society (126)
Long Island Postal History Society (154)
Lundy Collectors Club (121)
Machine Cancel Society (24)
Mailer's Postmark Permit Club (100)
Malaria Philatelists International (115)
Maritime Postmark Society (37)
Masonic Study Unit (94)
Massachusetts Postal Research League (93)
Mathematical Study Unit (130)
Maximum Card Study Unit (106)
Meso-American Archaeology Study Unit (82)
Mexico-Elmhurst Philatelic Society International (43)
Mobile Post Office Society (64)
Modern Postal History Society (163)
Nepal and Tibet Philatelic Study Group (122)
New Jersey Postal History Society (95)
North Carolina Postal History Society (155)
Ohio Postal History Society (66)
Old World Archaeological Study Unit (92)
Oregon Postal History Society (147)
Pennsylvania Postal History Society (50)
Perfins Club (57)
Performing Arts Study Unit (102)
Petroleum Philatelic Society International (170)
Philatelic History Society (161)
Philatelic Music Circle (141)
Pictorial Cancellation Society (56)
Pitcairn Islands Study Group (46)
Polonus Philatelic Society (119)
Post Mark Collectors Club (62)
Postal History Society (44)
Postal History Society of Canada (67)
Postal History Society of Minnesota (84)
Postal Order Society (167)
Precancel Stamp Society (65)
Rhodesian Study Circle (107)
Romanian Philatelic Club (88)
Rossica Society of Russian Philately (171)

Rotary-on-Stamps (117)
Ryukyu Philatelic Specialist Society (47)
St. Helena, Ascension and Tristan Da Cunha Philatelic Society (85)
Sarawak Specialists' Society (110)
Scandinavian Collectors Club (79)
Scandinavian Philatelic Foundation (137)
Ships on Stamps Unit (152)
Society for Czechoslovak Philately (18)
Society for Hungarian Philately (34)
Society for Thai Philately (78)
Society of Australasian Specialists/ Oceania(22)
Society of Costa Rica Collectors (96)
Society of Indo-China Philatelists (38)
Society of Israel Philatelists (105)
Society of Philatelists and Numismatists (116)
Society of Philaticians (143)
Souvenir Card Collectors Society (149)
Space Topics Study Group (29)
Spanish Main (162)
Sports Philatelists International (39)
Stamps on Stamps Centenary Unit (127)
State Revenue Society (164)
Texas Postal History Society (76)
Tonga/Tin Can Mail Study Circle (128)
Turkey and Ottoman Philatelic Society (108)
Tuvalu Kiribati Philatelic Society (90)
Ukrainian Philatelic/Numismatic Society (134)
United Nations Philatelists (71)
United Postal Stationery Society (20)
United States Cancellation Club (75)
U.S. 1869 Pictorial Research Association (87)
United States Philatelic Classics Society (11)
United States Possessions Philatelic Society (99)
Vatican Philatelic Society (129)
Vermont Philatelic Society (156)
Virginia Postal History Society (41)
War Cover Club (19)
Western Cover Society (14)
Western Postal History Museum (148)
Wisconsin Postal History Society (61)
Women on Stamps Study Unit (118)
Zeppelin Collectors Club (135)
Zippy Collectors Club (97)

APS Convention Sites

The 91st annual APS convention, Stampshow 77, held Aug. 25-28 in San Francisco, Calif., was the first convention to be conducted by the society. Previously, the APS was the guest of a host club.

1886: New York, N.Y.
1887: Chicago, Ill.
1888: Boston, Mass.
1889: St. Louis, Mo.
1890: New York, N.Y.
1891: New York, N.Y.
1892: Niagara Falls, N.Y.
1893: Chicago, Ill.
1894: Niagara Falls, N.Y.
1895: Clayton, N.Y.
1896: Lake Minnetonka, Minn.
1897: Boston, Mass.
1898: New York, N.Y.
1899: Detroit, Mich.
1900: Milwaukee, Wis.
1901: Buffalo, N.Y.
1902: Springfield, Mass.
1903: Clayton, N.Y.
1904: Pittsburgh, Pa.
1905: Minneapolis, Minn.
1906: Boston, Mass.
1907: Denver, Colo.
1908: Columbus, Ohio
1909: Atlantic City, N.J.
1910: Detroit, Mich.
1911: Chicago, Ill.
1912: Springfield, Mass.
1913: Put-In-Bay, Ohio
1914: Niagara Falls, N.Y.
1915: San Francisco, Calif.
1916: Boston, Mass.
1917: Alexander Bay, N.Y.
1918: Cleveland, Ohio
1919: St. Louis, Mo.
1920: Providence, R.I.
1921: Milwaukee, Wis.
1922: Springfield, Mass.
1923: Washington, D.C.
1924: Detroit, Mich.
1925: Los Angeles, Calif.
1926: New York, N.Y.
1927: St. Louis, Mo.
1928: Toronto, Canada
1929: Minneapolis, Minn.
1930: Boston, Mass.
1931: Memphis, Tenn.
1932: Los Angeles, Calif.
1933: Chicago, Ill.
1934: Atlantic City, N.J.
1935: Washington, D.C.
1936: Omaha, Neb.
1937: Detroit, Mich.
1938: New Orleans, La.

1939: San Francisco, Calif.
1940: Buffalo, N.Y.
1941: Baltimore, Md.
1942: Cleveland, Ohio
1944: Milwaukee, Wis.
1945: Newark, N.J.
1946: Chicago, Ill.
1947: Pittsburgh, Pa.
1948: Denver, Colo.
1949: Boston, Mass.
1950: Washington, D.C.
1951: Toronto, Canada
1952: Philadelphia, Pa.
1953: Houston, Texas
1954: San Francisco, Calif.
1955: Norfolk, Va.
1956: St. Louis, Mo.
1957: Tampa, Fla.
1958: Cleveland, Ohio
1959: Los Angeles, Calif.
1960: Portland, Ore.
1961: Chicago, Ill.
1962: State College, Pa.
1963: Mexico City, Mexico
1964: Washington, D.C.
1965: Denver, Colo.
1966: Cincinnati, Ohio
1967: Newark, N.J.
1968: Rochester, N.Y.
1969: Baltimore, Md.
1970: Honolulu, Hawaii
1971: San Antonio, Texas
1972: New Haven, Conn.
1973: Los Angeles, Calif.
1974: Chicago, Ill.
1975: Columbus, Ohio
1976: Memphis, Tenn.
1977: San Francisco, Calif.
1978: Indianapolis, Ind.
1979: Boston, Mass.
1980: Spokane, Wash.
1981: Atlanta, Ga.
1982: Milwaukee, Wis.
1983: Pittsburgh, Pa.
1984: Dallas, Texas
1985: San Diego, Calif.
1986: Washington, D.C.
1987: Boston, Mass.
1988: Detroit, Mich.
1989: Anaheim, Calif.

Future Conventions

1990: Cincinnati, Ohio
1991: Philadelphia, Pa.

APS Spring Meeting Sites

1958: Cleveland, Ohio
1959: Detroit, Mich.
1960: Richmond, Va.
1961: Phoenix, Ariz.
1962: New York, N.Y.
1963: San Francisco, Calif.
1964: Salt Lake City, Utah
1965: Cleveland, Ohio
1966: Portland, Ore.
1967: New Orleans, La.
1968: San Diego, Calif.
1969: Tucson, Ariz.
1970: Memphis, Tenn.
1971: Atlantic City, N.J.
1972: New Orleans, La.
1973: Williamsburg, Va.
1974: Miami, Fla.
1975: Phoenix, Ariz.
1976: Philadelphia, Pa.
1977: New Orleans, La.
1978: Toronto, Canada
1979: Denver, Colo.
1980: London, England
1981: State College, Pa.
1982: Tucson, Ariz.
1983: Portland, Ore.
1984: Reno, Nev.
1985: Providence, R.I.
1986: Chicago, Ill.
1987: Toronto, Canada
1988: Reno, Nev.
1989: Cleveland, Ohio

Future Spring Meetings

1990: Phoenix, Ariz.
1991: Denver, Colo.

APS Presidents, Vice Presidents and Conventions

Term of Office	President	Vice President	Convention	Year
1886-88	*John K. Tiffany Missouri	R.R. Bogert New York	1st New York, N.Y. 2nd Chicago, Ill. 3rd Boston, Mass.	1886 1887 1888
1888-90	*John K. Tiffany Missouri	Willard C. Van Derlip Massachusetts	4th St. Louis, Mo. 5th New York, N.Y.	1889 1890
1890-92	*John K. Tiffany Missouri	Charles B. Corwin New York	6th New York, N.Y. 7th Niagara Falls, N.Y.	1891 1892
1892-93	*John K. Tiffany Missouri	Willard C. Van Derlip[1] Massachusetts	8th Chicago, Ill.	1893
1893-94	*John K. Tiffany Missouri	Hiram E. Deats New Jersey	9th Niagara Falls, N.Y.	1894
1894-96	*John K. Tiffany Missouri	Alvah Davison New York	10th Clayton, N.Y. 11th Lake Minnetonka, Minn.	1895 1896

Term of Office	President	Vice President	Convention	Year
		Board of Vice Presidents		
1896-98	*Col. Frank F. Olney Rhode Island	Boston, Mass. Willard C. Van Derlip John L. Kilbon George L. Toppan	12th Boston, Mass. 13th New York, N.Y.	1897 1898
1898-99	*Col. Frank F. Olney Rhode Island	Boston, Mass. Willard C. Van Derlip George L. Toppan Ernest M. Carpenter	14th Detroit, Mich.	1899
1899-00	*George L. Toppan Wisconsin	New York, N.Y. J.W. George P.F. Bruner Alexander Holland Albert Perrin[2]	15th Milwaukee, Wis.	1900
1900-02	*George L. Toppan Wisconsin	Chicago, Ill. Samuel Leland C.E. Severn P. M. Wolsieffer	16th Buffalo, N.Y. 17th Springfield, Mass.	1901 1902
1902-03	*Alexander Holland New York	Boston, Mass. Frank H. Burt Gordon Ireland J. F. Johnson Edwin F. Sawyer[3]	18th Clayton, N.Y.	1903
1903-04	*Alexander Holland New York	Boston, Mass. Frank H. Burt Willard O. Wylie Gordon Ireland	19th Pittsburgh, Pa.	1904
1904-05	*Hiram E. Deats New Jersey	Boston, Mass. Frank H. Burt Willard O. Wylie Gordon Ireland	20th Minneapolis, Minn.	1905
1905-06	*William C. Stone Massachusetts	Chicago, Ill. Henry N. Mudge Alexander Holland Henry A. Fowler	21st Boston, Mass.	1906
1906-07	*William C. Stone Massachusetts	Chicago, Ill. Henry N. Mudge Fred Michaels Henry A. Fowler	22nd Denver, Colo.	1907

Term of Office	President	Vice President	Convention	Year
1907-09	*John N. Luff	Boston, Mass.	23rd Columbus, Ohio	1908
	New York	Clifton A. Howes	24th Atlantic City, N.J.	1909
		Lorenzo L. Green		
		Edward deZ. Kelley		
1909-11	*Henry N. Mudge	St. Louis, Mo.	25th Detroit, Mich.	1910
	Illinois	Frederick R. Cornwall	26th Chicago, Ill.	1911
		Adelbert Strauss		
		Chester Myers		
1911-13	*Fredk. R. Cornwall	Detroit, Mich.	27th Springfield, Mass.	1912
	Missouri	Gen. Chas. A. Coolidge	28th Put-in-Bay, Ohio	1913
		Herbert Bowen		
		C. Frederic Heyerman		
1913-15	*Gen. C.A. Coolidge	Cleveland, Ohio	29th Niagara Falls, N.Y.	1914
	Michigan	Henry C. Crowell		
		John F. Rust	30th San Francisco,	1915
		Alvin Good	Calif.	
1915-17	*Clifton A. Howes	Brooklyn, N.Y.	31st Boston, Mass.	1916
	Massachusetts	Henry H. Wilson	32nd Alexandria Bay,	1917
		Dr. Carroll Chase	N.Y.	
		Wm. B. Sprague		
1917-19	*John W. Scott	Omaha, Neb.	33rd Cleveland, Ohio	1918
	New York	F.S. Parmelee[4]	34th St. Louis, Mo.	1919
		Dr. W.P. Wherry		
		H.A. Whipple		
1919-20	*Henry H. Wilson	Omaha, Neb.	35th Providence, R.I.	1920
	New York	F.S. Parmelee		
		Dr. W.P. Wherry		
		H.A. Whipple		
1920-22	*Dr. Carroll Chase	Springfield, Mass.	36th Milwaukee, Wis.	1921
	New York	Robert C. Munroe	37th Springfield, Mass.	1922
		John W. Prevost		
		H.P. Atherton		
1922-23	*C. Fred. Heyerman	Cleveland, Ohio	38th Washington, D.C.	1923
	Michigan	W.W. MacLaren		
		James A. Harris Jr.		
		Otto F. Moses		
1923-24	*C. Fred. Heyerman	Cleveland, Ohio	39th Detroit, Mich.	1924
	Michigan	W.W. MacLaren		
		W.H. Barnum		
		Otto F. Moses		
1924-25	*P.M. Wolsieffer	Kansas City, Mo.	40th Los Angeles, Calif.	1925
	Illinois	Wm. C. Michaels		
		Wilson D. Wood		
		Wm. Jerrems Jr.		
1925-27	*August H. Wilhelm	Milwaukee, Wis.	41st New York, N.Y.	1926
	California	Dr. Frederick A. Kraft	42nd St. Louis, Mo.	1927
		W.O. Staab		
		Dr. Samuel G. Keller		
1927-29	*August H. Wilhelm	Cincinnati, Ohio	43rd Toronto, Ont.	1928
	California	Wm. C. Kennett Jr.	44th Minneapolis, Minn.	1929
		Dr. L.G. Tedesche		
		Gustave M. Mosler		
1929-31	*Gustave M. Mosler	Chicago, Ill.	45th Boston, Mass.	1930
	Ohio	Chas. F. Mann	46th Memphis, Tenn.	1931
		Adolph F. Boehm		
		Dr. C.W. Hennan		
1931-33	*Dr. C.W. Hennan	Cleveland, Ohio	47th Los Angeles, Calif.	1932
	Illinois	Frank W. Grant	48th Chicago, Ill.	1933
		William D. Preston		
		Michael J. Lloyd		

Term of Office	President	Vice President	Convention	Year
1933-35	Roscoe B. Martin	Lynchburg, Va.	49th Atlantic City, N.J.	1934
	New York	Milton Moses	50th Washington, D.C.	1935
		Edward F. Haley		
		Don. P. Peters[5]		
		Carter Glass Jr.		
1935-37	*Eugene Klein	Washington, D.C.	51st Omaha, Neb.	1936
	Pennsylvania	Hugh M. Southgate	52nd Detroit, Mich.	1937
		Philip Simms Warren		
		Mrs. C.L. Manning		
1937-39	*Carter Glass Jr.	Buffalo, N.Y.	53rd New Orleans, La.	1938
	Virginia	Adolph Steeg	54th San Francisco,	1939
		Frederick L. Koepf	Calif.	
		Rollin E. Flower		
1939-43	*Rollin E. Flower	Cleveland, Ohio	55th Buffalo, N.Y.	1940
	New York	Donald W. Martin	56th Baltimore, Md.	1941
		Judge D.F. Lybarger	57th Cleveland, Ohio	1942
		Ralph E. Johnson	(no convention)	1943
1943-47	*Donald F. Lybarger	Baltimore, Md.	58th Milwaukee, Wis.	1944
	Ohio	Sol Glass	59th Newark, N.J.	1945
		Judge D.D. Caldwell	60th Chicago, Ill.	1946
		Mrs. D.B. McEntee	61st Pittsburgh, Pa.	1947
1947-49	*Donald F. Lybarger	New Orleans, La.	62nd Denver, Colo.	1948
	Ohio	Fred N. Billingsley	63rd Boston, Mass.	1949
		Douglas Watson		
		Leonard V. Huber		
1949-51	Wilbur F. Cannon	Milwaukee, Wis.	64th Washington, D.C.	1950
	Iowa	Clarence J. Gruhl	65th Toronto, Ontario	1951
		Burleigh E. Jacobs		
		Claude W. Degler		
1951-53	Wilbur F. Cannon	Philadelphia, Pa.	65th Philadelphia, Pa.	1952
	Iowa	Earl P.L. Apfelbaum	67th Houston, Texas	1953
		P. Harbot Sanville Sr.		
		Donald M. Steele		
1953-55	Burleigh E. Jacobs	Moline, Ill.	68th San Francisco,	1954
	Wisconsin	Chas. C. Cratsenberg	Calif.	
		Frank J. Patterson	69th Norfolk, Va.	1955
		Allen Seiffert[6]		
		Col. Guy W. Ade		
1955-57	*L.D. Shoemaker	Moline, Ill.	70th St. Louis, Mo.	1956
	Florida	Chas. C. Cratsenberg	71st Tampa, Fla.	1957
		Allen Seiffert[6]		
		Col. Guy W. Ade		
1957-61	C.C. Cratsenberg	San Francisco, Calif.	72nd Atlantic City, N.J.	1958
	Illinois	Joseph M. Clary	73rd Los Angeles, Calif.	1959
		Charles A. McKeown	74th Portland, Ore.	1960
		Fred B. Thomas	75th Chicago, Ill.	1961
1961-65	Fred B. Thomas	Washington, D.C.	76th State College, Pa.	1962
	California	George T. Turner	77th Mexico City, Mexico	1963
		Edward S. Conger	78th Washington, D.C.	1964
		Paul J. Plant	79th Denver, Colo.	1965
1965-69	*Edward L. Willard	Los Angeles, Calif.	80th Cincinnati, Ohio	1966
	Pennsylvania	Emerson A. Clark	81st Newark, N.J.	1967
		Stanley H. Beecher	82nd Rochester, N.Y.	1968
		W. Eugene Tinsley	83rd Baltimore, Md.	1969
1969-73	*Daniel W. Vooys	Phoenix, Ariz.	84th Honolulu, Hawaii	1970
	New York	Grant Bulkley	85th San Antonio, Tex.	1971
		Dr. Wm. C. Parker	86th New Haven, Conn.	1972
		Robert D. Corless	87th Los Angeles, Calif.	1973

Term of Office	President	Vice President	Convention	Year
1973-77	*Emerson Clark	New Orleans, La.	88th Chicago, Ill.	1974
	California	Henry H. Frenkle	89th Columbus, Ohio	1975
		Hubert C. Skinner	90th Memphis, Tenn.	1976
		William H. Bauer	91st San Francisco	1977
		John M. Kinabrew Jr.[7]		
1977-81	John Foxworth Jr.	New York Area	92nd Indianapolis, Ind.	1978
	Michigan	F. Burton Sellers	93rd Boston, Mass.	1979
		David L. Lidman	94th Spokane, Wash.	1980
		E.E. Fricks	95th Atlanta, Ga.	1981
1981-85	William H. Bauer	Boston Area	96th Milwaukee, Wis.	1982
	Texas	Lois M. Evans	97th Pittsburgh, Pa.	1983
		George S. Norton	98th Dallas, Texas	1984
		Guy R. Dillaway	99th San Diego, Calif.	1985
1985-89	F. Burton Sellers	New York Area	100th Washington, D.C.	1986
	Arizona	Ralph W. Walther		
		Joseph E. Foley		
		Patricia S. Siskin		

NOTE: In 1896 the society bylaws were changed to increase the number of vice presidents from one to three. They are now required to reside within a radius of 200 miles of each other. The chairman of the Board of Vice Presidents is listed first and the secretary, clerk or recorder (title has changed through the years) is listed last.

*—President deceased.

1—Elected in January 1892 to complete the term of Chas. B. Corwin.

2—Succeeded Alexander Holland who resigned as vice president in early 1900.

3—Succeeded J.F. Johnson who died Feb. 8, 1903.

4—Acting president for balance of term following death of John W. Scott on Jan. 4, 1919.

5—Succeeded Edward F. Haley who resigned as vice president in early 1935.

6—Succeeded Frank J. Patterson who resigned as vice president in March 1954.

7—Succeeded William H. Bauer who resigned as vice president in November 1976.

APS Hall of Fame

The APS Hall of Fame for outstanding contributors to philately was established in 1941 when 15 persons from years past were recognized. Except in 1943, 1965 and 1970, one to three individuals have been added annually. The date preceding the name of the individual indicates the year of nomination.

1941: Ralph A. Barry, Sir Rowland Hill, Beverly S. King, Edward S. Knapp, James L. Lindsay, John N. Luff, Frederick J. Melville, Charles Lathrop Pack, Charles J. Phillips, John W. Scott, Charles E. Severn, Hugh M. Southgate, Thomas K. Tapling, John K. Tiffany, Philip M. Wolsieffer
1942: W. Hamilton Barnum, Walter J. Conrath, Evelyn Severn
1944: Eugene Klein
1945: C.R. Richards, Franklin Delano Roosevelt, Willard O. Wylie
1946: J. Murray Bartels, Percy G. Doane
1947: William C. Stone
1948: Alfred F. Lichtenstein
1949: Edward H. Mason, James Starr
1950: Frederick R. Harris, Saul Newbury, Walter S. Scott
1951: Nicolas Sanabria, J.B. Seymour, Rev. William H. Tower
1952: Donald W. Martin, Walter R. McCoy
1953: David Caldwell, E.F. Hurt
1954: Theresa M. Clark, Dr. James Goodwin, Al Van Dahl
1955: Jere. Hess Barr, D.D. Berolzheimer
1956: Clarence W. Brazer, Dr. H.A. Davis, Dr. Clarence W. Hennan
1957: Hugh M. Clark, Max G. Johl, John W. Stowell
1958: Sidney F. Barrett, Theodore E. Steinway
1959: Stanley B. Ashbrook, Stephen G. Rich
1960: Dr. Carroll Chase, Adolph Steeg
1961: Rollin E. Flower, Morris Fortgang, Harry M. Konwiser
1962: F. Van Dyk MacBride, George B. Sloane
1963: L.H. Barkhausen, Hugh Barr, Hiram E. Deats
1964: Henry Chaloner, August Dietz, Howard H. Elliott
1966: Carl E. Pelander, Philip H. Ward
1967: William W. Hicks, George W. Linn, Harry Weiss
1968: Louise Boyd Dale, Vincent Domanski Jr., Francis Cardinal Spellman
1969: Charles S. Hamilton, Henry A. Meyer, Dr. Gregory B. Salisbury
1971: Richard McP. Cabeen, L.B. Gatchell, Donald F. Lybarger
1972: Edward Denny Bacon, Lester G. Brookman, C.H. Mekeel
1973: Edith M. Faulstich, Peter G. Keller, Elliott Perry
1974: Winthrop Boggs, Sol Glass, Edwin Mueller
1975: Henry M. Goodkind, Delf Norona
1976: Manuel M. Risueno, Sir John Wilson
1977: Alfred H. Caspary, James M. Chemi
1978: Alberto Diena, Irwin Heiman
1979: H.E. Harris, Harry L. Lindquist, Lowell Ragatz
1980: J.R.W. Purves, George T. Turner, Daniel W. Vooys
1981: William E. Gerrish, Dr. James J. Matejka Jr., Ethel B. McCoy
1982: Leon Dubs, Charles P. DeVolpi, Svend Yort
1983: Warren H. Colson, Mohamed Dadkhah, David Lidman
1984: George Hargest, Takaharu Mitsui, A. Earl Weatherly
1985: Eugene Costales, Mortimer L. Neinken, Joseph Schatzkes
1986: Robert P. Alexander, Richard H. Thompson, Lucien Berthelot
1987: Harrison D.S. Haverbeck, Soichi Ichida, Ernest Kehr
1988: James Beal, Herbert J. Bloch, William R. Ricketts

World Series of Philately

The World Series of Philately was introduced at the 82nd annual APS convention held in Rochester, N.Y., in September 1968. It has proved to be a success and has achieved increasing popularity.

The decision to have a competition that would enable grand award winners at major national stamp exhibitions to compete against each other to determine a Champion of Champions was the result of a demand by serious collectors voiced over many years.

From the first announcement, the novel idea earned wide and immediate acceptance. The quality of exhibits entered in competition at Rochester in 1968 and subsequent competitions has been outstanding.

Prior to the institution of the World Series of Philately, the assembling of a number of truly great award-winning exhibits in one place for viewing by the general public rarely occurred. Usually such exhibits were staged at huge international exhibitions.

To the average stamp collector unable to travel to the site of an international exhibition, the Champion of Champions competition offers an opportunity to see some of the most outstanding collections ever formed.

Because the APS holds the conventions in various sections of the United States, all stamp collectors may take advantage of an unparalleled philatelic experience by attending a World Series of Philately exhibition.

The opportunity to see such a wealth of superbly mounted, painstakingly prepared and hard-to-obtain material has attracted an ever-increasing number of collectors and non-collectors to each successive World Series exhibition.

The inevitable, long-range results of this high-level competition will be the upgrading of exhibits entered in regional or national shows and the opportunity, previously lacking, for large numbers of people in various parts of the country to see philately at its best.

Because of the obvious popularity of the program, the APS board of directors has adopted a set of rules designed to establish nationally recognized and accepted standards for entries in the World Series of Philately. It was decided that grand award winners of major national stamp exhibitions would be invited to exhibit their award-winning entries in competition with other winners of similar awards.

The rules were adopted to determine what exhibition will be considered as qualifying and to establish the criteria for the display to be entered in competition.

These WSP rules were updated at the end of 1989 and are available by sending a request and a stamped, addressed envelope to the APS.

An exhibition must first meet all of the requirements and be certified by the APS, and then the grand award winners of all subsequent exhibitions will be eligible to participate in the World Series of Philately as long as the exhibition continues to meet the minimum requirements.

If a certified exhibition falls below the minimum requirement, it must re-apply and requalify.

The following exhibitions have qualified and received certification for their grand award winners to compete in the World Series competition.

Airpex, Dayton Stamp Club

Aripex, Arizona Federation of Stamp Clubs

Balpex, Baltimore Philatelic Society

Chicagopex, Chicago Philatelic Society

Colopex, Columbus Philatelic Club

Florex, Florida Federation of Stamp Clubs

Frespex, Fresno Philatelic Society

Garfield Perry March Party, Garfield Perry Stamp Club

Indypex, Indiana Stamp Club

Interpex, American Stamp Dealers' Association

Midaphil, Collectors' Club of Kansas City

Milcopex, Milwaukee Philatelic Society

Napex, National Philatelic Exhibitions of Washington, D.C.

National Postage Stamp Show, American Stamp Dealers' Association

Nojex, North Jersey Federated Stamp Clubs

Okpex, Oklahoma City Stamp Club

Philatelic Show, Northeast Federation of Stamp Clubs

Pipex, Northwest Federation of Stamp Clubs

Plymouth Show, West Suburban Stamp Club

Rompex, Rocky Mountain Philatelic Exhibition

Ropex, Rochester Philatelic Association

Sandical, San Diego County Philatelic Council

Sarapex, Sarasota Philatelic Club

Sepad, Associated Stamp Clubs of Southeast Pennsylvania and Delaware

Sescal, Federated Philatelic Clubs of Southern California

Stamporee, Southeast Florida Stamp Exhibition Inc.

Stampshow, American Philatelic Society

Sunpex, Sunnyvale Stamp Society

Texpex, Texas Philatelic Association

Vapex, Virginia Federation of Stamp Clubs

Westpex, Association for Western Philatelic Exhibitions

Previous winners of the Champion of Champions crown are ineligible for further competition except in international competition. They may, however, exhibit non-competitively or in a Court of Honor.

Champion of Champions

Winners of the Champion of Champions follow with the year of competition, the exhibition they represent, the name of the exhibitor and residence, and the name of the exhibit.

1968, CPS, Robert H. Cunliffe, Pittsburgh, Pa., 19th-Century U.S. Revenues

1969, Sojex, Col. James T. DeVoss, State College, Pa., Via Panama Mail before 1881

1970, Sescal, Margaret L. Wunsch, Aurora, Ill., U.S. 1869 Issue

1971, Sojex, Wilber H. Schilling, Minneapolis, Minn., 19th-Century U.S.

1972, Nopex, Louis Grunin, Spring Valley, N.Y., U.S. 1847-1857

1973, Sescal, Robert P. Odenweller, Great Neck, N.Y., New Zealand 1855-1874

1974, APS-Stampede, Dr. Ludwig L. Simon, East Orange, N.J., The Aristocrats of Confederate Philately

1975, Nojex, Victor E. Engstrom, Upper Montclair, N.J., Postal History of the Danish West Indies

1976, CPS, Robert C. Magnesen, Elmhurst, Ill., Peru

1977, Florex, Edward J. Dormer, Miami, Fla., Mexico

1978, Westpex, Ryohei Ishikawa, Tokyo, Japan, U.S. 1¢ 1851-61

1979, CPS, George P. Trefonas, Park Ridge, Ill., Large Hermes Heads of Greece

1980, Frespex, Lynne S. Warm, Oceanside, Calif., United States First Bureau Issue 1894-1903

1981, Garfield Perry, Blake Myers, Canton, Ohio, Civil War Patriotic Covers

1982, Westpex, Joseph F. Rorke, Scottsdale, Ariz., Black Jacks

1983, Westpex, Harvey Warm, Greenwich, Conn., Postal History of Louisiana

1984, Milcopex, Eugene Bowman, Milwaukee, Wis., Cape of Good Hope, 1792-1910

1985, Stampshow, John Birkinbine II, Tucson, Ariz., Confederate States of America

1986, Sarapex, George Kramer, Clifton, N.J., Wells Fargo & Co., 1852-1895

1987, Aripex, Robert A. Paliafito, Phoenix, Ariz., Mexico, The First Designs, 1856-1867

1988, Frespex, Gene Scott, Iceland Numeral Issues, 1873-1903

John N. Luff Awards

The APS Luff awards are presented for meritorious contributions to philately by living philatelists.

1940: Stanley B. Ashbrook, August Dietz

1944: Dr. Carroll Chase, Elliott Perry, Col. Ralph A. Kimble

1946: Clarence W. Brazer, Lester G. Brookman, David Lidman

1948: Lester G. Brookman, Chester Smeltzer, Harry L. Lindquist

1950: Max G. Johl, Donald F. Lybarger, Laurence D. Shoemaker

1952: Winthrop S. Boggs, Van Dyk MacBride, James T. DeVoss

1954: Sol Glass, Dr. Holland A. Davis

1956: Barbara R. Mueller, Daniel W. Vooys

1958: James T. DeVoss, Henry Abt, Bernard Davis

1961: Herman Herst Jr., Frank J. Kovarik, Charles C. Cratsenberg

1962: Mortimer L. Neinken, Earl P.L. Apfelbaum, George A. Blizil

1964: Judge Edward I.P. Tatelman, James M. Chemi, Joseph M. Clary

1966: Richard McP. Cabeen, Henry E. Harris, H. Clay Musser

1968: Arnold H. Warren, Herbert J. Bloch, Anna D. Plant, Paul J. Plant

1970: Creighton C. Hart, Ezra Cole, Mrs. Arthur G. Lane

1972: Alex L. ter Braake, Edward N. Sampson, Frederick B. Thomas

1974: Horace W. Harrison, Eugene Costales, George M. Martin

1976: Denwood N. Kelly, Ernest A. Kehr, George T. Turner

1978: George W. Brett, John R. Boker Jr., Daniel W. Vooys

1979: Philip Silver, William W. Wylie

1980: Emerson A. Clark, George E. Hargest, Robson Lowe

1981: Charles A. Fricke, Enzo Diena, Cyrus R. Thompson

1982: Bernard A. Hennig, Richard H. Thompson, Carl H. Werenskiold

1983: Robert G. Stone, F. Burton Sellers, John E. Foxworth Jr.

1984: Gordon C. Morison, Soichi Ichida

1985: James H. Beal, Thomas J. Alexander, Robert L.D. Davidson

1986: Susan McDonald, Charles Starnes, Walter Eugene Tinsley

1987: Kenneth A. Wood, Henry M. Gobie, William H. Bauer

1988: Karl H. Schimmer, Charles J. Peterson, Wilbur F. Cannon

APS Slide Programs

1: U.S. Postal History, from the collection of the late Adolph Steeg.

6: Fancy U.S. Cancellations, by Burleigh E. Jacobs.

7: Alaska and the Mails, by Joseph J. Cavagnol.

9: Graf Zeppelin Flights of the World, Part 1, by Wolfgang Fritzsche.

10: Graf Zeppelin Flights of the World, Part 2, by Wolfgang Fritzsche.

11: Development of Postal History of East Germany, by Wolfgang Fritzsche.

12: Development of Postal History of

West Germany, French Zone and Saar, by Wolfgang Fritzsche.

13: Development of Postal History of West Germany, U.S. and British Occupation, by Wolfgang Fritzsche.

14: Maximum Postcards, by George A. Blizil.

20: The Frank C. Atherton Collection of Hawaiian Stamps, by E.M. Pickop.

21: Yugoslavia, Part 1, by Wolfgang Fritzsche.

22: Yugoslavia, Part 2, by Wolfgang Fritzsche.

23: Collecting Postal Stationery, Part 1, by Wolfgang Fritzsche.

24: Collecting Postal Stationery, Part 2, Pictorial Postcards, by Wolfgang Fritzsche.

25: Newfoundland Aerophilately, Part 1, by James J. Matejka Jr.

27: Philatelic Hiways and Byways, by James H. McMeen.

29: Selected Covers and Stamps of the Pan-American Exposition, created by Pitt Petri and the Buffalo Historical Society from the collection of Adolph Steeg.

33: How to Collect Airmail Covers, by Perham C. Nahl.

34: August Dietz Collection of Confederate Stamps.

The following programs are available with cassette tape recording:

35: Canal Zone Gems From the DeVoss Collection, by James T. DeVoss.

36: Norway, The Cancellations and Usages of the Skilling Issues, 1855-1875, by Svend Yort.

38: Errors, Varieties, Freaks and Oddities on U.S. Stamps, by Clyde Jennings Jr.

39: Postally Used Valentines of the 19th-Century, by Van Dyk MacBride.

40: Number Ones of the World, by Svend Yort.

41: Stamp Printing Methods, Identified and Illustrated, by O.L. Harvey.

42: The 1851-57 Issues, by the U.S. Philatelic Classics Society with J. David Baker as narrator.

43: Postmaster's Provisionals, by J. David Baker.

45: The Tale of the Kicking Mule, by Lee H. Cornell.

46: Cats on Stamps, by Betty Stevens.

47: Ships on Stamps, by Audrey Pankratz.

48: Guatemala, by Warren Stevens.

49: The U.S. 1847s, by Jacob J. Legeer.

50: Canada's Registry System (1827-1893), by Horace W. Harrison.

51: 1861 — A Year of Change, by J. David Baker.

52: The Universal Postal Union, by Alex L. ter Braake.

53: Stamps of the Trans-Mississippi or Omaha Issue of 1898, by Paul J. Wolf.

54: Story of the Penny Black, by Albert A. LeShane Jr.

55: Canada, Maple Leaf Issues of 1897-1898, by W.J. Banks.

56: Denmark, Wavy Lines, Typographed Issues, by W.J. Banks.

57: France, First Issue 1849-1850, by the France and Colonies Philatelic Society, Affiliate 45.

58: The Black Jack, by Paul J. Wolff.

59: The Postal History of the Commune Revolution in Paris, 1871, by the France and Colonies Philatelic Society.

60.1: Stamps of the Steamship Companies, Part I, by Denwood N. Kelly.

60.2: Stamps of the Steamship Companies, Part II, by Denwood N. Kelly.

61: The Postage Stamps of Prince Edward Island, by Robert V.C. Carr.

62: A History of Hawaii as Told Through Stamps, by Albert J. Schwalm.

63: Black Jack in the Foreign Mails, by Paul J. Wolf and John Hendrickson.

64: Swedish Postal History, by Swedish Postal Museum.

65: The Division of the Union, by Robert L.D. Davidson.

66: A Glimpse of the Confederate States of America, from the Harris S. Mueller collection.

67: The Postal History of the Civil War, Part 2, Federal Patriotics, by Robert L.D. Davidson.

68: The Cape Triangles, by Paul J. Wolff

69: Costa Rica, by the Society of Costa Rica Collectors.

70: Postal History of Switzerland, by Harlan F. Stone.

71: Canadian Postal Stationery as Used by the Canadian Pacific Railway, by Horace Harrison.

72: U.S. Private Die Proprietary Stamp Issues, by Richard Riley and Richard Willing.

73: The Ten-Cent Frameline of the Confederate States of America — Gems from the Wiseman Collection, by R.P. Gravely Jr.

74: French Balloon Posts, by Herman Herst Jr.

75: The Doctoring of Postage Stamps — Philatelists Beware, by G.S. Joseph.

76: The Mails of the Graf Zeppelin to and from Palestine, by Fred Blau.

77: The Wide-Wide World of Postal Stationery, Part 1, by Charles A. Fricke.

78: The Wide-Wide World of Postal Stationery, Part 2, by Charles A. Fricke.

79: The Wide-Wide World of Postal Stationery, Part 3, by Charles A. Fricke.

81: The World's Columbian Exposition, by James Doolin and Gordon Bleuler.

82: Postal Rarities from the National Postage Stamp Collection, by the Smithsonian Institution.

83: First Day Cover Collecting, A Primer, by Curtis Patterson.

84: Fascinating Highlights of FDC Collecting, by Curtis Patterson.

85: Seventy Years of Firsts on First Day Covers, by Marge Finger and Curtis Patterson.

86: Classic U.S. Air Mail Covers, by Phil Silver.

87: The Postal People FDC's of 1973, by Donald Crisman.

88: The 7-1-71 Affair, by Roy E. Mooney.

90: Postal History Panorama of Post WWII Germany, by A. Heinz.

91: U.S. Glider Mail Flights, by Simine Short.

92: France, Birth of the Third Republic, 1870-1871, Part I.

93: France, Birth of the Third Republic, 1870-1871, Part II.

94: Detecting Forgeries, by Mark Rowe.

95: Rotary International on Stamps, by Rotary on Stamps.

96: The Voskhod Program and Philately (Russian Space Program), by Peter Pesavento.

97: The Stamps and Postal History of Western Australia, by the Western Australia Study Group.

98: Plate Number Coils, by Ken Lawrence.

99: The First Five Years of Government Issued Air Mail Stamps of the World.

100: The APS Story.

101: U.N. Philately, by David S.J. Alexander.

102: Under-Rated First Day Covers, by Frank Raciti.

103: American Revolution Bicentennial Stamps and Cachets on International FDCs, by Gladys Vogel.

104: A Placid Winter, by Dorothy Gulick.

105: Maritime Mail, 1907 to 1980, Part I, from the Admiral Byrd Chapter of the Universal Ship Cancellation Society, by Eugene Peterson.

106: Maritime Mail, 1907 to 1980, Part II, from the Admiral Byrd Chapter of the USCS, by Eugene Peterson.

107: American Revolution Bicentennial: 1971-1984, by Allen Syler.

108: The 6.3 Story, by Les Lebo.

109: Irish Philately, by the James Hoban Chapter of the Eire Philatelic Association.

110: Today's Iran on Stamps, by Robert Kline.

111: Stamp Collecting Basics, by Anthony J. Torres Jr. and the Kodak Stamp Club.

112: Holyland Israel Revenues, by Larry Cohn.

113: Luminescent U.S. First Day Covers, by William Bayless.

Video Cassette No. 1: Timbromania, VHS only.

Video Cassette No. 2: Mexico, 1914 The Denver Eagles, by Ron Mitchell.

Video Cassette No. 3: The APS Story, VHS only.

Video Cassette No. 4: The Guernsey Collection, VHS only.

APS Sales Division

Many thousands of members of the APS have found the Sales Division to be the ideal system to dispose of their duplicates and to acquire stamps at reasonable prices.

The fact that the Sales Division has functioned since 1886 speaks for itself. Years of experience have resulted in an efficient service designed to produce the ultimate in satisfaction for the buyer and seller.

Multiple circuits are sent to members residing in the 48 contiguous states. They are designed to offer a group of collectors (not more than 10) a selection of up to 10 sales books containing stamps of the same country or category.

No minimum purchase is required. Multiple circuits are usually sent to members living in relatively close proximity to each other. This speeds transmission of the circuit and reduces parcel post costs.

Each member may retain the circuit up to seven days. Requests for circuits are processed in the order received.

Some multiple circuits of extremely popular material in short supply have long waiting lists. A member is placed on the circuit list according to his geographical location. Thereafter, his name moves upward on the list each time the same circuit (composed entirely of a new selection) is remailed from the Sales Division.

Eventually, every member has the opportunity to receive the circuit first. Once this happens, his name reverts to the bottom of the list and the process begins anew. There is no relationship between the order of the names on different circuits. Each circuit operates entirely independent of others.

Direct circuits are sent to Hawaii, Alaska, U.S. possessions and foreign countries. They may contain books of more than one country or category, depending upon the availability of the material requested. They may be retained by the member for a maximum of 20 days.

Chapter circuits are available to APS chapters upon request. These circuits must be mailed to the APS representative or an APS member specially designated by the chapter.

Chapter circuits consist of sales books of countries or categories requested by the chapter and are mailed automatically on a schedule furnished by the chapter. These circuits may be retained for a maximum of 30 days.

There are three types of sales books. One contains 192 spaces designed for single stamps or sets, while another consists of 14 pages, with a pocket on each page designed to hold a maximum of two covers per pocket. The third consists of 96 spaces for blocks of four and plate blocks.

Stamps may be mounted in the sales books as singles or sets, mint or used. Each sales book contains detailed regulations for purchasers and rules for owners, as well as many helpful hints. Low-cost mounts in three sizes are available to members who wish to mount never-hinged material.

Every page of every sales book is photographed on microfilm before the book is dispatched. This is done for the protection of the sales book's owner and to resolve disputes.

The Sales Division accepts no responsibility for items that overlap or are mounted in glassine or other cloudy coverings, since stamps so mounted cannot be properly photographed for identification purposes.

All sales books entered in the Sales Division are checked by competent stamp collectors. Sales books containing stamps of exceptional value or stamps known to have been counterfeited are sent to qualified examiners. The examiners are recognized specialists and authorities in their particular fields of philately.

Members questioning the authenticity of any stamp may submit it for examination to the Philatelic Foundation or the American Philatelic Expertizing Service providing the Sales Division is notified of this action within 10 days of purchase of the stamp.

If the item is found to be fraudulent or not as described, the purchase price of the stamp will be refunded to the purchaser. The society will not, however, pay the cost of the examination.

A set of rules has been developed as a result of many decades' experience in handling sales circuits. These have been refined many times. Those not needed have been discarded. For each rule now published within the sales books, there exists a definite need or reason.

Included here are some of the more important rules.

Regulations for Purchasers

1. On receipt of circuit, the member must check to be sure that all books

listed on the invoice are present. He should note missing stamps showing no purchaser's mark. If circuit has missing books or stamps, he should notify the individual from whom he received the circuit and send a copy of the letter to the Sales Division.

The member should attach the note to the sales book indicating to the next member that the discrepancy has been reported.

The member must not hold up the circuit, but should retain the postal receipt or signed receipt, if hand carried, for at least four months. The Sales Division will request a copy should it be necessary to file an insurance claim.

2. Members are not permitted to write in the sales book. Only the Sales Division and the sales examiners are permitted to correct or change the owner's original entries.

Any change by a member will make that member responsible for the net value of the item corrected.

If an obvious mistake was overlooked by the Sales Division or sales examiner, the member should attach a separate note to the sales book and give page and space number of the discrepancy over his signature.

Revisions will be made when the circuit is finally returned to the Sales Division and the sales book has been checked against the microfilm.

3. A purchaser may not make any handwritten additions to any sales book. Nor is it permissible to sign a name or initials in the space from which an item is removed.

Instead, a rubber-stamp symbol showing the chapter's name, or member's name or initials and APS membership number will be handstamped in the appropriate space to identify the purchaser. The rubber stamp must not be over one inch in length, and may be purchased locally or from one of the advertisers in the *American Philatelist.*

When an item occupying more than one space is removed from a sales book, the symbol must be placed only in one space — the space where the net value is given.

4. Members are fully responsible for the entire value of the circuit from the time of receipt until (a) the circuit, properly packed and addressed to next authorized recipient, is placed in the United States mails, insured or registered for not less than $100, and a receipt obtained therefor;

Or (b) is placed in the foreign mails, registered in accordance with instructions on the invoice, and a receipt obtained therefor;

Or (c) the circuit is hand delivered to the next recipient and a written receipt obtained therefor. Member shall remain liable if the circuit is hand delivered to anyone other than the authorized recipient.

5. Remittance for purchases must be made in full directly to the Sales Division at the same time the circuit is forwarded. Credit and partial payments are not permitted. The circuit invoice or report sheet must be sent to the Sales Division at that time, and the insurance fee paid regardless of method of delivery, even though no stamps are purchased.

6. Members must forward circuits promptly. A fine of 50¢ per day per circuit will be imposed against members who retain a circuit beyond the period authorized.

7. Circuit must be wrapped securely before being placed in the mails. Member must follow mailing instructions that accompany every circuit. He must treat every book with the utmost care.

The member must keep the circuit away from heat and moisture. It must be kept in a safe place where it will not be lost, damaged or stolen. Any losses that result from obvious neglect or carelessness in failing to protect a circuit properly will be the responsibility of the sender, and he shall be completely liable for that portion of the value above whatever reimbursement may be obtained from postal insurance.

8. Failure to comply with any of the aforementioned regulations will be sufficient reason to discontinue the privilege of receiving sales circuits. Violations of a serious nature will be reported to the APS board of vice presidents for necessary action.

Mounting Rules for Owners

1. Arrange stamps by country and in

catalog numerical order.

2. Ink must be used for all net prices. For the protection of the owner, books with net prices changed will be rejected, except where the item has been completely removed and space left blank.

3. If a stamp has an imperfection of any sort (i.e., thin, crease, tear, clipped perforation, pin hole, unused but gum missing, etc.), it must be so labeled in the space occupied by that stamp.

4. Write legibly. Prices must be entered in the space provided only. It is best if net values are visible with the stamp in place, but under no condition will a book be accepted in which a stamp or block covers the net value of another item.

5. Mount stamps securely.

6. Special mounts are permitted.

7. The Sales Division accepts no responsibility for items that overlap or are mounted in glassine or other cloudy coverings since stamps so mounted cannot be properly photographed for identification purposes.

8. Do not use rubber cement or any adhesives that leave a residue that will adhere to other stamps or pages once the item is removed.

9. Blank spaces not used in the sales book need not be marked out. Leave them completely blank.

Pricing

10. Prices must be competitive if the member desires good results.

11. Do not waste time mounting material that belongs in penny approvals.

12. Sets may be offered as a unit.

13. Do not submit books with a total net value of less than $30 or more than $300 (maximum limit of insurance coverage).

Charges

14. An insurance charge of 2 percent of the total net value (minimum 60¢) provides complete coverage against loss or damage while sales book is in the hands of the Sales Division.

15. Commission on sales is 20 percent with a minimum of $3 per book.

16. Charges cannot be paid in advance. Together with any fines and cost of return postage and insurance, they will be deducted when settlement is made at time sales book is retired and returned to its owner.

Fines

17. Any stamp judged to be reperforated, regummed, repaired, cleaned, fiscally used, or otherwise altered, unless clearly identified as such by marking in ink in the space where the stamp is mounted, shall subject the owner to a fine of $2 per stamp if the stamp is priced more than $10 and a fine of $1 if priced $10 or less. Counterfeit stamps, even if identified as such, or material offered "as is," will not be accepted.

18. Fines at the same rate may be levied where items are not labeled as required in Rule No. 3, provided the owner has been previously warned in writing by the Sales Division.

Liability

19. The APS accepts no responsibility for sales books until they are initially received from the owner for entry in the Sales Division. The society liability ceases when the book is retired and delivered to the last known address of the owner.

20. The APS accepts no liability for any loss or damage to sales book caused by climatic conditions unless there is conclusive proof of human negligence, and accepts no liability for decrease in value of multiple stamps due to perforation separation.

Rejection

21. The Sales Division reserves the right to reject any book for any reason it deems appropriate. Reasons most frequently the cause for rejection are stamps overpriced, not properly or securely mounted, or oversupply of material.

Classification Guide

Experience has revealed that more than 90 percent of the buyers submitting requests for sales books are for specific individual countries or categories.

General or worldwide collectors are becoming scarce. Books containing an unrelated hodgepodge are poor sellers. Likewise, their circulation is limited since buyers do not ask for material mounted in this manner.

To increase sales, U.S. material should be subdivided so that a single book contains only one of the following categories:

19th-century postage, regular and/or commemoratives
20th-century postage, regular and/or commemoratives
Mint singles
Used singles
Booklet panes
Coil pairs
Airmail, singles and/or blocks
Blocks of four, mint and/or used
Plate blocks
Plate number singles
Cancellations
19th-century covers
First-day covers
First-flight covers
Stationery or cut squares
Revenues
Departments
Postage dues and special delivery
Precancels
U.S. possessions (individual possession preferred)

If books cannot be limited to an individual country or colony, the following categories or combinations of countries may be accepted:

British North America
British West Indies
British America
British Africa
British Asia
British Oceania
British Europe
British Middle East (including sheikdoms)
Central America
Latin West Indies
South America
French Colonies
Benelux (Belgium, Netherlands, Luxembourg)
Scandinavia (including Finland, Greenland, Faroes, Iceland)
Central Europe (Germany, Saar, Austria, Switzerland, Liechtenstein)
Southern Europe (including Greece, Italy, Spain, Portugal)
Eastern Europe (U.S.S.R.-dominated countries)
Baltic States (Estonia, Latvia, Lithuania)
Balkans (Albania, Bosnia, Serbia)
Europe
Middle East (including Iraq, Iran, Turkey, Saudi Arabia, Jordan)
Far East (including Japan, China, Korea)
Southeast Asia (Laos, Cambodia, Vietnam, Thailand)
Asia
Africa (Independent)

Colonies and offices abroad of any country may be included with the mother country if necessary. Europe, Asia and Africa (Independent) categories should be used only if an earlier listed category will not suffice.

Books of an individual country are definitely preferred to any of the aforementioned categories. Further limiting each book to 19th- or 20th-century is also desirable but not required.

Better results can be obtained if mint and used are mounted in separate books. Special books are now available for covers. Low-cost mounts for never-hinged material are also available in three sizes.

Sellers should clearly identify the country, countries or category contained in each sales book. The Sales Division cannot ensure that your books will be included in the right classification unless the appropriate information is filled in on the front cover of each sales book.

The supply of sales books of certain countries sometimes exceeds the demand, and for temporary periods are not accepted by the Sales Division. Those countries urgently needed and those in oversupply are published at frequent intervals in the column Sales Talk appearing in the *American Philatelist.*

Collectors Club, Inc.

In 1896, a group of New York stamp collectors discussed the possibility of forming an association of men interested in stamps, incorporating it, and establishing a headquarters where collectors and dealers could meet at any time and "where the privileges of a club could be enjoyed by city and country members."

These discussions resulted in the formation of a committee, which on June 24, 1896, sent a circular letter to a selected list of 100 men, 50 of whom resided in the city and 50 of whom resided in the country, outlining its tentative plan and canvassing a favorable response.

In addition to J.M. Andreini, William Herrick, and Charles Gregory, this founding committee included two philatelic patriarchs, John N. Luff and John W. Scott.

Sixty-two of the men became shareholders and leased quarters for the Collectors Club at 351 4th Ave., New York City on Sept. 26, 1896.

The first meeting was held in the club rooms on Oct. 5, and the first exhibition followed on Oct. 19 when John N. Luff showed his collection of United States stamps, essays and proofs.

The number of members increased steadily, and at the sixth meeting of the board of governors, it was announced that the Collectors Club had incorporated on Dec, 14, 1896.

In addition to the founding committee, the first board included H.L. Calman, F.E.P. Lynde, H.E. Deats and F.A. Nast.

Present membership numbers about 1,100 worldwide.

Although founded primarily as an association whose members shared the privileges of a club and the club-like atmosphere generated from their common interest, the Collectors Club did not neglect the more serious aspects of the hobby.

The letters of incorporation state that one of the particular objectives of the club "is to encourage the best interests of philately by all proper means." The constitution reaffirms this objective.

The club has been faithful to this objective through the establishment and maintenance of a library and reading rooms, the publication of the *Collectors Club Philatelist* and studies by authorities in their field, lectures at regular meetings, and participation in the extra-curricular activities devoted to developing greater appreciation of stamp collecting.

Since 1936, the Collectors Club has occupied 22 E. 35th St., in the Murray Hill section of New York City. The club's five-story brownstone rowhouse, faced with red and gray block laid up in Flemish bond with contrasting stone and metal detail, has been designated a National Historical Landmark.

The facilities are made available to other stamp associations and societies, as well as to Scouts and similar organizations who wish to hold exhibitions (public or private) or other gatherings of a philatelic nature.

The John N. Luff reference collection, the property of the Philatelic Foundation, is housed in the John N. Luff Room of the Collectors Club building.

Meetings

Regular meetings of the Collectors Club are held the first and third Wednesday of the month at 8 p.m. in the Stephen G. Rich Memorial Room. No meetings are held during the summer months.

With the exception of the annual meeting on the second Wednesday in January, which is devoted to the business of operating the club, the meetings are devoted to the scheduled subject.

J. Brace Chittenden Memorial Library

The Collectors Club library has more than 140,000 manuscripts, maps, pictures, slides, microforms, tear sheets, books, reports, dissertations, pamphlets and journals. With the exception of certain unique periodicals, rare limited editions and presentation copies, all items in the collection are available for loan to members in accordance with the rules of the library. Conditions for the use of the rarer material are also outlined in the rules.

The names of early benefactors, several of whom served as librarian of the J. Brace Chittenden Memorial Library, include Hiram Deats, Joseph S. Rich, John W. Scott, William R. Ricketts, Abraham Hatfield, Alfred F. Lichtenstein, Charles J. Phillips, Theodore E. Steinway, and Dr. J. Brace Chittenden.

Dr. Chittenden did much to elevate the library to its present state from its earlier status of "a mere collection of books." The board of governors designated the library as the J. Brace Chittenden Memorial on June 6, 1928.

Among the collections in the library are the Victor Suppantschitsch collection of printed matter on stamp collecting up to 1900 including some 28,000 items; Pablo Busch collection containing philatelic publications issued in Argentina and near completion for many other South American countries; and Joseph S. Rich collection of postal guides and postmasters' reports of the United States.

The library catalog is cross-indexed so that an author, country or subject can be located. The library contains two major divisions of material— periodicals and handbooks, catalogs and subdivisions. Great emphasis is placed on the completion of periodical collections.

The reference material is open to the general public Monday, Wednesday and Friday, 10 a.m. to 5 p.m. by appointment.

The major portion of the catalog collection is housed in the Joseph S. Rich Room, including auction catalogs.

Steinway Memorial Publications Fund

Theodore E. Steinway was a dedicated member of the Collectors Club who shook the club loose from the doldrums of World War I, revitalizing its organization and its purpose.

Steinway gave numerous gifts to the library's collection, including the Suppantschitsch collection that embraced any literature printed on stamps and stamp collecting during the 19th century.

The literature of the hobby was to Steinway the keystone to successful research in philately. The Collectors Club established the Steinway Memorial Publications Fund for the publication of philatelic handbooks. This fund has been in operation since June 1957.

'Collectors Club Philatelist'

The *Collectors Club Philatelist* is the bimonthly periodical published for members of the Collectors Club. The periodical was established as a quarterly in January 1922 and became a bimonthly in 1950.

The *Collectors Club Philatelist* contains selected articles from members of the club and details of regular meetings and business matters.

Translations from the *Kohl Handbook*, to which the Collectors Club has English-language rights, appear as space and interest permit.

Awards

The Collectors Club program committees have, on occasion, scheduled a competitive display limited to the members present at meetings with appropriate certificates for first, second and third awards.

In recent years, this event has been scheduled annually. Silver awards are given to the top exhibits.

Collectors Club medals have been awarded to members since 1925 for outstanding achievements. Collectors Club medals are also awarded annually to the author of the best article published in the *Collectors Club Philatelist* during the previous year.

Certificates of merit are awarded to the articles ranking second.

The program that, in the opinion of the Awards Committee, has been the best of the season's scheduled meetings is also awarded a Collectors Club medal.

Lichtenstein Medal

The Alfred F. Lichtenstein memorial award was established in 1952 to honor this great American collector. The Lichtenstein medal is given in recognition of distinguished philatelic service.

Study Groups

The Collectors Club has maintained a

program supporting any valid study group. It is not required that all members of these groups be members of the club, but it is requested that a member of the club, who is also a member of the individual group, act for the Collectors Club in matters pertaining to the club and its home.

The chief contribution of the club to study groups is providing a meeting place. It has also been arranged for individual or collective displays by members of the study group at regularly scheduled meetings of the Collectors Club

The pages of the *Collectors Club Philatelist* have been made available for publication of such groups' studies as are consistent with members' wishes and editorial policy.

Activities

The Collectors Club supplies stamps and philatelic supplies to schools, hospitals, and other institutions, and offers advice and cooperation to qualified institutions.

Lectures are provided on request both nationally and internationally.

The club has actively supported national and international exhibitions devoted to philately.

Membership

No person under 21 years of age is eligible for membership. A resident member is such person who resides, has a business address, or is employed within a radius of 50 miles from the club house.

A non-resident member is such person who resides and is employed entirely outside the areas previously mentioned, including Canada and Mexico.

Annual dues are $50 for resident members, $15 for non-resident members and $15 for overseas members.

Applications should not be accompanied by remittance; dues are payable upon notification of election. Applications may be obtained from Collectors Club, 22 E. 35th St., New York, N.Y. 10016.

Board of Governors

Governors are men and women elected by voting members to administer the services, functions, activities and maintenance of the Collectors Club. The officers of the club are elected from among the board of governors.

Each governor has an assigned responsibility, such as membership, maintenance of the physical plant, club's publications, library, and study groups, and is required to account for the charge at each scheduled meeting of the board.

Governors

1989

Joseph E. Foley
Jerold M. Massler
Robert M. Rosende
Martin F. Stempien Jr.
Scott Trepel
Ira S. Zweifach

1990

Ernest E. Fricks
Helen M. Galatan
Kenneth Kutz
Thomas Mazza
Robert Odenweller

1991

Louis Grunin
Keith Harmer
Louis E. Repeta
Louis K. Robbins
Michael E. Ruggiero

Trustees

Helen M. Galatan
Louis Grunin
Martin F. Stempien Jr.

Officers

President: Robert Odenweller
Vice president: Kenneth Kutz
Secretary: Robert M. Rosende
Treasurer: Keith Harmer

American Association of Philatelic Exhibitors

Founded in the summer of 1986, the American Association of Philatelic Exhibitors was the creation of a small group of dedicated collectors who sought to fill a void in organized philately.

This founding council was comprised of Randy L. Neil, John Hotchner, William Bauer, Leo John Harris, Clyde Jennings, Mary Ann Owens, Steven Rod and Steve Schumann. The AAPE was formed to bring together stamp exhibitors from all levels, as well as those collectors who are supportive of exhibiting and stamp shows in general.

Interest in this new organization was widespread, and within three years the membership roster swelled to 1,200. AAPE is dedicated to helping its membership stay abreast of all facets of exhibiting at the local, regional, national and international levels.

AAPE publishes a quarterly journal, *The Philatelic Exhibitor*. It contains a wide variety of features, articles, illustrations and news of the world of philatelic exhibiting. AAPE members may use the Exhibitor's Critique Service, which enables exhibitors to have their exhibits evaluated by qualified APS judges free of charge.

The exhibitor mails a photocopy of the exhibit to the critique service and receives the exhibit via return mail marked with constructive criticisms. The service is designed to encourage and motivate collectors to exhibit by providing hands-on guidance.

AAPE provides all stamp shows with the AAPE awards of honor. These awards were created to provide recognition to exhibits that are presented in an excellent manner, regardless of the exhibits' contents. These awards have been helpful in encouraging philatelic exhibiting among collectors who may not necessarily want to spend a great deal of money to acquire items that some exhibits require.

An Exhibit Archive Service was established to encourage exhibitors to deposit photocopies of their exhibits at the American Philatelic Research Library so they will be available for reference to all interested collectors.

To encourage youth exhibiting, AAPE established the American Youth Stamp Exhibiting Championships, which will debut in 1990.

AAPE Officers

President: Randy Neil
Vice president: Mary Ann Owens
Secretary: Steven J. Rod
Treasurer: Paul Rosenberg

Board of Directors

Class of 1990
Darrell Ertzberger
Cheryl Ganz
Stephen Schumann
Class of 1992
Dane Claussen
Richard Drews

Committees and Committee Chairpersons

Local/Regional Exhibiting: Cheryl Ganz
National Exhibiting: Clyde Jennings, Stephen Schumann
International Exhibiting: William Bauer
Youth Exhibiting: Dane Claussen, Cheryl Edgecomb
Thematic/Topical Exhibiting: Mary Ann Owens, George Guzzio
Show Management: Steven Rod
Association Attorney: Leo John Harris

Annual Convention Sites

Midaphil 86, Kansas City, Mo.
Indypex 87, Indianapolis, Ind.
Chicagopex 88, Chicago, Ill.
Vapex 89, Virginia Beach, Va.

Membership

Membership dues are $12.50 annually in the United States and Canada, and $20 elsewhere. Information is available from AAPE, Box 432, South Orange, N.J. 07079.

American Topical Association

The American Topical Association was founded Sept. 12, 1949, to promote the hobby of topical stamp collecting. Its current address is Box 630, Johnstown, Pa. 15907.

The collecting of stamps for the subject portrayed on the stamp rather than for the country that issued it or its postal use is not new. At the beginning of the 20th century, stamp collectors in the United States and in Europe put together collections of stamps depicting animals, ships, mountains, architecture and famous people.

But topical collecting made little headway for decades because there was only a comparatively small number of pictorial stamps available to collect on particular themes. This was remedied with the revolution in lithography and color printing methods.

In 1944, Phebe B. Boothe authored an 86-page handbook listing more than 1,250 different topical subjects. With this stimulus, Jerome Husak, a 12-year-old youngster from Milwaukee, Wis., attended his first stamp show in search of topical stamps. A faint germ of an idea of expanding topical collecting and exchanging information with others grew over the next five years.

At the age of 17, Husak founded the American Topical Association, using a bedroom in his parents' home as an office. Within the first two months, ATA had recruited 203 members; incorporated as a non-profit organization; and published the first issue of *Topical Time*. At the end of ATA's first year, *Topical Time* had become a bimonthly journal, and in another six months the membership had risen to 1,000.

ATA now has more than 7,000 members in more than 90 countries around the world, and whole number 233 of *Topical Time* features 96 pages of topical articles, checklists, topical new issues, publication reviews, philatelic current events, study unit reports, news of members, and a question-and-answer column titled Clearing House of Knowledge, which has answered more than 4,000 questions from topicalists worldwide.

Topical Time whole number issues 1 through 148 have been reprinted, excluding all advertising matter, and are now available in 13 handbooks, while entire issues from 149 to date are still available from ATA. Commencing with a 10-year cumulative index (1949-59), five-year cumulative indexes through 1979 have been published as a reference source of all topical information published in the ATA bimonthly journal. The computer printout of topical new issues appearing in each issue of *Topical Time* is compiled annually by topical categories and published in separate handbooks. The latest in this series provides a listing of more than 175,000 stamps in 25 volumes.

Another series of ATA handbooks consists of the cream of the crop of thousands of topical articles appearing in hundreds of philatelic and non-philatelic journals. There are now nine *Topical Digests* — some in their second edition, but all available.

The majority of ATA handbooks are definitive studies with comprehensive checklists for specific topics. These illustrated handbooks include such topics as aircraft; American flag; Americana; animals; astronomy; birds; cooking; education; fairy tales; fish; Holy Family; insects; Lions International; maps; Masons; medicine; music; pharmacy; plants; railways; religion; Roosevelt; science; shells; ships; space; stamps on stamps; Statue of Liberty; theater; United Nations; U.S. bicentennial; and women.

On April 29, 1950, the Casey Jones Railroad Unit was founded as the first American Topical Association Study Unit. Today, ATA has more than 50 active study units, most of which publish their own bulletin.

The scope of the topics covered in this abundance of philatelic literature includes Americana; archaeology; astronomy; automobiles; aviation; bicycles; biology; birds; Canadiana; cats; chemistry; chess;

Christmas; Churchill; Columbus; cooking; dogs; Durer; Europa; fairy tales; fine arts; gay and lesbian history; graphics; journalists; lighthouses; Lions International; malaria; maps; Masons; mathematics; medical subjects; minerology; Napoleon; performing arts; petroleum; railroads; Roosevelt; Rotary; ships; space; sports; stamps; telecommunications; textiles; United Nations; UPU; windmills; women; and World's Fairs.

The first ATA chapter chartered was the Thematic Stamp Club of South Africa, making ATA truly international in scope. Today, chapters are scattered throughout the United States and in various other countries.

The first ATA co-sponsored, all-topical stamp exhibit was held in January 1950, at the National Philatelic Museum in Philadelphia. The first all-ATA meeting was held in September 1950, in Chicago. The first combined ATA annual convention and ATA topical exhibit (Topex) was held in Johnstown, Pa., June 20-22, 1952. Topex remains the largest all-topical stamp exhibit held in the United States. The grand award winner is eligible for the annual APS Champion of Champions competition.

The *ATA Membership Directory* provides in alphabetical order the names and addresses of members, and lists collectors by topics. Overseas members are listed by country so that ATA members can contact topicalists with similar interests in various parts of the world. A Language Translation Service is staffed by 46 members, translating 22 languages for ATA members. Other ATA services described in the directory include:

An Information Board where some 425 members offer specific information on 250 different topics; a Biography Service that offers thumbnail bio-sketches of some 13,000 persons pictured on postage stamps; a slide-lecture library offering more than 60 programs to members as well as stamp clubs; Heirs and Estates Service with members in various sections of the country to assist heirs in disposing of collections and labels available for members' collections explaining the service; Claims Service to arbitrate claims of $25 or more of members against other members, dealers or vice versa; Judges Accreditation Service with procedures for accrediting topical judges and suggesting judges for various stamp shows; best-in-topical awards available to any stamp show that includes a topical classification; Sales Service to assist members in disposing of duplicates and in locating needed stamps; and a Checklist Service to provide shorter checklists at cost.

ATA Accredited Judges

Alusio, Frank, Ontario, Canada
Baum, Werner J., Pittsford, N.Y.
Beuthel, Donald G., Denver, Colo.
Fisher, Ingeburg, Spokane, Wash.
Fitz, Charles M., Elizabeth, N.J.
Garabrant, Lauretta, New Port Ritchey, N.J.
Garabrant, Melvin, New Port Ritchey, N.J.
Green, Jack H., Madison, Wis.
Griffenhagen, George, Vienna, Va.
Griffiths, John O., Vista, Calif.
Guzzio, George T., Brooklyn, N.Y.
Hackett, Margaret, R., Whiting, N.J.
Hellard, Ruth E., Lake Katrine, N.Y.
Hess, Winand, Del Mar, Calif.
Johnston, Hugh W., Spokane, Wash.
Luster, Stephen, Sterling, Va.
Mueller, Barbara, Jefferson, Wis.
Oesch, Robert, San Diego, Calif.
Owens, Mary Ann, Brooklyn, N.Y.
Smith, Donald W., Johnstown, Pa.
Weinberg, Irving, Philadelphia, Pa.
Wetmore, Ruth, Brevard, N.C.
Winick, Lester, Homewood, Ill.

For information on judges for your topical show, contact the ATA.

ATA Chapters

Ajax Philatelic Society, Ajax, Ontario, Canada
Arizona Society of Topical Philatelists, Phoenix, Ariz.
Aurora (Colo.) Stamp Club
Cedar Rapids (Iowa) Stamp Club
Central Coast Stamp Club, Lompoc, Calif.
Chelmsford (Mass.) Stamp Club
Chicagoland Chapter, Chicago, Ill.
China Topical Club, Taipei, China
Collectors Club of Seattle (Wash.)
Collectors Club of Washington (D.C.)
Columbus (Ohio) Philatelic Club
Corn Belt Philatelic Society Inc.,

Bloomington, Ill.
Cuy-Lor Stamp Club, Westlake, Ohio
Fremont (Calif.) Stamp Club
Glen Ellyn (Ill.) Philatelic Club
Greater Los Angeles (Calif.) Chapter
Hazlet (N.J.) Stamp Club
Inland Empire Philatelic Society, Spokane, Wash.
Johnstown (Pa.) Chapter
Junior Topicalists of Johnstown (Pa.)
Kent Philatelic Society, Grand Rapids, Mich.
Lincoln (Neb.) Stamp Club
Lombard (Ill.) Woman's Stamp Club
New York Area Chapter
Northern Indiana Philatelic Society, Mishawaka, Ind.
Northern Toronto (Canada) Stamp Club
Oxford Chapter, Woodstock, Ont., Canada
Philadelphia (Pa.) Chapter
San Diego (Calif.) Topical and Thematic Club
San Jose (Calif.) Stamp Club
Stamp Collector's Club of Toledo (Ohio)
Thematic Philatelic Society of Victoria (Australia)
Thematic Society of Australia, Sydney, Australia
Thematic Stamp Club, Cape Town, South Africa
Topical Philatelists in Colorado
Tucson (Ariz.) Stamp Club
Virginia Topical Association
West Suburban Stamp Club, Plymouth, Mich.

ATA Study Units

Americana Unit
Astronomy Study Unit
Biblical Topics Study Unit
Bicycle Stamp Club
Biology Unit
Butterfly and Moth Stamp Society
Capt. Cook Study Unit
Carto-Philatelists (Maps)
Casey Jones Railroad Unit
Cats on Stamps Study Unit
Chemistry and Physics Study Unit
Chess on Stamps Study Unit
Christmas Philatelic Club
Christopher Columbus Philatelic Society
Churchill Philatelic Society
Dogs on Stamps Study Unit
Albrecht Durer Study Unit
Earth's Physical Features Study Unit
Embroidery-Stitchery-Textile Unit
Europa Study Unit
Fairy Tales/Folklore Unit
Fine Arts Philatelists
Gay and Lesbian History on Stamps Study Unit
Gems, Minerals & Jewelry Study Unit
Graphics Philately Association
Law Enforcement Study Unit
Lighthouse Unit
Lions International Stamp Club
Masonic Study Unit
Mathematical Study Unit
Medical Subjects Unit
Meso-American Archaeology Study Unit
Old World Archaeological Study Unit
Performing Arts Study Unit
Petroleum Philatelic Society International
Rotary on Stamps Unit
Ships on Stamps Unit
Space Unit
Sports Philatelists International
Stamps on Stamps — Centenary Unit
United Nations Philatelists
Windmill Study Unit
Women on Stamps Study Unit
World's Fair Collectors Society Inc.

TOPEX Convention Sites

1952: Johnstown, Pa.
1953: Philadelphia, Pa.
1954: Dayton, Ohio
1955: Decatur, Ill.
1956: Detroit, Mich.
1957: Chicago, Ill.
1958: Little Rock, Ark.
1959: New York, N.Y.
1960: Minneapolis, Minn.
1961: Johnstown, Pa.
1962: Colorado Springs, Colo.
1963: Phoenix, Ariz.
1964: Camden, N.J.
1965: Aurora, Ill.
1966: Boston, Mass.
1967: Rochester, N.Y.
1968: Milwaukee, Wis.
1969: Chicago, Ill.
1970: Montreal, Canada
1971: Syracuse, N.Y.
1972: Portland, Maine
1973: Denver, Colo.
1974: Rochester, N.Y.
1975: Lincoln, Neb.

1976: Philadelphia, Pa.
1977: Dallas, Texas
1978: Atlantic City, N.J.
1979: Spokane, Wash.
1980: Portland, Maine
1981: Chicago, Ill.
1982: Baltimore, Md.*
1983: San Antonio, Texas
1984: Lincoln, Neb.
1985: Reno, Nev.
1986: Chicago, Ill.
1987: Columbia, S.C.
1988: Toronto, Canada
1989: Spokane, Wash.
1990: Providence, R.I.

* Topex was not held in 1982, but an ATA convention was held at Balpex.

ATA Presidents

Past ATA presidents are listed by the year in which they succeeded to the presidency.

1949: Rudolph J. Kasta
1950: Charles J. Keenan
1954: Homer L. Jones
1956: Allyn H. Wright
1958: Harvey E. Johnson
1962: John H. Groet
1964: Margaret R. Hackett
1968: Fred Korotkin
1972: Henry Peterson
1976: George B. Griffenhagen
1980: Donald W. Smith
1984: Alan J. Hanks
1988: David A. Kent

Current ATA Officers

President: David A. Kent

First vice president: Donald G. Beuthel

Second vice president: Hugh W. Johnston

Secretary: Dorothy Smith

Treasurer: Donald B. Brenke

Executive director: Donald W. Smith

Directors: George B. Griffenhagen, Alan J. Hanks and Jerome Husak

Advisory board: Homer L. Jones, Alan J. Hanks, Margaret R. Hackett, Fred Korotkin, Donald W. Smith and George B. Griffenhagen

Special Activity Directors

Chapters director: Hugh W. Johnston

Units director: Donald B. Brenke

Topical awards director: Arlene Crosby

Catalog number conversion director: Howard J. Burkhalter

Checklist director: Joan Bleakley

Claims director: A. Michael Knapp

Distinguished Topical Philatelist Award director: Margaret R. Hackett

ATA historian: Homer L. Jones

Information director: Edna B. Cummins

Biography service director: Paul G. Partington

Judges accreditation director: George T. Guzzio

Slide-lecture director: Frank J. Gomba

Translation director: Dmytro Bykovetz Jr.

Sales service operator: William J. Thomas

Topical Time editor: Glen Crago

Youth activities director: Melvin Garabrant

Editorial board: Edna B. Cummins, John Henry Richter, Ruth Y. Wetmore, Robert S. Oesch, George B. Griffenhagen, Glen Crago, Marshall Whitehead, Fred Foldvary, R. Hal Holden, Ann Shoemake, Donald Brenke, Jerome Husak and Marilyn Schafstall.

Distinguished Topical Philatelist Award Winners

The Distinguished Topical Philatelist award has been presented to ATA members since 1952 for service to topical philately and the ATA.

1952: Jerome Husak, Homer L. Jones, Charles J.Keenan, Allyn H. Wright

1953: S.C. Becker, George Bourgraf, Catherine D. Caspary Fechner

1954: John H. Groet, Ernest A. Kehr

1955: Willard F. Stanley, Wilson A. Swanker

1956: Margaret R. Hackett, Walter W. Sievers

1957: Clare McAlister, Sidney R. Esten

1958: Jal Cooper, Edward J. Flath

1959: M.P. Polson, Louis K. Sievert

1960: Ennis C. Cleveland, Harvey E. Johnson

1961: Shirley C. Tucker, Edgar W. Spurgeon

1962: O. Frank Freedner, Fred Korotkin

1963: John Henry Richter, M.F. Stern

1964: Fred H. Campbell, Mr. and Mrs. A.H. Pritzlaff Jr.

1965: Robert S. Oesch, H.F. Rayl

1966: Melvin J. Andrews, Henry Peterson

1967: Brother Camillus Casey, E. Willis Hainlen

1968: Clarence Beltmann, John Thomas

1969: Mary Ann Owens, Cyril C. Ranschaert

1970: Dorothy F. Smith, George Griffenhagen

1971: K.D. Dinshah, Sophia Webb

1972: Charles S. Diamant (posthumously), Lester E. Kufahl

1973: Edna Cummins, Melvin Garabrant, Lauretta Garabrant

1974: George T. Guzzio, Margaret M. Wurtz

1975: Myrtle I. Watt, Ruth Y. Wetmore

1976: Franklin R. Bruns Jr., Donald W. Smith

1977: Sam Wilkinson III, Jack H. Green

1978: Lester E. Winick, Robert F. Kante

1979: Donald B. Brenke, Kenneth A. Wood

1980: Paul G. Partington, Walter L. Tasker

1981: Ann Shoemake, Henry J. Rajewski

1982: Dulcie Apgar, Robert A. Kyle

1983: Sally A. Husak, Lawrence Black

1984: Arlene A. Crosby, Elaine Durnin Boughner

1985: Alan J. Hanks, Marshall Whitehead

1986: David A. Kent, Donald G. Beuthel

1987: Hugh W. Johnston, William A. Coffey

1988: Fred E. Foldvary, Betty Killingbeck

ATA Exhibiton Award

The ATA will present either a best in topicals gold medal or certificate to any annual philatelic show. This award will be given to the exhibitor of the best topical exhibit. Criteria for the award are:

1. The show must provide a separate classification for topicals.

2. The following ATA definition for topicals must be used: "Topical collecting is defined as forming a collection of philatelic material selected and arranged by subject, design or theme rather than by country or issuance or type of postal service rendered."

3. Brochures on ATA and topical collecting must be distributed at the show.

4. The exhibition chairman must supply the name and address of the winner as well as the title of the winning exhibit to the ATA director of awards.

5. The basis of topical judging shall be: presentation, 15 points; topical/thematic knowledge — originality, 5 points; development of theme, 25 points; topical research, 15 points; philatelic elements — condition, 5 points; philatelic items, 15 points; scarcity, 10 points; philatelic information, 10 points. Total, 100 points.

For the medal, the show must have more than 500 pages on exhibit. In addition, the ATA medal winner must earn a bronze or better in the competition.

For the certificate, any annual show meeting the five aforementioned criteria and not qualifying for an ATA gold medal will qualify for a best in topicals certificate.

Silver and bronze ATA medals are also available for purchase.

The following stamp shows are eligible for the ATA youth award for the best youth topical/thematic exhibit: all regional or national shows with three or more youth exhibitors, all youth exhibitions with five or more youth exhibitors, or all local shows with five or more youth exhibitors.

All inquiries concerning ATA awards should be directed to Arlene Crosby, ATA Director of Awards, 1348 Union N.E., Grand Rapids, Mich. 49505.

ATA Topical Publications

Publications of the ATA will be found listed in this almanac under Literature.

ATA Slide Program Loan Service

ATA full-color slide programs include more than 60 titles and more than 5,000 slides. Each show consists of 30 to 100 slides and may run from 25 to 45 minutes. All are complete with a written script. Several also have audio cassette taped scripts. This service is open to members and non-members in the 50 states.

For information on any of the following programs, contact the ATA Slide Librarian, Fred Gomba, Box 674, Sverna Park, Md. 21146. Please include a stamped, addressed envelope.

Shows are listed in alphabetical order. Those with single asterisks (*) are available with audio cassette tapes. Titles with double asterisks are available in a Kodak carousel tray and mailer.

50: Adventures in Topical Philately*
1: Americana on Foreign
61: American Revolution
2: Animals*
46: Astronomy
29: Bible Stories*
54: Bicycles on Stamps
6: Birds*
30: Christian Faith
64: Church Architecture
62: Columbian Exposition
53: Dogs on Stamps*
48: Drugs and Pharmacy
44: Easter, The Story of
32: English Religion
55: Europa*
57: Fairy Tales*
7: Fine Arts*
8: Fish and Fishing
11: Flowers, Series B*
12: Flowers, Series C
39: Geology
31: Helpers of Mankind
56: Hive and Honeybee
40: Horses*
67: Ice Age Art*
13: Insects and Butterflies
42: Lincoln's Life and Monuments*
43: Lions International*
14: Maps*
33: Masonic*
37: Medical History
15: Medical Subjects
65: Microscopes and Magnifying Glasses*
18: Music
41: National Parks and Monuments
36: Nurses
16: Nutrition
45: Old Glory Around the World
25: Olympic Games
63: Owls
19: Plants and Fruits
60: Prehistory*
68: Pyramids — Old and New*
20: Religion
49a: Rotary International*
49b: Rotary International**
52: Royalty on Stamps*
21: St. Benedict
22: Scouts

23: Ships*
35: Space*
24: Sports
26: Stamps on Stamps
66: That's Entertainment*
27: Trains
17: Tuberculosis
28: United Nations (World)
59: Jules Verne
70: Women on Stamps

ATA Information Service

The ATA's free Information Service consists of nearly 500 advanced collectors who have volunteered to answer ATA members' questions on more than 300 different topical subjects on stamps. First organized in 1951 for only 45 subjects and constantly expanded by new volunteers, the ATA Information Service aids members in obtaining information needed to write up their collections.

The complete list of service volunteers is available to ATA members.

Translation Service

The Translation Service is available to ATA members for philatelic correspondence and short articles in 24 different languages. This valuable service to ATA members is free of charge except for return postage.

The 46 linguists who serve as translators are proficient in Bulgarian, Chinese, Czech, Danish, Dutch, Esperanto, Estonian, French, German, Hebrew, Hungarian, Italian, Latin, Latvian, Norwegian, Portuguese, Romanian, Russian, Slovak, Spanish, Swedish, Tagalog, Thai and Ukranian.

Heirs and Estates Service

The vital Heirs and Estates Service has a worldwide committee willing to help evaluate philatelic holdings of deceased ATA members and make recommendations on the disposal of such collections. ATA urges collectors to keep records of the purchase prices and/or current estimated value of their collections, and to record instructions for disposition upon death to be placed with the person's will so that the wishes of the deceased may be followed.

A specific method of liquidation cannot be recommended until the collection has been evaluated. Once this is completed, an ATA Heirs and Estates Committee member will recommend methods of disposition best suited to the particular collection. These may include sale at auction, private sale to a dealer, private sale of various individual parts of a collection to different dealers, ATA sales service, or private negotiation to interested collectors.

Gummed labels for insertion in stamp albums to make heirs aware of this service are available at cost from the ATA. Additional information is available from the ATA.

Checklist Service

The ATA Checklist Service director serves as a resource person for those checklists for which no handbook has been published. In addition, information to older handbooks is updated, and data for shorter lists that have a more limited interest and are not published in the ATA's journal is provided.

Normally, the checklists consist of country, date of issue, catalog number and brief description. Most lists are from one to 10 pages in length and are available to ATA members for 15¢ per page. More than 200 checklists are on file.

Catalog Number Conversion Service

This service for ATA members is aimed at providing catalog numbers to collectors who do not have access to certain catalogs other than the one they regularly use.

The service is particularly helpful to non-U.S. members who need Scott catalog numbers, but have only some other catalog as a reference, and for U.S. members seeking various European catalog numbers. The service charges only $1 or two International Reply Coupons per 25 conversions.

Council of Philatelic Organizations

The Council of Philatelic Organizations is composed of nearly 450 national, regional and local stamp clubs, societies and dealers united to promote stamp collecting. COPO is the largest umbrella group ever assembled within the hobby.

The council was formed for the sole purpose of promoting stamp collecting by providing a means for cooperation, information exchange, and interaction among member organizations and the public.

Membership is open only to organizations; individuals are not eligible to join. Commercial firms and businesses may hold associate memberships with the same rights and privileges as non-commercial groups.

There is no membership fee or required annual membership dues. However, all COPO activities are funded by voluntary contributions from its members.

Every stamp organization is eligible to become a member of COPO, with equal voting privileges. Each member organization, regardless of size, has one vote and one official delegate, who is eligible to help elect COPO's governing body, the board of directors.

The annual election meeting is usually held in the fall in New York City, at the ASDA National Postage Stamp Show.

COPO has received tax-exempt status under Section 501 (c) (3) of the Internal Revenue Code, which means all donations of money or philatelic property are completely deductible on individual Federal Income Tax returns.

The council does not compete for membership with any stamp group already established and devotes its full efforts and resources to bringing people into stamp collecting.

The council plans a variety of efforts — publicity campaigns, educational programs and special stamp exhibitions — to draw the attention of the non-collector and interest him in collecting stamps.

COPO is a united front, representing diverse elements of stamp collecting. It cooperates with the United States Postal Service to promote the hobby. COPO and the USPS jointly sponsored the first National Stamp Collecting Month in October 1981.

The theme of the first National Stamp Collecting Month was "Discover Stamp Collecting — The Hobby of a Lifetime." COPO considered its 1981 effort to be the largest, most concentrated promotional venture on behalf of the hobby ever attempted in the United States up to that time.

The USPS, in addition to providing post office lobby displays, banners and posters, distributed more than 750,000 copies of "Introduction to Stamp Collecting," a 32-page basic informational booklet.

Each October since then, COPO has issued a cacheted cover for National Stamp Collecting Month, and the Postal Service has provided a special cancellation.

Formation

The need for an effective organization to represent the hobby as a whole became apparent in the past 10 years, when significant changes in the hobby had been observed.

Despite many individual promotional efforts, there was no unified effort being made until the late 1970s to advocate the hobby and its educational benefits or to guide its development.

The need for cohesive action was discussed by a group of prominent stamp collectors at the National Postage Stamp Show in November 1978. There, the seeds of COPO were sown.

Nine major national stamp organizations were again invited to a discussion in March 1979 in New York, during INTERPEX. As a result, a non-profit "stamps council" was proposed.

Preliminary organizational work continued, and on Oct. 6, 1979, a draft copy of the articles of incorporation was signed by representatives of the nine organizations at the Sheraton Hotel in Philadelphia during SEPAD.

The nine organizations and their representatives were:

American Academy of Philately: Milton Mitchell

American Philatelic Congress: Sidney Schneider

American Philatelic Society: John E. Foxworth Jr.

American Stamp Dealers' Association: Lewis F. Shull

American Topical Association: George B. Griffenhagen

Bureau Issues Association: E. Ray Shank

Collectors Club of New York: F. Burton Sellers

The Philatelic Foundation: John C. Chapin

Society of Philatelic Americans: Milton Mitchell

It was decided that these nine organizations would constitute the acting board of directors for COPO, and the first meeting was set for the following month in New York. The nine representatives elected Foxworth acting president and Shank acting secretary.

COPO was officially voted into existence in New York on Nov. 10, 1979, as the articles of incorporation had been signed by the presidents of eight of the nine organizers. The ninth signature was obtained later.

The first meeting of COPO was held Nov. 22, 1980, in New York. By that time, bylaws had been adopted, an application for federal tax exemption had been filed, and COPO membership had grown to 124 organizations.

The original nine-member board was enlarged to include 15 organizations. Information about COPO is available from Box COPO, State College, Pa. 16803-8340.

Leadership

Organizations, not individuals, are elected to the COPO board of directors. Each organization appoints a representative to act on its behalf.

Officers are elected from the membership of the board of directors for two-year terms. The next election is scheduled for fall 1989.

Representatives are listed in parentheses.

Officers

President: American Philatelic Society (Patricia A. Siskin)

Vice President: Universal Ship Cancellation Society (David A. Kent)

Secretary: Eire Philatelic Association (Patricia S. Walker)

Treasurer: American Topical Association (George Griffenhagen)

Member at Large: Junior Philatelists of America (Kenneth P. Martin)

Board of Directors

Term expires 1989

American Philatelic Society (Patricia A. Siskin)

Bureau Issues Association (John Hotchner)

Collectors Club of New York (Robert P. Odenweller)

Universal Ship Cancellation Society (David Kent)

Postal History Society (W. Danforth Walker)

Term expires 1991

American Air Mail Society (Stephen Reinhard)

American First Day Cover Society (E. Lee Howard)

American Topical Association (George B. Griffenhagen)

Junior Philatelists of America (Kenneth P. Martin)

Virginia Philatelic Federation (Allen D. Jones)

Term expires 1993

American Philatelic Congress (Diane Boehret)

American Stamp Dealers' Association (Lewis F. Shull)

Eire Philatelic Association (Patricia S. Walker)

Philatelic Foundation (Roberto Rosende)

Nojex (Samuel S. Goldsticker)

COPO Membership

Aeronutronic Stamp Club, Irvine, Calif.

Aerophilatelic Federation of the Americas

Aksarben Stamps, Omaha, Neb.

Albuquerque (N.M.) Philatelic Society

Aldrich School Stamp Club, Howell, N.J.

Allison (Iowa) Stamp Club

Ambler Stamp Club

American Air Mail Society
American Festivals
American First Day Cover Society
American First Day Cover Foundation
American Philatelic Brokerages
American Philatelic Congress
American Philatelic Research Library
American Philatelic Society
American Stamp Dealers' Association
American Topical Association
Americana Unit (ATA/APS)
Arge U.S./Canada
Arizona Philatelic Rangers
Arizona Society of Topical Philatelists, Tempe, Ariz.
Armstrong Activities Association
Art Cover Exchange
Artex Stamps
Asheville (N.C.) Stamp Club Inc.
Athens (Ga.) Philatelic Society
Athens (Ohio) Stamp Club
Atlanta (Ga.) Stamp Collectors Club
Atoz Stamp Club
Augsburg American Stamp and Coin Club
Austin Philatelic Club, Chicago, Ill.
Austin (Texas) Stamp Club
Badger Stamp Club
Baltimore (Md.) Philatelic Society
Bandon (Ore.) Stamp Club
Baraboo (Wis.) Area Stamp Club
Basilic Philatelic Society, Bronx, N.Y.
Ben Franklin Stamp Club, Long Beach, Calif.
Ben Franklin Stamp Club, Santa Ana, Calif.
Ben Franklin Stamp Club, Albert City, Iowa
Bicentennial Stamps and Covers
Bick International, Van Nuys, Calif.
Black Heritage and History, Chicago, Ill.
Black River Stamp Club, Elyria, Ohio
Bloomfield (N.J.) Philatelic Society
Boca (Fla.) Century Stamp and Coin Club
Boeing Employees Stamp Club, Kent, Wash.
Bowie (Md.) Stamp Club
Boys Club Sarasota (Fla.)
Branford (Conn.) Philatelic Society
Brattleboro (Vt.) Stamp Club
Brazil Philatelic Association
Bright Ideas, Washington, D.C.
Brookhaven (Pa.) Stamp Club
Brower's Stamp and Coins, Florence, Ore.
Buffalo Stamp Club, Apollo, Pa.
Bureau Issues Association
Bux-Mont Stamp Club, Warminster, Pa.
CAP Townsend Stamp Club, Clearwater, Fla.
California Collectors Club
Calvary Lutheran Philatelic Society, Lincoln Park, Mich.
Cardinal Spellman Philatelic Museum
Carto Philatelists, New York, N.Y.
Casey Jones Rail Road Unit (ATA)
Castle Country Coin and Stamp, Price, Utah
Centerville Stamp Club, Winchester, Ind.
Central Coast Stamp Club, Lompoc, Calif.
Central Florida Stamp Club, Orlando, Fla.
Central Michigan Philatelic Society, Lansing, Mich.
Central Suffolk Auction Inc., Patchogue, N.Y.
Chai Chapter SIP, Rockaway Park, N.Y.
Champaign-Urbana (Ill.) Stamp Club
Christmas Philatelic Club, Long Beach, Calif.
Christopher Columbus Philatelic Society
Cincinnati (Ohio) Philatelic Society
The Classic Collector, Albuquerque, N.M.
Clearwater (Fla.) Stamp Club
Clermont County (Ohio) Stamp Club
Club of Channel Islands Collectors
Club Filatelico of Barranguilla (Colombia)
Club Philatelique de St. Leonard (Quebec)
Cobb County (Ga.) Stamp Club
Collectors Club of Akron (Ohio)
Collectors Club of Chicago (Ill.)
Collectors Club of Dallas (Texas)
Collectors Club of Kansas City (Kan.)
Collectors Club of New York
Collier County (Fla.) Stamp Club
Colorado Springs (Colo.) Stamp Club
Company B Limited, England
Confederate Stamp Alliance
Connecticut Philatelic Society
Corn Belt Philatelic Society, Bloomington, Ill.
Cortlandt Stamp Club, Montrose, N.Y.
Coryell's Ferry Stamp Club, Yardley, Pa.
Council of Northern California Philatelic Society
Crireq Stamp Club, Canada
Criterien Philatelic Service, Forestville, Conn.
Croatian Philatelic Society

Dallas (Texas) Philatelic Society
Dana Okey, San Diego, Calif.
Dan'l Webster Stamps, Portales, N.M.
Dayton (Ohio) Stamp Club
Dearborn (Mich.) Stamp Club
Delray Beach (Fla.) Stamp Club
Dilltown (Pa.) Stamp Club
Dogs on Stamps Unit
Dolley Madison Stamp Club, Falls Church, Va.
DuPont Stamp Club, Hockessin, Del.
E. and C. August, Walpole, N.H.
Eastern Prince William Stamp Club, Fredericksburg, Va.
Edmonton (Alberta, Canada) Stamp Club
Eire Philatelic Association
Ellyson Collectors Club, Pensacola, Fla.
Empire State Postal History Society
Errors, Freaks and Oddities Collectors Club
Euclid (Ohio) Stamp Club
Europa Study Unit
Evansville (Ind.) Stamp Club
F. Abel Elementary School, Sarasota, Fla.
Fairfield (Conn.) Philatelic Society
Fall River (Mass.) Philatelic Society
Fargo Moorhead (Minn.) Philatelic Society
Federated Philatelic Clubs of Southern California
Ferndale Stamp Club, Palm Beach Garden, Fla.
Fire Service in Philately
First Day Cover Collectors of Wisconsin
Ned Fishkin Ltd., Chicago, Ill.
Flint Hills Stamp Club, Manhattan, Kan.
Fond du Lac (Wis.) Stamp Club
Fort Findlay (Ohio) Stamp Club
Fort Lauderdale (Fla.) Stamp Club
Fort Steuben Stamp Club, Steubenville, Ohio
Fox Valley Stamp Club, Aurora, Ill.
Franklin D. Roosevelt Philatelic Society
Fulton (N.Y.) Stamp Club
Garden City Stamp Club, Missoula, Mont.
German Philatelic Society, Milwaukee Chapter No. 18
Germany Philatelic Society
Glen Ellyn (Ill.) Stamp Club
Golden Gate Stamp Club, San Francisco, Calif.
Gopher Stampers, Prior Lake, Minn.
Graphics Philately Association
Greater Hazleton (Pa.) Area Stamp Club
Greater Pittsburgh First Day Cover Club
Green Bay (Wis.) Philatelic Society
Guam Stamp Club
Haiti Philatelic Society
Hardware City Stamp Club, New Britain, Conn.
Harold Herman, Bayside, N.Y.
Harrison Stamp and Coin Club, White Plains, N.Y.
Hattiesburg (Miss.) Stamp Club
Hawthorne Stamp Club, Oak Park, Ill.
Heart of Texas Stamp Club, Waco, Texas
Hendersonville (N.C.) Stamp Club
Hereford (Texas) Stamp Club
Hollywood (Fla.) Stamp Club
Holston Stamp Club, Johnson City, Tenn.
Horace Harrison and Associates, Stevenson, Md.
Howard County Stamp Club, Columbia, Md.
Humboldt Collectors Club, Eureka, Calif.
Huntington Stamp Club, East Northport, N.Y.
Illinois Math and Science Academy
Illinois Postal History Society
Indiana Stamp Club
Intercontinental Philatelics
Inter-Governmental Philatelic Corp.
International Association of Space Philatelists
International Guild of Vatican Philatelists
International Society of Worldwide Stamp Collectors
International Stamp Collectors Society
Iowa Women's Philatelic Society, Des Moines, Iowa
Irvine (Calif.) Stamp and Coin Club
Italian American Stamp Club, Milwaukee, Wis.
J. & D. Paschke, Marblefaus, Texas
J & L Stamp Co., Lovington, N.M.
J.P. Philatelics, Salt Lake City, Utah
Jacques C. Schiff Jr. Inc., Ridgefield Park, N.J.
Jamaica Bay West Stamp Club, Fort Myers, Fla.
JAPOS Study Group
Jockey Hollow Stamp Club, Morristown, N.J.
Johnstown (Pa.) Stamp Club
Johnstown (Pa.) Junior Stamp Club
Joplin (Mo.) Stamp Club
Joseph E. Krois Jr. Inc., Southampton, N.Y.
Junior Ambassadors
Junior Philatelists of America

Joseph Kenton, Kansas City, Mo.
Kalamazoo (Mich.) Stamp Club
Kenneth F. Chapman, England
Korea Stamp Society Inc., Lebanon, Pa.
Laguna Hills (Calif.) Stamp Club
Lake County (Ill.) Philatelic Society
Lake Minnetonka (Minn.) Stamp Club
Lansdowne-Upper Darby Stamp Club, Yeadon, Pa.
Latin American Philatelic Society
Law Enforcement Study Unit
Learning With Stamps, Orwell, Ohio
Lerner's, Suisun, Calif.
Lewis and Clark Stamp Club, Bismark, N.D.
Liberty Philatelic, Brewster, N.Y.
Linn's Stamp News, Sidney, Ohio
Lions Club of Sea Point (South Africa) Stamp Club
Lions International Stamp Club
Lions Stamp Club Chapter No. 2, Rockville, Md.
Littleton (N.H.) Stamp and Coin Co.
Local Post Collectors Society
Long Beach (Calif.) Stamp Club
Los Alamos (N.M.) Stamp Collectors Association
Louisville (Ky.) Stamp Society Inc.
Lowell School Ben Franklin Stamp Club, Waukesha, Wis.
Lynchburg (Va.) Stamp Club
M.S. Roe, Morganville, N.J.
MacIntosh Middle School, Sarasota, Fla.
Madison County Bicentennial Stamp Club, Anderson, Ind.
Maggie's Mart, Baytown, Texas
Mailer's Postmark Permit Club
Main Exchange, Waukesha, Wis.
Malaria Philatelists International
Manatee Stamp Club, Holmes Beach, Fla.
Manchester Philatelic Society, Rockville, Conn.
Manchester Stamp Club, North Salem, N.H.
George Martin, Yakima, Wash.
Maryland Stamp Club
Masonic Stamp Unit, Ogden, Utah
Mathematical Study Unit
Maximum Card Study Unit
Meadville (Pa.) Stamp Club
Medina County (Ohio) Stamp Club
Memphis (Tenn.) Stamp Collectors Society
Merchantville Stamp Club, Cherry Hill, N.J.
Mesa (Ariz.) Stamp Club
Meso-American Archaeology Study Unit
Metropolitan Air Post Society, Bloomfield, N.J.
Mexico-Elmhurst Philatelic Society International
Mille Cachets, Canton, Texas
Miller Elementary School, Sarasota, Fla.
Milwaukee (Wis.) Philatelic Society
Missile Stamp Club, Melbourne, Fla.
Mobile Post Office Society
Modern Postal History Society
Monadnock Stamp Club, Keene, N.H.
Montgomery (Ala.) Area Stamp Club
Motor City Stamp and Cover Club, Hazel Park, Mich.
Mound City Stamp Club, St. Louis, Mo.
Mount Joy (Pa.) Stamp Club
Mountainside (N.J.) Stamps, Coins
Mountain State Stamp Club, Elkins, W.Va.
Mulready Research Foundation, Laguna Hills, Calif.
Mystic Stamp Co. Inc., Camden, N.Y.
Nancy L. Davis, Hurst, Texas
Napoleon Age Philatelists
National Philatelic Collection
National Wildlife Galleries
Nevada (Mo.) Coin and Stamp Club
Nevada Stamp Study Society
Newburgh (N.Y.) Stamp Club
New Jersey Stamp Dealers' Association
New Mexico Philatelic Association
Niagara Frontier Stamp Club, Lewiston, N.Y.
Nippon Philatelics, Carmel-by-the-Sea, Calif.
Nippon Stamp Club of New England
Norfolk (Va.) Philatelic Society
North Central Stamp and Coin Club, Hermansville, Mich.
Northeastern Federation of Stamp Clubs
North Chautauqua Philatelic Society
Northern Colorado Philatelic Society
Northern Neck Stamp Club, Windmill Point, Va.
North Georgia Chapter, AFDCS
North Jersey Federated Stamp Clubs
North Jersey Stamp Club
North Shore Philatelic Society, Chicago, Ill.
NPIMCO (Cachet Makers), Sarasota, Fla.
Oak Ridge North Ben Franklin Club, Conroe, Texas
Ohio Postal History Society

Old Colony Philatelists, South Easton, Mass.
Old World Archaeological Study Unit
Olean (N.Y.) Area Stamp Club
Oneco Elementary School, Sarasota, Fla.
Orange County (Calif.) Philatelic Society
Oregon Stamp Society Inc.
Oswego (N.Y.) Stamp Club
Outgamie Philatelic Society, Appleton, Wis.
Oxford Philatelic Society, Philadelphia, Pa.
Palmdale Stamp Club, Lancaster, Calif.
Palo Duro Stamp Club, Albuquerque, N.M.
Park Cities Philatelic Society, Dallas, Texas
Park Forest Stamp Club, Homewood, Ill.
Patchogue (N.Y.) Stamp Club
Peachtree Stamp and Study Club, Elkhart, Ind.
Penn State Stamp Club
Pennsylvania Postal History Society
Pennyrile Philatelic Society, Hopkinsville, Ky.
Penpex, San Carlos, Calif.
Pensacola (Fla.) Philatelic Society
Perfins, El Paso, Texas
Perfins Club
The Perforation Gauge, West Hartford, Conn.
H.S. Perlin Co. Inc., La Jolla, Calif.
Permit Imprint Collectors Society
Philatelic Emporium, Rumford, Maine
Philatelic Foundation
The Philatelic Journalist
Philatelic Society of Atascadero (Calif.)
Philatelic Society of Pittsburgh (Pa.)
Philippine Stamp Dealers' Association
Pine Tree Stamp Club, Caribou, Maine
Pleasure Ridge Park Philatelic Society, Louisville, Ky.
Polonus Philatelic Society
Port St. Lucie Stamp Club, Stuart, Fla.
Postal History Society Inc.
Poster Editor
Potomac (Md.) Philatelic Society
Pottstown (Pa.) Area Stamp Club
Poway (Calif.) Stamp Club
Prall Stamp Club, Staten Island, N.Y.
Promenade Stamp Co., Pompano Beach, Fla.
Public School No. 8 Stamp Club, Staten Island, N.Y.
Puerto Rico Philatelic Society
Pugh Cachets, The Woodlands, Texas
Quail Trail Mail Stamp Co., Tucson, Ariz.
Queen City-Warren Stamp and Cover Club
R.G. Simpson and Co., St. Petersburg, Fla.
R.J. Stamps, Albertson, N.Y.
Raleigh (N.C.) Stamp Club
Razorback Stamp Club
Rhode Island Philatelic Society
Richard Novick, Uniondale, N.Y.
Roadrunner Stamp Club
Robert J. Murrin Inc., St. Petersburg, Fla.
Rochester (N.Y.) Philatelic Association
Routing Labels Society
Rubber City Stamp Club, Akron, Ohio
Rumex Stamp Club, Rumford, Maine
Rushstamps, Lyndhurst, England
Sacramento (Calif.) Philatelic Society
Saginaw Valley (Mich.) Stamp Society
St. Augustine YMCA Stamp Club
St. Helena and Dependencies Philatelic Society
St. Mary's Stamp Club, Lee, Mass.
St. Petersburg (Fla.) Stamp Club
Sam Houston Auction
Samuel Brown School, Peabody, Mass.
Samuel Osgood Stamp Club, Methuen, Mass.
San Antonio (Texas) Philatelic Association
San Diego (Calif.) Stamp Club
San Francisco Pacific (Calif.) Philatelic Society
San Joaquin Philatelic Society, Manteca, Calif.
Santa Fe (N.M.) Stamp Club
Scandinavian Collectors Club No. 5, Beverly, Mass.
Scandinavian Collectors Club, Newtonville, Mass.
Scandinavian Collectors Club Chapter 17
Scandinavian Philatelic Foundation
Scott Publishing Co.
Scouts on Stamps Society International
Selwyn Stamps, Arlington, Va.
Sepad, Horsham, Pa.
Sharon Stamp Club, Hermitage, Pa.
Shrub Oak (N.Y.) Library Stamp Club
Shull Service, Crofton, Md.
Silver Spring Shores Stamp Club, Ocala, Fla.
Slater Stamp Club, Pawtucket, R.I.

Sociedad Filatelica Regiomontana
Society of Australian Specialists/Oceania
Society of Costa Rica Collectors
Society of Olympic Collectors
Sodus (N.Y.) Stamp Club
South Metro Stamp Club, Atlanta, Ga.
Southern Nevada Stamp Club
Southern New Jersey Stamp Club
Souvenir Card Collectors Society
Space Topics Study Group
Sperry Stamp Club, Great Neck, N.Y.
Sports Philatelists International
Springfield Delco Stamp Club, Yeadon, Pa.
Springfield (Va.) Stamp Club
Springfield (Mo.) Stamp and Coin Collectors Club
SRL Stamps, New York, N.Y.
Stamp and Coin Exchange, St. Louis, Mo.
Stamp Club of Friendship, Monterey Park, Calif.
Stamp Collector, Albany, Ore.
Stamp Expo, Van Nuys, Calif.
Stampic Olympics, Simi Valley, Calif.
Stamps Are Fun Club, Dalton, Ga.
Stamps on Stamps Centenary Unit
Stamptrotters Society of Kingston (N.Y.)
Stampworld, Albuquerque, N.M.
Stanislaus Stamp Society, Modesto, Calif.
Stanley Piller and Associates, Oakland, Calif.
State Revenue Society
Sullivan County (N.Y.) Philatelic Society
Sun City West (Ariz.) Coin and Stamp Club
Suncoast Philatelic Society
Susquehanna Valley Stamp Study Club
Taconic Philatelic Society, Poughkeepsie, N.Y.
Texas Stamp Dealers' Association
TRW Stamp Club, Redondo Beach, Calif.
Tucson (Ariz.) Stamp Club
Tuscora Stamp Club, New Philadelphia, Ohio
Tuvalu Kiribati Philatelic Society
U Sivado — Geo Phila, Glendale, Calif.
Ukrainian Philatelic and Numismatic Society
U.S. Cancellation Club
United Postal Stationery Society
United States 1869 Pictorial Research Associates
USS Arizona Chapter 78, USCS
U.S. Souvenir Page Society
Universal Ship Cancellation Society, Chapter 78
Universal Ship Cancellation Society, Edgewater, Md.
University City Stamp Club, Gainesville, Fla.
Upper Keys Collectors Club, Key Largo, Fla.
VA Medical Center Stamp Club, Brooklyn, N.Y.
Valdosta (Ga.) Stamp Club
Vancouver Island Philatelic Society
Vidiforms Co. Inc., Congers, N.Y.
Virginia Beach Stamp Club
Virginia Philatelic Federation
Virginia Postal History Society
Visalia (Calif.) Philatelic Society
Walla Walla Valley (Wash.) Philatelic Society
Wallace Stamp Co., Port Washington, N.Y.
Waltham Stamp Club, Newton Centre, Mass.
WaMarVa Philippine Philatelic Study Group
War Cover Club
Washington Crossing (Pa.) Card Collectors Club
Washington Philatelic Society
Washington Press, Florham Park, N.J.
Waukesa County (Wis.) Philatelic Society
Wauwatosa (Wis.) Philatelic Society
Westfield Stamp Club, Granby, Conn.
Westpex, San Carlos, Calif.
West Suburban Stamp Club, Plymouth, Mich.
White Rose Philatelic Society, Glen Rock, Pa.
Wilkinsburg (Pa.) Stamp Club
Winston A. Ross Co., Baldwin Place, N.Y.
Wisconsin Federation of Stamp Clubs
Wisconsin Postal History Society
Wisconsin Valley Philatelic Society
Women's History Series of FDCS
Yakima Valley (Wash.) Stamp Club
Ye Olde King's Highway Stamp Club, Darien, Conn.
Yellowstone Stamp and Coin Collectors Society, Canada
Yucca Stamp Club, Hobbs, N.M.
Zane's Trace Philatelic Society, Zanesville, Ohio
Zippy Collectors Club

Philatelic Writers' Organizations

Philatelic writers' organizations are established to promote journalism in the field of philately as well as to give recognition to worthy philatelic writers.

American Philatelic Society Writers Unit No. 30

Sixteen interested, nationally known philatelic writers held a breakfast meeting on Sept. 24, 1967, at the Hotel Robert Treat, during the 81st annual convention of the American Philatelic Society at Newark, N.J. At this meeting, the Writers Unit was formed.

An immediate application was made to the American Philatelic Society for "unit" status, which was obtained. The writers requested that the society be issued the number 30 in recognition of the newsman's symbol for the termination of a story. Writer's Unit No. 30 was born.

It was the consensus of those present that a national organization be formed that would bring this nation's philatelic writers into one group for the mutual exchange of knowledge and assistance at a very low annual cost.

By unanimous approval of those present, the following were named as the new organization's officers:

Chairman (later changed to president), David Lidman;

Vice chairman (vice president), James M. Chemi;

Secretary-treasurer, C.C. Cratsenberg.

The new officers formulated a constitution and bylaws, and established a meeting, or seminar, on philatelic writing at all future APS spring meetings and annual conventions. This has become the annual WU seminar at Stampshow and the twice-yearly WU breakfasts.

At the Writers Unit meeting during the 1968 APS spring meeting, positive steps were taken to establish a National Philatelic Literature Exhibition as part of the APS annual convention. The first National Literature Exhibition was held in Rochester, N.Y., in September 1968. There has been a philatelic literature exhibition in each APS Stampshow since that time.

A committee composed of Daniel Vooys, James Chemi and George T. Turner agreed to set up the rules of the classification and the entry of exhibits. The committee's work was completed in time to allow 75 entries, far beyond the expectation of all concerned.

Over the years, the WU has worked with the APS Judges Accreditation Committee to help establish guidelines for judging philatelic literature. It has supported the establishment of literature exhibitions at stamp shows across the country.

Officers

David Lidman was the unit's first president, followed by George M. Martin and James M. Chemi. Upon Chemi's death in 1976, vice president John E. Foxworth Jr. became president and served until his election as APS president in 1977. William Bauer was elected president to succeed Foxworth.

Previous vice presidents of the unit have been James Chemi, George Martin, John Foxworth, Barbara W. de Violini, and Charles O. Emery. C.C. Cratsenberg was the sole occupant of the office of secretary-treasurer from the inception of the unit until 1979, when the office was separated into its two components. The position of secretary was filled by Barbara W. de Violini and that of treasurer by Ray Crow.

Current officers are Robert de Violini, president; John T. Nugent, vice president (east); Thomas Current, vice president (west); George Griffenhagen, secretary-treasurer; and Ken Lawrence, editor.

During 1970, the three unit officers found that additional experienced help was required to properly carry out the increasing number of new projects and expand those already introduced. The membership, by individual ballots, overwhelmingly approved the addition of an advisory council with a minimum of four members, up to a maximum of nine, with the immediate past president serving as the council chairman. The work of the council is most evident in the progress of many of the new unit programs and services.

The present council members are Joe Frye, chairman; George Martin; John Foxworth Jr.; Ernst Cohn; Diane Manchester; Randolph Neil; Steven Rod; and William Welch.

Broken Pen Award

In 1970, at Honolulu, Hawaii, as a spur-of-the-moment gag award, a hastily made plaque was made from the end of a corrugated packing box for canned pineapple juice. Properly inscribed with a felt tip pen, it became the first of the now-traditional Broken Pen awards, given each year at the fall APS convention Writer's Breakfast.

Edward L. Willard, then APS president, was the first recipient. Until his death, his Broken Pen award was hung in a prominent place in his office, treasured as a tongue-in-cheek award that represented a special honor. Each recipient since the original presentation receives a much more attractive plaque. Subsequent winners of the Broken Pen award, by year and site of the award, have been:

1971 — Herman Herst Jr., San Antonio, Tex.
1972 — C.C. Cratsenberg, New Haven, Conn.
1973 — C.W. Christian, Los Angeles, Calif.
1974 — Dr. Charles W. Wunsch, Chicago, Ill.
1975 — William T. Amos, Columbus, Ohio
1976 — Maryette B. Lane, Memphis, Tenn.
1977 — Fred S. Wolfe, San Francisco, Calif.
1978 — Barbara W. de Violini, Indianapolis, Ind.
1979 — Irwin Weinberg, Boston, Mass.
1980 — Ernst Cohn, Spokane, Wash.

Although the award has not been presented for a number of years, there are plans to resurrect it at a future WU breakfast.

'Philatelic Communicator'

As with any widespread organization, an informative journal is a primary means of retaining membership. In the Writers Unit, the journal is the *Philatelic Communicator*. Originally called the *News Bulletin*, it was first edited by James Chemi and contained only four pages.

Following the first issue, Klass van Ingen was appointed editor and David C. Stump publisher. After 18 months, Stump became both editor and publisher until 1973, when Joe F. Frye became editor-publisher. The publication was edited by Barbara R. Mueller from 1981 to 1988. In 1989, the editorship was assumed by Ken Lawrence. Joe Frye continues as the publisher.

The Writers Unit is proud of the fact that it was the early donor of a $1,000 pledge for the new American Philatelic Research Library building at State College, Pa., and continues to support this project.

Hall of Fame

In 1974, the National Philatelic Writers Hall of Fame was established. A large plaque was obtained with 100 individual nameplates, and the initial list of honorees was unveiled at the Writer's Breakfast in Chicago. Each honoree's name, principal writing field, and the year of selection for the Hall of Fame is engraved on the individual plates. Deceased honorees are further noted by dates of birth and death.

The plaque is hung permanently in the new American Philatelic Building Central Office in State College, Pa. It is updated yearly with the addition of new honorees, announced at the APS spring meeting Writer's Breakfast. A list of honorees follows, divided by date named to the Hall of Fame.

1974, Chicago, Ill.

Stanley Ashbrook
Winthrop S. Boggs
Lester G. Brookman
Richard McP. Cabeen
Dr. Caroll Chase
August A. Dietz Sr.
Edith M. Faulstich
Max G. Johl
George W. Linn

John N. Luff
Delf Norona
Elliot Perry
John W. Scott
Al Van Dahl
Prescot H. Thorp
William W. Wylie
Harry L. Lindquist
James B. Hatcher
Herman Herst Jr.
George F. Stilpen

1975, Columbus, Ohio

Henry M. Goodkind
Ralph A. Kimble
Harry Weiss
Daniel W. Vooys
Belmont Faries
Robert M. Spaulding Jr.

1976, Philadelphia, Pa.

Ralph A. Barry
Kent B. Stiles
Stephen G. Rich
James M. Chemi
Everett C. Erle
Douglas A. Patrick
Alex ter Braake

1977, New Orleans, La.

Thomas D. Perry
Bertram W. Poole
Willard O. Wylie
Ernest A. Kehr
Fred Jarrett
Mortimer Neinken

1978, Toronto, Ontario, Canada

Dr. L. Seale Holmes
William R. Stewart
Lyons F. Livingston
Edith R. Doane
Barbara R. Mueller
Dr. Felix D. Bertalanffy

1979, Denver, Colo.

Franklin R. Bruns Jr.
Henry W. Holcombe
Melvin H. Schoberlin
Lucius Jackson
George W. Brett
Earl P.L. Apfelbaum
Charles E. Foster

1980, London, England

George Turner
Frederick J. Melville
Maurice Williams
Robson Lowe
L. Norman Williams

1981, State College, Pa.

Lowell J. Ragatz
David Lidman

1982, Tucson, Ariz.

Edwin Mueller
Dr. William Reiner-Deutsch
Maryette B. Lane

1984, Denver, Colo.

Kenneth Wood

1986, Chicago, Ill.

Robert P. Alexander
James H. Baxter
Kenneth F. Chapman
Susan M. McDonald

1987, Toronto, Ont., Canada

Perham C. Nahl
Charles Towle
Roy White

1988, Reno, Nev.

R. Felix Ganz
Allen Kerr

1989, Cleveland, Ohio

J.W.R. Purves
Charles Fricke
C.W. Christian

Membership

From its start with 16 members in 1967, the Writers Unit has grown to more than 300 members, most of whom reside in the United States, Canada and Mexico, although many are from Western Europe, South and Central America, Africa, Asia and the Pacific Islands.

At the WU board meeting in 1986 at Ameripex, a new set of bylaws was approved and subsequently ratified by the membership. A significant change in these new bylaws was the elimination of the requirement that WU members had to be APS members.

The annual membership dues are $10 for members in the United States, $12.50 for those elsewhere in North America and $17 for all others. Membership is open to all philatelic authors, publishers, editors or columnists, regardless of membership in other philatelic organizations.

Further information and an application is available from George Griffenhagen, 2501 Drexel St., Vienna, Va. 22180.

Association Internationale des Journalistes Philateliques

Association Internationale des

Journalistes Philateliques (AIJP) was established in 1962 in Prague, Czechoslovakia, for the advancement of philatelic journalism.

The association conducts annual congresses and publishes a bulletin at intervals.

President of the AIJP is Dr. Anton van der Flier of The Netherlands; vice president (east), Jan Witkowski of Poland; vice president (west), Dr. Werner Bohne of the United States; secretary general, Fritz E. Baeker of West Germany; treasurer, Jean Frising of Luxembourg; and press secretary, Adolf Hujer of Czechoslovakia.

Recognized philatelic writers should contact Dr. Werner Bohne, Box 915678, Longwood, Fla. 32791-5678.

Philatelic Press Club, Inc.

The Philatelic Press Club Inc. was organized in 1964 as a guild dedicated to raising the standards of professional philatelic writing and to cooperate with postal administration members of the Universal Postal Union in exercising integrity in policies related to or affecting the stamp hobby.

By 1975, so many distinguished overseas writers had been invited and admitted that "International" was added to the corporate name.

Membership is by invitation only and is offered to recognized writers who contribute regular columns to stamp periodicals, metropolitan newspapers and other mass media, including radio and television.

The guild periodically publishes and distributes a *Report to Members*, which relays worldwide news information and leads received from correspondents on the six continents.

For several years, the IPPC presented annual awards to those postal administrations that provided members with outstanding news services.

Further membership information is available from David Kent, Box 127, New Britain, Conn. 06050.

Junior Philatelists of America

The Junior Philatelists of America was formed Jan. 1, 1976, with the merging of the Junior Philatelic Society of America and the Junior Division of the American Philatelic Society Writer's Unit No. 30.

The JPSA was founded July 10, 1963, by Robert J. Osterhoff, the organization's first president. The society fought an uphill battle for recognition and was refused APS affiliation in 1964.

The JPSA participated in its first national or international exhibition at Sipex held in Washington, D.C., in 1966. The society was established as an APS unit in 1967.

The Junior Division of the APS Writer's Unit was formed in 1971, the year the JPSA was granted national branch status by the Society of Philatelic Americans. The two groups co-existed until Jan. 1, 1976, when the merger was completed.

Since 1976, the JPA has participated to a great extent at Interphil 76 held in Philadelphia, Pa.; Capex 78 held in Toronto, Ont., Canada; and Ameripex 86 in Chicago, Ill. The society was also the only junior society that held meetings at Stampshow 79 held in Boston, Mass. The JPA plans to increase its involvement with national and regional exhibitions.

The society is incorporated as a non-profit corporation in Pennsylvania and has been recognized as a Section 501(c)(3) organization by the Internal Revenue Service since 1988.

There are three classes of membership in the JPA. Junior members are age 18 and younger when joining. The services and benefits of membership are geared towards these members. Many of the services and committees in the group are operated by the junior members. Chapter membership for junior stamp clubs and special junior contributing memberships are also available.

Adult supporting members are those older than age 18 when joining. These members show their support of the group's efforts and assist in an advisory and administrative capacity.

Graduate members are former members who have passed the age of 18 and have the same status as adult supporting members. The JPA has more than 700 active members and has issued more than 4,500 memberships since 1963.

Through a grant provided by the Council of Philatelic Organizations, the JPA publishes a series of informational pamphlets on stamp collecting. These are distributed through the mail, by clubs and at shows. The four titles currently in print are *Ten Easy Ways to Start Collecting Stamps*, *Search 'n' Find Puzzles for Stamp Collectors*, *How to Avoid Common Mistakes as a Beginning Stamp Collector*, and *Getting Started in Stamp Collecting*.

Many of these pamphlets are distributed outside of philatelic channels, using a wide variety of publications geared towards young people and school teachers. Copies of these pamphlets are sent along with information on the JPA and a glassine envelope with 20 worldwide stamps. Nearly 10,000 requests were received in 1988.

Services available to JPA members include an auction service, an exchange department, educational projects, library service, pen-pal service, stamp identification service, chapters and study groups. Current study groups include first-day covers, topicals, Europe and United States.

The society's bimonthly, illustrated publication is the *Philatelic Observer*.

Junior JPA Officers (Elected through 1990)

President: David Flack
First vice president: Martha Cunnings
Second vice president: David Bodnick
Directors-at-large: Angelo Martinez, Shan Peters
Past president: Glen Rivenbark

Committee Chairmen

Auction department: vacant
Awards chairman: vacant
Europe Study Group: Angelo Martinez

Editor, *Philatelic Observer:* Karen Weigt
Publicity chairman: Maria Sarantopoulos
Library services: Mark H. Winnegrad
Pen Pal chairman: vacant
Stamp identification: Kenneth Martin
United States Study Group: Mark Kaufman
Exchange service: Victor Pawlak

JPA Advisory Council (Appointed through 1989)

Chairman: Daniel Siegel
Executive secretary: John G. Taddy
Treasurer: Jeffrey D. Kaye
Educational projects: MaryAnn Bowman
Members-at-large: Victor Pawlak, Mark Winnegrad, MaryAnn Bowman, Dorothy B. Blaney, Cheryl B. Edgecomb, Steven J. Rod

JPA Awards

JPA exhibition awards include the JPA blue ribbon and the JPA research award, which are available to any local, regional or national shows upon request.

The JPA H.E. Harris medal, made available through a grant from H.E. Harris & Co. stamp firm, is awarded at all regional and national, as well as international shows.

The only requisite for receiving this award is a minimum of four youth entries in a show. Award recipients need not be JPA members.

These awards are presented free of charge by the JPA.

Membership

Further information concerning JPA membership and/or awards is available by sending a No. 10 stamped, addressed envelope to the JPA, Central Office, Box 701010, San Antonio, Texas 78270-1010.

Local Stamp Clubs

Following is a listing of stamp clubs that are registered with *Linn's* Club Center. Included are meeting days, location, time and contact person's name and address. *Linn's* urges groups omitted to contact the Club Center, Linn's Stamp News, Box 29, Sidney, Ohio 45365.

ALABAMA

DOTHAN: Wiregrass Stamp Club, first Monday, September to June, Northside Mall Community Room, Ross Clark Circle, 7 p.m. Roger Tuttle, 600 Highland St., Dothan, Ala. 36301.

FAIRHOPE: Eastern Shore Stamp Collectors, first and third Tuesday, Trinity Presbyterian Church, 7:15 p.m. Ian L. Robertson, Secretary-Treasurer, 117 Kiefer Ave., Fairhope, Ala. 36532.

HOOVER: Hoover Stamp Club, third Tuesday, Hoover Public Library, Conference Room, Hoover City Hall building. Bill Carlin, 2431 Titonka Road, Birmingham, Ala. 35244.

HUNTSVILLE: Huntsville Philatelic Club, first Monday and third Tuesday, Trinity United Methodist Church, Room A201, 607 Airport Road, 7:30 p.m. Ed Kazmierczak, Box 4395, Huntsville, Ala. 35815.

JACKSONVILLE: Calhoun County Stamp Club, second and fourth Tuesdays, Central Bank N.A., South Pelham, 7 p.m. R.C. Effinger, Box 279, Jacksonville, Ala. 36265-0279.

MONTGOMERY: Montgomery Area Stamp Club, second and fourth Thursdays, except for November and December (second Thursday), Highland Avenue Community Center, 1735 Highland Ave., 7 p.m. George D. Wall, 5741 Ainsworth Drive, Montgomery, Ala. 36117.

ALASKA

ANCHORAGE: Anchorage Philatelic Society, second and fourth Wednesdays, Z.J. Loussac Library, 3600 Denali St., 7:30 p.m. Judy Ireton, 505 Jordt Circle, Anchorage, Alaska 99504.

— Ptarmigan Coin & Stamp Society, second and fourth Mondays, 111 E. Fifth Ave., 7 p.m. Joe or Lorraine Russo, Box 91090, Anchorage, Alaska 99509-1090.

MISCELLANEOUS

Gastineau Philatelic Society, meeting on third Tuesday, Mountain View Senior Center, 7 p.m. Don Hitchcock, President, Box 20641, Juneau, Alaska 99802.

ARIZONA

GLENDALE: Germany Philatelic Society, Kachina Chapter 25, second Tuesday, Recreation Hall, Royal Glen Mobile Home Court, 7200 N. 43rd Ave., 7 p.m. Len Thumann, Box 1601, Sun City, Ariz. 85372-1601.

— Glencroft Stamp Club, third Thursday, 6510 W. Butler Drive, Apt. 100, 2 p.m. Robert A. Hartig, 6510 W. Butler Drive, Apt. 100, Glendale, Ariz. 85302.

PHOENIX: Arizona Precancel Club, fourth Monday, except December, Yucca Branch, Phoenix Public Library, 5648 N. 15th Ave., 7 p.m.-9. John T. Moore, Secretery, 7507 E. Latham St., Scottsdale, Ariz. 85257.

— Phoenix Philatelic Association, second Monday and fourth Wednesday, Los Olivos Center, 2802 E. Devonshire, 7 p.m. Steve Butler, Box 10337, Phoenix, Ariz. 85016.

SIERRA VISTA: Roadrunner Stamp Club, third Wednesday, Oscar Yrun Community Center, 7 p.m. Douglas Syson, 300 East Vista, Bisbee, Ariz. 85603.

SUN CITY: Sun City Stamp Club, first Monday and third Tuesday, (June to September, third Tuesday only), Marinette Recreation Center, 7 p.m. Fran Hoyt, 9413 Sandstone Drive, Sun City, Ariz. 85351.

TEMPE: Mesa Stamp Club, second and fourth Tuesdays, various locations in members homes, 7 p.m. Mary Thompson/Fred Scheuer, Box 2356, Mesa, Ariz. 85214.

TUCSON: The Armory Park Stamp Club, first and third Wednesday, 220 S. Fifth Ave., 2:30 p.m. Grace H. Martin, 7441 Calle Toluca, Tucson, Ariz. 85710.

— Tucson Stamp Club, first and third Tuesday, Armory Park Senior Citizens' Center, 220 5th Ave., 7 p.m. Carl H. Spitzer, 610 N. Bedford Drive, Tucson, Ariz. 85710.

— VAMC Stamp and Coin Club, Tuesdays and Thursdays, VAMC Stamp Room (auditorium), 9 a.m.-5 p.m. Charles R. Carn/Cora Tannenbaum, VAMC Stamp and Coin Club, c/o Chief Voluntary Suc., Tucson, Ariz. 85723.

ARKANSAS

FAYETTEVILLE: Fayetteville Stamp Club, third Thursday, Sequoyah United Methodist Church hall, 1910 Old Wire Road N., 7 p.m. Donald E. Cook, 1715 Horseshoe Drive, Springdale, Ark. 72764.

LITTLE ROCK: Pinnacle Stamp Club, fourth Thursday, Community Room, University Mall, 7 p.m. Nita Carter, 5 Leawood Circle, Little Rock, Ark. 72205.

CALIFORNIA

ALAMEDA: Alameda Stamp Club, first Tuesday, McKinley Park Recreation Center, Walnut Street and Buena Vista Avenue, 7:30 p.m. Albert R. Muller, Box 861, Oakland, Calif. 94604.

ARCADIA: Arcadia Stamp Club, second and fourth Tuesday, except December (second Tuesday only), Our Savior Lutheran Church, 512 W. Duarte Road, 7 p.m.-9. Walter P. Esparza, Box 787, Azusa, Calif. 91702-0787.

ATASCADERO: Atascadero Stamp Club, Wednesday, Atascadero State Hospital, Room NJA-1, 7 p.m. Tammy West, Atascadero State Hospital, Box 7001, Atascadero, Calif. 93423.

BURLINGAME: Peninsula Stamp Club, first and third Thursday, Burlingame Library Community Room, 480 Primrose Road, 8 p.m. J.W. Conner, Box 69, Burlingame, Calif. 94011.

CAMARILLO: Camarillo Stamp Club, second Thursday, Camarillo Senior Center, 1605 E. Burnley St.; fourth Thursday, Mercury Savings, 1656 Arneill Road, 7:30 p.m. Ruth G. Cox, 1708 Burnley St., Camarillo, Calif. 93010.

CULVER CITY: Philatelic Society of Los Angeles, first Tuesday, Culver City Library, 4975 Overland Blvd., 7:45 p.m.-9:45; fourth Tuesday, Westside Pavilion, 10800 W. Pico Blvd., third floor community room, 7:45 p.m.-9:45. Harold Wasserman, 11740 Wilshire Blvd., Apt. A-1809, Los Angeles, Calif. 90025.

DAVIS: Davis Stamp Club, first and third Wednesdays, Heart Savings and Loan, community room, Third and F streets., 7 p.m.-9. Anne Hance, Box 658, Davis, Calif. 95616.

DOWNEY: Downey Stamp Club, first Wednesday, Youth Hut, Maude Price School, 9525 Tweedy Lane, 7:30 p.m. Francis A. Bartolomeo, 9184 Buell St., Downey, Calif. 90241.

EL CAJON: East County Stamp Club, first and third Sundays, Home Savings, 396 N. Magnolia, 11 a.m. Jim Stewart, 4625 Calavo Drive, La Mesa, Calif. 92041.

EL TORO: Saddleback Stamp Club, second and fourth Wednesday, Mercury Savings and Loan, 23021 Lake Center Drive, 7 p.m. Eleanor A. Taylor, 1405 S. Ola Vista, San Clemente, Calif. 92672.

FORT BRAGG: Mendocino Coast Stamp Club, first Thursday, Fort Bragg Library, 7:30 p.m. Dennis M. Tuomala, Box 753, Fort Bragg, Calif. 95437.

FRESNO: Fresno Philatelic Society, first Sunday - 2 p.m., third Thursday - 7:30 p.m., Best by Far Restaurant, 3777 N. Clovis Ave. Terry Miller, President, Box 5694, Fresno, Calif. 93755.

GRASS VALLEY: Gold Country Stamp Club, first and third Thursday, Lyman Gilmore School library, Rough and Ready Highway, 7:30 p.m. R. Douglas Wright, Box 1076, Grass Valley, Calif. 95945.

LAGUNA HILLS: Laguna Hills Stamp Club, second and fourth Tuesday, Clubhouse 3, Leisure World, 1:30 p.m. President, Box 2142, Laguna Hills, Calif. 92653.

LAKEPORT: Lake County Stamp & Coin Club, first Friday, Gibraltar Savings meeting room, 890 Lakeport Blvd., 7:30 p.m. Art Thompson, President, 5830 Robin Hill Drive, No. 45, Lakeport, Calif. 95453.

LA MESA: La Mesa Philatelic Society, second and fourth Thursdays, Vista La Mesa Christian Church, 4210 Massachusetts Ave., 7:30 p.m. Larry Elliott, 10670 Snyder Road, La Mesa, Calif. 92041.

LONG BEACH: Long Beach Stamp Club, first and third Tuesday, including school holidays, Millkan High School cafeteria, 2800 Snowden Ave., 7:30 p.m. Beryl Z. Norris, Box 90042, Long Beach, Calif. 90809.

LOS ANGELES: Mexico-Elmhurst Philatelic Society International, Chapter One, Southern California, fourth Wednesday, California Federal Savings and Loan, 1900 E. Sunset Blvd., 7:30 p.m. Robert R. Jones, 2350 Bunker Hill Way, Costa Mesa, Calif. 92626.

— United Postal Stationery Society, Chapter No. 2, third Wednesday, 1900 Sunset Blvd., 7:30 p.m. Arthur Thomas, Box 48, Redlands, Calif. 92373.

MAGALIA: Paradise Stamp Club, second Tuesday, American Savings, 7 p.m. Thomas C. Ferrara, Box 3181, Chico, Calif. 95927-3181.

MODESTO: Stanislaus Stamp Club, second Tuesday, Homewood Village Mobile Home Park, 2000 Mable Ave., 7:30 p.m. Box 4742, Modesto, Calif. 95352-4742.

MONTROSE: Glendale Stamp Club, fourth Monday, Glendale Federal Savings, 2350 Honolulu Ave., 7 p.m. Forrest B. Evans, Box 8465, La Crescenta, Calif. 91214.

NAPA: Napa Valley Stamp Club, first and third Mondays, also fifth Monday, Senior Center, 1500 Jefferson, 7:30 p.m. Arthur A. McAuley, 1077 Lorraine Drive, Napa, Calif. 94558.

OAKLAND: Japanese American Society for Philately, third Sunday except December, Sumitomo Bank, 20th and Franklin, 1:30 p.m. John R. Shively, 1231 King Drive, El Cerrito, Calif. 94530.

ORANGE: Orange Senior Citizens Stamp Club, every Wednesday, Orange Senior Center, 170 S. Olive St., 10 a.m.-noon. Thelma Darrow, 445 N. Lincoln St., Orange, Calif. 92666.

PALM SPRINGS: Palm Springs Philatelic Society, first Wednesday, Pomona First Federal Savings and Loan meeting room, 39950 Date Palm Drive, Cathedral City, 7:30 p.m; third Wednesday, Pomona First Federal Savings and Loan, 1111 Tahquitz, 1:30 p.m. Charles C. Kirshbaum, 845 Calle De Flora Vista, Palm Springs, Calif. 92262.

PASA ROHLES: Golden Gate Precancel Society, April and October each year, Pasa Rohles Inn. Roberta M. Coltman, Box 102, Clearlake, Calif. 95422.

PETALUMA: Petaluma Philatelic Society, first and third Saturday, Westamerica Bank, community room, Washington Square, 7:30 p.m. Marty Wallach, Secretary, 2056 Willow Drive, Petaluma, Calif. 94952.

REDONDO BEACH: Hawthorne Elks Coin and Stamp Club, first and third Monday, Home Federal Savings and Loan, 1670 S. Pacific Coast Highway, 7:30 p.m.-9:30. Martin Trouillon, 12209 S. Hawthorne Way, Hawthorne, Calif. 90250.

REDWOOD CITY: Sequoia Stamp Club, second and fourth Tuesday, Community Activity Center, 1400 Roosevelt Ave. Stuart J. Phillips, 219 Stilt Court, Foster City, Calif. 94404.

RIVERSIDE: Riverside Stamp Club, first Monday, 9391 California Ave., 7:30 p.m. Arthur Thomas, Box 48, Redlands, Calif. 92373.

SACRAMENTO: Sacramento Philatelic Society, every Wednesday except fifth Wednesdays, Easter Seals Facility, 3205 Hurley Way, 7 p.m.-9. Anson B. Stout, 1399 Sacramento Ave., No. 71, West Sacramento, Calif. 95605.

SALINAS: Monterey County Stamp Club, fourth Thursday, Steinbeck Library, Lincoln and San Luis streets, 7:30 p.m. Paul DeBord, 947 San Vincente, Salinas, Calif. 93901.

SAN BERNARDINO: Arrowhead Stamp Club, second Wednesday, Arrowview Jr. High auditorium, Highland and G streets, 7 p.m. Bill Brooks, Box 2698, San Bernardino, Calif. 92406.

— TRW Stamp Club, third Wednesday, Building 524, Room 431, Norton AFB, noon. Richard C. Carlston, Box 1310, San Bernardino, Calif. 92402-1310.

SAN FRANCISCO: San Francisco Pacific Philatelic Society, third Tuesday, except July, Homestead Savings, 5757 Geary Blvd., 7 p.m. Laura E. Smith, 986 Guerrero St., San Francisco, Calif. 94110.

— California Collectors Club, every Friday except holidays, First United Lutheran Church, 30th Avenue and Geary Boulevard, 7 p.m. Preston Pope, President, Box 5625, San Mateo, Calif. 94402.

SAN LEANDRO: The Philatelic Society of San Leandro Inc., third Tuesday, San Leandro Community Library, 8 p.m. Don

MacDougall, Box 633, San Leandro, Calif. 94577.

SAN LUIS OBISPO: San Luis Obispo County Philatelic Society, third Wednesday and last Friday, no July meeting, Wednesday only in November, December dates change, Senior Citizens Building, Santa Rosa and Buchon, 7:30 p.m. Chris Weigle, 3960 S. Higuera, No. 6, San Luis Obispo, Calif. 93401.

SAN PABLO: San Pablo Pines Stamp Club, Mondays, 100 Austin Court, 7:30 p.m. Erik Albertsen, 7125 Blake St., El Cerrito, Calif. 94530.

SANTA BARBARA: Santa Barbara Stamp Club, first and third Tuesdays, Recreation Center, 7:30 p.m.-9:30. Ogden Monks, 3929 Harrold Ave., Santa Barbara, Calif, 93110.

SANTA MARIA: Central Coast Stamp Club, first and third Thursday, Veteran's Memorial Cultural Center, Pine and Tunnell streets, 7:30 p.m. Al Hardy, Box 814, Lompoc, Calif. 93438.

SEAL BEACH: Leisure World Stamp Club, first Wednesday, Leisure World. Alfred Pickhardt, 13962 El Dorado 60J, Seal Beach, Calif. 90740.

SEBASTOPOL: Sonoma County Philatelic Society, first and third Thursdays, Glendale Savings and Loan, community room, 201 Main St., 8 p.m. Arthur A. Reynor, Box 2081, Guerneville, Calif. 95446.

SHERMAN OAKS: Scandinavian Collectors Club, Southern California Chapter 17, second Tuesday, Union Federal Savings and Loan, 13300 Ventura Blvd., 8 p.m. P.A. Nelson, Box 57397, Los Angeles, Calif. 90057.

SIMI VALLEY: The Ultimate Collectors' Society, irregular in members' homes. Jim Ellsworth, Box 3695, Simi Valley, Calif. 93063.

— Simi Valley Stamp Club, first Monday and third Thursday, Simi Valley Presbyterian Church, 4832 Cochran St., 7 p.m.-10. Frank Rudiger, President, 1709 Wychoff Ave., Simi Valley, Calif. 93063.

SONORA: Tuolumne County Stamp Club, second Wednesday, Tuolumne County Library, 7:30 p.m. Jack E. Amundsen, 1235 Shaws Flat Road, Sonora, Calif. 95370.

SUN CITY: Sun City Stamp Club, second and fourth Tuesdays, community room, Coast Savings and Loan Association, 27190 Sun City Blvd., 2 p.m. Pat Bonning, 25810 Baltrustral, Sun City, Calif. 92381.

SUNNYVALE: Friends of the Western Philatelic Library, Stu Leven, Box 2219, Sunnyvale, Calif. 94087.

— Lera Stamp Club, every Tuesday, Sunnyvale Public Library, 7:30 p.m. N. Papson, 104 Amber Oak Court, Los Gatos, Calif. 95030.

— Sunnyvale Stamp Society, Tuesdays, Sunnyvale Community Center auditorium, 550 E. Remington Ave., 7:30 p.m.-10. Lois Bertelson, 114 Cirrus Ave., Sunnyvale, Calif. 94087.

VALLEJO: Vallejo Stamp Club, second and third Tuesdays, Vallejo Community Center, 225 Amados St., 7:30 p.m.-9:30. Kayde England, 155 Kit Carson Way, Vallejo, Calif. 94589.

VENTURA: Ventura County Philatelic Society, first and third Monday, E.P. Foster Library, 651 E. Main St., 8 p.m. Robert W. Thompson, Box 42148, Point Nuon, Calif. 93042.

VICTORVILLE: Hi-Desert Stamp Society, second and fourth Thursdays, Gold West Mobile Park Clubhouse, 15-252 Seneca Road, 7:30 p.m. Jo Ann James, 15-252 Seneca Road, No. 190, Victorville, Calif. 92392.

WALNUT CREEK: Diablo Valley Stamp Club, second and fourth Thursdays, Leisure Services building, 1650 N. Broadway, 7:30 p.m. C.M. Kimpton, 825 Oak Grove Road, No. 17, Concord, Calif. 94518.

WATSONVILLE: Pajaro Valley Stamp Club, fourth Saturday, All-Saints Episcopal, 2 p.m. Don Spence, 720 Oregon St., Watsonville, Calif. 95076.

YUBA CITY: Yuba-Sutter Philatelic Club, fourth Monday, Sutter County Library, Clark and Forbes streets, 7 p.m. John J. Anderson, Box 2592, Marysville, Calif. 95901.

MISCELLANEOUS

The Western Arm (U.N. Philatelists), Regional shows in the San Francisco Bay area. Don Bakos, Box 70263, Sunnyvale, Calif. 94086.

— Scandinavian Collectors Club,

Golden Gate Chapter 21, Saturdays, stamp exhibitions in the Bay Area, 10 a.m.- noon. Helmer Nielsen, Secretary-Treasurer, 1980 Laver Court, Los Altos, Calif. 94022.

— Federated Philatelic Clubs of Southern California, four times a year at various philatelic exhibitions. James A. Bowman, President, 3459 Township Ave., Santa Susana, Calif. 93063.

— American First Day Cover Society Claude C. Ries Chapter, Saturdays, various stamp shows in Southern California. Rick Range. 16212 S. Menlo Ave., Gardena, Calif. 90247.

— C and E Stamp Club, first Saturday, 11 a.m.-noon, may vary. Cale J. Whitehouse, 12343 Cliff Ave., Bakersfield, Calif. 93306.

— Clear Lake Stamp Club, second Tuesday, members' homes, 6 p.m.-8. Scott Klynstra, Drawer 1050, Clearlake Park, Calif. 95424.

— Ben Franklin Stamp Club, Anita Morris, 1900 E St., Fresno, Calif. 93706.

— ECHO, Expo Collectors Historians Organization, Edward J. Orth, 1436 Killarney Ave., Los Angeles, Calif. 90065.

— Nippon Philatelic Society, fourth Sunday, alternate months, 2 p.m. Donald W. Polhemus, 800 S. Windsor Blvd., Los Angeles, Calif. 90005.

— Scouts on Stamps Society International Sunset Trail Chapter 10, meetings vary. Kenneth Weber, Box 2542, Oxnard, Calif. 93034.

— Jet Propulsion Laboratory Stamp Club, second Tuesday, JPL facility, noon. James Rose, Jet Propulsion Laboratory, 4800 Oak Grove Drive, Pasadena, Calif. 91107.

— Southern California Precancel Club, third Sunday, various places, noon. Charles Lewis, Box 3246, Beaumont, Calif. 92223.

— Council of Northern California Philatelic Society, meets quarterly at shows. Charles R. Waller, Box 1992, Pittsburg, Calif. 94565.

— TRW Stamp Club, second and fourth Tuesday, TRW, 1 Space Park, Redondo Beach, noon. G.C. Sozio, 5303 Holt Ave., Los Angeles, Calif. 90056.

— California Mens Colony Philatelic Society, Tuesday, California Mens Colony-East, Highway 101, San Luis Obispo. Club Sponsor, Box 8101, San Luis Obispo, Calif. 93409-0001.

COLORADO

DENVER: Denver Germany Stamp Club, Chapter 27, first Wednesday, VFW Hall, Denver Post, 1545 S. Broadway, 7 p.m. Charles A. Wilkinson, 12987 W. 20th Ave., Golden, Colo. 80401.

— Denver Stamp Club, third Tuesday except June-August, Church of the Ascension, Sixth Avenue and Gilpin Street, 7:30 p.m. Mike Milam, Box 10644, Denver, Colo. 80210.

— Rocky Mountain Stamp Club, fourth Wednesday, Southwest State Bank, 1380 S. Federal Blvd., 7:30 p.m. Stan McAlister, 13553 W. Virginia Drive, Lakewood, Colo. 80228.

— West Side Stamp Club Inc., first Tuesday and third Thursday, First Presbyterian Church, 8210 W. 10th Ave., 7:30 p.m. Lorraine Hackman, 11840 W. 30th Place, Lakewood, Colo. 80215.

ENGLEWOOD: Cherrelyn Stamp Club, second Monday, except August, Grace Evangelical Lutheran Church, 4750 S. Clarkson. Attn: Secretary, Box 1621, Englewood, Colo. 80150.

FT. COLLINS: Northern Colorado Philatelic Society, third Wednesday, St. Luke's Episcopal Church, 2000 S. Stover, 7:30 p.m. Ted Beers, Box 823, Ft. Collins, Colo. 80522.

GRAND JUNCTION: Stamp Club of Grand Junction, second Monday, Mesa County Public Library, Fifth and Grand, 7 p.m. Secretary, Box 1494, Grand Junction, Colo. 81502.

LITTLETON: Arapahoe Stamp Club, first Wednesday, Bemis Library, 6014 S. Datura, 7 p.m. Malcolm Komitor, 8006 S. Logan Drive, Littleton, Colo. 80122.

MISCELLANEOUS

Rocky Mountain Aerophilatelic Club, American Air Mail Society, Chapter 39, quarterly meeting, S.V. Reeder, 1003 Geneva St., Aurora, Colo. 80010-3944.

— U.S.S. Colorado (BB-45), Chapter 95, U.S.C.S., Saturdays every other month. Jerry Crow, 1011 S. Ironton St., No. 110, Aurora, Colo. 80012.

CONNECTICUT

BRANFORD: Branford Philatelic

Society, first and third Monday, Branford Community House, Church Street, 7:30 p.m. Frederick L. Chidester Jr., 304 Twin Lakes Road, North Branford, Conn. 06471-1220.

BRIDGEPORT: Bridgeport Philatelic Club, first Sunday, Main Post Office, Middle Street, 1 p.m. Mike Conway, 74 Woodside Circle, Fairfield, Conn. 06430.

BROOKLYN: Apple Hill Stamp Club, January, May, August and October, 547 Pomfret Road. Michael A. Belliveau, 547-A Pomfret Road, Brooklyn, Conn. 06234.

CHESHIRE: Cheshire Philatelic Society Inc., first and third Friday, Connecticut Bank, South Main Street, 8 p.m. A.C. Abbatiello, Box 206, Cheshire, Conn. 06410.

DARIEN: Ye Olde Kings Highway Stamp Club, second and fourth Tuesday, Noroton Presbyterian Church, 8 p.m. Fran Conley, 83 Bayne St., Norwalk, Conn. 06851.

FAIRFIELD: Fairfield Philatelic Society, second Sunday except July and August, 197 Reef Road, 1:30 p.m. Arthur Lang, 522 High St., Fairfield, Conn. 06430.

MANCHESTER: Manchester Philatelic Society Inc., second and fourth Tuesday, Whiton Memorial Library, 100 N. Main St., 6 p.m.-8:30. Secretary, Box 448, Manchester, Conn. 06040.

MILFORD: Universal Ship Cancellation Society USS Nathan Hale Chapter, first Sunday except July and August, Plymouth building of the First United Church of Christ, 18 West Main St. David Kent, Secretary, Box 127, New Britain, Conn. 06050.

NEW BRITAIN: Hardware City Stamp Club, first and third Tuesday except July and August, Holy Trinity Church School, 305 Washington St., Gene Sessaman, 15 Glen Hollow Drive, Unionville, Conn. 06085.

NORTH HAVEN: North Haven Stamp Club, second and fourth Mondays, Recreation Center, 7 Linsley St., 7 p.m. James Haglind, 111 Frost Drive, North Haven, Conn. 06473.

NORWALK: Norwalk Stamp Club, first and third Mondays, Nathan Hale Middle School, 176 Strawberry Hill Ave., 8 p.m. John Murphy, Box 267, Norwalk, Conn. 06840.

PORTLAND: Middletown-Portland Stamp Club, first and third Tuesday except July and August, Portland Library, Freestone Avenue, 7:30 p.m.-9:30. Lou Damiata, Box 1014, Middletown, Conn. 06457.

SHELTON: Valley Stamp Club, third Thursday except July and August, Methodist Convalescent Home, Recreation Room, Wicke Health Center, 584 Long Hill Ave., 7:30 p.m.-9:30. Kay Don Kahler, President, 63 Lynne Terrace, Shelton, Conn. 06484.

WATERBURY: Waterbury Stamp Club, first, third and fourth Monday, Salvation Army, 74 Central Ave. Pat Rinaldi, Box 581, Waterbury, Conn. 06720.

WATERFORD: Thames Stamp Club, second and fourth Wednesdays, September thru June, Clark Lane Junior High School, Clark Lane, 7:30 p.m. George G. Ryan, Box 244, Waterford, Conn. 06385.

DELAWARE

DOVER: Dover Stamp Club. Bill Kircher, Box 300, Camden, Del. 19934.

MILFORD: Milford Stamp and Coin Club, second Wednesday, Kiwanis Building, First Street, 7:30 p.m. Michael K. Drummond, Box 493, Scaford, Del. 19973.

WILMINGTON: DuPont Stamp Club, first Wednesday except July and August, location changes. F.S. Dickson, 640 Woodview Drive, Hockessin, Del. 19707.

— Wilmington Stamp Club, 2nd Wednesday, Calvary United Methodist Church, 36th & Washington, 8 p.m. W.T. Connelly, 213 Trinity Avenue, Wilmington, Del. 19804.

DISTRICT OF COLUMBIA

WASHINGTON, D.C.: Capitol Hill Philatelic Club, second Tuesday, Rayburn House Office Building, Room 2203, noon-1 p.m. Roland J. Williams, Room B-394A, Rayburn HOB, Washington, D.C. 20515.

— Mr. Beasley Stamp Club of Chevy Chase, first Thursday, September thru May, Blessed Sacrament Church, 6001 Western Ave. N.W., .7:30 p.m. David S. Orem, 7 Leland Court, Chevy Chase, Md. 20815.

— Washington Philatelic Society, second and. fourth Wednesday, September thru June, St. John's Parish House, 1525 H St. N.W., 8 p.m. Joel Fassler, President, Box 28414, Washington, D.C. 20038-8414.

MISCELLANEOUS

Washington D.C. Chapter International Society of Japanese Philately, first Tuesday, Lee R. Wilson, Secretary, 4216 Jenifer St. N.W., Washington, D.C. 20015.

FLORIDA

BOCA RATON: Century Village Boca Stamp and Coin Club, second Tuesday, Century Village Club House, 10 a.m. Louis Hess, President, Box 2789, Boca Raton, Fla. 33427.

BRANDON: Brandon Stamp Club, first and third Tuesday, Fort Brooke Savings & Loan Association building, Route 574 and Parsons Road, 8 p.m. Jacques A. Musy, Drawer A, Valrico, Fla. 33594.

CAPE CORAL: Cape Coral Stamp Club, second Wednesday, First Federal Savings & Loan Bank, community room, Cape Coral Parkway and Del Prado Boulevard, 7:30 p.m. Wilma Marik, Box 42, Cape Coral, Fla. 33910.

CLEARWATER: Cap Townsend Stamp Club, Robby's Pancake House, 1617 Gulf to Bay, meets once a month, 11:30 a.m.-1:30. Charles D. Seaman, 48 Dogwood Court, Safety Harbor, Fla. 34695.

— Clearwater Stamp Club, first and third Monday, G.T.E. Building, 1280 Cleveland St., 7 p.m. E. Walter Parker, Box 5442, Clearwater, Fla. 33518.

— Florida West Coast Chapter 23, Scandinavian Collectors Club, every third Monday, Poseidon Restaurant, 2370 U.S. 19 N., 6:30 p.m. J. Edward Evan, Box 2533, Clearwater, Fla. 34617.

DELAND: West Volusia Stamp Club, first and third Tuesday, 7 p.m., second and fourth Tuesday, 2 p.m., Faith Lutheran Church, 509 E. Pennsylvania Ave. Gerald Lane, c/o Faith Church, 509 E. Pennsylvania Ave., Deland, Fla. 32724.

DELRAY BEACH: Delray Beach Stamp Club, first and third Wednesday, Atlantic High School, 2501 Seacrest Blvd., 7 p.m. Louis Lerner, Normandy G 295, Delray Beach, Fla. 33484.

DUNNELLON: Rainbow Stamp Club, Rainbow Lake Estates, Rainbow Lake Boulevard, third Tuesday, 7 p.m., no summer meetings. Roberta Schwartz, 7867 S.W. 203 Court, Dunnellon, Fla. 32630.

FERNANDINA BEACH: Fernandina Beach Stamp Club, second Tuesday, Prince of Peace Lutheran Church, 2600 Atlantic Ave., 7 p.m. Dwight E. Wiles, Box 131, Fernandina Beach, Fla. 32034.

FT. LAUDERDALE: Oakland Park Stamp Club, second and fourth Thursday, Collins Community Center, 3900 N.E. Third Ave., 7 p.m. F. Louis Wolff, 3006 E. Commercial Blvd., Ft. Lauderdale, Fla. 33308.

HALLANDALE: South Florida Chapter, Society of Israel Philatelists, second Thursday, Hallandale Ingall's Park Center, 735 S.W. One St., 8 p.m. Dan Piver, 8851 Carlyle Ave., Surfside, Fla. 33154.

HOLLY HILL: Halifax Area Philatelic Society, second and fourth Friday, Clubhouse, behind city hall, 7:30 p.m. Emery D. Bowman, Box 1361, Ormond Beach, Fla. 32074.

HOLLYWOOD: Hollywood Stamp Club, every Tuesday evening, Multi-Purpose Building, 2030 Polk St. Violet Montalto, 2030 Polk St., Senior Citizen Center, Hollywood, Fla. 33020.

KISSIMMEE: Florida Precancel Club, second Thursday, 9 a.m.-9 p.m. Wilson World, 7491 W. Spacecoast Parkway. James Estes, Box 256, Goldenrod, Fla. 32733-0256.

— Osceola Stamp Club, third Wednesday, Senior Citizens Resource Center, 1099 Shady Lane, 1:30 p.m. Frances Purcell, 4425 Pleasant Hill Road, Lot 313, Kissimmee, Fla. 32741.

LAKELAND: Germany Philatelic Association, Chapter 23, second Sunday, St. Paul Lutheran Church, 3020 S. Florida Ave., 2 p.m. Mason S. Curran Jr., 10095 60th Court N., Pinellas Park, Fla. 34666.

MARGATE: Margate Stamp Club, every third Sunday, Teen Center, 6111 N.W. 10th St., 1 p.m.-4. Daniel Caust, 4342 Acaca Circle, Coconut Creek, Fla. 33066.

MELBOURNE: Missile Stamp Club, first Wednesday and third Tuesday, USPS Postal Annex, 1515 Elizabeth St., 7:30 p.m. David L. Moore, Box 362321, Melbourne, Fla. 32936.

MIAMI BEACH: Miami Beach Stamp Club, every second and fourth Monday,

Miami Beach Public Library, 2100 Collins Ave., 5:30 p.m. Charles R. Loeb, 1495 N.E. 167th St. No. 4, N. Miami Beach, Fla. 33162.

NEW PORT RICHEY: New Port Richey Stamp Club, first and third Sunday, People's State Bank, U.S. 19 and Main Street, 1 p.m. Murray Kober, 57 S. Shore Drive, New Port Richey, Fla. 34652.

OCALA: Silver Springs Shores Stamp Club, fourth Thursday, Silver Springs Shores, 7 p.m. Florence Kleinert, 12 Silver Way, Ocala, Fla. 32672.

PALM COAST: Florida First Coast Stamp Club, first and third Wednesdays (September thru June), Belle Terre Middle School, 7:30 p.m. Gary G. Heiser, Box 353277, Palm Coast, Fla. 32035-3277.

PANAMA CITY: Bay County Stamp Club, first and third Thursday, Junior Museum Annex, Maureen Knipper, 303 Alexander Drive, Lynn Haven, Fla. 32444.

PEMBROKE PINES: Century Village Stamp Club, every Friday, Century Village, 7:30 p.m. Abe Katz, 1301 S.W. 135th Terrace, Ivanhoe J No. 213, Pembroke Pines, Fla. 33027.

PENSACOLA: Pensacola Philatelic Society, first and third Monday, downtown Pensacola Library, 7:30 p.m. Jeanna S. Valmus, 316 Chattman St., Pensacola, Fla. 32507.

POMPANO BEACH: Gold Coast Stamp Club, second Wednesday, Pompano Beach Recreation Center, 1801 N.E. 6th St. (just west of Federal Highway No. 1), 7 p.m. Robert E. Reton, 750 N. Orchard Blvd., Pompano Beach, Fla. 33062.

PORT RICHEY: Pasco Stamp Club, second and fourth Tuesday, St. Petersburg Times Building (Pasco Times), 11321 U.S. Highway 19 N., 7 p.m. Sheldon Rogg, Box 1076, Port Richey, Fla. 34673-1076.

PORT ST. LUCIE: Port St. Lucie Stamp Club, second Thursday, PSL Community Building, 200 S.W. Prima Visa Blvd., 7:30 p.m. Lois M. Gross, 274 N.E. Soleda Drive, Port St. Lucie, Fla. 34983.

ST. AUGUSTINE: St. Augustine Stamp Club, first Tuesday (except June, July and August), Coquina Plaza, YMCA Center. Sandie Stratton, 160 1/2 Avenida Menendez, St. Augustine, Fla. 32084.

ST. PETERSBURG: St. Petersburg Stamp Club, every Wednesday, Trinity Lutheran Church, 401 Fifth St. N., 7:30 p.m. Club President, Box 546, St. Petersburg, Fla. 33731-0546.

SUNRISE: Sunrise Stamp Club, second and fourth Sunday, Roarke Center, 1720 N.W. 60th Ave., noon-3 p.m. S.J. Cohan, 1101 N.W. 58 Terrace, Sunrise, Fla. 33313.

TAMPA: Tampa Collectors Club, second and fourth Mondays, Galley Room of Red Lobster Restaurant, 11601 N. Dale Mabry Highway, 7:30 p.m. Walter Nazarenko, 8314 W. Pocahontas St., Tampa, Fla. 33615.

TITUSVILLE: Titusville-Moonport Stamp Club, first Monday, library, Hopkins Avenue. Russell Smith, Box 6071, Titusville, Fla. 32782.

VERO BEACH: Indian River Stamp Club, second and fourth Monday (except July and August), First Presbyterian Church, 7:30 p.m. Edward D. Oulund, Box 842, Vero Beach, Fla. 32961.

WEST PALM BEACH: Cresthaven Stamp Club, second and fourth Tuesday, Dudley Center. Herman W. Steeg, 4637 Kirk Road, Lake Worth, Fla. 33461.

MISCELLANEOUS

Florida Federation of Stamp Clubs, semi-annual meetings in conjunction with Florida exhibits. Helen Krasne, 4801 Taylor St., Hollywood, Fla. 33021.

GEORGIA

ATLANTA: Atlanta Chapter, Society of Israel Philatelists, second Thursday, Atlanta Jewish Community Center, 1745 Peachtree St., 8 p.m. Lewis Willner, 1654 Anita Place N.E., Atlanta, Ga. 30306.

— Atlanta Stamp Collectors Club, second and fourth Wednesday (except December, second only), First United Methodist Church, 360 Peachtree St. N.E, 7:30 p.m. A.C. Roozen, 133 Carnegie Way, Room 812, Atlanta, Ga. 30303.

— Stamp Dealers Association of Georgia, first Thursday, 800 Peachtree St., second floor, 6:30 p.m. David Kirtley, Box 56981, Atlanta, Ga. 30343-0981.

KENNESAW: Cobb County Stamp Club, fourth Sunday, Outlet Square Mall community room, Busbec Parkway, 1:30 p.m. John or Phyllis Kruse, 4587 Danna Drive, Austell, Ga. 30001.

LEXINGTON: Oglethorpe County Ben

Franklin Stamp Club, second Wednesday, Oglethorpe County Elementary School, Room 301, 3:30 p.m.-5. Gregory Frederick, O.C.E.J., Comer Road, Lexington, Ga. 30648.

LILBURN: Button Gwinnett Stamp Club, third Tuesday, Lilburn City Hall, 7:30 p.m. Joseph E. Treadway, 2010 Hunter's Walk Court, Lawrenceville, Ga. 30244-5322.

MACON: Macon Philatelic Society, first Thursday, Liberty Savings Bank, 201 Second St., 7:30 p.m. Edgar E. Maxwell, 1903 Upper River Road, Macon, Ga. 31211-1101.

STONE MOUNTAIN: Stone Mountain Philatelic Society, second and fourth Thursday, Central Congregational Church, 2627 Clairmont Road N.E., 7:30 p.m. George E. Wampole, 1381 Saxony Square, Stone Mountain, Ga. 30083.

VALDOSTA: Valdosta Stamp Club, second Monday, South Georgia Regional Library, 7:30 p.m. Bernard L. Lenz, 3110 Northfield Road, Valdosta, Ga. 31601.

HAWAII

HONOLULU: Hawaiian Philatelic Society, second Monday, 7:30 p.m., fourth Monday, 7 p.m., YMCA, 1441 Pali Highway. Secretary, Box 10115, Honolulu, Hawaii 96816-0115.

KAILUA: Windward Oahu Philatelic Society, fourth Monday, Kailua Library. Clarence E. McIntosh, 1416 Mokolea Drive, Kailua, Hawaii 96734.

IDAHO

BOISE: Silver Star Stamp Club, every Saturday, Idaho Stamp Collectors Library, 5612 W. State St., 1 p.m.-3. June Davies or Michael Uhl, 5612 W. State St., Boise, Idaho 83703.

EMMETT: Valley of Plenty Stamp Club, last Monday (except July and August), Public Library meeting room, 7 p.m. Jean Burr, 511 S. Commercial, Emmett, Idaho 83617.

POCATELLO: Pocatello Stamp Club, fourth Wednesday, lower level Public Library, 812 E. Clark, 7 p.m. William Atteberry, Box 4485, Pocatello, Idaho 83201-4485.

TWIN FALLS: O'Leary Stamp Club, every other Monday (when school is in session), O'Leary Junior High, Room A19, 2350 Elizabeth Blvd., 3:15 p.m.-4. Bill White, O'Leary Junior High, 2350 Elizabeth Blvd., Twin Falls, Idaho 83301.

ILLINOIS

ARLINGTON HEIGHTS: Northwest Stamp Club, twice monthly, first and third or second and fourth Tuesday or Thursday, Arlington Heights Memorial Library, 500 N. Dunton Ave., 7:30 p.m. Peter J. Zachar, Box 322, Mt. Prospect, Ill. 60065.

AURORA: Fox Valley Stamp Club, second Tuesday (except July and August), McCollough Park Recreation Center, Route 31 and Illinois Avenue, 7:30 p.m. Earl Button, McCollough Park Recreation Center, Route 31 and Illinois Avenue, Aurora, Ill. 60506.

BELLEVILLE: Belleville Sott Stamp Club, second and fourth Wednesday (except June, July and August), Nichols Community Center, 515 E. D Street, 7 p.m. Kay W. Potts, 427 N. 39th St., Belleville, Ill. 62223.

BERWYN: Chicagoland Czechoslovak Philatelic Society, first Sunday (except July and August). Mrs. Joe F. Sterba Jr., 6624 Windsor Ave., Berwyn, Ill. 60402-3550.

BLOOMINGTON: The Bloomington Stampers, second and fourth Thursday, 6:30 p.m.-7:30. Larry Schwab, 2507 Newport Drive, Bloomington, Ill. 61704.

BROOKFIELD: Suburban Collectors Club of Chicago, second and fourth Wednesday (July, August and December: second Wednesday only), Sokol Brookfield Hall, 3909 Prairie Ave., 8 p.m. Secretary, Box 207, Brookfield, Ill. 60513.

CARBONDALE: Southern Illinois Stamp Club, second and fourth Thursday (the fourth is omitted in June, July, November and December), Xavier Hall, Walnut and Poplar streets, 7:30 p.m. Bill Ashwell, Box 2152, Carbondale, Ill. 62902.

CHAMPAIGN: Champaign-Urbana Stamp Club, first and third Monday, Champaign Public Library, 7 p.m. Michael J. Carson, R.R. 2, Box 27, Tuscola, Ill. 61953-9802.

CHICAGO: Chicago Air Mail Society, fourth Tuesday, Oriole Park Field House, 5430 N. Olcott, 7:30 p.m. Stephen

Neulander, Box 25, Deerfield, Ill. 60015.

— Chicago Philatelic Society, first and third Thursday, Bismarck Hotel, 171 W. Randolph St., 7:30 p.m. Jacquelyn S. Alton, Box A-3953, Chicago, Ill. 60690-3953.

— Fermi Stamp Club, Mondays and Wednesdays, Fermi School, 1415 E. 70th St., 2:45 p.m.-3:45. Philip A. Peffley, 1415 E. 70th St., Chicago, Ill. 60637.

— Lithuania Philatelic Society, Sunday, three times a year (spring, fall, winter), Lithuanian Youth Center, 5620 S. Claremont Ave., noon. John Variakojis, 3715 W. 68th St., Chicago, Ill. 60629.

— North Shore Philatelic Society, second and fourth Saturday, Warren State Park, 6601 N. Western Ave. Ron Schloss, 7001 N. Clark St., Room 210, Chicago, Ill. 60626.

— Roosevelt Philatelic Society, first and third Tuesday, Francis D. Hayes Park Fieldhouse, 2936 W. 85th St., 8 p.m. Bob Bosserdet, 1131 Jefferson St., Lockport, Ill. 60441.

— Tower Stamp Club, first and third Tuesday (except June, July and August), 23rd floor of Sears Tower, noon-1 p.m. John Jirgenson, Sears Tower, D/696, BSC 5-26, Chicago, Ill. 60684.

— Universal Ship Cancellation Society Moffett Chapter No. 6, Sundays about 9 months per year at homes of members. Lawrence Groh, 9648 S. Major Ave., Oak Lawn, Ill. 60453.

ELGIN: Collectors Club of Steamwood High School, Wednesdays, Streamwood High School, 7 a.m.-7:30. James Sedivec, Route 4, Box 307, Elgin, Ill. 60120.

GALESBURG: Galisburg Philatelic Society, third Tuesday, Galesburg Community Center, 150 E. Simmons St., 7 p.m. Charles L. McCullock, 212 Highland Ave., Galesburg, Ill. 61401.

GLEN ELLYN: Glen Ellyn Philatelic Club, first and third Monday (except August, first Monday only), Glen Ellyn Civic Center, 535 Duane St., 7:30 p.m. Ron Baumgardner, Box 217, Glen Ellyn, Ill. 60138.

LAGRANGE: Southwest Surburban Center on Aging, first and third Tuesday, Southwest Surburban Center on Aging, 111 W. Harris Ave., 9 a.m. William E. Wollney, 111 W. Harris Ave., Lagrange Park, Ill. 60525.

LIBERTYVILLE: North Suburban Stamp Club, second Thursday, Cook Memorial Library, 413 N. Milwaukee Ave., 7:30 p.m. President, Box 353, Libertyville, Ill. 60048.

LOCKPORT: Fairmont Junior High School, Thursdays, Fairmont Junior High School, Green Garden Place, 3 p.m. Ross Margentina, Green Garden Place, Lockport, Ill. 60441.

MOLINE: Quad-City Stamp Club, second Thursday, Moline Township Hall, 620 18th St., 7 p.m.-10. Box 10301, Moline, Ill. 61265-9301.

NAPERVILLE: Naperville Stamp Club, first and third Wednesday, John Greene Realtor, 1111 S. Washington Ave., 7:30 p.m. Randy Meyle, 506 Old Indian Trail, Aurora, Ill. 60506.

OTTAWA: LaSalle County Stamp Club, second Wednesday except July and August, JoAnn Bruce, 1117 Howard St., Ottawa, Ill. 61350.

QUINCY: Quinsippi Stamp Club, first Wednesday (except January), Good Samaritan Home, 2130 Harrison St., 7 p.m. Paul S. Gabriel, 1019 Klondike Road, Quincy, Ill. 62301.

ROCKFORD: Rockford Stamp Club, first Wednesday, Home Federal Savings & Loan, 1107 E. State St., 8 p.m. George W. Finn, 3236 Liberty Drive, Rockford, Ill. 61103.

ROXANA: Community Stamp Club, second and fourth Mondays, Rox-Arena, 7 p.m. Donald C. Landis, 5111 Williams Place, Godfrey, Ill. 62035.

SKOKIE: Israel-Palestine Philatelic Society of America, Chicago Chapter of Society of Israel Philatelists, second Thursday (except July and August), Skokie Library, 5215 W. Oakton Ave., 7:30 p.m. Justin R. Gordon, Box 322, Skokie, Ill. 60076.

— Smith Center Stamp Club, first and third Wednesday, Smith Activities Center, Lincoln and Galitz Avenues, 1:30 p.m. Robert L. Klein, 5033 Dobson St., Skokie, Ill. 60077-2822.

SPRINGFIELD: Springfield Philatelic Society, fourth Tuesday, Security Federal Savings & Loan (basement), 510 E. Monroe St., 7:30 p.m. Larry E. Barregarye, 410 Amherst Drive, Sherman, Ill. 62684.

SOUTH ELGIN: Clinton Stamp Club, second and fourth Wednesday, Clinton School, 2 p.m. Lewis Sampson, 4 N. Jackson, Elgin, Ill. 60123.

WAUKEGAN: Lake County Philatelic Society, second and fourth Tuesday, Belvidere Recreation Center, 7p.m.-9. Marilyn Bardonner-Dee, Box 1129, Waukegan, Ill. 60079-1129.

MISCELLANEOUS

Illinois Postal History Society, annual meetings at fall exhibits in Illinois. Marilyn Bardonner-Dee, Box 1129, Waukegan, Ill. 60079-1129.

— Illini Precancel Stamp Club, approximately six swap sessions per year, held in members' homes. J. Austin Eckstein, 14 Valley Drive, Route 7, Streator, Ill, 61364.

— Quail Creek Stamp Club, informal get togethers, most members correspond via mail. Howard Shaughnessy, 1600 Deer Run, Gurnee, Ill. 60031.

INDIANA

EVANSVILLE: Evansville Stamp Club Inc., first and third Tuesday, Main Post Office, 800 Sycamore St., 7:30 p.m. Paul Adam, Box 161, Evansville, Ind. 47702.

INDIANAPOLIS: Indiana Stamp Club Inc., first Monday, Children's Museum, 30th and Meridian streets, 7:30 p.m. J. Adams, Box 40792, Indianapolis, Ind. 46240.

KOKOMO: Kokomo Stamp Club, second Wednesday, Howard County Library, 7 p.m. Ned P. Booher, 421 S. Philips St., Kokomo, Ind. 46901.

LAPORTE: LaPorte County Stamp Club, second and fourth Monday, LaPorte Public Library, 7 p.m. Samuel C. Zerbe, 1008 E. Michigan Blvd., Michigan City, Ind. 46360.

LOGANSPORT: Logansport Stamp Club, third Wednesday, Logansport Public Library, 7:30 p.m. Helen L. Wagner, Route 4, Box 26, Logansport, Indiana 46947.

MUNCIE: Muncie Coin & Stamp Club Inc., second Tuesday, Minnetrista Cultural Center, 1200 N. Minnetrista Parkway, Box 1527, 7 p.m. Larry Crouch, Box 1184, Muncie, Ind. 47302.

— Update Learning Stamp Club, first Thursday, Youth Lounge, High Street Methodist Church, 219 S. High St., 10 a.m. Jean Nicklin, 8505 W. Butternut Road, Muncie, Ind. 47304.

ROSELAND: Northern Indiana Philatelic Society, second and fourth Thursday, basement, Trust Corp. Bank building, Bus. 31 North at Darden Road, 7:30 p.m. Joseph Bellina Jr., Box 393, Mishawaka, Ind. 46544.

SEYMOUR: Seymour High School Stamp Club. Arthur Jones, 1350 W. Second St., Seymour, Ind. 47274.

TERRE HAUTE: Wabash Valley Stamp Club, last Thursday (except third Thursday in November and no meeting in December), Vigo County Public Library, 1 Library Square, 7 p.m. Harmon Rose, Box 2, St. Mary-of-the-Woods, Ind. 47876.

MISCELLANEOUS

Indiana Postal History Society, annual meeting at Indypex, Indianapolis, Ind. (usually in September). Arthur Hadley, 9635 S. Randal St., Columbus, Ind. 47203.

IOWA

ALLISON: Allison Stamp Club, second Saturday, REC meeting room, 521 North Main St., 7:30 p.m. (except August - 6:30 p.m.). Ruth Miller, Box 24, Allison, Iowa 50602.

CEDAR RAPIDS: Cedar Rapids Postcard Club, third Thursday (except July and August), Northwest Bank, 101 Third Ave. S.W. 7:30 p.m. Vivian Rinaberger, 4548 Fairlane Dr. N.E., Cedar Rapids, Iowa 52402.

DES MOINES: Federation of Iowa Stamp Clubs, annual meeting, CIAPEX. Wilma Hinrichs, 4200 S.E. Indianola Road, Des Moines, Iowa 50320.

GRINNELL: Grinnell Philatelic Society, fourth Tuesday (except December). Irving Y. Fishman, Grinnell College, Grinnell, Iowa 50112.

WATERLOO: Cedar Valley Stamp Club, second and fourth Wednesday, National Bank of Waterloo building, Crossroads Boulevard, 7:30 p.m. Maurice Johnson, 2304 Valley Park Drive, Cedar Falls, Iowa 50613.

MISCELLANEOUS

Iowa Postal History Society, in conjunction with Federation of Iowa Stamp Clubs (FISC). Norman Erickson, 1298 29th St. N.E., Cedar Rapids, Iowa 52402.

KANSAS

GREAT BEND: Cheyenne Stamp Club, second Sunday, Ralph Wallace Cafe, 2:30 p.m. Lester Spong, 2408 16th St., Great Bend, Kan. 67530.

HAYS: Fort Hays Stamp Club, third Sunday (September-May), last Sunday (June and July), 2 p.m. James E. Thorns, Coronado Estates, 500 W. 36th St., Hays, Kan. 67601.

LAWRENCE: Lawrence Stamp Club, first Thursday, Watkins Community Museum, 1047 Massachusetts St., 7 p.m. Gordon Longbach, 3612 Boulder Court, Lawrence, Kan. 66044.

LEAVENWORTH: Stamp Club of Leavenworth, third Thursday (except July and August), community room, First National Bank, Seventh and Deleware, 7:30 p.m. Bernie Duree, c/o Box 11, Leavenworth, Kan. 66048.

MANHATTAN: Flint Hills Stamp Club, second and fourth Thursday (no meeting fourth Thursday of November or December), Civil Service Room, Manhattan Post Office, 7:30 p.m. Karen Mayse, 2417 Charolais, Manhattan, Kan. 66502.

TOPEKA: Topeka Stamp Club, third Thursday, Topeka Savings basement, Eighth and Quincy, 6:30 p.m. James H. Parker, 2926 S.W. Arrowhead Road, Topeka, Kan. 66614.

WICHITA: Cessna Employees Stamp Club, second Thursday, Cessna Employees Activity Center, 2744 S. George Washington Blvd. Michael Barkley, 329 Maynard, Haysville, Kan. 67060.

— Kansas Precancel Society, third Thursday of even months, University Friends Church, 7 p.m. Dilmond D. Postlewait, Box 1335, Wichita, Kan. 67201-1335.

— Wichita Postcard Club, alternates between first Tuesday 7 p.m.-9 and first Saturday 2 p.m.-5, downtown Wichita public library. Hal N. Ottaway, Box 780282, Wichita, Kan. 67278-0282.

— Wichita Stamp Club, first and third Thursday, except July, August and December, University Friends Church, 1840 University, 7:30 p.m. Mark Burnett, Box 1427, Wichita, Kan. 67201.

KENTUCKY

FRANKFORT: Kentucky Stamp Club, first Thursday, Church of the Ascension, 311 Washington St., 7 p.m. Mike Howard, Box 1203, Frankfort, Ky. 40602-1203.

HOPKINSVILLE: Pennyrile Philatelic Society, third Tuesday, city/county library, 6:30 p.m. Marie Chandler, 2917 Seminole Drive, Hopkinsville, Ky. 42240.

LEXINGTON: Henry Clay Philatelic Society, third Monday, Second Presbyterian Church, 1200 Ransom Ave., 7 p.m. David Kluch, Box 24086, Lexington, Ky. 40524.

LOUISVILLE: Shelby Street Stamp Society, second Wednesday, 1404 S. Shelby St., 3 p.m. R. Paul Baker, 1310 Tycoon Way, Louisville, Ky. 40213.

— Philatelic Club of Louisville, first Thursday, location may vary, 7 p.m. Billy M. Adams, 1822 Oehrle Drive, Louisville, Ky. 40216.

OWENSBORO: Owensboro Area Stamp Club, first Friday, Trinity Episcopal Church, Ford Avenue, 7:30 p.m. Sister Emma Cecelia Busam, Mount St. Joseph, Maple Mount, Ky. 42356.

PADUCAH: Purchase Area Philatelic Society, fourth Monday except June, July, August and December, Paducah Main Post Office, conference room, South Fourth Street, 7 p.m. Walter Whinnery, 245 Oriole Lane, Paducah, Ky. 42001-6119.

LOUISIANA

ALEXANDRIA: Cenla Stamp Club, last Tuesday except December, Main Post Office, 1715 Odum St., 6 p.m. Charles D. Preuett, Rt. 1 Box 345-A, Dry Prong, La. 71423.

BATON ROUGE: Baton Rouge Stamp Club, first and third Wednesday, East Baton Rouge Parish Library, 7711 Goodwood Blvd., 7 p.m.-9. Edith H. Stevens, 5323 Heatherstone Drive, Baton Rouge, La. 70820.

LAFAYETTE: Aladiana Stamp Club, second Thursday, conference room of the Main Post Office, 1105 Moss St., 7 p.m. Ken Johnstone, Box 3939, Lafayette, La. 70502-3939.

LAKE CHARTER: Southwest Louisiana Philatelic Society, second Thursday, Main Post Office, conference room, Moss Street,

6:30 p.m.-7:30. George Carr, 1000 Royal St., Lake Charter, La. 70605.

MONROE: Twin City Stamp Club, first Monday, Post Office, Sterlington Road, 7 p.m. Pauline Hendrixson, 4106 Roger St., Monroe, La. 71201.

NEW ORLEANS: Dixiana Stampers, first Friday, Eucharistic Missionary, 1101 Aline St., 7 p.m. Henry Koberg, 2825 St. Charles Ave. No. 114, New Orleans, La. 70115-4436.

SHREVEPORT: Red River Stamp Club, first Thursday, General Mail Facility conference room, Texas Street, 7 p.m. Billy D. Culver, Box 3352, Shreveport, La. 71133.

SLIDELL: Slidell Scouting Collectors, first Saturday, 1465 Eastridge Drive, 10 a.m. Tom Holmes, 1465 Eastridge Drive, Slidell, La. 70458.

MAINE

AUBURN: Twin Rivers Stamp Club, second and fourth Tuesday, Auburn YMCA. Ray Gagnon, 23 Sylvan Ave., Lewiston, Maine 04240.

FAIRFIELD: Waterville Stamp Club, September to May first and third Friday; June, July and August third Friday, 6:30 p.m.-9. Richard Williams Jr., RFD 2, Box 700, Fairfield, Maine 04937.

PORTLAND: Pine Tree Post Card Club, second Monday, Public Safety Building, 7:30 p.m. John J. Verra Sr., Box 6783, Portland, Maine 04101

SANFORD: York County Stamp Club, second and fourth Thursday, People's Heritage Bank basement, Ames Plaza, 7 p.m. Arthur Martineau, 5 Stilson St., Sanford, Maine 04073.

SOUTH PARIS: Twin Town Stamp Club, first and third Thursday, Paris Community Room, 7 p.m. c/o Mimi Bell, Rt. 1, Norway, Maine 04268.

WOODLAND: Saint Croix Valley Stamp Club, second Monday, Woodland Elementary School. Ralph J. Ryan Sr., 64 Broadway, Box 547, Woodland, Maine 04694.

MISCELLANEOUS

Rumex Stamp Club, first Sunday, location varies. Al Dalbec, 550 Kennebec St., Rumford, Maine 04276.

MARYLAND

ADELPHI: Beltway Stamp Club, first and third Wednesdays, 8508 Adelphi Road, 7:30 p.m. David H. Elliott, 8508 Adelphi Road, Adelphi, Md. 20783.

ARBUTUS: The Arbutus Stamp Club, third Saturday, Holy Nativity Lutheran Church, 1200 Linden Ave., 1 p.m.-4. Van Baker, 5555 Oregon Ave., Baltimore, Md. 21227.

BALTIMORE: Germany Philatelic Society Baltimore Chapter 16, third Sunday, except July and August, 1224 N. Calvert St., 1:30 p.m. Christopher Deterding, Box 779, Arnold, Md. 21012.

— Baltimore Philatelic Society, first Friday, next Thursday, next Wednesday and next Tuesday, 1224 N. Calvert St., 8 p.m. K. Illyefalvi, 8207 Daren Court, Baltimore, Md. 21208.

— Scouts On Stamps Society International, third Thursday, Jerusalem Evangelical Lutheran Church, 4605 Belair Road, 7:30 p.m. Dennis James Boland, 4202 Belmar Ave., Baltimore, Md. 21206-1943.

— Southwestern Stamp Club, third Monday, Robert J. Lock, 521 S. Longwood St., Baltimore, Md. 21223.

BEL AIR: Harford County Stamp Club, second and fourth Wednesday, Bob's Big Boy, Route 1, 7:30 p.m. Judy Laylon, Box 163, Bel Air, Md. 21014.

CHEVY CHASE: The Fossils Stamp and Coins Group, third Wednesday, Chevy Chase United Methodist Church, 2 p.m. Alfred T. Wellborn, 5011 Brookeway Drive, Bethesda, Md. 20816.

COLUMBIA: Howard County Stamp Club, first and third Thursday, except July and August, Howard Community College, 7:30 p.m. Edmund Midura, 5311-C Columbia Road, Columbia, Md. 21044.

CUMBERLAND: Tri-State Stamp Club, second Wednesday, South Cumberland Library, 7 p.m. Garnett E. Fazenbaker, 811 Gephart Drive, Cumberland, Md. 21502.

GAITHERSBURG: Rockville/Gaithersburg Stamp Club, second and fourth Thursday, Gaithersburg High School, 314 S. Frederick Ave., 7:30 p.m. Thomas W. Smith, 7533 Tarpley Drive, Derwood, Md. 20855.

GREENBELT: NASA/Goddard Space Flight Center Stamp Club, second Tuesday except for July and August, GSFC,

Building No. 22, 11:30 a.m. Manfred Owe, President, Goddard Space Flight Center, Code 624, Greenbelt, Md. 20771.

HAGERSTOWN: Hagerstown Stamp Club, second Tuesday, St. Johns Lutheran Church, Education Building, 7:30 p.m. Vernon B. Downey, 116 Holly Terrace, Hagerstown, Md. 21740.

OXON HILL: Oxon Hill Philatelic Society, first Monday, Oxon Hill Library, 6200 Oxon Hill Road, 7:30 p.m. Pat Fowler, 9915 Williamsburg Drive, Upper Marlboro, Md. 20772.

SALISBURG: Eastern Shore Stamp Club, first and third Wednesday except July and August, Wicomico Youth and Civic Center, 7:30 p.m. Gail C. Vaughn, Box 298, Fruitland, Md. 21826.

SUITLAND: NOAA Space Philatelic Society, second Monday, Jesse M. Rodriguez, Box 559, Suitland, Md. 20746-0559.

WESTMINSTER: Carroll County Philatelic Association, third Thursday, Carroll County Office Building, 225 N. Center St., 8 p.m. Herman S. Beck Jr., 501 Beck Drive, Mount Airy, Md. 21771.

MISCELLANEOUS

James Hoban Chapter/Eire Philatelic Society, Robert E. Moskowitz, Secretary, 3313 Southern Ave., Baltimore, Md. 21214.

— North Arundel Philatelic Society, first, third and fifth Thursday, 6 p.m.-8:30. Harold Netzer, 860 Swift Road, Pasadena, Md. 21122.

— Plate Number Coil Collectors Club, meetings held as needed. Larry Thibodeau, 634 Derringer Drive, Bel Air, Md. 21014-4815.

MASSACHUSETTS

AMHURST: Amherst Stamp Club, fourth Tuesday (September-May), Jones Library. Siegfried Feller, 8 Amherst Road, Pelham, Mass. 01002

BOXBOROUGH: Stamp Hunters, first Friday, Shearaton, 7:30 p.m. P.E. Hunter, Drawer K, Shaker Road, Harvard, Mass. 01451.

BROOKLINE VILLAGE: Boston Philatelic Society, first and third Thursdays September-June, Brookline Public Library (main), 361 Washington St., 7 p.m.-9. John W. McGovern, 67 Perry St., Brookline, Mass. 02146.

CHELMSFORD: Chelmsford Stamp Club, second Wednesday and fourth Tuesday, except July and August, Carriage House, Boston Road, 7:30 p.m. Len Andexler, Box 163, Chelmsford, Mass. 01824.

FALL RIVER: Henry Lord Stamp Club, every Tuesday, Henry Lord Middle School, Room 3, 9 a.m. Edward J. Davis Jr., 615 Tucker St., Fall River, Mass. 02721.

FITCHBURG: Wachusett Philatclic Society, third Tuesday (September-November, January-May), second Tuesday (December and June), Chapel of All Saints, 1469 Main St. (Whalom), 7:30 p.m. Edward T. Donnelly, 225 North St. (Whalom), Fitchburg, Mass. 01420.

HARWICH: Harwich Stamp Club, first and third Wednesday, except July and August, Pine Oaks Community Center, Bank Street, 1:30 p.m. Caxton C. Foster, Box 488, East Orleans, Mass. 02643.

LAWRENCE: Samuel Osgood Stamp Club, first and third Wednesday, Lawrence Public Library South Branch, 135 Parker St., 7 p.m.-9. Charles MacBride, 9 Bellevue Road, Andover, Mass. 01810.

LYNN: Lynn Phiatelic Society Youth Group, last Tuesday, Sisson Elementary School, 56 Comono Ave., 1:45 p.m.-2:45. Michael J. Bourgault, 17 Lake View Place, East Lynn, Mass. 01904-2347.

NEEDHAM: Needham Stamp Club, third Friday, Steven Palmer Center, basement, 83 Pickering Road. Alice Ungethuem, 58 Chickering Road, Dedham, Mass. 02026.

OXFORD: Clara Barton Stamp Club, first Thursday, Episcopal Church Hall, Main Street. Peter Pierce, Box 560, Oxford, Mass. 01540-0560.

PITTSFIELD: Berkshire Museum Stamp Club, second and fourth Tuesdays, September thru June, Berkshire Museum, 39 South St., Stanley E. Moore, Corresponding Secretary, 39 South St., Pittsfield, Mass. 01201.

QUINCY: Granite City Stamp Club, first and third Tuesday, Lincoln Hancock School, 7:30 p.m. John J. Murphy, 4 Angus St., North Quincy, Mass. 02171.

STOUGHTON: Stoughton Stamp Club, first and third Monday, First Congregational Church, 76 Pierce St., 7 p.m.-9. John C. Nasuti, 36 Deerfield Road, Sharon, Mass. 02067.

WESTON: Waltham Stamp Club, first and third Tuesday, Cardinal Spellman Philatelic Museum, 7:30 p.m. John Seidl, 121 Cocasset St., Apt. 6, Foxboro, Mass. 02035.

MICHIGAN

ANN ARBOR: Ann Arbor Stamp Club, third Monday, Salvation Army Citadel, 100 Arbana Ave., Catherine Rector, Secretary, Box 2012, Ann Arbor, Mich. 48106.

BERRIEN SPRINGS: Redbud Philatelic Society, first Thursday except July and August, Senior Citizen Center, Shawnee Road, 7:30 p.m. Verda Trickett, 8846-1 Maplewood, Berrien Springs, Mich. 49103.

DEARBORN: Dearborn Stamp Club, second and fourth Wednesday, Dearborn Youth Center, Michigan at Greenfield, 7 p.m. Joan Klimchalk, 4488 Merrick, Dearborn Hts., Mich. 48125.

— Ford Stamp Club, first Monday, Ford P and A Building, 7:30 p.m. Robert L. Hyzy, Box 2388, Dearborn, Mich. 48123.

— Michigan Stamp Club, second and fourth Monday, Prince of Peace Lutheran Church, 19100 Ford Road, 7 p.m. Robert F. Rinke, secretary, 31890 Hoover Road, Warren, Mich. 48093.

— Motor City Stamp and Cover Club, last Sunday, Prince of Peace Lutheran Church, Ford Road, 3 p.m. October thru April; 4 p.m. May thru September. Robert Quintero, 22608 Poplar Court, Hazel Park, Mich. 48030-1928.

EAST LANSING: Central Michigan Philatelic Society, second and fourth Thursday, East Lansing Community Center, 201 Valley Court, 7 p.m. William C. Allen, Box 80946, Lansing, Mich. 48908.

FERNDALE: Ferndale Stamp Club, first and third Tuesday, Ferndale Community Center, 400 E. 9-Mile Road, 7 p.m. Robert K. Helbig, 22191 Morton, Oak Park, Mich. 48237.

GRAND RAPIDS: Kent Philatelic Society, second and fourth Wednesday, Grand Rapids Public Museum, South Jefferson at State Street, 7 p.m. Charles Miller, Box 1156, Grand Rapids, Mich. 49501.

GROSSE POINTE WOODS: Wayne Stamp Society, second and fourth Wednesday, Standard Federal Savings, basement, Mack near Cook Road, 7:30 p.m. Tom DeBoever, 6364 Hereford, Detroit, Mich. 48224.

HIGHLAND PARK: Liberty School Stamp Club, Wednesday, Liberty School Science Room, Liberty School, 16535 Joslyn, 3 p.m.-4:30. James Fostey, 16535 Joslyn, Highland Park, Mich. 48203.

INDIAN RIVER: Northern Michigan Stamp Club, last Monday, First of America Bank, 7:30 p.m. Harold R. Heintz, Box 33, Harbor Springs, Mich. 49740.

KALAMAZOO: Kalamazoo Stamp Club, fourth Tuesday, Fidelity Federal Saving and Loan basement, 5018 W. Main St., 7 p.m. Darlene Pylar, Box 121, Portage, Mich. 49081.

— Southwestern Michigan Post Card Club, first Monday, Hope Reformed Church Annex, 910 Jenks, 7 p.m. Louise B. Northam, 1833 Waite Ave., Kalamazoo, Mich. 49008.

KINGSFORD: Lindquist Stamp Club, second Wednesday, 804 Hamilton Ave., 7 p.m. Frank N. Kangas, 804 Hamilton Ave., Kingsford, Mich. 49801.

— Northwoods Philatelic Society, third Tuesday, Queen of Peace Church, 7 p.m. Mel Degroot, 527 Millie St., Iron Mt., Mich. 49801.

LINCOLN PARK: Hoover World Stamp Club, Monday, Hoover School Library, 3:15 p.m. Pat Cavanaugh, 3750 Howard, Lincoln Park, Mich. 48146.

MONROE: Floral City Stamp Club, second Monday, Monroe Bank & Trust, community room, Monroe Shopping Center, South Monroe Street, 7:30 p.m. Adele Rottenbucher, Secretary, 3785 Heiss Road, Monroe, Mich. 48161.

MUSKEGON: Muskegon Stamp Club, first and third Wednesday, McGraft Memorial Congregational Church, 1617 Palmer Ave., 7:30 p.m. Robert G. Gust, President, 2495 LeTart, Muskegon, Mich. 49441.

OAK PARK: Collectors Club of Michigan, first Monday, Oak Park Community Center, 13500 Oak Park Drive. Donald Nelson, Secretary, 19126 Devonshire Road, Birmingham, Mich. 48009.

— Northwest Stamp Society, second Tuesday, except July and August, Oak Park Community Center, 14300 Oak Park Blvd., 7 p.m.-10. Wilmont V. Osborn, 27501 Somerset, Inkster, Mich. 48141.

— Detroit/Oak Park Stamp Club of Michigan, second Tuesday, Oak Park Community Center, 13600 Oak Park Blvd., 7:30 p.m. Henry C. Lenhoff, 27451 Fairfax, Southfield, Mich. 48076.

— Oak Park Stamp Club, second Tuesday, Oak Park Community Center, Room B, Oak Park Blvd., 8 p.m. Henry C. Lenhoff, 27451 Fairfax, Southfield, Mich. 48076.

— Scandinavian Collectors Club of Detroit, Chapter 3, second Tuesday, except July and August, Oak Park Community Center, Room 1, 14300 Oak Park Blvd., 7 p.m.-9:30 Petter A. Poppe, 1028 Montrose, Royal Oak, Mich. 48073-2746.

— Society of Israel Philatelists Detroit Oak Park Chapter, second Tuesday, Oak Park Community Center, Room B, Oak Park Blvd., Irvin Girer, 27436 Aberdeen, Southfield, Mich. 48076.

PLYMOUTH: West Suburban Stamp Club, first and third Friday, Plymouth Township Meeting Hall, 42350 Ann Arbor Road, 8 p.m. Hal Williams, Box 643, Plymouth, Mich. 48170.

PONTIAC: Pontiac Stamp Club, second and fourth Tuesdays, Don O. Tatroe Instructional Materials Center, 1325 Crescent Lake Road, 8 p.m.-10. Michael R. Miley, 5923 Pleasant Drive, Drayton Plains, Mich. 48020.

SAGINAW: Saginaw Valley Stamp Society, first and third Wednesday, Chemical Bank Building, 2300 Midland Road, 7:30 p.m. P.A. Walters, Box 413, Freeland, Mich. 48623.

WARREN: USS Michigan Chapter 80, Universal Ship Cancellation Society, third Friday, GM Personnel Development Center, 6464 E. 12-Mile Road, 7 p.m Robert Quintero, Secretary, 22608 Poplar Court, Hazel Park, Mich. 48030-1928.

WESTLAND: Grandparent/Grandchildren Stamp Club, Dyer Center, 36745 Marquette Road. Alexander Velasco, 33728 Tawas Trail, Westland, Mich. 48185.

MISCELLANEOUS

USS Kalamazoo Chapter, Universal Ship Cancellation Society, James E. Smith, Box 336, Gobles, Mich. 49055.

— KCS Collectors Club, noon, various days. Duane Brummel, 624 52nd St. S.E., Kentwood, Mich. 49508.

— Scouts on Stamps Society International Great Lakes Chapter 8, Friday, April and November, members' homes, 7:30 p.m.-10. George. V. Holland, 32164 St. Anne's Drive, Warren, Mich. 48092.

MINNESOTA

ALBERT LEA: Interstate Stamp and Coin Club of Albert Lea, third Wednesday, American Legion Club, 142 N. Broadway, 7:30 p.m. Warren W. Rosenau, Secretary-Treasurer, Box 747, Albert Lea, Minn. 56007-0747.

DULUTH: Arrowhead Stamp Club, second Monday, St. Mary's Hall, 11th Street and Weeks Avenue, Superior, Wis., 7:30 p.m.; fourth Monday, Duluth Community Center, 211 N. Third Ave. E., Duluth, Minn., 7:30 p.m. Howard Pramann, 2137 Appalachian St., Duluth, Minn. 55811.

EXCELSIOR: Lake Minnetoka Stamp Club, second Tuesday, except June, July and August, Excelsior Elementary School, 7:30 p.m. Chris A. Juhl, 15 Bay St., Tonka Bay, Minn. 55331.

MANKATO: Mankato Area Stamp Club, first Wednesday and third Thursday, Minnesota Valley Regional Library, 6:30 p.m. Winston Grundmeier, 1331 North St., Mankato, Minn. 56001.

MARSHALL: Lyon County Philatelic Society, third Monday, September thru May, Marshall Middle School, 7 p.m. Stephen Klein, 401 Charles Ave., Marshall, Minn. 56258.

MINNEAPOLIS: Minnehaha Stamp Club, second Thursday, Pearl Park Neighborhood Center, 414 E. Diamond Lake Road, 7 p.m. George Breiner, 6844 Upton Ave. S., Minneapolis, Minn. 55423.

— Twin City Philatelic Society, first Thursday, Christ Lutheran Church, University Avenue, St. Paul; third Thursday, Bryant Park Center, 34th and Bryant, 7 p.m. Jim Wilbur, Box 27274, Minneapolis, Minn. 55427.

OWATONNA: Owatonna Coin and Stamp Club, third Thursday, Park and Recreation Building, West Hills, Mark

D. Rasmussen, 556 McIndoe St. E., Owatonna, Minn. 55060-3529.

RED WING: Red Wing Area Coin and Stamp Club, second Tuesday, Red Wing Public Library, 7 p.m. Mark L. Dugstad, 600 1/2 W. Lyon Ave., Lake City, Minn. 55041.

ST. CLOUD: St. Cloud Stamp Club, first and third Thursday, St. Cloud Public Library, 7:30 p.m. Robert B. Phillips, 1525 Northway 333, St. Cloud, Minn. 56303.

ST. PAUL: 3M Stamp Club, first or second Tuesday or Wednesday (except June-August), 3M Center, Bryan J. McGinnis, 3M Center, Building 230-3G-07, St. Paul, Minn. 55144.

— Maplewood Stamp Club, first Monday, except July and August, White Bear Fire Station, McKnight Road and East County Road E, 6:45 p.m. John Federowicz, Box 16507, St. Paul, Minn. 55116-0507.

WILLMOR: West Central Minnesota Stamp Club, second Thursday and fourth Tuesday, (except June-August), Senior High School library, 7:30 p.m. Johan F. Mattson, 8 Woodcock Drive, Spicer, Minn. 56288.

MISCELLANEOUS

North Star Stamp Club, Bill Norberg, 3101 Kentucky Ave. N., Crystal, Minn. 55427.

MISSISSIPPI

JACKSON: Jackson Philatelic Society, second Friday, Power and Light Building, Pearl Street, 7:30 p.m. Jim Scrivener, Box 1000, Ackerman, Miss. 39735.

PICAYUNE: Space Center Stamp Club, first and third Wednesday, Navy Library, conference room, Stennis Space Center, 11:30 a.m.-12:30. J. Houston Costolo III, 215 Boley Drive,, Picayune, Miss. 39466.

MISSOURI

COLUMBIA: Columbia Philatelic Society, first Monday, Columbia Mall meeting room, 7 p.m.-9. John Marquardt, 804 N. Ann St., Columbia, Mo. 65201.

GLADSTONE: Gladstone Philatelic Club, second Thursday, Gladstone Community Building, 69th and North Holmes, 7:15 p.m. John Burt, President, 3028 Swift, N. Kansas City, Mo. 64116.

JOPLIN: Joplin Stamp Club, first and third Tuesday except June, July and August, Park Apartment's Clubhouse, 1763 Campbell Parkway, 7 p.m. Frederic L. Roesel, 4225 E. 25th, Joplin, Mo. 64804.

KANSAS CITY: Midwest Philatelic Society, first Saturday, Plaza Library, 4801 Main St. John M. Hamilton, 6611 N. Platte Hills Road, Kansas City, Mo. 64152.

ROLLA: Rolla Philatelic Society, third Thursday, Rolla Public Library, 900 Pine St., 7 p.m. Glendell L. Maples, 605 Shady Acres Court, Rolla, Mo. 65401.

ST. LOUIS: Mound City Stamp Club, first and third Monday (July and August, third Monday only), Olivette Community Center, 9723 Grandview Drive, 8 p.m. James W. Adler, 6452 Nashville Ave., St. Louis, Mo. 63139.

— Society of Israel Philatelists St. Louis Chapter, last Tuesday, Covenant House on J.C.C.A. grounds, 10 Millstone Campus, 7:30 p.m. Bernard Schram, 1732 Chouteau Ave., St. Louis, Mo. 63103.

WEBSTER GROVES: Webster Groves Stamp Club, first and third Friday, 75 W. Lockwood, 8 p.m. Hans Stoltz, 34 North Gore, Webster Groves, Mo. 63119.

MISCELLANEOUS

Missouri Precancel Club, one Mulefest per year, usually in the summer or fall. Edwin Swafford, 714 Delchester Lane, Kirkwood, Mo. 63122-1006.

— Shell Knob Lakers Stamp Club, Ruth Huff, Drawer M, Shell Knob, Mo. 65747.

MONTANA

BILLINGS: Billings Stamp Club, first Tuesday, except July and August, St. Vincent's Hospital, Training Rooms 1 and 2. Claude Wilson, 1106 Main St., Suite 2, Billings, Mont. 59105.

KALISPELL: Glacier Stamp Club, first Monday, Montana Power Building, North Meridian Road, 6:30 p.m. youth, 7:30 p.m. adults. George T. Hanson, Box 1727, Columbia Falls, Mont. 59912-1727.

MISSOULA: Garden City Stamp Club, first Tuesday and third Thursday, September thru June, Montana Power Building, 1903 Russell St., 8 p.m. Oliver E. White, 200 Whitaker Drive, Missoula, Mont. 59803.

MISCELLANEOUS

Great Falls Stamp Club, last Monday and second and third Thursday, 7 p.m. Joseph C. Merrifield, Secretary, 614 Sixth Ave. N., Great Falls, Mont. 59401.

NEBRASKA

GRAND ISLAND: Central Nebraska Stamp Club, second Sunday, except June thru August, Grace Abbott Library, 211 N. Washington. Doris M. Sundermeier, Secretary/Treasurer, Box 248, Cairo, Neb. 68824.

LINCOLN: Lincoln Stamp Club, first and third Friday, Southeast High School, 37th and Van Dorn, 7:30 p.m. Lawrence Kinyon, Box 2412, Lincoln, Neb. 68502.

OMAHA: Omaha Philatelic Society, second Friday, Omaha Public Library, 210 S. 15 St.; fourth Friday, St. Timothy Lutheran Church, 930 W. Dodge Road, 7:30 p.m. Allen R. Hendricksen, Box 12411, Omaha, Neb. 68112.

— West Omaha Stamp Club, third Thursday, 11334 Elm St. Herb Eveland, 203 S. 72nd St., Suite 3, Omaha, Neb. 68114.

NEVADA

INDIAN SPRINGS: Southern Desert Stamp Group, first and third Monday, Clark County School District, Cold Creek Road, 6:15 p.m. J. Hardacre or T. Townsen, Box 208, Hobbycraft Program, Indian Springs, Nev. 89018-0208.

NEW HAMPSHIRE

DOVER: Great Bay Stamp Club, second Tuesday, September thru June, Seacoast Savings Bank conference room, 240 Locust St., 7 p.m. Vincent S. Cahill Jr., 6 Tri City Road, Apt. 4, Dover, N.H. 03820.

HANOVER: Ray School Stamp Club, first Monday, Ray School, Rosquick Road, 3 p.m.-4:30. Isaac Oelgart, 24 School St. No. 12, Hanover, N.H. 03755.

LITTLETON: Profile Stamp Club, second Monday, Community Center, Main Street, 7 p.m. Sandra Willey, 25 Richmond St., Littleton, N.H. 03561.

MADISON: White Mountain Stamp Club, third Monday, Barbara Savary, Route 16, next to Metz Engineering, 7 p.m. Sharon Morrill, Box 121, North Conway, N.H. 03860.

MANCHESTER: Manchester Stamp Club, fourth Monday, except June thru August, first floor Conference Room, Public Service of New Hampshire, 1000 Elm St., 7:30 p.m. Robert Dion, President, Box 1, North Salem, N.H. 03073.

PEMBROKE: Pembroke Stamps, Larry W. Young Sr., 5 Donald Ave., Pembroke, N.H. 03275.

NEW JERSEY

BERGENFIELD: Roy W. Brown Collectors Club, Roy W. Brown Middle School, 130 S. Washington Ave., Thomas P. Neats, 362 Wildrose Ave., Bergenfield, N.J. 07621.

BLOOMFIELD: North Jersey Federated Stamp Clubs Inc., fourth Wednesday, Bloomfield Recreation Center, 7:30 p.m. Nathan Zankel, Box 267, New Brunswick, N.J. 08903.

BRIDGETON: Bridgeton Stamp Club, second and fourth Thursday, except November and December, Oakview Heights Recreation Center, Oakview Heights Senior Citizens Development, North West Avenue and Greenwich Road, 8 p.m. Don Hart, Treasurer, 41 Preston Ave. Extension, Bridgeton, N.J. 08302.

CINNAMINSON: Riverfront Philatelic Society, fourth Monday, Cinnaminson Public Library, Riverton Road, 7:30 p.m. James Natale, 3307 Concord Drive, Cinnaminson, N.J. 08077.

CLARK: Garden State Post Card Collectors Club, first Sunday except October, American Legion Hall, 76 Westfield Ave., noon-5. Dolores Kirchgessner, 421 Washington St., Hoboken, N.J. 07030.

CLIFTON: American First Day Cover Society, Chapter 41, first Monday, except July and August, Clifton Recreation Center, 1232 Main Ave., 8 p.m.-9. Robert F. Drummond, Lake Forest RD 1, Lake Hopatcong, N.J. 07849.

— Clifton Stamp Society, first, third and fifth Mondays, Clifton Recreation Center, 1232 Main Ave., 7 p.m. Gerard Neufeld, 33 Comfort Place, Clifton, N.J. 07011.

ENGLEWOOD: Englewood Stamp Club, David B. Popkin, Box 528, Englewood, N.J. 07631-0528.

FAIR LAWN: American Helvetia Philatelic Society, Northern New Jersey Chapter No. 1, third Tuesday, Old Library

Theatre, 12-56 River Road, 8 p.m. George H. Wettach, Box 261, Fair Lawn, N.J. 07410.

— Fair Lawn Stamp Club, second and fourth Tuesday, Fair Lawn Arts Center, River Road, 8:30 p.m. John J. O'Neil, 11-06 Third St., Fair Lawn, N.J. 07410.

HAMILTON TWP.: Hamilton Township Stamp Club, third Tuesday, Hamilton Twp. Main Library, 1 Municipal Drive, 7:30 p.m. Richard Marolda, 4 Kruger Lane, Trenton N.J. 08620.

HAZLET: Hazlet Stamp Club, second and fourth Tuesdays, Hazlet Recreation Center, Veterans Park, Union Avenue, 8 p.m. Robert W. Henry, Chapter Representative, Box 12, Hazlet, N.J. 07730.

HIGHLAND PARK: Central Jersey Chapter Society of Israel Philatelists, second Tuesday, except July and August, YM and YWHA, 2 S. Adelaide Ave. Nathan Zankel, Box 267, New Brunswick, N.J. 08903.

JERSEY CITY: Five Corners Library Ben Franklin Stamp Club, every Friday, Five Corners Branch, Jersey City Public Library, 678 Newark Ave., 3:30 p.m.-4:30. Anne Byrne, Five Corners Library, 678 Newark Ave., Jersey City, N.J. 07303.

LAKEHURST: Leisure Village West Stamp & Coin Club, first and third Wednesdays, (July and August meetings held on first Wednesday), Willow Hall, Rooms A & B, 10 a.m. Arthur Poppe, 24 B. Edinburgh Lane, Lakehurst, N.J. 08733.

MADISON: North Jersey Chapter of Society of Israel Philatelists, fourth Monday, library, 39 Keep St., 8 p.m. Chester S. Callen, 27 Marmon Terrace, West Orange, N.J. 07052.

MONTCLAIR: West Essex Philatelic Society, second and fourth Monday, Montclair Public Library, 50 S. Fullerton Ave., 7:30 p.m. Raymond Laplace, Box 443, Elmwood Park, N.J. 07407.

MORGANVILLE: Molly Pitcher Stamp Club, second and fourth Monday, September thru June, Grace Lutheran Church, Park Avenue (Route 33). Paul Sherman, 50 Highway 9, Morganville, N.J. 07751.

MORRISTOWN: Jockey Hollow Stamp Club, first and third Monday, Morristown Memorial Hospital, Mt. Kemble Division, cafeteria, 95 Mt. Kemble Ave., 8 p.m. David Ahl, Box 2411 R, Morristown, N.J. 07960.

PENNSAUKEN: Merchantville Stamp Club, first Thursday and third Wednesday, Temple Lutheran Church, Route 130 and Merchantville Avenue, 7 p.m.-8:30. Paul Schumacher, Box 2913, Cherry Hill, N.J. 08034.

RIDGEWOOD: North Jersey Stamp Club, second and fourth Wednesday, except July and August, Bethlehem Lutheran Church, Room 124, 155 Linwood Ave., 8 p.m. Marguerite J. Doney, 65 New St., Allendale, N.J. 07401-2122.

SOUTH PLAINFIELD: Roosevelt School, after school, Mario C. Barbiere, Roosevelt School, Jackson Avenue, South Plainfield, N.J. 07090.

TEANECK: Teaneck Stamp Club, first and third Thursdays, Townhouse, Teaneck Road and Forest, 8 p.m. Philip E. Lilgeberg, 77 Lexington Ave., Rochelle Park, N.J. 07662.

TOMS RIVER: Holiday City at Berkeley Stamp Club, every other Wednesday, Club House No. 1, 631 Jamaica Blvd., 10 a.m. Alfred A. Glatz, Box 3254, Toms River, N.J. 08756.

WARREN: Queen City - Warren Stamp and Cover Club, first and third Mondays, First National Bank of Central Jersey, 59 Mountain Blvd., 8 p.m. George Gray, Box 4503, Warren, N.J. 07060-0503.

WESTFIELD: Westfield Stamp Club, fourth Thursday, September thru June, Westfield Municipal Center, East Broad Street. Thomas M. Jacks, Box 1116, Mountainside, N.J. 07092.

MISCELLANEOUS

Crestwood Coin and Stamp Club, second Wednesday, Hilltop Club House, Crestwood Village, 7 p.m.; fourth Tuesday, Unity Club House, Crestwood Village, 1:30 p.m. President, Box 154, Whiting, N.J. 08759.

NEW MEXICO

ALAMOGORDO: Chaparral Coin/ Stamp Club, first and third Tuesday, during school term, Chaparral Junior High, 1401 College Ave., 3:30 p.m.-4:15. Elise Haley, 2413 Princeton, Alamogordo, N.M. 88310.

ALBUQUERQUE: Great Britain Stamp

Club of New Mexico, Mail Boxes of New Mexico, 3232 San Mateo N.E., Albuquerque, N.M. 87111. Paul D. Gaffan, 3709 Erbbe St. N.E., Albuquerque, N.M. 87111.

— Palo Duro Philatelic Society, Mondays, Palo Duro Senior Center, 5221 Palo Duro Ave. N.E., 12:30 p.m.-2:30. Earlene Brinegar, 8907 Fairbanks Road N.E., Albuqurque, N.M. 87112.

FARMINGTON: Animas Valley Stamp Club, fourth Tuesday, Farmington Civic Center, Jack E. Robb, 170 W. 32nd St., Farmington, N.M. 87401.

LAS CRUCES: Mesilla Valley Stamp Club, first and third Thursdays except August, Branigan Library, 200 E. Picacho Ave., 7:30 p.m. Arthur Dudenhoeffer, Box 546, Mesilla, N.M. 88046.

NEW YORK

ALBANY: Fort Orange Stamp Club, second and fourth Tuesday, except June thru August, First Lutheran Church, 646 State St., Jack Haefeli, Secretary, Box 8645, Albany, N.Y. 12208.

— Heritage Stamp & Coin, every other Saturday, 1871 Central Ave., 11 a.m.-4 p.m. J.F. McEnerney, 1871 Central Ave., Albany, N.Y. 12205.

AUBURN: Auburn Stamp Club, first Tuesday and third Wednesday (first Tuesday in July and August), Westminister Church, 17 William St., 7 p.m. Debbi Goodelle, 3 Seymour St., Auburn, N.Y. 13021.

BATAVIA: Batavia-Genesee Country Coin & Stamp Club, third Thursday, YMCA Building, East Main Street, 7:30 p.m. Dennis Kane, 268 Ross St., Batavia, N.Y. 14020.

BROOKLYN: Brooklyn Caribe Stamps Club, first Sunday, 301 Third St., Apt. 2, Brooklyn, N.Y. 11215.

— Geshromim Society, third Wednesday, even months except August, Queens Midtown Tunnel, George Michaels, 350 65th St., Apt. 18J, Brooklyn, N.Y. 11220.

— John Dewey High School Stamp Club, daily meeting during school year, John Dewey High School. Ronald Broth, 50 Ave. X, Brooklyn, N.Y. 11223.

— Midwood High School Stamp Club, Thursday, Room 235, Period 9. S. Milstein and M. Ort, Bedford Avenue and Glenwood Road, Brooklyn, N.Y. 11210.

— Public School 16 Ben Franklin Stamp Club, Friday, 157 Wilson St., Room 418, 3 p.m.-4. Steven J. Braunstein, 157 Wilson St., Brooklyn, N.Y. 11211.

— St. Matthew-Emmanuel Stamp Club, first and third Wednesday, Community Center, 415 Seventh St., 7:30 p.m. Alice Britt, 461 Eighth St., Brooklyn, N.Y. 11215.

BUFFALO: Plewacki Post Stamp Society, every Tuesday, American Legion Post 799, 385 Paderewski Drive, 8 p.m. Stanley A. Keane, 385 Paderewski Drive, Buffalo, N.Y. 14212.

CANISTEO: Steuben Stamp Club, second Monday, Canisteo Central School, Room 322, 84 Greenwood St., 7 p.m. John S. Babbitt, 84 Greenwood St., Canisteo, N.Y. 14823.

CHEEKTOWAGA: Senior-Pex Stamp Club of Cheektowaga, last Wednesday, Senior Center of Cheektowaga, 1 p.m. Dominick A. Zaccagnino, President, 68 Constance Lane, Cheektowaga, N.Y. 14227.

COHOCTON: Cohocton Central Ben Franklin Stamp Club, first Monday during school year, Cohocton Central School, Mr. Palmer's room, 3 p.m. Barbara F. Sick, Box 94, Cohocton, N.Y. 14826-0094.

COMMACK: Commack High School Stamp Club, varied days during school year, Commack High School. Joseph Walter, Scholar Lane, Commack, N.Y. 11725.

DANSVILLE: Dansville Area Coin & Stamp Club, third Sunday, Dansville Town Hall, Clara Barton Street, 2 p.m. Robert L. Stickeny, Box 574, Dansville, N.Y. 14437.

DUNKIRK: Northern Chautauqua Philatelic Society, first Monday and third Wednesday, VFW Club, Post 1017, 113 Deer St., 7:30 p.m. Richard W. Long, Club Representative, 419 Robin St., Dunkirk, N.Y. 14048.

EAST AURORA: East Aurora Philatelic Society, alternate Wednesday, East Aurora Middle School, Main Street, 7 p.m.-9. Nannette Walterich, 52 Shearer Ave., East Aurora, N.Y. 14052.

EAST MEADOW: Long Island Cover Society, first Monday, Eisenhower Park

Golf Course, 19th Hole Meeting Room, Parking Field 7, 7:45 p.m. Charles Breyer, Box 325, Valley Stream, N.Y. 11582.

ELMIRA: Elmira Stamp Club, third Tuesday, Community Room, Columbia Banking Federal Saving and Loan Association, 351 North Main St., 7:30 p.m. Alan Parsons, APS Representative, 809 Holley Road, Elmira, N.Y. 14905.

FULTON: Fulton Stamp Club, second and fourth Wednesday, except July and August, one meeting in December, Fulton Municipal Building community room, 141 S. First St., John A. Cali, 613 W. Fourth St., Fulton, N.Y. 13069.

GENEVA: Finger Lakes Stamp Club, second and fourth Wednesday, January thru May, October and November; second Wednesday, June and December; fourth Wednesday, September, Jordan Hall, N.Y. State Agriculture Experiment Station, West North Street, 7 p.m. Gil Lewis, 502 Route 88 S., Newark, N.Y. 14513-9015.

HAMILTON: Chenango Valley Stamp Club, third Monday, All-American Room of Huntington Gymnasium, Colgate University, 7:45 p.m. Robert H. Betz, RD 1 Box 135, Earlville, N.Y. 13332.

HARRISON: Harrison Stamp and Coin Club, first three Wednesdays, Solazzo Recreation Center, 270 Harrison Ave., 8 p.m.-10. Howard Basterl, President, Box 851, Harrison, N.Y. 10528.

INDIAN LAKE: Ben Franklin Stamp Club, Wednesdays, Indian Lake Central School, third grade classroom, 2:50 p.m.-3:50. Marcia Breakey, Indian Lake Central School, Indian Lake, N.Y. 12842.

KODAK PARK: Kodak Stamp Club, fourth Tuesday, except December and April, Recreation Building 28, second floor cafeteria, Kodak Park, 7:30 p.m. Bob Najjar, Secretary, Recreation Club Building 28, Eastman Kodak Co., Rochester, N.Y. 14650.

LOCKPORT: Lockport Coin and Stamp Club, second and fourth Tuesday, Emmanuel Methodist Church, 75 East Ave., 7 p.m. Betty Steimer, Secretary, 4233 Hartland Road, Box 361, Gasport, N.Y. 14067-0361.

LYNBROOK: Professional Coin and Stamp Dealers' Association of Long Island Inc., second Tuesday, Bob's Big Boy Restaurant, Commack Road, 8 p.m. Stan Roe, Box 354, Lynbrook, N.Y. 11563.

MONTICELLO: Sullivan County Philatelic Society, first Sunday, afternoon meetings in December thru March, Temple Sholom, 7:30 p.m. or 1:30 p.m. Art Rosenzweig, Box 230, Monticello, N.Y. 12701.

NEWBURGH: Newburgh Stamp Club, fourth Monday (December, third Monday), First Baptist Church, South and West streets, 7:30 p.m. William T. McCaw, Box 1361, Newburgh, N.Y. 12550.

NEW HARTFORD: Utica Senior and Junior Stamp Club, first Tuesday, September thru June, Zion Lutheran Church, Frenich Road, 7:30 p.m. Janet Collmer, Secretary, Box 85, Franklyn Springs, N.Y. 13341.

NEW YORK: France and Colonies Philatelic Society, first Tuesday, Collectors Club of New York, 22 E. 35th St., 8 p.m. Walter E. Parshall, Corresponding Secretary, 103 Spruce St., Bloomfield, N.J. 07003.

— Club of Channel Islands Collectors, first Thursday, except July and August, Colletors Club, 22 E. 35th St. Matthew Trachinsky, Box 579, New York, N.Y. 10028.

— City Hall Stamp Club, Saturdays, 180 Varick St., 14th floor, 8 a.m.-3 p.m. Jacob Habib, Secretary, 150 Nassau St., New York, N.Y. 10038.

— New York Chapter, American Revenue Association, first Thursday, except July and August, Collectors Club, 22 E. 35th St., 8 p.m. Terence Hines, Box 629, Chappaqua, N.Y. 10514-0629.

— American Topical Association New York Chapter, second Thursday, Collectors Club, 22 E. 35th St., 7:15 p.m.-9:30. Harlan Hamilton, President, 170 E. 83 St., Apt 3-L, New York, N.Y. 10028.

— Hellenic Philatelic Society of America, second Friday, except July and August, Collectors Club, Dr. N. Asimakopulos, 541 Cedar Hill Ave., Wyckoff, N.J. 07481.

— International Stamp Club, first Tuesday, 7 p.m.; third Sunday, 1 p.m., International House, 155 Claremont Ave. Farnsworth Lobenstine, 80 LaSalle St., No. 3G, New York, N.Y. 10027.

— Italy and Colonies Study Circle, last Friday, Studio of Domenico Facci,

248 West 14th St., 8 p.m. Gregory Carrubba, 215 Adams St., Brooklyn, N.Y. 11201.

— Judaica Historical Philatelic Society, third Tuesday, August thru May, Collectors Club, 22 E. 35 St., 7:30 p.m. Sam Simon, 80 Bruce Ave., Yonkers, N.Y. 10705.

— Masonic Stamp Club of New York, second Wednesday, except July and August, Collectors Club, 22 E. 35th St., 2 p.m. Allan Boudreau, Director, Masonic Hall, Box 10, 46 W. 24th St., New York, N.Y. 10010.

— New York Estonian Philatelic Society, second Sunday, Estonia House, 243 E. 34th St., 11 a.m.-2 p.m. Rudolf Hamar, 31 Addison Terrace, Old Tappan, N.J. 07675.

— U.S. Philatelic Classics Society, New York Chapter, third Tuesday, except July and August, Collectors Club, 22 E. 35 St., 7:30 p.m. Irving Adams, c/o Collectors Club, 22 E. 35 St., New York, N.Y. 10016-3806.

OSWEGO: Oswego Stamp Club, second and fourth Monday, Roy McCrobie Building, West Lake Street, 7:30 p.m. Patricia Piersall, President, 57 E. 10th St., Oswego, N.Y. 13126.

PLATTSBURGH: Plattsburgh Stamp Club, second and fourth Mondays, September thru May; fourth Monday, June thru August, Clinton County Government Center, Margaret Street. Glen A. Estus, Box 451, Westport, N.Y. 12993.

REGO PARK: Long Island Stamp Club, first, second and third Tuesday, Lost Battalion Hall, 93-29 Queens Blvd., 7 p.m.-10. Anton Zorn, 60-11 59 Drive, Maspeth, N.Y. 11378.

RIVERHEAD: Riverhead Stamp Club, second and last Thursday, Riverhead Library, 7 p.m. Mildred Wright, 1161-276 Old Country Road, Riverhead, N.Y. 11901.

ROCHESTER: Rochester Philatelic Association Inc., second and fourth Thursdays, September thru June, St. Paul's Episcopal Church, East Avenue and Vick Park B, 7:30 p.m. Joseph K. Doles, 34 Carlisle St., Rochester, N.Y. 14615-2043.

— Society of Israel Philatelists Rochester Chapter, third Monday, Jewish Community Center, Edgewood Avenue, Dr. Sherwin M. Morris, 1840 Monroe Ave., Rochester, N. Y. 14618.

ROCKVILLE CENTRE: Long Island Hinges, third Thursday, Church of the Ascension, 71 N. Village Ave., 8 p.m. Charles W. Machovec, 117 Lawson Ave., East Rockaway, N.Y. 11518.

ROME: Fort Stanwix Stamp Club, second and fourth Thursday, except June thru August, Rome City Hall, second floor, 7:30 p.m. Franklyn Rudd, 614 N. James St., Rome, N.Y. 13440.

SCHENECTADY: Schenectady Stamp Club, first and third Mondays, third Monday September thru June, Union Presbyterian Church, 1068 Park Ave., 7:30 p.m. Stephen E. Gray, 10 C-1 Hillcrest Village W., Schenectady, N.Y. 12309.

SHERRILL: Community Stamp Club, third Thursday, except June thru August, CAC Club House, Hamilton Avenue, Don Connelly, Vice President, 68 Glenwood Ave., RD 1 Box 461, Oneida, N.Y. 13421.

SHRUB OAK: Shrub Oak Stamp Club, first and third Monday, John C. Hart Memorial Library, 7:30 p.m. Alfred F. Schaum, Box 616, Shrub Oak, N.Y. 10588.

SIDNEY: Tri-County Stamp Club, third Monday, September thru June, Sidney Civic Center, second floor, 7 p.m. Clifford Tuttle, 20 Pear St. E., Sidney, N.Y. 13838.

— Tri-County Stamp Club, third Monday, Civic Center, Room 204, 7 p.m. Owen R. Dewey, 10 Hatfield Ave., Sidney, N.Y. 13838.

STATEN ISLAND: Public School 8 Stamp Club, Tuesdays, Public School 8, Lindenwood Road, 3 p.m.-4. Fred Sprague, 503 King George Road, Basking Ridge, N.J. 07920.

— Staten Island Philatelic Society, first and third Mondays, except July and August, Faith United Methodist Church, 221 Heberton Ave., Port Richmond, 7:30 p.m. Edward Hochuli, President, Box 231, Staten Island, N.Y. 10314.

SYRACUSE: Syracuse Stamp Club, first and third Fridays, The Reformed Church of Syracuse, 1228 Teall Ave. Richard W. Finzer, Secretary, Box 6, Cato, N.Y. 13033.

TROY: Uncle Sam Stamp Club of Troy, first and third Wednesday, September thru May, Holmes and Waton, 450 Broadway, Terrill S. Miller, Box 335, Troy, N.Y. 12180.

VESTAL: Johnson City Stamp Club, first and third Monday, New York State Electric and Power Plant Building, Stage Road, 7 p.m.-9. Steve Malack, Box 628 Union Station, Endicott, N.Y. 13760.

WESTBURY: Westbury Stamp Club, second Thursday, Westbury Library, Rockland Street at School Street, 7:30 p.m. Vernon L. Brenner, 70 Cameron Ave., Hempstead, N.Y. 11550.

MISCELLANEOUS

Bell Park Gardens Stamp Club, second and fourth Friday, members' homes, 7:30 p.m. Charles Amira, 218-06 68 Ave., Bayside, N.Y. 11364.

— Central New York First Day Cover Society Chapter 53, annual meeting at Ropex. Richard A. Kase, Secretary, 6 Starwood Drive, Rochester, N.Y. 14625-2631.

— Collectors Club, 22 E. 35th St., New York, New York 10016, open to public Monday, Wednesday and Friday 10 a.m.-4 p.m., first and third Wednesday from 1 p.m.-8. Closed holidays and June 15-September 15. Meetings, lectures during year.

— Empire State Postal History Society, Maris Tirums, Secretary-Treasurer, Box 5475, Albany, N.Y. 12205.

— Federation of Central New York Philatelic Societies Inc., meets biannually, Sundays, usually June and October, Karrat's Restaurant, 1 p.m. John A. Cali, 613 W. Fourth St., Fulton, N.Y. 13069.

— Mark Twain Stamp Club, during school day, Helene Alalouf, Mark Twain JHS, Woodlawn Avenue, Yonkers, N.Y. 10704.

NORTH CAROLINA

ASHEVILLE: Asheville Stamp Club Inc., third Monday, meeting place varies, 7 p.m.-9. Carl W. Greene, Vice President, Box 8317, Asheville, N.C. 28814.

CHAPEL HILL: Triangle Stamp Club, third Thursday except December, Commons Room, Chapel of the Cross, 304 E. Franklin St., 7:30 p.m. George Gretz, Box 75, Carrboro, N.C. 27514.

CHARLOTTE: Charlotte Philatelic Society, first and third Sunday, Metrolina Association for the Blind, 704 Louise Ave., Robert R. Reeves, President, Box 30101, Charlotte, N.C. 28230.

FAYETTEVILLE: Cape Fear Philatelic Society, first and third Thursday, Sears Conference Room, Cross Creek Mall, 7 p.m. Charlotte M. Brooks, 627 Danforth Place, Fayetteville, N.C. 28303.

GREENSBORO: Tarheel Post Card Club, Saturdays, except July and August, 1614 Helmwood Drive, 1 p.m.-5. Roberta S. Greiner, 1614 Helmwood Drive, Greensboro, N.C. 27410.

RALEIGH: Raleigh Stamp Club, first Monday, Jaycee Center, Wade Avenue, 7:30 p.m. Anne T. Carson, 2411 Lake Drive, Raleigh, N.C. 27609.

WINSTON-SALEM: Winston-Salem Stamp Club, last Tuesday, Miller Park Recreation Center, 7:30 p.m. Miriam C. Bumgarner, 2448 Maplewood Ave., Winston-Salem, N.C. 27103.

MISCELLANEOUS

Tarheel Chapter, Scouts on Stamp Society International, Scout shows and other various times. W.C. Coinen, Box 31242, Raleigh, N.C. 27622-1242.

OHIO

AKRON: Rubber City Stamp Club Inc., first and third Friday September thru June, Montrose Zion United Methodist Church, 565 N. Cleveland-Massillon Road, 8 p.m. R. Morris Frost, 238 Meadowview Road, Northfield, Ohio 44067-2419.

BEACHWOOD: Society of Israel Philatelists Cleveland Chapter, first Tuesday (September thru June), Congregation Shaarey Tikvah, 26811 Fairmount Blvd., 8 p.m. Albert Friedberg, 3813 Bushnell Road, University Heights, Ohio 44118.

CANTON: Stark County Stamp Club, second Wednesday, Sippo Lake Park Clubhouse, 5300 Tyner St. N.W., 7:30 p.m. Brian Mumford, 1210 31st St. N.W., Canton, Ohio 44709-2929.

CINCINNATI: The Greater Cincinnati Philatelic Society, second Monday, Lifton First National (Star) Bank, 425 Ludlow Ave.; fourth Wednesday, Roselawn First National (Star) Bank, 7660 Reading Road. Virginia Fisher, 3091 Riddle View Lane, Cincinnati, Ohio 45220.

CLEVELAND: Cuy-Lor Stamp Club, second and fourth Friday, West Park United Church of Christ, 3909 Rocky River Drive, 8 p.m. Tom Kacmarcik, Box 45042, Cleveland, Ohio 44145.

— Garfield Perry Stamp Club, every Friday, Holiday Inn-Lakeside, 1111 Lakeside Ave. and East 12th Street, 8 p.m. R.H. Parker, 1111 Lakeside, Cleveland, Ohio 44114.

COLUMBUS: Columbus Philatelic Club Inc., second and fourth Monday, Radisson Hotel Columbus, 4900 Sinclair Road, 7 p.m. Paul H. Gault, Box 16036, Columbus, Ohio 43216.

— Germany Philatelic Society, Edward E. Kuehn Chapter 20, third Sunday, Upper Arlington Public Library, 2 p.m. Paul H. Gault, 140 W. 18th Ave., Columbus, Ohio 43210.

CUYAHOGA FALLS: Cuyahoga Falls Stamp Club, first and third Monday, Fraternal Order of Eagles Hall, Front Street Mall, 7:30 p.m. Bob Patetta, Box 104, Cuyahoga Falls, Ohio 44222-0104.

DAYTON: Dayton Stamp Club, first and third Monday, Wegerzyn Garden Center, 1301 E. Siebenthaler Ave., 7:30 p.m. Michael J. Komiensky, Box 1574, Dayton, Ohio 45401.

— Gettysburg VA Stamp Club, every Thursday, VAMC conference room, 5N. 20, 7 p.m. Walter J. Strobel Jr., VAMC SN. 20 4100 W. Third St., Dayton, Ohio 45428.

ELYRIA: Black River Stamp Club, first Friday, Elyria Savings & Trust (branch office), 1000 Lowell St., 8 p.m. James M. Forbes, 6443 Lake Ave., Elyria, Ohio 44035.

FINDLAY: Fort Findlay Stamp Club, second and fourth Wednesday, Trust Corp., 1600 Tiffin Ave., 7:30 p.m. Donald M. Yeager, 3312 Ridgeview Drive, Findlay, Ohio 45840.

KINGSVILLE: Ashtabula County Stamp Club Inc., second Monday (except December), Kingsville Public Library, 8:05 p.m. Edward Fiala, 175 McKinley Ave., Conneaut, Ohio 44030.

MARION: Marion Hobby Club, second Thursday, First United Church of Christ, South Prospect and West Columbia streets, 7:30 p.m. Berneice Smith White, 3487 Firstenberger Road, Marion, Ohio 43302.

MEDINA: Medina County Stamp Club, first Thursday, Medina Community Library, Public Square, 7:30 p.m. Jack W. Ryan, 140 W. Lafayette Road No. 3, Medina, Ohio 44256.

MIDDLETOWN: Miami Valley Stamp Club, third Thursday, First National Bank of S.W. Ohio Sunset Branch, 1300 Sunset St., 7:30 p.m. Larry L. Neal, 403 Brelsford Ave., Trenton, Ohio 45067.

MILFORD: Clermont County Stamp Club, third Thursday, Old Library, 19 Water St., 7 p.m. Janet Klug, RR 1, Box 370-B, Pleasant Plain, Ohio 45162.

NEW PHILADELPHIA: Tuscora Stamp Club, first and third Wednesday, Emmanuel Lutheran Church, 202 E. High Ave., 7 p.m. (winter), 7:30 p.m. (summer). Jim Shamel, 605 Buckeye Hollow Road, Uhrichsville, Ohio 44683.

NORWOOD: Norwood Middle School Stamp Club, every other Wednesday (during school year), Norwood Middle School, Room 308, 3 p.m. Dave Moore, 2020 Sherman Ave., Norwood, Ohio 45212.

ST. CLAIRSVILLE: Belmont County Stamp Club, third Sunday, Buckeye Savings Bank, Perimeter of Ohio Valley Mall, 2 p.m. Charles Snider, 54300 East Road Dix Add., Martins Ferry, Ohio 43935.

SANDUSKY: Sandusky Stamp Club, first Thursday (except June, July and August), Sandusky High School, Room 111, Hayes Avenue, 7:30 p.m. Yvonne M. Fievet, 910 Carr St., Sandusky, Ohio 44870.

SIDNEY: Sidney Stamp Club, third Monday, Northtown Branch Star Bank, 1222 Wapak Road, 7 p.m. Paul F. Amann, Box 357, Fort Loramie, Ohio 45845.

STEUBENVILLE: Fort Steuben Stamp Club, fourth Monday, Ohio Valley Towers, 500 Market St., 7:30 p.m. Verna Tarr, Box 1131, Steubenville, Ohio 43952.

TIFFIN: Tiffin Stamp Club, third Thursday, Tiffin-Seneca Public Library, 7:30 p.m. Raymond J. Turck, 165 Hampden Park, Tiffin, Ohio 44883.

TOLEDO: Stamp Collector's Club of Toledo, second and fourth Thursday (except Thanksgiving and Christmas), Medical College of Ohio, Mulford Public Library cafeteria, Arlington Avenue, 7:30

p.m. Allan M. Cunningham, 706 Spring Grove Ave., Toledo, Ohio 43605.

WOOSTER: Wooster Stamp Club, third Thursday, United Methodist Church, North Market Street, 7:30 p.m. Helen Keptner, Box 444, Wooster, Ohio 44691.

WORTHINGTON: Worthington Stamp Club, first and third Monday (September thru June), Sharon Twp. Hall, 137 E. Dublin-Granville Road, (S.R. 161). Stanley P. Bednarczyk, 5303 N. High St., Columbus, Ohio 43214.

YOUNGSTOWN: Mahoning Valley Stamp Club, second and fourth Thursday (one in November and December), Martin Luther Church, 420 Clearmont Drive, 7:30 p.m. Ernest F. Neptune, 49 South Edgehill, Youngstown, Ohio 44515.

MISCELLANEOUS

China Stamp Society Inc., KoLunPu Chapter, fourth Sunday, (quarterly, January, April, July, October). Paul H. Gault, 140 W. 18th Ave., Columbus, Ohio 43210.

— Ohio Postal History Society, dates vary, Airpex, Dayton; Colopex, Columbus; Tolpex, Toledo. Michael J. Morrissey, Box 441, Worthington, Ohio 43085.

— Ohio Precancel Club, Charles Pearson, 1004 Pinehollow Lane, Cincinnati, Ohio 45231.

— Shaker Heights Philatelic Society, third Monday (except July and August), members' homes, 8 p.m. Larry Cohn, 23351 Chagrin Blvd., No. 403, Beachwood, Ohio 44122.

OKLAHOMA

ARDMORE: Southern Oklahoma Stamp Club, first and third Thursday, Ardmore Public Library, Grand & E Northwest, 7 p.m. Ruth Young, Box 1446, Ardmore, Okla. 73401.

BARTLESVILLE: Washington County Philatelic Society, fourth Thursday (except July, August and December), Disciples Christian Church, Douglas Lane, 7:30 p.m. J.F. Copeland, Box 741, Bartlesville, Okla. 74005.

EDMOND: Edmond Junior Stamp Club, second and fourth Saturday, Edmond Public Library, 10 S. Boulevard, 9:30 a.m.-11:30. Alma Benedict, 601 Vista Lane, Edmond, Okla. 73034.

LAWTON: Lawton-Ft. Sill Stamp Club, first and third Tuesday, Town Hall, 5th and B streets, 7:30 p.m. Hildegard Taylor, 1703 N.W. Cedarwood Drive, Lawton, Okla. 73505.

OKLAHOMA CITY: Oklahoma City Stamp Club, first and third Tuesday, 3333 North Meridian, 7:45 p.m. Alma Benedict, Box 26542, Oklahoma City, Okla. 73126.

MISCELLANEOUS

Chelsea Stamp Club, Herb R. Schibelle, Box 63, Chelsea, Okla. 74016-0063.

OREGON

ALBANY: Linn County Philatelic Society, second Thursday, Albany Post Office, Second and Washington streets, 7:30 p.m.-9. Arnold Swirbul, 2810 N.W. Monterey Drive, Corvallis, Ore. 97330.

COOS BAY: Bandon Stamp Club, third Friday, North Bend Medical Center, 1900 Woodland Drive, 8 p.m. Charlotte Casey, 2678 Stanton St., North Bend, Ore. 97459.

CORVALLIS: Corvallis Stamp Club, first Wednesday (except July and August), Highland View School, Room 23, 1920 N.W. Highland Drive, 7:30 p.m.-9. Arnold Swirbul, 2810 N.W. Monterey Drive, Corvallis, Ore. 97330.

EUGENE: Greater Eugene Stamp Society, second and fourth Wednesday, Main Post Office Building, Fifth and Williamette streets, 7:30 p.m. Gary Schweiger, Box 734, Eugene, Ore. 97440.

GRANTS PASS: Rogue Valley Stamp Club, first Tuesday, 300 Greenfield Road, 7 p.m. Blair T. Smith, 245 Blue Bell Lane, Grants Pass, Ore. 97527.

MEDFORD: Southern Oregon Philatelic Society, first Thursday, B.L.M. Building, 7:30 p.m.; and second or third Sunday, 2 p.m. Len Lukens, Box 117, Phoenix, Ore. 97535.

PORTLAND: Oregon Stamp Society Inc., second and fourth Tuesday, society clubhouse, 4828 N.E. 33rd Ave., 8 p.m. Secretary, Box 82121, Portland, Ore. 97282-0121.

SALEM: Junior Stamp Collectors Club of Salem, third Tuesday, Grant School, 725 Market St. N.E., 7:30 p.m.-9. H. Douris, Box 3685, Salem, Ore. 97302.

— Willamette Valley Stamp Club, fourth Tuesday, Willamette Savings & Loan building, community room, 600 Center St., 7 p.m. Thomas D. Pomeroy, 1909

Nut Tree Drive N.W., Salem, Ore. 97304-1110.

MISCELLANEOUS

Benton County Stamp Club, second Tuesday. Thomas D. Pomeroy, 1909 Nut Tree Drive N.W., Salem, Ore. 97304-1110.

PENNSYLVANIA

AMBLER: Ambler Stamp Club, first and third Wednesday, First Presbyterian Church of Ambler, Ridge and Butler Pike, 7:30 p.m. James H. O'Mara, 1230 Lois Road, Ambler, Pa. 19002.

ASTON: Brookhaven Stamp Club, third Thursday except July and August, Aston Township Building, Route 452. Thomas R. Ogden III, 924 East 18th St., Chester, Pa. 19013.

BRADFORD: Bradford Stamp Club, second Wednesday, hospitality room, Northwest Savings & Loan, 33 Main St., 7 p.m. Ronald J. Yeager, 214 Jackson Ave., Bradford, Pa. 16701.

BRYN ATHYN: Bryn Athyn Elementary School Stamp Club, every Friday, Glencairn Museum, 1001 Papermill Road, 1:30 p.m. Ivan K. Smith, 625 Woodward Drive, Huntingdon Valley, Pa. 19006.

ERIE: Erie Stamp Club, first and fourth Thursday, Sacred Heart School Library, 25th and Plum streets. Robert F. Smith, 5108 Mill St., Erie, Pa. 16509.

EASTON: Bi-State Stamp Club, fourth Tuesday (except December), Merchants Bank community room (in the basement), 25th and Northampton streets. Barbara E. Snyder, 4000 Green Pond Road, Palmer, Pa. 18042.

GETTYSBURG: Blue & Gray Stamp Club, first Wednesday and third Thursday, library of St. James Church, 7:30 p.m. Donald Reimer, 154 South Howard Ave., Gettysburg, Pa. 17325.

GREENSBURG: Westmoreland County Philatelic Society, second Sunday (third Sunday in May), community room, Greengate Mall, Route 30, 2:15 p.m. Beverly G. Vaughn, RD 5, Box 549, Mt. Pleasant, Pa. 15666.

HOLLIDAYSBURG: Blair County Stamp Club, first Thursday, 7 p.m.-9; third Sunday, 2 p.m.-4, First Presbyterian Church of Hollidaysburg, Clark and Walnut streets. Elvin Liebegott, 530 W. 14th St., Duncansville, Pa. 16635.

JOHNSTOWN: Johnstown Junior Stamp Club, first Thursday, Community Room, First United Federal building, 227 Franklin St., 7 p.m. Donald W. Smith, Box 576, Johnstown, Pa. 15907.

KANE: Kane Ben Franklin Stamp Club, first Wednesday (except June, July and August), Friends Memorial Library, 2 Greeves St., 7 p.m. Ronald E. Swanson, 633 Biddle St., Kane, Pa. 16735.

KING OF PRUSSIA: Associated Stamp Clubs of Southeastern Pennsylvania and Delaware Inc. (SEPAD), first Friday (except July and August), 7 p.m. Alan Warren, Box 731, Horsham, Pa. 19044.

LANCASTER: Armstrong Activities Association Stamp Club, second Thursday (except June, July and August), Armstrong World Industries Innovation Center, 2500 Colombia Ave., 7 p.m. Thomas A. Ream, Box 3511, Lancaster, Pa. 17604.

LEBANON: Lebanon Stamp Collectors Club, second Tuesday, Chamber of Commerce Meeting Room. Jerome G. Laconis, Box 114, Palmyra, Pa. 17078-0114.

LEMOYNE: Susquehanna Valley Stamp Club, second and fourth Tuesday, West Shore Stamps, 829 State St., 7 p.m. Catherine E. McAlister, 2145 Lambs Gap Road, Enola, Pa. 17025.

LYNDORA: Butler County Philatelic Society, first and third Wednesday, Dunbar Community Center, 7 p.m.-9. Joyce M. Freshcorn, 226 Eighth Ave., Butler, Pa. 16001.

MONTOURSVILLE: Williamsport Stamp Club, fourth Wednesday, American Legion Post 104, 1312 Broad St., 8 p.m. Harold Gottshall, 1009 Weldon St., Montoursville, Pa. 17754-1529.

MORRISVILLE: Summerseat Stamp Collectors, fourth Wednesday, Summerseat, Hillcrest and Legion avenues, 7:30 p.m. Doris G. Burkhardt, 216 Osborne Ave., Morrisville, Pa. 19067.

MOUNT JOY: Mount Joy Stamp Club, first Wednesday, Trinity Lutheran Church, 47 W. Main St., 7:30 p.m. Anne Zimmerman, 263 Park Ave., Mount Joy, Pa. 17552.

PHILADELPHIA: American Topical Association Philadelphia Chapter 6, first Thursday (except July and August), Jefferson Medical College, Room 213,

1015 Walnut St., 7:30 p.m. George M. Gerhart, 7130 Chew Avenue, Philadelphia, Pa. 19119.

— Delaware Valley Chapter of American First Day Cover Society, third Thursday, Bethany Baptist Church, Rhawn and Rockwell streets, 7:30 p.m. George J. Mullen, Box 11485, Philadelphia, Pa. 19111.

— Frankford Arsenal Stamp Club, second Thursday, Bridesburg Recreation Center, Richmond and Ash streets, 7:30 p.m. Michael A. Stefanowicz, 7610 Lexington Ave., Philadelphia, Pa. 19152.

— Germantown-Chestnut Hill Stamp Club, first Tuesday and third Wednesday, Watertower Recreation Center, Hartwell Lane and Ardleigh Street, 7:45 p.m. Dorothy L. Moore, Box 128, Flourtown, Pa. 19031.

— Greater Northeast Stamp Club, third Thursday, Recreation Center, Solly and Bustleton avenues, 7:30 p.m. Sam Rothkoff, 3177 Kensington Ave., Philadelphia, Pa. 19134.

— Society of Israel Philatelists Philadelphia Chapter, fourth Monday (September thru May), Kaiserman Jewish Community Center, City Line and Haverford avenues, Daniel J. Siegel, 532 Circle Drive, Havertown, Pa. 19083.

PITTSBURGH: Greater Pittsburgh First Day Cover Club, fourth Monday, Carnegie Library of Squirrel Hill, 6 p.m. Carol Ann Remmick, 336 Lime Hollow Road, Verona, Pa. 15147.

— Kelton Stamp Club, every Friday (during school year), Curt Buchanan, 1098 Kelton Ave., Pittsburgh, Pa. 15216.

— The Philatelic Society of Pittsburgh, first and third Monday, First Lutheran Church, 615 Grant St., 7:30 p.m. W.K. Schomburg, 5296 Range Drive, Pittsburgh, Pa. 15236-2865.

POTTSTOWN: Pottstown Area Stamp Club, first Monday, Leader Nursing and Rehabilitation Center, activities room, 724 N. Charlotte St., 7 p.m. Valeria F. Bell, 2048 Yarnall Road, Pottstown, Pa. 19464.

QUAKERTOWN: North Penn Stamp Club, first Tuesday, St. John's Evangelical Lutheran Church, 19 S. 10th St. Paul V. Scheetz, 145 S. 10th Street, Quakertown, Pa. 18951.

ROCKLODGE: Germany Philatelic Society Chapter 2, third Thursday (except July and August), library, Ukrainian Cultural Center. Chris Kulpinski, Box 464F, Feasterville, Pa. 19047.

SCHUYLKILL: Schuylkill Stamp & Coin Club, second Tuesday (except June and July), Senior Citizens Building, 7:30 p.m. Fred Koch, 155 Avenue E, Schuylkill Haven, Pa. 17972.

STATE COLLEGE: Mt. Nittany Philatelic Society Inc., first Wednesday and third Thursday, APS Building. President, Box 902, State College, Pa. 16804.

WARMINSTER: Bux-Mont Stamp Club, second and fourth Tuesday, Grace Lutheran Church, Street Road, 8 p.m.-10. Michael Fesnak, 6733 N. Lawrence St., Philadelphia, Pa. 19126.

WARREN: Warren County Stamp Club, third Tuesday, First Presbyterian Church, corner Third and Market streets, 7 p.m. Doris A. Brennan, 101 Home St., Warren, Pa. 16365.

WASHINGTON CROSSING: Coryell's Ferry Stamp Club, first Monday, Lambertville Baptist Church, Bridge Street, Lambertville, N.J. 08530, third Monday, Methodist Church, 8 p.m. Bertha Davis, Box 7005, Wrightstown, Pa. 18940-0800.

WAYNE: Pennsylvania Postal History Society, third Saturday, Northeast Regional Library, Philadelphia, Pa. (September, November, January, March and May), Radnor Twp. Library (October, December, February, April and June), 2 p.m. John L. Kay, 329 Milne St., Germantown, Pa. 19144-4205.

WESTFIELD: Ben Franklin Stamp Club, first Thursday, Westfield Boro Elementary School, 3:15 p.m.-4:30. Cheryl B. Edgcomb, Box 59, Knoxville, Pa. 16928-0059.

WILKES-BARRE: Wyoming Valley Stamp Club, first and third Tuesday (except July and August), YMCA, 40 W. Northampton St. Verna Kovach, 77 Kent Lane, Wilkes-Barre, Pa. 18702.

WILKINSBURG: Wilkinsburg Stamp Club, second and fourth Sunday, Wilkinsburg Borough Building, 2 p.m. Thomas F. Shaw, Box 8711, Pittsburgh, Pa. 15221-0711.

YORK: Colonial York Junior Stamp

Club, third Saturday (September thru May), Martin Memorial Library, 10 a.m. L.B. Zemaitis, 696 Maryland Ave., York, Pa. 17404.

— White Rose Philatelic Society of York, first and third Wednesday, United Way Building, 800 E. King St., 7:30 p.m. John C. Hufnagel, Box 85, Glenrock, Pa. 17327-0085.

MISCELLANEOUS

Ben Franklin Stamp Club, Leslie W. Goldstein, 345 Barclay Ave., Pittsburgh, Pa. 15221-4058.

— China Stamp Society, first Wednesday (September thru December and February thru May), 7:30 p.m. John G. Glenn Jr., Box 997, Fort Washington, Pa. 19034.

— Daniel Boone Chapter, Scouts on Stamps Society International, first or second Sunday (January, April and October). Walter M. Creitz, 830 Berkshire Drive, Reading, Pa. 19601.

— Meadville Stamp Club, third or fourth Wednesday. Conrad Fisher, RD 6, Box 198, Meadville, Pa. 16335.

— Montandon Ben Franklin Stamp Club, first or second Tuesday, 6:30 p.m. James Terry Baldwin, 8 Wilson Circle, Milton, Pa. 17847.

— Western Pennsylvania Precancel Society, first Sunday (March thru October). Scott A. Shaulis, 119 W. Sanner St., Somerset, Pa. 15501.

PUERTO RICO

PUERTO NUEVO: Puerto Rico Philatelic Society, Sundays, Ave. Andalucia 773, 9:30 a.m.-12 p.m. Luis Gonzalez Perez, Box 1500, Hato Rey, Puerto Rico 00919.

RHODE ISLAND

CRANSTON: Rhode Island Philatelic Society, Inc., first and third Tuesday, Meshanticut Park Baptist Church Hall, 180 Oaklawn Ave. Raymond L. Gaillaguet, Box 9345, Providence, R.I. 02940.

JAMESTOWN: Jamestown Ben Franklin Stamp Club, Wednesdays, Jamestown School, 6:30 p.m.-7:30. William R. McCarthy, 18 Bryer Ave., Jamestown, R.I. 02835.

PAWTUCKET: Slater Stamp Club, first and third Wednesday, Centennial Towers, 35 Goff Ave. V. Guy Moreau, 44 Slater Park Ave., Pawtucket, R.I. 02861-2910.

WARWICK: Kent County Philatelic Society, second and fourth Tuesday, St. Barnabas Church, 7:30 p.m. Frank C. McCardell, 91 Barnold St., West Warwick, R.I. 02893.

SOUTH CAROLINA

COLUMBIA: Columbia Philatelic Society Inc., second Tuesday and fourth Thursday, Columbia Newspapers Plant, Shop Road, 7:30 p.m. Secretary, Box 1675, Columbia, S.C. 29202.

NORTH CHARLESTON: Charleston Stamp Club, first and third Thursday, Armory Park Recreation Building, Mixon Avenue. Charles Kolb, Box 5711, N. Charleston, S.C. 29406.

SPARTANBURG: Spartanburg Stamp Club, first Thursday, Woodland Heights Recreation Center, Reidville Road, 7:30 p.m. Larry Vincent, 335 Weblin St., Spartanburg, S.C. 29301.

SUMTER: Sumter Philatelic Society, third Tuesday, Sumter County Library, 7 p.m. N.L. Parnes, 17 Brooks St., Sumter, S.C. 29150.

MISCELLANEOUS

Germany Philatelic Society Chapter 37, Piedmont, one Saturday, 11 a.m.-5 p.m. Erik B. Nagel, Box 65, Taylors, S.C. 29687-0065.

— Greenville Stamp Club, fourth Tuesday, President, Box 1871, Greenville, S.C. 29602.

SOUTH DAKOTA

ABERDEEN: Ringneck Coin and Stamp Club, second Monday, First Bank-Aberdeen, 320 S. 1st, 8 p.m. Mark Zimmerman, 323 S. Boyd St., Aberdeen, S.D. 57401.

HURON: Fair City Coin & Stamp Club, fourth Monday, Beadle County Court House, 7:30 p.m. Bernadine Paulsen, 1285 Idaho S.E., Huron, S.D. 57350.

MOBRIDGE: Bridge City Coin and Stamp Club, first Thursday, Citizens Bank social room, Main Street, 7:30 p.m. Stan Mack, Box 91, Mobridge, S.D. 57601.

PIERRE: Pierre Coin and Stamp Club, third Tuesday, State Library, 7:30 p.m. Les Mord, Box 211, Pierre, S.D. 57501.

SIOUX FALLS: Sioux Falls Stamp Club, first and third Thursday, Old County Courthouse, Sixth Street and Dakota

Avenue, 7:30 p.m. Donna Kappenman, 516 Melrose St., Sioux Falls, S.D. 57106.

TENNESSEE

AUBURNTOWN: The Collectors, Thursday, Auburn School. Derrick Hughes, Route 1, Box 228, Auburntown, Tenn. 37016.

BRENTWOOD: Brentwood Philatelic Society, third Tuesday, seminar room, Brentwood Library, 5055 Maryland Way. 6:30 p.m. Deborah L. Allen, President, Box 1791, Brentwood, Tenn. 37024-1791.

JACKSON: West Tennessee Stamp Club, third Tuesday, Jackson-Madison Co. Library, 7 p.m. Frank E. Kos, Box 204, Medina, Tenn. 38355-0204.

KINGSPORT: State of Franklin Stamp Club, third Tuesday, Children's Dept., Kingsport Public Library, 4 p.m.-5. Josephine S. Wang, Kingsport Public Library, Broad and New streets, Kingsport, Tenn. 37660.

MEMPHIS: Memphis Stamp Collectors Society, first and third Tuesdays, West Meeting Room, Pink Palace Museum, 8 p.m. Frank Tilghman, 1598 Staunton, Southaven, Miss. 38671.

NASHVILLE: Nashville Philatelic Society, second and fourth Mondays, 4312 Gallatin Road at Inglewood Branch Library, 7 p.m. Terry Chaney, Secretary, Box 60531, Nashville, Tenn. 37206.

OOLTEWAH: White Oak Stamp Club, first Sunday, Draper Building of S.D.A. Church, Amos Road, 9:30 a.m. W. Troy McDougal, 8540 Rancho Drive, Ooltewah, Tenn. 37363.

MISCELLANEOUS

Holston Stamp Club, third Thursday, alternating in Bristol, Tenn.; Johnson City, Tenn.; Kingsport, Tenn.; 7 p.m. C.L. Overstreet, 413 Robin Road, Bristol, Tenn. 37620.

TEXAS

AMARILLO: Amarillo Golden Spread Stamp Club, third Thursday, General Mail Facility third floor, 2300 Ross, 7:30 p.m. Thomas H. Stich, Box 31016, Amarillo, Texas 79120.

ARLINGTON: Mid-Cities Stamp Club, first Wednesday, Community Center, 7:30 p.m. Jerry Mertz, 3004 Amberway Drive, Arlington, Texas 76014.

AUSTIN: Austin Stamp Club, first and third Tuesday, Howson Branch Library, 2500 Exposition Blvd., 7:30 p.m. John G. Karabaic, 9409 Queenswood Drive, Austin, Texas 78748.

— Austin-Texas Stamp Club, first and third Tuesday, Howson Branch, Austin Public Library, 2500 Exposition, 7:30 p.m. Romaine Flanagin, Secretary, 6802 Duquesne Drive, Austin, Texas 78723.

— Shady Hollow Stamp Club, second and fourth Wednesday, Shady Hollow Community Center, 7 p.m. Mike Aldrige, 11505 Brodie Lane, Austin, Texas 78748.

BORGER: Borger Stamp Club, first and third Tuesday, Hutchinson County Library, club rooms, 7:30 p.m. Eleanor Gonser, 1515 Pellinore St., Borger, Texas 79007.

DALLAS: East Dallas Stamp Club, second and fourth Thursday, Casa Linda Presbyterian Church, 9353 Garland Road. Fred Hollenbeck, 11341 Earlywood Drive, Dallas, Texas 75218.

— Society of Israel Philatelists Dallas Chapter, third Tuesday, Jewish Community Center, 7800 N. Haven Road, 7:30 p.m. Jerome L. Byer, President, 1114 N. Bishop, Dallas, Texas 75208.

EDINBURG: Pan American University Stamp Club, first Monday, Pan American University, 1201 W. University Drive, Room BA 220C, 6 p.m. Walter E. Greene, 1201 W. University Drive, Edinburg, Texas 78539-2999.

EL PASO: El Paso Philatelic Society, first and third Wednesday, Christ The King Episcopal Church, 3416 Atlas Drive, 7:30 p.m. John W. Panke, 1656 Bert Green, El Paso, Texas 79936.

FORT WORTH: Panther City Philatelic Society, second and fourth Tuesdays, Panther Boys Club, 1519 Lipscomb St., 7:30 p.m. Charles W. Brock, 4633 El Campo Ave., Fort Worth, Texas 76107-4913.

— William James Stamp Club, Fridays, Room 323, William James Middle School. Camille Thomason, 1101 Nashville, Fort Worth, Texas 76105.

HEREFORD: Hereford Stamp Club, second and fourth Tuesday, except summer, Hereford Community Center, 400 E. Park Ave., 7:30 p.m. Marian R. Kreig, 405 Ave. J, Hereford, Texas 79045.

KILLEEN: Central Texas Philatelic

Society, third Tuesday, the Oveta Culp Hobby Memorial Library, Central Texas College campus, 4:30 p.m. Kathleen Gray, Box 988, Copperas Cove, Texas 76522.

MARSHALL: Marshall Stamp Club, second Tuesday, Swepco Hospitality Room, 7:30 p.m. Barney Wyatt, 2701 Cedar Crest, Marshall, Texas 75670.

NACOGDOCHES: Nacogdoches Stamp Club, first Thursday, Westminister Presbyterian Church, 903 North St., 7:30 p.m. William Gibson, 3601 Logansport Road, Nacogdaches, Texas 75961.

RICHARDSON: Germany Philatelic Society, Dallas Chapter, Wineburgh Philatelic Research Library, McDermott Library, The University of Texas at Dallas. Peter R. Thompson, 2616 Teakwood Lane, Plano, Texas 75075.

SNYDER: White Buffalo Stamp Club, second Monday, TU Electric, 2301 Ave. R, 7:30 p.m. Robert Patterson, Snyder Health Mart Drug, 3609 College, Snyder, Texas 79549.

WACO: Heart of Texas Stamp Club Inc., third Thursday, Main Post Office, Highway 6 and Sanger Avenue, 7 p.m. George Kubal, Box 1196, Hewitt, Texas 76643.

VERMONT

BENNINGTON: Green Mountain Stamp Society, second and fourth Wednesday (September-June), Crescent Manor Nursing Home, Crescent Boulevard, 7 p.m. Stuart E. Libby, Box 571, Bennington, Vt. 05201.

BRATTLEBORO: Brattleboro Stamp Club, third Monday, meeting room, Brooks Memorial Library, Main Street, 7 p.m. Irene Kirchheimer, Secretary, RD 2, Box 34, Brattleboro, Vt. 05301.

GROTON: Groton Stamp Club, Tuesday, Groton Public Library, 6:30 p.m.-8. M. Ross McLeod, RR 1, Box 42A, Groton, Vt. 05046.

MONTPELIER: Washington County Stamp Club, third Tuesday, First Baptist Church, School and St. Paul streets, 7:30 p.m. Herbert H. Storm, Secretary, Box 269, Randolph, Vt. 05060.

RUTLAND: Rutland County Stamp Club Inc., every other Thursday, Laurence Recreation Center, Center and Court streets, 7 p.m. Nick Nikolaidis, RFD 1, Box 720, Bethel, Vt. 05032.

SOUTH BURLINGTON: Chittenden County Stamp Club, second Monday, New England Telephone Co., Hinesburg Road, 7 p.m. Ruth M. Henson, 102 Adams St., Burlington, Vt. 05401.

VIRGINIA

COLONIAL HEIGHTS: Appomattox Stamp Club, fourth Wednesday, Colonial Heights Public Library, 7:30 p.m. Iris Schwartz, Box 832, Colonial Heights, Va. 23834.

COVINGTON: Boys' Home Stamp Club, third Wednesday, Boys' Home Library, 5 p.m. R.A. Huddleston, Route 2, Box 121, Covington, Va. 24426.

DANVILLE: Dan River Philatelic Society, third Tuesday, Downtown Sovran Bank, 341 Main St., 7:30 p.m. Charles Fowlkes, Secretary, 124 Winston Road, Danville, Va. 24541.

HARRISONBURG: Rockingham Stamp Club, fourth Wednesday, Rockingham Public Library meeting room, 7:30 p.m. Eldon Layman, 85 E. Elizabeth St., Harrisonburg, Va. 22801.

LYNCHBURG: Lynchburg Stamp Club, second Tuesday, First Colony Life Building, Seventh and Main, 7 p.m. Terry D. Bailey, Box 901, Lynchburg, Va. 24505-0901.

MANASSAS: Postcard Club Federation, third Sunday except August, Manassas School of Dance, Manassas Shopping Center, 1 p.m.-5. John H. McClintock, Box 1765, Manassas, Va. 22110.

MCLEAN: Dolley Madison Stamp Club, first and third Fridays, McLean Government Center, 1437 Balls Hill Road, John M. Hotchner, Box 1125, Falls Church, Va. 22041-0125.

NORFOLK: Tidewater Chapter No. 1, Armed Forces Stamp Exchange Club, last Thursday, Dehare Coins & Stamps, 6500 Virginia Beach Blvd., 7 p.m. Joseph Coulbourne, Sam Division USS John F. Kennedy CV-67, F.P.O. New York, N.Y. 09538.

RADFORD: New River Valley Stamp Club, third Tuesday, Radford City Library, 7:30 p.m. C.W. Nye, Box 582, Dublin, Va. 24084.

ROANOKE: Big Lick Stamp Club of Roanoke Valley, every second Sunday, Room 182, Post Office, 419 Rutherford

Ave. N.E., 2:30 p.m. Ranes Chakravorty, 5049 Cherokee Hills Drive, Salem, Va. 24153-9848.

SPRINGFIELD: Springfield Stamp Club, second and fourth Wednesday (except July and August), Lynbrook Elementary School, 5801 Backlick Road, 7 p.m. Joe Schoen, Box 544, Springfield, Va. 22150.

VIENNA: Ayrhill Stamp Club of Vienna, first and third Thursday, Vienna Branch of Fairfax County Public Library, Maple Avenue and Center Street, 7:30 p.m. Miles Manchester, 9508 Rockport Road, Vienna, Va. 22180.

WINCHESTER: Trojan Stamp Club, last Thursday, Frederick County Middle School, time varies. Michael Hough, c/o Frederick County Middle School, 441 Linden Drive, Winchester, Va. 22601.

WOODBRIDGE: Eastern Prince William Stamp Club, every first and third Monday, Potomac Library, 2201 Opitz Blvd., 7:30 p.m. Joan Bleakley, 15906 Crest Drive, Woodbridge, Va. 22191.

MISCELLANEOUS

Lions International Stamp Club, Dennis A. Clark, 8174 Electric Avenue, Vienna, Va. 22180.

— Virginia Philatelic Federation Inc. executive board meets four times a year at various locations. Leroy P. Collins III, Secretary, Box 2183, Norfolk, Va. 23501.

WASHINGTON

BELLEVUE: Greater Eastside Stamp Society, second and fourth Thursday, Lake Hills Library conference room, 15228 Lake Hills Boulevard, 7 p.m.-9. Eric Baker, 13724 N.E. 72nd Place, Redmond, Wash. 98072.

BREMERTON: Olympic Philatelic Society, the second and fourth Tuesdays, First United Methodist Church, 1150 Marine Drive, 7:30 p.m. Alanson Powell, Box 4266, South Colby, Wash. 98394.

OAK HARBOR: Whidbey Island Stamp Club, first and third Tuesday, Harbor Tower Retirement Community, 7330 700th Ave W. Lee Dougherty, 6195 600 Ave. W., Oak Harbor, Wash. 98277.

RICHLAND: Tri City Stamp Club, third Wednesday, Frontier Federal Savings and Loan, 7 p.m. James Durham, 300 Adams, Richland, Wash. 99352.

SEATTLE: Collectors Club of Seattle, every Tuesday, noon to 3 p.m.; every Friday, 7 p.m. to 10. George G. Barry, Box 15205, Seattle, Wash. 98115.

SEQUIM: Strait Stamp Society, first Thursday, Sequim Library, 7 p.m.-9. Cathleen F. Osborne, Box 1781, Sequim, Wash. 98382.

SUNNYSIDE: Lower Valley Stamp Club, second Thursday, Sunnyside Library, Seventh and Grant, 7:30 p.m.-9. Gerald Bird, 725 Victory Way, Sunnyside, Wash. 98944.

WALLA WALLA: Walla Walla Philatelic Society, third Thursday, Berney School, Pleasant and School streets, 7:30 p.m. Louis Ruzicko, 47 E. Main, Walla Walla, Wash. 99367.

MISCELLANEOUS

Serbia Study Group, Larry O. Sundholm, W. 448 27th Ave., Spokane, Wash. 99203.

— Sno-King Stamp Club, second Wednesday, except August, United States Post Office, 8120 Hardeson Road; third Wednesday, except July, Florence Anderson Center, Seventh and Main. Donna Samuelsen, Secretary, 14220 Three Lakes Road, Snohomish, Wash. 98290.

WEST VIRGINIA

BUCKHANNON: Upshur County Coin & Stamp Club, third Wednesday of the month, Social Hall of the Episcopal Church, South Kanawha Street, 7:30 p.m. Kay Sienkiewec, 26 Meade St., Buckhannon, W.Va. 26201.

CHARLESTON: Kanawha Stamp Club, first Sunday, Conference Room, Main Post Office, 1002 Lee St., 2:30 p.m. Sam N. Poolos, 604 S. Park Road, Charleston, W.Va. 25304.

CLARKSBURG: Harrison County Stamp Club, third Monday, Senior Citizens Center, 7:30 p.m. Michael Ravis, Box 405, Clarksburg, W.Va. 26301.

PARKERSBURG: Blennerhassett Stamp Society, first Thursday and third Monday, Trinity Hall, Fifth and Juliana streets. Evert L. Whitlatch, Secretary, Box 4293, Parkersburg, W.Va. 26104.

SISTERSVILLE: Middle Island Stamp Club, second Tuesday, Sistersville Public Library, 8 p.m. Donald D. Slider, 115 Rural St., Paden City, W.Va. 26159.

WISCONSIN

APPLETON: Outagamie Philatelic Society, third Thursday Sept.-May, Valley Fair Mall conference room, 3145 S. Memorial Drive, 6:30 p.m. Verna Shackleton, 208 E. Circle St., Appleton, Wis. 54911.

BROOKFIELD: Germany Philatelic Society, Milwaukee Chapter 18, fourth Sunday, Equitable Savings & Loan Association, 14545 W. Capitol Drive, 7 p.m. Roger J. Szymanski, Box 1690, Milwaukee, Wis. 53201.

EAU CLAIRE: Chippewa Valley Stamp Club, third Thursday, London Square Mall, Community Room, 7 p.m. Melanie Reimann, 872 Broadview Blvd., Eau Claire, Wis. 54703.

ELKHORN: Walworth County Stamp Club, second Wednesday, Civic Center, 7:30 p.m. Howard Powell, 14 W. Geneva, Elkhorn, Wis. 53121.

FOND DU LAC: Fond Du Lac Stamp Club, first Tuesday and third Thursday, Petries Bavarian Inn, 84 N. Main St., 7:30 p.m. Fred L. Ericksen, Box 821, Fond Du Lac, Wis. 54936-0821.

GREEN BAY: Green Bay Philatelic Society Inc., third Thursday, Steiner's Family Restaurant, North Webster and Radison. Kirk E. Becker, Box 33053, Green Bay, Wis. 54303.

MADISON: Badger Stamp Club, first and third Saturday, Bethany United Methodist Church, 3910 Mineral Point Road, 2 p.m. Karen Weigt, 4184 Rose Court, Middleton, Wis. 53562.

MANITOWA: Manitowa Philatelic Society, second Tuesday, Rohr-West Museum, Eighth and Park. Mary Lou Wagner, Secretary, 15 S.C. Trunk St., Cato, Wis. 54206.

MILWAUKEE: Milwaukee Philatelic Society Inc., third Saturday, Howard Johnson Lodge, 1716 W. Layton Ave., 7 p.m. Irene Orz, Secretary, Box 1980, Milwaukee, Wis. 53201.

— North Shore Philatelic Society, first Wednesday, Security Savings and Loan Office, 5555 N. Port Washington Road, 7:30 p.m. Ronald J. Gorski, 5820 N. 34th St., Milwaukee, Wis. 53209.

— Temple Stamp Club, fourth Wednesday, except July and August, Scottish Rite Cathedral, 790 N. Van Buren St. Carl H. Cerull, 4420 S. Dora Lane, New Berlin, Wis. 53151.

— The Philatelic Society at the University of Wisconsin-Milwaukee, third Monday, University of Wisconsin-Milwaukee Student Union, 2200 E. Kenwood Blvd., 6 p.m. Bruce Ramme, Box 407, Okauchee, Wis. 53069.

OSHKOSH: Oshkosh Philatelic Society, first Tuesday and third Monday, except June, July and August, Evergreen Manor, 1130 N. Westfield St., 7:30 p.m. Herbert E. Burgett, 600 Merritt Ave., Apt. 311, Oshkosh, Wis. 54901.

RHINELANDER: Northwoods Stamp & Coin Club, second and fourth Tuesday, Oneida County Senior Center, 1103 Thayer St. Carol L'Herault, President, 4169 Pine Point Drive, Rhinelander, Wis. 54501.

RIPON: Ripon Philatelic Stamp Club, second Thursday, Braun's Restaurant, Blackburn Street, 7:30 p.m. Hilda M. Casetta, 834 Newbury St., Ripon, Wis. 54971.

SHEBOYGAN: Sheboygan Stamp Club, every other Wednesday, Rehabilitation Center of Sheboygan Inc., 1305 St. Clair Ave., 7:30 p.m. Perry Harris, 2313 Broadway Ave., Sheboygan, Wis. 53081.

SHULLSBURG: Ben Franklin Stamp Club, once a month in school cafeteria, date varies. M. M. Spillane, 444 N. Judgement St., Shullsburg, Wis. 53586.

WAUKESHA: Waukesha County Philatelic Society, second and fourth Thursday, except July and August, First Financial Savings, 100 E. Sunset Drive, 7:30 p.m. MaryAnn Bowman, Box 1451, Waukesha, Wis. 53187.

WAUSAU: Wisconsin Valley Philatelic Society, second Monday, except summer months, Old Town Hall, Marathon County Park. Robert Ashe, Box 71, Wausau, Wis. 54401.

WAUWATOSA: Pilgrim Lutheran School Stamp Club, first and third Wednesday, Pilgrim Lutheran School, 6717 W. Center St., 3:15 p.m.-4:30. Jan Koopman, 6717 W. Center St., Wauwatosa, Wis. 53210.

— Wauwatosa Philatelic Society Inc., first Thursday and third Wednesday, September thru May; June, July and August, third Wednesday, Wauwatosa

Civic Center, North 76th and West North Avenue, 7:30 p.m. Walter Jaglowski, 1304 N. 123, Wauwatosa, Wis. 53226.

WEST BEND: Kettle Moraine Coin & Stamp Club, second Thursday, Recreation Center, 724 Elm St., 7 p.m. Ed Pawlowski, 1245 Jefferson St., West Bend, Wis. 53095.

MISCELLANEOUS

Antigo Stamp Club, Toni Thomas, 113 E. 10th Ave., Antigo, Wis. 54409.

— Central Wisconsin Stamp Club, first Thursday each month, St. Paul's United Methodist Church, 600 Wilshire Blvd., 7 p.m.; third Thursday each month, Port Edwards Credit Union, Market Avenue 7 p.m. c/o Deanna Juhnke, 3701 Jordan Lane, Stevens Point, Wis. 54481.

— Northwestern Mutual Life Stamp Club, third Tuesday, location varies, 7:30 p.m. Donald H. Arndt, 7816 N. Edgeworth Drive, Milwaukee, Wis. 53223.

— Wisconsin Blue & Gray Society, yearly, Wisconsin Federation of Stamp Clubs Show. Roger H. Oswald, 2514 Sheridan Place, Manitowoc, Wis. 54220.

— Wisconsin Christmas Seal and Charity Society, Chapter IV. Herbert E. Burgett, 600 Merritt Ave., Apt. 311, Oskkosh, Wis. 54901.

— Wisconsin Postal History Society, annual Wisconsin Federation of Stamp Clubs show. 10 a.m. on Sunday of the show. Frank Moertl, N95 W32259 County Line Rd., Hartland, Wis. 53029.

WYOMING

GILLETTE: Gillette Stamp Club. Marty and Steve Hamby, 4 M Court, Gillette, Wyo. 82716.

National Stamp Clubs

Following is a list of National Stamp Clubs that are registered with Linn's Club Center. Societies affiliated with other organizations are indicated in parentheses: APS, American Philatelic Society; ATA, American Topical Association. The numbers in parentheses are codes for the National Stamp Club index that follows this section.

(1)
Aerophilatelic Federation of the Americas
Fred L. Wellman
Box 1239
Elgin, Ill. 60121-1239

(2)
Alaska Collector Club
Bob McKain
2337 Giant Oaks Drive
Pittsburgh, Pa. 15241

(3)
Americana Unit
(APS, ATA)
Donald Brenke
Box 179
Washington, D.C. 20044

(4)
American Air Mail Society
(APS)
Simine Short, Secretary
Box 291
Downers Grove, Ill. 60515

(5)
American-Belgian Philatelic Society
(APS)
Donald L. Whitwell
8604 S. Yakima Ave.
Tacoma, Wash. 98444

(6)
American Bicentennial Study Group
June B. Bancroft
Secretary/Treasurer
1 Scott Circle N.W., No. 404
Washington, D.C. 20036

(7)
American Helvetia Philatelic Society
(APS)
Richard T. Hall
Box 666
Manhattan Beach, Calif. 90266-0666

(8)
American Philatelic Society
Executive Director
Box 8000
State College, Pa. 16803

(9)
American Plate Number Single Society
Thomas Yano
Box 375
Glen Echo, Md. 20812-0375

(10)
American Society for Netherlands Philately
(APS)
Marinus Quist
124 Country Club Drive
Covington, La. 70433

(11)
American Topical Association
(APS)
Donald W. Smith
Box 630
Johnstown, Pa. 15907

(12)
Armed Forces Stamp Exchange Club
Karl Bielenberg
Executive Secretary
Box 1337
Omaha, Neb. 68101

(13)
Associated Collectors of El Salvador
(APS)
Jeff Brasor
Secretary-Treasurer
2 Howard Road
Chelmsford, Mass. 01824

(14)
Belize Philatelic Study Circle
Peter Bylen
Box 411238
Chicago, Ill. 60641

(15)
Buildings Study Group
(Germany Philatelic Society)
Anthony J. Torres Jr.
107 Hoover Road
Rochester, N.Y. 14617-3611

(16)
Chess-On-Stamps Study Unit
(ATA)
Russ Ott
Box 157470
Irving, Texas 75015

(17)
Cheswick Historical Society
Steve Pavlina
208 Allegheny Ave.
Cheswick, Pa. 15024

(18)
Christmas Philatelic Club
(APS, ATA)
Vaughn H. Augustin
Secretary/Treasurer
Box 77
Scottsbluff, Neb. 69361

(19)
Christopher Columbus Philatelic Society
(APS, ATA)
David E. Nye
Box 1492
Frankenmuth, Mich. 48734

(20)
Collectors of Religion on Stamps
(COROS)
Verna Shackleton
208 E. Circle St.
Appleton, Wis. 54911

(21)
Confederate Stamp Alliance Inc.
(APS)
Jerry S. Palazolo
5010 Raleigh LaGrange Road
Memphis, Tenn. 38128

(22)
Cousin's Stamp Club
Richard H. Thiel Sr.
6618-44 Ave.
Kenosha, Wis. 53142

(23)
Cover Collectors Club
Barbara White
237A Rossway Road
Pleasant Valley, N.Y. 12569

(24)
Croatian Philatelic Society
(APS)
James T. Lee
Box 770913
Cleveland, Ohio 44107

(25)
Czeslaw Slania Study Group
Edith Ann Malson
Secretary
Box 1382
Milwaukee, Wis. 53201

(26)
Deltiologists of America
James Lewis Lowe
Box 8
Norwood, Pa. 19074

(27)
Earth's Physical Features Study Unit
(ATA)
Fred Klein
Secretary-Treasurer
515 Magdalena
Los Altos, Calif. 94022

(28)
Eire Philatelic Association
(APS)
Robert Jones
8 Beach St.
Brockton, Mass. 02402

(29)
EFO Collectors Club
(APS)
James McDevitt
1903 Village Road W.
Norwood, Mass. 02062-2524

(30)
Fairytale/Folklore Study Unit
(APS, ATA)
Karen Cartier
2509 Buffalo Drive
Arlington, Texas 76013

(31)
Fine Arts Phiatelists
(APS, ATA)
Tom Ulrich, Secretary
7502 E. 80th St.
Indianapolis, Ind. 46256

(32)
Gay & Lesbian History on Stamps Club
(ATA)
Ed S. Centeno
Box 3940
Hartford, Conn. 06103

(33)
Gems, Minerals and Jewelry Study Unit
(ATA)
George G. Young
Secretary-Treasurer
Box 632
Tewksbury, Mass. 01876

(34)
George Washington Masonic Stamp Club
Ralph F. Knisely
Recording Secretary
7400 Skyline Drive
Frederick, Md. 21701-3652

(35)
Graphics Philately Association
(APS, ATA)
Dulcie Apgar
Secretary-Editor
Box 1513
Thousand Oaks, Calif. 91360

(36)
Great Britain Correspondence Club
Tom Current
Box 4586
Portland, Ore. 97208

(37)
Haiti Philatelic Society
(APS)
Dwight Bishop
16434 Shamhart Drive
Granada Hills, Calif. 91344

(38)
Hamex Stamp Club
Stephen J. Rudolph Jr.
3465 MacClymont Court
Palm Harbor, Fla. 34684

(39)
International Federation of Postcard Dealers
(APS)
John H. McClintock, Secretary
Box 1765
Manassas, Va. 22110

(40)
International Philippine Philatelic Society
(APS)
Eugene A. Garrett
President, International Operations
446 Stratford Ave.
Elmhurst, Ill. 60126

(41)
International Society for Japanese Philately
(APS)
Kenneth Kamholz
Box 1283
Haddonfield, N.J. 08033

(42)
Iran Philatelic Study Circle
A. John Ultee
Secretary, American Chapter
816 Gwynne Ave.
Waynesboro, Va. 22980

(43)
Israel Plate Block Society
David Lebson
5902 Winner Ave.
Baltimore, Md. 21215

(44)
Isthmian Collectors Club (ICC)
Bob Karrer
Box 6094
Alexandria, Va. 22306

(45)
Jugoslavia Study Group (JSG)
Michael Lenard
1514 N. Third Ave.
Wausau, Wis. 54401

(46)
Jack Knight Air Mail Society
Fred L. Wellman
Box 1239
Elgin, Ill. 60121-1239

(47)
Korea Stamp Society Inc.
(APS)
Forrest W. Calkins
Box 1057
Grand Junction, Colo. 81502

(48)
Latin American Philatelic Society
(APS)
Richard E. Taylor
5200 Brittany Drive S., No. 901
St. Petersburg, Fla. 33715

(49)
Law Enforcement Study Unit
(APS, ATA)
Stephen F. O'Conor
Box 858
Vernon, N.J. 07462-0858

(50)
Local Post Collectors Society
(APS)
Joseph J. Frasketi Jr.
2019 Maravilla Circle
Fort Myers, Fla. 33901-7232

(51)
Lundy Collectors Club
(APS)
Roger S. Cichorz
3925 Longwood Ave.
Boulder, Colo. 80303

(52)
Machine Cancel Society
(APS)
Arthur Hadley
9635 E. Randal St.
Columbus, Ind. 47203

(53)
Mailer's Postmark Permit Club
(APS)
Florance M. Sugarberg
Box 5793
Akron, Ohio 44372-5793

(54)
Mathematical Study Unit
(APS, ATA)
Estelle A. Buccino
135 Witherspoon Court
Athens, Ga. 30606

(55)
Maximum Card Study Unit
(APS)
Scott Henault
22 Denmark St.
Dedham, Mass. 02026

(56)
Metropolitan Air Post Society
(MAPS)
Robert S. Miller
126 Drake Ave.
Staten Island, N.Y. 10314-3012

(57)
Metropolitan Postcard Club
Leah Schnall
6700 192 St.
Flushing, N.Y. 11365

(58)
Monumental Postcard Club
John Corliss
Box 20899
Baltimore, Md. 21209

(59)
Napoleon Age Philatelists
Donald W. Smith
Box 576
Johnstown, Pa. 15907

(60)
National Association of
Precancel Collectors Inc.
G.W. Dye
5121 Park Blvd.
Wildwood, N.J. 08260-0121

(61)
New England Precancel Club
Philip Cayford
Box 387
Dublin, N.H. 03444

(62)
Northwest Federation of Stamp Clubs
James W. Graue
East 11911 Connor Road
Valleyford, Wash. 99036

(63)
Old World Archaeological Study Unit
(APS, ATA)
Heinz D. Schwinge
1516 Hinman Ave., No. 503
Evanston, Ill. 60201

(64)
The Perfins Club
(APS)
Edward S. Hoyt
225 W. Coover, No. 2
Mechanicsburg, Pa. 17055

(65)
Petroleum Philatelic Society International
(APS, ATA)
H. Victor Copeland
615 Orion Drive
Colorado Springs, Colo. 80906-1016

(66)
Philatelic Music Circle
(APS)
Cathleen F. Osborne
Box 1781
Sequim, Wash. 98382

(67)
Philippine Study Group
Donald J. Peterson
7408 Alaska Ave. N.W.
Washington, D.C. 20012

(68)
Pitcairn Islands Study Group
(APS)
Anne A. Hughes
Box 466
Concordia, Kan. 66901

(69)
Postmark Collectors Club
(APS)
Wilma Hinrichs
4200 S.E. Indianola Road
Des Moines, Iowa 50320

(70)
Precancel Stamp Society Inc.
(APS)
Arthur Damm
Pine Manor Apt. B-3
8215 Pine Road
Philadelphia, Pa. 19111

(71)
Rotary-On-Stamps
(APS, ATA)
Donald E. Fiery
Box 333
Hanover, Pa. 17331

(72)
St. Helena, Ascension, and Tristan Da Cunha Philatelic Society
(APS)
Mrs. V. Finne
Box 366
Calpella, Calif. 95418

(73)
The Samuel Gompers Stamp Club
Edwin M. Schmidt
Box 1233
Springfield, Va. 22151

(74)
Scandinavian Collectors Club
(APS)
Executive Secretary
Box 302
Lawrenceville, Ga. 30246-0302

(75)
Society For Hungarian Philately
(APS)
Thomas Phillips
Box 1162, Samp Mortar Station
Fairfield, Conn. 06430

(76)
Society of Australasian Specialists/Oceania
(APS)
James Cary
Box 484
Battle Creek, Mich. 49016

(77)
Society of Costa Rica Collectors (APS)
T.C. Willoughby
6400 Arthur St.
Merrillville, Ind. 46410

(78)
Society of Indochina Philatelists (APS)
Paul Blake
1466 Hamilton Way
San Jose, Calif. 95125

(79)
Society of Philatelists and Numismatists (APS)
Joe R. Ramos
1929 Millis St.
Montebello, Calif. 90640-4533

(80)
South Africa Study Group
Sidney Goldfield
309 W. 72nd St., No. 3D
New York, N.Y. 10023

(81)
Souvenir Card Collectors Society (APS)
Dana M. Marr
Box 4155
Tulsa, Okla. 74159-0155

(82)
Spanish Philatelic Society
A.J. Orville
29 Shadow Lane
Great Neck, N.Y. 11021

(83)
Telegraph & Telephone Study Circle
Syl C. Tully
Box 5627
Hamden, Conn. 06518

(84)
Tonga/Tin Can Mail Study Circle (APS)
Larry Benson
1832 Jean Ave.
Tallahassee, Fla. 32308

(85)
Trans-Mississippi Philatelic Society, Inc.
Patricia A. Loec
1714 S. 94 St.
Omaha, Neb. 68124

(86)
Turkish & Ottoman Philatelic Society (APS)
Menachim Mayo
Box 289
Ivy, Va. 22945

(87)
Tuvalu & Kiribati Philatelic Society (APS)
Michael A. Butkiss
Box 1209
Temple Hills, Md. 20772

(88)
Ukrainian Philatelic and Numismatic Society (APS)
George M.J. Slusarczuk
Box C
Southfields, N.Y. 10975

(89)
Ukrainian Philatelic & Numismatic Society (UPNS)
Ingert Kuzych
7758 Condor Court
Alexandria, Va. 22306-2929

(90)
United Postal Stationery Society (APS)
Joanne Thomas
Box 48
Redlands, Calif. 92373

(91)
The U.S. Philatelic Classics Society, Inc. (APS)
Robert R. Hegland
Box 1011
Falls Church, Va. 22041

(92)
United States Possessions Philatelic Society
(APS)

William T. Zuehlke
8100 Willow Stream Drive
Sandy, Utah 84093

(93)
War Cover Club
(APS)

Chris Kulpinski
Box 464-F
Feasterville, Pa. 19047

(94)
Windmill Study Unit
(ATA)

John J. Blocker
17060 Jodave St.
Hazel Crest, Ill. 60429

(95)
World's Fair Collectors Society
(ATA)

Mike Pender
6639 Waterford Lane
Sarasota, Fla. 34238

National Stamp Clubs Specialized Index

Find your collecting speciality in the following listing, then turn back to the preceding pages covering National Stamp Clubs to determine which group is best suited to your needs. Example: Persons interested in aerophilately will find that subject followed by numbers 1, 4, 46 and 56. Turn back to the national club list and find the clubs with those numbers.

Foreign Stamp Clubs

AUSTRALIA

Dalby Stamp Club
Colyn Juillerat
Box 590
Dalby, Queensland
4403 AUSTRALIA

Eastern Districts Philatelic Society
Box 240
Magill, South Australia
5076 AUSTRALIA

Gladstone and District Philatelic Society
Rosemary Hunt
Box 1089
Gladstone, Queensland
4680 AUSTRALIA

Junction Park Stamp Club
Dell Luxton
Box 177, Annerley
Brisbane, Queensland
4103 AUSTRALIA

Manly-Warringah Philatelic Society
G.C. Morriss
Box 80
Manly, NSW
2095 AUSTRALIA

Philatelic Society of Canberra
Secretary
GPO Box 1840
Canberra, ACT
2601 AUSTRALIA

Sherwood (Afternoon) Stamp Society
Barbara Mullard
Box 99, Corinda
Brisbane, Queensland
4075 AUSTRALIA

CANADA

Alberni Valley Stamp Club
Box 1237
Port Alberni, British Columbia
CANADA
V9Y 7M1

Burma Philatelic Study Circle
Alan Meech
7127 87 St.
Edmonton, Alberta
CANADA
T6C 3G1

Calgary Philatelic Society
Philip Wolf
Box 1478
Calgary, Alberta
CANADA
T2P 2L6

Canadiana Study Unit
John G. Peebles
Box 3262, Station A
London, Ontario
CANADA
N6A 4K3

Canadian Aerophilatelic Society
Maj. R.K. Malott, Rtd.
16 Harwick Crescent
Nepean, Ontario
CANADA
K2H 6R1

Credit Valley Philatelic Society
R. Laker, Secretary
2118 Dickson Road
Mississauga, Ontario
CANADA
L5B 1Y6

Crireq Stamp Club
Raymond Rajotte
Box 1000
Varennes, Quebec
CANADA
J0L 2P9

Delta Stamp Club (British Columbia, Canada)
Bill Heather
Box 507
Point Roberts, Wash. 98281

East Toronto Stamp Club
Raymond Reakes
188 Woodmount Ave.
Toronto, Ontario
CANADA
M4C 3Z4

Electrohome Stamp Club
Ron Heimpel
86 River Road E.
Kitchener, Ontario
CANADA
N2B 2G2

Essex County Stamp Club
A. Mancinone
Box 1503, Station A
Windsor, Ontario
CANADA
N9A 6R5

Fort George Philatelic Society
Mrs. B. McMurray
Box 1812
Prince George, British Columbia
CANADA
V2L 4V7

Fraser Valley Junior Stamp Club
Arthur H. Holmes
3364 248 St., R.R. 4
Aldergrove, British Columbia
CANADA
V0X 1A0

Fraser Valley Philatelic Club (British Columbia, Canada)
Norman C. Holden
Box 1314
Sumas, Wash. 98295

Hamilton Philatelic Society
Barry Hong
Box 205, Station A
Hamilton, Ontario
CANADA
L8N 3A2

Kelowna & District Stamp Club
Carol Ross
Box 1185
Kelowna, British Columbia
CANADA
V1Y 7P8

La Societe Philatelique de Quebec
Roland Arsenault
Box 2222
Quebec City, Quebec
CANADA
G1K 7N8

Lakehead Stamp Club
A.J. Sparks
1813 McGregor Ave.
Thunder Bay, Ontario
CANADA
P7E 5G1

Lakeshore Stamp Club Inc.
Jim Manton, President
Box 1
Pointe Claire, Quebec
CANADA
H9R 4N5

Latvian Philatelic Society
Rudolfs Zalamans
608-315 Glendale Ave.
St. Catharines, Ontario
CANADA
L2T 2L7

London Philatelic Society
Arnold Benjaminsen
298 Neville Drive
London, Ontario
CANADA
H6G 1E3

Middlesex Stamp Club
William L. Sanders
1897 Parkhurst Ave.
London, Ontario
CANADA
N5V 2C4

Niagara Philatelic Society
David L. Hill
78 Jefferson Drive
St. Catharines, Ontario
CANADA
L2N 3V4

North Shore Stamp Club
Neil Worley
2500 Kilmarnock Crescent
North Vancouver, British Columbia
CANADA
V7J 2Z5

North York Philatelic Society
Alan J. Hanks
34 Seaton Drive
Aurora, Ontario
CANADA
L4G 2K1

Nova Scotia Stamp Club
George A. MacKenzie
1333 S. Park St., Apt. 515
Halifax, Nova Scotia
CANADA
B3J 2K9

Okanagan Mainline Philatelic Association
Fred R. Arnot
Site 37, Comp. 1 - R.R. No. 3
Penticton, British Columbia
CANADA
V2A 7K8

Oxford Philatelic Society
Gib Stephens
Box 1131
Woodstock, Ontario
CANADA
N4S 8P6

Petroleum Philatelic Society International
Brenda Curtis
16 Carnarvon Way N.W.
Calgary, Alberta
CANADA
T2K 1W4

Polish Philatelic Society of Canada
Jozef Podejko
510 St. George St.
New Westminster, British Columbia
CANADA
V3L 1L2

Prince Edward County Stamp Club
Alan R. Capon
Box 2122
Picton, Ontario
CANADA
K0K 2T0

"RA" Stamp Club
Steven Mulvey
2441 Ogilvie Road
Gloucester, Ontario
CANADA
K1J 7N3

Regina Philatelic Club Inc.
Ken W. Arndt
3829 20th Ave.
Regina, Saskatchewan
CANADA
S4S 0P3

Royal City Stamp Club
Josef Ochs
Box 145
Milner, British Columbia
CANADA
V0X 1T0

St. Catharines Stamp Club
Roy W. Houtby
Box 2145, Station B
St. Catharines, Ontario
CANADA
L2M 6P5

St. Thomas Stamp Club
Bernard J. Key, Secretary
9 Stokes Road
St. Thomas, Ontario
CANADA
N5R 5V5

Sydney Stamp Club
Fred R. Guy
56 Trinity Ave.
Sydney, Nova Scotia
CANADA
B1P 4Z5

Three Valleys Stamp Club
Audrey S. Mercer
96 Fenelon Drive
Don Mills, Ontario
CANADA
M3A 3K6

Toronto Estonian Philatelic Club
H. Maeste, Chairman
91 Old Mill Drive
Toronto, Ontario
CANADA
M6S 4K2

Toronto Stamp Collectors' Club
Ted Nixon
255 Cortleigh Blvd.
Toronto, Ontario
CANADA
M5N 1P8

West Toronto Stamp Club
H. Fordham, Secretary
37 Hayward Crescent
Agincourt, Ontario
CANADA
M1S 2T7

Women on Stamps Study Unit (ATA)
Betty Killingbeck
905 Birch Ave.
Peterborough, Ontario
CANADA
K9H 6G7

World Stamp Exchange Club
Elvin Person, Director
Esther, Alberta
CANADA
T0J 1H0

Yellowhead Stamp & Coin Collectors Society
Piet Steen
Box 820
Hinton, Alberta
CANADA
T0E 1B0

DENMARK

SAS Philatelic Club, Denmark
Bent Okstoft
Lundeberggardsvej 132
Dk 2740 Skovcunde
DENMARK

DOMINICAN REPUBLIC

Sociedad Filatelica Dominicana
Apartado 1930
Santo Domingo
DOMINICAN REPUBLIC

EAST GERMANY

Newst Issue Stamp Club
Holger Kaufhold
Wilhelm-Pieck-Str. 22
1254 Schoneiche b. Berlin
GERMAN DEMOCRATIC REPUBLIC

FINLAND

Aihefilatelistit ry. (The Finnish Thematic Association)
Seppo Laaksonen
Runeberginkatu 4 c B 28
00100 Helsinki
FINLAND

GREAT BRITAIN

Austrian Stamp Club of Great Britain
Martin H.K. Brumby
9 Heath Moor Drive
York Y01 4NE
GREAT BRITAIN

Captain Cook Study Unit
D. Seymour
38 Sherwood Road
Meols, Wirral, Merseyside L47 9RT
GREAT BRITAIN

Concorde Study Circle
Brian Asquith
Alandale, Radcliffe Gardens, Carshalton Beeches
Surrey SM5 4PQ
GREAT BRITAIN

Ethiopia Collector's Club
The Rev. F.G. Payne
83 Penn Lea Road
Bath BA1 3RQ
GREAT BRITAIN

Indian Ocean Study Circle
Mrs. S. Hopson
Field Acre, Hoe Benham
Newbury, Berkshire RG16 8PD
GREAT BRITAIN

Judaica Philatelic Society
Clive H. Rosen
Harold Poster House
Kingsbury Circle
London NW9
GREAT BRITAIN

King George VI Collectors' Society
Richard Lockyer
24 Stourwood Road, Southbourne
Bournemouth BH6 3QP
GREAT BRITAIN

Malta Study Circle
Frank A. Gray
69 Stonecross Road
Hatfield, Herts. AL10 OHP
GREAT BRITAIN

Pacific Islands Study Circle of Great Britain
J.D. Ray
24 Woodvale Ave.
London SE25 4AE
GREAT BRITAIN

The Psywar Society
Rod Oakland
21 Metchley Lane, Harborne
Birmingham BI7 0HT
GREAT BRITAIN

South African Collectors' Society
Mr. W.A. Page
138 Chastilian Road
Dartford, Kent DA1 3LG
GREAT BRITAIN

GUAM

Guam Combined Stamp Clubs
Phill Mendel
165 Marata St., No. 411
Tumon Bay 96911
GUAM

Guam Stamp Club
Steve Lander
Box 10571
Tamuning 96911
GUAM

GUATEMALA

Asociacion Filatelica De Guatemala
Romeo J. Routhier
U.S. Milgp (Guatemala)
APO Miami, Fla. 34024

HONG KONG

St. Joseph's College Philatelic Society
Brother Patrick
7 Kennedy Road
Central
HONG KONG

INDIA

Phil Club
C. Abraham Jos
Cheeran House
P.O. Chowannoor (via) Kunnamkulam
Trichur (DT)
Kerala-680503
INDIA

United Philatelists
B.J. Kumar
3-A/149 Azad Nagar
Kanpur-208002
INDIA

JAPAN

Toyonaka Stamp Club
Yoshiharu Kada
2-13-10 Shinsenri-Kita
Toyonaka, Osaka
565 JAPAN

KOREA

Chasun Stamp Club (Seoul)
Pamela Warm
SAES-DODDS Box 7
APO San Francisco 96301-0005

MALAYSIA

Philatelic Society of Malaysia
C. Nagarajah
Box 10588 GPO
50718 Kuala Lumpur
MALAYSIA

NEW ZEALAND

New Zealand Junior Stamp Club
A. F. Watters
Post Box 812
New Plymouth
4601 NEW ZEALAND

PHILIPPINES

FIL-AM Stamp Club
Jack Cullivan
PSC No. 1, Box 5436
APO San Francisco, Calif. 96286

PORTUGAL

Tap-Air Portugal Philatelic Club
F. Lemos Da Silveira
Box 5194
P-1777 Lisbon Codex
PORTUGAL

SOUTH AFRICA

Pretoria Philatelic Society
E. Hansen, Secretary
Box 514
ZA0001 Pretoria
REPUBLIC OF SOUTH AFRICA

SWITZERLAND

Frick Valley Stamp Club
Robert Harper
IM Hard 4
4310 Rheinfelden
SWITZERLAND

Chapter 16

Stamp Exhibiting

What the Judge Looks For

A stamp exhibit is a story told by stamps, covers, and/or other postal emissions such as meters, cancellations and postmarks, preferably those most difficult to acquire. The exhibit has an introduction, a body of the story, and a logical ending. It should be presented neatly, the material described, but the description should not overshadow the material.

Recently, an additional requirement was added. The exhibit is required to have a title page and an outline to help the viewer and the judge understand the subject and intent of the exhibit.

The judge, therefore, breaks down the exhibit into certain components and then sees how well the exhibitor has fulfilled those requirements.

The criteria into which the exhibit is broken down are as follows:

1. Treatment & importance of exhibit	30/35
2. Knowledge & research	35
3. Condition & rarity	25/30
4. Presentation	5
Total	100

The relative importance of each of these criteria is indicated by the points or percentile attributed to each as indicated above.

Treatment and importance of exhibit, knowledge and research, and condition and rarity need further definition and refinement depending on what type of exhibit is being considered.

The International Federation of Philately (FIP), through its various commissions, has further refined these criteria for each of the specialties such as traditional philately, postal history, postal stationery, aerophilately, maximaphily, and others.

These can be found in the Special Regulations for the Evaluation of Philatelic Exhibits in this chapter. In addition, many of the commissions have published guidelines and definitions to assist the judge in each particular specialty.

Judges consider the following:

Treatment of Philatelic Material

Is it presented in a logical sequence? Has proper consideration been given to issuing bodies or the proper historical events giving rise to the issue? What material is missing or should be there to properly cover the subject of the exhibit? Is the exhibit balanced? Is it loaded with easily acquired material but sparse in more difficult-to-acquire material?

How important is the specific material shown when compared to the philately of the entire country that issued the material? Is it a small insignificant part of the whole, or is it significant?

Knowledge

Does the exhibitor show philatelic knowledge through the exhibit? How much? How significant?

Research

What philatelic research is shown in the exhibit? Is it correct? Is there new and original research shown? Is the research secondary research (namely, adapting previous research to this particular exhibit)? This should not reduce the medal level.

Condition

What is the condition of the material shown? If it is early material that usually comes in poor condition, is it in pristine condition? If it is of more recent times, is it torn, smudged, dirty?

How rare is the material? How difficult is it to find, not considering its value?

Presentation

Is the story line promoted by the philatelic material, or does the exhibit require cachets, newspaper clippings and pictures to promote the story line?

Is the sequence logical? If not logical, does the exhibit explain why the story line is different? Do the title page and outline tell the viewer what the exhibit story is, and does the story told actually follow the outline?

In the United States, the judge applies these criteria mentally. In some foreign countries, the judge is required to complete an evaluation sheet detailing the points given to the exhibit by the judge for each of the criteria. While presently the completion of an evaluation sheet is not mandatory for all countries that are members of the FIP, it is anticipated that gradually pressure will build on all countries not using the evaluation sheet to introduce and use it in all stamp shows.

The reasoning is that until now the older judges have come from the ranks of collectors who, at some time during their lives, have collected the whole world and thus became familiar with the postal emissions of all of the countries of the world and thus have a basis of comparison when judging exhibits.

In recent years, however, most judges come from a more limited specialty. They have collected only one country, only one portion of a country or only thematics. Therefore, it is argued that a judge has no basis of comparison and, therefore, will be helped by the use of the evaluation sheet.

FIP Regulations

The International Federation of Philately was founded in 1926 as a non-profit association to promote stamp collecting on an international level. The registered office of the FIP is in Zurich, Switzerland. FIP membership is comprised of national federations with one representative for each country. Where no national federation exists, FIP membership is granted to the most representative stamp organization in the country on a temporary basis until a national federation is formed. The American Philatelic Society is the member for the United States.

Besides giving patronage to international stamp exhibitions held by FIP members, the FIP is empowered to organize on its own initiative international stamp exhibitions with the agreement of the national federation concerned.

The following are the FIP general regulations for international stamp exhibitions.

Additional information on the FIP and its special regulations can be obtained from secretary-general Marie-Louise Heiri, Zollikerstrasse 128, CH-8008 Zurich, Switzerland.

General Regulations Of The FIP For The Evaluation Of Competitive Exhibits At FIP Exhibitions

Article 1 : Competitive Exhibitions

1.1 The FIP promotes international philatelic exhibitions in accordance with its Statues (Article 5 and 43-45) and the General Regulations of the FIP for Exhibitions (GREX). The FIP may extend its patronage to world exhibitions, its auspices to international exhibitions and its support to other exhibitions.

1.2 The principles defined in the following General Regulations of the FIP for the Evaluation of the Exhibits at FIP Exhibitions (GREV) are applicable to all competitive exhibitions. They are intended to serve the Jury as regulations and as a guide to the collector for the development of the exhibits.

1.3 The GREV apply to all competitive classes at FIP exhibitions.

1.4 The Special Regulations of the FIP for the Evaluation of Competitive exhibits at FIP Exhibitions (SREV) for each competitive class are based upon and developed from the GREV. The Commissions of FIP may supplement or adapt these principles considering the peculiarities of their respective classes.

Article 2: Competitive Exhibits

2.1 The limit of the frame space allocated at exhibitions as per Article 6 of the GREX does not normally allow the collector to display his entire collection. Therefore, he must select that suitable material, which will insure continuity and understanding of the subject and show the most relevant aspects of knowledge and condition.

2.2 The evaluation of the exhibit will only take into consideration the material displayed.

2.3 The composition of an exhibit in the respective classes will be defined in the SREV.

Article 3: Principles of Exhibit Composition

3.1 An exhibit shall consist solely of appropriate philatelic material.

3.2 Appropriate philatelic material is that which, for the purpose of transmitting mail or other postal communications, has been issued, intended for issue, or produced in the preparation for issue, used, or treated as valid for postage by governmental, local or private postal agencies, or by other duly commissioned or empowered authorities.

3.3 The exhibit shall show a clear concept of the subject treated, developed according to the characteristics of the respective competitive class, as defined by the SREV for that class. The exhibit shall be developed according to a well-laid-out plan as well as personal research. The title must agree with the contents of the exhibit. The concept shall be laid out in an introductory statement, and must be written in one of the FIP official languages.

3.4 The material displayed should be fully consistent with the subject chosen.

The selection should express the concept in the most appropriate manner, showing the level of understanding of the subject and the personal research of the exhibitor. It should also include the fullest range of relevant philatelic material of the highest available quality.

3.5 The presentation and the accompanying text of the exhibit should be simple, tasteful and well-balanced. A short explanation is required when the material is not self explanatory or there is a need to illustrate special research.

Article 4: Criteria for Evaluating Exhibits

4.1 The evaluation of the exhibit is made by a jury, which will be constituted and shall perform its duties in accordance with the provisions of Section V of the GREX.

4.2 General criteria for the evaluation of competitive exhibits at FIP exhibitions are as follows:

— Treatment of the exhibit
— Importance of the exhibit
— Knowledge and research
— Condition and rarity of material
— Presentation of the exhibit

4.3 The criterion of "Treatment of the Exhibit" requires an evaluation of the completeness and correctness of the selected material made by the exhibitor to illustrate his chosen subject.

4.4 The criterion of "Importance of the Exhibit" requires an evaluation of the general significance of the subject chosen by the exhibitor, in terms of its scope, and the philatelic interest of the exhibit.

4.5 The criteria of "Knowledge and Research" require an evaluation of the degree of knowledge of the exhibitor, as expressed in the exhibit by the items chosen for display and their related comments, and of the personal research work shown in the exhibit by the way in which the facts related to the chosen subject are developed.

4.6 The criteria of "Condition and Rarity" require an evaluation of the quality of the displayed material considering the standard of the material that exists for the chosen subject, the rarity and the relative difficulty of acquisition of the selected material.

4.7 The criterion of "Presentation" requires an evaluation of the clarity of the display, the text as well as the overall aesthetic balance of the exhibit.

Article 5: Judging of Exhibits

5.1 The judging of an exhibit will be carried out in general accordance with Section V (Articles 31-47) of the GREX.

5.2 The Judgement of the exhibits is based on the criteria laid out in Article 4 above. The following relative terms are presented to lead the Jury to a balanced evaluation:

— Treatment and Importance of exhibit	30/35
— Knowledge and Research	35
— Condition and Rarity	25/30
— Presentation	5
— Total not to exceed	100

The definite weight to be given for "Treatment and Importance" and "Condition and Rarity" will be defined in the SREV to reflect the characteristics of each respective class. No evaluation sheet will be required to be completed unless otherwise specifically provided for by the SREVs.

5.3 Prizes will be awarded according to Article 7 of the GREX.

5.4 Medals will be awarded as per the following table, based on the total of the relative terms obtained by the exhibit (ref.: Article 7.4 of the GREX).

Large Gold	95
Gold	90
Large Vermeil	85
Vermeil	80
Large Silver	75
Silver	70
Silver Bronze	65
Bronze	60

5.5 The Grand Prizes are awarded to the exhibits with the greatest philatelic merit, from among those exceeding the requirement of a large gold medal (ref.: Art. 7.3 of GREX).

5.6 Special prizes may be placed at the disposal of the Jury in accordance with Article 7.5 of GREX. The Jury may award these prizes, at its discretion, to exhibits having received at least a large vermeil medal in appreciation of outstanding philatelic merits and exceptional material. This should not create another intermediary medal level.

5.7 The Jury may express Felicitations, in addition to the medal awarded, for exhibits distinguishing themselves by philatelic research or originality. Feliciations cannot be given to the same exhibit twice. (ref.: Article 7.6 of the GREX)

5.8 The owner of an exhibit which has been downgraded by a Jury, because it contains faked and forged material not properly identified by him, will be duly notified through the national federation and the commissioner. This information should also be passed to the FIP Commission for Expertizing and the Prevention of Forgeries.

5.9 The provisions of Article 5 may be varied as necessary for the Literature and Youth Classes because of their nature. These variations will be shown in the SREV of the concerned classes.

Article 6: Concluding Provisions

6.1 In the event of any discrepancies in the text arising from translation, the English text shall prevail.

6.2 The General Regulations of the FIP for the Evaluation of Competitive Exhibits at FIP Exhibitions have been approved by the 54th FIP Congress on 5th November, 1985 in Rome. They came into force on 5th November, 1985 and apply to those exhibitions that are granted FIP patronage, auspices or support at the 54th FIP Congress and thereafter.

Special Regulations For The Evaluation Of Traditional Philately At FIP Exhibitions

Article 1: Competitive Exhibitions

In accordance with Article 1.5 of the General Regulations of the FIP for the Evaluation of Competitive Exhibits at FIP Exhibitions (GREV) these Special Regulations have been developed to supplement those principles with regard to Traditional Philately. Also refer to Guidelines to Traditional Philately Regulations.

Article 2: Competitive Exhibits

Traditional philately embraces all aspects of philately. An exhibition will be considered to be traditional philately unless it is otherwise entered as an exhibit in one of the specialized FIP classes. It is based on the collecting of all postal items, including items related to the production of postage stamps in as specialized or as generalized a nature as the collector desires (ref. GREV, Art. 2.3).

Article 3: Principles of Exhibit Composition

Material appropriate to traditional philately includes, among other things, (ref. GREV, Art. 3.2)

1. Postage stamps, whether unused or used, singles or multiples, and stamps used on cover.

2. Varieties of all kinds, such as those of watermark, gum, perforation, paper and printing.

3. Essays and proofs, whether of adopted or rejected designs.

4. Pre-stamp and stampless items as appropriate, but normally not to exceed 15% of the exhibit space.

5. Other specialized items, including postal forgeries, postally used fiscal stamps, or unused postal/fiscal stamps valid for postal use.

The plan or concept of the exhibit shall be clearly laid out in an introductory statement which may take any form. (ref. GREV, Art. 4.5)

Article 4: Criteria for Evaluating Exhibits

"Knowledge and Research" (ref. GREV, Art. 4.5) Exhibits which cover areas which have been extensively researched and the findings published should not be penalized for a lack of personal research.

Article 5: Judging of Exhibits

5.1 Traditional philately exhibits will be judged in accordance with Section V (Art. 31-47) of GREX (ref. GREV, Art: 5.1).

5.2 For Traditional Philately exhibits, the following relative terms are presented to lead the Jury to a balanced evaluation (ref. GREV, Art. 5.2)

Treatment (10) and Importance (20) of the exhibits	30
Knowledge and Research	35
Condition and Rarity	30
Presentation	5
Total	100

Article 6: Concluding Provisions

1. In the event of any discrepancies in the text arising from translation, the English text shall prevail.

2. These Special Regulations for the Evaluation of Traditional Philately Exhibits at FIP Exhibitions have been approved at the 54th Congress on 5th November, 1985, in Rome. They came into force on 5th November, 1985 and apply to those exhibitions which are granted FIP patronage, auspices or support at the 54th FIP Congress and thereafter.

Special Regulations For The Evaluation Of Postal History Exhibits At FIP Exhibitions

Article 1: Competitive Exhibitions

In accordance with Art. 1.5 of the General Regulations of the FIP for the Evaluation of Competitive Exhibits at FIP Exhibitions (GREV), these Special Regulations have been developed to supplement those principles with regard to Postal History. Also refer to Guidelines to Postal History Regulations.

Article 2: Competitive Exhibits

A postal history exhibit is an exhibit of documents or postal items, which have been carried by a postal service whether official, local or private. Such exhibits will show either routes, rates and markings and/or the classification and study of postal markings on covers or stamps applied by those services or institutions, and of the marks of obliteration on postal items (ref. GREV, Art. 2.3).

Article 3: Principles of Exhibit Composition

3.1 A postal history exhibit consists of used covers, used postal stationery, used postage stamps, and postal documents so arranged as to illustrate a balanced plan as a whole or to develop among other things any one of the following aspects of postal history:

1. Pre-adhesive postal services.
2. The development of postal services national or international.
3. Postal rates.
4. Routes for transportation of mails.
5. Postal markings (marcophily).
6. Military mail: field post, siege mail, POW and concentration camp mail.
7. Maritime mail.
8. Disaster mail.
9. Disinfected mail.
10. Railway mail.
11. Censorship of mail.
12. Postage due mail.
13. Automation of the mails.
14. Forwarding agents markings.

The plan or concept of the exhibit shall be clearly laid out in an introductory statement (ref. GREV, Art. 3.3).

3.2 A postal history exhibit may contain, where strictly necessary, maps, prints, decrees and similar associated materials. Such items must have direct relation to the chosen subject and to the postal services described in the exhibit (ref. GREV, Art. 3.4).

Article 4: Criteria for Evaluating Exhibits (ref. GREV, Art. 4)

"Presentation" (ref. GREV, Art. 4.7)

The importance of understanding a postal history exhibit can mean that more text is included. However, this text must be concise and clear.

Article 5: Judging of Exhibits

5.1 Postal history exhibits will be judged by the approved specialists in their respective fields and in accordance with Section V (Art. 31-47) of GREX (ref. GREV. 5.1)

5.2 For postal history exhibits, the following relative terms are presented to lead the jury to a balanced evaluation (ref GREV. 5.2)

Treatment and Importance of the exhibit	35
Knowledge and Research	35
Condition and Rarity	25
Presentation	5
Total	100

Article 6: Concluding Provisions

6.1 In the event of any discrepancies in the text arising from translation, the English text shall prevail.

6.2 These Special Regulations for the Evaluation of Postal History Exhibit at FIP Exhibitions have been approved by the 54th Congress on 5th November, 1985 in Rome. They came into force on November, 1985 and apply to those exhibitions which are granted FIP patronage, auspices or support at the 54th FIP Congress and thereafter.

Special Regulations For The Evaluation Of Postal Stationery Exhibits At FIP Exhibits

Article 1: Competitive Exhibitions

In accordance with Article 1.5 of the

General Regulations of the FIP for the Evaluation of Competitive Exhibits at FIP Exhibitions (GREV), these Special Regulations have been developed to supplement those principles with regard to postal stationery. Also refer to Guidelines to Postal Stationery Regulations.

Article 2: Competitive Exhibits

A postal stationery exhibit should comprise a logical and coherent assembly of postal matter which either bears an officially authorized pre-printed stamp or device or inscription indicating that a specific face value rate of postage has been pre-paid (ref. GREV Art. 2.3).

Article 3: Principles of Exhibit Composition

A postal stationery exhibit should be arranged using appropriately chosen unused and/or postally used items of postal stationery from a particular country or associated group of territories to illustrate one or more of the categories set out below.

3.1 Postal Stationery can be classified according to either:

1) The manner of its availability and usage;

2) The physical form of the paper or card; or

3) The postal or associated service for which it is intended.

3.2 The manner and availability and usage may be defined as follows:

1) Post Office Issues:

2) Official Service Issues:

3) Forces (Military) Issues:

4) Stamped to Order (Private) Issues: Stamped stationery bearing stamps applied with postal administration approval and within specified regulations but to the order of private individuals or organizations.

3.3 The physical form of the paper or card on which the stamps etc. has been printed can be subdivided as follows:

1) Letter sheets including Aerogrammes.

2) Envelopes including Registration envelopes.

3) Post Cards.

4) Letter Cards.

5) Wrappers (Newapaper Bands)

6) Printed Forms of various kinds.

3.4 Postal Stationery has been produced for a variety of postal and associated services including the following:

1) Postal: Surface — local, inland, foreign; Air — local, inland, foreign.

2) Registration: Inland, foreign.

3) Telegraph: Inland, foreign.

4) Receipt of Miscellaneous Fees etc.: Certificate of posting of letters or parcels; Money Orders; Postal Orders, and other documents bearing impressions of postage stamp designs etc.

3.5 Formula items sold bearing adhesive stamps, covering the relevant country, may be included.

3.6 Postal Stationery exhibits should normally be of entire items. Where certain items are very rare in entire form or are only known to exist in cut-down (cut-square) form they would be acceptable as part of an exhibit as would a study for example of variations in the stamp dies used or those with rare cancellation etc. The use of postal stationery stamps as adhesives could also properly be included.

3.7 Essays and proofs, whether of adapted or rejected designs, can also be included.

The plan or concept of the exhibit shall be clearly laid out in an introductory statement which may take any form, (ref. GREV, Art. 3.3)

Article 4: Criteria for Evaluating Exhibits
(ref. GREV, Art. 4)

Article 5: Judging of Exhibits

5.1 Postal Stationery exhibits will be judged by the approved specialists in their respective fields and in accordance with Section V (Articles 31-47) of GREX (ref. GREV, Article 5.1).

5.2 For Postal Stationery exhibits, the following relative terms are presented to lead the Jury to a balanced evaluation (ref. GREV, Article 5.2)

Treatment and Importance of the exhibit	35
2) Knowledge and Research	35
3) Condition and Rarity	25
4) Presentation	5
Total	100

Article 6: Concluding Provisions

6.1 In the event of any discrepancies in the text arising from translation, the English text shall prevail.

6.2 The Special Regulations for the Evaluation of Postal Stationery Exhibits at FIP Exhibitions have been approved by the 54th FIP Congress on 5th November 1985 in Rome. They came into force on 5th November, 1985 and apply to those exhibitions which are granted FIP patronage, auspices, or support at the 54th FIP Congress and thereafter.

Special Regulations For The Evaluation Of Aerophilatelic Exhibits At FIP Exhibitions

Article 1: Competitive Exhibitions

In accordance with Art. 1.5 of the General Regulations of FIP for the Evaluation of Competitive Exhibits at FIP Exhibitions (GREV), these Special Regulations have been developed to supplement those principles with regard to Aerophilately. Also refer to Guidelines to Aerophilatelic Regulations.

Article 2: Competitive Exhibits

An Aerophilatelic exhibit is composed, essentially, of postal documents transmitted by air bearing evidence of having been flown (ref. GREV Art. 2.3).

Article 3: Principles of Exhibit Composition

3.1 An Aerophilatelic exhibit has as basic contents:

1. Postal documents dispatched by air.

2. Official and semi-official stamps issued especially for use on airmail, mint or used but principally on cover.

3. All types of postal and other marks, vignettes and labels relating to aerial transport.

4. Postal items connected with a particular means of aerial transport, not conveyed through a postal service, but with official sanction of a qualified authority.

5. Leaflets, messages and newspapers dropped from the air, as a way of normal postal delivery or on the occasion of postal services interrupted by unforeseen events.

6. Mail recovered from aircraft accidents and incidents.

3.2 The arrangement of an aerophilatelic exhibit derives directly from its intended structure following basic patterns:

1. Chronological
2. Geographical
3. Means of transport:
a) Pigeon
b) Lighter than air
c) Heavier than air
d) Rocket (ref. GREV. Art. 3.2)

3.3 Aerophilatelic exhibits may include ancillary items, such as maps, photographs, timetables and the like, as long as they are considered vital to illustrate and draw the attention to, a particular point or situation. They should not overpower the material and accompanying text on display. (ref. GREV. Art, 3.4).

3.4 The plan or the concept of the exhibit shall be clearly laid out in an introductory statement (ref. GREV. Art. 3.3)

Article 4: Criteria for Evaluating Exhibits
(ref. GREV. Art. 4)

Article 5: Judging of Exhibits

5.1 Aerophilatelic exhibits will be judged by the approved specialist in their respective field and in accordance with Section V (Art. 31-47) of GREX (ref. GREV Art. 5.1).

5.2 For Aerophilatelic exhibits, the following relative terms are presented to lead the Jury to a balanced evaluation (ref. GREV. Art. 5.2).

Treatment and Importance of the exhibit	30
Knowledge and Research	35
Condition and Rarity	30
Presentation	5
Total	100

Article 6: Concluding Provision

6.1 In the event of any discrepancies in the text arising from translation, the English text shall prevail.

6.2 These Special Regulations for the Evaluation of Aerophilatelic Exhibits at FIP Exhibitions have been approved by the 54th FIP Congress on 5th November, 1985 in Rome. They came into force on 5th November, 1985 and apply to those exhibitions which are granted FIP patronage, auspices or support at the 54th FIP Congress and thereafter.

Special Regulations For The Evaluation Of Astrophilatelic Exhibits At FIP Exhibitions

Article 1: Competitive Exhibitions

In accordance with Article 1.5 of the General Regulations of FIP for the Evaluation of Competitive Exhibits at FIP exhibitions (GREV) these special regulations have been developed to supplement those principles with regard to Astrophilately. Also refer to Guidelines to Astrophilately Regulations.

Article 2: Competitive Exhibits

An Astrophilatelic Exhibit is built up on historical, technical and scientific aspects related to space research and space programs.

Article 3: Principles of Exhibit Composition

Appropriate philatelic material of an astrophilatelic exhibit includes the following:

1. Documents handed over by a postal administration for dispatch by stratosphere balloons, rockets, spaceships, stratoplanes, recovery ships, rescue helicopters & vice versa, and to their related precursors.

2. Stamps, vignettes and leaflets, special envelopes and cards, postal stationeries and Mailgrams with reference to the different parts of space program — including the start, the flight landing of space traveling objects, and the participating tracking stations, ships and other supporting aircraft.

3. Some of the special characteristics of Astrophilately are envelopes and cards canceled by the post office at the place and exact date on which the special events took place.

4. The text should contain all aspects to the exact technical data, the dates, the place and the purpose of the rocket flight including the special work of the Astronauts and Cosmonauts involved.

5. An Astrophilatelic Exhibit may encompass all aspects related to or a self-containing section of:

a) Astronomy in connection with space research

b) The history of space research

c) Stratosphere flights referring to space research

d) Rocket Mail

e) Exploration of the earth and other planets by manned and unmanned satellites.

f) Transmission of news from the early days until used by satellites.

g) Manned space flights.

6. The plan or the concept of the exhibit shall be clearly laid out in an introductory statement (ref. GREV Art. 3.3)

Article 4: Criteria for Evaluating Exhibits (ref. GREV Art. 4)

Treatment of the exhibit (ref. GREV Art 4.3)

Special value is given on the exact technical and chronological evaluation of the events.

Knowledge and Research (ref. GREV Art. 4.5)

It also requires a high degree of knowledge in history, astronomy, space and rocket research.

Article 5: Judging of Exhibits

1. Astrophilatelic exhibits will be judged by the approved specialists in their respective field and in accordance with section V (Art. 31-47) of GREX (ref. GREV Art. 5.1).

2. For Astrophilately exhibits the following relative terms are presented to lead the Jury to a balanced evaluation (ref. GREV, Art. 5.2)

Treatment and importance of the exhibit	35
Knowledge and research	35
Condition and Rarity	25
Presentation	5
Total	100

Article 6: Concluding provisions

6.1 In the event of any discrepancies in the text arising from translation, the English text shall prevail.

6.2 The Special Regulation for the Evaluation of Astrophilatelic Exhibits at FIP Exhibitions have been approved by the 54th FIP Congress on 5th November, 1985 in Rome. They came into force on 5th November, 1985 and apply to those exhibitions which are granted FIP patronage, auspices or support at the 54th FIP Congress and thereafter.

Special Regulations For The Evaluation Of Philatelic Literature Exhibits At FIP Exhibitions

Article 1: Competitive Exhibitions

In accordance with Art. 1.5 of the General Regulations of FIP for the Evaluation of Competitive Exhibits at

FIP Exhibitions (GREV), these Special Regulations have been developed to supplement those principles with regard to Philatelic Literature. Also refer to Guidelines to Philatelic Literature Regulations.

Article 2: Competitive Exhibits

Philatelic literature includes all printed communications available to collectors related to postage stamps, postal history, and their collecting, and to any of the specialized fields connected therewith (ref. GREV Art. 2.3).

Article 3: Principles of Exhibit Composition

Philatelic literature will be subdivided as follows:

(1) Handbooks and Special Studies

a) Handbooks

b) Monographs

c) Specialized research articles

d) Bibliographies and similar special works

e) Exhibition catalogs

f) Specialized catalogs which besides philatelic issues of one or more countries treat varieties, cancellations or other specialized aspects.

g) Transcripts of philatelic lectures presented to the public (including radio, television, film and slide show scripts).

h) Similar special works.

(2) General Catalogs

Worldwide, regional and single area catalogs whose depth of coverage does not qualify them as specialized catalogs.

(3) Philatelic Periodicals

Philatelic journals and newspapers, society organs, house organs, yearbooks and similar publications.

(4) Articles

Articles of a general nature, in philatelic or non-philatelic publications.

Article 4: Criteria for Evaluating Exhibits

4.1 Literature exhibits will be evaluated according to following criteria:

— Treatment of contents

— Originality, significance and depth of research

— Technical matters

— Presentation

4.2 The criterion "treatment of contents" requires an evaluation of the literary style, clarity, and skill in communication shown in the exhibit.

4.3 The criterion "originality, significance and depth of research" requires an evaluation of the overall significance of the subject matter presented in the exhibit, as well as the degree to which the exhibit displays original discoveries, research, analysis or approaches to a comprehensive understanding of the subject matter.

4.4 The criterion "technical matters" requires an evaluation of such aspects as title page and imprint, pagination, credits, bibliography, index, and use of illustrations.

4.5 The criterion "presentation" requires an evaluation of the effect of binding, typography, and similar production factors on the usability of the publication. To avoid the impact of purely commercial aspects, this criterion will only be evaluated to the degree that it represents a negative factor.

Article 5: Judging of Exhibits

5.1 Literature exhibits will be judged by the approved specialists in their respective fields and in accordance with Section V. (Art. 31-47) of GREX (ref. GREV, Art. 5.1).

5.2 For Literature exhibits, the following relative terms are presented to lead the Jury to balanced evaluation (ref. GREV, Art. 5.2).

Treatment of contents	40
Originality, significance and depth of research	40
Technical matters	15
Presentation	5
Total	100

Article 6: Concluding Provisions

6.1 In the event of any discrepancies in the text arising from translation, the English text shall prevail.

6.2 These Special Regulations for the Evaluation of Philatelic Literature Exhibits at FIP Exhibitions have been approved by the 54th FIP Congress on 5th November, 1985 in Rome. They came into force on 5th November, 1985 and apply to those exhibitions which are granted FIP patronage, auspices or support at the 54th FIP Congress and thereafter.

Supplementary Rules For The Philatelic Literature Class In FIP Exhibitions

Rule 1: These supplementary rules for the admission of Literature Exhibits have been developed under Art. 4.9 of the General Regulations of the FIP for Exhibitions (GREX) and will apply too all literature entries in General and Special Exhibitions of FIP (GREX Art. 2).

Rule 2: In amplification of Art. 16.1 (GREX), entries may be exhibited by the author, compiler, editor, publisher, sponsoring organization or society, or any other individual holding proprietary rights.

Rule 3: The exhibit will meet the qualification requirement of Art. 9.1 of GREX if previously met by any one of the authorized exhibitors under Rule 2. Newer publications which have not had the opportunity to exhibit at a national exhibition may directly participate in an FIP exhibition.

Rule 4: A separate application form will be used for entries in the literature class. In addition to the other information needed by the Exhibition Management, this form should also include the publication date, publisher, number of pages, frequency of publication (for periodicals) and means of ordering the publication (address, price).

Rule 5: Two copies of each literature exhibit shall be provided by the exhibitor: one copy for judging, and the other for a reading room as per Art. 6.7 of GREX following the exhibition. One copy shall be sent by the Exhibition Management to the FIP Secretariat for the FIP library and the other shall go to a library designated by the member federation hosting the exhibition, unless the exhibitor specifically asks for the return of these copies.

Rule 6: The entry fee for a literature exhibit shall be equivalent to the price of one frame in the general competition class of the same exhibition.

Rule 7: The Exhibition Management shall furnish the judges a list of literature entries at least three months prior to the exhibition.

Rule 8: Handbooks and special studies must have been published not earlier than 5 years prior to the exhibition year. For all other entries the publication date should be not earlier than 2 years prior to the exhibition year.

— For multi-volume works, the date of publication of each volume shall govern.

— Revised editions will be considered as new publications.

— For periodicals, the most recent complete volume or year shall be exhibited.

— A selection of at least ten different newspaper articles is required for exhibition.

Rule 9: Medals in the literature class will bear the word "Literature" either abbreviated or in full. Literature entries are also eligible for the FIP medal (Art. 8 GREX) and special awards (Art. 7-5 GREX).

Rule 10: Literature judges must have a reading ability in at least two languages, one of which must be any of the five official FIP languages (Art. 27.1 of the Statues).

Rule 11: In the event of any discrepancies in the text arising from translation, the English text shall prevail.

Rule 12: These Supplementary Rules for the Evaluation of the Philatelic Literature Class in FIP Exhibitions have been approved by the 54th Congress of the FIP on 5th November, 1985 in Rome, and replace all previous special regulations for literature. They came into force on 5th November, 1985 and apply to those exhibitions which are granted FIP patronage, auspices or support at the 54th FIP Congress and thereafter.

Special Regulations For The Evaluation Of Thematic Exhibits At FIP Exhibitions

Article 1: Competitive Exhibitions

In accordance with Art. 1.5 of the General Regulations of the FIP for the Evaluation of Competitive Exhibits at FIP Exhibitions (GREV), these Special Regulations have been developed to supplement those principles with regard to Thematic Exhibits. Also refer to Guidelines to Thematic Regulations.

Article 2: Competitive Exhibits

A Thematic collection, of which the exhibit is a part develops a theme according to the plan, demonstrating the best knowledge of the theme through the philatelic items chosen.

Article 3: Principles of Exhibit Composition

3.1 The thematic collection uses all types of related appropriate philatelic material. Non-philatelic items cannot be admitted.

3.2 A thematic exhibit comprises the following thematic elements:

3.2.1. **The plan**

The plan defines the structure of the work and its subdivision into parts. It has to be logical, correct and balanced, and cover all aspects related to the title. Furthermore, it has to be fully consistent with the title chosen and should be structured according to thematic criteria.

— The plan may:

* be freely chosen in order to make the synthesis of a theme or an idea.

* derive naturally from the theme, for instance when this describes analytically organizations, institutions and recurrent events.

A plan based on a classification by issuing date, country, type of material, is not considered suitable.

The plan must be provided at the beginning of the exhibit. It should detail the contents of the collection, its subdivision, and their relative size. That should enable a clear understanding of the relation between the exhibit and the whole collection. However, evaluation will take into account only the displayed material.

3.2.2 **The development of the theme**

Demonstrates the personal research for depth and originality. Depth of development requires the detailed analysis and synthesis of each aspect of the theme. Originality is expressed by the personal development of an uncommon subject or a new elaboration of a well-known one.

A successful development requires a thorough knowledge of the chosen theme and a high degree of philatelic knowledge, to identify all the items related thereto. This results in the adequate selection, positioning and sequence of the items, and accuracy of the thematic text. This text must be correct, concise and relevant, to introduce the items shown and ensure the thematic link.

The elaboration utilizes the thematic information obtainable from:

— the purpose of issue

— the primary and secondary elements of the design

— other postal (not privately originated) characteristics.

3.2.3 **The philatelic material**

Each item selected must be strictly related to the chosen theme and show its thematic information in the clearest way. In the case of canceled documents, preference will be given to genuine postal usage and conforming with contemporary postal rates. Philatelic studies may be included in a thematic exhibit, as long as they are consistent with the thematic development and the degree of specialization of the exhibit.

Article 4: Criteria for Evaluating Exhibits

The general criteria, as specified in Art. 4 of the GREV, are applied according to the peculiarities of the thematic exhibition.

4.1 The criterion of treatment of an exhibit requires the evaluation of the plan and the size of the collection, as reflected in the exhibit.

The plan will be evaluated considering the:

— presence and adequacy of the plan page

— consistency of the plan with the title

— correct, logical and balanced sub-division in parts

— coverage of all the parts necessary to develop the plan

The size will be evaluated considering the one of the factual treatment against that which can be achieved by a thorough development.

4.2 The criterion of development requires the evaluation of thematic research and thematic importance, the latter being expressed by the successful elaboration considering the specific scope and interest of the theme developed.

The development of the theme will be evaluated considering the:

— originality of the research

— depth and balance of the elaboration

— thematic importance

— correct thematic knowledge

4.3 The criterion of philatelic knowledge requires the evaluation of the degree of knowledge expressed in the exhibit also with reference to the philatelic importance of the items displayed as related to the chosen theme.

Philatelic knowledge will be evaluated considering the:

— presence of the different types of philatelic items

— correct adherence to the rules of philately

— philatelic importance

— postal characteristics of the documents

— correct philatelic comments, when required

— valid philatelic study, when consistent with the plan.

4.4 Condition and Rarity (ref. GREV, Art. 4-6).

4.5 Presentation (ref. GREV, Art. 4-7).

Article 5: Judging of Exhibits

5.1 Thematic exhibits will be judged by the approved specialists in their respective fields and in accordance with the section V (Act. 31 to 47) of GREX (ref. GREV, Art. 5.1)

5.2 For Thematic exhibits, the following relative terms are presented to lead the Jury to a balanced evaluation (ref. GREV, Art. 5.2).

Treatment	25
Plan 20	
Size 5	
Development of the theme	25
Philatelic knowledge	20
Condition & Rarity	25
Presentation	5
Total	100

Article 6: Concluding Provisions

6.1 In the event of any discrepancies in the text arising from translation, the English text shall prevail.

6.2 These Special Regulations for the Evaluation of Thematic Exhibits at FIP Exhibitions have been approved by 54th FIP Congress on 5th November, 1985 in Rome. They came into force on 5th November 1985 and apply to those exhibitions which are granted FIP patronage, auspices or support at the 54th FIP Congress and thereafter.

Special Regulations For The Evaluation Of Maximaphily Exhibits At FIP Exhibitions

Article 1: Competitive Exhibitions

In accordance with Article 1.5 of the General Regulations of the FIP for the Evaluation of Competitive Exhibits at FIP Exhibitions (GREV) these Special Regulations have been developed to supplement those principles with regard to Maximaphily. Also refer to Guidelines to Maximaphily Regulations.

Article 2: Competitive Exhibits

The maximaphily items should conform to the principles of maximum possible concordance between:

a) The postage stamp

b) The picture postcard

c) Postmark

Article 3: Principles of Exhibit Composition

The constituent elements of maximum card should conform to the following characteristics:

1. The postage stamp should be postally valid and affixed only on the view side of the picture postcard. (Postage due, pre-cancels, fiscals, and official stamps are not admissible).

2. The picture postcard dimensions must conform to Universal Postal Convention. Chapter 1 Art. 19 para 1 (Max. 105 x 148 mm - Min. 90 x 140 mm + 2 mm) and at least 75% of its area must be used for the picture and the illustration should show the best possible concordance with the subject of the stamp design or with one of these subjects if there are several. Picture postcards with mere reproduction of the stamps are forbidden.

3. Postmark and time. The pictorial design of the cancellation and the place of cancellation (name of the post office) should have a close and direct connection with the subject of the stamp and of the picture postcard, and within the validity of the stamp and as close as possible to the date of its issue.

4. Maximaphily exhibits can be classified by:

a) Country

b) Specialized or study

c) Thematic

5. The plan or the concept of the exhibit shall be clearly laid out in an introductory statement.

(ref. GREV, Art. 3.3).

Article 4: Criteria for Evaluating Exhibits (ref. GREV Article 4).

Knowledge and Research (ref. GREV, Art. 4.5)

For maximaphily exhibits special significance is given to the maximum possible concordance shown.

Article 5: Judging of Exhibits

1. Maximaphily exhibits will be judged by the approved specialists in their respective field and in accordance with Sec. V (Art. 31-47) of GREX (ref. GREV Art. 5.1).

2. For Maximaphily exhibits, the following relative terms are presented to lead the Jury to a balanced evaluation. (ref. GREV, Art. 5.2).

Treatment and Importance of the exhibit	30
Knowledge and Research	35
Condition and Rarity	30
Presentation	5
Total	100

Article 6: Concluding Provisions

6.1 In the event of any discrepancies in the text arising from translation, the English text shall prevail.

6.2 These Special Regulations for the Evaluation of Maximaphily Exhibits at FIP Exhibitions have been approved by the 54th FIP Congress on 5th November, 1985 in Rome. They came into force on 5th November, 1985 and apply to those exhibitions which are granted FIP patronage, auspices or support at the 54th FIP Congress and thereafter.

Special Regulations For The Evaluation Of Youth Exhibits At FIP Exhibitions

Article 1: Competitive Exhibitions

In accordance with Art. 1.5 of the General Regulation of FIP for the Evaluation of Competitive Exhibits at FIP Exhibitions (GREV), these Special Regulations have been developed to supplement those principles with regard to Youth Philately. Also refer to Guidelines to Youth Philately Regulations.

Article 2: Competitive Exhibits

The Exhibit of young philatelists aged from 14 to 21, assigned to age classes A to D form the youth class (ref. 2-3).

Article 3: Principles of Exhibit Composition

1. The principles defined in the special regulations of the various competitive classes are, in general, also valid for the exhibits of young philatelists.

2. Each young exhibitor will introduce a title page for his exhibit and clearly define the scope of his exhibit.

Article 4: Criteria for Evaluating Exhibits

The following four main criteria are valid for exhibits of young philatelists:

— Treatment (philatelic/thematic)
— Philatelic knowledge
— Philatelic material
— Presentation of the collection

In accordance with article 4 of the GREV, these criteria are from case to case modified to comply with the conditions for youth.

Article 5: Judging of Exhibits

1. For the evaluation of exhibits of young philatelists, the following number of points will be allocated for the criteria mentioned in the various age classes:

Criteria — Age Class	A	B	C	D
Treatment	20	24	29	35
Knowledge	15	21	28	35
Material	20	20	20	20
Presentation	45	35	23	10

2. The allocation of points for the various criteria in the respective age classes corresponds to the philatelic degree of advancement of young philatelists and takes into consideration their progressing qualification. Moreover, this allocation of points facilitates a gradual adjustment to the relative terms of the GREV, Art. 5.2.

3. Medals, diplomas and certificates of participation are attributed upon the evaluation of exhibits. The following medals are awarded:

45 points — diploma
60 points — bronze medal
65 points — silver-bronze medal
70 points — silver medal
75 points — large silver medal
80 points — vermeil medal
85 points — large vermeil medal

A large vermeil medal is the highest award awarded to a young philatelist.

4. Youth exhibits will be judged by the FIP approved jurors who interest themselves regularly in youth philately and in accordance with Sec. V (Art. 31-47) of GREX.

5. The Jury will establish for each exhibitor a short critical evaluation sheet prepared by the FIP Commission for Youth Philately. The exhibitor is entitled

to receive his valuation sheet through his national commissioner.

Article 6: Concluding Provisions

6.1 In the event of any discrepancies in the text arising from the translation, the English text shall prevail.

6.2 These Special Regulations for the Evaluation of Youth Exhibits at FIP Exhibitions have been approved by the 54th FIP Congress on 5th November, 1985 in Rome. They came into force on 5th November, 1985 and apply to those exhibitions which are granted FIP patronage, auspices or support at the 54th FIP Congress and thereafter.

Supplementary Rules For The Divisions Of Youth Exhibitions In FIP Exhibitions

Rule 1: These supplementary rules for the admission of Youth Exhibits have been developed under Art. 4.9 of the General Regulations of the FIP for Exhibitions (GREX) and will apply to Youth Section of philately in general as well as Special Exhibitions of FIP.

Rule 2: Young exhibitors aged from 14 to 21 years belong in the category of young philatelists.

Rule 3: The exhibit of young philatelists will be assigned to one of the four age classes A, B, C and D according to the age of the young philatelist:

Age class A: 14 and 15 years old
Age class B: 16 and 17 years old
Age class C: 18 and 19 years old
Age class D: 20 and 21 years old

Collective exhibits shall be included in age class C.

The age attained on January 1st of the year in which the exhibition takes place applies.

Rule 4: Each exhibit shall be allocated the following number of frames in conformity with its assignment to the respective age class:

Age class	Minimum	Maximum
A	24 to 32 pages	60 to 64 pages
B	24 to 32 pages	60 to 64 pages
C	32 to 36 pages	72 to 80 pages
D	48 pages	72 to 88 pages

Rule 5: Young philatelists are exempt from fees.

Rule 6 : Only such exhibits shall be admitted which have obtained at least a Silver Bronze medal in a National Exhibition.

Rule 7: An exhibit will be able to participate only once in a competition class of the Youth section of a FIP Exhibition (Article 2 GREX) during the same year.

Rule 8: An exhibit having gained a Large Vermeil medal twice, will not be able to compete in the same age class again.

Rule 9: Literature entries of the Youth class, both in general and special exhibition, will be evaluated according to the following criteria:

— devoted to young philatelists
— written by young philatelists
— periodicals, journals and magazines of interest to young philatelists

Rule 10: Exhibits will only be displayed under the name of the exhibitor.

Rule 11: At special Youth FIP exhibitions, the FIP Coordinator will propose in consultation with the President of Youth Commission of the FIP the list of members of the Jury to the FIP Board, according to Article 32 (GREX).

The President of the FIP Commission for Youth Philately is a member of the Jury for a special exhibition of Youth. If he is unable to attend, he may propose a representative.

Rule 12: The following medals are awarded in a competition of collections of young philatelists:

Large vermeil medal
Vermeil medal
Large silver medal
Silver medal
Silver-bronze medal
Bronze medal

In addition, there are diplomas and certificates of participation.

Rule 13: At a special FIP exhibition of Youth philately, a grand prize of the exhibition (Grand Prix d'Exposition) is awarded to the best exhibit which clearly exceeds the minimum requirement of the Large Vermeil medal.

The grand prize may only be awarded once to the same exhibit.

In addition, special prizes may be awarded; however, the collections involved must also have obtained a Large Silver medal beforehand.

Felicitations of the Jury may be expressed according to Art. 6 of the General Regulations (GREX).

Rule 14: At a special exhibition of Youth philately all publicity material as well as the catalog has to contain names and addresses of the President of the FIP Commission for Youth Philately.

Rule 15: The organizer of a special exhibition of Youth philately will make arrangements for a conference of the FIP Commission for Youth Philately on occasion of the exhibition and to put at disposal suitable rooms.

Rule 16: These supplementary rules replace the special regulations for exhibitions of young philatelists dated April 14, 1975.

Rule 17: In the event of any discrepancies in the text arising from translation, the English text shall prevail.

Rule 18: These Supplementary Rules for the Division of Youth Exhibits at FIP Exhibitions have been approved by the 54th Congress of the FIP on 5th November, 1985 in Rome. They came into force on 5th November, 1985 and apply to those exhibitions which are granted FIP patronage, auspices, or support at the 54th FIP Congress and thereafter.

International Stamp Shows

The following list includes a number of the outstanding international stamp shows held around the world during the past century. Although hardly complete, it does represent a compilation of information available from research at the American Philatelic Research Library, State College, Pa., and *Linn's* Philatelic Library.

1881: First World Philatelic Exhibition, held in Vienna, Austria, Nov. 13-20. Largely national in character.

1890: International Postage Stamp Exhibition, held in Vienna, Austria, under auspices of Austrian Philatelic Club. Marked 50th anniversary of introduction of postage stamps and 40th anniversary of first Austrian postage stamps.

1897: London Philatelic Exhibition, held in London, England, July 22-Aug. 5.

1905: Exhibition of British Colonial Fiscal and Telegraph stamps, held in London, England, April 7-8.

1906: International Philatelic Exhibition, held in London, England, May 23-June 1.

1910: International Postage Stamp Exhibition (Internationale Postwertzeichen Ausstellung), held in Bern, Switzerland, Sept. 3-12.

1911: International Exhibition of Stamps, held in Sydney, Australia, October 1911, under auspices of the First Philatelic Congress of Australia.

1913: International Philatelic Exhibition, held in New York City, Oct. 27-Nov. 1, under auspices of the Association for Stamp Exhibitions, Inc.

1923: International Postage Stamp Exhibition (Internationale Postwertzeichen Ausstellung) held in Vienna, Austria. Held at a time of great emergency following World War I.

1925: International Postage Stamp Exhibition (Exposition Internationale de Timbres-Poste) held in Paris, France, May 2-12.

1926: International Philatelic Exhibition (second in the United States), held in New York City, Oct. 16-23, under auspices of Association for Stamp Exhibitions, Inc.

1929: International Philatelic Exhibition held at LeHavre, France, May 18-26, under patronage of the president of the French Republic.

1932: International LuPosta — International Air Mail Exhibition held in Danzig, July 23-31.

1933: WIPA 1933: Vienna International Postage Stamp Exhibition held in Vienna, Austria, in June 1933, sponsored by the Union of Austrian Philatelic Clubs.

1934: National Stamp Exhibition held in New York City, Feb. 10-18, sponsored by the New York American and endorsed by Association for Stamp Exhibitions, American Philatelic Society and Collectors Club of New York.

1936: TIPEX: Third International Exhibition in the United States held in New York City, May 9-17. Sponsored by the Association for Stamp Exhibitions. Occasion for release of the TIPEX sheet.

1937: PEXIP 1937: International Postage Stamp Exhibition held in Paris, France, in June. Occasion for release of the special sheet of four stamps (Ceres type) on June 18.

1938: International Philatelic Exposition held in Rio de Janeiro, Brazil, Oct. 22-30.

1940: Stamp Centenary Exhibition held in London, England, May 6-11 under the auspices of the Royal Philatelic Society.

— International Centennial Stamp Exhibition held at the British Pavilion, World's Fair in New York City, in cooperation with the New York World's Fair Corp. and British Commission to the World's Fair.

1943: GEPH: Exposition Philatelique Nationale held in Geneva, Switzerland, Aug. 17-26.

1947: Centenary International Stamp Exhibition held in New York City, May 17-25, under auspices of the Association for Stamp Exhibitions, Inc. Recognized the 100th anniversary of the first U.S. postage stamps.

1948: IMABA: International Postage Stamp Exhibition held Aug. 21-29 in Basel, Switzerland.

1949: CITEX 1949: Centenary International Exhibition held in June in Paris, France.

1950: London International Stamp Exhibition held in London, England, May 6-13.

— EFIRA 1950: Exposicion Filetelica International held Oct. 6-12 in Buenos Aires, Argentina.

— ESCE: Centenary Exhibition of the first Spanish postage stamp held in Madrid, Spain, Oct. 12-22.

1951: Canadian International Philatelic Exhibition held in Toronto, Sept. 21-25, under auspices of Canadian Association for Philatelic Exhibitions.

1952: REINTAX: International Philatelic Exhibition held in Monaco, April 26-May 4. FIP patronage.

— CENTILUX 1952: International Centenary Stamp Exhibition held in Luxembourg City, Luxembourg, May 24-June 4.

— ITEP: International Centenary Stamp Exhibition held in Utrecht, The Netherlands, June 28 to July 5.

1953: International Stamp Exhibition honoring centenary of postage stamps in Portugal held in Lisbon, Portugal, Sept. 26-Oct. 5. Recognized by the FIP.

1954: INDIPEX: International Stamp Exhibition observing the India postage stamp centenary held in New Delhi, India, Oct. 1-15.

1955: NORWEX: International Stamp Exhibition honoring centenary of Norwegian postage stamps held in Oslo, Norway, June 4-12. Recognized by FIP.

— STOCKHOLMIA '55: International Stamp Exhibition held in Stockholm, Sweden, July 1-10, observing centenary of Swedish postage stamps.

— International Postage Stamp Exhibition held in Prague, Czechoslovakia, Sept. 10-25. FIP patronage.

— International Philatelic Exposition held in Havana, Cuba, Nov. 12-19.

1956: PHICIPEX: Philippine Centenary International Philatelic Exhibition in Manila, Philippines, April 25-May 9.

1956: JUFIZ: Yugoslavia International Philatelic Exhibition held in Zagreb, Jugoslavia, May 20-27.

1956: FIPEX: Fifth International Philatelic Exhibition in the United States held in New York City, April 28-May 6, under auspices of the Association of Stamp Exhibitions, Inc.

— FINLANDIA 1956: International Stamp Exhibition held in Helsinki, Finland, July 8-16, honoring the centenary of Finnish postage stamps.

— EXMEX 1956: International Philatelic Exhibition held in Mexico City, Mexico, Aug. 1-15.

1957: TABIL: International Postage Stamp Exhibition held in Tel Aviv, Israel, Sept. 17-23. FIP patronage.

1958: EFICON: Exposicion Filatelica InterAmericana Confederacion held in Parana, Argentina, April 19-27.

— TEMATICA 1958: International Postage Stamp Exhibition in Buenos Aires, Argentina, Aug. 16-23.

— International Aero Philatelist Exhibition held in Philadelphia, Pa., Oct. 10-12, in connection with the Aero Philatelists convention.

1959: INTERPOSTA 1959: International Postage Stamp Exhibition held in Hamburg, Germany, May 22-31, recognizing the centenary of the stamps of Hamburg and Lubeck. FIP sanctioned.

— SICILIA 1959: International Philatelic Exhibition held in Palermo, Sicily, Oct. 10-26, celebrating the centenary of the stamps of Sicily. FIP sanctioned.

1960: First International Philatelic Congress in Spain, held in Barcelona, March 26-April 5.

— UNIPEX 1960: International Philatelic Exhibition held in Johannesburg, South Africa, May 30-June 4, observing Golden Jubilee of Union of South Africa.

— London International Stamp Exhibition, held in London England, July 9-16. Sponsored by Royal Philatelic Society and British Philatelic Association.

— POLSKA '60: International Philatelic Exhibition held in Warsaw, Poland, Aug. 27-Sept. 9, honoring the 100th anniversary of first Polish postage stamp. FIP patronage.

— International Exhibition of Postage Stamps held in Bratislava, Czechoslovakia, Sept. 24-Oct. 9. Sponsored by

Federation of Czechoslovak Philatelists.

1961: BUDAPEST 1961: International Postage Stamp Exhibition held in Budapest, Hungary, Sept. 23-Oct. 3.

— TEMEX '61: Exposicion Internationale de Filatelia Tematica held in Buenos Aires, Argentina, Oct. 14-24.

1962: Canadian National Philatelic Exhibition held in Windsor, Ont., Canada, May 3-5, sponsored by the Royal Philatelic Society of Canada.

— PRAGA 1962: World exhibition held in Prague, Czechoslovakia, Aug. 18-Sept. 2. Sponsored by Federation of Czechoslovak Philatelists and the Ministry of Transport and Communications. FIP recognized.

— LUPOSTA 1962. International Air Post Exhibition held in Berlin, Germany, Sept. 12-16.

1963: MELUSINA '63: International Exhibition in Luxembourg, organized by the Federation of Philatelic Societies of Luxembourg. Held April 13-21. FIP sponsored.

— AEROPHILA '63: International Airmail Exhibition held in Brussels, Belgium, Sept. 1-8. Third congress of the FISA.

— ISTANBUL '63: International Stamp Exhibition held in Istanbul, Turkey, Sept. 7-15, sponsored by the Federation of Philatelic Clubs of Turkey, honoring the first Turkish stamps. FIP patronage.

1964: PHILATEC 1964: International Philatelic and Postal Techniques Exhibition held in Paris, France, June 5-12.

1965: WIPA 1965: The Vienna International Postage Stamp Exhibition held in Vienna, Austria, June 4-13. FIP patronage.

— NABRA '65: International Postage Stamp Exhibition held in Bern, Switzerland, Aug. 27-Sept. 5.

1966: SIPEX: Sixth International Philatelic Exhibition in the United States, held in Washington, D.C., May 21-30. FIP patronage.

— AEROPEX: International Airmail and Aerospace Exhibition held in New York City, June 10-12. Sixth FISA congress.

1967: AMPHILEX '67: International Philatelic Exhibition held in Amsterdam, The Netherlands, May 11-21, sponsored by The Netherlands Federation of Philatelic Societies.

— FILEX '67: International Exhibition held in Reykjavik, Iceland, Sept. 2-10.

— International Aerophilatelic Exhibition held in Budapest, Hungary, Sept. 7-8. National Association of Hungarian Philatelists in association with FISA.

1968: EUROPA '68: International Philatelic Show held in Naples, Italy, April 26-May 5.

— Red Crescent Thematic Exhibition held in Istanbul, Turkey, June 11-30.

— IFA WIEN 1968: International Airmail Exhibition held in Vienna, Austria, May 30-June 4. Held under FISA sponsorship and marked by the Eighth FISA congress.

— PRAGA 1968: World Stamp Exhibition held in Prague, Czechoslovakia, June 22-July 7. Marked by the 37th congress of the FIP.

— TEMATICA-POZNAN '68: International Philatelic Exhibition held in Poznan, Poland, July 28-Aug. 11. Organized by the Polish Philatelic Federation. FIP patronage.

— EFIMEX '68: Exposicion Filatelica International held in Mexico City, Mexico, Nov. 1-9. Under FIP patronage.

1969: Centenary Exhibition, Royal Philatelic Society, London, England, held April 11-20.

— JUVENTUS 1969: First International Philatelic Exhibition for FIP juniors, held in Luxembourg City, April 3-8. FIP patronage.

— SOFIA '69: World Philatelic Exhibition held in Sofia, Bulgaria, May 31-June 8.

— LUPO '69: First Airmail Exhibition in Switzerland, held in Lucerne, Switzerland, April 26-28, sponsored by the International Federation of Aerophilatelic Societies.

— TORINO '69: International Postage Stamp Exhibition held in Turin, Italy, June 26-29.

— JOEPEX '69: International Stamp Exhibition held in Colombo, Ceylon, July 3-6.

— EXFILBO '69: International Postage Stamp Exhibition held in Bogota, Colombia, Nov. 28-Dec. 7. First exposition of Filatelica InterAmericana.

1970: ANPEX 1970: Australian National Philatelic Exhibition held in Sydney, New South Wales, April 27-May 1.

— PHILYMPIA: London International Stamp Exhibition held in London, Sept. 18-26. Sponsored by Royal Philatelic Society, British Philatelic Association, and Philatelic Traders' Society.

— XII Philatelic Exhibition held in Barcelona, Spain, Oct. 25-31.

— EXFILCA '70: Second Exposicion Filatelica InterAmericana held in Caracas, Venezuela, Nov. 27 to Dec. 6. Under FIAF sponsorship.

— Malta Philatelic Exhibition, organized by the General Post Office of Malta, held Dec. 28 to Jan. 9, 1971.

1971: PHILATOKYO '71: International Philatelic Exhibition held in Tokyo, Japan, April 20-30, commemorating a century of Japanese Posts. Under FIP patronage.

— International Stamp Exhibition held in Capetown, South Africa, May 22-31, under auspices of the Philatelic Federation of South Africa.

— International Luposta: International Airmail Exhibition held in West Berlin, Germany, June 10-13. 11th FISA congress.

— BUDAPEST '71: International Philatelic Exhibition held in Budapest, Hungary, Sept. 4-12.

— EXFILIMA '71. International Philatelic Show held in Lima, Peru, Nov. 6-14. Held under FIAF patronage.

— ANPHILEX: Commemorating the 75th year of the Collectors Club of New York City. Held Nov. 26-Dec. 1 at the Waldorf-Astoria Hotel in New York City.

1972: COPEX '72: International Philatelic Exhibition held in Kerala, India, Feb. 24-27.

— EFIME '72: International Philatelic Exhibition held in Medellin, Colombia, April 20-27.

— BELGICA '72: International Philatelic Exhibition held in Brussels, Belgium, June 24-July 9, sponsored by the Royal Federation of Belgian Philatelic Societies. FIP patronage.

— LIBA: International Show held in Vaduz, Liechtenstein, Aug. 18-27.

— INTERJUNEX 1972: Second international philatelic exhibition for juniors. FIP sponsorship. Held in Kristiansand, Norway, Aug. 25-Sept. 3.

— EXFILBRA '72: Fourth Exhibition under FIAF sponsorship, held in Rio de Janeiro, Brazil, Aug. 26-Sept. 2.

— ROCPEX '72: Republic of China Philatelic Exhibition, held in Taipei, Oct. 24-Nov. 2. Organized by the Directorate General of Posts.

1973: IBRA-MUNCHEN '73: International Postage Stamp Exhibition held in Munich, West Germany, May 11-20, under sponsorship of the FIP with the Federation of German Philatelists.

— POLSKA '73: World Postage Stamp Exhibition held in Poznan, Poland, Aug. 19-Sept. 3, marking the 500th anniversary of the birth of Nicolaus Copernicus. Held with FIP patronage.

— INDIPEX '73: India International Philatelic Exhibition held in New Delhi, India, Nov. 11-14.

— JERUSALEM '74: International Stamp Exhibition held March 25-April 2, 1974, under FIP patronage, celebrating the 25th anniversary of Israeli stamps.

1974: INTERNABA 1974: International Postage Stamp Exhibition held in Basel, Switzerland, June 6-17. Under FIP patronage. Marked the centenary of the Universal Postal Union.

— INJUNPEX '74: First International All-Junior Stamp and Literature Exhibition, July 5-7. Held in New York City.

— STOCKHOLMIA '74: International Postage Stamp Exhibition held in Stockholm, Sweden, Sept. 21-29. Sponsored by the Philatelic Society of Sweden and the Royal Swedish Post, with FIP patronage.

— EXFILMEX '74-UPU: Fifth Exposicion Filatelica InterAmericana held in Mexico City, Mexico, Oct. 26-Nov. 3. FIAF sponsorship.

— LUBRAPEX '74: Fifth Lubrapex Exposicion Filatelica Luso Brazileira held in Sao Paulo, Brazil, Nov. 26-Dec. 4.

1975: ESPANA '75: International Philatelic Exhibition held in Madrid, Spain, April 4-13, in cooperation with Spanish Philatelic Societies. FIP sponsorship. Forty-fourth congress of FIP.

— NORDIA '75: Nordic Stamp Exhibition held in Helsinki, Finland, April 26-May 1. Held with cooperation of the Philatelic Society of Finland and Administration of Posts and Telegraph.

— ARPHILA '75: International Philatelic Exhibition held in Paris, France, June 6-16. Sponsored by Federation of French Philatelic Societies, marking the 50th anniversary of the first stamp exhibition in Paris in 1925.

— INJUNPEX '75: Second International All-Junior Stamp and Literature Exhibition, July 6-12. Held in Guadalajara, Mexico.

— EXFILMO '75: Inter-American Philatelic Exhibition held in Montevideo, Uruguay, Oct. 10-19. Organized by Club Filatelico del Uruguay and Circulo Filatelico de Montevideo.

— EXFIVIA '75: First Exhibition of Filatelica Boliviana held in La Paz, Bolivia, Nov. 15-22.

— THEMABELGA: World Exhibition of Thematic Philately held in Brussels, Belgium, Dec. 13-21. First world exhibition of thematic philately held under FIP patronage.

1976: INTERPHIL '76: International Philatelic Exhibition held in Philadelphia, Pa., May 29-June 6. Forty-fifth congress of the FIP.

— HAFNIA '76: First International Postage Stamp Show in Denmark. Held in Copenhagen, Aug. 20-29, marking 125th anniversary of first Danish stamp. FIP patronage.

— ITALIA '76: World Stamp Exhibition held in Milan, Italy, Oct. 14-24. Organized by the Federation of Italian Philatelic Societies and held as part of the Milan Fair, FIP patronage.

1977: JUPHILEX '77: International Exhibition for Juniors held in Bern, Switzerland, April 7-11.

— International Philatelic Youth Exhibition held in Antwerp, Belgium, Aug. 6-16. Sponsored by the Royal Federation of Belgium Philatelic Societies and Pro-Post, under the auspices of the FIP Youth Commission.

— LUPOSTA '77: International Air Post Exhibition held in West Berlin, West Germany, Aug. 19-21.

— SAN MARINO: International Philatelic Exhibition held Aug. 28-Sept. 4 in honor of the centenary of the first San Marino stamps.

— PORTUCALE '77: Second International Thematic Stamp Exhibition held Nov. 19-28 in Portugal. FIP patronage.

1978: CAPEX '78: International Philatelic Exhibition held June 9-18 in Toronto, Ont., Canada. FIP patronage.

— PRAGA 1978: World Postage Stamp Exhibition held Sept. 8-17 in Prague, Czechoslovakia. FIP patronage.

1979: PHILASERDICA '79: International Philatelic Exhibition held in Sofia, Bulgaria, May 8-27, noting the 100th anniversary of the first Bulgarian postage stamps. FIP patronage.

— BRASILIANA '79: First Inter-American Exhibition of Classic Philately and Third World Exhibition of Thematic Philately, held Sept. 15-23 in Rio de Janeiro, Brazil. FIP patronage.

1980: INDIA '80: International Philatelic Exhibition held in New Delhi, India, Jan. 25-Feb. 3. FIP patronage.

— LONDON 1980: International Philatelic Exhibition held in London, England, May 6-14. FIP patronage.

— NORWEX '80: International Philatelic Exhibition held June 13-22 in Oslo, Norway. FIP patronage.

— JUPOSTEX: Youth Exhibition held in Eindhoven, The Netherlands, May 23-27. Sponsored by Netherlands Federation of Philatelic Societies and Foundation of Philatelic Youthwork, FIP patronage.

— BUENOS AIRES '80: International Philatelic Exhibition held Oct. 24-Nov. 2 in Buenos Aires, Argentina, under FIP patronage in conjunction with annual meeting of Inter-American Philatelic Federation.

1981: LURABA 1981: Organized by Managing Board of Federation of Swiss Philatelic Societies. Held March 20-29 in Lucerne, Switzerland. Sponsored by Foundation Pro Aero and the Funds for Promotion of Philately. FIP patronage.

— WIPA '81: International Philatelic Exhibition held in Vienna, Austria, May 22-31. FIP patronage.

— PHILATOKYO '81: International Stamp Exhibition, held Oct. 9-18 in Tokyo, Japan. FIP patronage.

1982: CANADA 82: International

Philatelic Youth Exhibition held May 20-24 in Toronto, Canada. Sponsored by Royal Philatelic Society of Canada and Canada Post. FIP patronage.

— PHILEXFRANCE '82: held June 11-21 in Paris, France.

— BELGLICA '82: International Stamp Show held Dec. 11-19 in Brussels, Belgium. FIP patronage.

1983: TEMBAL 83: International Stamp Show held May 21-29 in Basel, Switzerland. FIP patronage.

— BRASILIANA 83: International Stamp Show held July 29-Aug. 7 in Rio de Janeiro, Brazil. FIP patronage.

— BANGKOK 1983: International Stamp Show held Aug. 4-13 in Bangkok, Thailand. FIP patronage.

1984: ESPANA 84: International Stamp Show held April 27-May 6 in Madrid, Spain. FIP patronage.

— AUSIPEX 84: International Stamp Show held Sept. 21-30 in Melbourne, Australia. FIP patronage.

— PHILAKOREA 1984: International Stamp Show held Oct. 22-31 in Seoul, Korea. FIP patronage.

1985: ISRAPHIL 85: International Stamp Show held May 14-22 in Tel Aviv, Israel. FIP patronage.

— ARGENTINA '85: International Stamp Show held July 5-14 in Buenos Aires, Argentina. FIP patronage.

— ITALIA '85: International Stamp Show held Oct. 25-Nov. 3 in Rome, Italy. FIP patronage.

1986: AMERIPEX 86: International Stamp Show held May 22-June 1 in Chicago, Ill. FIP patronage.

— STOCKHOLMIA 86: International Stamp Show held Aug. 28-Sept. 7 in Stockholm, Sweden. FIP patronage.

1987: CAPEX 87: International Stamp Show held June 13-21 in Toronto, Canada. FIP patronage.

— HAFNIA 87: International Stamp Show held Oct. 16-25 in Copenhagen, Denmark. FIP patronage.

1988: FINLANDIA 88: International Stamp Show held June 1-12 in Helsinki, Finland. FIP patronage.

— PRAGA 88: International Stamp Show held Aug. 26-Sept. 4 in Prague, Czechoslovakia. FIP patronage.

— JUVALEX 88: International Youth Exhibition held March 28-April 3 in Luxembourg. FIP patronage.

— OLYMPHILEX 88: International Stamp Show held Sept. 19-28 in Seoul Korea. FIP patronage.

1989: INDIA 89: International Stamp Show held Jan. 20-29 in New Delhi, India. FIP patronage.

— IPHLA 89: International Literature Exhibition held April 19-23 in Frankfurt, Germany. FIP patronage.

— BULGARIA 89: International Stamp Show held May 21-30 in Sofia, Bulgaria. FIP congress convened May 31-June 1. FIP patronage.

— PHILEXFRANCE 89: International Stamp Show held July 7-17 in Paris, France. FIP patronage.

Future FIP Shows

1990: STAMP WORLD LONDON 1990: International Stamp Show to be held May 3-12 in London England. FIP congress convening May 13-15. FIP patronage.

— DUSSELDORF 90: International Youth Exhibition to be held June 20-24 in Dusseldorf, Germany. FIP patronage.

— NEW ZEALAND 90: International Stamp to be held Aug. 24-Sept. 2 in Auckland, New Zealand. FIP patronage.

1991: ISTANBUL 91: International Stamp Show to be held in August in Istanbul, Turkey. FIP patronage.

— PHILANIPPON 91: International Stamp Show to be held Nov. 15-24 in Tokyo, Japan. FIP patronage.

1992: MONTREAL 92: International Stamp Show to be held March 25-29 in Montreal, Canada. FIP patronage.

— ESPANA 92: International Stamp Show to be held April 10-19 in Granada, Spain. FIP patronage.

— GENOVA 92: International Stamp Show to be held June 5-14 in Genoa, Italy. FIP status has not been established.

— URUGUAY 92: International Stamp Show to be held Oct. 15-22 in Montevideo, Uruguay. FIP status has not been established.

1993: WARSZWA 93: International Stamp Show to be held in Warsaw, Poland. FIP status has not been established.

1994: BULGARIA 94: International Youth Exhibition to be held in Bulgaria. FIP status has not been established.

1995: EXPO 95: International Stamp Show to be held in Budapest, Hungary. FIP status has not been established.

1996: GREECE 96: International Stamp Show to be held in Athens, Greece. FIP status has not been established.

— CANADA 96: International Stamp Show to be held in Toronto, Canada. FIP status has not been established.

1997: NORWEX 97: International Stamp Show to be held April 10-20 in Oslo, Norway. FIP status has not been established.

— PACIFIC 97: International Stamp Show to be held in California. FIP status has not been established.

1998: ISRAEL 98: International Stamp Show to be held in Israel. FIP status has not been established.

— PRAGA 98: International Stamp Show to be held in Prague, Poland. FIP status has not been established.

— PORTUGAL 98: International Stamp Show to be held in Portugal. FIP status has not been established.

1999: FRANCE 99: International Stamp Show to be held in France. FIP status has not been established.

2000: U.K.: International Stamp Show to be held in London, England. FIP status has not been established.

— WIPA 2000: International Stamp Show to be held June 1-11 in Vienna, Austria. FIP status has not been established.

2001: HAFNIA 01: International Stamp Show to be held in Copenhagen, Denmark. FIP status has not been established.

— TOKYO 01: International Stamp Show to be held in Tokyo, Japan. FIP status has not been established.

2002: NETHERLAND 02: International Stamp Show to be held in Netherlands.

Grand Prix Winners

The following is a list of grand-prix-award winners at FIP shows since 1968. Three top awards are given at FIP shows: The grand prix d'honneur is awarded to the best exhibit in the FIP class of honor. To be entered in the class of honor, the exhibit must have previously won three international large golds at FIP shows. The grand prix d'honneur may only be won once by a particular exhibit. The grand prix international goes to the best exhibit from outside the sponsoring country. The grand prix national is awarded to the best exhibit from the sponsoring country.

PRAGA 1968

Grand Prix d'Honneur

Prieto Provera of Italy, "Austria and Lombardy-Venetia: 1850-1880"

Grand Prix International

Horst Knapp of West Germany, "Germany: Saxony"

Grand Prix National

Zdenek Kvasnicka of Czechoslovakia, "Czechoslovakia: 1918-1938, Specialized"

SOFIA 1969

Grand Prix d'Honneur

Stig Ljunggren of Sweden, "Norway 1855-1875"

Grand Prix International

Roberto Tomasini of Italy, "Romania: First Issue"

Grand Prix National

Theodor V. Popov of Bulgaria, "Bulgaria: 1879-1890"

BUDAPEST 1971

Grand Prix d'Honneur

Michel Liphschutz of France, "Russia: Two Hundred Years of the Mails"

Grand Prix International

Rolf Rothmayr of Switzerland, "Switzerland: Classics"

Grand Prix National

Gyula Madarasz of Hungary, "Hungary: 1871"

BELGICA 1972

Grand Prix d'Honneur

Emile Antonini of Switzerland, "France: 1849-1875"

Grand Prix International

Conte Alfredo Gerli of Italy, "Italy — Tuscany: Specialized"

Grand Prix National

Dr. de Mons Xhigne of Belgium, "Belgium: 1865, 1866 and 1869 Issues"

IBRA 1973

Grand Prix d'Honneur

W.G. Scheller of Switzerland, "Bavaria: Specialized"

Grand Prix International

Conte Alfredo Gerli of Italy, "Italy: Sicily"

Grand Prix National

Arthur Salm of the United States, "Germany: Thurn and Taxis"

POLSKA 1973

Grand Prix d'Honneur

Gunnar Roos of Sweden, "Sweden: 1855-1872"

Grand Prix International

Samad Khorshid of Iran, "Persia: Lion Stamps 1868-1879"

Grand Prix National

Stanislaw Dolinski of Poland, "Kingdom of Poland 1858-1870"

JERUSALEM 1974

Grand Prix d'Honneur

(No honor class)

Grand Prix International

Louis Abrams of South Africa, "German South-West Africa: Postal History"

Grand Prix National

Dr. Hans Georg Sladowsky of West Germany, "Palestine: 1730-1918"

INTERNABA 1974

Grand Prix d'Honneur

Luis Cervera of Spain, "Spain: Specialized 1850-1865"

Grand Prix International

Dr. Anton Jerger of Austria, "Hungary: 1850-1871"

Grand Prix National

Rolf Rothmayr of Switzerland, "Switzerland: Classics"

STOCKHOLMIA 1974

Grand Prix d'Honneur

John Griffiths of Great Britain, "Great Britain: Line Engraved 1840-1880"

Grand Prix International

Simone Rubeli of Switzerland, "Switzerland: Canton and Federal Stamps 1842-1856"

Grand Prix National

Lawson Stone of the United States, "Sweden: 1880"

ESPANA 1975

Grand Prix d'Honneur

Joaquin Galvez N. of Spain, "Chile: 1853-1866"

Grand Prix International

Prieto Provera of Italy, "Austria and Lombardy-Venetia: 1850-1880"

Grand Prix National

Antonio Perpina Sebria of Spain, "Spain: 1850-1854"

ARPHILA 1975

Grand Prix d'Honneur

Samad Khorshid of Iran, "Persia: Lions Stamps 1868-1879"

Grand Prix International

Hiroyuki Kanai of Japan, "Mauritius: Local Issues 1847-1862"

Grand Prix National

Plastiras N. Foster of France, "France: 1849-1876"

THEMABELGA 1975

Grand Prix d'Honneur

(No honor class)

Grand Prix International

Hans Paikert of West Germany, "Universal Postal Union"*

Grand Prix National

(No national class)

INTERPHIL 1976

Grand Prix d'Honneur

Wallace Knox of the United States, "Great Britain: Classics"

Grand Prix International

Horst Dietrich of West Germany, "Afghanistan: 1842-1878"

Grand Prix National

Louis Grunin of the United States, "United States: 1847-1857"

HAFNIA 1976

Grand Prix d'Honneur

Einar Lundstrom of Sweden, "Iceland"

Grand Prix International

Tevfik Kuyas of Turkey, "Brazil: 1843-1850"

Grand Prix National

Hans Mott of Sweden, "Denmark: 1851-1863"

ITALIA 1976

Grand Prix d'Honneur

Jose Gonzales Garcia of Portugal, "Portugal: Classics"

Grand Prix International

Emil Capellaro of West Germany, "Austria and Lombardy-Venetia: First Issues"

Grand Prix National

Giuseppe Barcella of Italy, "Italy: Romagne"

AMPHILEX 1977

Grand Prix d'Honneur

Gary S. Ryan of Great Britain, "Hungary: 1867-1874"

Grand Prix International

Henri van der Auwera of Belgium, "Belgium: First Three Issues 1849-1866"

Grand Prix National

G.C. van Balen Blanken of the Netherlands, "Netherlands: 1852 Issue"

PORTUCALE 1977

Grand Prix d'Honneur

(No honor class)

Grand Prix International

Walter Grob of Switzerland, "Scouting Worldwide"*

Grand Prix National

(No national class)

CAPEX 1978

Grand Prix d'Honneur

Hiroyuki Kanai of Japan, "Mauritius Local Issues 1847-1862"

Grand Prix International

John Jacob Engelau of Sweden, "Denmark: Classics"

Grand Prix National

John DuPont of the United States, "British North America: Imperforate Pence Issus"

PRAGA 1978

Grand Prix d'Honneur

Ryohei Ishikawa of Japan, "United States: Hawaii"

Grand Prix International

Giuseppe Barcella of Italy, "Italy: Romagne"

Grand Prix National

Max Mahr of West Germany, "Czechoslovakia"

PHILASERDICA 1979

Grand Prix d'Honneur

Fritz Heimbuechler of West Germany, "Romania: Moldavia-Walachia 1822-1864"

Grand Prix International

Enrique Martin de Bustamante of Spain, "Peru: Classics"

Grand Prix National

Vassil Karaivanov of Bulgaria, "Bulgaria: Large and Small Lions"

BRASILIANA 1979

Grand Prix d'Honneur

(No honor class)

Grand Prix International

Michel Hecq of Belgium, "Railroads"*

Grand Prix National

(No national class)

INDIA 1980

Grand Prix d'Honneur

Giuseppe Barcella of Italy, "Italy: Romagne"

Grand Prix International

Ryohei Ishikawa of Japan, "Hong Kong: Victoria Issue 1862-1903"

Grand Prix National

S.N. Poddar of India, "India: 19th Century"

LONDON 1980

Grand Prix d'Honneur

Reynaldo B. Pracchia of Brazil, "Brazil: 1843-1866"

Grand Prix International

Antonio Perpina Sebria of Spain, "Spain: 1850-1854"

Grand Prix National

Henri Grand of Switzerland, "Great Britain: Queen Victoria"

NORWEX 1980

Grand Prix d'Honneur

Marcel Decerier of France, "France: 1849-1870"

Grand Prix International

Isac Seligson of Luxembourg, "Luxembourg: 1852-1865"

Grand Prix National

F.C. Moldenhauer of Norway, "Norway: Specialized 1845-1880"

BUENOS AIRES 1980

Grand Prix d'Honneur

Robert P. Odenweller of the United States, "New Zealand: 1855-1874"

Grand Prix International

Enrique Martin de Bustamante of Spain, "Venezuela: Classics"

Grand Prix National

G.A. Sanchez of Argentina, "Argentina: Classics"

LURABA 1981

Grand Prix d'Honneur

(No honor class)

Grand Prix International

Zbigniew Mikulski of Switzerland, "USSR: Airmails"*

Grand Prix National

(No national class)

WIPA 1981

Grand Prix d'Honneur

Antonio Perpina Sebria of Spain, "Spain: 1850-1854"

Grand Prix International

Ryohei Ishikawa of Japan, "United States: 1847-1869"

Grand Prix National

Emil Capellaro of West Germany, "Austria and Lombardy-Venetia: First Issues"

PHILATOKYO 1981

Grand Prix d'Honneur

Enrique Martin de Bustamante of Spain, "Peru: Classics"

Grand Prix International

Giuseppe Barcella of Italy, "Italy: Papal States"

Grand Prix National

Yoshio Watanabe of Japan, "Japan: Hand Engraved 1871-1876"

PHILEXFRANCE 1982

Grand Prix d'Honneur

Emile Antonini of Switzerland, "Egypt: 1800-1875"

Grand Prix International

Henry Grand of Switzerland, "Switzerland: 1843-1900"

Grand Prix National

Fernand Pineau of France, "France: Postal Reform of 1848"

BELGICA 1982

Grand Prix d'Honneur

(No honor class)

Grand Prix International

Andre Bollen of Belgium, "Great Britain: Offices in the Americas"*

Grand Prix National

(No national class)

TEMBAL 1983

Grand Prix d'Honneur

(No honor class)

Grand Prix International

Luciano Viti of Italy, "Venice — A Millenium"*

Grand Prix National

(No national class)

BRASILIANA 1983

Grand Prix d'Honneur

Purnendu Gupta of India, "Nepal"

Grand Prix International

Feridoun N. Farahbakhsh of Iran, "Iran: Lions Issues"

Grand Prix National

Dr. Norman Hubbard of the United

States, "Brazil: 1843"

BANGKOK 1983

Grand Prix d'Honneur

John O. Griffiths of the United States, "Australia: South Australia"

Grand Prix International

John E. duPont of the United States, "Samoa: 1877-1900"

Grand Prix National

Prakaipet Indhusophon of Thailand, "Thailand: -1908"

ESPANA 1984

Grand Prix d'Honneur

Antonio Perpina Sebria, "Spain: 1855-1860"

Grand Prix International

Saverio Imperato of Italy, "Italy: Tuscany 1851-1860"

Grand Prix National

Juan M. Alfaro Caballero of Spain, "Spanish Postal Dependency"

AUSIPEX 1984

Grand Prix d'Honneur

John H. Levett of Great Britain, "French Colonies: 1859-1881"

Grand Prix International

John E. duPont of the United States, "British North America: Imperforate Pence Issues"

Grand Prix National

Rodney A. Perry of Australia, "Australia: Victoria 1850-1858"

PHILAKOREA 1984

Grand Prix d'Honneur

Gerhard Blank of Switzerland, "Chile: Classics"

Grand Prix International

Peng Hian Tay of Singapore, "Straits Settlements"

Grand Prix National

Ichiro Kondoh of Japan, "Korea: 1884-1903"

ISRAPHIL 1985

Grand Prix d'Honneur

Jochen Heddergott of West Germany, "India"

Grand Prix International

Leonard Kapiloff of the United States, "United States: 1847 Issue"

Grand Prix National

Silvano Sorani of Italy, "Palestine: The Holy Land"

ARGENTINA 1985

Grand Prix d'Honneur

(No honor class)

Grand Prix International

Franco Pellegrini of Italy, "Olympics 1896-1906"*

Grand Prix National

(No national class)

ITALIA 1985

Grand Prix d'Honneur

Saverio Imprato of Italy, "Italy: Tuscany 1851-1860"

Grand Prix International

Meiso Mizuhara of Japan, "China: Customs Posts 1878-1897"

Grand Prix National

Giuseppe Barcella, "Italy: Parma"

AMERIPEX 1986

Grand Prix d'Honneur

Enrique Martin de Bustamante of Spain, "Venezuela: Classics"

Grand Prix International

John E. duPont of the United States, "British Guiana"

Grand Prix National

Ryohei Ishikawa of Japan, "United States: 1847-1869"

STOCKHOLMIA 1986

Grand Prix d'Honneur

John E. duPont of the United States, "British North America: Imperforate Pence Issues"

Grand Prix International

Hugo Josefson of Sweden, "Sweden: 1855-1872"

Grand Prix National

Christian Sundman of Finland, "Finland: 1637-1885"

CAPEX 1987

Grand Prix d'Honneur

Ryohei Ishikawa of Japan, "United States: 1847-1869"

Grand Prix International

Hassan Shaida of Great Britain, "Great Britain: 1d and 2d Line Engraved"

Grand Prix National

Gerald Wellburn of Canada, "British Columbia Specialized"

HAFNIA 1987

Grand Prix d'Honneur

Rolf-Dieter W. Jaretzky of West Germany, "Germany: Brunswick"

Grand Prix International

Ronald A.G. Lee of Great Britain, "Cape of Good Hope: 1853-1863"

Grand Prix National

Peter Meyer of Denmark, "Danish West Indies: Postal History"

FINLANDIA 1988

Grand Prix d'Honneur

Rolf-Dieter W. Jaretzky of West Germany, "United States: Postmasters, Carriers and Local Issues"

Grand Prix International

Giuseppe Barcella of Italy, "Italy: Parma"

Grand Prix National

Hiroyuki Kanai of Japan, "Finland: 1856-1875"

PRAGA 1988

Grand Prix d'Honneur

Albert Fillinger of France, "France: Postal History of French Army Campaigns 1689-1830"

Grand Prix International

Zbigniew Mikulski of Switzerland, "Russia: 1846-1913"

Grand Prix National

Fred W. Hefer of West Germany, "Czechoslovakia: 1918-1938"

INDIA 1989

Grand Prix d'Honneur

Praikaipet Indhusophon of Thailand, "Siam: 19th Century and Post Offices Abroad"

Grand Prix International

Samir Amin Fikry of Egypt, "The Nile Collection: 200 B.C. to 1872"

Grand Prix National

Dilip Shah of India, "Indian Classics"

* Grand prix of the specialized exhibition.

U.S. Winners at FIP Shows

The following is a list of U.S. exhibitors at FIP-sponsored shows who have won a vermeil prize or higher. The listing includes all international exhibitions held under the patronage of the FIP from 1968 through 1988.

Abelson, Robert, "United States: Florida Manuscript Postmarks," AMERIPEX 86, vermeil

Ackerman, G. Adolph, "USSR: Airmails," PRAGA 88, large vermeil with special prize

Adams, James R., "United States: New York Postal History," ISRAPHIL 85, vermeil

Adams, Jeanette K., "Great Britain: Scotland Postal History 1711-1857," ISRAPHIL 85, vermeil

Adler, Kurt, "Russia: 18th and 19th Century Pre-Adhesives," PRAGA 68, vermeil; SOFIA 69, vermeil

Adlerblum, Burton, "Palestine: Turkish and British Periods," IBRA-MUNCHEN 73, vermeil with felicitations; INTERPHIL 76, vermeil; AMERIPEX 86, vermeil

Alexander, Thomas J., "United States: Three Cent 1851-1857," PHILATOKYO 81, gold

Alton, Jacquelyn, "Germany: Cologne — 1899," AMERIPEX 86, vermeil

Anderson, David, "United States: Twenty-four Cent 1861 Issue," PHILATOKYO 81, vermeil; PHILEXFRANCE 82, gold

Andrews, James C., "Guatemala: Postal Stationery 1875-1930," AMERIPEX 86, large vermeil

Anttila, Kaarlo E., "Ecuador: 1865-1872," FINLANDIA 88, gold with special prize

Arfken, George B., "Canada: Postal History Small Queen Era," AMERIPEX 86, large vermeil

Arlen, Samuel, "United States: Western Express Franks," INTERPHIL 76, vermeil; LONDON 1980, vermeil

Arnould, Howard L., "Danish West Indies: Postal History," STOCKHOLMIA 86, large vermeil; CAPEX 87, gold; HAFNIA 87, gold

Artander, Steffen, "Denmark: Fire RBS and 2 RBS," HAFNIA 76, vermeil

Asimakopulos, Nicholas, "Greece: Large Hermes Head Varieties," ESPANA 84, large vermeil; ISRAPHIL 85, large vermeil; ITALIA 85, vermeil; AMERIPEX 86, vermeil; CAPEX 87, vermeil; FINLANDIA 88, large vermeil with felicitations; PRAGA 88, large vermeil

Aussprung, H. Leon, "United States: 1851-1857," INTERPHIL 76, vermeil

Banchik, Seymour and Barbara, "Israel," INDIA 80, vermeil; WIPA 81, vermeil; PHILEXFRANCE 82, vermeil; ISRAPHIL 85, gold with special prize; AMERIPEX 86, large vermeil; STOCKHOLMIA 86, large vermeil; CAPEX 87, vermeil

Barovick, Fred, "Number One Stamps of the World on Cover," PRAGA 78, vermeil

Bauer, William H., "United States: Colorado Postal History," INTERPHIL 76, vermeil; LONDON 1980, vermeil; NORWEX 80, vermeil

Beals, David T. III, "United States: Western Covers 1820-1861," INTERPHIL 76, gold

Belknap, Thomas L., "New Guinea and Papua: 1885-1931," CAPEX 78, gold with felicitations; AUSIPEX 84, gold; PHILAKOREA 84, gold; AMERIPEX 86, large vermeil; "Gilbert and Ellice Islands," CAPEX 87, vermeil

Berecz, Victor G., "Hungary: Airmails," CAPEX 87, vermeil; PRAGA 88, vermeil

Birkinbine, John II, "Confederate States of America: 1861-1865," AUSIPEX 84, large gold; AMERIPEX 86, gold; STOCKHOLMIA 86, large gold; CAPEX 87, large vermeil with special prize

Blau, Fred F., "Holy Land: The Airmails History," JERUSALEM 74, gold; ESPANA 75, gold; ARPHILA 75, gold; INTERPHIL 76, gold; AMPHILEX 77, gold; CAPEX 78, gold with special prize and felicitations; INDIA 80, gold with special prize; LONDON 1980, gold; BUENOS AIRES 80, gold; LURABA 81, gold; WIPA 81, large gold; PHILEXFRANCE 82, gold with felicitations; BELGICA 82, large gold; BRASILIANA 83, large gold; ESPANA 84, prix d'honneur; AUSIPEX 84, prix d'honneur;

PHILAKOREA 84, prix d'honneur; ISRAPHIL 85, prix d'honneur; ITALIA 85, prix d'honneur; AMERIPEX 86, prix d'honneur; STOCKHOLMIA 86, prix d'honneur; CAPEX 87, prix d'honneur; HAFNIA 87, prix d'honneur; "Palestine: Allied Military Airmail," AMERIPEX 86, gold with felicitations; STOCKHOLMIA 86, gold; CAPEX 87, gold; HAFNIA 87, large vermeil; PRAGA 88, gold

Blinn, Christine, "Danish West Indies: Specialized Including Pre-Adhesive," INTERPHIL 76, vermeil; CAPEX 78, vermeil with felicitations; LONDON 1980, vermeil

Boehret, Diane D., "Germany: Offices in China: Boxer Rebellion 1900-1906," BRASILIANA 83, vermeil with special prize; AMERIPEX 86, vermeil; STOCKHOLMIA 86, large vermeil; FINLANDIA 88, vermeil; "Germany: Offices in Turkish Empire 1914-1918," ISRAPHIL 85, vermeil

Boksenbom, J.P., "Ethiopia," INTERNABA 74, vermeil; ESPANA 75, vermeil with special prize; ARPHILA 75, vermeil

Bormann, Gordon, "United States: Airmails," CAPEX 87, vermeil; FINLANDIA 88, vermeil

Boshwit, Buck, "Confederate States: Tennessee Postal History 1861-1864, AMERIPEX 86, large vermeil with felicitations

Bowden, R. Renee, "Germany: Thurn and Taxis," INTERPHIL 76, vermeil; AMERIPEX 86, large vermeil

Bowman, Eugene E., "Cape of Good Hope: 1792-1910," AMERIPEX 86, large vermeil; CAPEX 87, gold

Bowman, James A., "Olympic Games 1936," FINLANDIA 88, vermeil

Brambilla, Louis, "Israel," SOFIA 69, vermeil

Brandon, Ralph, "Confederate States of America," AMERIPEX 86, gold

Brichacek, Robert J., "United States: Columbian Issue 1893," AMERIPEX 86, vemeil; STOCKHOLMIA 86, large vermeil

Brooks, Walter, "France: Paris Siege 1870-1871," ISRAPHIL 85, vermeil; ITALIA 85, vermeil; AMERIPEX 86, vermeil; STOCKHOLMIA 86, large vermeil

Brown, Gardner L., "Franco-Prussian War: Aftermath 1871-1872," AMERIPEX 86, gold

Brown, Gardner L. and Ruth M., "France: Balloon Mail," PHILEXFRANCE 82, vermeil

Bushnell, Edward, "United States: 19th Century Domestic Registered Mail," INTERPHIL 76, vermeil

Byers, Jerome, "Holy Land: Forerunners," ISRAPHIL 85, large gold with special prize; AMERIPEX 86, gold; CAPEX 87, large vermeil with special prize; HAFNIA 87, gold with special prize and felicitations; "Palestine: Airmails," CAPEX 87, vermeil

Carr, Grace, "Canada: Nova Scotia and New Brunswick," INTERNABA 74, large gold; INTERPHIL 76, gold; CAPEX 78, gold; LONDON 1980, vermeil; "Canada: New Brunswick," CAPEX 87, vermeil; "Canada: Nova Scotia," CAPEX 87, vermeil

Carr, Laura K., "Liberia: 19th Century," JERUSALEM 74, gold; INTERNABA 74, vermeil; INTERPHIL 76, vermeil; ISRAPHIL 85, vermeil

Carr, Robert V.C., "Canada: British Columbia," ESPANA 75, gold; INTERPHIL 76, vermeil; CAPEX 78, gold; ISRAPHIL 85, gold; CAPEX 87, gold; "Canada: Prince Edward Island," JERUSALEM 74, large gold; INTERNABA 74, gold with special prize; STOCKHOLMIA 74, vermeil with felicitations; CAPEX 78, vermeil; LONDON 1980, vermeil; CAPEX 87, gold

Chesloe, Charles J., "Czechoslovakia: Forerunners Scout and Siberia Post," INTERPHIL 76, vermeil; PRAGA 78, vermeil; AMERIPEX 86, gold; "Czechoslovakia: 1918-1939," PRAGA 78, gold with special prize; ISRAPHIL 86, vermeil; PRAGA 88, large vermeil with special prize

Christian, C.W., "United States: One and Three Cent of 1861 Issue," INTERPHIL 76, gold; "United States: Three Cent 1861 Issue," CAPEX 78, vermeil with felicitations; NORWEX 80, vermeil; "United States: One Cent 1861 Issue," CAPEX 78, gold; "United States: Ten Cent 1861 Issue," AMERIPEX 86, gold; CAPEX 87, vermeil

Cipolla, Ronald H. II, "United States: One Cent 1851-1857 Imperforate," PHILATOKYO 81, large gold; PHILEXFRANCE, large gold

Clague, Brian H., "United States: Proprietary Stamps," AMERIPEX 86, vermeil

Clarke, Cortlandt, "United States: Postage Dues," AMERIPEX 86, vermeil; FINLANDIA 88, vermeil

Clatterbuck, W.C., "Canada: 1851-1897," CAPEX 87, vermeil

Cohen, Arthur, "Israel: 1947-1949," JERUSALEM 74, gold

Cohn, Ernst M., "France: Paris, Siege 1870-1871," BELGICA 72, vermeil; CAPEX 78, vermeil with felicitations; ISRAPHIL 85, gold; HAFNIA 87, gold with special prize

Cooley, Robert J., "Great Britain: Line Engraved Issues," CAPEX 87, large vermeil; FINLANDIA 88, vermeil

Corwin, Richard A., "United States: Civil War 1861-1865," AUSIPEX 84, gold; PHILAKOREA 84, gold with special prize; ISRAPHIL 85, gold; AMERIPEX 86, gold; HAFNIA 87, large vermeil with special prize; "United States: Airmails 1910-1939," FINLANDIA 88, large vermeil; PRAGA 88, large vermeil

Cowan, Bennie, "Greece: Small Hermes Heads 1886-1900," INTERPHIL 76, vermeil

Cowitt, Richard I., "United States: One Cent 1851-1857 Imperforate," AMERIPEX 86, large vermeil

Crow, Ray B., "United States: Postal Publicity Covers," INTERPHIL 76, vermeil

Cryer, James C.M., "United States: 1869 Issue," INTERPHIL 76, vermeil; LONDON 1980, gold

Cuesta, Ernesto, "Cuba: 1876-1888," ESPANA 84, large vermeil; AMERIPEX 86, large vermeil; CAPEX 87, vermeil

Cunliffe, Robert H., "Stamps with Inverted Centers," INTERPHIL 76, large gold; CAPEX 78, vermeil; "United States: Revenues 1755-1902," INTERPHIL 76, large gold; CAPEX 78, large gold

Dalum, Wilbert, "United States: Mail from China," INTERPHIL 76, vermeil; CAPEX 78, vermeil with felicitations; PRAGA 78, vermeil; INDIA 80, vermeil; AMERIPEX 86, gold

Danzer, Robert C., "Luxembourg: Postal History," PHILEXFRANCE 82, vermeil with special prize; AMERIPEX 86, large vermeil

Dean, L. Wallace III, "Haiti: Postal History French Colonial Period—1881," AMERIPEX 86, large gold; CAPEX 87, gold with special prize

D'Eliaa, Robert A., "Ecuador: Postal History," FINLANDIA 88, gold; PRAGA 88, large gold

Dennison, Ellery, "China: Postal Stationery," AMERIPEX 86, large vermeil; CAPEX 87, large vermeil

DeRidder, Frederik C.J., "Tibet," INDIA 80, vermeil

deViolini, Barbara W., "Ryukyu Islands: U.S. Administration 1945-1952," HAFNIA 76, vermeil; CAPEX 78, vermeil

DeVoss, James T., "Via Panama Postal History," BELGICA 72, large gold; IBRA-MUNCHEN 73, large gold; STOCKHOLMIA 74, prix d'honneur; INTERPHIL 76, prix d'honneur; CAPEX 78, prix d'honneur

Diamond, J. Leonard, "United States: Spanish American War Covers," INTERPHIL, vermeil with special prize

Dickgiesser, Robert W., "United States: One Cent Pan American Issue," CAPEX 87, vermeil

Dillaway, Guy, "Great Britain: 2d Blue 1840-1880," AMERIPEX 86, large vermeil

Dinger, Paul C., "Airmail: Dornier DO-X," ESPANA 84, large vermeil; ISRAPHIL 85, large vermeil; AMERIPEX 86, gold; CAPEX 87, gold; HAFNIA 87, gold

Dixon, Michael D., "Peru: Postal Stationery 1862-1895," LONDON 1980, vermeil; NORWEX 80, vermeil; FINLANDIA 88, vermeil

Doolittle, Frederick W., "United States; Parcel Post," INTERPHIL 76, vermeil

Dorfman, David, "Palestine: 1917-1948," JERUSALEM 74, vermeil with special prize; INTERPHIL 76, vermeil

DuPont, John, "British North America: Imperforate Pence Issues," CAPEX 78, grand prix national; LONDON 1980, large gold with special prize; ESPANA 84, large gold with special prize; AUSIPEX 84, grand prix international; PHILAKOREA 84, large gold with special prize; AMERIPEX 86, prix d'honneur; STOCKHOLMIA 86, grand prix d'honneur; "Samoa: 1877-1900," PHILATOKYO 81, large gold; BANGKOK 83, grand prix international; "British Guiana," AMERIPEX 86, grand prix international

Dupuy, Peter, "United States: Columbian Issue 1893," ESPANA 75, gold; INTERPHIL 76, gold

Eggen, John A. Jr., "United States:

Waterways Markings," PHILATOKYO 81, vermeil; AMERIPEX 86, vermeil

Elnen, Thomas, "United States: Ocean Mail before July 1, 1876," AMPHILEX 77, vermeil with felicitations; "United States: Postal Rates 1847-1869," INDIA 80, vermeil with special prize

Engel, Arnold, "Latvia: Postal History — 1940," CAPEX 87, vermeil

Engstrom, Victor F., "Danish West Indies: 1794-1917," STOCKHOLMIA 74, gold; HAFNIA 76, gold with special prize; CAPEX 78, gold; NORWEX 80, large gold with special prize; "Norway: Skilling Issue 1855-1875," JERUSALEM 74, vermeil with special prize; INTERPHIL 76, gold; "Danish West Indies: Postal Stationery," ISRAPHIL 85, gold; AMERIPEX 86, large vermeil; STOCKHOLMIA 86, gold

Epstein, Norman, "Russia: Imperial 1857-1913," INTERPHIL 76, gold; LONDON 1980, vermeil with special prize; WIPA 81, gold

Evans, Don L., "United States: One Cent Franklin 1861-1867," AMERIPEX 86, vermeil

Evans, Lois M., "Japan: 19th Century," INTERPHIL 76, vermeil

Falk, Helga, "France: Military Postmarks 1756-1763," INTERPHIL 76, vermeil; HAFNIA 76, vermeil

Farrington, Jeremiah A., "United States: Postmaster Provisionals 1845," AMERIPEX 86, vermeil; STOCKHOLMIA 86, large vermeil; FINLANDIA 88, gold

Feltus, Peter R., "Egypt: Second Issue," ISRAPHIL 85, vermeil

Fernando, Quintus, "Mexico: Guadalajara 1867-1868," PHILAKOREA 84, gold; "Mexico: 1864-1866," AUSIPEX 84, gold with special prize; AMERIPEX 86, gold

Finkelburg, Falk, "United States: Essays and Proofs 1861-1867 Issues," INTERPHIL 76, gold; "United States: Essays and Proofs 1869 Issue," CAPEX 78, gold

Firby, Charles G., "Canada: 1851-1868," WIPA 81, gold

Fischel, Albert, "Germany: Mannheim Postal History," ISRAPHIL 85, vermeil; AMERIPEX 86, large vermeil

Fischmeister, Ladislav, "Austria: First Five Issues," INTERPHIL 76, vermeil; "Czechoslovakia: 1918-1925," CAPEX 78, vermeil; PRAGA 78, gold; LONDON 1980, gold; NORWEX 80, gold with special prize; WIPA 81, gold; AMERIPEX 86, gold; PRAGA 88, large vermeil with special prize; "Austria: 1850-1867," PRAGA 88, large vermeil

Fitch, William M., "United States: Private Proprietary Stamps," INTERPHIL 76, gold; AMERIPEX 86, vermeil

Fitz, Charles, "Philately and Murder," ISRAPHIL 85, vermeil; ARGENTINA 85, vermeil; AMERIPEX 86, large vermeil; STOCKHOLMIA 86, large vermeil with special prize; CAPEX 87, gold; HAFNIA 87, gold

Fitzgibbons, Wayne, "Zeppelin Flights: Switzerland," HAFNIA 87, vermeil

Flickinger, Lloyd, "Guam," INTERPHIL 76, vermeil

Forster, Donald E., "Australia: New South Wales Classics," LONDON 1980, gold

Fluck, John G., "Austria: Vienna Pneumatic Post," AMERIPEX 86, large vermeil with felicitations

Forester, Dale E., "Australia: New South Wales Classics," LONDON 1980, gold; AMERIPEX 86, large gold; "Australia/New Zealand: Routes/Rates via Marseilles/Brindisi," AUSIPEX 84, large vermeil

Forster, Jeffrey M., "United States: 1869 Issue and Re-issues," PHILATOKYO 81, gold; PHILEXFRANCE 82, large gold; ESPANA 84, large gold; AMERIPEX 86, large gold; HAFNIA 87, prix d'honneur

Fox, J. Eugene, "Peru: Development of the Mails," AMERIPEX 86, vermeil

Frater, Stephen I., "Hungary: 1871," ESPANA 84, gold; AUSIPEX 84, gold with special prize; ISRAPHIL 85, gold; AMERIPEX 86, gold with special prize; STOCKHOLMIA 86, large gold; CAPEX 87, large gold; "Hungary: 1850-1875," ITALIA 85, gold; PRAGA 88, gold; "Hungary: Austrian Post in 1850-1867," FINLANDIA 88, gold

Fricke, Charles, "United States: Postal Card 1873-1875," INTERPHIL 76, vermeil with special prize

Friedberg, Albert, "Israel: Forerunners," JERUSALEM 74, vermeil; "Palestine: Forerunners," ISRAPHIL 85, large vermeil; "Palestine: British Army Post Offices 1917-1919," ISRAPHIL 85, large vermeil

Friedman, Deborah, "Colombia: SCADTA," ITALIA 85, large vermeil; AMERIPEX 86, gold; STOCKHOLMIA 86, gold; CAPEX 87, gold with special prize; FINLANDIA 88, large vermeil

Friend, Maurice, "Crete: 1898-1899," JERUSALEM 74, vermeil with special prize; CAPEX 78, gold; PRAGA 78, vermeil with felicitations; "Greece: Hermes Heads 1861-1862," ARPHILA 75, vermeil; PRAGA 78, vermeil; LONDON 1980, vermeil; NORWEX 80, vermeil; "Crete: Postal History —1899," LONDON 1980, vermeil; NORWEX 80, vermeil; BUENOS AIRES 80, vermeil with special prize

Frigstad, Roger K., "Guatemala: 19th Century," ESPANA 75, large gold; INTERPHIL 76, vermeil

Gaillaguet, Denise S., "France: Sower Issues 1903-1944," AMERIPEX 86, large vermeil; CAPEX 87, vermeil; FINLANDIA 88, vermeil

Gaillaguet, Raymond L., "France: Siege of Paris 1870-1871," BELGICA 72, vermeil with special prize; "France: Third Republic 1871-1875," IBRA-MUNCHEN 73, vermeil; INTERPHIL, 76, vermeil; CAPEX 78, vermeil; "France: Sower Issues 1903-1944," PHILEXFRANCE 82, vermeil with special prize

Gallagher, D. Scott, "Caribbean Mail: — 1900," STOCKHOLMIA 86, vermeil; CAPEX 87, vermeil; FINLANDIA 88, vermeil

Ganz, Cheryl, "Zeppelin Mail," AMERIPEX 86, vermeil

Garcia-Frutos, Silvia, "Cuba: 18th and 19th Centuries," CAPEX 78, vermeil; LONDON 1980, vermeil; BUENOS-AIRES 80, vermeil; PHILATOKYO 81, vermeil with special prize; BRASILIANA 83, vermeil with special prize; AMERIPEX 86, large vermeil; "Ecuador: Airmails," BUENOS-AIRES 80, vermeil; BRASILIANA 83, vermeil

Garfinkel, M.D., "Holy Land: Forerunners," JERUSALEM 74, large gold with special prize; INTERPHIL 76, large gold

Garrett, Duane, "United States: 1847 Issue," CAPEX 78, vermeil; PHILATOKYO 81, large gold with special prize

Gilbart, Kenneth D., "United States: Ten Cent 1861 Issue," WIPA 81, gold; PHILATOKYO 81, vermeil; AUSIPEX 84, gold; AMERIPEX 86, large vermeil

Gobie, Henry, "United States: Special Delivery 1885-1902," INTERPHIL 76, vermeil; CAPEX 78, gold; AMERIPEX 86, gold; CAPEX 87, large vermeil

Goldsmith, Edward, "Spanish Antilles," AMERIPEX 86, gold; CAPEX 87, gold

Gornish, Stanley, "Israel: Postal History of Rishon Le Zion," ISRAPHIL 85, vermeil

Gough, James P., "Postage Dues," FINLANDIA 88, large vermeil

Grabowski, Edward J.J., "French Colonies," AMERIPEX 86, gold; CAPEX 87, large vermeil

Green, Brian, "Confederate States of America 1860-1865," ESPANA 75, vermeil; INTERPHIL 76, vermeil; CAPEX 78, vermeil with felicitations; PHILASERDICA 79, gold; LONDON 1980, gold; WIPA 81, gold; PHILATOKYO, gold; PHILEXFRANCE 82, gold; BRASILIANA 83, gold; AUSIPEX 84, large vermeil with special prize; PHILAKOREA 84, gold; ISRAPHIL 85, gold; AMERIPEX 86, gold; STOCKHOLMIA 86, large vermeil

Green, Howard P., "Confederate States of America: Postal History," STOCKHOLMIA 86, large gold; CAPEX 87, gold with special prize; PRAGA 88, large gold

Green, Richard, "Austria: Pre-adhesive and Classics," PRAGA 78, gold; PHILATOKYO 81, vermeil; "Austria: Inflation Issues 1919-1924," ISRAPHIL 85, vermeil; PRAGA 88, large vermeil

Griffiths, John O., "Great Britain: Line Engraved 1840-1880," BUDAPEST 71, large gold with special prize; BELGICA 72, large gold with special prize; IBRA-MUNCHEN, prix d'honneur; POLSKA 73, prix d'honneur; INTERNABA 74, prix d'honneur; STOCKHOLMIA 74, grand prix d'honneur; HAFNIA 76, prix d'honneur; AMPHILEX 77, prix d'honneur; "Great Britain: Victoria Issues 1855-1900," HAFNIA 76, gold; AMPHILEX 77, large gold; INDIA 80, large gold; LONDON 1980, large gold; NORWEX 80, large gold; "South Australia: 1855-1875," INTERPHIL 76, large gold; AMPHILEX 77, large gold; CAPEX 78, large gold; INDIA 80, prix d'honneur; LONDON 1980, prix d'honneur; WIPA 81, prix d'honneur;

PHILATOKYO 81, prix d'honneur; BANGKOK, grand prix d'honneur; "Australia: South Australia 1867-1912," AUSIPEX 84, gold; PHILAKOREA 84, large vermeil; "United States: Postal History 1837-1870," ISRAPHIL 85, gold; AMERIPEX 86, large gold; STOCKHOLMIA 86, large gold; CAPEX 87, gold; "History of Railways during the Steam Era," STOCKHOLMIA 86, large vermeil; CAPEX 87, large vermeil; HAFNIA 87, large vermeil; "Leeward Islands: 1757-1956," PRAGA 88, vermeil

Grigaliunas, J., "Lithuania: Airmails," IBRA-MUNCHEN 73, vermeil with felicitations

Groton, Arthur H., "St. Helena: Napoleon to UPU Postal History," FINLANDIA 88, large vermeil

Grunin, Louis, "United States: 1847-1857," BELGICA 72, gold; INTERPHIL 76, grand prix national; "United States: Covers 1847-1870," CAPEX 78, large gold with special prize; "United States: Covers 1851-1857," LONDON 1980, large gold; AMERIPEX 86, large gold with special prize

Guzzio, George T., "Penguinalia," AUSIPEX 84, large vermeil; STOCKHOLMIA 86, gold; FINLANDIA 88, gold

Hahn, Charless, "Great Britain: Mulreadys," LONDON 1980; AMERIPEX 86, gold; HAFNIA 87, large vermeil; "Great Britain: Scotland Local Cancellations," ISRAPHIL 85, vermeil

Hahn, Henry, "Czechoslovakia: 1918-1939," PRAGA 78, gold; LONDON 1980, vermeil; AMERIPEX 86, large vermeil; CAPEX 87, large vermeil

Hahn, Joseph, "El Salvador: 1780-1899," INTERPHIL 76, vermeil

Harmer, Bernard, "Colombia: Airmails," STOCKHOLMIA 74, vermeil with felicitations; INTERPHIL 76, vermeil with special prize; PRAGA 78, vermeil with special prize

Harris, Leo J., "Ecuador: Specialized," SOFIA 69, vermeil; INTERNABA 74, vermeil; ESPANA 75, vermeil with special prize; INTERPHIL 76, vermeil; CAPEX 78, gold; LONDON 1980, gold; BRASILIANA 83, vermeil; AMERIPEX 86, large vermeil; "Nicaragua," PRAGA 78, vermeil; LONDON 1980, vermeil; PHILEXFRANCE 82, vermeil; "Ecuador: Postal History 1674-1865," BELGICA 82, vermeil; "Central America: Postal History," CAPEX 87, vermeil with felicitations; "Peru: Postal History," HAFNIA 87, vermeil

Harrison, Horace W., "Canada: Postal Stationery," AMERIPEX 86, gold; CAPEX 87, vermeil; FINLANDIA 88, gold with special prize; PRAGA 88, gold; "Canada: Registry System—1904," STOCKHOLMIA 86, large vermeil; CAPEX 87, gold with special prize; FINLANDIA 88, gold; PRAGA 88, gold

Hart, Creighton C., "United States: Free Franks of Presidents and Widows," INTERPHIL 76, gold; ITALIA 76, gold; AMERIPEX 86, gold; "United States: 1847 Issue," INTERPHIL 76, large gold; CAPEX 78, large gold with special prize; LONDON 1980, large gold; ESPANA 84, prix d'honneur

Hart, Ralph A., "Canada: Newfoundland 1857-1861," INTERNABA 74, large gold; ESPANA 75, vermeil; INTERPHIL 76, gold

Haverbeck, Harrison D.S., "Labuan," PHILASERDICA 79, vermeil

Hayward, Lhoyd, "United States: Vermont Pre-adhesives 1788-1855," INTERPHIL 76, vermeil

Heath, Edgar A., "Germany: Wurttemburg Postal History 1558-1851," CAPEX 87, large vermeil

Heinz, Alfred, "Germany: Local Posts 1945-1946," IBRA-MUNCHEN 73, gold; "Germany: Provisional Cancellations after World War II," INTERPHIL 76, vermeil

Helme, James, "Canal Zone: Overprints on Fourth Provisional Issue," INTERPHIL 76, large gold; AMPHILEX 77, vermeil; CAPEX 78, gold; PRAGA 78, gold with special prize; LONDON 1980, gold with special prize; NORWEX 80, gold; BUENOS-AIRES 80, gold with special prize and felicitations; WIPA 81, gold with special prize; PHILEXFRANCE 82, gold with felicitations "Panama: Airmails," BELGICA 72, vermeil; "Panama: Overprints," INTERPHIL 76, vermeil; "Panama: Registration Covers—1907," BELGICA 82, vermeil; ESPANA 84, gold; AUSIPEX 84, vermeil with felicitations; PHILAKOREA 84, large vermeil; ISRAPHIL 85, large vermeil; "Panama: 1887 Issue," AMERIPEX 86, large vermeil with felicitations; CAPEX 87, large vermeil;

HAFNIA 87, large vermeil with special prize; FINLANDIA 88, gold

Hennig, Bernard A., "Germany: Danzig Airmails," IBRA-MUNCHEN 73, vermeil with felicitations; LONDON 1980, gold; LURABA 81, gold; PHILEXFRANCE, gold with special prize; "Germany: Danzig Research Collection 1640-1938," PRAGA 68, vermeil; IBRA-MUNCHEN 73, gold; JERUSALEM 74, gold; ESPANA 75, gold with special prize; AMPHILEX 77, large gold; LONDON 1980, gold with special prize; PHILEXFRANCE 82, large gold; BRASILIANA 83, large gold; CAPEX 87, prix d'honneur; "Germany: World War I and Packet Mail," IBRA-MUNCHEN 73, vermeil

Herbert, Greg, "Pursuit of Butterflies," AMERIPEX 86, vermeil; FINLANDIA 88, vermeil

Herschkowitz, Erwin, "Bolivia: Postal History," CAPEX 78, gold; LONDON 1980, gold; NORWEX 80, gold with special prize; WIPA 81, large gold; PHILATOKYO 81, large gold; AUSIPEX 84, gold with special prize; PHILAKOREA 84, large gold; "Bolivia: Airmail and Flights," BELGICA 82, vermeil with special prize; "Bolivia: Postal Stationery," BELGICA 82, vermeil; AMERIPEX 86, gold; "Bolivia: Pre-adhesive 1780-1890," ESPANA 84, large vermeil; CAPEX 87, gold with special prize; "Bolivia: Airmails 1924-1936," FINLANDIA 88, large vermeil with special prize

Hess, Winand, "Wine, from the Vine to the Glass," AMERIPEX 86, vermeil; FINLANDIA 88, vermeil

Herzog, William K., "United States: 1861-1868," ESPANA 75, vermeil; INTERPHIL 76, gold

Hillmer, Duane, "Canada: 1851-1870," INTERNABA 74, large gold; INTERPHIL 76, large gold; "France: 1849-1876," ESPANA 75, gold; ARPHILA 75, gold with special prize; INTERPHIL 76, gold with special prize

Hochheiser, Arthur M., "Palestine: 1918-1948," ISRAPHIL 85, vermeil

Hooper, R. Malcolm, "United States: Precancels," AMERIPEX 86, vermeil

Horner, J. King, "United States: Postmasters, Carriers and Local Stamps," LONDON 1980, large gold

Hotchner, John M., "Stamp Separation: Worldwide Development," AMERIPEX 86, vermeil

Houser, Gary H., "Luxembourg: Classics," FINLANDIA 88, vermeil

Houser, Henry W., "Turkey: Austrian Post Offices in," BUDAPEST 71, vermeil; INDIA 80, gold with special prize; LONDON 1980, gold; BUENOS-AIRES 80, gold; WIPA 81, gold; PHILATOKYO 81, large gold; ESPANA 84, gold; AUSIPEX 84, large gold; PHILAKOREA 84, large gold; ISRAPHIL 85, large gold; AMERIPEX 86, prix d'honneur; STOCKHOLMIA 86, prix d'honneur; CAPEX 87, prix d'honneur; HAFNIA 87, prix d'honneur; "United States: Waterbury Cancellations," WIPA 81, gold; ISRAPHIL 85, large vermeil; CAPEX 87, gold with special prize; "Catapult Flights," HAFNIA 87, vermeil

Hubbard, Norman, "Brazil: 1843," INTERNABA 74, large gold; WIPA 81, large gold; BRASILIANA 83, grand prix national; "Colombia 1859-1880," ARPHILA 75, gold; AMPHILEX 77, large gold; CAPEX 78, gold; "El Salvador: 1867-1889," INTERPHIL 76, large gold; "Haiti: 1881-1887," CAPEX 78, gold; "Peru: 1857-1873," ESPANA 75, gold; INTERPHIL 76, large gold; AMERIPEX 86, large gold; "Chile: 1853-1865," PHILATOKYO 81, large gold; "Uruguay: Classics 1856-1864," BRASILIANA 83, large gold with special prize; "Argentina: 1858-1863," ITALIA 85, gold with special prize; CAPEX 87, large gold with special prize; HAFNIA 87, large gold with special prize

Huggins, Roland C. Jr., "United States: Official Stamps," AMERIPEX 86, large vermeil

Hvidonov, Michael E., "Finland: 1638-1891," AMERIPEX 86, gold; FINLANDIA 88, large vermeil with special prize

Hyzen, Leon, "United States: 1861 Issue," AMPHILEX 77, vermeil; CAPEX 78, vermeil; PRAGA 78, vermeil; LONDON 1980, gold; PHILATOKYO 81, gold; BRASILIANA 83, large gold; ESPANA 84, gold with special prize; ISRAPHIL 85, large gold; AMERIPEX 86, large gold

Iglesias, Fernando J., "Cuba: Postal History," BUENOS-AIRES 80, vermeil; BRASILIANA 83, large gold; ESPANA 84, gold; CAPEX 87, gold with special prize; HAFNIA 87, gold with special prize

Ireland, Philip, "China: First Issue

and Forerunners," INTERPHIL 76, vermeil; HAFNIA 76, gold; AMPHILEX 77, vermeil; LONDON 1980, gold with special prize; NORWEX 80, gold with special prize; PHILATOKYO 81, large gold; AUSIPEX 84, large gold; STOCKHOLMIA 86, large gold; CAPEX 87, prix d'honneur; COPENHAGEN 87, prix d'honneur; FINLANDIA 88, prix d'honneur

Isaacs, Mark, "Indo-China: 1862-1908," INDIA 80, vermeil; PHILEXFRANCE 82, vermeil; ESPANA 84, large vermeil; ISRAPHIL 85, large vermeil; AMERIPEX 86, gold

Jenich, Frank A., "United States: Inland Waterway Markings," INDIA 80, vermeil with special prize

Jennings, Clyde, "United States: Color Cancellations 1847-1925," AMERIPEX 86, gold with felicitations; "United States: Postal History —1900," HAFNIA 87, vermeil

Jersey, Stanley C., "South Pacific: Postal History," POLSKA 73, vermeil with special prize; "New Hebrides," PHILEXFRANCE 82, gold; AUSIPEX 84, gold; PHILAKOREA 84, large vermeil; "British Solomon Islands," AUSIPEX 84, gold; PHILAKOREA 84, large vermeil with special prize; "New Caledonia: 1857-1912," ISRAPHIL 85, vermeil; AMERIPEX 86, large vermeil; CAPEX 87, large vermeil; HAFNIA 87, large vermeil; "United States: Six Cent Airmail," ISRAPHIL 85, vermeil

Johnson, Nicholas J., "Confederate States of America," CAPEX 78, gold

Jones, Allen D., "United States: Airmails Pioneer Period," AMERIPEX 86, large vermeil; CAPEX 87, large vermeil; HAFNIA 87, large vermeil; FINLANDIA 88, large vermeil; "United States: Airmails 1918-1924," CAPEX 87, large vermeil; PRAGA 88, large vermeil

Jordan, Richard, "United States: Rhode Island Postal History," AUSIPEX 84, gold; ITALIA 85, gold; AMERIPEX 86, gold; STOCKHOLMIA 86, gold

Kahn, William, "Greenland," HAFNIA 76, vermeil

Kapiloff, Leonard, "United States: 1847 Issue," AUSIPEX 84, large gold with special prize; ISRAPHIL 85, grand prix international; AMERIPEX 86, large gold with special prize; CAPEX 87, large gold with special prize; FINLANDIA 88, large gold with special prize

Kaposta, Julius, "Hungary: Airmails 1898-1938," LURABA 81, vermeil

Kayfetz, Paul, "Gibraltar: 1903-1938," PRAGA 88, vermeil

Kent, Victor, "Russia: Livonia-Weden Postal District," ITALIA 76, vermeil; CAPEX 78, vermeil; PRAGA 78, vermeil; STOCKHOLMIA 86, vermeil

Kestenbaum, Louis, "Israel: First Issues," ISRAPHIL 85, large vermeil; CAPEX 87, large vermeil

Kilgas, Carl A., "China: 1863-1911," AMERIPEX 86, vermeil

Kner, Albert, "Hungary: 1850-1914," PRAGA 68, vermeil

Knox, Wallace, "Great Britain: Classics," BELGICA 72, large gold with special prize; STOCKHOLMIA 74, large gold with special prize; ARPHILA 75, large gold, prix d'honneur Europe; INTERPHIL 76, grand prix d'honneur; "Great Britain: Pictorial Covers," STOCKHOLMIA 74, vermeil; "United States: Campaign Covers, Pearce Against Scott," INTERPHIL 76, vermeil

Kocheisen, Joseph, "Zeppelin Stamps," ESPANA 75, vermeil; ARPHILA 75, vermeil; CAPEX 78, gold; PRAGA 78, gold; WIPA 81, vermeil; AMERIPEX 86, large vermeil

Kohn, Frank, "Czechoslovakia: Prague Postal History 1527-1875," WIPA 81, gold; CAPEX 87, vermeil

Kohn, Milton M., "Concentration Camp Mail," BUDAPEST 71, vermeil; AMPHILEX 77, vermeil

Korn, Gerhard, "Germany: Booklets," FINLANDIA 88, vermeil

Kramer, George, "United States: Wells, Fargo & Co. 1852-1895," AUSIPEX 84, gold; ISRAPHIL 85, gold; AMERIPEX 86, large gold; CAPEX 87, large gold with special prize; PRAGA 88, large gold; "United States: Telegraph Stamps 1846-1865," AUSIPEX 84, vermeil with felicitations; ISRAPHIL 85, large vermeil; AMERIPEX 86, gold; CAPEX 87, gold; PRAGA 88, vermeil

Krieger, Richard, "Confederate States of America: Five-cent Issues," BRASILIANA 83, vermeil; AUSIPEX 84, vermeil

Krievins, Victor B., "United States: Three Cent 1851-1857," AMERIPEX 86, large vermeil

Kuderwicz, Josef, "Poland: Disinfected Mail," INTERPHIL 76, vermeil; WIPA 81, vermeil with special prize; "Poland: Napoleon and Postal History," JERUSALEM 74, vermeil; STOCKHOLMIA 74, vermeil; ARPHILA 75, vermeil; HAFNIA 76, vermeil; AMPHILEX 77, vermeil; "Poland: Siege of Przemysl 1914-1915," PHILASERDICA 79, vermeil; NORWEX 80, vermeil; WIPA 81, vermeil; FINLANDIA 88, vermeil; "Nicolas Copernicus," POLSKA 73, vermeil with special prize; "Poland: Postal History —1900," ISRAPHIL 85, large vermeil; AMERIPEX 86, large vermeil; "Austria-Hungary: Disinfected Mail," CAPEX 87, vermeil; PRAGA 88, large vermeil with felicitations

Kunzmann, George, "Germany: 1889-1900," BELGICA 72, vermeil with special prize; IBRA-MUNCHEN 73, vermeil

Kutz, Kenneth J., "Gold Fever 1849-1910," AMERIPEX 86, gold with felicitations; CAPEX 87, gold with special prize

Larkin, Richard F., "United States and Possessions: Booklet Panes," AMERIPEX 86, vermeil; CAPEX 87, vermeil

Larsen, Paul, "Leeward Islands: 1890-1935," ESPANA 84, large vermeil; ISRAPHIL 85, vermeil; AMERIPEX 86, vermeil; "Germany: Togo 1885-1914," HAFNIA 87, large vermeil

Laurence, Michael M., "United States: Ten Cent 1869 Issue," AMERIPEX 86, gold with felicitations; STOCKHOLMIA 86, gold

Leds, David J., "Canal Zone: Overprinted on Panama 1904-1924," AMERIPEX 86, large vermeil; CAPEX 87, vermeil

Lefton, G.Z., "Hungary: 1850-1867," PRAGA 68, gold

Lell, Adolph, "Estonia: 1918-1920," STOCKHOLMIA 74, vermeil; BUENOS-AIRES 80, vermeil

Lettick, Edward, "Philippines: Airmail Flights 1919-1945," FINLANDIA 88, large vermeil

Levitsky, Frederick J., "Italy: Roman States," AMERIPEX 86, large vermeil; CAPEX 87, vermeil

Lieberman, Eugene, "Afghanistan," BUENOS-AIRES 80, vermeil with special prize; ESPANA 84, large vermeil; AUSIPEX 84, gold; PHILAKOREA 84, large vermeil

Lievsay, John E., "France: 25c Ceres 1871," PHILEXFRANCE 82, vermeil with special prize; "France: Paris Cancellations 1863-1876," AMERIPEX 86, large vermeil

Light, Theodore, "Afghanistan: Classics," PRAGA 68, vermeil with special prize; BELGICA 72, vermeil; IBRA-MUNCHEN 73, vermeil; JERUSALEM 74, gold; INTERNABA 74, vermeil with special prize; ESPANA 75, vermeil; ARPHILA 75, vermeil; INTERPHIL 76, gold; AMPHILEX 77, gold with special prize

Likins, Floyd L. Jr., "United States: Flat Plate Booklets," INTERNABA 74, vermeil; INTERPHIL 76, vermeil

Litt, Nathaniel, "Paraguay," SOFIA 69, vermeil

Lloyd, Carroll, "Haiti: The Liberty Head Issues," AMERIPEX 86, large gold

Login, Jerry, "United States: Columbian Issue 1893," AMERIPEX 86, large vermeil

Longfellow, Harold H., "United States: Arizona Postal Markings 1850-1864," INTERPHIL 76, gold

Longo, Antonio H., "Spain: Puerto Rico Postal History —1898," ESPANA 84, vermeil; CAPEX 87, large vermeil

Lopez, Frederick W., "United States: Essays and Proofs 1869 Issue," AMERIPEX 86, large vermeil

Lubke, Henry G. Jr., "Canada: Numeral Cancellations 1857-1896," CAPEX 87, gold with special prize

Lucas, Vincent P., "Lepidopteran Love Affair," CAPEX 87, vermeil

Luft, Stanley J. and Anita N., "France: Revolutionary and Napoleonic Armies 1792-1814," PHILEXFRANCE 82, large gold; AUSIPEX 84, gold with special prize; ITALIA 85, gold with special prize; AMERIPEX 86, gold; STOCKHOLMIA 86, large gold; CAPEX 87, gold with special prize; FINLANDIA 88, gold

Lussey, Harry W., "Canada: Federal Revenues," CAPEX 87, large vermeil with special prize

Madden, Henry B., "Guatemala: Pre-adhesive 1881," INTERPHIL 76, vermeil; "Guatemala: Pre-adhesive 1770-1870," ESPANA 84, large vermeil; ISRAPHIL 85, gold; AMERIPEX 86, gold; STOCKHOLMIA 86, gold; CAPEX 87, gold; FINLANDIA

88, gold

Magnesen, Robert C., "Peru: 1769-1873," ESPANA 84, vermeil; AUSIPEX 84, large vermeil; PHILAKOREA 84, large vermeil; ISRAPHIL 85, gold; AMERIPEX 86, large vermeil; HAFNIA 87, vermeil; FINLANDIA 88, large vermeil; "Peru: 1874-1895," ISRAPHIL 85, large vermeil

Maher, James, "Ireland: Overprinted Stamps of Great Britain 1922-1937," AMERIPEX 86, large vermeil; CAPEX 87, large vermeil with special prize

Marcovitch, Jacques, "Russia: Zemstvo Postal Service," PHILEXFRANCE 82, gold with special prize; ESPANA 84, large gold

Mardiguian, Steven, "Turkey: 1863-1935," INTERPHIL 76, vermeil; PRAGA 78, vermeil

Martin, Marc W., "France: Maritime Mail 1784-1900," ARPHILA 75, vermeil; CAPEX 78, vermeil; LONDON 1980, vermeil; PHILEXFRANCE 82, vermeil; AMERIPEX 86, gold; "France: 1849-1870," INTERPHIL 76, gold; AMPHILEX 77, vermeil; PHILEXFRANCE 82, vermeil with special prize

Martin, Paul, "United States: Maritime Mail," INTERPHIL 76, vermeil

Mason, James H., "Korea: 19th and Early 20th Century," INTERPHIL 76, vermeil; PRAGA 78, vermeil

Massler, Jerold M., "Monaco: Albert I Issues," PHILEXFRANCE 82, vermeil; "Monaco: Postal History 1729-1924," ITALIA 85, large vermeil; AMERIPEX 86, large vermeil; CAPEX 87, large vermeil; FINLANDIA 88, vermeil

Matejka, James J., "Czechoslovakia: 1918-1939," PRAGA 78, large gold with special prize; "United States: Alaska Postal History," PRAGA 78, vermeil with felicitations; "Canada: Newfoundland Airmails," BELGICA 72, prix d'honneur; ESPANA 75, prix d'honneur; INTERPHIL 76, prix d'honneur; PRAGA 78, prix d'honneur

Mayer, George C., "Seebeck Era," CAPEX 78, vermeil with felicitations; ESPANA 84, large vermeil; AUSIPEX 84, vermeil; PHILAKOREA 84, vermeil; ISRAPHIL 85, large vermeil; "Turkey: Cilicia 1919-1921," INDIA 80, vermeil with special prize

Mazepa, James, "Poland: Semi-official and Official Airmails —1939," LURABA 81, vermeil with special prize; ESPANA 84, gold; ISRAPHIL 85, gold; CAPEX 87, gold; "Poland: 1858-1865," ESPANA 84, gold; ISRAPHIL 85, gold with special prize; AMERIPEX 86, gold

McCann, Peter P., "Turks and Caicos Islands," FINLANDIA 88, vermeil

McClellan, Robert G., "United States: Two Cent Black Jack 1863," PRAGA 78, vermeil

McDonald, Susan M., "British North America: Cross Border Mails 1875," INTERPHIL 76, gold; CAPEX 87, gold; "Transatlantic Mail," CAPEX 78, gold; LONDON 1980, vermeil; "United States: Treaty Mails 1845-1875," AMERIPEX 86, large vermeil; CAPEX 87, large vermeil

Meier, Eileen, "The Olympian Gods," ARGENTINA 85, vermeil; AMERIPEX 86, large vermeil; CAPEX 87, large vermeil; FINLANDIA 88, large vermeil

Meier, Harry C., "Germany: Postal Reconstruction After WW II," AMERIPEX 86, vermeil

Meyersburg, Robert, "United States: Carrier Service 1847-1856," WIPA 81, gold; AMERIPEX 86, large vermeil

Miller, William H. Jr., "New Zealand: Great Barrier Island Pigeon Posts 1897-1908," INTERPHIL 76, vermeil; CAPEX 78, vermeil; PHILASERDICA 79, gold; INDIA 80, vermeil with special prize; LONDON 1980, vermeil

Mishrick, Adballah, "Egypt: Second Issue 1867-1872," INTERNABA 74, vermeil with special prize; INTERPHIL 76, gold with special prize

Mitchell, Milton, "United States: Three Cent 1861 Issue," PRAGA 88, vermeil with felicitations

Moolenaar, Willy, "A Parade of Penguins," AUSIPEX 84, vermeil; ISRAPHIL 85, vermeil; AMERIPEX 86, large vermeil; CAPEX 87, large vermeil; HAFNIA 87, large vermeil

Moyer, Joseph W., "United States: Columbian Issue 1893," INTERPHIL 76, vermeil

Murphy, William, "Confederate States of America," AMERIPEX 86, large vermeil; CAPEX 87, vermeil; FINLANDIA 88, large vermeil

Myer, John N., "Colombia: States and Departments 1868-1896," ESPANA 75, gold; INTERPHIL 76, gold

Myers, Blake, "United States: Civil War Patriotics," INTERPHIL 76, gold; CAPEX 78, vermeil; LONDON 1980, gold; ISRAPHIL 85, gold; AMERIPEX 86, gold; CAPEX 87, gold

Nahra, Joseph A., "Lebanon," ISRAPHIL 85, large vermeil; AMERIPEX 86, vermeil; CAPEX 87, vermeil

Neil, Randolph L., "United States: Two Cent 1883 Issue," AMERIPEX 86, gold

Neufeld, Gerard, "United States: 19th Century Ship Markings," HAFNIA 76, vermeil

Nicholson, Drew A., "German South-West Africa: Postal History 1903-1907," AMERIPEX 86, large vermeil

Nortum, Rose, "Siam: First and Second Issues," INTERPHIL 76, gold

Nowak, Henry, "United States: Postal History One Cent Usage 1861-1865," AMERIPEX 86, vermeil

Odenweller, Robert P., "Australia: Tasmania 1826-1870," CAPEX 78, vermeil; PRAGA 78, gold; PHILASERDICA 79, gold; INDIA 80, gold; LONDON 1980, gold; NORWEX 80, gold; "New Zealand: 1855-1874," ARPHILA 75, large gold; INTERPHIL 76, large gold; CAPEX 78, large gold; PRAGA 78, large gold; PHILASERDICA 79, prix d'honneur; INDIA 80, prix d'honneur; LONDON 1980, prix d'honneur; NORWEX 80, prix d'honneur; BUENOS-AIRES 80, grand prix d'honneur; "Samoa: 1836-1914," IBRA-MUNCHEN 73, vermeil; STOCKHOLMIA 74, vermeil with felicitations; ESPANA 75, gold with special prize

Ortiz-Patino, Jaime, "Bolivia: 1863-1878," AMERIPEX 86, vermeil; FINLANDIA 88, large gold

Owens, Mary Ann, "Elephant," STOCKHOLMIA 74, vermeil; PORTUCALE 77, vermeil; AMERIPEX 86, gold with special prize; HAFNIA 87, large gold with special prize; "Beautiful Blue Danube," INDIA 80, vermeil; AUSIPEX 84, gold; CAPEX 87, gold with special prize; PRAGA 88, gold

Paliafito, Robert A., "United States: Thirty Cent 1861 Issue," CAPEX 78, gold; PRAGA 78, gold with special prize; PHILATOKYO 81, large gold; PHILEX-FRANCE 82, large gold with felicitations; ESPANA 84, large gold with special prize; "United States: Civil War Patriotics," PHILATOKYO 81, gold; AUSIPEX 84, large gold

Pamel, James P., "Greece: Large Hermes Heads 1861-1886," PHILEX-FRANCE 82, gold with special prize; ESPANA 84, gold; AMERIPEX 86, gold; CAPEX 87, gold; FINLANDIA 88, large gold

Pernes, Patricia J., "Spain and Colonies: Postal Stationery 1873-1973," STOCKHOLMIA 86, large vermeil

Pernes, Rufino R., "Portugal: Postal History," PRAGA 78, vermeil; PHILA-SERDICA 79, vermeil; "Portugal and Colonies: Airmail," AUSIPEX 84, vermeil; PHILAKOREA 84, vermeil; ISRAPHIL 85, large vermeil; ITALIA 85, large vermeil with special prize; AMERIPEX 86, gold; "Search for the Sea Route to India," ISRAPHIL 85, vermeil; STOCKHOLMIA 86, vermeil; CAPEX 87, vermeil; "Portuguese India," CAPEX 87, large vermeil; HAFNIA 87, large vermeil; FINLANDIA 88, vermeil

Peter, Harold E., "Allied Occupation: Germany," ESPANA 75, vermeil; ESPANA 84, large vermeil; AMERIPEX 86, large vermeil; CAPEX 87, vermeil

Pildes, Robert B., "Israel: Interim Period," CAPEX 87, vermeil

Piller, Stanley M., "United States: Three Cent 1851-1857," PHILATOKYO 81, gold; PHILEXFRANCE 82, gold with special prize; ESPANA 84, gold with special prize; ISRAPHIL 85, gold with special prize; AMERIPEX 86, large gold; CAPEX 87, gold with special prize; FINLANDIA 88, gold

Plass, Gilbert N., "Canal Zone: 1909-1912," INTERPHIL 76, large gold

Plyler, Earle F., "France: Paris Star Cancellations 1852-1876," AMERIPEX 86, vermeil

Pogue, Jeanne B., "Pakistan: Provisional Overprints 1947-1949," CAPEX 87, vermeil

Politis, Constantine, "Greece: Airmails," ISRAPHIL 85, large vermeil; AMERIPEX 86, vermeil; CAPEX 87, vermeil

Prats, Ignacio, "Cuba: First Issue," AMERIPEX 86, large gold with special prize; CAPEX 87, large gold with special prize

Pratt, Robert H., "Canada: Newfoundland Pence and First Cent Issues," IBRA-MUNCHEN 73, large gold; INTERNABA 74, large gold with special prize; ESPANA 75, prix d'honneur; INTERPHIL 76, prix d'honneur; AMPHILEX 77, prix d'honneur; CAPEX 78, prix d'honneur; "Canada: St. Pierre Postal History," LONDON 1980, vermeil with felicitations; CAPEX 87, large vermeil; "St. Pierre and Miquelon," WIPA 81, gold; "Canada: Newfoundland First Cent Issue 1865-1880," BRASILIANA 83, gold; CAPEX 87, large gold with special prize

Pulver, Dale R., "Mexico: Forwarded Transatlantic Mail," ISRAPHIL 85, vermeil; "Mexico: 1856-1867," AMERIPEX 86, vermeil

Ramkissoon, Reuben A., "Trinidad: 1803-1896," ISRAPHIL 85, large vermeil; AMERIPEX 86, vermeil; CAPEX 87, gold; "Trinidad and Tobago: Postal Stationery," ISRAPHIL 85, vermeil; AMERIPEX 86, vermeil; CAPEX 87, vermeil; HAFNIA 87, vermeil

Ray, Samuel, "Italy: Sardinia Lettersheets," PRAGA 68, vermeil

Reed, Eugene C., "United States: Classics," INTERPHIL 76, vermeil; HAFNIA 76, gold; CAPEX 78, vermeil with felicitations; PHILASERDICA 79, gold; LONDON 1980, gold; "United States: One Cent 1851 Issue," AMERIPEX 86, gold

Reich, Louis H., "Trans-Atlantic Mail," CAPEX 78, vermeil; INDIA 80, vermeil; AUSIPEX 84, vermeil; AMERIPEX 86, vermeil

Rendon, Alex, "Bolivia: Postmarks 1793-1867," CAPEX 78, vermeil; "Bolivia: 1863-1875," BELGICA 72, gold; IBRA-MUNCHEN 73, gold; POLSKA 73, gold with special prize; INTERNABA 74, gold; STOCKHOLMIA 74, gold with special prize; INTERPHIL 76, large gold; AMPHILEX 77, large gold; CAPEX 78, large gold; "Colombia: Insured Letters," CAPEX 78, vermeil; "Spain: Postal Forgeries 1854-1874," ESPANA 75, vermeil; "Colombia: Pioneer Airmails," LONDON 1980, gold with special prize; LURABA 81, gold with felicitations; WIPA 81, gold with special prize; PHILATOKYO 81, large gold; PHILEXFRANCE 82, large gold; BELGICA 82, large gold with special prize; BRASILIANA 83, large gold; ITALIA 85, prix d'honneur; AMERIPEX 86, prix d'honneur; "Colombia: 1868-1881," ITALIA 85, gold; FINLANDIA 88, gold

Richardson, Edward A., "Canada: Airmails," INTERPHIL 76, gold

Richardson, Martin D., "United States: Postal History D.O. Blood and Co.," AMERIPEX 86, gold with felicitations

Richter, Jared H., "Norway: 1855-1876," AMERIPEX 86, large gold with special prize; STOCKHOLMIA 86, gold

Robbins, William C. III, "United States: California: Solano County," INTERPHIL 76, gold

Robertson, Peter A., "Cuba: The War of Independence 1895-1902," BUENOS-AIRES 80, large gold; PHILEXFRANCE 82, gold; BRASILIANA 83, gold; ESPANA 84, gold with special prize; AUSIPEX 84, gold; PHILAKOREA 84, gold; ISRAPHIL 85, large gold; AMERIPEX 86, large gold with special prize; STOCKHOLMIA, large gold

Rochlin, Phillip, "United States: John Charles Fremont," INTERPHIL 76, vermeil

Rockett, Wilmer C., "Canada: Revenues," CAPEX 87, vermeil

Rohloff, Mildred, "United States: Connecticut Waterbury Cancel, Soldier's Head," INTERPHIL 76, gold

Rohloff, Paul C., "Jamaica: Ship Letters," INTERPHIL 76, gold; "United States: Waterway Markings 1847," INTERPHIL 76, gold

Rorke, Joseph F., "United States: Black Jacks 1863-1867," CAPEX 78, vermeil with felicitations; BRASILIANA 83, gold; AMERIPEX 86, large gold; CAPEX 87, large gold

Rose, Jonathan W., "United States: 1869 Issue and Reissues," AMERIPEX 86, gold; "Canada: 1851-1868," CAPEX 87, large vermeil

Rosen, Morris, "Olympic Games 1896-1932," ISRAPHIL 85, large vermeil with special prize; AMERIPEX 86, vermeil

Rosenberg, Paul, "United States: Abraham Lincoln Stamps and Covers," AMERIPEX 86, vermeil

Rosende, Roberto M., "Cuba: Postal History," ESPANA 75, large gold with felicitations; ARPHILA 75, gold with felicitations; INTERPHIL 76, large gold;

ITALIA 76, gold with special prize and felicitations; AMPHILEX 77, gold with felicitations; CAPEX 78, large gold; LONDON 1980, prix d'honneur

Rosendorf, Samuel S. Jr., "United States: Precancels," INTERPHIL 76, vermeil

Rothman, Stephen, "Israel: Doar Ivri Issue," ISRAPHIL 85, gold; AMERIPEX 86, large vermeil

Rozman, Sol, "Palestine: Forerunners," INTERPHIL 76, gold

Ruggeiro, Michael E., "Japan: Classics," INTERPHIL 76, vermeil; PHILATOKYO, gold with special prize; AMERIPEX 86, large vermeil

Rustad, Roland, "United States: 1861 and 1867 Issues," CAPEX 78, gold; "United States: 1861 Issue," LONDON 1980, gold; AMERIPEX 86, vermeil

Salm, Arthur, "Germany: Bergedorf Postal History," IBRA-MUNCHEN 73, gold; ESPANA 75, vermeil; INTERPHIL 76, vermeil; "Germany: Bremen Postal History," IBRA-MUNCHEN 73, vermeil; ESPANA 75, gold; "Germany: Thurn and Taxis," IBRA-MUNCHEN 73, grand prix national; ESPANA 75, large gold; INTERPHIL 76, large gold with special prize; AMPHILEX 77, prix d'honneur; CAPEX 78, prix d'honneur; INDIA 80, prix d'honneur

Sandrik, William Anton, "Austria: Post Offices Abroad," PRAGA 78, vermeil; "Disinfected Mail," AMERIPEX 86, vermeil with felicitations

Sawyer, Charles E., "United States: Boston, Massachusetts, Postal Markings," CAPEX 78, gold; LONDON 1980, vermeil; AMERIPEX 86, large vermeil

Scamp, Lee, "Hong Kong: Postal History," AMERIPEX 86, vermeil

Schaffling, Otto, "Hungary: Classics," BUDAPEST 71, gold with special prize; ESPANA 75, gold; INTERPHIL 76, gold; PRAGA 78, gold with special prize; AUSIPEX 84, large vermeil with special prize; "Hungary: Watermark Study 1881-1914," AMERIPEX 86, vermeil with felicitations; CAPEX 87, large vermeil; FINLANDIA 88, vermeil

Schilling, Wilber H. Jr., "United States: 19th Century and Airmails of 20th Century," IBRA-MUNCHEN 73, gold

Schnell, Roger G., "Norway: No. One," AMERIPEX 86, large vermeil with felicitations; STOCKHOLMIA 86, large vermeil; "Danish West Indies: Postal Stationery," FINLANDIA 88, large vermeil with special prize

Schuessler, Leo, "Israel," JERUSALEM 74, vermeil; ESPANA 75, vermeil; ARPHILA 75, vermeil; "Holy Land: Forerunners," INTERPHIL 76, vermeil; AMPHILEX 77, vermeil; CAPEX 78, vermeil; LONDON 1980, vermeil; NORWEX 80, vermeil; BUENOS-AIRES 80, vermeil with special prize; WIPA 81, gold; PHILATOKYO 81, gold; PHILEXFRANCE 82, gold; BRASILIANA 83, gold with special prize; ISRAPHIL 85, large gold

Schuman, William O., "United States: First One Thousand Plate Numbers," INTERPHIL 76, gold with felicitations

Schumann, Stephen D., "Sarawak: Postal History," AMERIPEX 86, vermeil

Schwartz, Joseph D., "Germany: Offices in Turkey," CAPEX 78, vermeil; CAPEX 87, vermeil; "Palestine: 1917-1918," JERUSALEM 74, vermeil; CAPEX 78, vermeil; AMERIPEX 86, large vermeil; CAPEX 87, vermeil

Scott, Gene, "Denmark: Skilling Issues 1851-1874," AMERIPEX 86, large gold; STOCKHOLMIA 86, large gold; FINLANDIA 88, large gold; "Germany: Bavaria Numeral and Arms Issues 1849-1911," AMERIPEX 86, gold with special prize; "Uganda: 1895-1896," CAPEX 87, gold with special prize and felicitations; "Iceland: 1873-1904," HAFNIA 87, large gold with special prize

Seebacher, Ira, "A Century of Sport Philately 1838-1937," INTERPHIL 76, vermeil

Sellers, F. Burton, "Haiti: The Liberty Head Issues," INTERNABA 74, vermeil; ARPHILA 75, gold; CAPEX 78, gold; AUSIPEX 84, large gold; STOCKHOLMIA 86, large gold; CAPEX 87, gold with special prize; HAFNIA 87, gold; FINLANDIA 88, large gold

Selzer, Howard J., "Singapore: Postal History," INDIA 80, vermeil with special prize

Shachat, Norman, "United States: Philadelphia Postal History," AMERIPEX 86, vermeil

Sharghi, Ali, "Iran: 1865-1878," AMERIPEX 86, gold; STOCKHOLMIA 86, gold with special prize; CAPEX 87, large gold; HAFNIA 87, large gold; FINLANDIA 88, large gold with special prize; PRAGA 88, large gold with special prize

Shek, Peter, "Hong Kong: Preadhesive," ARPHILA 75, vermeil; CAPEX 78, vermeil with felicitations; NORWEX 80, gold

Sicking, Richard A., "United States: Guam Navy Department Issue," INTERPHIL 76, gold

Silver, Philip, "Uruguay: Airmails," ESPANA 75, vermeil with felicitations; PRAGA 78, gold; PHILASERDICA 79, gold; INDIA 80, gold; LONDON 1980, gold with special prize; WIPA 81, gold; PHILATOKYO 81, gold

Simon, Ludwig L., "Confederate States of America: Aristocrats," INTERPHIL 76, large gold

Simon, Sam, "Germany: Concentration and Displaced Persons Camp Mail 1933-1947," JERUSALEM 74, vermeil; "Israel: Postal History of Concentration Camps 1933-1945," ISRAPHIL 85, vermeil

Singer, Armand E., "Tibet: 1809-1962," CAPEX 78, vermeil

Siskin, Patricia A., "United States: Washington/Franklin Stamps of Third Bureau Issue," AMERIPEX 86, vermeil

Skinner, Hubert C., "United States: New Orleans, Louisiana, Postal History 1792-1865," INTERPHIL 76, gold; CAPEX 78, gold with felicitations; LONDON 1980, gold; AMERIPEX 86, gold with special prize; CAPEX 87, large vermeil with special prize; "United States: New Orleans Postmaster Provisionals 1861-1865," AMERIPEX 86, large gold; CAPEX 87, gold

Smith, Julian C., "Canada: 1851-1931," IBRA-MUNCHEN 73, vermeil; INTERNABA 74, vermeil; CAPEX 78, gold; LONDON 1980, vermeil; PHILEXFRANCE 82, gold; AMERIPEX 86, large vermeil

Smith, Peter A.S., "Egypt: Early Post," ITALIA 76, vermeil; LONDON 1980, vermeil; AMERIPEX 86, gold

Soderberg, Ralph B., "Switzerland: Standing Helvetia 1882-1907," AMERIPEX 86, vermeil; CAPEX 87, large vermeil

Staal, Frits, "India: Jammu and Kashmir," BANGKOK 83, large gold

Staub, Louis, "Italy and Colonies: Aerogrammes," BELGICA 72, vermeil; INTERPHIL 76, gold with special prize

Stein, Robert C., "Nauru: —1924," CAPEX 87, vermeil

Stempien, Martin F. Jr., "Franco-British Accountancy Marks," CAPEX 78, vermeil with felicitations

Stets, Robert J., "United States: Philadelphia, Pennsylvania, Postal History," CAPEX 78, vermeil

Stevens, Richard M., "Serbia: 1916-1918," CAPEX 87, large vermeil

Stever, Rex H., "United States: Three Cent 1869 Issue," AMERIPEX 86, gold

Stieg, Carl, "Victorian Lettercards," AMERIPEX 86, large vermeil

Stilwell, George W., "Canal Zone: 1904-1929," INTERPHIL 76, gold

Stollnitz, Henry, "United States: Offices in China: Shanghai," INTERPHIL 76, vermeil; "United States: Postal Markings 1845-1851," AMERIPEX 86, gold with special prize; STOCKHOLMIA 86, large vermeil

Stone, Harlan F., "Switzerland: Postal History 1621-1814," INTERPHIL 76, vermeil; CAPEX 78, vermeil; LONDON 1980, vermeil; PHILEXFRANCE 82, vermeil; "Switzerland: Sitting Helvetia 1862-1883," STOCKHOLMIA 86, large vermeil; CAPEX 87, large vermeil

Stone, Lawson, "Sweden: —1880," STOCKHOLMIA 74, grand prix national; INTERPHIL 76, large gold with special prize and felicitations; LONDON 1980, large gold with special prize; "Sweden: Postal Rates 1855-1875," AMERIPEX 86, large gold; STOCKHOLMIA 86, large gold with special prize

Stone, Robert G., "Saint Pierre and Miquelon 1765-1892," AMERIPEX 86, gold

Stral, Harold M., "Great Britain: Mulreadys," ISRAPHIL 85, vermeil; AMERIPEX 86, vermeil; CAPEX 87, gold

Stromberg, Henry, "Estonia: Provisionals 1918-1920," ITALIA 76, vermeil with special prize

Swanson, Roger, "Iceland: Aurar Issue 1876-1901," INTERPHIL 76, vermeil

Theimer, Ernst T., "Austria and Lombardy-Venetia," AMPHILEX 77, vermeil; PRAGA 78, gold; LONDON 1980, gold; WIPA 81, gold with felicitations; ESPANA 84, gold with special prize;

AUSIPEX 84, large gold; ISRAPHIL 85, large gold; AMERIPEX 86, large gold; CAPEX 87, prix d'honneur; PRAGA 88, prix d'honneur; "Austria: Postal Stationery," CAPEX 87, large vermeil with special prize; PRAGA 88, large gold

Thompson, Richard H., "U.S. Imperforate Issues 1906-1926," STOCKHOLMIA 74, vermeil; INTERPHIL 76, gold

Tinsley, W. Eugene, "Australia: Tasmania 1822-1912," INTERPHIL 76, gold with special prize; CAPEX 78, gold; WIPA 81, gold; AUSIPEX 84, gold; "Australia: Tasmania Postal Stationery," AMERIPEX 86, vermeil

Tobias, A.L.T., "Confederate States: Petersburg, Virginia, 1861-1865," AMERIPEX 86, large vermeil

Torrey, Gordon H., "Turkey: Ottoman," INTERPHIL 76, vermeil; "Saudi Arabia: —1930," INDIA 80, vermeil; "Russia: Offices Abroad," STOCKHOLMIA 86, large vermeil

Towle, Charles L., "U.S.: Railway Route Agent Markings 1837-1861," AMERIPEX 86, vermeil with felicitations

Trefonas, George, "Greece: Airmails," JERUSALEM 74, vermeil; ESPANA 75, vermeil; INTERPHIL 76, vermeil with special prize; AMPHILEX 77, vermeil; PRAGA 78, vermeil with special prize; LURABA 81, vermeil; "Greece: Large Hermes Heads," INTERPHIL 76, vermeil; AMPHILEX 77, vermeil; CAPEX 78, gold; PRAGA 78, large gold; INDIA 80, large gold; LONDON 1980, gold; BUENOS-AIRES 80, large gold; WIPA 81, large gold; PHILATOKYO 81, large gold; PHILEXFRANCE 82, prix d'honneur; BRASILIANA 83, prix d'honneur; AUSIPEX 84, prix d'honneur; PHILAKOREA 84, prix d'honneur; ISRAPHIL 85, prix d'honneur; "Greece: Small Hermes Heads," ISRAPHIL 85, gold; AMERIPEX 86, gold; CAPEX 87, vermeil; HAFNIA 87, large vermeil; PRAGA 88, gold with special prize

Triggle, Ann M., "Great Britain: Postal History of Machynlleth, Wales," CAPEX 87, large vermeil with special prize

Trowbridge, John B., "United States: Trans-Atlantic Mail," CAPEX 78, vermeil

Turner, George T., "United States: Mourning Covers —1870," INTERPHIL 76, vermeil; CAPEX 78, gold

Twigg-Smith, Thurston, "United States: Hawaii Classics," INTERPHIL 76, large gold, prix d'honneur; AMPHILEX 77, large gold, prix d'honneur; CAPEX 78, large gold, prix d'honneur

Verner, Jaroslav J., "Czechoslovakia: Classics," PRAGA 68, gold; POLSKA 73, vermeil; INTERPHIL 76, vermeil with special prize; NORWEX 80, gold; STOCKHOLMIA 86 large vermeil; PRAGA 88, gold; "Czechoslovakia: Siberian Field Post 1917-1920," PRAGA 78, gold with special prize; LONDON 1980, gold; STOCKHOLMIA 86, gold

Vignola, Frank, "Nepal: 1881-1907," JERUSALEM 74, vermeil; INTERPHIL 76, vermeil; INDIA 80, gold; BANGKOK 83, large gold with felicitations; AMERIPEX 86, large gold; CAPEX 87, large gold

Vogel, Raymond, "United States: Postal History 1861-1867," AUSIPEX 84, vermeil; ISRAPHIL 85, gold with special prize; AMERIPEX 86, large gold; CAPEX 87, gold with special prize; HAFNIA 87, large vermeil with special prize; FINLANDIA 88, gold

Vondrak, Joseph, "Austria: Offices in the Levant," PRAGA 78, vermeil with felicitations; BUENOS-AIRES 80, vermeil with felicitations; WIPA 81, vermeil; ESPANA 84, large vermeil; PHILAKOREA 84, vermeil; ISRAPHIL 85, vermeil; AMERIPEX 86, vermeil; CAPEX 87, vermeil; HAFNIA 87, vermeil

Walker, Patricia W., "Ireland: Postal History —1900," BELGICA 82, vermeil with special prize; AUSIPEX 84, gold; AMERIPEX 86, gold; CAPEX 87, vermeil; HAFNIA 87, large vermeil

Walker, W. Danforth, "Grenada: Postal History 1752-1913," PHILEXFRANCE 82, gold; BELGICA 82, gold with special prize and felicitations; BRASILIANA 83, large gold; AUSIPEX 84, large gold; CAPEX 87, large vermeil; HAFNIA 87, large vermeil with special prize; FINLANDIA 88, gold; "India: Barwani," AUSIPEX 84, large vermeil; ISRAPHIL 85, large vermeil; AMERIPEX 86, large vermeil

Warm, Lynne S., "United States: First Bureau Issue," INTERPHIL 76, vermeil; AMPHILEX 77, gold; CAPEX 78, gold; INDIA 80, gold; LONDON 1980, gold with special prize and felicitations; NORWEX 80, vermeil with special prize;

AUSIPEX 84, gold; ISRAPHIL 85, large vermeil; AMERIPEX 86, gold; CAPEX 87, gold; HAFNIA 87, gold with special prize; "United States: Used Abroad 1894-1904," LONDON 1980, vermeil with felicitations

Warm, Harvey R., "United States: Louisiana Postal History," PHILATOKYO 81, gold; BANGKOK 83, large gold with special prize; ESPANA 84, large gold

Warren, Daniel C., "United States: Virginia Postal History 1788-1865," INTERPHIL 76, vermeil

Washburne, Stephen S., "Portugal: 1862-1889," AMERIPEX 86, vermeil; PRAGA 88, vermeil; "Portugal: Postal History 1799—," PRAGA 88, vermeil

Waud, Morrison, "United States: Lincoln Collection," INTERPHIL 76, vermeil; AMERIPEX 86, large vermeil; "United States: Postage Dues 1879-1893," CAPEX 78, vermeil; "United States: Three Cent 1861 Issue," CAPEX 78, vermeil

Weeks, Harvey C., "Chile: Occupation of Peru 1879-1884," LONDON 1980, vermeil with felicitations

Weimer, John R., "United States: Postal Stationery 1861," CAPEX 87, large vermeil with special prize and felicitations; "United States: Postal Stationery 1853," CAPEX 87, large vermeil

Weismann, William, "United States: Postal History Ten Cent 1861," AMERIPEX 86, large vermeil with special prize

Weiss, Gary B., "Canal Zone: Officials," INTERPHIL 76, vermeil

Weiss, Sonja, "From Madrigal to Modern Music," AMERIPEX 86, large vermeil; FINLANDIA 88, vermeil

Wenk, Henry L.C. III, "United States: 1847 Issue," ARPHILA 75, vermeil; INTERPHIL 76, gold; LONDON 1980, gold

Wenz, Charles E., "Germany: Inflation Period 1921-1923," BELGICA 82, vermeil

Williams, J. Edgar, "New Zealand Dependencies: Cook Islands, Niue and Western Samoa," CAPEX 87, vermeil; FINLANDIA 88, vermeil

Willing, Richard S., "Germany: Bergedorf," AMERIPEX 86, large vermeil

Winick, Lester E., "Evolution of Space Mail," LURABA 81, gold; PHILEXFRANCE 82, vermeil; "Iceland: Airmails," BELGICA 82, vermeil; ISRAPHIL 85, vermeil; AMERIPEX 86, vermeil

Wolf, Paul J., "United States: Black Jacks Abroad," INTERPHIL 76, vermeil; CAPEX 78, vermeil; PRAGA 78, vermeil; LONDON 1980, vermeil

Wolff, Gerhardt S., "Zeppelin Mail," JERUSALEM 74, vermeil; INTERPHIL 76, vermeil; HAFNIA 76, vermeil; AMPHILEX 77, vermeil; CAPEX 78, vermeil; PRAGA 78, vermeil; PHILASERDICA 79, vermeil; INDIA 80, vermeil; LONDON 1980, vermeil; AUSIPEX 84, large vermeil; PHILAKOREA 84, large vermeil; AMERIPEX 86, large vermeil; CAPEX 87, large vermeil; PRAGA 88, vermeil; "Zeppelin Mail from Scandinavia," NORWEX 80, vermeil; HAFNIA 87, large vermeil; "Liechtenstein and Switzerland: Zeppelin Mail," LURABA 81, vermeil; PHILATOKYO 81, vermeil; "Zeppelin Mail from Austria," WIPA 81, vermeil; "Zeppelin Mail from France, Monaco and Andorra," PHILEXFRANCE 82, vermeil

Wunderlich, R.G., "United States: Bank Note Issues 1870-1889," INTERPHIL 76, large gold; CAPEX 78, gold; PHILATOKYO, gold; "United States: 1847-1857," INTERNABA 74, large gold; ESPANA 75, large gold; "United States: 1861 Issue," INTEPHIL 76, large gold; AMERIPEX 86, large gold with special prize; "United States: 1869 Issue," CAPEX 78, gold

Wunsch, Charles, "United States: Columbian Issue 1893," ESPANA 75, gold; AMPHILEX 77, vermeil; "United States: 19th Century Postal Stationery," INTERPHIL 76, gold; CAPEX 78, gold

Wunsch, Margaret L., "United States: 1869 Issue," IBRA-MUNCHEN 73, gold; STOCKHOLMIA 74, large gold; ESPANA 75, gold; INTERPHIL 76, gold; AMPHILEX 77, gold; "United States: Columbian Issue 1893," ISRAPHIL 85, large vermeil; AMERIPEX 86, gold; STOCKHOLMIA 86, gold; CAPEX 87, gold; FINLANDIA 88, gold

Yort, Svend, "Danish West Indies," CAPEX 78, vermeil

Zagorsky, Dragomir, "Bulgaria: Classics," AMERIPEX 86, vermeil

Zalstein, Harold N., "Netherlands Indies: Cancellations 1864-1868," AMPHILEX 77, vermeil; "Netherlands Indies: Postal History," CAPEX 78, gold; PRAGA 78, gold; LONDON 1980, vermeil; ISRAPHIL 86, large vermeil

Chapter 17

Flaws and Repairs

The connection between a stamp's condition and its value cannot be overemphasized.

This crucial relationship is difficult for many beginning stamp collectors (and a good many longstanding ones) to fully appreciate. Relatively common stamps in exceptional condition regularly sell for many times the price of a scarce but defective issue with a much higher catalog value.

Always influential, the emphasis on condition has grown even more pointed in recent years. All-but-undetectable shortcomings that would once have been overlooked are now sufficient to reduce the value of an otherwise valuable stamp by hundreds of dollars. At the same time, perfect copies of otherwise inexpensive early definitives now enjoy unprecedented demand and attract record prices.

Things were much different 120 years ago, in the early years of the stamp hobby. Collectors simply wanted stamps — as many different stamps as they could acquire.

Eager collectors diligently tore early issues off all incoming mail, frequently leaving part of the stamp behind. Stamp dealers on the Paris bourse stuck pins through their wares to hang them on ribbons for more prominent display. When stamp albums arrived, some early collectors trimmed away what they deemed to be excess paper around the printed portion of the stamp designs, so what was left of the stamps would fit better when glued down firmly to the printed page.

The consequences of these and other such practices were twofold. First, many of the earliest postage stamps that were saved, including some great rarities, survive in what collectors today consider to be defective or damaged condition. Even the famous 1856 British Guiana 1-penny magenta, renowned as the world's most valuable stamp, has thin spots in the paper and trimmed margins that give it its distinctive octagonal shape.

The second consequence is that, from the time that collectors began to take an interest in stamp condition, faulty stamps have been repaired. The aim has been to minimize their flaws, improve their appearance and make them more palatable to the collector and more salable in the marketplace.

As recently as the early years of this century, the repair and alteration of stamps was advertised in the philatelic press as a service to collectors. For a modest fee, a repairer could transform a damaged, disfigured stamp into a good-looking, collectible copy. Of course, it was easier simply to replace common and inexpensive stamps, so that the more elusive and valuable ones tended to be those most frequently repaired.

While some of the early repair work was crude and easy to detect, there were also many talented craftsmen in this labor-intensive field. One Belgian stamp dealer in the 1920s advertised his willingness to take "any postage stamp, without philatelic value, thinned, perforation missing, torn, with a piece missing, etc., etc., and you will receive it without being able to see where it is repaired." He further claimed to be able to indetectably fabricate a tete-beche pair out of any two stamps.

This repair artist was later also found to be a forger and convicted of fraud — and, indeed, fraud has always been the problem with philatelic repairs and alterations.

Even when a stamp is repaired for a small fee and returned to its proper owner as such, there is no guarantee that it will not one day be resold as a sound, fault-free copy at a much higher price than was originally paid for it, whether out of ignorance or otherwise.

Though there is no need for extraordinary alarm, collectors should remain alert to the possible existence of repairs and alterations, especially on earlier and more valuable stamps.

There is nothing wrong with adding a repaired stamp to a collection — provided both buyer and seller are aware of its status, and arrive at a sensible price for it on that basis. Even the most skillfully repaired stamp is generally worth much less than a sound one, though it is usually worth more than a faulty but unrepaired copy. Some rebacked stamps, for example, are very attractive.

For virtually every flaw there is a repair, and the skilled collector can detect flaws and repairs alike. Though it is impossible to identify every kind of flaw and repair, the following are some of the most commonly encountered ones, accompanied by hints on their detection.

Stamp Flaws and Repairs

Soiling, stains and discoloration

Dirty, stained, faded or toned stamps are understandably beloved by few collectors. Any number of soaps, solvents and similar concoctions have been formulated and used over the years to try and restore such stamps to collectible condition. This process is complicated by the fact that what removes dirt very well from one stamp will sometimes remove the design from another.

Surface dirt can often be removed gently with a soft gum eraser, taking care to work outward from the center of the stamp only in slow strokes to prevent damage to the perforations or margins.

Dirt and grease have been treated with a variety of solutions of commercial soaps, detergents and cleaners, with varying degrees of success.

Solvents, such as an equal admixture of cyclohexane and tolune, can be applied to remove tape stains. The success of this treatment is largely limited by the number of repetitions, the nature of the stamp, and the extent and age of the stain. Many other techniques are described in some detail in *The Dealers' Guide to Chemical Restoration of Postage Stamps.*

Toned stamps — those where the stamp paper has taken on an unattractive yellowish or brownish cast — are most often the result of long-term continuous exposure to high heat and humidity, tobacco smoke or an otherwise inclement or polluted atmosphere. While a bleaching agent may lighten the toning, it is likely to have a similar effect on the colors of many stamps.

A color-affected stamp or color changeling can result from this or exposure to any other chemical agent. A color changeling is a stamp in a color in which it was never originally issued, sometimes dramatically different from the issued color. Like badly toned or stained stamps, such changelings are of little interest or value to most collectors.

Though it cannot cure all ills, proper cleaning can restore much of the attractiveness of a soiled or stained stamp, and should be essentially undetectable. The use of cleaning agents that contain optical brighteners may leave residue in the stamp paper that will react abnormally under ultraviolet light.

The term "cleaning" is used here in its general sense as defined by the Philatelic Foundation: "The removal of foreign substance from a stamp by any cleaning method." It is noteworthy that on the expertizing certificates of the Philatelic Foundation, cleaning "is only mentioned when there is a noticeable change in appearance" of a stamp.

This use of the term is also distinct from the expression "cleaned stamps" used in reference to stamps from which postal or other cancellations have been removed. Removal of cancellations is an alteration, and is listed in that section of this chapter.

Thins

A thin is one of the most frequently encountered stamp flaws, produced when paper is accidentally sheared from the front or back of a stamp. It is most frequently found on used stamps peeled from envelopes or pulled from paper that had not soaked sufficiently to fully loosen the gum. Thins can also occur on unused stamps when the gum has been accidentally moistened on all or part of the back and then roughly separated. Many thins on used and unused stamps alike have resulted from the use of improper adhesives in mounting. The majority of thins, however, probably arise from careless hinge removal, and are called hinge thins.

A thin can run the gamut from the removal of virtually all paper from the back of a stamp to a slightly thinned pinpoint. The inadvertent moistening of perforation tips when hinging gummed stamps can result in perf thins at the very tips of the perforations, typically towards the top of the stamp.

Thins can be repaired or disguised in many ways. Small and superficial thins can be masked by filling the thinned areas with paper pulp, egg white, liquid paper or some other light-colored compound. Massive thins on scarce stamps are sometimes disguised by grafting a new thin piece of matching paper onto the back of the thinned stamp, producing what is known as a rebacked stamp. This takes great skill, and frequently yields pleasing results.

At the opposite extreme, one of the laziest and most common methods of disguising hinge thins is to apply a hinge over the thinned area and then tear the loose portion off, leaving a hard-to-remove hinge remnant to mask the previous damage.

The first step in detecting thins is to examine the back of the stamp illuminated from behind by (though at a safe distance from) a strong source of light. Thins can often be detected as irregular bright spots in the paper.

A better check is to immerse the stamp in watermark fluid in a black watermark tray. Viewed in the tray, thins are seen as unusually dark spots. Check perforation tips carefully. Any that are abnormally dark may be thinned.

Filled thins in watermark fluid will generally appear as unusually light or opaque white spots because most of the compounds used to fill thins are denser in composition than stamp paper.

Unused stamps with thins have sometimes been cleverly repaired by filling them with a matching color of paper pulp that is sanded smooth when dry, then blended into the back of the stamp by regumming the stamp. Such sophisticated repair work can sometimes be seen under an ultraviolet lamp if the pulp used reacts differently to UV light than does the original stamp paper.

This same method can also sometimes detect rebacked stamps, particularly if UV-reactive optical brighteners have been used in the new paper. Careful examination of the edges or perforations of the stamp immersed in watermark fluid or with a strong magnifying glass will otherwise usually reveal the presence of two separate pieces of paper.

When a hinge remnant is left on the back of a used stamp, it is easy to soak and remove it to determine whether it covers a thin. On an unused stamp, when preservation of the original gum may be a financial consideration, hinge remnants may be softened for removal by use of a stamplift, which uses the high humidity of a small enclosed container to soften the adhesive and release the hinge. It is always wise to see what is under a hinge remnant before you purchase a stamp.

Scrapes

Scrapes are the same as thins, though they occur on the front rather than the back of the stamp. To the extent that they mar the printed design, they are very serious flaws. On used stamps, they are generally caused by abrasion in the mailstream. Facial scrapes on unused stamps may be caused when the accidentally moistened gum of one stamp adheres to and removes ink from the face of another.

A lesser but similar flaw is the surface rub, usually also caused by abrasion and especially common on British Commonwealth issues printed on chalk-coated papers.

Scraped and surface-rubbed stamps are generally shunned by collectors, and most are unrepairable. Scraped copies of scarcer monochrome or bicolored stamps, where the scrape is not extensive, have sometimes been repaired by carefully painting in the missing or affected portion of the stamp design. Another technique is to use black ink to hide the scrape under what appears to be a cancellation, though this is of course actually a deceptive alteration rather than a repair.

Scrapes are detected in the same manner as thins. Careful scrutiny will usually soon detect even the most skillfully painted design.

Paper Inclusions

Paper inclusions are pieces of foreign material incorporated into the paper at the time of its manufacture. Though they are perfectly natural, many collectors feel that they are flaws when they are visible on the front of the stamp. (On primitive stamps produced on handmade native papers, where inclusions are ubiquitous, they are generally tolerated.)

Inclusions may be abnormally light or dark, and can sometimes actually be felt on the surface of the stamp. They could be masked in the same way as scrapes, but attempts are seldom made to repair them. Attempts to remove such inclusions usually result in even greater damage to the stamp, visible as a pinhole or small tear.

Tears

Many kinds of tears can afflict postage stamps, though many are quite small and difficult for the untutored eye to detect. For example, the Philatelic Foundation defines a tiny tear as 1 millimeter in length or smaller, a small tear as 1mm to 2.5mm, and a tear as 2.5mm or longer.

Perf tears are fairly common, and are often produced in the course of stamp separation. They are usually quite small and, as the name implies, are generally found at or near a perforation, often near one corner of a stamp.

A pinhole is self-explanatory, though frequently very difficult to detect. Internal tears can also be difficult to recognize, occurring in the body of the stamp and not reaching any of its margins. These are often produced in the same ways as thins.

Repairers use any of a number of adhesives to close tears, including epoxy and other glues, collodion and liquid paper compounds.

In a watermarking tray, tears will generally show as very thin black lines in the stamp, with sealed tears showing as thicker, lighter lines. Collodion shows as an opaque white substance. A 10-power or stronger magnifying glass should be used to determine whether a tear is actually present. On the face of the stamp, tears will always break the printed design. Pinholes are usually most easily detected by viewing the stamp against a strong light source.

Creases

Perhaps the most common of stamp flaws, a crease can severely reduce the value of a stamp. Creases range from small, minor and scarcely detectable to large and disfiguring. They do not include natural folds in the paper produced during or before the printing process, which leave uninked areas when they later open. These are called pre-printing paper folds and are considered freaks rather than flaws.

Creases most frequently occur at the corners of a stamp, accordingly referred to as corner creases. Minute but heavy creases across corner perforations can be very serious. Although they can be difficult to see and may appear to be trivial, such creases are likely to eventually lead to paper separation that will seriously devalue the stamp.

The only real treatment for creases is to press or iron them out using heat, moisture or pressure. They will still be visible as faint straight dark lines in watermark fluid, or as straight white lines when dry. Holding the back of the stamp at a very acute angle to a strong source of light from behind will often show creases as well.

Creases should not be confused with minor wrinkles or gum bends created in production or through natural gum expansion and contraction. These are seldom perfectly straight and generally disappear when a stamp is immersed in watermark fluid.

Margin Flaws

The appearance of the perforations or margins and their visual relation to the printed design of a stamp, known as its centering, have an important bearing on stamp value. The ideal, for perforated and imperforate stamps alike, are large, even and equal margins all around. Few stamps reach this standard, and many have margin flaws that significantly diminish their desirability.

Imperforate stamps often have unbalanced margins, and may have been cut up to or even slightly into the printed design in the course of stamp separation. A corner may be clipped diagonally, and opposite margins may not be parallel.

On perforated stamps perf faults are the most common complaint. Perfs may be clipped, shortened or even removed by scissor separation. Careless manual separation of the stamps can result in the absence of a perforation, referred to as a pulled or short perf.

The stamp may simply be badly centered, which is actually a flaw only to the extent that collectors generally shun such copies.

All of these flaws should be detectable by simple visual examination. The repair for all of them is generally to create new margins by adding new paper to the stamp.

The expert addition of a margin or part of a margin is generally easy to detect. It usually leaves a small but visible seam and a double thickness of paper where the newly added margin and the old paper overlap.

A more convincing and less detectable repair is to reback the stamp completely. This involves sanding or shaving the stamp and a matching sample of paper, which is sometimes obtainable from a piece of original selvage or from a common stamp of the same paper type. The two pieces are then carefully grafted together and new perforations or margins added to give the stamp a pleasing appearance. On used stamps, cancels are sometimes painstakingly extended onto the new paper of the margin by pen or brush.

As mentioned under thins, examination of the perforations or margins of a rebacked stamp immersed in watermark fluid or under magnification will usually disclose the addition of new paper. This often appears as a double or ghost image at the edges or perforation tips of a rebacked stamp.

Stamp Alterations

It is important to distinguish between a stamp repair and a stamp alteration, even though the techniques employed in each are sometimes identical.

Repairs include filling a thin, mending a tear or flattening a crease. The intention of such treatments is to enhance the appearance of a defective stamp. Though many may disagree, such repairs may be defended as restorative or preservative in nature. They become fraudulent only if the repaired stamp is offered as a sound, unrepaired copy.

The alteration of stamps — an attempt to make them appear to be something that they are not — has no such defense. For example, the addition of horizontal perforations to an imperforate 1908 5¢ Lincoln is an undeniable attempt to simulate a rare coil variety, to turn a copy of Scott 315 into what appears to be a copy of Scott 317. Such an alteration is clearly intended only to deceive and defraud.

This distinction between repairs and alterations is not an attempt to vindicate fraud. To offer a repaired stamp as a sound copy is every bit as unethical and illegal as it is to offer an altered copy of a common stamp as a more valuable variety. It is also true that repairs are often combined with alterations with fraudulent intent, as in the addition of gum (an alteration) to hide filled thins (a repair).

At one time, fraud in philately was chiefly confined to the creation and sale of forgeries. But the decline of the skills required to produce successful philatelic forgeries in the latter part of the 20th century has been paralleled by the growing discovery by criminals of simpler ways to fleece collectors. Some of these are examined in the following section.

Almost every conceivable alteration that could enhance the apparent value of a stamp has probably been attempted at one time or another. Some of these alterations are easy for the alert collector to detect. Others are not, and may require authentication by an expertizing service.

Gum

The manipulation or addition of gum is a relatively modern type of stamp alteration, and may be the most prevalent of all such practices today. Its rise is a direct consequence of the post-World War II demand for unused stamps.

Collectors expect unused stamps of recent vintage to be "mint, never-hinged" (MNH), possessing their original gum with no trace of any kind of disturbance.

Older, unused stamps, typically issued prior to World War II, are acceptable to many collectors in "mint, lightly hinged" (MLH, or LH) condition, or with "disturbed gum" (DG), though MNH copies of the same stamps often command considerably higher prices and are in greater demand.

Many unused examples of the earliest postage stamps, including the 19th-century classics, are offered with only part of their "original gum" (OG), or may be uncanceled but have "no gum" (NG). Removal of remnants of the old hinges often found on these stamps can be very difficult and may result in damage to the stamp. Hinges can be soaked off, but only at the cost of removing whatever original gum may remain.

Well-centered OG, MNH copies of 19th- and many early 20th-century stamps are extremely scarce. Their existence in MNH condition is virtually an accident, since any collector who came across such a stamp prior to the 1940s would surely have hinged it into an album. Thus MNH copies of many stamps issued prior to World War I often sell for considerable premiums or even multiples of the prices of their LH, DG or NG counterparts.

Fakers have not been slow to appreciate that the appearance of undisturbed gum can mean a difference of as much as hundreds or even thousands of dollars in the price a stamp brings. And since most early stamp gum was composed of simple and widely known organic compounds, it was not long before seemingly MNH stamps with decidedly non-original gum began to surface. Today they are ubiquitous, and these so-called regummed (RG) stamps are noted as such in many sales lists and auction catalogs.

The application of gum to an ungummed, uncanceled stamp is a practice unambiguously intended to boost its resale value. It does nothing to make the stamp more attractive, nor to restore or preserve it.

The existence of sophisticated clandestine laboratories that offer not merely to gum stamps, but to match in every respect the original gum found on genuine copies of a specific issue attests to the true intent of these practices. So does the fact that the fees charged by such firms are pegged to the catalog value of the stamp to be gummed rather than fixed at a flat rate. (In a flat-rate system, for example, it should cost no more to put gum on a $4 Columbian than a 2¢ Columbian.)

Fortunately, much regumming has been fairly unsophisticated, and many regummed stamps are readily detectable.

Many professionals and dealers claim to achieve reliable results in judging the authenticity of gum by its color and tone. They use their experience in handling many hundreds of similar stamps to judge which of them have been regummed.

Regrettably, few ordinary collectors are likely to have comparable hands-on experience on which to rely. However, collectors can often acquire low-value OG, LH stamps and use the undisturbed portion of their gum as a basis for comparison with that of valuable stamps from the same issue.

The presence of tiny bubbles, brushstrokes or even brush hairs in the gum is usually a sure sign of regumming. These can be detected by shining a light on the stamp from behind at an acute angle or by using a magnifying glass.

Sometimes these signs will be limited to a small area towards the top and center of the stamp, indicating that an attempt has been made to alter an LH, OG stamp to one that appears to be MNH by masking the small area of disturbed gum that even skillful hinging leaves behind. The visible result of this deceptive practice is euphemistically referred to as "redistributed original gum."

Many authentic OG stamps curl up on their long axis when laid face up on a flat surface. This gum curl is the natural result of the differential contraction of the gum and paper on the stamp. By contrast, regummed copies of the same stamps often lie perfectly flat.

Some 20th-century U.S. stamps display gum breakers on the back of the stamps, a regular pattern of ridges in the gum intended to minimize gum curl. These ridges are absent on regummed stamps.

But the most dependable way to detect most regumming jobs is by carefully examining the perforation tips and holes at the edges of the stamp.

Since stamps are gummed before they are perforated, authentic MNH stamps have cleanly punched holes that are regular in size, spacing and appearance. When the stamps are separated, the tips of the perforation teeth show many individual paper fibers where the paper of the perforation bridge between adjoining stamps has been torn.

Fakers usually apply gum to individual stamps that have already been perforated. Some of the bogus gum almost invariably laps over into the perforation holes and onto the perf tips.

On poorly regummed stamps, the perf tips may feel stiff and sharp from the additional gum, like the serrations on a bread knife. The overlapping gum and gum-matted fibers at the tips of the perforations are usually clearly visible under 10-power to 30-power magnification.

More cunning fakers sometimes intentionally tease or fray the tips of the perforations to simulate the natural appearance of a MNH OG stamp, but few are able to eliminate all traces of excess gum in the perforation holes.

Still other clever regummers lightly hinge their work, seeking to allay suspicion that the stamp has been regummed. After all, who would hinge a regummed stamp? In fact, the often substantial difference in price between NG and LH copies of a valuable stamp can make this practice fairly profitable.

There is serious concern today that expert regumming of early stamps by skilled workers in purpose-dedicated facilities may be indetectable even by experts. A significant number of European experts will no longer offer opinions on whether a stamp is NH or has previously been hinged.

Buyers are urged to be cautious if they intend to pay a substantial premium for a stamp principally on the basis of its gum.

Perforations

Alterations of perforations — their addition, removal and modification — have proven a rich source of stamp frauds.

Wherever a relatively inexpensive stamp can be manipulated to simulate a scarcer perforation gauge, variety or error, it has probably been attempted. Many collectors have been taken in by such frauds.

As with gum alteration, altered perforations may or may not be easy to detect. Simple comparison will detect many of the more obvious attempts to simulate or alter perforations.

Fake perforations probably have been added most frequently to eliminate the straight edges that occur naturally on many early U.S. stamps. Straight edged copies aesthetically displease many collectors, who will pay more for fully perforated copies of the same stamp, and stamp fakers have been happy to cater to this bias. The fact that straight edged $1 to $5 Columbians are now almost unheard of even though 10 percent of them were originally printed with straight edges attests to the prevalence of this practice.

With very limited exceptions, genuinely perforated stamps show holes of nearly identical width, spacing, appearance and gauge on parallel sides of each stamp. Lines of perforations on opposite sides of a stamp will be almost perfectly parallel with one another.

In addition, close scrutiny will show that the holes on authentically perforated stamps are rarely perfectly round, but generally are slightly oval in appearance.

Seldom are all these characteristics perfectly reproduced on a stamp with altered or added perforations.

Fake perfs generally are perfectly round. They are often irregular in appearance, and may not run in a straight line parallel with the perforations on the opposite side of the stamp.

Stamps with two or three sides perforated normally and one or two sides that do not match are almost invariably straight edges with added perforations.

As with gum, the perforations on low-value stamps can be used as a basis for comparison with the perforations of more valuable stamps and varieties known to exist from the same issue and to have been perforated in the same manner. Any variation in perforation when the stamps are overlapped should be cause for concern.

There are, unfortunately, a lot of exceptions to this rule, and it is important to know the material. For example, perforations and stamp sizes are known to vary significantly on genuine copies of some 19th-century issues. Many stamps have been perforated by a variety of different machinery and techniques, giving rise to subtle and perfectly normal variations.

The removal of perforations to simulate an imperforate variety or error has been frequently attempted. Even where stamps were regularly issued in imperforate form, such as the U.S. commemoratives of 1909, neatly trimming the perforations from large-margined perforated stamps and selling the result as imperforate can prove profitable. A used imperforate 1909 2¢ Lincoln Memorial, for example, has more than 10 times the catalog value of its perforated counterpart.

Collectors serious about protecting the value of their investment should purchase imperforate stamps only in pairs or larger multiples.

While adherence to this rule undoubtedly rejects some authentic single off-cover imperforates, there is absolutely no way to tell those that are good from those that are not. Thousands of very plausible imperforate singles have been created by trimming perforations from wide-margined singles and booklet stamps. Single imperforates cannot be expertized.

Neither can single flatbed press-printed U.S. coil stamps, as elaborated in detail by George W. Brett in *The Congress Book of 1987*.

Bogus single copies of valuable early U.S. coil stamps, mostly faked by adding or altering perforations on less expensive Washington-Franklins, probably outnumber genuine copies by a substantial margin.

Some of these alterations are easily indentified, but many are not. Especially where more valuable varieties are concerned, authentication by a reputable expertizing authority is a must.

An extensive and helpful treatment of faked U.S. coils is available in *How to Detect Damaged, Altered and Repaired Stamps* by Paul W. Schmid. Read thoroughly and applied rigorously, it will help root out the vast majority of dangerous faked coils. It is highly recommended to any collector with an interest in early U.S. coil issues and fraudulent stamp alterations in general.

Other kinds of perforation fakery can be much more difficult to detect, and many collectors lack the knack for it altogether. As a defensive measure, however, collectors should be extremely wary of any so-called perforation error or rarity offered at suspiciously low prices.

In philately as elsewhere, deals that seem too good to be true generally are. No payment should be made for such stamps until they have been submitted to an acknowledged expertizing service and determined to be authentic.

Overprint

The addition of false overprints and surcharges to stamps is a fairly simple way to convert many inexpensive stamps into plausible imitations of more valuable ones. The work is much less than that involved in producing a complete forgery from scratch, and often makes use of cheap, extensive stocks of common remainders.

For many nations there is a rich literature on overprint and surcharge fakes, although their numbers doubtless continue to grow.

Where a series or set of stamps is involved, authentically overprinted lower values may again prove useful as comparison copies in detecting counterfeits of more valuable denominations. However, forged overprints are known on stamps cataloging as little as 50¢ or less. (Where the stamp they have been added to catalogs 5¢ or 10¢, this still represents a considerable profit for the faker, particularly if the overprints are being added to full sheets of otherwise unsalable stamps.)

For knowledgeable collectors, some overprint alterations are easy to spot. Amateur fakers often choose the wrong ink, type font or size for their creations, and can rarely match the original in every respect. Sometimes forged overprints are added on top of the cancellations on used or canceled-to-order stamps, which may be detectable.

An extension of the addition of overprints or surcharges is their alteration. Lettering may be transposed, deleted, doubled or inverted, as indeed may be the entire overprint, in attempting to simulate a scarce variety. Crooks have shown a great love of such concoctions, including the creation of entirely new variations.

Collectors should approach with caution any overprint or surcharge that is not listed in a current specialized catalog of a given nation's issues. Many collectors, duped into believing that they have stumbled across a hitherto undescribed rarity, pay significant sums for such items. In fact, as it often later develops, these seeming errors are unlisted because they do not legitimately exist.

Another kind of amateur overprint alteration is the physical or chemical modification of a genuine overprint on a genuine stamp. A sharp knife can be used to gently pare away overprint ink on an uninked background, leading to what may seem to be "missing period" or "comma omitted" varieties. The fraudulent nature of such creations is usually visible under strong magnification.

As a general rule, unless you are thoroughly acquainted with such forgeries and the reference works that describe them, it is wise to have any valuable overprinted or surcharged issue expertized when it is purchased. It is also wise to resist unlisted varieties altogether, or at least to have them authenticated before any money changes hands.

Cancellation

Virtually all of the preceding commentary on overprints and surcharges applies equally well to cancellations.

For a variety of reasons, some stamps are much scarcer and more valuable in used condition than they are mint. Where there is a premium for used copies, however, collectors should realize that the premium only applies to stamps with legible cancellations identifiable as having been applied postally during the period of issue of the stamp.

Copies showing part of a ring, a line, an inked smudge or some similar unidentifiable marking should be regarded as uncanceled, NG copies and valued accordingly. Stamps showing partial cancels or postmarks clearly from a different era than that of the stamp, referred to as non-contemporary cancellations, are much less desirable.

Evaluating cancellations is complicated by the fact that some stamps have been canceled with post office ink and genuine (though misappropriated) canceling devices, cleverly backdated to simulate an authentic scarce postmark. Fortunately, most such post office thieves have been content to use a single date die in their cancellations, which collectors can sometimes learn to recognize and avoid.

Cancellations may also be lightened, enhanced or partially altered to increase stamp value and salability. While the lightening of a cancel by chemical or mechanical means verges on restoration (assuming the attempt has not been to remove it), enhancing or changing the marking are obvious alterations.

The most common so-called enhancement is the inking or painting in of uninked or underinked portions of a postmark. The same techniques have been used to alter a cancel from a common to a scarce variety, to transform an early date to the rare first date of issue and so forth.

Cancellations can also be removed for philatelic fraud (as distinct from the removal of cancellation to defraud the post office).

Where the cancellation is light or minimal, stamps with removed cancellations can be gummed and sold as mint. Heavy cancellations that permanently mar or indelibly stain the surface of the stamp can be removed and replaced with more attractive, scarce or otherwise desirable postmarks. Fake markings are often placed to overlap and disguise the traces of the original cancel.

Fiscal cancellations often have been removed from British Commonwealth stamps that were used both for postal and revenue purposes. Many of the higher values of such issues were commonly used to pay taxes, and are exceptionally scarce and valuable with genuine postal cancellations. Fiscal manuscript cancels and purple revenue handstamps sometimes have been bleached from such stamps and their remnants hidden under bogus postmarks to defraud collectors.

Some postal markings, such as U.S. classic-era fancy cancels, are often worth considerably more than the relatively common stamps on which they most frequently appear. The simulation of these valuable markings on otherwise nondescript copies of inexpensive stamps is yet another variety of cancellation alteration for which collectors should be alert.

While close scrutiny, a critical eye and a working knowledge of the postmarks of the era, issue and nation in question will detect many such alterations, there is some evidence to suggest that frauds of this nature are on the rise. Valuable stamps should be expertized.

Watermark

Designed as security devices well before the advent of the postage stamp, watermarks are difficult to alter, although they sometimes have been simulated.

The cleverest and most convincing way to simulate a scarce watermark variety is to reback a common unwatermarked stamp with paper showing the desired watermark from a second stamp. This in effect adds the second stamp's watermark to the first stamp's design. Fortunately, the same inspection used to detect rebacked stamps will usually uncover such alteration.

Fakers and forgers have sometimes impressed a waxy or greasy pattern similar to that of a desired watermark onto the back of a common unwatermarked stamp, but the apparent watermark vanishes when immersed in watermarking fluid.

Color

It is difficult to alter the color of a stamp deliberately from its original shade to a plausibly scarcer one. Although stamps frequently change color due to soaking, washing, bleaching or some entirely unintended photochemical exposure, most of the color changelings so produced are obviously altered. The color of the paper on such changelings is frequently different from that of a normal stamp as well.

At least one limited issue for which colors have been intentionally altered are the U.S. bluish paper issues of 1909. Copies of the 1908-09 definitives they otherwise resemble have been soaked in solutions of bluing or other coloring agents to simulate the distinctive appearance of their valuable bluish paper counterparts. Given the high value of genuine bluish paper stamps, it is prudent to purchase only authenticated copies.

Identity

Though believed to be relatively uncommon, it is possible to alter the identity of a stamp entirely by painting or inking in details of its design or by removing them. The presence of a few minute ornaments, for example, is all that distinguishes U.S. Scott 5, with a used catalog value of $22,500, from Scott 7, which catalogs $85.

Alterations of identity have been largely confined to classic issues. New examples appear to be seldom encountered today, although dangerous early alterations may linger from the past. They are generally detected by microscopic inspection of the critical portions of the stamp design.

A Critical Approach To U.S. Covers

The majority of fake covers are readily exposed by a simple process of elimination. If you ask yourself the right questions regarding a cover, the answers often lead to conclusions that either reveal it as a fake or support its authenticity.

The steps in the process of determining fake covers and the questions to be asked are basic and simple.

To begin with, what is the actual date or probable period of the cover? Sometimes no precise date is available from a datestamp, a dateline, the contents or a docketing marking. If all these are unavailable, the period can still be narrowed down by determining the period of usage of the stamps, the postal rate indicated and any other markings that appear on the cover. Narrow down the period during which the cover could have been used as much as possible. Subsequent steps in establishing authenticity will rely heavily on accurately determining this period.

The next step is to determine if all aspects of the cover are internally consistent with the date or period established. The paper, the ink, the stamps, the markings — even whether the item is an envelope or a folded letter — all should be consistent with the period of use you have established.

Where did the item originate, and where was it sent? Determine if the cover is consistent with the kinds of mail service and the usual methods of handling between these two points during the period you have established.

Sometimes the point of origin is unknown, as is frequently the case with steam, route agent and other classes of mail. Even when you do not know the exact point where the item originated, you can usually determine the most likely area or region of origin. Contents, if available, can provide useful clues. A letter remarking on a bountiful cotton crop will have a different region of origin than one that alludes to the local availability of fresh lobster.

The address may hint at the origin. A letter addressed simply to a town and county will usually have originated in the same state or territory. Letters sent from abroad to the United States are usually so inscribed, while those originating within the country seldom are.

If the letter was forwarded, returned or not delivered as originally addressed, try to determine why this may have been so. If the letter is from a known correspondence, comparing the stamps and markings with others found in the same correspondence may prove fruitful.

Some items, such as ship and steamship usages, almost invariably originated at a point different from that at which they entered the government mails. Such mail may have been carried by an independent mail carrier, a ship captain or even a friend.

Attempt to determine what other kind of service may have been involved. This may be signaled by non-government rates or pencil notations, which may indicate handling by an express service or a carrier delivery.

For the period, the method of handling, the point of origin and the destination of the cover, what should the postal rates have been? Prepayment in whole or in part was mandatory for some items and impossible for others. Knowing which is usual, the presence of stamps or paid markings on a cover, becomes important evidence of its authenticity.

Especially in the early adhesive period, not all prepayment was by postage stamps. Some mail went to those who had the privilege of receiving it free, but the privilege may have been limited to certain classes or weights of mail.

Determining the correct rate for a given item is crucial. Although there were some errors by postal clerks, especially where calculations were complicated by compound rates, the vast majority of covers are correctly rated. Overpayments occur frequently in mail to foreign countries.

Were postage stamps required, optional or exceptional during the period for the type of service the item received? Some early stamps were limited in the kinds of mail they could prepay. Some kinds of mail could not be prepaid by stamps. This information can be important in learning whether a cover is genuine.

If a cover with a postage stamp was sent during a period when the use of stamps was optional, check to ensure that its markings are consistent with stamp use rather than direct prepayment. Markings on a stamped cover that would appear on it if it were posted without a stamp should have a plausible explanation. Otherwise, they suggest that it is a stampless cover to which a postage stamp has been fraudulently added to increase its apparent value.

If stamps were required during the period indicated by a cover that lacks stamps paying the full rate, check for signs that a stamp has been removed or has accidentally come off. Some such covers originated at U.S. territorial post offices, where stamps were often unavailable, and may have been prepaid in cash rather than stamps.

Does the item bear markings consistent with its usage? It should be possible to account for all rate markings and handstamps on a cover. Datestamps should reflect a logical or explicable progression from the cover's point of origin to its destination.

The markings on the cover should match other known genuine examples in appearance. The inks of the markings should match as well. Cancellations and other postal markings are subject to alteration. They can also be fraudulently added to an item carried outside of the government mails.

If possible, check to see that markings applied at the same post office are consistent with other known genuine examples of the period. For example, some offices routinely used one color of ink for the postmark and another for the cancellation. If both are in the same color, check to see if the inks match. If the stamp is tied by the cancel to the cover, check to see whether the tie has been enhanced or added.

Has the item been altered in any way that might conceal manipulation? If a dateline has been removed, or differs from the remainder of the contents, determine if the markings on the cover could be explained by a different point of origin than the apparent one. Repairs are also sometimes hidden by sealing a cover closed.

Finally, has a consistent and logical explanation been developed for the markings on the item? If any inconsistencies exist, it is always possible that they can be explained by starting over in your analysis with a different assumption.

Assume, for example, that a different stamp was originally on the cover, or that the cover was originally a stampless cover. If either premise explains all the markings, you may have good reason to suspect fakery.

If there is more than one logical explanation for the item, carefully review the rates and regulations of the period. If that fails, you may seek information about additional or similar covers that would tend to favor one explanation.

If you go through these steps on several troublesome covers, you will find you have spent a lot of time reading and studying postal laws and regulations. The more you know about these, the less likely you are to be deceived. Proper reference materials will make your task easier.

Chapter 18

Worldwide Philatelic Expertizing Services

Expertizing is the use of an independent source to arrive at an opinion on the authenticity of a stamp, cover or other philatelic item.

As a collector, expertizing offers you the peace of mind of knowing that you get what you pay for. The cost of expertization is relatively modest.

Expertization can trace its origins back to well before the turn of the century.

Amid a proliferation of 19th-century forgeries, facsimilies, reprints and bogus issues, early collectors often consulted a dealer or specialist who was known to be knowledgeable on the stamps of a given nation.

The initials or signatures of these individuals are often seen on the backs of early issues. The practice is still continued by a few experts, signifying their opinion that the stamps are genuine.

As time passed, stamp collecting became more refined and the number of worldwide issues escalated. So too did the variety and sophistication of the fakes.

Many of the great rarities of the hobby were copied, with results ranging from amusing to dangerously convincing. By the same token, many cheap and common stamps were counterfeited for use in the packet trade over the years as well.

In some respects, the development of the hobby can be likened to a foot race, in which the ceaseless struggle to detect frauds strives to keep pace with the cunning efforts of those who produce them.

In the heyday of the greatest fakers, notorious names such as Fournier and Sperati, entire covers came into existence that were bogus in all respects, from stamps to envelopes to markings. But it clearly takes less skill to slightly modify an existing stamp than to create an accurate forgery from scratch. That is why fraudulent modification has become the principal activity of most fakers of the last half-century.

Stamps have been trimmed, perforated and reperforated to simulate valuable varieties. Where an overprint or cancel increases the value of a stamp, fakers have often added one. Where the premium is for stamps without such markings, other fakers have removed them.

Many early collectors, including some of the greatest names in the annals of the hobby, were satisfied with any genuine copy of a sought-after stamp, often irrespective of condition. However, the ascendancy of highly quality- and condition-conscious collectors, especially in the postwar era, has led to a second kind of fakery.

Indisputably genuine copies of high-value stamps have been altered to appear to be more attractive, desirable and hence vastly more valuable than they actually are. At the low end of this kind of fakery, a straight edge on a stamp can be perforated to create what appears to be an evenly margined, fully perforated adhesive. At the other extreme, margins may be augmented, cancels removed, tears sealed, a new back added to disguise a thin spot and the entire concoction regummed to yield a plausible simulation of a rare, mint, never-hinged gem.

Modifying a stamp is, in itself, not illegal. In theory, there is nothing wrong with any of this, provided that the seller fully apprises all potential buyers of the repairs and alterations that have been made. In practice, however, sooner or later someone lacking either knowledge or scruples will attempt to pass the item off as something it is not.

Expertizing is an important line of defense against both bogus stamps and deceptive alterations. The techniques employed by most experts or expertizing committees are part comparison, part technology and part educated instinct.

The most important tool for nearly all experts is a reference collection. Comprehensive reference collections contain examples of both genuine and bogus stamps, varieties, markings and covers. Such collections are usually supplemented by documentary and photographic records, as well as a basic reference library.

By comparing an item with the wide variety of authentic and fake copies in such a collection, it is often possible to reach a quick determination. For example, many otherwise excellent forgeries have an incorrect cancellation, which stands out like a sore thumb when compared with the authentic postmarks in a reference collection.

There are many technological means to detect forgeries as well. Though it is probable that far more frauds can be detected with a good perforation gauge, a watermark detector and an ultraviolet lamp than with the services of a refracting spectrometer or an optical comparator, all these tools and many others have roles to play in finding fakes.

Educated instinct, or expertise, is a feel for stamps and especially covers that can come only from having handled hundreds or even thousands of such items. At a glance, many experts get a sense that a specific cover is or is not authentic. Their experience in having handled many other such items tells them what details need to be cross-checked to confirm or disprove their hunch.

Those interested in a closer look at the expertizing process — its procedures, processes and limitations — should look into *Opinions*, an annual anthology of various cases submitted to the Philatelic Foundation. Primarily focusing on stamps and covers of the United States, the case studies presented demonstrate how expertizers arrive at their decision.

Taken in total, the services offered by expertizers can help keep you safe from the predators in the philatelic jungle.

The accompanying chart lists most North American experts and expertizing committees, as well as a selection of those abroad. This list is by no means comprehensive. Many of the numerous expertizing services available around the world were not contacted.

Many other experts not listed here offer considerable expertise in narrowly circumscribed areas. For various German and related issues, for example, the Michel Germany specialized catalog lists 108 experts, several of whom specialize in a single stamp or even a specific category of postmark.

While such services are beyond the scope of this presentation, they are well worth seeking out and consulting for their opinions on relevant material.

The chart gives the name, address, area of expertise, basic fee schedule and turn-around time for various expertizing services. Costs for items determined to be authentic vary considerably from expert to expert. They are generally either a percentage or a flat fee pegged to the catalog value of the item in question. For bogus items or items on which no opinion can be reached, the price spread is even more dramatic, though most expertizers process such material at a nominal cost.

The letters in the column at the far right in the chart refer to other important expertizing features, as detailed in the Key to Additional Services.

An opinion is an expert or a committee judgment regarding whether an item is or is not genuine. It is interesting to note what experts will and will not cover in their opinions.

While virtually all services provide opinions on stamp condition (B) and the presence of original gum (D), only two of the North American services we consulted, and 16 of 25 overall, are willing to provide an opinion on whether a stamp was previously hinged (E).

Only a few firms give opinions on value (C), supplied on request in respect to particularly unusual items.

A total of 11 services guarantee their opinions (A). The extent of the indemnity implied in such a claim presumably varies from service to service.

Expert services may be divided into those provided by individuals (F) and those administered by committee (G). Virtually all of these services verify the description of stamps on request (J), which is the principal activity of experts.

However, in spite of several well-funded but abortive efforts in the United States to promote professional stamp-grading, only nine foreign respondents and none of the larger U.S. services will verify the grade of a stamp (I).

Most expert services are accepted as authoritative by auction houses (K), which furnish experts with a great deal of their business. Auction firms rely upon expert opinions as the bona fides for valuable stamps prior to sale and as confirmations of authenticity for customers who request it after a sale. Most auctions and mail bid sales list rules governing the use of experts in the terms and conditions printed in their sale catalogs.

Photographic certificates are now issued for authentic stamps by virtually all expertizing services. Experts' handstamps and signatures can and have been forged. But it is nearly impossible to precisely match the centering, appearance, cancel and perforation pattern of a stamp as recorded with perfect fidelity in a photograph.

Photographic certificates include either a black and white (L) or a color photograph (M) tied by an embossed seal to a written description the stamp and the expert's opinion of it. These certificates are signed either by the expert, one or more members of the expert committee or the secretary of the organization.

Some services register certificates to the submitting party (H), and some acknowledge the receipt of material submitted for expertization (Q).

A solitary European firm makes sales offers (P). Though several experts are affiliated with stamp firms or are dealers themselves, they take pains to rigorously segregate stamp dealing from expertizing activities.

Name and address of service	Area of expertise	Schedule of Fees: Found to be genuine:	Schedule of Fees: Not genuine:	Turnaround time for U.S. clients	Additional services (consult key)
North America					
American First Day Cover Society Expertizing Committee Box 29544 Columbus, Ohio 43229	First-day covers (stamps and cachets)	up to $200 Scott catalog value, $10; $201 to $500, $15; $501 to $1,000, $20; more than $1,000, $20 plus 1 percent of catalog value	$5	60 days	G J K
American Philatelic Expertizing Service Box 8000 State College, Pa. 16803	United States, worldwide	$12 to $25 for items up to $1,700 catalog value; 1 1/2 percent of value for items above $1,700; 33-percent discount for APS members	costs of service and postage	45-90 days	B D G J K L Q
John Bulat Box 91 Yonkers, N.Y. 10702-0091	Ukraine, Western Ukraine, Carpatho-Ukraine	4 percent of catalog value (minimum 25¢ per stamp) plus postage and insurance	1/4 percent of catalog value	10 days	A B C D E F H I J K O
Germany Philatelic Society Expert Committee Box 915678 Longwood, Fla. 32791-5678	Germany and area, states and colonies	4 percent of catalog value	reduced fee	about 30 days	A B D F G J K M N

Name and address of service	Area of expertise	Schedule of Fees		Turnaround time for U.S. clients	Additional services (consult key)
		Found to be genuine:	Not genuine:		
Vincent Graves Greene Philatelic Research Foundation Box 100 — First Canadian Place Toronto, Canada M5X 1B2	British North America	$10 to $15	no response	56-84 days	B D G H K M
International Society for Japanese Philately Michael E. Ruggiero 264 Westminster Road Brooklyn, N.Y. 11218	Japan	$5 per stamp, $15 per cover, plus postage; special low-cost service that does not provide certificates also available	no response	60-90 days	B D G J K L
The Philatelic Foundation 21 E. 40th St. New York, N.Y. 10016	Pre-1940 United States and foreign	up to $450 catalog value, $15; 3 1/2 percent of catalog value above $450; 4 percent of value for stamps on cover, 4 1/2 percent for cancellations and overprints. Maximum fee $750.	$15	60 days	B D E G H J K L M Q
Professional Stamp Expertizing 12651 S. Dixie Highway Suite 326 Miami, Fla. 33156	United States, Confederate States, U.S. possessions	six-step flat fee scale from $32 for items of less than $700 catalog value to $200 for items of more than $25,000 catalog value	$32	30-60 days; 14-day express service available	B D G J K M Q

Name and address of service	Area of expertise	Schedule of Fees		Turnaround time for U.S. clients	Additional services (consult key)
		Found to be genuine:	Not genuine:		
Stamp Institute of America Box 48 Jericho, N.Y. 11753	Germany and area states and colonies	standard fee is $40 or 5 percent of market value, whichever is higher	reduced fee	14 days	B D E F H J K L
Foreign					
Dr. Dante Bolaffi Cso. Duca d. Abruzzi 32 I-10129 Turin Italy,	Italy, Italian states and colonies	3,000 lira per stamp (five-stamp minimum) plus postage; color photo certificates 20,000 lire plus postage	3,000 lira per stamp plus postage	3-4 days plus travel time	A B C D E F J K M
BPA Expertising Ltd. Box 163 Carshalton Surrey, England SM5 4QR	worldwide	£14 for single stamps up to £700 Gibbons catalog value, 2 percent of catalog value thereafter; £42 for sets of stamps up to £3,000 catalog value, 2 percent thereafter	same as for genuine stamps	42-56 days	B D G H K L Q
Brun & Fils 85 Galerie Beaujolais Palais Royale F-75001 Paris, France	France and French colonies, worldwide classics	3 percent of catalog value or market value (10-franc minimum); black & white photo certificates 120fr, color certificates 220fr	same as for genuine stamps	no response	B D E F H I J K L O P
Roger Calves 8 Rue Drouot F-75009 Paris, France	France and French colonies	no response	no response	21 days	A B D E F H I J K L Q

Name and address of service	Area of expertise	Schedule of Fees		Turnaround time for U.S. clients	Additional services (consult key)
		Found to be genuine:	Not genuine:		
F.W. Collins Stoborough Croft, St. Cross Winchester, England SO23 9RX	Cape of Good Hope	up to $250 Scott catalog value, $15; $251 to $1,000 catalog value, $20; more than $1,000, 2 percent of catalog value	$15	30 days	B D E F H K L Q
Comision de Expertos Filatelicos Pau Claris 106 08009 Barcelona, Spain	Spain and Spanish area	up to 100,000 pesetas Edifil catalog value, 3,000ptas; 100,000ptas and above, 3 percent of catalog value	postage and insurance only	21 days	B G K M Q
Dr. Arno Debo Laufzorner Strasse 5 D-8000 Munich 90 Federal Republic of Germany	Denmark, Danish Virgin Islands, Greenland, Iceland, Faroes	3 percent of Michel catalog value (minimum 20 marks); reduced fees for faulty stamps	20 marks per item	7-30 days	A B D E F K L M
Horst G. Dietrich Ludgerusstrasse 33 D-4044 Kaarst- Buettgen Federal Republic of Germany	Afghanistan	up to 4 percent of catalog value for stamps; 3 percent to 4 percent of market value for covers	costs of service and postage	14-42 days	A B D E F H I J K N
Paul Morgoulis 8 Rue Drouot F-75009 Paris, France	Portugal and Portuguese colonies	2 percent of catalog value	costs of postage	30 days	B C D E F J K L

Name and address service	Area of expertise	Schedule of Fees		Turnaround time for U.S. clients	Additional services (consult key)
		Found to be genuine:	Not genuine:		
Horst Proschold Raimundstrasse 151 D-6000 Frankfurt 1 Federal Republic of Germany	Great Britain, Ireland, Cyprus Gibraltar, Malta, Saxony	no response	no response	30 days	A B D E F H I J K M N
Raybaudi Experts Box 756 I-00184 Rome, Italy	Italy and Italian colonies, overprints	30,000 to 125,000 lire on a 12-step fee scale, plus 30,000l per certificate	3,000 lire each	15-20 days	B C D E F I J K M
Emil Rellstab Widenbuel 50 CH-8617 Moenchaltorf Switzerland	Switzerland	25 Swiss francs plus 3 percent of market value (certificate included)	20-50fr	14-30 days	A B D E F I J K L M O
Dr. H. Rommerskirchen Nernstrasse 23-25 D-4150 Krefeld Federal Republic of Germany	Albania, Croatia, German occupation of Channel Is.	2 percent to 4 percent of Michel catalog value	1 percent of catalog value	14 days	A B C D E F H I J L N
Bruno Rupp Postfach 88 FL-9491 Ruggell, Liechtenstein	Liechtenstein	the greater of 2 percent of catalog or market value, plus 20-franc certificate fee; lower cost without certificates	no response	3 days plus travel time	A B C D E F I J K L M N

Name and address of service	Area of expertise	Schedule of Fees		Turnaround time for U.S. clients	Additional services (consult key)
		Found to be genuine:	Not genuine:		
Hermann E. Sieger Box 1160 D-7073 Lorch, Wurttemberg Federal Republic of Germany	Zeppelin mail, rocket mail and airmail	4 percent of catalog value	1/2 percent of catalog value	60 days	A B C D E F H K L M N Q
Dr. Laszio Steiner Oktober hat utca 8 H-1051 Budapest, Hungary	Hungary	no response	no response	60 days	B D F J L
Zumstein & Cie. Postfach 2585 CH-3001 Bern Switzerland	Switzerland	1/2 percent to 2 percent of market value, depending on time required, plus photo certificate fee of 35 Swiss francs	no response	30-60 days	B C D E F H J K L M

Key to Additional Services

A: All opinions are guaranteed; B: Provide opinions on condition; C: Provide opinions on value; D: Provide opinions on original gum; E: Provide opinions on hinging; F: Authentication/certificate signed by individual; G: Authentication/certificate signed by committee; H: Certificates are registered to submitter; I: Verify grade of stamps on request; J: Vertify description of stamp on request; K: Opinions are accepted as authoritative by most auction houses; L: Black and white photograph sealed to certificate; M: Color photograph sealed to certificate; N: Fakes are marked indelibly; O: Fakes are marked indelibly on request only; P: Sales offers made; Q: Receipt of materials acknowledged.

Chapter 19

Dealers' Organizations

American Stamp Dealers' Association

Executive offices of the American Stamp Dealers' Association, Inc., are located at 3 School St., Glen Cove, N.Y. 11542. ASDA dealers are engaged in every facet of philately and are located throughout the United States and the world. No matter where a collector lives or visits, or what his collecting interests or needs, he is not far from an ASDA dealer who can serve him. The triangle insignia is the symbol of membership in the ASDA.

A membership application to ASDA is approved only after a thorough search has been made regarding the applicant. Before membership is granted, the applicant must agree in writing to abide by the ASDA pledge and code of ethics, which include the assurance of fair dealing to collectors.

To be admitted to regular membership in ASDA, an applicant must have at least four years of professional philatelic experience; for provisional membership at least two years.

Among the functions of ASDA are: sponsoring national and local chapter shows, sponsoring seminars for dealers, maintaining a credit file and information on hundreds of dealers and collectors, publishing a membership directory and encouraging junior collectors to exhibit.

The association also serves as a spokesperson when conflict arises with local, state or federal legislation.

ASDA Bylaws

Preamble

The purpose of this association is to provide an organization for the maintenance and development of high standards of business ethics among those engaged directly and indirectly in the merchandising of stamps and other materials for the hobby of philately, and thereby to promote mutual trust and friendship among its members and public confidence and respect for the trade; to provide a medium for the exchange of trade and credit information of philatelic interest through trade papers, releases, meetings and similar means; to arbitrate disputes, mediate, adjust and settle differences between members and the public;

To assist recognized governmental agencies in the prosecution of violations of law relating to philatelic matters; to do all within its power for the general good of philately and in connection therewith to aid in the establishment of local chapters throughout the United States; to so operate that no part of the income or earnings of the association inure to the benefit of any individual or member; and to insure that no officer, member or employee shall receive or be entitled to receive pecuniary profit from the operations thereof except reasonable compensation for services actually rendered.

Article I

Board of Directors

Section 1. Number of Members. The Board of Directors shall consist of nine members and shall include among its members the president, vice president, secretary and treasurer of the association. The four members elected to fill the respective active offices of the association and five other nominees for directorships receiving the greatest number of votes of the membership shall be deemed elected to the board. The president of the association shall be the chairman of the board. The immediate past president shall be ex-officio to the board and shall not have a vote.

Section 2. Qualifications. Only members of the association pursuant to Article VI, Section 1 of these bylaws shall be eligible for nomination and election as a director. Each officer and director of the board must present evidence of ability to be bonded at the time of acceptance of nomination for position and must be bondable throughout the entire term of service.

Section 3. Term of Office. Directors shall take office on the first day of January in the year following the year of their election and shall serve without compensation for two years and until their successors are elected and qualify. The board, by an affirmative vote of six members, may remove any director or officer with cause. A written petition by 200 members of the association in good standing or by 20 percent of the membership, whichever is greater, shall be sufficient to cause a recall referendum to be conducted for the removal of any officer or officers, director or directors, named therein. The board shall cause such referendum to be conducted within 90 days of receipt of a valid petition by the secretary of the association.

Section 4. Classes. Terms of directors shall be divided into two classes so that in the year in which officers are elected by the membership two directors shall also be elected. In the alternate year, the other three directors shall be elected.

Section 5. Regular and Special Meetings. Regular meetings of the board shall be held at least two times a year. Special meetings of the board may be called by the president, or upon the written request of five board members. The time and place for all regular meetings shall be fixed by the board and, 10 days prior notice thereof, shall be given by mail or publication in the newsletter. The time and place of all special meetings shall be fixed by the president and shall be given by mail unless less than seven days notice is given, in which event notice shall be given by telephone or telegraph not less than three days prior to the meeting date.

Section 6. Quorum. Five members of the board shall constitute a quorum at regular meetings as the board of directors and five shall constitute a quorum at special meetings. Except as provided in Article III, Section 2 of these bylaws, the act of a majority of the members present at a meeting at which a quorum is present shall be the act of the board.

Section 7. Action by Mail or Telephone Poll. If, in the opinion of the president, action upon any matter cannot reasonably be deferred until the next scheduled meeting of the board, he may direct that the members of the board be polled by mail or telephone. The secretary shall notify all board members of the result of each such poll in writing. The results of such poll shall be valid as if adopted at a meeting of the board.

Section 8. Reimbursement for Expenses. Reimbursement for expenses incurred in the performance of bona fide ASDA business as directed by the board, executive committee or executive officer may be authorized by the executive officer with the concurrence of the finance committee. Reimbursement of expenses may be requested by submitting such requests to the finance committee for approval. The finance committee shall, under the supervision of the treasurer, review and report to the executive committee on a continuing basis all expense accounts for the purpose of assuring such accounts have not been abused. Reimbursement of travel expenses is not to exceed the lowest regularly available economy coach air fare actually incurred by members of the board. The executive officer will administer the procedure for requesting reimbursement.

Article II

Officers

Section 1. Officers. The officers shall consist of a president, vice president, secretary and treasurer, each of whom shall perform the duties incidental to the office. They shall take office on the first day of January in the year following the year of their election and shall serve without compensation for a two-year term and until their successors are elected and qualify. Only members of the association pursuant to Article VI, Section 1 of these bylaws shall be eligible for nomination and election as an officer.

Section 2. President. The president shall be chief executive officer of the association. He shall preside over all meetings of the board and of the members pursuant to Article IV. He shall see that all duly adopted orders and resolutions of the association are carried into effect. He shall be ex-officio a member of all committees with the right to vote, except for the nominating committee, and shall have the general powers and duties of supervision, management and responsibilities usually vested in the office of president.

Section 3. Vice President. The vice president shall perform the duties and exercise the powers of the president during the absence, death or disability of the president, as well as such other duties as may be assigned by the president.

Section 4. Secretary. The secretary shall attend all meetings of the members pursuant to Article IV and of the board and shall preserve in books of the association true minutes of the proceedings of all such meetings. He shall keep in his custody the seal of the association and shall have authority to affix the same to all instruments where its use is required. He shall give all notices required by statute, these bylaws or any resolution of the board. He shall perform such other duties as may be delegated to him by the board.

Section 5. Treasurer. The treasurer shall have charge of the custody of all corporate funds and securities and the keeping of books belonging to the association, including full and accurate accounts of all receipts and disbursements; he shall also have charge of the deposit of all monies, securities and other valuable effects in the name of the association in such depositories as may be designated for that purpose by the board. He shall supervise the disbursement of the funds of the association as may be ordered by the board, taking proper vouchers for such disbursements, and shall render to the president and board at regular meetings of the board, and whenever requested by them, an account of all his transactions as treasurer and of the financial condition of the association.

Section 6. Number of Terms. No person shall be elected to any one office more than twice.

Article III

Elections and Vacancies

Section I. Election. Elections for officers and directors shall be held as follows:

A. On or before May 1 of each year the board shall appoint from among members of the association a nominating committee of not less than three (3) members, and designate the chairman thereof. The names of the appointees shall be published in an official publication. Not later than Sept. 15 of each year the president shall appoint such inspectors of election as the president shall deem necessary. Committee members or inspectors of the election may not be members of the board.

B. The nominating committee shall endorse at least one (1) candidate from among the members for each office. The endorsement shall be in writing, signed by the chairman of the nominating committee, and delivered to the secretary not later than Aug. 1.

C. A petition signed by twenty-five (25) members nominating an additional candidate or candidates for a specific office or as a director may be delivered to the secretary not later than Sept. 1.

D. Nominees for office shall immediately and not later than ten days thereafter present to the secretary of the association written evidence of ability to be bonded reasonably acceptable to the secretary and acceptance of the nomination for office.

E. The secretary shall prepare a printed ballot, which shall contain: (1) The name of each person endorsed and the method of endorsement; and (2) Sufficient space for the entry of other candidates by the member voting.

F. Not later than Sept. 30, the secretary shall cause a ballot to be mailed to each member entitled to vote. The ballot shall indicate that it must be returned to the secretary, first-class or airmail postage prepaid, by a date specified, which shall not be less than thirty (30) days subsequent to the date of mailing of the ballots. The ballot will be unsigned and transmitted in an unaddressed and sealed envelope marked "Ballot" and be contained in a regular envelope addressed to ASDA Headquarters. The unaddressed ballot envelope will remain sealed until opened by the inspectors of election.

G. Seven days subsequent to the specified date, or as soon thereafter as practicable, the inspectors of election shall tabulate the ballots and certify the results to the secretary, who shall cause a notice of election to be published in an official publication.

H. The board of directors may establish such additional election procedures as it may deem necessary so long as they are consistent with the provisions of the bylaws.

Section 2. Vacancies. Vacancies in any office or directorship shall be filled by appointment made by a majority of the remaining members of the board. Each person so appointed shall remain in that position until his successor has been elected by the members and shall qualify.

Section 3. Appointment and Removal of Employees and Agents.

A. The board may appoint such employees and agents as it may from time to time consider in the best interest of the association, and fix their powers and compensation. Appointees need not be members of the association.

B. Any officer or agent appointed pursuant to this Section 3 may be removed by the board whenever, in its judgment, the interests of the association will be served thereby.

C. No officer or director shall concurrently serve as executive officer or as a paid employee of the association.

Article IV

Meetings of Members

Section 1. Annual Meetings of Members. At least once during each calendar year, the board shall direct that an annual meeting of members be held, and fix the time and place thereof.

Section 2. Special Meetings of Members. Special meetings of members may be called by the president or any five members of the board acting together in writing.

Section 3. Notice. At least thirty (30) days prior to the date fixed, notice of the annual or a special meeting of members shall be published in an official publication of the association to all members.

Section 4. Attendance by Board. Unless excused by the president, all members of the board shall attend all annual and special meetings of members.

Section 5. Order of Business.

A. If a quorum is not present, meetings of members may adopt resolutions indicating the sense of the meeting, which shall be considered at the next meeting of the board.

B. Whether or not a quorum is present, all members shall be entitled to attend and discuss the affairs of the association with the board.

Section 6. Quorum. At any annual or special meeting, a quorum shall consist of the lesser of 50 voting members or five percent of the voting membership.

Article V

Committees

Section 1. Standing Committees. At the first meeting of the board held after Jan. 1 in each year, the president shall appoint after consultation with the board from among the members of the board to the extent possible:

A. A chairman of the Membership Committee.

B. A chairman of the Expert Committee.

C. A chairman of the Bylaws Committee.

D. A chairman of the Legal Committee.

The committee chairman shall name additional members to the Membership Committee, Expert Committee, Bylaws Committee and Legal Committee who need not be members of the board.

Section 2. Special Committees. The board may from time to time create special committees, and designate their function and term of office. Members of special committees shall be named by the chairman of the committee and need not be members of the board or members of the association unless so established by the board. The president shall designate after consultation with the board the chairman of the committee.

Section 3. Membership Committee. The Membership Committee shall exercise the functions assigned to it by Article VI of these bylaws.

Section 4. Expert Committee. The Expert Committee shall oversee all activities of the association in relation to the American Philatelic Expertization Service, and shall act as the association's liaison with the Philatelic Research Institute and Philatelic Foundation as well as other agencies involved in this service.

Section 5. Bylaws Committee. The Bylaws Committee shall keep the bylaws under continuous study for the good and welfare of the association.

Section 6. Legal Committee. The Legal Committee shall maintain general supervision over the Code of Ethics disciplinary actions and arbitration procedures under rules adopted by the board.

Section 7. Vacancies. Vacancies in the membership of any committee may be filled by appointments made in the same manner as original appointments.

Section 8. Term. The chairman and all members of the standing and special committees of the association serve at the discretion of the president of the association after consultation with the board.

Section 9. Quorum. Unless otherwise designated in the resolution creating a committee, a majority of the whole committee shall consititute a quorum and the act of a majority of the members present at a meeting at which a quorum is present shall be the act of the committee.

Section 10. Rules. Each committee may adopt rules for its own government consistent with these bylaws and the approved policy memorandums on file in the ASDA Policy Manual at ASDA Headquarters. Committee chairs shall review their respective policy memorandums for completeness and consistency with the bylaws for the good and welfare of the association.

Article VI

Membership

Section 1. Regular Member. Any individual natural person may apply for regular membership in the association if he or she:

A. has been a dealer in philatelic material, supplies, accessories and publications, or in the opinion of the board of directors is engaged in a trade, business or profession which directly advances and benefits the trade; and

B. furnishes documentary proof of four years of professional experience in the stamp business; and

C. subscribes to the Code of Ethics of the association; and

D. has attained the age of legal majority in the jurisdiction in which he resides.

Section 1a. Foreign Members.

A. Foreign applicants must be members of their respective country's IFSDA organization if such exists or an organization of equal status, with board approval.

Section 2. Other Membership Categories.

B. Honorary Member. The board may grant honorary memberships to any person or persons who have in their judgment served the trade and hobby of philately with distinction and honor. No dues shall be required of such memberships nor shall such honorary member be entitled to voting rights, and such memberships may be withdrawn by the board at any time for good cause shown. Such membership shall be non-transferable. An honorary member upon payment of regular membership dues will be entitled voting rights.

C. Retired Member. A member having reached 30 years continuous ASDA membership or having become 65 years of age may apply for retired member status. Retired members will receive all official correspondence, will pay reduced dues as set forth in Article VI and may wear the retired member lapel pin. Retired members may not vote or hold elected office in the association or in any of its chapters. They may not represent themselves professionally as a member of the association unless specifically authorized by the board.

Members who elect to apply for retired member status will not be eligible to participate as a boothholder in any of the shows sponsored by the association or any of its chapters. Retired member status may be withdrawn by action of the board for good cause shown.

D. Life Member. Persons who, as of Jan. 1, 1978, were life members pursuant to the bylaws prior to the adoption of this provision shall be life members as are persons granted such membership purusant to Article IX, Section 1 of these bylaws. Life members shall have all of the rights of members and be entitled to such voting rights so long as they may live (unless such membership shall be withdrawn by a vote of three-fourths of all the board of directors for good cause shown).

No portion of the life member's dues shall be refunded by the association in the event of such withdrawal. Such membership shall be non-transferable.

E. Provisional Membership. Any person that meets the criteria in Section 1 above, paragraph A and C, may apply for provisional membership. Provisional members will be upgraded to regular membership upon fulfilling the two years experience requirement unless in the opinion of the board other action should be taken.

Provisional members' dues will be 20 percent less than regular membership and shall be prorated during any year that upgrade action is taken. A provisional member shall have all the rights and privileges of a regular member except they may not vote nor display the ASDA logo. They may, however, indicate their ASDA provisional member status in advertising and correspondence. ASDA logo, plaque and a lapel pin will be furnished at the time of upgrading to regular status.

F. Subsidiary Membership. Any regular member in good standing may sponsor a member of his or her immediate family (spouse, parent, son, daughter, son-in-law, daughter-in-law) for subsidiary membership provided such family member has attained the age of legal majority in the jurisdiction in which he or she resides.

A subsidiary member will be entitled to all rights and privileges of members except voting rights and will be subject to all responsibilities of membership; however, the annual dues will be one half of the regular dues. A subsidiary member will receive all official correspondence except the newsletter and membership directory.

Applications for subsidiary membership will be processed in the same manner as those for regular membership. In the event a regular member is suspended, all subsidiary memberships under his or her sponsorship shall automatically be suspended. In the event a regular member is expelled, all subsidiary memberships under his or her sponsorship shall automatically be terminated.

A subsidiary member may apply for regular membership and shall be allowed prorated credit for any dues previously paid if application is made within 60 days subsequent to the termination of the sponsoring membership, provided such membership was in good standing on termination date. Failure to apply for regular membership upgrading within this 60-day grace period will result in automatic termination of the affected subsidiary membership.

Section 3. Applications. Applicants for membership shall submit their application on forms prescribed by the membership committee accompanied by the application fee and dues for one (1) year. The application fee shall not be refundable but the dues shall be refunded if the applicant is not accepted.

Section 4. Publication. Names of applicants for membership shall be published in an official publication of the association at least once prior to consideration by the membership committee. Such publication shall be mailed at least thirty (30) days prior to consideration of such applicants by the membership committee, it being intended that the membership of the association have time to comment on any applicant.

Section 5. Approval. The membership committee shall report to the board as follows: All applicants for membership and its recommendations as to each. If the report is accepted by at least five members of the board, the person recommended for membership by the committee shall become a member of the association as of the date of acceptance of the report.

Section 6. Non-acceptance. An applicant whose application for membership is not accepted may re-apply not earlier than one (1) year after the date of the applicant's notification of non-acceptance.

Section 7. Resignation. No member shall be permitted to resign from the association nor shall a member be dropped for non-payment of dues if charges against the member are pending under Article VII. If the board establishes procedures for the determination of complaints against members, no member shall be permitted to resign or be dropped for non-payment of dues while such complaint is unresolved, unless otherwise specifically ordered by the board.

Section 8. Any individual person, upon acceptance to membership, shall register with the association all corporations, partnerships, or other philatelic entities in which he holds a financial or stock interest of substantial nature or in which he holds a position as officer, director, or employee and shall take full responsibility for the obligation of the said entity to meet the same standards of dealing imposed upon him individually by the association and can be disciplined pursuant to the Article VII of the bylaws for the action of such entity.

Section 9. Reinstatement. A previous member having been dropped from the rolls for resignation or non-payment of dues may be automatically reinstated if:

a. Application for reinstatement is made during the same calendar year in which he was dropped from membership; and

b. Forwards with his application dues for the full year plus administrative fee as may be determined by the board of directors; and

c. Has not had charges filed against him as defined in Article VII which remain unresolved.

Section 10. An applicant having been expelled or denied membership for cause may apply for membership or reinstatement in the association if:

A. (1) A period of seven (7) years has elapsed since the completion of any sentence or probation period if such person has been convicted of a crime, and

(2) During said seven (7) year period the applicant has been active in the stamp business, and

(3) Applicant has, in the opinion of the board of directors, conducted his professional stamp and business activities in a manner consistent with the code of ethics and bylaws; or

B. (1) A period of seven (7) years has elapsed since the applicant has been discharged in bankruptcy, and

(2) During said seven (7) year period the applicant has been active in the stamp business, and

(3) Applicant has, in the opinion of the board of directors, conducted his professional stamp and business activities in a manner consistent with the code of ethics and bylaws; or

C. (1) A period of seven (7) years has elapsed since the applicant has settled and resolved all outstanding debts and claims made against him or her, which have not been discharged in bankruptcy, and

(2) During said four (4) year period the applicant has been active in the stamp business, and

(3) Applicant has, in the opinion of the board of directors, conducted his professional stamp and business activities in a manner consistent with the code of ethics and bylaws.

An individual applying for membership or reinstatement under this provision shall also meet all other criteria provided for regular membership in these bylaws.

Article VII

Ethics And Discipline

Section 1. Code of Ethics. The board shall establish a code of ethics for the association, which shall be binding upon all members. The board may amend the code of ethics at any time, provided that no change shall be effective until one (1) month after the amendment has been published in an official publication of the association.

Section 2. Action by Board of Directors. If any member is ruled by the board to have committed any of the acts prescribed in Section 3 of this article, the board may censure, suspend, expel or otherwise discipline the member. Notice of such action may be published in an official publication of this association. The board may establish and amend trade practice rules governing the procedure to be followed in such cases, provided that such rules shall afford the member of a fair hearing and the right to counsel. The board may delegate the conduct of the hearing to a committee of members.

Section 3. Violation. Any member may be subject to censure, suspension, expulsion or other action by the board who alone, or through the member's partners, employees, agents or servants:

(1) Violates the code of ethics or the bylaws;

(2) Fails to pay the member's lawful obligations within a reasonable time;

(3) Fails to answer communications addressed to the member by the association or its duly authorized officers or appointees;

(4) Fails to participate in any arbitration proceeding conducted by the association;

(5) Knowingly makes a false statement to the association or its representatives;

(6) So conducts the member's business affairs as to bring disrepute to the trade or to lessen public confidence in stamp dealers; or

(7) Is convicted or pleads nolo contendere (or the equivalent) to a crime involving moral turpitude under the laws of the jurisdiction in which the member is charged or resides;

Shall be subject to disciplinary action under Section 2 of this article. So long as charges are pending pursuant to subparagraph (7) of this Section 3 and all appeal rights shall not have been exhausted such member may be suspended from membership in the association.

Section 4. Suspension. So long as charges are pending pursuant to subparagraph A (7) of this Section 3 and all appeal rights shall not have been exhausted, such member may be suspended from membership in the association. During any period of suspension, a member shall not be eligible to receive any of the benefits of membership, nor to participate as a member in the affairs of the association.

Section 6. Costs of Complaints. Whenever a member shall have filed or outstanding three or more complaints or inquiries in any twenty-four (24) month period involving matters based upon which disciplinary action could be taken by the association, the board of directors may, in its sole but reasonable determination, assess against said member costs of the association related to the handling of these complaints or inquiries, including but not limited to legal fees, staff time and costs of communication.

Article VIII

Local Chapters

Section 1. Creation. Not less than ten (10) voting members may apply to the board for the establishment of a chapter of the association. The application shall contain the proposed name of the chapter and the geographic area which it proposes to encompass. Upon acceptance by the board, the members may proceed to establish the chapter.

Section 2. Regulation. Each chapter may establish its own bylaws and rules, not inconsistent with these bylaws and any resolution of the board, which shall include the following:

A. Only members of the association shall be members of the chapter.

B. The chapter shall file with the secretary the names and addresses of its officers as elected from time to time.

C. The chapter shall not hold less than three (3) meetings during each calendar year.

D. Copies of the minutes of all chapter meetings shall be sent to the executive officer at the principal offices of the association; and

E. No chapter shall be or hold itself out to be an agent of the association.

Section 3. Suspension or Revocation of Authority. The board may suspend or revoke the authority of any chapter for any cause which would result in like action against an individual member, or if the chapter in the sole discretion of the board of directors of the association becomes inactive.

Section 4. Chapter Shows. Chapters are encouraged to sponsor and support philatelic bourses and exhibitions. The board may by resolution agree to advance initial costs as a loan or guarantee a chapter against losses in the operation of a philatelic event, to the extent specified in its resolution.

Article IX

Dues And Fees

Section 1. Establishment of Dues. There shall be six classes of membership in the organization; to wit: regular, life, honorary, retirement, subsidiary and provisional. For each dues period the board of directors shall establish the annual rate to be paid by all members. Any regular member in good standing may, by paying 12 times the annual dues in one payment, become a life member, subject to the approval of the board and shall thereafter no longer be required to pay dues.

Section 2. Notice. If the annual dues established by the board exceeds the rates for the current period, notice of the new rates shall be published in an official publication not later than Nov. 15.

Section 3. Payment. All dues shall be payable on Jan. 1 for the year beginning on that date for all persons who are members on that date. Dues for new members after Jan. 1 shall be prorated on a quarterly basis to the beginning of the quarter preceding their admission to membership.

Section 4. Failure to Pay. If the dues of any member remain unpaid on March 1, the treasurer shall notify the member of the member's delinquency and assess the member a 10-percent surcharge on the amount due which shall also become a part of the amount due and payable by the member. If the member's dues remain unpaid on April 1, the member's membership shall then terminate and notice of termination shall be published in an official publication.

Section 5. Refunds. No dues shall be refunded to any member whose membership terminates for any reason.

Article X

Contracts, Checks And Deposits

Section 1. Contracts. The board may authorize any officer or officers, agent or agents, in addition to the officers authorized by these bylaws, to enter into any contract or execute and deliver any instrument in the name of and on behalf of the association, and such authority may be general or confirmed to specific instances.

Section 2. Checks, Drafts, etc. All checks, drafts or orders for the payment of money, notes or other evidences of indebtedness issued in the name of the association shall be signed by such officer or officers, agent or agents of the association and in such manner as shall from time to time be determined by resolution of the board. In the absence of such determination, such instruments shall be signed by the treasurer and countersigned by the president, vice president or secretary.

Section 3. Deposits. All funds of the association shall be promptly deposited from time to time to the credit of the association in such banks, trust companies or other depositories as the board may elect.

Article XI

Amendments

Section 1. Method of Proposal of Amendments. The board may propose amendments to these bylaws at any time or such amendments may be proposed by petition of 20 percent of the membership or 200 members thereof, whichever shall be greater, addressed to the board. All such proposed amendments if timely received will be presented by the board to the membership with or without recommendations not later than the next following annual meeting of the association.

Section 2. Publication. The proposed amendment shall be published in an official publication, and shall be accompanied by a ballot whereon voting members may vote to approve or disapprove the amendment.

Section 3. Voting. The inspectors of election shall establish a date, which shall be at least thirty (30) days after the date of publication, for the return of ballots. A simple majority vote of members voting is sufficient to adopt an amendment.

Section 4. Certification of Results. On or after the final date for the return of the ballots, the secretary or the secretary's designee shall tabulate the results, and certify the same to the president.

Section 5. Effective Date. An amendment shall become effective on the date specified in the amendment, if any. If no date is specified, the amendment shall be effective upon the date of certification of adoption which fact shall be included in the publication of the proposed amendment in an official publication.

Article XII

Miscellaneous

Section 1. Definitions. As Used in These Bylaws:

A. "Association" means the American Stamp Dealers' Association, Inc.

B. "Board" means the board of directors of the association.

C. "Official Publication" shall mean the ASDA Bulletin, Newsletter, or any other communication addressed to all of the members of the association.

D. "Qualify" when used with respect to election of officers and directors shall mean such time as the officer or director shall become eligible to serve under applicable law and the bylaws of the association.

E. "Member" unless otherwise stated means an individual natural person admitted to membership in the association pursuant to Article VI of these bylaws.

Section 2. Titles. The titles of articles and sections are used for reference only, and have no substantive effect.

Section 3. Fiscal Year. The fiscal year of the association shall be the calendar year unless otherwise determined by a two-thirds vote of the board.

Section 4. Notice. Any notice required to be given under these bylaws is effective upon deposit in the United States mails, postage prepaid.

Section 5. Audit. The accounts of the association shall be audited not less than annually by a Certified Public Accountant who shall be appointed by the board. A summary of such audit shall be published as soon as practicable after receipt and acceptance of same by the board in an official publication of the association.

Section 6. Quarterly Financial Reports. The treasurer of the association shall cause to be prepared and published in an official publication a summary of financial operations of the association in such form as may be determined by the board of directors, such summaries to be provided on a quarterly basis for all periods other than the year-end period for which an audit has been prepared in accordance with Section 5 of this Article XII.

Section 7. Association Sponsored Shows. No person who is under suspension or who has previously been expelled or denied membership for causes other than insufficient experience may be allowed to act as a dealer's assistant or otherwise appear behind a dealer's booth at any association or chapter sponsored show.

ASDA Code Of Ethics

Membership in the ASDA is a privilege extended to those persons and organizations deemed worthy, and is not a right. Membership may be continued unless the board of directors determines that the conduct of a member has been such that in the best interests of the ASDA, the member should be suspended or his or her membership terminated.

As a guide to all members, this code of ethics has been duly adopted by the board of directors under the authority vested in by the constitution and bylaws of the ASDA.

1. I will support and be subject to the constitution and bylaws of the ASDA and such amendments, resolutions and policies as may be established.

2. I will abide by all federal, state and local laws related to philatelic matters.

3. I will conduct myself so as to bring no discredit to the ASDA, or to diminish the prestige of the membership therein.

4. I will neither buy nor sell philatelic items of which the ownership is in doubt and will promptly report to the proper law enforcement agencies information

on suspected stolen material.

5. I will correct promptly any error I may make in any transaction.

6. I will assist in the prosecution of violations of law pertaining to philatelic matters of which I have knowledge, and will report promptly to the proper law enforcement agencies any violations.

7. I will properly, carefully and honestly grade and describe all merchandise offered for sale by me and indicate any faults, defects, restorations or alterations that may exist, to include indication of canceled to order material.

8. I will immediately refund on any item sold by me where the description was either inaccurate or misleading.

9. I will publish and make available my terms of sale so that all clients have an opportunity to become familiar with them.

10. I will hold intact, pending written acceptance from the seller, all merchandise sent to me for offer, and should the offer be unacceptable, promptly and carefully return it to its proper owner.

11. I will honor any buying prices that I have published within a reasonable period after their publication. Price lists will include a statement as to expiration of offer or give an actual expiration date and explain any limitations.

12. I will make prompt cash refund on all "out of stock" or returned merchandise.

13. I will advertise for sale only those items that are available to me at the time the advertisement is placed.

14. I will provide all consignors of merchandise with a contract stating my legal commitments.

15. I will pay for all material I purchase according to the terms of sale at the time of purchase.

16. I will not sell, produce, nor advertise counterfeit material in any form in violation of law.

17. I will never substitute or alter material submitted to me without the consent of the owner.

18. I will abide by the "terms of sale" and will publish prices realized within a reasonable time after a public auction.

19. I will conduct myself according to accepted standards of morality and courtesy in all philatelic activities not specifically cited in this code.

20. Insofar as possible I will use the ASDA logo in my advertising.

21. If I should be found guilty of unethical or unlawful conduct, the record thereof may be disclosed to other philatelic societies of which I am a member.

22. I will submit any dispute concerning philatelic transactions in which I may become involved to arbitrators mutually agreed upon by the parties.

ASDA Auction Firm Code of Ethics

As a guide to all ASDA members this code of ethics has been duly adopted by the board of directors:

1. I will provide proof of licensing in my principal location as required by my municipal and state regulations. If my local and/or state governments do not require licensing, I must provide a statement indicating this.

2. I will file the terms and conditions of sale as printed in my auction catalog with my application.

3. My terms and/or conditions of sale will provide for the return of misdescribed lots within the time specified therein.

4. My terms of sale will provide the conditions under which the purchaser shall have the right to seek authentication of my descriptions.

5. My auction catalogs will provide a specific time and place that lots to be auctioned may be viewed.

6. I will provide specific dates and starting times for my auctions.

7. People can personally attend my auctions.

8. A printed prices realized will be available (free or for purchase) for each auction I conduct.

9. I will maintain an adequate insurance policy to cover consignments I accept for public auction.

10. I will provide a written consignor's agreement to the consignor. I will provide ASDA with a copy of the form used.

11. The following statement must appear in the auction catalog: "This firm is a subscriber to the ASDA code of

ethics for auction firms."

ASDA Pledge

A member shall be required to subscribe to the following pledge upon joining the American Stamp Dealers' Association, Inc.:

As a member of the American Stamp Dealers' Association, Inc., I recognize my obligation to the public and pledge:

1. To buy and sell at prices commensurate with a reasonable return on my investment and at prevailing market conditions.

2. To give advice to my clientele in philatelic matters to the best of my ability.

3. To refrain from dealing in stolen philatelic and counterfeit material, and to furnish buyers for repaired, regummed, reperforated, restored, reprinted or otherwise altered philatelic material with a complete written statement showing in detail the nature of the changes and alterations in such material.

4. To purchase philatelic material from the public at reasonable prices, with due allowances for my risk and prevailing market conditions; to be truthful in my advertising; to refrain from denigrating my competitors; and to make no false claim to a policy or practice of generally underselling competitors.

Current Officers and Directors

Current officers of the American Stamp Dealers' Association are:

Diane Apfelbaum, president.
Robert Feldman, vice president.
Philip Bansner, treasurer.
Daniel Warren, secretary.
Aubrey Bartlett, director.
Bob Dumaine, director.
Lewis Kaufman, director.
L.W. Martin, Jr., director.
John Menary, director.

The executive officer is Joseph B. Savarese. Inquiries should be directed to American Stamp Dealers' Association, Inc., 3 School St., Glen Cove, N.Y. 11542.

ASDA Committees and Chairmen

Auction Committee
Jacques C. Schiff, Jr.

Bylaws Committee
Larry Martin

Ethics Committee
Lewis Shull and Philip Bansner

Finance Committee
Philip Bansner

Insurance Committee
Robert Feldman

Legal Committee
Christopher M. Houlihan

Membership Committee
Robert Feldman

Show Committee
Daniel Warren

Special Projects Committee
Lewis Kaufman

ASDA Chapters

Current contact persons for the chapters are:

MID-ATLANTIC
James C. Bird,
Box 2765,
Laurel, Md. 20708

NORTHERN CALIFORNIA
Stanley Piller
3351 Grand Ave.
Oakland, Calif. 94610

SOUTHERN CALIFORNIA
James H. Crum
2720 E. Gage Ave.
Huntington Park, Calif. 90255

NEW ENGLAND
Don Tocher
Box 582
Westboro, Mass. 01581

SOUTHERN FLORIDA
Ricardo Del Campo
14 N.E. First Ave.
Miami, Fla. 33132

INTERNATIONAL NORTHWEST
Harold Chevrier
Box 700
Yachats, Ore. 60064

LONG ISLAND
Marilyn Nowak
Box 66 Gravesend Station
Brooklyn, N.Y. 11223

SOUTHWEST CHAPTER
Bob Friedman
2504 W. Park Row
Arlington, Texas 76013

MIDWEST CHAPTER
Don Ebert
Box 807
North Chicago, Ill. 60064

Regional, Foreign Dealers' Associations

United States

Central Atlantic Stamp Dealers Association. The CASDA serves dealers in Pennsylvania, New Jersey, Delaware, Maryland, Washington, D.C., Virginia and West Virginia. Contact Jack Essig, Box 885, Fairfax, Va. 22030.

Florida Stamp Dealers Association. Box 4585, Clearwater, Fla. 33518.

New Jersey Stamp Dealers Association. Box 412, East Brunswick, N.J. 08816.

Professional Coin & Stamp Dealers' Association of Long Island. The association serves the Long Island, N.Y., area and is open to any legitimate stamp dealer with a tax resale number and the sponsorship of two members. Contact Box 354, Lynbrook, N.Y. 11563.

Stamp Dealers Association of Georgia. 133 Carnegie Way NW, Room 203, Atlanta, Ga. 30303.

Texas Stamp Dealers Association. Box 30442, Dallas, Texas 75230. The TSDA has approximately 70 members in Texas and nearby states.

Canada

The Canadian Stamp Dealers' Association is comprised of regular and honorary members. The organization is headed by a staff of four officers, including the president, vice president, secretary and treasurer. Membership in the Canadian organization is open to qualified dealers based in other countries. Additional information is available from any of the CSDA officials.

Officers

President: Erling S.J. van Dam, Box 300, Bridgenorth, Ontario K0L 1H0.

Vice president: Gary J. Lyon, Box 450, Bathurst, New Brunswick E2A 3Z4.

Secretary: Alan G. Burrows, Box 606, Station K, Toronto, Ontario M4P 2H1.

Treasurer: Russell Lott, Box 41, Guelph, Ontario N1H 6J6.

CSDA Code Of Ethics:

1. At all times to conduct myself in a businesslike and professional manner.

2. To advise my clients in philatelic matters to the very best of my ability and in questions of doubt to consult with other respected members of the association.

3. Not to sell, knowingly, repaired, improved, or in any way altered stamps as sound, or for anything else than what they are.

4. To refrain from misleading advertisements and statements.

5. To refrain from dealing in stolen material.

6. To honor and fulfill my contracts and undertakings.

7. To cooperate in all matters which tend to the betterment of the Canadian Stamp Dealers' Association and philately in general.

Foreign Organizations

Argentina: Sociedad de Comerciantes Filatelicos de la Republica Argentina (SOCOFIRA), Casilla de Correo Central 3296, Buenos Aires, Argentina.

Australia: Australasian Stamp Dealers Association (ASDA), G.P.O. Box 5378, Melbourne, Victoria 3001, Australia.

Austria: Oesterreichischer Briefmarkenhandler-Verband, Mariahilferstrasse 105, A-1060 Wien, Austria.

Belgium: Chambre Professionnelle Belge des Negociants en Timbres-Poste (CPBNTP), Galerie du Centre, Bureau 343, B-1000 Bruxelles, Belgium.

Brazil: Associacao Brasileria dos Comerciantes Filatelicos (ABCF), Caixa Postal 3577, 01051 Sao Paulo, Brazil.

Denmark: Danmarks Frimaerkenhandlerforening, Fuglebakkevej 9, DK-2000 Kobenhavn F, Denmark.

Finland: Suomen Postimerkkikauppiaiden Litto Ry., Fredrikinkatu 51-53, 00100 Helsinki, Finland.

France: Chambre Syndicale Francaise des Negociants et Experts en Philatelie (CNEP), 4 Rue Drouot, F-75009 Paris, France.

Germany: Bundesverband des Deutschen Briefmarkenhandels A.P.H.V. e.V., Geibelstrasse 4, D-5000 Koln 41 (Lindenthal), West Germany.

Great Britain: Philatelic Traders Society Ltd. 27 John Adam St., London WC2N 6HZ, England.

Greece: Greek Stamp Dealers' Association, 7 Stadiou Street, Athens 105 62, Greece.

India: India Stamp Dealers' Association (ISDA), 19 Chandi Chowk St., Calcutta 700 072, India.

Ireland: Irish Philatelic Traders' Association (IPTA), 102 Leinster Road, Dublin 6, Ireland.

Israel: Israel Stamp Dealers' Association (ISDA), Box 4944, Tel-Aviv 61040, Israel.

Italy: Federazione Nazionale Commercianti di Filatelici Italiani (FNCFI), c/o Dr. Camillo Pescatori, Piazza Mignanelli 3, I-00187 Rome, Italy.

Japan: Japan Stamp Dealers' Association (JSDA), Central Post Office 1003, Tokyo, Japan.

Netherlands: Nederlandsche Vereeniging van Postzegelhandelaren (NVPH), Weteringkade 45, NL-2515 AL Den Haag, Netherlands.

New Zealand: New Zealand Stamp Dealers' Association Inc., Box 4390, Auckland, New Zealand.

Norway: Norsk Frimerkenhandler Forening (NFHF), Box 65, N-5032 Minde, Norway.

Spain: Asociacion Nacional de Emprasarios de Filatelia de Espana (ANFIL), Calle Mayor No. 18, 2 Derecha, Madrid 28013, Spain.

South Africa: South African Philatelic Dealers' Association (SAPDA), Box 31193, Braamfontein 2017, Republic of South Africa.

Sweden: Sveriges Frimarkshand-arforbund, Box 30077, S-10425 Stockholm, Sweden.

Switzerland: Schweizerischer Briefmarkenhandlerverband/Association Suisse des Negociants en Timbres-Poste (SBHV/ASNP), Gallustrasse 22, CH-9000 St. Gallen, Switzerland.

Turkey: Pul Tuccarlari Dernegi (PTD), P.K. 129, Beyoglu - Istanbul, Turkey.

Venezuela: Asociacion de Comerciantes de Filatelia y Numismatica de Venezuela (ACOFINUVEN), Apartado de Correos 60581, Caracas 1060-A, Venezuela.

International

International Federation of Stamp Dealers' Associations. The groundwork for IFSDA was laid in London, England, in 1950 during the first postwar international stamp show. Representatives of stamp dealers' associations from Belgium, Denmark, the United States, France, Great Britain, the Netherlands and Switzerland felt that the time had come to unify and coordinate on a worldwide level the efforts that had been undertaken for several decades in their individual countries.

Committee meetings were held on May 8, 1950, Grosvenor House, London; on May 29, 1951, Waldorf Hotel, London; and on April 28, 1952, in the Hotel Metropole, Monte Carlo. The first General Assembly was held in Utrecht, Holland, on July 2, 1952. The federation currently comprises 27 national societies.

The objects of the federation are:

(a) To promote and maintain a high standard of professional integrity among philatelic dealers throughout the world.

(b) To promote the exchange among the member organizations of information and literature likely to be of service to the philatelic trade.

(c) To endeavor in all ways to reduce the barriers in international philatelic trade.

(d) To promote the exchange of information regarding stolen, forged, faked and repaired stamps.

(e) To take any action which may be thought to be fit to prevent or reduce the sale of stamps which, in the opinion of the federation, were not issued under satisfactory circumstances.

(f) To take any action which may be thought to be fit against new issues for speculative purposes or without any postal justification.

(g) To take any action which, in the opinion of the federation, would promote the interests of stamp dealers in any part of the world.

(h) To cooperate with the International Philatelic Federation or any other national or international organization for the attainment of any of the above objectives.

(i) To provide for the use of all the member organizations of the federation the necessary information and material to carry out the objectives of the federation. To endeavor to have a handbook published whenever it be necessary, which should contain the names and addresses of the members of all national organizations.

(j) To directly participate and cooperate in international exhibitions, and be responsible for the integrity and honesty of the commercial standholders. For this, IFSDA will charge a fee.

(k) To cooperate against robbery and terrorism when directed against the philatelic trade.

Membership

Membership of the IFSDA shall be confined to national trade organizations, and there will be only one member organization per country.

Any national organization with more than 30 members may become affiliated with IFSDA. Those national associations with less than 30 members may apply for affiliation.

State organizations can also be admitted. The same right may be given to postal administrations or their official representatives, provided that in the country in question there does not exist a trade society that is a member of IFSDA.

A dealer can join a foreign trade society only if he is a member of the trade society in the country where he lives. If there is no trade society in that country, he is free to join any trade society of his choice.

The general assembly shall normally meet every year, if possible, in a city where an international stamp exhibition or any other international philatelic function is being held. Extraordinary general assemblies may also be convened on request of one-third of the member organizations of the federation.

Each member organization of the federation may send a delegation to the general assembly. Organizations with up to 200 members will have two votes in the assembly and two additional votes for each additional 200 members. One country will not have more than six votes.

The general assembly may at every general assembly or extraordinary general assembly elect an honorary president and honorary vice presidents. It shall elect a chairman, three vice chairmen, a treasurer and nine members for two years, thus totaling 14 members for the constitution of an executive committee, and appoint an international firm of accountants as auditors. All voting shall be in writing and by secret ballot.

Official languages of the federation will be: English, German, French and Spanish.

Resolutions involving financial subscriptions and obligations of the member associations shall require a two-thirds majority vote of those present or represented, which should be 50 percent or more of all the members of IFSDA (individuals or organizations). All other business requires a simple majority of the members present or represented.

In the event of a tie, the chairman or vice chairman of the meeting may exercise a casting vote.

Voting by proxy shall be allowed, provided proxies are authorized in writing. Each national association can be the bearer of only one proxy vote.

Requests for interventions or suggestions to the general assembly or extraordinary general assembly have to be in the hands of the secretariat six weeks before the meetings.

Obligations of the national trade societies are:

(a) To inform IFSDA on their activities (bourses, exhibitions) before December of the preceding year.

(b) To be up to date with payment of subscriptions.

(c) To have prepared every year the membership list before Feb. 28; it is recommended that an equal system be used by all trade societies. Basic themes recommended for their elaboration:

1. Separate national members from foreign ones, and;
2. Place members in alphabetical order.

The national trade societies will ensure that their members comply with normal ethical standards and will act as impartial arbitrators in cases of a dispute among the members of their trade societies.

The IFSDA Secretariat may be contacted at 27 John Adam St., London WC2N 6HZ, England.

Vice president of honor in the United States is Kurt Weishaupt, Box 37, Flushing, N.Y. 11358. The American Stamp Dealers' Association is the U.S. member society of IFSDA.

How to Buy and Sell Stamps

Buying and selling are activities at the very heart of stamp collecting.

Much of the pleasure of the hobby is in the thrill of the chase — the pursuit of desirable philatelic material. In fact, many collectors find that they spend more hours gazing longingly at a single stamp they desire in a price list or an auction catalog than at all the hundreds they already have in their albums.

While thoughtful relatives, swaps with fellow collectors and the daily mail are sources of free stamps or covers that should not be overlooked, the needs of the developing stamp collector usually soon outstrip such no-cost sources. Collectors find themselves confronted with a wide variety of unfamiliar methods to use in building their collections, often with little idea of the best way to proceed.

This chapter attempts to meet that need. Read it carefully. Making the right choices early on can save you time, frustration and expense.

Begin by trying to form a clear idea of what kind of material you want to acquire and what kind of realistic budget you have available for your collecting interests.

Have you been collecting for years, or are you just starting out? Do you collect a fairly narrow range of specialized material or a broad spectrum of stamps from around the world? Is your album fresh from the printer and awaiting its first stamps or all filled except for those difficult final 100 spaces?

The answers to all these questions will help you choose the methods of buying and selling stamps that are likely to work best for you.

As to the question of which method of buying stamps is best, the answer is: it depends. All have merits and drawbacks, and we will examine both.

The fact is that a young boy with a dime to spend on a colorful new commemorative and the mature specialist contemplating buying an important old rarity are both stamp collectors. Each can find the right source for the stamp he seeks. So can you.

Above all, don't be afraid to experiment, to try new avenues in adding to your album. As broad as philately has become today, even the very best dealers cannot supply every collector's requirements. It can be well worth the effort to explore new sources of material.

As your hobby develops, you are likely to find that your needs change. Stamp sources ideal for the beginner often cannot meet the needs of more advanced collectors.

If you have philatelic friends or belong to a local stamp club, don't be shy when it comes to asking for suggestions, ideas and recommendations. Ask a good dealer you've patronized before; if he can't supply what you need, he often can and will suggest the name of someone who can.

The Post Office

The first and most obvious place to get stamps is, of course, the post office. Current stamps may be acquired straight from the source — the postal administration that issues them — not only in the United States and Canada but around the world.

Many U.S. post offices operate philatelic sales windows or postiques specifically to serve the needs of collectors. Many also operate sales booths at a host of stamp shows large and small around the country each year.

For added convenience, the U.S. Postal Service publishes a bimonthly *Philatelic Catalog*, listing all items currently in stock for retail sale to collectors. This is generally a wider range of material than is available even at most major post offices.

Items for sale in the catalog include all current issues from full coil rolls and complete panes down to single stamps. The catalog also offers position pieces such as plate blocks and coil strips, current postal stationery items, Official stamps and stationery unavailable at most post offices. It also offers migratory bird hunting and conservation stamps.

In addition, the catalog offers many items designed just for collectors. These include prepackaged sets of stamps from recent years, souvenir and maximum cards, stamp-collecting kits, specialty folders, albums, posters and other philatelic items. USPS even has its own basic stamp catalog, the color-illustrated *Postal Service Guide to U.S. Stamps*.

Orders may be prepaid by check, prior deposit or major credit cards. There is a modest charge for service, shipping and handling.

All of these items, including subscriptions to the *Philatelic Catalog*, are available from the U.S. Postal Service, Philatelic Sales Division, Washington, D.C. 20265-9997.

The Canadian postal administration, Canada Post, publishes a similar *National Philatelic Centre Product Catalogue*, also offering a broad range of material for collectors. Information and copies are available from the National Philatelic Centre, Canada Post Corporation, Antigonish, Nova Scotia, Canada B2G 2R8.

The United States and Canada both also maintain a standing-order service by which new issues will be sent to you directly after they are produced in any of a number of formats. Billing for the stamps is applied against a credit card or a previous deposit to your own philatelic account.

In 1988, USPS expanded its standing-order service to include single stamps, blocks of four, coil strips, booklets, plate number strips from panes or complete panes of commemorative, definitive, airmail and Official stamps.

In addition, U.S. Commemorative Stamp Club, Souvenir Page and Commemorative Panel subscriptions may also be acquired on a standing-order basis. Payment for these items is deducted from an advance-deposit account, with amounts determined in advance by the type and quantity of stamps desired. There are no service, shipping or handling charges for this service.

Collectors may obtain a free USPS *Standing Order Catalog* from the Standing Order Service, Philatelic Sales Division, Washington, D.C. 20265-9974.

Canada Post offers its own comparable Collectors' Subscription Service, which is also detailed in the *National Philatelic Centre Product Catalogue* previously mentioned.

Most other postal administrations around the world offer a version of this service for their own stamps, with varying degrees of sophistication and efficiency. For details, consult the comprehensive listing of worldwide postal administrations elsewhere in this almanac.

The advantages of these services, in efficiency, cost and insuring that you receive new issues as they are produced, are self-evident.

Rightly or wrongly, state-run philatelic services have been criticized for the proliferation of purpose-crafted collectibles designed purely to boost their own profits. Many of these popular and colorful souvenir items are peripheral to the hobby and successfully distract collectors from the traditional goal of building as complete a stamp collection as possible.

The only obvious disadvantage of postal administrations for stamp collectors is that while they can do a very good job in supplying the latest stamps, and may even stock and sell selected items from immediately preceding years, they are of no help whatever in filling the older spaces in an album. They can supply only a tiny fraction of the stamps most collectors seek.

Mixtures and Stamp Exchanges

One of the first sources many stamp collectors turn to are other stamp collectors, and a local stamp club can be a wonderful source of new material for your album. It is in the nature of the hobby that all collectors acquire duplicates, and trading or exchanging spare material for stamps you need just makes good sense. Building and maintaining a worthwhile stock of duplicates as your collection grows can thus be rewarding in more ways than one.

Stamp mixtures are the unrefined ore of the stamp hobby and a prime source of duplicates. Generalizing about mixtures is difficult due to their wide variety and value, but most mixtures consist of used stamps taken from incoming mail.

The stamps in mixtures may still be on paper from their original envelopes or they may be off paper — that is, previously soaked loose. Most are categorized, graded or described for the convenience of collectors: one pound of recent U.S. definitives including multiples and coils, for example, or four ounces of French semipostals off paper.

Mixtures build collections both in giving you attractive used copies of stamps you do not have and as a rich source of duplicates you can swap for other stamps you need. Mixtures are available in a wide range of prices, and many are quite inexpensive.

The disadvantages of mixtures are inherent in their limitations. If you like mint stamps or need stamps from the 1920s, you'll find little here. And though it may be relatively inexpensive, a pound of worldwide stamps on paper takes a lot of time to soak, examine, sort and organize, though many collectors enjoy the work.

It is also fair to say that some mixtures are no bargain at any price. Deep duplication in common definitives and heavily canceled or faulty copies of better stamps are problems that most of those who buy mixtures have encountered.

Collectors who do develop a good stock of duplicates frequently find a useful outlet for them in trading with their fellow collectors. One way to do this is through stamp exchanges.

A stamp exchange is basically a formalized arrangement in which one grouping of stamps is exchanged for another: 350 used U.S. commemoratives for five 3¢ plate blocks, for example, or $25 worth of Scott catalog-valued worldwide stamps for a U.S. coil plate number strip of five. These are examples of individual exchange offers such as those advertised in *Linn's*.

Other than such one-to-one offers, there are also exchange clubs or networks in which larger numbers of collectors pick and choose among one another's offers. Such exchanges generally have a common or shared basis of exchange, such as any mint or used stamp with a catalog value of 25¢ or more.

These can be a great way to trade duplicates, and by adding attractive stamps to the exchange you should attract an equally interesting selection of material from other participants.

Every exchange is different, and each has its own rules and guidelines. Each can supply you with details on how it operates.

A potential disadvantage of a stamp exchange is that, human nature being what it is, some members in some exchanges can try to take advantage of others. If your used foreign high-value pictorials cataloging 50¢ to $1.75 each bring you a like number of poorly centered, overcanceled common definitives cataloging exactly 25¢ apiece, demand an explanation. You may want to consider taking your trade elsewhere; there are many exchange networks, and those that rip off their members seldom last very long.

The Local Stamp Dealer

Until the early 1980s, most North American cities and towns and even a good many neighborhoods had a local retail stamp dealer. Though many such local dealers remain in business, especially in larger population centers, their heyday has now largely passed.

Should you be fortunate enough to have such a stamp dealer near you, he can be a tremendous asset, especially in the beginning and intermediate stages of stamp collecting.

An informed dealer can provide the basic tools of the hobby at fair prices, answer questions, give sound advice and can help build your collection — if you let him know what you are looking for.

Unlike hobby shops that carry a few packets of stamps between plastic models and macrame kits, retail-based storefront stamp dealers generally travel fairly widely and acquire fresh philatelic stock from a broad range of sources. If you make such a dealer aware that you are looking for early Central American stamps or U.S. first-day covers of the 1930s, he can get the word out to his contacts, who in turn go to their contacts for the material.

The benefit for you is your ability to buy items for your collection from a much greater range of sources than you could probably find for yourself. You get convenience, ease and selection, and the local dealer generally adds a modest mark-up to his material as the price of providing you with these services.

For the casual hobbyist interested in filling out a basic collection, a good working relationship with a friendly and knowledgeable local dealer can be the perfect match and a real complement to his enjoyment of the hobby.

Because of the limited size of the local dealer's clientele and his face-to-face familiarity with your wants and needs, he can offer you a level of personalized service unobtainable anywhere else in the hobby.

The disadvantages of the local dealer also arise from the size of his business. Because of the immense postwar growth in value of older stamps and the enormous number and expense of the new issues constantly being produced, the average small dealer can no longer afford to maintain a stock of stamps comparable in depth or breadth to those of dealers of a generation ago.

Naturally enough, most of today's storefront stamp dealers stock what the majority of their customers ask for most. Typically, U.S. stamps priced at under $25 comprise most of their stock, followed in rapidly descending order by Canadian, British Commonwealth and a smattering of other foreign issues.

If you develop a special interest in collecting Swedish stamps, or become serious about filling the more expensive spaces even in a U.S. collection, you may find little in a local dealer's stock to interest you.

Stamp Shows and Bourses

What a single dealer cannot supply, several dealers often can. That is the principle behind the stamp show or bourse.

A bourse is an event at which a number of dealers come together to sell their wares. A stamp show, generally presented by a stamp club, usually also holds a bourse in addition to offering displays of stamps and other hobby-related activities.

Shows and bourses offer the collector an opportunity to browse through the stocks of a number of dealers in search of the stamps or covers they desire. Selection is greater, and the opportunity to comparison shop can save you money.

Bourses also can help you make contact with dealers familiar with your area of interest whom you would otherwise never meet. Especially in towns or cities with few or no local dealers, bourses and shows are an excellent opportunity not only to buy stamps but to sell them as well, taking the best deal you can make among a number of knowledgeable dealers.

Stamp shows and bourses can be a thoroughly enjoyable way to make significant additions to your stamp collection and cultivate new sources of supply.

The disadvantages of the show or bourse are that, like dealers, such events are mainly limited to larger population centers. Smaller communities and less populous regions may have one or two shows or bourses each year in a nearby city. However, most collectors find limiting their buying to a day or two annually an unsatisfactory arrangement.

Such collectors want more opportunities to add to their albums. The answer, for most of them, is as near as the local post office.

Most of the stamps that change hands each year in North America are bought and sold by mail. The post office gives collectors indirect access to thousands of potential stamp sources, which may be grouped in several different categories.

Sales Circuits

One of the principal member benefits of some national stamp organizations, such as the American Philatelic Society, are its sales circuits. These consist of a series of small books containing stamps, covers or other philatelic material from a category or categories chosen by you. The contents of each book — usually another collector's duplicates — are priced for sale.

You simply choose what you want, marking your choices in the circuit book, and forward the sales circuit on to the next name after yours on the list that is provided. Payment, usually with a small insurance fee, is made back to the society. The society in turn pays the original owner of the stamps.

The APS offers more than 150 different

categories of circuits, covering a broad range of different kinds of U.S. material, as well as individual countries and topics from around the world.

More than 13,000 APS members take advantage of sales circuits through the APS Sales Division, both as buyers and sellers. Annual circuit-book sales approach $2 million. While the APS clearly is the leading national philatelic society in sales circuits, many smaller societies offer similar sales-circuit services to their members.

Sales circuits offer the convenience of allowing you to examine stamps in your own home, with no obligation of any kind. You see the material before you pay for it and choose only the items you want. Many collectors speak with pride of some of the material purchased from sales circuits, proving that one man's duplicate is another man's gem.

Sales circuits also often include desirable stamps of very low price that no commercial dealer could afford to offer because of the slim profit margin.

One disadvantage of sales circuits is the sometimes erratic quality and caliber of material offered and the prices it is offered at.

Those who put together sales circuit books are free to price their stamps as they see fit, within reason. Some offer great bargains, while others overprice fairly common items. Some collectors unfortunately use circuit books as a dumping ground for damaged and unattractive spacefillers of nominally high catalog value but little real worth.

Mainly through inexperience, collectors also often overlook faults in their material, so it is wise to scrutinize the stamps you select carefully before you buy.

In attempting to be fair to everyone, sales circuits are sent out in such a way that the individual who gets first choice from one will be the last on the list to receive the next. New subscribers begin at the bottom of the list.

In time, this rotating order gives each circuit subscriber first crack at the books. After a book has gone to eight to 10 collectors, it is generally taken out of service and returned to its owner.

While this system is faultlessly fair, the last collector to receive the circuit is apt to find that the best circuit books have been picked clean, and that little of the material that remains is of interest.

Approval Services

The commercial counterpart of the sales circuit is the approval service. It is one of the oldest ways of buying stamps and remains one of the most popular as well.

Approvals are shipments of stamps or covers that are sent to you "on approval" — pending your selection and purchase of the ones you want.

Some approval dealers send a variety of material selected according to the general area of interest you specify, such as U.S. commemoratives prior to World War II or mint Canadian stamps. You look them over, make your selection, and return the stamps you don't want along with payment for those you do to the approval dealer.

For collectors who already have a good start on filling their album, many approval dealers have a second method.

You send them a want list indicating specific Scott catalog numbers of stamps from a given country and the condition (mint or used) in which they are desired. The dealer then sends you a priced selection of the stamps on that list, from which to make your choices.

Approval dealers of either method will often require your complete name, address and telephone number, along with membership numbers of any stamp collecting organizations to which you belong and the name and address of one or more business with which you have had successful dealings.

While this may seem like a lot of bother, bear in mind that approval dealers regularly entrust people they don't know on the other side of the country with thousands of dollars worth of their personal property. It would be foolhardy of them not to require some information about their clients.

Always indicate an approximate dollar value limit when requesting approvals. There is no need to be coy, since dealers recognize that all collectors have financial limitations, whether the limit is $10 or $1,000. If you can only afford to purchase

$5 to $10 worth of stamps per shipment, most approval dealers do not mind, but they would rather not tie up $250 worth of stamps in a shipment, most of which you cannot afford.

Handle any approvals you receive with care, packaging them securely and returning them promptly with payment as soon as you can after you receive them. Respect the deadline dates many dealers indicate on their approval invoices, and find out from the dealer what insurance, if any, is provided on his shipments.

The advantages of approvals are the same as those of the sales circuit, often in addition to the benefits of dealing with a professional stamp dealer. A good approval dealer who learns your tastes and requirements can be a powerful ally in building a good collection.

Approvals sent according to your specified budget limitations and your want list refine this advantage. You receive only those stamps you are looking for, in amounts that should not put a strain on your finances.

As a general rule, stamps purchased on approval tend to be somewhat more expensive than those available from some other sources.

Price Lists

One of the broadest categories from which stamps may be purchased are retail price lists, both those prepared by individual dealers and those advertised in the philatelic press.

Larger display advertisements in weekly stamp publications such as *Linn's* often consist of lists of stamps by Scott catalog number, a symbol or symbols specifying condition and a retail price. Some specialist dealers will use foreign catalog numbers in addition to or instead of Scott catalog numbers.

At the same time, many dealers place small classified advertisements in the back pages of the paper offering price lists. These may be similar to those mentioned, or offer a wide range of intriguing items up to entire intact collections. Prices can vary from a nickel up to several thousand dollars.

It is highly recommended, especially for the newcomer in the hobby, that you take the time to scrutinize published price lists carefully. Clip the ones that you see in print, and request as many of those that are offered as you can. By familiarizing yourself with these lists, you can develop a good sense of the current range of selling prices for the stamps you want to buy.

Purchases from price lists are a popular way of buying stamps, and are hard to top in terms of filling tough spaces in your album. Many good bargains are listed for those who take the time and trouble to ferret them out. In principle, you simply choose the item or items you want from the price list and send your check in.

The charge will include the costs of postage, insurance and handling, unless otherwise specified. If you pay by check, be sure to allow enough time for your check to clear and for the shipment to reach you.

In practice, as virtually all price lists point out, quantities are limited. This is obviously true of one-of-a-kind collections and better or scarcer stamps of which the dealer is likely to have only a single copy.

Many other readers and collectors see the same price list you do, and you should order promptly to avoid the disappointment of discovering that the stamp you wanted has already been sold. You can sometimes call by phone to confirm that a given item is still available, and dealers who know you will sometimes hold onto a given item pending the arrival of your check and order.

Another disadvantage of price lists is that you do not have the opportunity to examine the material before you pay for it. A prompt return of a stamp you decide you don't want will get your money refunded, but it is inconvenient and time-consuming for both parties.

Collectors must also take care to be very literal-minded in using price lists effectively. A stamp described as "fine, with one short perforation" will not magically become a very-fine stamp with all perforations intact when it gets to your door.

Disappointment inevitably results when the stamp that comes in the mail doesn't match the mental picture formed by the collector when he wrote out his check. However, the least expensive copy of a given stamp advertised anywhere may not be the stamp for you nor the best deal for your money.

Finding a dealer whose price lists offer you what you want at a price you are willing to pay can take time, but is generally well worth it. Most such dealers are quite consistent in their descriptions and in the quality of the stamps they offer, which means that you can send them repeat orders with confidence.

Auctions and Mail Bid Sales

Many stamp collectors are unaccountably reluctant to take part in mail bid sales or stamp auctions. This feeling may arise out of the misconception that these are games with difficult rules that only a chosen few can master.

In reality, nothing is further from the truth. In fact, a good many of those who get their feet wet as skeptical first-time bidders eventually go on to make the most of their philatelic purchases in this manner.

In both auctions and mail bid sales, stamps and covers are sold to the highest bidder at one bid above the level of the second-highest bid. While the majority of the world's great rarities are sold by bidding, so are many of the affordable single stamps and sets that most collectors want and need.

The difference between mail bid sales and auctions is that you or someone acting on your behalf can bid in person at an auction. The comparison of mailed bids received by a given deadline determines who wins a given lot in a mail bid sale.

Auctions also generally offer the opportunity for those who attend to view the material they intend to bid on, which is seldom available to mail bid sale patrons.

In fact, however, the overwhelming majority of lots offered in both public stamp auctions and mail bid sales are sold to individuals who are not in attendance when the sale is held. The tool that makes this possible is the mail sale or auction catalog.

How to Use the Catalog

There are four important parts of such a catalog. The most important of these is the listing of terms and conditions, a precise and detailed set of rules under which the sale is conducted.

Most of the questions that keep inexperienced collectors from bidding are answered in these terms and conditions. They specify the limitations, rights and responsibilities of all the parties involved in the sale.

Typically included in the terms and conditions is information about the buyer's commission, reserve prices, use of auction agents, payment procedures for successful bidders, arrangements for inspecting the material in person or by mail, resolution of disputes arising over the descriptions of items in the sale, procedures for expertizing items offered in the sale and many other important details.

Reading and understanding the terms and conditions is absolutely indispensable to making the most of a public auction or mail sale. Since these terms and conditions will vary from firm to firm, it pays always to read them in detail for each sale you take part in. This is especially true of foreign auctions, where the rules may be radically different.

Reputable public auction and mail bid sale firms are more than happy to answer any questions you may have that are not covered in the terms and conditions.

The second part of most mail sale and public auction catalogs consists of specifications, which can really be considered as an extention of the terms and conditions. The precise philatelic meaning of the abbreviations used in describing stamps and covers is explained, as are the firm's bidding increments.

Bidding increments are the steps in bidding. For example, if a lot opens with a bid of $30, it may proceed in $2 increments to $50. In the same sale, a lot where the bidding begins at $300 will proceed in $25 steps to $750, and in $50 increments thereafter. This is important information because bids that do not conform to this system are always rounded down to the nearest correct interval, making it less likely that they will be successful.

The third part of most catalogs is the

bid sheet. Read yours carefully. Some offer additional services you may wish to take advantage of. One of these offered by some firms is a limit service that allows you to specify a ceiling for your expenditures in the sale. For example, such a service allows you to bid on $150 worth of various lots while specifying that your total purchases in the sale will not exceed $100.

Note also that your bid sheet requires your signature to a statement that you have read the terms and conditions of the sale as specified and place your bids in acceptance of them. An unsigned bid sheet is invalid. A signed one is a contract to buy the lots indicated as described at or below the prices you specify and in keeping with the rules of the firm.

If you do choose to bid by mail, print neatly and clearly on the bid sheet. Be sure to double check your bid sheet carefully before you send it, including the lot numbers as well as the bids. Many people have won items they never wanted by transposing two digits on a bid sheet, and the responsibility for such errors is entirely yours. It may be wise to keep a photocopy of your bid sheet for future reference.

Also, be careful not to bid on too many lots in a sale just because you only expect to win a few of them. Many collectors have been philatelically pleased and financially horrified to discover that all $500 of their bids succeeded when they only expected to win $75 worth of stamps!

Finally there are the actual mail bid sale or public auction listings. These may consist of anything from a catalog number augmented by a few symbols and abbreviations up to a lengthy paragraph of description complete with a color enlargement of the stamp or cover.

The description for most lots falls somewhere between these extremes. Due to the high costs of photography, printing and mailing, illustrations of lots in most sales are confined to the more valuable and unusual items, including the depiction of only the most valuable stamp to illustrate a set. Many public auctions will furnish copies of a lot that is not illustrated in the catalog for the price of photocopying and postage.

A description usually concludes with either the current catalog value of the item offered or an estimate of its value according to the auctioneer.

How to Bid

Many first-time bidders are understandably unsure of how much to bid. They are intimidated by the prospect of bidding too much or too little. But another tool is available to assist the collector in this regard — auction prices realized.

Prices realized consist of a printed list of the lots by number and the prices that were paid for them in previous sales. Under the American Stamp Dealers' Association's auction code of ethics (which appears with the information on ASDA elsewhere in this almanac), all ASDA-sanctioned public auctions must provide prices realized, though some do so at additional cost to the customer.

Others include them for free bound into subsequent auction catalogs. Even a few mail bid sales publish lists of prices from prior sales, though this remains the exception rather than the rule.

Prices realized give the collector a benchmark by which to judge his probable chances of success in purchasing a given stamp at a given price in a public auction.

For example, imagine that you are planning to bid for an unused fine-to-very-fine copy of the $3 Columbian commemorative, Scott 243. Looking through the prices realized for one auction firm, you discover that it recently sold two such copies for $650 and $675, respectively. Another firm sold a fine-to-very-fine copy for $725, and a very-fine copy for $900. Still another auction gallery sold a very-fine copy for $1,150.

You now have not only a basis on which to plan your bid, but perhaps an indication of which firm you would like to bid with. (You also have a fairly telling indication of how exceptional centering can boost the price of a stamp.) You now know that a bid of $600 is unlikely to be successful for the stamp you desire, but that you should probably not have to spend more than about $725, either. By referring to current published retail price lists mentioned previously, you should also be able to find one or more retail prices for the $3 Columbian. There is little point in bidding more than that retail price for a stamp of comparable quality.

Because of the high cost of production and postage, many North American public auction firms now charge a nominal subscription price for their auction catalogs and prices realized. Generally this fee amounts to little more than the cost of postage. Others still offer their catalogs and prices realized for free, or offer sample copies in advertisements in the philatelic press.

It is well worthwhile subscribing to auction catalogs and prices realized for one or more firms, provided you take the time to study the results and use them to guide your bidding.

Of course, no bid is guaranteed. A fine-to-very-fine $3 Columbian may sell for $575 next month and $850 the month after that. The point is that by studying a range of prices drawn from different sources, and by adding new information as you receive it, you can build an accurate picture of what a winning bid should be. When you do finally get that stamp, you'll get it at a price you know to be fair.

That is one of the advantages offered by a public auction. Relatively few price lists, fewer dealers and virtually no circuit books have $3 Columbians. It is a valuable stamp, and a dealer can't afford to have his money tied up owning a copy for a year in hopes that a buyer for it will send in a want list or walk into his store. Even if he does have a copy, it may not be the stamp you want.

Yet 100 or more copies of this and other comparably valuable stamps trade hands in public auctions and mail bid sales each month, giving you the opportunity to pick and choose one you like and bid at a level that suits you. If your bid is successful, you have your stamp; if not, there's always another auction next month, giving you an opportunity to readjust your bid should you wish to do so.

Most public auctions and a good many mail bid sales can afford to offer as many as several thousand lots of valuable material because, unlike a conventional stamp dealer, they may not own all or even much of what they are selling. Rather, they are acting as sales agents on behalf of consignors, the individuals — often collectors like yourself — to whom the material actually belongs.

For the service of offering his stamps or covers, the auctioneer charges the consignor a commission of 10 percent to 20 percent of whatever the final bid may be. In addition, most public auctions charge a buyer's commission of 10 percent to 15 percent.

Take the public sale of a stamp for which $200 is the so-called hammer price — the final high bid when the auctioneer's gavel falls. The auctioneer might receive a 20-percent seller's commission ($40) plus a 10-percent buyer's commission ($20), thereby making a total of $60 on the sale. The buyer's $20 comission is added onto his bid, his final price being $220 plus any additional sales tax or postage and handling fees.

Most mail bid sales, by comparison, have no buyer's commission. Of those that accept consignments — and many do not — seller's commissions are sometimes lower than for public auction consignments.

However, most mail bid sales predominantly offer stamps and covers owned by the firm conducting the sale; many do so exclusively. Their profit is the difference between what they paid for a given item and what the bidder pays for it. The same $200 stamp purchased from a mail bid sale instead of a public auction thus saves you $20 in commission fees. You pay only the $200 you originally bid if you are the winning bidder. An additional benefit to mail bid sales is that, with lower overhead and often less lavish catalogs, they can afford to offer stamps and covers worth only $10 to $50, which most auction firms would offer only in large mixed lots.

As mentioned previously, most lots in public auctions sell to bidders who are not in attendance through the use of bid sheets. All bids received by mail are matched up with their corresponding lots to furnish what is referred to as the auction book — a list of bidders and the bids at which each lot in a sale will begin.

Returning to the example of the $3 Columbian, imagine that an auctioneer receives three bids for a copy of this stamp in his next public sale: one for $550, one for $600 and your bid of $725.

The $550 bid is discarded; it is lower than the second-highest bid, and will therefore play no role in this sale (nor would any other bids under $600.) With bidding in increments of $25 at this level, as things stand the stamp will be sold to you for $625 — one step above the second-highest bid.

On the day of the sale, the auctioneer calls out the lot in question and announces that he has a bid (yours) of $625 for the stamp. If there is no offer from those who have come to bid — the floor, in auction parlance — the stamp will sell to you at $625 plus the auctioneer's commission.

To contest it, a floor bidder must bid $650. If someone does, the auctioneer will announce that he has a book bid (yours, again) of $675. A floor bid of $700 would bring your final book bid of $725 — though the bidder on the floor does not know that.

If he bids again, the stamp will be his for $750. If he does not, the stamp will be hammered down to you for your full original bid of $725 plus commission.

If two comparable copies of the $3 Columbian are offered in the same auction, you may hedge your bet by placing "or" bids on both of them: a bid of $725 on lot No. 123 or lot No. 124. This may increase your likelihood of success.

A mail bid sale functions in essentially the same manner but without any floor bidders. Comparing the bid sheets determines the winner, with tie mail bids (as in auctions) being awarded to the bidder whose bid was received first.

For customers who dislike the impersonality of mail bidding but are unable to attend a sale, some auction firms offer the option of bidding by telephone just as they would if they were actually in the room.

Though not all collectors get the opportunity, many feel that there is just no substitute for attending an auction in person. It is unquestionably the most exciting way to buy stamps. It can be almost as enthralling to watch the competition for lots you're not bidding for as it is to take part yourself.

If you've never bid before at a public auction and plan to do so, by all means enjoy yourself, but plan ahead to make sure your purchases will be sensible ones. Make a list of lots you're interested in and what you feel each is worth, based on your research of auction prices realized and retail price lists.

Form a total budget for the sale and stick to it. In the heat of the moment it is easy to bid $20, $50 or even $100 more on an item than you originally intended, or to find you have to forego a lot you really wanted because you spent too much in earlier bidding for items of lesser value. To the extent that an auction is a game, it pays to come to it equipped with a game plan.

Some bidders prefer to place their bids through an auction agent. An auction agent is a professional who attends auctions to bid on behalf of a number of other interested parties, usually in exchange for a percentage of the hammer price. One or more agents are usually in attendance at most major public stamp auctions, and auction firms are usually happy to recommend one or more should you so desire.

Since mail bidders have to rely on written descriptions, and mistakes in grading or identification do happen, a period of three to five days after receipt is usually allowed in which a successful bidder can return lots that are not satisfactory.

Reputable firms generally are willing to accept returns for any good reason though, again, the sale terms and conditions are the final authority in any dispute on this matter. In most sales, large lots containing 10 or more items are not returnable for any reason.

Persons who bid from the floor at any public auction usually do not have the same return privilege that mail bidders enjoy, since they have the opportunity to inspect lots before bidding, and it is deemed their responsibility to do so.

Many collectors eschew public auctions and mail bid sales alike out of fear that the sale can be manipulated in such a way as to cause them to have to pay more than they should.

But there are measures you can take to protect yourself. You can start by confining your bidding to firms whose sales are advertised in *Linn's* and other philatelic journals, which do not accept advertising from firms with a record of unresolved complaints.

You can limit your bidding to those auction companies that subscribe to the ASDA auction code of ethics.

If you have other collector friends who share your interests and have bid in auctions, ask for their recommendations of firms with which they have had the greatest success.

But probably the best way to ensure your satisfaction with a public auction or mail bid sale firm is by knowing as much as you can about what you are bidding on. If you plan to bid on a stamp that your research has shown regularly sells for about $200 in price lists and as recorded in auction prices realized, and you win a stamp of comparable condition and quality with a $160 bid, you will know that you have done well.

By the same token, don't delude yourself, either. A $50 bid won't win that stamp, even if the auction firm has to buy it back for the consignor for $55 to top your bid.

Some auctions and mail bid sales specify reserve prices or minimum bids — a bottom price level for a given lot below which bids will not be entertained. Others do not specify them, but have them in mind just the same, and few sales or auctions any longer describe themselves as unreserved.

How to Consign

If you wish to consign stamps to a public auction or mail bid sale, it is often wise to write first to find out if the auctioneer can use what you have to offer. A stamped, self-addressed envelope may encourage a prompt reply.

As a general rule, the bigger the auction, the better the material it offers in both quality and rarity. Less valuable stamps will probably be accepted in a major sale only as part of a large wholesale or remainder lot, and many entire collections are offered intact as a single lot.

When packing your consignment, be sure to include in the package a statement of your full name, address, telephone number and the contents of the shipment, and keep a copy of this homemade invoice for your own records.

It may be wise as a minimal precaution to buy a "return receipt requested" slip for the package, if only for your own peace of mind, as the auctioneer may be too busy to acknowledge receipt of your consignment right away.

With rare exceptions, consignments must be sent in well ahead of the actual date of the auction to allow time for your material to be processed. This consists of organizing, cataloging, describing, listing by lot number and publishing your material in an auction or sale catalog, which must then be printed and sent well in advance of the sale date to give bidders the chance to bid. Some auctions are prepared many months in advance, and as much as a year may be needed for the preliminary work for some of the most important auctions.

Once the consignor has sent in his material, he will sometimes be sent a preliminary or "proof" copy of the auction list, or the part of the catalog with his consignment in it, so that he can check it for accuracy.

Following the sale, there is usually a period of about 30 days that is needed to notify the high bidders, obtain their payments, and then be assured of their satisfaction with the lots. Consignors are usually not settled with until the money for the entire auction is in hand, and it may be wise to allow for a delay of at least 30 to 60 days between the sale date and the arrival of your check.

When all is said and done, the purpose of a successful auction is to sell material at a price that will please the bidder, satisfy the consignor and maintain the auctioneer in business with something to show for his efforts. If you bear these practical considerations in mind, whether as a bidder or a consignor, you're likely to have little trouble finding an auction firm that satisfies your requirements.

Mailing Stamps

Whether you return approvals, take part in sales circuits, consign stamps to an auction or mail them out for expertization, correct mailing procedures can be important to you.

On its long and often arduous journey from sender to addressee, mail is subjected to much handling by many people. The current volume of mail handled by the USPS amounts to billions of pieces per year. With that kind of volume, the postal employee simply cannot give attention to each separate piece of mail.

This being the case, it behooves you to provide as much protection as possible for your letters and packages.

Enclose the stamps on a manila stockcard within a glassine envelope. This may be placed between two pieces of stout cardboard for added protection and as stiffeners to help prevent bending or folding in the mailstream.

Include a letter identifying yourself as well as the stamp or stamps and stating the reason they are being sent. Your accompanying letter should also include complete instructions for the return of the stamps (if desired) and, of course, sufficient return postage to provide for whatever level of protection you desire in its return.

Registered mail provides signature protection for the contents. That means that anyone handling the package en route must sign for it. Registered mail also provides for a declared value up to the amount specified by the sender upon payment of the proper fee. The fee structure is a complex one. Registered mail is strictly a first-class service.

A note of caution: USPS liability for loss on registered parcels addressed to foreign countries is limited to $24.60, except Canada, for which the maximum liability for goods is $1,000 and $200 for cash.

Insured mail goes via third- or fourth-class. It too provides indemnity for declared value but only up to a limit of $500.

Contrary to popular belief, insuring a package does not guarantee delivery. It guarantees only that the sender will be reimbursed for loss in transit. Further, the sender is not guaranteed to recover the amount declared.

Priority mail may be used for heavier pieces that are charged at the first-class rate, but may be insured at third-class insurance rates, rather than the much higher first-class registration rates.

The USPS will often attempt to establish a value for the lost stamps based on findings of a disinterested authority. This is its common practice, and one of the ways in which the USPS attempts to protect itself against fraud.

If the stamp has no intrinsic value, it can be sent via certified mail. A receipt is issued to the sender, and for an additional fee, a return receipt can be obtained showing when, where and to whom the mail was delivered.

Both registered and certified mail are traceable from initial mailing to ultimate delivery.

Whatever means of mailing is selected, be certain that the package is securely sealed. An auctioneer's nightmare begins with the receipt of a package that is empty because the sender neglected to seal it properly. If you have additional questions, be sure to ask the personnel at your post office, most of whom can and do cheerfully provide free, knowledgeable and professional advice.

Chapter 20

Major Stamp Auctions

Sale	Auction house	Year
Stanley Ashbrook	Edson J. Fifield	1958
	Herman Herst Jr.	1958
	Harmers of New York	1958
	Samuel C. Paige	1959
Ameer of Bahawalpur	Stanley Gibbons Ltd.	1968
L.H. Barkhausen	Harmers of New York	1955, 1956
Robert W. Baughman	Robert A. Siegel Auctions	1971
Arthur W. Bingham Jr.	Robert A. Siegel Auctions	1967
John Boker	Heinrich Koehler	1985-88
Alvaro Bonilla-Lara	Harmers of New York	1961
Stephen D. Brown	Harmer, Rooke & Co.	1939
Dr. John A. Buchness	Harmers of New York	1971
Maurice Burrus	Shanahan	1959
	Robson Lowe	1962-67
	Harmer, Rooke & Co.	1963
King Carol II	Harmer, Rooke & Co.	1951
Alfred H. Caspary	Harmers of New York	1955, 1958
Carroll Chase	Daniel F. Kelleher	1925-26
	Herman Toaspern	1926
	Harmers of New York	1944
	Samuel C. Paige	1961
	Felix Brunner	1963
William H. Crocker	Harmer, Rooke & Co.	1938-39
Caroline Prentice Cromwell	Harmers of New York	1957, 1958
	Irwin Heiman	1957-58
	Carl E. Pelander	1957
Dale-Lichtenstein	Harmers of New York	1968-1971
		1989-1991
Hiram Deats	Scott Stamp Co.	1900-01
	New England Stamp Co.	1905-06
	Frank Brown	1909
Harold G. Duckworth	Harmer, Rooke & Co.	1962

Sale	Auction house	Year
Clarence Eagle	Bertrand L. Drew	1922
	J. Murray Bartels	1922, 1924
	J.C. Morgenthau	1923
	Percy G. Doane	1923
	Kelton and Sloane	1923
	Max Ohlman	1923
Judge Robert Emerson	Daniel F. Kelleher	1937-51
	Percy G. Doane	1937-39
	Harmer, Rooke & Co.	1944
Agathon Faberge	Harmers of London	1939
	Robson Lowe	1939
Count Ferrari	M.A. Broquelet and M.G. Gilbert	1921-25
	E. Luder Edelmann	1929
King Fouad	Harmers of London	1954
Henry C. Gibson	Eugene Klein	1923, 1944
	Philip H. Ward Jr.	1944
	Christie's/Robson Lowe	1984
Gen. Robert Gill	Robson Lowe	1957, 1965
	Mercury Stamp Co.	1960
	Behr and Robineau	1967
	Harmers of New York	1970
Henry M. Goodkind	Harmers of New York	1971
Col. Edward H.R. Green	Barr, Doane, Harmer-Rooke, Kelleher, Morgenthau, Heiman, Laurence & Stryker, Fifield and Costales	1942-46
Louis Grunin	Robert A. Siegel	1971, 1975, 1981
	Harmers of New York	1976
	American Philatelic Brokers	1978
	Christie's/Robson Lowe	1987-88
Marc Haas	Robert A. Siegel	1972, 1980, 1983
	Stanley Gibbons	1980
Mr. and Mrs. John H. Hall	Harmers of New York	1971
Harrison D.S. Haverbeck	Harmers of New York	1973
Maj. Charlton T. Henry	Harmer, Rooke & Co.	1961
		1961
Henry W. Hill	John A. Fox	1956
	Samuel C. Paige	1959
	Robert A. Siegel	1961
Arthur Hind	Charles J. Phillips and William C. Kennett	1933
Isleham	Robert A. Siegel Auctions	1986
	Christie's/Robson Lowe	1986-87

Sale	Auction house	Year
Fred Jarrett	J.N. Sissons Ltd.	1959-61
Ralph A. Kimble	Sylvester Colby	1953, 1954, 1955
Edward S. Knapp	Parke-Bernet	1940-41
David Kohn	Robert A. Siegel Auctions	1970
Harry M. Konwiser	Sylvester Colby	1953
Emmerson C. Krug	Robert A. Siegel Auctions	1958
Col. Hans Lagerloef	Harmers of New York	1953
John Lek	Harmers of New York & London	1959
	J.L. Van Dieten	1962
Josiah K. Lilly	Robert A. Siegel Auctions	1967-68
John N. Luff	Sylvester Colby	1970
Edwin Mayer	Harmers of New York	1967
Charles F. Meroni	Eugene N. Costales	1949
	John A. Fox	1952-53
William L. Moody III	Harmers of New York	1950-58
Mortimer L. Neinken	Robert A. Siegel Auctions	1970
Saul Newbury	Robert A. Siegel Auctions	1961-62
Charles L. Pack	Harmer, Rooke & Co.	1944-47
Baron Alphonse de Rothschild	Harmers of London & New York	1939, 1941-44, 1968
	J. Murray Bartels	1941
	Mercury Stamp Co.	1947, 1953
	Shanahan Stamp Co.	1958
Franklin D. Roosevelt	Harmers of New York	1946
Oscar A. Schenck	Harmer, Rooke & Co.	1950-51
Norman Serphos	Harmer, Rooke & Co.	1941
John F. Seybold	J.C. Morgenthau & Co.	1910
Theodore Sheldon	Mercury Stamp Co.	1970
Max L. Simon	Robert A. Siegel Auctions	1965
	Equitable Stamp Co.	1965
	Mercury Stamp Co.	1965
	Irwin Heiman	1966
	Vahan Mozian	1966
Y. Souren	Harmers of New York	1951
	Harmer, Rooke & Co.	1952

Major Stamp Auctions

Sale	Auction house	Year
W. Parsons Todd	Robert A. Siegel Auctions	1977
		1978
		1978
Ferrars H. Tows	Carl E. Pelander	1948-50
George Walcott	Robert Laurence	1935
Philip H. Ward Jr.	J.&H. Stolow	1954
	Harmer, Rooke & Co.	1958
	Parke-Bernet Galleries	1964
	Robert A. Siegel Auctions	1964-65, 1968
	Sylvester Colby	1965, 1966, 1967
Waterhouse Collection	Harmers of London	1955

Top 100 Auction Records

The following list includes record-breaking prices at auction for philatelic items. These prices include auction realizations only. Private sales are not included.

$935,000

British Guiana 1856 1¢ magenta. Robert A. Siegel Auction Galleries 1980.

$680,500

Baden 1851 9-kreuzer black on blue-green error of color on folded letter from Altdorf to the Barons of Turckheim. Heinrich Koehler March 16, 1985.

$657,140

Wurttemberg 1873 70-kreuzer red-lilac, sheet position 1 from second printing with double dividing lines, together with 1kr and 3kr in the later oval design each with black "HEILBRONN" pen cancellation on cover insured for 5,700 gulden addressed to Munich. Heinrich Koehler Nov. 12, 1988.

$455,000

Sweden 1855 3-skilling-banco error of color. David Feldman SA March 29-30, 1984.

$434,780

Lubeck 1862 1/2-schilling lilac block of four canceled LUEBECK BAHNHOF 14/3 IIZ on blue folded letter addressed to Procurator Reppenhagen in Bergedorf with BERGEDORF 14 3/IVT arrival mark. Heinrich Koehler March 14, 1987.

$418,000

United States 1867 1¢ blue "Z" grill. Superior Galleries Nov. 10-11, 1986.

$407,000

Oldenburg 1859 1/3-groschen black on green unused block of 12. Heinrich Koehler Nov. 14, 1987.

$380,000

Mauritius cover with two copies of 1847 1-penny Post Office Mauritius. Harmers of New York Oct. 21, 1968.

$343,200

Mecklenburg-Strelitz 1864 1/4-silbergroschen pair and two singles in yellow-orange shade on cover to Neubrandenburg canceled "FURSTENBERG." Heinrich Koehler March 19, 1988.

$314,000

Schleswig-Holstein 1850 1-schilling blue horizontal pair canceled "12" and with departure marking "HOLST: P. HAMBURG 29 10" on folded letter to Rendsburg. Heinrich Koehler Nov. 14, 1987.

$302,300

Oldenburg 1859 3-groschen black on yellow strip of four canceled with blue Brake FRANCO. Heinrich Koehler Nov. 14, 1987.

$302,300

Lubeck 1859 1/2-schilling deep lilac, 2 1/2s lilac-rose and 4s deep green canceled "LUBECK 21.2" on registered front to Schwerin with red double-framed RECOM. Heinrich Koehler Nov. 14, 1987.

$298,800

Saxony 1851-52 1/2-neugroschen black on pale blue in counter sheet of 10. Heinrich Koehler March 19, 1988.

$295,860

Bavaria 1849 1-kreuzer black in complete counter sheet of 90 with interpanneau pairs. Heinrich Koehler March 19, 1988.

$282,600

Saxony 1850 3-pfennig cherry-red plate II block of four showing types 4 to 5, 9 to 10 with double-circle MNITZ cancel. Heinrich Koehler March 14, 1987.

$275,000

Brazil "Pack" strip consisting of two 1843 30-reis and one 60r stamps. Robert A. Siegel Auction Galleries May 25, 1986.

$266,670

Bavaria 1849 1-kreuzer black tete-beche marginal unused block of 12. Heinrich Koehler March 15, 1986.

$255,800

Thurn and Taxis 1865 1/2-silbergroschen orange bisected diagonally used together with 1/2 silbergroschen orange canceled 221 on cover front with APOLDA 10.6.1865 departure mark addressed to Buttstedt. Heinrich Koehler Nov. 14, 1987.

$244,200

Schleswig-Holstein 1865 1 1/4-schilling gray bisected diagonally and canceled

OLDESLOE 28.9.67 as 1/2-schilling rate on local cover. Heinrich Koehler Nov. 14, 1987.

$244,186

Oldenburg 1859 2-groschen black on deep rose in horizontal strip of three canceled HEPPENS on piece. Heinrich Koehler Nov. 14, 1987.

$240,000

United States Running Chicken fancy cancellation cover bearing three strikes of the cancellation over three 1¢ 1869 stamps. Sotheby Parke Bernet Oct. 30, 1979.

$230,000

Hawaii 1851 2¢ Missionary. Sotheby Parke Bernet Nov. 18, 1980.

$220,000

United States 1901 2¢ Pan American invert, block of four. Sotheby Parke Bernet April 29, 1980.

$220,000

Lubeck 1859 2 1/2-schilling red-brown error together with 2-schilling red-brown on cover to Neustrelitz with red "HAGENOW-ROSTOCK 1 IT" railway and Sterlitz arrival marking on reverse. Heinrich Koehler Dec. 7, 1985.

$211,400

Brunswick 1864 1-silbergroschen black on yellow in horizontal strip of six from bottom of the sheet on cover with black-green double circle GREENE datestamp addressed to Bolkenhain in Silesia. Heinrich Koehler Nov. 12, 1988.

$210,000

Bermuda 1848 1-penny Perot provisional on cover. Robert A. Siegel Auction Galleries April 5, 1980.

$207,100

Bergedorf 1861-67 4-schilling block on brown horizontal pair on complete cover to Streideldorf near Freystadt in Schlesien. Heinrich Koehler March 19, 1988.

$207,000

France 1849-50 1-franc vermillion tete-beche in block of four. David Feldman SA May 30, 1986.

$206,500

Bergedorf 1861-67 1/2-schilling block on deep blue vertical pair with upper sheet margin on complete wrapper addressed to Neuburg a/d Donau in Bavaria with DONAUWORTH transit and NEUBURG arrival marks. Heinrich Koehler March 15, 1987.

$197,700

Lubeck 1859-62 1/2-schilling deep lilac unused block of 35. Heinrich Koehler Nov. 14, 1987.

$194,300

Bergedorf 1861-67 1-schilling black canceled with bars in mixed franking with Hamburg 2 schilling red perforated, partly affixed over the Bergedorf stamp with Hamburg bar cancellation on small cover to Cuxhaven with "BERGEDORF 6 3/IIIT" departure mark "HAMBURG 16.3.66 transit and blue "RITZEBUTTEL 17.3.66" arrival marking on reverse. Heinrich Koehler Nov. 12, 1988.

$192,500

United States 1918 24¢ inverted Jenny, "Princeton" block of four. Harmers of New York Dec. 13, 1982.

$180,000

United States 1869 15¢ invert. Robert A. Siegel Auction Galleries April 24, 1982.

$177,300

Saxony 1850 3-pfennig red-brown, plate 1, types 14-15, 1920, block of four. Heinrich Koehler Nov. 14, 1987.

$177,000

Bergedorf 1861-67 3-schilling blue on rose together with 4-schilling black on red-brown, canceled with double bars on cover to Rotterdam with "BERGEDORF 20 7/IVT" departure mark. "HAMBURG 21.7.65" transit and "ROTTERDAM 22.7.65" arrival markings on reverse. Heinrich Koehler Nov. 12, 1988.

$176,000

Confederate States of America 1861 5¢ Livingston (Alabama) postmaster's provisional pair on cover. Christie's/ Robson Lowe June 18, 1985.

$160,000

Lubeck 1862 1/2-schilling deep lilac horizontal strip of five probably from the top of the sheet, tied by bar cancellation on cover with "LUBECK" departure mark addressed to Malchin in Mecklensburg "HAGENOWROSTOCK 1 IT" railway cancellation on reverse. Heinrich Koehler Nov. 12, 1988.

$152,200

Baden 1862-65 3-kreuzer pale dull lilac-rose, the imperforate Stockach Provisional, canceled double circle

FREIBURG 22 JAN (1866) on cover with FREIBURG/THIENGEN Postablage handstamp addressed to Herr Constantin Dandler in Stockach. Heinrich Koehler March 14, 1987.

$150,000

United States 1901 4¢ Pan American invert, block of four. Sotheby Parke Bernet April 29, 1980.

$142,900

Mecklenburg-Sterlitz 1864 1-schilling violet, the only known horizontal pair canceled "NEUSTRELITZ" on cover to Stargard with additional framed "STARGARD i. Macklbg." cancellation. Heinrich Koehler Nov. 12, 1988.

$141,300

Bergedorf 1861-67 1 1/2-schilling black on yellow tete-beche pair, tied by bar cancellations to piece with semicircular BERGEDORF datestamp alongside. Heinrich Koehler March 14, 1987.

$137,000

Brunswick 1852 2-silbergroschen black on blue, the upper right half, canceled "18" in bars on folder letter Osterode with "HALLEA.D.WESER 23.2." (1865) departure and arrival mark of the same day. Heinrich Koehler Nov. 12, 1988.

$135,000

United States 1857-61 5¢ brick red Jefferson, block of four. Robert A. Siegel Auction Galleries 1983.

$135,000

Bergedorf 1861-67 3-schilling blue on rose and 4 schilling black on red-brown canceled. BERGEDORF 1/7 IIIT" departure datestamp, oval red "PD" and "LONDON PAID 3JY 66" arrival markings. Heinrich Koehler Nov. 15, 1986.

$126,500

Canada 1851 12-penny black. Greg Manning Auctions May 10, 1980.

$125,000

United States 1869 30¢ invert. Robert A. Siegel Auction Galleries April 29, 1981.

$125,700

Mecklenburg-Schwerin 1864 4 1/2-schilling red rouletted together with 3-schilling orange imperforate as additional franking on 1 schilling postal stationery envelope, the 5-schilling+3-silbergroschen Postal Union rate canceled two-line "HEIL.DAMM.B.D." (Heilegendamm bei Dobran) addressed to Berlin. Heinrich Koehler Nov. 12, 1988.

$120,000

Bergedorf 1861-67 1-schilling black horizontal pair from right of sheet as additional franking on Hamburg 1/2-schilling postal stationery envelope registered to Hamburg. Heinrich Koehler Nov. 15, 1986.

$120,000

Oldenburg 1861 1/4-groschen yellow-orange horizontal strip of four with framed "BLEXEN" cancellations on cover with official seal of the Blexen authority on reverse addressed to "den Deichgeschworenen Ritter zu Alttrevenfeld." Heinrich Koehler Nov. 12, 1988.

$120,000

Bergedorf 1861-67 1/2-schilling black on pale blue in a vertical strip of four canceled on cover addressed to the "Expedition der Eisenbahn-Zeitung" in Lubeck. "BERGEDOEF 15 4/IVT" departure mark and on reverse Lubeck "No. 3" arrival marking. Heinrich Koehler Nov. 12, 1988.

$120,000

Baden 1851-52 1-kreuzer black on buff horizontal pair with interpanneau gutter, each stamp canceled "57" of Heidelberg on small piece. Heinrich Koehler Nov. 12, 1988.

$118,300

Oldenburg 1852-55 1/10-thaler black on yellow horizontal strip of four canceled blue FRANCO on complete folded letter to Adelaide, Australia, with blue framed BRAKE 18/4(1860) alongside. Oldenburg transit mark dated 18.4 on reverse. Red LONDON PAID date 21.4 transit and G.P.O. ADELAIDE dated 4.7.1860 arrival marks on front. Heinrich Koehler March 19, 1988.

$115,000

United States 1870 24¢ grill. Superior Galleries Oct. 29-31, 1984.

$114,300

Hamburg 1859 9-schilling pale yellow from the first printing, four copies affixed to cover with red "HAMBURG PAID APRIL 6 1859" addressed to New York, routed via Aachen with red double circle "AACHEN PAID 50 CTS" and "N.YORK BR. PKT60 PAID" tax mark. Heinrich Koehler Nov. 12, 1988.

$110,000

Nova Scotia three 1851 1-shilling stamps on mourning cover to Madras. Christie's/Robson Lowe Oct. 4, 1984.

$107,000

Greece 1871 40-lepta Solferino error of color on piece. David Feldman SA March 29-30, 1984.

$106,500

Bergedorf 1861-67 2 1/2-schilling olive-green as additional franking on 1 1/2-schilling postal stationery envelope with watermark canceled semicircular BERGEDORF 1.10./VT as a 3-schilling franking to Wehner near Oldenburg with OLDENBURG 2.10. (1867) arrival datestamp. Heinrich Koehler March 19, 1988.

$105,000

British Guiana "Miss Rose" 1877 2¢ Cottonreel cover. Stanley Gibbons Ltd. April 21, 1977.

$104,500

United States 5¢ red-brown, block of four. Christie's/Robson Lowe Oct. 7, 1987.

$102,900

Mecklenburg-Sterlitz 1864 3-silbergroschen pale brown, a horizontal pair with central cancellation and a 2-silbergroschen blue affixed as a strip on complete folded letter from "FRIEDLAND MBG." as a double-weight registered letter addressed to Munich. Heinrich Koehler Nov. 12, 1988.

$100,600

Saxony 1850 3-pfennig deep red, plate V, horizontal strip of three, types 11 to 13, canceled with two strikes of double circle LEIPZIG 10.APR.51 6 1/2-7 on contrasting blue wrapper from the deutsche Nationalverein fur Handel und Gewerbe addressed to Woldegk in Mecklenburg-Sterlitz. Prussian MAGDE-BURG-LEIPZIG and BERLIN-MAGDE-BURG railway cancellation on reverse. Heinrich Koehler March 19, 1988.

$100,000

Oldenburg 1861 1/3-groschen black on green horizontal strip of three canceled small framed "BERNE" on cover to Loningen, "DELMENHORST" transit and "LONINGEN" arrival marks on reverse. Heinrich Koehler Nov. 12, 1988.

$99,000

Sweden 1856-62 1-skilling-banco Stockholm local. Frimarkshuset Sept. 2, 1986.

$95,900

Hamburg 1864-65 3-schilling ultramarine horizontal strip of four, canceled in pairs with light circular HELIGOLAND 2 SP 1866 datestamp paying the double rate for an overweight letter to Halle and with blue HELIGOLAND alongside. Stadtpostamt Hamburg transit and Halle arrival marking on reverse. Heinrich Koehler March 19, 1988.

$94,600

Bavaria 1850-58 9-kreuzer bluish-green strip of four with horizontal interpanneau gutter, dividing lines and frame lines of adjoining stamps at places canceled "243" on large piece. Heinrich Koehler March 15, 1986.

$93,300

Oldenburg 1852-55 1/3-silbergroschen black on green, unused block of nine. Heinrich Koehler March 15, 1986.

$92,500

Mecklenburg-Strelitz 1864 1/4-silbergroschen red-orange, two copies together with 2-silbergroschen blue affixed as a strip and canceled with a single strike of the NEU-BRANDENBURG segmented datestamp and as usual with blue manuscript cancellation on registered wrapper addressed to G. Wilhelm in Broda in Mecklenburg-Strelitz. Heinrich Koehler Nov. 15, 1986.

$91,400

Saxony 1850 3-pfennig cherry red, plate II, type 20, canceled framed "LEIPZIG 15 AUG 50" on wrapper to Hungary with complete address. "EPERIES 22.8" ornamental handstamp on reverse. Heinrich Koehler Nov. 12, 1988.

$90,000

Oldenberg 1852-55 1/30-thaler black on blue in block of 12 showing types III + I + III + I/I + III + I + III/III + I + III + I. Heinrich Koehler.

$89,000

Bergedorf 1861-67 3-schilling blue on rose with right sheet margin, canceled with two strikes of BERGEDORF 15.12. arrival marks on reverse. Heinrich Koehler March 19, 1988.

$88,900

Bergedorf 1861-67 1/2-schilling black on deep blue and 3-schilling black on rose, both with double bar cancellations on overweight and taxed cover to Steinkirchen in Alten Lande, HAMBURG transit and JORK arrival marks on reverse. Heinrich Koehler March 15, 1986.

$88,700

Brunswick 1852 3-silbergroschen orange-red horizontal strip of three on official cover from the Brunswick patent office to the Staatsministerium in Dormstadt. Heinrich Koehler March 19, 1988.

$88,600

Bremen 1856-60 7-grote black on yellow, canceled "BREMERHAVEN" key datestamp in red on cover to the Lubeck enclave of Stockelsdorf. "BREMEN" transit and Lubeck "No. 2" arrival marks on reverse. Heinrich Koehler Nov. 12, 1988.

$88,600

Bergedorf 1861-67 1/4-schilling black, two copies affixed as a pair with "BERGEDORF 3/8" town cancellation on cover to the editor of the "Eisenbahn-Zeitung" in Bergedorf. Heinrich Koehler Nov. 12, 1988.

$87,200

Schleswig-Holstein 1865 4-schilling brown, canceled double circle KIEL 25.10.65 and black FRANCO on the famous cover to Karajan, Vienna. Heinrich Koehler Nov. 14, 1987.

$87,000

Oldenburg 1861 1/2-groschen moss green and a second issue 1-groschen black on deep blue each tied by double circle OLDENBURG datestamp to wrapper addressed to Goldenstedt and with VECHTA arrival date. Heinrich Koehler March 14, 1987.

$85,800

Baden 1862-65 3-kreuzer pale lilac-rose imperforate with frame lines of the adjoining stamps above and below used together with 1-kreuzer black on small piece, each canceled double circle STOCKACH 28 DEZ. datestamp. Heinrich Koehler March 19, 1988.

$82,900

Bergedorf 1861-67 1-schilling black and 3-schilling blue on rose, both with bar cancellations on cover with "BERGEDORF" departure mark addressed to Vienna. Prussian "HAMBURG-BERLIN" railway, "WIEN" transit and "WIEDEN IN WIEN" arrival markings on reverse. Heinrich Koehler Nov. 12, 1988.

$82,900

Thurn and Taxis 1852-53 3-kreuzer black on deep blue horizontal strip of three, canceled with two red strikes of the GAMMERTINGEN 11 JUL 1852 datestamp. Heinrich Koehler March 19, 1988.

$81,500

Lubeck 1859 2-schilling red-brown showing the error "ZWEI EIN HALB" schilling, tied by bar cancellation to folded letter, double circle LUBECK 27/5 departure mark and Hamburg arrival mark dated 28.5.62. Heinrich Koehler March 14, 1987.

$80,000

Australia 1854-57 4-penny inverted swan. Harmers of Sydney Oct. 6, 1980.

$80,000

United States 1901 1¢ Pan American invert, block of four. Sotheby Parke Bernet April 29, 1980.

$78,500

Thurn and Taxis 1862-63 1-silbergroschen rose bisected diagonally and canceled "322" on cover front with HORN 25 6 departure mark addressed to the Stadlgericht in Detmold. Heinrich Koehler Nov. 14, 1987.

$77,000

United States 1846 5¢ Millbury postmaster's provisional on cover. Harmers of New York Oct. 27, 1983.

$76,000

Oldenburg 1861 1/3-groschen blue-green horizontal strip of three, the third stamp with small "o" in Oldenburg on thin "G" in Groschen tied by framed APEN cancellations to complete folder letter with handstamp of the "Oldenburgische Eisenhuttengesellschaft zu Augustfehn" addressed to Steinhausen near Varel dated 8 August 1862. Heinrich Koehler Nov. 14, 1987.

$75,000

Japan 1871 500 mon with inverted characters. Waverly Trading Co. Dec. 9, 1973.

$73,900

Saxony 1850 3-pfennig brick-red in a horizontal strip of three from plate 11, positions 18-20, on cruciform wrapper canceled "LEIPZIG 25.SEP.50" datestamp to Altenburg. Heinrich Koehler March 16, 1985.

$73,400

Bremen 1861-63 10-grote black on white horizontal pair, with two single copies as a 40-grote quadruple rate franking canceled BREMEN 14.7. * 5-6 (1866) on folded letter from the Unkart correspondence, red framed Bremen PAID and manuscript "40." Heinrich Koehler March 14, 1987.

$72,700

Bavaria 1862 1-kreuzer yellow horizontal strip of six from the upper sheet margin with gutter between first and second stamp, with right sheet margin. The left stamps are canceled with double circle NURNBERG 20 APR 1867, the right strip of five with open cogwheel "356." Heinrich Koehler Nov. 14, 1987.

$71,400

Bavaria 1862 3-kreuzer carmine horizontal strip of three, the so-called "Brucke," canceled open "145" cogwheel on folded letter from Furth to Sigmar near Chemnitz with "1. Auagabe 20/XI" arrival mark on reverse. Heinrich Koehler Nov. 12, 1988.

$71,100

Bremen 1861-63 10-grote black pair and two singles (one with left sheet margin) tied to cover to New York by framed BREMEN datestamp. This 40-grote franking is the highest rate recorded for a prepaid letter. Heinrich Koehler March 15, 1986.

$70,700

Mecklenburg-Schwerin 1864-67 2-schilling brownish-gray, two copies, and 4 1/2-schilling red all canceled double circle "ROSTOCK 29.10" (1867) on complete folded letter with contents to Berlin. On reverse Berlin machine arrival cancellation dated 30.10. Heinrich Koehler March 15, 1986.

$70,000

Canada 1959 5¢ Seaway invert. John W. Kaufmann Inc., Nov. 27, 1979.

$70,000

Bremen 1866-67 5-silbergroschen bluish-green together with 5-grote black on rose type I as a registered franking on cover to Liverpool. Red boxed "Registered" and tax mark and the only recorded example of the "BREMEN REGISTERED" datestamp. Heinrich Koehler March 15, 1986.

$68,900

Bremen 1866-67 7-grote black on yellow in mixed franking with 1862 5-grote black on rose rouletted and 1866 3-grote black on gray-blue perforated canceled "BREMEN 9.2" (1867) on cover via New York to Havana (roulettes and perforations irregular). Heinrich Koehler March 15, 1988.

$67,500

Baden 1851-52 9-kreuzer black on lilac-rose vertical block of eight used on piece in combination with second issue 6-kreuzer black on orange-yellow placed over the center of the block all canceled "24." Heinrich Koehler Nov. 15, 1986.

$67,000

Oldenburg 1861 1/3-groschen black on green tied by double circle OLDENBURG datestamp to wrapper with complete original contents addressed to Barschlute. BERNE arrival mark. Heinrich Koehler March 14, 1987.

$67,000

Bergedorf 1861-67 3-schilling blue on rose, fresh color, canceled blue Prussian railway HAMBURG/7 4 IR/BERLIN datestamp on cover with manuscript "Bergedorf 7/4" departure marking addressed to Gustrow in Mecklenburg. Another strike of the railway datestamp and arrival mark of the same date on reverse. Heinrich Koehler March 14, 1987.

$66,700

Lubeck 1-schilling orange, two singles, together with 2-schilling brown and 4-schilling deep green with bar cancellations on cover from Lubeck dated 14.4 to Reval with arrival datestamp on front and "RIGA 6 APR 1861" transit datestamp on reverse. Heinrich Koehler March 15, 1986.

$66,700

Oldenburg 1/15-thaler black on rose type I strip of four with wide margins on all sides tied to registered letter by framed HEPPENS datestamp addressed to Hanover with arrival mark. Heinrich

Koehler March 15, 1986.

$66,700

Schleswig-Holstein 1-schilling blue block of four with margins on all sides canceled with two strikes of the barred "3" on cover to Hameln, "ALTONA 24.6.51" datestamp and HAMELN arrival mark dated 25.6 on reverse. Heinrich Koehler March 15, 1986.

Chapter 21

Famous Stamp Collectors

Personalities of the Past

Over the years countless men and women have contributed immeasurably to stamp collecting, helping to make it the great hobby it is today, enjoyed by millions throughout the world. The following list of famous stamp collectors does not include any living person.

-A-

Ernest R. Ackerman
(1863-1931) New Jersey

Congressman from New Jersey, he was serving his 14th term in the House of Representatives at the time of his death and was credited with bringing about much favorable action on legislation of benefit to stamp collectors. His collections included outstanding presentations of U.S. Departmentals on cover, U.S. proofs and 20th-century issues. A collector from boyhood, he recalled late in his life that during an 1883 visit to the national capital he purchased the reissues of the 1869 pictorials, using them on covers addressed to himself.

William L. Alexander
(1903-1979) Arizona

Founder of the Western Postal History Museum and the Arizona Philatelic Rangers, William L. Alexander, Tucson, Ariz., was frequently recognized for his efforts in the development of a free philatelic education course for asthmatic and underprivileged children throughout the state of Arizona. Auctions and other activities of the history museum and the Arizona Philatelic Rangers, which he headed, raised more than $100,000 for the National Foundation for Asthmatic Children. On his retirement as a director of the Western Postal History Museum in 1976, he was given the title of director emeritus.

In 1963, he was elected a member of the Arizona Philatelic Hall of Fame and presented a community service award in Tucson in 1969.

Spencer Anderson
(1907-1947) New York

One of New York's best-known stamp dealers during the 1930s and 1940s, working for the Reliant Stamp Company before going into business for himself. His sudden death during the Centenary Philatelic Exhibition (Cipex) cast a shadow over that event.

Frank Applegate
(1879-1964) Oregon

Pioneer student of state revenue stamps, contributing many articles about them to the stamp papers and compiling some of the first catalogs and checklists of such material.

Stanley B. Ashbrook
(1882-1958) Kentucky

One of the most distinguished of American philatelic scholars, famed for his monumental handbook on the 1¢ U.S. stamp of 1851-57, which brought him the Crawford medal of the Royal Philatelic Society of London in 1937. However, he explored all aspects of the production and use of 19th-century U.S. stamps and issues of the Confederate States, writing many articles for philatelic journals on the physical characteristics of stamps and the postal markings found on covers.

Sir William Avery
(1854-1908) England

Sir William Avery began one of the most comprehensive philatelic collections, under the guidance of stamp dealer Charles J. Phillips. He began by purchasing the Australian collection of T. Henry Bullock and the W.W. Blest collection of British Colonies. In 1839 he purchased two of the most valuable stamps in the world, a set of the unused 1-penny and 2-penny Post Office Mauritius for $3,400. Arthur Hind later purchased them for $30,000. Avery's collecting interests included Ceylon, India, the British Colonies, Switzerland, and

North and South America. He accumulated between 90,000 and 100,000 specimens of used and unused stamps. However, he never attempted to display the priceless material in any orderly fashion. Upon his death, his philatelic adviser, William Peckitt purchased the entire Avery collection for a record $120,000. Peckitt did not catalog the prices realized from the dispersal of the items. Some of the material found its way into the Ferrari and the Royal Philatelic Collections.

-B-

Edward Denny Bacon
(1860-1938) England

This great philatelic scholar was commissioned by the Earl of Crawford, James Lindsay, to catalog his philatelic library and to later catalog his collection of 1895 plate impressions. Bacon later received the Crawford medal for his contribution to the advancement of stamp collecting. He was also responsible for the sorting, mounting and arranging of the Thomas Tapling collection for the British Museum. It took Bacon and an assistant working four days a week seven years to finish. He held every position in the Philatelic Society of London and was elected in 1917 to the highest office. Bacon also was elected to the Roll of Distinguished Philatelists in 1921. For 25 years, he was employed in Buckingham Palace as the keeper of the Royal Philatelic Collection.

Sidney F. Barrett
(1893-1958) New York

One of New York's leading professionals during the 1940s and 1950s. In the stamp trade for 49 years, he first worked for Eustace B. Power. He later joined Ed Stern as a proprietor of the Economist Stamp Company and opened his own shop in 1951.

Ralph A. Barry
(1891-1939) New York

Engineer whose articles on stamp collecting appearing in the *New York Herald-Tribune* after the 1929 stock market crash attracted favorable attention and led the newspaper's management to engage him to write a weekly column of philatelic news and comment.

J. Murray Bartels
(1872-1944) New York

In the collecting of U.S. embossed stamped envelopes, the name of Bartels is as esteemed as that of Ashbrook, Chase and Luff to the collector of adhesives. A stamp dealer in Washington, D.C., and Boston before locating to New York. Bartels took a special interest in U.S. envelopes and postal cards and provided philately with much authoritative literature on this material, particularly after purchasing the comprehensive stock of cut squares and entires assembled by Victor Berthold. He contributed many articles to the stamp papers, many dealing with postal stationery, but others providing sound information on the stamps of the Canal Zone, Danish West Indies, Puerto Rico and New York foreign mail postal markings.

James Beal
(1922-1987) Ohio

The theft of his award-winning collection of Mexican classics and postal history in 1974 prompted James Beal to work closely with the FBI on identifying stolen items and to later become head of the APS stamp theft program. He was a major factor in the recovery of two copies of the Jenny invert, which were stolen from the New York Public Library. Beal was also an internationally accredited judge and served as an APS director-at-large for four years. In 1985, he garnered the APS Luff award.

C.W. Bedford
(1884-1932) Ohio

A chemical engineer by profession, Bedford delighted in the search for plate varieties of U.S. stamps and shared his findings with fellow enthusiasts in the Shift Hunter Letters, which appeared under his byline in philatelic periodicals during the 1920s and 1930s.

Fritz Billig
(1902-1986) New York

Born in Vienna, Fritz Billig traveled throughout Europe buying and selling stamps. He was the publisher of a series of studies on forgeries and a series of handbooks on postmarks. His index book named *Mondial* appeared in German, French and English and was an index to stamp periodicals. Unfortunately, the

200-page loose-leaf index was abandoned due to a lack of collector appreciation for its importance. Billig founded the Billig's Stamp Co. in 1945 and was joined by Fred Rich in 1945. Billig & Rich Inc. conducted regular auctions. Billig's contribution to philatelic literature also included the publishing of six specialized catalogs. He did not undertake publishing as a commercial venture, but strictly as a hobby.

Julian Blanchard, Ph.D.
(1885-1967) New York

Julian Blanchard, a physicist associated with the Bell Laboratories, was one of the founders of the Essay-Proof Society and produced many significant studies on the use of bank note vignettes on adhesive stamps.

Herbert J. Bloch
(1907-1987) New York

Often called the ultimate philatelist by friends, Bloch joined H.R. Harmer Inc. of New York in 1943 and became a partner of the Mercury Stamp Co. in 1956. He received the first annual J.W. Scott award for his outstanding contributions to philately and was named head of the American Philatelic Awards Council in 1979. He received every top philatelic honor, including the Alfred F. Lichtenstein and Luff awards. He also signed the Roll of Distinguished Philatelists in England. Bloch served as a judge in many international exhibitions and as honorary judge in Milan in 1976 and Prague in 1978. He was the last surviving member of the Friedl Expert Committee and chairman of the Philatelic Foundation's Expert Committee. He retired from the latter post April 30, 1987, due to continuing health problems.

Bloch's reference collection contained material covering the entire world, from early classic issues to some of the most difficult 20th-century stamps.

Paul Bluss
(—1949) New York

Considered the premier philatelic literature auctioneer in the United States between 1945-49, Paul Bluss conducted more than 500 auction sales. Most of these were weekly office auctions with no catalogs issued. On Aug. 18, 1945, he sold a major portion, 1,013 lots, of the William R. Ricketts philatelic library. He sold his remaining stock of literature to L.R. Stadtmiller in 1949. The stock contained the philatelic literature of Arnold Auerbach, which included the duplicates of the Collectors Club of New York.

Bill Bogg
(1928-1986) Florida

Said to be one of the great cover dealers, William Bogg was also a postal history expert and former American Stamp Dealers' Association president. Bogg bought the New England Stamp Co. in the early 1950s and moved it to Naples, Fla., in 1975. He served the ASDA as vice president, president and director. Bogg and Kenneth Laurence acquired rights to publish the *Dietz Confederate States Catalog and Handbook*, the standard reference source for Confederate stamps.

Clarence Wilson Brazer
(1880-1956) New York

Doyen of specialists on proofs and essays, particularly those of the United States and Canada, he was responsible for much of the published literature on this material. He was founder and first president of the Essay-Proof Society.

John J. Britt
(1900-1980) New York and Florida

A lawyer by profession and for many years a member of the New York board conducting bar examinations, John J. Britt was the recipient of many philatelic awards during his early residency in New York state and in Florida in later years. A past president of the Collectors Club of New York, he was the winner of its Lichtenstein award in 1961 for distinguished service to philately. Other honors included the Collectors Club medal and the Bohn award.

After locating in Florida, he was one of the founders of the Hollywood Stamp Club, one of the largest in the country, and also helped establish the School of Philately in that city. He was much in demand as a judge, speaker and master of ceremonies at stamp shows. In 1974, the John J. Britt Philatelic Foundation was created as a trust to further philatelic knowledge and promote and encourage stamp collecting.

William P. Brown
(1842-1930) New York

Pioneer stamp dealer, his activity dated

from about 1860 and continued until he closed his Nassau Street shop in New York City in 1920 and retired. Originally a dealer in coins and curios, he was inspired to begin selling stamps at an outdoor stand in City Hall Park, where he displayed stamps pinned to a board from which his customers could take those they wanted. The first of several price lists he published appeared in 1868. During his early years in the stamp trade Brown handled many adhesives that are rarities today, including a 2¢ Hawaii "Missionary" that he sold to Count Ferrari in Paris for $5.

Emil Bruechig
(1903-1947) New York

Alumnus of the Scott Stamp and Coin Co. (where many stamp dealers of the 1920s and 1930s learned the ins and outs of the stamp trade), he enjoyed distinction as a specialist dealer in airpost material.

Franklin R. Bruns Jr.
(1912-1979) Washington D.C.

Supervisor and curator of the Smithsonian Institution's Division of Postal History, Franklin R. Bruns Jr. was also a nationally known philatelic writer. His journalistic career began in 1932 as stamp editor for the *New York Sun.* During the succeeding 40 years, he developed his own nationally syndicated stamp and coin column. He was also the author of a number of philatelic books.

A native of New York City, he went to Washington in 1951 to assume the position of curator of the Smithsonian Institution's philatelic collection. He also served as the initial curator of the Cardinal Spellman Philatelic Museum, Weston, Mass., serving from 1957 to 1962. He was appointed to the Citizens' Stamp Advisory Committee in 1957 and again in 1971. In 1972 he returned to the Smithsonian as a research associate. He was elevated to the position of supervisor and curator of the Division of Postal History in 1977.

A guiding spirit in the formation of the American Philatelic Congress, he served as its president from 1944 to 1947, and editor of the organization's official organ, *The Congress Books*, from 1952 to 1955. He received the society's special service award in 1966.

Gerald H. Burgess
(1881-1938) Minnesota

Organizer of a course in stamp collecting at the University of Minnesota in the mid-1930s. The course is identified as the first such course for which college credit was given in an American educational institution.

George E. Burghard
(1874-1963) New York

Specialist in the stamps of Hong Kong and Switzerland, he made pioneer broadcasts on stamp collecting from New York radio stations in the 1920s.

Al Burns
(1892-1948) Oregon

Best known as editor of *Weekly Philatelic Gossip* from 1927 to 1940 and of *Western Stamp Collector* from 1942 to 1948. While associated with the Rotnem Stamp Company in Minneapolis, he was involved in the compilation of its precancel catalogs. During his years as editor of *Gossip*, he was very much involved in the editing and production of the *Dworak Catalogue of Air Mail Covers.*

Maurice Burrus
(1882-1959) Switzerland

This warm-hearted, courtly man assembled one of the premier collections in the world. The collection contained representatives of almost every known rarity. He became interested in stamps at the age of 7, and extensive travel in later years enabled him to acquire rare stamps. He battled with Arthur Hind for many of the gems of the 1922 Ferrari auction. Twelve years later, Burrus obtained many of the Ferrari items from the dispersal of the Hind collection. When his fingers became crippled with arthritis, Burrus decided to sell his collection. Raymond Weill's offer of $4 million was refused, as was an American dealer's $5 million offer. The eventual sale of the Burrus collection took five years and 75 separate auctions or private sales. Although the cumulative value of the collection is not known, Robson Lowe Auctions, which conducted 38 of the 75 sales, alone totaled $5,560,000 in three years.

-C-

Alfred H. Caspary (1878-1955) New York

Wall Street personality who quietly assembled a superlative collection of classic stamps of the world that realized a record $2,895,146 when dispersed in a series of 16 auction sales after its owner's passing. Caspary avoided the limelight, although he served as a judge at the International Exhibition in 1913. Only his most intimate friends knew of his interest in stamps or the extent of his holdings. Although he loaned fine items from his collections for Court of Honor showings in international exhibitions, such as CIPEX in 1947, he did so anonymously. Caspary rarities illustrated in *Life* magazine's philatelic issue of 1954 were identified simply as items from collections owned by "Pacificus."

Theodore Champion (?) France

In the first Ferrari sale in 1921, Theodore Champion bought a collection of stamps from Uruguay comprised of 2,222 items for $10,400. A great French dealer, his France collection was obtained by Arthur Hind for $63,000. He also had in his collection, for a time, the famous cover addressed to Miss Rose with the vertical pair of 2¢ rose British Guiana issue of 1851. The cover is considered one of the top 10 rarities of the world.

Carroll Chase (1878-1960) New Hampshire

Because of Chase's intensive study and publication of its production and use, the 3¢ U.S. stamp of 1851-57 may be described accurately as the United States postal adhesive that has given more solid pleasure to serious philatelists than any other. Beginning his studies of this first U.S. 3¢ stamp early in the century, he assembled thousands of copies and devoted many hours to their study. His initial monograph, published by the American Philatelic Society in 1909, reported his first efforts to plate the issue. Eventually he was able to complete this plating, and his handbook detailing this work received the Crawford medal of the Royal Philatelic Society of London in 1930.

Returning to this country from France just before World War II, he took up the study of the territorial postmarks of the United States, collaborating with Richard McP. Cabeen in a series of articles in the *American Philatelist*, which were published as a handbook in 1953.

James M. Chemi (1912-1976) Arizona

A professional newspaperman by vocation, James M. Chemi became the first full-time paid editor of the *American Philatelist* when the official publication of the American Philatelic Society was put on a full-time basis in 1965. When David Lidman relinquished the editorship of the *American Philatelist* in 1960, Chemi took over that post on a part-time basis, and five years later became the first full-time editor.

He was the recipient of the John N. Luff award and was elected a member of the Arizona State Philatelic Hall of Fame, serving two terms as president of the Phoenix Philatelic Association. A founding member and trustee of the American Philatelic Research Library, he was also serving as president of the APS Writers Unit No. 30 at the time of his death. He was an accredited judge in the categories of Great Britain and Colonies, France, British North America, topicals, general and literature.

In 1960, he organized the first Arizona Philatelic Workshop and helped to re-activate the Arizona Federation of Stamp Clubs in 1969. He was an avid supporter of juniors in philately and, along with his other activities, compiled two stamp columns each week for the non-philatelic press, appearing in Phoenix newspapers.

Hugh M. Clark (1886-1956) New York

Editor of the Scott catalog from 1936 to 1946, he was intimately involved in its production for a dozen years before that. A young stamp dealer in Chicago during the early years of the century, Clark joined the staff of the Scott Stamp and Coin Co. in 1912 and became its proprietor in 1935. Trained in the fine art of philatelic catalog editorship by John N. Luff, he gradually relieved Luff of much of the routine work of producing the annual editions so that there were no problems when Luff died in 1938.

Clark's major contribution to the Scott catalog was the development of the new system of catalog numbers introduced in the 1940 edition. Under Clark's administration of the Scott organization, publication of the *Scott Specialized U.S. Catalogue* and the *Scott Air Post Catalogue* began, and a variety of new albums were introduced. Failing health made it necessary for Clark to restrict his activities and in 1946 he sold Scott Publications Inc. to Gordon Harmer, who was proprietor until its sale in 1960 to Esquire Inc. Clark was active in organized philately and was a prime mover in the establishment of the Philatelic Foundation in the 1940s.

Sylvester Colby
(1904-1984) New York

A humorous stamp auctioneer who cried many important New York stamp sales, Sylvester "Sy" Colby often said that non-bidders came to his sales just to hear his jokes. He ran a stamp office at 505 Fifth Ave., in New York for many years. His specialty in later years was philatelic literature. He handled the libraries of Philip Ward Jr., David Lidman and Frank Rossi, among others. His own library was sold at auction by Robert A. Siegel. Colby was a former American Stamp Dealers' Association president and a life member of the American Philatelic Society.

Charles B. Corwin
(— 1891) New York

One of the founders of the American Philatelic Association (now the American Philatelic Society) in 1886 and a leading spirit in the establishment of the Collectors Club of New York in 1896, Corwin was one of the first collectors in this country to take watermark and perforation varieties seriously. He had the distinction of being the first collector in history to pay more than $1,000 for a single postage stamp when he bid $1,010 for the 2¢ British Guiana "Cottonreel" of 1851 when the DeCoppet collection was dispersed at auction by John Walter Scott.

Eugene N. Costales
(1894-1984) New York

Eugene N. Costales began collecting at age 9 and became a stamp dealer at age 14 when he went to work for the Scott Stamp and Coin Co. He compiled the first *Scott Specialized Catalog of United States Stamps* in 1922. A stamp dealer on Nassau Street for many years. Mr. Costales joined Scott Publications Inc. in 1955 and edited the *Scott Standard Postage Stamp Catalogue* until his retirement in 1971. Among the awards he received during his long philatelic career were the John Luff award, the Dr. Carroll Chase cup and the Philatelic Foundation award for lifelong service to philately.

W.H. Crocker
(1861-1937) California

William H. Crocker was a successful banker in San Francisco who became interested in stamps when he bought the collection of Edward A. Craig in 1884. He was the regional vice president of the Third International Philatelic Exhibition in New York in 1936, despite the fact that he rarely displayed his extensive collection. The 42 albums in the Crocker collection included 15 albums of Great Britain and colonies. The highlight of the nine separate Crocker collection sales in 1938-39 was a used block of four of the 24¢ 1869 Pictorial issue with inverted center, which went to Y. Souren for $11,625.

-D-

Louise Boyd Dale
(1905-1967) New Jersey

Dale was the first woman to be invited by the Philatelic Congress of Great Britain to sign its Roll of Distinguished Philatelists. Daughter of Alfred F. Lichtenstein, she inherited her father's love for stamps and mastered the fine art of philately under his tutelage. Chairman of the Philatelic Foundation, she headed its Expert Committee for many years. She was the first woman to serve as a member of the jury at an international philatelic exhibition at Fipex in 1956.

Hiram E. Deats
(1870-1963) New Jersey

Last survivor of the group that organized the American Philatelic Association (now the American Philatelic Society) on Sept. 14, 1886. He began collecting about 1880 and selected the development of the U.S. postal service as the subject for his graduation thesis at Princeton University. His purchase of U.S. Treasury Department waste paper in the 1890s put him in possession of information on the production of U.S. revenue stamps, which he used in the writing of what is known as the *Boston Revenue Book*. He is also famous in philately as the discoverer of the unique Boscawen, N.H., postmaster's provisional stamp of 1845.

Baron Anthony de Worms
(1869-1938) England

A 50-year member of the Royal Philatelic Society, London, Baron Anthony de Worms was placed on the Roll of Distinguished Philatelists at its inauguration in 1921. His collection of Ceylon issues was well-known among collectors of the time. Baron de Worms also collected unused stamps of Great Britain. His Ceylon collection was first shown in 1893 and later won many high awards at international exhibitions. He was elected to the Royal Philatelic Society, London, council in 1916 and was awarded the society's Tilleard medal in 1932.

August Dietz Sr.
(1870-1963) Virginia

As the doyen of specialists in the stamps and postal history of the Confederate States of America, he was known affectionately as "The General" by members of the Confederate Stamp Alliance. The CSA was the organization of collectors of Confederate States material in whose formation he played an active role. His *Postal Service of the Confederate States of America*, published in 1929, is an established reference book. Editions of his *Confederate Catalogue and Handbook*, which began appearing in 1936, are an invaluable source of information.

Henry Duveen
(1854-1919) New York and England

The aim of Henry Duveen was to secure mint, fresh stamps in the most perfect condition possible, with the exception of certain rare used issues for which no mint copy was available. He was known mainly for his collection of British Guiana and British Colonies. His entire collection included between 200,000 and 250,000 items. Edward D. Bacon assisted Duveen in assembling his collection, which eventually won a silver medal at the International Philatelic Exhibition of 1906 and the grand prize trophy at the International Philatelic Exhibition in New York City in 1913.

Duveen also won numerous other gold medals for his Mauritius and Great Britain entries. Upon Duveen's death, his collection was auctioned by Charles Phillips over a four-year period. His family received $680,000 from the sales.

A.V. Dworak
(1879-1931) Kansas

Proprietor of a printing establishment that published a variety of philatelic literature, notably the periodical *Weekly Philatelic Gossip* and the *Dworak Catalogue of U.S. Air Mail Covers*, Dworak was a skilled printer and a stamp collector. He launched a journal known as *Philatelic Gossip* in 1915, publishing it monthly until weekly publication began in 1923. The airmail cover catalog developed from information on the expanding U.S. airmail service appearing in the weekly in the 1920s. After Dworak's death his widow, Dorothy E. Dworak, carried on the business and *Philatelic Gossip*, with Al Burns, Charles S. Thompson, Charless Hahn and Harry Weiss as editors. The publication appeared weekly until 1960.

-E-

The Rev. Robert Earee
(1846-1928) England

The Rev. Earee wrote *Album Weeds*, a classic two-volume book that describes every forged stamp known to the author. The books were dedicated to the then prince of Wales and later King George V. The books were later reprinted in eight volumes. The Rev. Earee signed the Roll of Distinguished Philatelists in its inaugural year, 1921. The philatelic press gave little if any mention when he died in Cheltenham, England, in 1928.

-F-

Agathon Faberge
(— 1951) Russia

Often called the Tsar of Philately, Agathon Faberge was also known for his fabulous collections of jewelry, precious stones and beautiful Easter eggs. He accumulated enormous collections of stamps and was the founder of the Sterky Correspondence, an archive of tens of thousands of letters from Finland, the Scandinavian countries, Russia and the Far East. At a Ferrari auction, Faberge paid a Berlin stamp dealer 20,000 francs in gold to not compete with him for the Zemstvo stamps of Russia. His Russian collection consisted of everything from proofs to the largest blocks. He also had collections of the old Italian States, Argentina and New South Wales. His Finnish collection was so large that he received an advanced deposit on it of more than 18,000 English pounds.

Count Philippe Ferrari
(1850-1917) France

As a frail and sickly child of inestimably wealthy parents, Philippe Ferrari was introduced to stamp collecting at age 10. By the 1880s, he was credited with having the most complete stamp collection known. One of his most important purchases was the Judge Frederick Philbrick collection, which he paid $45,000 for in 1882. In 1878 he acquired the 1¢ black on magenta British Guiana stamp of 1856, known as the world's most valuable stamp.

Due to his great wealth and eagerness to acquire rarities, Count Ferrari had every prominent European dealer commissioned to buy him any unique items they encountered. The enormity and pricelessness of his collection became an international legend that helped to propel stamp collecting from just another hobby to a major avocation.

Count Ferrari seldom showed his collection to individuals and never exhibited in philatelic competitions. A reclusive and private man, he died of a heart attack while attempting to acquire a rare Swiss stamp.

In 30 years of collecting, it is estimated that he spent close to $1,250,000. Following his death, his collection was confiscated by France and sold, with proceeds being credited to the German War Reparations Account. His material was auctioned in 14 separate sales. It is suspected that a portion of his collection was not sold in auction, as many rarities that he was known to own never surfaced publicly.

-G-

King George V
(1865-1936) England

Probably the best-known collector of his era, King George the V was dubbed "The Premier Collector of the World" by the philatelic press. He formed the Red Collection section of the Royal Philatelic Collection, which today consists of 350 volumes and is kept in the Stamp Room of Buckingham Palace. When he was known as the Duke of York, he was made honorary vice president of the Philatelic Society of London in 1893 and eventually held the position of president for 14 years. After he became king, he became a patron of the society for the remainder of his life.

King George V entered his Mauritius and Hong Kong collections at the International Philatelic Exhibition in 1906 and won two silver medals. This was the only time he chose to compete. In 1921, his name was added to the Roll of Distinguished Philatelists.

Stanley Gibbons
(1856-1981) Great Britain

As a young lad in England, Stanley Gibbons began selling stamps in a corner of his father's pharmacy. Within two years he had moved to a room above the shop and was working full-time at his stamp dealings. In 1865 he published *Descriptive Price List and Catalogue of British, Colonial and Foreign Postage Stamps For Sale by E. Stanley Gibbons*, of which only two copies now exist. In 1874 he moved his stamp business to London, and for the next 14 years, he built up his business, published his 100-page *Catalogue and Price List* and produced stamp albums. He also introduced catalog numbers for the stamps of each country.

At the age of 50, Stanley Gibbons retired and sold his business to Charles Phillips. In 1890 the first *Gibbons Monthly Journal* was published, a forerunner to today's *Gibbons Stamp Monthly*. In 1893 Stanley Gibbons Ltd. was moved to 391 Strand in London.

Henry C. Gibson Sr.
(1885-1987) Pennsylvania

Widely known as one of the first serious

cover collectors, Henry Gibson Sr. assembled one of the finest collections of early United States stamps in the 1920s and 1930s. His exhibit of U.S. 1847s received a gold medal at the New York International Philatelic Exhibition in 1926. He began his collecting career by buying many covers from the John Seybold sale in 1910. The sale of his own U.S. cover collection in 1944 by Philip H. Ward was heralded as one of the most important auctions of its time. In 1982, Gibson's family found many of his items that had not been seen for decades. Among the finds were 1847 covers, postmasters' provisionals and 1869 covers. A rare block of the 1854 4-anna India issue was also discovered.

Col. E.H.R. Green
(1868-1936) New York and Texas

As the son of the famous frugal Hetty Green, Edward H. Green was known for his eccentric, philandering lifestyle. He preferred stamps with inverted centers and acquired 360 varieties. Col. Green often purchased his material from his Pierce-Arrow on Nassau Street. His most famous acquisition was a complete sheet of bicolored 24¢ inverted Jennies, for which he paid $20,000. His mass accumulation of stamps was auctioned between 1942 and 1946 in 28 separate sales. Col. Green's collection, which proved to be a potpourri of both expensive and cheap material, realized a record $1,800,000.

Vincent Graves Greene
(1893-1988) Canada

Known as a dean of Canadian philatelists, he co-authored *The Stamps of New Brunswick and Nova Scotia* with John Young. Greene studied the importance of postal rates as represented on covers and began compiling a cover collection going back to the 1700s. He was an international judge and also served as the chairman of Capex in Toronto. Among many philatelic honors, he was a signatory of the Roll of Distinguished Philatelists, a fellow of the Royal Philatelic Society and recipient of the Alfred F. Lichtenstein memorial award. In 1975, he used $50,000 from the sale of his major collection to form the Vincent Graves Greene Philatelic Foundation, one of the foremost expertizing services in Canada.

-H-

Mannel Hahn
(1895-1954) Illinois

Prolific contributor to the stamp papers in the 1930s and 1940s, he produced the chapter on postal markings in Stanley Ashbrook's handbook on the 1¢ U.S. 1851-57. Trained as an engineer, he was a flier during World War I, holding a pilot's license signed by Orville Wright. His publications include a handbook on U.S. postal markings of 1847-51 and the how-to-do-it book *So You're Collecting Stamps*, published in 1940.

Henry Revell Harmer
(1869-1966) England

The auction firm of H.R. Harmer Inc. was started in 1918 in London, England. The business is now worldwide and is carried on by H.R. Harmer's sons and grandsons. A leading stamp dealer Henry Harmer was known for being brilliant and shrewd. His company made the public auction important in stamp collecting and revolutionized the stamp market. He became a member of the Collectors Club of New York in 1924.

Henry E. Harris
(1902-1977) Massachusetts

Recognized by many as the "Grand Master of Philately," Henry E. Harris was the founder in 1916 of H.E. Harris and Co., a business that developed into "The World's Largest Stamp Firm." He started the Boston-based company at the age of 14 years, carrying on the business from the family home, first in Washington and later in Boston. What had once been a one-man operation in a bedroom had grown to include a payroll of approximately 400 permanent employees. Harris sold the business to General Mills in 1973. It has been sold several times since then.

In 1933, Harris conceived the idea of packaging stamps for sale in packets in chain and variety stores. The following year, he came up with the marketing coup of offering stamps as premiums, and in three years was credited with distributing more than 400 million stamps.

A legal victory that prevented Canal

Zone postal authorities from reprinting the Thatcher Bridge commemorative "error" brought him the Luff award from the American Philatelic Society in 1966. He also received a special citation in the same year from the Society of Philatelic Americans. In 1976 he was presented the American Stamp Dealers' Association Service to Philately award.

Clarence W. Hennan, M.D.
(1894-1955) Illinois

A collector since boyhood, this Chicago physician became intensely interested in U.S. precancels in the 1920s and wrote about them extensively. Later he became interested in the stamps of Curacao. He also produced a specialized catalog and formed an important collection of Haiti. Hennan was president of the American Philatelic Society from 1931 to 1933, and was active in the American Philatelic Congress, heading it in 1951.

Arthur Hind
(1856-1933) New York

Wealthy manufacturer of upholstery plush, he began building a fabulous collection of the world's postage stamps after buying his doctor's collection as an investment in 1891. He was a heavy buyer of rarities during the Ferrari sales in Paris in the 1930s, making headlines by paying the highest price ever paid for a single postage stamp when he acquired the unique 1¢ British Guiana provisional of 1856 for the equivalent of $34,000 in U.S. funds. This showpiece and other rarities from his albums were the cynosure of the 1926 International Philatelic Exhibition in New York City. After Hind's death the U.S. material in his collection realized $244,810 at auction sales in New York City. The balance of the collection, with the exception of the British Guiana rarity, was sold to a syndicate. The collection realized the equivalent of $680,544 at a series of auction sales in London in 1934 and 1935.

-J-

Lucius J. Jackson
(1915-1978) Vermont

A well-known authority in the stamp hobby, Lucius J. Jackson had been owner and publisher of *Stamp Wholesaler* for more than 41 years at the time of his death in August 1978. Although probably best known for his interests in the publication field, other philatelic accomplishments include his role as a founder of the Cardinal Spellman Philatelic Museum Corp. He was a member of the Collectors Club of New York and a life member of the American Stamp Dealers' Association.

Jackson took over publication of the *Stamp Wholesaler* in the summer of 1937 from Ray D. Fisher. Established by Harold C. Theba, the first issue was designed to serve principally the wholesale stamp trade and had appeared in April a year earlier. It ceased publication after seven issues. In his 25th anniversary issue, Jackson noted that Fisher had acquired the magazine from Theba for $5, but after five issues suspended publication and sold out to Jackson for the same price.

Max G. Johl
(1901-1957) Connecticut

Thread manufacturer whose specialized interest in U.S. postage stamps of the 20th century inspired many articles in the stamp papers about his discoveries. These articles led to the eventual publication of handbooks that provide authoritative material about those issues. The first of these handbooks, covering U.S. stamps from 1901 to 1922, was produced in collaboration with Beverly S. King. After King's death, the series was continued by Johl. Its fourth volume, covering commemoratives of the 1930s, received the Crawford medal in 1938. The first volume of the series was revised by Johl after modification of U.S. regulations restricting the picturing of postage stamps made possible publication of adequately illustrated philatelic reference works. In 1947 Johl authored a two-volume handbook on U.S. commemoratives, which received the American Philatelic Society's Luff award in 1950.

Albert I. Jones
(— 1956) Indiana

Pioneer in the serious collecting of U.S. precancels. His checklist of known varieties printed in *Mekeel's Weekly Stamp News* in 1898 was one of the first such listings published.

-K-

Ernest Kehr
(1911-1986) New York

The philatelic writing career of this noted collector began in 1937 when he became the hobby news editor of the New York *World-Telegram*. Kehr moved to the New York *Herald-Tribune* in 1939 as stamps news editor. After the paper closed, he worked for the Long Island *Newsday* and was that paper's stamp columnist at the time of his death. He was the author of *Hints for Stamp Collectors, Guide to Stamp Collecting* and *The Romance of Stamp Collecting*. In addition, Kehr broadcast radio programs on stamp collecting on the NBC radio network, as well as on local stations in New York City. Franklin D. Roosevelt often called upon him for philatelic advice. He belonged to many philatelic organizations and founded the Philatelic Press Club in 1964. An internationally qualified judge, he was also the director of the International Stamp Exhibit for the New York World's Fair in 1940.

Col. Ralph A. Kimble
(1893-1974) Michigan

Editor of the *American Philatelist* from 1936 to 1951 with leave of absence during World War II for service in the U.S. Army. He was active in the philatelic life of Chicago during the 1920s, organizing some of the first radio broadcasts calculated to stimulate interest in stamp collecting. His writings include books on stamp collecting, stamps as an investment and U.S. commemoratives, which were published by Grosset and Dunlap in the early 1930s. His impressive philatelic library, one of the largest ever formed by an individual, was dispersed by Sylvester Colby in a series of auction sales in the 1950s.

Beverly S. King
(1879-1935) New York

Engineer whose interest in 20th-century U.S. stamps led to his collaboration with Max G. Johl in the writing of articles about these stamps. King's death in a traffic accident ended the collaboration, but Johl continued the articles under his own byline. They eventually appeared in a series of four handbooks published by H.L. Lindquist.

Eugene Klein
(1878-1944) Pennsylvania

Philadelphia stamp dealer whose activities included purchase of the unique sheet of the 24¢ U.S. airmail invert of 1918 from W.T. Robey of Washington, D.C., and its sale to Col. E.H.R. Green. He was founder and first president of the American Philatelic Congress. Klein contributed many articles to the stamp papers and published the definitive handbook on the postal markings of U.S. inland waterways.

John Klemann
(1879-1955) New Jersey

Known as the greatest dealer for U.S. essays and proofs, John Klemann handled many great collections, including the William Smith Jr. collection and the Henry Mandel collection. He was president of the Nassau Stamp Co. He won numerous first-place awards for his exhibits at philatelic competitions. Klemann also served on the Expert Committee of the Philatelic Foundation and was the editor of the *Philatelic Gazette* for five years. After his retirement in 1939, his stock of U.S. and British North American essays and proofs were auctioned by Eugene Costales and Harmer, Rooke and Co. for $50,000.

Edward Knapp
(1878-1940) New York

This prominent collector of 19th-century United States covers, Confederates, locals, cancels, Pony Express and Western Express material was known for his plating of the 5¢ New Orleans issue. He won awards at the international exhibitions held in New York in 1926 and 1936. Knapp also wrote a book on the Pony Express and frequently contributed to the philatelic press.

Roger Koerber
(1934-1988) Michigan

Active as a stamp dealer for 37 years, Roger Koerber founded the Roger Koerber Auction Galleries of Southfield, Mich. In the 1970s, his firm was among the first in the hobby to use computers in auction and inventory management. Two of the largest American philatelic libraries, those of George Turner and Herbert Bloch, were offered in Koerber sales in 1981 and 1985, respectively.

Koerber assembled a specialized collection of Austria's 1933 WIPA semipostals early in his career. He was also known for his interest in Zeppelin airmail covers.

Harry M. Konwiser
(— 1960) New York

Konwiser was best known for his *U.S. Stampless Cover Catalogue*, listing postal markings of the era before stamps came into use and prepayment of postage became mandatory. Student of postal history and a prolific writer for the stamp papers, his publications include monographs on Colonial postal service and the postal service of the Texas Republic and the *American Stamp Collector's Dictionary*.

-L-

Maryette Lane
(1910-1986) Florida

Maryette Lane was instrumental in the establishment of the American Philatelic Society Stamp Theft Committee in the mid-1960s after a rash of stamp thefts, including Harry Allen's collection of Black Jacks that was in her possession at the time of its disappearance. She served as chairwoman of the committee until 1981. Mrs. Lane was a founding member of the American Philatelic Research Library, a fellow of the Royal Philatelic Society of London and a member of the National Philatelic Writers Hall of Fame. Most likely, she will be remembered for her discovery of the "star on cheek" on later Black Jack plates, which aids in identifying the reissues of 1875.

Henry Lapham
(1875-1939) Massachusetts

Henry Lapham's remarkable collection of New York postmasters' provisionals won a gold medal at the 1926 New York International Philatelic Exhibition. A grand award was garnered by his U.S. postmaster's provisionals collection at Tipex. The showing featured 200 examples of the stamp, including a half dozen examples of the rare "R.H.M." signature. It is believed that John Boker acquired most of Lapham's postmasters' provisionals and much of his U.S. material by private treaty.

Alfred F. Lichtenstein
(1876-1947) New York

Lichtenstein ranks as one of philately's greatest proponents and valued enthusiasts. Described as a philatelist in the fullest sense of the term, he collected stamps and devoted many hours to the study of them and the circumstances under which they were issued. He developed an intimate knowledge of philatelic art that was unrivaled. Only the finest specimens satisfied him and his collections represented the superlative in condition.

His specialized presentations of Mauritius, British Guiana, Canada, the Cape of Good Hope, Switzerland, the United States and other countries received many awards in international competition. At the 1926 international show in New York City, his Uruguay received the grand award as best in the show, and his Newfoundland, Nova Scotia and Cape of Good Hope received gold medals.

He began collecting as a schoolboy in Brooklyn and had amassed impressive holdings in 1917 when he paid $445,000 for the outstanding collection formed by George Worthington. This collection had received major awards at the 1913 international exhibition in New York City. Lichtenstein joined the Collectors Club in 1911 and was one of its most generous patrons, financing many of its projects, including the acquisition of its permanent home at 22 E. 35th St. in New York City. Just before his death in 1947, he was a prime mover in the establishment of the Philatelic Foundation. As a tribute to his standing as a philatelist, the Court of Honor at the Centenary International Philatelic Exhibition (Cipex) was dedicated to Alfred F. Lichtenstein, and the Collectors Club gave his name to its annual award for distinguished contributions to philately by living philatelists.

David Lidman
(1905-1982)

A newspaperman by profession for more than 50 years, David Lidman wrote and edited philatelic columns for numerous newspapers including the *New York Herald-Tribune*, the *Chicago Sun* and the *New York Times*. He helped found and was editor of the weekly stamp journal *Philately* in 1946, and also was a contributor and editor for the *Chambers Stamp Journal* and the *Western Stamp Collector*. Books authored by Lidman were *The New York Times Guide to Collecting Stamps, Treasury of Stamps* and *The World of Stamps and Stamp Collecting*.

Numerous philatelic honors were bestowed on him. Among these were the APS Luff award, Writers Unit No. 30 silver medal, American Philatelic Congress scroll of honor and the Sepad award. In 1981 he was named to the Philatelic Writers Hall of Fame. In the 1960s he was a member and chairman of the Citizens' Stamp Advisory Committee of the U.S. Post Office Department.

Josiah Lilly Jr.
(1893-1966) Indiana

A man of many collecting interests and the grandson of the pharmaceutical giant, Eli Lilly, Josiah Lilly Jr. collected stamps of the world in mint condition. He quietly accumulated 77,000 stamps into one of the finest collections ever assembled. Robert Siegel Auction Galleries auctioned Lilly's collection in a 10-part sale that began in 1967. The Lilly material realized a record $3,144,752.

Harry L. Lindquist
(1884-1978) New York City

Although Harry L. Lindquist is probably best known as the founder of *Stamps* magazine, he served in many capacities in the philatelic world, as well as in other fields in which he had an interest. As a youth, he developed a taste for many hobbies, especially stamp collecting. At the age of 17 he was editor of the magazine of the American Society of Curio Collectors.

When the family moved to Chicago, he began meeting some of the famous philatelic personalities he had read about, and the field of philately dominated his interests. He joined the Chicago Philatelic Society and later edited its monthly publication. Moving to New York, he began publishing *Stamps* magazine, the first issue appearing under date of Sept. 17, 1932.

Lindquist served on the first Citizens' Stamp Advisory Committee and also served as president of the People to People Hobby Committee Inc., appointed by President Eisenhower in 1956 to promote friendship and understanding between Americans and citizens of other lands.

A life member of the Collectors Club of New York, he served as the group's president from 1927 to 1930. He was an honorary member of many philatelic societies and held regular membership in others, including the American Philatelic Society and the Society of Philatelic Americans. In 1952, he founded the National Federation of Stamp Clubs and was its president for a number of years.

James Lindsay
(1847-1914) Great Britain

Also known as the Earl of Crawford, James Lindsay became an enthusiastic stamp collector in middle age, acquiring an incredible collection of philatelic literature, and postal issues from Britain, Italian States and the United States. He purchased the philatelic library of John Tiffany, a distinguished American philatelic author and bibliophile. A book titled *The Catalogue of the Philatelic Library of the Earl of Crawford* was 923 pages long and was printed in a limited edition of 300.

A famous acquisition by the Earl was the Mandel collection of U.S. essays and proofs, which he elaborately classified with detailed notes. King George V proposed that the Earl be elected president of the Royal Philatelic Society of London in 1903. Prior to his death, he sold some of his extensive collection to W.H. Peckitt. A medal in his honor is awarded to original contributions to philately published in book form.

George Ward Linn
(1884-1966) Ohio

Philatelic publisher and editor, famed for the vigor of his writings. With decided opinions on most philatelic subjects, he voiced them in language that even those who disagreed with him admitted was never dull. Linn was the son of a country printer. His first essays in stamp paper publishing were produced in his father's shop in connection with a stamp business he had started. Developing an interest in philatelic literature, Linn made a pioneer effort to launch a philatelic literature society in 1910 and held literature auctions in 1911 and 1912. When interest in Revolutionary issues of Mexico dominated the philatelic scene in the second decade of the century, Linn produced a monograph on the Coach Seal issues of Sonora that is still authoritative.

Linn's Stamp News, first published in Dayton, Ohio, and later in Columbus, Ohio, adopted a tabloid newspaper format when its office was moved to Sidney, Ohio, in 1943. Linn retired in 1965 and moved to Florida, with Carl P. Rueth succeeding him as editor of the weekly until 1969. The newspaper was then sold to Amos Press Inc. Linn's publishing efforts include a checklist of philatelic publications in English in 1909, a catalog of the patriotic covers of World War II and a definitive monograph on the "Paid" markings found on the 3¢ U.S. 1851.

Frances C. Locey, M.D.
(— 1932)

Virginia Navy medical officer whose interest in the postal markings of naval establishment postal installations led to his creation of the system for classifying U.S. Navy postmarks bearing his name.

John N. Luff
(1860-1938) New York

Probably the most distinguished of American philatelic scholars, whose competent editorship of the Scott *Standard Postage Stamp Catalogue* during the first three decades of the 20th century made it one of the world's most prestigious philatelic reference books. He was one of the first Americans invited to sign the Roll of Distinguished Philatelists when the Philatelic Congress of Great Britain created it in 1921.

Active in organized philately, Luff was president of the American Philatelic Society from 1907 to 1909 and served two terms as president of the Collectors Club, in whose formation in 1896 he had been a prime mover. He served as a judge at international exhibitions in Europe in the 1920s and was chairman of judges at the 1936 show in New York City.

The Luff reference collection, which was formed to provide a basis for the listings in the Scott catalog during Luff's editorship, became an asset of the Philatelic Foundation when it was established after World War II. Luff was a prolific writer in the stamp papers, and his major production in hard covers is the handbook on 19th-century U.S. stamps, based on articles appearing under his byline in the *American Journal of Philately* at the turn of the century.

-M-

F. Van Dyk MacBride
(1893-1961) New Jersey

F. Van Dyk MacBride was an investment banker whose presentations of the U.S. 1869 series and 19th-century Valentines received many awards in stamp shows. He is best known in philately for his activity as a specialist in Confederate States material. He was a founder and past president of the Confederate Stamp Alliance and a prolific contributor to its journal. He joined the American Philatelic Society in 1908, after exhibiting as a 14-year-old collector at one of its conventions. In 1947 he produced a monograph, which was published in the *American Philatelist*, on Barnabas Bates, leader of the campaign for postal service reform in this country that led to the issuance of the 5¢ and 10¢ U.S. stamps of 1847.

Henry Mandel
(1857-1902) New York

Henry Mandel's job as a counterfeit and color expert at the American Bank Note Co. made him an authority on the process of stamp design and manufacture. From various close sources, he was able to obtain numerous rare philatelic material. Mandel coordinated the U.S. Post Office Department Exposition in Paris in 1900. He also served as adviser to the Bureau of Printing and Engraving during the 1903 reprinting of small die proofs that had been commissioned as state gifts to political dignitaries. After Mandel's death, the bulk of his essay and proof collection was sold for $30,000 to James Lindsay, the Earl of Crawford.

Catherine L. Manning
(1881-1957) Washington, D.C.

Curator of the National Stamp Collection at the Smithsonian Institution in Washington D.C. during the last two decades of her life. Beginning her business career soon after the turn of the century in John Bartels' stamp shop in Washington, she joined the Smithsonian staff on a temporary basis to mount stamps the U.S. Post Office had received from the Universal Postal Union and had turned over to the Smithsonian. Manning spent the next 40 years building the National Postage Stamp Collection.

Dr. James J. Matejka Jr.
(— 1979) Illinois

A general practitioner in Chicago for 39 years, James J. Matejka Jr. was a world-renowned stamp collector. He played a major role in the hobby as a collector, a judge and a commissioner for international exhibitions. Shortly before his death, he was honored by being asked to sign the Roll of Distinguished Philatelists at the Congress of the British Philatelic Federation, the highest honor in international philately.

He was a member of the Citizens' Stamp Advisory Committee for eight years. He served as U.S. commissioner to international stamp shows in Belgium and Czechoslovakia, and as an international judge in Taiwan, Berlin and England. His personal collections of Newfoundland airmails, Czechoslovakia, United States and Austria were outstanding.

Among his numerous philatelic affiliations were: Society of Philatelic Americans (past president), American Philatelic Society, Royal Philatelic Society of London, Collectors Club of New York, Collectors Club of Chicago, charter member of the Cardinal Spellman Philatelic Museum. A member of the American Philatelic Congress and past president of the American Air Mail Society. He was a co-founder and life member of Compex — the Combined Philatelic Exhibition of Chicagoland.

Charles Haviland Mekeel
(1864-1921) Missouri

Dominant figure in American philately in the 1890s whose C.H. Mekeel Stamp and Publishing Co. is said to have placed stamp collecting in this country on a dollar, rather than a penny, basis. The firm, established in 1890 with a capitalization of $100,000, carried on an aggressive trade in stamps, published three editions of a general catalog of stamps of the world and a variety of albums, and became headquarters for Mexican stamps after the firm made a deal with a revolutionary government and acquired the holdings of Mexico's dead letter office. Acquisition of the fabulous Louisville find of St. Louis "Bears" was another of its coups.

Mekeel, who had published a stamp paper as a boy in Chicago in 1881, began publishing the *American Journal of Philately* in 1883 after moving to St. Louis and published it monthly until 1895. In 1891 he launched *Mekeel's Weekly Stamp News* and in 1896 began publishing the *Daily Stamp Item*. Mekeel kept the daily coming out for a year, but confided to his friends that he was some $5,000 out of pocket as a result.

The Mekeel Co. experienced financial difficulties in 1897 and in a re-organization Mekeel's brother, Isaac A. Mekeel, took over the weekly and published it as an in-depth journal. After Isaac's death in 1913, Charles E. Severn, Willard Otis Wylie and Charles Jewett organized the Severn-Wylie-Jewett Co. to continue its publication. C.H. Mekeel left St. Louis after 1900 and located in Virginia where he launched and published the *Albemarle Stamp Collector*.

William Claire Menninger, M.D.
(1899-1967) Kansas

Probably the most distinguished of the many medical men who found stamp collecting a satisfying avocation. One of the country's leading psychiatrists, Menninger began collecting as a boy and never lost his enthusiasm for the hobby. He sought the stamps of all countries in postally used condition, stamps of the U.S. regularly used on cover and stamps with medical subjects.

Benjamin Miller Jr.
(1849-1928) Wisconsin

An authority on United States stamps, Benjamin Miller Jr. donated his collection to the New York City Public Library in 1925. One of the most valuable items in his collection at the time was the 30¢ 1869 invert.

Walton I. Mitchell, M.D.
(1878-1960) California

Though best known as editor of the *Official Catalogue of U.S. Bureau Precancels*, Mitchell was a distinguished student of postal stationery of the world, particularly postal cards and the revenue stamps of Canada. A physician in practice in Kansas and Colorado before locating in California in the 1920s, Mitchell's studies made possible the publication of the first catalog of bureau precancels in 1925. He edited annual editions of the catalog until failing eyesight made it necessary for him to discontinue the activity in the late 1950s.

Edwin Mueller
(1891-1962) New York

A professional in Austria for many years, associated with the distinguished Otto Friedl and administrator of the impressive WIPA exhibition in Vienna in 1933, Mueller came to this country in 1938 and established the Mercury Stamp Co. in New York City. His special field was 19th-century Europe with emphasis on Austria and imperforate stamps. His published works include the monograph on Austrian postmarks that he published in Vienna in 1927, a bilingual specialized catalog on Austria, published in 1927, and a monograph on the pre-stamp postmarks of Austria that appeared in 1950.

-N-

Perham Nahl
(1909-1988)

Known to many as the dean of aerophilately, Perham Nahl joined the American Air Mail Society in 1927 and was elected as a director several years later. He served the society as director or vice president until 1969, when he became president. Nahl's major claim to fame was his research and writings. He was an editor of a section of the *Dworak Airmail Catalogue*, editor of the *West Coast Airmail Society Catalogue* and editor-in-chief of the *American Air Mail Catalogue*. The AAMS presented numerous awards to him, including the Walter Conrath memorial award. He was inducted into the APS Writers Unit No. 30 Hall of Fame in 1987 and received a gold medal from the International Federation of Aerophilatelic Societies for his outstanding service to aerophilately.

Mortimer Neinken
(1896-1984) New York

One of this honored philatelic writer's most significant contributions was his book *The United States One Cent Stamp of 1851 to 1861*, which was published in 1972. A devoted student of U.S. classic stamps, Mortimer Neinken won the John Luff award in 1962, was inducted into the APS Writers Unit Hall of Fame in 1977 and received the Eugene Klein memorial award from the American Philatelic Congress three times. The Collectors Club of New York presented him with its Alfred E. Lichtenstein award in 1971 and its Cryer research award. In addition, he received all four prizes offered by the U.S. Philatelic Classics Society. He devoted many hours of voluntary service to philately and was involved with the Philatelic Foundation and its expert committee for many years.

Saul Newbury
(— 1950) Illinois

Chicago department store executive who formed a collection of 19th-century Brazil featuring the Bull's-Eyes of 1851, which earned many major awards in international competition. He later assembled the collection of 19th-century U.S. that received the grand award at the Centenary International Philatelic Exhibition (Cipex) in 1947.

-O-

Max Ohlman
(1881-1957) New York

Nassau Street stamp dealer for many years, holding auction sales in which many collections were dispersed during the 1920s and 1930s. Franklin D. Roosevelt was one of his clients, and while the late president was serving as New York's governor, Ohlman sponsored his application for membership in the American Philatelic Society.

Ross O'Shaughenessy
(— 1954) California

One of San Francisco's stamp dealers at the turn of the century and the only one to resume business after the 1906 earthquake and fire. A pioneer collector of Western Express covers and related material.

-P-

Elliott Perry
(1884-1972) New Jersey

Inspired to take up stamp collecting by the appearance of the Columbian commemoratives in 1893, Perry spent his life in philatelic activity, functioning as a full-time stamp dealer after 1915. While his most spectacular achievement was his successful plating of the 10¢ U.S. stamp of 1847, something Luff and other students had feared was impossible because of the dearth of material available for study, Perry also made significant contributions to philatelic understanding of 19th-century postage and revenue stamps and their use. Notable are his studies of the distribution of the 1847 stamps to post offices, the demonetization of the 1857 series in 1861, issues of Sanitary Fairs and U.S. locals and carrier stamps. He produced many articles for the stamp papers, using the pseudonym Christopher West on some of his contributions, and published a house organ, *Pat Paragraphs*, in which he recorded facts developed by his research.

Thomas Doane Perry
(1878-1958) New Jersey

Perry's philatelic interests centered on U.S. embossed stamp envelopes. He made signal contributions to the literature of envelope collecting.

James Petrie
(1844-1918) New Jersey

This part-time dealer from New Jersey also worked as a philatelic scout for J.W. Scott and Co. His cunning and questionable ethics earned him an unsavory reputation. He openly bragged about selling fakes and counterfeits to Ferrari. His famous acquisition of four sheets of the 100 subjects on card of the 15¢, 24¢, 30¢ and 90¢ Pictorial issues of 1869 with inverted centers was a philatelic coup. It is believed that he purchased the panes from a government agent at the American Bank Note Co. With few kind feelings for his fellow collectors, Petrie died quietly with only a brief mention of his passing in one American philatelic journal.

Reginald Phillips
(?) England

Founder of the National Postal Museum in London, England, Reginald Phillips hoped to establish a national home for postal history. The material he presented from his collection in 1965 commemorated the history of British stamps from Queen Victoria's reign. The assemblage included unique official documents, artists' drawings, proofs and issued stamps. Phillips spent 30 years assembling the most complete historical study of 19th-century British stamps. In 1960, in an international exhibition in London, he exhibited a select portion of his collection for the first time and garnered the grand prix.

Sidney G. (Sid) Pietzsch
(— 1978) Texas

A newspaperman by profession, the interests of Sidney G. (Sid) Pietzsch in philately carried him into extensive writings in the hobby, both for the philatelic and non-philatelic press. He began his writing career as editor of the University of Texas humor magazine, later returning to his hometown of Beaumont, Texas, to work as a reporter and as city editor of the *Beaumont Journal*.

For five years prior to his death, his writings for *Linn's Stamp News* included the popular feature Cinderellas and compilation of the first *Linn's Basic Knowledge For The Stamp Collector*. He compiled a stamp column for the *Dallas Morning News*, along with other writings. He was a member of most major philatelic organizations, as well as several local clubs.

Bertram W.H. Poole
(1880-1957) California

Emigrating to this country from England in 1900, Poole located in Los Angeles where he operated a stamp shop and found time to produce many articles on stamps and stamp collecting for the stamp papers. Many of these articles were published in some 30 pamphlet handbooks by *Mekeel's Weekly Stamp News*. He was one of the first professionals to call attention to the interest of subject-matter (topical) collecting. Late in his life he assembled a *Philosophy of Collecting* presentation, which was exhibited at the National Philatelic Museum in Philadelphia and was described in a handbook appearing with the museum's imprint.

Eustace B. Power
(1872-1939) New York

A stamp dealer who is said to have restored sanity to U.S. collecting by publication in the 1920s and 1930s of a series of *Philatelic Horse Sense* pamphlets in which he detailed a commonsense approach to the collecting of U.S. adhesives. Born in England, Power came to this country in the 1890s and was associated with J.C. Morgenthau in Chicago before going to New York, where he managed the U.S. branch of Stanley Gibbons Ltd. of London for a time before going into business under his own name.

J.W.R. Purves
(1903-1979) Australia

This dedicated stamp collector became a fellow of the Royal Philatelic Society of London in 1929 and received the A.F. Lichtenstein Memorial Award in 1960. He was elected to the British Roll of Distinguished Philatelists in 1937 and received the Tapling medal in 1953. Purves served as an international judge and also exhibited on numerous occasions, winning high awards in Vienna, Paris, Prague and Stockholm. He wrote numerous handbooks, articles and two books on such subjects as the postal history of Fiji, Victoria, Queensland and Tasmania.

Purves succeeded in financing a clubhouse for The Royal Philatelic Society of Victoria in Melbourne, Australia, of which he was a member for more than 30 years and also president. He also contributed to the creation of *Philately From Australia*, a quarterly journal devoted to serious philatelic research of Australasian stamps and postal history.

-R-

Joseph S. Rich
(1860-1931) New York

A collector from the age of 16, Rich was a dominant figure in American philately for more than half a century. One of the proprietors of the Scott Stamp and Coin Co. from 1895 to 1913 he was intimately involved in the production of the Scott catalog as it assumed stature as a major reference work. Rich was one of the founders of the Collectors Club and active in its affairs until his death. Rich had a special interest in U.S. Telegraph stamps, and his 1897 monograph on them, revised by his son for publication by the Society of Philatelic Americans in 1946, is a standard reference book.

Stephen G. Rich
(1890-1958) New Jersey

A leading spirit in half a dozen stamp organizations, a publisher and contributor to nearly all the stamp papers of his era, Stephen G. Rich is probably the best-known philatelic personality of the 1940s and '50s. Son of Joseph S. Rich, Stephen Rich grew up in a philatelic atmosphere. He was active in the American Philatelic Society, the Collectors Club of New York, the Society of Philatelic Americans, the France and Colonies Philatelic Society, the Precancel Stamp Society and New Jersey stamp clubs. He published a dozen editions of the *Mitchell-Hoover Bureau Precancel Catalogue* and three editions of Harry Konwiser's *Stampless Cover Catalogue*, as well as the monthly *Precancel Bee* and *Postal Markings* journal. He was a prolific writer. His byline appeared in the stamp papers over articles dealing with almost every aspect of philatelic activity with special emphasis on his particular interests: the stamps of France, Poland's first adhesive and South African philately.

Franklin Delano Roosevelt
(1882-1945) New York

Because he was an enthusiastic collector and was always willing to talk about his interest in stamps and stamp collecting, Roosevelt is generally believed to have done more than anyone else to give the hobby of stamp collecting the prestige it enjoys in this country. No one could say that stamp collecting was a juvenile activity when the president of the United States let it be known that he regularly spent happy hours working with his stamp collections.

It was while he occupied the White House that federal statutes limiting the illustration of stamps were changed, making possible publication of more useful albums, catalogs and philatelic literature.

Roosevelt developed an interest in stamp collecting as a youngster and continued a collection formed by his mother. His enthusiasm for the hobby continued, and by the time he was elected governor of New York, his collection filled many volumes. Though he was interested in all stamps, he had a special affection for the issues of Hong Kong, Haiti, Argentina, Venezuela and British Colonies in the Caribbean.

Following his death, his heirs decided to sell most of his collections, and the property was appraised at $80,000 by the late George B. Sloane, a Nassau Street stamp dealer. However, Roosevelt's stamps brought $221,000 when sold at auction in 1946. Certain collections that were retained by the late president's family are on exhibit in the Roosevelt Library in Hyde Park, N.Y.

-S-

Waller A. Sager
(1929-1977) California

Leading spirit in the Collectors of Religion on Stamps Society (COROS), Waller Sager was editor of its journal, *COROS Chronicle*, for 23 years. His more significant contributions to the literature of topical collecting include monographs on stamps illustrating the life of Martin Luther, U.S. stamps with religious subjects and Christmas stamps.

Nicolas Sanabria
(1890-1945) New York

A native of Venezuela, Sanabria came to the United States in 1922 and went to work in Victor Weiskopf's stamp shop. In 1927 he went into business for himself, specializing in airmail material and launching the catalog of airpost stamps bearing his name.

John Walter Scott
(1842-1919) New York

Generally identified as the Father of American Philately, Scott came to this country in 1861, bringing with him a stamp collection he had assembled as a youth in England. Within a decade he was one of New York City's foremost stamp dealers, had issued the first of the detailed price lists that were to develop into the Scott *Standard Postage Stamp Catalogue*, had held the world's first auction sale of postage stamps and had published the first of the more than 30 stamp albums bearing his imprint.

In 1886 he sold his prosperous business, including the right to use the Scott name, to George C. Calman and went back to England. Returning to the United States in a few years, Scott resumed activity as a stamp dealer. He was a dominant figure on the philatelic scene until his death in 1919. He was one of the founders of the Collectors Club in 1896 and, at the time of his death, was president of the American Philatelic Society.

Charles E. Severn
(1872-1929) Illinois

A contributor to *Mekeel's Weekly Stamp News* from its beginning in 1891, Severn became proprietor of the periodical when the Mekeel organization was reorganized in 1897 and was its editor until he retired in 1926. He was one of the Americans invited to sign the Roll of Distinguished Philatelists when it was created in 1921 by the Philatelic Congress of Great Britain.

John Seybold
(1858-1909) New York

Often referred to as the father of postal history, John Seybold accumulated a major world postal history collection with strengths in Confederate States postmasters' provisionals. In 1897, his philatelic library numbered more than 500 volumes. After he took his own life at the age of 51, Seybold's collection was sold in three auctions by J.C. Morgenthau in 1910.

George I. Silberberg
(1911-1982) New York

George I. Silberberg, founder of Philatelic Hobbies for the Wounded and chairman of Hobbies for All Ages, died in New York City, Feb. 14, 1982. His voluntary crusade to rebuild the spirits of those ill and confined grew out of a personal tragedy in 1942, when his legs were severely crushed in an accident.

Silberberg was a member of the American Philatelic Society, the Society of Philatelic Americans, the Bronx County Stamp Club and the American Stamp Dealers' Association. He was also an honorary member of many school clubs, which he visited on a trip around the world.

James N. Sissons
(1914-1980) Ontario, Canada

A leading Canadian philatelic authority, James Normart Sissons was credited with having sponsored Canada's first postage stamp auction in 1946. He was president of J.N. Sissons Ltd., a stamp auction firm in Toronto. He was the founding president of the Canadian Stamp Dealers' Association.

A native of Pennsylvania, Sissons went to Toronto as a child and entered law school in Canada. His interest turned to stamps, however, and his philatelic career began before his law studies were completed. He was a leading auctioneer in Canada and was described by some as "the world's foremost authority on Canadian stamp collecting."

George C. Slawson
(1905-1969) Vermont

Student of stamps, postal stationery and postal history whose publications include the catalog of postal stationery of U.S. possessions brought out in 1958 by Van Dahl Publications, and *Postal History of Vermont*. The latter appeared in 1969 with the imprint of the Collectors Club's Theodore E. Steinway Memorial Publications Fund.

Hugh M. Southgate
(1871-1940) Washington, D.C.

Most of what collectors know about the production of U.S. stamps during the 1920s and through the 1940s stems from Hugh Southgate's rapport with responsible personnel at the Bureau of Engraving and Printing during that period. A dedicated stamp collector, trained as an engineer, Southgate enjoyed the friendship of Bureau personnel at a time when the introduction of the rotary press and other sophisticated equipment was revolutionizing U.S. stamp production. He was alert to every development there and communicated his observations to the stamp world through articles in the stamp papers.

Southgate was a leading spirit in the organization of the Philatelic Plate Number Association in 1926, and four years later, when this organization expanded its activity to cover everything produced in the Bureau and assumed the style of Bureau Issues Association, Southgate was named president. He held that office for a decade. His services to stamp collecting brought him the Washington Philatelic Society's Michael Eidsness award in 1939.

Francis Cardinal Spellman
(1889-1967) New York

A collector since boyhood in Massachusetts, Cardinal Spellman built an exceptional collection of mint U.S. singles and added Vatican City issues to his interests while stationed in Rome and before returning to New England. In his numerous global travels as a bishop, archbishop and cardinal, he acquired collections from every corner of the earth.

Coming to New York, he led the campaign for the Al Smith stamp. When he was named a cardinal in 1946, he donated his entire collection to Regis College, where it first was housed in the college library. Subsequently, through a contribution by a personal friend and benefactor, a special building was designed to become the Cardinal Spellman Philatelic Museum, constructed on the campus.

His collection was first displayed at the 1947 Cipex international stamp show at Grand Central Palace, N.Y. After that, it was displayed at numerous international shows in Europe, Argentina, the Philippines and other nations.

John Stark
(1918-1987) Ohio

John Stark was a recognized authority on U.S. experimental stamps and a regular contributor to *Linn's Stamp News* from 1970-74, writing primarily on luminescent U.S. stamps. He co-authored the *Handbook on U.S. Luminescent Stamps* with Al Boerger. Stark was presented the Society of Philatelic Americans' top award for literature for his article The Mail Code Sorting System, which was published in the *SPA Journal*.

Theodore E. Steinway
(1883-1957) New York

Member of the distinguished family of piano manufacturers, Steinway has been identified as the "Renaissance Man" of American philately because of the scope of his philatelic interests and enthusiasms. Though his collections of Hamburg and other German States and the "Sydney Views" of New South Wales demonstrated his scholarship adequately, he formed outstanding presentations of stamps with socked-on-the-nose postmarks and stamps with musical subjects. He ignored no aspect of philately.

Joining the Collectors Club of New York in 1912, he was one of its most generous patrons, providing the funds for its purchase in 1922 of the outstanding philatelic library formed by Chief Justice Suppantschitsch. It was because of his interest in philatelic literature that the Collectors Club established the Theodore E. Steinway Memorial Publications Fund after his death. He was a judge at many international exhibitions and was chairman of the jury at the Centenary International Exhibition (Cipex) in 1947.

Byron F. Stevens
(1903-1970) Illinois

Student of the stamps of Mexico and a leading spirit in the formation in 1935 of the specialist organization now known as the Mexico-Elmhurst Philatelic Society International.

Kent B. Stiles
(1887-1951) New York

American philately's most active publicist, he produced regular columns of news and comment about stamp collecting for many years in popular periodicals such as *American Boy, Youth's Companion* and *Boy's Life*, produced a syndicated column appearing in many newspapers and served as stamp news editor for the *New York Times* during the last two decades of his life. He was one of the editors of the *Scott Monthly Journal* from its beginnings in 1920, writing many features dealing with the stories suggested by stamp designs and the personalities portrayed on postal adhesives. His *Stamps, An Outline of Philately*, was published by Harpers in 1929 and his *Geography and Stamps* was brought out in 1932 by McGraw-Hill.

David C. Stump
(— 1982) Pennsylvania

David C. Stump, of Devon, Pa., a past president of the American Philatelic Congress Inc. and a founder of the Perfins Club, died Jan. 5, 1982. Active for years in philatelic circles, he edited the *Congress Book* from 1964 through 1971, in addition to serving the APC Council.

Stump edited the Perfins Club bulletin for 15 years, was the group's treasurer for 20 years and served as president from 1976, resigning the latter position shortly before his death. A past president of the Philatelic Press Club, he served as vice president of Interphil 76 and as chairman of the Association International des Journalistes Philatelique.

-T-

Thomas Tapling
(1855-1891) Great Britain

Thomas Tapling accumulated one of the finest collections of 19th-century stamps in the world, surpassed in exellence only by the Ferrari material. He joined the London Philatelic Society in 1871 and became its vice president 10 years later. Tapling succeeded in acquiring the finest items of many major collections.

Unlike other 19th-century stamp collectors, he collected stamps on pieces and entire covers with postmarks of exceptional interest. Tapling's collection was estimated to comprise at least 200 volumes of material. After Tapling's early death at age 36, the collection was sorted, mounted and arranged for the British Museum by Edward Denny Bacon. It was first exhibited in 1904.

John K. Tiffany
(1847-1907) Missouri

St. Louis business man and pioneer collector who was one of the organizers of the American Philatelic Association (now the American Philatelic Society) and its president from 1886 through 1896. He wrote a history of U.S. stamps that was published in the French language by Moens in Belgium in 1883 and in the English language in this country in 1887.

George T. Turner
(1906-1979) Washington, D.C.

A past curator of the Smithsonian Institution's Division of Philately, Turner was perhaps America's leading philatelic bibliophile. He amassed a philatelic library of immense scope and was instrumental in the publication of several works, most notably *Sloane's Column*, a collection of columns by philatelic writer George Sloane.

A graduate of Cornell University with

bachelor's and master's degrees in chemistry, he left a 27-year career in business to head up the Post Office Department's Division of Philately in 1958. Turner retired in 1962, devoting his time to stamp collecting pursuits.

He was chairman of the Sixth International Philatelic Exhibition in 1966 and was a director of the APS from 1951-61 and from 1971-75. He served as vice president of the organization from 1961-65 and was its director of international affairs from 1975-78. He was a signatory of the Roll of Distinguished Philatelists in 1978.

-V-

Daniel W. Vooys
(1914-1978) New York

A collector of philatelic literature in his association with the hobby, Vooys was serving as president of the American Philatelic Research Library at the time of his death. He joined the American Philatelic Society in 1937 and served two terms as president of the association from 1969-73. He founded the Philatelic Literature Association in 1942 and was instrumental in merging that group into the present American Philatelic Research Library.

Vooys was inducted into the Writers Hall of Fame in 1975 and received the Luff Award for meritorious contributions to philately by living philatelists in 1956 and again in 1978, on the weekend of his death. Deeply interested in financial policies of the APS, he served as a member or chairman of the Finance Committee for almost 25 years. He was also a major financial benefactor of the APRL. He represented the APS at a number of FIP (International Federation of Philately) congresses, the first APS president to attend such sessions.

-W-

Philip H. Ward Jr.
(1890-1963) Washington, D.C.

A member of the American Philatelic Society for almost 60 years, Philip H. Ward Jr. was a widely known dealer and stamp columnist.

He joined the APS in 1906 and for some years was a columnist for *Meekel's Weekly Stamp News*. He embarked on an autograph collecting project at the age of 10, a project that later developed into one of the world's finest assemblages of presidential letters and American historical documents. Reportedly, it was a letter from former President Grover Cleveland, sent in response to one sent by Ward to Cleveland, about the turn of the century, that was the start of his collection.

Sir Nicholas Waterhouse
(1877-1964) England

This philatelic scholar was the author of *A Comprehensive Catalogue of the Postage Stamps of the U.S.* A specialist in U.S. collecting, Waterhouse was a gold medal winner at the 1936 Third International Philatelic Exhibition in New York. He was present at the third and final sale of his own rarities on June 27, 1955, in London by H.R. Harmer. The cumulative sales of his material totaled $97,230.

Richard Wolffers
(1924-1986) California

A stamp collector since age 5 and founder of the auction house Richard Wolffers Inc., Richard Wolffers began in the retail stamp business in 1961 with $500 in capital. He built the auction house to one of the top three in the country in sales by the mid-1980s. A member of the American Stamp Dealers' Association, he served as a director in 1976.

P.M. Wolsieffer
(1857-1934) New York

Prominent figure in the stamp trade, operating retail shops and staging auctions in Philadelphia and New York City in the years after World War I. He is said to have begun operating as a stamp dealer in Chicago at the age of 12 and was one of the Windy City's leading dealers before shifting his operations to Philadelphia. He is famed as the inventor of the approval card.

George Worthington
(1850-1924) Ohio

A wealthy businessman born in Canada, George Worthington accumulated so many stamps that he hired a full-time philatelic secretary. His Cleveland, Ohio, office became a mecca for international dealers seeking to sell him their materials. He became the first American stamp collector to own a Post Office Mauritius after he bought the two singles of the 1-penny issue on cover. Stamp Collector Worthington employed John Luff to handle his auction bids in New York. His purchases totaled approximately $50,000 per year. Worthington's collection was kept in 75 albums and included every U.S. issue in blocks of four.

In 1911, he displayed a $260,000 section of his collection at the American Philatelic Exhibition in Chicago. In 1913 he was elected honorary president of the International Philatelic Exhibition in New York City. Worthington's business investments began to fail in 1914, and he was forced to eventually sell off his collection. Alfred Lichtenstein purchased the Worthington collection for $445,000 in 1917.

Willard Otis Wylie
(1862-1945) Massachusetts

Editor of *Mekeel's Weekly Stamp News* from 1927 to 1940 and a dominant figure in American philately during the first four decades of the 20th century. He began writing for Mekeel's in 1902 while carrying on a stamp business in Boston. Later he became a proprietor of the *Philatelic Era*. This periodical was consolidated with Mekeel's in 1922 and the Wylie-Severn-Jewett Co. was set up to publish it. Wylie and Charles E. Severn shared editorship of the weekly until Severn retired.

William W. Wylie
(1905-1982) Nebraska

William W. Wylie, one of the nation's outstanding stamp journalists, was the recipient of many philatelic awards, including the Luff Award presented by the American Philatelic Society in 1979.

A member of the Arizona Hall of Fame, the National Writers Hall of Fame and the Writers Unit No. 30 of the APS, he also held memberships in the Bureau Issues Association, the Society of Philatelic Americans, the Precancel Stamp Society, the United Postal Stationery Society and the Collectors Club of New York.

A journalist by profession, working for newspapers in Kansas, Missouri and New York, he turned to writing for the philatelic press. He joined the staff of *Western Stamp Collector* in 1948 and continued that association for some 20 years.

Joining the Scott Publishing Co., he served as editor of the *Scott Monthly Journal* until the publication was sold by Duane Hillmer. On his retirement from active writing, Wylie continued his philatelic work by acting as a consultant to the PhilaMatic Center at Boys Town (Neb.) until he was hospitalized in 1978.

-Z-

Helen Kingsbury Zirkle
(1902-1976) Pennsylvania

A graduate of Bryn Mawr College, Helen Kingsbury Zirkle took up stamp collecting in 1945 and, since she had spent her youth in Japan, took a special interest in East Asian material. She was one of the founders of the International Society for Japanese Philately and was its secretary-treasurer for many years. Besides definitive monographs on the stamps of Korea and Manchukuo, she produced the Philately article in the *Encyclopedia Britannica* and a series of articles on the problems of the newcomer in stamp collecting.

Chapter 22

Infamous Forgers

The first forgery, described by Rowland Hill as "a miserable thing which could not possibly deceive any except the most stupid and ignorant," followed hard on the heels of the release of the Penny Black in 1840. Like all of the very earliest forged postage stamps, it was intended to defraud the post office.

The philatelic forgery, intended to defraud the collector, accompanied the rise in popularity of stamp collecting in the 1860s and '70s. It followed what had been intended as a benign creation, the facsimile: a convincing simulation of a hard-to-find stamp, created and sold for a nominal sum to fill an album space that would otherwise remain empty. Many of the earliest forgeries mentioned here were clearly intended only as facsimilies, as indicated by their very modest prices and frequently cartoonlike designs.

Inevitably, as collectors began to pay significant sums for scarce and unusual varieties, forgers endeavored to manufacture and market their creations as the genuine items at ever-escalating prices. Some of the most eminent early collectors were among their favorite victims.

The following listing, by no means exhaustive, is a greatly abbreviated and condensed version of Varro Tyler's highly recommended volume on *Philatelic Forgers: Their Lives and Works*. Tyler's text furnishes considerably more detail on these fascinating individuals and their bogus creations, as well as a useful bibliography of references to each of them.

Unlike the famed stamp collectors listed elsewhere in this text, the birth and death dates of many of these shadowy characters are unknown, nor is it likely they would be widely celebrated. Philatelic forgery continues to be a scourge of the hobby to this day, the following being but a very short list of some of its more notorious practitioners.

-A-

Bernard Assmus (a.k.a. A. Bernard)

A well-educated French novelist and journalist, Bernard Assmus was arrested in the course of one of several unsuccessful attempts to sell a forgery of the unissued British Penny Black V.R. Official stamp in London in 1890. A subsequent search of his residence uncovered 800 forged and altered stamps of British colonies, German states and Mexico. He was convicted in 1891-92 and sentenced to three years in prison.

A. Alisaffi

A Constantinople stamp dealer who produced photolithographic forgeries of the Greek Hermes Head issues in Paris in 1902. When the forgeries were condemned to the police in Athens as fakes, Alisaffi subsequently and successfully applied for a permit to sell the ungummed items as "simple images," since the Hermes Head stamps were by then no longer postally valid.

-B-

E.C.W. Bredemeyer

A Hamburg stamp dealer who in 1878 commissioned 75,000 counterfeits of the 1855-67 stamps of the German state of Bremen from the original printers. He also had a role in perforating and marketing reprint forgeries of the 1865 issue of Ecuador during the 1890s.

-C-

George Carion

A French stamp dealer and editor of philatelic journals in Paris in 1879, Carion later moved to Tahiti where he came to the attention of authorities in connection with forged Tahitian overprints. He moved to San Francisco in 1895, and was condemned in 1896 for the production of bogus Cochin China overprints. He was also linked to forged overprints of Obock, forgeries of Brazil's 1867 Condor issues and the production of a vast number of faked or altered United States Western Express covers, most of which are now well known to be fraudulent. He eventually returned to Paris, and remained active as a dealer and self-proclaimed expert until at least 1909.

Joseph J. Casey

Casey prepared a bogus "3 aspers" issue of Egypt in 1866 and, at about the same time, a stamp for a non-existent U.S. local service, Walker's Penny Post. J.W. Scott condemned and fired Casey from his position as editor of *The American Journal of Philately* in 1874 after he promoted bogus reprints of Berford & Co. California Express stamps. Casey later falsely represented himself as an official of the 1876 Philadelphia Centennial Exhibition, soliciting donations of stamps ostensibly to be exhibited there.

Andrien Champion (a.k.a. Henri Bauche, Hauf, Jules Rapin, Oscar Rapin, E. Wessler)

A Swiss stamp dealer based in Geneva in the 1880s, Champion's businesses dissolved or went bankrupt three times before 1900 under suspicions that he made off with substantial stocks of stamps, his own facsimiles and some very good forgeries. Champion subsequently sold these throughout Europe under numerous aliases.

Charged with fraud involving Swiss Cantonal forgeries in London in 1901, Champion jumped bail and fled. He was arrested in France and tried and convicted in Switzerland in 1902 for bankruptcy irregularities. Through an intermediary, he repurchased his own forgery stock, outbidding a Swiss stamp club that had hoped to acquire and destroy it. He was briefly a stamp dealer in the French town of Gex, later returning to set up shop in Switzerland under the name Frederic Champion.

Yong Chu Chee (a.k.a. George Gee, Alan Gee, Ma)

A Chinese restauranteur and stamp dealer in Sydney, Australia. In 1961, a police search of Chee's premises for pornography instead turned up zinc linecuts of some 250 postal overprints and surcharges of China, Australia's B.C.O.F. issues, Malaya, Burma, Papua and elsewhere. Chee was convicted in 1963 on two counts of possession of forged postage stamp plates, but was given a suspended sentence.

James M. Chute

A member of the infamous Boston Gang of forgers and swindlers associated with S. Allan Taylor, Chute specialized in developing false stories and documents used to make plausible the bogus stamps that the gang created and sold. In 1892, Chute represented himself as the agent of a non-existent Grand International Postal Exhibition in hopes of luring foreign governments into giving him stamp exhibits.

David Cohn

Berlin stamp dealer, reprinter and forger, responsible for an enormous number of reprints of the 1867-68 Roman States issues and reprint-forgeries of the 3-groschen 1859-64 issues of the German state of Hanover.

-E-

Ferdinand Elb

A stamp dealer in Dresden, Germany, in the early 1860s, Elb was an ingenious and resourceful forger and faker, best known for skillful facsimiles of German States, private local post and steamship issues. Elb's forged errors in reversed colors of Finland's 1845 stamped envelope imprints were so masterful that they convinced the Helsinki postmaster that official reprints of them should be made.

-F-

Henry Flachskamm

Operating as the Standard Stamp Co. of St. Louis, Mo., the Alsatian-born Flachskamm had a hand in a number of dangerous reprints and forgeries of classic Mexican stamps between 1897 and the early 1900s, marketing them and perhaps preparing them as well. Convicted of mail fraud for unrelated offenses in 1906, Flachskamm served a three-year sentence before re-entering the stamp trade in St. Louis. The stock of the Standard Stamp Co., which was dispersed in 1912, included vast quantities of reprints and forgeries from around the world.

Englehardt Fohl

Born in Dresden, Germany, Fohl's career as a forger spanned at least 36 years, beginning with forgeries and facsimiles of Moldavia, Mexico and Luzon that were exposed in 1871. More than 160,000 forgeries produced for him by a printing firm in Gera were seized following that company's bankruptcy in 1898, including classic German states, Portuguese, Serbian, Canadian, Romanian and steamship company issues. Fohl avoided prosecution in Germany by selling his wares only to customers abroad. He remained active upon his return to Dresden until at least 1906.

Georges Foure

Described by Tyler as "one of the most notorious philatelic forgers of all time" yet "scarcely known to modern collectors," Georges Foure was a Paris-born stamp dealer and publisher in Berlin, where he founded the highly regarded *Berliner Illustrierte Philatelisten-Zeitung* in 1878. Foure became a close friend of H.G. Schilling — a neighbor who, as fate would have it, turned out to be an engraver for the Prussian and later the Imperial German Printing Office. Schilling's private collection of dies and overprint cliches and access to printing facilities and equipment proved an irresistible temptation to Foure. Foure prevailed upon Schilling to produce forged German States envelopes with North German Confederation overstamps.

The combination of Schilling producing fakes with the original dies on state presses and Foure announcing them in his authoritative journal proved to be devastating. Other stamp experts and journalists were understandably also taken in, and many reputable dealers offered Foure's fakes in good faith to collectors such as Ferrari, who purchased many of them. Foure even acquired authentic postal canceling devices at post office auctions with which excellent bogus covers could be fabricated.

Schilling died in 1890, but not before a host of Prussian, North German Confederation and early German Imperial postal stationery frauds had been disseminated. In 1893 Foure was exposed, and three years later he deserted his family to return to Paris, where he is reputed to have continued as a faker until his death in 1902.

Francois Fournier

The best known of all the forgers, the Swiss-born Fournier became a French citizen but returned to Geneva following the Franco-Prussian War. In 1904 he purchased the stock of the bankrupt Louis-Henri Mercier, and for the next decade Fournier published extensive price lists of what he referred to as "facsimile reproductions" of stamps from around the world. His 64-page 1914 price list offered 3,671 different forgeries, though many of these were the products of other forgers. Fournier offered a stamp repair clinic, published a combination house organ and stamp journal and did a booming business until World War I brought the European stamp trade to a standstill. He died in 1917, and what was left of his business perished 10 years later.

Fournier's enduring renown is due to the fate of his forgeries, printing and perforating equipment. These were ultimately purchased by the Geneva Philatelic Union from the widow of one of Fournier's employees in 1927. The forgeries were overprinted as such and mounted in 480 albums, not all of which were complete. Intact copies of these albums are now highly sought-after by collectors of the very sort Fournier once victimized, an irony he would certainly have savored.

Sigmund Friedl

An Austrian stamp dealer of the 1870s and operator of a postal museum in Vienna, Friedl sold dangerous forgeries of Colombia's 1865 Cubiertas as early as 1875. In the 1890s an Austrian court forced Friedl to make restitution to all customers who had purchased his photolithographic forgery of the rare Austrian newspaper stamp of 1856. An acknowledged philatelic expert, Friedl also produced very dangerous forgeries on early Moldavian and Romanian issues.

-G-

Enrique Gainsboro

Gainsboro was a part-time stamp dealer and Bolivian Legation employee in Paris who created an entirely fictitious issue of Bolivian newspaper stamps in 1892. He later made unauthorized reprints and fraudulent printings of the 1894

Coat of Arms issues.

Stanley Gibbons

One of the greatest of the early stamp dealers of Great Britain, Gibbons also produced unofficial reprints of the 1862 5-centavo Seal issue of Argentina and, by modifying the figures of value, forgeries of the 10c and 15c values as well.

Konrad and Johan Gjuric

Yugoslavian stamp dealers arrested in 1930 in Zagreb for production of counterfeit early Yugoslavian overprints, forged cancellations and stamps of 1918-33. The brothers were convicted and given stiff sentences.

Julius Goldner

A prominent 19th-century stamp dealer in Hamburg, Germany, Goldner was responsible for an enormous number of reprints of Hamburg and Heligoland, which he produced over a period of 15 years. Among his outright forgeries were several different Heligoland stamped wrappers and stamps of Bergedorf and Romagna. His firm was an important outlet for the products of other forgers of the age as well.

-H-

Mizra Hadi

A Paris stamp dealer of Persian background, Hadi purchased an extensive stock of remainders and reprints of the Transvaal issues of 1885-96 from the Dutch firm of Enschede & Son in 1911. Hadi had forged overprints and bogus cancellations added to massive numbers of these reprints, which he continued to offer as recently as 1967 from the Transvaal Stamp Co. of Monaco. Hadi also had a plausible forged numeral cancel added to remaindered 1894 issues of the Italian offices abroad sometime prior to World War I.

William B. Hale

A traveling stamp salesman and philatelic raconteur late in the gay '90s, Hale was primarily a forger of cancellations, though he also forged the 5¢ Confederate postmaster's provisional of Mobile, Ala. Following a career of illegal activities, Hale died in prison in 1936.

Rodolfo Hensel

A first-rate Genoese forger of stamps and postmarks of the Italian State of Parma, Roman States and Two Sicilies, Hensel was active during the years around 1895.

Hirose

Hirose was a masterful Japanese forger of the mid-1890s who produced dangerously deceptive forgeries of Japanese classics, including the 1871-72 Dragon stamps and 1872-76 Cherry Blossom issues.

George A. Hussey

Operator of a New York City local postal service during 1854-73, Hussey was quick to capitalize on collector interest in postmaster's provisional, carrier and local issues of the day. These he reprinted whenever it was possible and forged whenever it was not. Hussey produced well-known forgeries of the 5¢ and 10¢ postmaster's provisionals of Providence, R.I., and is alleged to have been involved in numerous other reprinted and counterfeit creations.

-I-

N. Imperato

Imperato was a prolific Genoese disseminator of forgeries whose house organ of 1920-22 advertised many of them. His own specialities were "Venezia Giulia" and "Venezia Tridentina" overprints on Italian occupation of Austria issues of 1918, the 1908 offices in the Turkish Empire issues, Batum, Fiume, Spain's 1905 Don Quixote commemorative, as well as a good many 19th-century issues of Eritrea, Two Sicilies, Honduras, Cape of Good Hope and others. He is also said to have found fresh markets for the forgeries of Erasmus Oneglia of Turin, which had been produced years before.

-J-

George Kirke Jeffreyes

At the age of 16 in 1883, Jeffreyes was already an accomplished creator of fake overprints on stamps of the British Empire and South America. He later turned to engraved forgeries of classic stamps of British Australasia, Ceylon and Grenada, the latter produced with forged surcharges, as well as lithographed forgeries of Victoria. He was also behind a pair of fantasy stamps purported at the time to be Hawaiian. The chief purveyor of Jeffreyes' wares was the London firm of Benjamin and Sarpy. Jeffreyes, Benjamin and Sarpy were arrested and convicted of conspiracy to defraud in an 1891 court case, and the trio was sentenced to six months at hard labor.

-K-

Kamigata

Kamigata was a turn-of-the-century Tokyo stamp dealer who ordered and disseminated forged stamps and postal stationery of Japan, China, Shanghai, Taiwan and Korea. Most of his lithographed imitations, which range in quality from crude to sophisticated, were sold as copyrighted imitations, but many were later resold as authentic issues. Kamigata also sold from an extensive stock of forged issues of India, Mexico, Liberia, the United States, Hawaii, England, Russia, France and Borneo, as well as rare stationery, all believed to have been imported by him from abroad.

Rheinhold Krippner

Dealer of Freiburg, Germany, in the 1880s and the mid-'90s, Krippner was an expert in the fakery of valuable varieties of German States issues, most of which he created by modifying genuine existing stamps or remainders. This was typically done by the addition of rouletting, perforations and a host of forged cancels, and he also simulated a scarce blue paper error of Saxony by boiling stamps in ink. Tried and convicted on 23 counts of fraud, Krippner was subject to a two-and-one-half year prison term and the seizure of all his forgeries and equipment.

H. Kuroiwa

A Korean stamp dealer in the first decade of the 20th century, Kuroiwa specialized in Tai Han overprints simulating the Korean issue of 1897 and the 1900 3-cheun issue.

-L-

John Stewart Lowden (a.k.a. F. Moore, George Ellis)

Lowden was the creator of forged Central South African Railways overprints on issues of Orange River Colony and the Transvaal circa 1905. Under a variety of different stamp shop names, Lowden also commissioned forgeries of the North Borneo issue of 1887-92 from a Parisian printer. In and out of court as a principal in a variety of cases, Lowden was finally convicted for the 1913 sale of more than 2,600 forged British £1 stamps and cancels and sentenced to a three-year prison term.

Charles A. Lyford

Another member of S. Allan Taylor's notorious Boston Gang and one of Taylor's intimates, Lyford is said by some to have been the source of a bogus Prince Edwards Island 10¢ Ship stamp. The versatile Lyford posed as an interpreter in commissioning a first (and bogus) issue of Guatemala, was a distributor of a Hawaiian Taylor forgery and edited *The New England Journal of Philately* — apparently a sales tool for the Boston gang's fraudulent fabrications — during 1869.

-M-

Maximilian Maitret

An orchestra musician when he emigrated to the United States from France in 1891, Maitret founded the Loyalty Stamp Co. in New York City in 1894. A search of his residence and a printing shop owned by Maitret after his arrest the following year brought to light plates, woodcuts and forged stamps of Haiti and British Columbia. It was determined that he had produced more than two million forgeries, mainly of South American and West Indian stamps.

Arthur Maury

Already an accomplished stamp dealer while still in his teens in 1860, Maury went on to found one of the first monthly philatelic journals in 1864 and one of the best early standard stamp catalogs the year following. Maury also added "T" postage due perforated initials to Tunisian stamps and chronicled bogus "D.S."-overprinted French stamps purported to be provisionals of Diego Suarez. Maury sold bogus Persian postage dues as well as certain suspicious early Ethiopian issues, and his pioneering 1865 catalog advertised reprints and imitations of U.S. local issues.

Maury went on to become honorary president of the French Philatelic Society and to author a landmark study of the development of French stamps prior to his death in 1907.

Louis-Henri Mercier (Henri Goegg)

A self-described craftsman "of absolute perfection in the reproduction of old Swiss stamps," Henri Goegg opened a forgery business in Geneva in 1890. His facsimilies were as good as he claimed, too, winning awards for their superior craftsmanship all over France during 1895-98. Goegg changed his name to Louis-Henri Mercier in 1893 or 1894, and in 1897 issued a 32-page price list of facsimilies under that name. Mercier never achieved notoriety during his career, but after Mercier's bankruptcy shortly before the turn of the century, Francois Fournier purchased Mercier's remaining stock of forgeries and successfully used Mercier's awards and reputation to boost his own standing within philately.

Gustave Michelsen

Turn-of-the-century Colombian collector and diplomatic representative to Germany, in 1889 Michelsen used high government connections to secure a stock of soon-to-be-demonetized Colombian issues of 1868-81, plus a hoard of related material including excellent forgeries and printings on colored paper. A small portion of this material Michelsen gave to his larcenous partner, American engineer William T. Curtis, and together they flooded the philatelic world with these forgeries and fakes.

Jean-Baptiste Phillipe Constant Moens

One of Europe's greatest pioneer stamp dealers, Moens founded his business in Brussels in 1852. He published a monthly philatelic journal from 1863 to 1900 and in 1864 produced one of the world's first illustrated stamp catalogs of comprehensive scope and scale. Moens also commissioned restored cliches of Romagna stamps, from which he produced forgeries in 1892 and 1897. It is alleged that the blocks used to illustrate Moens' 1864 catalog and subsequent editions were used to produce facsimilies, though whether these were made by Moens or by someone else at a later date is unclear.

C.M. Moriou (a.k.a. Paul Paulescu, G. Matheesco)

Moriou was a talented Bucharest forger of scarce early Moldavian stamps. By selling his creations exclusively to foreigners, Moriou managed to remain within the bounds of Romanian law despite an 1889 arrest, but his well-executed creations were exposed definitively in 1903.

Charles Mottes

A lieutenant-colonel with the Austrian Legation in Persia late in the 19th century, Mottes occupied himself by producing forged and fakes stamps, postal stationery and cancellations of his host country. In spite of clever and innovative attempts to conceal his swindles, Mottes was finally exposed in about 1894.

-N-

Alwin Nieske

The creator in 1872-74 of lithographic forgeries of stamps and postal stationery of the German States of Brunswick, Hanover and Saxony.

-O-

Erasmus Oneglia

A creator and dealer in numerous fakes, Oneglia is described by Tyler as "the first link in a long chain of Italian forgers." Active in Turin, Italy, in the 1890s and early 1900s, Oneglia offered regular catalogs of his engraved, photogravure, and photolithographic wares, which seem to have spanned most of the stamp-issuing world. For example, his U.S. forgeries include copper-engraved counterfeits of the 90¢ values of 1860 and 1869 and the 1869 24¢, and the inverted-center varieties of both these 1869 values. Oneglia cooperated closely with other prolific Italian forgers of his day, most of whom freely sold one another's fakes in addition to their own.

Adolph Otto

The German printer of 1869-74 stamps for Transvaal, Otto went on to print his own stock for sale to dealers, eventually including bogus cancellations and his own forgeries of later issues never originally printed by him at all. An agent of the Transvaal government paid a visit to Otto's shop in Mecklenburg-Schwerin in 1882, confiscating sheets of forgeries and the plate from which they were printed.

-P-

Angelo Panelli

Operator of a major forgery operation, chiefly in San Remo, Italy, in the years between the world wars, Panelli began as an independent salesman of fakes, including those of Fournier and Oneglia, but soon began to create his own engraved forgeries. Convicted of counterfeiting French colonial stamps in 1926, Panelli served a seven-month jail term, following which he built an elaborate network of sales operatives to avoid further brushes with the law. Panelli, or those whom he commissioned, is believed responsible for many forged stamps of the European colonies, Italy, Belgium and Norway. A well-engraved forgery of the U.S. 1930 $2.60 Zeppelin issue is attributed by some to Panelli. He was still in business at least as late as 1938, selling forged overprints and cancellations of Italy and colonies.

Louis Pasche

A European stamp forger and consummate repair artist active circa 1910-30, Pasche is known to have operated in France, Belgium and Switzerland. Responsible for forgeries of Serbia, Sweden, Surinam, Haiti and Transvaal, Pasche was eventually convicted of stamp fraud in France in 1927.

Giovanni Patroni

A prolific forger, Patroni was arrested in Philadelphia in 1875 and charged with producing postal forgeries of Nicaraguan stamps, his defense being that they were for sale to collectors. He was found guilty but not sentenced, and later moved to South America. Patroni made lithographic forgeries of stamps of Angola, St. Thomas, British Guiana, Japan, Luxembourg, Cuba, French Colonies, Hyderabad, Tolima, Cundinamarca, Iceland, Baden, Hanover and the Pacific Steam Navigation Co.

James A. Petrie

A former Civil War naval surgeon and an occasional employee of J.W. Scott, Petrie became a dangerous specialist in Confederate States fakes, including non-existent Confederate postmasters' provisionals as well as forged general issues. His greatest success was a concocted 5¢ Greenville, Ala., provisional adhesive that appeared in the Scott catalog until the authentic issue finally displaced it in the the early decades of this century. Petrie also was adept at the simulation of valuable U.S. stamps through the modification of inexpensive proofs. He sold many counterfeits, not least to some of Europe's greatest collectors, and was still active up to the turn of the century.

-R-

"Mr. Re ——"

His complete name unrecorded, "Mr. Re ——" was an Antwerp collector and the first individual known to have created, in 1856-57, forgeries for the express purpose of deceiving stamp collectors. He hoped to profit from lithographed simulations of scarce early Brazilian issues, but his fakes were too crude to successfully dupe anyone.

Manual Rivadeneira

Printer of the first issues of Ecuador in 1865, Rivadeneira produced reprints and forgeries of the same in 1890 and 1893.

Miguel Rodriguez (a.k.a. Miguel Rodriguez Sanchez)

Forger of the Spanish issues of 1850-51 that were marketed by fellow Spaniard Placido Ramon de Torres during the mid-1880s.

-S-

Saatjian

A Parisian stamp dealer who managed to acquire the original stone used to print the 40-centime Suez Canal stamp in 1907. From this he eventually produced reprints and forgeries of the other issued denominations.

Salama

Following an abortive attempt to sell genuine watermarked paper and canceling devices for Egypt's 1866 issues to Stanley Gibbons, Salama of Alexandria went on to produce his own Egyptian first-issue forgeries. Caught and confronted, he nevertheless managed to sell many of his fakes to dealers in Cairo and Alexandria, while others reached the stamp trade in Paris. Because they possess the authentic watermark found on the original stamps, Salama's counterfeits are more dangerous than most.

Frederico Saureck

This turn-of-the-century stamp dealer in Guatemala was shot to death in a barroom dispute by a fellow expatriate German. A search of his lodgings by officials turned up fake "OFICIAL" overprint and cancel dies of Uruguay and counterfeit "VIA PUERTO BARRIOS"-overprinted Guatemalan issues. Saureck is also known to have produced forged 1898 surcharged Guatemala postage and fiscal stamps.

Julius Schlesinger

A stamp dealer and expertizer from the late 1870s on, first in Breslau and later in Berlin, Schlesinger forged overprints of South Bulgaria's 1885 issues. To these and other questionable items he applied his expert's backstamp, which was also forged and used by the Spetsiotis Brothers of Athens on their own Hermes Head fakes.

Oswald Schroder

Schroder was a partner in a Leipzig printing firm that offered 56 collotype forgeries of stamps of British Guiana, Cape of Good Hope, Colombia, Finland, France, Guadalajara, Hanover, Philippines and the United States in its 1891 price list. Among Schroder's most notorious creations were excellent and broadly circulated fakes of the Buenos Aires 1858 Ship issues, and his forgery of Saxony's 3-pfennig first issue in tete-beche sheets of 17, which he created for a Dresden stamp dealer. Later in the 1890s Schroder moved to Zurich, steadfastly disavowing any knowledge of these earlier fabrications.

John Walter Scott

Following his fruitless pursuit of the California Gold Rush, this 22-year-old London-born immigrant returned to New York in 1867 to open the stamp business for which he became famous. In the mid-1870s Scott actively sought the plates that had been used to print earlier U.S. local and express stamps in order to create private reprints. When these proved mainly unobtainable, he printed forgeries of some of them from the cliches used in his catalogs and albums, as well as offering sets of 116 Hamburg local post forgeries. He is said to have ceased these practices by 1886. Scott's best-known creation was a lithographed Confederate States adhesive similar to the De La Rue & Co. 10¢ issue of 1862 and probably made from part of the original plate, but in a 5¢ denomination different from the genuine issues.

Miguel Segui

Owner of one of the most renowned restaurants in Spain in the early 1900s, Segui was a painstaking stamp forger on the side. By 1905, his dangerous counterfeits of classic stamps of Spain, Cuba, Fernando Po, the Philippines and Puerto Rico were offered throughout Barcelona in spite of their denunciation at about the same time.

Charles M. Seltz
(Frederick Henry King)

There is considerable doubt that Charles M. Seltz ever existed as anything more substantial than a consistent pseudonym for Frederick Henry King, yet another crony of S. Allan Taylor and the Boston Gang. Seltz was reputed to have been one of the earliest Boston stamp dealers. Two 1865 price lists were issued in the name of Seltz, and he was credited as author of *The Stamp Collector's Hand Book* and a stamp catalog in 1866-67. He played a part in the Boston gang's woodcut forgery of an 1864 Philippines issue and as an important marketer of some of Taylor's concoctions.

Louis and Richard Senf

In the 1870s and '80s, the brothers operated Gebruder Senf, then a world-renowned stamp dealership and philatelic publishing firm in Leipzig, Germany. Beginning in 1884, the firm's esteemed philatelic magazine, *Illustriertes Briefmarken-Journal*, began including clearly marked facsimiles in each issue. These proved popular and were eventually supplied in quantity to dealers as well. As stamp collectors began finally to recognize the damage that decades of such creations by others had done, a poll of the journal's subscribers led to the suspension of facsimile supplements in 1890.

In all, the brothers Senf produced facsimiles of 112 different stamps and four stamped envelopes, including 1-penny and 2d Mulready envelopes, some of the dollar denominations of the U.S.

State Department Official stamps and cents and dollar values of the U.S. newspaper stamps of 1875.

Rudolf Siegel

This highly regarded Berlin stamp dealer and auctioneer of the early 20th century sold remarkable numbers of Baden, Hamburg, Heligoland and Thurn and Taxis issues with scarce cancellations, as well as rare roulettes of some imperforate Brunswick issues. Another prominent German auctioneer, Heinrich Kohler, exposed these as Siegel's own fabrications, many of which also had counterfeit expert's backstamps. In 1926, Siegel was arrested and jailed, though he was soon released due to ill health and, according to Tyler, "to avoid a public scandal in philately."

Jean de Sperati

The finest stamp forger who ever lived, the Italian de Sperati learned his trade from his mother and elder brothers in the first years of the 20th century. His technical virtuosity and attention to detail made his fakes exceptionally dangerous.

The family set up a booming business in mail-order forgeries in Pisa, Italy, in 1909, later fleeing just ahead of the police who arrived to confiscate two wagon-loads of material. Jean moved to Paris and married in 1914, becoming a factory worker by day and a stamp forger by night. Forgery became his full-time profession following his relocation to Aix-les-Bains in 1930.

Between 1909 and 1953, de Sperati produced 566 forged stamps of more than 100 countries. With a boundless capacity for work and an ego to match, he also authored *La Philatelie sans experts?* mainly to express his deep contempt for the experts whom he claimed his products had so frequently fooled. A second book, in which de Sperati explained how he had done so, was written but never published.

De Sperati observed the letter of the French law, which specified that the production of stamp forgeries was legal if they were sold only as such. His marking to that effect appeared on the back of each item — written lightly and in pencil.

Charged with exporting a number of valuable stamps in violation of French wartime currency export regulations in 1943, de Sperati proved each of the stamps to be entirely his own creation in a celebrated court case.

A decade later at age 70, de Sperati sold his forgeries, reference collections, cliches and copyrighted formulas to the British Philatelic Association for an undisclosed five-figure sum and agreed to make no new fakes. The BPA in 1954 sponsored an exhibition of the forgeries and published *The Work of Jean de Sperati*, a two-volume study now highly sought-after by specialists. Some of his better individual forgeries now bring prices of more than $100 when they are offered as such in public auctions.

Jan Spetsiotis (a.k.a. L. Papastathopoulos, Helleniades

An Athenian forger of the 1908 Hellas overprints of Crete as well as the Greek Olympic Games issue of 1896 and its subequent "A.M." surcharges of 1900-01, Spetsiotis also offered his fakes with a wide variety of forged cancels.

Edoardo Spiotti

A Genoese forger specializing in Italian States issues in the latter half of the 1890s, Spiotti was also a distributor if not the author of a wide variety of other bogus issues, probably including those of Erasmus Oneglia.

Philip Spiro

Philip Spiro was the head of Spiro Brothers, a professional lithographic printing house in Hamburg, Germany, which added stamp facsimilies to its product line beginning in 1864. Over the next decade and a half, Spiro manufactured about 500 forgeries, offered either mint or canceled. He viewed his fakes as harmless and said he intended to deceive no one.

However, Spiro's forgeries prompted the publication of *The Spud Papers, or Notes on Philatelic Weeds*, which appeared in 67 serialized installments in the British philatelic press beginning in 1871. These described more than 400 forgeries, most of which were Spiro's work, and illustrated them with 140 specimens. *The Spud Papers* marked a turning point in the long, uneasy relationship of forgeries to stamp collecting, following which counterfeits such as those of Spiro were regarded as a menace to the hobby that no reputable dealer should sell. Faced with a shrunken market, the Spiro Brothers made no more facsimilies after 1879 or 1880.

Bela Szekula

A Budapest-born stamp dealer, swindler and scofflaw, Szekula was already notorious prior to his arrival in Geneva in 1902. One year later he purchased remaindered mint Dominican Republic stamps, which he offered to collectors with forged cancellations on and off cover. He also sold forgeries of a Nicaraguan stamp before a 1904 return to Budapest, where he soon churned out fakes of Bolivia's 1894 issue. Back in Switzerland during World War I, he saturated the world stamp market with large quantities of mint stamps seized during the German invasion of Belgium. Szekula surfaced again in 1935 with reprint forgeries and fake errors of Ethiopia's 1919 commemoratives.

-T-

Jonoski Takuma

A Japanese craftsman in Sydney, Australia, Takuma was convicted in 1898 and sentenced to a year at hard labor for producing skillful fakes of scarce New South Wales numeral watermark errors, which he made by carefully laminating the thinned fronts and backs of two different stamps together. Takuma also marketed forged Fiji overprints and New South Wales Official overprints. His 1895 postal forgery of the 1888 2-penny Emu of New South Wales was so expert that it was cataloged as genuine for almost half a century.

Samuel Allan Taylor

Fascinated with stamps beginning in his teenage years, the Scottish-born Taylor created hundreds of different fakes, forgeries and wholly spurious issues in North America from the 1860s to the early 1890s.

In Montreal, Canada, in 1864 Taylor published the first philatelic magazine in the Americas, *The Stamp Collector's Record.* He later moved to Albany, N.Y., and then to Boston, Mass., where he gained his greatest notoriety. His prodigious output of counterfeits of all countries and types, including his many fantasy creations, was aided and abetted by the likes of Ferdinand M. Trifet, and later members of Taylor's so-called Boston gang, including William E. Skinner, Chute, Lyford, and Seltz.

Taylor's most noteworthy concoctions include imaginary Canadian locals, and entirely bogus stamps of the Dominican Republic, Prince Edward Island and Guatemala. He also produced what was purported to be an adhesive for a non-existent Crosby's City Post, which was listed as an authentic U.S. local for nearly a century.

Taylor was charged with counterfeiting three times during 1887-91, which convinced him to give up his career as a forger. He died in 1913.

Though Taylor was presumably as crooked and avaricious as any other forger of his era, a good many of his creations are viewed with nostalgic good humor today. Many were conceived with creative and fanciful designs that could not now be confused with those of any genuine stamp, and some are avidly sought after.

Rudolph Thomas (a.k.a. "Greasy Dick")

A sleazy Chicago stamp dealer, forger and ne'er-do-well of the interwar years, Thomas' first appearance was a 1912 advertisement to exchange stamps in Fournier's, *Le Fac-Simile,* described by Tyler as " a journal not representative of the highest standards of the hobby." Thomas' stamp shop was said to have been dimly lit in order to keep customers literally in the dark about the nature of the material he was selling.

It was only with the death of Thomas and an examination of his premises in 1941 that the extent of his fraudulent deceptions was fully revealed. The tools of his nefarious trade that were found included scores of woodcut cancelers for the United States, Latin America, Italian and German States and a host of other European colonies, in addition to a perforation machine and five grill-embossing devices.

W.R. Thomas

Allegedly the creator of forged British

colonial and other overprints and surcharges that surfaced in Boston in 1902.

Raoul Ch. de Thuin

A prolific philatelic forger, de Thuin began his career in Brussels in the mid-1920s. Posing as a specialist in art objects, he evidently found greater profit in eliminating fiscal cancels from high-value British issues and producing forged overprints on stamps of Siam.

He moved to Merida on Mexico's Yucatan Peninsula in 1931. Over the next three decades, de Thuin peddled his forgeries through a variety of non-existent companies located at the addresses of relatives and friends, specializing in Latin America generally and Mexico in particular. The most dangerous and deceptive of his fraudulent practices was to enhance the value of otherwise genuine covers and stamps by adding desirable overprints, cancellations and markings, sometimes including excellent counterfeit backstamps of some of the noted experts of the day.

In 1966 the American Philatelic Society purchased de Thuin's equipment, 1,636 cliches and most of his stock of fakes. Mexico, Honduras and other Latin lands accounted for about 75 percent of the material, but the balance ran the gamut from Afghanistan and Albania to Nova Scotia and the Native States of India.

Honoring his agreement with the APS to refrain from further fakery, de Thuin sold some samples of his earlier forgeries as such from the private collection he retained prior to his death in 1975.

Placido Ramon de Torres (a.k.a. Rosendo Fernandez)

A Spanish stamp dealer who attempted to sell forgeries of Spain's 1850-51 issues, de Torres was convicted of fraud in a German court in 1886, but fled with his stock of 4,000 counterfeits before he could be imprisoned.

Under the alias Fernandez, he made a selling trip to Cuba, Mexico and the United States in 1892. Alerted by a stamp dealer in Galveston, Texas, to the bogus nature of the material, St. Louis stamp dealer C.H. Mekeel tipped off the authorities following a visit from de Torres, whose stock of fakes was confiscated for nonpayment of customs duties.

De Torres also took part in an 1893-94 scam in which phantom stamps supplied by him and added with the connivance of a postal employee to envelopes from Spanish soldiers serving in Morocco were given false cancellations. The intention was to later represent these letters as bearing valuable and esoteric military mail issues, but the scheme was uncovered and foiled by his arrest in 1894.

Harold Treherne (a.k.a. G. Arnold, M. Melville, T. Morton, R. Newman, A. West)

This teen-aged loan clerk from Brighton, England, commissioned zinc cliches of overprints, cancels and postage stamps from a London photolithographer in 1902. From these he both forged stamps outright and added forged overprints to genuine stamps of at least 15 different British Empire nations. These were sold at shops all over Brighton and, through a contact, in Bombay, India, as well.

Entrapped through a plan by the Stamp Trade Protective Association into obtaining money on false pretences, Treherne was arrested, tried and pleaded guilty in 1907, receiving a deferred sentence. Counterfeiting charges brought later that year resulted in his imprisonment at hard labor for five months.

Ferdinand Marie Trifet

A French immigrant, the 18-year-old Trifet founded a stamp business in 1866 in Boston, where he was initially befriended by S. Allan Taylor. Trifet toyed with forgeries briefly, counterfeiting Hawaii's Numeral issues and, with the Boston gang, preparing a woodcut forgery of an 1864 3 1/8-cuarto Philippines issue. When he parted company with Taylor, he took dies of some Hamburg forgeries with him.

In 1867, Trifet forswore further forgeries, establishing a pioneer U.S. stamp journal, *The American Stamp Mercury*. He did, however, make the most of his commission to arrange an authorized U.S. collection for the 1876 Centennial, removing from the archives, with full if thoughtless official approval, rare 1870 issues on experimental chemical papers, which he later sold. Trifet died in 1899.

-U-

Samuel C. Upham

A Philadelphia salesman, in 1862 Upham became perhaps the first forger of Confederate currency and stamps. These included postmasters' provisionals of Memphis and Nashville, Tenn., Mobile, Ala., and New Orleans, La., as well as facsimiles of the Confederate States 5¢ and 10¢ general issues.

Upham cloaked his activities in the flag of Union patriotism, claiming his creations would cause economic hardship to the rebel cause.

According to contemporary accounts, Tyler contends that Upham's facsimiles may have had an unintended and ironic benefit. Widely circulated and sold as novelties by newsboys and stationery stores, the fakes "were said to be instrumental in popularizing stamp collecting in the United States."

E. Carlo Usigli

A Florentine forger and reprinter of the 1870s and '80s, Usigli's principal products were fakes of the Italian States, including Parma, Roman States and the imprinted Sardinian lettersheets of 1820 that are better known as Cavallini.

-V-

A. Venturini

Operating from addresses in Pisa, Turin and Florence, Venturini was one of the major marketers of forgeries in Europe at the dawn of the 20th century. He is thought by some to have been a cooperative contemporary competitor of the prominent Turin forger Erasmus Oneglia, and by others to have been little more than a successful marketer of Oneglia's products and, later, a manufacturer of fresh fakes made from Oneglia's original dies.

Whether Venturini actually produced forgeries or not, he was a superb salesman for them, taking to heart the maxim that the customer is always right. Venturini supplied his enormous range of merchandise gummed or ungummed, canceled or uncanceled, perforated or imperforate at the request of his clientele, these services said to have been supplied to order by Oneglia in Turin.

-W-

Wada Kontaro

Owner of a Tokyo curio shop and, from the 1890s to 1911, the greatest forger of Japanese stamps, Wada prepared hundreds of thousands of high-quality counterfeits of the classic issues of 1871-79. While his earlier copper-engraved forgeries frequently contained the Japanese characters for "imitation" in the form of small letters or a cancellation, many of his later and more dangerous fabrications did not.

Not content with selling massive numbers of fakes to gullible American and European tourists, Wada's most ambitious project was the creation of two forged editions of the government's own *Postage Stamp History of the Japanese Empire*, which contained genuine early Japanese stamps and postal stationery. Most of Wada's counterfeit editions were seized, and the few that survive are rare and remarkable.

Wada stopped selling forgeries in 1911, and his printing plates were later destroyed during the disastrous Tokyo earthquake and fire of 1923.

Even eminent philatelists and Japanese specialists have sometimes been stung by the superlative workmanship of many of Wada's fakes, which live on undetected in countless stamp collections. Tyler estimates that Wada forgeries may outnumber authentic classic stamps of Japan in general collections by as much as 10 to 1.

George Whitehurst

A Birmingham, England , stamp dealer who, with John D. Harris, produced forged 1937 Coronation Day covers with first-day cancels of 10 different remote nations of the British Empire. Harris, a stamp dealer in Smethwick, supplied stamps, envelopes and genuine first-day covers to copy, while Whitehurst applied the fake cancels with dies he'd commissioned for the purpose. Exposed in a series of articles by Robson Lowe in 1937-38, Whitehurst and Harris were convicted of fraud and sent to prison.

R.P.H. Wolle

A turn-of-the-century faker in the United States, Wolle specialized in clever conversions of cheap proofs and common stamps into rare varieties. Tricks of his fraudulent trade included excising framelines and handpainting in new ornaments to convert an 1851 1¢ Franklin type II to the much rarer type III. He engineered numerous fraudulent bisect covers of the classic era by forging the cancellations that tied them and was also adept at simulating the valuable inverted-center errors of the 1869 Pictorial and 1901 Pan-American commemorative issues.

Wolle spent 1900-03 in a Missouri penitentiary for turning $1 bills into $5 bills, having previously been jailed for his stamp swindles. While incarcerated, he surreptitiously continued his trade in bad and forged stamps, for which he was convicted of grand larceny in 1904 and given yet another prison sentence, this time for four years.

-Y-

Chauncey L. Young

An Iowa minister and spare-time bookbinder, Young modified U.S. stamped envelopes into rare and sometimes otherwise unknown varieties. Most of his manipulations were to the envelopes themselves, his bookbinding talents enabling him to rearrange flaps, gum ungummed varieties and even add convincing windows where none had ever existed. His most dangerous work was in indetectably transforming common stamped envelopes into rarer and more profitable exotic sizes.

Confronted with the evidence of his frauds, largely through the efforts of J. Murray Bartels, then the leading dealer in U.S. stamped envelopes, Young agreed to cease their production in 1921 in exchange for supression of the scandal. It was only after Young's death that full details of the story were published in 1969.

-Z-

Georg Zechmeyer

A Bavarian toy dealer and later a stamp dealer too, Zechmeyer maintained a profitable trade in packets of common stamps. In the 1870s he supplemented his business with even more profitable sales of pictures designed to look like stamps, though these adhesives were not intended to deceive and were printed on brightly colored paper. He also sold booklets of colored wet transfers of classic stamps.

In a major failure of his generally good sense, Zechmeyer foolishly offered a selection of common forgeries in an exchange with a respected stamp dealer in England in 1872, for which he was blacklisted by the then-influential *Philatelical Journal.*

His stamp business in packets and mixtures grew and prospered through the remainder of the 19th century, succeeding to the extent that Zechmeyer was able to open a branch in Paris. He purchased from Bavaria the 3.5 million stamps and vast quantities of postal stationery of 1849-75 that were made obsolete when that German state converted to Imperial currency in 1876. He died wealthy and respected in 1899.

Chapter 23

Philatelic Honor Roll

Outstanding service awards have been established by several stamp organizations to recognize individual contributions to the hobby. The following is a list of these awards and thier recipients.

American Philatelic Congress Fawcett Award

An award established in the name of James Waldo Fawcett by the American Philatelic Congress in 1959 for meritorious service to the APC.

1960 Zirkle, Mrs. Conway
1961 Shaner, James B. Jr.
1962 Lidman, David
1963 Yort, Svend
1964 Brandeberry, Robert B.
1965 DeVoss, James T.
1966 Bruns, Franklin R. Jr.
1967 Glass, Sol
1968 Turner, George T.
1969 Davidson, Robert L. D.
1970 Stump, David C.
1972 McCoy, Ethel
1975 Harris, James P.
1981 Schneider, Sidney
1987 Mueller, Barbara

American Philatelic Society Hall of Fame

Established by the American Philatelic Society in 1941 to posthumously recognize outstanding individuals for significant contributions to philately.

1941 Barry, Ralph A.
Hill, Sir Rowland
King, Beverly S.
Knapp, Edward S.
Lindsay, James Ludovic
Luff, John N.
Melville, Frederick J.
Pack, Charles Lathrop
Phillips, Charles J.
Scott, John Walter
Severn, Charles E.
Southgate, Hugh M.
Tapling, Thomas Keay
Tiffany, John Kerr
Wolsieffer, Philip M.
1942 Barnum, W. Hamilton
Conrath, Walter J.
Severn, Evelyn
1944 Klein, Eugene
1945 Richards, C.R.
Roosevelt, Franklin D.
Wylie, Willard O.
1946 Bartels, J. Murray
Doane, Percy G.
1947 Stone, William C.
1948 Lichtenstein, Alfred H.
1949 Mason, Edward H.
Starr, Maj. James
1950 Harris, Adm. Frederick R.
Newbury, Saul
Scott, Walter S.
1951 Sanabria, Nicolas
Seymour, J.B.
Tower, Rev. William R.
1952 Martin, Donald W.
McCoy, Walter R.
1953 Caldwell, Judge David
Hurt, E.F.
1954 Clark, Theresa M.
Goodwin, Dr. James
Van Dahl, Al
1955 Barr, Jere. Hess
Berolzheimer, D.D.
1956 Brazer, Clarence W.
Davis, Dr. Holland A.
Hennan, Dr. Clarence W.
1957 Clark, Hugh M.
Johl, Max G.
Stowell, John W.
1958 Barrett, Sidney F.
Steinway, Theodore E.
1959 Ashbrook, Stanley B.
Rich, Stephen G.
1960 Chase, Dr. Carroll
Steeg, Adolph
1961 Flower, Rollin E.
Fortgang, Morris
Konwiser, Harry
1962 MacBride, F. Van Dyk
Sloane, George B.

1963 Barkhausen, L.H.
Barr, Hugh
Deats, Hiram E.
1964 Chaloner, Henry
Dietz, August
Elliott, Howard H.
1966 Pelander, Carl E.
Ward, Philip H.
1967 Hicks, William W.
Linn, George W.
Weiss, Harry
1968 Dale, Louise Boyd
Domanski, Vincent Jr.
Spellman, Francis Cardinal
1969 Hamilton, Col. Charles S.
Meyer, Henry A.
Salisbury, Dr. Gregory B.
1971 Cabeen, Richard McP.
Gatchell, L.B.
Lybarger, Donald F.
1972 Bacon, Edward Denny
Brookman, Lester
Mekeel, Charles H.
1973 Faulstich, Edith
Keller, Peter G.
Perry, Elliott
1974 Boggs, Winthrop S.
Glass, Sol
Mueller, Edwin
1975 Goodkind, Henry M.
Norona, Delf
1976 Risueno, Manuel M.
Wilson, Sir John
1977 Caspary, Alfred
Chemi, James
1978 Diena, Alberto
Heiman, Irwin M.
Morgenthau, Julius C.
1979 Harris, Henry E.
Lindquist, Harry L.
Ragatz, Lowell
1980 Purves, J.R.W.
1981 Gerrish, William E.
Matejka, Dr. James J. Jr.
McCoy, Ethel B.
1982 DeVolpi, Charles P.
Dubs, Leon
Yort, Svend
1983 Colson, Warren H.
Dadkhah, Mohamed
Lidman, David
1984 Hargest, George
Mitsui, Takaharu
Weatherly, A. Earl
1985 Costales, Eugene
Neinken, Mortimer L.
Schatzkes, Joseph
1986 Alexander, Robert P.
Berthelot, Lucien
Thompson, Richard H.
1987 Haverbeck, Harrison D.S.
Ichida, Soichi
Kehr, Ernest
1988 Beal, James
Bloch, Herbert J.
Ricketts, William R.

American Topical Association
Distinguished Topical Philatelist

A hall of fame established in 1952 by the American Topical Association for annual recognition of outstanding contributions in the field of topical collecting.

1952 Husak, Jerome K.
Jones, Homer L.
Keenan, Charles J.
Wright, Allyn H.
1953 Becker, Rev. S.C.
Bourgraf, George
Fechner, Catherine D.
1954 Groet, John
Kehr, Ernest A.
1955 Stanley, Willard F.
Swanker, Dr. Wilson A.
1956 Hackett, Margaret
Lievers, Walter W.
1957 Esten, Sidney R.
McAlister, Clare
1958 Cooper, Jal
Flath, Edward J.
1959 Polson, M.P.
Sievert, Louis K.
1960 Cleveland, Ennis C.
Johnson, Harvey E.
1961 Spurgeon, Edgar W.
Tucker, Shirley C.
1962 Freedner, O. Frank
Korotkin, Fred
1963 Richter, John H.
Stern, Capt. M.F.
1964 Campbell, Lt. Col. Fred H.
Pritzlaff, Mr. and Mrs. A.H. Jr.
1965 Oesch, Robert S.
Rayl, H.F.
1966 Andrews, Dr. Melvin J.
Peterson, Henry
1967 Casey, Brother Camillus, O.S.F.
Hainlen, Dr. E. Willis
1968 Beltmann, Clarence

Thomas, John
1969 Owens, Mary Ann
Ranschaert, Cyril C.
1970 Griffenhagen, George B.
Smith, Dorothy F.
1971 Dinshah, K.D.
Webb, Sophia
1972 Diamant, Charles S.
Kufahl, Lester E.
1973 Cummins, Edna
Garabrant, Mr. and Mrs. Melvin
1974 Guzzio, George T.
Wurtz, Margaret M.
1975 Watt, Myrtle
Wetmore, Ruth
1976 Bruns, Franklin R. Jr.
Smith, Donald W.
1977 Green, Jack H.
Wilkinson, Sam III
1978 Kante, Robert F.
Winick, Lester E.
1979 Brenke, Donald B.
Wood, Kenneth A.
1980 Partington, Paul G.
Tasker, Walter L.
1981 Rajewski, Henry J.
Shoemake, Ann
1982 Apgar, Dulcie
Kyle, Robert A.
1983 Black, Lawrence
Husak, Sally A.
1984 Boughner, Elaine Durnin
Crosby, Arlene A.
1985 Hanks, Alan J.
Whitehead, Rev. Marshall J.
1986 Beuthel, Donald G.
Kent, David A.
1987 Coffey, William A.
Johnston, Hugh W.
1988 Foldvary, Fred. E.
Killingbeck, Betty

Angers Award

An award in the name of George W. Angers, past president of the American Air Mail Society, for outstanding contributions to aerophilately.

1963 Angers, Margaret
1965 Klemann, J.J.
1966 Kronstein, Dr. Max
1967 Leigh, Dr. Southgate
1972 Rowe, Basil L.
1976 Kohl, Richard F.
1978 Muller, Frank
1980 Silver, Philip
1982 Wellman, Earl H.
1984 Dahmann, Kurt
1986 Malott, Richard K.
1988 da Silveira, L. Lemos

Arizona Hall of Fame

An honor role established in 1961 by the Phoenix Philatelic Association, primarily honoring philatelic achievement in the Southwest.

Alexander, William L.
Brown R.D.
Bulkley, Grant
Cate, Richard W.
Chemi, James
Coless, Robert E.
Coyne, Bernard V.
Cratsenberg, Charles C.
Di Violini, Robert
Ditzler, Robert E.
Evans, Albert
Finch, Wilfred J.
Fine, Harry L.
Fitzgerald, Edwin G.
Flagg, May
Fleishman, Leo
Fricke, Ellsworth C.
Hilton, Hugh
Ihms, James
Jacquemin, Ralph E.
James, Milo
King, Oliver
Metzong, Debs
Nelson, Hildegarde
O'Brien, Emma
Shreve, Forrest
Smith, Rev. James L.
Springer, Arthur
Theobald, John and Lillian
Wilde, Donald E.
Williamson, Omega
Wylie, William W.
Yag, Otto

Barr Award

An award established in the name of Jere. Hess Barr by the American Philatelic Congress in 1959 for the best presentation at that organization's annual Writers' Forum.

1959 DeVoss, Col. James T.
1960 Murch, Robert W.

1961 Doane, Edith R.
1962 Norona, Delf
1963 Murch, Robert W.
1964 Fricke, Charles A.
1965 ter Braake, Alex
1966 Sellers, F. Burton
1967 ter Braake, Alex
1968 Doane, Edith R.
1969 Griffenhagen, George B.
1970 Green, Brian and Patricia
1971 Odenweller, Robert P.
1972 Resnick, Larry
1973 Cohn, Ernst M.
1974 Sellers, F. Burton
1975 Jennings, Clyde
1976 Fricke, Charles A.
1977 Hahn, Joseph D.
1978 Crow, Ray
1979 Cohn, Ernst M.
1981 Cohn, Ernst M.
1983 Wald, Kimber A.
1984 Wald, Kimber A.
1985 Lloyd, Carroll L.
1986 Clemente, John

Bohn Award

Award in the name of Richard S. Bohn, a leader in Aero-Philatelists, Inc., for outstanding contributions in airpost collecting.

1961 Goodkind, Henry M.
1962 Britt, John J.
1965 Silver, Phil
1966 Braunstein, Ila
1968 Rice, Stanley R.
1969 Eisendrath, Joseph
1970 Staub, Louis N.

Broken Pen Award

An accolade for activity as a philatelic writer established by the APS Writer's Unit in 1970 and presented intermittently since then.

1970 Willard, Edward L.
1971 Herst, Herman Jr.
1972 Cratsenberg, Charles C.
1973 Christian, C.W.
1974 Wunsch, Dr. Charles W.
1975 Amos, William T.
1978 De Violini, Barbara W.
1979 Weinberg, Irwin
1980 Cohn, Ernest

Bureau Issues Association Hall of Fame

Established by the Bureau Issues Association to posthumously honor members who made outstanding contributions to the association and to the collecting of United States postal paper.

Glass, Sol
Lundy, Mrs. J.W.
McCoy, Walter R.
McIntyre, Walter A.
Owen, Arthur E.
Southgate, Hugh M.
Turner, George T.
Bryant, Roger A.

Cabeen Award

Award established in 1988 in the name of the late Richard McP. Cabeen by the Collectors Club of Chicago, honoring excellence in philatelic literature. The winner is chosen from annual nominations by a 10-member panel of authors, journalists and critics.

1988 Wierenga, Theron

Colby Award

An award established in the name of Dorothy Colby by the American Philatelic Congress in 1973 for the best article or pamphlet published during the past year.

1973 French, Loran C.
1975 Schoberlin, Melvin H.
1976 Hart, Creighton C.
1978 LaBlonde, Maj. Charles J.
1979 Milgram, James W., M.D.
1980 Reed, Eugene C.
1982 Lutz, Abbot
1983 Silver, Philip

Conrath Award

Award in the name of Walter Conrath, one of the founders of the American Air Mail Society, presented intermittently for service to philately by a member of the society.

1943 Angers, George W.
1944 Gatchell, L.B.
1945 Singley, Richard, L.
1946 Kehr, Ernest A.
1947 Kingdom, George D.
1948 Warns, Dr. M.O.
1951 Conrath, Grace
1953 Johnson, Adm. Jesse

1955 Heinmuller, John F.V.
Smith, John J.
1957 Orio, Rafael
1959 Smith, Ruth J.
1961 Eisendrath, Joseph
Murch, Robert W.
1963 Matejka, Dr. James J. Jr.
1964 Manning, Lester F.
1966 Harring, Robert
1968 Nahl, Dr. Perham C.
1971 Dickason, Donald E.
Wynn, William T.
1973 Ware, William R.
1975 Alley, William R.
Blumenthal, Frank H.
1979 Kleinart, Herman
1981 Mead, William N.
1983 Lussky, Don
1985 O'Sullivan, Thomas J.
1987 Outlaw, Robert

Crawford Medal

Award established in 1923 by the Royal Philatelic Society of London, made in the name of the distinguished philatelic bibliographer the Earl of Crawford, for a significant contribution to philatelic literature.

1923 Pack, Charles Lathrop
1929 Woodward, Tracy
1930 Chase, Dr. Carroll
1937 Ashbrook, Stanley B.
1938 Johl, Max G.
1945 Thorp, Prescott Holden
1947 Boggs, Winthrop S.

Dietz Award

Presented in the name of August Dietz, a pioneer in Confederate philately, the award is presented annually by the Confederate Stamp Alliance for distinguished service to that specialty in the field of research and writing by a CSA member.

1962 Lemley, Harry J.
1963 Phillips, Robert S.
1964 McGee, M. Clinton
1965 Antrim, Earl
1966 McGee, M. Clinton
1967 Sheppard, Harvey E.
1968 Werner, Robert W.
1969 Rooke, Harry F.
1970 Crown, Francis J. Jr.
1971 Green, Brian M. and Patricia A.
1972 Milgram, James, M.D.
1973 Weatherly, A. Earl
1974 Cooper, Everett
1975 Crown, Francis J. Jr.
1976 Giron, Raymond
Taylor, Edwin
1977 Lemley, Harry J.
1978 Kohlhepp, John D.
1979 Skinner, Dr. Hubert C.
1980 Hensel, Henry
1981 Green, Brian M.
1982 Everett, Morris
1983 Green, Brian M.
1984 Crown, Frank
Krieger, Richard
1985 Jaronski, Stefan T.
1986 Gunter, Erin
Sanders, Warren
Skinner, Hubert
1987 Byne, Richard S.

Drossos Award

An award established in the name of Erani P. Drossos by the American Philatelic Congress in 1981 for the best foreign article in *The Congress Book*, the organization's annual publication.

1981 Boehret, Jesse and Diane
1982 Washburne, Stephen S.
1983 Laessig, Henry
1984 Sellers, F. Burton
1985 Washburne, Stephen S.
1986 Sellers, F. Burton
1987 Stone, Robert G.

Eidsness Award

Made by the Washington Philatelic Society in the name of "Mike" Eidsness, for many years in charge of the philatelic activities of the U.S. Post Office Department.

1938 Klein, Eugene
1939 Southgate, Hugh M.
1940 Clark, Hugh M.
1942 Brazer, Clarence W.

Klein Memorial Award

American Philatelic Congress award made in the name of its founder, Eugene Klein.

1961 Neinken, Mortimer
1962 Tatelman, Judge Edward I.P.
1963 Koeppel, Adolph

1964 Neinken, Mortimer
1965 Zirkle, Mrs. Conway
1967 Doane, Edith R.
1968 Altmann, Solomon
1969 Towle, Charles L.
1970 ter Braake, Alex
1971 Willard, Edward L.
1972 Hargest, George E.
1973 Neinken, Mortimer L.
1975 Turner, George T.
1976 Thompson, R.R.
1978 Sloat, Ralph L.
1979 French, Loren C.
1983 Engstrom, Victor E.

Lagerloef Award

Established in 1938 by the Society of Philatelic Americans in the Name of Hans Lagerloef, a distinguished patron of that now-defunct organization. The award was made annually for outstanding service to the society and to philately.

1944 Vining, J. Edward
1945 Zinsmeister, J. Elmer
1946 Diamond, Alfred
1947 Best, Hil F.
1948 Rich, Stephen G.
1949 Reeves, Ben
1950 Myer, Henry A.
1951 Bledsoe, Arthur
1952 Zinsmeister, Marian C.C.
1953 Reiner, Ignatz
1954 Vrendenburgh, Walter
1955 Longinotti, Helen
1956 Sloan, Louis
1957 Nouss, Henry O.
1958 Moorefield, Emily
1959 Jacobson, Gerald A.
1960 Yant, Robert
1961 Barovick, Fred
1962 Alkema, Ward
1963 Meyer, Charles E.
1964 Yant, Hilda P.
1965 Bailey, Stewart T.
1966 Domanski, Vincent Jr.
1967 Edmunds, Larry
1968 Hennig, Bernard
1969 Faries, Belmont
1970 Matejka, Dr. James J. Jr.
1971 Papa, Inez
1972 Bruns, Franklin R. Jr.
1973 Selzer, Howard
1974 Mitchell, Milton

Lichtenstein Award

The accolade of the Collectors Club of New York, made annually in the name of the late Alfred F. Lichtenstein, distinguished philatelist and patron, for outstanding service to philately by a living individual.

1952 Steinway, Theodore E.
1953 Hennan, Dr. Clarence W.
1954 Chase, Dr. Carroll
1955 Dietz, August
1956 Wilson, John
1957 Lindquist, Harry L.
1958 Boggs, Winthrop S.
1959 Wickersham, Gen C.W.
1960 Purves, J.R.W.
1961 Britt, John J.
1962 Dale, Louise Boyd
1963 Goodkind, Henry M.
1964 Greene, Vincent G.
1965 Lara, Alvaro Bonilla
1966 Haverbeck, Harrison D.S.
1967 Boker, John R. Jr.
1968 Bloch, Herbert
1969 Holmes, H.R.
1970 Lowe, Robson
1971 Neinken, Mortimer
1972 Ichida, Soichi
1973 Silver, Phil
1974 Kehr, Ernest A.
1975 Schatzkes, Joseph
1976 Turner, George T.
1977 Sellers, F. Burton
1978 DeVoss, Col. James T.
1979 Diena, Dr. Enzo
1980 Mueller, Barbara R.
1981 Stone, Robert G.
1982 Brett, George W.
1983 Pratt, Robert H.
1984 Miller, William H.
1986 South, George
1987 Hennig, Bernard A.
1988 Marriott, John B.
1989 McDonald, Susan M.

Luff Award

Established in 1940 by the American Philatelic Society in the name of John N. Luff, dean of American philatelists during the first decades of the 20th century. The award is presented for meritorious contributions to philately by living collectors.

1940 Ashbrook, Stanley B.
Dietz, August
1944 Chase, Dr. Carroll

Kimble, Col. Ralph A.
Perry, Elliott
1946 Brookman, Lester
Brazer, Clarence W.
Lidman, David
1948 Brookman, Lester
Lindquist, Harry L.
Smeltzer, Chester
1950 Johl, Max G.
Lybarger, Donald F.
Shoemaker, Laurence D.
1952 DeVoss, Col James T.
Boggs, Winthrop S.
MacBride, F. Van Dyk
1954 Davis, Dr. Holland A.
Glass, Sol
1956 Vooys, Daniel W.
Mueller, Barbara R.
1958 Abt, Henry
Davis, Bernard
DeVoss, Col. James T.
1961 Cratsenberg, Charles C.
Herst, Herman Jr.
Kovarik, Frank J.
1962 Apfelbaum, Earl P.L.
Blizil, George A.
Neinken, Mortimer
1964 Chemi, James
Clary, Joseph M.
Tatelman, Judge Edward I.P.
1966 Cabeen, Richard McP.
Harris, Henry E.
Musser, H. Clay
1968 Bloch, Herbert
Plant, Anna and Paul J.
Warren, Arnold H.
1970 Cole, Ezra
Hart, Creighton C.
Lane, Maryette B.
1972 Sampson, Edward
ter Braake, Alex
Thomas, Frederick B.
1974 Costales, Eugene
Harrison, Horace
Martin, George M.
1976 Kehr, Ernest A.
Kelly, Denwood
Turner, George T.
1978 Boker, John R. Jr.
Brett, George W.
Vooys, Daniel W.
1979 Silver, Philip
Wylie, William W.
1980 Clark, Emerson A.
Hargest, George E.
Lowe, Robson
1981 Diena, Dr. Enzo
Fricke, Charles A.
Thompson, Cyrus R.
1982 Hennig, Bernard A.
Thompson, Richard H.
Werenskiold, Carl H.
1983 Foxworth, John E. Jr.
Sellers, F. Burton
Stone, Robert G.
1985 Alexander, Thomas J.
Beal, James H.
Davidson, Robert L.D.
1986 McDonald, Susan
Starnes, Charles J.
Tinsley, Walter E.
1987 Bauer, William H.
Gobie, Henry M.
Wood, Kenneth A.
1988 Cannon, Wilbur F.
Peterson, Charles J.
Schimmer, Karl H.

McCoy Award

An annual American Philatelic Congress award established in 1953 in the name of Walter R. McCoy for the best article in *The Congress Book*, the organization's annual publication.

1953 Kaiser, J.B.
1954 Wagner, C. Corwith
1955 Mueller, Barbara R.
1956 Perry, Thomas Doane
1957 Myee, John N.
1958 Stone, Robert G.
1959 DeVoss, Col. James T.
1960 McKenzie, Vernon L.
1961 Schag, Gustave
1962 Stone, Robert G.
1963 Hutcheson, Robert J.
1965 Stevens, Warren C.
1966 DeVoss, Col. James T.
1968 Doane, Edith R.
1969 Birkinbine, John II
1970 Clark, Lawrence S.
1971 ter Braake, Alex
1972 Turner, Craig J.
1973 Warm, Harvey R.
1974 Towle, Charles L.
1975 Doane, Edith R.
1976 Waud, Morrison
1977 Hahn, Joseph D.
Sousa, Joseph M.
1978 Skinner, Hubert C.
1979 Cohn, Ernest M.

1980 Heinz, Alfred
1981 Boehret, Jesse and Diane
1982 Washburne, Stephen S.
1983 Wald, Kimber A.
1984 Jaronski, Stefan T.
1985 Washburne, Stephen S.
1986 Sellers, F. Burton
1987 Pulver, Dale R.

Mexico Hall of Fame

Established in 1969 by the Mexico-Elmhurst Philatelic Society International to honor individuals who have made outstanding contributions to the collection and study of the stamps and postal history of Mexico.

Bash, John K.
Benson, Gunnar
Billings, R.R.
Follansbee, Nicholas
Hamilton, Col. Charles S.
Havemeyer, John T.
Linn, George W.
Schimmer, Dr. Karl
Stevens, Byron F.
Yag, Otto

Neinken Medal

Presented annually since 1981 by the Philatelic Foundation to an individual whose conduct and dedication over a long period of time best exemplify the spirit exhibited by the late Mortimer L. Neinken, a pre-eminent student of classic U.S. issues.

1981 Brett, George W.
1982 Costales, Eugene N.
1983 Boker, John R. Jr.
1984 Neinken, Mortimer L.
1985 Miller, William H. Jr.
1986 Bloch, Herbert J.
1987 Siegel, Robert A.
1988 Weill, Raymond H. and Roger G.

Newbury Award

The Chicago Philatelic Society accolade for outstanding service to philately by a living philatelist in the Chicago area, in the name of one such distinguished collector, Saul Newbury.

1945 Lidman, David
1946 Strait, Walter G.
1947 Kenworthy, Waldo V.
1951 Hennan, Dr. Clarence W.
1952 Stuart, Elmer
1953 Cabeen, Richard McP.
1954 Reeves, Ben
1955 Pollock, Dr. Herbert C.
1956 Zinsmeister, J. Elmer and Marian
1957 Russo, Anthony C.
1958 Jacobs, Ernest R.
1959 Matejka, Dr. James J. Jr.
1961 Schulze, William H. and Anna
1962 Schrader, Col. Otto
1964 Fergus, W. Lee
1965 Kovarik, Frank J.
1966 Ray, Samuel
1967 Canman, Richard W.
1968 Hennig, Bernard
1969 Love, L. Cecil
1970 Light, Theodore
1972 Hahn, Charless
1973 Wellman, Earl H.
1975 Janecka, Joseph J. Jr.
1978 Fuerst Thomas
1979 Isaacs, Mark R.
1980 Ganz, P. Felix
1981 Berman, Aubrey
1982 Winick, Lester
1983 Outlaw, Robert
1984 Alton, Jacquelyn S.
1985 Karlen, Dr. Harvey M.
1986 Drews, Richard E.
1987 Ganz, Cheryl
1988 Berg, Charles

Pacific Northwest Distinguished Philatelist

Member of a hall of fame established in 1960 by the Northwestern Federation of Stamp Clubs to honor residents of the Pacific Northwest who made significant contributions to philately in that region.

1960 Binks, Bury C.
Carver, Fred E. and Margaret
Hitt, Henry C.
Payne, Edwin R.
Thiele, R.R.
Van Dahl, Al
Van Dahl, Arlene
Wellburn, Gerald
Wylie, William W.

1961 Blogg, Cecil A.
1962 Martin, George M.
1963 Slough, J. Burton
1964 Smith, Dr. Gerald B.
1965 Marston, C.L.
1966 Bartley, Deane C.

	Bates, Jack B.
1967	Newcomer, Ewald J.
1968	Long, Russell A.
1969	Barnet, Alexander A.
1970	Topping, William E.
1972	Melvin, George H.
1973	Fraser, R. Thurlow
1975	Small, Lester E.
1976	Taylor, J. Pascoe
1977	Wanderer, Fred E.
1978	Robinson, H.R.
1980	Steernberg, Peter
1981	Cochran, Louise
1982	Waldron, Florence M.
1983	Fisher, Ingeburg L.
1985	Flansburgh, W.H.
	Jones, Dr. C.T.
	Whittaker, Henry W.
1986	Current, Thomas G.
	Robinson, William G.
1988	White, John W.
1989	Wood, Kenneth
	Young, Winnifred H.

Roll of Distinguished Philatelists

Established at the 1920 Philatelic Congress of Great Britain. King George V was the first signatory to a scroll on which the signatures of outstanding philatelists are added annually.

1920	King George V
1921	Howes, Clifton A.
	Luff, John N.
	Pack, Charles Lathrop
	Richetts, William R.
	Severn, Charles E.
1924	Chase, Dr. Carroll
1925	Hatfield, A.
1927	Lichtenstein, Alfred H.
1929	Henry, C. Charlton
1933	Deats, Hiram E.
1935	Jarrett, Fred
1947	Calder, Sen. James A.
	Clark, Hugh M.
	Lindquist, Harry L.
	Starr, Maj. James
	Steinway, Theodore E.
1950	Ashbrook, Stanley B.
	Brookman, Lester
	Chafter Bey, Ibrahim
1951	Wellburn, Gerald
1953	Caspary, Alfred
	Holmes, H.R.
1954	DeBeer, W.S. Wolff
1956	Dale, Louise Boyd
	Wichersham, Gen. C.W.
1957	Johl, Max G.
1959	Boggs, Winthrop S.
1962	Blake, Maurice C.
1963	Burghard, George E.
	Greene, Vincent G.
	Schatkes, Dr. Joseph
1964	Boker, John R. Jr.
	Buhler, Joshua I.
1965	Lee, R.A.G.
1966	Bojanowicz, M.A.
	Goodkind, Henry M.
1967	Bonilla-Lara, Alvaro
	Langois, Pierre
1968	Bloch, Herbert
	Field, Francis J.
	Lipschutz, M. Michel
	Rivolta, Dr. Achille
1969	Campbell, H.M.
	Harmer, C.H.C.
	Rider, John F.
	Towsend, W.A.
1970	Green, Mrs. Doris M.
	Haverbeck, Harrison D.S.
1971	Ichida, Dr. S.
	Stanley, Marcel
1972	Berthelot, Lucien
	Caroe, Sir E.A.G., CBE
	Crustin, J.H.E.
	Marriott, John B.
1973	Van der Willigen, Dr. A.M.A.
1974	Fromaigeat, Dr. J.
	Pearson, P.C.
	South, George
1975	Butler, A.R.
	Kehr, Ernest A.
	Plancquaert, Jules L.J.
1976	Gartner, John
	Guggenheim, Max
	Morgan, Mrs. E.L.
	Wolter, K.K.
1977	Diena, Dr. Enzo
	Dromberg, D.A.
	Palmer, Derek
	Ringstrom, Sigge
1978	Bjaringer, Tomas
	McNaught, Kenneth John
	Michael, A.L.
	Morgan, A.L.
	Silver, Philip
	Turner, George T.
1979	Hunziker, Hans
	Levett, John H.
	Matejka, Dr. James J. Jr.
	Messenger, John L.

1980 Andersen, Stig
Kuyas, Tevfik
Pennycuick, Kenneth
Purves, J.R.W.
Ryan, Gary S.
Salm, Arthur
1981 Aisslinger, Horst
Bolaffi, Dr. Giulio
DeVoss, Col. James T.
Fisher, H.W.
1982 Branz, Hermann
Hennig, Bernard
1983 Hertsch, Max
Huggins, Alan K.
Jatia, Deoki N.
Tinsley, Walton E.
1984 Jaeger, Anton
Mondolfo, Renato
Rapkin, Leon V.
Stone, Robert G.
1985 Bruhl, Carlrichard
Rosende, Roberto M.
Wellsted, W. Raife
1986 Fosbery, John A.L.
Sellers, F. Burton
Vollmeier, Paolo O.
1987 Chapman, Ray
Griffiths, John
Jaeger, Heinz
Stibbe, Jacques
1988 Ellott, Gerald J.
Jensen, Paul H.
1989 de Bustamente, Enrique M.
Indhusophon, Prakaipet
Loeuillet, Roger
Sundman, Christian C.
Willcocks, R. Martin

Wagner Award

An American Philatelic Congress award extablished in 1981 in the name of C. Corwith Wagner for the best American postal history article for the period 1776-1876 in *The Congress Book*, the organization's annual publication.

1981 Wierenga, Theron
1982 Newman, Lowell S.
1984 Jaronski, Stefan T.

Writers' Hall of Fame

The National Philatelic Writers' Hall of Fame was established by the Writers' unit of the American Philatelic Society in 1974 to honor outstanding philatelic writers of the past and present.

1974 Ashbrook, Stanley B.
Boggs, Winthrop S.
Brookman, Lester
Cabeen, Richard McP.
Chase, Dr. Carroll
Chemi, James
Dietz, August
Faulstich, Edith
Hatcher, James B.
Herst, Herman Jr.
Johl, Max G.
Lindquist, Harry L.
Linn, George W.
Luff, John N.
Norona, Delf
Perry, Elliott
Rich, Stephen G.
Scott, John Walter
Stilpen, George
Thorp, Prescott Holden
Van Dahl, Al
Wylie, William W.

1975 Faries, Belmont
Goodkind, Henry M.
Kimble, Col. Ralph A.
Spaulding, Robert M.
Vooys, Daniel W.
Weiss, Harry
1976 Barry, Ralph A.
Erle, Everett
Patrick, Douglas A.
Stiles, Kent B.
1977 Jarrett, Fred
Kehr, Ernest A.
Perry, Thomas Doane
Poole, Bertram W.H.
Wylie, Willard O.
1978 Bertalanffy, Dr. Felix D.
Doane, Edith R.
Holmes, Dr. L. Seales
Livingston, Lyons F.
Mueller, Barbara R.
Stewart, William R.
1979 Apfelbaum, Earl P.L.
Brett, George W.
Bruns, Franklin R. Jr.
Foster, Charles
Holcombe, Henry W.
Jackson, Lucius
Schoberlin, Melvin H.
1980 Lowe, Robson
Meville, Frederick J.
Turner, George T.
Williams, L. Norman

Williams, Maurice
1981 Lidman, David
Ragatz, Lowell J.
1982 Lane, Maryette B.
Mueller, Edwin
Reiner-Deutsch, William
1984 Wood, Kenneth
1986 Alexander, Robert P.
Baxter, James H.
Chapman, Kenneth F.
McDonald, Susan M.
1987 Nahl, Perham C.
Towle, Charles
White, Roy
1988 Ganz, R. Felix
Kerr, Allen
1989 Christian, C.W.
Fricke, Charles
Purves, J.W.R.

Chapter 24

Museums and Libraries

National Philatelic Collections

Smithsonian Institution, Washington, D.C.

The National Philatelic Collections, which include the United States National Postage Stamp Collection and various foreign-area holdings, is maintained by the Smithsonian Institution, and is housed in the National Museum of American History, Constitution Avenue (between 12th and 14th streets), Washington, D.C.

The National Philatelic Collections include more than 16 million objects — stamps, covers, and postal history objects — and new material is added each year.

An excellent representation of the material embraced within the National Philatelic Collections are displayed in the Hall of Postal History and Philately. The exhibit area is located on the third floor of the National Museum of American History.

The exhibition may be visited seven days a week (except Christmas Day), between 10 a.m. and 5:30 p.m. Admission is free.

History

The cornerstone for the first Smithsonian Institution building was laid May 1, 1847 — two months before official United States postage stamps appeared.

James Smithson, an English scientist, bequeathed his fortune to the United States of America in 1846 for the "increase and diffusion of knowledge." Congress acted quickly, and on Aug. 10, 1846, President James K. Polk signed the act establishing the Smithsonian Institution.

The first philatelic donation — including a pane of 10¢ Confederate stamps (four had been removed) — was made in 1886. A short time later the Smithsonian received 1,733 stamps bequeathed by Spencer Fullerton Baird, secretary from 1878 to 1887. By 1908, some 2,500 stamps had been received as gifts or bequests.

David W. Cromwell, then a prominent New York collector, gave the Smithsonian's philatelic holdings a substantial boost through a series of donations that totaled 20,000 stamps by 1915.

Some of Cromwell's stamps were exhibited in the Smithsonian's Arts and Industries Building as early as 1911. This display was not pretentious; open albums were placed in glass-topped cases.

A major addition to the collection came in 1911-12 when the United States Post Office Department closed down a postal museum it had operated for roughly 20 years. The collection — representing about 20,000 stamps, postal stationery items, proofs, post office equipment, and related items — was transferred to the Smithsonian Institution.

To manage the collection, Joseph B. Leavy became the Smithsonian's first philatelic specialist in 1913 and, with the help of Catherine L. Manning, who later succeeded him, completed a display of stamps in specially constructed pullout frames. This exhibit, which was opened to the public in early 1915, was housed in the Arts and Industries building.

Manning became government philatelist (later curator) when Leavy died in 1921, and continued in that capacity for 30 years.

Succeeding Manning as curators were Franklin R. Bruns Jr. (1951-57), George T. Turner (1958-62), Francis J. McCall (1962-63), Carl H. Scheele (1963-75), Franklin R. Bruns Jr. again (1975-79), Reidar Norby (1966-1988) and James H. Bruns (1984-present).

In November 1979, the Division of Postal History was elevated to a department level headed by executive director Robert Tillotson. The present executive director, Herbert R. Collins, succeeded Tillotson in 1982.

Other members of the staff are: Nancy Pope, librarian; Virginia Kilby, collections manager; Gisela Cooke, assistant collections manager; James O'Donnell, vault supervisor; Joseph Geraci, museum specialist; and Marge Porter, office manager.

Hall of Postal History and Philately

Since 1908, representative portions of the nation's philatelic collection have been on public display. Although initially housed in cramped quarters in the Arts and Industries building, the exhibit was moved to the newly completed National Museum of History and Technology in 1964. The building was subsequently renamed the National Museum of American History.

On display are a variety of different items and replicas that trace the growth of postal communications from the Sumerian cunieform to modern mail-handling processes. This exhibit utilizes prints and photographs, models, actual postal objects and covers to show advances in mail transportation from foot carriers to airmail service.

Among the postal objects on display are mailbags and pouches, mailboxes, locks, cancels, metering devices and uniforms of mail carriers.

Also on display is a full-size replica of Ben Franklin's colonial post office/print shop.

One highlight of the Hall of Postal History and Philately is a representative worldwide collection of postal issues. This collection is housed in 473 double-sided pullout frames and numbers about 85,000 stamps.

The Hall of Postal History and Philately holds a learning center manned by retired postmasters, railway mail clerks and postal inspectors. At the learning center, visitors can dress in vintage postal uniforms, investigate stamp collecting, practice sorting and canceling mail and examine objects related to postal history. Special tours of the hall also are conducted from the learning center. The learning center is open on Tuesdays and Thursdays from 1 p.m. to 3 p.m.

In addition, there is an area devoted to United States stamp production. On display is an engraver's booth, with tools and an actual die. Also represented are a transfer press and a small Stickney rotary press, both circa 1912, and early perforating machines, circa 1918-39.

To illustrate the various stages in the production of a postage stamp, color transparencies trace each step from design and die engraving to transfer, printing and perforating.

A separate area is also dedicated to the prodution of postal stationery. On display is a hub die, a master die and a frame die prepared for governmental embossed envelopes by George F. Nesbitt & Company between 1853 and 1861. Also on display are the preliminary and final stages of dies for United States postal cards of 1910 (McKinley) and 1911 (Lincoln).

Another attraction in the hall is a rarities alcove. Among the items frequently on display are such rarities as the 24¢ inverted Jenny airmail; one of two existing panes of the Canal Zone Thatcher Ferry Bridge stamp with the missing bridge error; panes of the Washington 5¢ in 2¢ sheet error; the only *Balloon Jupiter* cover with message; the 1869 and 1901 United States inverts; the $1 CIA invert; and exceptional United States covers and postal memorabilia.

Reference Collections

Only representative samples of the National Philatelic Collection are on public display. Present exhibit facilities, large though they currently are, do not permit the display of every postage stamp issued, nor the many stamp varieties of interest to specialists.

The museum does maintain one of the largest philatelic reference collections. Collectors interested in stamps produced by the Bureau of Engraving and Printing, for example, can examine certified plate proofs of every plate from No. 1 on, as well as essays and die proofs of 19th-century United States postage and revenue stamps.

Also available are the U.S. Post Office Department/U.S. Postal Service stamp files for much of this century.

United States postal historians and researchers also have access to full panes of many items, multiple pieces and a strong representation of plate number strips and plate block numbers, precancels, stamps with perforated initials (perfins), meter markings, and Christmas and Easter seals.

Cover and postal stationery collectors can examine corner cards, special markings and backstamps, and die varieties.

Also in this area are first-day covers, flight covers and war covers.

Postal stationery of the world is also well-represented. The museum's collection of worldwide postal stationery references is probably the largest in the world.

The reference area also contains various collections covering booklet panes and souvenir sheets of the world, Austrian fiscals, Mexican revenues and Swiss military adhesives, plus one of the finest collections of Israeli ever assembled.

Other notable reference strengths are Afghanistan, Albania, Australia, 20th-century Belgium, Chile, Colombia, Ecuador, Egypt, France and Germany.

Also included are materials on India and the Indian Feudatory States, Indonesia, Ireland, Italian States, Japan, Latvia, Nepal, Panama, Peru, the Philippines, Ryukyus, Saar, Salvador, Spain, Tibet, Transvaal, Trieste, Ukraine and Venezuela.

There are also thematic areas of note, including United Nations stamps of the world, Rotary and Red Cross issues, and Lincoln and Kennedy material, to name just a few.

Those wishing to refer to any of the reference materials in the National Philatelic Collections should request permission to use the collection at least four weeks in advance of the projected visit. Such a request should clearly state the area to be researched. Requests should be addressed to: Executive Director, National Philatelic Collection, Room 4300, National Museum of American History, Washington, D.C. 20560.

Use of the reference area is restricted to 10 a.m. to 4:30 p.m. Monday through Friday. Access is subject to the availability of staff for supervision and assistance.

Research Library

With the addition of the renowned collection of reference materials amassed by the late George T. Turner, the museum's philatelic library is among the largest in the world.

The research library includes 2,000 linear feet of shelf space. The monographs, serials, catalogs, manuscripts and documents cover the stamps and postal history of virtually every country of the world.

Library stacks are open. Specialized and selected files are available upon request. The library also houses various microfilmed philatelic and postal periodicals, auction catalogs, stamp catalogs, stamp albums and international philatelic exhibition programs. Serials from 1863 to the most current, including all important U.S. and foreign philatelic and postal history journals, are available. Publications of the United States Post Office Department and the United States Postal Service are in the library. They offer a vast amount of information.

The National Philatelic Collection reference library has implemented a new computerized library system designed to assist in making publications accessible. The system is known as SIBIS (Smithsonian Institution Bibliographic Information System). Through SIBIS, the National Philatelic Collection provides quick and efficient access to this large and most comprehensive library. Through inter-library loan, most items, depending on their condition and rarity, can be made available to researchers throughout the country. For more information on local inter-library loan practices, researchers should consult their public library or a college or university library.

A notable strength of the philatelic reference library is the photographic collection. It includes more than 10,000 prints and slides of philatelic and postal history subjects. Each year the collection acquires approximately 300 additional prints, slides and photographs. Reproductions are available for research, publication and educational purposes. A price list of reproductive photographic work is available from the librarian.

The photographic collection has been categorized and arranged in file cabinets and slide cases. Of the slides and photographs, transportation is the largest single category, embracing all methods of moving mail, from the runner to rockets.

A collection of audio recordings of observations by philatelic experts and American postal workers is being established. Recordings of Gregory Stolow, Lester Brookman and Sylvester Colby are among those included in this new collection.

A wide selection of slide programs has been developed by the National Philatelic Collection. These are lent, free of charge, for a one-week period. The slide sets are provided as a service. Borrowers may not charge admission to slide programs nor may the programs be used to solicit funds in any way. Scripts are provided with each presentation. No order form is necessary to borrow one of the sets. Simply send a letter or card indicating the tentative date when your group would like to present a slide program. A list of the slide programs and a brief description of each presentation is available from the librarian of the National Philatelic Collection.

The Headsville Post Office

To complement the philatelic collection, the museum maintains a country store/ post office. The structure stood in Headsville, W.Va., from about 1861 to 1914. It was carefully taken apart, transported to Washington, D.C., and assembled on the first floor of the museum building.

The Headsville Post Office (now designated as the Smithsonian Station) is operated by the United States Postal Service. Museum visitors may purchase current postal issues and have them postmarked with a special Smithsonian Station pictorial cancellation.

The Headsville Post Office looks much as it did about 100 years ago. It served as the basis for the 8¢ U.S. postage stamp honoring the 100th anniversary of mail order.

National Air and Space Museum

The National Air and Space Museum is located on the Independence Avenue side of the Smithsonian's museum complex in Washington, D.C. It contains a variety of airmail vehicles and other items relating to postal history.

Library hours are Monday through Friday, 10 a.m. to 4:30 p.m., by appointment only. The museum itself is open daily on the same schedule as the rest of the Smithsonian complex.

National Archives and Records Service

The permanently valuable documents and records of the United States are housed in the National Archives Building, Eighth and Pennsylvania Avenue N.W., Washington, D.C.

The National Archives comprises almost 800,000 cubic feet of historic and important documents, records, maps, recordings, motion pictures and photographs dating from around 1774 to the present.

Included are displays of such original documents as the Declaration of Independence and the Constitution. Also included are the records of the former U.S. Post Office Department. All archival records are available to philatelists and researchers, subject to the regulations for the public use of materials in the National Archives and Records Service.

The hours for the Central Research Room and Microfilm Research Room are 8:45 a.m. to 10 p.m. Monday through Friday, and 8:45 a.m. to 5 p.m. Saturday. Records to be used on Saturday must be requested by 5 p.m. on Friday; those to be used after 5 p.m. Monday through Friday must be requested by 4 p.m. of the day on which they are to be used.

Library of Congress

The nation's library, the Library of Congress, consists of three buildings on Capitol Hill in Washington, D.C. The oldest, and the one often considered the main Library of Congress building, is the Thomas Jefferson Building completed in 1897. The other two are the John Adams Building (1939) and the James Madison Memorial Building (1980). The Jefferson building is featured on the 1982 U.S. Library of Congress commemorative stamp. The Madison building includes more space than the Jefferson and Adams buildings combined.

The Library of Congress contains more than 80 million items on virtually any subject and is likely to contain the largest general reference collection of philatelic materials available anywhere.

Researchers can also make good use of the more than 1,200 newspapers in the permanent collection as reference sources. Official documents relating to many presidents and postmasters general are also contained in the Library of Congress.

Researchers should consult with library officials for information on hours and regulations. Interested persons may contact the Library of Congress, Information Office, 10 First St. S.E., Washington, D.C. 20540.

U.S. Libraries and Museums

Philatelic museums and libraries in the United States, except those in the nation's capital previously listed, are presented here alphabetically by state, and by city within each state listing. This listing is as complete and comprehensive as possible, with information current through March 1989. Some changes to this listing are the result of questionnaires sent to all known and previously listed museums and libraries. Directors of philatelic libraries and museums are asked to send updates and corrections to *Linn's*.

Travelers planning a visit to any of these museums or libraries might be advised to make advance contact to confirm hours, location and availability of material. A visit to a postal museum can be a fascinating aspect of any business or pleasure trip. Researchers may also benefit from the resources of libraries with specialized holdings that may not be available elsewhere. There are endless hours of learning and entertainment encompassed in the pages of this U.S. listing, and countless more in the foreign listing which follows afterwards.

Arizona

TUCSON. Western Postal History Museum, Box 40725, Tucson, Ariz. 85717-0725.

Founded in 1960. Complete U.S. type collection. Postmarks from 13 Western states. Territorial Arizona and New Mexico covers pertaining to "long-gone" camps, forts and mining towns. Also, State of Arizona revenue collection, specialized collections from other countries, including Mexico, Canada and a United Nations collection.

Exhibits prepared periodically and for special occasions. Permanent exhibit areas are located in the Arizona Heritage Center, 949 E. Second St., while the museum's offices, library, Sales Department, Youth Philatelic Education Department and some additional exhibits are located only two blocks away at 920 N. First Ave. The permanent exhibits include Western dioramas and paintings and an old-time territorial-days post office formerly used in Naco.

Museum exhibits at the Arizona Heritage Center open to the public Monday through Saturday 10 a.m. to 4 p.m., Sunday 12 to 4 p.m. Free.

The museum's Philatelic Education Department conducts regular courses in local and outlying public schools, coordinating a study of stamps with history, geography and social studies. The museum has philatelic-related publications of its own. The museum's "The Heliograph" — published quarterly — is one of the benefits of museum membership. The Philatelic Research Library — the largest west of the Mississippi — is located along with the museum offices.

The museum offices and library are open to the public weekdays 8:30 a.m. to 4:30 p.m., or by appointment (602) 623-6652. Closed on most Federal holidays. Facilities available at the discretion of the executive director.

California

FRESNO. Henry Madden Library, California State University, Shaw Avenue at Cedar.

Collection includes U.S. regular, commemorative, airmail and official adhesive postage stamps, 1847-1956; some Panama-Pacific International Exposition cancels, 1910-15. The collection is no longer on display, but it is available for viewing with one day's notice.

Hours are 9 a.m. to 5 p.m. Monday through Friday. Closed weekends and all official holidays. Free.

LOS ANGELES. Scandinavian Philatelic Library of Southern California Inc.

Library list of Scandinavian books, monographs, catalogs and periodicals available through club address.

Library materials available on special request by mail or in person. Direct inquiries to Scandinavian Philatelic Library of Southern California Inc., Box 57397, Los Angeles, Calif. 90057.

—Wells Fargo Bank History Museum, 333 S. Grand Ave., in the Wells Fargo Center.

Museum exhibit covers staging, express, banking, mining, gold and early Southern California. Also on exhibit is an original Concord stagecoach.

Open to the public, Monday through Friday, 9 a.m. to 5 p.m. Closed all bank holidays. Free.

REDLANDS. The Lincoln Shrine, 125 W. Vine St., in Smiley Park at the rear of the A.K. Smiley Public Library.

Stamps relating to Lincoln and the Civil War period, Lincoln commemoratives, stampless covers and Civil War envelopes. Collection also includes foreign stamps.

Lincoln Log, publication of the Lincoln Society of Philately, available.

All materials noncirculating.

Open 1 p.m. to 5 p.m., Tuesday through Saturday. Closed Sunday, Monday and holidays, except Lincoln's birthday. Visitors asked to call or write for special appointments for tour groups during morning hours.

— United Postal Stationery Society. Books related to postal stationery. Information available from the UPSS Central Office, Box 48, Redlands, Calif. 92373.

SAN FRANCISCO. Wells Fargo Bank History Museum, 420 Montgomery St.

The Wiltsee Memorial Collection of Western Stamps, Franks and Postmarks, left in trust by Ernest A. Wiltsee for public display, more than 1,300 covers giving examples from 235 different express companies.

Pony Express stamps, covers, postal markings from California communities, many now ghost towns.

Entire exhibit centered around an original Concord stagecoach.

Open to the public Monday through Friday, 9 a.m. to 5 p.m. Closed all bank holidays. Free.

SUNNYVALE. Western Philatelic Library, philatelic section of the Sunnyvale Public Library, 665 W. Olive Ave., Sunnyvale, Calif. 94086.

Established in 1969 by the Friends of the South Bay Philatelic Library, Inc. A 1971 merger with the trustees of the Philatelic Research Library resulted in the sponsor's change of name to the Friends of the Western Philatelic Library, Inc.

Most materials are available through your public library inter-library loan system. Contact your local library for details.

Over 750 linear feet in the philatelic section contain more than 2,500 books and 2,700 bound volumes of 300 periodical titles.

More than 800 books now available for library use; circulated to library card holders. Occasional in-library lobby displays of philatelic material.

Open Monday through Thursday 10 a.m. to 9 p.m.; Friday-Saturday, 10 a.m. to 6 p.m.; Sunday, 1 p.m. to 5 p.m. Closed holidays.

Florida

FORT LAUDERDALE. International Swimming Hall of Fame Inc., 1 Hall of Fame Drive, Fort Lauderdale, Fla. 33316.

The late Axel Nordquist's sports stamp collection features swimming. All stamps, including other sports, displayed and organized by major events — Olympics, World Championships, Pan American and others.

Stamps displayed in leatherbound books by country and subject as permanent part of the hall's special exhibits room.

Open daily 10 a.m. to 5 p.m.; Sunday, 11 a.m. to 4 p.m. Admission, $4 for adults; $2 for students, military personnel and senior citizens. Family rate $10. Group rates for 10 or more people; 300-seat auditorium available for regular meetings or special events.

Illinois

CHICAGO. Balzekas Museum of Lithuanian Culture, 6500 S. Pulaski Road., Chicago, Ill. 60629. Complete collection of Lithuanian stamps on permanent exhibit, letters and envelopes, periodicals and history of Lithuanian stamps and designers; also philatelic books.

The museum is a center for philatelic activities, offers lectures and has a traveling philatelic exhibit. Materials available to scholars and the general public.

Open seven days a week 10 a.m. to 4 p.m.; closed Christmas and New Year's Day. Admission, $3; children, $1; senior citizens, $2.

Massachusetts

WESTON. Cardinal Spellman Philatelic Museum, 235 Wellesley St., Weston, Mass. 02193.

Items include the original Cardinal Spellman collection, President Dwight D. Eisenhower, Gen. Matthew Ridgway, and Jascha Heifitz collections, and extensive worldwide stamps.

Also, 30,000 volumes of philatelic and collateral material, extensive acquisitions of letters and envelopes. Three galleries of exhibits always open.

Museum has philatelic publications, teaching facilities, traveling exhibits. Materials available to scholars and general public; museum members have room use and library privileges.

Open to the public Sunday, 1 p.m. to 5 p.m.; Tuesday through Thursday, 10 a.m. to 4 p.m. Other times by appointment.

Admission is free by donation.

Michigan

PLYMOUTH. West Suburban Stamp Club, Plymouth.

Growing library includes reference books, periodicals, auction and show catalogs. No permanent site at present. Several hundred volumes in library for use by membership. Open on request basis only. Contact Box 643, Plymouth, Mich. 48170.

Montana

HELENA. Montana Historical Society, 225 N. Roberts St., Helena, Mont. 59620.

Covers from territorial days, early post offices in Montana, early Montana territorial letters.

Open Monday through Friday, 8 a.m. to 5 p.m. Closed holidays.

Nebraska

BOYS TOWN. The Stamp Center is located in the Visitor's Center at Father Flanagan's Boys' Home, just west of Omaha.

Contains a major exhibit on the Father Flanagan stamp and topical displays with a child-related theme. Sales area and youth exhibit area.

Open to the public year round, Monday through Saturday, 8 a.m. to 4:30 p.m.; Sundays and holidays, 9 a.m. to 4:30 p.m. Closed Thanksgiving, Christmas, New Year's Day and Good Friday afternoon. Free. Group reservations can be made by calling the center in advance: (402) 498-1140.

GOTHENBURG. Original Pony Express Station, Ehmen Park, Gothenburg, Neb. 69198.

Authentic Pony Express items in the museum. Open to the public May through September, 9 a.m. to 6 p.m.; June through August, 8 a.m. to 9 p.m. Free.

New Hampshire

HINSDALE. Hinsdale Post Office, Hinsdale, N.H. 03451.

Established Jan. 24, 1815. According to records, it is the oldest continuously operated post office building in the United States and is still operating.

New Jersey

WILDWOOD. Chester Davis Memorial Library, 5121 Park Blvd., Wildwood, N.J. 08260-0121.

Precanceled postage stamps from the United States, England, France, Canada, United Nations; also letters, envelopes, philatelic publications.

Revolving exhibits; otherwise shown at Precanex stamp shows.

Open only to paid members of the National Association of Precancel Collectors.

New York

HYDE PARK. The Franklin D. Roosevelt Library/Museum, Hyde Park.

Variety of albums given President Roosevelt by other heads of state. Holdings also include singles, sheets, proofs, postcards, envelopes and covers. Museum items available to the public and scholars on a limited basis.

The library has correspondence and literature relating to Roosevelt's interests in the post office, stamps and stamp collecting. There is no charge for those doing research in the presidential papers.

Museum hours, 9 a.m. to 5 p.m. every day except Christmas and New Year's. General admission fee (including fee for Vanderbilt Historic Site and home of Franklin D. Roosevelt).

NEW YORK. The Collectors Club, 22 E. 35th St., New York, N.Y. 10016.

Extensive philatelic library. Open to the public Monday, Wednesday and Friday from 10 a.m. to 4 p.m., except every first and third Wednesday of the month from 1 p.m. to 8 p.m. Closed legal holidays and during the summer, June 15 through Sept. 15. Appointment necessary for research purposes. Meetings and lectures scheduled during the year.

— Library/Malloch Rare Book Room, New York Academy of Medicine, 2 E. 103rd St., New York, N.Y. 10029.

Library has three substantial collections of stamps. The Denker collection consists of six volumes of stamps related to health and medicine. It is international in scope and has stamps dating from 1897-1962. The Simon collection comprises 21 framed displays and six volumes of stamps related to radiology, cancer and public health, primarily modern and international. The Abeloff collection consists of seven volumes and contains international stamps relating to cancer, smoking, blood donors, leprosy and malaria. Stamps in the Abeloff collection date from 1925 to 1986.

The library's catalog also lists 32 articles and nine books on the subject of stamps and medicine.

Open to the general public Monday, noon to 5 p.m.; Tuesday through Friday, 9 a.m. to 5 p.m., except holidays.

— Philatelic Foundation, 21 E. 40th St., 14th Floor, New York, N.Y. 10016.

An extensive collection of Luff reference material including comprehensive U.S. and worldwide reference stamp collections and covers with a variety of postal markings, extensive library, photographic reference files, and records of postal services from many countries.

Educational program includes publication of analysis of Foundation's expertizing work, periodic counterfeit advisory leaflets and audio-visual programs.

Materials available to the public Monday through Friday, 10:30 a.m. to 4 p.m. by appointment to facilitate service. Closed evenings and legal holidays.

Ohio

BELLEVUE. Margie Pfund Postmark Museum.

Owned by Post Mark Collectors Club. Extensive and growing collection of postal cancellations, items related to post offices and postal service.

Located in the Historic Lyme Village post office building, part of the restored complex at the intersection of Ohio Routes 4 and 113.

The Village is open Tuesday through Sunday, 1p.m. to 5 p.m., June through August; open weekends May and September. Village admission: adults, $2.50; senior citizens, $2.25; students, $1.25; children under 12 (accompanied by adult), free.

For further information, contact Bernice Mittower, curator, RR 2, Box 136, Republic, Ohio 44867.

CLEVELAND. Society of Israel Philatelists Slide Library, 3813 Bushnell Road, Cleveland, Ohio 44118.

Library has more than 4,500 philatelic slides encompassing 95 different lectures. A written text accompanies all SIP slide lectures.

These slide lectures are available at no charge to responsible philatelic clubs and organizations, as well as non-philatelic groups.

Request for use of slides must be made at least three weeks prior to meeting date. State exact meeting date when requesting use of a slide lecture.

All slides must be returned by registered or first-class insured mail or United Parcel Service with a declared value of $1 per slide within two days after meeting date.

Slide lectures may not be held for longer periods without prior permission from the slide library's chairman, Albert Friedberg.

SIDNEY. George W. Linn Memorial Research Library, Amos Press Inc., 911 Vandemark Road, Sidney, Ohio 45365.

Approximately 5,000 volumes, 200 current periodicals covering all phases of philately. Non-circulating.

All issues of *Linn's Stamp News* on microfilm; printouts available. Photocopy services available.

Open year round Monday through Friday, 8 a.m. to 5 p.m. Closed seasonal holidays.

Pennsylvania

PHILADELPHIA. American Swedish Historical Museum, 1900 Pattison Ave., Philadelphia, Pa. 19145.

Museum has an extensive Swedish collection, 1650-present.

Materials are used on a regular basis for exhibits, publications and teaching.

Open Tuesday through Friday, 10 a.m. to 4 p.m.; Saturday, noon to 4 p.m. Closed Sundays and Mondays.

— The Franklin Institute, 20th Street and Benjamin Franklin Parkway, Philadelphia, Pa. 19103. Collections include U.S. classics, rarities, covers, Wells Fargo and other non-governmental carriers. Numismatic collection. Collections not available to public. Scholars may apply for permission to view collection only by writing at least three weeks in advance to the Institute, Attention: Curatorial Assistant.

Museum open weekdays 9:30 a.m. to 4:30 p.m. and weekends 10 a.m. to 5 p.m. Closed some holidays. Summer schedule may differ.

Admission: adults $5.50, children 4-11 $4.50. Children under 4 not charged. Group rates available.

— B. Free Franklin Post Office, 311 Market St., Philadelphia, Pa. 19106-9996. In an authentically restored house once owned by Benjamin Franklin.

Postal Museum located on second floor houses the pictorial history of the beginning of the postal service with Benjamin Franklin to the present postmaster general. Seasonal and topical displays are changed periodically.

B. Free Franklin Post Office is open daily 9 a.m. to 5 p.m. Closed Christmas and New Year's Day.

— The Free Library of Philadelphia, Logan Square.

Extensive collection of books, periodicals and catalogs on stamps and stamp collecting with continuous acquisitions.

Holdings based on two major collections: The Eugene Klein collection is strong in European books. The Hiram Deats collection includes philatelic literature of American origin.

Philatelic literature available to general public for in-house reference consultation. Library is charged with statewide resource responsibility for philately.

Open 9 a.m. to 9 p.m., Monday through Wednesday; 9 a.m. to 6 p.m., Thursday and Friday; 9 a.m. to 5 p.m., Saturday; and 1 to 5 p.m., Sunday (except in summer). Free for in-person reference use.

STATE COLLEGE. American Philatelic Research Library, 100 Oakwood Ave., State College, Pa.

Incorporated in 1968 as the research and educational arm of the American Philatelic Society.

Materials include handbooks, catalogs, price lists, periodicals, auction catalogs, bibliographies and indexes on all aspects of philately and the history of stamp collecting.

Persons interested in doing philatelic research are encouraged to visit the library for maximum use of the facilities. Persons not able to visit State College may contact the library to receive a listing of materials available on their collecting interest or topic.

Members of the American Philatelic Society or the American Philatelic Research Library may receive materials directly from the library. Persons not affiliated with either of these organizations are encouraged to make use of the resources of the APRL through their public library's inter-library loan system.

The library charges standardized fees that reflect the cost of shipping all materials. Changes in the fee structure are announced in the *American Philatelist* and the *Philatelic Literature Review*. Fees in effect March 31, 1989, are: Shipping and handling, $2 per shipment; additional fee per book loaned, 75¢; photocopy charges per page, 20¢.

The library's card catalog has been converted to a computerized system. Print-outs of specific topics are available.

The charge for the initial search, including up to four pages of print-out, is $8. Additional pages of print-out are 20¢ per page. There is no shipping and handling fee when the print-out is the only item requested.

The mailing address for the APRL is: Box 8338, State College, Pa. 16803-8338. Materials may be requested by writing to the library.

The library is open Monday through Friday, 8 a.m. to 4:30 p.m., and Saturdays, 8 a.m. to noon. There are no Saturday hours from Nov. 1 to March 1.

Texas

RICHARDSON. University of Texas at Dallas, Wineburgh Philatelic Research Library, Box 830643, Richardson, Texas 75083-0643. Extensive collection of books, periodicals and catalogs on stamps and stamp collecting with emphasis on postal history, counterfeits, forgeries and airmail. Continuous acquisition of new material. All material available to public for in-house reference.

On permanent display are panels of U.S. postal history, stampless covers and panels of "The Language of Philately." Other exhibits continually changing.

Members may borrow items directly from the library. Non-members may utilize the facilities through their public library's inter-library loan program.

Open year round 9 a.m. to 6 p.m., Monday thru Thursday; 9 a.m. to 5 p.m. Friday; 1 p.m. to 5 p.m. on first Saturday of each month; other hours by appointment.

Virginia

NORFOLK. Gen. Douglas MacArthur Memorial, MacArthur Square, Norfolk, Va. 23510.

Stamps primarily of the Philippines, others of World War II and later origin; first-day covers, letters and envelopes. Materials available to scholars and general public.

Open Monday through Saturday, 10 a.m. to 5 p.m.; Sunday, 11 a.m. to 5 p.m. Closed Thanksgiving, Christmas and New Year's Day.

Wyoming

CHEYENNE. National First Day Cover Museum, 702 Randall Blvd., Cheyenne, Wyo. 82001.

On display are first-day covers, including one of Great Britain's Penny Black.

The museum is open to the public

Foreign Libraries and Museums

Throughout the world, public and private museums maintain and display stamps and covers for the delight of visiting collectors. These holdings range from the massive offerings of national postal museums to the small postal history displays of local historical societies.

Philatelic libraries may also be found worldwide. Some have extensive holdings and unusual or specialized philatelic significance.

The following list includes foreign libraries and museums known to be of interest to stamp collectors. This listing has been updated with the cooperation of curators and library directors throughout the world. Future additions and corrections will be appreciated, as will information on any museums and libraries that may not be included here.

One interesting aspect of postal museums outside the United States is the frequent inclusion of the telephone, telegraph and other means of communication in the same historical offering. This is because the major means of communication are under one government department. Aspects of technology frequently are government monopolies, managed by the postal administration or a general telecommunications department.

Argentina

BUENOS AIRES. Empresa Nacional de Correos y Telegrafos, Encotel, Buenos Aires 1000, Argentina. General Post Office: library on sixth floor, Room 631. Museum at 851 Avenida de los Italianos.

Philatelic booklets, letters, stamps and envelopes with historical postal markings.

Open to the general public throughout the year. Hours: library, 11:30 a.m. to 7 p.m.; museum, 10 a.m. to 6 p.m. Free.

Austria

VIENNA. Post und Telegraphen-museum, Technisches Museum, Mariahilfer Strasse 212, A-1140 Vienna, Austria.

Collection considers the development of mail and telecommunications in Austria. Also shows a few stamps and their production, letters, covers, postal markings and other materials. Founded 1889.

A library covering the history of Austrian communications is also available for use.

The collection is open Tuesday through Friday from 9 a.m. to 4 p.m.; Saturday from 9 a.m. to 1 p.m. The library is open Tuesday through Friday from 9 a.m. to noon. Closed Monday with the exception of Easter Monday and Whit Monday, also closed Jan. 1, Good Friday, May 1, Corpus Christi, Nov. 1 and 2, and Dec. 25.

The Technical Museum building charges 3 schillings for adults; reductions for certain persons and groups. Free admission for children under 10 years and members of ICOM. Free for all on every last Saturday of the month.

Museum guidebook available for 24 shillings.

Belgium

BRUSSELS. Musee Postal, Place du Grand Sablon 40, B-1000 Brussels, Belgium.

Collection deals with the stamps of Belgium and of other Universal Postal Union members.

Also a large variety of postal markings on covers and cards. A library of philatelic works is also available. Original drawings, cliches, and other printing materials are also held.

The collection was founded in 1928, and the first museum opened in 1936.

Included in the collection are three major subdivisions: postal history, philately, and the evolution of the telegraph and telephone.

Hours are Tuesday through Saturday, 10 a.m. to 4 p.m., Sundays and holidays, 10 a.m. to 12:30 p.m. The building is closed Mondays, Christmas Day and New Year's Day. Free.

Canada

Manitoba

BRANDON. John E. Robbins Library, Brandon University, 18th and Princess Ave., Brandon, Manitoba, Canada R7A 6A9.

The Gordon Jory collection of 19th-century covers and postmarks housed in the library.

Hours, Monday through Thursday 8:30 a.m. to 9:30 p.m.; Friday 8:30 a.m. to 5 p.m.; Saturday 1 p.m. to 4:30 p.m.; Sunday (fall/winter term only) 1 p.m. to 4:30 p.m.

Ontario

KINGSTON. Queen's University Archives, Kathleen Ryan Hall, University Avenue, Kingston, Ontario, Canada K7L 3N6.

The Austin stamp collection covering Canada, British West Indies, Cape of Good Hope, Great Britain, Gibraltar and Malta; other holdings.

Open Monday through Friday, 9 a.m. to 5 p.m. Closed between Christmas and New Year's Day and on civic holidays. Free.

OTTAWA. Canadian Postal Archives, 365 Laureen Ave. W., Ottawa, Ontario, Canada K1A 0N3.

Extensive collection of Canadian, British North American and foreign stamps. Archival holding relating to Canadian postage stamps.

Material at the Canadian Postal Archives (a section of the National Archives of Canada) is available to researchers, subject to ordinary limitations applicable to archival holdings. The CPA also contains a specialized library of 10,000 books on philately and postal history. Hours: Tuesday to Saturday, 10 a.m. to 5 p.m. Free.

Denmark

COPENHAGEN. Dansk Post- og Telegrafmuseum, Danish Post and Telegraph Museum, 9 Valkendorfsgade, 1151 Copenhagen K., Denmark.

Founded in 1907. Collection includes a wide variety of materials dealing with the Danish posts.

Examples of the displays include a reconstruction of the famed "ball-post" vehicle of the 19th century, and the interior of a post office from about 1845.

The collection also includes designs and printing materials for Danish stamps, as well as postal history covers.

Open May-October: Tuesday-Sunday 1 p.m. to 4 p.m., closed Monday. November-April: Tuesday, Thursday, Saturday and Sunday 1 p.m. to 4 p.m. Admission is free.

Finland

HELSINKI. Postal Museum of Finland, Tehtaankatu 21 B, Box 167, 00151 Helsinki, Finland.

Collection represents development of Finnish postal service over the past 350 years. On display are examples of all stamps issued by Finland and Universal Postal Union issues from 1941.

Philatelic library of the museum contains approximately 10,000 works; manuscripts on different subjects.

Rotating exhibits of the collections. The museum also participates in national and international stamp exhibitions.

Collections open to the public according to general usage of museums. Library manuscripts available to scholars and the public. Very old books not circulated.

Open year round Tuesday to Friday, noon to 3 p.m.; Wednesday, noon to 6 p.m.

Admission: adults 4 Finnish markka, children 2 Finnish markka.

France

AMBOISE. Musee de la Poste, 6 rue Joyeuse, F-37400 Amboise, France.

Collection dealing with postal communications. Special material on the horse-drawn post, including badges, artwork and examples of vehicles.

Exhibits on the posts offer France's first stamp, Paris siege material, maritime post information and airmail artifacts. Military mails and services in foreign countries. Means of urban communications. Housed in 16th-century building.

Open all year, daily except Monday. Closed Jan. 1, May 1, the Thursday of Ascension, Nov. 1, and Dec. 25.

Hours from April 1 to Sept. 30 are 9:30 a.m. to noon, and 2 p.m. to 6:30 p.m. From Oct. 1 to March 31, 10 a.m. to noon and 2 p.m. to 5 p.m. Admission, adults, 10 francs; children 5fr.

NANTES. Musee Postal, Direction Regionale des Postes, 10 boulevard Auguste Pageot, F-44038 Nantes, France.

Collection ranging from 1426, with documents, artwork, posters, letters, stamps. Postal relay maps from 1632, 1676 and 1712.

Founder served in Germany after World War II and has collected some holdings relating to the German posts.

Many almanacs about life in Nantes during 17th, 18th and 19th centuries.

NICE. Cosmos-Museum Philatelique, Villa Cimarosa, Avenue Michel de Cimiez, F-06000 Nice, France. A facility of Lollini Timbres-Poste.

Emphasis on conquest of space, collections, first-day covers. Philatelic literature.

Publications include catalog of stamps and first-day covers, *Conquest of Space*, 13-volume album, monthly information.

PARIS. Musee de la Poste. Maison de la Poste et la Philatelic. 34 Boulevard de Vaugirard, F-75731 Paris Cedex 15, France.

A public institution under the authority of the Ministry of Posts, Communication and Space.

The permanent museum collections are presented in 15 rooms arranged in a spiral format, with the formal tour beginning on the sixth and proceeding to the second floor. The general theme of the permanent exhibit is human communication through the ages.

Individual rooms are devoted to a wide variety of displays, including postal uniforms, the signs of the postillions and early mail carriages. Early mailboat and airmail service is presented, along with the teleplone, postal history and military mails.

Other exhibits deal with stamp production, the history of the letter before and after the introduction of the postage stamp, and France and French community issues since 1849. The Musee de la Poste houses the national philatelic collection of France.

Other rooms are devoted to foreign post offices, practices and uniforms. The final room in the exhibit presents current postal and philatelic affairs.

The Musee de la Poste serves as a research center, produces photocopies and photographs and acts as a consultancy on important historical and philatelic collections.

In addition, it operates a temporary exhibition gallery. The Musee de la Poste boutique offers philatelic books, material and official documents. The Musee is open Monday through Saturday from 10 a.m. to 5 p.m. and is closed national holidays. There is a 10-franc admission fee.

RIQUEWIHR. Musee d'Histoire des PTT d'Alsace, F-68340 Riquewihr, France.

Collection dealing with the history of posts and telecommunications in the northeast part of France, located in the Chateau de Wurtemberg-Montbeliard. Collection of the Amis de l'Histoire des PTT d'Alsace.

Six rooms show the history of letter post, means of transport (railway, automobile, postal aviation), telecommunications (Chappe's aerial telegraph system, the electric telegraph, the telephone, wireless telegraphy, space communications).

Hours: March 11 to Nov. 12, from 10 a.m. to noon and 2 p.m. to 6 p.m. daily, except Tuesdays. In July and August, open every day.

Entrance fee: adults 18 francs, children and students 7 francs. Groups (minimum 20 persons) 14 francs per person. Family ticket (parents and children) 45 francs.

German Democratic Republic

BERLIN. Postmuseum der DDR, Leipziger Strasse, D-1066 Berlin, East Germany.

Museum has been under renovation since 1983. Selected parts of the collection on display. Library is open.

Collection includes German States, Germany 1871-1945, the German Democratic Republic, foreign nations and associated materials.

The library includes 20,000 volumes. First-day covers, postal history materials, postal stationery and documentary materials may be seen.

Exhibits show the development of communications through the ages.

Hours are 10 a.m. to 6 p.m., Tuesday through Saturday. Entry is 1.05 marks; 20 pfennigs for students; 50pf for student groups of 10.

Germany, Federal Republic of

BERLIN. Berliner Post- und Fernmeldemuseum, Berlin Postal and Telecommunications Museum, An der Urania 15, Urania-Haus, D-1000 Berlin 30, West Germany.

Collections of stamps of the world since 1945 on exhibit. Various letters and envelopes, Prussian and Berlin area.

Philatelic literature included in Postgeschichtliche und Philatelistische Bibliothek, D-1000 Berlin 21, West Germany.

The Museum is open to the general public, Monday through Thursday, 9 a.m. to 5 p.m.; Saturday and Sunday, 10 a.m. to 5 p.m. The Library is open to the general public, Friday, 10 a.m. to 6 p.m.

BONN. Postwertzeichenausstellung im Bundesministerium fur das Post- und Fernmeldewesen, Adenauerallee 81, Postfach 8001, D-5300 Bonn 1, West Germany.

Special exhibitions in conjunction with the postal museum in Frankfurt. Open Sunday 9 a.m. to 12:30 p.m.; Wednesday 10 a.m. to 3 p.m. Free.

FRANKFURT am MAIN. Bundespost-museum, Schaumainkai 53, D-6000 Frankfurt 70, West Germany.

Opened in 1958, contains some of the collections of the former Reichspost-museum in Berlin.

Museum traces the history of postal and telecommunications with uniforms, works of art, post-house signs, postboxes, models, telegraph devices, telephones, radios and other equipment.

Stamps, covers, and printing items are also displayed. Many special exhibits.

The collection also includes substantial archival and library holdings.

The Bundespostmuseum is closed at present (1989) because of construction work. It will be re-opened in autumn 1990 as the Deutsches Postmuseum.

FRIEDRICHSDORF im TAUNUS. Philipp-Reiss-Sammlung, Hugenottenstrasse 93, Friedrichsdorf im Taunus, West Germany.

This collection is associated with the postal museum in Frankfurt. It is open to visitors Saturday from 10 a.m to noon.

HAMBURG. Philatelistische Bucherei, Hohenfelder Strasse 10, D-2000 Hamburg 76, West Germany.

A library of philatelic publications, open to public use. Hours are Tuesday from 2 p.m. to 6 p.m., Thursday from 2 p.m. to 7 p.m. Open every first Saturday in the month from 9 a.m. to noon.

Books may be used in the building, or in most cases withdrawn for circulation. A moderate charge is made for circulation to persons who are not members of the library.

Catalog available for 9.50 marks.

KOBLENZ. Oberpostdirektion Postal Museum, Friedrich-Ebert-Ring 14-20, D-5400 Koblenz, West Germany.

A few stamps on envelopes, postcards and stampless covers on permanent exhibition.

Open to the public Monday through Friday by appointment. Closed Sundays and holidays.

MUNICH. Philatelistische Bibliothek (corner of Blumenstrasse and Pestilozzistrasse). A part of the Stadtbibliothek Munchen, founded by Christoph Otto Muller.

Library contains 22,000 volumes with 8,000 titles on philately of all countries. Books on specialized subjects, cancellations, forgeries, topicals, postal history; 320 volumes of philatelic periodicals in all languages.

Stamp catalogs of leading German and international publishers; auction catalogs of most European firms. Card file index of philatelic articles in international magazines, with 80,000 entries on all countries.

Open to the public Monday, 8 a.m. to noon; Tuesday, noon to 7 p.m.; Thursday and Friday, 8 a.m. to 3:30 p.m. Closed holidays. Free. Data and hours uncertain.

NURNBERG. Verkehrsmuseum Nurnberg, Bahnpost, Lessingstrasse 6, D-8500 Nurnberg 70, West Germany.

Exhibition rooms closed for rebuilding. Archives and library are accessible to the public.

Exhibit scheduled to re-open in fall 1990 and will show the postal service in Bavaria, a specialized collection of Bavarian stamps and a general collection of more than 100,000 worldwide stamps.

Open Monday through Friday, October through March, 10 a.m. to 4 p.m., April through September, 10 a.m. to 5 p.m. Open Saturday and Sunday, 10 a.m. to 5 p.m. Closed certain German holidays.

REGENSBURG. Furst Thurn und Taxis Zentralarchiv und Hofbibliothek, Emmeramsplatz 5; mailing address Postfach 11 02 46, D-8400 Regensburg 11, West Germany.

The collection deals with the famed Thurn and Taxis postal system, including the pre-stamp period and markings on the stamps of Prussia, the North German Confederation, and the German State.

Among the items to be found are documents and artifacts dealing with the communications of the period. Library is available for use, with a card catalog that also permits access through the Bavarian central library catalog in Munich.

Hours are Monday through Thursday, 7:30 a.m. to noon and 1 p.m. to 4:45 p.m., closing at 3:30 p.m. on Friday. It is possible to obtain photocopies and microfilm copies of material in the archives. This is primarily a research facility.

STUTTGART. Post- und Fernmeldemuseum, Friedrichstrasse 13, D-7000 Stuttgart 1, West Germany. The museum is located near the America-House.

Displays focus on the posts of yesterday, today and the future. Displays of Wurttemberg postal history. Also displays on communications in general, including radio and the telegraph, as well as the future means of communications.

Open Monday through Friday, 10 a.m. to 4 p.m., extended hours on Thursday until 6 p.m. Free admission.

Liechtenstein

VADUZ. Postmuseum Landesverwaltung, Furstentum Liechtenstein, FL-9490 Vaduz, Liechtenstein. In the same building as the prince's art collection.

The collection, founded in 1930, includes all the stamps of Liechtenstein, with printing and other specialty items, as well as periodic special exhibitions.

Letters, pre-stamp materials and entires are also on display as space permits.

Open daily 10 a.m. to noon and 2 p.m to 6 p.m. Free.

Luxembourg

LUXEMBOURG. Musee des Postes et Telecommunications, 19 rue de Reims, L-2020 Luxembourg. The museum is located on the ground floor of the main post office building.

It traces the history of postal communications with postal collection boxes, uniforms, devices and other equipment. Stamps, covers and printing items are also displayed, along with documents relating to the establishment of the Luxembourg postal system. Many special exhibits.

Monday through Friday, 2 p.m. to 5 p.m. Free.

Malta

VALLETA. General Post Office, Merchants Street, Valleta, Malta.

Stamps and philatelic material, including color proofs, progressive sheets and original designs, reportedly may be available in the near future for viewing at the post office.

Monaco

MONACO-VILLE. Musee du Palais Princier, MC Monaco-Ville, Monaco. Opened to the public in 1970.

Permanent exhibits include all stamps issued in the Principality of Monaco, the Prince Rainier III collection, letters and envelopes relating to postal history of the principality.

Open December 6, 1988, to May 31, 1989: daily 10:30 a.m. to 12:30 p.m., 2 p.m. to 5 p.m., except Monday; June 1, 1989 to September 30, 1989: daily 9:30 a.m. to 6:30 p.m.; October 1 to October 22, 1989: daily 10 a.m. to 5 p.m. Admission: adults 15 francs, tourist group 10fr, children 7fr.

Netherlands

THE HAGUE. PTT Museum, Zeestraat 82 2518 AD, 's-Gravenhage, Netherlands. Founded 1929.

General, documentary and specialized collections of the Netherlands, also world collection, on permanent display.

Extensive collection of letters, some bearing what are reported to be oldest known postal markings of the world.

Museum also has collection of designs, engraving materials of Dutch stamps, catalogs, periodicals, books on Dutch philately.

The museum participates in approximately 20 major philatelic exhibitions each year in the Netherlands and abroad.

Open to general public; scholars have access to research material by appointment.

Weekdays 10 a.m. to 5 p.m.; Sundays and public holidays, 1 p.m. to 5 p.m. Closed Jan. 1 and Dec. 25.

Norway

OSLO. The Post Office Museum of Oslo, Tollbugata 17 I, Oslo 1, Norway.

Norway's largest collection of Norwegian and foreign postage stamps, datestamps and postal objects illustrating the 340-year history of the Norwegian Post Office.

Open to the public Monday through Friday, 10 a.m. to 3 p.m. Closed New Year's Eve, Christmas, Easter, Pentecost, May 1 and May 17. Free.

Peru

LIMA. Museo Postal y Filatelico, Hall del Correo Central de Lima, Jr. Conde de Superunda No. 170, Lima, Peru.

Official collections of the Peruvian posts, exhibited chronologically. Philatelic souvenirs are available.

Hours are 7:45 a.m. to 4 p.m. Monday through Saturday, April to December. Sundays and holidays, 10 a.m. to noon. January to March 7:45 a.m. to 1:30 p.m., 10 a.m. to 12:30 p.m. on Sundays and holidays.

English-speaking personnel available.

Poland

WROCLAW. Museum of Post and Telecommunication, ul. Krasinskiego nr 1, skr. poczt 2030, 50-954 Wroclaw, Poland.

Deals with Polish stamps, and with foreign emissions as received through the Universal Postal Union. Library of works in Polish and foreign languages.

Collection includes approximately 5,000 letters and covers, and also proofs and other printing process materials.

The museum takes part in numerous philatelic expositions and also organizes thematic exhibitions of its own. Special programs cater to students, teachers and tour guides.

Founded after World War I and opened to the public in Warsaw in 1928, the collection suffered serious losses during the World War II occupation of Poland. The museum was opened in Wroclaw in 1956.

Hours are 10 a.m. to 3 p.m., Sundays 11 a.m. to 2:30 p.m., closed Tuesdays. Entry is 70 zloty, 50zl for students, 30zl for tours. Free on Sunday.

Portugal

LISBON. Museo de Correos e Telecommicacoes, Avenida Casal Ribeiro 28-2, P-1000 Lisboa, Portugal.

Includes materials relating to the posts, telephone, telegraph and radio.

The collection includes a wide variety of postal and telecommunications devices, including mail coaches, mailboxes and canceling devices. Also on display are stamps of Portugal and colonies.

Open Tuesday through Saturday, 10 a.m. to noon, and 3 p.m. to 6 p.m. Closed Sunday, Monday and holidays. Free.

San Marino

SAN MARINO. Museo Postale e Filatelico di Borgo Maggiore, Casella Postale 1, 47031 Republic of San Marino.

Early San Marino issues exhibited including sketches, proofs and essays.

A topical display features Olympic Games, airmail history and the like. Museum also has complete collection of Universal Postal Union issues since 1920.

Highly modern design of display area.

South Africa

JOHANNESBURG. Public Library, Market Square, 26/2643, Johannesburg, South Africa.

Comprehensive collection of books, journals, periodicals and catalogs on philately, both general and specialist in nature.

Certain books are loaned to members of the philatelic societies of Johannesburg and Germiston on presentation of a membership card.

Open Monday through Thursday, 9 a.m. to 7 p.m.; Friday through Saturday, 9 a.m. to 5 p.m.

The library building also houses the Africana Museum, with a general collection of South African postage stamps and some adjacent territories; also the Curle collection of Transvaal stamps; a collection of postal covers, post and censor marks illustrating the postal history of World War II as it affected South Africa; also, Johannesburg postmarks, Boer War letters, and postal stationery.

Museum hours are Monday through Friday, 9 a.m. to 5:30 p.m.; Saturday 9 a.m. to 5 p.m.; Sunday and public holidays, 2 to 5:30 p.m. Closed Good Friday, Christmas Day and Day of Goodwill. Professional staff not available Saturday, Sunday and public holidays. All closings May through August are at 5 p.m. Free.

Spain

BARCELONA. Museu Gabinet Postal Rambla 99, Palau de la Virreina, 3a planta, E-0800 Barcelona 2, Spain.

Contains postal history, pre-philatelic items, stamps.

Library of more than 1,600 volumes.

Open Monday through Thursday 9 a.m. to 3 p.m.

Switzerland

BERN. General Directorate PTT, Library and Documentation, Viktoriastrasse 21, CH-3030 Berne 30, Switzerland.

The facility is open to the public weekdays during office hours. It features books, catalogs, price lists, about 400 titles of philatelic reviews, and a file of postal markings since 1849.

The PTT-Library also serves as the central library of the Association of Swiss Philatelic Societies. Most works circulate. Research facilities.

A photocopy service is available.

— Swiss PTT-Museum, Helvetiaplatz 4, CH-3005, Switzerland. Founded in 1907.

Museum collection arranged in three parts, stamps of Switzerland, the world and special collections. Updated yearly. Housed in specially equipped room in the museum basement. A worldwide selection of postage stamps on display in 45 steel cases, each consisting of 50 sliding panels.

Philatelic highlights are provided by special collections such as Old Switzerland, Swiss airmails, international airmails, zeppelin mails, old United States; also, letters and envelopes with Swiss markings.

Postcard sets, individual postcards, copper plate print, variety of books can be bought.

Open mid-May through mid-October: Monday 2 p.m. to 5 p.m., Tuesday through Sunday, 10 a.m. to 5 p.m. Winter: Monday 2 p.m. to 5 p.m., Tuesday through Sunday, 10 p.m. to noon, 2 p.m. to 5 p.m. Closed on public holidays.

The museum is to be transferred to a new building by 1990.

GENEVA. United Nations Philatelic Museum, Palais des Nations, CH-1211 Geneva 10, Switzerland.

Featured are the 11,000-item Prof. Charles Misteli collection — stamps, first-day covers and postal documents, strong in League of Nations, early International Labour Office and other specialized material from U.N. agencies.

Also, all U.N. postage stamps issued in Swiss franc, dollar and Austrian schilling values, first-day covers and related material, thematic collections.

An audio-visual program is available on request. Reader's corner containing international philatelic magazines, handbooks and catalogs open to visitors.

Open to the public Monday through Friday 9 a.m. to noon and 2 p.m. to 4:30 p.m. Free.

Turks and Caicos Islands

GRAND TURK. Government Library, Grand Turk, Turks and Caicos Islands.

Open Monday through Friday, 8:30 a.m. to 5 p.m.; Saturday, 8:30 a.m. to 1 p.m.

United Kingdom

COLNE (LANCASHIRE). British in India Museum, Sun Street, Colne BB8 0JJ, England.

Cancellations and stamps issued during British rule; the first air flight between India and the United Kingdom.

Open to the public Saturday and Sunday, May 1 to Sept. 30, 2 to 5 p.m. Parties of more than 20 persons welcome during the "closed season," by appointment. Details upon application.

Admission, adults £1.20; children 50 pence.

LONDON. The British Library, Philatelic Collections, Great Russell Street, London WC1, England.

An extensive display of 6,000 sheets is shown in the King's Library gallery, including part of the Tapling collection (worldwide to 1890), the Mosely collection of British Africa to 1935, the Bonjanwicz collection (Polish postal history 1938-49), the Model collection (Germany 1945-46 provisional issues), the Chinchen collection (Lundy Island), the Row collection (Thailand 1883-1918), the Fitzgerald collection of airmails, and other collections.

Items on display include Hawaiian Missionary stamps, U.S. Confederate locals, early postmasters' provisionals, Post Office Mauritius, early British Guiana, and more.

Collections not on display are available for study by appointment. These include Crown Agents and Inland Revenue Archives; UPU and Fitzgerald (airmail) collections together with artwork, proofs, specimens, covers, airmails, revenues, locals, and cinderellas from most countries. Also Pre-issue Publicity and Photograph Collections; British National Collections of Manuscripts, Maps, Newspapers (Colindale NW9): all countries and periods; India Office Library and Records (Blackfriars Road SE1) printed books containing philatelic literature including the Crawford Library. Readers Pass required for access.

Great Russell Street museum open Monday through Saturday, 10 a.m. to 5 p.m.; Sunday, 2 p.m. to 6 p.m. Closed Good Friday, First Monday in May, Christmas Eve and Day, Boxing Day and New Year's Day. Free.

— British National Postal Museum, King Edward Building, King Edward Street, London EC1A 1LP, England.

Established with the Reginald M. Phillips collection tracing the history of stamps and postal services of Great Britain from 1837-1900.

Also, the post office collection, all postage stamps issued in Great Britain and worldwide offices under control of the British GPO, the Universal Postal Union Collection, and the De La Rue Philatelic Archives.

Open Monday through Thursday, 9:30 a.m. to 4:30 p.m.; Friday, 9:30 a.m. to 4 p.m.; closed weekends and all bank holidays.

— Bruce Castle Museum, Bruce Castle Park, Lordship Lane, London N17 8NU, England.

Collections on local and postal history, material on history of the British Post Office extending from the 16th century to the present day with emphasis on the period 1700-1840.

Postal history collection divided into 10 sections: miscellanea; general history; organization of the postal service; staff; finance; collection; distribution and delivery of mails; communications; telegraphs; wireless services and telephones; other services as savings banks, money orders and pensions; and foreign post offices.

Material ranges from 16th-century letters, 17th-century newspapers, 18th-century official notices, 19th-century post horns and coaching prints, to books, pamphlets and periodicals on postal history.

The major portion of postal history, the Morten collection, is on permanent loan from the Union of Communication Workers.

Bulk of postal history collection is not on display; specific items for study can be seen by appointment.

Hours: daily 1 p.m. to 5 p.m. Closed winter bank holidays and Good Friday. Free.

— Imperial War Museum, Lambeth Road, London SE1 6HZ, England.

Extensive holdings of material relating to 20th-century warfare, collections of postage stamps, paper money, censorship marks, coins and medallions.

The collection can be viewed on application to the Department of Art.

Open Monday through Saturday, 10 a.m. to 6 p.m.; Sunday, 2 p.m. to 6 p.m. Closed Christmas Eve, Christmas Day, Boxing Day, New Year's Day. Admission charge beginning June 30, 1989.

— The Royal Philatelic Society, 41 Devonshire Place, London W1N 1PE, England.

A membership organization offering philatelic lectures and displays, expertization and a library that circulates among United Kingdom members. Founded 1869.

YORK. The York Castle Museum, York YO1 1RY, England.

Considered an outstanding folk museum, including reconstructed Victorian streets. Exterior of a subpost office can be seen and the Victorian wall-mounted postbox can be used for posting letters. A Victorian pillar-box can be seen outside the William IV Hotel in Half Moon Court, an Edwardian street.

Open all year except Christmas Day, Boxing Day and New Year's Day. Further details from the secretary.

Yugoslavia

BELGRADE. National Postal Museum, Majke Jevrosime Street 13, YU-11001 Belgrade, Yugoslavia. Operated by the Yugoslav Postal Administration, displays feature postal history of the country.

Zimbabwe

HARARE. The National Archives, Private Bag 7729, Causeway, Harare, Zimbabwe. Founded 1935. Gun Hill location.

Holdings include sheets of every postage stamp issue from 1913 and single specimens of all earlier issues from the first in 1890. Also some revenues, specimen cancellations, draft designs, covers and other postal history material, and relevant archival and published sources.

Written application to the director is required for access to the stamps.

Open to the public Monday through Friday, 8 a.m. to 4:30 p.m.; Saturday, 8 a.m. to noon. Closed public holidays and Sundays.

Chapter 25

Philatelic Literature Stamp Periodicals

This is a selected list of stamp collecting newspapers, magazines and journals. It includes works in many languages but is primarily a list of English language periodicals. The major sections of the listing are general periodicals, topical periodicals and periodicals relating to specific countries or collecting regions.

The subsection that lists periodicals by country is in alphabetical order by country name. Works under a given country are about that country's stamps or postal history and are not necessarily published in that country. A section of periodicals covering the stamps of more than one country appears at the beginning of the country section.

Each subdivision under the major subsections is in alphabetical order by periodical title. Each periodical is in the language of its title unless otherwise stated. Following the title is a number in parentheses noting the publishing frequency per year. Weeklies use (52), bimonthlies (6), quarterlies (4), biannuals (2) and so on. Following frequency is the name of the publisher of the periodical. Most publishers are stamp collector societies or private companies. The address of the publisher or the society's secretary follows the name of the publisher. The last item in each listing is the periodical's editor.

A question mark follows some information or is used in place of any information that the editors were unable to confirm.

Some stamp periodicals have an annual index in one of their issues during a year. Listings in this chapter for periodicals having extensive indexes that cover an interval of years include a reference for the index.

Information for each periodical is believed to be current as of spring 1989. Some stamp collector societies have permanent addresses. Others elect a new secretary at regular intervals and have address changes at the same time. The editor's position and issuing frequency also can change. New society journals or new private publications can last only a few issues or a few years, if they find no audience.

Most societies and publishers will send a sample copy of their publication for the cost of postage and handling. Inquire first before remitting any money. Include an addressed, stamped envelope with any inquiry. Inquiries to foreign addresses should include an addressed envelope and two International Reply Coupons.

Please send any corrections, additions or deletions to this list to *Linn's* Almanac, Periodicals Editor, Box 29, Sidney, Ohio 45365.

Linn's Stamp News reviews stamp collector periodicals regularly. Editors and society officers are requested to send copies of their society journal to *Linn's*, Journal Reviews, at the address in the previous paragraph.

General Philatelic Press

The Australian Stamp Monthly (12), Ramsey Ware Stockland Pty Ltd., Box 178, Carlton South, Victoria 3053, Australia; R.J. Cooper, managing ed.

Austria-Philatelist (4), Osterreichische Briefmarken-Zeitung, Verlag Adolf Kosel, Postfach 55, A-1095 Vienna, Austria; Leopold Sander, ed.

Belgica (4), R-Editions PVBA, St.-Katelijnevest 34, B-2000 Antwerpen, Belgium.

Berner Briefmarken-Zeitung/Journal Philatelique de Berne, Zumstein und Cie, Zeughausgasse 24, CH-3001 Berne,

Switzerland.

Boletin Filatelico (6), Chiaveri 3051, Ap. 2, Montevideo, Uruguay. William Marino, ed.

Canadian Stamp News (26), The Mirror Division, 10 Tempo Ave., North York, Ontario M2H 2N8, Canada; Don Atanasoff, ed.

Cefico (12), Centra Filatelico Cordoba — Filatelico y Numismatics, C.C. 241, Cordoba 5000, Republic of Argentina; Daniel A. Hernandez, ed.

DBZ — Deutsche Briefmarken Zeitung (52), DBZ Verlag, Postfach 1363, D-5408 Nassau, West Germany; Werner Rittmeier, ed.

La Filatelia (4), Av. de las Rosas 182, Colonia Chapalita, Guadalajara, Jal., Mexico; Manuel Pardo Morato, ed.

Filateliai Szemle (12), Pf: 4, Budapest, H-1387 Hungary; subscription to: Kultura Foreign Trade Enterprise, Pf. 149, Budapest H-1389, Hungary.

Ind Dak (12) L. G. Shenoi, 190 Defence Colony, Indira Nagar, Bangalore 560 038, India.

Irish Stamp News (4), MacDonnell Whyte Ltd., 102 Leinster Rd., Dublin 6, Ireland; Ian W. Whyte, ed.

Israeli Philatelic Monthly (12), 9 Kahanstam Street, Tel Aviv, Israel.

Korean Stamp Review (4), Korean Philatelic Center, 5th floor, Central Post Office Blvd., Chunk-Ku, C.P.O. Box 5122, Seoul 150 Korea; Jae-Keon Yoon, ed.

L'Echo de la Timbrologie (12), 37 rue des Jacobins, F-80036 Amiens, France; Jacques Gervais, ed.

Le Monde des Philatelists (12), 24 rue Chanchat, F-75009 Paris, France; Jean-Toussaint Stofati, ed.

Linn's Stamp News (52), Amos Press, Inc., Box 29, Sidney, Ohio 45365; Michael Laurence, ed. and pub.

Mekeel's Weekly Stamp News (52), Philatelic Communications Corp., Box 5050, White Plains, N.Y. 10602; John F. Dunn, ed. and pub.

New Zealand Stamp Monthly (12), Len Jury Ltd., Box 174, New Plymouth, New Zealand.

Sammler Express (24), Transpress VEB Verlag fur Verkehrswesen, Franzosische Str. 13/14, Berlin DDR-1086, East Germany; Afred Peter, ed.

Schweizer Briefmarken-Zeitung (12), Verband Schweizerischer Philatelisten-vereine, A. Guggisberg, Alpenstrasse 15, CH-2502 Biel, Switzerland.

Scottish Stamp News (12), 34, Gray Street, Glasgow G3 7TY, Scotland, UK; Stanley K. Hunter, ed. and pub.

SD — Sammlerdienst (12), R.V. Decker's Verlag, In Weiter 10, D-6900 Heidelberg, West Germany; Dieter Stein, ed.

SFT (?), Klostergatan 15, S-53200 Skara, Sweden.

Stamp Collector (52), Van Dahl Publications Inc., Box 10, Albany, Ore. 97321-0006; James A. Magruder III, ed. and pub.

Stamp Digest (?), P70 C1T-VIM, Calcutta 700054, India.

Stamp Journal (?), Standard Building, D. Naoroje Road, Bombay, India.

Stamp Magazine (12), Link House Magazines Ltd., Dingwall Avenue, Croydon, Surrey CR9 2TA, England; Richard West, ed.

Stamp News Australasia (12), Macquarie Publications Pty. Ltd., Box 1410, Dubbo, New South Wales 2830, Australia; Michael Sanig, consulting ed.

Stamps (52), H.L. Lindquist Publications, 85 Canistee St., Hornell, N.Y. 14843; Albert W. Starkweather, ed.

Stamps World (4), 107/2 Amherst Street, Calcutta 700 009, India; Dipok Dey, ed.

Timbroloisirs (11), Timbropresse, 33 rue de Chazelles, F-75017 Paris, France; Georges Bartoli, ed.

Timbroscopie (11), Timbropresse, 33 rue de Chazelles, F-75017 Paris, France; Georges Bartoli, ed.

Yushi (12), Japan Philatelic Society, Inc., Box 1, Shinjuku, Tokyo 160-91, Japan.

Philatelic Writers

AIJP Bulletin (4), Association Internationale des Journalistes Philateliques, Am Osterberg 19, D-3122, Hankensbuttel 1, West Germany.

The Philatelic Communicator (4), Writers Unit No. 30 of the American Philatelic Society, 2501 Drexel St., Vienna, Va. 22180; Ken Lawrence, ed.

The Philatelic Quill (4), Philatelic Writers' Society, 8 King St., St. James's, London SW1Y 6QT, England; D. Lang, ed.

Stamp Catalog Related

Gibbons Stamp Monthly (12), Stanley Gibbons Magazines Ltd., 5 Park Side, Christchurch Road, Ringwood, Hampshire BH24 3SH, England; Hugh Jeffries, ed.

Il Collezionista (?), Alberto Bolaffi, via Cavour 17/F, 10123, Torino, Italy.

Michel Rundschau (12), Schwaneberger Verlag GmbH., Muthmannstrasse 4, D-8000 Munich 45, West Germany.

Scott Stamp Monthly, with Scott Catalogue update (12), Scott Publishing Co., Box 828, Sidney, Ohio 45365; Richard L. Sine, ed.

International Organizations

Flash (4), Federation Internationale de Philatelie (FIP), Zollikerstrasse 128, CH-8008 Zurich, Switzerland; Marie-Louise Heiri, Secretary General.

IFSDA Report (4), International Federation of Stamp Dealers' Associations, 27 John Adam Street, London WC2N 6HZ, England; Otto Hornung, ed.

Union Postale (6), Universal Postal Union International Bureau, Case Postale, CH-3000 Bernc 15, Switzerland.

National Societies

AFRA Boletin Informativo (26), Asociacion Filatelica de la Republica, Argentina, Tucuman 672, 1 Piso, Depto. 2, 1049 Buenos Aires, Argentina.

Alhambra: Revista Filatelica Internacional (12), Club International Alhambra, Box 109, Granada, Spain; F. del Darro, ed.

The American Philatelist (12), American Philatelic Society, Box 8000, State College, Pa. 16803; Bill Welch, ed.

Briefmarke (12), Oesterreichischer Philatelisten-Vereine, Getreidemarkt 1, A-1060 Vienna, Austria; Karl-Heinz Wagner, ed.

CAC Newsletter (4), American Philatelic Society, Chapter Activities Committee, Box 8000, State College, Pa. 16803.

Clube Filatelico de Portugal Boletim (6), Clube Filatelico de Portugal, Av. Almirante Reis 70, 5 Dto., 1100 Lisbon, Portugal; Silva Gama, ed.

COPO Contact (4), Council of Philatelic Organizations, Box COPO, State College, Pa. 16803-8340; Patricia S. Walker, ed.

Dansk Filatelistisk Tidsskrift (9), Danmarks Filatelist Forbund, Box 36, Vinrosevej 8, 8541 Skodstrup, Denmark; Tol Norby, ed.

Filatelen Pregled (12), Ministerstvo na Informatsiiata i Suobshteniiata, 8 Ul. Graf Ignatiev, Sofia, Bulgaria; I. Kostov, ed.

Filatelia (12), Asociatia Filatelistilor din Republica Socialista Romania, Strada Botenu Nr. 6, Bucharest 1, Rumania; Nicolse Neagu, ed.

Filatelia Cubana (3), Federacion Filatelica Cubano, Edciones Cubanas, Departmento de Exportaciones, Obispo No. 461, Apdo. 605, Havana 1, Cuba.

Filatelie (24), Svaz Ceskoslovenskych Filatelistu, Nakladatelstvi Dopravy a Spoju, Hybernska 5, 115 78 Prague 1, Czechoslovakia; Vitezslav Houska, ed.

Filatelija (3), Hrvatski Filatelisticki Savez, Habdeliceva 2, 41000 Zagreb, Yugoslavia; Velimir Ercegovic, ed.

Filateliya SSSR (12), Vsesoyuznoe Obshchestvo Filatelistov, Moscow, Russian SFSR, USSR; B. Balashov, ed.

Filotelico (6), Sociedad Filatelica Dominicana, Artes Graficas Sordomudez, Apartado 1930, Santo Domingo, Dominican Republic.

Guatemala Filatelica (1), Asociacion Filatelica de Guatemala, Apdo. Postal 39, Guatemala; Romeo J. Routhier, ed.

Japan Philatelist (12), Japan Philatelic Society, Inc., Box 1, Shinjuku, Tokyo 160-91, Japan.

Korean Stamps (12), Philatelists Union of the Democratic People's Republic of Korea, Pyongyang, North Korea.

Norsk Filatelistisk Tidsskrift (10), Norsk Filatelistforbund, Postboks 2517, 7001 Trondheim, Norway; Erling Sjong, ed.

Pemungut Setum Malasia/ Malaysian Philatelist (4), Philatelic Society of Malaysia, Box 10588 GPO, Kuala Lumpur 01-02, Malaysia; C. Nagarajah, ed.

Philatelia Fennica (12), Suomen Filatelistiliitto r.y., Mannerheimintie 40 A 15, Box 202, 00101 Helsinki 10, Finland; August Leppa, ed.

The Philatelic Exhibitor (4), The American Association of Philatelic

Exhibitors, Box 432, South Orange, N.J. 07079; John M. Hotchner, ed.

The Philatelic Observer (4), Junior Philatelists of America, Box 701010, San Antonio, Texas 78770-1010; Karen L. Weigt, ed.

Philatelie (6), Bund Deutscher Philatelisten e.V., Mainzer Landstrasse 221-223, D-6000 Frankfurt am Main 1, West Germany; Wolf J. Pelikan, ed.

Philatelie (11), Nederlandsch Maandblad voor Philatelie, Lis 20, NL-1273 CD Huizen, Netherlands; Index op de Jaargangen 1922 t/m 1950, 195p, Willem de Ruiter, comp.

Philatelie Francaise (12), Federation des Societes Philateliques Francaises, 7 rue Saint-Lazare, F-75009 Paris, France; Raymond Duxin, ed.

Philatelie Quebec (10), Editions Phibec Inc., Box 1000, Stn. M., Montreal, Quebec H1V 3R2, Canada; Dennis Cottin, ed.

Philately from Australia (4), Royal Philatelic Society of Victoria, Box 2071, Melbourne, Victoria 3001, Australia; H.L. Chisholm, ed.

Philately in Japan (12), Japan Philatelic Society Foundation, Box 1, Shinjuku, Tokyo 16391, Japan; Meiso Mizuhara, president.

Philotelia (6), Hellenic Philotelic Society, 57 Akadimias St., GR-106 79, Athens, Greece. J. Halvatzidopoulos, ed.

Postales de Bolivia (4), Federacion Filatelica Boliviana, Apartado 8013, La Paz, Bolivia.

The SA Philatelist (12), The Philatelic Federation of South Africa, Box 4430, Pretoria 0001, South Africa; Joh Groonewald, ed.

Stamp Lover (6), National Philatelic Society, 107 Charterhouse St., London EC1M 6PT, England; Peter E. Collins, ed.

Stamp Mail (12), The British Philatelic Federation, 107 Charterhouse St., London EC1M 6PT, England; Allan M. Daniell, ed.

Svensk Filatelistisk Tidskrift (10), Sveriges Filatelist-Foerbund, Vasavaegen 86, S-181 41 Lidingoe, Sweden; Gosta Karlsson, ed.

Trinidad and Tobago Philatelic Society Bulletin (4), Philatelic Society of Trinidad and Tobago, 33 Verbena Row, Victoria Gardens, Diego Martin, Trinidad; J. Chay, ed.

Uruguay Filatelico (4), Club Filatelico del Uruguay, Box 518, Montevideo, Uruguay.

Stamp Trade

ASDA Newsletter (12), American Stamp Dealers' Association, 3 School St., Glen Cove, N.Y. 11542.

Philatelic Exporter Ltd. (12), Box 21, Radlett, Herts. WS7 7EF, England; G.R. Phillips, ed.

PTS Journal (6), Philatelic Traders Society, 27 John Adam St., London WC2N 6H2, England.

Stamp Auction News (12), H.L. Lindquist Publications, 85 Canisteo St., Hornell, N.Y. 14343; Albert W. Starkweather, ed.

The Stamp Wholesaler (26), Van Dahl Publications Inc., Box 706, Albany, Ore. 97321; James A. Magruder III, ed. and pub.

Libraries, Museums and Related

The Bay Phil (6), The Friends of the Western Philatelic Library, Inc., Box 2219, Sunnyvale, Calif. 94087-2219; Virginia Burey, temporary ed.

British Philatelic Bulletin (6), National Postal Museum, King Edward Street, London EC1A 1LP, England; John Holman, ed.

Literatur Nachtrichten (1), Bundesstelle Literatur im Bund Deutscher Philatelisten e. V., Koln, West Germany.

Luren (12), Scandinavian Philatelic Library of Southern Californa Inc., Box 57397, Los Angeles, Calif. 90057; Paul Nelson, ed.

Museum Post Rider (12), Cardinal Spellman Philatelic Museum Inc., 235 Wellesley St., Weston, Mass. 02193.

Philatelic Literature Review (4), American Philatelic Research Library, Box 8338, State College, Pa. 16803; Bill Welch, ed.

Posted! (4), Friends of Bath Postal Museum, 8 Broud Street, Bath BA1 5LJ, England.

Miscellaneous General Periodicals

The American Philatelic Congress Book

(1), The American Philatelic Congress, Box 61774, Virginia Beach, Va. 23462; Index to the Congress Books of the American Philatelic Congress, Vols. 1-52, 1935-86, in the Philatelic Literature Review, third quarter 1987, compiled by Kathleen Wolsiffer.

The Collectors Club Philatelist (6), Collectors Club, 22 E. 35th St., New York, N.Y. 10016; E.E. Fricks, ed.; Cumulative Index 1922-1971.

The London Philatelist (6), The Royal Philatelic Society, London, 41 Devonshire Place, London W1N 1PE, England; George E. Barker, ed.

New Zealand Stamp Collector (4), Royal Philatelic Society of New Zealand, 1269, Wellington, New Zealand; G.B. Vincent, ed.

The Philatelist and PJGB (6), Robson Lowe Ltd., 39 Poole Hill, Bournemouth BH2 5PX, England; Robson Lowe, ed.

Post Office

American Postal Worker (12), American Postal Workers Union, AFL-CIO, 1300 L St., N.W., Washington, D.C. 20005.

Courier (12), British Post Office Headquarters, 33 Grosvenor Place, London SW1X 1PX, England.

Dak Tar (4), Department of Posts & Telecommunication, Parliament St., New Delhi 110001, India.

Deutsche Post (6), Transpress VEB Verlag fur Verkehrswesen, Franzosische Str. 13-14, DDR-1086 Leipzig, East Germany.

Domestic Mail Manual (1), United States Postal Service, Washington, D.C. 20260.

International Mail Manual (1), United States Postal Service, Washington, D.C. 20260.

National Rural Letter Carrier (4), National Rural Letter Carriers Association, 1448 Duke St., Alexandria, Va. 22311.

Postal Bulletin (52), United States Postal Service, Washington, D.C. 20260-1571.

Postal Life (12), United States Postal Service, 475 L'Enfant Plaza S.W., Washington, D.C. 20260.

Postal Supervisor (12), National Association of Postal Supervisors, 490 L'Enfant Plaza, S.W., No. 3200, Washington, D.C. 20024.

Postmasters Advocate (4), National League of Postmasters, 1023 N. Royal St., Alexandria, Va. 22314.

Postmasters Gazette (12), National Association of Postmasters of the United States, Box 16868, Alexandria, Va. 22302; Marilyn Duhigg, ed.

Airmail

Air Mail News (4), British Aerophilatelic Federation, 174 Westwood Road, Tilehurst, Reading RG3 6LN, England; A.G. Mathieson, ed.

The Airpost Journal (12), American Air Mail Society, Box 291, Downers Grove, Ill. 60515; Frank H. Blumenthal, ed.; Index to the Airpost Journal, Vol. 1-50 (November 1929-September 1979), David H. Eyman and Frank H. Blumenthal, comps.; Charles J. Peterson, ed.

Concorde Study Circle Newsletter (4), Brian L. Asquith, Alandale, Radcliffe Gardens, Carshalton Beaches, Surrey SM5 4PQ, England.

Slipstream (12), Hovermail Collectors' Club, 15 The Twitton, Southwick, Brighton BN4 4DB, England; J.K. Pemberton, ed.

Cinderellas

Atalaya (2), Christer Brunstrom, Kungsgatan 23, S-30245 Halmstad, Sweden.

The Cinderella Philatelist (4), Cinderella Stamp Club, 24 Sidney Road, Staines, Middx. TW18 4LX, England; L.N. Williams and M.K. Williams, eds.; Index to the Cinderella Philatelist, Vols. 1-25, 1961-1985, issues 1-100, and to The Private Post, 8 issues 1977-85, Ian D. Crane, comp.

The Private Post (1), British Private Post Study Group, published by Cinderella Stamp Club, 44 The Ridgeway, London NW11 8QS, England.

Seal News (10), Christmas Seal & Charity Stamp Society, 5825 Dorchester Ave., Chicago, Ill. 60637; Henry Irwin, ed.

Postal History

Modern Postal History Journal (4), Modern Postal History Society, Box 629, Chappaqua, N.Y. 10514-0629; Terence Hines, ed.

P.S. — A Quarterly Journal of Postal History (4), aGatherin', Box 175, Wynantskill, N.Y. 12198, Diane De Blois, ed.

Postal History Journal (3), Postal History Society, Box 61774, Virginia Beach, Va. 23462; Harlan F. Stone, ed.

Postal History Quarterly (4), The Postal History Society, Box 3, St. Neots, Cambs. PE19 2HQ, England; O.W. Newport, ed.

Postscript (4), Society of Postal Historians, J.L. Grimwood-Taylor, c/o Argyll Etkin Ltd., 48 Conduit Street, London W1R 9FB, England; I. Owen, ed.

Other Specialties

The Circuit (6), International Society of Worldwide Stamp Collectors, 85 E. Torrey, New Braunfels, Texas 78130; Arlene Futrell, ed.

Civil Censorship Study Group Bulletin (6), L.D. Mayo Jr., 4305 Wyandotte Dr., Indianapolis, Ind. 46220-5765; A.R. Torrance and William Barker, eds.

Essay Proof Journal (4), Essay-Proof Society, Inc., 225 S. Fischer Ave., Jefferson, Wis. 53549; Barbara R. Mueller, ed.

The Interleaf (4), Booklet Collectors Club, 1016 E. El Camino Real, No. 107, Sunnyvale, Calif. 94087; Gerhard G. Korn, ed.

Maximaphily (4), Maximum Card Study Unit, 4702 D. Main St., Skokie, Ill. 60076; Gary Denis, ed.

Meter Stamp Society Bulletin (4), Meter Stamp Society, Box 1345, Jackson, N.J. 08527; Richard Stambaugh, ed.

The Obliterator (4), Pictorial Cancellation Society, Box 306, Hancock, Md. 21750; Nicholas Shestople, ed.

Pantograph of Postal Stationery (6), United Postal Stationery Society, Box 48, Redlands, Calif. 92373; Joann Thomas, ed.

The Perfins Bulletin (10), The Perfins Club, Rural Route 1, Box 5645, Dryden, Maine 04225; John F. Lyding, ed.

Philatelic Paraphernalia (4), Philatelic History Society, Hunters Lodge, Cottesmoore Road, Ashwell, Oakham, Leicestershire, LE15 7LJ, England; Victor Short, ed.

Postal Stationery (6), United Postal Stationery Society, Redlands, Calif. 92373; John Weimer, ed.

Pratique (4), Disinfected Mail Study Circle, 39 Lullington Garth, London N12 7LT, England; V. Denis Vandervelde, ed.

Reply Coupon Collector (2), International Society of Reply Coupon Collectors, Box 165, Somers, Wis. 53171-0165; Allan Hauck, ed.

Seaposter (6), Maritime Postmark Society, Box 1264, Absecon, N.J. 08201; Tom Hirschinger, ed.

Transit Postmark Collector (6), Mobile Post Office Society, Box 502, Bedford Park, Ill. 60499; Douglas N. Clark, ed.

War Cover Club Bulletin, War Cover Club, Box 464, Feasterville, Pa. 19047; Richard W. Helbock, ed.

Topical Periodicals

Topicals - General

Themes (4), Thematic Society of Australia, Box 956, Parramatta, NSW 2150, Australia; W. Banks, ed.

Themescene (4), British Thematic Association, 3 Stockfield Road, Claygate, Surrey KT10 0QG, England; M.I. Morris, ed.

Topical Time (6), American Topical Association, Box 630, Johnstown, Pa. 15907; Glen Crago, ed.; Five-Year Cumulative Index to Topical Time and ATA Handbooks 1975-79, 42p, 1984.

Topicals - Animals

The DOSSU Journal (4), Dogs on Stamps Study Unit, 3208 Hana Road, Edison, N.J. 08817-2552. Morris Raskin; ed.

Flight (4), The Bird Stamp Society, Lynnmoor, Ampney Crucis, Glos. GL7 5RY, England; A. Pollock, ed.

The Swallowtail (3), Butterfly and Moth Stamp Society, 63 Dorchester Rd., Garstang, Preston, Lancs. PR3 1HH, England; T. Lloyd, ed.

Topicals - The Arts

The Baton (3), Philatelic Music Circle, 92 Beechwood Park Road, Solihull, West Midlands B91 1EU, England; I. Lawford, ed.

Codex Filatelica, Mesoamerican Archeology Study Unit, Box 1442, Riverside, Calif. 92502; Chris L. Moser interim ed.

Disnemation (4), William Silvester, 378C Cotlow Rd., Victoria, British Columbia V9C 2G1, Canada.

Durer Journal (4), Albrecht Durer Study Unit, Box 477, Temple RD No. 1, Temple, Pa. 19560; Jack A. Denys, ed.

FAP Journal (4), Fine Arts Philatelists, 2502 E. 80th St., Indianapolis, Ind. 46256;

David W. Christel, ed.

Old World Archaeologist (4), Old World Archaeological Study Unit, 1516 Hinman Ave., No. 503, Evanston, Ill. 60201; David A. Detrich, ed.

Philateli-Graphics (4), Graphics Philately Association, Box 1513, Thousand Oaks, Calif. 91360; Dulcie M. Apgar, ed.

Topicals - The Earth & Exploration

The Carto-Philatelist (4), 303 S. Memorial Drive, Appleton, Wis. 54911; Mark D. Larken, ed.

Cook's Log (4), Captain Cook Study Unit, 38 Sherwood Road, Meols, S. Wirral L47 9RT, England. I. Boreham, ed.

Discovery! (4), Journal of the Christopher Columbus Philatelic Society, 9880 Junction Rd., Frankenmuth, Mich. 48734; Donald R. Ager, ed.

Ice Cap News (6), American Society of Polar Philatelists, Box 945, Skokie, Ill. 60077; Russ Ott, ed.

Nature's Wonders (4), Earth's Physical Features Study Unit, 515 Magdalena, Los Altos, Calif. 94022.

One Half Fathom (11), Oceanographic Philately, 4004 Bay to Bay Boulevard, Tampa, Fla. 33609; Irene Fager, ed.

The Petro-Philatelist (4), Petroleum Philatelic Society International, 1896 Mount Baker Highway, Bellingham, Wash. 98225; Feitze Papa, ed.

Polar Post (4), Polar Postal History Society of Great Britain, 12 Longlands Spinney, Charmandean, Worthing, West Sussex BN14 9NU, England; G.R. Garbutt, ed.

Windmill Whispers (6), Windmill Study Unit, 17060 Jodaue St., Hazel Crest, Ill. 60429; Wim Bosman, ed.

Topicals - Medicine

Collections/Connections Newsletter (4), Club for Philately in Gerontology, 2525 Centerville Road, Dallas, Texas 75228; Herbert Shore, ed.

Medi-Theme, Medical Thematic Circle, 162 Canterbury Road, Kennington, Ashford, Kent TN24 9QD, England; T. Wilson, ed.

Miasma Philatelist (4), Malaria Philatelists International, Box 486, Harlowton, Mont. 59036.

Scalpel and Tongs (6), Medical Subjects Unit, 5049 Cherokee Hills Dr., Salem, Va. 24153; Ranes Chakravorty, ed.

Topicals - Miscellaneous

Americana Philatelic News (6), Americana Unit, No. 1 Scott Circle, N.W., Washington D.C. 20036; August Mark Vaz, ed.

The Blotter (4), Law Enforcement Study Unit, Box 858, Vernon, N.J. 07462; Steve O'Conor, ed.

The Blue Lamp (4), Constabulary Study Group, 9 Queensway, Tiptree, Colchester CO5 0LP, England; R. Holdeman, ed.

The Canadian Connection (4), The Canadian Study Unit, Box 3262, Station A, London, Ontario N6A 4K3, Canada; John G. Peebles, ed.

Europa News (6), Europa Study Unit, 6408 South Troy St., Chicago, Ill. 60629-2809; Stephen Luster, ed.

Exspansion (6), Society of Philatelists and Numismatists, 1929 Millis St., Montebello, Calif. 90640. Ralph A. Holmes, ed.; philatelic-numismatic combinations.

Impress (4), The Newsletter of the International Mensa Philatelists Society, Box 9033, Winter Haven, Fla. 33883-9033; Samuel A. Shaffe, ed.

SOS (4), Stamps on Stamps Centenary Unit, 855 Stonehenge Rd., Cherry Hill, N.J. 08003; Robert L. Graves, ed.

Topicals - Organizations

Lions International Philatelist (4), 8174 Electric Ave., Vienna, Va. 22180; F.S. Bill Taft, ed.

The Masonic Philatelist (4), Masonic Stamp Club of New York, Masonic Hall, Box 10, 46 W. 24th St., New York, N.Y. 10010; Irwin M. Yarry, ed.

Newsletter (4), Masonic Philatelic Club, 76 Merrivale Road, Beacon Park, Plymouth PL2 2RP, England; T.J. Fray, ed.

The Philatelic Freemason (6), Masonic Study Unit, 59 Greenwood Road, Andover, Mass. 01810; Robert A. Dominigue, ed.

Topicals - People

Campaign (4), Napoleonic Age Philatelists, 7315 Clayton Drive, Oklahoma City, Okla. 73132; Ken Berry, ed.

Finest Hour (4), International Churchill Society, 1847 Stonewood Drive, Baton Rouge, La. 70816; Richard M. Langworth, ed.

JFK FDC Study Group Newsletter (4), Box 535-J, Madison Square Station, New York, N.Y. 10010; Henry B. Scheuer, ed.

Lambda Philatelic Journal (4), Gay and Lesbian History on Stamps Club, Box 3940, Hartford, Conn. 06103; Paul Hennefeld, ed.

The Topical Woman (6), Women on Stamps Study Unit, 1345 Sleep Hollow Dr., Coshocton, Ohio 43812; Davida Kristy, ed.

Topicals - Religion

Biblical Philately (4), Biblical Topics Study Unit, 802 Hidden Valley Drive, Houston, Texas 77088; Bob Woodworth, ed.

Bulletin of the Guild of St. Gabriel (4), Guild of St. Gabriel, 133 Waldegrave Road, Teddington TW11 8LL, England; C. Hughes, ed.

Coros Chronicle (6), Collectors of Religion on Stamps, 208 E. Circle St., Appleton, Wis. 54911; Augustine Serafini, ed.

Judaica Philatelic Journal (4), Judaica Historical Philatelic Society, 80 Bruce Ave., Yonkers, N.Y. 10705; Murray Frost, ed.

Yule Log (6), Christmas Philatelic Club, Box 77, Scottsbluff, Neb. 69361; Kathy Ward, ed.

Topicals - Science & Technology

Astrophile (6), Space Topics Study Unit, Box 2579, Marathon Shores, Fla. 33052; David Chudwin, ed.

Bio-Philately (4), Biology Unit, 4310 Indian Creek Road, Marion, Iowa 52302; George A. Ball, ed.

The Compulatelist (4), Computers in Philately Committee, Box 1574, Dayton, Ohio 45401.

Explorer (6), International Association of Space Philatelists, Box 302, Yonkers, N.Y. 10710; Bill York, ed.

HAM-Stamps (4), International HAM Stamp Group, Eckstrasse 1, D-6792 Ramstein 2, West Germany; M.G. Bussemer, ed.

Philamath (4), Mathematic Study Unit, 135 Witherspoon Court, Athens, Ga. 30606; Randy Woodward, ed.

Philatelia Chimica et Physica (4), Chemistry and Physics on Stamps Study Unit, 3133 Glendale Ave., Pittsburgh, Pa. 15227; C.S. Kettler, ed.

Topicals - Scouting

Bulletin of the Scout and Guide Stamps Clubs (6), Scout and Guide Stamps Clubs, 16 Effingham House, Kingsnympton Park, Kingston Hill, Surrey KT2 7RU; P.J. Duck, ed.

Journal of the Scout and Guide Stamp Society (4), Scout and Guide Stamp Society, 7/3 Harrison Crescent, Hawthorn, Victoria 3122, Australia; M. Lambe, ed.

SOSSI Journal (4), Scouts on Stamps Society International, 20 Cedar Lane, Cornwall, N.Y. 12518; Michael S. Strother, ed.

Topicals - Sports & Recreation

Chesstamp Review (4), Chess on Stamps Study Unit, 7770 Annesdale Drive, Cincinnati, Ohio 45243; Russell E. Ott, ed.

Journal of Sports Philately (6), Sports Philatelists International, 322 Riverside Drive, Huron, Ohio 44839; John La Porta, ed.

MatchPoint (4), Box 424, Albuquerque, N.M. 87103; Les Yerkes, ed.

Newsletter of the International Guild of Rugby Theme Collectors (4), International Guild of Rugby Theme Collectors, Bay View, Penrice, Oxwich, Swansea SA13 1LN, England; D.R. Gwynn, ed.

Tee Time (4), International Philatelic Golf Society, Caberfeidh, Riverside, Poolewe, Ross-shire IV22 2LA, Scotland, United Kingdom.

Torchbearer (4), Society of Olympic Collectors, 152 Spring Road, Bournemouth BH1 4PX, England; F. Rapkin, ed.

Topicals - Transportation

Bicycle Stamps (irregular), Bicycle Stamp Club, 358 Iverson Place, East Windsor, N.J. 08320; Douglas Marchant, ed.

The Dispatcher (4), Casey Jones Railroad Unit, Box 31631, San Francisco, Calif. 94131; Oliver C. Atchison, ed.

The Pharos (12), Lighthouse Study Unit, 19735 Scenic Harbor Drive, Northville, Mich. 48167; Gary J. Kurylo, ed.

Railway Philately (4), Railway Philatelic Group, 50 Roberts Road, Prestbury, Cheltenham GL52 5DF, England; R. Wright, ed.

Transport Philately (4), Blake H. Sugarberg, 1415 De Witt Drive, Akron,

Ohio 44113.

Watercraft Philately (6), Ships on Stamps Unit, 186 Butler St., Fall River, Mass. 02724; William A. Coffey, ed.

Periodicals By Country

Periodicals Covering More Than One Country

British Caribbean Philatelic Journal (5), British Caribbean Philatelic Study Group, 12 Massey Place S.W., Calgary, Alberta T2V 2G3, Canada; Mark Swetland, ed.

Bulletin of the British West Indies Study Circle (4), British West Indies Study Circle, Timbers, Chequers Lane, Tharston, Norwich NR15 2YA, England; D.W. Atkinson, ed.

Bulletin of the East Africa Study Circle (3), East Africa Study Circle, Chantry Court, 1 The Close, Warminster, Wilts. BA12 9AC, England; R. Dunstan, ed.

Cameo (2), West Africa Study Circle, 1/12 The Paragon, Blackheath, London SE3 0NZ, England; J.J. Martin, ed.

Central American Newsletter (4), Central American Group of the Spanish Main Society, Box 105, Peterborough PE3 87Q, England; Michael P. Birks, ed.

Indo-China Philatelist (6), Society of Indo-China Philatelists, 1466 Hamilton Way, San Jose, Calif. 95125; George Demeritte III, ed.

The Informer (12), Society of Australasian Philatelists-Oceania, Box 484-FW, Battle Creek, Mich. 49016.

IO (3), Indian Ocean Study Circle, The Vineyard, Garden Close Lane, Newbury, Berkshire RG14 6PR, England; P.T.E. Bradshaw, ed.

The Latin American Post (4), Latin American Philatelic Society, Box 820, Hinton, Alberta, T0E 1B0 Canada; Piet Steen, ed.

Mainsheet (4), Spanish Main Society, 16 Lynwood Close, Gordon Road, London E18 1DP, England.

Newsletter (4), Transatlantic Study Group, British North American Philatelic Society, Box HM1263, Ham, Bermuda.

North Atlantic Philately (4), Publishing House 5F, Sandknosen 51, DK-5250 Odense SV, Denmark; Kristian Hopballe, ed.

OPAL Journal (3), Oriental Philatelic Association of London, 2 Blenheim Road, Westbury Park, Bristol BS6 7JW, England; J.R. Ertughrul, ed.

Pacifica (4), Pacific Islands Study Circle of Great Britain, 24 Woodvale Ave., London SE25 4AE, England; B.A. Jones, ed.

Postal Himal (4), Nepal and Tibet Study Circle, 12 Charnwood Close, Peterborough, Cambs. PE2 9BZ, England; C.T. Hepper, ed.

The Posthorn (4), Scandinavian Collectors Club, Box 302, Lawrenceville, Ga. 30246; Gene Lesney, ed.; The Posthorn: 40 Year Index Vols. 1-40, November 1943-November 1983, by Robert C. Gross, 32p, 1984

Scandinavian Contact (4), Scandinavia Philatelic Society, Flat 8, 126 Castelnau, Barnes, London SW13 9ET, England; G. Wewiora, ed.

The Seebecker (4), International Seebeck Study Society, 188 Center St., Brewer, Maine 04412; Bill Welch, ed.

South Atlantic Chronicle, St. Helena, Ascension and Tristan da Cunha Philatelic Society, Box 366, Calpalla, Calif. 95418; Everett C. Parker, ed.

The Trumpeter (4), Croatian Philatelic Society, 1512 Lancelot Road, Borger, Texas 79007; Eck Spahich, ed., covers Balkan countries.

Ascension

Wideawake (4), Ascension Study Circle, Greys, Tower Road, Whitstable, Kent CT5 2ER, England; R.W. Atkinson, ed.

Australia

Australian Forces Mail Research Group Newsletter (6), Box 201, Gladesville, New South Wales 2111, Australia; David J. Collyer, ed.

Bulletin of the British Society of Australian Philately (6), The British Society of Australian Philately, 86 Clarence Road, Fleet, Hants. GU13 9RS, England; B.R. Peace, ed.

NSW Philatelist (4), Box 601, GPO Sydney 2001, Australia; N.J. Sheppard, ed.

Philas News (4), Philatelic Association of N.S.W., Box A495, Sydney South, NSW-2000, Australia; B.J. Hancock, ed.

Stamp Hinges (6), Philatelic Society of Western Australia, Box 886, Subiaco, Western Australia 6008, Australia; R.A.L. Wood, ed.

Sydney Views, Australian States Study

Circle of the Royal Sydney Philatelic Circle, Box C300, Clarence St., NSW 2001, Australia.

Austria

Austria (4), Austrian Stamp Club of Great Britain, 9 Heath Moor Drive, York YO1 4NE, England; John F. Giblin, ed.

Austria Bulletin (4), Austria Philatelic Society of New York, 150 Rumson Road, Rumson, N.J. 07760; Anthony Pisano, ed.

Bechuanaland

The Runner Post (4), Bechuanalands and Botswana Study Group, 18 Goldsmid Road, Hove, E. Sussex BN3 1QA, England; A. Macgregor, ed.

Belgian Congo

Belgian Congo Study Circle Bulletin (4), Belgian Congo Study Circle, 5 Ascham Lane, Whittlesford, Cambs. CB2 4NT, England; R.E. Jacquemin, ed.

Belgium

Belgapost (2), Belgian Congo Study Circle, 5 Sutherland Grove, Southfields, London SW18 5PS, England; J.B. Horne, ed.

The Belgiophile (4), American Belgian Philatelic Society, 8604 S. Yakima Ave., Tacoma, Wash. 98444; Albert B. de Lisle, ed.

Belize

The Belize Collector (4), Belize Philatelic Study Circle, Box 411238, Chicago, Ill. 60641-1238; Bob Chenault, ed.

Bermuda

Bermuda Post (4), Bermuda Collectors Society, 86 North Road, Purdys, N.Y. 10578; Reid L. Shaw, ed.

Brazil

Bull's Eyes (4), Brazil Philatelic Association, 118 Park Ave., Holly, Mich. 48442; William P. Krieble, ed.

Burma

Burma Peacock (4), Burma Philatelic Study Circle, 7127 87 St., Edmonton, Alberta T6C 3G1, Canada; Alan Meech, ed.

Canada

B.N.A. Topics (6), British North American Philatelic Society, 6312 Carnarvon St., Vancouver, British Columbia V6N 1K3, Canada; H. Michael Street, ed.

The Canadian Philatelist (6), The Royal Philatelic Society of Canada, 5320 Station F, Ottawa, Ontario K2C 3J1, Canada; Jim Haskett, ed.

Maple Leaves (5), Canadian Philatelic Society of Great Britain, 3 Rutherford Way, Tonbridge, Kent TN10 4RH, England; D.F. Sessions, ed.

PHSC Journal (4), Journal of the Postal History Society of Canada, 216 Mailey Drive, Carleton Place, Ontario K7C 3X9, Canada.

Ceylon

Bulletin of the Ceylon Study Circle (4), Ceylon Study Circle, 42 Lonsdale Road, Cannington, Bridgwater, Somerset, England; R.W.P. Frost, ed.

Channel Islands

Channel Islands Reporter (4), The Club of Channel Islands Collectors Inc., Box 579, New York, N.Y. 10028; Robert Ausubel, ed.

Channel Islands Specialists Bulletin (3), 17 Westlands Ave., Huntercombe, Slough, Berks. SL1 6AG, England; O.W. Newport, ed.

Les Iles Normandes (4), 17 Westlands Ave., Huntercombe, Slough, Berks. SL1 6AG, England; O.W. Newport, ed.

Chile

Chile Newsletter (4), Chile Group of the Spanish Main Society, Box 105, Peterborough PE3 8TQ, England; John Fosbery, ed.

China

The China Clipper (6), China Stamp Society, 140 W. 183 Ave., Columbus, Ohio 43210; Donald R. Alexander, ed.

China Philately (6), China Philatelic Publishing House, 27 Dong Chang An St., Beijing, China; Zhao Wonyi, ed.

Colombia and Panama

Copacarta: The Journal of Copaphil (4), The Colombia-Panama Philatelic Study Group, Box 2245, El Cajon, Calif. 92021; Jim Cross, ed.

Isthmian Collectors Club Journal (4), Box 6094, Alexandria, Va. 22306; Robert J. Karrer Jr., ed.

Costa Rica

The Oxcart (4), The Society of Costa Rica Collectors, 6400 Arthur St., Merillville, Ind. 46410; T. Edwards, ed.

Cuba

The Cuban Philatelist (4), Cuban Philatelic Society of America, Box 450207, Miami, Fla. 33245-0207; Silvia Garcia Frutos, ed.

Cyprus

Cyprus Circular Post (3), Cyprus Study Circle, Hill Cottage, Slinfold, W. Sussex RH13 7SN England; P. Ellis, ed.

Cyprus Philately (4), Cyprus Philatelic Society, Box 1151, Nicosia, Cyprus; G. Stavrinos, ed.

Czechoslovakia

The Czechoslovak Specialist (10), Society for Czechoslovak Philately Inc., 6624 Windsor Ave., Berwyn, Ill. 60402; Mirko L. Vondra, managing ed.

Czechout (4), 146 Old Shoreham Road, Shoreham-by-Sea, West Sussex BN4 5TE, England; A. Knight, ed.

Egypt

Quarterly Circular of the Egypt Study Circle (4), 6 Urlwin Walk, Myatts Fields South, London SW9 6QG, England; J.A. Grimmer, ed.

Estonia

Eesti Filatelist/The Estonian Philatelist/ Der Esnische Philatelist (1), Estonian Philatelic Society, 31 Addison Terrace, Old Tappan, N.J. 07675; Elmar Ojaste, ed.

Ethiopia

The Lion (4), Ethiopian Collectors' Club, 83 Penn Lea Road, Weston, Bath BA1 3RQ, England; Norman Cape, ed.

Menelik's Journal (4), Ethiopian Philatelic Society, 5710 S.E. Garnet Way, Milwaukee, Ore. 97267; Huguette Gagnon, ed.

Falkland Islands

Upland Goose (4), Falkland Islands Study Group, Sandle Manor, Fordingbridge, Hants. SP6 1NS, England; M.G. Wharton, ed.

France

Les Feuilles Marcophiles (4), Union Marcophile, 19 avenue de Chatelet, F-77330 Lesigny, France.

France & Colonies Philatelist (4), France & Colonies Philatelic Society, 103 Spruce St., Bloomfield, N.J. 07003; Robert G. Stone, ed.; France & Colonies Philatelist 40-Year Cumulative Index to Whole Nos. 1-182, Volumes 1-36, 1941-80, Robert G. Stone, comp.

Journal of the France and Colonies Philatelic Society of Great Britain (4), 34 Traps Lane, New Maiden, Surrey KT3 4SA, England; D.J. Richardson, ed.

Germany

Archiv fur deutsche Postgeschichte (2), Gesellschaft fur deutsche Postgeschichte e.V., Schaumainkai 53, D-6000 Frankfurt 70, West Germany; Gottfried North, ed.

Bavaria Study Group Bulletin (6), Bavaria Study Group of the Germany Philatelic Society, Box 65, Taylors, S.C. 29687; Douglas Syson, ed.

German Postal Specialist (12), Germany Philatelic Society, Box 779, Arnold, Md. 21012; Austin H. Dulin, ed.

Germania (6), Germany and Colonies Philatelic Society of Great Britain, "The Oaks," Hook Cross, Rotherwick, Hants RG27 9BZ, England.

Inflation Study Group Bulletin (4), Inflation Study Group of the Germany Philatelic Society, Box 3128, Columbus, Ohio 43210; Diana Manchester, ed.

Plebiscite Memel Saar Bulletin (4), Plebiscite, Memel, Saar Study Group, 203 Bucket Post Court, Bel Air, Md. 21014; Michael D. Jolly, ed.

Gibraltar

Calpe (4), Gibraltar Philatelic Society, Box 270, Gibraltar; R.J.M. Garcia, ed.

The Rock (4), Gibraltar Study Circle, 36 Starkholmes Road, Matlock, Derby DE4 3DD, England; E.D. Holmes, ed.

Great Britain

The Bookmark (5), Decimal Stamp Book Study Circle, 7 Old Farm Close, Needingworth, Huntingdon, Cambs. PE17 3SG, England; D.G.A. Myall, ed.

British Decimal Stamp Study Circle Newsletter (6), The British Decimal Stamp Study Circle, 70 Moor Park Close, Rainham, Gillingham, Kent ME8 8QT, England; A. Gleave, ed.

British Royal Portraits Study Group Newsletter (3), British Royal Portraits Study Group, 62a Bridge Street, Pershore, Worcs. WR10 1AX, England; L.E. Young, ed.

British Postmark Society Quarterly Bulletin (4), British Postmark Society, 9 Gainsborough Ave., Marple Bridge, Stockport, Cheshire SK6 5BW, England; C.G. Peachey ed.

Forces Postal History Society Newsletter (4), 71 Victory Road, London SW19 1HP, England. A.J. Brown, ed.

GB Journal (6), Great Britain Philatelic

Society, Ferndown, Doggetts Wood, Close, Chalfont, St. Giles, Bucks. HP8 4TL, England; M. Jackson, ed.

Geosix (4), King George VI Collectors' Society, 24 Stourwood Road, Southbourne, Bournemouth BH6 3QP, England; F.R. Huxley, ed.

Great Britain Collectors Club Quarterly Newsletter (4), Great Britain Collectors Club, Box 4586, Portland, Ore. 97208; Tom Current, ed.

L&P Bulletin (4), London and Provincial Society, 189 Wamstead Park Road, Ilford 1G1 3TW, England; R. Negus, ed.

London Postal History Group Notebook (5), London Postal History Group, 24 Dovercourt Road, Dulwich SE22 85T, England; Peter Forrestier Smith, ed.

The Overprinter (4), The Great Britain Overprints Society, Bunkers, Titlarks Hill, Sunningdale, Berks. SL5 0JD, England; D.A.S. Stotter, ed.

Perfins Society of Great Britain Bulletin (6), Perfins Society of Great Britain, 13 Moncrieffe Road, Sheffield S7 1HQ, England; F.S. Tully, ed.

Postal Mechanisation Study Circle Newsletter (12), Postal Merchanisation Study Circle, 16 Crawshay Drive, Emmer Green, Berks., RG4 8SX, England; J. Peach, ed.

Postal Order News (4), The Postal Order Society, 15 Witch Close, east Stour, Gillingham, Dorset SP8 5LB, England; R.H. Lunn, chairman.

Precancels (6), Precancel Stamp Society, 42 Westville Road, Thames Ditton, Surrey KT7 0UJ, England; G.R. Eveleigh, ed.

Raflet Review (1), Raflet (Royal Air Force), Swiss Cottage, Sutton Road, Huttoft, Alford, Lines. LN13 9RG, England; L.R.C. Haward, ed.

Greece

H.P.S.A. News Bulletin (4), Hellenic Philatelic Society of America, 541 Cedar Hill Ave., Wyckoff, N.J. 07481; N. Asimakopulos, Peter Gondis, William C. Stavides, eds.

Quarterly Bulletin of the Hellenic Philatelic Society of Great Britain (4), Hellenic Philatelic Society of Great Britain, 37 Alders View Drive, East Grinstead, W. Sussex RH19 2DN, England; W.G. Mosely, ed.

Guatemala

El Quetzal (4), International Society of Guatemala Collectors, 5023 Klingle St. N.W., Washington, D.C. 20016; Stuart A. Johnson, ed.; Cumulative Index to El Quetzal, Vols. 1-30, Roberta Palen and Deborah Brown, comps., 66p, 1981.

Haiti

Haiti Philately (4), Haiti Philatelic Society, 16434 Shamhat Drive, Granada Hills, Calif. 91344; Gerald L. Boarino, ed.

Hong Kong

Bulletin of the Hong Kong Study Circle (4), Hong Kong Study Circle, 34 Old Butt Lane, Talke, Stoke-on-Trent ST7 1N1, England; C.R. Riding, ed.

Hungary

News of Hungarian Philately (4), Society for Hungarian Philately, Box 1162, Samp-Mortar Sta., Fairfield, Conn. 06430; Victor Berecz, ed.

Stamps of Hungary (4), Hungarian Philatelic Society of Great Britain, 4 Chequers Place, Headington, Oxford OX3 8LR, England; D. Williams, ed.

India

India Post (4), India Study Circle, 2 St. Georges Road, Great Yarmouth, Norfolk NR30 2JR, England; R.A. Mockford, ed.

India's Stamp Journal (12), Empire of India Philatelic Society, c/o Jasavala & Co., Uco Bank Buildings, 359 DN Road, Bombay 400001, India; V.S. Dastur, ed.

Iran

Bulletin of the Iran Philatelic Study Circle (3), Iran Philatelic Study Circle, 99 Moseley Wood Drive, Cookridge, Leeds LS16 7HD, England; B. Lucas, ed.

Ireland

Irish Philately (4), Irish Philatelic Circle, 3 Cleves Way, Hampton, Middx. TW12 2PL, England; O.M. Richards, ed.

The Revealer (4), Eire Philatelic Association, 8 Beach St., Brockton, Mass. 02402; Patrick J. Ryan, ed.

Isle of Man

Isle of Man Postal History Society Bulletin (?), Isle of Man Postal History Society, 6 Eairy Terrace, East Foxdale, Isle of Man, United Kingdom; B.G.F. Osborne, ed.

Israel

BAPIP Bulletin (4), British Association of Palestine-Israel Philatelists, 21 High

Meadows, Chigwell, Essex IG7 5JY, England; W. Loebl, ed.

Holy Land Postal History (4), Society of the Postal History of Eretz-Israel, Box 10175, Jerusalem 91-101, Israel; E. Glassman, Z. Shimony, eds.

The Israel Philatelist (6), Society of Israel Philatelists Inc., 31715 Vine St., Willowick, Ohio 44094; Oscar Stadtler, ed.

Israel Plate Block Journal (4), Israel Plate Block Society, Box 10496, Baltimore, Md. 21209; Sam Aaron, Benjamin J. Fishman, Michael Kaplan, David Libson, Max Peisach and Earl M. Yavner, eds.

WPC Newsletter (2?), World Philatelic Congress of Israel Holy Land Judaica Societies, 102 Sierra Place, Warm Mineral Springs, Fla. 34287.

Italy

Fil-Italia (4), 6 Marston Road, Teddington, Middx. TW11 9JU, England; C. Pilkington, ed.

Japan

Japanese Philately (6), International Society for Japanese Philately, Box 1283, Haddonfield, N.J. 08033; Robert M. Spaulding, ed.

Kitte Shimbun (3), International Society for Japanese Philately - United Kingdom Chapter, 23 Britannia Road, Norwich NR1 4HP, England; D.H. Hubbard, ed.

Korea

Korean Philately (4), Korea Stamp Society, Inc., Forrest W. Calkins, Box 1057, Grand Junction, Colo. 81501; Gordon H. Lazerson, ed.

Latvia

Latvian Collector (3), Box 5403, San Mateo, Calif. 94402; Maris Tirums, ed.

Liberia

Liberian Philatelic Society Newsletter (4), Liberian Philatelic Society, 9027 S. Oakley Ave., Chicago, Ill. 60620; Henry Chlanda, ed.

Liechtenstein

Liechtenstudy (4), Liechtenstein Study Group, 100 Elizabeth St., No. 112, Duluth, Minn. 55803; Max Rheinberger, ed.

Lithuania

Bulletin of the Lithuanian Philatelic Society of New York (4), 2647 Eddington St., Philadelphia, Pa. 19137; Walter E. Norton, ed.

Lundy

L.C.C. Philatelic Quarterly (4), Lundy Collector's Club, 2021 Ridge Rd., Homewood, Ill. 60430; Roger Cichorz, ed.

Malawi

Cleft Stick (12), Philatelic Society of Malawi, Box 1443, Blantyre, Malawi; A. Hawken, ed.

Malaysia

The Malaysian Philatelist (4), Philatelic Society of Malaysia, Peti Surat, 10588 Pejabat Pes Besar, 50718 Kuala Lumpur, Malaysia; C. Nagarajah, ed.

Malta

The PSM Magazine (4), The Philatelic Society (Malta), 5 Oleander St., St. Julians, Malta; A. Bonnici, ed.

Malta Study Circle Newsletter (3), Malta Study Circle, 69 Stonecross Road, Hatfield, Herts. AL10 0HP, England; R.E. Martin, ed.

Mexico

Amexfil (6), Asociacion Mexicana de Filatelia Ac., Apartado Postal 1313, 06000 Mexico, DF, Mexico; Carlos Fernandez, director of publications.

Mexicana (4), Mexico-Elmhurst Philatelic Society International, 2350 Bunker Hill Way, Costa Mesa, Calif. 92626; Edward M. Nissen, ed.

Natal

Philatelic Society of Natal Newsletter (11), Philatelic Society of Natal, 34 Portland Place, Durban North, South Africa; R. Osborne, ed.

Netherlands

The Netherlands Philatelist (3), Netherlands Philatelic Circle, 202A Old Bath Road, Cheltenham, Glos. GL53 9EQ, England; L.G. Jobbins, ed.

Netherlands Philately (4), American Society for Netherlands Philately, 2354 Roan Lane, Walnut Creek, Calif. 94596; Paul E. van Reyen, ed.; also Newsletter (4), Frans H.A. Rummens, ed.

New Zealand

C.P. Newsletter (12), Campbell Patterson Ltd., Box 5555 Auckland 1, New Zealand.

The Kiwi (6), New Zealand Society of Great Britain, 24a Tarrant St., Arundel, West Sussex BN18 9DJ, England; A.P. Berry, ed.

Mail-Coach (4), Postal History Society of New Zealand Inc., Box 38-503, Howick, Auckland 1130, New Zealand; R.M. Startup, ed.

N.Z. Stamp Collector (4), Royal Philatelic Society of New Zealand Inc., Box 1269, Wellington, New Zealand; B.G. Vincent, ed.

The New Zealand Stamp Magazine (6), New Zealand Philatelic Brokers Publishing, Box 80-226, Green Bay 7, Auckland, New Zealand.

Orange Free State

O.F.S. Bulletin (4), Orange Free State Study Circle, 28 Oxford Street, Burnham-on-Sea, Somerset, England; D. Hepworth, ed.

OFS Philatelic Magazine (12), Orange Free State Philatelic Society, Box 702, Bloemfontein 9300, South Africa; J.A. van Beukering, ed.

Papua New Guinea

New Guinea Calling (4), Papuan Philatelic Society, 12 Main St., Gorebridge, Midolothian EH23 4BX, England; R. Lee, ed.

The Philippines

IPPS News (4), International Philippines Philatelic Society, Box 437, Manila, Philippines; Robert F. Yacano, ed.

Philippines New Issue Updates (4?), IPPS, Box 1936, Manila, Philippines; Ngo Tiong Tak and Linda Stanfield, eds.

Philippine Philatelic News (4), International Philippine Philatelic Society, Box 437, Manila, Philippines; Robert F. Yacano, ed.

Philippine Philatelic Society Journal (4), Philippine Philatelic Society, 7408 Alaska Ave. N.W., Washington, D.C. 20012.

Pitcairn Island

Pitcairn Log (4), Pitcairn Islands Study Group, Box 343, Little Current, Ontario P0P 1K0, Canada; Everett L. Parker, ed.

Poland

Bulletin of the Union of Polish Philatelists in Great Britain (6), Union of Polish Philatelists in Great Britain, 17 Denbigh Road, London W13, England.

Polish Philatelic Review (4), Polish Philatelic Federation of Great Britain, 40 Ansell Road, London SW17 7LS, England; Z.R. Bojakowski and W.Z.J. Nowicki, eds.

Bulletin of the Polonus Philatelic Society (6), Box 1217, Oak Park, Ill. 60304, Chester Schafer, ed.; Index to the Bulletin of the Polonus Philatelic Society: Issue Nos. 1-410, Aug. 1942-Dec. 1983, and Thirteen Issues of Polonus Magazine, Nov. 1940-Apr. 1942, Marion J. Dudeck, 192p, 1984.

Portugal

Bulletin of the Portuguese Philatelic Society of Great Britain (4), Portuguese Philatelic Society of Great Britain, 7 Carisbrooke Avenue, Mapperley Park, Nottingham NG3 5DT, England; G.R. Pearson, ed.

Portu-Info (4), International Society for Portuguese Philately, Box 3229, Syracuse, N.Y. 13220; Stephen S. Washburne, ed.

Rhodesia

The Journal of the Rhodesian Study Circle (4), Rhodesian Study Circle, 25 Exe View, Exminster, Devon EX6 8AZ, England; C.M. Hoffman, ed.

Russia

British Journal of Russian Philately (1), British Society of Russian Philately, Freefolk Priory, Freefolk, Whitchurch, Hants. RG28 7NL, England; I. Steyn, ed.

The Journal of the Rossica Society of Russian Philately (1), Rossica Society of Russian Philately, 7415 Venice St., Falls Church, Va. 22043; Kennedy L. Wilson, ed.

Ryukyus Islands

From the Dragon's Den (4), Ryukyu Philatelic Specialist Society Ltd., Box 381, Clanton, Calif. 94517-0381; Russ W. Carter, ed.; From the Dragon's Den: Cumulative Index, Vols. 1-19, 1969-1980, 33p, 1981.

Sarawak

Sarawak Journal (4), Sarawak Specialists, 77 Ingram Ave., Bedgrove, Aylesbury, Bucks. HP21 9DH, England; B. Cave, ed.

Scotland

Scottish Stamp News (6), Alba Stamp Group, 27 Gilmore Road, Edinburgh EH16 5NS, Scotland; T. Rielly, ed.

South Africa

Forerunners: Journal of the Pre-Union South Africa Study Group (4), Pre-Union South Africa Study Group, Box 2632, San Bernardino, Calif. 92406.

Springbok (6), South African Collectors, 138 Chastilian Road, Dartford DA1 3LG, England; C.P. Ravilious, ed.

The Springbok Philatelist (3), South Africa Study Group, 309 W. 72nd St., No. 3d, New York, N.Y. 10023; Sidney Goldfield, ed.

Spain

Espana (2), Spanish Study Circle, 16 Fairford Avenue, Luton, Beds. LU2 7ER, England; B. Burch, ed.

Sudan

Camel Post (2), Sudan Study Group, Bemerton, Lingfield Road, East Grinstead, West Sussex RH19 2EJ, England; H.R.J. Davies, ed.

Switzerland

Tell (6), American Helvetia Philatelic Society, Box 666, Manhattan Beach, Calif. 90266; Steven S. Weston, ed.; Cumulative Index of Tell and Forerunners 1958-1985, Karl E. Henson, ed., 135p, 1986.

Newsletter of the Helvetia Philatelic Society of Great Britain (12), 8 Rhodesia Ave., Stafford Road, Halifax, W. Yorks. HX3 0PB, England; P. Hobbs, ed.

Taiwan

Postal Service Today (6), Director General of Posts, Republic of China, 55 Chinshan South Road, Sec. 2, Taipei 10603, Taiwan; Charles C.Y. Wang, pub.

Thailand

Thai Philately (4), Society for Thai Philately, Box 370, Bryn Mawr, Calif. 92318; Carlos Swanson, ed.

Thai Times (3), Thailand Philatelic Society, 53 Wattisham Road, Bildeston, Ipswich, Suffolk IP7 7EG, England; A.G. Smith, ed.; 1978 reprint by Carlos Swanson of Vols. 1-20; also 1981 revision with cumulative index to Vols. 1-22, 1958-1980.

Tonga

Tin Canner (6), Tonga/Tin Can Mail Study Circle Inc., 1050 N.W. 128th, Portland, Ore. 97229-5545, Janet Klug, ed.

Turkey

The Tughra Times (4), The Turkey and Ottoman Philatelic Society, 19 W. Flagler St., No. 1103, Miami, Fla. 33130; Charles G. Maki, ed.

Tuvalu

Maneapa (4), The Tuvalu and Kiribati Philatelic Society, Box 1209, Temple Hills, Md. 20748; Frank Caprio, ed.

Newsletter of the Kiribati and Tuvalu Philatelic Society (4), 6 Urlwin Walk, Myatts Field South, London SW9 6GC, England; H. Bennet, ed.

Ukraine

Trydent Visnyk (6), Ukrainian Philatelic and Numismatic Society (6), Box 14163, Washington, D.C. 20044; Wes Capan, ed.

United Nations

Bulletin of the United Nations Study Group (4), 86 Liverpool Road, Ashton-in-Makerfield, Wigan WN4 9LP, England; R. Goodey, ed.

The Journal of the United Nations Philatelists (6), 3724 Greentree Drive, Wantagh, N.Y. 11793; Richard Powers, ed.

United Nations Philately Supplement and Journal (4), Box 351, Spring Valley, N.Y. 10977; Arleigh Gaines, ed.

United States - General

The Chronicle of the U.S. Classic Postal Issues (4), U.S. Philatelic Classics Society, Box 1011, Falls Church, Va. 22041; Susan M. McDonald, editor in chief; also The Chairman's Chatter (4) Louise van Ingen, ed.

The Confederate Philatelist (6), Confederate Stamp Alliance, Box 14, Manitowac, Wis. 54220; Stefan T. Jaronski, Genevieve Gwynne, eds.

1869 Times (4), U.S. 1869 Pictorial Research Associates, 3348 Clubhouse Rd., Virginia Beach, Va. 23452; Jonathan W. Rose, ed.

The Heliograph (4), Western Postal History Museum, Box 40725, Tucson, Ariz. 85717; Charles L. Towle, ed.

La Posta: A Journal of American Postal History (6), La Posta Publications, Box 135, Lake Oswego, Ore. 97034; Richard W. Helbock, ed.

Mayflower (4), American Stamp Club of Great Britain, 16 Sutherland Avenue, Leeds LS8 1BZ, England; M.A. Inger, ed.

Modern Postal History Journal (4), Modern Postal History Society, Box 629, Chappaqua, N.Y. 10514-0629; Terence Hines, ed.

Postal History U.S.A. (irregular), 430 Ivy Ave., Crete, Neb. 68333; William F. Rapp, ed.

The Trans-Mississippian (5), Trans-Mississippi Philatelic Society, Box 164, Council Bluffs, Iowa 51502; Robert J. Lambert, coordinating ed.

United States Specialist (12), Bureau Issues Association Inc., Box 1047, Belleville, Ill. 62231; Charles A. Yeager, ed.

U.S. Stamp Prices (?), Wynmoor, 8453 Millwood Place, Springfield, Va. 22152; Jeremy A. Lifsey, compiler and publisher.

United States - Airmails

Air Mail Northwest (4), American Air Mail Society, Northwest Chapter, 725 S.E. Davidson, No. 30, Albany, Ore. 97321; Sherman L. Pompey, ed.

The Beacon Newsletter (4), The Beacon Air Mail Study Group, 520 Pike St., Suite 2360, Seattle, Wash. 98101-4005; Philip Silver, ed.

Chicago Air Mail Society Bulletin (4), Chicago Air Mail Socity, Box 25, Deerfield, Ill. 60015-0025; Stephen Neulander, ed.

The Jack Knight Air Log (4), Jack Knight Air Log, AFA News and Aerophilatelic Federation of the Americas, Box 1239, Elgin, Ill. 60121-1239; Fred L. Wellman, ed.

Metropolitan Air Post Society Quarterly (4), 126 Drake Ave., Staten Island, N.Y. 10314; Robert S. Miller, ed.

NAMWITS Journal (4), National Air Mail Week Historical Society, 1501 Quincy St., Piscataway, N.J. 48854-1657.

United States - Postal Markings

Commemorative Cancellation Catalog (10), General Image Inc., Box 335, Maplewood, N.J. 07040.

Machine Cancel Forum (4), Machine Cancel Society, 9635 E. Randall St., Columbus, Ind. 47203-9340; Bart Billings, ed.; includes some foreign.

PMCC Bulletin (11), Post Mark Collectors Club Inc., 4200 S.E. Indianola Road, Des Moines, Iowa 50320; Kimberlee K. Terry, ed.

U.S.C.S. Log (12), Universal Ship Cancellation Society, 35 Montague Circle, East Hartford, Conn. 06118; Robert D. Rawlins, ed.

U.S. Cancellation Club News (6), U.S. Cancellation Club, Box 545, Clearfield, Pa. 16830; Roger D. Curran, ed.

United States - Revenues

The American Revenuer (10), The American Revenue Association, 701 S. First Ave., Arcadia, Calif. 91006; Kenneth Trettin, ed.; cumulative index to The American Revenuer, Sept. 1947 to Dec. 1983, Whole Nos. 1-143, in the association's 1984 biennial directory.

State Revenue Newsletter (6), The State Revenue Society, Box 629, Chappaqua, N.Y. 10514-0629; Terence Hines, ed.

United States - Specialties

The Ceremonial (8), American Ceremony Program Society, 436 E. Thirwell Ave., Hazleton, Pa. 18201-7719; Donald Ludwig, ed.

Coil Line (12), Plate Number Coil Collectors Club, 1604 Bardale Ave., San Pedro, Calif. 90731; Tom Maeder, ed.

EFO Collector (6), EFO Collector Club, 1903 Village Road W., Norwood, Mass. 02062-2524; Howard Gates, ed.

First Days (8), American First Day Cover Society, 203 Village Way, Brick, N.J. 08724; Sol Koved, ed.; Cumulative Index of Each Volume of First Days: Volume 1 through Volume 25, Sept./Dec. 1955 to Nov./Dec. 1980, reprinted from the annual indexes.

Official Mail Journal (4), Official Mail Study Group, 725 S.E. Davidson, No. 30, Albany, Ore. 97321; Sherman Lee Pompey, ed.

The Page and Panel Journal (4), American Society for Philatelic Pages and Panels, 4116 Kilmer Ave., Allentown, Pa. 18104; Ron Walenciak, ed.

Permit Patter (6), Mailer's Postmark Permit Club, Box 5973, Akron, Ohio 44372-5793.

The Plate Number (6), Box 20130, Shaker Heights, Ohio 44120-0130; Stephen G. Estrati, ed.

Plate Numbers (6), American Plate Number Single Society, 10926 Annette Ave., Tampa, Fla. 33612; Martin L. Wilson, ed.

The Poster (6), Local Post Collectors Society, 2019 Maravilla Circle, Fort Myers, Fla. 33901; Howard J. Wunderlich, ed.

The Precancel Forum (12), Precancel Stamp Society Inc., Box 160, Walkersville, Md. 21793; Dilmond D. Postlewait, ed.; coverage is mostly U.S. but includes some foreign.

The Souvenir Card Journal (4), Souvenir Card Collectors Society, Box 4155, Tulsa,

Okla., 74159-0155; Doug Holl, ed.

United States - State Federations

Across The Fence (12), Wisconsin Federation of Stamp Clubs, 1017 Chieftain Lookout, Madison, Wis. 53711; Howard Sherpe, ed.

Arizona Philatelist (12), Arizona Federation of Stamp Clubs Inc., Box 10337, Phoenix, Ariz. 15016; Dave Pikul, ed.

The Florida Philatelist (5), Florida Federation of Stamp Clubs, 4801 Taylor St., Hollywood, Fla. 33021; Stephen Patrick, ed.

Stamp Insider (10), Federation of Central New York Philatelic Societies Inc., Box 44, Fulton, N.Y. 13069; John Cali, ed.

The Texas Philatelist (6), The Texas Philatelic Association, 6802 Dusquesne Drive, Austin, Texas 78723; Jane King Fohn, ed.

Virginia Philatelic Forum (4), Virginia Philatelic Federation, Box 2183, Norfolk, Va. 23501; James B. Gouger, ed.

United States - State Postal History

The periodicals in this section are alphabetic by state rather than by title.

The Alaskan Philatelist (4), Alaska Collectors Club, 2337 Giant Oaks Drive, Pittsburgh, Pa. 15241; Robert W. Collins, ed.

The Roadrunner (4), The Arizona-New Mexico Postal History Society, 370 Deer Pass Drive, Sedona, Ariz. 86336; Owen Kriege, ed.

Western Express (4), Western Cover Society, 1615 Rose St., Berkeley, Calif. 94703; Alan H. Patera, ed.; coverage is primarily California.

The Journal of the Postal History Society of Connecticut (3), Box 276, Bloomfield, Conn. 06002; Frank Reischerl, ed.

G.P.H.S. Bulletin (irregular), Box 51, Lexington, Ga. 30648; Douglas N. Clark, ed.

Po'Oleka O Hawaii (4), Hawaiian Philatelic Society, Box 10115, Honolulu, Hawaii 96816-0115.

Illinois Postal Historian (4), Illinois Postal History Society, Box 1129, Waukegan, Ill. 60085; Jack Hilbing, ed.

Indiana Postal History Society Newsletter (?), 9635 E. Randall St., Columbus, Ind. 47201.

Iowa Postal History Society Bulletin (4), Iowa Postal History Society, 1298 29th St. N.E., Cedar Rapids, Iowa 52402; James Williamson, ed.

Maryland Postal History Society Publication (irregular), Maryland Postal History Society, Box 13430, Baltimore, Md. 21203; Roy Cox, ed.

Massachusetts Spy (6), Massachusetts Postal Research Society, Box 202, North Abington, Mass. 02351; Robert S. Borden, ed.

Minnesota Postal History Society Newsletter (?), 55 Idaho Ave. N., Golden Valley, Minn. 55427.

Montana Postcard/Paper Club Newsletter (2), Box 814, East Helena, Mont. 59635; Tom Mulvaney, ed..

Granite Posts (4), The New Hampshire Postal History Society, Box 1532, Dover, N.H. 03820; Russell White IV, ed.

NJPH (4), New Jersey Postal History Society, 28 Briar Lane, Basking Ridge, N.J. 07920; E.E. Fricks, ed.

New Mexico: See Arizona.

Long Island Postal Historian (4), Long Island Postal History Society, 97-1071st Ave., Forest Hills, N.Y. 11375; J. Fred Rodriguez, ed.

NCPHS Newsletter (4), North Carolina Postal History Society, 602 Pearson Circle, New Bern, N.C. 28560; Tony Crumbley and Darrell Ertzberger, eds.

Dakota Collector (4), North Dakota Postal History Society, Box 280, Maddock, N.D. 58348; Gordon Twedt, ed.

Ohio Postal History Journal (4), Ohio Postal History Society, Box 441, Worthington, Ohio 43085; Martin Richardson and George J. Bell, eds.

Northern Ohio Postmark Circle Postscript (?), Richard H. Parker, 1526 Mainview Drive, Westlake, Ohio 44145.

Oregon Postal History Journal (4), The Oregon Postal History Society, 201 Iowell St., Klamath Falls, Ore. 97601; Bernie Griffin, ed.

Pennsylvania Postal Historian (6), Pennsylvania Postal History Society, 329 Milne St., Philadelphia, Pa. 19144; Tom Clark, ed.

The RI Phil Newsletter (6), Rhode Island Philatelic Society, Box 9385, Providence, R.I. 02940.

The Texas Postal History Society

Journal (4), 5825 Caldwell, Waco, Texas 76710.

The Vermont Philatelist (4), The Vermont Philatelic Society, Oak Terrace Apts., No. 10C, Colchester, Vt. 05446; Jason J. Granger, ed.

Way Markings (4), Virginia Postal History Society, 2703 Dellrose Ave., Richmond, Va. 23228; Tom Stanton, ed.

Badger Postal History (4), Wisconsin Postal History Society, N95 W32259 County Line Road, Hartland, Wis. 53029; William B. Robinson, ed.

The Wyoming Collector (4), Box 2093, Lake Grove, Ore. 97034; Alan H. Patera, ed.

United States - Territories

Boletin Filatelico (4), Sociedad Filatelica de Puerto Rico, Apartado 1500, Hayo Rey, Puerto Rico 00919; Luis Gonzales Perez, ed.

Canal Zone Philatelist (4), Canal Zone Study Group, 408 Redwood Lane, Schaumbeg, Ill. 60193; Gary B. Weiss, ed.

Philatelically Yours (4), Guam Stamp Club, Tumon Holiday Manor, No. 411, 165 Marata St., Tumon Bay, Guam 96911; Phill Mendel, ed.

Possessions (4), United States Possessions Philatelic Society, 8100 Willow Stream Drive, Sandy Utah, 84092; Gilbert N. Plass, editor in chief.

Official Business (?), United States Possessions Philatelic Society, 8100 Willow Stream Drive, Sandy, Utah 84092.

Vatican City

Vatican Notes (6), Vatican Philatelic Society, 165-15 Union Turnpike, Flushing, N.Y. 11366; William M. Wickert Sr., ed.

Wales

Welsh Philatelic Society Newsletter (3), 27 Tan-y-Bryn, Llanbedr D.C., Ruthin, Clwyd, LL15 1AQ, Wales, United Kingdom; D.R. Gwynn, ed.

Yugoslavia

Jugoposta (4), Yugoslavia Study Group, 2 Thorn Street, Earlston, Berwickshire TD4 6DP, England.

Zimbabwe

Magnify (4), Box 803, Bulawayo, Zimbabwe; P. Tucker, ed.

U.S. Philatelic Literature

Stamp and cover collectors learn about what they collect mainly by examining actual stamps and covers and by discussing them with other collectors.

Philatelic literature, both books and periodicals, records the findings and thoughts of collectors about what they have seen and collected.

The literature of stamp collecting is vast. It includes introductions for beginners, worldwide catalogs, topical handbooks and specialized handbooks for specific countries. Although the listing in this chapter is long, it is still only a selected bibliography of items related to United States stamps and covers.

The listing serves two purposes: to record the basic U.S. catalogs and to present a reliable list of handbooks that can be consulted by specialists.

As much as possible, the listings in this bibliography are based on examining actual books and pamphlets. The list in the previous edition of *Linn's World Stamp Almanac* was a starting point, but that list is reorganized and updated. Much use was made of the literature lists and reviews published in the *Philatelic Literature Review*, the quarterly journal of the American Philatelic Research Library, a part of the American Philatelic Society.

Except for basic catalogs, individual entries in the bibliography are by author's last name in alphabetical order. In some cases, works have corporate authors. Works with no authors are entered under title, also in alphabetical order.

Following the author is the work's title from the title page, edition for second or higher editions, number of volumes for multivolume works, number of pages and year of publication.

A work is in the language of its title unless noted otherwise. The year of publication is the year or latest copyright year given on the front or back of the title leaf. In reality, a work sometimes is initially distributed before or after the year on its title page. For reprints, the original year of publication is given in parentheses before the year of the reprint.

Often, philatelic literature is published without a printed year of publication. Undated works are noted with the abbreviation "n.d.," except where the compiler of this bibliography is certain of the year of publication. Year of publication is sometimes given with a question mark (?) for undated works when there is uncertainty. To make this bibliography as accurate as possible, comments on uncertain information or inaccuracies are invited.

Entries without a page count, without "n.d.," or without a date of publication have not been seen by the compiler. The entry is based on an incomplete entry in another source or from a book review.

The number of pages specified for a given work is the number of the last page with information that is part of the work, whether that page has a printed number or not. Blank pages or pages with advertising following the last page of the work are not included.

No consideration has been given to preliminary pages numbered with small Roman numerals. Pages are totaled for multivolume works. Collectors or bibliophiles who need an exact collation of a work must examine the actual volume or volumes.

Bibliophiles and stamp collectors seeking philatelic literature are advised to join the American Philatelic Research Library. Members receive its quarterly journal, *Philatelic Literature Review*. The journal includes advertising from literature dealers and has a clearinghouse for members selling or seeking to buy specific literature.

Linn's thanks those individuals who offered suggestions and corrections to the literature chapter in the previous edition. Other corrections and additions are welcome, especially on data listed with a question mark or missing.

Collectors having questions related to philatelic literature are requested to include a stamped, addressed envelope with their inquiry.

United States

GENERAL WORKS

Brookman Stamp Co., **Comprehensive Price Guide to United States Stamps**, annual, title varies.

Michel USA-Spezial-Katalog, published every few years.

Scott Specialized Catalogue of United States Stamps, annual.

Scott U.S. Pocket Stamp Catalogue and Checklist, regularly updated.

Stanley Gibbons, **United States**, regularly updated.

* * *

Cowitt, Richard, **United States Stamp Compendium**, 17p, 1974, stamp and stationery quantities.

French, Loran C., **Encyclopedia of Plate Varieties on U.S. Bureau-Printed Postage Stamps**, 338p, 1979.

H.E. Harris & Co. Inc., **Postage Stamp Prices of the United States, United Nations, Canada & Provinces, plus: Confederate States, U.S. Possessions,...**, regularly updated, title varies.

Kersey, Judy M., **Bogus United States Stamps Produced by S. Allan Taylor**, 1983.

Kimble, Ralph A., **Commemorative Postage Stamps of the U.S.**, 350p, 1933.

Konwiser, Harry, **The American Stamp Collector's Dictionary: United States Stamps and Postal History**, 309p, 1949.

Konwiser, Harry, **American Philatelic Dictionary and Colonial and Revolutionary Posts**, 152p and 208p, 1947.

McDonald, Susan M., **American Philatelic Miscellany**, 569p, 1976 reprint, articles from *The Stamp Specialist*.

Micarelli, Charles N., **Manual and Identification Guide to the United States Regular Issues, 1847-1934**, 116p, 1981.

Minkus Specialized American Stamp Catalogue, 28th ed., 473p, 1988.

Marzulla, Elena, ed., **Pictorial Treasury of U.S. Stamps**, 223p, 1974.

Mueller, Barbara, **United States Postage Stamps: How to Collect, Understand and Enjoy Them**, 343p, 1958.

Perry, Elliott, **Pat Paragraphs**, compiled and arranged by George T. Turner and Thomas E. Stanton, 648p, 1987.

Phillips, David, **American Illustrated Cover Catalog**, 259p, 1981, also price supplement.

Reynolds, J.H. Davis, **U.S. Guide Lines**, 16p, 1947.

Sloane, George B., **Sloane's Column**, articles from *Stamps Magazine*, 1932-58, compiled and arranged by George T. Turner, 467p, 1961.

Smith, Chester M., **American Philatelic Periodicals**, 78p, 1979.

United States Postal Service, **Exploring the World of Stamps in your Classroom: A Teacher's Guide to Stamp Collecting**, 1982.

United States Postal Service, **The Postal Service Guide to U.S. Stamps**, annual editions 1-8 were published as **Stamps and Stories**.

White, Roy H., **Encyclopedia of the Colors of United States Postage Stamps, 1847-1918**, five vols., 1981/86.

White, Roy H., **The Papers and Gums of United States Postage Stamps 1847-1909**, 118p, 20 plates, 1983.

19TH CENTURY

Ashbrook, Stanley B., **Special Service**, Nos. 1-81, 658p, 319 illustrations on other sheets, 1951/57.

Baker, Hugh J., and J. David Baker, **Baker's U.S. Classics: Compiled and Arranged by Subject from the Columns in Stamps, 1962-1969**, 343p, 1985.

Boggs, Winthrop S., **Early American Perforating Machines and Perforations 1857-67**, 32p, (1954) 1982 reprint.

Brookman, Lester G., **Notes on the Grilled Issues**, 72p, (1940) 1980 reprint.

Brookman, Lester, **Notes on the Grilled Issues of the United States and U.S. Grills**, 87p, 1980 reprint; see also Stephenson.

Brookman, Lester G., **The United States Postage Stamps of the 19th Century**, three vols., 882p, 1966/67, two-volume edition, 624p, 1947.

Chapin, John C., **A Census of U.S. Classic Plate Blocks**, 116, 1982, errata slip; supplement in March 1984 *Collectors Club Philatelist*.

Chase, Carroll, **Classic United States Stamps, 1845-1869**, 45p, 1962.

Ishikawa, Ryohei, **The United States Stamps 1847-1869: Ryohei Ishikawa Collection**, 1981.

Luff, John N., **The Postage Stamps of the United States**, 417p, 1902; 320p, 1937; *Weekly Philatelic Gossip* edition, 320p, Nov. 8, 1941 to May 8, 1943, as bound volume, 1944?; 320p, (1902) 1981 reprint.

Rohrbach, Peter T., and Lowell S. Newman, **American Issue: The United States Postage Stamp, 1842-1869**, 231p, 1984.

Stevenson, William L., **U.S. Grills**, 15p, 1910?

20TH CENTURY

Armstrong, Martin A., **United States Definitive Series, 1922-38**, 2nd ed., 115p, 1980.

Armstrong, Martin A., **United States Coil Issues, 1906-1938**, 2nd ed., 124p, 1980.

Armstrong, Martin A., **Washington-Franklins, 1908-21**, 2nd ed., 224p, 1979.

Barrett, L.G., **United States 3¢ Violet War and Victory**, 14p.

Boerger, Alfred G., **Handbook on U.S. Luminescent Stamps**, 143p, 1975.

Denson, Ed, **Denson's Specialized Catalog of Plate Number Coils on First Day Covers, Souvenir Pages and Ceremony Programs**, 156p, 1988?

Esrati, Stephen G., ed., **Catalog of Plate Number Coils**, 5th ed., 60p, 1989.

Glass, Sol, **United States Postage Stamps, 1945-1952**, 180p, 1954.

Hahn, George, **United States Famous American Series of 1940**, 193p, 1950.

Helbock, Richard W., ed., **Prexie Postal History**, 100p, 1988.

Howard, George P., **The Stamp Machines and Coiled Stamps**, 127p, 1943.

Johl, Max, **United States Postage Stamps 1902-1935**, 5 vols., 1,245p, (1932/38), 1976 reprint of 566 pages includes chapters from the revised Vol. I (1937) and Vol. III; Beverly King co-authored volumes I and II.

Johl, Max, **The United States Commemorative Stamps of the 20th Century**, two vols., 738p, 1947.

Linn's U.S. Stamp Yearbook, annual volumes, 1983 to date.

Mosher, Bruce, **Discovering U.S. Rotary Booklet Pane Varieties 1926-1978**, 128p, 1979.

Mosher, Bruce, **U.S. EFO Booklet Panes from Multiple Processing Mistakes**, 1981.

Schoen, R.H., and James T. DeVoss, **Counterfeit Kansas-Nebraska Overprints on 1922-34 Issues**, 34p, 1976 reprint.

Segal, Stanley B., **Errors, Freaks and Oddities on U.S. Stamps**, 88p, 1979.

Silberberg, B., **U.S. Stamp Pan-American Issue Series of 1901**, 120p, 1976.

Sloat, Ralph L., **Farley's Follies**, 108p, 1979.

POSTMASTERS' PROVISIONALS

Hatcher, James Brush, **A Forerunner of the 1847s. The New York Postmaster Stamp of 1845**, 8p.

Luff, John N., **The Postage Stamps of the United States — Part One: Postmasters' Provisional Stamps**, revised by Hugh M. Clark, 70p, 15 plates, 1937.

Means, Carroll Alton, **The New Haven Provisional Envelope**, 51p.

Slater, A.B., **The Stamps of the Providence, Rhode Island, Postmaster, 1846-1847**, 104p, 1930.

1847 ERA

Boggs, Winthrop S., **Ten Decades Ago 1840-1850. A Study of the Work of Rawdon, Wright, Hatch and Edson of New York City...**, 100p, 1949.

Brookman, Lester G., **The 1847 Issue of U.S. Stamps**, 77p, 1942.

Hart and McDonald, **Directory of 10¢ 1847 Covers**, 2nd ed., 155p, 1970.

1851 ERA

Ashbrook, Stanley B., **The United States One Cent Stamp of 1851-1857**, two vols., 692p, 1938.

Ashbrook, Stanley B., **The United States Ten Cent Stamp of 1855-1857**, 87p, 1936.

Chase, Carroll, **The 3¢ Stamps of the United States 1851-1857 Issue**, 374p, (1942) 1975 reprint, 375p.

Cole, Maurice, **The Black Jacks of 1863-67**, 12p, 1950.

Hill, Henry W., **The United States Five Cent Stamps of 1856-1861**, 79p, 1955.

Lane, M.B., **The Harry F. Allen Collection of Black Jacks**, 148p, 1969.

Neinken, Mortimer L., **The United States One Cent Stamp of 1851 to**

1861, 552p, 1 plate, 1972.

Neinken, Mortimer L., **The United States Ten Cent Stamps of 1855-59**, 252p, 1960.

Neinken, Mortimer L., **The 1851-57 Twelve Cent Stamp**, 74p, 1964.

1869 ERA

Ashbrook, Stanley B., **The United States Issue of 1869 Preceded by Some Additional Notes on "The Premieres Gravures of 1861,"** 77p (including the 5-page addendum that was removed from many copies), 1943.

Rose, Jonathon W., and Richard M. Searing, **The 1869 Issue on Cover: A Census and Analysis**, 223p, 1986.

Schueren, Fred P., **The United States 1869 Issue: An Essay Proof History**, 127p, 1947.

U.S. 1869 Pictorial Research Associates, **Interphil 1976 Publication**, 112p, 1976.

U.S. 1869 Pictorial Research Associates, **The 1977 Register**, 94p, 1977.

U.S. 1869 Pictorial Research Associates, **The 1978 Register**, 113p, 1978.

U.S. 1869 Pictorial Research Associates, **The 1982 Register**, 124p, 1983.

BANK NOTES THROUGH EARLY BUREAU ISSUES

Brookman, Lester G., **The Bank Note Issues of U.S. Stamps, 1879-93**, 98p, (1941) 1981 reprint.

Davis, H.A., **U.S. 1887 3 Cent Vermilion**, 22p, (1922) 1979 reprint.

Lauzon, A.A., **The United States Columbian Issue 1893**, 67p, 1942.

Sampson, J.W., **Seven Cent Vermilion U.S. 1871-1873 Issue**, 16p, 1920?

Stanton, F.E., **Relief Breaks on the 2¢ Stamp of 1890**, 17p, 1935.

Wiley, H.L., **The U.S. 3¢ Green 1870-1887**, 21p, 1951, reprinted 1979 with Davis.

Willard, Edward L., **The United States 2¢ Red Brown of 1883-1887**, two vols., 328p, 1970.

AIRMAIL, AIRMAIL STAMPS AND SPACE

American Air Mail Society, **American Air Mail Catalogue**, 5th ed., Vol. 1, 474p, 1974; Vol. 2, 509p, 1977; Vol. 3, 509p, 1979; Vol. 4, 618p, 1981; Vol. 5, 555p, 1985; pricing supplement for Volumes 1-3, 96p, 1983.

Amick, George, **Jenny!**, 251p, 1986, the 24¢ inverted center airmail stamps.

Boughner, Fred, **Airmail Antics**, 186p, 1988.

Crampon, L.J., **Aerophilatelic Flights: Hawaii and Central Pacific 1913-1946**, 69p, printed on one side, 1980.

Curley, Walter, **Amelia Earhart**, 28p, 1966.

Curley, Walter, **Charles A. Lindbergh, A Biographical and Philatelic Study**, 44p, 1978.

Fidelma, Sister M., **Catalog of the Charles A. Lindbergh Collection of the Cardinal Spellman Museum**, 75p, 1968.

Goodkind, Henry M., **The First Airmail Stamps of the U.S.**, 12p, 1940?

Goodkind, Henry M., **United States RF (French) Overprints 1944-45 on Air Mail Stamps and Stationery**, 63p, 1958.

Goodkind, Henry M., **U.S.: The 5¢ Beacon Airmail Stamp of 1928**, 61p, 1965.

Goodkind, Henry M., **The 24¢ Air Mail Inverted Center of 1918**, 32p, 1956.

Jackson, Donald, **Flying the Mail**, 176p, 1982.

Leary, William M., **Aerial Pioneers: The U.S. Airmail Service, 1918-1927**, 1985.

O'Sullivan, Thomas J., **The Pioneer Airplane Mails of the United States**, 338p, 1985.

O'Sullivan and Weber, **History of the U.S. Pioneer ... Air Mail Service 1910-28**, 180p, 1973.

Ramkissoon, Reuben A., and Lester E. Winick, **A Philatelic History of Space Exploration: U.S.A. Space Cover Catalog and Pricing Guide. Part 1 — The Pioneer Years, 1904-1960**, 56p, 1986.

Ronson, William, **United States Navy Missile Mail,** 32p, 1966.

Schoendorf, Robert, **The Buffalo Balloon Mail 1873-1877 Including a Specialized History with Prices**, 30p, 1979.

Schoendorf, Robert, **Catalog of Classic American Airposts and Aeronautics 1784-1900**, 99p, 1982.

Stein, E.P., **Flight of the Vin Fiz**, 1985.

SPECIAL SERVICES

Gobie, Henry M., **The Speedy: A**

History of the U.S. Special Delivery, 296p, 1976.

Gobie, Henry M., **U.S. Parcel Post — A Postal History**, 250p, 1979.

Markovits, Robert L., **U.S. 10¢ Registry Stamp of 1911**, 32p, 1973.

Sloat, Ralph L., **The Airmail Special Delivery Stamps of the United States**, 86p.

LOCALS

Brooks, Edward, **American Letter Express Co., Louisville and Nashville 1861**, 60p, 1946.

Chautauqua Lake Local Post: A Unique Mail Delivery Service on Chautauqua Lake Since 1970, 22p, 1979.

Cooper, Lowell B., **The Fresno and San Francisco Bicycle Mail of 1894**, 134p, 1982.

Edelis, Tadas, **Catalog of Modern U.S. Locals**, two vols., 1975.

Patton, Donald S., **The Private Local Posts of the United States**, Vol. I, New York State, 350p, 1967; no other volumes published.

Perry and Hall, **100 Years Ago 1842-1942: Centenary of the First Adhesive Postage Stamp in the U.S.**, 68p, 1942, city despatch post.

Perry, Elliot, **Byways of Philately: Privately Owned Posts and Early Locals**, 270p, 1966.

Perry, Elliot, **The Chatham Square Post Office and Swarts' City Despatch Post**, 34p, 1941.

Schultz, William R., **Catalog of Rattlesnake Island Local Post Stamps**, 4th ed., 1985.

Standen, Jack C., **Rattlesnake Island: The Story of a Local Post**, 1980.

ESSAYS AND PROOFS

Brazer, Clarence, **A Historical Catalog U.S. Stamp Essays and Proofs. The 1847 Issue**, 32p, 1947.

Brazer, Clarence, **A Historical Catalog of U.S. Stamp Essays and Proofs. Trans-Mississippi Issue 1898**, 48p, 1939.

Brazer, Clarence, **Essays for U.S. Adhesive Postage Stamps**, 236p, (1941); 295p, 1977 reprint.

Markovits, Robert L., **Dr. Clarence W. Brazer Essays Proof Price Lists 1937-1956**, 128p, 1982.

PRINTING OF STAMPS

Bureau of Engraving and Printing, Treasury Department, **History of the Bureau of Engraving & Printing**, 199p, (1962) 1978 reprint.

Griffiths, William G., **The Story of the American Bank Note Company**, 92p, 16 plates, 1959.

Morris, Thomas F. II, **The Life and Work of Thomas F. Morris, 1852-1898, Designer of Bank Notes and Stamps**, 159p, 1968.

REVENUE STAMPS AND PRIVATE DIE ISSUES

Aldrich, Michael E., **Match and Medicine Census**, 14p, 1987.

Beaumont, Howard, **Printed Cancellations 1862-1883**, 40p, 1972.

Bidwell, Ray W., **Series of 1941 Wine Revenue Stamps of the U.S.**, 44p, 1965.

Black, George, comp., **Shift Hunter Letters: U.S. Revenue Varieties**, originated by C.W. Bedford, 35p, 1983.

Burt, Randall E., **Adhesive Revenue Stamps of Hawaii: Their History and Use**, 114p, 1986.

Cass, Harry, and Joseph Bush, **The Bush-Cass Catalog of AMG Revenue Stamps of the Allied Military Government in Europe, 1945-1954**, 54p, 1958, third printing (1978) has revised collation.

Chappell, C.H., **Proprietary Revenues of 1898, Precanceled Varieties**, 89p, 1957.

Combs, W.V., **First Federal Issue 1798-1801, U.S. Embossed Revenue Stamped Paper**, 124p, 1979.

Einstein, Kingsley and DeKay, **Handbook of U.S. Revenue Stamped Paper**, 88p, 1979.

Hines, Terence, **Revenue Study of U.S. Federal Special Tax Stamps Unlisted in Scott and Beginning with the Issues of 1873** 140p.

Holcombe, Henry W., **Patent Medicine Tax Stamps: A History of the Firms Using U.S. Private Die Proprietary Medicine Tax Stamps**, 604p, (1936/57) 1979 reprint.

Joyce, Morton Dean, **The Case of Dr. Kilmer**, 28p, 1954, the Dr. Kilmer and Co. proprietary overprints on the 1895 postage stamps.

King, Beverly S., Justin L. Bacharach

and George T. Turner, eds., **Revenue Unit Columns from the American Philatelist**, 237p, 1981 reprint.

McBride, David P., **The Federal Duck Stamps: A Complete Guide**, 206p, 1984.

Priester, Thomas W., **United States Beer Stamps**, 95p, 1979.

Rickerson, Wildey C., **United States Revenue Stamps: Collect Them for Fun and Profit**, 64p, 10 two-sided plates, 1973?

Shellabear, H.P., **Railroad Company Cancellations on U.S. Revenue Stamps of 1862-1883**, 52p, 1943.

Toppan, Deats and Holland, **An Historical Reference List of the Revenue Stamps of the United States Including Private Die Proprietary Stamps**, 423p, 1 plate, (1899) 1980 reprint, known as The Boston Revenue Book; Gossip reprint has 440p.

Turner, George T., **Essays and Proofs of United States Internal Revenue Stamps**, 446p, 1974.

U.S. Fish and Wildlife Service, **The Duck Stamp Collection**, 59p, 1988, update sheets; the successor to Duck Stamp Data.

Vecchairelli, Carlo, **U.S. Duck Stamps**, 104p, 1979.

Wald, Kimber A., **A Centennial Survey of the United States Civil War Revenue Stamped Paper Issues, 1865-1883**, 1983.

West, Christopher, **Private Die Match Stamps: A History of the Stamps and the Firms Using Them**, 262p, 1980 reprint of articles by Elliot Perry.

West, Christopher, **The Revenue Stamps of the United States**, 102p, 16 plates, 1979 reprint.

West, Christopher, **U.S. Match and Medicine Stamps**, 56p, 64 plates, 1980 reprint.

STATE REVENUES

Hines, Terrence, **The Revenue Stamps of the New England States**, 76p, 1984.

Hubbard, Elbert, **U.S. State Revenue Catalog**, 280p.

Vanderford, E.L., **Handbook of Fish and Game Stamps**, 195p plus supplementary pages for many states, 1973.

CINDERELLAS

Koeppel, Adolph, **Stamps That Caused the American Revolution: Stamps of the 1765 British Stamp Act for America**, 193p, 1976.

Mosbaugh's U.S. All Funds Seal Catalog, sections 1-11, 1976/81.

Rich, J., and S. Rich, **U.S. Telegraph Stamps**, 76p, 1947.

Springer, Sherwood, **Springer's Handbook of North American Cinderella Stamps**, 10 editions, 1962/85, 6th through 10th editions are current.

POSTAL STATIONERY

Barrett, L.G., **Retouched 2 Cent Envelope Dies of 1903**, 22p, 1911.

Beachboard, John H., ed., **United States Postal Card Catalog**, 6th ed., 278p, 1980, 1983 price supplement.

Chamberlin, Taylor M., **A Checklist of U.S. Penalty Overprinted Envelopes**, 74p, 1984.

Ellis, F.L., and W.H. Maisel, **United States Commemorative Stamped Envelopes 1876-1965**, 86p, 1974.

Fricke, Charles A., **1973 Centennial Handbook of the First Issue United States Postal Card 1873-75**, Vol. 1: A Complete Plating of the 72 Subject Plates, 70p, 1973; Vol. 2: Chronological Presentation of Contemporary [Documents] During the Period 1870-1875, 146p, 1973.

Fricke, Charles A., **Transitive Relationship to Family Tree of Proofs**.

Fricke, Charles A., **The United States International Single Postal Cards of 1879, 1897 and 1898**, Vol. 1: Plating, 60p, 1974.

Haessler, Rob, **A List of the U.S. Columbian Stamped Envelopes of 1893**, 2nd ed., 1984.

Haller, Austin P., **Private Printed Franks on U.S. Government Envelopes**, 128p, 1988.

Hedding, Benjamin D., **Precancelled Envelopes of the United States**, 2nd ed., 104p, 1981.

Ross, Leroy L., **Penalty Overprinted United States Envelopes**, 147p, 1982.

Thorp, Prescott H., **Catalogue of 20th Century Stamped Envelopes and Wrappers of the United States**, 206p, 1968.

Thorp, Prescott H., and J.M. Bartels, **Thorpe-Bartels Catalogue of the Stamped Envelopes and Wrappers of the United States and Possessions**,

5th ed., two vols., 420p, 1943; 6th ed., 597p, 1954, latter called the Century Edition.

McGovern, Edmund C., ed., **UPSS Catalog of the 19th Century Stamped Envelopes and Wrappers of the United States**, 340p, 1984.

PRECANCELS

Einstein, Joseph S., **Scott #513 13¢ Apple Green Precancel Catalog**, 20p, 1981.

Hooper, R. Malcolm, **A Historical Survey of Precancels**, 109p, 1979.

Jones, Raymond E., ed., **U.S. Classic Precancel Town and Type Catalog**, 66p, 1982.

Klein, George, and Dilmond D. Postlewait, **Precancel Stamp Society Bureau Precancel Catalog**, 2nd ed., 64p, 1982.

Klein, George, comp., **Catalog of the Elite Precancels**, 60p, 1982, PSS town and type catalog items with $25 value and higher.

Noble, Gilbert W., **The Noble Official Catalog of U.S. Bureau Precancels**, 64th ed., 236p, 1983.

Noble, Gilbert W., **The Official Printed Dated Control Precancel Catalog**, 5th ed., 164p, 1981, Dale E. Besom ed.

Precancel Stamp Society, **The Precancel Stamp Society's Town and Type Catalog of the U.S. & Territories**, 4th ed., 1985.

Trout, Horace Q., ed., **Specialists' Guide to Bureau Precancels**, 3rd ed., 1980.

OTHER SPECIALTIES

Balough, Joseph J., and Dorothy Balough, **Catalog of U.S. Perfins**, 547p, 1979.

Bruns, Franklin R., and James H. Bruns, **Catalog of United States Souvenir Cards with a Section on United Nations Souvenir Cards**, 98p, 1980.

Bruns, James, **The Philatelic Truck**, 108p, 1982.

Catalog of Plate Number Singles, Mint and Used, 1981.

Combs, W.V., **U.S. Departmental Specimen Stamps**, 48p, 1965.

Friedberg, Milton, **The Encyclopedia of U.S. Fractional and Postal Currency**, 158p, 11p price guide, 1978.

Godin, George H.V., Vahe Nazar and William G. Patten, eds., **Durland Standard Plate Number Catalog**, 304p, 1986.

Herbert's Catalogue of Plate Number Singles, 200p, 1988.

Perkal, Adam, and Seymour Kazman, **The Post Office Seals of the United States**, Vol. One: The Regular Issues, 161p, 1983.

Rapp, William F., and John H. Willard, **A Catalog of Telegraph Message Covers, 19th Century**, 77p, 1978.

Slabaugh, Arlie, **U.S. and Foreign Encased Postage Stamps: The Use of Stamps as Money**, 35p, 1967.

Walker, Doris, **Philatelic Numismatic Covers, 1970.**

Wasson, Stanley H., **Catalogue of U.S. Philatelic Exhibition Seals**, 23p, 1942.

Wilson, Jon M., **Handstamp Dated Control Handbook and Checklist**, Alabama-New Mexico, 3rd ed., 110p, 1988; New York-Wyoming, 2nd ed., 19?

CONFEDERATE STATES AND CIVIL WAR

Skinner, Hubert C., Erin R. Gunter and Warren H. Sanders, **The New Dietz Confederate States Catalog and Handbook**, 270p, 1986.

* * *

Antrim, Earl, **Civil War Prisons and Their Covers**, 215p, 1961.

Ashbrook, Stanley B., **Postal Legislation of the Confederate States of America 1861-65**, 54p, 1946.

Brannon, Peter A., **The Organization of the Confederate Post Office Department at Montgomery**, 165p, 1960.

Byne, Richard, **Confederate States of America Philatelic Subject Index and Bibliography, 1862-1984**, 352p, 1986.

Crown, Francis J. Jr., **Confederate Postal History,** anthology from *The Stamp Specialist*, 313p, 1976.

Crown, Francis J. Jr., ed., **Surveys of the Confederate Postmasters' Provisionals**, 726p, 1982.

Dietz, August, **The Postal Service of the Confederate States of America,** 439p, 1929.

Dietz, August, **Confederate States Catalog and Handbook**, 282p, 1959.

Everett, Morris, **Confederate Handstamped Paids**, 1981, addendum 1983.

Grant, R.W. **The Handbook of Civil**

War Patriotic Envelopes and Postal History, 286p, 1977.

Green, Brian M., **The Confederate States Two-Cent Red-Jack Intaglio Stamps: The Postage Stamp and Its Postal History**, 62p, 1983.

Green, Brian M., **The Typographs of the Confederate States of America**, 37p, 1981.

Green, Brian M., **The Confederate States Ten-Cent Blue Lithograph**, 1979.

Hubbell, Raynor, **Confederate Stamps, Old Letters and History**, 89p, 1959.

Krieger, Richard, **The Trans-Mississippi Mails After the Fall of Vicksburg**, 1984.

Laurence, Robert, comp., **The George Walcott Collection of Used Civil War Patriotic Covers**, 261p, (1934) 1975 reprint.

MacBride, Van Dyk, **Confederate Patriotic Covers**, 64p, (1943) 1979 reprint.

Malpass, George N., **The Jefferson Davis Postage Stamp Issues of the Confederacy**, 24p, 1954.

Milgram, James W., **Abraham Lincoln Illustrated Envelopes and Letter Paper, 1860-1865**, 1984.

Powell, Peter W.W., **Confederate States of America Markings and Postal History of Richmond, Virginia**, 186p, 1987.

Pratt, Thomas H., **The Postmaster's Provisionals of Memphis, Tennessee**, 43p, 1929.

Proctor, B., **Not Without Honor: The Life of John Reagan**, 381p, 1962, postmaster general of the Confederacy.

Quaife, M.M., ed., **Absalom Grimes: Confederate Mail Runner**, 216p, 1926.

Ramsey, Grover C., **Confederate Postmasters in Texas**, 71p, 1963.

Shenfield, Lawrence, **CSA: The Special Postal Routes**, 101p, 1961.

Wierenga, Theron, comp., **Official Documents of the Post Office of the Confederate States of America**, two vols., (1861-64) 1979 reprint.

Wishnietsky, Benjamin, **Confederate States of America Stampless Cover Catalog**, 93p, 1980.

POSTAL RATES

Hargest, George E., **History of Letter Post Communication Between the United States and Europe 1845-1875**, 234p, 1971; 2nd ed., 234p, 1975.

Post Office Department, **United States Domestic Postage Rates 1789-1956**, 138p, 1956.

Starnes, Charles J., **United States Letter Rates to Foreign Destinations, 1847 to GPU-UPU**, 74p, printed on one side, 38 plates, 1982.

United States Post Office Department, Division of Classification, **Postage Rates 1789-1930: Abstract of Laws Passed Between 1789 and 1930, Fixing Rates of Postage and According Free Mail Privileges**, 1982.

POSTAL LAWS AND GUIDES

Bower, Eli, **The United States Post Office Guide**, 345p, (1851) 1976 reprint.

Colton's United States Post Office Directory, 1856, 239p, 1985 reprint.

Laurence, Michael, ed., **U.S. Mail and Post Office Assistant, Oct. 1860 to Sept. 1872**, 585p, 1975.

List of Post Offices and Postal Laws and Regulations of the United States of America: 1857, 262p, 1980 reprint.

List of Post Offices in the United States, 1862, Including Various Postal Laws and Instructions of 1861, 1863, 1864 and 1865, 331p, 1981 reprint.

List of Post Offices in the United States for 1803 (and Additions to the 1805 List), reprint.

List of Post Offices in the United States on the 1st of July, 1836, 183p, reprint.

Postal Laws and Regulations of the United States of America, 1832 & 1843, 168p, 1980 reprint; 1847, 222p, 1980 reprint; 1852, 332p, 1980 reprint; 1866, 203p, 1981 reprint.

Postmaster General, **Report of the Postmaster General**, 19 sections, 1841/67, reprint.

Postmaster General, **Report of the Postmaster General,** reprints for 1868, 1872 and 1873.

United States Post Office Department, **Restriction on Transportation of Letters: The Private Express Statutes and Interpretations**, 4th ed., 28p, 1961.

United States. Congress, **American States Papers, Post Office Department, 1789-1833**, 361p, 1981 reprint.

The United States Postal Guide and Official Advertiser, two vols., 748p,

1982 reprint.

THE POST OFFICE

Bowyer, Mathew J., **They Carried the Mail**, 223p, 1972.

Cullinan, Gerald, **The Post Office Department**, 272p, 1968.

Cushing, Marshall, **The Story of Our Post Office**, 1,034p, 1892.

Day, J. Edward, **My Appointed Round: 929 Days as Postmaster General**, 152p, 1965.

Fuller, Wayne E., **The American Mail: Enlarger of the Common Life**, 378p, 1972.

Fuller, Wayne E., **RFD: The Changing Face of Rural America**, 361p, 1964.

Holbrook, J., **Ten Years Among the Mail Bags**, 432p, 1874.

Holbrook, Stewart H., **The Old Post Road**, 273p, 1962.

Kelly, Clyde, **United States Postal Policy**, 321p, 1932.

Leech, D., **The Post Office Department of the United States**, 109p, (1879) 1976 reprint.

Meluis, Louis, **The American Postal Service**, 2nd ed., 112p, 1917.

Moroney, Rita L., **History of the U.S. Postal Service, 1775-1984**, 1985.

Moroney, Rita L., **Montgomery Blair — Post Master General**, 44p, 1963.

Rich, W.E., **The History of the U.S. Post Office to 1829**, 190p, (1924) 1977 reprint.

Scheele, Carl H., **A Short History of the Mail Service**, 250p, 1970.

Scheele, Carl H., **Neither Snow, Nor Rain ... The Story of the U.S. Mails**, 99p, 1970.

Summerfield, Arthur E., **U.S. Mail**, 1960.

POSTAL INVESTIGATIONS

Barrslag, Karl, **Robbery by Mail**, 224p.

Clifton, Robert Bruce, **Murder By Mail and Other Postal Investigations**, 225p, 1979.

Makris, John, **The Silent Investigators**, 319p, 1959.

U.S. Government Printing Office, **History of the Postal Inspection Service**, 26p, 1987.

Woodward, P.H., **Guarding the Mails, or The Secret Service of the Post Office Department**, 583p, (1886) 1978 reprint.

Postal Markings

Alexander, Thomas, **Simpson's U.S. Postal Markings, 1851-61**, 2nd ed., 434p, 1979.

Chase and Cabeen, **The First Hundred Years of U.S. Territorial Postmarks 1781-1887**, 341p, (1950) 1980 reprint.

Cornell, Lee H. **Tale of the Kicking Mule**, 60p, 1949.

Doane, Edith R., **County Systems of RFD**, 199p, 1977.

Fishback, Hamilton R., and William C. Walker, **20th Century United States Fancy Cancellations Revised**, 244p, 1987, pricing guide by William R. Weiss Jr., 48p, 1987, see Loso and de Windt.

Helbock, Richard W., **Postmarks on Postcards: An Illustrated Guide to Early Twentieth Century United States Postmarks**, 248p, 1987.

Herst and Sampson, **Fancy Cancellations on U.S. 19th Century Stamps**, 4th ed., Billig Handbook No. 33, 288p, 1972.

Howell, John M., comp., **Checklist of Mailer's Postmarks First Used after Sept. 21, 1978**, 1983.

Konwiser, Harry M., **Postal Markings**, 762p, 1980 reprint, columns from *Stamps*.

Linn, George W., **The Paid Markings on the 3¢ United States Stamp of 1861**, 104p, 4 plates, 1955.

Loso and de Windt, **20th Century U.S. Fancy Cancellations**, 162p, 7p pricing guide, 1967, see Fishback.

Lounsbury, Jay W., **Discontinued and Renamed Post Offices in the Zip Era, 1963 through April 1986**, 179p, 1986.

Mailer's Postmark Permit Club, **Mailer's Postmarks Used Before September 21, 1978,** 1982; includes **U.S. Precancelled Cards**, 1970, by Steve Pendleton, and **Checklist of MPPs**, by John M. Howell,.

Norona, Delf, **Cyclopedia of United States Postmarks and Postal History**, two vols., 405p,(1933/35) 1975 reprint.

Konwiser, Harry M., **Norona's General Catalog of U.S. Postmarks**, 98p, revision of the 1935 volume, 1946.

Phillips, David, ed., **American Stampless Cover Catalog**, 4th ed., Vol. 1, 396p, 1985; Vol. 2, 306p, 1987.

Richow, Harold C., **Encyclopedia of R.F.D. Cancels**, 281p, 1983.

Salkind, Sol, **U.S. Cancels 1890-1900:**

with Special Emphasis on the Fancy Cancels Found on the 2-Cent Red Definitive Stamps of This Period, 120p, 1985.

Sampson, E.N., **U.S. Territorial Postmark Catalog**, 81p, 1950.

Weiss, William R. Jr., **Collecting United States Covers and Postal History**, 95p, 1987.

Skinner, Hubert, and Amos Enos, **United States Cancellations — 1845-1869: Unusual and Representative Markings**, 362p, 1980.

Stern, Edward, **The History of the Free Franking of Mail in the United States**, 236p, 1936; supplements 31p, 1943; 40p, 1944.

Van Vlissingen and Waud, **New York, Foreign Mail Cancellations**, 105p, 1968.

COLONIAL PERIOD

Bernstein, H., **The Ledger of Doctor Benjamin Franklin**, 126p, 1976 reprint.

Finlay, Hugh, **The Hugh Finlay Journal: Colonial Postal History 1773-1774**, 98p, (1867) 1975 reprint.

Holmes, Oliver W., and Peter T. Rohrbach, **Stage Coach East: Stagecoach Days in the East from the Colonial Days to the Civil War**, 220p, 1983.

Horowicz, Kay, and Robson Lowe, **The Colonial Posts in the United States of America 1606-1783**, 52p, 1967.

Konwiser, Harry M., **Colonial and Revolutionary Post: A History of the American Postal Systems, Colonial and Revolutionary Periods**, 81p, 1931.

Lowe, Robson, **Encyclopedia of Empire Postage Stamps, Vol. 5: North America**, 760p, 1973.

ter Braake, Alex, **The Posted Letter in Colonial and Revolutionary America 1628-1790**, 653p, 1975.

Wooley, Mary E., **The Early History of the Colonial Post Office**, 33p, (1894) 1969 reprint.

OCEAN MAIL

Cutler, C., **Queens of the Western Ocean: The Story of America's Mail and Passenger Sailing Lines**, 233p, 1970.

Lytle, William M., and Forrest R. Holdcamper, **Merchant Steam Vessels of the U.S. 1790-1868**, revised ed. by C. Bradford Mitchell and Kenneth R. Hall, 322p, 1975; supp. 1, 14p, 1978; supp. 2, 23p, 1982; supp. 3, 31p, 1984.

Rainey, Thomas, **Ocean Steam Navigation and the Ocean Post**, 224p, (1858) 1977 reprint.

Staff, Frank, **The Transatlantic Mail**, 191p, (1956) 1980 reprint.

Wierenga, Theron, **United States Incoming Steamship Mail 1847-1875**, 242p, 1983.

Wiltsee, Ernest, **Gold Rush Steamers of the Pacific**, 421p, (1938) 1976 reprint.

INLAND WATERWAY

Brown, A.C., **Steam Packets on the Chesapeake: A History of the Old Bay Line Since 1840**, 192p, 1961.

de Lisle, Kenneth R., **The W.L.L. Peltz Collection of Albany Postal History: The Hudson River Mail, 1804-58**, 59p, 1969.

Heath, D.R., **The Mail Boat of the Detroit River**, 25p, 1947.

Huber, Leonard, **Beginnings of Steamboat Mail on Lower Mississippi**, 14p, 1960.

Klein, Eugene **U.S. Waterway Packetmarks, 1832-99**, 208p, 1940, two supplements.

Milgram, James W., **Vessel-Named Markings on United States Inland and Ocean Waterways, 1810-1890**, 828p, 1985.

WESTERN AND EXPRESS

Coburn, Jesse L., **Letters of Gold: California Postal History Through 1869**, 389p, 1984.

Folkman, David J., **The Nicaragua Route**, 173p, 1972.

Forster, Dale E., **Oregon Express Companies**, 231p, 1985.

Harlow, Alvin F., **Old Waybills: The Romance of the Express Companies**, 504p, 1937.

Hatch, A., **American Express: A Century of Service**, 287p, 1950.

Hertz, A.J., **A Study of the Western Express**, 13p, 1952.

Inman, H., **The Old Santa Fe Trail**, (1897) 1987 reprint.

Kemble, John H., **The Panama Route**, 316p, (1943) 1972 reprint.

Kemble, John H., **The Panama Route, 1848-69**, 496p, (1938) 1976 reprint.

Lewis, Oscar, **Sea Routes to the Gold Fields**, 286p, 1949.

Lindquist, Harry L., ed., **The Story of Mormon Island**, 7p, 1929, in California.

Milgram, James W., **The Western Mails**, 62p, n.d., 1965?

Milgram, James W., **The Express Mail of 1836-1839 to Provide a Faster Mail Service Between the North and the South and the East and the West**, 214p, 1977.

Moody, Ralph, **Stagecoach West**, 341p, reprint.

Nathan, Mel C., **Franks of Western Expresses**, 281p, 1973.

Nevin, David, **The Expressmen**, 240p, 1974.

Settle, R., and M. Settle, **Saddles and Spurs**, 217p, 1955, also reprint.

Sloane, George B., **William F. Harnden: The Original Expressman**, 19p, 1932.

Smith, Wadell, **Stage Lines and Express Companies in California**, 24p, 1965.

Taylor, Morris F., **First Mails West: Stagecoach Lines on the Santa Fe Trail**, 253p 8 plates, 1971.

Tucker, T.W., **Waifs from the Waybills of an Expressman**, 143p, 1872.

Wiltsee, Ernest A., **The Joseph W. Gregory Express 1850-1853**, 29p, 1937.

Wiltsee, Ernest A., **Pioneer Miner and the Pack Mule Express**, 112p, 10 plates, (1931) 1976 reprint, 143p.

Wiltsee and Parker, **The Franks of the Everts Expresses**, 16p, 1931.

Winther, Oscar, **Via Western Express and Stagecoach**, 158p, 1954.

Wyman, W.D., **California Emigrant Letters**, 177p.

PONY EXPRESS

Bloss, Roy S., **Pony Express: The Great Gamble**, 159p, 1959.

Chapman, Arthur, **The Pony Express**, 319p, 1932.

Diggs, Howard R., **The Pony Express Goes Through**, 208p, 1935.

Knapp, Edward S., **Pony Express**, 27p, 1936.

Boggs, Winthrop S. and M.C. Nathan, **The Pony Express**, 105p, 1962.

Reinfeld, Fred, **Pony Express**, 127p.

Visscher, William L., **A Thrilling and Truthful History of the Pony Express**, 98p, 1946.

WELLS FARGO

Beebe and Clague, **U.S. West: The Saga of Wells Fargo**, 320p, (1949) 19? reprint.

Berthold, Victor M., **Handbook of the Wells, Fargo and Company's Handstamps and Franks Used in the U.S. and Dominion of Canada and Foreign Countries**, 85p, (1926) 1978 reprint.

Giblin, John, **Record of the Fargo Family**, 36p, 1968.

Hungerford, Edward, **Wells Fargo: Advancing the American Frontier**, 274p, 1949.

Jackson, W.T., **Wells Fargo Stagecoaching in Montana Territory**, 64p, 1979.

Leutzinger, John F., **The Handstamps of Wells, Fargo and Co. 1852-95**, 276p, 1968, supplement 1971.

Loomis, Noel M., **Wells Fargo**, 1968.

Theobald, John, and Lillian Theobald, **Wells Fargo in Arizona Territory**, 210p, 1978.

OVERLAND MAIL

Conkling and Conkling, **The Butterfield Overland Mail 1857-1869**, three vols., 858p, 1947.

Hafen, LeRoy. **The Overland Mail 1849-1869: Promoter of Settlement, Precursor of Railroads**, 361p, (1926) 1977 reprint.

Ormsby, Waterman, **The Butterfield Overland Mail**, 192p, (1942) 1972 reprint.

Overland to the Pacific, California Committee and Overland Mail Centennials, 1957-1958, 1956.

Pinkerton, Robert, **The First Overland Mail**, 185p, 1953.

Root, Frank A., and William E. Connelley, **The Overland Stage to California**, 645p, (1901) 1970 reprint.

Sloane, Eleanor, **The Butterfield Overland Mail Across Arizona**, 1958.

Wright, Muriel H., **The Butterfield Overland Mail One Hundred Years Ago**, 16p, 1957.

RAILROAD AND MOBILE POST OFFICES

Brenner, Clarence D., **Postmarks of Railway Post Offices and Route Agents in California**, 15p, 1973.

Bruns, James H., **Collection and Distribution Wagon Service, 1896-1904**, 1986.

Bruns, James H., **The First Highway Post Office: Introduction of Highway Post Office Service, Washington, D.C./ Harrisonburg, Virginia, a Compilation**

from Government Documents and Contemporary Accounts, 1985.

Dennis, William J., **The Travelling Post Offices: History and Incidents of the Railway Mail Service**, 125p, 1916.

Kay, John L., **Directory of Railway Post Offices, 1864 to 1977: A Listing of the Railway Post Offices, Operated by the United States Post Office Department and the United States Postal Service, over Railroads and Waterways, including the Dates of Establishments, Discontinuances and Changes of Names and Operation**, 1985.

Leet, Mervin, **Railway Mail Postmarks of Wisconsin and Upper Michigan**, 107p, 1978.

Long and Dennis, **Mail by Rail: The Story of the Postal Transportation Service**, 414p, 1951.

MacDonald, Frederick D., **Catalog of New Jersey Railway Postal Markings**, 1984.

McKee, Lewis, **Railroad Post Office History**, 218p, 49p index of railroad names.

Miller, **B&O Railroad Mail and Cancellations**, 1948.

Railway Mail Service: Sixth Division, Comprising Illinois, Iowa, Nebraska and Wyoming; Schedule of Mail Trains and List of Express Pouches, March 28, 1899, 120p, 1983 reprint of 40p.

Railway Mail Service — Schedule of Mail Trains No. 61. First Division. (Comprising Maine, New Hampshire, Vermont, Massachusetts, Rhode Island, and Connecticut) January 10, 1890, 1984 reprint.

Remele, C.W., **U.S. Railroad Postmarks 1837 to 1861**, 169p, 1958.

Riegel, **Story of the Western Railroads**, 345p, (1926) 19? reprint.

Towle, Charles L., **The Catalog of New Mexico Railway Postal Markings, 1881-1967**, 80p, 1981.

Towle, Charles L., **United States Transit Markings Catalog, 1837-1974**, four vols., 1975/77.

Towle, Charles L., **U.S. Route and Station Agent Postmarks**, 422p, 1986; also **Historical Supplement, Railway Historical Notes with Maps**, 122p, 1986.

Towle and Meyer, **Railroad Postmarks of the United States 1861-1886**, 379p, 1968.

White, James, **A Life Span and Reminiscences of Railway Mail Service**, 274p, (1910) 1973 reprint.

Votaw, C., **Jasper Hunnicutt of Jimpsonhurst**, 194p, 1907, aspects of railway mail service.

STREET RAILWAYS

Beardsley, Wallace R., and Robert W. Parkinson, **The Street Railway Postal Service in San Francisco**, 56p, 1984, includes Clark, **Seattle**.

Booth, Lloyd, **The Street Railway Post Offices of Pittsburgh**, 59p, 1983.

C.B. & Q.R.R.'s Fast Mail: The First 75 Years, 1959.

Clark, Douglas N., **Street Car R.P.O. Service in Rochester**, 16p, 1986, published with Stewart, **Cincinnati and Cleveland**.

Clark, Douglas N., and Lawton Gowey, **Seattle and Seattle R.P.O.**, 1984, published with Beardsley, **San Francisco**.

Clark, Douglas N., and F.E. Ruckle, **The Street Railway Post Offices of Baltimore**, 35p, 1979.

Heinen, Roger J., **The Street Railway Post Offices of Boston**, 46p, 1981.

Mason, John R. and Raymond A. Fleming, **Street Car R.P.O. Service in Chicago**, 73p, 1983.

Price, John M., **Street Car R.P.O. Service in Brooklyn and New York City**, 48p, 1979.

Schultz, Robert G., **The Street Railway Post Offices of Saint Louis**, 56p, 1984.

Stanton, Thomas E., and Robert A. Truax, **The Street Railway Post Offices of Washington, D.C.**, 214p, 1983.

Stets, Robert J., **Street Car R.P.O. Service in Philadelphia**, 41p, 1979.

Stewart, Kenneth T., **Street Car R.P.O. Service in Cincinnati and Cleveland**, 36p, 1986, includes Clark, **Rochester**.

Willard, J.H., **Some Early Railway Postal Routes: Colorado Postal History**, 61p, 1974.

MACHINE CANCELS

Bomar, William J., **Postal Markings of United States Expositions**, 210p, 1986, also includes hand cancels.

Brofos, Frederick, **The History of the Krag-Hansen Postmarking Machine and Its History**, 1981.

Funk, Eugene, and Arthur H. Bond,

Barry Machine Cancels, 1971.

Geschwindner, Louis, Reg Morris and John Koontz, **Time Marking Machine Co. and B.F. Cummins Co.**, 200p, 1982.

Hanmer, R.F., **U.S. Machine Postmarks, 1871-1925**, 2nd ed., 1984.

Langford, Frederick, **History of Flag Cancel Collecting 1940-1961**, 23p, 1966.

Langford, Frederick, **Standard Catalog of Doremus Machine Cancels**, 2nd ed., 60p, 1988.

Langford, Frederick, **Standard Flag Cancel Encyclopedia**, 3rd ed., 117p, 1976.

Luff, Moe, **United States Postal Slogan Cancel Catalog**, 2nd ed.,128p, 1975.

Morris, Reg, **American Machine Bar Cancels, 1884-1898**, 43p.

Olson, K.F., and V.M. Olson, **Rapid Canceling Machines, Manufacturers and Impressions**, 31p, 1946.

Stratton, Frank B., **Descriptive Catalog of the Leavitt Machine Cancellations**, 3rd ed., 42p, 1985.

VandenBoom, Vi, **Classifying the U.S. "Biplane and Monoplane" Slogan Cancels**, 1979.

MILITARY MARKINGS

Broderick and Mayo, **Civil Censorship in the U.S. During WWII**, 113p, 1980.

Bush, Joseph V., **A.M.G. Catalog-Handbook**, 44p, 1958.

Gruenzner, Norman, **Postal History of American POWs: World War II, Korea, Vietnam**, 138p, 1979.

Guthrie, William K., **Guthrie's Catalog of World War II Cartoon Patriotic Envelopes**, 113p, 1985.

Hollister, Paul E., **The Linn-Hollister Catalogue of World War Two Patriotic Envelopes**, 1981.

Jersey, Stanley, **Postal History of the U.S. and Japanese Military Forces in the Gilbert and Ellice Islands: World War II**, 39p, 1978.

Jersey, Stanley C., **Postal History of United States Forces in British Solomon Islands Protectorate during World War II**, 90p, 1968.

Linn, George W., **Catalogue of Patriotic Covers of World War II**, 88p, (1943) 1975 reprint.

Prucha, Francis Paul, **A Guide to the Military Post of the U.S. 1789-1895**, 178p, 1964.

Rawlins, R.D., **Naval Cover Cachet Makers Catalog**, 1985.

Sanford, Hennen M., **The Mail of the A.E.F.: American Expeditionary Forces 1917-21**, 56p, 1940.

Shaffer, James, ed., **Geographic Locations of U.S. APOs 1941-1984**, 5th ed., 127p, 1985.

van Dam, Theo., ed., **The Postal History of the AEF, 1917-1923**, 242p, 1980, price guide, 22p., 1983.

Wells, Stanley, **U.S. Army Post Offices & Navy Numbers in Cook Islands, Tonga and Fiji**.

FIRST-DAY COVERS AND CACHETS

August, Leo and Gerald Strauss, **Specialized Catalog of United States First Day Covers**, 53rd ed., 128p, 1988.

Brookman Stamp Co., **First Day Cover Price Guide: United States and United Nations**, regularly updated.

Mellone, Michael A., **Scott U.S. First Day Cover Catalogue and Checklist**, 224p, 1988.

* * *

Ansink, Hal, and Richard A. Monty, comps., **Mellone's First Cachets: An FDC Reference Catalog**, 2nd ed., 1983.

Baker, Philip R., **A Compilation of 200 Designers, Producers and Servicers of Identifiable Cachets, 1933-46**, 22p, 1978.

Boerger, Alfred, **Handbook of Alfred Boerger Cachets**, 1985.

Borges, John E., and Marge Finger, **Photo Cachet Catalog, Fulton Covers**, 50p.

Cusick, Allison W., **Linprint FDC Photo Catalog**, 64p, coverage is 1923/41.

Eiserman, Monte, **The Handbook for First Day Cover Collectors**, 100p, 1979.

Gasper, Wayne, **Specialized Catalogue of Henry Grimsland Cacheted FDCs and Covers**, 45p, 1977.

Harvey, Jack V., **First Day Covers of the Regular Issue of 1922-1935**, 2nd ed., 1985.

Helzer, James A., **Fleetwood's Standard First Day Cover Catalog**, various editions.

Hough, Joe D., **Theron Fox: Pioneer Cachet Maker**, 1984.

Ioor, Harry, **Special Envelopes for**

Special Purposes, 2nd ed., 193?

Krohn, Edward, **Noble's Catalog of Cacheted Presidential Inaugural Covers**, 1984.

Langer, Ernest, **Reference Manual on First Day Cancellations**, 64p, 1980.

Mack, Vincent H., **Specialized Catalogue of Aristocrat Cachets**, 1985.

Mellone, Michael A., **Mellone's Directory of Cachet Makers and Services**, 1980.

Mellone, Michael A., **Mellone's Specialized Cachet Catalog of Ducks and Express Mail First Day Covers**, 144p, 1988.

Mellone, Michael A., **Mellone's Specialized Cachet Catalog of First Day Covers of the 1940s**, 2nd ed., two vols., 256p, 1984.

Mellone, Michael A., **U.S. Early FDC Cachet Identifier**, 59p, 1976.

Mellone, Michael, and Monte Eiserman, **Mellone's Specialized Cachet Catalog of First Day Covers of the 1950s**, two vols., 1983.

Mellone, Eiserman and Zorn, **Mellone's Specialized Cachet Catalog of First Day Covers of the 1960s**, three vols., 1985?

Mellone and Newton, **The Cachet Identifier of U.S. Cacheted First Day Covers**, 2nd ed., 60p, 1979.

Mellone and Newton, **Discovering the Fun in First Day Covers**, 123p, 1979.

Monty, Richard, **Specialized Catalogue of Jacques Minkus FDCs and Patriotic Cachets**, 93p, 1977.

Mooney, Roy E., **The 7-1-71 Affair: Handbook and Catalog for July 1, 1971 FDC Issue**, 3rd ed., 1983.

Newton, Barry, **A.C. Roessler Photo Cachet Catalogue**, 111p, 1977.

Newton, Barry, **Winfred Grandy FDC Cachet Identifier**, 72p, 1980.

Parks, M. Douglas, **Photo Cachet Catalog, Harry Ioor**, 92p, 1976.

Parks, M. Douglas, **The Cachet Catalogue of Staehle and Knapp**, 1981.

Piscina, A., **Classic FDC Prices**, 47p.

Planty, Earl, **Cram Course in First Day Covers**, 32p, 1980.

Planty, Earl, **Planty's Photo Encyclopedia of Cacheted FDCs**, Vols. 1-10, coverage is 1923-39, including airmail stamps.

Russell, Gene H., **Handcrafted Cachets: The Make-Your-Own Cachet and Envelope Handbook**, 1984.

The Stamp Post, **Cachet Identifier for the Cachets of William J. Van Ohlen**, 1976.

Vero, A.J., **Those Incredible B2FDCs**, 121p, April 13, 1976, and July 4, 1976, $2 bill FDCs.

METERED MAIL

Cahn, William, **The Story of Pitney Bowes**, 262p, 1961.

Simon, Werner, and David P. Walsh, **The United States Postage Meter Stamp Catalog**, 2nd ed., 102p, 1982.

STAMP EXHIBITIONS

Ameripex Exhibition Catalog, 346p, 1986.

Anphilex 71 Anniversary Philatelic Exhibition, 128p, 1975.

Cipex 1947 Exhibition Catalog, 184p, 4p addendum, 1947.

Fipex Exhibition Catalogue, 176p, 1956.

Interphil 1976 Exhibition Catalog, 267p, 1976.

Official Catalogue of the Postage Stamp Exhibit...at the World's Columbian Exhibition, Chicago, 1893, 68p, 1893, reprint.

Postal History by State

ALABAMA

Penny, Gilbert, and Patricia Penny, **Alabama: A Glimpse at Its Postal History**, 22p, 1969.

ALASKA

Cavagnol, Joseph J., **Postmarked Alaska: A Saga of the Early Alaska Mails**, 107p, 1957.

Couch, James, **A Postal History of Alaska**, 81p, 1957.

Helbock, Richard W., and D.S. Dimpsey, **Naval Postmarks of Territorial Alaska**, 262p, 1979.

Helbock, Richard W., **Postmarks of Territorial Alaska**, 3rd ed., 258p, 1986.

Helbock, Richard W., **Military Postmarks of Territorial Alaska**, 197p, 1979.

Ricks, M.B., **Directory of Alaska's Postmasters and Post Offices 1867-1963**, 72p, 1965.

ARIZONA

Kriege, Owen H., **Arizona Territorial Postmark Catalog**, 4th ed., 103p, 1985.

Patera, Alan H., and John S. Gallagher, **Arizona Post Offices**, 244p, 1988.

Theobald, John, and Lilian Theobald, **Arizona Territory Post Offices and Postmasters**, 178p, 1961.

Towle, Charles L., **The Centennial Catalog of Arizona Railway Postal Markings**, 47p, 1979.

ARKANSAS

Patera, Alan H., and John S. Gallagher, **Checklist of Arkansas Post Offices**, 51p, 1983.

Phillips, George H., **Handling the Mail in Benton County, Arkansas, 1836-1976**, 136p, 1979.

CALIFORNIA

Helbock, Richard W., Randy Stehle and John Williams, **California Doanes**, 56p, 1983.

Frickstad, Walter N., **A Century of California Post Offices**, 395p, 1955.

Salley, Harold E., **History of California Post Offices 1849-1976**, 302p, 1977.

COLORADO

Bauer, Ozment and Willard, **Colorado Postal History: The Post Offices**, 248p, 1971.

Dike, Sheldon, **The Territorial Post Offices of Colorado**, 16p, 1957.

Harlan, George, **Colorado Postmarks & Places**, 211p, 1976.

Jarrett, David L., **Colorado Territorial and Pre-Territorial Postmarks**, 207p, 1976.

CONNECTICUT

Leonard, P.L., ed., **Stamford Post Offices and Postmasters 1790-1977**, 22p, 1977.

Patera, Alan H., **The Post Offices of Connecticut**, 55p, 1977.

Rohloff, Paul C., **The Waterbury Cancellations 1865-1890**, 264p, 1979.

Warmsley, Arthur J., **Connecticut Post Offices and Postmarks**, 257p, 1977.

DELAWARE

Bounds, Harvey C., **Postal History of Delaware** , 111p, 1938.

Crowther, Frank M., and Laurence M. Merolla, **The Post Offices of Delaware and the District of Columbia**, 44p, 1978.

FLORIDA

Bradbury and Hallock, **A Chronology of Florida Post Offices**, 91p, 1962.

Dike, Sheldon, **The Territorial Post Offices of Florida**, 12p, 1963.

Pickett, Rice and Spelman, **Florida Postal History and Postal Markings During the Stampless Period**, 1957.

GEORGIA

Goff, John H., **Placenames of Georgia**, 1975.

Krahow, Kenneth K., **Georgia Place Names**, 1975.

HAWAII

Pukai, Mary Kawena, **Place Names of Hawaii**, 2nd ed., 1974.

For more Hawaii, see U.S. Possessions.

IDAHO

Landis, Robert L., **Post Offices of Oregon, Washington and Idaho**, 251p, 1969.

ILLINOIS

Duncan, Wilbur, comp., **Pre-1830 Post Office Business: Excerpts from the Postmaster General Letter Books Pertaining to Illinois and Surrounding Areas 1801-1829**, 100p, 1984.

Karlen, Harvey M., **Chicago Postal History**, 191p, 1971.

Russell, Richard, **Illinois 19th Century Cancels**, 92p, 1984.

Teeman, Charles M., **The Postal Saga of Jo Daviess County Illinois**, 109p, 1985.

INDIANA

Baker, J. David, **Postal History of Indiana**, two vols., 1,061p, 1976.

Ryle, Russell G., **Ohio County, Indiana, Postal History**, 118p, 1983.

IOWA

Kirkpatrick, Inez E., **Stagecoach Trails in Iowa**, 232p, 1975.

Kirkpatrick, Inez E., **A Postal History of Sioux City**, 20p, 1977.

Patera, Alan H., and John S. Gallagher, **Iowa Post Offices, 1833-1986**, 232p, 1987.

KANSAS

Baughman, Robert W., **Kansas Post Offices 1828-1961**, 2nd ed., 256p, 1977.

KENTUCKY

Atkins, A.T., **Postmarked Kentucky...1792-1900**, 163p, 1975.

McCarter, John G., comp., **A Postal History Reference for the State of Kentucky 1790 thru 1855**, 170p, 1985.

LOUISIANA

Huber, Leonard V., and C. Corwith Wagner, **The Great Mail: A Postal History**

of New Orleans, 200p, 1949.

Wagner, C. Corwith, **Postal Facilities and Postmarks, District of Louisiana, Territory of Louisiana and Territory of Missouri 1804-1821**, 38p, 1960, reprint from 20th APC book with addition of **St. Louis Postal Facilities and Postmarks 1821-61**.

MAINE

Dow, Sterling T., **Maine Postal History and Postmarks**, 167p, (1943) 1976 reprint with additions, 235p.

MARYLAND

Smith, Chester M. Jr., and John L. Kay, **The Postal History of Maryland, the Delmarva Peninsula and the District of Columbia: The Post Offices and First Postmasters from 1775 to 1984**, 327p, 1984.

Kendall, Homer D., **Maryland Postal History and Handstamped Markings of the Stampless Period**, 275p, 1984.

MASSACHUSETTS

Blake, Maurice C., and Wilbur W. Davis, **Postal Markings of Boston, Massachusetts, to 1890**, 367p, (1949) 1974 reprint.

Lincoln, Leo L., and Lee C. Drickamer, **Postal History of Berkshire County, Massachusetts, 1790-1981**, 183p, 1982.

Ernst, Carl W., **Postal Service in Boston 1639-1893**, 70p, (1894) 1975 reprint.

Merolla and Crowther, **The Post Offices of Massachusetts**, 159p, 1981.

MICHIGAN

Cole, Maurice F., **Michigan Postal Markings**, 198p, 1955.

Cole, Maurice F., **Voices in the Wilderness**, 336p, 1961.

Dodge, Roy L., **Michigan Ghost Towns**, three vols., 612p, 1970/73.

Hennig, Sister Marciana, ed., **Post Offices of Michigan 1802-1976**, 995p, 1977.

Romig, Walter, **Michigan Place Names**, 673p, (1973) 1987 reprint.

MINNESOTA

Patera, Alan, and John S. Gallagher, **Post Offices of Minnesota**, 279p, 1978.

Risvold, Floyd E., **The Minnesota Territory in Postmarks, Letters and History**, 329p, 1985.

MISSISSIPPI

Oakley, Bruce C. Jr., **A Postal History of Mississippi**, two vols., 938p, 1969/80.

MISSOURI

Schultz, Robert G., **Missouri Post Offices 1804-1981**, 107p, 1982.

MONTANA

Lutz, Dennis J., **Montana Post Offices and Postmasters**, 243p, 1986.

NEBRASKA

Rapp, William F., **The Post Offices of Nebraska, Part 1: Territorial Post Offices**, 17p, 1971.

Rapp, William F., **The Postal History of Nebraska, Part 2**, 150p, 1985.

Rapp, William F., **Discontinued Post Offices of Nebraska**, 11p, 1967.

NEVADA

Frickstad, Thrall and Meyers, **A Century of Nevada Post Offices 1852-1957**, 40p, 1958.

Gamett, James, and Stanley W. Paher, **Nevada Post Offices: An Illustrated History**, 176p, 1983.

Harris, Robert R., **Nevada Postal History 1861-1972**, 64p, 1973.

NEW HAMPSHIRE

Hunt, Elmer, **New Hampshire Town Names**, 282p, 1970.

Smith, Chester M. Jr., and John L. Kay, **The Postal History of New Hampshire: The Post Offices and Postmasters from 1775 to 1985**, 1986.

NEW JERSEY

Arch, Brad, ed., **Handbook and Checklist of New Jersey DPOs**, 1981.

Coles, William C. Jr., **The Postal Markings of New Jersey Stampless Covers**, 287p, 1983.

Kay, John L., and Chester M. Smith Jr., **New Jersey Postal History: The Post Offices and First Postmasters, 1776-1976**, 199p, 1977.

NEW MEXICO

Dike, Sheldon, **New Mexico Territorial Postmark Catalog**, 8th ed., 145p, 1981.

Helbock, Richard W., **The Post Offices of New Mexico**, 70p, 1980.

NEW YORK

Boggs, Winthrop S., **Postmaster Robert Morris of New York, Being Letters for the Period June 11, 1847, to February 28, 1848**, 206p, 1960.

Chlanda, Henry, and Chester E. Wilcox, **Manuscript Post Offices of New York State**, 3rd ed., 1983.

Kay, John L., and Chester M. Smith Jr., **New York Postal History: The Post Offices and First Postmasters from 1775 to 1980**, 556p, 1982.

NORTH CAROLINA

Johnson, L.C., and P.H. Perkinson, **North Carolina Post Office Catalog**, 1984.

Ridgeway, Richard F., **Self-Sufficiency at All Costs: Confederate Post Office Operations in North Carolina 1861-65**, 78p, 1988.

NORTH DAKOTA

Patera, Alan H., and John S. Gallagher, **North Dakota Post Offices**, 188p, 16p checklist, 1982.

OHIO

Ball, George J., **The Toledo Strip**, 73p, 1985.

Billings, Bart, **A History of Postmarking Machines Used in Ohio**, 34p, 93 plates, 1982.

Gallagher, John S., and Alan Patera, **Post Offices of Ohio**, 320p, 1979.

Grabb, John R., **A History of the Chillicothe and Other Ross County, Ohio, Post Offices, 1799-1987**, 76p, 1987.

Kelly, Sophia Nutter, **The Western Reserve-Maumee Stage**, 1942.

West, Robert D., **Chillicothe, Ohio: A Postal History**, 81p, 1959.

OKLAHOMA

Shirk, George H., **Oklahoma Place Names, 1965.**

Shirk, George H., **First Post Offices Within the Boundaries of Oklahoma Indian and Oklahoma Territory**, 61p, 1948.

OREGON

Helbock, Richard W., **Oregon Post Offices 1847-1982**, 2nd ed., 160p, 1985.

Helbock, Richard W., **Portland Area Postal History**, 46p, 1983.

Whittlesey, Charles A., and Richard W. Helbock, **Oregon Postmarks: A Catalog of 19th Century Usage**, 244p, 1985.

PENNSYLVANIA

Flack, Wylie H., **Introduction to the Postal History of Philadelphia and Philadelphia County**, 1978.

Heisey, M. Luther, **A Brief Postal History of Lancaster County**, 38p, 1944.

Kay, John L., and Chester M. Smith Jr., **Pennsylvania Postal History**, 564p, 1976.

Stets, Robert J., **An Illustrated Catalog of Philadelphia Postal Markings Found on Stampless Covers 1728-1863**, 1983.

Stets, Robert J., and John L. Kay, comps., **Independent Post Offices of Philadelphia County 1800-1867**, 1979.

RHODE ISLAND

Gallagher, John S., **The Post Offices of Rhode Island**, 36p, 1977.

Merolla, Lawrence M., Frank M. Crowther and Arthur B. Jackson, **Rhode Island Postal History: The Post Offices**, 136p, 1977.

SOUTH DAKOTA

Phillips, G.H., **Post Offices of South Dakota, 1861-1930**, 66p, 1975.

TENNESSEE

Frazier, D.R., **Tennessee Post Offices and Postmaster Appointments 1789-1984**, 834p, 1984, errata sheet.

TEXAS

Day, J.M., **Post Office Papers of the Republic of Texas, 1836-1840**, two vols., 479p, 1966-67.

Deaton, Charles, **Texas Postal History Handbook**, 245p, 1980.

Deaton, Charles, **A Philatelic Guide to the 1936 Texas Centennial Celebration**, 95p, 1984.

Konwiser, Harry M., **Texas Republic Postal System**, 72p, 1933.

ter Braake, Alex, **Texas: The Drama of Its Postal Past**, 298p, 1970.

Wheat, **Post Offices & Postmasters of Texas 1846-1930**, 2,000p, 1982.

UTAH

Gallagher, John, **Post Offices of Utah**, 84p, 1977.

Gruber, Ted, **Postal History of Utah 1849-1976**, 45p, 1978.

Whall, Les **The Salt Lake City Post Office (1849-1869)**, 1982.

VERMONT

Jolley, Max W., **The Postmasters of Vermont**, 1986.

Jolley, Max W., **Notes on Berkshire, Vermont, Post Office and Early Postal Roads**, 12p, 1961.

McMorrow, Michael J., **A Scarcity and Value Rating of the Postmarks and Cancellation from the Discontinued Post Offices of Vermont**, 40p, 1970.

Slawson, Bingham and Drenan, **The**

Postal History of Vermont, 308p, 1969; index, 56p, 1971, by Chester M. Smith Jr.

VIRGINIA

Hall, Virginius C., **Virginia Post Offices 1798-1859**, 49p, (1973) 1985 reprint.

Virginia Postal History Society **Catalog of Virginia Postal Markings and Postmasters' Provisionals: Colonial—1865**, various sections.

WASHINGTON

Boardman, Tim, and Richard W. Helbock, **Washington Post Offices**, 148p, 1986.

Ramsey, Guy Reed, **Postmarked Washington**, Island County & San Juan County, 62p, 1976; Lewis & Cowlitz Counties, 240p, 1978; Jefferson, Clallam & Mason Counties, 192p, 1978.

WISCONSIN

Bournique, Raymond A., **County & Postmaster Postmarks of Wisconsin**, 12p, 1985.

Buckland, Andrew, **Flag and Doane Postmarks of Wisconsin**, 10p, 1986.

Hale, James B., comp., **Wisconsin Post Office Handbook**, 49p, 1988.

Hale, James B., **Straight Line Postmarks of Wisconsin**, 2nd ed., 12p, 1984.

Moertl, Frank, comp., **Nineteenth Century Fancy Cancellations of Wisconsin**, 28p, 1987.

Richow, Harold, **Rural Free Delivery Postmarks of Wisconsin**, 8p, 1985.

Richow Harold, **Territorial Post Offices of Wisconsin**, 38p, 1963.

Segnitz, Paul H., and Ray Van Handel, **Wisconsin Federation of Stamp Clubs Postal History Project**, 1946/1958.

WYOMING

Gallagher, John S., and Allan H. Patera, **Wyoming Post Offices, 1850-1980**, 176p, 1980, 16p checklist.

Meschter, Daniel Y., **Wyoming Territorial and Pre-Territorial Post Offices**, 17p, 1971.

States in General

Adams, Harrington, **Comparative Values of Ghost Towns**, 7th ed.

Devol and Graham, **Establishment of the First U.S. Government Post Offices in the Northwest Territory**, 48p, 1975.

Helbock, Richard W., **Western Postmaster Compensation in the 1880s**, 160p, 1980.

Phillips, G.H., **Post Offices and Postmarks of Dakota Territory**, 74p, 1973.

Helbock, Richard W., **Frontier Centennial Western Postal Route Atlas**, 132p, 1981.

Helbock, Richard W., **Pacific Northwest Doanes**, 68p, 1985.

U.S. Possessions

Napp, Joseph M., **A Study of the Plate Number Combinations Created by the Overprinting of U.S. Postage Stamps for Use in the United States Possessions and Administrative Areas 1899-1946**, Vol. 1, 190p, 1988?

PACIFIC

Mizuhara, Meiso, **U.S. Postal Activities in China: M. Mizuhara Collection**, 1982.

Murphy, Robert T., **Postal History/Cancellation Study of the U.S. Pacific Islands Including the Trust Territories**, 2nd ed., 359p, 1983.

Riddell, John D., and Sheila Riddell, **U.S.A. Consular Post Offices in Japan**, 12p, 1972.

HAWAII

Burns, Edward J., **Additions to Hawaiian Postal History**, two vols., 92p, 1980.

D'Assis, Joe, **Hawaii: The I.D.C., an Informative and Descriptive Catalogue of Hawaii Stamps and Related Issues**, 1983.

Dutton, Meiric K., **Henry M. Whitney: Pioneer Printer-Publisher & Hawaii's First Postmaster**, 1955.

Gill, Charles, **Hawaii Censored Mail 1941-45**, 66p, 1975.

Hawaii Postal Stationery Study Group, **The Postal Stationery of Hawaii**, 134p, 1982.

Hogan, Pat, **A History of the Stamps of Hawaii: 1851-1900**, 22p, 1980.

Meyer, Harris, et al., **Hawaii: Its Stamps and Postal History**, 412p, 1948.

Schwalm, A.J., **Plating Hawaii 1894-1899 Two Cent Stamp**, 20p, 1973.

Westerburg, J.F., **Plating the Hawaiian Numerals**, 85p, 1968.

PHILIPPINES

Blessington, John J., ed., **The Postal Stationery of the Philippines, Under United States Administration 1898-**

1946, 48p, 1983, 7p price supplement, 1984.

RYUKYU ISLANDS

Askins, Arthur L., **Bibliography of Source Material for the Study of the Provisional Postal Items of the Gunto Governments of the Ryukyu Islands, 1945-1951**, 28p, 1977.

Faries, Belmont, **The Postal Stationery of the Ryukyu Islands.**

Kenkichi, Tachikawa, **Handbook of Ryukyu Postage Stamps**, 174p, 1973.

Kenkya Kai Kanyo, **The Postal Stationery Catalog of Ryukyu.**

Mori and Chinen, eds., **Post Offices in Ryukyu Islands**, 24p, 1966.

Schoberlin, Melvin, ed., **Handbook and Specialized Catalogue of the Postal Issues of the Ryukyu (Lin Ch'iu) Islands (Issued under United States Administrations)**. Part I: Postal Stationery of the Gunto Governments, 2nd ed., revised and updated by Arthur L.-F. Askins, 88p, 1978; Part II: Postal Stationery of the Central Governments 1948-1972, 2nd ed., revised and updated by Arthur L.-F. Askins, 218p, 1979; Part III: The Nansei Shoto Provisional Postage Stamps, 2nd ed., revised and updated by Arthur L.-F. Askins, 148p, 1983; Part VII, Fascicle 1: War Diary of Military Government Detachment B-101-X (Subsequently Kume Shime District of Military Government), 40p, 1981, by William C., Lassiter and Billie A. Caler; Part VII, Fascicle 2: Immediate Postwar History of the Okinawa Postal Administration, by Hirata Shiichi, translated by Nobu Vogel; Part VII, Fascicle 3: History of the Development of the Communications Service in Amami Oshima after Its Separation from Japan, 55p, 1983, by Shigemura Kuniyoshi, translated by Nobu Vogel; Part VII, Fascicle 4: Miyako Island Postal History During and After the War, 27p, 1985, by Tomiyama Jojin; Part VII, Fascicle 5: Battle Records of the Former Communications Employees of Okinawa: Kumishima Post Office Portion, 35p, 1988.

Schoberlin, Melvin, **Provisional Postal Stationery**, 85p, 1968.

Schoberlin, Melvin, **Standard List of Post Offices**, 40p.

Sera, Minoru, **Ryukyu Handbook: Philatelic and Historic**, 238p, 1962.

CANAL ZONE

Blessington, John J., ed., **The Postal Stationery of the Canal Zone**, 62p, 1985, 4p price supplement.

Brett, George, **Canal Zone Essays and Proofs**, 27p, 1955.

Karrer, Robert J., **Mails Across the Isthmus 1840-1955**, 1984.

Plass, Gilbert N., Geoffrey Brewster and Richard H. Salz, **Canal Zone Stamps**, 345p, 1986.

Entwistle, Lawson, **The Postal Markings of the Canal Zone**, 222p, 1982, two supplements.

Tatelman, Edward, **Canal Zone Postal Stamps**, 439p, 1961.

Weiler, Rodolf, **Canal Zone First Issue on Cover**, 19?

PUERTO RICO

Garcia-Lomas, Jose I., **Resera Inventario de Marcas, Sellos, Pruebas y Enteros Postales de Puerto Rico Como Dependencia Postal Espanola**, 256p, 1977, errata sheet.

Preston and Sanborn, **The Postal History of Puerto Rico**, 100p, 1950.

Storer, Hugo D., **Philatelic Catalog of Puerto Rico.**

VIRGIN ISLANDS

Birch, J. Alfred, **Postal History of the U.S. Virgin Islands**, 40p, 1966.

Stamp Columnists

Following is a list of names and addresses of columnists who write for the non-philatelic press.

George Amick
Trenton Times
500 Perry Street
Trenton, N.J. 08618

Ronald Anders
Arcadia Features Syndicate
Box 411115
Chicago, Ill. 60641

Bob Ankeny
Detroit News
615 Lafayette Street
Detroit, Mich. 48231

Larry Birger
Miami Herald
2 Herald Plaza
Miami, Fla. 33101

Lea Blauvelt
Copley News Service
1104 Loyola Drive
Libertyville, Ill. 60048

George Brown
Asbury Park Press
Press Plaza
Asbury Park, N.J. 07712

Richard Carr
Ft. Lauderdale News & Sun Sentinel
Box 14430
Fort Lauderdale, Fla. 33302

Donald Chafetz
Morris County Daily Record
Box 225
Mt. Freedom, N.J. 07970

Al Collins
Houston Chronicle
Box 4260
Houston, Texas 77210

Jim Collins
Willoughby News Herald
38879 Mentor Ave.
Willoughby, Ohio 44094

Jeff Csatari
Boys' Life
Box 152079, 1325 Walnut Hill Lane
Irving, Texas 75015-2079

Walter Czubay
Metro News
Box 41
Kerhonkson, N.Y. 12446

Edward Davis, Jr.
The Providence Journal
847 Main Road
Tiverton, R.I. 02878

Peg Dow
The Florida Times-Union
Features Department
Box 1949-F
Jacksonville, Fla. 32231

David Fine
Where New Orleans
200 Ridgewood Drive
Metairie, La. 70005

John Foxworth, Jr.
Detroit Free Press
25600 Lone Pine Road
West Bloomfield, Mich. 48033

Robert Frederick
Chronicle Telegram
276 Dowd Street
Elyria, Ohio 44035

Jesse Glasgow
Baltimore Sun
4904 Wilmslow Road
Baltimore, Md. 21210

Fred Greene
Dallas Morning News
11316-B Park Central
Dallas, Texas 75230

J.R. Greene
Athol Daily News
Exchange Street
Athol, Mass. 01331

Charless Hahn
Chicago Sun Times
370 Walnut Street
Winnetka, Ill. 60093

Wayne Hassell
St. Paul Pioneer Press Dispatch
345 Cedar Street
St. Paul, Minn. 55101

Bradford A. Hathway
New Bedford Standard Times
87 Aucoot Road
Mattapoisett, Mass. 02739

Barth Healey
New York Times
229 West 43rd Street
New York, N.Y. 10036

Charles Ireland
Santa Barbara News
Drawer NN
Santa Barbara, Calif. 93702

David Kent
Hartford Courant
Box 127
New Britain, Conn. 06050

Dick King
Topeka Capital-Journal
616 Jefferson Street
Topeka, Kan. 66607

Tom Koch
The Dallas Times Herald
1013 Spring Brook Drive
De Soto, Texas 75115

Fred Korotkin
Keeping Posted, The Enterprise
4925 Minnetonka Blvd., #512
Minneapolis, Minn. 55416

Barry Krause
Los Angeles Times
Times Mirror Square
Los Angeles, Calif. 90012

Syd Kronish
A.P. Newsfeatures
11918 Suellen Circle
West Palm Beach, Fla. 33411

Alex Lutgendorf
Green Valley News & Sun
5260 Sweetwater Drive
Tucson, Ariz. 85745

Russell MacKendrick
Manchester Herald
Box 390
Manchester, Conn. 06040

James Martin
The Sacramento Bee
Box 279
Greenville, Calif. 95947

Denis Masse
La Presse
Box 1212, Place d'Armes Station
Montreal, Que., Canada H2Y 3K2

Tom Mayhill
Antique Week
Box 90
Knightstown, Ind. 46148

Bill McAllister
The Washington Post
1150 15th Street NW
Washington, D.C. 20071

Bill McCloskey
Associated Press
2021 K Street NW, Room 606
Washington, D.C. 20006

Larry McInnis
The Gazette
Box 4300 Place d'Armes
Montreal, Que., Canada H2Y 3S1

Gene Mierzejewski
The Flint Journal
200 East First Street
Flint, Mich. 48502

Ralph Mitchener
Ottawa Citizen
1101 Baxter Road
Box 5020
Ottawa, Ont., Canada K2C 3M4

James Montagnes
Toronto Star
11 Burton Road
Toronto, Canada M5P 1T6

Alfred Moses
Collectors News
Box 156
Grundy Center, Iowa 50638

Jim Nichols
Dayton Daily News
4th & Ludlow
Dayton, Ohio 45401

Michael Pauly
The Des Moines Register
Route 2, Box 210
Des Moines, Iowa 50003

Andre Pellerin
Le Nouvelliste
1850, Bellefeuille St.
C.P. 668
Trois-Rivieres, Que.
Canada G9A 5J6

Mike Read
The Houston Post
Box 4747
Houston, Texas 77210

Delbert Reason
New Castle Courier-Times
Box 97
Shirley, Ind. 47384

Bernadine Rechner
Daily Herald
Box 75
Prospect Heights, Ill. 60070

Morris Rothblum
Camden Courier-Post
103 Leconey Circle
Palmyra, N.J. 08065

Dominick Sama
Philadelphia Enquirer
400 North Broad Street
Philadelphia, Pa. 19101

Nicholas Shestople
European Stars & Stripes
DEH USMCA NEU-ULM
APO New York, N.Y. 09035

Eck Spahich
Borger News Herald
1512 Lancelot Road
Borger, Texas 79007

F. Lee Stegemeyer
Palm Beach Post
Box 4082
West Palm Beach, Fla. 33402

Charles Teed
Daily Sentinel
Box 668
Grand Junction, Colo. 81502

Les Winick
COPO Syndicate
2121 Maple Road
Homewood, Ill. 60430

Maurice Wozniak
The Milwaukee Journal
Box 661
Milwaukee, Wis. 53201-0661

Joseph Zollman
Stamping Groups
Box 632
Long Beach, N.Y. 11561

Chapter 26

Computers and Stamps

Stamp Inventory Programs

The following table lists stamp inventory programs available during the past six years. No prices are included with this list since prices may be out of date or the software may no longer be marketed. Collectors may contact the vendors at the addresses listed. Some vendors offer demonstration versions of their software for a $5 or $10 charge, which usually can be applied to the purchase price.

Computer types are abbreviated. IBM includes compatible machines, such as Compact, Leading Edge, AST, and newer Tandy machines. Apple refers to Apple II and Mac to Macintosh. Comm is Commodore and usually includes C64 and C128 machines. RS refers to older Radio Shack machines, such as the TRS-4 and Model 100s. CPM refers to those machines, such as Kaypro, that use the CPM operating system.

The JV Technologies software consists of templates that can be used with spreadsheet programs. Supported programs are VisiCalc, Lotus 123 and SynCalc.

Some programs are limited. Philatelic Management System, from SoftStyle, for example, uses a proprietary operating system and does not support a hard disk. This is a severe restriction for most computer owners.

Program	Computer	Supplier
Stamps	Comm	Batteries Included, 17875 Sky Park North, Suite P, Irvine, Calif. 92714
The Collector	Apple	CNC Galleries, 2 Majestic Lane, South Merrimack, N.II. 03054
Stamps	Apple/Mac/IBM	Compu-Quote, 6914 Berquist Ave., Canoga Park, Calif. 91307
U.S. Stamp Inventory Management System	RS Color Computer	Crockett Software, Box 1221, St. Ann, Md. 63074
Custom Business Series	IBM/Apple/RS/Atari	Custom Business System, 1293 Lavall Drive, Gambrills, Md. 21054
Stamp Expert	IBM	DGS Systems, 33 Ticonderoga, Mills, Mass. 02054
Collector's Friend	IBM	Ecosoft, 6413 N. College Ave., Indianapolis, Ind. 45220
Stamp Record	IBM	Fisher Software, Box 3513-5B, Hemet, Calif. 92343
Philasoft	Comm	Gagneron, Box 340033, Boca Raton, Fla. 33434
Stamps	Apple	Gordon Trotter, 10626 Fable Row, Columbia, Md. 21044
Collector's Software	IBM	Hence EDP, 2021 Sperry Ave., Suite 17, Ventura, Calif. 93003
Stamp Gallery	Atari/Apple/IBM	JV Technologies, Box 563, Ludington, Mich. 49431
First Base Software	Apple/IBM/RS	McGraw Hill, software stores or bookstores
Stamp Collector	Comm	MicroClear, Box 9368, Raytown, Md. 64133
Stampkeeper	Apple/Mac/IBM	MSL Software, Box 11700, Pittsburgh, Pa. 15237
Collector's Database	Atari	Munroe Software, Box 2, Allen Park, Mich. 48101
Supercat	IBM/CPM systems	Progressive Software, 1710 Buena Vista

Stamp Inventory Computer Programs

Program	Computer	Supplier
		Ave., Spring Valley, Calif. 92077
Stamp Inventory	Comm	Robert Gear, Box 427P, Hinsdale, Ill. 60522
Stamp Collector's Database	IBM	Roger Edelman, 3001 Veazey Terrace NW, Washington, D.C. 20008
Philatelist	IBM/Apple/Comm/RS	SciEd Software, Box 1511, Elmhurst, Ill. 60126
Philapal	Apple	SixR Software, 1116A Eighth St., Suite 120, Manhattan Beach, Calif. 90266
Stamp Masstore	Apple	SoftShoe Enterprises, 10959 Kane Ave., Whittier, Calif. 90604
Philatelic Management System	IBM	SoftStyle, 7192 Kalanianaola Highway, Suite 200, Honolulu, Hawaii 96825
Ben Franklin	IBM/Apple	1Step Software, Suite 1300, Charlotte Plaza, Charlotte, N.C. 28244

Chapter 27

Linn's Stamp News Customer Service

Linn's Basic Advertising Policy

Linn's Stamp News offers advertising space for the purpose of bringing buyer and seller together for their mutual benefit. Years of publishing experience indicate the reader must be able to expect satisfactory service from the advertiser in order to respond to future advertisements. It is by giving such satisfactory service that advertisers can expect to continue productive advertising. Readers are reminded that all transactions are "two-way streets," and equity must exist for both parties for a satisfactory transaction.

Advertisements submitted that are not in the best interests of the advertiser specifically, and of the trade generally, in the opinion of the publishers, or which may mislead readers, will be rejected.

Customer checks of advertisers are periodically made by the publishers in a practical effort to assure accuracy and reliability of all advertisements. However, it is impossible to guarantee the reader's satisfaction with the advertiser's manner of doing business, and the reader is therefore reminded to exercise common sense in responding to any advertisement.

Remember: There is no Santa Claus in philately! The reader is also urged to exercise patience in awaiting response from an advertiser, making allowances for sufficient mail transit time.

Return Period

Stamps or philatelic material, which the buyer finds to be in unsatisfactory condition, may be returned to the seller for full refund or replacement if returned as sent. Returns must be made within five days of receipt by the buyer, unless other return periods are specified in the advertisement. Refund, or replacement, will be made by the seller within three days of receipt of the returned item(s).

All trades must be held intact for two weeks following shipment of material sent in exchange, to allow time for receipt and acceptance of material shipped.

Return Postage on Buy and Trade Ads

All advertisers who do not state "write first" in their ads are expected to return stamps at no expense to the seller or trader. Unless an ad states "write first" or similarly indicates that confirmation is needed before shipping, refusal of packages at the post office may be grounds for suspension of advertising privileges. If overgraded stamps are to be returned at seller's or trader's expense, advertisement must so state.

Prompt Handling of Orders

Advertisers are normally expected to fill orders within three to five days of receipt of good remittance. In cases where shipment is withheld pending clearance of check (which varies from five to 16 days, depending on location), advertisers will so notify the buyer, giving approximate shipping date, unless check clearance terms are stated in the advertisement.

Layaway Sales

Advertiser must have in his possession, and have good title to, any merchandise offered for sale on any layaway plan.

Advance Orders

Advertisements for offerings of stamps or philatelic material which are not physically delivered into the hands of dealers at time of placing the advertisements will not be accepted. EXCEPTION: Advertisements will be accepted from Governments or their officially appointed agents or distributors for future issues. Dealers may offer officially announced new issues and new-issue services.

Stamp Descriptions

Stamps offered for sale shall be accurately described. Damaged or repaired stamps should be properly noted in advertisements. Verification by *Linn's* Customer Checking Service of an advertiser shipping damaged or repaired stamps in response to orders for better grade material will be sufficient cause for declining or suspension of further advertisements.

Sold Out

In the event an item is sold out, remittance will be returned within 48 hours. The advertiser will not hold the remittance pending arrival of a new supply without obtaining permission of the buyer.

Complaints

All advertisers will be notified of complaints received in writing from the readers, and prompt adjustment by the advertiser, if warranted, and notification to the publisher will be expected as a condition of continued acceptance of advertising. Failure of an advertiser to adjust the cause of a complaint, or satisfactorily explain the same, will be considered sufficient reason for declining or suspending further advertising.

Authenticity

The submission of an advertisement for publication is considered a warranty by the seller that all items offered are genuine. Any buyer of a fake or spurious item shall be entitled to full refund. Any purchaser who doubts the authenticity of an item may request an opinion from mutually acceptable authority.

It is the responsibility of the purchaser to (A) advise the seller of action undertaken within 25 days of purchase and (B) submit the item to a mutually acceptable authority promptly.

Expenses incurred shall be borne by the purchaser except where the lot is other than described, when the dealer shall accept responsibility of the actual cost of the opinion up to $10 or 5 percent of the sale price (if the cost of the opinion is in excess of $10) with a maximum of $50.

Proof of the inability of a mutually acceptable authority to express a definite opinion is not grounds for the return of an item.

Copy Regulations

All advertisements submitted are subject to copy regulations contained in the rate card. By submitting advertising, advertiser acknowledges that he is familiar with the advertising contract and copy regulations then in effect. Additional copies will be furnished upon request.

Customer Checking Service

This checking service has been established to secure verification of certain types of customer complaints received. Collectors living in various parts of the United States, upon instruction from the publishers, place orders for merchandise advertised. The parcels are forwarded, unopened, to the publishers for examination of the contents.

Reserved Right to Reject Advertising

All advertising is submitted subject to publishers' approval. The publishers reserve the right to reject, or decline, advertising, or suspend advertising privileges for such periods of time as in their discretion they see fit, for any reason whatsoever, irrespective of the validity of reasons for rejection or declination of advertising, or suspension of advertising privileges.

Liability for Contents of Ads

Advertiser assumes liability for all contents (including text representation and illustrations) of advertisement printed and also assumes responsibility for any claims arising therefrom made against the publishers.

Verification, Inspection Financial Statement

Acceptance of advertising for any item or service is subject to investigation and verification of the product or service, and of the claims made for it in the advertisement submitted for publication. All such investigations and verifications shall be to the publishers' satisfaction.

The publishers reserve the right to require a current financial statement from any advertiser at any time.

Use of Post Office Box

California law requires complete legal

company name and full street address from which the business is actually being conducted. A post office box or phone number is not considered sufficient.

Linn's urges that complete information be included in all ads to promote uniformity and fairness between advertiser and reader.

Customer Service Department

A carefully organized Customer Service Department handles and answers each customer complaint received. Operation of this department is costly. However, its effectiveness is very important to you, the reader, and to the bona fide stamp dealer.

Your assurance of good service from a *Linn's* advertiser (or prompt intervention by our complaint department) will keep you a continued *Linn's* reader and an active supporter of our advertisers.

If you have a problem with an advertiser, *Linn's* will be happy to assist you in resolving the matter.

Linn's suggests you follow these basic steps in placing orders and in tracing them:

Ordering

Be specific in listing what you are ordering, including all pertinent information, such as lot or order number if used, catalog number, price, and from which issue or publication you are ordering. Be sure to list any descriptive information that might identify the stamp, such as grade, condition, etc. The dealer may have two similar stamps with different prices. Type or neatly print your order. Be sure that your address is included inside the package. Always keep a carbon, making notes of mailing dates etc., for your own records.

Order Arrivals

A wait of two weeks prior to inquiry is in order. If you have included a personal check, the dealer may negotiate your check and wait for it to clear before shipping. This could require an additional 10 days.

If you have not received your order during this time or a postcard from the dealer advising of a shipping date, write to the dealer, giving full information included in original order, asking for his shipping date. If you are unable to secure a satisfactory response and your merchandise still has not arrived, forward a letter to Linn's Stamp News, Attention Customer Service Department, Box 29, Sidney, Ohio 45365. List full details or, better yet, send copies of your correspondence if they can be readily obtained.

Be patient in ordering by mail and don't be too quick to blame the dealer for slow delivery. Uncle Sam's mail service is usually fast and efficient, but it is not unusual to experience delays ranging from days to weeks, depending on the area and type of mailing.

Return Privileges

All *Linn's* advertisers must offer a five day return privilege. If you are unhappy with the merchandise received, and feel that it is not as advertised, just return it for a full refund (less postage), or for a replacement.

When receiving stamps, open the package immediately upon receipt. Carefully inspect each stamp, comparing the copy received with the carbon of your original order. If it is necessary to return them, carefully package them and return insured or registered.

There may be special instances where the usual five day return privilege is not in force. Some advertisers offer seven, 10 or up to 30 days for returns. When these variations occur, they will be listed in the advertisement. In a few instances, there may be no return privilege. However, it must be so stated in the ad. An example might be a listing of several poor grade stamps as a lot. The advertiser may indicate these are purchased "as is" and cannot be returned.

Stamps Lost or Stolen in Shipment

If after following the steps outlined above you determine that your order has been lost or stolen in shipment, ask the dealer to place a "tracer" on the package. Again, patience is in order, as postal regulations require a 30-day waiting period before a tracer can be placed. The post office will contact you to verify that the package did not arrive and will ask you to sign a form indicating it has not. This form will be returned to the dealer for him to file an insurance claim.

The dealer is unable to take any steps

until this form has been returned. Once this form has been returned, he is obligated to refund your money or replace the shipment and wait to receive the insurance claim.

Fake, Altered and Spurious Stamps

What should you do if you think the stamp or philatelic item you purchase through the mail is altered or an outright fabrication: There is nothing more embarrassing than to falsely accuse a dealer or another collector and then find we have been mistaken. It is always best to seek a second authoritative opinion before taking any further action.

After being reasonably sure that your suspicions are well-founded, it is advisable to send the material in question to a recognized expert committee, having first advised the seller of your action and secured his agreement to the authority chosen to rule on the item's authenticity. This should be done within 25 days of purchase.

The major expertizing committees are listed elsewhere in this almanac.

Some groups guarantee their certificates; some will indelibly mark any items found to be fraudulent. It is important that the owner carefully read all of the regulations before submitting items for expertization.

Should the expertizer determine that the item is not as advertised, it should be returned, with the certificate, to the seller, who is required to refund the cost of the stamp and the expertization fee, within the guidelines of *Linn's* Basic Advertising Policy. If the item is shown to be as described, the expertization fee must be paid by the buyer.

Suspected stamps or philatelic material should not be sent to *Linn's*. The expertization of stamps requires equipment and detailed philatelic knowledge that are best found in the established expertizing committees.

Responding to Buy Ads

This can be a satisfying experience for both collector and dealer or it can be a difficult transaction when a few basic steps are not followed.

Package stamps securely, since they may receive some rough treatment in the mails. Be sure to insure or register the package for its full value. Remember, you may be paid this amount should the package be lost. Should the dealer's prices be unacceptable to you, it is his obligation to return to you insured or registered for this same amount.

When preparing your package, be sure to include a shipping invoice listing all items sent, including catalog numbers, grades, any special features, etc. If you are shipping for an offer, your invoice should include this statement. If you are shipping in response to a specific buy ad, be sure to mention which ad, issue date, etc. Dealers may have several buy ads running in different publications. Since deadlines vary from the weekly to monthly publications, prices in the ads may differ somewhat.

It is always wise to re-examine your material before sending. In most instances, overgraded or misdescribed stamps will be returned to you at your expense.

Read all instructions carefully. Quantities or conditions may be limited. Remember, dealers are reaching over 90,000 readers. They are not necessarily obligated to buy everything sent to them.

However, they are obligated to return the unneeded items to you, at their expense, unless the ad stated, "write first," if you have followed instructions on grades and quantities.

Many dealers will make commitments by telephone. Such a commitment is binding on both parties under *Linn's* policy and could be a wise approach in selling your stamps.

Linn's Writers' Guidelines

General

The goal at *Linn's Stamp News* is to create a weekly publication that is indispensable to stamp collectors. Everything we do, from the broadest editorial policy to the most trivial stylistic idiosyncrasy, is thought out in the light of this one overriding goal.

We try to achieve indispensability in various ways:

Every collector, from the beginner to the most sophisticated, wants to know the news. Our aim is to provide all the news, as conveniently and as accessibly as we can. In this regard, we feel we are the *New York Times* of philately.

In stamp collecting, the news is not just club and show announcements, new issues and auction realizations.

New discoveries are constantly being made, sometimes involving material that is decades or even centuries old. We cover this news too, relying on the worldwide network of columnists and correspondents who contribute to our pages.

Of course, we rely on these contributors for much more than hard news. Many of the feature items in *Linn's*, which make up the bulk of our editorial content, originate with free-lance contributors in the collector community.

Here *Linn's* performs an important educational function by bringing to the attention of more than 75,000 subscribers (and hundreds of thousands of readers) a diverse selection of facts, thoughts and observations about stamps, postal markings, covers and stamp-related subjects.

Writing in *Linn's*, the free-lance contributor has the opportunity to share his specialized knowledge with the largest stamp collector audience of any periodical in the world.

It should go without saying, then, that *Linn's* features are aimed at a broad group of relatively novice collectors, whose average level of sophistication, on any given subject, is less than that of the specialist author.

Linn's writers should keep this general interest level of the audience uppermost in mind. Advanced or more sophisticated collectors, as many of our columnists tend to be, must also avoid writing down to the reader.

The goal in writing for the *Linn's* audience is to provide information that makes stamp collecting more interesting to more people. Ideally, every feature we run promotes the hobby.

A *Linn's* article is not the appropriate place to showcase everything the author knows, nor is it a lofty podium from which to speak over people's heads.

The *Linn's* writer must strive to reach out and embrace the reader, to invite him in, even to hold his hand along the path. This attitude of friendliness and openness in one's prose is difficult to articulate, but it's extremely important. It is very much a part of our desire to make *Linn's* accessible to all collectors, and to help them grow as philatelists.

Without condescending, the *Linn's* writer should assume that the reader knows little or nothing about the specific subject at hand. Complicated terms or unfamiliar words should be defined, even if they might be familiar to the more advanced philatelist.

The *Wall Street Journal* is a good model here: Every time they use the phrase "short sale," they define what it is. *Linn's* strives to be similarly introductory in its approach to the jargon of philately.

The ideal *Linn's* feature would contain enough new (or newly presented) information to instruct even the specialist in the field, written in a way to capture the attention (and hold the interest) of the beginning collector.

While the scope of our editorial interest ranges as widely as philately itself, many of our features focus on U.S. and U.S.-related material. No matter what his collecting specialty, the *Linn's* reader still maintains an interest in the stamps and postal history of his own country. Week after week, *Linn's* offers the most complete coverage of the U.S. philatelic scene available anywhere.

This is not to say that we ignore the philately of the rest of the world — quite the contrary. We have regular columns in many non-U.S. areas; we record and notice the new issues of the entire world; and our feature writers routinely range the globe, writing on subjects from classic to contemporary.

Linn's is also big enough to accommodate a wide range of writing styles. Many of our columnists have individual voices, and we don't discourage this. We will always try to preserve a writer's style, assuming that he is a writer and has a style.

Terms

We purchase first worldwide periodical rights plus a non-exclusive right to anthologize or otherwise re-use on a proportionate royalty basis.

In other words, we want to be the first periodical to publish the work. The author is subsequently free to resell the work elsewhere, 60 days after we've published it; but here we'd like to be credited. We reserve the right to re-use all works published in *Linn's* (in our almanac or in an anthology, for instance), and we will pay an appropriate royalty for such re-uses.

The specific legal details of our purchase are spelled out in our "standard terms and conditions" section of this guideline.

Articles submitted should be exclusive to *Linn's*. We are not interested in material that is simultaneously submitted to other publications (except press releases, of course, which are not part of this discussion). Thus, we want to see original typescripts, and we tend to look unfavorably on photocopies or carbon copies.

We reserve the right to edit, cut or reject anything submitted. Unsolicited materials will be returned only if accompanied by an addressed envelope, suitably franked.

Articles accepted may not appear immediately. Please be patient. The rejection process is fairly quick (three weeks at most), but accepted pieces sometimes sit for months before publication.

Payment for features and columns is made upon publication. Checks are mailed monthly, shortly after the 5th of the month. Thus, in the ordinary course of events, writers should have received, by the middle of the month, our check for whatever of their works was published in the issues of *Linn's* cover-dated the previous month.

Rates vary, generally between $10 and $40 per feature. We do strive to pay every contributor who produces original work for us. This is more by way of saying "thank you" than providing a livelihood, since the economics of newspaper publishing don't sustain magazine rates.

Payment varies according to quality, craft, degree of difficulty, previous work done for *Linn's*, number and quality of visuals, and length.

We do not pay by the word. Longer is not necessarily better. In fact, the longer a feature, the less likely we'll have room for it.

We usually have a large inventory of half- to full-page features (over 750 words) and a screaming need for shorter items (200-500 words).

Illustrations

Include illustrations wherever possible: stamps, covers, postmarks or whatever other visual material supports your text.

Many would-be contributors seem to break down here. For *Linn's*, a picture is indeed worth, if not 1,000 words, at least 250. More frequently than we would prefer, we find ourselves returning otherwise publishable work because it lacks the necessary visual support.

As a general rule, the best way to write an article on almost any philatelic subject is to have the photos in front of you before you begin. That way you are sure to properly illustrate your subject, and your text is fairly certain to explain what's in its pictures.

Conversely, an easy way to get into trouble is to write an article with no visual support, in the expectation of finding a photo after the article is done. Nine times out of ten, the result is a text that lacks illustrations or doesn't connect to them.

On the other hand, bear in mind that

in final page make-up there must be a balance between illustrations and text. Too many illustrations can overpower a skimpy text and make it difficult (sometimes impossible) for us to lay out the words.

We prefer crisp, sharp-focus, high-contrast glossy black and white photos. A few items that have no tonal gradations, postmarks or surcharges for instance, can be reproduced adequately from photocopies. Stamps and covers cannot.

If you can't provide decent photos, send us the material and we'll make the photos here. (Clear this with us first if the value is substantial.)

Please don't expect us to seek out your visuals for you; we don't have the time or the resources.

Our typical purchase includes the acquisition of the illustrations. If you want your photos returned, we should discuss this beforehand. Include your name and full address on the reverse of each photo.

Along with illustrations, we expect you to provide captions. Please provide captions on a separate sheet of paper, not imbedded within your manuscript. The ideal caption should explain what the picture shows and make the reader want to read the accompanying text. At the very least, a caption should explain what's in the picture. Identify all people and everything else that would provoke reader curiosity. "Figure 1" with no explanation is not an acceptable caption.

Don't paste visuals or captions onto your manuscript. Keep them separate.

Copy Preparation

Copy should be typewritten, double spaced with ample margins, on one side only of sheets of white 8 1/2- by 11-inch bond paper. Put your name and the page number in the upper right corner of each page.

Avoid typewritten strikeovers, especially with figures. Better to cross it out and say it again. Clarity is more important than neatness, because everything we publish must be retyped anyway.

Footnotes and bibliographies are not appropriate to our newspaper style. If attribution or citation is essential, then it's important enough to be worked into the text.

Refer to illustrations as Figure 1, Figure 2, etc. Avoid eye directions such as above and below, which might be contradicted by page makeup.

For similar reasons, charts in the text should be avoided. They typically run wider than one column width, and cause difficult (sometimes impossible) make-up problems. If you must include a chart, prepare and discuss it separately, as if it were a photo.

Style: General

Linn's is a weekly magazine in newspaper format. Our editorial style is designed to communicate information as quickly and as clearly as possible. Stylistic quirks that hinder rapid communication are discouraged. Our basic reference in matters of editorial style is The Associated Press Stylebook, available from AP at 50 Rockefeller Plaza, New York, N.Y. 10020.

Even though your subject might be specialized, write it understandably. Always explain terms. Remember that *Linn's* is read by tens of thousands of readers who don't know your subject as well as you do. Reach out and help them.

Avoid lengthy paragraphs. One typewritten line makes two lines of type in *Linn's*. Our newspaper style calls for very short paragraphing. This also aids readership.

Don't use lengthy sentences. Two or three short sentences are easier to read than one long one. Never use parentheses or dashes when commas or separate sentences will serve the same end. Never use a comma when a period will do. That saves ink.

Avoid cliches. Don't try to be cute. Re-read your sentences to see if you can express the same thoughts in fewer words.

Check and double check all facts, especially names, addresses, catalog numbers and other critical bits of information. We rely on you for the accuracy of your prose.

Don't be afraid of the first person. We'll be publishing your work under your name. "We" or "this writer" are pedantic and often confusing. Say "I" if it's appropriate.

Use a dictionary or a spelling guide.

Frequent misspellings suggest a lack of attention to detail that is inappropriate to the craft of journalism. The back pages of Webster are useful regarding punctuation and grammar.

Avoid jarring repetition of the same words or phrase. There are many ways to say the same thing.

Style: *Linn's*

Never refer to a stamp by Scott number only. Describe it first and then add the Scott number if needed. As an example: "The U.S. 10¢ 1869 stamp (Scott 116) . . ." In a series, it's Scott 51-58; 233-37.

Spell out numerals one through nine, then use figures for 10 and higher. Don't use decimals after an even number of dollars (ie: we say $20, not $20.00). For large numbers, insert the comma beginning with 1,000. Generally, figures are used in ages; always in percentages.

No comma after a month without a day (March 1983); adding the day requires the comma (March 13, 1983). The reverse "13 March 1983" takes no comma, but is difficult to read and should be avoided.

We abbreviate months when used with days (Aug. 12, 1869) but not without days (August 1869). We never abbreviate the five short months: March, April, May, June, July.

We never use italics or quotation marks for emphasis. If you want to emphasize a word or a point, write emphatically. Don't use quotation marks to indicate anything other than a quotation. Periods and commas go inside the quotation marks; semicolons go outside.

Abbreviations: We use the old style state abbreviations. We don't abbreviate Alaska, Hawaii, Idaho, Iowa, Maine, Ohio, Texas, Utah. Two-word states are abbreviated with no space: W.Va.

Mr. is used only with Mrs. or when the man is dead. Mrs. and Miss are generally unnecessary. We never use Ms.

We don't use periods with most well-known organizations: USS, HMS, UPU, USPS, UNPA, APS, APO, GPO, etc. However, we do use periods with country initials: U.S., U.N., U.S.S.R.

Postal administrations and other organizations take the singular: APS will stage its spring meeting, UNPA will announce its 1984 stamps.

Note the punctuation and separation of the following: American Stamp Dealers' Association, Citizens' Stamp Advisory Committee, bank note, price list. The following are all one word: mailcoach, handcancel, handstamp, datestamp, semipostal, multicolor, steamship.

Our general style is lowercase. When in doubt over whether a word should be capitalized, leave it down.

Standard Terms Governing Acceptance of Original Material

Linn's Stamp News, a division of Amos Press Inc. (the "publisher"), accepts original copy and/or artwork subject to the following terms and conditions:

1. **First Worldwide Periodical Rights**. The contributor grants to publisher the exclusive right to be the first to publish the article and supporting artwork in whole or edited fashion (sometimes referred to collectively as the "work") in *Linn's Stamp News* and to use said work in advertising and/or promotion.

2. **Subsequent Use**. The contributor retains the right to sell the work elsewhere provided such subsequent sale occurs no sooner than sixty (60) days after publication by *Linn's Stamp News*. The contributor agrees that any subsequent reprint will appropriately reference *Linn's Stamp News* copyright. The contributor grants to publisher a right to re-use said work in any publication of the publisher, subject to publisher's payment of an appropriate fee to the contributor.

3. **Copyright**. The contributor grants to the publisher the right to obtain copyright on the work in the publisher's name in the United States and any other country, subject to the contributor's retained non-exclusive right to re-use as set forth above.

4. **Indemnity**. The contributor warrants and guarantees that he is the sole proprietor of the work; that said work violates no existing copyright, in whole or part, that it contains no libelous or otherwise injurious matter; that the work has not heretofore been published; that he is the sole and exclusive owner of the rights granted herein to the publisher; and that he has not heretofore assigned, pledged, or otherwise encumbered said work. At his own expense, the contributor

will protect and defend said work from any adverse claim of copyright infringement, and shall indemnify, defend and hold the publisher harmless from asserted claims of whatever nature, damages, costs and expenses that the publisher may incur as a result of the publication of said work and/or subsequent re-use.

5. **Payment**. The contributor accepts such amount as is tendered by separate check from the publisher as payment in full for the rights in the work granted herein to the publisher; provided, however, that it is agreed that additional monies may be due only as a result of subsequent re-use as set forth in paragraph 2 hereof.

6. **Rights Reserved**. All rights in the work not specifically granted to the publisher are expressly reserved to the contributor.

7. **Applicable Law**. The agreement between the contributor and publisher shall be governed by the law of Ohio and shall be deemed to have been entered into at Sidney, Ohio, as of the date of the issuance of publisher's check in payment of the amount due to the contributor pursuant to paragraph 5.

8. **Arbitration**. Any claim, dispute or controversy arising out of or in connection with the agreement between the contributor and publisher or any breach thereof, shall be arbitrated by the parties before the American Arbitration Association under the rules then applicable of that association. The arbitration shall be held in the city of Sidney, Ohio.

9. **Successors and Assigns**. The agreement of the contributor and publisher shall be binding upon, and inure to the benefit of each of their respective heirs, successors, administrators, and assigns.

10. **Entire Agreement**. It is understood by the contributor and publisher that these Standard Terms And Conditions and publisher's check tendered in payment in accordance with paragraph 5 set forth the parties' entire agreement regarding this work and may not be varied except by an additional writing signed by the contributor and the publisher.

Index

- G -

- I -

- J -

- M -

- O -

- P -

- S -

- U -

- X -

Useful Addresses

American Philatelic Research Library
Box 8338
State College, Pa. 16803

American Philatelic Society
Box 8000
State College, Pa. 16801

American Philatelic Society
Insurance Program
Box 157
Stevenson, Md. 21153

American Philatelic Society
Stamp Theft Committee
Box 293
Cuyahoga Falls, Ohio 44222
(216)923-6811

American Stamp Dealers' Association
3 School St.
Suite 205
Glen Cove, N.Y. 11542

American Topical Association
Box 630
Johnstown, Pa. 15907

Bureau of Engraving and Printing
14th and C Streets SW
Washington, D.C. 20228

Citizens' Stamp
Advisory Committee
Stamp Information Branch
U.S. Postal Service
Washington, D.C. 20260-6352

Collectors Club of New York
22 E. 35th St.
New York, N.Y. 10016

COPO
Box COPO
State College, Pa. 16803-8340

First-day covers, U.S.

Collectors affixing stamp:
Postmaster
(City)
(State and ZIP Code-9991)

USPS affixing stamp:
Postmaster
(City)
(State and ZIP Code-9992)

International Federation of Philately
Zollikerstrasse 128
CH-8008 Zurich, Switzerland

International Federation of
Stamp Dealers' Associations
27 John Adam St.
London WC2N 6HZ, England

Linn's Stamp News
Box 29
Sidney, Ohio 45365

Pacific 97
International Stamp Show
Quinby Building
Top Floor
650 S. Grand Ave.
Los Angeles, Calif. 90017

Philatelic Foundation
21 E. 40th St.
New York, N.Y. 10016

Philatelic Traders Society
27 John Adam St.
London WC2N 6HZ, England

Scott Publishing Co.
Box 828
Sidney, Ohio 45365

Smithsonian Institution
National Philatelic Collection
Room 4300
National Museum of American History
Washington, D.C. 20560

U.S. Postal Service Headquarters
475 L'Enfant Plaza SW
Washington, D.C. 20260-6753

U.S. Postal Service
Philatelic Sales Division
Washington, D.C. 20265-9997

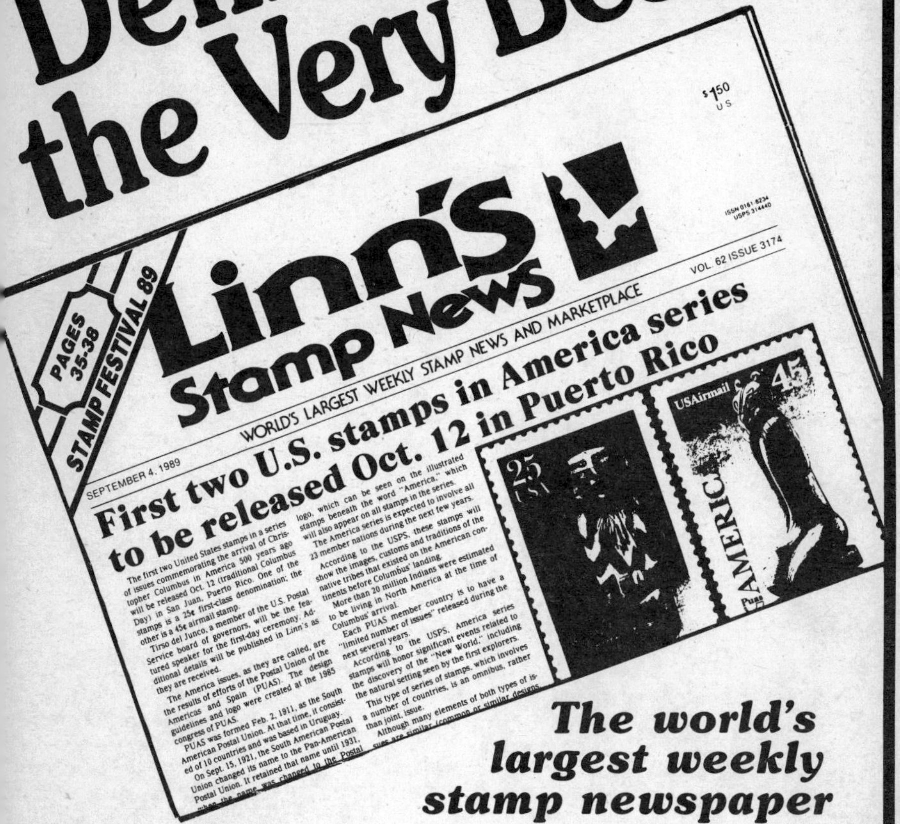